What are the obstacles to treatment for the mentally ill? **p. 479**

How many scents can humans smell? **p. 128**

Why do some dogs seem to know when it's dinnertime? **p. 210**

What is the relationship between behavior and reward? **p. 217**

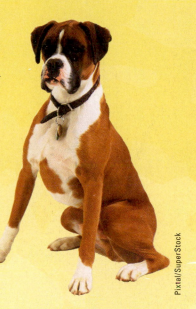

Can we decide not to stereotype? **p. 405**

What is it to be self-actualized? **p. 364**

What's the first step in helping someone with a psychological disorder? **p. 441**

When is anxiety harmful, and when is it helpful? **p. 448**

Introducing Psychology

Introducing Psychology

THIRD EDITION

Daniel L. Schacter
Harvard University

Daniel T. Gilbert
Harvard University

Daniel M. Wegner
Harvard University

Matthew K. Nock
Harvard University

WORTH
PUBLISHERS

A Macmillan Education Imprint

Senior Vice President, Editorial and Production: Catherine Woods
Vice President, Editorial, Sciences and Social Sciences: Charles Linsmeier
Publisher: Rachel Losh
Senior Acquisitions Editor: Daniel DeBonis
Senior Development Editor: Valerie Raymond
Assistant Editor: Katie Garrett
Editorial Assistant: Kimberly Morgan
Marketing Manager: Lindsay Johnson
Marketing Assistant: Alli Greco
Executive Media Editor: Rachel Comerford
Director of Editing, Design, and Media Production for the Sciences and Social Sciences:
    Tracey Kuehn
Managing Editor: Lisa Kinne
Project Editor: Rob Errera
Production Manager: Sarah Segal
Photo Editor: Cecilia Varas
Photo Researcher: Elyse Rieder
Art Director: Diana Blume
Text and Cover Designer: Blake Logan
Chapter Opener Researcher: Lyndall Culbertson
Art Manager: Matthew McAdams
Illustrations: Evelyn Pence, Jackie Heda, Matthew McAdams, Matt Holt, Christy Krames,
    Don Stewart, and Todd Buck
Composition: MPS Ltd.
Printing and Binding: RR Donnelley

Cover: © Tim Noble and Sue Webster. All Rights Reserved, DACS, ARS, NY 2014;
Photo: Andy Keate
Chapter Opening Art Credits: p. xxxiv, Yagi Studio/Getty Images; p. 26, photosindia/Getty
Images; p. 54, Cary Wolinsky/Getty Images; p. 94, Andrew Geiger; p. 134, Chad Baker/
Getty Images; p. 170, David Johnston/Getty Images; p. 206, Gandee Vasan/Getty Images; p. 244,
Image Source/agefotostock; p. 272, Kalium/AgeFotostock; p. 312, Tooga/Getty Images; p. 348,
Copyright Karim Parris; p. 378, Tim Macpherson/Getty Images; p. 410, © Fotosearch/age
footstock; p. 438, © easyFotostock/age footstock; p. 476, © 2008 Lívia Fernandes/Getty Images
Data Visualization Icons: Roman Sotola/Shutterstock

Library of Congress Preassigned Control Number: 2014954299

ISBN-13: 978-1-4641-0781-8
ISBN-10: 1-4641-0781-5

Worth Publishers
41 Madison Avenue
New York, NY 10010
www.worthpublishers.com

We dedicate this edition to the memory of
Dan Wegner, our co-author, colleague,
and deeply missed friend.

About the Authors

Daniel Schacter is William R. Kenan, Jr. Professor of Psychology at Harvard University. Dan received his B.A. degree from the University of North Carolina at Chapel Hill. He subsequently developed a keen interest in amnesic disorders associated with various kinds of brain damage. He continued his research and education at the University of Toronto, where he received his Ph.D. in 1981. He taught on the faculty at Toronto for the next six years before joining the psychology department at the University of Arizona in 1987. In 1991, he joined the faculty at Harvard University. His research explores the relation between conscious and unconscious forms of memory, the nature of distortions and errors in remembering, and how we use memory to imagine future events. Many of Schacter's studies are summarized in his 1996 book, *Searching for Memory: The Brain, The Mind, and The Past,* and his 2001 book, *The Seven Sins of Memory: How the Mind Forgets and Remembers*, both winners of the APA's William James Book Award. Schacter has also received a number of awards for teaching and research, including the Harvard-Radcliffe Phi Beta Kappa Teaching Prize, the Warren Medal from the Society of Experimental Psychologists, and the Award for Distinguished Scientific Contributions from the American Psychological Association. In 2013, he was elected to the National Academy of Sciences.

Daniel Gilbert is Edgar Pierce Professor of Psychology at Harvard University. After attending the Community College of Denver and completing his B.A. from the University of Colorado, Denver, he went on to earn his Ph.D. from Princeton University. From 1985 to 1996, he taught at the University of Texas, Austin, and in 1996, he joined the faculty of Harvard University. He has received the American Psychological Association's Distinguished Scientific Award for an Early Career Contribution to Psychology, the Diener Award for Outstanding Contributions to Social Psychology, and has won teaching awards that include the Phi Beta Kappa Teaching Prize and the Harvard College Professorship. His research focuses on how and how well people think about their emotional reactions to future events. He is the author of the international best seller *Stumbling on Happiness*, which won the Royal Society's General Prize for best popular science book of the year, and he is the co-writer and host of the PBS television series, *This Emotional Life*.

Daniel Wegner was the John Lindsley Professor of Psychology in Memory of William James at Harvard University. He received his B.S. in 1970 and Ph.D. in 1974, both from Michigan State University. He began his teaching career at Trinity University in San Antonio, Texas, before his appointments at the University of Virginia in 1990 and then Harvard University in 2000. He was a Fellow of the American Academy of Arts and Sciences, and the recipient of the William James Award from the Association for Psychological Science, the Award for Distinguished Scientific Contributions from the American Psychological Association, and the Distinguished Scientist Award from the Society of Experimental Social Psychology. His research focused on thought suppression and mental control, transactive memory in relationships and groups, and the experience of conscious will. His work on thought suppression and consciousness served as the basis of two popular books, *White Bears and Other Unwanted Thoughts* and the *Illusion of Conscious Will*, both of which were named Choice Outstanding Academic Books. He died in 2013.

Matthew Nock is a Professor of Psychology at Harvard University. Matt received his B.A. from Boston University (1995) and his Ph.D. from Yale University (2003), and he completed his clinical internship at Bellevue Hospital and the New York University Child Study Center (2003). Matt joined the faculty of Harvard University in 2003 and has been there ever since. While an undergraduate, Matt became very interested in the question of why people do things to intentionally harm themselves, and he has been conducting research aimed at answering this question ever since. His research is multidisciplinary in nature and uses a range of methodological approaches (e.g., epidemiologic surveys, laboratory-based experiments, and clinic-based studies) to better understand how these behaviors develop, how to predict them, and how to prevent their occurrence. He has received multiple teaching awards at Harvard and also four early career awards recognizing his research, and in 2011, he was named a MacArthur Fellow.

Brief Contents

Contents

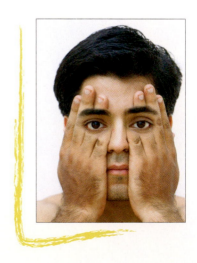

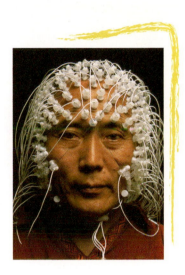

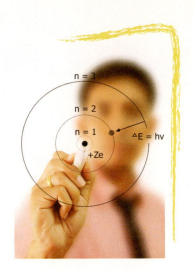

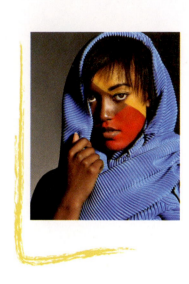

PREFACE

Why are you reading the preface? The book really gets going in about 10 pages, so why are you here instead of there? Are you the kind of person who can't stand the idea of missing something? Are you trying to justify the cost of the book by consuming every word? Did you just open to this page out of habit? Are you starting to think that maybe you made a big mistake?

For as long as we can remember, we've been asking questions like these about ourselves, about our friends, and about anyone else who didn't run away fast enough. Our curiosity about why people think, feel, and act as they do drew each of us into our first psychology course, and though we remember being swept away by the lectures, we don't remember much about our textbooks. That's probably because those textbooks were little more than colorful encyclopedias of facts, names, and dates. Little wonder that we sold them back to the bookstore the moment we finished our final exam.

When we became psychology professors, we did the things that psychology professors often do: we taught classes, we conducted research, and we wore sweater vests long after they stopped being fashionable. We also wrote stuff that people truly enjoyed reading, and that made us wonder why no one had ever written an introductory psychology textbook that students truly enjoyed reading. After all, psychology is the single most interesting subject in the known universe, so why shouldn't a psychology textbook be the single most interesting object in a student's backpack? We couldn't think of a reason, so we sat down and wrote the book that we wished we'd been given as students. The first edition of *Psychology* was published in 2008 and the reaction to it was nothing short of astounding. We'd never written a textbook before so we didn't know exactly what to expect, but never in our wildest dreams did we imagine that we would *win the Pulitzer Prize*!

Which was good, because we didn't. But what did happen was even better: We started getting letters and emails from students all over the country who just wanted to tell us how much they liked reading our book. They liked the content, of course, because as we may have already mentioned, psychology is the single most interesting subject in the known universe. But they also liked the fact that our textbook didn't *sound* like a textbook. It wasn't written in the stodgy voice of the announcer from one of those nature films that we all saw in 7th grade biology ("Behold the sea otter, nature's furry little scavenger"). Rather, it was written in *our* voices—the same voices in which we talk to our students, our spouses, our kids, and our pets (which explains why Chapter 16 is titled "Get Your Paws Off the Couch!"). We made a conscious effort to tell the *story* of psychology—to integrate topics rather than just list them, to illustrate ideas rather than just describe them. We realized that because science is such a complicated and serious business, some teachers might think that a science textbook should be complicated and serious too. We didn't see it that way. We think writing is the art of making complicated things seem simple and making serious things seem fun. The students who sent us nice letters seemed to agree (even if the Pulitzer Prize committee didn't).

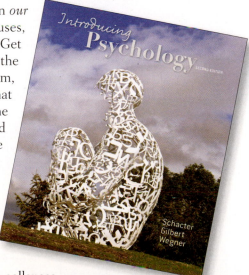

The last edition of our book was a hit—so why have we replaced it? Two reasons. First, we got tired of being asked about the guy on the cover. He is gone now, and we're only going to say this one more time: No, we have no idea where his face went, and yes, if you remove all the L's from his torso, he collapses into a big pie of meta. The second and somewhat more important reason for bringing out a new edition is that things change. Science changes (psychologists know all sorts of things about the mind and the brain that they didn't know just a few years ago), the world changes (when we wrote the second edition, no one had heard of twerking or shot a Vine), and we change (our research and reading give us new perspectives on psychological issues, and our writing and teaching show us new ways to help students learn). With all of these changes happening around us and to us, we felt that our book should change as well.

Changes to the Third Edition

New Focus on Critical Thinking

As sciences uncover new evidence and develop new theories, scientists change their minds. Some of the facts taught in a science course will still be facts a decade later, and others will require qualification or turn out to have just been plain wrong. That's why you need not only to learn the facts, but also how to *think* about facts—how to examine, interrogate, and weigh the evidence that scientists produce. We emphasize this sort of critical thinking throughout our text, of course, but in this edition we have included a new section dedicated entirely to helping you think about the mistakes we humans make when we try to consider evidence (see "Thinking Critically about Evidence" in Chapter 2: Methods in Psychology, page 44). We hope this section will help you learn how to use empirical evidence to develop well-grounded beliefs—not only about psychological science, but also about the stuff of everyday life.

New Section "Learning in the Classroom"

Like other psychology textbooks, the first two editions of our text provided in-depth coverage of many different kinds of learning, ranging from classical conditioning to observational learning. We still do. But strangely enough, the Learning chapters in most psychology texts, including the previous two editions of this text, haven't said much about the very kind of learning that is most relevant to our readers: learning in the classroom. We think that it is about time to change this puzzling state of affairs, and so we have. Chapter 7 now includes a new section cleverly titled "Learning in the Classroom, " page 237, that summarizes some of the exciting recent developments in this area, including evaluation of the most effective study techniques, insights into cognitive illusions that can mislead us into studying ineffectively, research on how to improve attention and learning during lectures, and discussion of the prospects for online learning. The Learning chapter should be relevant to your life as a student, and we've done our best to make it so.

New Research

A textbook should provide a complete tour of the classics, of course, but it should also dance on the cutting edge. We want you to see that psychology is not a museum piece—not just a collection of past events but also of current events—and that this young and evolving science has a place for you if you want it. So we've packed the third edition with information about what's happening in the field today. Not only have we included more than 400 new citations, but we've featured some of the hottest new findings in the "Hot Science" boxes that you'll find in every chapter.

CHAPTER NUMBER	HOT SCIENCE
1	Psychology as a Hub Science, p. 22
2	Do Violent Movies Make Peaceful Streets?, p. 42
3	Epigenetics and the Persisting Effects of Early Experiences, p. 81
4	Music Training: Worth the Time, p. 123
5	The Mind Wanders, p. 141
6	Sleep on It, p. 181
7	Dopamine and Reward Learning in Parkinson's Disease, p. 227
8	The Body of Evidence, p. 255
9	Dumber and Dumber?, p. 304
10	A Statistician in the Crib, p. 321
11	Personality on the Surface, p. 356
12	The Wedding Planner, p. 403
13	Can Discrimination Cause Stress and Illness?, p. 414
14	Optimal Outcome in Autism Spectrum Disorder, p. 466
15	"Rebooting" Psychological Treatment, p. 488

Fully Updated Coverage of *DSM-5*

One area where there has been a lot of new research—and lots of big changes—is in the study of psychological disorders. As you will learn, psychologists use a manual called the *Diagnostic and Statistical Manual of Mental Disorders (DSM)* to make decisions about which behaviors should be formally considered "disordered." For instance, we all get sad from time to time, but when should extreme sadness be classified as a psychological disorder that should be treated? The *DSM* answers questions like this. After nearly 20 years of using the fourth edition of the *DSM* (*DSM-IV*), psychologists now have an updated fifth edition (*DSM-5*), which was just published in 2013. Psychologists have learned a lot about psychological disorders over the past 20 years, and this third edition of our book contains updated information about how psychologists think about, define, and classify psychological disorders.

New Organization

We've also rearranged our table of contents to better fit our changing sense of how psychology is best taught. Specifically, we've moved the chapter on Stress and Health forward so that it now appears before the chapters on Psychological Disorders and Treatment of Psychological Disorders. We think this improves the flow of the book in several ways. First, as you will learn, the experience of stress has a lot to do with interpersonal events and how we respond to them, information that you will have just learned about in the chapters on Personality and Social Psychology. Second, current models of psychological disorders view them as resulting from an interaction between some underlying predisposition (e.g., genetic or otherwise) and stressful life events. Such models will be much more intuitive if you first learn about the body's stress response. Third, this chapter has information about health-promoting behaviors that could come in handy during exam season, and moving the chapter forward ensures you'll learn about them before the end of the semester!

New Other Voices Feature

Long before psychologists appeared on Earth, the human nature business was dominated by poets, playwrights, pundits, philosophers, and several other groups beginning with P. Those folks are still in that business today, and they continue to have deep and original insights into how and why people behave as they do. In this edition, we decided to invite some of them to share their thoughts with you via a new feature that we call "Other Voices." In several of the chapters, you will find a short essay by individuals who have three critical qualities: (a) They think deeply, (b) they write beautifully, and (c) they know things we don't. For example, you will find essays by leading journalists David Brooks, Ted Gup, and Tina Rosenberg; essayist and cartoonist Tim Kreider; best-selling novelist Alice Randall; award-winning educators Linda Moore and Robert H. Frank; and renowned legal scholars Gustin Reichbach and Elyn Saks. And just to make sure we aren't the only psychologists whose voices you hear, we've included essays by Tim Wilson, Chris Chabris, Daniel Simons, and Charles Fernyhough. Every one of these amazing people has something important to say about human nature, and we are delighted that they've agreed to say it in these pages. Not only do these essays encourage students to think critically about a variety of psychological issues, but they also demonstrate both the relevance of psychology to everyday life and the growing importance of our science in the public forum.

CHAPTER NUMBER	OTHER VOICES
2	Is Psychology a Science?, p. 50
3	Neuromyths, p. 89
5	A Judge's Plea for Pot, p. 166
6	Early Memories, p. 202
8	Fat and Happy, p. 263
9	Americans' Future Has to Be Bilingual, p. 283
10	You Are Going to Die, p. 344
12	91% of All Students Read This Box and Love It, p. 397
13	Freedom to Be Unhealthy?, p. 435
14	Successful and Schizophrenic, p. 463
15	Diagnosis: Human, p. 497

Less Still Is More: A Focus on Core Topics

Every teacher knows that it is easier to prepare an hour-long talk than a five-minute one. It is easy to carry on at great length about things you understand in great depth, but when asked to deliver a concise talk with a time restriction, you have to make hard decisions about what's important, how it can be conveyed with interest, and how the benefit to the audience can be maximized. These are the same challenges we faced in writing *Psychology*, and even more so in writing this briefer text, *Introducing Psychology*. We found that in a briefer edition, you can't say all the same things, but you can say them in the same way. For us, that meant retaining the aides, the touches of humor, and the broader story of psychology that is so important to understanding its influence. We have always felt that in presenting psychology to a new audience, we have to ensure that the stories carry the facts, not vice versa. So, we have stayed true to the approach that so many found appealing in *Psychology*, asking our students to read, engage, think, and (we hope) enjoy their first encounter with psychology.

Additional Student Support

Practice

- *Cue questions* encourage critical thinking and help identify the most important concepts in every major section of the text.
- Research shows that regular, short quizzes improve memory, so a *Key Concept Quiz* follows each major section within the chapters.
- *Bulleted summaries* are included at the end of every chapter to reinforce key concepts and make it easier to study for the test.
- *Critical thinking questions* are offered throughout the chapters within a number of the photo captions, offering the opportunity to apply various concepts.

Practical Application

What would the facts and concepts of psychology be without real world application? And, culture influences just about everything we do—from how we perceive lines to how long we'll stand in them—and this edition continues to celebrate the rich diversity of human beings both in Culture & Community boxes and throughout the text, as detailed below.

> How do people respond when they know they're being observed?

© Clément Philippe/Arterra Picture Library/Alamy

According to the theory of natural selection, inherited characteristics that provide a survival advantage tend to spread throughout the population across generations. Why might sensory adaptation have evolved? What survival benefits might it confer to a predator trying to hunt prey?

CHAPTER NUMBER	THE REAL WORLD
1	The Perils of Procrastination, p. 4
1	Improving Study Skills, p. 6
2	Oddsly Enough, p. 41
3	Brain Plasticity and Sensations in Phantom Limbs, p. 76
4	Multitasking, p. 100
5	Drugs and the Regulation of Consciousness, p. 163
6	Is Google Hurting Our Memories?, p. 192
7	Understanding Drug Overdoses, p. 212
8	Jeet Jet?, p. 261
9	Look Smart, p. 296
10	Walk This Way, p. 326
11	Are There "Male" and "Female" Personalities?, p. 357
12	Making the Move, p. 388
15	Types of Psychotherapists, p. 479

CHAPTER NUMBER	CULTURE & COMMUNITY

CULTURE AND MULTICULTURAL EXPERIENCE

Focus on Learning Outcomes

Teaching with the APA Learning Goals and Outcomes

In an effort to develop greater consensus on goals and learning outcomes for undergraduate education in psychology, the American Psychological Association (APA) created a task force on Undergraduate Psychology Major Competencies to provide a framework for educators. The task force subsequently published comprehensive recommendations in the *APA Guidelines for the Undergraduate Psychology Major*, revised for version 2.0 released in May 2013. These revised guidelines present a rigorous standard for what students should gain from foundational courses and from the psychology major as a whole. They comprise five goals relating to the following:

Goal 1: Knowledge Base in Psychology
Goal 2: Scientific Inquiry and Critical Thinking
Goal 3: Ethical and Social Responsibility in a Diverse World
Goal 4: Communication
Goal 5: Professional Development

The intent of the APA Task Force is to provide overarching goals without dictating exactly how students and teachers should achieve them. In that spirit, Worth Publishers offers a wide variety of resources to support students and teachers in achieving the APA outcomes. Most important, a concordance of the content in *Introducing Psychology*, Third Edition, to the APA goals is available for download from the Resources area of LaunchPad at http://www.macmillanhighered.com/launchpad/schacterbrief3e. To assist with assessment, all of the items included in the Test Bank to accompany *Introducing Psychology*, Third Edition, are tagged to the relevant outcomes, and in addition, the Instructor's Resources and LaunchPad learning system feature a variety of activities and additional content items that contribute to the APA goals. All of these resources combined offer instructors a powerful set of tools for achieving their course outcomes.

Preparing for the MCAT 2015

From 1977 to 2014, the Medical College Admission Test (MCAT) focused on biology, chemistry, and physics, but starting with the test to be administered in 2015, 25 percent of its questions will cover "Psychological, Social, and Biological Foundations of Behavior," with most of those questions concerning the psychological science taught in introductory psychology courses. According to the *Preview Guide for the MCAT 2015 Exam*, Second Edition, the addition of this content "recognizes the importance of socio-cultural and behavioral determinants of health and health outcomes." The psychology material in the new MCAT covers the breadth of topics in this text, and the table below offers a sample of how the topics in this text's Sensation and Perception chapter correspond precisely to the topics laid out in the MCAT *Preview Guide*. A complete correlation of the MCAT psychology topics with this book's contents is available for download from the Resources area of LaunchPad at http://www.macmillanhighered.com/launchpad/schacterbrief3e. In addition, since the MCAT represents a global standard for assessing the ability to reason about scientific information, the Test Bank for *Introducing Psychology*, Third Edition, features a new set of data-based questions for each chapter that are designed to test students' quantitative reasoning. These questions are available for preview in LaunchPad.

MCAT 2015 Category	SGWN, *Introducing Psychology*, Third Edition, Correlations	
Content Category 6A: Sensing the environment	Section Title or Topic	Page Number
Sensory Processing		
Sensation	Chapter 4: Sensation & Perception	95–130
• Thresholds	Measuring Thresholds	98–99
• Weber's Law (PSY)	Measuring Thresholds	98–99
• Signal detection theory (PSY)	Signal Detection	99
• Sensory adaptation	Sensory Adaptation	100–101
• Sensory receptors	Sensation & Perception are Distinct Activities	96–101
	Vision I: How the Eyes and Brain Convert Light Waves to Neural Signals	101–103
	Touch	123–124
• Sensory pathways	Pathways for What, Where, and How	108
	Touch	123–124
• Types of sensory receptors	The Body Senses	123–126
	Vision I: How the Eyes and Brain Convert Light Waves to Neural Signals	101
Vision		
Structure and function of the eye	The Human Eye	102–104
Visual processing	Vision II: Recognizing What We Perceive	109–117
• Visual pathways in the brain	The Visual Brain	106–108
• Parallel processing (PSY)	The Visual Brain	106–108
• Feature detection (PSY)	The Visual Brain	106–108
Hearing		
Auditory processing	Audition: More Than Meets the Ear	118–122
• Auditory pathways in the brain	Perceiving Pitch	120–121
Sensory reception by hair cells (PSY)	The Human Ear	119–120

MCAT 2015 Category	SGWN, *Introducing Psychology*, Third Edition, Correlations	
Content Category 6A: Sensing the environment	Section Title or Topic	Page Number
Other Senses (PSY, BIO)		
Somatosensation	The Chemical Senses: Adding Flavor	127–130
• Pain perception (PSY)	Pain	124–125
Taste	Taste	129–130
• Taste buds/chemoreceptors that detect specific chemicals	Taste	129–130
Smell	Smell	127–129
• Olfactory cells/chemoreceptors that detect specific chemicals	Smell	127–129
• Olfactory pathways in the brain (BIO)	The Chemical Senses: Adding Flavor	127–130
Kinesthetic sense	Body Position, Movement, Balance	125–126
Vestibular sense	Body Position, Movement, Balance	125–126
Perception		
Perception	Chapter 4 (mentioned throughout)	95–130
• Bottom-up/Top-down processing	Pain	124–125
	Smell	127–129
• Perceptual organization (e.g., depth, form, motion, constancy)	Vision II: Recognizing What We Perceive	109–117
• Gestalt principles	Vision II: Recognizing What We Perceive	109–117

Media and Supplements

LaunchPad with LearningCurve Quizzing

A comprehensive Web resource for teaching and learning psychology
LaunchPad combines Worth Publishers' award-winning media with an innovative platform for easy navigation. For students, it is the ultimate online study guide with rich interactive tutorials, videos, e-Book, and the LearningCurve adaptive quizzing system. For instructors, LaunchPad is a full course space where class documents can be posted, quizzes are easily assigned and graded, and students' progress can be assessed and recorded. Whether you are looking for the most effective study tools or a robust platform for an online course, LaunchPad is a powerful way to enhance your class.

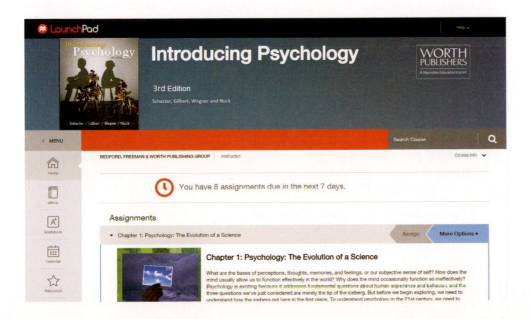

LaunchPad to Accompany *Introducing Psychology*, Third Edition, can be previewed and purchased at http://www.macmillanhighered.com/launchpad/schacterbrief3e.

Psychology, Third Edition, and LaunchPad can be ordered together with ISBN-10: 1-319-01490-9 / ISBN-13: 978-1-319-01490-2.

LaunchPad for *Introducing Psychology*, Third Edition, includes all the following resources:

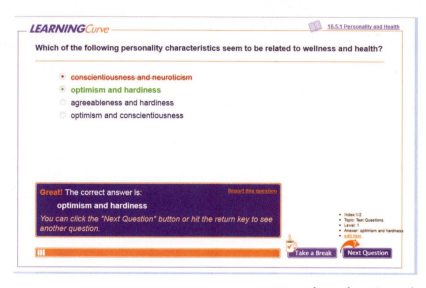

- The **LearningCurve** quizzing system was designed based on the latest findings from learning and memory research. It combines adaptive question selection, immediate and valuable feedback, and a gamelike interface to engage students in a learning experience that is unique to them. Each LearningCurve quiz is fully integrated with other resources in LaunchPad through the Personalized Study Plan, so students will be able to review with Worth's extensive library of videos and activities. And state-of-the-art question analysis reports allow instructors to track the progress of individual students as well as their class as a whole.

- New! **Data Visualization Exercises** offer students practice in understanding and reasoning about data. In each activity, students interact with a graph or visual display of data and must think like a scientist to answer the accompanying questions. These activities build quantitative reasoning skills and offer a deeper understanding of how science works.

- **An interactive e-Book** allows students to highlight, bookmark, and make their own notes, just as they would with a printed textbook. Google-style searching and in-text glossary definitions make the text ready for the digital age.

- **Concept Practice**, created by award-winning multimedia author Thomas Ludwig (Hope College), helps students solidify their understanding of key concepts. With these in-depth tutorials, students explore a variety of important topics, often in an experimental context, in the role of either researcher or subject. Tutorials combine animations, video, illustrations, and self-assessment.

- **Student Video Activities** include more than 100 engaging video modules that instructors can easily assign and customize for student assessment. Videos cover classic experiments, current news footage, and cutting-edge research, all of which are sure to spark discussion and encourage critical thinking.

- **Investigations** offer an interactive lab experience that fortifies the most important concepts and content of introductory psychology. In these activities, students participate in classic and contemporary experiments, generating real data, and they review the broader implications of those findings. A virtual host makes this a truly interactive experience.

- **The *Scientific American* Newsfeed** delivers weekly articles, podcasts, and news briefs on the very latest developments in psychology from the first name in popular science journalism.

- **Deep integration** is available between LaunchPad products and Blackboard, Brightspace by D2L, Canvas, and Moodle. These deep integrations offer educators single sign-on and gradebook sync now with auto refresh. Also, these best-in-class integrations offer deep linking to all Macmillan digital content at the chapter and asset level, giving professors ultimate flexibility and customization capability within their LMS.

Additional Student Supplements

- The **CourseSmart e-Book** offers the complete text of *Introducing Psychology*, Third Edition, in an easy-to-use format. Students can choose to purchase the CourseSmart e-Book as an online subscription or download it to a personal computer or a portable media player, such as a smartphone or iPad. The CourseSmart e-Book for *Introducing Psychology*, Third Edition, can be previewed and purchased at **www.coursesmart.com.**

- *Pursuing Human Strengths: A Positive Psychology Guide* by Martin Bolt of Calvin College is a perfect way to introduce students to the amazing field of positive psychology as well as to allow them to discover their own personal strengths.

- *The Critical Thinking Companion for Introductory Psychology* by Jane S. Halonen of the University of West Florida and Cynthia Gray of Beloit College contains both a guide to critical thinking strategies as well as exercises in pattern recognition, practical problem solving, creative problem solving, scientific problem solving, psychological reasoning, and perspective-taking.

- Worth Publishers is proud to offer several readers of articles taken from the pages of *Scientific American*. Drawing on award-winning science journalism, the **Scientific American Reader to Accompany *Introducing Psychology*, Third Edition, by Daniel L. Schacter, Daniel T. Gilbert, Daniel M. Wegner, and Matthew K. Nock** features pioneering and cutting-edge research across the fields of psychology. Selected by the authors themselves, this collection provides further insight into the fields of psychology through articles written for a popular audience.

- *Psychology and the Real World: Essays Illustrating Fundamental Contributions to Society,* **Second Edition,** is a superb collection of essays by major researchers that describe their landmark studies. Published in association with the not-for-profit FABBS Foundation, the new edition of this engaging reader includes Alan Kazdin's reflections on his research on treating children with severe aggressive behavior, Adam Grant's look at work and motivation, and Steven Hayes's thoughts on mindfulness and acceptance and commitment therapy. A portion of all proceeds is donated to FABBS to support societies of cognitive, psychological, behavioral, and brain sciences.

> **Take advantage of our most popular supplements!**
>
> Worth Publishers is pleased to offer cost-saving packages of *Introducing Psychology*, Third Edition, with our most popular supplements. Below is a list of some of the most popular combinations available for order through your local bookstore.
>
> *Psychology*, 3rd Ed. & LaunchPad Access Card
> ISBN-10: 1-319-01490-9 / ISBN-13: 978-1-319-01490-2
>
> *Psychology*, 3rd Ed. & iClicker
> ISBN-10: 1-319-01491-7 / ISBN-13: 978-1-319-01491-9
>
> *Psychology*, 3rd Ed. & *Scientific American* Reader
> ISBN-10: 1-319-01492-5 / ISBN-13: 978-1-319-01492-6
>
> *Psychology*, 3rd Ed. & *Psychology and the Real World*
> ISBN-10: 1-319-02255-3 / ISBN-13: 978-1-319-02255-6

Course Management

- Worth Publishers supports multiple Course Management Systems with enhanced cartridges for upload into Blackboard, Canvas, Angel, Brightspace by D2L, Sakai, and Moodle. Cartridges are provided free upon adoption of *Introducing Psychology*, Third Edition, and can be downloaded from Worth's online catalog at www.worthpublishers.com. Deep integration is also available between LaunchPad products and Blackboard, Brightspace by D2L, Canvas, and Moodle. These deep integrations offer educators single sign-on and gradebook sync now with auto refresh.

Assessment

- The **Computerized Test Bank,** powered by Diploma, includes a full assortment of test items from author Chad Galuska of the College of Charleston. Each chapter features over 200 multiple-choice, true/false, and essay questions to test students at several levels of Bloom's taxonomy. The new edition also features a new set of data-based reasoning questions to test advanced critical thinking skills in a manner similar to the MCAT. All the questions are matched to the outcomes recommended in the 2013 *APA Guidelines for the Undergraduate Psychology Major*. The accompanying grade book software makes it easy to record students' grades throughout a course, sort student records, view detailed analyses of test items, curve tests, generate reports, and add weights to grades.

- The **iClicker** 2 Classroom Response System is a versatile polling system developed by educators for educators that makes class time more efficient and interactive. iClicker 2 allows you to ask questions and instantly record your students' responses, take attendance, and gauge students' understanding and opinions. iClicker 2 is available at a 10% discount when packaged with *Introducing Psychology*, Third Edition.

Presentation

- **Interactive Presentation Slides** are another great way to introduce Worth's dynamic media into the classroom without lots of advance preparation. Each presentation covers a major topic in psychology and integrates Worth's high quality videos and animations for an engaging teaching and learning experience. These interactive presentations are complimentary to adopters of *Introducing Psychology*, Third Edition, and are perfect for technology novices and experts alike.

- The **Instructor's Resources** by Jeffrey Henriques of the University of Wisconsin–Madison features a variety of materials that are valuable to new and veteran teachers alike. In addition to background on the chapter reading and suggestions for in-class lectures, the manual is rich with activities to engage students in different modes of learning. The Instructor's Resources can be downloaded at http://www.macmillanhighered.com/launchpad/schacterbrief3e.

- **The Video Anthology for Introductory Psychology** includes over 150 unique video clips to bring lectures to life. Provided complimentary to adopters of *Introducing Psychology*, Third Edition, this rich collection includes clinical footage, interviews, animations, and news segments that vividly illustrate topics across the psychology curriculum.

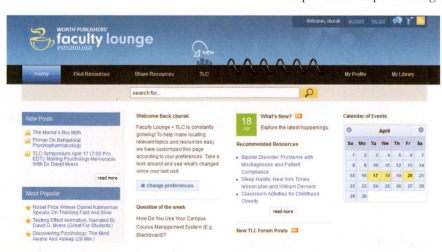

- **Faculty Lounge** is an online forum provided by Worth Publishers where teachers can find and share favorite teaching ideas and materials, including videos, animations, images, PowerPoint slides, news stories, articles, Web links, and lecture activities. Sign up to browse the site or upload your favorite materials for teaching psychology at www.worthpublishers.com/facultylounge.

Acknowledgments

Despite what you might guess by looking at our photographs, we all found women who were willing to marry us. We thank Susan McGlynn, Marilynn Oliphant, and Keesha Nock for that particular miracle and also for their love and support during the years when we were busy writing this book.

Although ours are the names on the cover, writing a textbook is a team sport, and we were lucky to have an amazing group of professionals in our dugout. We greatly appreciate the contributions of Martin M. Antony, Mark Baldwin, Michelle A. Butler, Patricia Csank, Denise D. Cummins, Ian J. Deary, Howard Eichenbaum, Sam Gosling, Paul Harris, Catherine Myers, Shigehiro Oishi, Arthur S. Reber, Morgan T. Sammons, Dan Simons, Alan Swinkels, Richard M. Wenzlaff, and Steven Yantis.

We are grateful for the editorial, clerical, and research assistance we received from Molly Evans and Mark Knepley.

In addition, we would like to thank our core supplements authors. They provided insight into the role our book can play in the classroom and adeptly developed the materials to support it. Russ Frohardt, Chad Galuska, and Jeff Henriques, we appreciate your tireless work in the classroom and the experience you brought to the book's supplements.

We would like to thank the faculty who reviewed the manuscript. These individuals showed a level of engagement we have come to expect from our best colleagues and students:

Reviewers

Eileen Achorn,
University of Texas–San Antonio

Jim Allen,
SUNY Geneseo

Randy Arnau,
University of Southern Mississippi

Kristin Biondolillo,
Arkansas State University

Stephen Blessing,
University of Tampa

Jeffrey Blum,
Los Angeles City College

Richard Bowen,
Loyola University of Chicago

Nicole Bragg,
Mt. Hood Community College

Michele Brumley,
Idaho State University

Josh Burk,
College of William and Mary

Richard Cavasina,
California University of
Pennsylvania

Amber Chenoweth,
Kent State University

Stephen Chew,
Samford University

Chrisanne Christensen,
Southern Arkansas University

Jennifer Daniels,
University of Connecticut

Joshua Dobias,
University of New Hampshire

Dale Doty,
Monroe Community College

Valerie Farmer-Dugan,
Illinois State University

Diane Feibel,
University of Cincinnati-Raymond
Walters College

Chad Galuska,
College of Charleston

Afshin Gharib,
Dominican University of California

Jeffrey Gibbons,
Christopher Newport University

Adam Goodie,
University of Georgia

John Governale,
Clark College

Patricia Grace,
Kaplan University Online

Sarah Grison,
University of Illinois at
Urbana-Champaign

Deletha Hardin,
University of Tampa

Jason Hart,
Christopher Newport University

Lesley Hathorn,
Metropolitan State College of
Denver

Jacqueline Hembrook,
University of New Hampshire

Allen Huffcutt,
Bradley University

Mark Hurd,
College of Charleston

Linda Jackson,
Michigan State University

Lance Jones,
Bowling Green State University

Linda Jones,
Blinn College

Don Kates,
College of DuPage

Martha Knight-Oakley,
Warren Wilson College

Ken Koenigshofer,
Chaffey College

Neil Kressel,
William Paterson University

Josh Landau,
York College of Pennsylvania

Fred Leavitt,
California State University–East Bay

Tera Letzring,
Idaho State University

Ray Lopez,
University of Texas–San Antonio

Jeffrey Love,
Penn State University

Greg Loviscky,
Penn State–University Park

Lynda Mae,
Arizona State University–Tempe

Caitlin Mahy,
University of Oregon

Gregory Manley,
University of Texas–San Antonio

Karen Marsh,
University of Minnesota–Duluth

Robert Mather,
University of Central Oklahoma

Wanda McCarthy,
University of Cincinnati–Clermont
College

Daniel McConnell,
University of Central Florida

Mignon Montpetit,
Miami University

Todd Nelson,
California State University–
Stanislaus

Aminda O'Hare,
University of Kansas

Brady Phelps,
South Dakota State University

Raymond Phinney,
Wheaton College

Claire St. Peter Pipkin,
West Virginia University–
Morgantown

Christy Porter,
College of William and Mary

Douglas Pruitt,
West Kentucky Community and
Technical College

Elizabeth Purcell,
Greenville Technical College

Celia Reaves,
Monroe Community College

Diane Reddy,
University of Wisconsin–
Milwaukee

Cynthia Shinabarger Reed,
Tarrant County College

David Reetz,
Hanover College

Tanya Renner,
Kapi'olani Community College

Wendy Rote,
University of Rochester

Larry Rudiger,
University of Vermont

Sharleen Sakai,
Michigan State University

Matthew Sanders,
Marquette University

Phillip Schatz,
Saint Joseph's University

Vann Scott,
Armstrong Atlantic State
University

Colleen Seifert,
University of Michigan–Ann Arbor

Wayne Shebilske,
Wright State University

Elisabeth Sherwin,
University of Arkansas–Little Rock

Kenith Sobel,
University of Central Arkansas

Genevieve Stevens,
Houston Community College

Mark Stewart,
American River College

Holly Straub,
University of South Dakota

Mary Strobbe,
San Diego Miramar College

William Struthers,
Wheaton College

Lisa Thomassen,
Indiana University

John Wright,
Washington State University

Keith Young,
University of Kansas

We are especially grateful to the extraordinary people of Worth Publishers. They include our publisher, Rachel Losh; our acquisitions editor, Dan DeBonis, who managed the project with intelligence, grace, and good humor; our development editors, Valerie Raymond and Mimi Melek; director of editing, design, and media production for the sciences and social sciences Tracey Kuehn, project editor Robert Errera, production manager Sarah Segal, and editorial assistant Kimberly Morgan, who through some remarkable alchemy turned a manuscript into a book; our designer Blake Logan, photo editor Cecilia Varas, and photo researcher Elyse Rieder, who made that book an aesthetic delight; our media editors Rachel Comerford and Anthony Casciano, and production manager Stacey Alexander, who guided the development and creation of a superb supplements package; and our marketing manager Lindsay Johnson, and associate director of market development Carlise Stembridge, who served as tireless public advocates for our vision. Thank you one and all. We look forward to working with you again.

Daniel L. Schacter   Daniel T. Gilbert   Matthew Nock

Cambridge, 2014

1

Psychology: Evolution of a Science

A lot was happening in 1860. Abraham Lincoln had just been elected president of the United States, the Pony Express had just begun to deliver mail between Missouri and California, and a woman named Anne Kellogg had just given birth to a child who would one day grow up to invent the cornflake. But none of this mattered very much to William James (1842–1910), a brilliant but taciturn 18-year-old who loved philosophy, science, art, and music, but who had no idea what to do with his life. Like many young people faced with similar decisions, William decided to do something in which he had little interest but of which his family heartily approved: He decided to become a doctor. Alas, within a few months after arriving at Harvard Medical School, he found himself depressed and uninspired. So he put his medical studies on hold and took off for Europe, where he learned about a new field that was using modern, scientific methods to answer age-old questions about human nature. That field was called *psychology* (from a combination of the Greek *psyche* [soul] and *logos* [to study]). Excited about this new discipline, William returned to America, finished his medical degree, and became a professor at Harvard University, where he devoted the rest of his life to philosophy and psychology. His landmark book, *The Principles of Psychology*, is still widely read today and remains one of the field's most important and influential works (James, 1890).

Throughout his youth, William James (1842–1910) seemed seriously mixed up. He began college as a chemistry major, then switched to anatomy, and then traveled to Europe, where he became interested in the new science of psychology. Luckily for us, he stuck with it for a while.

Letters to William James from various correspondents and photograph album, 1865–1929. MS Am 1092 (1185) #8, Houghton Library, Harvard University

psychology The scientific study of mind and behavior.

mind The private inner experience of perceptions, thoughts, memories, and feelings.

behavior Observable actions of human beings and nonhuman animals.

Keith Jarrett is a virtuoso who has been playing piano for more than 60 years. Compared to the brain regions of a novice, those that control Jarrett's fingers are relatively *less* active when he plays.

Jacques Munch/AFP/Getty Images

Emotions allow us to react quickly to potentially dangerous events. For example, fear leads many animals to freeze so that their enemies can't see them—as it did these young women who were touring a "haunted house" in Niagara Falls.

CB2/ZOB/WENN.com/Newscom

Psychology is *the scientific study of mind and behavior*. The **mind** refers to *the private inner experience of perceptions, thoughts, memories, and feelings,* an ever-flowing stream of consciousness. **Behavior** refers to *observable actions of human beings and nonhuman animals,* the things that we do in the world— by ourselves or with others. As you will see in the chapters to come, psychology is an attempt to use scientific methods to address fundamental questions about mind and behavior that have puzzled people for millennia. The answers to these questions would have astonished William James. Let's take a look at three key examples:

1. *Where does the mind come from?*

For thousands of years, philosophers tried to understand how the objective, physical world of the body was related to the subjective, psychological world of the mind. Today, psychologists know that all of our subjective experiences arise from the electrical and chemical activities of our brains. As you will see throughout this book, some of the most exciting developments in psychological research focus on how our perceptions, thoughts, memories, and feelings are related to activity in the brain. Psychologists and neuroscientists are using new technologies to explore this relationship in ways that would have seemed like science fiction only 20 years ago.

For example, the technique known as *functional magnetic resonance imaging* (fMRI) allows scientists to scan a brain to determine which parts are active when a person reads a word, sees a face, learns a new skill, or remembers a personal experience. In a recent study, the brains of both professional and novice pianists were scanned as they made complex finger movements, like those involved in piano playing. The results showed that professional pianists have *less* activity than novices in the parts of the brain that guide these finger movements (Krings et al., 2000). This finding suggests that extensive practice at the piano changes the brains of professional pianists and that the regions controlling finger movements operate more efficiently for them than they do for novices. You'll learn more about how the brain learns in the Memory and Learning chapters, and you'll see in the coming chapters how studies using fMRI and related techniques are beginning to transform many different areas of psychology.

2. *What is the mind for?*

Human beings are animals, and like all animals, they must survive and reproduce. Minds help us accomplish those goals. For example, the ability to sense and perceive allows us to recognize our families, see predators before they see us, and avoid stumbling into oncoming traffic. Our linguistic abilities allow us to organize our thoughts and communicate them to others. Our ability to remember allows us to avoid solving the same problems every time we encounter them. Our capacity for emotion allows us to react quickly to events that have life or death significance. The list goes on, but the point is that each of these psychological processes serves a purpose or, as William James would have said, each "has a function." That function becomes quite obvious the moment the process stops working. Consider, for example, the function of emotions.

Elliot was a middle-aged husband and father with a good job when his doctor discovered a tumor in the middle of his brain (Damasio, 1994). Surgery to remove the tumor both saved his life and ruined it. Why? Because after the surgery, Elliot had a hard time making decisions. He couldn't prioritize tasks at work because he couldn't decide what to do first. Eventually, this problem led to his being fired, which led to a series of risky business ventures, which led to bankruptcy. His wife divorced him, he married again, and his second wife divorced him too.

Why was Elliot unable to make decisions after having brain surgery? After all, his intelligence was intact, and his ability to speak, think, and solve logical problems was every bit as sharp as ever. The problem, it turned out, was that Elliot was no longer able to experience emotions because the surgery to remove the tumor disrupted a part of Elliot's brain tucked deep in the frontal lobes that plays a role in emotional experience (for further discussion of Elliot, see Chapter 9). For example, he didn't experience anger when his boss gave him the pink slip, anxiety when he risked his life savings, or sorrow when his wives packed up and left. Most of us have wished from time to time that we could be as stoic and unflappable as that; after all, who needs anxiety, sorrow, and anger? The answer is that we all do.

3. *Why does the mind fail?*

The mind is an amazing machine that can do many things quickly and well. We can guide a car through heavy traffic while talking to the person sitting next to us while keeping our eye out for the restaurant while listening to music. But like all machines that do many things at once, the mind occasionally makes mistakes. Consider these entries from the diaries of people who volunteered to keep track of all the mistakes they made in an ordinary day (Reason & Mycielska, 1982, pp. 70–73):

> I meant to get my car out, but as I passed the back porch on my way to the garage, I stopped to put on my boots and gardening jacket as if to work in the yard.

> I put some money into a machine to get a stamp. When the stamp appeared, I took it and said, "Thank you."

> On leaving the room to go to the kitchen, I turned the light off, although several people were there.

These mistakes are familiar and amusing, but they are also potentially useful clues about the way the mind works. For example, the person who bought a stamp said, "Thank you," but she did not say, "How do I find the subway?" The person said the wrong thing but did not say just *any* wrong thing: rather, the comment was simply wrong in that particular context (when buying stamps from a machine), but it would have been right in another (when buying stamps from a person). This tells us something quite interesting about the mind—namely, that it relies on well-learned habits that it executes without fully considering the context. The mind's mistakes are interesting to a psychologist primarily because they tell us so much about how the mind operates. (See the Real World box on procrastination).

Psychology's Roots: The Path to a Science of Mind

Psychology is a young science. William James once noted that "[t]he first lecture in psychology that I ever heard was the first I ever gave" (quoted in Perry, 1996, p. 228). Of course, that doesn't mean no one had ever thought about human nature before psychology came along. For more than 2,000 years, philosophers have thought deeply and carefully about many of the issues with which modern psychology is concerned.

Psychology's Ancestors: The Great Philosophers

Plato (428 BCE–347 BCE) and Aristotle (384 BCE–322 BCE) were among the first philosophers to struggle with fundamental questions about how the mind works (Robinson, 1995). They and other Greek philosophers debated many of the questions that psychologists continue to debate today. For example, Plato was a strong proponent of **nativism,** *the view that certain kinds of knowledge are innate or inborn.* Aristotle, on the

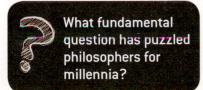

> **What fundamental question has puzzled philosophers for millennia?**

nativism The philosophical view that certain kinds of knowledge are innate or inborn.

Mistakes can teach us a lot about how people think . . . or fail to think, as the case may be.

AP Photo/Kalamazoo Gazette, Jill McLane Baker

How do young children learn about the world? Plato believed that certain kinds of knowledge are innate, whereas Aristotle believed that the mind is a blank slate on which experiences are written.

Geo Martinez/Feature Pics

The Real World

The Perils of Procrastination

William James understood that the human mind and human behavior are fascinating in part because they are not error free. Let's consider a malfunction that can have significant consequences in your own life: procrastination.

At one time or another, most of us have avoided carrying out a task or we have put it off to a later time. The task may be unpleasant, difficult, or just less entertaining than other things we could be doing at the moment. For college students, procrastination can affect a range of academic activities, such as writing a term paper or preparing for a test.

Some procrastinators defend the practice by claiming that they tend to work best under pressure or by noting that as long as a task gets done, it doesn't matter all that much if it is completed just before the deadline. Is there any merit to such claims, or are they just feeble excuses for counterproductive behavior?

A study of 60 undergraduate psychology college students provided some intriguing answers (Tice & Baumeister, 1997). At the beginning of the semester, the instructor announced a due date for the term paper and told students that if they could not meet the date, they would receive an extension to a later date. About a month later, students completed a scale that measures tendencies toward procrastination. At that same time and then again during the last week of class, students recorded health symptoms and levels of stress that they had experienced during the past week.

Students who scored high on the procrastination scale tended to turn in their papers late. One month into the semester, these procrastinators reported less stress and fewer symptoms of physical illness than did nonprocrastinators.

But at the end of the semester, the procrastinators reported more stress and more health symptoms than did the nonprocrastinators, and the procrastinators also reported more visits to the health center. The procrastinators also received lower grades on their papers and on course exams. More recent studies have found that higher levels of procrastination are associated with poorer academic performance (Moon & Illingworth, 2005) and higher levels of psychological distress (Rice, Richardson, & Clark, 2012). Therefore, in addition to making use of the tips provided in the Real World box on improving study skills (p. 6), you would be wise to avoid procrastination in this course and others.

---

philosophical empiricism The view that all knowledge is acquired through experience.

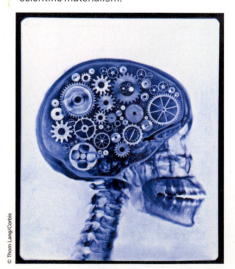

Rene Descartes believed that the physical body was a container for the non-physical thing called the mind. Centuries later, the philosopher Gilbert Ryle (1949) argued that Descartes was wrong, that there is no "ghost in the machine," and that all mental activity is simply the result of the physical activity of the brain. Most modern scientists reject Descartes's "dualism" and embrace Ryle's "scientific materialism."

© Thom Lang/Corbis

other hand, believed that the child's mind was a "blank slate" on which only experience could write, and he was a strong proponent of what we now call **philosophical empiricism,** *the view that all knowledge is acquired through experience.* Interestingly, the debate between these two great thinkers is still alive today as modern psychologists work to understand the roles that "nature" and "nurture" play in determining our thoughts, feelings, and actions. The main difference is that whereas Plato and Aristotle were quite good at formulating positions, they couldn't settle their debates because they had no objective means of testing those positions. As you will see in the Methods chapter, the ability to devise a theory and then test it is the cornerstone of the scientific approach that separates psychology and philosophy.

From the Brain to the Mind: The French Connection

We all know that the brain and the body are physical objects that we can see and touch; we also know that the subjective contents of our minds—our perceptions, thoughts, and feelings—are not visible or tangible. Inner experience is perfectly real, but where in the world is it? French philosopher René Descartes (1596–1650) argued that body and mind are fundamentally different things—that the body is made of a material substance, whereas the mind (or soul) is made of an immaterial or spiritual substance. But if the mind and the body are different things made of different substances, then how do they interact? How does the mind tell the body to put its foot forward, and when the body steps on a rusty nail, why does the mind say, "Ouch!"? This is the problem of *dualism,* or how mental activity can be reconciled and coordinated with physical behavior.

These kinds of questions proved to be difficult to answer, and the British philosopher Thomas Hobbes (1588–1679) argued that the reason they were difficult is that they were defective questions to begin with. The mind and body aren't different things at all, he claimed. Rather, the mind *is* what the brain *does.* From Hobbes's perspective, looking for a "place" where the mind meets the body is like looking for the place where heat and fire meet. It sounds like a sensible question only if you don't think too much about it! The best support for Hobbes's view came centuries later, when physicians discovered that specific changes in the brain led to specific changes in the mind. For example, the French surgeon Paul Broca (1824–1880) worked with a patient known as Monsieur Leborgne, who had suffered damage to a small part of the left side of the brain (now known as *Broca's area*). Leborgne was virtually unable to speak and could utter only the single syllable "tan." And yet, he understood everything that was said to him and was able to communicate using gestures. Broca had the crucial insight that damage to a specific part of the brain impaired a specific psychological func-

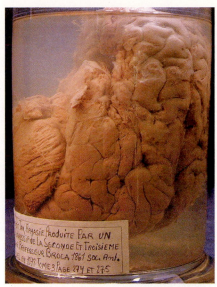

tion, demonstrating clearly that our mental lives are the products of the physical workings of one of the body's major organs: the brain. This may seem obvious to you now, but it was a radical idea in the 19th century when most people believed, as Descartes had, that the mind and the body are different things made of different substances and obeying different rules.

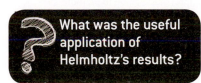

How did work involving patients with brain damage help demonstrate the relationship between mind and brain?

Mr. Leborgne was nicknamed "Tan" because it was the only word he could say. When he died in 1861, Paul Broca dissected his brain and found a lesion in the left hemisphere which, he concluded, had been responsible for Leborgne's loss of speech. Today, Leborgne's brain lives in a jar at the Musée Dupuytren in Paris, France. And to this day, no one knows his first name.

Structuralism: From Physiology to Psychology

In an 1867 letter to a friend, William James wrote, "It seems to me that perhaps the time has come for psychology to begin to be a science. Helmholtz and a man called Wundt at Heidelberg are working at it." So who were these guys?

Hermann von Helmholtz (1821–1894) was a physiologist who had developed a method for measuring the speed of nerve impulses. He gave participants a mild electric shock on different parts of their bodies and then recorded their **reaction times,** or *the time it takes to respond to a specific stimulus*. Helmholtz found that people generally took longer to respond when he shocked their toes than when he shocked their thighs. He concluded that it must take longer for the nerve impulse to travel from the toe to the brain than from the thigh to the brain because the toe is farther away from the brain. And because he knew exactly how much farther away it was, he knew exactly how fast a nerve impulse could travel! These

reaction time The amount of time taken to respond to a specific stimulus.

consciousness A person's subjective experience of the world and the mind.

structuralism The analysis of the basic elements that constitute the mind.

results were astonishing to 19th-century scientists because, at that time, just about everyone thought that mental processes occurred instantaneously. Helmholtz not only showed that this wasn't true, but he also showed that something as simple as a reaction time could help scientists unravel the mysteries of the brain and mind.

What was the useful application of Helmholtz's results?

The other fellow whom William James admired was Wilhelm Wundt (1832–1920), who had been a student of Helmholtz's. Wundt taught the first formal course in psychology in 1867 at the University of Heidelberg, and he opened the first psychology laboratory in 1879 at the University of Leipzig. Wundt believed that psychology should focus on analyzing **consciousness,** *a person's subjective experience of the world and the mind*. Wundt noted that chemists try to understand the structure of matter by breaking down natural substances into basic elements, and so he developed an approach to psychology known as **structuralism,** *the analysis of the basic elements that constitute the mind*. Wundt made good use of reaction times, as his mentor had taught him to do,

By measuring a person's reaction times to different stimuli, Hermann von Helmholtz (1821–1894) estimated the length of time it takes a nerve impulse to travel to the brain.

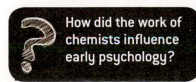

How did the work of chemists influence early psychology?

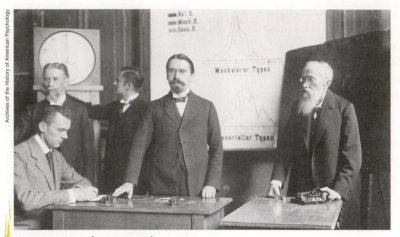

Archives of the History of American Psychology

Wilhelm Wundt (1832–1920), far right, founded the first laboratory devoted exclusively to psychology at the University of Leipzig in Germany. He sought to understand consciousness by breaking it down into its basic parts, including individual sensations and feelings.

but his primary research method involved **introspection,** which is *a method that asks people to report on the contents of their subjective experience.* In a typical experiment, Wundt's participants were exposed to a color or a sound and were simply asked to describe its brightness or its loudness. By analyzing the relationship between different aspects of these verbal reports, Wundt hoped to discover the basic elements of conscious experience.

James and the Functional Approach

William James agreed with Wundt on the importance of immediate experience and the usefulness of introspection as a technique (Bjork, 1983). But he disagreed with Wundt's claim that consciousness could be broken down into separate elements. James believed that trying to isolate and analyze a particular moment of consciousness was absurd because consciousness was like a flowing stream that could only be understood in its entirety. Furthermore, he felt that Wundt was asking the wrong question: He was asking what consciousness was *made of* rather than

The Real World

Improving Study Skills

Our minds don't work like video cameras, recording everything that happens and then faithfully storing the information. In order to retain new information, you need to take an active role in learning by doing such things as rehearsing, interpreting, and testing yourself. These activities initially might seem difficult, but in fact they are what psychologists call *desirable difficulties* (Bjork & Bjork, 2011): Making an activity more difficult by actively engaging during learning will increase your retention and ultimately result in improved performance. Here are four specific suggestions:

- **Rehearse.** One useful type of active manipulation is rehearsal: repeating to-be-learned information to yourself. For example, suppose you want to learn the name of a person you've just met. Repeat the name to yourself right away; wait a few seconds and think of it again; wait a bit longer (maybe 30 seconds), and bring the name to mind once more; then rehearse the name again after a minute and once more after 2 or 3 minutes. This type of spaced rehearsal improves long-term learning more than rehearsing the name without any spacing between rehearsals (Landauer & Bjork, 1978). You can apply this technique to names, dates, definitions, and many other

kinds of information, including concepts presented in this textbook.

- **Interpret.** If we think deeply enough about what we want to remember, the act of reflection itself will virtually guarantee good memory. The Changing Minds scenarios at the end of each chapter require you to review what you've learned in the chapter and to relate it to other things you already know about, which in turn will make you more likely to remember the information.

- **Test.** Don't just look at your class notes or this textbook; test yourself on the material as often as you can. Actively testing yourself helps you to later remember that information more than just looking at it again. The Cue Questions that you will encounter throughout the text (highlighted by green question marks) are designed to test you and thereby increase learning and retention. Be sure to use them.

- **Hit the main points.** Take some of the load off your memory by developing effective note-taking and outlining skills. Realize that you can't write down everything an instructor says, so try to focus on making detailed notes about the main ideas, facts, and people mentioned in the lecture. Later, organize your

notes into an outline that clearly highlights the major concepts. This will force you to reflect on the information in a way that promotes retention and will also provide you with a helpful study guide to promote self-testing and review.

These four activities may seem difficult or demanding at first, but they will result in improved retention and ultimately will make learning easier for you.

Anxious feelings about an upcoming exam may be unpleasant, but as you've probably experienced yourself, they can motivate much-needed study.

Superstudio/Getty Images

? **How does functionalism relate to Darwin's theory of natural selection?**

what consciousness was *for*. So James developed an approach now known as **functionalism,** which is *the study of the purpose that mental processes serve.* (See the Real World box for some strategies to enhance one of the functions of mental processes—learning.)

James was inspired not only by Helmholtz and Wundt, but also by the naturalist Charles Darwin (1809–1882),who had recently published a groundbreaking book on the theory of evolution. In that book, Darwin proposed the principle of **natural selection:** *The features of an organism that help it survive and reproduce are more likely than other features to be passed on to subsequent generations.* James realized that like all other animals, human beings must avoid predators, locate food, build shelters, attract mates, and so on. Applying Darwin's principle of natural selection, James (1890) reasoned that the ultimate function of all psychological processes must be to help people survive and reproduce, and he suggested that psychology's mission should be to find out exactly how different psychological processes execute that function. James's arguments attracted much attention, and by the 1920s, functionalism was the dominant approach to psychology in North America.

Yuri Kadobnov/AFP/Getty Images

You don't have to look at this photo for more than a half-second to know that Vladimir Putin, the president of Russia, is not feeling very happy. William James suggested that your ability to read emotional expressions in an instant serves an important function that promotes your survival and well-being.

SUMMARY QUIZ [1.1]

1. In the 1800s, Paul Broca conducted research that demonstrated a connection between
   a. animals and humans.
   b. the mind and the brain.
   c. brain size and mental ability.
   d. skull indentations and psychological attributes.

2. What was the subject of the famous experiment conducted by Hermann von Helmholtz?
   a. reaction time
   b. childhood learning
   c. structuralism
   d. functions of specific brain areas

3. Wundt and his students sought to analyze the basic elements that constitute the mind, an approach called
   a. consciousness.
   b. introspection.
   c. structuralism.
   d. objectivity.

4. William James developed _____, the study of the purpose mental processes serve in enabling people to adapt to their environments.
   a. empiricism
   b. nativism
   c. structuralism
   d. functionalism

introspection The subjective observation of one's own experience.

functionalism The study of the purpose mental processes serve in enabling people to adapt to their environment.

natural selection Charles Darwin's theory that the features of an organism that help it survive and reproduce are more likely than other features to be passed on to subsequent generations.

The Development of Clinical Psychology

While experimental psychologists were busy developing structuralism and functionalism, clinical psychologists were busy helping and studying people with mental disorders, and the observations of these clinical psychologists had an important influence on the development of psychology.

In this photograph, Sigmund Freud (1856–1939) sits by the couch reserved for his psychoanalytic patients, where they would be encouraged to recall past experiences and bring unconscious thoughts into awareness.

The Path to Freud and Psychoanalytic Theory

In the mid-19th century, the French physician Jean-Martin Charcot (1825–1893) became interested in studying patients who had developed an unusual condition then known as **hysteria,** which is a *temporary loss of cognitive or motor functions, usually as a result of emotionally upsetting experiences.* Some of these patients were blind, some were paralyzed, and others were unable to remember their pasts—and yet, there was no obvious physical cause for any of these symptoms. Charcot discovered that when he put these patients into a trancelike state by using hypnosis, their symptoms disappeared—the blind could see, the paralyzed could walk, and the amnesiac could remember! But after coming out of their trances, their symptoms reappeared. In short, patients in a normal waking state and a trancelike hypnotic state behaved like two different people.

Charcot's striking observations made a big impression on a young physician from Vienna, Austria, named Sigmund Freud (1856–1939). Freud theorized that hysteria was caused by painful childhood experiences that the patient could not remember. Freud suggested that these memories resided in the **unconscious,** which is *the part of the mind that operates outside of awareness but that influences thoughts, feelings, and actions.* This idea led Freud to develop **psychoanalytic theory,** *an approach that emphasizes the importance of unconscious mental processes in shaping feelings, thoughts, and behaviors.* Psychoanalytic theory formed the basis for a therapy that Freud called **psychoanalysis,** which focuses on *bringing unconscious material into conscious awareness to better understand psychological disorders.* Freud's theory suggested that the key to curing psychological problems was to help people remember the early experiences that were causing those problems. During psychoanalysis, patients were led to recall past experiences ("When I was a toddler, I was frightened by a masked man on a black horse") and to articulate their dreams and fantasies ("Sometimes I close my eyes and imagine not having to pay for this session"). Making unconscious material conscious was the key to the psychoanalytic cure.

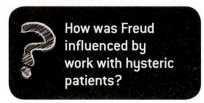

? How was Freud influenced by work with hysteric patients?

By the early 1900s, Freud's ideas had attracted a large number of followers in Europe, including soon-to-be-famous psychologists such as Carl Gustav Jung (1875–1961) and Alfred Adler (1870–1937). But his ideas were quite controversial in America because they suggested that understanding mental life required a thorough exploration of a person's early sexual experiences and unconscious sexual desires—topics that in those days were considered far too racy for discussion. In addition, Freud and most of his followers were physicians who neither conducted psychological experiments in the laboratory nor held positions at universities, so their ideas developed in isolation from the more academic and research-based approaches of people like William James.

hysteria A temporary loss of cognitive or motor functions, usually as a result of emotionally upsetting experiences.

unconscious The part of the mind that operates outside of conscious awareness but influences conscious thoughts, feelings, and actions.

psychoanalytic theory An approach that emphasizes the importance of unconscious mental processes in shaping feelings, thoughts, and behavior.

psychoanalysis A therapeutic approach that focuses on bringing unconscious material into conscious awareness to better understand psychological disorders.

September 1909 Clark University Worcester (Mass.) Celebration of the Psychological Department

Bull Seashore Jastrow   Holt Whipple Kirkpatrick   Wilson Goddard
Boas   Titchener   James Mc.Keen Cattell Katzenellenbogen Sanford Jung Burnham A. Meyer Chamberlain
                            Stern Burgerstein Stanley Hall Jones Freud   Jennings

Corbis

This famous psychology conference, held in 1909 at Clark University, brought together many notable figures, such as William James and Sigmund Freud. Both men are circled, with James on the left.

Influence of Psychoanalysis and the Humanistic Response

Most historians consider Freud to be one of the most influential thinkers of the 20th century, and the psychoanalytic movement influenced everything from literature and history to politics and art. Within psychology, psychoanalysis had its greatest im-

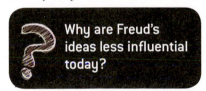

Why are Freud's ideas less influential today?

pact on clinical practice, but that influence has been considerably diminished over the past 40 years. This is partly because Freud's ideas were difficult to test, and a theory that can't be tested is of limited interest to scientists. But it was also because Freud's vision of human nature was such a dark one, emphasizing limitations and problems rather than possibilities and po-

tentials. He saw people as hostages to their forgotten childhood experiences and primitive sexual impulses, and the inherent pessimism of his perspective frustrated those psychologists who had a more optimistic view of human nature.

That's why in the second half of the 20th century, psychologists such as Abraham Maslow (1908–1970) and Carl Rogers (1902–1987) pioneered a new movement called **humanistic psychology,** *an approach to understanding human nature that emphasizes the positive potential of human beings.* Humanistic psychologists focused on the highest aspirations that people had for themselves. Rather than viewing people as prisoners of events in their remote pasts, humanistic psychologists viewed people as free agents who have an inherent need to develop, grow, and attain their full potential. This movement reached its peak in the 1960s when a generation of "flower children" found it easy to see psychological life as a kind of blossoming of the spirit. Humanistic therapists sought to help people realize their full potential; in fact, such therapists called them *clients* rather than *patients*. In this relationship, the therapist and the client (unlike the psychoanalyst and the patient) were on equal footing. The development of the humanistic perspective was one more reason why Freud's ideas eventually became less influential.

humanistic psychology An approach to understanding human nature that emphasizes the positive potential of human beings.

Humanistic psychology offered a positive view of human nature that matched the zeitgeist of the 1960s.

© United Archives GmbH/Alamy

behaviorism An approach that advocates that psychologists restrict themselves to the scientific study of objectively observable behavior.

stimulus Sensory input from the environment.

response An action or physiological change elicited by a stimulus.

reinforcement The consequences of a behavior determine whether it will be more or less likely to occur again.

SUMMARY QUIZ [1.2]

1. To understand human behavior, Jean-Martin Charcot studied people
    a. who appeared to be completely healthy.
    b. with psychological disorders.
    c. with damage in particular areas of the brain.
    d. who had suffered permanent loss of cognitive and motor function.

2. Building on the work of Charcot and others, Sigmund Freud developed
    a. psychoanalytic theory.
    b. the theory of hysteria.
    c. humanistic psychology.
    d. physiological psychology.

3. The psychological theory that emphasizes the positive potential of human beings is known as
    a. structuralism.
    b. psychoanalytic theory.
    c. humanistic psychology.
    d. functionalism.

The Search for Objective Measurement: Behaviorism Takes Center Stage

The schools of psychological thought that had developed by the early 20th century—structuralism, functionalism, and psychoanalysis—differed substantially from one another. But they shared an important similarity: Each tried to understand the inner workings of the mind by examining what the owners of those minds had to say about them. People reported on their perceptions, thoughts, memories, and feelings, and psychologists used those data to figure out what was going on inside. But some psychologists found these kinds of data to be distressingly imprecise and subjective, and as the 20th century unfolded, these psychologists developed a new approach. **Behaviorism** was *the idea that psychology should restrict itself to studying objectively observable behavior,* and it represented a dramatic departure from previous schools of thought.

Watson and the Emergence of Behaviorism

John Broadus Watson (1878–1958) believed that private experience could never be a proper object of scientific inquiry. Science required replicable, objective measurements of phenomena that are accessible to all observers, and verbal reports of subjective experience did not pass that test. So instead of asking people to report on their mental lives, Watson proposed that psychologists should instead study behavior—what people *do,* rather than what people *say*—because behavior can be measured reliably and objectively.

> **? How did behaviorism help psychology advance as a science?**

Watson was deeply interested in the work of Russian physiologist Ivan Pavlov (1849–1936), who studied digestion in dogs. In the course of his work, Pavlov had noticed that his dogs not only salivated at the sight of food, but they also salivated at the sight of the person who fed them. The feeders were not dressed in Alpo suits, so why should the mere sight of people trigger a basic

In 1894, a student of Titchener's, Margaret Floy Washburn (1871–1939) published an influential book, The Animal Mind. She reviewed what was then known about perception, learning, and memory in different animal species. She argued that nonhuman animals, much like human animals, have conscious mental experiences (Scarborough & Furumoto, 1987). Watson vehemently disagreed.

Archives of the History of American Psychology

digestive response? To answer this question, Pavlov developed a procedure in which he sounded a tone every time he fed the dogs, and then he looked to see what happened when he sounded the tone but didn't feed them. And what happened was this: They drooled! Pavlov went on to develop a hugely important theory to explain how the sound of a tone could cause a dog to drool (and you'll learn all about it in Chapter 7). He referred to the tone as the **stimulus** (which is *a sensory input from the environment*) and to salivation as the **response** (which is *a reaction to a stimulus*). Watson made these ideas the building blocks of behaviorism, which is sometimes called *stimulus–response* (S–R) psychology.

B. F. Skinner and the Development of Behaviorism

Burrhus Frederick Skinner (1904–1990) admired Pavlov's experiments and Watson's theories, but he thought something important was still missing. Pavlov's dogs had been passive participants that stood around, listened to tones, and drooled. Skinner recognized that in everyday life, animals don't just stand there—they do something! Animals *act* on their environments in order to find shelter, food, or mates, and Skinner wondered if he could develop behaviorist principles that would explain how animals learned to do all those things.

Skinner built what he called a *conditioning chamber* but that the rest of the world would forever call a *Skinner box*. The box had a lever and a food tray, and a hungry rat could get food delivered to the tray simply by pressing the lever. But rats can't read instruction manuals, so how do they learn to do this? Skinner noticed that when a rat was put in the box, it would wander around for a bit, sniffing, touching, and exploring the box. After a while, the rat would accidentally lean on the bar and then—viola!—a food pellet would appear in the tray. So the rat would lean again—and again be fed.

> **What did Skinner learn by observing the behavior of hungry rats?**

Once that happened a few times, the rat would start pressing the bar like a bongo player, stopping only when it was full. Skinner used this observation to postulate the principle of **reinforcement,** which states that *the consequences of a behavior determine whether it will be more or less likely to occur again.*

The concept of reinforcement became the foundation for Skinner's "new behaviorism" (Skinner, 1938), and he used it to solve problems in everyday life. For example, one day he was visiting his daughter's fourth-grade class when he realized that he could improve classroom learning by breaking complicated tasks into small bits and then using the principle of reinforcement to teach children each bit (Bjork, 1993). To learn a complicated math problem, for instance, students would first be asked an easy question about the simplest part of the problem. They would then be told whether the answer was right or wrong, and if a correct response was made, they would move on to a more difficult question. Skinner thought that the satisfaction of knowing they were correct would be reinforcing and help students learn.

If fourth graders and rats could be successfully trained, then why stop there? In a series of controversial popular books (Skinner, 1986; 1971), Skinner laid out his vision of a utopian society in which behavior was controlled by the judicious application of the principle of reinforcement. Skinner claimed that our subjective sense of free will is an illusion and that when we think we are exercising free will, we are actually responding to present and past patterns of reinforcement. We do things in the present that have been rewarding in the past, and our sense of "choosing" to do them is nothing more than an illusion. Not surprisingly, these claims sparked an outcry from critics who believed that Skinner was calling for a repressive society that manipulated people for its own ends. According to the great intellectual magazine, *TV Guide*,

Inspired by Watson's behaviorism, B. F. Skinner (1904–1990) investigated the way an animal learns by interacting with its environment. Here, he demonstrates the Skinner box, in which rats learn to press a lever to receive food.

Nina Leen/Time Life Pictures/Getty Images

Skinner's well-publicized questioning of such cherished notions as free will led to a rumor that he had raised his own daughter in a Skinner box. This urban legend, while untrue, likely originated from the climate-controlled, glass-encased crib that he invented to protect his daughter from the cold Minnesota winter. Skinner marketed the crib under various names, including the "Air-crib" and the "Heir Conditioner," but it failed to catch on with parents.

Bettmann/Corbis

illusions Errors of perception, memory, or judgment in which subjective experience differs from objective reality.

Gestalt psychology A psychological approach that emphasizes that we often perceive the whole rather than the sum of the parts.

cognitive psychology The scientific study of mental processes, including perception, thought, memory, and reasoning.

Skinner was advocating "the taming of mankind through a system of dog obedience schools for all" (Bjork, 1993, p. 201). In fact, Skinner was merely suggesting that knowledge of the principles that govern human behavior could be used to increase human well-being. In any case, the controversy certainly increased Skinner's well-being: A popular magazine that listed the 100 most important people who ever lived ranked him just 39 points below Jesus Christ (Herrnstein, 1977).

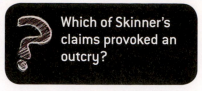
Which of Skinner's claims provoked an outcry?

SUMMARY QUIZ [1.3]

1. Behaviorism involves the study of
   a. observable actions and responses.
   b. the potential for human growth.
   c. unconscious influences and childhood experiences.
   d. human behavior and memory.

2. The experiments of Ivan Pavlov and John Watson centered on
   a. perception and behavior.
   b. stimulus and response.
   c. reward and punishment.
   d. conscious and unconscious behavior.

3. Who developed the concept of reinforcement?
   a. B. F. Skinner
   b. Ivan Pavlov
   c. John Watson
   d. Margaret Floy Washburn

Return of the Mind: Psychology Expands

Behaviorism dominated psychology from the 1930s to the 1950s. As the psychologist Ulric Neisser recalled, "Behaviorism was the basic framework for almost all of psychology at the time…That was the age when it was supposed that no psychological phenomenon was real unless you could demonstrate it in a rat" (quoted in Baars, 1986, p. 275). But behaviorism wouldn't dominate the field forever, and Neisser himself would play an important role in developing the perspective that replaced it.

The Pioneers of Cognitive Psychology

Even at the height of behaviorism, a few psychologists continued to study mental processes. For example, the German psychologist Max Wertheimer (1880–1943) studied psychological **illusions,** which are *errors of perception, memory, or judgment in which subjective experience differs from objective reality.* In one of Wertheimer's experiments, two lights flashed quickly on a screen, one after the other. When the time between the two flashes was relatively long (one fifth of a second or more), observers correctly reported seeing two lights going on and off in sequence. But when Wertheimer reduced the time between flashes to around one twentieth of a second, observers incorrectly

What do you see when you look at this image? Why do you see more than just random markings?

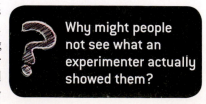
Why might people not see what an experimenter actually showed them?

reported seeing a single light moving back and forth (Fancher, 1979; Sarris, 1989). Wertheimer argued that during perception, the mind brings many disparate elements together and combines them into a unified whole, which in German is called a *gestalt*. Wertheimer's ideas led to the development of **Gestalt psychology,** *a psychological approach that emphasizes the active role that the mind plays in generating perceptual experience.* According to Gestalt psychology, the mind imposes organization on what it perceives. The German psychologist Kurt Lewin (1890–1947) was strongly influenced by Gestalt psychology and argued that the best way to predict a person's behavior was not to understand the stimuli to which they were responding, but to understand their subjective interpretation or *construal* of those stimuli. A pinch on the cheek can be pleasant or unpleasant depending on who we think has administered it and under what circumstances (as well as to which set of cheeks). For Lewin, the person's inner experience was paramount.

In the 1930s and 1940s, most psychologists ignored Wertheimer and Lewin—and ignored mental processes as well. In the 1950s, that was changed—not by yet another German psychologist, but by the invention of the computer. Although people and computers differ in important ways, both seem to register, store, and retrieve information, which led some psychologists to wonder whether the computer might be useful as a model for the human mind. Computers are information-processing systems, and the flow of information through their circuits is clearly no fairy tale. If mental events—such

Kurt Lewin argued that people react to the world as they see it and not to the world as it is.

as remembering, thinking, believing, evaluating, feeling, and assessing—were simply words we use to describe different kinds of information processing, then the events that took place inside a human mind could be studied as objectively as the events that took place inside a computer. This way of thinking gave rise to a new approach called **cognitive psychology,** which is *the scientific study of mental processes, including perception, thought, memory, and reasoning.*

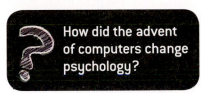

? How did the advent of computers change psychology?

For example, during World War II, the military turned to psychologists to help understand how soldiers could best learn to use new technologies, such as radar. Radar operators had to pay close attention to their screens for long periods while trying to decide whether blips were friendly aircraft, enemy aircraft, or flocks of wild geese in need of a good chasing (Ashcraft, 1998; Lachman, Lachman, & Butterfield, 1979). How could radar operators be trained to make quicker and more accurate decisions? The British psychologist Donald Broadbent (1926–93) observed that pilots can't attend to many different instruments at once and must actively move the focus of their attention from one to another (Best, 1992). Broadbent (1958) showed that the limited capacity to handle incoming information is a fundamental feature of human cognition and that this limit could explain many of the errors that pilots (and other people) made. At about the same time, the American psychologist George Miller (1956) pointed

This 1950s computer was among the first generation of digital computers. How was the computer analogy helpful in the early days of cognitive psychology?

out a striking consistency in our capacity limitations across a variety of situations—we can pay attention to and briefly hold in memory about seven (give or take two) pieces of information. Cognitive psychologists began conducting experiments

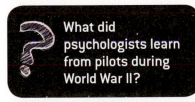

? What did psychologists learn from pilots during World War II?

and devising theories to better understand the mind's limited capacity.

The emergence of cognitive psychology was made possible by the advent of the computer, but it was also energized by the appearance of a book by B. F. Skinner called *Verbal Behavior,* which offered a

Shutterstock

Noam Chomsky (b. 1928) pointed out that even young children generate sentences they have never heard before—and therefore could not possibly be learning language by reinforcement. This critique of Skinner's theory signaled the end of behaviorism's dominance in psychology and helped spark the development of cognitive psychology.

behaviorist analysis of language (Skinner, 1957). But linguist Noam Chomsky (b. 1928) thought that Skinner's unwillingness to talk about the mind had led him to seriously misunderstand the nature of human language. Chomsky argued that just as a computer program contains a set of step-by-step rules for generating output, language relies on mental rules that allow people to understand and produce novel words and sentences. The ability of even the youngest child to generate new sentences that he or she had never heard before flew in the face of Skinner's claim that children learn to use language the same way that rats learn to press levers—namely, by reinforcement. Chomsky provided a clever, detailed, and thoroughly cognitive account of language that explained many of the phenomena that Skinner's account could not (Chomsky, 1959). These and other developments set the stage for an explosion of research in cognitive psychology, which dominated the landscape of academic psychology for the next 25 years.

The Brain Meets the Mind: The Rise of Cognitive Neuroscience

If cognitive psychologists studied the software of the mind, they had little to say about the hardware of the brain. And yet, as any computer scientist knows, the relationship between software and hardware is crucial: Each element needs the other to get the job done. Our mental activities often seem so natural and effortless—noticing the shape of an object, using words in speech or writing, recognizing a face as familiar—that we fail to appreciate the fact that they depend on intricate operations carried out by the brain. This dependence is revealed by dramatic cases in which damage to a particular part of the brain causes a person to lose a specific cognitive ability. Recall Broca's patient who, after damage to a limited area in the left side of the brain, could not produce words, even though he could understand them perfectly well. Such striking—sometimes startling—cases remind us that even the simplest cognitive processes depend on the brain.

Karl Lashley (1890–1958), a psychologist who studied with John Watson, conducted a famous series of studies in which he trained rats to run mazes, surgically removed parts of their brains, and then measured how well they could run the maze again. Lashley hoped to find the precise spot in the brain where *learning* occurred. Alas, no one spot seemed to uniquely and reliably eliminate learning (Lashley, 1960). Rather, Lashley simply found that the more of the rat's brain he removed, the more poorly the rat ran the maze. Lashley was frustrated by his inability to identify a specific site of learning, but his efforts inspired other scientists to take up the challenge. They developed a research area called *physiological psychology*. Today, this area has grown into **behavioral neuroscience,** *an approach to psychology that links psychological processes to activities in the nervous system and other bodily processes.* To learn about the relationship between brain and behavior, behavioral neuroscientists observe animals' responses as the animals perform specially constructed tasks, such as running through a maze to obtain food rewards. The neuroscientists can record electrical or chemical responses in the brain as the task is being performed, or they can later remove specific parts of the brain to see how performance is affected.

Of course, experimental brain surgery cannot ethically be performed on human beings; thus, psychologists who want to study the human brain often have to rely on nature's cruel and inexact

behavioral neuroscience An approach to psychology that links psychological processes to activities in the nervous system and other bodily processes.

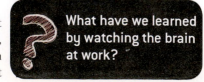
What have we learned by watching the brain at work?

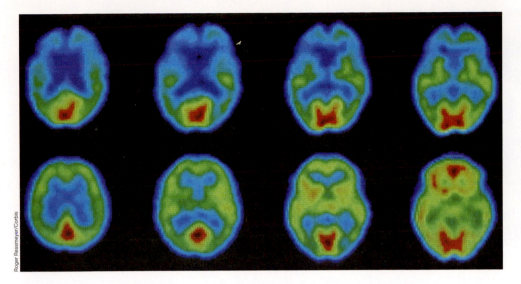

FIGURE 1.1 PET Scans of Healthy and Alzheimer's Brains PET scans are one of a variety of brain imaging technologies that psychologists use to observe the living brain. The four brain images on the top each come from a person suffering from Alzheimer's disease; the four on the bottom each come from a healthy person of similar age. The red and green areas reflect higher levels of brain activity compared to the blue areas, which reflect lower levels of activity. In each image, the front of the brain is on the top, and the back of the brain is on the bottom. You can see that the person with Alzheimer's disease, compared with the healthy person, shows more extensive areas of lowered activity toward the front of the brain.

Roger Ressmeyer/Corbis

experiments. Birth defects, accidents, and illnesses often cause damage to particular brain regions, and if that damage disrupts a particular ability, then psychologists deduce that the region is involved in producing the ability. For example, in the Memory chapter, you'll learn about a patient whose memory was virtually eliminated by damage to a specific part of the brain, and you'll see how this tragedy provided scientists with remarkable clues about how memories are stored (Scoville & Milner, 1957). But in the late 1980s, technological breakthroughs led to the development of noninvasive brain scanning techniques that made it possible for psychologists to watch what happens inside a human brain as a person performs a task such as reading, imagining, listening, and remembering (see **FIGURE 1.1**). Brain scanning is an invaluable tool because it allows us to observe the brain in action and to see which parts are involved in which operations (see the Neuroscience and Behavior chapter). In fact, there's a name for this area of research. **Cognitive neuroscience** is the *field of study that attempts to understand the links between cognitive processes and brain activity* (Gazzaniga, 2000).

The Evolved Mind: The Emergence of Evolutionary Psychology

Psychology's renewed interest in mental processes and its growing interest in the brain were two developments that led psychologists away from behaviorism. A third development also pointed them in a different direction. Recall that one of behaviorism's key claims was that organisms are blank slates on which experience writes its lessons, and hence any one lesson should be as easily written as another. But in experiments conducted during the 1960s and 1970s, psychologist John Garcia and his colleagues showed that rats can learn to associate nausea with the smell of food much more quickly than they can learn to associate nausea with a flashing light (Garcia, 1981). Why should this be? In the real world of forests, sewers, and garbage cans, nausea is usually caused by spoiled food and not by lightning, and although these particular rats had been born in a laboratory and had never left their cages, millions of years of evolution had prepared their brains to learn the natural associations causing nausea more quickly than the artificial one. In other words, it was not only the rat's learning history but the rat's *ancestors'* learning histories that determined the rat's ability to learn.

cognitive neuroscience The field of study that attempts to understand the links between cognitive processes and brain activity.

In 1925, schoolteacher John Scopes was arrested for teaching students about Darwin's theory of evolution. Today, that theory is the centerpiece of modern biology—and of evolutionary psychology.

Behaviorists explain behavior in terms of organisms learning to make particular responses that are paired with reinforcement (and to avoid responses that are paired with punishment). Evolutionary psychology focuses on how abilities are preserved over time if they contribute to an organism's ability to survive and reproduce. How might a proponent of each approach explain the fact that a rat placed in an unfamiliar environment will tend to stay in dark corners and avoid brightly lit open areas?

Although that fact was at odds with the behaviorist doctrine, it was the credo for a new kind of psychology. **Evolutionary psychology** *explains mind and behavior in terms of the adaptive value of abilities that are preserved over time by natural selection.* Evolutionary psychology has its roots in Charles Darwin's theory of natural selection, which, as we saw earlier, holds that the features of an organism that help it survive and reproduce are more likely than other features to be passed on to subsequent generations. Evolutionary psychologists think of the mind as a collection of specialized "modules" that are designed to solve the human problems our ancestors faced as they attempted to eat, mate, and reproduce over millions of years. According to evolutionary psychology, the brain is not an all-purpose computer that can do or learn one thing just as easily as it can do or learn another; rather, it is a computer that was built to do a few things well and everything else not at all. It is a computer that comes with a small suite of built-in applications that are designed to do the things that previous versions of that computer needed to have done.

Consider, for example, how evolutionary psychology treats the emotion of jealousy. All of us who have been in romantic relationships have experienced jealousy, if only because we noticed our partner noticing someone else. Jealousy can be a powerful, overwhelming emotion that we might wish to avoid, but according to evolutionary psychology, it exists today because it once served an adaptive function. If some of our hominid ancestors experienced jealousy and others did not, then the ones who experienced it might have been more likely to guard their mates and aggress against their rivals and thus may have been more likely to reproduce their "jealous genes" (Buss, 2000, 2007; Buss & Haselton, 2005).

Critics of the evolutionary approach point out that many current traits of people and other animals probably evolved to serve different functions than those they currently serve. For example, biologists believe that the feathers of birds probably evolved initially to perform such functions as regulating body temperature or capturing prey and only later served the entirely different function of flight. Likewise, people are reasonably adept at learning to drive a car, but nobody would argue that such an ability is the result of natural selection; the learning abilities that allow us to become skilled car drivers must have evolved for purposes other than driving cars.

Complications such as these have led the critics to wonder how evolutionary hypotheses can ever be tested (Coyne, 2000; Sterelny & Griffiths, 1999). We don't have a record of our ancestors' thoughts, feelings, and actions, and fossils won't provide much information about the evolution of mind and behavior. Testing ideas about the evolutionary origins of psychological phenomena is indeed a challenging task, but it is not an impossible one (Buss et al., 1998; Pinker, 1997a, 1997b).

Start with the assumption that evolutionary adaptations should also increase reproductive success. So if a specific trait or feature has been favored by natural selection, it should be possible to find some evidence of natural selection at work in the numbers of offspring that are produced by the trait's bearers. Consider, for instance, the hypothesis that men tend to have deep voices because women prefer to mate with baritones rather than sopranos. To investigate this hypothesis, researchers studied a group of modern hunter–gatherers, the Hadza people of Tanzania. Consistent with the evolutionary hypothesis, the researchers found that the pitch of a man's voice did indeed predict how many children he would have, but the pitch of a woman's voice did not (Apicella, Feinberg, & Marlowe, 2007). This kind of study provides evidence that allows evolutionary psychologists to test their ideas. Not every evolutionary hypothesis can be tested, of course, but evolutionary psychologists are becoming increasingly inventive in their attempts.

SUMMARY QUIZ [1.4]

1. The study of mental processes such as perception and memory is called
   a. behavioral determinism.
   b. Gestalt psychology.
   c. social psychology.
   d. cognitive psychology.

2. During World War II, cognitive psychologists discovered that many of the errors pilots make are the result of
   a. computer errors in processing detailed information.
   b. limited human cognitive capacity to handle incoming information.
   c. pilot inattention to incoming information.
   d. lack of behavioral training.

3. The use of scanning techniques to observe the brain in action and to see which parts are involved in which operations helped the development of
   a. evolutionary psychology.
   b. cognitive neuroscience.
   c. behaviorism.
   d. cognitive accounts of language formation.

4. Central to evolutionary psychology is the _____ function that minds and brains serve.
   a. emotional
   b. adaptive
   c. cultural
   d. physiological

Beyond the Individual: Social and Cultural Perspectives

Although psychologists often focus on the brains and minds of individuals, they have not lost sight of the fact that human beings are fundamentally social animals who are part of a vast network of family, friends, and acquaintances. Trying to understand people in the absence of that fact is a bit like trying to understand an ant or a bee without considering the function and influence of the colony or hive. People are the most important and most complex organisms that we ever encounter, so it is not too surprising that our behavior is strongly influenced by their presence—or their absence. The two areas of psychology that most strongly emphasize these facts are social and cultural psychology.

Social psychology is *the study of the causes and consequences of sociality.* Social psychology's development began in earnest in the 1930s and was driven by several historical events. The rise of Nazism led many of Germany's most talented scientists (such as Kurt Lewin) to flee to America and to watch from another shore as their homeland was commandeered by a madman who turned their former friends and neighbors into genocidal soldiers. Philosophers had speculated about the nature of

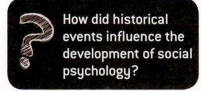

How did historical events influence the development of social psychology?

evolutionary psychology A psychological approach that explains mind and behavior in terms of the adaptive value of abilities that are preserved over time by natural selection.

social psychology The study of the causes and consequences of sociality.

Social psychology studies how the thoughts, feelings, and behaviors of individuals can be influenced by the presence of others. Members of the Reverend Sun Myung Moon's Unification Church are often married to one another in ceremonies of 10,000 people or more; in some cases, couples didn't know each other before the wedding began. Social movements such as this have the power to sway individuals.

Ap Photo/Ahn Young-Joon

cultural psychology The study of how cultures reflect and shape the psychological processes of their members.

The symptoms of some mental disorders can be reported differently across different cultures. Cultural psychology studies the similarities and differences in psychological processes that arise between people living in different cultures.

Deco/Alamy

sociality for thousands of years, and political scientists, economists, anthropologists, and sociologists had been studying social life scientifically for some time. But these German refugees were the first to generate theories of social behavior that resembled the theories generated by natural scientists, and more importantly, these refugees were the first to conduct experiments to test their social theories. For example, social psychologists who studied conformity discovered that most people will say something they know to be untrue if they see other people doing the same thing (Asch, 1956). Most people will do something that they know to be immoral if they are ordered to do so by an authority figure (Milgram, 1974).

Of course, "most people" meant "most White college-educated North Americans" because those were the people whom early psychologists could most easily study. But people in different places often think, feel, and behave differently, and modern psychologists are interested in those differences. Culture refers to the values, traditions, and beliefs that are shared by a particular group of people. Although we usually think of culture in terms of nationality and ethnic groups, cultures can also be defined by age (youth culture), sexual orientation (gay culture), religion (Jewish culture), or occupation (academic culture). **Cultural psychology** is *the study of how cultures reflect and shape the psychological processes of their members* (Shweder & Sullivan, 1993). Cultural psychologists study a wide range of phenomena, ranging from visual perception to social interaction, as they seek to understand which of these phenomena are universal and which vary from place to place and time to time (Cole, 1996; Segall, Lonner, & Berry, 1998). For example, the age of a person's earliest memory differs dramatically across cultures (MacDonald, Uesiliana, & Hayne, 2000), whereas judgments of facial attractiveness do not (Cunningham et al., 1995). We'll highlight the work of cultural psychologists throughout the text and in Culture & Community boxes like the one in this section concerning cultural differences in analytic and holistic styles of processing information.

Culture & Community

Analytic and Holistic Styles in Western and Eastern Cultures

The study of cultural influences on mind and behavior has increased dramatically over the past decade. An especially intriguing line of research has revealed differences in how the world is viewed by people from Western cultures, such as North America and Europe, and Eastern cultures, such as China, Japan, Korea, and other Asian countries. One of the most consistently observed differences is that people from Western cultures tend to adopt an *analytic* style of processing information, focusing on an object or person without paying much attention to the surrounding context, whereas people from Eastern cultures tend to adopt a *holistic* style that emphasizes the relationship between an object or person and the surrounding context (Nisbett & Miyamoto, 2005).

This difference is illustrated nicely by a study in which American and Japanese participants performed a novel task, called the *framed-line test*, which assesses how well an individual incorporates or ignores contextual information when making a judgment about a simple line stimulus (Kitayama et al., 2003). As shown in the accompanying figure, participants saw a line inside a square. They were asked to draw the line again in a new square. Either the line had to be exactly the same length as the original stimulus (the absolute task), or the length of the line in the new square had to be in the same proportion to the height of its frame as the length of the original line relative to the height of the original frame (the relative task). The absolute task engages analytic processing, whereas the relative task draws on holistic processing. The researchers found that American participants living in the United States were more accurate on the absolute task than on the relative task, whereas Japanese participants living in Japan were more accurate on the relative task than on the absolute task. Interestingly, Americans living in Japan performed more like Japanese participants, and Japanese living in the United States performed more like American participants. While we don't yet know how long it takes for a culture to produce a shift from an analytic style to a holistic style or vice versa, research on cultural influences continues to develop rapidly, and we are even beginning to obtain some clues about how differences between individuals from Eastern and Western cultures are realized in the brain (Kitayama & Uskul, 2011).

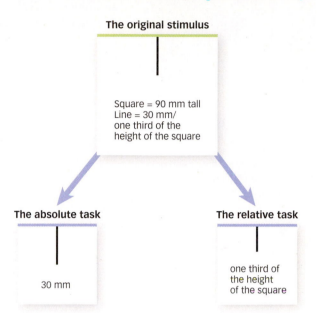

The original stimulus

Square = 90 mm tall
Line = 30 mm/
one third of the
height of the square

The absolute task

30 mm

The relative task

one third of
the height
of the square

SUMMARY QUIZ [1.5]

1. Social psychology differs most from other psychological approaches in its emphasis on
   a. human interaction.
   b. behavioral processes.
   c. the individual.
   d. laboratory experimentation.

2. Cultural psychology emphasizes that
   a. all psychological processes are influenced to some extent by culture.
   b. psychological processes are the same across all human beings, regardless of culture.
   c. culture shapes some but not all psychological phenomena.
   d. insights gained from studying individuals from one culture will only rarely generalize to individuals from other cultures, who have different social identities and rituals.

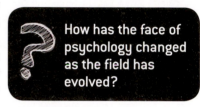

Mary Whiton Calkins (1863–1930), the first woman elected APA president, suffered from the sex discrimination that was common during her lifetime. Despite academic setbacks (such as Harvard University refusing to grant women an official PhD), Calkins went on to a distinguished career in research and teaching at Wellesley College.

The Profession of Psychology: Past and Present

In 1892, William James and six other psychologists came together for a meeting at Clark University. Although there were too few of them to make up a jury or even a respectable hockey team, these seven men decided that it was time to form an organization that represented psychology as a profession, and on that day, the American Psychological Association (APA) was born. The seven psychologists could scarcely have imagined that today their little club would have more than 150,000 members from all over the world. Although all of the original members were professors, 70% of the current members work in clinical and health-related settings instead of colleges and universities. Because the APA is no longer as focused on academic psychology as it once was, the Association for Psychological Science (APS) was founded in 1988 to focus specifically on the needs of research psychologists. Today, it has about 12,000 members.

The Growing Role of Women and Minorities

In 1892, the APA had 31 members, all of whom were White men. Today, about half of all APA members are women, and the percentage of non-White members continues to grow. Surveys of recent PhD recipients reveal a picture of increasing diversification in the field. In 1950, women represented only 15% of all students receiving PhDs in psychology, but that proportion had grown to 70% in 2010, and the proportion of racial minorities grew from a very small number to 24% during that same period. Clearly, psychology is increasingly reflecting the diversity of American society.

How has the face of psychology changed as the field has evolved?

The current involvement of women and minorities in the APA and in psychology more generally can be traced to early pioneers who blazed a trail that others followed. In 1905, Mary Whiton Calkins (1863–1930) became the first woman to serve as president of the APA. Calkins studied with William James at Harvard and later became a professor of psychology at Wellesley College. In her presidential address to the APA, Calkins described her theory of the role of the "self" in psychological function. Arguing against Wundt's structuralist ideas that the mind can be dissected into components, Calkins claimed that the self is a single unit that cannot be broken down into individual parts. Calkins wrote four books and published over 100 articles during her illustrious career (Calkins, 1930; Scarborough & Furumoto, 1987; Stevens & Gardner, 1982). Today, women play leading roles in all areas of psychology. Some of the men who formed the APA might have been surprised by the prominence of women in the field today, but we suspect that William James, a strong supporter of Mary Calkins, would not be one of them.

Kenneth B. Clark (1914–2005) studied the developmental effects of prejudice, discrimination, and segregation on children. Clark's research was cited by the U.S. Supreme Court in its decision for the landmark *Brown* v. *Board of Education* case that ended school segregation.

Just as there were no women at the first meeting of the APA, there weren't any non-White people either. The first member of a minority group to become president of the APA was Kenneth Clark (1914–2005), who was elected in 1970. Clark studied the self-image of African American children and argued that segregation of the races creates great psychological harm. Clark's conclusions had a large influence on public policy, and his research contributed to the Supreme Court's 1954 ruling (*Brown* v. *Board of Education*) to outlaw segregation in public schools (Guthrie, 2000). Clark's interest in psychology was sparked as an undergraduate at Howard University, when he took a course offered by Francis Cecil Sumner (1895–1954), who was the first African American to receive a PhD in psychology (from Clark University in 1920). Sumner's main interest was on the education of African American youth (Sawyer, 2000).

William E. Sauro/New York Times Co/Getty Images

What Psychologists Do: Research Careers

Before describing what psychologists do, it should be noted that most people who major in psychology do not go on to become psychologists. Psychology has become a major academic, scientific, and professional discipline with links to many other disciplines and career paths (see the Hot Science box). That being said, what should you do if you *do* want to become a psychologist, and what should you fail to do if you desperately want to avoid it? You can become "a psychologist" by a variety of routes, and the people who call themselves psychologists may hold a variety of different degrees. Students intending to pursue careers in psychology typically finish college and enter graduate school in order to obtain a PhD (or doctor of philosophy) degree in some particular area of psychology (e.g., social, cognitive, developmental). During graduate school, students generally gain exposure to the field by taking classes and learn to conduct research by collaborating with their professors. Although William James was able to master every area of psychology because the areas were so small during his lifetime, today a student can spend the better part of a decade mastering just one.

After receiving a PhD, students often go on for more specialized research training by pursuing a postdoctoral fellowship under the supervision of an established researcher in his or her area, or they apply for a faculty position at a college or university or a research position in government or industry. Academic careers usually involve a combination of teaching and research, whereas careers in government or industry are typically dedicated to research alone.

FIGURE 1.2 The Major Subfields in Psychology Psychologists are drawn to many different subfields in psychology. Here are the percentages of people receiving PhDs in various subfields. Clinical psychology makes up almost half of the doctorates awarded in psychology. *Source:* 2004 Graduate Study in Psychology. Compiled by APA Research Office.

Clinical neuropsychology 3%; Counseling 7%; Health 1%; School/Educational 8%; Other applied subfields 5%; Cognitive 3%; Developmental 5%; Experimental 1%; Industrial/Organizational 4%; Neuroscience/Physiological/Biological 3%; Social & personality 4%; Other research subfields 7%; Clinical 47%

The Variety of Career Paths

But research is not the only career option for a psychologist. Most people who call themselves psychologists neither teach nor do research, but rather, they assess or treat people with psychological problems. Most of these *clinical psychologists* work in private practice, often in partnerships with other psychologists or with psychiatrists (who have earned an MD, or medical degree, and are allowed to prescribe medication). Other clinical psychologists work in hospitals or medical schools, some have faculty positions at universities or colleges, and some combine private practice with an academic job. Many clinical psychologists focus on specific problems or disorders, such as depression or anxiety, whereas others focus on specific populations, such as children, ethnic minority groups, or older adults (see **FIGURE 1.2**). Just over 10% of APA members are *counseling psychologists,* who assist people in dealing with work or

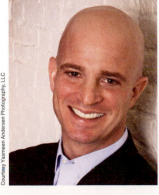
Michael Friedman

Shirley Wang

Betsy Stevens

A person earning a PhD in psychology can go on to a wide range of fields, like these three: a practicing clinical psychologist in New York City, a science and health journalist for a major news outlet, and a behavioral scientist for an international affairs consulting firm.

Hot Science

Psychology as a Hub Science

This chapter describes how psychology emerged as a field of study and illustrates some of the ways in which psychology is indeed a *scientific* field of study. But where does psychology stand in relation to other areas of science? With recent advances in computing and electronic record keeping, researchers are now able to literally create maps of science. Information about scientific articles, about the journals in which they are published, and about the frequency and patterns with which articles in one field are cited by articles in another field is now fully electronic and available online (in the Science Citation and Social Science Citation Indexes).

As an example, in an article called "Mapping the Backbone of Science," Kevin Boyack and his colleagues (2005) used data from more than 1 million articles, with more than 23 million references, published in more than 7,000 journals, to create a map showing the similarities and interconnectedness of different areas of science based on how frequently journal articles from different disciplines cite each other. The results are fascinating. As shown in the figure, seven major fields, or "hub sciences," emerged in the data: math, physics, chemistry, earth sciences, medicine, *psychology*, and social science. There were also smaller subfields that fell between the hub sciences: public health and neurology fall between psychology and medicine, statistics between psychology and math, and economics between social science and math.

Another study, which used data from more than 6 million citations found in more than 6,000 journals, led to the creation of a map of citation patterns focusing only on citations to articles published in a recent five-year period (in this case from 2000–2004; Rosvall & Bergstrom, 2008). In that analysis, psychology again emerged as a major scientific hub (see the figure on the right), with strong links (based on the frequency of citations of work in journals in each field) to neuroscience, psychiatry, education, sociology, business and marketing,

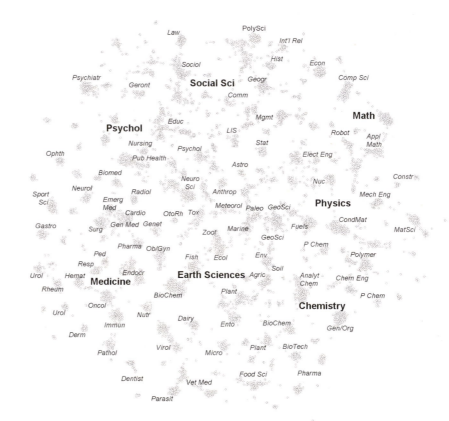

Boyack, Kevin W. Klavans, Richard, and Borner, Katy. Mapping the backbone of science. Scientometrics, Vol. 64, No. 3 (2005) 351-374. ©2005, Springer-Verlag/Akademiai Diado

career issues and changes or help people deal with common crises such as divorce, the loss of a job, or the death of a loved one.

Psychologists are also quite active in educational settings. About 5% of APA members are *school psychologists,* who offer guidance to students, parents, and teachers. A similar proportion of APA members, known as *industrial/organizational psychologists,* focus on issues in the workplace. These psychologists typically work in business or industry and may be involved in assessing potential employees, finding ways to improve productivity, or in helping staff and management to develop effective planning strategies for coping with change or

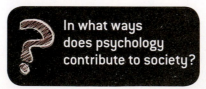

In what ways does psychology contribute to society?

and medicine. More recent and larger studies continue to support the overall structure of these maps of science (Börner et al., 2012).

Studies like these are useful to university administrators, funding agencies, and also to students to help them understand the relationships between different academic departments and how the scientific work of one field relates to the scientific field more broadly. They also show the reach of psychology to other disciplines and support the idea that knowledge about psychology has relevance for many related disciplines and career paths. Good thing you are taking this class!

Roswall, Martin and Bergstrom, Carl T., Maps of random walks on complex networks reveal community structure. PNAS, Jan. 29, 2008, Vol. 105, No. 2, p. 1118

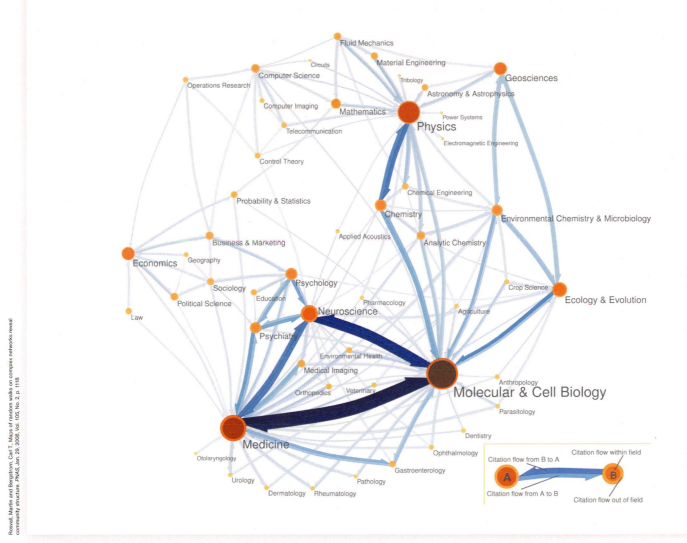

anticipated future developments. Of course, this brief list doesn't begin to cover all the different career paths that someone with training in psychology might take. For instance, sports psychologists help athletes improve their performances, forensic psychologists assist attorneys and courts, and consumer psychologists help companies develop and advertise new products. Indeed, we can't think of any major enterprise that *doesn't* employ psychologists.

Even this brief and incomplete survey of the APA membership provides a sense of the wide variety of contexts in which psychologists operate. You can think of psychology as an international community of professionals devoted to advancing scientific knowledge; assisting people with psychological problems and disorders; and trying to enhance the quality of life in work, school, and other everyday settings.

DATA VISUALIZATION

Understanding How to Read and Use (or misuse!) Data

www.macmillanhighered.com/ schacterbrief3e

SUMMARY QUIZ [1.6]

1. Mary Whiton Calkins
   a. studied with Wilhelm Wundt in the first psychology laboratory.
   b. did research on the self-image of African American children.
   c. was present at the first meeting of the APA.
   d. became the first woman president of the APA.

2. Kenneth Clark
   a. did research that influenced the Supreme Court decision to ban segregation in public schools.
   b. was one of the founders of the APA.
   c. was a student of William James.
   d. did research that focused on the education of African American youth.

CHAPTER REVIEW

SUMMARY

Psychology's Roots: The Path to a Science of Mind

> Philosophers have pondered and debated ideas about human nature for millennia, but they did not provide empirical evidence to support their claims.

> Some of the earliest successful efforts to develop a science linking mind and behavior came from studies showing that damage to the brain can result in impairments of behavior and mental functions.

> Helmholtz furthered the science of the mind by developing methods for measuring reaction time. His student Wundt is credited with founding psychology as a scientific discipline, and he espoused structuralism: the idea that the mind could be understood by analyzing its basic elements.

> William James applied Darwin's theory of natural selection to the study of the mind. His functionalist approach focused on how mental processes serve to enable people to adapt to their environments.

The Development of Clinical Psychology

> Psychologists have often focused on patients with psychological disorders as a way of understanding human behavior.

> Freud developed psychoanalysis, which emphasized the importance of unconscious influences and childhood experiences in shaping thoughts, feelings, and behavior.

> Humanistic psychologists suggested that people are inherently disposed toward growth and can usually reach their full potential with a little help from their friends.

The Search for Objective Measurement: Behaviorism Takes Center Stage

> Behaviorism advocated the study of observable actions and responses and held that inner mental processes were private events that could not be studied scientifically.

> Pavlov and Watson studied the association between a stimulus and a response and emphasized the importance of the environment in shaping behavior.

> Skinner developed the concept of reinforcement, which states that animals and humans repeat behaviors that generate pleasant results and avoid performing those that generate unpleasant results.

The Return of the Mind: Psychology Expands

> Cognitive psychologists study the inner workings of the mind and focus on inner mental processes such as perception, thought, memory, and reasoning.

> Cognitive neuroscience attempts to link the brain with the mind by studying individuals with and without brain damage.

> Evolutionary psychology both focuses on the adaptive function that minds and brains serve and seeks to understand the nature and origin of psychological processes in terms of natural selection.

Beyond the Individual: Social and Cultural Perspectives

> Social psychology recognizes that people exist as part of a network of other people and examines how individuals influence and interact with one another.

> Cultural psychology is concerned with the effects of the broader culture on individuals and with similarities and differences among people in different cultures.

The Profession of Psychology: Past and Present

> The American Psychological Association (APA) was formed in 1892 and now includes over 150,000 members working in clinical, academic, and applied settings.

> Through the efforts of pioneers such as Mary Whiton Calkins, women have come to play an increasingly important role in the field and are now as well represented as men.

> Minority involvement in psychology took longer, but the pioneering efforts of Sumner, Clark, and others have led to increased participation of minorities in psychology.

> Psychologists prepare for research careers through graduate and postdoctoral training and work in a variety of applied settings, including schools, clinics, and industry.

KEY TERMS

psychology (p. 2)
mind (p. 2)
behavior (p. 2)
nativism (p. 3)
philosophical empiricism (p. 4)
reaction time (p. 5)
consciousness (p. 5)

structuralism (p. 5)
introspection (p. 6)
functionalism (p. 7)
natural selection (p. 7)
hysteria (p. 8)
unconscious (p. 8)
psychoanalytic theory (p. 8)

psychoanalysis (p. 8)
humanistic psychology (p. 9)
behaviorism (p. 10)
stimulus (p. 11)
response (p. 11)
reinforcement (p. 11)
illusions (p. 12)

gestalt psychology (p. 13)
cognitive psychology (p. 13)
behavioral neuroscience (p. 14)
cognitive neuroscience (p. 15)
evolutionary psychology (p. 16)
social psychology (p. 17)
cultural psychology (p. 18)

CHANGING MINDS

1. One of your classmates says that she's only taking this class because it's required for her education major. "Psychology is all about understanding mental illness and treatment. I don't know why I have to learn this stuff when I'm going to be a teacher, not a psychologist." Why should your friend reconsider her opinion? What subfields of psychology are especially important for a teacher?

2. One of your friends confesses that he really enjoys his psychology courses, but he's decided not to declare a major in psychology. "You have to get a graduate degree to do anything with a psychology major," he says, "and I don't want to stay in school for the rest of my life. I want to get out there and work in the real world." Based on what you've read in this chapter about careers in psychology, what might you tell him?

3. On May 6, you spot a news item announcing that it's the birthday of Sigmund Freud, "the father of psychology." How accurate is it to call Freud the "father of psychology"? Having read about psychol-

ogy's subfields, are there other people who are as important—or more important—than Freud?

4. One of your classmates has flipped ahead in the book and notices that there is going to be a lot of material—including an entire chapter—on the brain. "I don't see why we have to learn so much biology," he says. "I want to be a school counselor, not a brain surgeon. I don't need to understand the parts of the brain or chemical reactions in order to help people." How are the brain and the mind connected? In what specific ways might knowing about the brain help us to understand the mind?

5. Another classmate is very unsettled after reading about B. F. Skinner's claim that free will is an illusion. "Psychology always tries to treat human beings like lab rats, whose behavior can be manipulated. I have free will, and I decide what I'm going to do next." What would you tell your friend? Does an understanding of the basic principles of psychology allow us to predict every detail of what individual humans will do?

ANSWERS TO SUMMARY QUIZZES

Summary Quiz 1.1: 1. b; 2. a; 3. c; 4. d
Summary Quiz 1.2: 1. b; 2. a; 3. c
Summary Quiz 1.3: 1. a; 2. b; 3. a
Summary Quiz 1.4: 1. d; 2. b; 3. b; 4. b
Summary Quiz 1.5: 1. a; 2. c
Summary Quiz 1.6: 1. d; 2. a

Need more help? Additional resources are located in LaunchPad at:
http://www.worthpublishers.com/launchpad/schacterbrief3e

Methods in Psychology

You Can Heal Your Life has sold over 35 million copies. Its author, Louise Hay, suggests that everything that happens to us is a result of the thoughts we choose to think. She claims that she cured herself of cancer simply by changing her thoughts, and says that others can learn to do the same by buying her books, CDs, DVDs, and by attending her seminars. In a recent television interview, Hay explained how she knows that her technique is effective.

Interviewer: How do you know what you're saying is right?

Hay: Oh, my inner ding.

Interviewer: Ding?

Hay: My inner ding. It speaks to me. It feels right or it doesn't feel right. Happiness is choosing thoughts that make you feel good. It's really very simple.

Interviewer: But I hear you saying that even if there were no proof for what you believed, or even if there were scientific evidence against it, it wouldn't change.

Hay: Well, I don't believe in scientific evidence, I really don't. Science is fairly new. It hasn't been around that long. We think it's such a big deal, but it's, you know, it's just a way of looking at life.

Louise Hay says she doesn't "believe" in scientific evidence, but what could that possibly mean? After all, if Hay's techniques really do cure cancer, then even she would have to expect cancer victims who practice her techniques to have a higher rate of remission than cancer victims who don't. That isn't "a way of looking at life." It's just plain, old-fashioned, common sense—exactly the kind of common sense that lies at the heart of science.

Science tells us that the only way to know for sure whether a claim is true is to go out and have a look. But that sounds easier than it is. For example, where would you look to see whether Louise Hay's claims are true? Would you go to one of her seminars and ask people in the audience whether or not they'd been healed?

Louise Hay says she doesn't believe in scientific evidence and instead trusts her "inner ding."

Michele Asselin/Contour by Getty Images

Would you examine the medical records of people who had and hadn't bought her books? Would you invite people to sign up for a class that teaches her techniques and then wait to see how many got cancer? All of these might sound reasonable, but the fact is that none of them would be particularly informative. There are a few good ways to test claims like Louise Hay's and a whole lot of bad ways, and in this chapter, you will learn to tell one from the other. Scientists have developed powerful tools for determining when an inner ding is right and when it is wrong, and it is these tools that make science special. As the philosopher Bertrand Russell (1945, p. 527) wrote, "It is not *what* the man of science believes that distinguishes him, but *how* and *why* he believes it." That, it turns out, goes for women of science too.

We'll start by examining the general principles that guide scientific research. Next, we'll see that the methods of psychology are meant to answer two basic questions: *What* do people do, and *why* do they do it? Psychologists answer the first question by observing and measuring, and they answer the second question by looking for relationships between the measurements they make. Finally, we'll consider the unique ethical questions that confront scientists who study people and other animals.

Empiricism and the Scientific Method

When ancient Greeks sprained their ankles, caught the flu, or accidentally set their togas on fire, they had to choose between two kinds of doctors: dogmatists (from *dogmatikos,* meaning "belief"), who thought that the best way to understand illness was to develop theories about the body's functions, and empiricists (from *empeirikos,* meaning "experience"), who thought that the best way to understand illness was to observe sick people. The rivalry between these two schools of medicine didn't last long because the people who went to see dogmatists tended to die, which was bad for business. Today we use the word *dogmatism* to describe the tendency for people to cling to their assumptions, and the word **empiricism** to describe *the belief that accurate knowledge can be acquired through observation*. The fact that we can answer questions about the natural world by examining it may seem painfully obvious to you, but for most of human history, people mainly trusted authorities to answer important questions, and it is only in the last millennium (and especially in the past three centuries) that people have begun to trust their eyes and ears more than their elders.

Empiricism is the essential element of the **scientific method,** which is *a procedure for finding truth by using empirical evidence*. In essence, the scientific method suggests that when we have an idea about the world—about how bats navigate, or about why people can't forget traumatic events— we should gather empirical evidence relevant to that idea and then, if necessary, modify the idea to fit with the evidence. Scientists usually refer to an idea of this kind as a **theory,** which is *a hypothetical explanation of a natural phenomenon*. For example, we might theorize that bats navigate by making sounds and then listening

The astronomer Galileo Galilei (1564–1642) was excommunicated and sentenced to prison for sticking to his own observations of the solar system rather than accepting the teachings of the church. In 1597 he wrote to his friend and fellow astronomer Johannes Kepler (1571–1630), "What would you say of the learned here, who, replete with the pertinacity of the asp, have steadfastly refused to cast a glance through the telescope? What shall we make of this? Shall we laugh, or shall we cry?" As it turned out, the answer was *cry*.

Bettmann/Corbis

empiricism The belief that accurate knowledge can be acquired through observation.

scientific method A procedure for finding truth by using empirical evidence.

theory A hypothetical explanation of a natural phenomenon.

hypothesis A falsifiable prediction made by a theory.

empirical method A set of rules and techniques for observation.

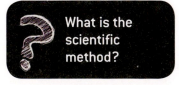

What is the scientific method?

for the echo, or that traumatic events cause the body to release chemicals that burn memories into the brain.

How do we decide if a theory is right? Theories make specific predictions about what we should observe. For example, if bats really do navigate by making sounds and then listening for echoes, then we should observe that deaf bats can't navigate. That "should" statement is technically known as a **hypothesis,** which is *a falsifiable prediction made by a theory*. The word *falsifiable* is a critical part of that definition. Some theories, such as "God created the universe," simply do not specify what we should observe if they are or are not true, and thus no observation can ever falsify them. Because these theories do not give rise to hypotheses, they can never be the subject of scientific investigation. That doesn't mean they're wrong—it just means that we can't evaluate them by using the scientific method.

So what happens when we test a hypothesis? Albert Einstein is reputed to have said: "No amount of experimentation can ever prove me right, but a single experiment can prove me wrong." Why should that be? Well, just imagine what you could learn about the navigation-by-sound theory by observing a few bats. If you saw the deaf bats navigating every bit as well as the

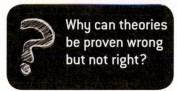

Why can theories be proven wrong but not right?

hearing bats, then the navigation-by-sound theory would instantly be proved wrong; on the other hand, if you saw the deaf bats navigating more poorly than the hearing bats, your observation would be *consistent* with the navigation-by-sound theory but would not prove it. After all, even if you didn't see a deaf bat navigating perfectly today, it is still possible that you will see one tomorrow. When evidence is consistent with a theory, it increases our confidence in that theory, but it never makes us completely certain. The next time you see a news headline that says, "Scientists prove theory *X* correct," you are hereby authorized to roll your eyes.

The scientific method suggests that the best way to learn the truth about the world is to develop theories, derive hypotheses from them, test those hypotheses by gathering evidence, and then use that evidence to modify the theories when necessary. Gathering evidence properly requires an **empirical method,** which is *a set of rules and techniques for observation*. Because human behavior is fairly easy to observe, you might expect psychology's empirical methods to be fairly simple. In fact, the methodological challenges facing psychologists are among the most daunting in all of modern science because three things make humans especially difficult to study:

> *Complexity:* No galaxy, particle, molecule, or machine is as complicated as the human brain. Scientists can describe the birth of a star or the death of a cell in exquisite detail, but they can barely begin to say how the 500 million interconnected neurons that constitute the brain give rise to the thoughts, feelings, and actions that are psychology's core concerns.

> *Variability:* In almost all the ways that matter, one *E. coli* bacterium is pretty much like another. But people are as varied as their fingerprints. No two individuals ever do, say, think, or feel exactly the same thing under exactly the same circumstances, which means that when you've seen one, you've most definitely not seen them all.

> *Reactivity:* An atom of cesium-133 oscillates 9,192,631,770 times per second regardless of whether anyone is watching. But people often think, feel, and act one way when they are being observed and a different way when they are not. When people know they are being studied, they don't always behave as they otherwise would.

Classical thinkers like Euclid and Ptolemy believed that our eyes work by emitting rays that travel to the objects we see. Ibn al-Haytham (965–1039) reasoned that if this were true, then when we open our eyes, it should take longer to see something far away than something nearby. And guess what? It doesn't. And with that single observation, a centuries-old theory vanished—in the blink of an eye.

People behave differently when they are and are not being observed. For example, President Obama might have inhibited that neck swivel if he'd realized that a photographer (as well as a rather amused French President Sarkozy) was watching him.

The fact that human beings are complex, variable, and reactive presents a major challenge to the scientific study of their behavior, but two kinds of methods allow us to meet these challenges head-on: *methods of observation* which allow us to determine what people do, and *methods of explanation* which allow us to determine why people do it. We'll examine both kinds of methods in the sections that follow.

SUMMARY QUIZ [2.1]

1. The belief that accurate knowledge can be acquired through observation is known as
   a. complexity
   b. dogmatism.
   c. empiricism.
   d. scientific research.

2. Which of the following is the best definition of a hypothesis?
   a. empirical evidence
   b. a scientific investigation
   c. a falsifiable prediction
   d. a theoretical idea

3. When people know they are being studied, they don't always behave as they otherwise would. This is known as
   a. reactivity
   b. complexity
   c. variability
   d. methodology

Observation: Discovering What People Do

To *observe* means to use one's senses to learn about the properties of an event (e.g., a storm or a parade) or an object (e.g., an apple or a person). For example, when you observe a round, red apple, your brain is using the pattern of light that is coming into your eyes to draw an inference about the apple's identity, shape, and color. That kind of informal observation is fine for buying fruit but not for doing science. Why? First, casual observations are notoriously unstable. The same apple may appear red in the daylight and crimson at night or spherical to one person and elliptical to another. Second, casual observations can't tell us about all of the properties that might interest us. No matter how long and hard you look, you will never be able to discern an apple's crunchiness or pectin content simply by watching it. Luckily, scientists have devised techniques to overcome these problems.

Measurement

The last time you said, "Can you give me a second?" you probably didn't know you were talking about atomic decay. Every unit of time has an **operational definition,** which is *a description of a property in concrete, measurable terms.* The operational

operational definition A description of a property in concrete, measurable terms.

definition of a second is *the duration of 9,192,631,770 cycles of microwave light absorbed or emitted by the hyperfine transition of cesium-133 atoms in their ground state undisturbed by external fields* (which takes roughly 6 seconds just to say). To count the cycles of light emitted as cesium-133 decays requires an **instrument,** which is *anything that can detect the condition to which an operational definition refers.* An instrument known as a "cesium clock" can count cycles of light, and when it counts 9,192,631,770 of them, one second has officially passed.

The steps we take to measure the psychological properties of a person are the same steps we take to measure the physical properties of an apple. For example, if we wanted to measure a person's intelligence, or shyness, or happiness, we would have to start by generating an operational definition of that property—that is, by specifying some concrete, measurable event that indicates it. A key feature of an operational definition is **validity,** which refers to *the goodness with which a concrete event defines a property.* For example, the concrete event called *frequency of smiling* is a valid way to define the property called *happiness* because, as we all know, people tend to smile more often when they feel happy. Do they eat more or talk more or spend more money? Well, maybe. But maybe not. And that's why food consumption or verbal output or financial expenditures would probably be regarded by most people as invalid measures of happiness (though perfectly valid measures of something else).

Once we have a valid operational definition of happiness, we just need a smile-detecting instrument, such as a computer loaded with facial-recognition software or maybe just an attentive research assistant with a pencil and a clipboard. Whatever instrument we use, it needs to have two features. First, it needs to have **reliability,** which is *the tendency for an instrument to produce the same measurement whenever it is used to measure the same thing.* For example, if a person smiles just as much on Tuesday as on Wednesday, then a smile-detecting instrument should produce identical results on those two days. If it produced different results (i.e., if the instrument detected differences that weren't actually there), it would lack reliability. Second, a good instrument needs to have **power,** which is *an instrument's ability to detect differences or changes in the property.* If a person smiled more often on Tuesday than on Wednesday, then a good smile-detector should produce different results on those two days. If it produced the same result (i.e., if it failed to detect a difference that was actually there), then it would lack power (see **FIGURE 2.1**).

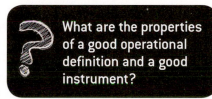

What are the properties of a good operational definition and a good instrument?

Demand Characteristics

Once we have a valid definition and a reliable and powerful instrument, we still have some work to do, because while we are trying to discover how people normally behave, normal people will be trying to behave as they think we want or expect them to. **Demand characteristics** are *those aspects of an observational setting*

Define the Property

Generate an operational definition that has validity

Detect the Property

Design an instrument that has reliability and power

FIGURE 2.1 Measurement There are two steps in the measurement of a property.

instrument Anything that can detect the condition to which an operational definition refers.

validity The goodness with which a concrete event defines a property.

reliability The tendency for an instrument to produce the same measurement whenever it is used to measure the same thing.

power An instrument's ability to detect small magnitudes of the property.

demand characteristics Those aspects of an observational setting that cause people to behave as they think someone else wants or expects.

Culture & Community

Best Place to Fall on Your Face Are most people prejudiced against people with disabilities? People rarely admit to being prejudiced when asked, and they generally won't behave in prejudiced ways if someone is watching. So how could you measure prejudice in a way that minimized demand characteristics?

Robert Levine of California State University–Fresno sent his students to 23 large international cities for an observational study in the field. Their task was to observe helping behaviors in a naturalistic context. In two versions of the experiment, students pretended to be either blind or injured while trying to cross a street, while another student stood by to observe whether anyone would come to help. A third version involved a student dropping a pen to see if anyone would pick it up.

The results showed that people helped in all three events fairly evenly within cities, but there was a wide range of response between cities. Rio de Janeiro, Brazil, came out on top as the most helpful city in the study with an overall helping score of 93%. Kuala Lampur, Malaysia, came in last with a score of 40%, and New York City placed next to last with a score of 45%. On average, Latin American cities ranked as most helpful (Levine, Norenzayan, & Philbrick, 2001).

Rex Features via AP Photo

Are most people prejudiced against people with disabilities? People rarely admit to being prejudiced when asked, and they generally won't behave in prejudiced ways if someone is watching. So how could you measure prejudice in a way that minimized demand characteristics?

that cause people to behave as they think someone else wants or expects. We call these demand characteristics because they seem to "demand" or require that people say and do certain things. When someone you love asks, "Do these jeans make me look fat?" the right answer is always no, and if you've ever been asked this question, then you have experienced demand. Demand characteristics make it hard to measure behavior as it typically unfolds.

One way that psychologists avoid the problem of demand characteristics is by observing people without their knowledge. **Naturalistic observation** is *a technique for gathering scientific information by unobtrusively observing people in their natural environments.* For example, naturalistic observation has shown that the biggest groups leave the smallest tips in restaurants (Freeman et al., 1975), that hungry shoppers buy the most impulse items at the grocery store (Gilbert, Gill, & Wilson, 2002), and that men do not usually approach the most beautiful woman at a singles' bar (Glenwick, Jason, & Elman, 1978). Each of these conclusions is the result of measurements made by psychologists who observed people who didn't know they were being observed. It seems unlikely that the same observations could have been made if the diners, shoppers, and singles had realized that they were being watched.

Unfortunately, naturalistic observation isn't always a viable solution to the problem of demand characteristics. First, some of the things psychologists want to observe simply don't occur naturally. If we wanted to know whether people who have undergone sensory deprivation perform poorly on motor tasks, we would have to hang around the shopping mall for a very long time before a few dozen blindfolded people with earplugs just happened to wander by and started typing. Second, some of the things that psychologists want to observe can only be gathered from direct interaction with a person—for example, by administering a survey, giving a test, conducting an interview, or hooking someone up to a machine. If we wanted to know how often people worry about dying, how accurately they can remember their high school graduations, or how much electrical activity their brains produce when they feel jealous, then simply watching them from the bushes won't do.

Luckily, there are ways to avoid demand characteristics. For instance, people are less likely to be influenced by demand characteristics when they are allowed to respond privately (e.g., completing questionnaires when they are alone) or anonymously (e.g., when their names or addresses are not recorded). A second technique that psychologists often use to avoid demand characteristics is to measure behaviors that cannot easily be controlled. You may not want a psychologist to know that you are extremely interested in the celebrity gossip magazine that she's asked you to read, but you can't prevent your pupils from dilating, which is what they do when you are mentally engaged.

A third way to avoid demand characteristics is to keep the people who are being observed from knowing the true purpose of the observation. When people are "blind" to the purpose of an

What are some of the limits of naturalistic observation?

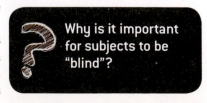

Why is it important for subjects to be "blind"?

naturalistic observation A technique for gathering scientific information by unobtrusively observing people in their natural environments.

double-blind An observation whose true purpose is hidden from both the observer and the person being observed.

observation, they can't behave the way they think they should behave because they don't *know* how they should behave. For instance, if you didn't know that a psychologist was studying the effects of music on mood, you wouldn't feel obligated to smile when music was played. This is why psychologists typically don't reveal the true purpose of an observation to the people who are being observed until the study is over.

Observer Bias

The people being observed aren't the only ones who can make measurement a bit tricky. Consider what happened when students in a psychology class were asked to measure the speed with which a rat learned to run through a maze (Rosenthal & Fode, 1963). Some students were told that their rats had been specially bred to be slow learners and others were told that their rats had been specially bred to be fast learners. Although all the rats were actually the same breed, the students who *thought* they were measuring the speed of a slow learner reported that their rats took longer to learn the maze than did the students who *thought* they were measuring the speed of a fast learner. In other words, the measurements revealed precisely what the students expected them to reveal.

Why did this happen? First, *expectations can influence observations*. It is easy to make errors when measuring the speed of a rat, and our expectations often determine the kinds of errors we make. Does putting one paw over the finish line count as learning the maze? If the rat falls asleep, should the stopwatch be left running, or should the rat be awakened and given a second chance? If a rat runs a maze in 18.5 seconds, should that number be rounded up or rounded down before it is recorded in the logbook? The answers to these questions may depend on whether one thinks the rat is a slow or fast learner. The students who timed the rat probably tried to be honest, vigilant, fair, and objective, but their expectations influenced their observations in subtle ways that they could neither detect nor control. Second, *expectations can influence reality*. Students who expected their rats to learn quickly may have unknowingly done things to help that learning along, for example, by muttering, "Oh no!" when the fast learner looked the wrong direction or by petting the slow learner less affectionately. (We'll discuss these phenomena more in the Social Psychology chapter.)

Observers' expectations, then, can have a powerful influence on both the observations they make and on the behavior of those whom they observe. Psychologists use many techniques to avoid these influences, and one of the most common is the **double-blind** observation, which is *an observation whose true purpose is hidden from both the observer and the person being observed.* For example, if the students had not been told which rats were fast learners and which were slow learners, then the students wouldn't have *had* any expectations about the rats, thus their expectations couldn't have influenced their measurements. That's why it is common practice in psychology to keep the observers as blind as the participants. For example, measurements are often made by research assistants who do not know what is being studied or why, and who therefore don't have any expectations about what the people being observed will or should do.

One way to avoid demand characteristics is to measure behaviors that people are unable or unlikely to control. For example, our pupils contract when we are bored (*left*) and dilate when we are interested (*right*), which makes pupillary dilation a useful measure of a person's level of engagement in a task.

People's expectations can cause the phenomena they expect. In 1929, investors who expected the stock market to collapse sold their stocks and thereby caused the very crisis they feared. In this photo, panicked citizens stand outside the New York Stock Exchange the day after the crash, which the *New York Times* attributed to "mob psychology."

variable A property whose value can vary across individuals or over time.

correlation Two variables are said to "be correlated" when variations in the value of one variable are synchronized with variations in the value of the other.

natural correlations A correlation observed in the world around us.

SUMMARY QUIZ [2.2]

1. When a measure produces the same measurement whenever it is used to measure the same thing, it is said to have
   a. validity.
   b. reliability.
   c. power.
   d. concreteness.

2. Aspects of an observational setting that cause people to behave as they think they should are called
   a. observer biases.
   b. reactive conditions.
   c. natural habitats.
   d. demand characteristics.

3. In a double-blind observation,
   a. the participants know what is being measured.
   b. people are observed in their natural environments.
   c. the purpose is hidden from both the observer and the person being observed.
   d. only surveys are used.

Explanation: Discovering Why People Do What They Do

It would be interesting to know whether happy people are healthier than unhappy people, but it would be even more interesting to know why. Does happiness make people healthier? Does being healthy make people happier? Does being rich make people healthy and happy? Scientists have developed some clever ways of using their measurements to answer questions like these. In the first section (Correlation), we'll examine techniques that can tell us whether two variables, such as health and happiness, are related; in the second section (Causation), we'll examine techniques that can tell us whether this relationship is one of cause and effect; in the third section (Drawing Conclusions), we'll see what kinds of conclusions these techniques allow us to draw; and in the fourth section (Thinking Critically about Evidence), we'll discuss the difficulty that most of us have drawing such conclusions.

Correlation

How much sleep did you get last night? Okay, now, how many U.S. presidents can you name? If you asked a dozen college students those two questions, you'd probably get a pattern of responses like the one shown in **TABLE 2.1**. Looking at these results, you'd probably conclude that students who got a good night's sleep tend to be better president-namers than students who pulled an all-nighter.

When you asked college students questions about sleep and presidents, you actually did three things:

> First, you measured a pair of **variables,** which are *properties whose values can vary across individuals or over time.* You measured one variable (number of hours slept) whose value could vary from *0* to *24,* and you measured a second variable (number of presidents named) whose value could vary from *0* to *43.*

Table 2.1 Hypothetical Data Showing Relationship Between Sleep and Memory

Participant	Hours of Sleep	No. of Presidents Named
A	0	11
B	0	17
C	2.7	16
D	3.1	21
E	4.4	17
F	5.5	16
G	7.6	31
H	7.9	41
I	9	40
J	9.1	35
K	9.6	38
L	9	43

> Second, you did this again and again. That is, you made a *series* of measurements, not just one.

> Third, you looked for a pattern in your series of measurements. If you looked at the second and third columns, you would notice that the values generally increase as you move from top to bottom. In other words, the two variables show a **correlation** (as in "co-relation"), meaning that *variations in the value of one variable are synchronized with variations in the value of the other.*

What's so cool about this is that simply by looking for synchronized patterns of variation, we can use measurement to discover the relationships between variables. For example, you know that people who smoke generally die younger than people who don't, but this is just a shorthand way of saying that as the value of *cigarette consumption* increases, the value of *longevity* decreases. Correlations not only describe the world as it is, they also allow us to predict the world as it will be. For example, given the correlation between smoking and longevity, you can predict with some confidence that a young person who starts smoking today will probably not live as long as a young person who doesn't. In short, when two variables are correlated, knowledge of the value of one variable allows us to make predictions about the value of the other variable.

A correlation can be positive or negative. When two variables have a "more-is-more" or "less-is-less" relationship, then they are positively correlated. So, for example, when we say that *more sleep* is associated with *more memory* or that *less sleep* is associated with *less memory,* we are describing a positive correlation. Conversely, when two variables have a "more-is-less" or "less-is-more" relationship, then they are negatively correlated. When we say that *more cigarette smoking* is associated with *less longevity* or that *less cigarette smoking* is associated with *more longevity,* we are describing a negative correlation. (See Appendix: Statistics for Psychology for more details on how correlation is measured.)

Researchers have found a positive correlation between mental illness and smoking. Can you think of three reasons why this correlation might exist?

Causation

We observe correlations all the time: between automobiles and pollution, between bacon and heart attacks, between sex and pregnancy. **Natural correlations** are *the correlations observed in the world around us,* and although such observations can tell us whether two variables have a relationship, they cannot tell us what *kind* of relationship these variables have. For example, many studies (Anderson & Bushman, 2001; Anderson et al., 2003; Huesmann et al., 2003) have found a positive correlation between the amount of violence to which a child is exposed through media such as television, movies, and video games (variable *X*) and the aggressiveness of the child's behavior (variable *Y*). The more media violence a child is exposed to, the more aggressive that child is likely to be. These variables clearly have a relationship—they are positively correlated—but why?

It isn't always easy to detect causal relationships accurately. For centuries, people sacrificed their enemies without realizing that doing so doesn't actually cause rain, and they smoked cigarettes without realizing that doing so actually does cause illness.

The Third-Variable Problem

One possibility is that exposure to media violence (*X*) causes aggressiveness (*Y*). For example, media violence may teach children that aggression is a reasonable way to vent anger and solve problems.

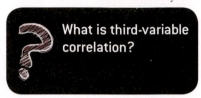

FIGURE 2.2 **Causes of Correlation**
If *X* (exposure to media violence) and *Y* (aggressiveness) are correlated, then there are at least three possible explanations: *X* causes *Y*, *Y* causes *X*, or *Z* (some other factor, such as lack of adult supervision) causes both *Y* and *X*, neither of which causes the other.

third-variable correlation Two variables are correlated only because each is causally related to a third variable.

In 1949, Dr. Benjamin Sandler noticed a correlation between the incidence of polio and ice cream consumption, and he concluded that sugar made children susceptible to the disease. Public health officials issued warnings. As it turned out, a third variable—warm weather—caused both an increase in disease (viruses become more active in the summer) and an increase in ice cream consumption.

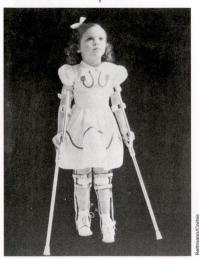

A second possibility is that aggressiveness (*Y*) causes children to be exposed to media violence (*X*). For example, children who are naturally aggressive may be especially likely to seek opportunities to play violent video games or watch violent movies. A third possibility is that a *third variable* (*Z*) causes children to be aggressive (*Y*) and to be exposed to media violence (*X*), neither of which is causally related to the other. For example, lack of adult supervision (*Z*) may allow children to get away with bullying others and to get away with watching television shows that adults would normally not allow. In other words, the relation between aggressiveness and exposure to media violence may be a case of **third-variable correlation**, which means that *two variables are correlated only because each is causally related to a third variable.* **FIGURE 2.2** shows three possible causes of any correlation.

What is third-variable correlation?

How can we determine by simple observation which of these three possibilities best explains the relationship between exposure to media violence and aggressiveness? Take a deep breath. The answer is: *We can't.* When we observe a natural correlation, the possibility of third-variable correlation can never be dismissed. But don't take this claim on faith. Let's try to dismiss the possibility of third-variable correlation and you'll see why such efforts are always doomed to fail.

The most straightforward way to determine whether a third variable, such as lack of adult supervision (*Z*), causes both exposure to media violence (*X*) and aggressive behavior (*Y*) is to eliminate differences in adult supervision (*Z*) among a group of children and see if the correlation between exposure (*X*) and aggressiveness (*Y*) is eliminated too. For instance, we could measure children who have different amounts of adult supervision, but we could make sure that for every child we measure who is exposed to media violence and is supervised *Q*% of the time, we also observe a child who is not exposed to media violence and is supervised *Q*% of the time, thus ensuring that children who are and are not exposed to media violence have the same amount of adult supervision *on average.* So if those who were exposed are on average more aggressive than those who were not exposed, we can be sure that lack of adult supervision was not the cause of this difference.

But don't applaud just yet. Because even if we used this technique to eliminate a *particular* third variable (such as lack of adult supervision), we would not be able to dismiss *all* third variables. For example, as soon as we finished making these observations, it might suddenly occur to us that emotional instability could cause children to gravitate toward violent television or video games and to behave aggressively. Emotional instability would be a new third variable (*Z*), and we would have to design a new test to investigate whether this variable explains the correlation between exposure (*X*) and aggression (*Y*). Unfortunately, we could keep dreaming up new third variables all day long without ever breaking a sweat, and every time we dreamed one up, we would have to rush out

and do a new test to determine whether *this* third variable was the cause of the correlation between exposure and aggressiveness. Because we can't rule out every possible third variable, we can never be absolutely sure that the correlation we observe between *X* and *Y* is evidence of a causal relationship between them. The **third-variable problem** refers to the fact that *a causal relationship between two variables cannot be inferred from the naturally occurring correlation between them because of the ever-present*

(a)   (b)

possibility of third-variable correlation. In other words, if we care about causality, then naturally occurring correlations just won't tell us what we really want to know. Luckily, another technique will. That technique is called an **experiment,** which is *a technique for establishing the causal relationship between variables.* The best way to understand how an experiment eliminates all possible third variables is by examining its two key features: *manipulation* and *random assignment*.

Manipulation

The most important thing to know about experiments is that you've been doing them all your life. Imagine that you are scanning Facebook on a laptop when all of a sudden you lose your wireless connection. You suspect that another device—say, your roommate's new smartphone—has somehow bumped you off the network. What would you do to test your suspicion? Observing a natural correlation wouldn't help much. You could carefully note when you did and didn't have a connection and when your roommate did and didn't use his phone, but even if you observed a correlation between these two variables, you still couldn't conclude that the phone was *causing* you to lose your network connection. After all, if your roommate was afraid of loud noises and called his mommy for comfort whenever there was an electrical storm, and if that storm interfered with your wireless network, then the storm (*Z*) would be the cause of both your roommate's phone usage (*X*) and your connectivity problem (*Y*).

So how could you test your suspicion? Well, rather than *observing* the correlation between phone usage and connectivity, you could try to *create* a correlation by intentionally making calls on your roommate's phone and observing changes in your laptop's connectivity as you did so. If you observed that "wireless connection off" only occurred in conjunction with "phone on," then you could conclude that your roommate's phone was the *cause* of your failed connection, and you could sell the phone on eBay and then lie about it when asked. The technique you used to solve the third-variable problem is called **manipulation,** *which involves changing a variable in order to determine its causal power.*

Manipulation can solve scientific problems too. For example, imagine that our passive observation of children revealed a positive correlation between exposure to violence and aggressive behaviors, and that now we want to design an experiment to determine whether the exposure is the cause of the aggression. We could ask some children to participate in an experiment, have half of them

third-variable problem The fact that a causal relationship between two variables cannot be inferred from the naturally occurring correlation between them because of the ever-present possibility of third-variable correlation.

experiment A technique for establishing the causal relationship between variables.

manipulation Changing a variable in order to determine its causal power.

> How does manipulation solve the third-variable problem?

How do you determine whether eating 60 hot dogs will make you sick? You eat them one day, don't eat them the next day, and then see which day you barf. *That's* manipulation! BTW, in 2013, world champion Joey Chestnut ate 69 hot dogs in 10 minutes by folding them up. *That's* manipulation too!

AP Photo/Henny Ray Abrams

independent variable The variable that is manipulated in an experiment.

experimental group The group of people who are exposed to a particular manipulation, as compared to the control group, in an experiment.

control group The group of people who are not exposed to the particular manipulation, as compared to the experimental group, in an experiment.

dependent variable The variable that is measured in a study.

play violent video games for an hour while the other half does not, and then, at the end of the hour, we could measure their aggression and compare the measurements across the two groups. When we compared these measurements, we would essentially be computing the correlation between a variable that we manipulated (exposure) and a variable that we measured (aggression). But because we *manipulated* rather than *measured* exposure, we would never have to ask whether a third variable (such as lack of adult supervision) caused children to experience different levels of exposure. After all, we already *know* what caused that to happen. *We* did!

Experimentation involves three critical steps (and several ridiculously confusing terms):

> First, we manipulate. We call *the variable that is manipulated* the **independent variable** because it is under our control, and thus it is "independent" of what a participant says or does. When we manipulate an independent variable (such as exposure to media violence), we end up with two groups of participants: an **experimental group,** which is *the group of people who experience a stimulus*, and a **control group,** which is *the group of people who do not experience that stimulus*.

> Second, having manipulated one variable (exposure), we now measure another variable (aggression). We call *the variable that is measured* the **dependent variable** because its value "depends" on what the participant says or does.

> Third and finally, we look to see whether our manipulation of the independent variable produced changes in the dependent variable. **FIGURE 2.3** shows exactly how manipulation works.

What are the three main steps in doing an experiment?

Random Assignment

Once we have manipulated an independent variable and measured a dependent variable, we've done one of the two things that experimentation requires. The second thing is a little less intuitive but equally important. Imagine that we began our exposure and aggression experiment by finding a group of children and asking each child whether he or she would

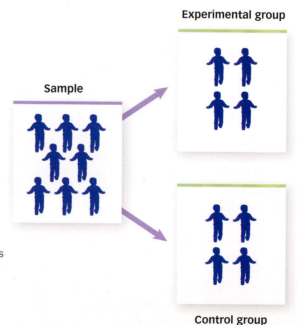

FIGURE 2.3 **Manipulation** The independent variable is exposure to media violence and the dependent variable is aggression. When we compare the behavior of participants in the experimental and control groups, we are essentially computing the correlation between the independent variable and the dependent variable. Notice how the chart to the right looks just like the chart shown in Table 2.1.

Sample

Experimental group

Exposed to media violence?	Aggression
Yes	High
Yes	High
Yes	High
Yes	High

Control group

Exposed to media violence?	Aggression
No	Low
No	Low
No	Low
No	Low

like to be in the experimental group or the control group. Imagine that half the children said that they'd like to play violent video games and the other half said they would rather not. Imagine that we let the children do what they wanted to do, measured aggression some time later, and found that the children who had played the violent video games were more aggressive than those who had not. Would this experiment allow us to conclude that playing violent video games causes aggression? Definitely not—but *why* not?

Because we let the children decide for themselves whether or not they would play violent video games, and children who ask to play such games are probably different in many ways from those who ask not to. They may be older, or stronger, or smarter—or younger, weaker, or dumber—or less often supervised or more often supervised. The list of possible differences goes on and on. The whole point of doing an experiment was to divide children into two groups that differed *in only one way*— namely, in terms of their exposure to media violence. The moment we let the children decide for themselves whether they would be in the experimental group or the control group, we had two groups that differed in countless ways, and any of those countless differences could have been responsible for any differences we observed in their aggression. **Self-selection** is *a problem that occurs when anything about a person determines whether he or she will be included in the experimental or control group.*

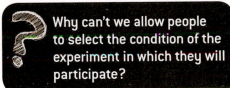

Why can't we allow people to select the condition of the experiment in which they will participate?

There is no evidence that Louise Hay's techniques can cure cancer. But even if cancer victims who bought her books *did* show a higher rate of remission than those who didn't, there would *still* be no evidence because buyers are self-selected and thus may differ from nonbuyers in countless ways.

If we want to be sure that there is one and only one difference between the children in our study who are and are not exposed to media violence, then their inclusion in the experimental or control groups must be *randomly determined*. One way to do this is to flip a coin. For example, we could walk up to each child in our experiment, flip a coin, and assign the child to play violent video games if the coin lands heads up and not to play violent video games if the coin lands heads down. **Random assignment** is *a procedure that lets chance assign people to the experimental or the control group.*

What would happen if we assigned children to groups with a coin flip? As **FIGURE 2.4** shows, we could expect the experimental group and the control group to

self-selection A problem that occurs when anything about a person determines whether he or she will be included in the experimental or control group.

random assignment A procedure that lets chance assign people to the experimental or control group.

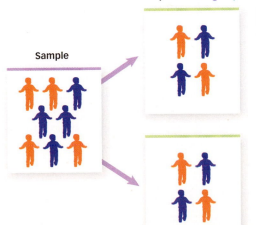

Sample

Experimental group

Exposed to media violence?	Adult supervision?	Aggression
Yes	Yes	High
Yes	No	High
Yes	Yes	High
Yes	No	High

Exposed to media violence?	Adult supervision?	Aggression
No	Yes	Low
No	No	Low
No	Yes	Low
No	No	Low

Control group

FIGURE 2.4 Random Assignment Children with adult supervision are shown in orange and those without adult supervision are shown in blue. The independent variable is exposure to media violence and the dependent variable is aggression. Random assignment ensures that participants in the experimental and the control groups are on average equal in terms of all possible third variables. In essence, it ensures that there is no correlation between a third variable and the dependent variable. You can see this clearly if you compare the chart to the right with the chart shown in Figure 2.3.

Robert Daly/Getty Images

Do strawberries taste better when dipped in chocolate? If you dip the big juicy ones and don't dip the small dry ones, then you won't know if the chocolate is what made the difference. But if you randomly assign some to be dipped and others not to be dipped, and if the dipped ones taste better on average, then you will have demonstrated scientifically what every 3-year-old already knows.

internal validity An attribute of an experiment that allows it to establish causal relationships.

external validity An attribute of an experiment in which variables have been defined in a normal, typical, or realistic way.

have roughly equal numbers of supervised kids and unsupervised kids, roughly equal numbers of emotionally stable and unstable kids, roughly equal numbers of big kids and small kids, of active kids, fat kids, tall kids, funny kids, and kids with blue hair named Harry McSweeny. Because the kids in the two groups would be the same *on average* in terms of height, weight, emotional stability, adult supervision, and every other variable in the known universe *except the one we manipulated*, we could be sure that the variable we manipulated (exposure) was the one and only cause of any changes in the variable we measured (aggression). After all, if exposure was the *only* difference between the two groups of children then it *must* be the cause of any differences in aggression we observe.

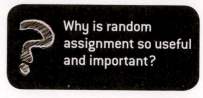

? Why is random assignment so useful and important?

Significance

Random assignment is a powerful tool, but like a lot of tools, it doesn't work every time, we use it. If we randomly assigned children to play or not to play violent video games, we could expect the two groups to have roughly equal numbers of supervised and unsupervised kids, roughly equal numbers of emotionally stable and unstable kids, and so on. The key word in that sentence is *roughly*. Coin flips are inherently unpredictable, and every once in a long while by sheer chance alone, a coin will assign more unsupervised, emotionally unstable kids to play violent video games and more supervised, emotionally stable kids to play none. When this happens, random assignment has failed—and when random assignment fails, the third-variable problem rises up out of its grave like a guy with a hockey mask and a grudge.

How can we tell when random assignment has failed? Unfortunately, we can't for sure. But we can calculate the *odds* that random assignment has failed each time we use it. Psychologists perform a statistical calculation every time they do an experiment, and they do not accept the results of those experiments unless the calculation tells them that there is less than a 5% chance that they would have found differences between the experimental and control groups if random assignment had failed. Such differences are said to be *statistically significant*, which means they were unlikely to have been caused by a third variable.

Drawing Conclusions

If we applied all the techniques discussed so far, we would have designed an experiment that had **internal validity,** which is *an attribute of an experiment that allows it to establish causal relationships.* When we say that an experiment is internally valid, we mean that everything *inside* the experiment is working exactly as it must in order for us to draw conclusions about causal relationships. But what exactly are those conclusions? If our imaginary experiment revealed a difference between the aggressiveness of children in the experimental and control groups, then we could conclude that media violence *as we defined it* caused aggression *as we defined it* in the people *whom we studied.* Notice those phrases in italics. Each corresponds to an important restriction on the kinds of conclusions we can draw from an experiment, so let's consider each in turn.

Representative Variables

The results of any experiment depend, in part, on how the independent and dependent variables are defined. For instance, we are more likely to find that exposure to media violence causes aggression when we define exposure as "playing

The Real World

Oddsly Enough

A recent Gallup survey found that 53% of college graduates believe in extrasensory perception, or ESP. Very few psychologists share that belief. What makes them such a skeptical lot is their understanding of the laws of probability.

The Nobel laureate Luis Alvarez was reading the newspaper one day, and a particular story got him thinking about an old college friend whom he hadn't seen in years. A few minutes later, he turned the page and was shocked to see the very same friend's obituary. But before concluding that he had an acute case of ESP, Alvarez decided to use probability theory to determine just how amazing this coincidence really was.

First he estimated the number of friends an average person has, and then he estimated how often an average person thinks about each of those friends. With these estimates in hand, he did a few simple calculations and determined the likelihood that someone would think about a friend five minutes before learning about that friend's death. The odds were astonishing. In a country the size of the United States, for example, Alvarez predicted that this amazing coincidence should happen to 10 people every day (Alvarez, 1965).

"In 10 years there are 5 million minutes," says statistics professor Irving Jack. "That means each person has plenty of opportunity to have some remarkable coincidences in his life" (quoted in Neimark, 2004). For example, 250 million Americans dream for about two hours every night (that's a half billion hours of dreaming!), so it isn't surprising that two people sometimes have the same dream, or that we sometimes dream about something that actually happens the next day. As mathematics professor John Allen Paulos (quoted in Neimark, 2004) put it, "In reality, the most astonishingly incredible coincidence imaginable would be the complete absence of all coincidence."

If all of this seems surprising to you, then you are not alone. Research shows that people routinely underestimate the likelihood of coincidences happening by chance (Diaconis & Mosteller, 1989; Falk & McGregor, 1983;

"Idaho! What a coincidence—I'm from Idaho."

Hintzman, Asher, & Stern, 1978). If you want to profit from this fact, assemble a group of 24 or more people, and bet anyone that at least two of the people share a birthday. The odds are in your favor, and the bigger the group, the better the odds. In fact, in a group of 35, the odds are 85%. Happy fleecing!

Grand Theft Auto for 10 hours" rather than "playing Pro Quarterback for 10 minutes," or when we define aggression as "interrupting another person" rather than "smacking someone silly with a tire iron." The way we define variables can have a profound influence on what we find, so which of these is the *right* way?

One answer is that we should define variables in an experiment as they are defined in the real world. **External validity** is *an attribute of an experiment in which variables have been defined in a normal, typical, or realistic way.* It seems pretty clear that the kind of aggressive behavior that concerns teachers and parents lies somewhere between an interruption and an assault, and that the kind of media violence to which children are typically exposed lies somewhere between sports and felonies. If the goal of an experiment is to determine whether the kinds of media violence to which children are typically exposed cause the kinds of aggression with which

Does piercing make a person more or less attractive? The answer, of course, depends entirely on how you operationally define *piercing*.

Do Violent Movies Make Peaceful Streets?

In 2000, the American Academy of Pediatrics and five other public health organizations issued a joint statement warning about the risks of exposure to media violence. They cited evidence from psychological experiments in which children and young adults who were exposed to violent movie clips showed a sharp increase in aggressive behavior immediately afterward. These health organizations noted that "well over 1,000 studies . . . point overwhelmingly to a causal connection between media violence and aggressive behavior" (American Academy of Pediatrics, 2000).

Given the laboratory results, we might expect to see a correlation in the real world between the number of people who see violent movies in theaters and the number of violent crimes. When economists Gordon Dahl and Stefano Della Vigna (2009) analyzed crime statistics and box office statistics, they found just such a correlation—except that it was negative! In other words, on evenings when more people went to the

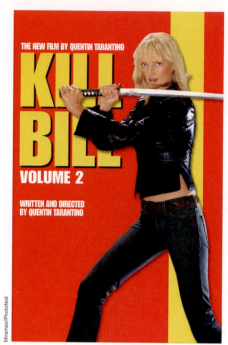

Miramax/Photofest

theater to watch violent movies, there were *fewer* violent crimes. Why? The researchers suggested that violent movies are especially appealing to the people who are most likely to commit violent crimes. Because those people are busy watching movies for a few hours, violent crime drops. In other words, blood-and-bullet movies take criminals off the street by luring them to the theater!

Laboratory experiments clearly show that exposure to media violence *can* cause aggression. But as the movie theater data remind us, experiments are a tool for establishing the causal relationships between variables and are not meant to be miniature versions of the real world, where things are ever so much more complex.

Quentin Tarantino is a director known for making violent movies, such as *Kill Bill 2*. Did seeing this movie cause anyone to commit murder? We can't say for sure, but one thing we do know is that while people were busy watching the movie, they weren't busy shooting each other.

---

societies are typically concerned, then external validity is essential. When variables are defined in an experiment as they typically are in the real world, we say that the variables are *representative* of the real world.

External validity sounds like such a good idea that you may be surprised to learn that most psychology experiments are externally *in*valid—and that most psychologists don't mind. The reason for this is that psychologists are rarely trying to learn about the real world by creating tiny replicas of it in their laboratories. Rather, they are usually trying to learn about the real world by using experiments to test hypotheses derived from theories, and externally invalid experiments can often do that quite nicely (Mook, 1983). For example, the idea that exposure to media violence causes aggression (a theory) suggests that children in a laboratory should behave more aggressively after being exposed to media violence (a hypothesis), and thus their behavior in the laboratory serves to test that theory (see the Hot Science box, Do Violent Movies Make Peaceful Streets?).

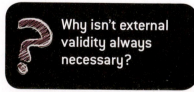

? Why isn't external validity always necessary?

Representative People

Our imaginary experiment on exposure to media violence and aggression would allow us to conclude that exposure as we defined it caused aggression as we defined it in the people *whom we studied*. That last phrase represents another important restriction on the kinds of conclusions we can draw from experiments.

Who are the people whom psychologists study? Psychologists rarely observe an entire **population,** which is *a complete collection of people*, such as the population of human

population A complete collection of participants who might possibly be measured.

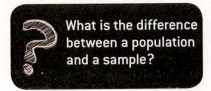

? What is the difference between a population and a sample?

beings (about 7 billion), the population of Californians (about 38 million), or the population of people with Down syndrome (about 1 million). Rather, psychologists observe a **sample**, which is *a partial collection of people drawn from a population.*

The size of a sample can be as small as 1. For example, some individuals are so remarkable that they deserve close study, and psychologists study them by using the **case method,** which is *a procedure for gathering scientific information by studying a single individual.* We can learn a lot about memory by studying Akira Haraguchi, who can recite the first 100,000 digits of pi, or about creativity by studying Jay Greenburg whose 5th symphony was recorded by the London Symphony Orchestra when he was just 15 years old. Cases like these are not only interesting in their own right, but can also provide important insights into how the rest of us work.

Of course, most of the psychological studies you will read about in this book included samples of ten, a hundred, a thousand, or even several thousand people. So how do psychologists decide which people to include in a sample? One way to select a sample from a population is by **random sampling,** which is *a technique for choosing participants that ensures that every member of a population has an equal chance of being included in the sample.* When we randomly sample participants from a population, the sample is said to be *representative* of the population. Random sampling allows us to *generalize* from the sample to the population—that is, to conclude that what we observed in our sample would also have been observed if we had measured the entire population. You probably already have solid intuitions about the importance of random sampling. For example, if you stopped at a farm stand to buy a bag of cherries and the farmer offered to let you taste a few that he had handpicked from the bag, you'd be reluctant to generalize from that sample to the population of cherries in the bag. But if the farmer invited you to pull a few cherries from the bag at random, you'd probably be willing to take those cherries as representative of the cherry population.

Random sampling sounds like such a good idea that you might be surprised to learn that most psychological studies involve nonrandom samples—and that most psychologists don't mind. Indeed, virtually every participant in every psychology experiment you will ever read about was a volunteer, and most were college students who were significantly younger, smarter, healthier, wealthier, and Whiter than the average Earthling. About 96% of the people whom psychologists study come from

When Jay Greenburg was just 15 years old, his first CD was released and his Violin Concerto premiered at Carnegie Hall.

sample A partial collection of people drawn from a population.

case method A procedure for gathering scientific information by studying a single individual.

random sampling A technique for choosing participants that ensures that every member of a population has an equal chance of being included in the sample.

Generalizing from nonrandom samples can lead to mistaken conclusions. In the presidential election of 1948, the *Chicago Tribune* mistakenly predicted that Thomas Dewey would beat Harry Truman. Why? Because polling was done by telephone, and Dewey Republicans were more likely to have telephones than were Truman Democrats. In the presidential election of 2004, exit polls mistakenly predicted that John Kerry would beat George Bush. Why? Because polling was done by soliciting voters as they left the polls, and Kerry supporters were more willing to stop and talk.

countries that have just 12% of the world's population, and 70% come from the United States alone (Henrich, Heine, & Norenzayan, 2010). This is because most psychology experiments are conducted by professors and graduate students at colleges and universities in the Western hemisphere, and as much as they might *like* to randomly sample the population of the planet, they are pretty much stuck studying the folks who volunteer for their studies.

So how can we learn *anything* from psychology experiments? Isn't the failure to sample randomly a fatal flaw? No, it's not, and there are three reasons why.

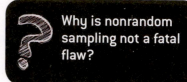

? Why is nonrandom sampling not a fatal flaw?

1. Sometimes the similarity of a sample and a population doesn't matter. If one pig flew over the Statue of Liberty just one time, it would instantly disprove the traditional theory of porcine locomotion. It wouldn't matter if all pigs flew or if any other pigs ever flew. One flying pig is enough. An experimental result can be illuminating even when the sample isn't typical of the population.

2. When the ability to generalize an experimental result *is* important, psychologists perform new experiments that use the same procedures with different samples. For example, after measuring how a nonrandomly selected group of American children behaved after playing violent video games, we might try to replicate our experiment with Japanese children, or with American teenagers, or with deaf adults. If the results of our study were replicated in these other samples, then we would be more confident (but never completely confident) that the results describe a basic human tendency.

3. Sometimes the similarity of the sample and the population is a reasonable starting assumption. Few of us would be willing to take an experimental medicine if a nonrandom sample of seven participants took it and died, and that would be true even if the seven participants were mice. Although these nonrandomly sampled participants would be different from us in many ways (including tails and whiskers), most of us would be willing to generalize from their experience to ours because we know that even mice share enough of our basic biology to make it a good bet that what harms them can harm us too. By this same reasoning, if a psychology experiment demonstrated that some American children behaved violently after playing violent video games, we should ask whether there is any compelling reason to suspect that Ecuadorian college students or middle-aged Australians would behave any differently? If the answer is yes, then experiments provide a way for us to investigate that possibility.

This mouse died after drinking the green stuff. Want to drink the green stuff? Why not? You're not a mouse, are you?

David J. Green/Alamy

Thinking Critically about Evidence

As you've seen in this chapter, the scientific method produces empirical evidence. But empirical evidence is only useful if we know how to think about it, and the fact is that most of us don't. Using evidence requires *critical thinking*, which involves asking ourselves tough questions about whether we have interpreted the evidence in an unbiased way, and about whether the evidence tells not just the truth, but the *whole* truth. Research suggests that most people have trouble doing both of these things and that educational programs designed to teach or improve critical thinking skills are not particularly effective (Willingham, 2007). Why do we have so much trouble thinking critically? There are two reasons: First, we tend to see what we expect to see, and second, we tend to ignore what we can't see. Let's explore each of these tendencies in turn.

We See What We Expect to See

People's beliefs can color their views of evidence and cause them to see what they expected to see. For instance, participants in one study (Darley & Gross, 1983) learned about a little girl named Hannah. One group of participants was told that Hannah came from an affluent family, which led the participants to expect her to be a good student. Another group of participants was told that Hannah came from a poor family, which led them to expect her to be a bad student. All participants were then shown a video of Hannah taking a reading test and were asked to rate Hannah's performance. Although both groups saw exactly the same video, those participants who believed that Hannah was from an affluent family rated her performance more positively than did those who believed that Hannah was from a poor family. What's more, both groups of participants defended their conclusions by citing evidence from the video. Numerous experiments show that people tend to look for evidence that confirms their beliefs (Hart et al., 2009; Snyder & Swann, 1978) and tend to stop looking when they find it (Kunda, 1990). What's more, when people do encounter evidence that disconfirms their beliefs, they hold it to a very high standard (Gilovich, 1991; Ross, Lepper, & Hubbard, 1975).

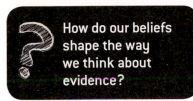

How do our beliefs shape the way we think about evidence?

Because it is so easy to see what we expect to see, the first step in critical thinking is simply to doubt your own conclusions—and one the best ways to doubt yourself is to talk to other people! Scientists go out of their way to expose themselves to criticism by sending their papers to the colleagues who are most likely to disagree with them or by presenting their findings to audiences full of critics, and they do this mainly so they can achieve a more balanced view of their own conclusions. If you want to be happy, take your friend to lunch; but if you want to be right, take your enemy.

Sir Francis Bacon (1561–1626) not only devised the scientific method, but also identified the two tendencies that make critical thinking so difficult. He bemoaned the fact that "human understanding, once it has adopted opinions ... draws everything else to support and agree with them," and also that "little or no attention is paid to things invisible."

We Consider What We See and Ignore What We Don't

Not only do people see what they expect to see, but they fail to consider what they can't see. For example, participants in one study (Newman, Wolff, & Hearst, 1980) played a game in which they were shown a set of trigrams, which are three-letter combinations such as *SXY*, *GTR*, *BCG*, and *EVX*. On each trial, the experimenter pointed to one of the trigrams in the set and told the participants that *this* trigram was the special one. The participants' job was to figure out what made the special trigram so special. For half the participants, the special trigram was always the one that contained the letter *T*, and participants in this condition needed to see about 34 sets of trigrams before they figured out that the presence of *T* was what made the trigram special. But for the other half of the participants, the special trigram was always the one that *lacked* the letter *T*. How many trials did it take before participants figured it out? In fact, they *never* figured it out! Experiments like this one suggest that people consider what they see, but rarely consider what they don't.

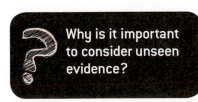

Why is it important to consider unseen evidence?

This tendency can cause us to draw all kinds of erroneous conclusions. Consider a study in which participants were randomly assigned to play one of two roles in a game (Ross, Amabile, & Steinmetz, 1977). The "quizmasters" were asked to make up a series of difficult questions, and the "contestants" were asked to answer them.

No matter how well the contestants perform, *Jeopardy* host Alex Trebek always seems like the smartest guy on the stage. But would you still get that impression if contestants were given an opportunity to ask him a few questions?

If you give this a quick try, you will discover that it's very easy to generate questions that you can answer but that most other people cannot. For example, think of the last city you visited. Now give someone the name of the hotel you stayed in and ask him or her what street it's on. They're not likely to know.

So participants who were cast in the role of quizmaster naturally asked lots of clever-sounding questions, and participants who were cast in the role of contestant naturally gave lots of wrong answers. Now comes the interesting part. Quizmasters and contestants played this game while another participant—the observer—watched. After the game was over, the observer was asked to make some guesses about what the players were like in their everyday lives. The results were clear: Observers consistently concluded that the quizmaster was a more knowledgeable person than the contestant. Observers *saw* the quizmaster asking sharp questions and *saw* the contestant saying, "Um…er…uh…I don't know," and observers considered this evidence. What they failed to consider was the evidence they did *not* see. Specifically, they failed to consider what would have happened if the person who had been assigned to play the role of quizmaster had instead been assigned to play the role of contestant, and vice versa. If that had happened, then surely the contestant would have been the one asking clever questions, and the quizmaster would have been the one struggling to answer them. Bottom line? The first step in critical thinking is to doubt what you do see, and the second step is to consider what you don't.

The Skeptical Stance

Winston Churchill once said that democracy is the worst form of government, except for all the others. Similarly, science is not an infallible method for learning about the world; it's just a whole lot less fallible than the other methods. Science is a human enterprise, and humans make mistakes. They see what they expect to see, and they rarely consider what they can't see at all.

What makes science different from most other human enterprises is that scientists actively seek to discover and remedy these biases. Scientists are constantly striving to make their observations more accurate and their reasoning more rigorous, and they invite anyone and everyone to examine their evidence and challenge their conclusions. As such, science is the ultimate democracy—one of the only sports in which the lowliest nobody can triumph over the most celebrated someone. When an unknown patent clerk named Albert Einstein challenged the greatest physicists of his day, he didn't have a famous name, a fancy degree, powerful friends, or a fat wallet. He just had evidence. And he prevailed for one reason: His evidence was right.

So think of the remaining chapters in this book as a report from the field—a description of the work that psychological scientists have done as they stumble toward knowledge. These chapters tell the story of the men and women who have put their faith in the scientific method and used it to pry loose small pieces of the truth about who we are, how we work, and what we are all doing here together on the third stone from the sun. Read it with interest but also with skepticism. Think critically about what you read here—and everywhere else.

SUMMARY QUIZ [2.3]

1. When we observe a natural correlation, what keeps us from concluding that one variable is the cause and the other is the effect?
   a. the third-variable problem
   b. random assignment
   c. random sampling
   d. statistical significance

2. A researcher administers a questionnaire concerning attitudes toward global warming to people of both genders and of all ages who live all across the country. The dependent variable in the study is the participant's _____.
   a. age
   b. gender
   c. attitudes toward global warming
   d. geographic location

3. The characteristic of an experiment that allows conclusions about causal relationships to be drawn is called
   a. external validity.
   b. internal validity.
   c. generalization.
   d. self-selection.

4. When people find evidence that confirms their beliefs, they often
   a. tend to stop looking their beliefs.
   b. seek additional evidence that disconfirms them.
   c. consider what they cannot see.
   d. think critically about it.

The Ethics of Science: First, Do No Harm

Somewhere along the way, someone probably told you that it isn't nice to treat people like objects. And yet, it may seem that psychologists do just that by creating situations that cause people to feel fearful or sad, to do things that are embarrassing or immoral, and to learn things about themselves and others that they might not really want to know. Don't be fooled by appearances. The fact is that psychologists go to great lengths to protect the well-being of every research participant, and they are bound by a code of ethics that is as detailed and demanding as the professional codes that bind physicians, lawyers, and accountants. That code requires psychologists to show respect for people, for animals, and for the truth. Let's examine each of these obligations in turn.

Respecting People

During World War II, Nazi doctors performed truly barbaric experiments on human subjects, such as removing organs from living people or submerging people in ice water just to see how long it would take them to die. When the war ended, the international community developed the Nuremberg Code of 1947 and then the Declaration of Helsinki in 1964, which spelled out rules for the ethical treatment of human subjects. Unfortunately, not everyone obeyed them. For example, from

informed consent A written agreement to participate in a study made by an adult who has been informed of all the risks that participation may entail.

debriefing A verbal description of the true nature and purpose of a study.

1932 until 1972, the U.S. Public Health Service conducted the infamous Tuskegee experiment in which 399 African American men with syphilis were denied treatment so that researchers could observe the progression of the disease.

In 1979, the U.S. Department of Health, Education, and Welfare (HEW) released what came to be known as the Belmont Report, which described three basic principles that all research involving human subjects should follow. First, research should show *respect for persons* and their right to make decisions for and about themselves without undue influence or coercion. Second, research should be *beneficent*, which means that it should attempt to maximize benefits and reduce risks to the participant. Third, research should be *just*, which means that it should distribute benefits and risks equally to participants without prejudice toward particular individuals or groups.

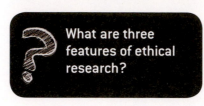
What are three features of ethical research?

The specific ethical code that psychologists follow incorporates these basic principles and expands them. Here are a few of the most important rules that govern the conduct of psychological research:

> *Informed consent:* Participants may not take part in a psychological study unless they have given **informed consent,** which is *a written agreement to participate in a study made by an adult who has been informed of all the risks that participation may entail.* This doesn't mean that the person must know everything about the study (e.g., the hypothesis), but it does mean that the person must know about anything that might potentially be harmful or painful. If people cannot give informed consent (e.g., because they are minors or are mentally incapable), then informed consent must be obtained from their legal guardians.

> *Freedom from coercion:* Psychologists may not coerce participation. Coercion not only means physical and psychological coercion but monetary coercion as well. It is unethical to offer people large amounts of money to persuade them to do something that they might otherwise decline to do.

> *Protection from harm:* Psychologists must take every possible precaution to protect their research participants from physical or psychological harm. If there are two equally effective ways to study something, the psychologist must use the safer method.

> *Risk-benefit analysis:* Although participants may be asked to accept small risks, such as a minor shock or a small embarrassment, they must not even be *asked* to accept large risks, such as severe pain or psychological trauma. The psychologist must also demonstrate that even the small risks are outweighed by the social benefits of the new knowledge that might be gained from the study.

> *Deception:* Psychologists may only use deception when it is justified by the study's scientific, educational, or applied value and when alternative procedures are not feasible.

> *Debriefing:* If a participant is deceived in any way before or during a study, the psychologist must provide a **debriefing,** which is *a verbal description of the true nature and purpose of a study.*

> *Confidentiality:* Psychologists are obligated to keep private and personal information obtained during a study confidential.

These are just some of the rules that psychologists must follow. But how are those rules enforced? Almost all psychology studies are done by psychologists who work at colleges and universities. These institutions have institutional review boards (IRBs) that are composed of instructors and researchers, university staff, and laypeople from the community (e.g., business leaders or members of the clergy). A psychologist may conduct a study only after the IRB has reviewed and approved it. The code of ethics and the procedure for approval are so strict that many studies simply cannot be performed anywhere, by anyone, at any time because doing so would require unethical experiments that violate basic human rights.

Respecting Animals

Not all research participants have human rights because not all research participants are human. Some are chimpanzees, rats, pigeons, or other nonhuman animals. The psychologist's ethical code specifically describes the special rights of these nonhuman participants, and some of the more important ones are these:

© American Broadcasting Companies, Inc.

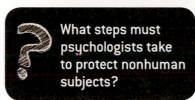

> All procedures involving animals must be supervised by psychologists who are trained in research methods and experienced in the care of laboratory animals and who are responsible for ensuring appropriate consideration of the animal's comfort, health, and humane treatment.

What steps must psychologists take to protect nonhuman subjects?

The man in this photo just saw another man slip a drug into a woman's drink, and he is alerting the bartender. What he doesn't know is that all the people at the bar are actors and that he is being filmed for the television show *What Would You Do?* Was it ethical for ABC to put this man in such a stressful situation without his consent? And how did men who didn't alert the bartender feel when they turned on their televisions months later and were confronted by their own shameful behavior?

> Psychologists must make reasonable efforts to minimize the discomfort, infection, illness, and pain of animals.

> Psychologists may use a procedure that subjects an animal to pain, stress, or privation only when an alternative procedure is unavailable and only when the procedure is justified by the scientific, educational, or applied value of the study.

> Psychologists must perform all surgical procedures under appropriate anesthesia and must minimize an animal's pain during and after surgery.

That's good—but is it good enough? Some Americans consider it unethical to use nonhuman animals in research, and some believe that nonhuman animals should have the same fundamental rights as humans (Singer, 1975). On the other hand, a majority of Americans consider it morally acceptable to use nonhuman

PAUL MCERLANE/Reuters/Corbis

Some people consider it unethical to use animals for clothing or research. Others see an important distinction between these two purposes.

animals in research and say they would reject a governmental ban on such research (Kiefer, 2004; Moore, 2003). Science is not in the business of resolving moral controversies, and every individual must draw his or her own conclusions about this issue. But whatever position you take, it is important to note that only a small percentage of psychological studies involve animals, and only a small percentage of those studies cause animals pain or harm. Psychologists mainly study people, and when they do study animals, they mainly study their behavior.

Respecting Truth

Institutional review boards ensure that data are collected ethically. But once the data are collected, who ensures that they are ethically analyzed and reported? No one does. Psychology, like all sciences, works on the honor system. You may find that a bit odd. After all, we don't use the honor system in stores ("Take the television set home and pay us next time you're in the neighborhood"), banks ("I don't need to look up your account—just tell me how much money you want to withdraw"), or courtrooms ("If you say you're innocent, well then, that's good enough for us"), so why would we expect it to work in science? Are scientists more honest than everyone else?

Definitely! Okay, we just made that up. But the honor system doesn't depend on scientists being especially honest as much as it depends on the fact that science is a community enterprise. When scientists claim to have discovered something important, other scientists don't just applaud; they start studying it too. When physicist

Other Voices

Is Psychology a Science?

Timothy D. Wilson is a professor of psychology at the University of Virginia and the author of several popular books, including *Redirect: The Surprising New Science of Psychological Change* (2011).

Photo by Jen Fariello, Courtesy Timothy D. Wilson

Nobody can dispute that you are taking a course in psychology, but are you taking a science course? Some critics maintain that psychology fails to meet accepted criteria for what constitutes a science. Timothy Wilson, a psychology professor at the University of Virginia, took on the critics by drawing from an appropriate source: the scientific literature (Wilson, 2012).

Once, during a meeting at my university, a biologist mentioned that he was the only faculty member present from a science department. When I corrected him, noting that I was from the Department of Psychology, he waved his hand dismissively, as if I were a Little Leaguer telling a member of the New York Yankees that I too played baseball.

There has long been snobbery in the sciences, with the "hard" ones (physics, chemistry, biology) considering themselves to be more legitimate than the "soft" ones (psychology, sociology). It is thus no surprise that many members of the general public feel the same way. But of late, skepticism about the rigors of social science has reached absurd heights. The U.S. House of Representatives recently voted to eliminate funding for political science research through the National Science Foundation (NSF). In the wake of that action, an opinion writer for the *Washington Post* suggested that the House didn't go far enough. The NSF should not fund any research in the social sciences, wrote Charles Lane, because "unlike hypotheses in the hard sciences, hypotheses about society usually can't be proven or disproven by experimentation."

Lane's comments echoed ones by Gary Gutting in the Opinionator blog of the *New York Times*. "While the physical sciences produce many detailed and precise predictions," wrote Gutting, "the social sciences do not. The reason is that such predictions almost always require randomized controlled experiments, which are seldom possible when people are involved."

This is news to me and the many other social scientists who have spent their careers doing carefully controlled experiments on human behavior, inside and outside the laboratory. What makes the criticism so galling is that those who voice it, or members of their families, have undoubtedly benefited from research in the disciplines they dismiss.

Most of us know someone who has suffered from depression and sought psychotherapy. He or she probably benefited from therapies such as cognitive behavioral therapy that have been shown to work in randomized clinical trials.

Problems such as child abuse and teenage pregnancy take a huge toll on society. Interventions developed by research psychologists, tested with the experimental method, have been found to lower the incidence of child abuse and reduce the rate of teenage pregnancies.

Ever hear of stereotype threat? It is the double jeopardy that people face when they

Jan Hendrik Schön announced in 2001 that he had produced a molecular-scale transistor, other physicists were deeply impressed—that is, until they tried to replicate his work and discovered that Schön had fabricated his data (Agin, 2007). Schön lost his job and his doctoral degree was revoked, but the important point is that such frauds can't last long because one scientist's conclusion is the next scientist's research question. This doesn't mean that all frauds are uncovered, but it does mean that the *important* frauds are.

What exactly are psychologists on their honor to do? At least three things. First, when they write reports of their studies and publish them in scientific journals, psychologists are obligated to report truthfully on what they did and what they found. They can't fabricate results (e.g., claiming to have performed studies that they never really performed) or fudge results (e.g., changing records of data that were actually collected), and they can't mislead by omission (e.g., by reporting only the results that confirm their hypothesis and saying nothing about the results that don't). Second, psychologists are obligated to share credit fairly by including as co-authors of their reports the other people who contributed to the work, and by mentioning in their reports the other scientists who have done related work. And third, psychologists are obligated to share their data. The fact that anyone can check up on anyone else is part of why the honor system works as well as it does.

> **What are psychologists expected to do when they report the results of their research?**

are at risk of confirming a negative stereotype of their group. When African American students take a difficult test, for example, they are concerned not only about how well they will do but also about the possibility that performing poorly will reflect badly on their entire group. This added worry has been shown time and again, in carefully controlled experiments, to lower academic performance. But fortunately, experiments have also showed promising ways to reduce this threat. One intervention, for example, conducted in a middle school, reduced the achievement gap by 40%.

If you know someone who was unlucky enough to be arrested for a crime he didn't commit, he may have benefited from social psychological experiments that have resulted in fairer lineups and interrogations, making it less likely that innocent people are convicted.

An often-overlooked advantage of the experimental method is that it can demonstrate what doesn't work. Consider three popular programs that research psychologists have debunked: Critical Incident Stress Debriefing, used to prevent posttraumatic stress disorders in first responders and others who have witnessed horrific events; the D.A.R.E. antidrug program, used in many schools throughout America; and Scared Straight programs designed to prevent at-risk teens from engaging in criminal behavior.

All three of these programs have been shown, with well-designed experimental studies, to be ineffective or, in some cases, to make matters worse. And as a result, the programs have become less popular or have changed their methods. By discovering what doesn't work, social scientists have saved the public billions of dollars.

To be fair to the critics, social scientists have not always taken advantage of the experimental method as much as they could. Too often, for example, educational programs have been implemented widely without being adequately tested. But increasingly, educational researchers are employing better methodologies. For example, in a recent study, researchers randomly assigned teachers to a program called My Teaching Partner, which is designed to improve teaching skills, or to a control group. Students taught by the teachers who participated in the program did significantly better on achievement tests than did students taught by teachers in the control group.

Are the social sciences perfect? Of course not. Human behavior is complex, and it is not possible to conduct experiments to test all aspects of what people do or why. There are entire disciplines devoted to the experimental study of human behavior, however, in tightly controlled, ethically acceptable ways. Many people benefit from the results, including those who, in their ignorance, believe that science is limited to the study of molecules.

Wilson's examples of psychological investigations that have had beneficial effects on society are excellent, but perhaps even more important is his point that much of psychology is based on carefully controlled experimentation using randomization procedures that the critics apparently believe—mistakenly—cannot be applied to the study of human beings. Should psychology strive to come up with general laws like those of physics or try to make precise predictions like those made by the so-called hard sciences? Should psychologists focus on laboratory experimentation or spend more effort attempting to study behavior in everyday life? What methods seem most promising to you as tools for psychological investigations? There is room for debate about what kind of science psychology is and should be; we hope that you think about these questions as you read this book.

Wilson, T. D. (July 12, 2012). Stop Bullying the "Soft" Sciences. In *The Los Angeles Times.* Copyright 2012 Timothy D. Wilson and Sherrell J. Aston. Reproduced by permission.

CHAPTER REVIEW

SUMMARY

Empiricism and the Scientific Method

> Empiricism is the belief that the best way to understand the world is to observe it firsthand. It is only in the last few centuries that empiricism has come into prominence.

> Empiricism is at the heart of the scientific method, which suggests that our theories about the world give rise to falsifiable hypotheses, and that we can thus make observations that test those hypotheses. The results of these tests can disprove our theories but cannot prove them.

> Observation doesn't just mean "looking." It requires a method. The methods of psychology are special because human beings are especially complex, variable, and reactive.

Observation: Discovering What People Do

> Measurement involves defining a property in concrete terms and then constructing an instrument that can detect the things those terms specify.

> A good measure is valid (the things it measures are conceptually related to the property of interest), reliable (it produces the same measurement whenever it is used to measure the same thing), and powerful (it can detect changes in the dependent variable).

> Demand characteristics are features of a setting that suggest to people that they should behave in a particular way. Psychologists try to reduce or eliminate demand characteristics by making sure participants don't know they are being observed, by measuring things that the participant can't control, and by hiding their expectations from the participant.

> Observer bias is the tendency for observers to see what they expect to see or cause others to behave as they expect them to behave. Psychologists try to eliminate observer bias by making double-blind observations.

Explanation: Discovering Why People Do What They Do

> To determine whether two variables are causally related, we must first determine whether they are related at all. This can be done by measuring each variable many times and then comparing the patterns of variation within each series of measurements. If the patterns are synchronized, then the variables are correlated.

> When we observe a naturally occurring correlation between two variables, we can't conclude that they are causally related because there are an infinite number of third variables that might be causing them both.

> Experiments solve this third-variable problem. In experiments, we manipulate an independent variable, randomly assign participants to the experimental and control groups that this manipulation creates, and measure a dependent variable. These measurements are then compared across groups.

> An internally valid experiment establishes a causal relationship between variables as they were operationally defined and among the people who participated. An externally valid experiment mimics the real world.

> Thinking critically about evidence is difficult because people have a natural tendency to see what they expect to and to fail to consider what they don't see.

The Ethics of Science: First, Do No Harm

> Institutional review boards ensure that scientific research upholds the principles of respect for persons, beneficence, and justice.

> Psychologists are obligated to get informed consent from participants, to not coerce participation, to protect participants from harm, to weigh benefits against risks, to avoid deception, and to keep information confidential.

> Psychologists are obligated to respect the rights of animals and treat them humanely. Most people are in favor of using animals in scientific research.

> Psychologists are obligated to tell the truth about their studies, to share credit appropriately, and to let others examine their data.

KEY TERMS

empiricism (p. 28)
scientific method (p. 28)
theory (p. 28)
hypothesis (p. 29)
empirical method (p. 28)
operational definition (p. 30)
instrument (p. 31)
validity (p. 31)
reliability (p. 31)

power (p. 31)
demand characteristics (p. 31)
naturalistic observation (p. 32)
double-blind (p. 33)
variable (p. 34)
correlation (p. 35)
natural correlation (p. 35)
third-variable correlation (p. 36)
third-variable problem (p. 37)

experiment (p. 37)
manipulation (p. 37)
independent variable (p. 38)
experimental group (p. 38)
control group (p. 38)
dependent variable (p. 38)
self-selection (p. 39)
random assignment (p. 39)
internal validity (p. 40)

external validity (p. 41)
population (p. 42)
sample (p. 43)
case method (p. 43)
random sampling (p. 43)
informed consent (p. 48)
debriefing (p. 48)

CHANGING MINDS

1. Back in Psychology: Evolution of a Science, you read about the principle of reinforcement, which states that the consequences of a behavior determine whether it will be more or less likely to occur in the future. So, for example, a rat's rate of lever pressing will increase if it receives food reinforcement after each lever press. When you tell a classmate about this principle, she only shrugs. "That's obvious. Anyone who's ever owned a dog knows how to train animals. If you ask me, psychology is just common sense. You don't have to conduct scientific experiments to test things that everyone already knows are true." How would you explain the value of studying something that seems like "common sense"?

2. You're watching TV with a friend when a news program reports that a research study has found that Europeans who work longer hours are less happy but Americans who work long hours are more happy (Okulicz-Kozaryn, 2011). "That's an interesting experiment," he says. You point out that the news only said it was a research study, not an experiment. What would have to be true for it to be an experiment? Why aren't all research studies experiments? What can't you learn from this study that you *could* learn from an experiment?

3. After the first exam, your professor says she's noticed a strong positive correlation between the location of students' seats and their exam scores. "The closer students sit to the front of the room, the higher their scores on the exam," she says. After class, your friend suggests that the two of you should sit up front for the rest of the semester to improve your grades. Having read about correlation and causation, should you be skeptical? What are some possible reasons for the correlation between seating position and good grades? Could you design an experiment to test whether sitting up front actually causes good grades?

4. A classmate in your criminal justice class suggests that mental illness is a major cause of violent crimes in the United States. As evidence, he mentions a highly publicized murder trial in which the convicted suspect was diagnosed with schizophrenia. What scientific evidence would he need to support this claim?

5. You ask your friend if he wants to go to the gym with you. "No," he says, "I never exercise." You tell him that regular exercise has all kinds of health benefits, including greatly reducing the risk of heart disease. "I don't believe that," he replies, "I had an uncle who got up at 6 a.m. every day of his life to go jogging, and he still died of a heart attack at age 53." What would you tell your friend? Does his uncle's case prove that exercise really doesn't protect against heart disease after all?

ANSWERS TO SUMMARY

Summary Quiz 2.1: 1. c; 2. c; 3. a
Summary Quiz 2.2: 1. b; 2. d; 3. c
Summary Quiz 2.3: 1. a; 2. c; 3. b; 4. a
Summary Quiz 2.4: 1. c; 2. d; 3. d

Need more help? Additional resources are located in LaunchPad at:
http://www.worthpublishers.com/launchpad/schacterbrief3e

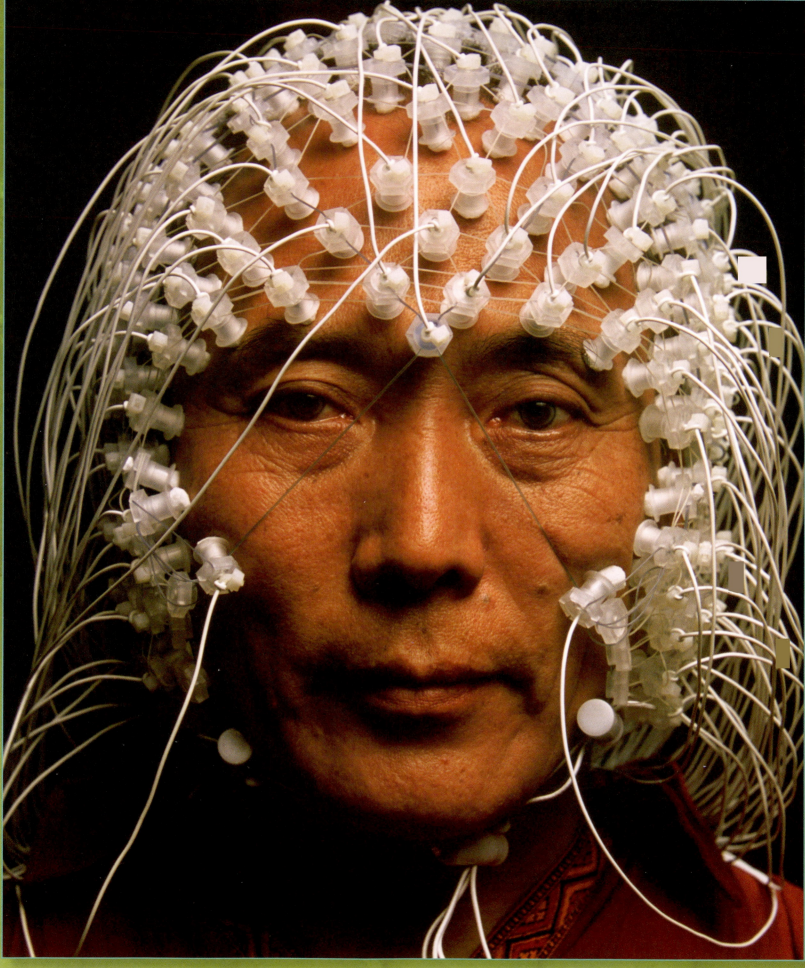

Neuroscience and Behavior

Ray Easterling and Dave Duerson came from different times and places, but both loved football and played the position of defensive back well enough to star in college and make it all the way to the National Football League—Easterling for the Atlanta Falcons during the 1970s, and Duerson for the Chicago Bears in the 1980s. Unfortunately, the parallels between Easterling and Duerson continued into their retirement years. Both men suffered from significant cognitive decline and depression, and both ended up taking their own lives: Duerson in 2011, Easterling in 2012. Postmortem analyses of their brains revealed the presence of a condition known as *chronic traumatic encephalopathy* (*CTE*), a form of progressive brain damage that has been linked to repeated concussions (McKee et al., 2012). Duerson and Easterling are just 2 of over 20 former NFL players who have been diagnosed with CTE, and the condition has also been observed after repeated head injuries in boxing, wrestling, hockey, and rugby (Costanza et al., 2011; Daneshvar et al., 2011; Lahkan & Kirchgessner, 2012; McKee et al., 2012).

We don't know whether CTE contributed to the demise of either Easterling or Duerson, but we do know that CTE is associated with an array of cognitive and emotional deficits in afflicted individuals, including an inability to concentrate, memory loss, irritability, and depression, usually beginning within a decade after repeated concussions and worsening with time (McKee et al., 2009). Fortunately, there is growing awareness of CTE and its consequences, which is leading professional sports organizations, as well as colleges, schools, and others involved in youth sports, to take steps to address the problem.

Ray Easterling (left) and Dave Duerson (right) had similarly outstanding NFL careers and similarly troubled retirements, perhaps associated with brain damage.

AP Photo/File

Michael J Minard/Getty Images

The symptoms of CTE, and the havoc they can wreak in the lives of affected individuals and their families, are stark reminders that our psychological, emotional, and social well-being depends critically on the health and integrity of the brain. The more we know about the brain, the better our chances of finding solutions to problems such as CTE. In this chapter, we'll consider how the brain works, what happens when it doesn't, and how both states of affairs determine behavior. First, we'll introduce you to the basic unit of information processing in the brain, the neuron. The electrical and chemical activities of neurons are the starting point of all behavior, thought, and emotion. Next, we'll consider the anatomy of the central nervous system, focusing especially on the brain, its overall organization, and its evolutionary development. Finally, we'll discuss methods that allow us to study both damaged and healthy brains.

DATA VISUALIZATION

Concussion Rates in High School and College Athletes

www.macmillanhighered.com/schacterbrief3e

Neurons: The Origin of Behavior

An estimated 1 billion people watch the final game of World Cup soccer every 4 years. That's a whole lot of people, but it's still only a little over 14% of the estimated 7 billion people or more currently living on Earth. But a really, really big number is inside your skull right now. There are approximately *100 billion* nerve cells in your brain that perform a variety of tasks to allow you to function as a human being. All of your thoughts, feelings, and behaviors spring from cells in the brain that take in information and produce some kind of output trillions of times a day. These cells are **neurons,** *cells in the nervous system that communicate with one another to perform information-processing tasks.*

Components of the Neuron

Neurons are complex structures composed of three basic parts: the cell body, the dendrites, and the axon (see **FIGURE 3.1**). Like cells in all organs of the body, neurons have a **cell body** (also called the *soma*), the largest component of the neuron that *coordinates the information-processing tasks and keeps the cell alive.* Functions such as protein synthesis, energy production, and metabolism take place here. The cell body contains a *nucleus*, which houses chromosomes that contain your DNA, or the genetic blueprint of who you are. The cell body is surrounded by a porous cell membrane that allows some molecules to flow into and out of the cell.

Unlike other cells in the body, neurons have two types of specialized extensions of the cell membrane that allow them to communicate: dendrites and axons. **Dendrites** *receive information from other neurons and relay it to the cell body.* The term *dendrite* comes from the Greek word for "tree"; indeed, most neurons have many dendrites that look like tree branches. The **axon** *carries information to other neurons, muscles, or glands.* Axons can be very long, even stretching up to a meter from the base of the spinal cord down to the big toe. The dendrites and axons of neurons do not actually touch each other. There's a small gap between the axon of one neuron and the dendrites or cell body of another. This gap is part of the **synapse,** *the junction or region between the axon of one neuron and the dendrites or cell body of another* (see **FIGURE 3.2**). Many of the 100 billion neurons in your brain have a few thousand synaptic junctions, so it should come as no shock that most adults have 100 to 500 trillion synapses. As you'll read shortly, the transmission of information across the synapse is fundamental to communication between neurons, a process that allows us to think, feel, and behave.

In many neurons, the axon is covered by a **myelin sheath,** *an insulating layer of fatty material.* The myelin sheath is composed of **glial cells** (named for the

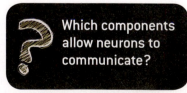

Which components allow neurons to communicate?

neurons Cells in the nervous system that communicate with one another to perform information-processing tasks.

cell body (or soma) The part of a neuron that coordinates information-processing tasks and keeps the cell alive.

dendrites The part of a neuron that receives information from other neurons and relays it to the cell body.

axon The part of a neuron that carries information to other neurons, muscles, or glands.

synapse The junction or region between the axon of one neuron and the dendrites or cell body of another.

myelin sheath An insulating layer of fatty material.

glial cells Support cells found in the nervous system.

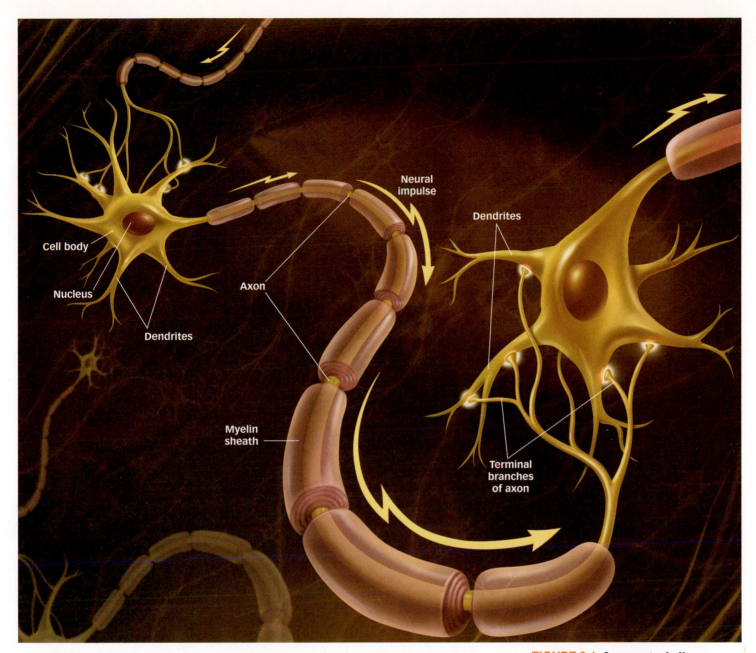

FIGURE 3.1 **Components of a Neuron**
A neuron is made up of three parts: a cell body that houses the chromosomes with the organism's DNA and maintains the health of the cell; dendrites that receive information from other neurons; and an axon that transmits information to other neurons, muscles, and glands.

Greek word for "glue"), which are *support cells found in the nervous system*. Although there are 100 billion neurons busily processing information in your brain, there are 10 to 50 times that many glial cells serving a variety of functions. Some glial cells digest parts of dead neurons, others provide physical and nutritional support for neurons, and others form myelin to help the axon carry information more efficiently. An axon insulated with myelin can more efficiently transmit signals to other neurons, organs, or muscles. In fact, with *demyelinating diseases*, such as multiple sclerosis, the myelin sheath deteriorates, slowing the transmission of information from one neuron to another (Schwartz & Westbrook, 2000). This kind of damage leads to a variety of problems, including loss of feeling in the limbs, partial blindness, and difficulties in coordinated movement and cognition (Butler, Corboy, & Filley, 2009).

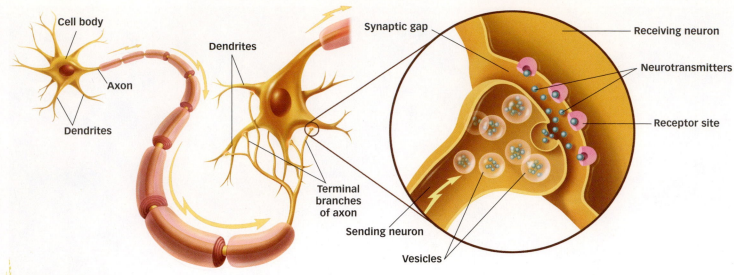

Cell body

Dendrites

Axon

Dendrites

Synaptic gap

Receiving neuron

Neurotransmitters

Receptor site

Terminal branches of axon

Sending neuron

Vesicles

FIGURE 3.2 The Synapse
The synapse is the junction between the dendrites of one neuron and the axon or cell body of another. Notice that neurons do not actually touch one another: There is a small synaptic space between them across which information is transmitted.

Major Types of Neurons

There are three major types of neurons, each performing a distinct function: sensory neurons, motor neurons, and interneurons. **Sensory neurons** *receive information from the external world and convey this information to the brain via the spinal cord.* They have specialized endings on their dendrites that receive signals for light, sound, touch, taste, and smell. **Motor neurons** *carry signals from the spinal cord to the muscles to produce movement.* These neurons often have long axons that can stretch to muscles at our extremities. However, most of the nervous system is composed of the third type of neuron, **interneurons,** which *connect sensory neurons, motor neurons, or other interneurons.* Some interneurons carry information from sensory neurons into the nervous system, others carry information from the nervous system to motor neurons, and still others perform a variety of information-processing functions within the nervous system.

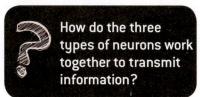

? How do the three types of neurons work together to transmit information?

sensory neurons Neurons that receive information from the external world and convey this information to the brain via the spinal cord.

motor neurons Neurons that carry signals from the spinal cord to the muscles to produce movement.

interneurons Neurons that connect sensory neurons, motor neurons, or other interneurons.

SUMMARY QUIZ [3.1]

1. Which of the following is NOT a function of a neuron?
    a. processing information
    b. communicating with other neurons
    c. nutritional provision
    d. sending messages to body organs and muscles

2. Signals from other neurons are received and relayed to the cell body by
    a. the nucleus.
    b. dendrites.
    c. axons.
    d. glands.

3. Signals are transmitted from one neuron to another
   a. across a synapse.
   b. through a glial cell.
   c. by the myelin sheath.
   d. in the cell body.

4. Which type of neuron receives information from the external world and conveys this information to the brain via the spinal cord?
   a. sensory neuron
   b. motor neuron
   c. interneuron
   d. axon

Information Processing in Neurons

Our thoughts, feelings, and actions depend on neural communication, but how does it happen? The communication of information within and between neurons proceeds in two stages. First, information has to travel inside the neuron via an electrical signal that travels from the dendrite to the cell body to the axon—a process called *conduction*. Then, the signal has to be passed from one neuron to another, usually via chemical messengers traveling across the synapse—a process called *transmission*. Let's look at both processes in more detail.

Electric Signaling: Conducting Information within a Neuron

The neuron's cell membrane has small pores that act as channels to allow small electrically charged molecules, called *ions*, to flow in and out of the cell. It is this flow of ions across the neuron's cell membrane that creates the conduction of an electric signal within the neuron. How does it happen?

The Resting Potential: The Origin of the Neuron's Electrical Properties

Neurons have a natural electric charge called the **resting potential,** *the difference in electric charge between the inside and outside of a neuron's cell membrane* (Kandel, 2000). The resting potential arises from the difference in concentrations of ions inside and outside the neuron's cell membrane (see **FIGURE 3.3a**). Ions can carry a positive (+) or a negative (−) charge. In the resting state, there is a high concentration of a positively charged ion, potassium (K^+), as well as negatively charged protein ions (A^-), *inside* the neuron's cell membrane compared to outside it. By contrast, there is a high concentration of positively charged sodium ions (Na^+) and negatively charged chloride ions (Cl^-) *outside* the neuron's cell membrane.

The concentration of K^+ inside and outside a neuron is controlled by channels in the cell membrane that allow K^+ molecules to flow in and out of the neuron. In the resting state, the channels that allow K^+ molecules to flow freely across the cell membrane are open, while channels that allow the flow of Na^+ and the other ions are generally closed. Because of the naturally higher concentration of K^+ molecules *inside* the neuron, some K^+ molecules move out of the neuron through the open channels, leaving the inside of the neuron with a charge of about −70 millivolts relative to

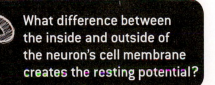

What difference between the inside and outside of the neuron's cell membrane creates the resting potential?

resting potential The difference in electric charge between the inside and outside of a neuron's cell membrane.

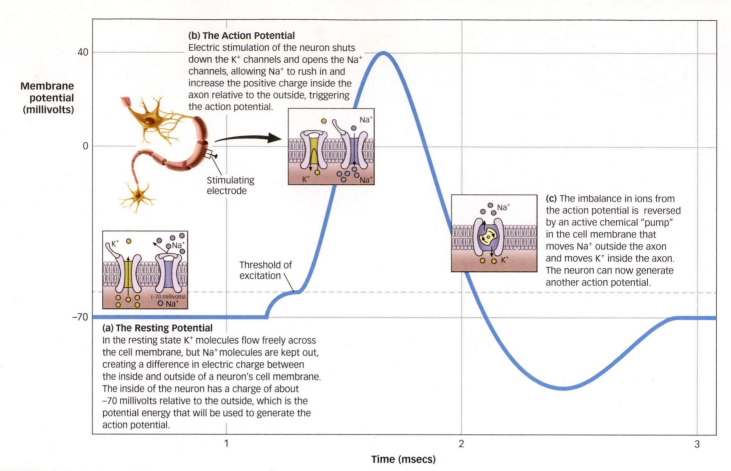

Membrane potential (millivolts)

40

0

−70

(b) The Action Potential
Electric stimulation of the neuron shuts down the K⁺ channels and opens the Na⁺ channels, allowing Na⁺ to rush in and increase the positive charge inside the axon relative to the outside, triggering the action potential.

Stimulating electrode

Threshold of excitation

(c) The imbalance in ions from the action potential is reversed by an active chemical "pump" in the cell membrane that moves Na⁺ outside the axon and moves K⁺ inside the axon. The neuron can now generate another action potential.

(a) The Resting Potential
In the resting state K⁺ molecules flow freely across the cell membrane, but Na⁺ molecules are kept out, creating a difference in electric charge between the inside and outside of a neuron's cell membrane. The inside of the neuron has a charge of about −70 millivolts relative to the outside, which is the potential energy that will be used to generate the action potential.

1   2   3

Time (msecs)

FIGURE 3.3 The Resting and Action Potentials Neurons have a natural electric charge called a resting potential. Electric stimulation causes an action potential.

the outside. Like the Hoover Dam that holds back the Colorado River until the floodgates are released, resting potential is potential energy, because it creates the environment for a possible electrical impulse.

The Action Potential: Sending Signals across the Neuron

The neuron maintains its resting potential most of the time. However, in the 1930s, biologists Alan Hodgkin and Andrew Huxley noticed that they could produce a signal by stimulating the axon with a brief electric shock, which resulted in the conduction of an electric impulse down the length of the axon (Hausser, 2000; Hodgkin & Huxley, 1939). This electric impulse is called an **action potential,** *an electric signal that is conducted along the length of a neuron's axon to a synapse.*

The action potential occurs only when the electric shock reaches a certain level, or *threshold*. The action potential is *all or none*: Electric stimulation below the threshold fails to produce an action potential, whereas electric stimulation at or above the threshold always produces the action potential. The action potential always occurs with exactly the same characteristics and at the same magnitude regardless of whether the stimulus is at or above the threshold.

Why is an action potential an all-or-nothing event?

The action potential occurs when there is a change in the state of the axon's membrane channels. Remember, during the resting potential, the channels that allow K⁺ to flow out are open, resulting in a net negative charge (−70 millivolts)

Like the flow of electricity when you turn on a light, the action potential is all or none. Either the switch is turned on or the room remains dark. Similarly, either the electrical stimulation in the neuron reaches the threshold to fire an action potential, or it remains at the resting potential.

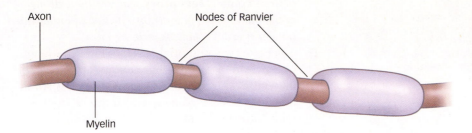

Axon

Nodes of Ranvier

Myelin

FIGURE 3.4 Myelin and Nodes of Ranvier
Myelin is formed by a type of glial cell, and it wraps around a neuron's axon to speed the movement of the action potential along the length of the axon. Breaks in the myelin sheath are called the nodes of Ranvier. The electric impulse jumps from node to node, thereby speeding the conduction of information down the axon.

relative to the outside. However, during an action potential, these channels briefly shut down, and channels that allow the flow of *positively* charged sodium ions (Na⁺) are opened (see **FIGURE 3.3b**). We've seen already that Na⁺ is typically much more concentrated outside the axon than inside. When the channels open, those positively charged ions (Na⁺) flow inside, increasing the positive charge inside the axon relative to the outside. This flow of Na⁺ *into* the axon pushes the action potential from negative (−70 millivolts) to positive (+40 millivolts).

After the action potential reaches its maximum, the membrane channels return to their original state, and K⁺ flows out until the axon returns to its resting potential. This leaves a lot of extra Na⁺ ions inside the axon and a lot of extra K⁺ ions outside the axon. During this period when the ions are imbalanced, the neuron cannot initiate another action potential, so it is said to be in a *refractory period*, the time following an action potential during which a new action potential cannot be initiated. The imbalance in ions is eventually reversed by an active chemical "pump" in the cell membrane that moves Na⁺ outside the axon and moves K⁺ inside the axon (the pump does not operate during the action potential; see **FIGURE 3.3c**).

So far, we've described how the action potential occurs at one point in the neuron. But how does this electric charge move down the axon? It's a domino effect. When an action potential is generated at the beginning of the axon, it spreads a short distance, which generates an action potential at a nearby location on the axon, and so on, thus conducting the charge down the length of the axon.

The myelin sheath facilitates the conduction of the action potential. Myelin doesn't cover the entire axon; rather, it clumps around the axon with little break points between clumps, looking kind of like sausage links. These break points are called the *nodes of Ranvier*, after French pathologist Louis-Antoine Ranvier, who discovered them (see **FIGURE 3.4**). When an electric current passes down the length of a myelinated axon, the charge seems to "jump" from node to node rather than traverse the entire axon (Poliak & Peles, 2003). This process is called *saltatory conduction*, and it helps speed the flow of information down the axon.

Chemical Signaling: Transmission between Neurons

When the action potential reaches the end of an axon, you might think that the action potential stops there. After all, the synaptic space between neurons means that the axon of one neuron and the neighboring neuron's dendrites do not actually touch one another. However, the electric charge of the action potential takes a form that can cross the relatively small synaptic gap by relying on a bit of chemistry.

Axons usually end in **terminal buttons,** *knoblike structures that branch out from an axon.* A terminal button is filled with tiny *vesicles,* or "bags," *that* contain **neurotransmitters,** *chemicals that transmit information across the synapse to a receiving neuron's dendrites.* The dendrites of the receiving

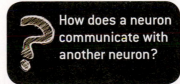

How does a neuron communicate with another neuron?

action potential An electric signal that is conducted along a neuron's axon to a synapse.

terminal buttons Knoblike structures that branch out from an axon.

neurotransmitters Chemicals that transmit information across the synapse to a receiving neuron's dendrites.

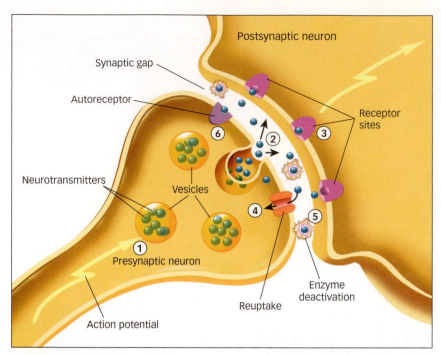

FIGURE 3.5 Synaptic Transmission
(1) The action potential travels down the axon and (2) stimulates the release of neurotransmitters from vesicles. (3) The neurotransmitters are released into the synapse, where they float to bind with receptor sites on a dendrite of a postsynaptic neuron, initiating a new action potential. The neurotransmitters are cleared out of the synapse by (4) reuptake into the sending neuron, (5) being broken down by enzymes in the synapse, or (6) binding to autoreceptors on the sending neuron.

receptors Parts of the cell membrane that receive the neurotransmitter and initiate or prevent a new electric signal.

agonists Drugs that increase the action of a neurotransmitter.

antagonists Drugs that block the function of a neurotransmitter.

neuron contain **receptors,** *parts of the cell membrane that receive neurotransmitters and either initiate or prevent a new electric signal.*

The action potential travels down the length of the axon of the sending neuron, or *presynaptic neuron,* to the terminal buttons, where it stimulates the release of neurotransmitters from vesicles into the synapse. These neurotransmitters float across the synapse and bind to receptor sites on a nearby dendrite of the receiving neuron, or *postsynaptic neuron.* A new electric signal is initiated in that neuron, which may in turn generate an action potential in that neuron. This electrochemical action, called *synaptic transmission* (see **FIGURE 3.5**), allows neurons to communicate with one another.

Neurotransmitters and receptor sites act like a lock-and-key system. Just as a particular key will only fit in a particular lock, so, too, some neurotransmitters will only bind to specific receptor sites on a dendrite. The molecular structure of the neurotransmitter must "fit" the molecular structure of the receptor site.

What happens to the neurotransmitters left in the synapse after the chemical message is relayed to the postsynaptic neuron? Something must make neurotransmitters stop acting on neurons; otherwise, there'd be no end to the signals that they send. Neurotransmitters leave the synapse through three processes (see Figure 3.5). First, neurotransmitters can be reabsorbed by the terminal buttons of the presynaptic neuron's axon, a process called *reuptake.* Second, neurotransmitters can be destroyed by enzymes in the synapse, in a process called *enzyme deactivation.* Third, neurotransmitters can bind to receptor sites called *autoreceptors* on the presynaptic neuron. Autoreceptors detect how much of a neurotransmitter has been released into a synapse and signal the presynaptic neuron to stop releasing the neurotransmitter when an excess is present.

Types and Functions of Neurotransmitters

You might wonder how many types of neurotransmitters are floating across synapses in your brain right now. Today, we know that some 60 chemicals play a role in transmitting information throughout the brain and body and differentially affect thought, feeling, and behavior, but a few major classes seem particularly important. We'll summarize those here, and you'll meet some of these neurotransmitters again in later chapters.

> *Acetylcholine (ACh)* is a neurotransmitter involved in a number of functions, including voluntary motor control. Acetylcholine is found in neurons of the brain and in the synapses where axons connect to muscles and body organs, such as the heart. Acetylcholine contributes to the regulation of attention, learning, sleeping, dreaming, and memory (Gais & Born, 2004; Hasselmo, 2006; Wrenn et al., 2006). Alzheimer's disease, a medical condition involving severe memory impairments (Salmon & Bondi, 2009), is associated with the deterioration of ACh-producing neurons.

> *Dopamine* is a neurotransmitter that regulates motor behavior, motivation, pleasure, and emotional arousal. Because of its role in associating actions with rewards, dopamine plays a role in drug addiction (Baler & Volkow, 2006). High levels of dopamine have been linked to schizophrenia (Winterer & Weinberger, 2004), whereas low levels have been linked to Parkinson's disease.

> *Glutamate* is the major excitatory neurotransmitter in the brain, meaning that it enhances the transmission of information between neurons. *GABA (gamma-aminobutyric acid)*, in contrast, is the primary inhibitory neurotransmitter in the brain, meaning that it tends to stop the firing of neurons. Too much glutamate, or too little GABA, can cause neurons to become overactive, causing seizures.

> Two related neurotransmitters influence mood and arousal: norepinephrine and serotonin. *Norepinephrine* is involved in vigilance, or a heightened awareness of dangers in the environment (Ressler & Nemeroff, 1999). *Serotonin* is involved in the regulation of sleep and wakefulness, eating, and aggressive behavior (Dayan & Huys, 2009; Kroeze & Roth, 1998). Because both neurotransmitters affect mood and arousal, low levels of each have been implicated in mood disorders (Tamminga et al., 2002).

> *Endorphins* are chemicals that act within the pain pathways and emotion centers of the brain (Keefe et al., 2001). Endorphins help dull the experience of pain and elevate moods. The "runner's high" experienced by many athletes as they push their bodies to painful limits of endurance can be explained by the release of endorphins in the brain (Boecker et al., 2008).

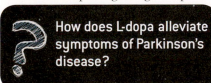 How do neurotransmitters create the feeling of runner's high?

Sandra Wallenhorst of Germany began a 112-mile bicycle ride, just one part of the 2009 Ironman World Championship in Hawaii. When athletes such as Wallenhorst engage in extreme sports, they may experience subjective highs that result from the release of endorphins—chemical messengers acting in emotion and pain centers that elevate mood and dull the experience of pain.

How Drugs Mimic Neurotransmitters

Each of these neurotransmitters affects thought, feeling, and behavior in different ways, so normal functioning involves a delicate balance of each. Even a slight imbalance—too much of one neurotransmitter or not enough of another—can dramatically affect behavior. People who smoke, drink alcohol, or take drugs, legal or not, are altering the balance of neurotransmitters in their brains.

Many drugs that affect the nervous system operate by increasing, interfering with, or mimicking the manufacture or function of neurotransmitters (Cooper, Bloom, & Roth, 2003; Sarter, 2006). **Agonists** are *drugs that increase the action of a neurotransmitter*. **Antagonists** are *drugs that block the function of a neurotransmitter* (see **FIGURE 3.6**).

For example, the drug L-dopa was developed to treat Parkinson's disease, a movement disorder characterized by tremors and difficulty initiating movement and caused by the loss of neurons that use the neurotransmitter dopamine. Dopamine is created in neurons by a modification of a common molecule called L-dopa. Ingesting L-dopa will spur the surviving neurons to produce more dopamine. In other words, L-dopa acts as an agonist for dopamine. The use of L-dopa has been reasonably successful in the alleviation of Parkinson's disease symptoms (Muenter & Tyce, 1971; Schapira et al., 2009).

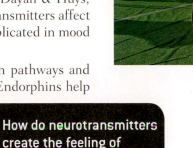 How does L-dopa alleviate symptoms of Parkinson's disease?

Michael J. Fox vividly described his struggles with Parkinson's disease in his 2009 memoir. Fox's visibility has increased public awareness of the disease and spurred greater efforts toward finding a cure.

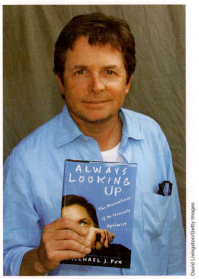

As another example, *amphetamine* is a popular drug that stimulates the release of norepinephrine and dopamine. In addition, both amphetamine and *cocaine* prevent the reuptake of norepinephrine and dopamine. The combination of increased release of norepinephrine and dopamine and the prevention of their reuptake floods the synapse with those neurotransmitters, resulting in increased activation of their receptors. Both of these drugs, therefore, are strong agonists, although the psychological effects of the two drugs differ somewhat because of subtle distinctions in where and how they act on the brain. Norepinephrine and dopamine

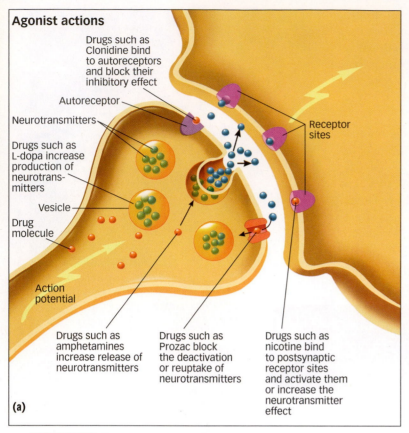

Agonist actions

Drugs such as Clonidine bind to autoreceptors and block their inhibitory effect

Autoreceptor

Neurotransmitters

Drugs such as L-dopa increase production of neurotransmitters

Vesicle

Drug molecule

Action potential

Receptor sites

Drugs such as amphetamines increase release of neurotransmitters

Drugs such as Prozac block the deactivation or reuptake of neurotransmitters

Drugs such as nicotine bind to postsynaptic receptor sites and activate them or increase the neurotransmitter effect

(a)

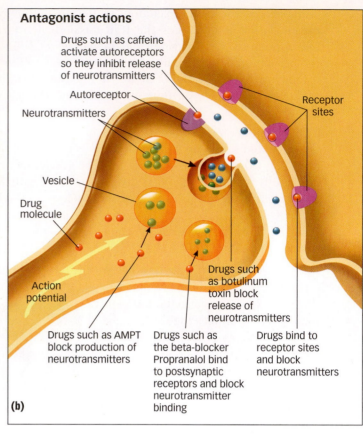

Antagonist actions

Drugs such as caffeine activate autoreceptors so they inhibit release of neurotransmitters

Autoreceptor

Neurotransmitters

Vesicle

Drug molecule

Action potential

Receptor sites

Drugs such as botulinum toxin block release of neurotransmitters

Drugs such as AMPT block production of neurotransmitters

Drugs such as the beta-blocker Propranalol bind to postsynaptic receptors and block neurotransmitter binding

Drugs bind to receptor sites and block neurotransmitters

(b)

FIGURE 3.6 **The Actions of Agonist and Antagonist Drugs** Agonist and antagonist drugs can enhance or interfere with synaptic transmission at every point in the process: in the production of neurotransmitters, in the release of neurotransmitters, at the autoreceptors, in reuptake, in the postsynaptic receptors, and in the synapse itself.

play a critical role in mood control, such that increases in either neurotransmitter result in euphoria, wakefulness, and a burst of energy. However, norepinephrine also increases heart rate. An overdose of amphetamine or cocaine can cause the heart to contract so rapidly that heartbeats do not last long enough to pump blood effectively, leading to fainting and sometimes death.

Other drugs that mimic neurotransmitters, such as antianxiety and antidepression drugs, will be discussed later, in the Treatment of Psychological Disorders chapter.

SUMMARY QUIZ [3.2]

1. An electric signal that is conducted along the length of a neuron's axon to the synapse is called
   a. a resting potential.
   b. an action potential.
   c. a node of Ranvier.
   d. an ion.

2. The chemicals that transmit information across the synapse to a receiving neuron's dendrites are called
   a. vesicles.
   b. terminal buttons.
   c. postsynaptic neurons.
   d. neurotransmitters.

The Organization of the Nervous System

We've seen how individual neurons communicate with each other. What's the bigger picture? Neurons work by forming circuits and pathways in the brain, which in turn influence circuits and pathways in other areas of the body. Neurons are the building blocks that form *nerves*, or bundles of axons and the glial cells that support them. The **nervous system** is *an interacting network of neurons that conveys electrochemical information throughout the body.*

There are two major divisions of the nervous system: the central nervous system and the peripheral nervous system (see **FIGURE 3.7**). The **central nervous system (CNS)** is *composed of the brain and spinal cord.* The central nervous system receives sensory information from the external world, processes and coordinates this information, and sends commands to the skeletal and muscular systems for action. The **peripheral nervous system (PNS)** *connects the central nervous system to the body's organs and muscles.* Let's look at each more closely.

The Peripheral Nervous System

The peripheral nervous system is itself composed of two major subdivisions, the somatic nervous system and the autonomic nervous system (see Figure 3.7). The **somatic nervous system** is *a set of nerves that conveys information between voluntary muscles and the central nervous system.* Humans have conscious control over this system and use it to perceive, think, and coordinate their behaviors. For example, reaching for your morning cup of coffee involves the elegantly orchestrated activities of the somatic nervous system: Information from the receptors in your eyes travels to your brain, registering that a cup is on the table; signals from your brain travel to the muscles in your arm and hand; feedback from those muscles tells your brain that the cup has been grasped; and so on.

In contrast, the **autonomic nervous system (ANS)** is *a set of nerves that carries involuntary and automatic commands that control blood vessels, body organs, and*

nervous system An interacting network of neurons that conveys electrochemical information throughout the body.

central nervous system (CNS) The part of the nervous system that is composed of the brain and spinal cord.

peripheral nervous system (PNS) The part of the nervous system that connects the central nervous system to the body's organs and muscles.

somatic nervous system A set of nerves that conveys information between voluntary muscles and the central nervous system.

autonomic nervous system (ANS) A set of nerves that carries involuntary and automatic commands that control blood vessels, body organs, and glands.

FIGURE 3.7 The Human Nervous System The nervous system is organized into the peripheral and central nervous systems. The peripheral nervous system is further divided into the autonomic and somatic nervous systems.

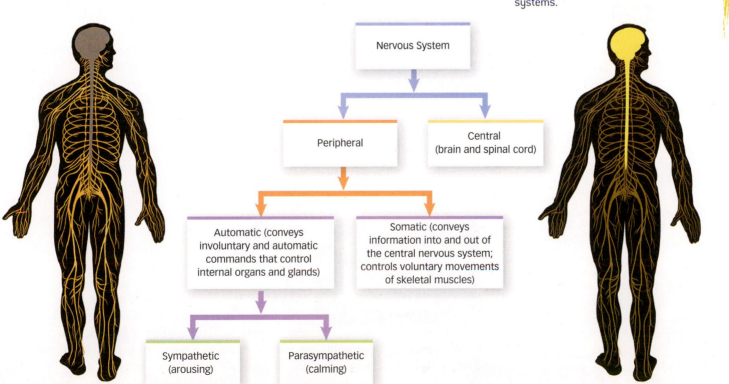

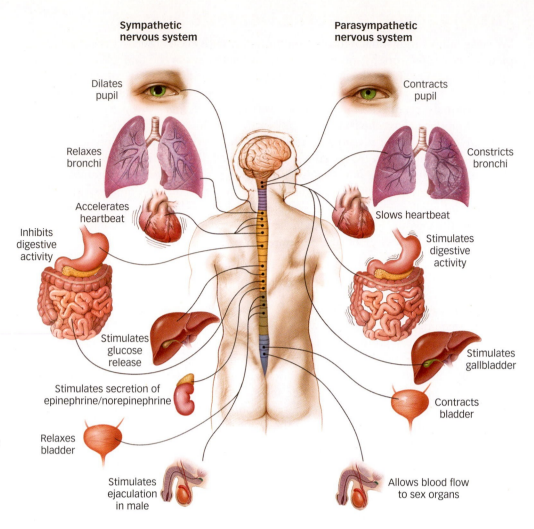

Sympathetic nervous system

Dilates pupil

Relaxes bronchi

Accelerates heartbeat

Inhibits digestive activity

Stimulates glucose release

Stimulates secretion of epinephrine/norepinephrine

Relaxes bladder

Stimulates ejaculation in male

Parasympathetic nervous system

Contracts pupil

Constricts bronchi

Slows heartbeat

Stimulates digestive activity

Stimulates gallbladder

Contracts bladder

Allows blood flow to sex organs

FIGURE 3.8 Sympathetic and Parasympathetic Systems The autonomic nervous system is composed of two subsystems that complement each other. Activation of the sympathetic system serves several aspects of arousal, whereas the parasympathetic nervous system returns the body to its normal resting state.

sympathetic nervous system A set of nerves that prepares the body for action in challenging or threatening situations.

parasympathetic nervous system A set of nerves that helps the body return to a normal resting state.

spinal reflexes Simple pathways in the nervous system that rapidly generate muscle contractions.

glands. As suggested by its name, this system works on its own to regulate bodily systems, largely outside of conscious control. The ANS has two major subdivisions, the sympathetic nervous system and the parasympathetic nervous system. Each exerts a different type of control on the body. The **sympathetic nervous system** is *a set of nerves that prepares the body for action in challenging or threatening situations,* and the **parasympathetic nervous system** *helps the body return to a normal resting state* (see **FIGURE 3.8**). For example, imagine that you are walking alone late at night and frightened by footsteps behind you in a dark alley. Your sympathetic nervous system kicks into action at this point: It dilates your pupils to let in more light, increases your heart rate and respiration to pump more oxygen to muscles, diverts blood flow to your brain and muscles, and activates sweat glands to cool your body. To conserve energy, the sympathetic nervous system inhibits salivation and bowel movements, suppresses the body's immune responses, and suppresses responses to pain and injury. The sum total of these fast, automatic responses is that they increase the likelihood that you can escape. When you're far away from your would-be attacker, your body doesn't need to remain on red alert. Now the parasympathetic nervous system kicks in to reverse the effects of the sympathetic nervous system and return your body to its normal state. The parasympathetic nervous system generally mirrors the connections of the sympathetic nervous system. For example, the parasympathetic nervous system constricts

> **?** **What triggers the increase in your heart rate when you feel threatened?**

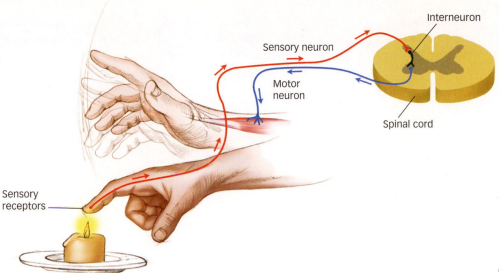

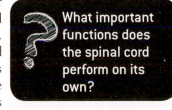

FIGURE 3.9 **The Pain Withdrawal Reflex** Many actions of the central nervous system don't require the brain's input. For example, withdrawing from pain is a reflexive activity controlled by the spinal cord. Painful sensations (such as the heat of fire) travel directly to the spinal cord via sensory neurons, which then issue an immediate command to motor neurons to retract the hand.

your pupils, slows your heart rate and respiration, diverts blood flow to your digestive system, and decreases activity in your sweat glands.

The Central Nervous System

Compared to the many divisions of the peripheral nervous system, the central nervous system may seem simple. After all, it has only two elements: the brain and the spinal cord. But those two elements are ultimately responsible for most of what we do as humans. The brain supports the most complex perceptual, motor, emotional, and cognitive functions of the nervous system. The spinal cord branches down from the brain to relay commands to the body.

The spinal cord often seems like the brain's poor relation: The brain gets all the glory and the spinal cord just hangs around, carrying out the brain's orders. But for some very basic behaviors, the spinal cord doesn't need input from the brain at all. Connections between the sensory inputs and motor neurons in the spinal cord mediate **spinal reflexes,** *simple pathways in the nervous system that rapidly generate muscle contractions.* If you touch a hot stove, the sensory neurons that register pain send inputs directly into the spinal cord (see **FIGURE 3.9**). Through just a few synaptic connections within the spinal cord, interneurons relay these sensory inputs to motor neurons that connect to your arm muscles and direct you to quickly retract your hand.

More elaborate tasks require the collaboration of the spinal cord and the brain. The peripheral nervous system sends messages from sensory neurons through the spinal cord into the brain. The brain sends commands for voluntary movement through the spinal cord to motor neurons, whose axons project out to skeletal muscles. Damage to the spinal cord severs the connection from the brain to the sensory and motor neurons that are essential to sensory perception and movement. The location of the spinal injury often determines the extent of the abilities that are lost. As you can see in **FIGURE 3.10**, different regions of the spinal cord control different systems of the body. Individuals with damage at a particular level of the spinal cord lose sensations of touch and pain in body parts below the level of the injury, as well as a loss of motor control of the muscles in the same areas. A spinal injury higher up the cord usually predicts a much poorer prognosis, such as quadriplegia (loss of sensation and motor control over all limbs), breathing through a respirator, and lifelong immobility. On a brighter note, researchers are making progress in understanding the nature of spinal cord injuries and

> **?** What important functions does the spinal cord perform on its own?

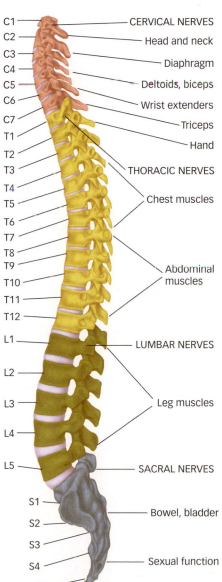

FIGURE 3.10 **Regions of the Spinal Cord** The spinal cord is divided into four main sections; each controls different parts of the body. Damage higher on the spinal cord usually means greater impairment.

how to treat them by focusing on how the brain changes in response to injury (Blesch & Tuszynski, 2009; Dunlop, 2008), a process that is closely related to the concept of brain plasticity that we will examine later in this chapter.

SUMMARY QUIZ [3.3]

1. The _____ automatically controls the organs of the body.
   a. autonomic nervous system
   b. parasympathetic nervous system
   c. sympathetic nervous system
   d. somatic nervous system

2. When you feel threatened, your _____ nervous system prepares you to either fight or run away.
   a. central
   b. somatic
   c. sympathetic
   d. parasympathetic

Structure of the Brain

Right now, your neurons and glial cells are busy humming away, giving you potentially brilliant ideas, consciousness, and feelings. But which neurons in which parts of the brain control which functions? To answer that question, neuroscientists had to find a way of describing the brain. It can be helpful to talk about areas of the brain from "bottom to top," noting how the different regions are specialized for different kinds of tasks. In general, simpler functions are performed at the "lower levels" of the brain, whereas more complex functions are performed at successively "higher" levels (see **FIGURE 3.11**). The brain can also be approached in a "side-by-side" fashion: Although each side of the brain is roughly analogous, one half of the brain specializes in some tasks that the other half doesn't. Although these divisions make it easier to understand areas of the brain and their functions, keep in mind that none of these structures or areas in the brain can act alone: They are all part of one big, interacting, interdependent whole.

Let's look first at the divisions of the brain and the responsibilities of each part, moving from the bottom to the top. Using this view, we can divide the brain into three parts: the hindbrain, the midbrain, and the forebrain (see Figure 3.11).

The human brain weighs only three pounds and isn't much to look at, but its accomplishments are staggering.

Omikron/Science Source

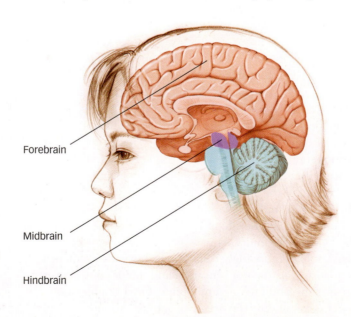

FIGURE 3.11 The Major Divisions of the Brain The brain can be organized into three parts, moving from the bottom to the top, from simpler functions to the more complex: the hindbrain, the midbrain, and the forebrain.

Forebrain

Midbrain

Hindbrain

The Hindbrain

If you follow the spinal cord from your tailbone to where it enters your skull, you'll find it difficult to determine where your spinal cord ends and your brain begins. That's because the spinal cord is continuous with the **hindbrain**, *an area of the brain that coordinates information coming into and out of the spinal cord.* The hindbrain looks like a stalk on which the rest of the brain sits, and it controls the most basic functions of life: respiration, alertness, and motor skills. The structures that make up the hindbrain include the medulla, the reticular formation, the cerebellum, and the pons (see **FIGURE 3.12**).

The **medulla** is *an extension of the spinal cord into the skull that coordinates heart rate, circulation, and respiration.* Beginning inside the medulla and extending upward is a small cluster of neurons called the **reticular formation,** which *regulates sleep, wakefulness, and levels of arousal.* In one early experiment, researchers stimulated the reticular formation of a sleeping cat. This caused the animal to awaken almost instantaneously and remain alert. Conversely, severing the connections between the reticular formation and the rest of the brain caused the animal to lapse into an irreversible coma (Moruzzi & Magoun, 1949). The reticular formation maintains the same delicate balance between alertness and unconsciousness in humans. In fact, many general anesthetics work by reducing activity in the reticular formation, rendering the patient unconscious.

Behind the medulla is the **cerebellum,** *a large structure of the hindbrain that controls fine motor skills.* (*Cerebellum* is Latin for "little brain," and the structure does look like a small replica of the brain.) The cerebellum orchestrates the proper sequence of movements when we ride a bike, play the piano, or maintain balance while walking and running. It contributes to the fine-tuning of behavior: smoothing our actions to allow their graceful execution rather than initiating the actions (Smetacek, 2002). The initiation of behavior involves other areas of the brain; as you'll recall, different brain systems interact and are interdependent with one another.

The last major area of the hindbrain is the **pons,** *a structure that relays information from the cerebellum to the rest of the brain.* (*Pons* means "bridge" in Latin.) Although the detailed functions of the pons remain poorly understood, it essentially acts as a relay station or bridge between the cerebellum and other structures in the brain.

The Midbrain

Sitting on top of the hindbrain is the *midbrain*, which is relatively small in humans. As you can see in **FIGURE 3.13,** the midbrain contains two main structures: the *tectum* and the *tegmentum*. These structures help orient an organism in the environment, and they guide movement towards or away from stimuli. For example, when you're studying in a quiet room and you hear a *click* behind and to the right of you, your body will swivel and orient to the direction of the sound; this is your *tectum* in action.

The midbrain may be relatively small, but it's important. In fact, you could survive if you had only a hindbrain and a midbrain. The structures in the hindbrain would

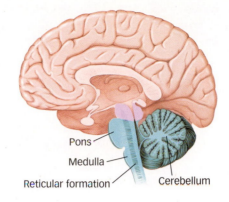

FIGURE 3.12 The Hindbrain The hindbrain coordinates information coming into and out of the spinal cord and controls the basic functions of life. It includes the medulla, the reticular formation, the cerebellum, and the pons.

Pons
Medulla
Reticular formation
Cerebellum

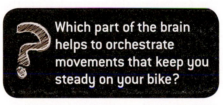

Which part of the brain helps to orchestrate movements that keep you steady on your bike?

High wire artist Freddy Nock relied on his cerebellum to coordinate the movements necessary to walk on the rope of the Corvatsch cable car from more than 10,000 feet over sea level down to the base station in Silvaplana, Switzerland on January 29, 2011. Nock set a new mark that day for the Guinness World Records.

AP Photo/Keystone, Arno Balzarini

hindbrain An area of the brain that coordinates information coming into and out of the spinal cord.

medulla An extension of the spinal cord into the skull that coordinates heart rate, circulation, and respiration.

reticular formation A brain structure that regulates sleep, wakefulness, and levels of arousal.

cerebellum A large structure of the hindbrain that controls fine motor skills.

pons A brain structure that relays information from the cerebellum to the rest of the brain.

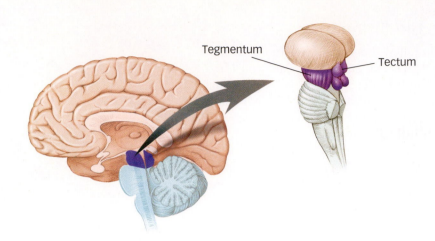

FIGURE 3.13 **The Midbrain** The midbrain is important for orientation and movement. It includes structures such as the tectum and tegmentum.

subcortical structures Areas of the forebrain housed under the cerebral cortex near the very center of the brain.

thalamus A subcortical structure that relays and filters information from the senses and transmits the information to the cerebral cortex.

take care of all the bodily functions necessary to sustain life, and the structures in the midbrain would orient you toward or away from pleasurable or threatening stimuli in the environment. But this wouldn't be much of a life. To understand where the abilities that make us fully human come from, we need to consider the last division of the brain.

The Forebrain

When you appreciate the beauty of a poem, plan to go skiing next winter, or notice the faint glimmer of sadness on a loved one's face, you are enlisting the forebrain. The *forebrain* is the highest level of the brain—literally and figuratively—and controls complex cognitive, emotional, sensory, and motor functions. The forebrain itself is divided into two main sections: the subcortical structures and the cerebral cortex. Let's look at each.

Subcortical Structures

The **subcortical structures** are *areas of the forebrain housed under the cerebral cortex near the center of the brain* (see **FIGURE 3.14**). They include the thalamus, hypothalamus, pituitary gland, hippocampus, amygdala, and basal ganglia, and these structures play an important role in relaying information throughout the brain, as well as performing

FIGURE 3.14 **The Forebrain** The forebrain is the highest level of the brain and is critical for complex cognitive, emotional, sensory, and motor functions. The forebrain is divided into two parts: the cerebral cortex and the underlying subcortical structures. The cerebral cortex, the outermost layer of the brain, is divided into two hemispheres, connected by the corpus callosum (see Figure 3.16). The subcortical structures include the thalamus, hypothalamus, pituitary gland, amygdala, hippocampus, and basal ganglia.

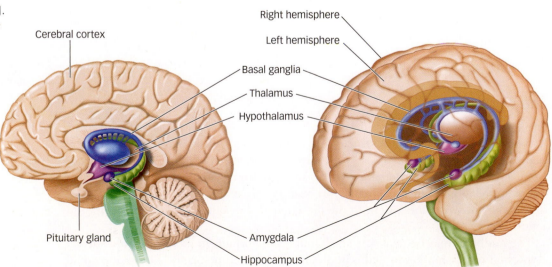

Cerebral cortex

Right hemisphere

Left hemisphere

Basal ganglia

Thalamus

Hypothalamus

Pituitary gland

Amygdala

Hippocampus

specific tasks that allow us to think, feel, and behave as humans. If you imagine sticking an index finger in each of your ears and pushing inward until they touch, that's about where you'd find the subcortical structures (see Figure 3.14). Let's take a quick look at each.

The **thalamus** *relays and filters information from the senses and transmits the information to the cerebral cortex.* The thalamus receives inputs from all the major senses except smell, and it acts as a kind of computer server in a net-worked system, taking in multiple inputs and relaying them to a variety of locations (Guillery & Sherman, 2002). However, unlike the mechanical operations of a computer ("send input A to location B"), the thalamus actively filters sensory information, giving more weight to some inputs and less weight to others. The thalamus also closes the pathways of incoming sensations during sleep, providing a valuable function in *not* allowing information to pass to the rest of the brain.

> **How is the thalamus like a computer?**

The thalamus receives inputs from all the major senses except smell. You can thank your thalamus when you see the red apple, feel its smoothness in your hand, hear the crunch as you bite into it, and taste its sweetness.

The **hypothalamus,** located below the thalamus (*hypo-* is Greek for "under"), *regulates body temperature, hunger, thirst, and sexual behavior.* For example, lesions to some areas of the hypothalamus result in overeating, whereas lesions to other areas leave an animal with no desire for food at all (Berthoud & Morrison, 2008).

Located below the hypothalamus is the **pituitary gland,** *the "master gland" of the body's hormone-producing system, which releases hormones that direct the functions of many other glands in the body.* The hypothalamus sends hormonal signals to the pituitary gland, which in turn sends hormonal signals to other glands to control stress, digestive activities, and reproductive processes. For example, when we sense a threat, sensory neurons send signals to the hypothalamus, which stimulates the release of adrenocorticotropic hormone (ACTH) from the pituitary gland. ACTH, in turn, stimulates the adrenal glands (above the kidneys) to release hormones that activate the sympathetic nervous system (Selye & Fortier, 1950). As you read earlier in this chapter, the sympathetic nervous system prepares the body to either meet the threat head-on or flee from the situation.

The **hippocampus** (from Latin for "sea horse," due to its shape) is *critical for creating new memories and integrating them into a network of knowledge so that they can be stored indefinitely in other parts of the cerebral cortex.* Individuals with damage to the hippocampus can acquire new information and keep it in awareness for a few seconds, but as soon as they are distracted, they forget the information and the experience that produced it (Scoville & Milner, 1957; Squire, 2009). This kind of disruption is limited to everyday memory for facts and events that we can bring to consciousness; memory of learned habitual routines or emotional reactions remains intact (Squire, Knowlton, & Musen, 1993). As an example, people with damage to the hippocampus can remember how to drive and talk, but they cannot recall where they have recently driven or a conversation they have just had.

The **amygdala** (from Latin for "almond," also due to its shape), *located at the tip of each horn of the hippocampus, plays a central role in many emotional processes,*

> **Why are you likely to remember details of a traumatic event?**

particularly the formation of emotional memories (Aggleton, 1992). When we are in emotionally arousing situations, the amygdala stimulates the hippocampus to remember many details surrounding the situation (Kensinger & Schacter, 2005). For example, people who lived through the terrorist

hypothalamus A subcortical structure that regulates body temperature, hunger, thirst, and sexual behavior.

pituitary gland The "master gland" of the body's hormone-producing system, which releases hormones that direct the functions of many other glands in the body.

hippocampus A structure critical for creating new memories and integrating them into a network of knowledge so that they can be stored indefinitely in other parts of the cerebral cortex.

amygdala A part of the limbic system that plays a central role in many emotional processes, particularly the formation of emotional memories.

A haunted house is designed to stimulate your amygdala, but only a little.

basal ganglia A set of subcortical structures that directs intentional movements.

cerebral cortex The outermost layer of the brain, visible to the naked eye and divided into two hemispheres.

corpus callosum A thick band of nerve fibers that connects large areas of the cerebral cortex on each side of the brain and supports communication of information across the hemispheres.

occipital lobe A region of the cerebral cortex that processes visual information.

parietal lobe A region of the cerebral cortex whose functions include processing information about touch.

attacks of September 11, 2001, remember vivid details about where they were, what they were doing, and how they felt when they heard the news, even years later (Hirst et al., 2009).

There are several other structures in the subcortical area, but we'll consider just one more. The **basal ganglia** are *a set of subcortical structures that directs intentional movements*. The basal ganglia receive input from the cerebral cortex and send outputs to the motor centers in the brain stem. One part of the basal ganglia, the *striatum*, is involved in the control of posture and movement. People who suffer from Parkinson's disease typically show symptoms of uncontrollable shaking and sudden jerks of the limbs and are unable to initiate a sequence of movements to achieve a specific goal. This happens because the dopamine-producing neurons in the tegmentum of the midbrain have become damaged (Dauer & Przedborski, 2003). The undersupply of dopamine then affects the striatum in the basal ganglia, which in turn leads to the visible behavioral symptoms of Parkinson's. This unfortunate disease provides a nice illustration of how hindbrain, midbrain, and forebrain structures all interact.

The Cerebral Cortex

Our tour of the brain has taken us from the very small (neurons) to the somewhat bigger (major divisions of the brain) to the very large: the **cerebral cortex,** which is *the outermost layer of the brain, visible to the naked eye, and divided into two hemispheres.* The cortex is the highest level of the brain, and it is responsible for the most complex aspects of perception, emotion, movement, and thought (Fuster, 2003). It sits over the rest of the brain, like a mushroom cap shielding the underside and stem, and it is the wrinkled surface you see when looking at the brain with the naked eye. The cerebral cortex occupies roughly the area of a newspaper page. Fitting that much cortex into a human skull is a tough task. But if you crumple a sheet of newspaper, you'll see that the same surface area now fits compactly into a much smaller space. The cortex, with its wrinkles and folds, holds a lot of brainpower in a relatively small package that fits comfortably inside the human skull (see **FIGURE 3.15**). The cerebral cortex can be best understood by studying its functions according to three levels of its organization: 1) across its two hemispheres; 2) within each hemisphere; and 3) within the specific cortical areas.

1. Organization across Hemispheres. The first level of organization divides the cortex into the left and right hemispheres. The two hemispheres are more or less symmetrical in their appearance and, to some extent, in their functions. However, each hemisphere controls the functions of the opposite side of the body. This is called *contralateral control*, meaning that your right cerebral hemisphere perceives stimuli from and controls movements on the left side of your body, whereas your left cerebral hemisphere perceives stimuli from and controls movement on the right side of your body.

The cerebral hemispheres are connected to each other by bundles of axons that make possible communication between parallel areas of the cortex in each half. The largest of these bundles is the **corpus callosum,** which *connects large areas of the cerebral cortex on each side of the brain and supports communication of information across the hemispheres*

Crumpling a newspaper allows the same amount of surface area to fit into a much smaller space, just like the wrinkles and folds in the cortex allow a great deal of brain power to fit inside the human skull.

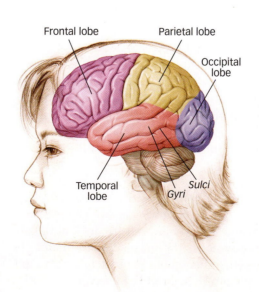

FIGURE 3.15 Cerebral Cortex and Lobes The four major lobes of the cerebral cortex are the occipital lobe, the parietal lobe, the temporal lobe, and the frontal lobe. The smooth surfaces of the cortex are called gyri and the indentations are called sulci.

Frontal lobe   Parietal lobe

Occipital lobe

Temporal lobe   Sulci

Gyri

(see **FIGURE 3.16**). This means that information received in the right hemisphere, for example, can pass across the corpus callosum to the left hemisphere.

2. Organization within Hemispheres.
The second level of organization in the cerebral cortex distinguishes the functions of the different regions within each hemisphere of the brain. Each hemisphere of the cerebral cortex is divided into four areas, or *lobes*: From back to front, these are the occipital lobe, the parietal lobe, the temporal lobe, and the frontal lobe, as shown in Figure 3.15.

The **occipital lobe,** located at the back of the cerebral cortex, *processes visual information.* Sensory receptors in the eyes send information to the thalamus, which in turn sends information to the primary areas of the occipital lobe, where simple features of the stimulus are extracted, such as the location and orientation of an object's edges (see the Sensation and Perception chapter for more details). These features are then processed still further, leading to comprehension of what's being seen. Damage to the primary visual areas of the occipital lobe can leave a person with partial or complete blindness. Information still enters the eyes, but without the ability to process and make sense of the information in the cerebral cortex, the information is as good as lost (Zeki, 2001).

The **parietal lobe,** located in front of the occipital lobe, carries out functions that include *processing information about touch.* The parietal lobe contains the *somatosensory cortex*, a strip of brain tissue running from the top of the brain down to the sides (see **FIGURE 3.17**). Within each hemisphere, the somatosensory cortex represents the skin areas on the contralateral surface of the body. Each part of the somatosensory cortex maps onto a particular part of the body. If a body area is more sensitive, a larger part of the somatosensory cortex is devoted to it. For example, the part of the somatosensory cortex that corresponds to the lips and tongue is larger than the area corresponding to the feet. The somatosensory cortex can be illustrated as a distorted figure, called a *homunculus* ("little man"), in which the body parts are rendered according to how much of the somatosensory cortex is devoted to them (Penfield & Rasmussen, 1950). Directly in front of the somatosensory cortex, in the frontal lobe, is a parallel strip of brain tissue called the *motor cortex*. Like the somatosensory cortex, the motor cortex has different parts that correspond to different body parts. The motor cortex initiates voluntary movements and sends messages to the basal ganglia, cerebellum, and spinal cord. The motor and somatosensory cortices, then, are like sending and receiving areas of the cerebral cortex, taking in information and sending out commands.

The **temporal lobe,** located on the lower side of each hemisphere, is *responsible for hearing and language.* The *primary auditory cortex* in the temporal lobe is analogous to the somatosensory cortex in the parietal lobe and the primary visual areas of the occipital lobe: It receives sensory information from the ears based on the frequencies of sounds (Recanzone & Sutter, 2008). Secondary areas of the temporal lobe then process the information into meaningful units, such as speech and words. The temporal lobe also houses the visual association areas that interpret the meaning of visual stimuli and help us recognize common objects in the environment (Martin, 2007).

The **frontal lobe,** which sits behind the forehead, has *specialized areas for movement, abstract thinking, planning, memory, and judgment.* As you just read, it contains the motor cortex, which coordinates movements of muscle groups throughout the body. Other areas

> **Why is the part of the somatosensory cortex relating to the lips bigger than the area corresponding to the feet?**

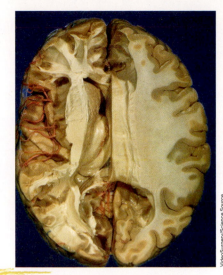

FIGURE 3.16 **Cerebral Hemispheres** The corpus callosum connects the two hemispheres and supports communication between them.

VideoSurgery/Science Source

temporal lobe A region of the cerebral cortex responsible for hearing and language.

frontal lobe A region of the cerebral cortex that has specialized areas for movement, abstract thinking, planning, memory, and judgment.

The homunculus is a rendering of the body in which each part is shown in proportion to how much of the somatosensory cortex is devoted to it.

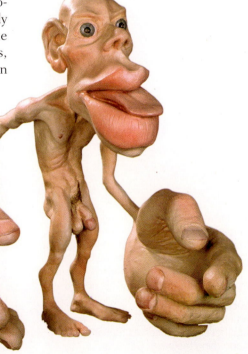

©The NATURAL HISTORY Museum/The Image Works

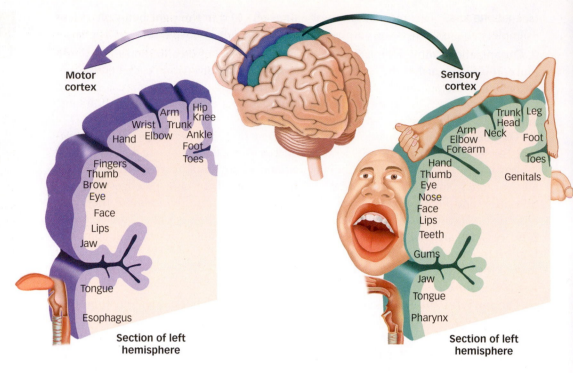

FIGURE 3.17 Somatosensory and Motor Cortices The motor cortex, a strip of brain tissue in the frontal lobe, represents and controls different skin and body areas on the contralateral side of the body. Directly behind the motor cortex, in the parietal lobe, lies the somatosensory cortex. Like the motor cortex, the somatosensory cortex represents skin areas of particular parts on the contralateral side of the body.

in the frontal lobe coordinate thought processes that help us manipulate information and retrieve memories, which we can use to plan our behaviors and interact socially with others. In short, the frontal cortex allows us to do the kind of thinking, imagining, planning, and anticipating that sets humans apart from most other species (Schoenemann, Sheenan, & Glotzer, 2005; Stuss & Benson, 1986; Suddendorf & Corballis, 2007).

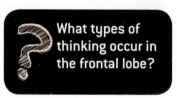

What types of thinking occur in the frontal lobe?

3. Organization within Specific Lobes. The third level of organization in the cerebral cortex involves the representation of information within specific lobes in the cortex. There is a hierarchy of processing stages from primary areas that handle fine details of information all the way up to **association areas,** which are *composed of neurons that help provide sense and meaning to information registered in the cortex.* For example, neurons in the primary visual cortex are highly specialized: Some detect features of the environment that are in a horizontal orientation, others detect movement, and still others process information about human versus nonhuman forms. Secondary areas interpret the information extracted by these primary areas (shape, motion, etc.) to make sense of what's being perceived—in this case, perhaps a large cat leaping toward your face. Similarly, neurons in the primary auditory cortex register sound frequencies, but it's the association areas of the temporal lobe that allow you to turn those noises into the meaning of your friend screaming, "Look out for the cat!" Association areas, then, help stitch together the threads of information in the various parts of the cortex to produce a meaningful understanding of what's being registered in the brain.

A striking example of this property of association areas comes from the discovery of mirror neurons. **Mirror neurons** are *active when an animal performs a behavior, such as reaching for or manipulating an object, and they are also activated when another animal observes the first animal as it performs the same behavior.* Mirror neurons are found in the frontal lobe (near the motor cortex) and in the parietal lobe

association areas Areas of the cerebral cortex that are composed of neurons that help provide sense and meaning to information registered in the cortex.

mirror neurons Neurons that are active when an animal performs a behavior, such as reaching for or manipulating an object, and are also activated when another animal observes that animal performing the same behavior.

(Rizzolatti & Craighero, 2004; Rizzolatti & Sinigaglia, 2012). Neuroimaging studies have shown that mirror neurons are active when people watch someone perform a behavior, such as grasping in midair, and seem to be related to recognizing the goal someone has in carrying out an action (Hamilton & Grafton, 2006, 2008; Iacoboni, 2009; Rizzolatti & Sinigaglia, 2012).

Finally, neurons in the association areas are usually less specialized and more flexible than neurons in the primary areas. As such, they can be shaped by learning and experience to do their job more effectively. This kind of shaping of neurons by environmental forces allows the brain flexibility, or plasticity, our next topic.

When one animal observes another engaging in a particular behavior, some of the same neurons become active in the observer as well as in the animal exhibiting the behavior. These mirror neurons seem to play an important role in social behavior.

Brain Plasticity

The cerebral cortex may seem like a fixed structure, one big sheet of neurons designed to help us make sense of our external world. Remarkably, though, sensory cortices are not fixed. They can adapt to changes in sensory inputs, a quality researchers call *plasticity* (i.e., the ability to be molded). As an example, if you lose your middle finger in an accident, the part of the somatosensory area that represents that finger is initially unresponsive (Kaas, 1991). After all, there's no longer any sensory input coming from that location to that part of the brain. You might expect the left middle-finger neurons of the somatosensory cortex to wither away. However, over time, that area in the somatosensory cortex becomes responsive to stimulation of the fingers *adjacent* to the missing finger. The brain is plastic: Functions that were assigned to certain areas of the brain may be capable of being reassigned to other areas of the brain to accommodate changing input from the environment (Feldman, 2009). This suggests that sensory inputs "compete" for representation in each cortical area. (See the Real World box for a striking illustration of phantom limbs.)

? What does it mean to say that the brain is plastic?

Plasticity doesn't only occur to compensate for missing digits or limbs, however. An extraordinary amount of stimulation of one finger can result in that finger "taking over" the representation of the part of the cortex that usually represents other, adjacent fingers (Merzenich et al., 1990). For example, concert pianists have highly developed cortical areas for finger control: The continued input from the fingers commands a larger area of representation in the somatosensory cortices in the brain. Consistent with this observation, recent research indicates greater plasticity within the motor cortex of professional musicians compared with nonmusicians, perhaps reflecting an increase in the number of motor synapses as a result of extended practice (Rosenkranz, Williamon, & Rothwell, 2007).

Plasticity is also related to a question you might not expect to find in a psychology text: How much exercise have you been getting lately? A large number of studies in rats and other nonhuman animals indicates that physical exercise can increase the number of synapses and even promote the development of new neurons in the hippocampus (Hillman, Erickson, & Kramer, 2008; van Praag, 2009). Studies also document beneficial effects of cardiovascular exercise on aspects of brain function and cognitive performance (Colcombe et al., 2004, 2006). It should be clear by now that the plasticity of the brain is not just an interesting theoretical idea; it has potentially important applications to everyday life (Bryck & Fisher, 2012).

Everyday forms of exercise, such as running, can benefit not only your heart, but also your brain.

The Real World

Brain Plasticity and Sensations in Phantom Limbs

Long after a limb is amputated, many patients continue to experience sensations where the missing limb would be, a phenomenon called *phantom limb syndrome*. Some even report feeling pain in their phantom limbs. Why does this happen? Some evidence suggests that phantom limb syndrome may arise in part because of plasticity in the brain.

Researchers stimulated the skin surface in various regions around the face, torso, and arms while monitoring brain activity in amputees (Ramachandran & Blakeslee, 1998; Ramachandran, Brang, & McGeoch, 2010; Ramachandran, Rodgers-Ramachandran, & Stewart, 1992). Brain imaging techniques displayed the cortical areas activated when the skin was stimulated. Stimulating areas of the face and upper arm activated an area in the somatosensory cortex that previously would have been activated by a now-missing hand. The face and arm were represented in the somatosensory cortex in an area adjacent to where the person's hand—now amputated—would have been represented. Stimulating the face or arm produced phantom limb sensations in the amputees; they reported "feeling" a sensation in their missing limbs.

Brain plasticity can explain these results (Pascual-Leone et al., 2005). The somatosensory areas for the face and upper arm were larger in amputees and had taken over the part of the cortex normally representing the hand. Indeed, the new face and arm representations were now contiguous with each other, filling in the space occupied by the hand representation. Some of these new mappings were quite concise. For example, in some amputees, when specific areas of the facial skin were activated, the patient reported sensations in just *one finger* of the phantom hand!

This idea has practical implications for dealing with the pain that can result from phantom limbs (Ramachandran & Altschuler, 2009). Researchers have used a "mirror box" to teach patients a new mapping to increase voluntary control over their phantom limbs. For example, a patient would place his intact right hand and phantom left hand in the mirror box such that when looking at the mirror, he sees his right hand reflected on the left—where he has placed his phantom—creating the illusion that the phantom has been

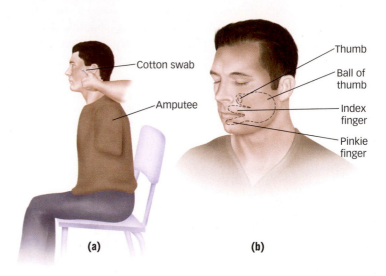

(a) Cotton swab — Amputee

(b) Thumb, Ball of thumb, Index finger, Pinkie finger

Mapping Sensations in Phantom Limbs (*a*) Researchers lightly touch an amputee's face with a cotton swab, eliciting sensations in the "missing" hand. (*b*) Touching different parts of the cheek can even result in sensations in particular fingers or the thumb of the missing hand.

restored. The phantom hand thus appears to respond to motor commands given by the patient, and with practice, the patient can become better at "moving" the phantom in response to voluntary commands. As a result, when feeling the excruciating pain associated with a clenched phantom hand, the patient can now voluntarily unclench the hand and reduce the pain. This therapeutic approach based on brain plasticity has been applied successfully to a variety of patient populations (Ramachandran & Altschuler, 2009). In one of the most striking applications, researchers used mirror box therapy with survivors of the destructive 2010 earthquake in Haiti who were experiencing phantom limb pain after

amputation of lower limbs (Miller, Seckel, & Ramachandran, 2012). Seventeen of the 18 amputees in that study reported a significant reduction in experienced pain following mirror box therapy.

A mirror box creates the illusion that the phantom limb has been restored.

V. S. Ramachandran et al., 2009

SUMMARY QUIZ [3.4]

1. Which part of the hindbrain coordinates fine motor skills?
   a. the medulla
   b. the cerebellum
   c. the pons
   d. the tegmentum

2. What part of the brain is involved in movement and arousal?
   a. the hindbrain
   b. the midbrain
   c. the forebrain
   d. the reticular formation

3. The _____ regulates body temperature, hunger, thirst, and sexual behavior.
   a. cerebral cortex
   b. pituitary gland
   c. hypothalamus
   d. hippocampus

4. What explains the apparent beneficial effects of cardiovascular exercise on aspects of brain function and cognitive performance?
   a. the different sizes of the somatosensory cortices
   b. the position of the cerebral cortex
   c. specialization of association areas
   d. neuron plasticity

The Development and Evolution of Nervous Systems

Far from being a single, elegant machine, the human brain is instead a system comprised of many distinct components that have been added at different times during the course of evolution. The human species has retained what worked best in earlier versions of the brain, then added bits and pieces to get us to our present state through evolution.

To understand the central nervous system, it is helpful to consider two aspects of its development. Prenatal development (growth from conception to birth) reveals how the nervous system develops and changes within each member of a species. Evolutionary development reveals how the nervous system in humans evolved and adapted from other species.

Prenatal Development of the Central Nervous System

The nervous system is the first major bodily system to take form in an embryo (Moore, 1977). It begins to develop within the 3rd week after fertilization, when the embryo is still in the shape of a sphere. Initially, a ridge forms on one side of the sphere and then builds up at its edges to become a deep groove. The ridges fold together and fuse to enclose the groove, forming a structure called the *neural tube*. The tail end of the neural tube will remain a tube, and as the embryo grows larger, this tube forms

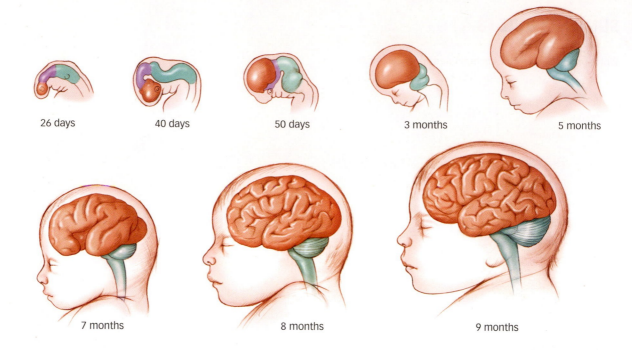

26 days   40 days   50 days   3 months   5 months

7 months   8 months   9 months

FIGURE 3.18 **Prenatal Brain Development**
The more primitive parts of the brain, the hindbrain and midbrain, develop first, followed by successively higher levels. The cerebral cortex with its characteristic fissures doesn't develop until the middle of the pregnancy. The cerebral hemispheres undergo most of their development in the final trimester.

the basis of the spinal cord. The tube expands at the opposite end, so that by the 4th week, the three basic levels of the brain are visible. During the 5th week, the forebrain and hindbrain further differentiate into subdivisions. During the 7th week and later, the forebrain expands considerably to form the cerebral hemispheres.

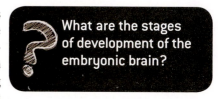

What are the stages of development of the embryonic brain?

As the embryonic brain continues to grow, each subdivision folds onto the next one and begins to form the structures easily visible in the adult brain (see **FIGURE 3.18**). The hindbrain forms the cerebellum and medulla, the midbrain forms the tectum and the tegmentum, and the forebrain subdivides further, separating the thalamus and hypothalamus from the cerebral hemispheres. In about half the time it takes you to complete a 15-week semester, the basic structures of the brain are in place and rapidly developing.

Evolutionary Development of the Central Nervous System

The central nervous system evolved from the very simple one found in simple animals to the elaborate nervous system in humans today. Even the simplest animals have sensory neurons and motor neurons for responding to the environment (Shepherd, 1988). For example, single-celled protozoa have molecules in their cell membrane that are sensitive to food in the water. Those molecules trigger the movement of tiny threads called *cilia,* which help propel the protozoa toward the food source. The first neurons appeared in simple invertebrates, such as jellyfish; the sensory neurons in the jellyfish's tentacles can feel the touch of a potentially dangerous predator, which prompts the jellyfish to swim to safety. The first central nervous system worthy of the name, though, appeared in flatworms. The flatworm has a collection of neurons in the head—a simple kind of brain—that includes sensory neurons for vision and taste and motor neurons that control feeding behavior.

During the course of evolution, a major split in the organization of the nervous system occurred between invertebrate animals (those without a spinal column) and vertebrate animals

Flatworms don't have much of a brain, but then again, they don't need much of a brain. The rudimentary brain areas found in simple invertebrates eventually evolved into the complex brain structures found in humans.

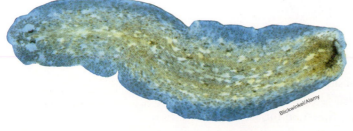

Blickwinkel/Alamy

(those with a spinal column). In all vertebrates, the central nervous system is organized into a hierarchy: The lower levels of the brain and spinal cord execute simpler functions, while the higher levels of the nervous system perform more complex functions. As you saw earlier, in humans, reflexes are accomplished in the spinal cord. At the next level, the midbrain executes the more complex task of orienting toward an important stimulus in the environment. Finally, a more complex task, such as imagining what your life will be like 20 years from now, is performed in the forebrain (Addis, Wong, & Schacter, 2007; Schacter et al., 2012; Szpunar, Watson, & McDermott, 2007).

The forebrain undergoes further evolutionary advances in vertebrates. In lower vertebrate species such as amphibians (frogs and newts), the forebrain consists only of small clusters of neurons at the end of the neural tube. In higher vertebrates, including reptiles, birds, and mammals, the forebrain is much larger, and it evolves in two different patterns. Reptiles and birds have almost no cerebral cortex. By contrast, mammals have a highly developed cerebral cortex, which develops multiple areas that serve a broad range of higher mental functions. This forebrain development has reached its peak—so far—in humans (**FIGURE 3.19**). This refinement allows for some remarkable, uniquely human abilities: self-awareness, sophisticated language use, abstract reasoning, and imagining, among others.

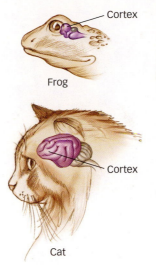

FIGURE 3.19 Development of the Forebrain Reptiles and birds have almost no cerebral cortex, whereas mammals such as rats and cats do have a cerebral cortex, but their frontal lobes are proportionately much smaller than the frontal lobes of humans and other primates. How might this explain the fact that only humans have developed complex language, computer technology, and calculus?

> **What distinguishes the brain of a mammal from the brain of an amphibian?**

Genes and Epigenetics

Is it genetics (nature) or the environment (nurture) that reigns supreme in directing a person's behavior? The emerging picture from current research is that both nature *and* nurture play a role in directing behavior, and the focus has shifted to examining the interaction of the two rather than the absolute contributions of either alone (Gottesman & Hanson, 2005; Rutter & Silberg, 2002; Zhang & Meaney, 2010).

What Are Genes?

A **gene** is *the major unit of hereditary transmission*. Historically, the term *gene* has been used to refer to two distinct but related concepts. Genes are sections on a strand of DNA (deoxyribonucleic acid) that are organized into large threads called **chromosomes,** *strands of DNA wound around each other in a double-helix configuration* (see **FIGURE 3.20**). Chromosomes come in pairs, and humans have 23 pairs each. These pairs of chromosomes are similar but not identical: You inherit one of each pair from your father and one from your mother.

As a species, we share about 99% of the same DNA (and almost as much with other apes), but there is a portion of DNA that varies across individuals. Children share more of this variable portion of DNA with their parents than with more distant relatives or with nonrelatives: Such children share half their genes with each parent, a quarter of their genes with their grandparents, an eighth of their genes with cousins, and so on. The probability of sharing genes is called *degree of relatedness*. The most genetically related people are *monozygotic twins* (also called *identical twins*), who develop from the splitting of a single fertilized egg and therefore share 100% of their genes. *Dizygotic twins (fraternal twins)*

> **Why do dizygotic twins share 50% of their genes, just like siblings born separately?**

gene The major unit of hereditary transmission.

chromosomes Strands of DNA wound around each other in a double-helix configuration.

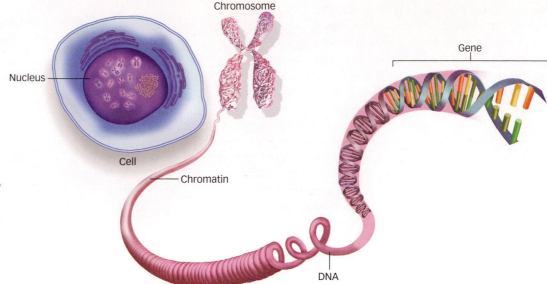

Chromosome

Gene

Nucleus

Cell

Chromatin

DNA

FIGURE 3.20 Genes, Chromosomes, and Their Recombination The cell nucleus houses chromosomes, which are made up of double-helix strands of DNA. Every cell in our bodies has 23 pairs of chromosomes. Genes are segments on the strand of DNA.

develop from two separate fertilized eggs and share 50% of their genes, the same as any two siblings born separately.

Many researchers have tried to determine the relative influence of genetics on behavior. One way to do this is to compare a trait shown by monozygotic twins with that same trait among dizygotic twins. This type of research usually enlists twins who were raised in the same household, so that the impact of their environment (their socioeconomic status, access to education, parental child-rearing practices, environmental stressors) remains relatively constant. Finding that monozygotic twins have a higher presence of a specific trait suggests a genetic influence (Boomsma, Busjahn, & Peltonen, 2002).

As an example, the likelihood that the dizygotic twin of a person who has schizophrenia (a mental disorder we'll discuss in greater detail in the Psychological Disorders chapter) will *also* develop schizophrenia is 27%. However, this statistic rises to 50% for monozygotic twins. That sounds frighteningly high . . . until you realize that 50% of monozygotic twins of people with schizophrenia will *not* develop the disorder. That means that environmental influences must play a role too. In short, genetics can contribute to the development, likelihood, or onset of a variety of traits. But a more complete picture of genetic influences on behavior must always take the environmental context into consideration. Genes express themselves within an environment, not in isolation.

Monozygotic twins (*left*) share 100% of their genes in common, whereas dizygotic twins (*right*) share 50% of their genes, the same as other siblings. Studies of monozygotic and dizygotic twins help researchers estimate the relative contributions of genes and environmental influences on behavior.

Paul Avis/Getty Images

JBphoto1/Alamy

A Role for Epigenetics

The idea that genes are expressed within an environment is central to an important and rapidly growing area of research known as **epigenetics**: *environmental influences that determine whether or not genes are expressed, or the degree to which they are expressed, without altering the basic DNA sequences that constitute the genes themselves.* To understand how epigenetic influences work, think about DNA as analogous to a script for a play or a movie. The biologist Nessa Carey (2012) offers the example of Shakespeare's *Romeo and Juliet,* which was made into a movie in 1936 starring Leslie Howard and Norma Shearer, and in 1996 starring Leonardo DiCaprio and Claire Danes. Shakespeare's script formed the basis of both films, but the directors of the two films used the script in different ways, and the actors in the two films gave different performances. Thus, the final products were different from one another, even though Shakespeare's original script still exists.

Similarly, epigenetics provides a way for the environment to influence gene expression—without altering the underlying DNA code. Epigenetics are now known to play a role in several important functions, including learning and memory (Bredy et al., 2007; Day & Sweatt, 2011; Levenson & Sweatt, 2005), and responses to stress (Zhang & Meaney, 2010). For example, subjective levels of stress in a sample of 92 Canadian adults, as well as physiological signs of stress, were correlated with epigenetic markers in the subjects' DNA (Lam et al., 2012). Other studies have reported a link between gene expression and early life experience, with differences observed between individuals who grew up in relatively affluent households versus those who grew up in poverty, even when controlling for such factors as current socioeconomic status (Borghol et al., 2012; Lam et al., 2012). These observations fit well with an important line of research described in the Hot Science box, showing that gene

epigenetics Environmental influences that determine whether or not genes are expressed, or the degree to which they are expressed, without altering the basic DNA sequences that constitute the genes themselves.

Hot Science

Epigenetics and the Persisting Effects of Early Experiences

An exciting series of studies show that epigenetic processes play a critical role in the long-lasting effects of early life experiences. Much of this work has come from the laboratory of Michael Meaney and his colleagues at McGill University.

Back in the 1990s, Meaney's lab found that there are notable differences in the mothering styles of rats (Francis et al., 1999; Liu et al., 1997): Some mothers spend a lot of time licking and grooming their young pups ("attentive" mothers), whereas others spend little time doing so ("inattentive" mothers). The researchers found that pups of attentive mothers are much less fearful as adults when placed in stressful situations than the adult pups of inattentive mothers. Later, when placed in fear-inducing situations, adult rats raised by the attentive mothers showed lower levels of several stress-related hormones than adult rats that had been raised by inattentive mothers. There was also increased evidence of serotonin in the adult pups of attentive mothers; as you learned earlier in this chapter, increased levels of serotonin are associated with elevated mood. In other words, the pups raised by attentive mothers grow up to become "chilled out" adults. These pups appeared to have epigenetically determined increases in the expression of genes controlling responses to stress hormones, resulting in a corresponding ability to respond more calmly to stress (Weaver et al., 2004).

But can early experiences affect adult behavior in humans, too? Meaney's group examined samples taken from the brains of 24 men who had committed suicide around the age of 35 (McGowan et al., 2009). Twelve of those men had a history of childhood abuse, and 12 did not. Strikingly, the researchers found evidence for epigenetic changes in the 12 men who had suffered childhood abuse and committed suicide compared with the 12 men who had not been abused. And the specific changes in gene expression were very similar to those observed in adult pups of inattentive mothers. In other words, there seem to be similar epigenetic effects of adverse early experiences in rats and humans, suggesting that in order to understand the effects of early experiences on subsequent development and behavior, we need to look to the broad role played by epigenetic influences (Meaney & Ferguson-Smith, 2010).

Rodent pups raised by a mother that spends a lot of time licking and grooming them are less fearful as adults in stressful situations.

Juniors Bildarchiv GmbH/Alamy

expression plays a key role in the long-lasting effects of early experiences for both rats and humans. In short, genes set the range of possible characteristics that can be expressed, but the environment and experience—through mechanisms such as epigenetics—determine which of those possibilities actually occur.

SUMMARY QUIZ [3.5]

1. During the course of embryonic brain growth, the _____ undergoes the greatest development.
   a. cerebral cortex
   b. cerebellum
   c. tectum
   d. thalamus

2. The first true central nervous system appeared in
   a. flatworms.
   b. jellyfish.
   c. protozoa.
   d. early primates.

3. Genes set the _____ that a given individual can express.
   a. individual characteristics
   b. range of variation
   c. environmental possibilities
   d. behavioral standards

Investigating the Brain

So far, you've read a great deal about the nervous system: how it's organized, how it works, what its components are, and what those components do. But *how* do we know all of this? Anatomists can dissect a human brain and identify its structures, but they cannot determine which structures play a role in producing which behaviors by dissecting a nonliving brain.

Scientists use a variety of methods to understand how the brain affects behavior. Let's consider three of the main ones: studying people with brain damage; studying the brain's electrical activity; and using brain imaging to study brain structure and watch the brain in action.

Studying the Damaged Brain

To understand the normal operation of a process better, it is instructive to understand what happens when that process fails. Much research in neuroscience correlates the loss of specific perceptual, motor, emotional, or cognitive functions with specific areas of brain damage (Andrewes, 2001; Kolb & Whishaw, 2003). By studying these

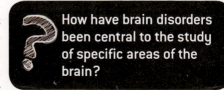
How have brain disorders been central to the study of specific areas of the brain?

instances of lost functions, neuroscientists can theorize about the functions those brain areas normally perform.

The Emotional Functions of the Frontal Lobes

As you've already seen, the human frontal lobes are a remarkable evolutionary achievement. However, psychology's first glimpse at some functions of the frontal lobes came from a rather unremarkable fellow—so unremarkable, in fact, that a single event in his life defined his place in the annals of psychology's history (Macmillan, 2000). Phineas Gage was a muscular 25-year-old railroad worker. On September 13, 1848, in Cavendish, Vermont, he was packing an explosive charge into a crevice in a rock when the powder exploded, driving a 3-foot, 13-pound iron rod through his head at high speed (Harlow, 1848). As **FIGURE 3.21** shows, the rod entered through his lower left jaw and exited through the middle top of his head. Incredibly, Gage lived to tell the tale. But his personality underwent a significant change.

Before the accident, Gage had been mild mannered, quiet, conscientious—and a hard worker. After the accident, however, he became irritable, irresponsible, indecisive, and given to profanity. The sad decline of Gage's personality and emotional life nonetheless provided an unexpected benefit to psychology. His case study was the first to allow researchers to investigate the hypothesis that the frontal lobe is involved in emotion regulation, planning, and decision making. Furthermore, because the connections between the frontal lobe and subcortical structures were affected, scientists were able to understand better how the amygdala, hippocampus, and related brain structures interacted with the cerebral cortex (Damasio, 2005).

Collection of Jack and Beverly Wilgus

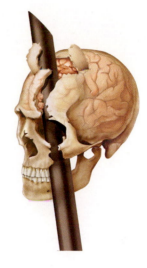

FIGURE 3.21 **Phineas Gage** Phineas Gage's traumatic accident allowed researchers to investigate the functions of the frontal lobe and its connections with emotion centers in the subcortical structures. The likely path of the metal rod through Gage's skull is reconstructed here.

The Distinct Roles of the Left and Right Hemispheres

You'll recall that the cerebral cortex is divided into two hemispheres, although typically the two hemispheres act as one integrated unit. Sometimes, though, disorders can threaten the ability of the brain to function, and the only way to stop them is with radical methods. This is sometimes the case for people who suffer from severe, intractable epilepsy. Seizures that begin in one hemisphere cross the corpus callosum (the thick band of nerve fibers that allows the two hemispheres to communicate) to the opposite hemisphere and start a feedback loop that results in a kind of firestorm in the brain. To alleviate the severity of the seizures, surgeons can sever the corpus callosum in a procedure called a *split-brain procedure*. The result is that

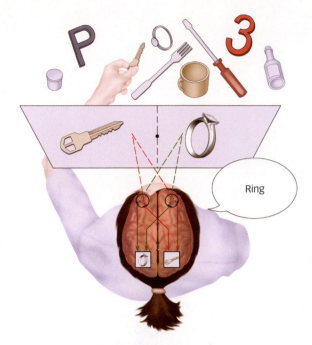

FIGURE 3.22 Split-Brain Experiment When a person with a split brain is presented with the picture of a ring on the right and that of a key on the left side of a screen, she can verbalize *ring* but not *key* because the left hemisphere "sees" the *ring* and language is usually located in the left hemisphere. She would be able to choose a key with her left hand from a set of objects behind a screen. She would not, however, be able to pick out a ring with her left hand because what the left hemisphere "sees" is not communicated to the left side of her body.

a seizure that starts in one hemisphere cannot cross to the other side. This procedure helps people with epilepsy, but it also produces some unusual, if not unpredictable, behaviors.

Normally, any information that initially enters the left hemisphere is also registered in the right hemisphere and vice versa: The information comes in and travels across the corpus callosum, and both hemispheres understand what's going on (see **FIGURE 3.22**). But in a person with a split brain, information entering one hemisphere stays there. Nobel laureate Roger Sperry (1913–1994) and his colleagues conducted a series of experiments in split-brain patients, showing that the hemispheres are specialized for different kinds of tasks. For example, language processing is largely a left-hemisphere activity. So imagine that some information came into the left hemisphere of a person with a split brain, and she was asked to describe verbally what it was. No problem: The left hemisphere has the information, it's the "speaking" hemisphere, so she should have no difficulty verbally describing what she saw. But this person's right hemisphere has no clue what the object was because that information was received in the left hemisphere and was unable to travel to the right hemisphere! So, even though she saw the object and could verbally describe it, she would be unable to use the right hemisphere to perform other tasks regarding that object, such as correctly selecting it from a group with her left hand (see Figure 3.22).

These split-brain studies reveal that the two hemispheres perform different functions and can work together seamlessly as long as the corpus callosum is intact. Without a way to transmit information from one hemisphere to the other, information remains in the hemisphere it initially entered, and we become acutely aware of the different functions of each hemisphere. Of course, a person with a split brain can adapt to this situation by simply moving her eyes a little so that the same information independently enters both hemispheres. Split-brain studies have continued over the past few decades and continue to play an important role in shaping our understanding of how the brain works (Gazzaniga, 2006).

Studying the Brain's Electrical Activity

A second approach to studying the link between brain structures and behavior involves recording the pattern of electrical activity of neurons. An *electroencephalograph (EEG)* is a device used to record electrical activity in the brain. Typically, electrodes are placed on the outside of the head, and even though the source of electrical activity in synapses and action potentials is far removed from these wires, the electric signals can be amplified several thousand times by the EEG. This provides a visual record of the underlying electrical activity, as shown in **FIGURE 3.23**. Using this technique, researchers can determine the amount of brain activity during different

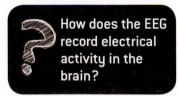

How does the EEG record electrical activity in the brain?

states of consciousness. For example, as you'll read in the Consciousness chapter, the brain shows distinctive patterns of electrical activity when awake versus asleep; in fact, there are even different brain-wave patterns associated with different stages of sleep. EEG recordings allow researchers to make these fundamental discoveries about the nature of sleep and wakefulness (Dement, 1978). The EEG can also be used to examine the brain's electrical activity when awake

Harley Schwadron

individuals engage in a variety of psychological functions, such as perceiving, learning, and remembering.

A different approach to recording electrical activity resulted in a more refined understanding of the brain's division of responsibilities, even at a cellular level. Nobel laureates David Hubel and Torsten Wiesel used a technique in which they inserted electrodes into the occipital lobes of anesthetized cats and observed the patterns of action potentials of individual neurons (Hubel, 1988). They discovered that neurons in the primary visual cortex are activated whenever a contrast between light and dark occurs in part of the visual field, such as a thick line of light against a dark background. They then found that each neuron responded vigorously only when presented with a contrasting edge at a particular orientation. Since then, many studies have shown that neurons in the primary visual cortex represent particular features of visual stimuli, such as contrast, shape, and color (Zeki, 1993).

These neurons in the visual cortex are known as *feature detectors* because they selectively respond to certain aspects of a visual image. For example, some neurons fire only when detecting a vertical line in the middle of the visual field, other neurons fire when a line at a 45° angle is perceived, and still others react in response to wider lines, horizontal lines, lines in the periphery of the visual field, and so on (Livingstone & Hubel, 1988). The discovery of this specialized function for neurons was a huge leap forward in our understanding of how the visual cortex works. Feature detectors identify basic dimensions of a stimulus ("slanted line . . . other slanted line . . . horizontal line"); those dimensions are then combined during a later stage of visual processing to allow recognition and perception of a stimulus ("Oh, it's a letter *A*").

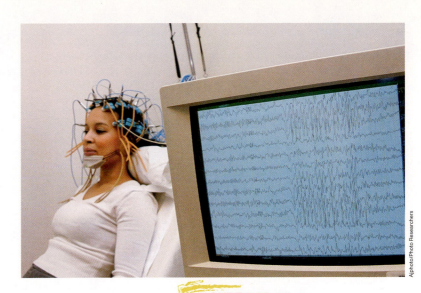

FIGURE 3.23 EEG The electroencephalograph (EEG) records electrical activity in the brain. Many states of consciousness, such as wakefulness and stages of sleep, are characterized by particular types of brain waves.

Using Brain Imaging to Study Structure and to Watch the Brain in Action

The third major way that neuroscientists can peer into the workings of the human brain involves *neuroimaging techniques* that use advanced technology to create images of the living, healthy brain (Posner & Raichle, 1994; Raichle & Mintun, 2006). *Structural brain imaging* provides information about the basic structure of the brain and allows clinicians or researchers to see abnormalities in brain structure. *Functional brain imaging*, in contrast, provides information about the activity of the brain when people perform various kinds of cognitive or motor tasks.

Structural Brain Imaging

One of the first neuroimaging techniques developed was the *computerized axial tomography (CT) scan*. In a CT scan, a scanner rotates a device around a person's head and takes a series of X-ray photographs from different angles. Computer programs then combine these images to provide views from any angle. CT scans show different densities of tissue in the brain. For example, the higher-density skull looks white on a CT scan, the cortex shows up as gray, and the least dense fissures and ventricles in the brain look dark (see **FIGURE 3.24**).

Magnetic resonance imaging (MRI) uses a strong magnetic field to line up the nuclei of specific molecules in the brain tissue. Brief, but powerful, pulses of radio waves cause the nuclei to rotate out of alignment. When a pulse ends, the nuclei snap back in line with the magnetic field and give off a small amount of energy in the

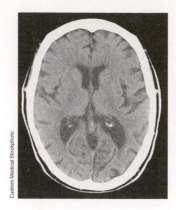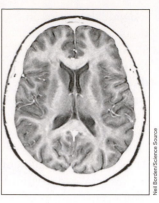

FIGURE 3.24 Structural Imaging Techniques (CT and MRI) CT (*left*) and MRI (*right*) scans are used to provide information about the structure of the brain and can help to spot tumors and other kinds of damage. Each scan shown here provides a snapshot of a single slice in the brain. Note that the MRI scan provides a clearer, higher-resolution image than the CT scan (see the text for further discussion of how these images are constructed and what they depict).

process. Different molecules have unique energy signatures when they snap back in line with the magnetic field, so these signatures can be used to reveal brain structures with different molecular compositions. MRI produces pictures of soft tissue at a better resolution than a CT scan, as you can see in Figure 3.24. Both CT and MRI scans give psychologists a picture of the structure of the brain and can help localize brain damage (as when someone suffers a stroke), but they reveal nothing about the functions of the brain.

Diffusion tensor imaging (DTI) is a relatively recently developed type of MRI that is used to visualize white matter pathways, which are fiber bundles that connect both nearby and distant brain regions to one another. DTI measures the rate and direction of diffusion or movement of water molecules along white matter pathways. Scientists can use measures based on the rate and direction of diffusion to assess the integrity of a white matter pathway, which is very useful in cases of neurological and psychological disorders (Thomason & Thompson, 2011). DTI plays a central role in an ambitious undertaking known as the Human Connectome Project, a collaborative effort funded by the National Institutes of Health beginning in 2009, that aims to provide a complete map of the connectivity of neural pathways in the brain: the human connectome (Toga et al., 2012). Researchers have made available some of their results at their Web site (www.humanconnectomeproject.org), which include fascinating colorful images of some of the connection pathways they have discovered.

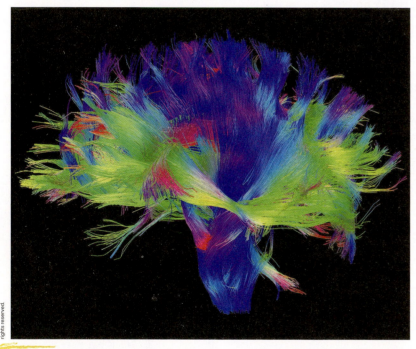

DTI allows researchers to visualize white matter pathways in the brain, the fiber bundles that play an important role by connecting brain regions to one another.

Functional Brain Imaging

Functional brain imaging techniques show researchers much more than just the structure of the brain by allowing us to watch the brain in action. These techniques rely on the fact that activated brain areas demand more energy for their neurons to work. This energy is supplied through increased blood flow to the activated areas. Functional imaging techniques can detect such changes in blood flow. In *positron emission tomography (PET)*, a harmless radioactive substance is injected into a person's bloodstream. Then the brain is scanned by radiation detectors as the person performs perceptual or cognitive tasks, such as reading or speaking. Areas of the brain that are activated during these tasks demand more energy and greater blood flow, resulting in a higher amount of the radioactivity in that region. The radiation detectors record the level of radioactivity in each region, producing a computerized image of the activated areas (see **FIGURE 3.25**).

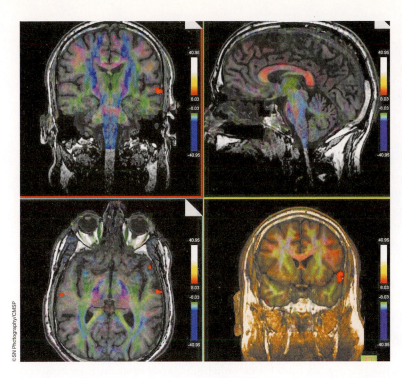

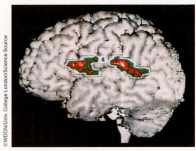

PET scan

FIGURE 3.25 Functional Imaging Techniques (PET and fMRI) PET and fMRI scans provide information about the function of the brain by revealing which brain areas become more or less active in different conditions. The PET scan (directly above) shows areas in the left hemisphere (Broca's area, left; lower parietal-upper temporal area, right) that become active when people hold in mind a string of letters for a few seconds. The red areas in the fMRI scans (all views to the left) indicate activity in the auditory cortex of a person listening to music.

For psychologists, the most widely used functional brain imaging technique nowadays is *functional magnetic resonance imaging (fMRI)*, which detects the difference between oxygenated hemoglobin and deoxygenated hemoglobin when exposed to magnetic pulses. Hemoglobin is the molecule in the blood that carries oxygen to our tissues, including the brain. When active neurons demand more energy and blood flow, oxygenated hemoglobin concentrates in the active areas; fMRI detects the oxygenated hemoglobin and provides a picture of the level of activation in each brain area (see Figure 3.25). Just as MRI was a major advance over CT scans, *functional* MRI represents a similar leap in our ability to record the brain's activity during behavior. Both fMRI and PET produce images that show activity in the brain while the person performs certain tasks. However, fMRI has a couple of advantages over PET. First, fMRI does not require any exposure to a radioactive substance. Second, fMRI can localize changes in brain activity across briefer periods than PET, which makes it more useful for analyzing psychological processes that occur extremely quickly, such as reading a word or recognizing a face. For example, when people look at faces, fMRI reveals strong activity in a region located near the border of the temporal and occipital lobes called the *fusiform gyrus* (Kanwisher, McDermott, & Chun, 1997). When this structure is damaged, people experience problems recognizing faces—even faces of friends and family they've known for years—although they don't have problems with their eyes and can recognize visual objects other than faces (Mestry et al., 2012). Finally, when people perform a task that engages emotional processing (e.g., looking at sad pictures), researchers observe significant activation in the amygdala, which you learned earlier is linked with emotional arousal (Phelps, 2006). There is also increased activation in parts of the frontal lobe that are involved in emotional regulation—in fact, in the same areas that were most likely damaged in the case of Phineas Gage (Wang et al., 2005).

Functional MRI can also be used to explore the relationship of brain regions with one another, using a recently developed technique referred to as *resting state functional connectivity*. As implied by the name, this technique does not require participants to

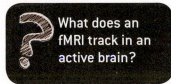

What does an fMRI track in an active brain?

perform a task; they simply rest quietly while fMRI measurements are made. Functional connectivity measures the extent to which spontaneous activity in different brain regions is correlated over time; brain regions whose activity is highly correlated are thought to be functionally connected with one another (Lee, Smyser, & Shimony, 2013). Functional connectivity measures have been used extensively in recent years to identify brain *networks*, that is, sets of brain regions that are closely connected to one another (Yeo et al., 2011). For example, functional connectivity helped to identify the *default network* (Gusnard & Raichle, 2001), a group of interconnected regions in the frontal, temporal, and parietal lobes that is involved in internally focused cognitive activities, such as remembering past events, imagining future events, daydreaming, and mind wandering (Andrews-Hanna, 2012; Buckner, Andrews-Hanna, & Schacter, 2008; see chapters on Memory and Consciousness). Functional connectivity, along with DTI (which measures structural connectivity), is used in studies conducted by the Human Connectome Project and will contribute important information to the map of the human connectome.

Transcranial Magnetic Stimulation

We noted earlier that scientists have learned a lot about the brain by studying the behavior of people with brain injuries. But, although brain damage may be related to particular patterns of behavior, that relationship may or may not be causal. Experimentation is the premier method for establishing causal relationships between variables, but scientists cannot ethically cause brain damage in human beings just to see how behavior might be affected. Functional neuroimaging techniques such as fMRI don't help on this point because they do not provide information about when a particular pattern of brain activity causes a particular behavior.

Happily, scientists have discovered a way to mimic brain damage with a benign technique called *transcranial magnetic stimulation* (TMS; Barker, Jalinous, & Freeston, 1985; Hallett, 2000). TMS delivers a magnetic pulse that passes through the skull and deactivates neurons in the cerebral cortex for a short period. Researchers can direct TMS pulses to particular brain regions (essentially turning them off) and then measure temporary changes in the way a person moves, sees, thinks, remembers, speaks, or feels. By manipulating the state of the brain, scientists can perform experiments that establish causal relationships.

For example, in an early study using TMS, scientists discovered that magnetic stimulation of the visual cortex temporarily impairs a person's ability to detect the motion of an object without impairing the person's ability to recognize that object (Beckers & Zeki, 1995). This intriguing discovery suggests that motion perception and object recognition are accomplished by different parts of the brain, but moreover, it establishes that activity in the visual cortex *causes* motion perception. More recent research has revealed that applying TMS to the specific part of the visual cortex responsible for motion perception also impairs the accuracy with which people reach for moving objects (Schenk et al., 2005) or for stationary objects when there is motion in the background of a visual scene (Whitney et al., 2007). These findings indicate that the visual motion area plays a crucial role in guiding actions when we're responding to motion in the visual environment.

Rather than relying solely on observational studies of people with brain injuries or the snapshots provided by fMRI or PET scans, researchers can also manipulate

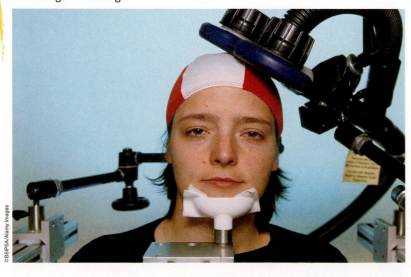

Transcranial magnetic stimulation (TMS) activates and deactivates regions of the brain with a magnetic pulse, temporarily mimicking brain damage.

©BSIP/SA/Alamy Images

Neuromyths

Christopher Chabris is an associate professor of psychology at Union College and **Daniel Simons** is a professor of psychology at the University of Illinois. Chabris and Simons co-authored *The Invisible Gorilla: And Other Ways Our Intuitions Deceive Us* (2010).

Photos: (left) Matt Milless; (Right) Courtesy Daniel S. Simons.

You've no doubt often heard the phrase "we only use 10% of our brains," and perhaps you've wondered whether there is anything to it. Chabris and Simons (2012) discussed this and other statements about the brain that they believe to be merely myths, based in part, on a recent study by Dekker, Howard-Jones, and Jolles (2012).

Pop quiz: Which of these statements is false?

1. We use only 10% of our brain.
2. Environments rich in stimuli improve the brains of preschool children.
3. Individuals learn better when they receive information in their preferred learning style, whether auditory, visual, or kinesthetic.

If you picked the first one, congratulations. The idea that we use only 10% of our brain is patently false. Yet it so permeates popular culture that, among psychologists and neuroscientists, it is known as the "10% myth." Contrary to popular belief, the entire brain is put to use—unused neurons die and unused circuits atrophy. Reports of neuroimaging research might perpetuate the myth by showing only a small number of areas "lighting up" in a brain scan, but those are just areas that have more than a base line level of activity; the dark regions aren't dormant or unused.

Did you agree with the other two statements? If so, you fell into our trap. All three statements are false—or at least not substantiated by scientific evidence. Unfortunately, if you got any of them wrong, you're hardly alone.

These "neuromyths," along with others, were presented to 242 primary and secondary school teachers in the Netherlands and the United Kingdom as part of a study by Sanne Dekker and colleagues at VU University Amsterdam and Bristol University, and just published in the journal *Frontiers in Psychology*. They found that 47% of the teachers believed the 10% myth. Even more, 76%, believed that enriching children's environments will strengthen their brains.

This belief might have emerged from evidence that rats raised in cages with amenities like exercise wheels, tunnels, and other rats showed better cognitive abilities and improvements in brain structure compared with rats that grew up isolated in bare cages. But such experiments show only that a truly impoverished and unnatural environment leads to poorer developmental outcomes than a more natural environment with opportunities to play and interact. It follows that growing up locked in a closet or otherwise cut off from human contact will impair a child's brain development. It does not follow that "enriching" a child's environment beyond what is already typical (e.g., by constant exposure to "Baby Einstein"-type videos) will boost cognitive development.

The myth about learning styles was the most popular: 94% of the teachers believed that students perform better when lessons are delivered in their preferred learning style. Indeed, students do have preferences about how they learn; the problem is that these preferences have little to do with how effectively they learn . . . .

Our own surveys of the U.S. population have found even more widespread belief in myths about the brain. About two-thirds of the public agreed with the 10% myth. Many also believed that memory works like a video recording or that they can tell when someone is staring at the back of their head.

Ironically, in the Dekker group's study, the teachers who knew the most about neuroscience also believed in the most myths. Apparently, teachers who are (admirably) enthusiastic about expanding their knowledge of the mind and brain have trouble separating fact from fiction as they learn. Neuromyths have so much intuitive appeal, and they spread so rapidly in fields like business and self-help, that eradicating them from popular consciousness might be a Sisyphean task. But reducing their influence in the classroom would be a good start.

If for some perverse reason you wanted to annoy the instructor of your psychology course, you probably could do no better than to claim that "we use only 10% of our brains." Even though, as pointed out by Chabris and Simon (2012), a surprisingly high proportion of elementary and secondary school teachers in the Netherlands and the United Kingdom subscribe to this myth, we don't know any psychologists teaching courses like the one you are taking who would endorse it, and we hope that there aren't any. How did the myth get started? Nobody really knows. Some think that it may have arisen from a quotation by the great psychologist William James ("We are making use of only a small part of our possible mental and physical resources") or that it possibly dates back to Albert Einstein's attempt to make sense of his own massive intellect (Boyd, 2008).

The key point for our purposes is that when you hear such bold claims made, say, by a friend who heard it from somebody else, it's time for you to put into action the kinds of critical thinking skills that we are focusing on in this text—and start asking questions: What's the evidence for the claim? Is there a specific study or studies that your friend can name to provide evidence in support of the claim? Are any such studies published in peer-reviewed scientific journals? What kind of sample was used in the study? Is it large enough to support a clear conclusion? Has the finding been replicated? Tall tales like the 10% myth don't stand much chance of surviving for long if claims for their existence are met head-on with critical thinking.

brain activity and measure its effects. Scientists have also begun to combine TMS with fMRI, allowing them to localize precisely where in the brain TMS is having its effect (Caparelli, 2007). Studies suggest that TMS has no harmful side effects (Anand & Hotson, 2002; Pascual-Leone et al., 1993), and this new tool has changed the study of how our brains create our thoughts, feelings, and actions.

In the Methods chapter you learned about the difference between correlation and causation—namely, that even if two events are correlated, it does not necessarily mean that one causes the other. Suppose a researcher designs an experiment in which participants view words on a screen and are asked to pronounce each word aloud, while the researcher uses fMRI to examine brain activity. First, what areas of the brain would you expect to show activity on fMRI while participants complete this task? Second, can the researcher now safely conclude that those brain areas are required for humans to perform word pronunciation?

Courtesy Vicki Gillis, Colorado State University

SUMMARY QUIZ [3.6]

1. Identifying the brain areas that are involved in specific types of motor, cognitive, or emotional processing is best achieved through
   a. recording patterns of electrical activity.
   b. observing psychological disorders.
   c. psychosurgery.
   d. brain imaging.

2. Split-brain studies have revealed that
   a. neurons in the primary visual cortex represent features of visual stimuli such as contrast, shape, and color.
   b. the two hemispheres perform different functions but can work together by means of the corpus callosum.
   c. when people perform a task that involves emotional processing, the amygdala is activated.
   d. brain locations for vision, touch, and hearing are separate.

3. Researchers can observe relationships between energy consumption in certain brain areas and specific cognitive and behavioral events using _____.
   a. functional brain imaging
   b. electroencephalography
   c. electrodes that are inserted into individual cells
   d. CT scans

CHAPTER REVIEW

SUMMARY

Neurons: The Origin of Behavior

> Neurons are the building blocks of the nervous system: They process information received from the outside world, communicate with one another, and send messages to the body's muscles and organs.

> Neurons are composed of three major parts: the cell body (which contains the nucleus and houses the organism's genetic material), the dendrites (which receive sensory signals from other neurons and transmit this information to the cell body), and the axon (which carries signals from the cell body to other neurons or to muscles and organs in the body).

> Neurons don't actually touch. They are separated by a small gap, which is part of the synapse across which signals are transmitted from one neuron to another.

> Glial cells provide support for neurons, usually in the form of the myelin sheath, which coats the axon to facilitate the transmission of information. In demyelinating diseases, the myelin sheath deteriorates.

Information Processing in Neurons

> The neuron's resting potential is due to differences in the potassium $(K+)$ concentrations inside and outside the cell membrane, resulting from open channels that allow $K+$ to flow outside the membrane while closed channels don't allow sodium ions $(Na+)$ and other ions to flow into the neuron.

> If electric signals reach a threshold, this event initiates an action potential, an all-or-none signal that moves down the entire length of the axon. After the action potential has reached its maximum, a chemical pump reverses the imbalance in ions, returning the neuron to its resting potential. For a brief refractory period, the action potential cannot be re-initiated.

> Communication between neurons takes place through synaptic transmission, where an action potential triggers release of neurotransmitters from the terminal buttons of the sending neuron's axon, which travel across the synapse to bind with receptors in the receiving neuron's dendrite.

> Neurotransmitters bind to dendrites on specific receptor sites. Neurotransmitters leave the synapse through reuptake, through enzyme deactivation, and by binding to autoreceptors.

> Some of the major neurotransmitters are acetylcholine (ACh), dopamine, glutamate, GABA, norepinephrine, serotonin, and endorphins.

> Drugs can affect behavior by acting as agonists, that is, by facilitating or increasing the actions of neurotransmitters, or as antagonists by blocking the action of neurotransmitters. Recreational drug use can have an effect on brain function.

The Organization of the Nervous System

> The nervous system is divided into the peripheral and the central nervous systems.

> The peripheral nervous system connects the central nervous system with the rest of the body, and it is itself divided into the somatic nervous system (which controls voluntary muscles) and the autonomic nervous system (which controls the body's organs).

> The autonomic nervous system is further divided into the sympathetic and parasympathetic nervous systems. The sympathetic nervous system prepares the body for action in threatening situations, and the parasympathetic nervous system returns the body to its normal state.

> The central nervous system is composed of the spinal cord and the brain. The spinal cord can control some basic behaviors such as spinal reflexes without input from the brain.

Structure of the Brain

> The brain can be divided into the hindbrain, midbrain, and forebrain.

> The hindbrain generally coordinates information coming into and out of the spinal cord with structures such as the medulla, the reticular formation, the cerebellum, and the pons. These structures respectively coordinate breathing and heart rate, regulate sleep and arousal levels, coordinate fine motor skills, and communicate this information to the cortex.

> The structures of the midbrain, the tectum and tegmentum, generally coordinate functions such as orientation to the environment and movement and arousal toward sensory stimuli.

> The forebrain generally coordinates higher-level functions, such as perceiving, feeling, and thinking. The forebrain houses subcortical structures, such as the thalamus, hypothalamus, hippocampus, amygdala, and basal ganglia; all of these structures perform a variety of functions related to motivation and emotion.

> Also in the forebrain, the cerebral cortex, composed of two hemispheres with four lobes each (occipital, parietal, temporal, and frontal), performs tasks that help make us fully human: thinking, planning, judging, perceiving, and behaving purposefully and voluntarily.

> Neurons in the brain can be shaped by experience and the environment, making the human brain amazingly plastic.

The Development and Evolution of Nervous Systems

> The nervous system is the first system that forms in an embryo, starting as a neural tube, which forms the basis of the spinal cord, then expands on one end to form the hindbrain, midbrain, and forebrain. Then, within each of these areas, specific brain structures begin to differentiate.

> Nervous systems evolved from simple collections of sensory and motor neurons in simple animals, such as flatworms, to elaborate centralized nervous systems found in mammals.

> The gene, or the unit of hereditary transmission, is built from strands of DNA in a double-helix formation that is organized into chromosomes. Humans have 23 pairs of chromosomes; half come from each parent.

> The study of genetics indicates that both genes and the environment work together to influence behavior. Genes set the range of variation in populations within a given environment, but these genes do not predict individual characteristics; experience and other environmental factors play a crucial role as well.

> Epigenetics, environmental influences that determine whether or not genes are expressed even when not altering the basic DNA sequences that constitute the genes, have been shown to play a critical role in persisting effects of early experiences in rats and humans.

Investigating the Brain

> The brain can be investigated by observing how perceptual, motor, intellectual, and emotional capacities are affected following brain damage; specific disruptions after damage in particular areas of the brain suggest that the brain area normally plays a role in producing those behaviors.

> Scientists can examine global electrical activity in large areas of the brain using the electroencephalograph (EEG), or they can examine the activity pattern of single neurons by recordings taken from specific neurons.

> Brain imaging, such as fMRI and PET, allow scientists to scan the brain as people perform different perceptual or intellectual tasks. Correlating energy consumption in particular brain areas with specific events suggests that those brain areas are involved in specific types of processing.

KEY TERMS

neurons (p. 56)
cell body (or soma) (p. 56)
dendrite (p. 56)
axon (p. 56)
synapse (p. 56)
myelin sheath (p. 56)
glial cells (p. 56)
sensory neurons (p. 58)
motor neurons (p. 58)
interneurons (p. 58)
resting potential (p. 59)
action potential (p. 60)
terminal buttons (p. 61)
neurotransmitters (p. 61)

receptors (p. 62)
agonists (p. 63)
antagonists (p. 63)
nervous system (p. 65)
central nervous system (CNS) (p. 65)
peripheral nervous system (PNS) (p. 65)
somatic nervous system (p. 65)
autonomic nervous system (ANS) (p. 65)
sympathetic nervous system (p. 66)
parasympathetic nervous system (p. 66)

spinal reflexes (p. 67)
hindbrain (p. 69)
medulla (p. 69)
reticular formation (p. 69)
cerebellum (p. 69)
pons (p. 69)
subcortical structures (p. 70)
thalamus (p. 71)
hypothalamus (p. 71)
pituitary gland (p. 71)
hippocampus (p. 71)
amygdala (p. 71)
basal ganglia (p. 72)

cerebral cortex (p. 72)
corpus callosum (p. 72)
occipital lobe (p. 73)
parietal lobe (p. 73)
temporal lobe (p. 73)
frontal lobe (p. 73)
association areas (p. 74)
mirror neurons (p. 74)
gene (p. 79)
chromosomes (p. 79)
epigenetics (p. 81)

CHANGING MINDS

1. Your friend has been feeling depressed and has gone to a psychiatrist for help. "He prescribed a medication that's supposed to increase serotonin in my brain. But my feelings depend on me, not on a bunch of chemicals in my head," she said. What examples could you give your friend to convince her that hormones and neurotransmitters really do influence our cognition, mood, and behavior?

2. A classmate has read the section in this chapter about the evolution of the central nervous system. "Evolution is just a theory," he says. "Not everyone believes in it. And, even if it's true that we're

all descended from monkeys, that doesn't have anything to do with the psychology of humans alive today." What is your friend misunderstanding about evolution? How would you explain to him the relevance of evolution to modern psychology?

3. A news program reports on a study (Hölzel et al., 2011) in which people who practiced meditation for about 30 minutes a day for 8 weeks showed changes in their brains, including increases in the size of the hippocampus and the amygdala. You tell a friend about this program, but he's skeptical. "The brain doesn't change like that," he responds. "Basically, the brain you're born with is

the brain you're stuck with for the rest of your life." Why is your friend's statement wrong? What are several specific ways in which the brain does change over time?

4. A friend of yours announces that he's figured out why he's bad at math. "I read it in a book," he says. "Left-brained people are analytical and logical, but right-brained people are creative and artistic. I'm an art major, so I must be right-brained, and that's why I'm not good at math." Why is your friend's view too simplistic?

ANSWERS TO SUMMARY QUIZZES

Summary Quiz 3.1: 1. c; 2. b; 3. a; 4. a.
Summary Quiz 3.2: 1. b; 2. d.
Summary Quiz 3.3: 1. a; 2. c.

Summary Quiz 3.4: 1. b; 2. b; 3. c; 4. d.
Summary Quiz 3.5: 1. a; 2. a; 3. b.
Summary Quiz 3.6: 1. d; 2. b; 3. a.

Need more help? Additional resources are located in LaunchPad at:
http://www.worthpublishers.com/launchpad/schacterbrief3e

Sensation and Perception

In 1946, a young designer named Donald Deskey helped to create the box design for Procter & Gamble's revolutionary new laundry detergent, Tide, which used, for the first time, synthetic compounds rather than plain old soap (Hine, 1995). Although extremely familiar to us today, in 1946, the bold, blue lettered "Tide" emblazoned on bull's-eye rings of yellow and orange marked the first use of eye-catching Day-Glo colors on a commercial product, and this mix of type and graphics was unlike any product design that anyone had seen before. The product would be impossible to miss on the shelves of a store, and as admirers of the design observed, "It was the box itself that most dynamically conveyed the new product's extraordinary power" (Dyer, Dalzell, & Olegario, 2004). Tide went to market in 1949, and Procter & Gamble never looked back.

Nowadays, we're used to seeing advertisements that feature exciting, provocative, or even sexual images to sell products. The notion is that the sight and sound of exciting things will become associated with what might be an otherwise drab product. This form of advertising is known as *sensory branding* (Lindstrom, 2005). Sensory branding often enlists sound, smell, taste, and touch as well as vision. In television commercials, these images are accompanied by popular music that advertisers hope will evoke an overall mood favorable to the product. That new-car smell you anticipate while you take a test drive? It's a manufactured fragrance sprayed into the car, carefully tested to evoke positive feelings among potential buyers. Singapore Airlines, which has consistently been rated "the world's best airline," has actually patented the smell of their airplane cabins (it's called Stefan Floridian Waters). Companies today, just like Procter & Gamble back in 1946, recognize the power of sensation and perception to shape human experience and behavior.

Donald Deskey recognized the power of perception back in 1946, when he grabbed the attention of consumers by using eye-catching colors and a striking design on the first box of Tide.

The Photo Works

sensation Simple stimulation of a sense organ.

perception The organization, identification, and interpretation of a sensation in order to form a mental representation.

transduction What takes place when many sensors in the body convert physical signals from the environment into encoded neural signals sent to the central nervous system.

You can enjoy a tempting ice cream sundae even if you do not know that its sweet taste depends on a complex process of transduction, in which molecules dissolved in saliva are converted to neural signals processed by the brain.

In this chapter, we'll explore key insights into the nature of sensation and perception. We'll look at how physical energy in the world around us is encoded by our senses, sent to the brain, and enters conscious awareness. Vision is predominant among our senses; correspondingly, we'll devote a fair amount of space to understanding how the visual system works. Then we'll discuss how we perceive sound waves as words or music or noise, followed by the body senses, emphasizing touch, pain, and balance. We'll end with the chemical senses of smell and taste, which together allow you to savor the foods you eat. But before doing any of that, we will provide a foundation for examining all of the sensory systems by reviewing how psychologists measure sensation and perception in the first place.

Sensation and Perception Are Distinct Activities

Sensation is *simple stimulation of a sense organ*. It is the basic registration of light, sound, pressure, odor, or taste as parts of your body interact with the physical world. After a sensation registers in your central nervous system, **perception** takes place in your brain: *the organization, identification, and interpretation of a sensation in order to form a mental representation*. Sensation and perception are related—but distinct—activities.

As an example, your eyes are coursing across these sentences right now. The sensory receptors in your eyeballs are registering different patterns of light reflecting off the page. Your brain is integrating and processing that light information into the meaningful perception of words. Your eyes—the sensory organ—aren't really seeing words; they're simply encoding different lines and curves on a page. Your brain—the perceptual organ—is transforming those lines and curves into a coherent mental representation of words and concepts.

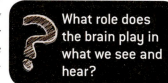

What role does the brain play in what we see and hear?

Sensory receptors communicate with the brain through **transduction,** which occurs *when many sensors in the body convert physical signals from the environment into encoded neural signals sent to the central nervous system*. In vision, light reflected from surfaces provides the eyes with information about the shape, color, and position of objects. In audition, vibrations (from vocal cords or a guitar string, perhaps) cause changes in air pressure that propagate through space to a listener's ears. In touch, the pressure of a surface against the skin signals its shape, texture, and temperature. In taste and smell, molecules dispersed in the air or dissolved in saliva reveal the identity of substances that we may or may not want to eat. In each case, physical energy from the world is converted to neural energy inside the central nervous system (see **TABLE 4.1**).

Psychophysics

Knowing that perception takes place in the brain, you might wonder if two people see the same colors in the sunset when looking at the evening sky. It's intriguing to consider the possibility that our basic perceptions of sights or sounds might differ fundamentally from those of other people. How can we measure such a thing objectively? Measuring the physical energy of a stimulus, such as the wavelength of a light, is easy enough: You can probably buy the

Fotoflare/istockphoto

Table 4.1 **Transduction**

The five senses convert physical energy from the world into neural energy, which is sent to the brain

Sense	Sensory Input	Conversion into Neural Energy
Vision	Light reflected from surfaces (for examples from a leaf) provides the eyes with information about the shape, color, and positions of objects.	(See Figure 4.3 for a more detailed view.)
Audition (hearing)	Vibrations (from a guitar string, perhaps) cause changes in air pressure that move through space to the listener's ears.	(See Figure 4.21 for a more detailed view.)
Touch	Pressure of a surface against the skin signals its shape, texture, and temperature.	(See Figure 4.24 for a more detailed view.)
Taste and Smell	Molecules dispersed in the air or dissolved in saliva reveal the identity of substances that we may or may not want to eat.	(See Figures 4.25 and 4.27 for more detailed views.)

necessary instruments online to do that yourself. But how do you quantify a person's private, subjective *perception* of that light?

In the mid-1800s, German scientist Gustav Fechner (1801–1887) developed an approach to measuring sensation and perception called **psychophysics:** *methods that measure the strength of a stimulus and the observer's sensitivity to that stimulus* (Fechner, 1860/1966). In a typical psychophysics experiment, researchers ask people to make a simple judgment—whether or not they saw a flash of light, for example. The psychophysicist then relates the measured stimulus, such as the brightness of the light flash, to each observer's yes-or-no response.

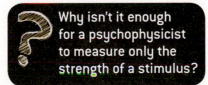

Why isn't it enough for a psychophysicist to measure only the strength of a stimulus?

psychophysics Methods that measure the strength of a stimulus and the observer's sensitivity to that stimulus.

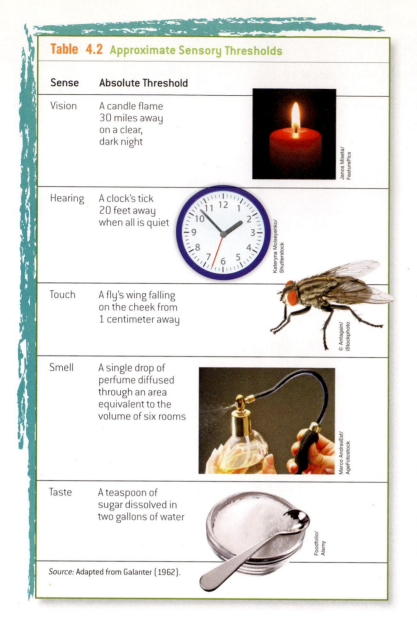

Table 4.2 Approximate Sensory Thresholds

Sense	Absolute Threshold	
Vision	A candle flame 30 miles away on a clear, dark night	
Hearing	A clock's tick 20 feet away when all is quiet	
Touch	A fly's wing falling on the cheek from 1 centimeter away	
Smell	A single drop of perfume diffused through an area equivalent to the volume of six rooms	
Taste	A teaspoon of sugar dissolved in two gallons of water	

Source: Adapted from Galanter (1962).

Measuring Thresholds

Psychophysicists begin the measurement process with a single sensory signal to determine precisely how much physical energy is required for an observer to become aware of a sensation. The simplest quantitative measurement in psychophysics is the **absolute threshold,** *the minimal intensity needed to just barely detect a stimulus in 50% of the trials.* A *threshold* is a boundary. The doorway that separates the inside from the outside of a house is a threshold, as is the boundary between two psychological states (awareness and unawareness, for example). In finding the absolute threshold for sensation, the two states in question are *sensing* and *not sensing* some stimulus. **TABLE 4.2** lists the approximate sensory thresholds for each of the five senses.

To measure the absolute threshold for detecting a sound, for example, an observer sits in a soundproof room wearing headphones linked to a computer. The experimenter presents a pure tone (the sort of sound made by striking a tuning fork) using the computer to vary the loudness or the length of time each tone lasts and recording how often the observer reports hearing that tone under each condition. The outcome of such an experiment is graphed in **FIGURE 4.1**. Notice from the shape of the curve that the transition from *not hearing* to *hearing* is gradual rather than abrupt.

If we repeat this experiment for many different tones, we can observe and record the thresholds for tones ranging from very low to very high pitch. It turns out that people tend to be most sensitive to the range of tones corresponding to human conversation. If the tone is low enough, such as the lowest note on a pipe organ, most humans cannot hear it at all; we can only feel it. If the tone is high enough, we likewise cannot hear it, but dogs and many other animals can.

The absolute threshold is useful for assessing how sensitive we are to faint stimuli, but the human perceptual system is better at detecting *changes* in stimulation than the simple onset or offset of stimulation. When parents hear their infant's cry, it's useful to be able to differentiate the "I'm hungry" cry from the "I'm cranky" cry from the "something is biting my toes" cry. The **just noticeable difference (JND)** is *the minimal change in a stimulus that can just barely be detected.*

The JND is not a fixed quantity; rather, it is roughly proportional to the intensity of the stimulus. This relationship was first noticed in 1834 by German physiologist Ernst Weber (Watson, 1978) and is now called **Weber's law:** *The just noticeable difference of a stimulus is a constant proportion despite variations in intensity.* As an example, if you picked up a 1-ounce

FIGURE 4.1 Absolute Threshold Absolute threshold is graphed here as the point where the increasing intensity of the stimulus enables an observer to detect it on 50% of the trials. As the intensity of a stimulus gradually increases, we detect the stimulation more frequently.

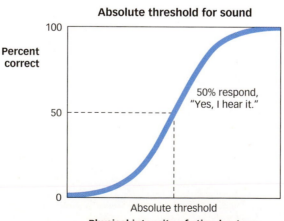

Absolute threshold for sound

Percent correct

100

50% respond, "Yes, I hear it."

50

0

Absolute threshold

Physical intensity of stimulus tone

envelope, then a 2-ounce envelope, you'd probably notice the difference between them. But if you picked up a 20-pound package and then a 20-pound, 1-ounce package, you'd probably detect no difference at all between them.

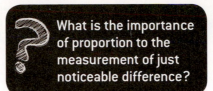

What is the importance of proportion to the measurement of just noticeable difference?

Signal Detection

Measuring absolute and difference thresholds requires a critical assumption: that a threshold exists! But humans don't suddenly and rapidly switch between perceiving and not perceiving; in fact, the very same physical stimulus, such as a dim light or a quiet tone, presented on several different occasions, may be perceived by the same person on some occasions but not on others (see Figure 4.1). Remember, an absolute threshold is operationalized as perceiving the stimulus 50% of the time, which means the other 50% of the time it might go undetected.

Our accurate perception of a sensory stimulus, then, can be somewhat haphazard. Whether in the psychophysics lab or out in the world, sensory signals face a lot of competition, or *noise,* which refers to all the other stimuli coming from the internal and external environment. Memories, moods, and motives intertwine with what you are seeing, hearing, and smelling at any given time. This internal "noise" competes with your ability to detect a stimulus with perfect, focused attention. Other sights, sounds, and smells in the world at large also compete for attention. As a consequence, you may not perceive everything that you sense, and you may even perceive things that you haven't sensed.

An approach to psychophysics called **signal detection theory** holds that *the response to a stimulus depends both on a person's sensitivity to the stimulus in the presence of noise and on a person's decision criterion.* That is, observers consider the sensory evidence evoked by the

How accurate and complete are our perceptions of the world?

stimulus and compare it to an internal decision criterion (Green & Swets, 1966; Macmillan & Creelman, 2005). If the sensory evidence exceeds the criterion, the observer responds by saying, "Yes, I detected the stimulus," and if it falls short of the criterion, the observer responds by saying, "No, I did not detect the stimulus."

Signal detection theory has practical applications at home, school, work, and even while driving. For example, a radiologist may have to decide whether a mammogram shows that a woman has breast cancer. The radiologist knows that certain features, such as a mass of a particular size and shape, are associated with the presence of cancer. But noncancerous features can have an appearance that is very similar to cancerous ones. The radiologist may decide on a strictly liberal criterion and check every possible case of cancer with a biopsy. This decision strategy minimizes the possibility of missing a true cancer but leads to many unnecessary biopsies. A strictly conservative criterion will cut down on unnecessary biopsies but will miss some treatable cancers. These different types of errors have to be weighed against one another in setting the decision criterion. For an example of a common everyday task that can interfere with signal detection, see the Real World box.

Crowds of people such as this one in New York City's Thanksgiving Day Parade present our visual system with a challenging signal detection task.

Blickwinkel /Alamy

The Real World

Multitasking

By one estimate, using a cell phone while driving makes having an accident four times more likely (McEvoy et al., 2005). In response to statistics such as this, state legislatures are passing laws that restrict—and sometimes ban—using mobile phones while driving. You might think that's a fine idea . . . for everyone else on the road. But surely *you* can manage to carry on a conversation while simultaneously driving in a safe and courteous manner. Right? In a word, *wrong*.

Talking on a cell phone while driving demands that you juggle two independent sources of sensory input—vision and audition—at the same time. This is problematic because research has found that when attention is directed to audition, activity in visual areas decreases (Shomstein & Yantis, 2004). This kind of *multitasking* creates problems when you need to react suddenly while driving. Researchers have tested experienced drivers in a highly realistic driving simulator, measuring their response times to brake lights and stop signs while they listened to the radio or carried on phone conversations about a political issue, among other tasks (Strayer, Drews, & Johnston, 2003). These experienced drivers reacted significantly more slowly during phone conversations than during the other tasks. This is because a phone conversation

requires memory retrieval, deliberation, and planning what to say and often carries an emotional stake in the conversation topic. Tasks such as listening to the radio require far less attention.

Whether the phone was handheld or hands-free made little difference, and similar results have been obtained in field studies of actual driving (Horrey & Wickens, 2006). This suggests that laws requiring drivers to use hands-free phones may have little effect on reducing accidents. The situation is even worse when text messaging is involved: Compared with a no-texting control condition, drivers spent dramatically less time looking at the road when either sending or receiving a text message in

the simulator, had a much harder time staying in their lane, missed numerous lane changes, and had greater difficulty maintaining an appropriate distance behind the car ahead of them (Hosking, Young, & Regan, 2009). A recent review concluded that the impairing effect of texting while driving is comparable to that of alcohol consumption and greater than that of smoking marijuana (Pascual-Ferrá, Liu, & Beatty, 2012).

So how well do you multitask in several thousand pounds of metal hurtling down the highway? Unless you have two heads with one brain each—one to talk and one to concentrate on driving—you would do well to keep your eyes on the road and not on the phone.

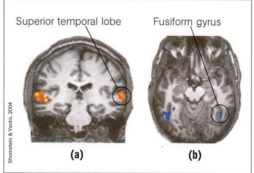

Superior temporal lobe   Fusiform gyrus

Shomstein & Yantis, 2004

(a)   (b)

Shifting Attention Participants received fMRI scans as they performed tasks that required them to shift their attention between visual and auditory information. (*a*) When focusing on auditory information, a region in the superior (upper) temporal lobe involved in auditory processing showed increased activity (yellow/orange). (*b*) But when participants focused on auditory information, a visual region, the fusiform gyrus, showed decreased activity (blue).

Sensory Adaptation

When you walk into a bakery, the aroma of freshly baked bread overwhelms you, but after a few minutes, the smell fades. If you dive into cold water, the temperature is shocking at first, but after a few minutes, you get used to it. When you wake up in the middle of the night for a drink of water, the bathroom light blinds you, but after a few minutes, you no longer squint. These are all examples of **sensory adaptation:** *Sensitivity to prolonged stimulation tends to decline over time as an organism adapts to current conditions.*

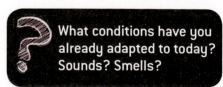

What conditions have you already adapted to today? Sounds? Smells?

Sensory adaptation is a useful process for most organisms. Imagine what your sensory and perceptual world would be like without it. (If you had to be constantly aware of how your tongue feels while it is resting in your mouth, you'd be driven to distraction.) Our sensory systems respond more strongly to changes in stimulation than to constant stimulation. A stimulus that doesn't change usually doesn't require any action; your car probably emits a certain hum all the time, one that you've gotten used to. But a change in stimulation often signals a need for action. If your car starts

sensory adaptation Sensitivity to prolonged stimulation tends to decline over time as an organism adapts to current conditions.

visual acuity The ability to see fine detail.

making different kinds of noises, you're not only more likely to notice them, but you're also more likely to do something about it.

According to the theory of natural selection, inherited characteristics that provide a survival advantage tend to spread throughout the population across generations. Why might sensory adaptation have evolved? What survival benefits might it confer to a predator trying to hunt prey?

SUMMARY QUIZ [4.1]

1. Sensation involves _____ , whereas perception involves _____ .
   a. organization; coordination
   b. stimulation; interpretation
   c. identification; translation
   d. comprehension; information

2. What process converts physical signals from the environment into neural signals carried by sensory neurons into the central nervous system?
   a. representation
   b. identification
   c. propagation
   d. transduction

3. The smallest intensity needed to just barely detect a stimulus is called
   a. proportional magnitude.
   b. absolute threshold.
   c. just noticeable difference.
   d. Weber's law.

Vision I: How the Eyes and the Brain Convert Light Waves to Neural Signals

You might be proud of your 20/20 vision, even if it is corrected by glasses or contact lenses. The expression *20/20* refers to a measurement of **visual acuity,** *the ability to see fine detail;* it is the smallest line of letters that a typical person can read from a distance of 20 feet. But hawks, eagles, owls, and other raptors have up to eight times greater visual acuity than humans, or the equivalent of 20/2 vision (meaning that what the normal human can just see from 2 feet away can be seen by these birds at a distance of 20 feet away). Your sophisticated visual system has evolved to transduce visual energy in the world into neural signals in the brain. Understanding vision, then, starts with understanding light.

Though controversial for other reasons, research has shown that action-shooter games improve attention and even basic visual acuity (Green & Bavelier, 2007; Li et al., 2009).

Sensing Light

Visible light is simply the portion of the electro-magnetic spectrum that we can see, and it is an extremely small slice of the pie (see **FIGURE 4.2**). You can think about light as waves of energy. Like ocean waves, light waves vary in height and in the distance between their peaks, or *wave-lengths*. There are three physical properties of

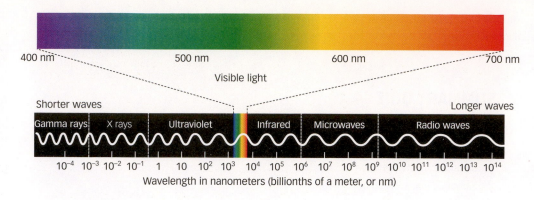

FIGURE 4.2 Electromagnetic Spectrum The sliver of light waves visible to humans as a rainbow of colors from violet-blue to red is bounded on the short end by ultraviolet rays, which honeybees can see, and on the long end by infrared waves, upon which night-vision equipment operates. Light waves are minute, but the scale along the bottom of this chart offers a glimpse of their varying lengths, measured in nanometers (nm; 1 nm = 1 billionth of a meter).

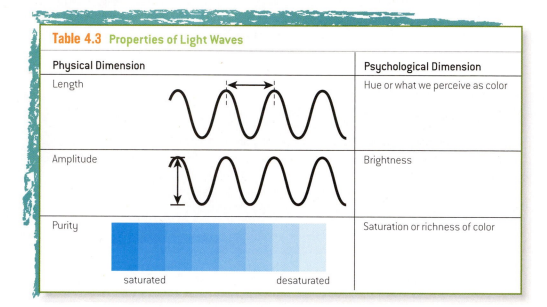

Table 4.3 Properties of Light Waves

Physical Dimension		Psychological Dimension
Length		Hue or what we perceive as color
Amplitude		Brightness
Purity	saturated desaturated	Saturation or richness of color

light waves, each of which produces a corresponding psychological dimension (see **TABLE 4.3**). The *length* of a light wave determines its hue, or what humans perceive as color. The intensity or *amplitude* of a light wave—how high the peaks are—determines what we perceive as brightness. *Purity* is the number of distinct wavelengths that make up the light, and it is purity that determines what we perceive as saturation, or the richness of colors.

The Human Eye

Eyes have evolved as specialized organs to detect light. **FIGURE 4.3** shows the human eye in cross-section. Light that reaches the eyes passes first through a clear, smooth outer tissue called the *cornea* and then continues through the *pupil*, a hole in the colored part of the eye. This colored part is the *iris*, which is a translucent, doughnut-shaped muscle that controls the size of the pupil and hence the amount of light that can enter the eye.

Immediately behind the iris, muscles inside the eye control the shape of the *lens* to bend the light and focus it onto the **retina**, *light-sensitive tissue lining the back of the eyeball*. The muscles change the shape of the lens to focus objects at different distances, making the lens flatter for objects that are far away or rounder for nearby objects. This is called **accommodation**, *the process by which the eye maintains a clear image on the retina*. **FIGURE 4.4a** shows how accommodation works.

If your eyeballs are a little too long or a little too short, the lens will not focus images properly on the retina. If the eyeball is too long, images are focused in front of the retina, leading to nearsightedness (*myopia*), which is shown in **FIGURE 4.4b**.

retina Light-sensitive tissue lining the back of the eyeball.

accommodation The process by which the eye maintains a clear image on the retina.

cones Photoreceptors that detect color, operate under normal daylight conditions, and allow us to focus on fine detail.

rods Photoreceptors that become active under low-light conditions for night vision.

fovea An area of the retina where vision is the clearest and there are no rods at all.

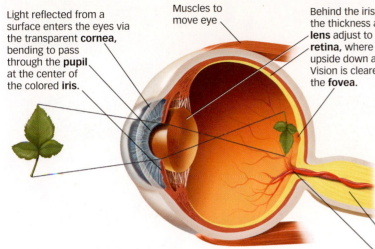

Light reflected from a surface enters the eyes via the transparent **cornea,** bending to pass through the **pupil** at the center of the colored **iris.**

Muscles to move eye

Behind the iris, the thickness and shape of the **lens** adjust to focus light on the **retina,** where the image appears upside down and backward. Vision is clearest at the **fovea.**

Light-sensitive receptor cells in the **retinal surface,** excited or inhibited by spots of light, influence the specialized neurons that signal the brain's visual centers through their bundled axons, which make up the **optic nerve.** The optic nerve creates the **blind spot.**

FIGURE 4.3 Anatomy of the Human Eye Specialized organs of the eye evolved to detect light.

How do eyeglasses actually correct vision?

If the eyeball is too short, images are focused behind the retina, and the result is farsightedness (*hyperopia*), as shown in **FIGURE 4.4c**. Eyeglasses, contact lenses, and surgical procedures can correct either condition. For example, eyeglasses and contacts both provide an additional lens to help focus light more appropriately, and procedures such as LASIK physically reshape the eye's existing lens.

From the Eye to the Brain

How does a wavelength of light become a meaningful image? The retina is the interface between the world of light outside the body and the world of vision inside the central nervous system. Two types of *photoreceptor cells* in the retina contain light-sensitive pigments that transduce light into neural impulses. **Cones** *detect color, operate under normal daylight conditions, and allow us to focus on fine detail.* **Rods** *become active under low-light conditions for night vision* (see **FIGURE 4.5**).

Rods are much more sensitive photoreceptors than cones, but this sensitivity comes at a cost. Because all rods contain the same photopigment, they provide no information about color and sense only shades of gray. Think about this the next time you wake up in the middle of the night and make your way to the bathroom for a drink of water. Using only the moonlight from the window to light your way, do you see the room in shades of gray? About 120 million rods are distributed more or less evenly around each retina except in the very center, the **fovea,** *an area of the retina where vision is the clearest and there are no rods at all.* The absence of rods in the fovea decreases the sharpness of vision in reduced light.

In contrast to rods, each retina contains only about six million cones, which are densely packed in the fovea and much more sparsely distributed over the rest of the retina, as you can see in Figure 4.5. This distribution of cones directly

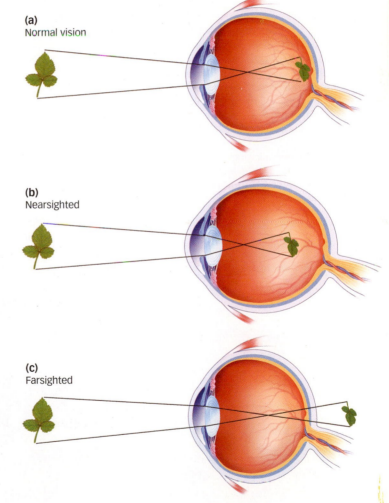

(a) Normal vision

(b) Nearsighted

(c) Farsighted

FIGURE 4.4 Accommodation Inside the eye, the lens changes shape to focus nearby or faraway objects on the retina. (*a*) People with normal vision focus the image on the retina at the back of the eye, both for near and far objects. (*b*) Nearsighted people see clearly what's nearby, but distant objects are blurry because light from them is focused in front of the retina, a condition called *myopia*. (*c*) Farsighted people have the opposite problem: Distant objects are clear, but those nearby are blurry because their point of focus falls beyond the surface of the retina, a condition called *hyperopia*.

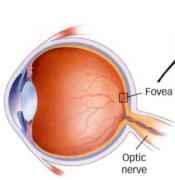

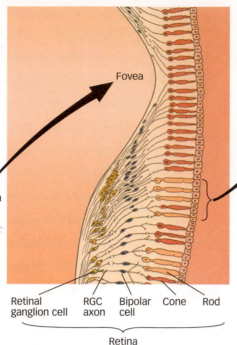

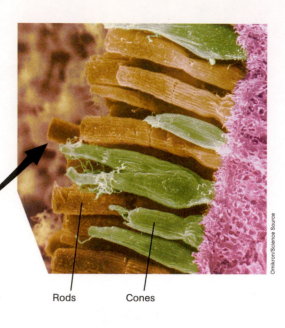

Fovea

Optic nerve

Fovea

Retinal ganglion cell   RGC axon   Bipolar cell   Cone   Rod

Retina

Rods   Cones

FIGURE 4.5 **Close-up of the Retina**
The surface of the retina is composed of photoreceptor cells, the rods and cones, beneath a layer of transparent neurons, the bipolar and retinal ganglion cells (RGCs). The axons of the RGCs form the optic nerve. Viewed close up in this cross-sectional diagram is the area of greatest visual acuity, the fovea, where most color-sensitive cones are concentrated, allowing us to see fine detail as well as color. Rods, the predominant photoreceptors activated in low-light conditions, are distributed everywhere else on the retina.

affects visual acuity and explains why objects off to the side, in your *peripheral vision,* aren't so clear. The light reflecting from those peripheral objects is less likely to land in the fovea, making the resulting image less clear.

As seen in Figure 4.5, the photoreceptor cells (rods and cones) form the innermost layer of the retina. Above them, the *bipolar cells* collect neural signals from the rods and cones and transmit them to the *retinal ganglion cells (RGCs),* which organize the signals and send them to the brain. The bundled RGC axons form the *optic nerve,* which leaves the eye through a hole in the retina. Because it contains neither rods nor cones and therefore has no mechanism to sense light, this hole in the retina creates a **blind spot,** *a location in the visual field that produces no sensation on the retina.* Try the demonstration in **FIGURE 4.6** to find the blind spot in each of your own eyes.

? What are the major differences between rods and cones?

The full-color image on the left is what you'd see if your rods and cones are fully at work. The grayscale image on the right is what you'd see if only your rods are functioning.

Perceiving Color

Sir Isaac Newton pointed out around 1670 that color is not something "in" light. In fact, color is nothing but our perception of wavelengths from the spectrum of visible light (see Figure 4.2). We perceive the shortest visible wavelengths as deep purple. As wavelengths increase, the color perceived changes gradually and continuously to blue, then green, yellow, orange, and, with the longest visible wavelengths, red. This rainbow of hues and accompanying wavelengths is called the *visible spectrum,* illustrated in **FIGURE 4.7**.

Cones come in three types; each type is especially sensitive to either red (long-wavelength), green (medium-wavelength), or blue

The image on the left was taken at a higher resolution than the image on the right. The difference in quality is analogous to light falling on the fovea versus the periphery of the retina.

FIGURE 4.6 Blind Spot Demonstration To find your blind spot, close your left eye and stare at the cross with your right eye. Hold the book 6 to 12 inches (15 to 30 centimeters) away from your eyes and move it slowly toward and away from you until the dot disappears. The dot is now in your blind spot. At this point, the vertical lines may appear as one continuous line because the visual system fills in the area occupied by the missing dot. To test your left eye's blind spot, turn the book upside down and repeat with your right eye closed.

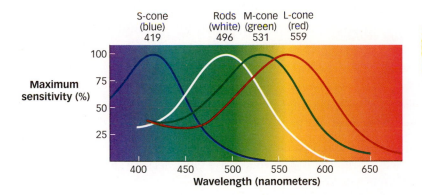

FIGURE 4.7 Seeing in Color We perceive a spectrum of color because objects selectively absorb some wavelengths of light and reflect others. Color perception corresponds to the summed activity of the three types of cones. Each type is most sensitive to a narrow range of wavelengths in the visible spectrum—short (bluish light), medium (greenish light), or long (reddish light). Rods, represented by the white curve, are most sensitive to the medium wavelengths of visible light but do not contribute to color perception.

(short-wavelength) light. Red, green, and blue are the primary colors of light; color perception results from different combinations of the three basic elements in the retina. For example, lighting designers add primary colors of light together, such as shining red and green spotlights on a surface to create a yellow light, as shown in **FIGURE 4.8**. Notice that in the center of the figure, where the red, green, and blue lights overlap, the surface looks white. This demonstrates that a white surface really is reflecting all visible wavelengths of light.

A genetic disorder in which one of the cone types is missing—and, in some very rare cases, two or all three—causes a *color deficiency*. This trait is sex-linked,

blind spot A location in the visual field that produces no sensation on the retina.

FIGURE 4.8 **Color Mixing** The millions of shades of color that humans can perceive are products not only of a light's wavelength, but also of the mixture of wavelengths a stimulus absorbs or reflects. Colored spotlights work by causing the surface to reflect light of a particular wavelength, which stimulates the red, blue, or green photo-pigments in the cones. When all visible wavelengths are present, we see white.

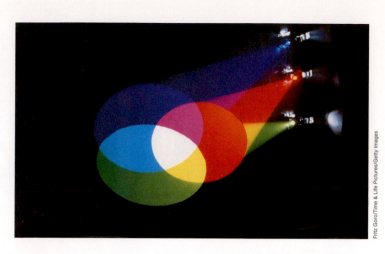

Many people (including about 5% of all males) inherit conditions in which either the "red" or the "green" photoreceptors do not transduce light properly. Such people have difficulty distinguishing hues that to typical individuals appear as red or green. Unfortunately, in the United States, traffic signals use red and green lights to indicate whether cars should stop or go through an intersection. Why do drivers with red–green blindness not risk auto accidents every time they approach an intersection?

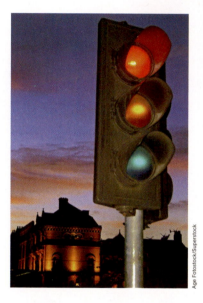

affecting men much more often than women. Color deficiency is often referred to as *color blindness*, but in fact, people missing only one type of cone can still distinguish many colors, just not as many as someone who has the full complement of three cone types. You can create a kind of temporary color deficiency by exploiting the idea of sensory adaptation. Staring too long at one color fatigues the cones that respond to that

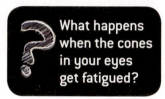

What happens when the cones in your eyes get fatigued?

color, producing a form of sensory adaptation that results in a *color afterimage*. To demonstrate this effect for yourself, follow these instructions for **FIGURE 4.9**:

> Stare at the small cross between the two color patches for about 1 minute. Try to keep your eyes as still as possible.

> After a minute, look at the lower cross. You should see a vivid color aftereffect that lasts for a minute or more. Pay particular attention to the colors in the afterimage.

Were you puzzled that the red patch produces a green afterimage and the green patch produces a red afterimage? When you view a color, let's say, green, the cones that respond most strongly to green become fatigued over time. Now, when you stare at a white or gray patch, which reflects all the colors equally, the green-sensitive cones respond only weakly compared with the still-fresh red-sensitive cones, which fire strongly. The result? You perceive the patch as tinted red.

FIGURE 4.9 **Color Afterimage Demonstration** Follow the accompanying instructions in the text, and sensory adaptation will do the rest. When the afterimage fades, you can get back to reading the chapter.

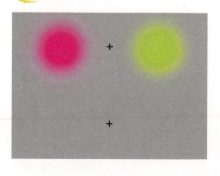

The Visual Brain

Streams of action potentials containing information encoded by the retina (neural impulses) travel to the brain along the optic nerve. Half of the axons in the optic nerve that leave each eye come from retinal ganglion cells (RGCs) that code information in the right visual field, whereas the other half code information in the left visual field. These two nerve bundles link to the left and right hemispheres of the brain, respectively (see **FIGURE 4.10**). The optic nerve travels from each eye to

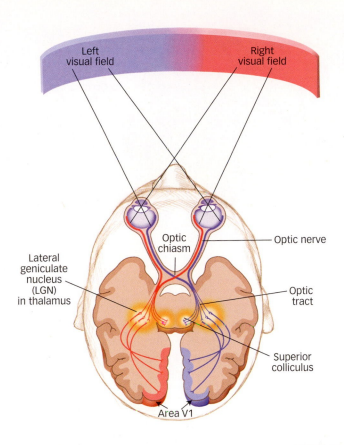

FIGURE 4.10 **Visual Pathway from Eye through Brain** Objects in the right visual field stimulate the left half of each retina, and objects in the left visual field stimulate the right half of each retina. The optic nerves, one exiting each eye, are formed by the axons of retinal ganglion cells emerging from the retina. Just before they enter the brain at the optic chiasm, about half the nerve fibers from each eye cross. The left half of each optic nerve (representing the right visual field) runs through the brain's left hemisphere via the thalamus, and the right half of each optic nerve (representing the left visual field) travels this route through the right hemisphere. So, information from the right visual field ends up in the left hemisphere, and information from the left visual field ends up in the right hemisphere.

the thalamus. From there, the visual signal travels to the back of the brain, to a location called **area V1,** *the part of the occipital lobe that contains the primary visual cortex.* Here the information is systematically mapped into a representation of the visual scene.

? What is the relationship between the right and left eyes, and the right and left visual fields?

area V1 The part of the occipital lobe that contains the primary visual cortex.

FIGURE 4.11 **Single-Neuron Feature Detectors** Area V1 contains neurons that respond to specific orientations of edges. Here a single neuron's responses are recorded (*left*) as the monkey views bars at different orientations (*right*). This neuron fires continuously when the bar is pointing to the right at 45°, less often when it is vertical, and not at all when it is pointing to the left at 45°.

Neural Systems for Perceiving Shape

One of the most important functions of vision involves perceiving the shapes of objects; our day-to-day lives would be a mess if we couldn't reliably differentiate between a warm doughnut with glazed icing and a straight stalk of celery. Perceiving shape depends on the location and orientation of an object's edges. As you read in the Neuroscience and Behavior chapter, neurons in the visual cortex selectively respond to bars and edges in specific orientations in space (Hubel & Wiesel, 1962, 1998). In effect, area V1 contains populations of neurons, each "tuned" to respond to edges oriented at each position in the visual field. This means that some neurons fire when an object in a vertical orientation is perceived, other neurons fire when an object in a horizontal orientation is perceived, still other neurons fire when objects in a diagonal orientation of 45° are perceived, and so on (see **FIGURE 4.11**).

Stimulus | Neuron's responses

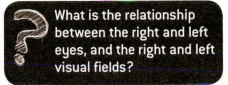

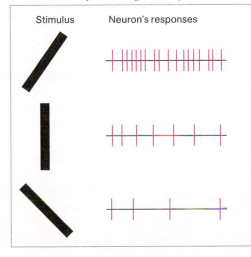

Fritz Goro/Time & Life Pictures/Getty Images

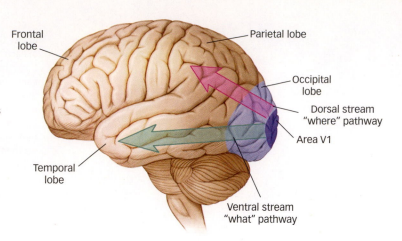

FIGURE 4.12 **Visual Streaming** The ventral pathway courses from the occipital visual regions into the lower temporal lobe and enables us to identify what we see. The dorsal pathway travels from the occipital lobe through the upper regions of the temporal lobe into the parietal regions and allows us to locate objects, to track their movements, and to move in relation to them.

The outcome of the coordinated response of all these feature detectors contributes to a sophisticated visual system that can detect where a doughnut ends and celery begins.

Pathways for What, Where, and How

Two functionally distinct pathways, or *visual streams,* project from the occipital cortex to visual areas in other parts of the brain (see **FIGURE 4.12**). One pathway, the *ventral* (below) *stream,* travels across the occipital lobes to the temporal lobe and includes brain areas that represent an object's shape and identity—in other words, what it is, essentially a "what" pathway (Kravitz et al., 2013; Ungerleider & Mishkin, 1982). The other pathway, the *dorsal* (above) *stream,* travels up from the occipital lobe to the parietal lobes (including some of the middle and upper levels of the temporal lobes), connecting with brain areas that identify the location and motion of an object—in other words, *where* it is (Kravitz et al., 2011). Because the dorsal stream allows us to perceive spatial relations, researchers originally dubbed it the "where" pathway (Ungerleider & Mishkin, 1982). Neuroscientists later argued that because the dorsal stream is crucial for guiding movements, such as aiming, reaching, or tracking with the eyes, the "where" pathway should more appropriately be called the "how" pathway (Milner & Goodale, 1995).

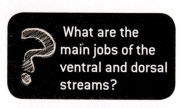

What are the main jobs of the ventral and dorsal streams?

Some of the most dramatic evidence for the existence of these two pathways comes from studying patients with brain injuries. For example, a woman known as D.F. suffered permanent damage to a large region of the lateral occipital cortex, an area in the ventral stream (Goodale et al., 1991). Her ability to recognize objects by sight was greatly impaired, although her ability to recognize objects by touch was normal. This suggests that her *visual representation* of objects, not her *memory* for objects, was damaged. D.F.'s condition is called **visual form agnosia,** *the inability to recognize objects by sight* (Goodale & Milner, 1992, 2004). Conversely, other patients with brain damage to the parietal lobe, a section of the dorsal stream, have difficulty using vision to guide their reaching and grasping movements (Perenin & Vighetto, 1988). However, their ventral streams are intact, meaning they recognize what objects are. We can conclude from these two patterns of impairment that the ventral and dorsal visual streams are functionally distinct; it is possible to damage one while leaving the other intact.

visual form agnosia The inability to recognize objects by sight.

SUMMARY QUIZ [4.2]

1. The world of light outside the body is linked to the world of vision inside the central nervous system by the
   a. cornea.
   b. lens.
   c. retina.
   d. optic nerve.

2. Light striking the retina, causing a specific pattern of response in the three cone types, leads to our ability to see
   a. motion.
   b. colors.
   c. depth.
   d. shadows.

3. In which part of the brain is the primary visual cortex, where encoded information is systematically mapped into a representation of the visual scene?
   a. the thalamus
   b. the lateral geniculate nucleus
   c. the fovea
   d. area V1

binding problem How features are linked together so that we see unified objects in our visual world rather than free-floating or miscombined features.

illusory conjunction A perceptual mistake where features from multiple objects are incorrectly combined.

Vision II: Recognizing What We Perceive

Our journey into the visual system has already revealed how it accomplishes some pretty astonishing feats. But the system needs to do much more in order for us to be able to interact effectively with our visual worlds. Let's now consider how the system links together individual visual features into whole objects, allows us to recognize what those objects are, organizes objects into visual scenes, and detects motion and change in those scenes. Along the way, we'll see that studying visual errors and illusions provides key insights into how these processes work.

Attention: The "Glue" That Binds Individual Features into a Whole

Specialized feature detectors in different parts of the visual system analyze each of the multiple features of a visible object: orientation, color, size, shape, and so forth. But how are different features combined into single, unified objects? What allows us to perceive that the young man in the photo is wearing a red shirt and the young woman is wearing a yellow shirt? Why don't we see free-floating patches of red and yellow? These questions refer to what researchers call the **binding problem** in perception: *how features are linked together so that we see unified objects in our visual world rather than free-floating or miscombined features* (Treisman, 1998, 2006).

Illusory Conjunctions: Perceptual Mistakes

In everyday life, we correctly combine features into unified objects so automatically and effortlessly that it may be difficult to appreciate that binding is ever a problem at all. However, researchers have discovered errors in binding that reveal important clues about how the process works. One such error is known as an **illusory conjunction,** *a perceptual mistake where features from multiple objects are incorrectly combined.* In one

We correctly combine features into unified objects; so, for example, we see that the young man is wearing a gray shirt and the young woman is wearing a red shirt.

Thomas Barwick/Getty Images

Presented

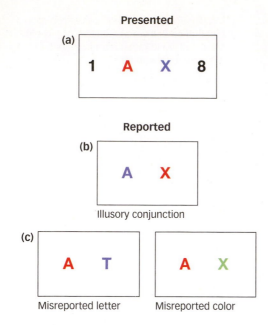

(a)

1   A   X   8

Reported

(b)

A   X

Illusory conjunction

(c)

A   T   A   X

Misreported letter   Misreported color

FIGURE 4.13 Illusory Conjunctions Illusory conjunctions occur when features such as color and shape are combined incorrectly. For example, when participants are shown a red *A* and blue *X*, they sometimes report seeing a blue *A* and red *X*. Other kinds of errors, such as a misreported letter (e.g., reporting *T* when no *T* was presented) or misreported color (reporting green when no green was presented) occur rarely, indicating that illusory conjunctions are not the result of guessing. (Information from Roberston, 2003.)

A quick glance and you recognize all these letters as *G*, but their varying sizes, shapes, angles, and orientations ought to make this recognition task difficult. What is it about the process of object recognition that allows us to perform this task effortlessly?

G g g
G g G G
G g g G g

study, researchers briefly showed participants visual displays in which black digits flanked colored letters, such as a red *A* and a blue *X*, then instructed participants first to report the black digits and second to describe the colored letters (Triesman & Schmidt, 1982). Participants frequently reported illusory conjunctions, claiming to have seen, for example, a blue *A* or a red *X* (see **FIGURE 4.13a** and **b**). These illusory conjunctions were not just the result of guessing; they occurred more frequently than other kinds of errors, such as reporting a letter or color that was not present in the display (see **FIGURE 4.13c**).

Why do illusory conjunctions occur? Psychologist Anne Treisman and her colleagues proposed a **feature-integration theory** (Treisman, 1998, 2006; Treisman & Gelade, 1980; Treisman & Schmidt, 1982), which holds that *focused attention is not required to detect the individual features that comprise a stimulus, such as the color, shape, size, and location of letters, but it is required to bind those individual features together*. From this perspective, attention provides the "glue" necessary to bind features together, and illusory conjunctions occur when it is difficult for participants to pay full attention to the features that need to be glued together.

For example, in the experiments we just considered, participants were first required to name the black digits, thereby reducing attention to the colored letters and allowing illusory conjunctions to occur. When experimental conditions are changed so that participants can pay full attention to the colored letters and they are able to correctly bind their features together, illusory conjunctions disappear (Treisman, 1998; Treisman & Schmidt, 1982).

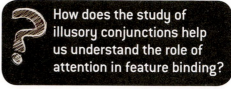

How does the study of illusory conjunctions help us understand the role of attention in feature binding?

The Role of the Parietal Lobe

The binding process makes use of feature information processed by structures within the ventral visual stream, the "what" pathway (Seymour et al., 2010; see Figure 4.12). But because binding involves linking together features that appear at a particular spatial location, it also depends critically on the parietal lobe in the dorsal stream, the "where" pathway (Robertson, 1999). For example, Treisman and others studied R.M., who had suffered strokes that destroyed both his left and right parietal lobes. Although many aspects of his visual function were intact, he had severe problems attending to spatially distinct objects. When presented with stimuli such as those in Figure 4.13, R.M. perceived an abnormally large number of illusory conjunctions, even when he was given as long as 10 seconds to look at the displays (Friedman-Hill, Robertson, & Treisman, 1995; Robertson, 2003).

Recognizing Objects by Sight

Take a quick look at the letters in the accompanying illustration. Even though they're quite different from one another, you probably effortlessly recognized them as all being examples of the letter *G*. Now consider the same kind of demonstration using your best friend's face. Suppose one day your friend gets a dramatic new haircut—or adds glasses, hair dye, or a nose ring. Even though your friend now looks strikingly different, you still recognize that person with ease. Just like the variability in Gs, you somehow are able to extract the underlying features of the face that allow you to accurately identify your friend.

This thought exercise may seem trivial, but it's no small perceptual feat. If the visual system were somehow stumped each time a minor variation occurred in an object, the inefficiency of it all would be overwhelming. We'd have to process information effortfully just to perceive our friend as the same person from one meeting to another, not to mention laboring through the process of knowing when a *G* is really a *G*. In general, though, object recognition proceeds fairly smoothly, in large part due to the operation of the feature detectors we discussed earlier.

How do feature detectors help the visual system accurately perceive an object in different circumstances, such as your friend's face? Some researchers argue for a *modular view*—namely, that specialized brain areas, or modules, detect and represent faces or houses or even body parts. Using fMRI to examine visual processing in healthy young adults, researchers found a subregion in the temporal lobe that responds most strongly to faces compared to just about any other object category, whereas a nearby area responds most strongly to buildings and landscapes (Kanwisher, McDermott, & Chun, 1997). This view suggests we have not only feature detectors to aid in visual perception but also "face detectors," "building detectors," and possibly other types of neurons specialized for particular types of object perception (Downing et al., 2006; Kanwisher & Yovel, 2006). Other researchers argue for a more *distributed representation* of object categories. In this view, it is the pattern of activity across multiple brain regions that identifies any viewed object, including faces (Haxby et al., 2001). Each of these views explains some data better than the other one, and researchers continue to debate their relative merits.

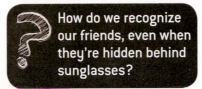

How do we recognize our friends, even when they're hidden behind sunglasses?

feature-integration theory The idea that focused attention is not required to detect the individual features that comprise a stimulus, but is required to bind those individual features together.

Our visual systems allow us to identify people as the same individual even when they change such features as hair style and skin color. Despite the extreme changes in these two photos, you can probably tell that they both portray Johnny Depp.

Principles of Perceptual Organization

Before object recognition can even kick in, the visual system must perform another important task: grouping the image regions that belong together into a representation of an object. The idea that we tend to perceive a unified, whole object rather than a collection of separate parts is the foundation of Gestalt psychology, which you read about in Chapter 1. Gestalt *perceptual grouping rules* govern how the features and regions of things fit together (Koffka, 1935). Here's a sampling:

> *Simplicity*: When confronted with two or more possible interpretations of an object's shape, the visual system tends to select the simplest or most likely interpretation. In **FIGURE 4.14a**, we see an arrow, rather than two separate shapes: a triangle sitting on top of a rectangle.

> *Closure*: We tend to fill in missing elements of a visual scene, allowing us to perceive edges that are separated by gaps as belonging to complete objects. In **FIGURE 4.14b**, we see an arrow despite the gaps.

> *Continuity*: When edges or contours have the same orientation, we tend to group them together perceptually. In **FIGURE 4.14c**, we perceive two (continuous) crossing lines instead of two V shapes.

> *Similarity*: Regions that are similar in color, lightness, shape, or texture are perceived as belonging to the same object. In **FIGURE 4.14d**, we perceive three columns—a column of circles flanked by two columns of triangles—instead of three rows of mixed shapes.

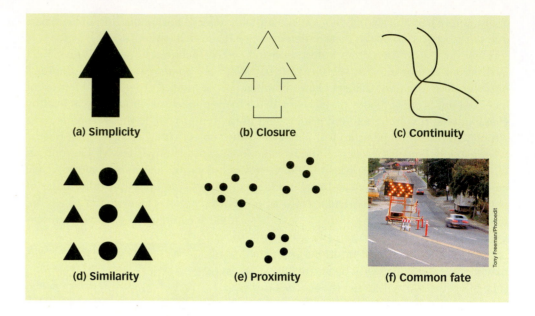

FIGURE 4.14 **Perceptual Grouping Rules** As noted by the Gestalt psychologists, the brain is predisposed to impose order on incoming sensations, such as by responding to patterns among stimuli and grouping like patterns together.

(a) Simplicity (b) Closure (c) Continuity

(d) Similarity (e) Proximity (f) Common fate

Tony Freeman/PhotoEdit

> *Proximity:* Objects that are close together tend to be grouped together. In **FIGURE 4.14e**, we perceive three groups or "clumps" of 5 or 6 dots each, not just 16 dots.

> *Common fate:* Elements of a visual image that move together are perceived as parts of a single moving object. In **FIGURE 4.14f**, the series of flashing lights in the road sign are perceived as a moving arrowhead.

Separating Figure from Ground

Perceptual grouping involves visually separating an object from its surroundings. In Gestalt terms, this means identifying a *figure* apart from the (back)*ground* in which it resides. For example, the words on this page are perceived as figural: They stand out from the ground of the sheet of paper on which they're printed. Similarly, your instructor is perceived as the figure against the backdrop of all the other elements in your classroom. You certainly can perceive these elements differently, of course: The words *and* the paper are all part of a thing called *a page*, and your instructor *and* the classroom can all be perceived as *your learning environment*. Typically, though, our perceptual systems focus attention on some objects as distinct from their environments.

Size provides one clue to what's figure and what's ground: Smaller regions are likely to be figures, such as tiny letters on a big sheet of paper. Movement also helps: Your instructor is (we hope) a dynamic lecturer, moving around in a static environment. Another critical step toward object recognition is *edge assignment*. Given an edge, or boundary, between figure and ground, which region does that edge belong to? If the edge belongs to the figure, it helps define the object's shape, and the background continues behind the edge. Sometimes, though, it's not easy to tell which is which.

Edgar Rubin (1886–1951), a Danish psychologist, capitalized on this ambiguity and developed a famous illusion called the *Rubin vase* or, more generally, a *reversible figure–ground relationship*. You can view this "face–vase" illusion in **FIGURE 4.15** in two ways, either as a vase on a black background or as a pair of silhouettes facing each other. Your visual system settles on one or the other interpretation and fluctuates between them every few seconds. This happens because the edge that would normally separate figure from ground is really part of neither: It equally defines the contours of the vase as it does the contours of the faces. Evidence from fMRIs shows, quite nicely, that when people are seeing the Rubin image as faces, there is greater activity in the face-selective region of the temporal lobe we discussed earlier than when they are seeing it as a vase (Hasson et al., 2001).

FIGURE 4.15 **Rubin's vase** Fixate your eyes on the center of the image and your perception will alternate between a vase and facing silhouettes, even as the sensory stimulation remains constant.

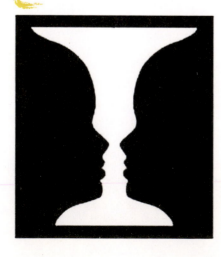

Perceiving Depth and Size

Objects in the world are arranged in three dimensions—length, width, and depth—but the retinal image contains only two dimensions, length and width. How does the brain process a flat, 2-D retinal image so that we perceive the depth of an object and how far away it is? The answer lies in a collection of *depth cues* that change as you move through space. Monocular and binocular depth cues all help visual perception (Howard, 2002).

Monocular Depth Cues

Monocular depth cues are *aspects of a scene that yield information about depth when viewed with only one eye.* These cues rely on the relationship between distance and size. Even when you have one eye closed, the retinal image of an object you're focused on grows smaller as that object moves farther away and larger as it moves closer. Our brains routinely use these differences in retinal image size, or *relative size,* to perceive distance. Most adults, for example, fall within a familiar range of heights (perhaps 5–7 feet tall), so retinal image size alone is usually a reliable cue to how far away they are. Our visual system automatically corrects for size differences and attributes them to differences in distance. **FIGURE 4.16** demonstrates how strong this effect is.

In addition to relative size, there are several more monocular depth cues, such as

> *Linear perspective*, the phenomenon that parallel lines seem to converge as they recede into the distance (see **FIGURE 4.17a**).

> *Texture gradient*, the fact that the size of the elements on a patterned surface grows smaller as the surface recedes from the observer (see **FIGURE 4.17b**).

FIGURE 4.16 Relative Size When you view images of people, such as the people in the left-hand photo, the object you perceive as smaller appears farther away. With a little image manipulation, you can see in the right-hand photo that the relative size difference projected on your retinas is far greater than you perceive. The image of the person in the blue vest is exactly the same size in both photos.

monocular depth cues Aspects of a scene that yield information about depth when viewed with only one eye.

(a)

(b)

(c)

(d)

FIGURE 4.17 Pictorial Depth Cues Visual artists rely on a variety of monocular cues to make their work come to life. You can rely on cues such as linear perspective (*a*), texture gradient (*b*), interposition (*c*), and relative height (*d*) in an image to infer distance, depth, and position, even if you're wearing an eye patch.

The View-Master has been a popular toy for decades. It is based on the principle of binocular disparity: Two images taken from slightly different angles produce a stereoscopic effect.

binocular disparity The difference in the retinal images of the two eyes that provides information about depth.

> *Interposition*, the fact that when one object partly blocks another (see **FIGURE 4.17c**), you can infer that the blocking object is closer than the blocked object.

> *Relative height in the image*, the fact that objects that are closer to you are lower in your visual field, whereas faraway objects are higher (see **FIGURE 4.17d**).

Binocular Depth Cues

We can also obtain depth information through **binocular disparity**, *the difference in the retinal images of the two eyes that provides information about depth*. Because our eyes are slightly separated, each registers a slightly different view of the world. Your brain computes the disparity between the two retinal images to perceive how far away objects are, as shown in **FIGURE 4.18**. Viewed from above in the figure, the images of the more distant square and the closer circle each fall at different points on each retina. The View-Master toy and 3-D movies both work by exploiting retinal disparity.

Illusions of Depth and Size

We all are vulnerable to *illusions,* which, as you'll remember from the Psychology: Evolution of a Science chapter, are errors of perception, memory, or judgment in which subjective experience differs from objective reality (Wade, 2005). A famous illusion that makes use of a variety of depth cues is the *Ames room,* which is trapezoidal in shape rather than square (see **FIGURE 4.19a**). A person standing in one corner of an Ames room is physically twice as far away from the viewer as a person standing in the other corner. But when viewed with one eye through the small peephole placed in one wall, the Ames room looks square because the shapes of the windows and the flooring tiles are carefully crafted to *look* square from the viewing port (Ittelson, 1952). The visual system perceives the far wall as perpendicular to the line of sight so that people standing at different positions along that wall appear to be at the same distance, and the viewer's judgments of their sizes are based directly on retinal image size. As a result, a person standing in the right corner appears to be much larger than a person standing in the left corner (see **FIGURE 4.19b**).

FIGURE 4.18 Binocular Disparity We see the world in three dimensions because the image of an object falls on the retinas of each eye at a slightly different place. In this two-object scene, the images of the square and the circle fall on different points of the retina in each eye. The disparity in the positions of the circle's retinal images provides a compelling cue to depth.

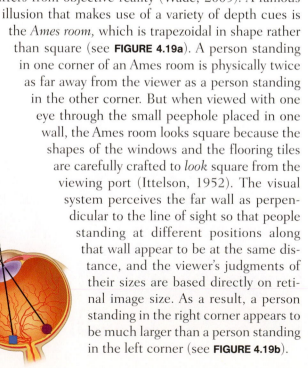

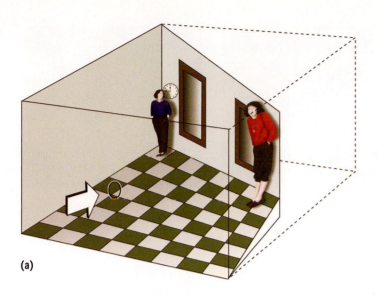

(a)

(b)

Phil Schermeister/Corbis

FIGURE 4.19 The Amazing Ames Room (*a*) A diagram showing the actual proportions of the Ames room reveals its secrets. The sides of the room form a trapezoid with a back wall that's way off square. The uneven floor makes the room's height in the far back corner shorter than the other. (*b*) Looking into the Ames room through the viewing port with only one eye, the observer infers a normal size–distance relationship—that both people are the same distance away. But the different image sizes they project on the retina leads the viewer to conclude, based on monocular cues, that one person is very small and the other is very large.

Perceiving Motion and Change

You should now have a good sense of how we see what and where objects are, a process made substantially easier when the objects stay in one place. But real life, of course, is full of moving targets. Birds fly, horses gallop, and trees bend in the wind. Understanding how we perceive motion and why we sometimes fail to perceive change can bring us closer to appreciating how visual perception works in everyday life.

Motion Perception

To sense motion, the visual system must encode information about both space and time. The simplest case to consider is an observer who does not move trying to perceive an object that does.

As an object moves across an observer's stationary visual field, it first stimulates one location on the retina, and then a little later it stimulates another location on the retina. Neural circuits in the brain can detect this change in position over time and respond to specific speeds and directions of motion (Emerson, Bergen, & Adelson, 1992). A region in the middle of the temporal lobe referred to as *MT* (part of the dorsal stream we discussed earlier) is specialized for the visual perception of motion (Born & Bradley, 2005; Newsome & Paré, 1988), and brain damage in this area leads to a deficit in normal motion perception (Zihl, von Cramon, & Mai, 1983).

Of course, in the real world, rarely are you a stationary observer. As you move around, your head and eyes move all the time. The motion-perception system must take into account the position and movement of your eyes—and ultimately of your head and body—in order to perceive the motions of objects correctly. The brain accomplishes this feat by monitoring your eye and head movements and "subtracting" them from the motion in the retinal image.

The movement of objects in the world is not the only event that can evoke the perception of motion. The successively flashing lights of a Las Vegas casino sign can evoke a strong sense of motion because people perceive a series of flashing lights as a whole, moving object (see again Figure 4.15f). This *perception of movement as a result of alternating signals appearing in rapid succession in different locations* is called **apparent motion**. Video technology and animation depend on apparent motion. Motion pictures flash 24 frames per second (fps). A slower rate would produce a much choppier sense of motion; a faster rate would be a waste of resources because we would not perceive the motion as any smoother than it appears at 24 fps.

How can flashing lights on a casino sign give the impression of movement?

apparent motion The perception of movement as a result of alternating signals appearing in rapid succession in different locations.

(a)　　　(b)　　　(c)

FIGURE 4.20 Change Blindness The white-haired man was giving directions to one experimenter (*a*), who disappeared behind the moving door (*b*), only to be replaced by another experimenter (*c*). Like many other people, the man failed to detect a seemingly obvious change.

change blindness When people fail to detect changes to the visual details of a scene.

inattentional blindness A failure to perceive objects that are not the focus of attention.

College students who were using their cell phones while walking through campus failed to notice the unicycling clown more frequently than students who were not using their cell phones.

Hyman et al., 2010

Change Blindness and Inattentional Blindness

Motion involves a change in an object's position over time, but objects in the visual environment can change in ways that do not involve motion (Rensink, 2002). You might walk by the same clothing store window every day and notice when a new suit or dress is on display. Intuitively, we feel that we can easily detect changes to our visual environment. However, our comfortable intuitions have been challenged by experimental demonstrations of **change blindness,** which occurs *when people fail to detect changes to the visual details of a scene* (Rensink, 2002; Simons & Rensink, 2005). One study tested this idea by having an experimenter ask a person on a college campus for directions (Simons & Levin, 1998). While they were talking, two men walked between them holding a door that hid a second experimenter (see **FIGURE 4.20**). Behind the door, the two experimenters traded places so that when the men carrying the door moved on, a different person was asking for directions than the one who had been there just a second or two earlier. Remarkably, only 7 of 15 participants reported noticing this change.

Although surprising, these findings once again illustrate the importance of focused attention for visual perception. Just as focused attention is critical for binding together the features of objects, it is also necessary for detecting changes to objects and scenes (Rensink, 2002; Simons & Rensink, 2005).

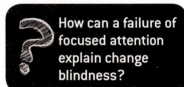

How can a failure of focused attention explain change blindness?

Change blindness is most likely to occur when people fail to focus attention on the changed object (even though the object is registered by the visual system) and is least likely to occur for items that draw attention to themselves (Rensink, O'Regan, & Clark, 1997).

The role of focused attention in conscious visual experience is also dramatically illustrated by the closely related phenomenon of **inattentional blindness,** *a failure to perceive objects that are not the focus of attention.* We've already seen that using cell phones has negative effects on driving (see The Real World: Multitasking). In another study, researchers asked whether cell phone use contributes to inattentional blindness in everyday life (Hyman et al., 2010). They recruited a clown to ride a unicycle in the middle of a large square in the middle of the campus at Western Washington University. On a pleasant afternoon, the researchers asked 151 students who had just walked through the square whether they saw the clown. Seventy-five percent of the students who were using cell phones failed to notice the clown, compared with less than 50% who were not using cell phones. Using cell phones draws on focused attention, resulting in increased inattentional blindness and emphasizing again that our conscious experience of the visual environment is restricted to those features or objects selected by focused attention.

Culture & Community

Does culture influence change blindness? The evidence for change blindness that we've considered in this chapter comes from studies using participants from Western cultures, mainly Americans. Would change blindness occur in individuals from other cultures? Think back to the Culture & Community box from the Psychology: Evolution of a Science chapter, where we discussed evidence showing that people from Western cultures rely on an *analytic* style of processing information (i.e., they tend to focus on an object without paying much attention to the surrounding context), whereas people from Eastern cultures tend to adopt a *holistic* style (i.e., they tend to focus on the relationship between an object and the surrounding context: Kitayama et al., 2003; Nisbett & Miyamoto, 2005).

With this distinction in mind, Masuda and Nisbett (2006) noted that previous studies of change blindness, using mainly American participants, had shown that participants are more likely to detect changes in the main or focal object in a scene, and less likely to detect changes in surrounding context. The researchers hypothesized that individuals from an Eastern culture would be more focused on—and therefore likely to notice—changes in surrounding context than individuals from a Western culture. To test their prediction, they conducted three experiments examining change detection in American and Japanese college students (Masuda & Nisbett, 2006). In each experiment, they made changes either to the main object in a scene or to the surrounding context (e.g., objects in the background).

The results of the experiments were consistent with predictions: Japanese students detected more changes to contextual information than did American students, whereas American students detected more changes to focal objects than did Japanese students. These findings extend earlier reports that people from Eastern and Western cultures see the world differently, with Easterners focusing more on the context in which an object appears and Westerners focusing more on the object itself.

SUMMARY QUIZ [4.3]

1. Our ability to visually combine details so that we perceive unified objects is explained by
   a. feature-integration theory.
   b. illusory conjunction.
   c. synesthesia.
   d. ventral and dorsal streaming.

2. The idea that specialized brain areas represent particular classes of objects is
   a. the modular view.
   b. attentional processing.
   c. distributed representation.
   d. neuron response.

3. What kind of cues are relative height and linear perspective?
   a. motion-based
   b. binocular
   c. monocular
   d. template

pitch How high or low a sound is.

loudness A sound's intensity.

timbre A listener's experience of sound quality or resonance.

Audition: More Than Meets the Ear

Vision is based on the spatial pattern of light waves on the retina. The sense of hearing, by contrast, is all about *sound waves*: changes in air pressure unfolding over time. Plenty of things produce sound waves: the collision of a tree hitting the forest floor, the vibration of vocal cords during a stirring speech, the resonance of a bass guitar string during a thrash metal concert. Understanding auditory experience requires understanding how we transform changes in air pressure into perceived sounds.

Sensing Sound

Striking a tuning fork produces a *pure tone,* a simple sound wave that first increases air pressure and then creates a relative vacuum. This cycle repeats hundreds or thousands of times per second as sound waves travel outward in all directions from the source. Just as there are three physical dimensions of light waves corresponding to three dimensions of visual perception, so, too, there are three physical dimensions of a sound wave that determine what we hear (see **TABLE 4.4**).

> The *frequency* (or wavelength) of the sound wave depends on how often the peak in air pressure passes the ear or a microphone, measured in cycles per second, or hertz (Hz). Changes in the physical frequency of a sound wave are perceived by humans as changes in **pitch,** *how high or low a sound is.*

> The *amplitude* of a sound wave refers to its height, relative to the threshold for human hearing (which is set at zero decibels, or dBs). Amplitude corresponds to **loudness,** or *a sound's intensity.* The rustling of leaves in a soft breeze is about 20 dB, normal conversation is measured at about 40 dB, shouting produces 70 dB, a Slayer concert is about 130 dB, and the sound of the space shuttle taking off 1 mile away registers at 160 dB or more.

> Differences in the *complexity* of sound waves, or their mix of frequencies, correspond to **timbre,** *a listener's experience of sound quality or resonance.* Timbre (pronounced "TAM-ber") offers us information about the nature of sound. The same note played at the same

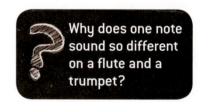
Why does one note sound so different on a flute and a trumpet?

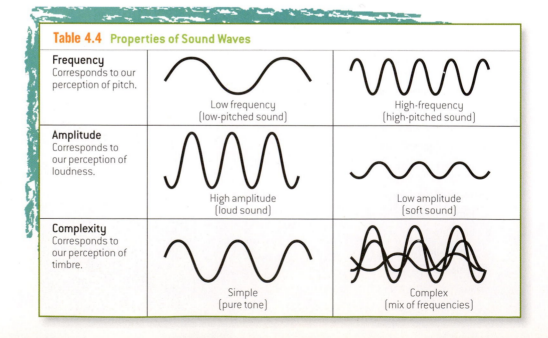

Table 4.4	Properties of Sound Waves	
Frequency Corresponds to our perception of pitch.	Low frequency (low-pitched sound)	High-frequency (high-pitched sound)
Amplitude Corresponds to our perception of loudness.	High amplitude (loud sound)	Low amplitude (soft sound)
Complexity Corresponds to our perception of timbre.	Simple (pure tone)	Complex (mix of frequencies)

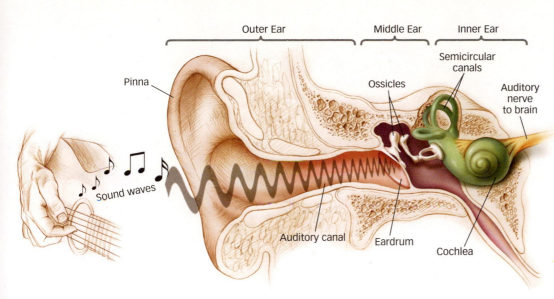

Outer Ear | Middle Ear | Inner Ear

Pinna

Ossicles

Semicircular canals

Auditory nerve to brain

Sound waves

Auditory canal

Eardrum

Cochlea

FIGURE 4.21 **Anatomy of the Human Ear** The pinna funnels sound waves into the auditory canal to vibrate the eardrum at a rate that corresponds to the sound's frequency. In the middle ear, the ossicles pick up the eardrum vibrations, amplify them, and pass them along by vibrating a membrane at the surface of the fluid-filled cochlea in the inner ear. Here fluid carries the wave energy to the auditory receptors that transduce it into electrochemical activity, exciting the neurons that form the auditory nerve leading to the brain.

loudness produces a perceptually different experience depending on whether it was played on a flute versus a trumpet, a phenomenon due entirely to timbre.

Most sounds—such as voices, music, the sound of wind in trees, the screech of brakes, the purring of a cat—are composed of not one, but many different frequency components. Although you perceive the mixture (the cat's purr, for example, not the 206 Hz component in the purr), the first thing the ear does to a sound is to break it down—to analyze it—into its separate component frequencies. The psychological attributes of pitch, loudness, and timbre are then "built up" by the brain from the separate frequency components that are represented in the inner ear, just as visual perceptions are "built up" from the spatial pattern of activity on the retina. The focus in our discussion of hearing, then, is on how the auditory system encodes and represents sound frequency (Kubovy, 1981).

cochlea A fluid-filled tube that is the organ of auditory transduction.

basilar membrane A structure in the inner ear that undulates when vibrations from the ossicles reach the cochlear fluid.

The Human Ear

How does the auditory system convert sound waves into neural signals? The process is very different from the visual system, which is not surprising, given that light is a form of electromagnetic radiation, whereas sound is a physical change in air pressure over time: Different forms of energy require different processes of transduction. The human ear is divided into three distinct parts, as shown in **FIGURE 4.21**: the *outer ear,* the *middle ear,* and the *inner ear.*

The outer ear consists of the visible part on the outside of the head (called the *pinna*); the auditory canal; and the eardrum, an airtight flap of skin that vibrates in response to sound waves gathered by the pinna and channeled through the canal. The middle ear, a tiny, air-filled chamber behind the eardrum, contains the three smallest bones in the body, called *ossicles*. Named for their appearance as hammer, anvil, and stirrup, the ossicles fit together into a lever that mechanically transmits and intensifies vibrations from the eardrum to the inner ear.

The inner ear contains the spiral-shaped **cochlea** (Latin for "snail"), *a fluid-filled tube that is the organ of auditory transduction.* The cochlea is divided along its length by the **basilar membrane,** *a structure in the inner ear that undulates when vibrations from the ossicles reach the cochlear fluid* (see **FIGURE 4.22**). Its wavelike

"The ringing in your ears—I think I can help."

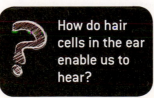

How do hair cells in the ear enable us to hear?

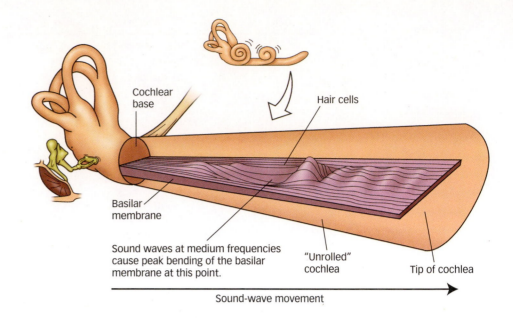

FIGURE 4.22 Auditory Transduction Inside the cochlea (shown here as though it were uncoiling), the basilar membrane undulates in response to wave energy in the cochlear fluid. Waves of differing frequencies ripple varying locations along the membrane, from low frequencies at its tip to high frequencies at the base, and bend the embedded hair cell receptors at those locations. The hair cell motion generates impulses in the auditory neurons, whose axons form the auditory nerve that emerges from the cochlea.

Cochlear base

Hair cells

Basilar membrane

Sound waves at medium frequencies cause peak bending of the basilar membrane at this point.

"Unrolled" cochlea

Tip of cochlea

Sound-wave movement

movement stimulates thousands of tiny **hair cells,** *specialized auditory receptor neurons embedded in the basilar membrane.* The hair cells then release neurotransmitter molecules, initiating a neural signal in the auditory nerve that travels to the brain.

Perceiving Pitch

From the inner ear, action potentials in the auditory nerve travel to the thalamus and ultimately to an area of the cerebral cortex called **area A1,** *a portion of the temporal lobe that contains the primary auditory cortex* (see **FIGURE 4.23**). Neurons in area A1 respond well to simple tones, and successive auditory areas in the brain process sounds of increasing complexity (see Figure 4.23, inset; Rauschecker & Scott, 2009; Schreiner, Read, & Sutter, 2000; Schreiner & Winer, 2007). For most of us, the auditory areas in the left hemisphere analyze sounds related to language and those in the right hemisphere specialize in rhythmic sounds and music. There is also evidence that the auditory cortex is composed of two distinct streams, roughly analogous to the dorsal and ventral streams of the visual system. Spatial ("where") auditory features, which allow you to locate the source of a sound in space, are handled by areas toward the back (caudal) part of the auditory cortex, whereas nonspatial ("what") features, which allow you to identify the sound, are handled by areas in the lower (ventral) part of the auditory cortex (Recanzone & Sutter, 2008).

How is the frequency of a sound wave encoded in a neural signal? Our ears have evolved two mechanisms to encode sound-wave frequency, one for high frequencies and one for low frequencies.

FIGURE 4.23 Primary Auditory Cortex Area A1 lies in the temporal lobe in each hemisphere. The left hemisphere auditory areas govern speech in most people. A1 cortex has a topographic organization (inset), with lower frequencies mapping toward the front of the brain and higher frequencies toward the back, mirroring the organization of the basilar membrane along the cochlea (see Figure 4.22).

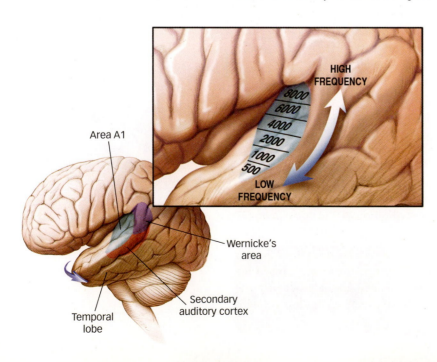

HIGH FREQUENCY

8000
6000
4000
2000
1000
500

LOW FREQUENCY

Area A1

Wernicke's area

Secondary auditory cortex

Temporal lobe

> The **place code,** used mainly for high frequencies, refers to the process by which *different frequencies stimulate neural signals at specific places along the basilar membrane.* Sounds of different frequencies cause waves that peak at different points on the basilar

membrane (see Figure 4.22). When the frequency is low, the wide, floppy tip (*apex*) of the basilar membrane moves the most; when the frequency is high, the narrow, stiff end (*base*) of the membrane moves the most. The movement of the basilar membrane causes hair cells to bend, initiating a neural signal in the auditory nerve. Axons fire the strongest in the hair cells along the area of the basilar membrane that moves the most, and the brain uses information about which axons are the most active to help determine the pitch you "hear."

> A complementary process handles lower frequencies. A **temporal code** *registers relatively low frequencies (up to about 5000 Hz) via the firing rate of action potentials entering the auditory nerve.* Action potentials from the hair cells are synchronized in time with the peaks of the incoming sound waves (Johnson, 1980). If you imagine the rhythmic *boom-boom-boom* of a bass drum, you can probably also imagine the *fire-fire-fire* of action potentials corresponding to the beats. This process supplements the information provided by the place code.

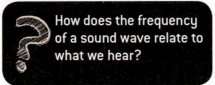

How does the frequency of a sound wave relate to what we hear?

hair cells Specialized auditory receptor neurons embedded in the basilar membrane.

area A1 A portion of the temporal lobe that contains the primary auditory cortex.

place code The process by which different frequencies stimulate neural signals at specific places along the basilar membrane, from which the brain determines pitch.

temporal code The cochlea registers low frequencies via the firing rate of action potentials entering the auditory nerve.

Localizing Sound Sources

Just as the differing positions of our eyes give us stereoscopic vision, the placement of our ears on opposite sides of the head gives us stereophonic hearing. The sound arriving at the ear closer to the sound source is louder than the sound in the farther ear, mainly because the listener's head partially blocks sound energy. This loudness difference decreases as the sound source moves from a position directly to one side (maximal difference) to straight ahead (no difference).

Another cue to a sound's location arises from timing: Sound waves arrive a little sooner at the near ear than at the far ear. The timing difference can be as brief as a few microseconds, but together with the intensity difference, this time difference is sufficient to allow us to perceive the location of a sound. When the sound source is ambiguous, you may find yourself turning your head from side to side to localize the source. By doing this, you are changing the relative intensity and timing of sound waves arriving in your ears and collecting better information about the likely source of the sound. Turning your head also allows you to use your eyes to locate the source of the sound—and your visual system is much better at pinpointing the location of things than your auditory system is.

Hearing Loss

Broadly speaking, hearing loss has two main causes. *Conductive hearing loss* arises because the eardrum or ossicles are damaged to the point that they cannot conduct sound waves effectively to the cochlea. In many cases, medication or surgery can correct the problem. Sound amplification from a hearing aid also can improve hearing through conduction to the cochlea via the bones around the ear directly.

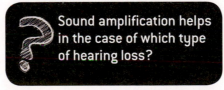

Sound amplification helps in the case of which type of hearing loss?

Sensorineural hearing loss is caused by damage to the cochlea, the hair cells, or the auditory nerve, and it happens to almost all of us as we age. Sensorineural hearing loss can be heightened in people regularly exposed to high noise levels (such as rock musicians or jet mechanics). Simply amplifying the sound does not help because the hair cells can no longer transduce sound waves. In these cases, a *cochlear implant* may offer some relief.

A cochlear implant works when a microphone picks up sounds and sends them to a small speech-processing computer worn on the user's belt or behind the ear. The electric signals from the speech processor are transmitted to an implanted receiver, which sends the signals via electrodes to the cochlea, where the signals directly stimulate the auditory nerve.

AP Photo/Rochester Post-Bulletin, Jerry Olson

A cochlear implant is an electronic device that replaces the function of the hair cells (Waltzman, 2006). The external parts of the device include a microphone and speech processor, about the size of a USB key, worn behind the ear, and a small, flat, external transmitter that sits on the scalp behind the ear. The implanted parts include a receiver just inside the skull and a thin wire containing electrodes inserted into the cochlea to stimulate the auditory nerve. Sound picked up by the microphone is transformed into electric signals by the speech processor, which is essentially a small computer. The signal is transmitted to the implanted receiver, which activates the electrodes in the cochlea. Cochlear implants are now in routine use and can improve hearing to the point where speech can be understood.

Marked hearing loss is commonly experienced by people as they grow older, but is rare in an infant. However, infants who have not yet learned to speak are especially vulnerable because they may miss the critical period for language learning (see the Learning chapter). Without auditory feedback during this time, normal speech is nearly impossible to achieve, but early use of cochlear implants has been associated with improved speech and language skills for deaf children (Hay-McCutcheon et al., 2008). Efforts are under way to introduce cochlear implants to children as young as 12 months old or younger to maximize their chances of normal language development (DesJardin, Eisenberg, & Hodapp, 2006; Holman et al., 2013). (For research on the importance of music and brain development, see the Hot Science: Music Training: Worth the Time.)

SUMMARY QUIZ [4.4]

1. What does the frequency of a sound wave determine?
   a. pitch
   b. loudness
   c. sound quality
   d. timbre

2. The placement of our ears on opposite sides of the head is crucial to our ability to
   a. localize sound sources.
   b. determine pitch.
   c. judge intensity.
   d. recognize complexity.

3. The place code works best for encoding
   a. high intensities.
   b. low intensities.
   c. high frequencies.
   d. low frequencies.

haptic perception The active exploration of the environment by touching and grasping objects with our hands.

Hot Science

Music Training: Worth the Time

Did you learn to play an instrument when you were younger? If so, there's good news for your brain. Compared to nonmusicians, musicians have greater plasticity in the motor cortex (Rosenkranz, Williamon, & Rothwell, 2007) and increased grey matter in motor and auditory brain regions (Gaser & Schlaug, 2003; Hannon & Trainor, 2007). But musical training also extends to auditory processing in nonmusical domains (Kraus & Chandrasekaran, 2010). Musicians, for example, show enhanced brain responses when listening to speech compared with nonmusicians (Parbery-Clark et al., 2012). Musicians also exhibit an improved ability to detect speech when it is presented in a noisy background (Parbery-Clark, Skoe, & Kraus, 2009).

Remembering to be careful not to confuse correlation with causation, you may ask: Do differences between musicians and nonmusicians reflect the effects of musical training, or do they reflect individual differences, perhaps genetic ones, that lead some people to become musicians in the first place? Maybe people blessed with enhanced brain responses to musical or other auditory stimuli decide to become musicians *because* of their natural abilities. Recent experiments support a causal role for musical training. One study compared two groups of 8-year-old children, one group with 6 months of musical training and the other with 6 months of painting training. Musical training produced changes in the brain's electrical responses to musical and speech stimuli, and those changes were correlated with enhanced performance on both musical and speech perception tasks (Moreno et al., 2009). More recent musical training studies indicate that neural changes produced by musical training in childhood persist into adulthood (Skoe & Kraus, 2012).

We don't yet know all the reasons why musical training has such broad effects on auditory processing, but one likely contributor is that learning to play an instrument demands attention to precise details of sounds (Kraus & Chandrasekaran, 2010). Future studies will no doubt pinpoint additional factors, but the research to date leaves little room for doubt that your hours of practice were indeed worth the time.

Thinkstock

The Body Senses: More Than Skin Deep

Vision and audition provide information about the world at a distance. By responding to light and sound energy in the environment, these "distance" senses allow us to identify and locate the objects and people around us. In comparison, the body senses, also called *somatosenses* (*soma* from the Greek for "body"), are up close and personal. **Haptic perception** is the *active exploration of the environment by touching and grasping objects with our hands.* We use sensory receptors in our muscles, tendons, and joints as well as a variety of receptors in our skin to get a feel for the world around us (see **FIGURE 4.24**).

Touch

Touch begins with the transduction of skin sensations into neural signals. Four types of receptors located under the skin's surface enable us to sense pressure, texture, pattern, or vibration against the skin (see Figure 4.24). The receptive fields of these specialized cells work together to provide a rich tactile (from Latin, "to touch") experience when you explore an object by feeling it or attempting to grasp it. In addition, *thermoreceptors,* nerve fibers that sense cold and warmth, respond when your skin temperature changes. All these sensations blend seamlessly together in perception, of course, but detailed physiological studies have successfully isolated the parts of the touch system (Hollins, 2010; Johnson, 2002).

There are three important principles regarding the neural representation of the body's surface. First, the left half of the body is represented in the right

This geodesic dome sits on the floor of the Exploratorium, a science museum in San Francisco. It was created in 1971 by August Coppola (brother of director Francis Ford Coppola and father of actor Nicolas Cage) and Carl Day, who wanted to create an environment in which only haptic perception could be used. The inside of the dome is pitch black; visitors must crawl, wiggle, slide, and otherwise navigate the unfamiliar terrain using only their sense of touch. How would you feel being in that environment for an hour or so?

© Exploratorium

FIGURE 4.24 Touch Receptors Specialized sensory neurons form groups of haptic receptors that detect pressure, temperature, and vibrations against the skin; their long axons enter the brain via the spinal or cranial nerves. Pain receptors populate all body tissues that feel pain; they are distributed around bones and within muscles and internal organs as well as under the skin surface. Different types of pain receptors transmit immediate, sharp pain sensations or signal slow, dull pain that lasts and lasts.

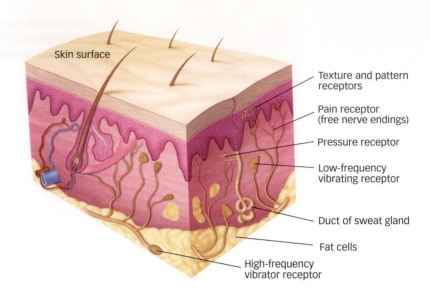

Skin surface

Texture and pattern receptors

Pain receptor (free nerve endings)

Pressure receptor

Low-frequency vibrating receptor

Duct of sweat gland

Fat cells

High-frequency vibrator receptor

half of the brain and vice versa. Second, just as more of the visual brain is devoted to foveal vision where acuity is greatest, more of the tactile brain is devoted to parts of the skin surface that have greater spatial resolution. Regions such as the fingertips and lips are very good at discriminating fine spatial detail, whereas areas such as the lower back are quite poor at that task. Think back to the homunculus you read about in the Neuroscience and Behavior chapter; you'll recall that different locations on the body project sensory signals to different locations in the somatosensory cortex in the pari-etal lobe. Third, there is mounting evidence for a distinction between "what" and "where" pathways in touch analogous to similar distinctions we've already considered for vision and audition. The "what" system for touch provides information about the properties of surfaces and objects; the "where" system provides information about a location in external space that is being touched or a location on the body that is being stimulated (Lederman & Klatzky, 2009). The evidence from fMRI studies suggests that the "what" and "where" touch pathways involve areas in the lower and upper parts of the parietal lobe, respectively (Reed, Klatzky, & Halgren, 2005).

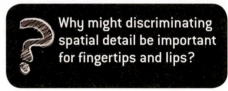

Why might discriminating spatial detail be important for fingertips and lips?

Touch information can have a powerful effect on our decisions and judgments. For example, recent research has shown that merely touching an object that we don't already own can increase our feeling of ownership and lead us to value the object more highly than when we view it but don't touch it (Peck & Shu, 2009); the longer we touch an object, the more highly we value it (Wolf, Arkes, & Muhanna, 2008). You might keep this "mere touch" effect in mind the next time you are in a shop and considering buying an expensive item. Retailers are probably aware of this effect: During a recent holiday shopping season, the office of the Illinois state attorney general warned shoppers to be cautious in stores that encouraged them to touch the merchandise (Peck & Shu, 2009).

Be warned for your next shopping trip: Touching the merchandise can lead you to value it more highly than just looking at it.

Ckd/Corbis

Pain

Although pain is arguably the least pleasant of sensations, it is among the most important for survival: Pain indicates damage or potential damage to the body. Without the ability to feel pain, we might ignore infections, broken bones, or serious burns. Children with congenital insensitivity to pain, a rare inherited disorder that specifically impairs pain perception, often mutilate themselves (e.g., by biting into their tongues or by gouging their skin while scratching) and are at increased risk of dying during childhood (Nagasako, Oaklander, & Dworkin, 2003).

Tissue damage is transduced by pain receptors, the free nerve endings shown in Figure 4.24. Fast-acting *A-delta fibers* transmit the initial sharp pain one might feel right away from a sudden injury, and slower *C fibers* transmit the longer-lasting, duller pain that persists after the initial injury. If you were running barefoot outside and stubbed your toe against a rock, you would first feel a sudden stinging pain transmitted by A-delta fibers that would die down quickly, only to be replaced by the throbbing but longer-lasting pain carried by C fibers. Both the A-delta and C fibers are impaired in cases of congenital insensitivity to pain, which is one reason why the disorder can be life threatening.

Neural signals for pain travel to two distinct areas in the brain and evoke two distinct psychological experiences (Treede et al., 1999). One pain pathway sends signals to the somatosensory cortex, identifying where the pain is occurring and what sort of pain it is (sharp, burning, dull). The second pain pathway sends signals to the motivational and emotional centers of the brain, such as the hypothalamus and amygdala, and to the frontal lobe. This is the aspect of pain that is unpleasant and motivates us to escape from or relieve the pain.

Pain typically feels as if it comes from the site of the tissue damage that caused it. If you burn your finger, you will perceive the pain as originating there. But we have pain receptors in many areas besides the skin: around bones and within muscles and internal organs as well. When pain originates internally—in a body organ, for example—we actually feel it on the surface of the body. This kind of **referred pain** occurs when *sensory information from internal and external areas converges on the same nerve cells in the spinal cord*. One common example is a heart attack: Victims often feel pain radiating from the left arm rather than from inside the chest.

One influential account of pain perception is known as the **gate-control theory of pain,** which holds that *signals arriving from pain receptors in the body can be stopped, or gated, by interneurons in the spinal cord via feedback from two directions* (Melzack & Wall, 1965). Pain can be gated by the skin receptors, for example, when you rub the affected area. Rubbing your stubbed toe activates neurons that "close the gate" to stop pain signals from traveling to the brain. Pain can also be gated from the brain by modulating the activity of pain-transmission neurons. This neural feedback comes from a region in the midbrain called the *periaqueductal gray* (PAG). Under extreme conditions, such as high stress, naturally occurring endorphins can activate the PAG to send inhibitory signals to neurons in the spinal cord that then suppress pain signals to the brain, thereby modulating the experience of pain. The PAG is also activated through the action of opiate drugs, such as morphine.

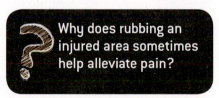

Why does rubbing an injured area sometimes help alleviate pain?

Although some details of the gate-control theory of pain have been challenged, a key concept underlying the theory—that perception is a two-way street—has broad implications. The senses feed information such as pain sensations to the brain, a pattern termed *bottom-up control*. The brain processes this sensory data into perceptual information at successive levels to support movement, object recognition, and eventually more complex cognitive tasks, such as memory and planning. But there is ample evidence that the brain exerts plenty of control over what we sense as well. Visual illusions and the gestalt principles of filling in, shaping up, and rounding out what isn't really there provide some examples. This kind of *top-down control* also explains how the brain influences the experience of touch and pain.

Body Position, Movement, and Balance

It may sound odd, but one aspect of sensation and perception is knowing where parts of your body are at any given moment. Your body needs some way to sense its position in physical space other than relying on the movement of your eyes constantly to visually check the location of your limbs. Sensations related to position, movement, and

referred pain Feeling of pain when sensory information from internal and external areas converges on the same nerve cells in the spinal cord.

gate-control theory of pain A theory of pain perception based on the idea that signals arriving from pain receptors in the body can be stopped, or *gated*, by interneurons in the spinal cord via feedback from two directions.

balance depend on stimulation produced within our bodies. Receptors in the muscles, tendons, and joints signal the position of the body in space, whereas information about balance and head movement originates in the inner ear.

Sensory receptors provide the information we need to perceive the position and movement of our limbs, head, and body. These receptors also provide feedback about whether we are performing a desired movement correctly and how resistance from held objects may be influencing the movement. For example, when you swing a baseball bat, the weight of the bat affects how your muscles move your arm as well as the change in sensation when the bat hits the ball.

Maintaining balance depends primarily on the **vestibular system,** *the three fluid-filled semicircular canals and adjacent organs located next to the cochlea in each inner ear* (see Figure 4.21). The semicircular canals are arranged in three perpendicular orientations and studded with hair cells that detect movement of the fluid when the head moves or accelerates. The bending of the hair cells generates activity in the vestibular nerve, which is then conveyed to the brain. This detected motion enables us to maintain our balance, or the position of our bodies relative to gravity (Lackner & DiZio, 2005).

Vision also helps us keep our balance. If you see that you are swaying relative to a vertical orientation, such as the contours of a room, you move your legs and feet to keep from falling over. Psychologists have experimented with this visual aspect of balance by placing people in rooms that can be tilted forward and backward (Bertenthal, Rose, & Bai, 1997; Lee & Aronson, 1974). If the room tilts enough—particularly when small children are tested—people will topple over as they try to compensate for what their visual system is telling them. When a mismatch between the information provided by visual cues and vestibular feedback occurs, motion sickness can result. Remember this discrepancy the next time you try reading in the back seat of a moving car!

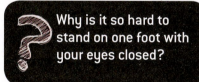

Why is it so hard to stand on one foot with your eyes closed?

Hitting a ball with a bat or racket provides feedback as to where your arms and body are in space, as well as how the resistance of these objects affects your movement and balance. Successful athletes, such as Serena Williams, have particularly well-developed body senses.

AP Photo/Rick Rycroft

vestibular system The three fluid-filled semicircular canals and adjacent organs located next to the cochlea in each inner ear.

SUMMARY QUIZ [4.5]

1. Which part of the body occupies the greatest area in the somatosensory cortex?
   a. calves.
   b. lips.
   c. lower back.
   d. hips.

2. The location and type of pain we experience is indicated by signals sent to
   a. the amygdala.
   b. the spinal cord.
   c. pain receptors.
   d. the somatosensory cortex.

The Chemical Senses: Adding Flavor

Somatosensation is all about physical changes in or on the body: Vision and audition sense energetic states of the world—light and sound waves—and touch is activated by physical changes in or on the body surface. The last set of senses we'll consider share a chemical basis to combine aspects of distance and proximity. The chemical senses of *olfaction* (smell) and *gustation* (taste) respond to the molecular structure of substances floating into the nasal cavity as you inhale or dissolving in saliva. Smell and taste combine to produce the perceptual experience we call *flavor*.

Smell

Olfaction is the least understood sense and the only one directly connected to the forebrain, with pathways into the frontal lobe, amygdala, and other forebrain structures (recall from the Neuroscience and Behavior chapter that the other senses connect first to the thalamus). This mapping indicates that smell has a close relationship with areas involved in emotional and social behavior. Smell seems to have evolved in animals as a signaling sense for the familiar: a friendly creature, an edible food, or a sexually receptive mate.

Countless substances release odors into the air, and some of their *odorant molecules* make their way into our noses, drifting in on the air we breathe. Situated along the top of the nasal cavity shown in **FIGURE 4.25** is a mucous membrane called the *olfactory epithelium*, which contains about 10 million **olfactory receptor neurons (ORNs),** *receptor cells that initiate the sense of smell*. Odorant molecules bind to sites on these specialized receptors, and if enough bindings occur, the ORNs send action potentials into the olfactory nerve (Dalton, 2003).

olfactory receptor neurons (ORNs) Receptor cells that initiate the sense of smell.

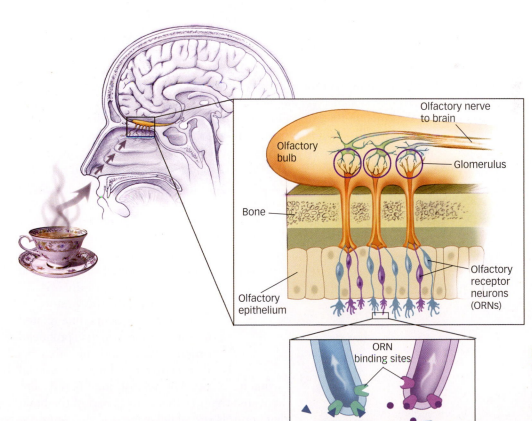

FIGURE 4.25 Anatomy of Smell Along the roof of the nasal cavity, odorant molecules may bind to olfactory receptor neurons (ORNs) embedded in the olfactory epithelium. ORNs respond to a range of odors and, once activated, relay action potentials to the olfactory bulb, located just beneath the frontal lobes. The olfactory nerve projects directly into the forebrain.

olfactory bulb A brain structure located above the nasal cavity beneath the frontal lobes.

pheromones Biochemical odorants emitted by other members of its species that can affect an animal's behavior or physiology.

taste buds The organ of taste transduction.

Taste and smell both contribute to what we perceive as flavor. This is why smelling the bouquet of a wine is an essential part of the wine-tasting ritual. The experience of wine tasting is also influenced by cognitive factors, such as knowledge of a wine's price.

Adam Gregor/Shutterstock

Each olfactory neuron has receptors that bind to some odorants but not to others, as if the receptor is a lock and the odorant is the key (see Figure 4.25). Humans possess about 350 different ORN types that permit us to discriminate among some 10,000 different odorants through the unique patterns of neural activity each odorant evokes. This setup is similar to our ability to see a vast range of colors based on only a small number of retinal receptor cell types or to feel a range of skin sensations based on only a handful of touch receptor cell types.

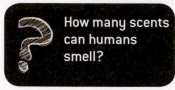

How many scents can humans smell?

Groups of ORNs send their axons from the olfactory epithelium into the **olfactory bulb,** *a brain structure located above the nasal cavity beneath the frontal lobes*. The olfactory bulb sends outputs to various centers in the brain, including the parts that are responsible for controlling basic drives, emotions, and memories. Odor perception includes both information about the identity of an odor, which involves relating olfactory inputs to information stored in memory (Stevenson & Boakes, 2003), as well as our emotional response to whether it is pleasant or unpleasant (Khan et al., 2007). The relationship between smell and emotion explains why smells can have immediate, strongly positive or negative effects on us. If the slightest whiff of an apple pie baking brings back fond memories of childhood, you've got the idea.

Our experience of smell is determined not only by bottom-up influences, such as odorant molecules binding to sites on ORNs, but also by top-down influences, such as our previous experiences with an odor (Gottfried, 2008). Consistent with this idea, people rate the identical odor as more pleasant when it is paired with an appealing verbal label such as *cheddar cheese* than when paired with an unappealing one such as *body odor* (de Araujo et al., 2005; Herz & von Clef, 2001). The evidence of fMRIs indicates that brain regions involved in coding the pleasantness of an experience, such as the orbiotofrontal cortex, respond more strongly to the identical odor when people think it is cheddar cheese than when they think it is a body odor (de Araujo et al., 2005).

Smell may also play a role in social behavior. Humans and other animals can detect odors from **pheromones,** *biochemical odorants emitted by other members of a species that can affect an animal's behavior or physiology*. Parents can distinguish the smell of their own children from other people's children. An infant can identify the smell of his or her mother's breast from the smell of other mothers. Pheromones play a role in reproductive behavior in insects and in several mammalian species, including mice, dogs, and primates (Brennan & Zufall, 2006). Research in humans has demonstrated no consistent tendency for people to prefer the odors of people of the opposite sex over other pleasant odors. Recent research, however, has provided a link between sexual orientation and responses to odors. Researchers used positron emission tomography (PET) scans to study the brain's response to two odors, one related to testosterone, which is produced in men's sweat, and the other related to estrogen, which is found in women's urine. The testosterone-based odor activated the hypothalamus (a part of the brain that controls sexual behavior; see the Neuroscience and Behavior chapter) in heterosexual women but not in heterosexual men, whereas the estrogen-based odor activated the hypothalamus

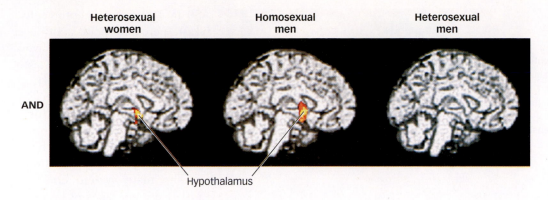

Heterosexual women   Homosexual men   Heterosexual men

AND

Hypothalamus

FIGURE 4.26 **Smell and Social Behavior** In a PET study, heterosexual women, homosexual men, and heterosexual men were scanned as they were presented with each of several odors. During the presentation of a testosterone-based odor (referred to in the figure as AND), there was significant activation in the hypothalamus for heterosexual women (*left*) and homosexual men (*center*) but not for (*right*) heterosexual men (Savic Berglund, & Lindstrom, 2005).

in heterosexual men but not in heterosexual women. Strikingly, homosexual men responded to the two chemicals in the same way as heterosexual women did (Savic, Berglund, & Lindstrom, 2005; see **FIGURE 4.26**). Other common odors unrelated to sexual arousal were processed similarly by all three groups. Taken together, the findings suggest that some human pheromones are related to sexual orientation.

Taste

One of the primary responsibilities of the chemical sense of taste is identifying things that are bad for you—as in poisonous and lethal. Some aspects of taste perception are genetic, such as an aversion to extreme bitterness (which can indicate poison), and some are learned, such as an aversion to a particular food that once caused nausea. In either case, the direct contact between a tongue and possible foods allows us to anticipate whether something will be harmful or palatable.

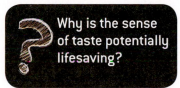

Why is the sense of taste potentially lifesaving?

The tongue is covered with thousands of small bumps, called *papillae,* which are easily visible to the naked eye. Within each papilla are hundreds of **taste buds,** *the organ of taste transduction* (see **FIGURE 4.27**). The mouth contains 5,000 to 10,000 taste buds fairly evenly distributed over the tongue, roof of the mouth, and upper throat (Bartoshuk & Beauchamp, 1994; Halpern, 2002). Each taste bud contains

FIGURE 4.27 **A Taste Bud** Taste buds stud the bumps ("papillae") on the tongue, shown here, as well as the back, sides, and roof of the mouth (*a*). Each taste bud contains a range of receptor cells that respond to varying chemical components of foods (*b*). Each taste bud contacts the branch of a cranial nerve at its base (*c*).

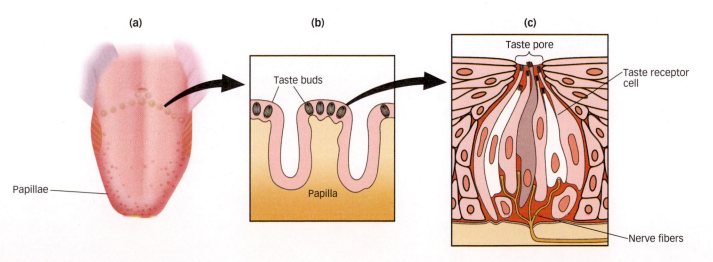

(a)

(b)

(c)

Taste pore

Taste buds

Taste receptor cell

Papillae

Papilla

Nerve fibers

Leslie Banks/iStockphoto

Fussy eater or just too many taste buds? Our taste perception declines with age: We lose about half of our taste receptors by the time we're 20 years old. That can make childhood a time of either savory delight or a sensory overload of taste.

DATA VISUALIZATION

Finding Best Fits/Models for Data Sets (Sensation and Perception Themed)

www.macmillanhighered.com/schacterbrief3e

50 to 100 taste receptor cells. Taste perception fades with age (Methven et al., 2012): On average, people lose half their taste receptors by the time they turn 20. This may help to explain why young children seem to be "fussy eaters," since their greater number of taste buds brings with it a greater range of taste sensations.

The taste system contains just five main types of taste receptors, corresponding to five primary taste sensations: salty, sour, bitter, sweet, and umami (savory). The first four are quite familiar, but *umami* may not be. In fact, perception researchers are still debating its existence. The umami receptor was discovered by Japanese scientists who attributed it to the tastes evoked by foods containing a high concentration of protein, such as meats and cheeses (Yamaguchi, 1998). If you're a meat eater and you savor the feel of a steak topped with butter or a cheeseburger as it sits in your mouth, you've got an idea of the umami sensation. The food additive *monosodium glutamate* (MSG), which is often used to flavor Asian foods, particularly activates umami receptors. Some people develop headaches or allergic reactions after eating MSG.

Of course, the variety of taste experiences greatly exceeds the five basic receptors discussed here. Any food molecules dissolved in saliva evoke specific, combined patterns of activity in the five taste receptor types. Although we often think of taste as the primary source for flavor, in fact, taste and smell collaborate to produce this complex perception. As any wine connoisseur will attest, the full experience of a wine's flavor cannot be appreciated without a finely trained sense of smell. Odorants from substances outside your mouth enter the nasal cavity via the nostrils, and odorants in the mouth enter through the back of the throat. This is why wine aficionados are taught to pull air in over wine held in the mouth: It allows the wine's odorant molecules to enter the nasal cavity through this "back door."

You can easily demonstrate the contribution of smell to flavor by tasting a few different foods while holding your nose, preventing the olfactory system from detecting their odors. If you have a head cold, you probably already know how this turns out. Your favorite spicy burrito or zesty pasta probably tastes as bland as can be.

Taste experiences also vary widely across individuals. About 50% of people report a mildly bitter taste in caffeine, saccharine, certain green vegetables, and other substances, whereas roughly 25% report no bitter taste. Members of the first group are called *tasters,* and members of the second group are called *nontasters.* The remaining 25% of people are *supertasters*, who report that such substances, especially dark green vegetables, are extremely bitter, to the point of being inedible (Bartoshuk, 2000). Children start out as tasters or supertasters, which could help explain their early tendency toward fussiness in food preference. There is evidence that genetic factors contribute to individual differences in taste perception (Kim et al., 2003), but much remains to be learned about the specific genes that are involved (Hayes et al., 2008; Reed, 2008).

Sam Gross/The New Yorker Collection/Cartoonbank.Com

"We would like to be genetically modified to taste like Brussels sprouts."

SUMMARY QUIZ [4.6]

1. What best explains why smells can have immediate and powerful effects?
   a. the involvement in smell of brain centers for emotions and memories
   b. the vast number of olfactory receptor neurons we have
   c. our ability to detect odors from pheromones
   d. the fact that different odorant molecules produce varied patterns of activity

2. People lose about half their taste buds by the time they are
   a. 20
   b. 40
   c. 60
   d. 80

CHAPTER REVIEW

SUMMARY

Sensation and Perception Are Distinct Activities

> Sensation is the simple stimulation of a sense organ, whereas perception organizes, identifies, and interprets sensation at the level of the brain.

> Transduction is the process which converts physical signals from the environment into neural signals carried by sensory neurons into the central nervous system.

> Psychophysics is an approach to studying perception that measures the strength of a stimulus and an observer's sensitivity to that stimulus. The just noticeable difference (**JND**) is the smallest change in a stimulus that can be detected.

> Sensory adaptation occurs because sensitivity to lengthy stimulation tends to decline over time.

Vision I: How the Eyes and the Brain Convert Light Waves to Neural Signals

> Two types of photoreceptor cells in the retina transduce light into neural impulses: cones, which operate under normal daylight conditions and sense color; and rods, which are active under low-light conditions for night vision.

> Light striking the retina causes a specific pattern of response in each of the three cone types that are critical to color perception: short-wavelength (bluish) light, medium-wavelength (greenish) light, and long-wavelength (reddish) light. The overall pattern of response across the three cone types results in a unique code for each color.

> Information encoded by the retina travels to the brain along the optic nerve, to the thalamus and then to the primary visual cortex (area V1) in the occipital lobe.

> Two pathways project from the occipital lobe to visual areas in other parts of the brain. The ventral stream projects to areas of the temporal lobes that represent an object's shape and identity. The dorsal stream projects to the parietal lobes that identify the location and motion of an object.

Vision II: Recognizing What We Perceive

> According to feature-integration theory, attention provides the glue necessary to bind features together. The parietal lobe is important for attention and contributes to feature binding.

> Some regions in the occipital and temporal lobes respond selectively to specific object categories, supporting the modular view that specialized brain areas represent particular classes of objects such as faces or houses or body parts.

> Gestalt principles of perceptual grouping, such as simplicity, closure, and continuity, govern how the features and regions of things fit together.

> Depth perception depends on monocular cues such as familiar size and linear perspective, binocular cues such as retinal disparity, and motion-based cues, which are based on the movement of the head over time.

> Change blindness and inattentional blindness occur when we fail to notice visible and even salient features of our environment, emphasizing that our conscious visual experience depends on focused attention.

Audition: More Than Meets the Ear

> Perceiving sound depends on three physical dimensions of a sound wave – frequency, amplitude, and complexity or mix of frequencies; respectively, these features determine our perception of pitch, loudness, and sound quality (timbre).

> Auditory pitch perception begins in the outer ear, which funnels sound waves toward the middle ear, which in turn sends the vibrations to the inner ear, which contains the cochlea.

> Action potentials from the inner ear travel along an auditory pathway through the thalamus to the primary auditory cortex (area A1) in the temporal lobe.

> Auditory perception depends on both a place code and a temporal code. Our ability to localize sound sources depends critically on the placement of our ears on opposite sides of the head.

The Body Senses: More Than Skin Deep

> Sensory receptors on the body send neural signals to locations in the somatosensory cortex, a part of the parietal lobe, which the brain translates as the sensation of touch.

> The experience of pain depends on signals that travel to the somatosensory cortex, which indicates the location and type of pain, and to the emotional centers of the brain, which result in unpleasant feelings.

> Balance and acceleration depend primarily on the vestibular system, but they are also influenced by vision.

The Chemical Senses: Adding Flavor

> Our experience of smell, or olfaction, is associated with odorant molecules binding to sites on specialized olfactory receptors, which send axons to the olfactory bulb. The olfactory bulb in turn sends signals to parts of the brain that control drives, emotions, and memories, which helps to explain why smells can have immediate and powerful effects on us.

> Smell is also involved in social behavior, as illustrated by pheromones, which are related to reproductive behavior and sexual responses in several species.

> Sensations of taste depend on taste buds, which are distributed across the tongue, roof of the mouth, and upper throat, and on taste receptors that correspond to the five primary taste sensations of salty, sour, bitter, sweet, and umami.

KEY TERMS

sensation (p. 96)
perception (p. 96)
transduction (p. 96)
psychophysics (p. 97)
absolute threshold (p. 98)
just noticeable difference (JND) (p. 98)
Weber's law (p. 98)
signal detection theory (p. 99)
sensory adaptation (p. 100)
visual acuity (p. 101)
retina (p. 102)

accommodation (p. 102)
cones (p. 103)
rods (p. 103)
fovea (p. 103)
blind spot (p. 104)
area V1 (p. 107)
visual form agnosia (p. 108)
binding problem (p. 109)
illusory conjunction (p. 109)
feature-integration theory (p. 110)
monocular depth cues (p. 113)

binocular disparity (p. 114)
apparent motion (p. 115)
change blindness (p. 116)
inattentional blindness (p. 116)
pitch (p. 118)
loudness (p. 118)
timbre (p. 118)
cochlea (p. 119)
basilar membrane (p. 119)
hair cells (p. 120)
area A1 (p. 120)
place code (p. 120)

temporal code (p. 121)
haptic perception (p. 123)
referred pain (p. 125)
gate-control theory of pain (p. 125)
vestibular system (p. 126)
olfactory receptor neurons (ORNs) (p. 127)
olfactory bulb (p. 128)
pheromones (p. 128)
taste buds (p. 129)

CHANGING MINDS

1. A friend of yours is taking a class in medical ethics. "We discussed a tough case today," she says. "It has to do with a patient who's been in a vegetative state for several years, and the family has to decide whether to take him off life support. The doctors say he has no awareness of himself or his environment, and he is never expected to recover. But when light is shined in his eyes, his pupils contract. That shows he can sense light, so he has to have some ability to perceive his surroundings, doesn't he?" Without knowing any of the details of this particular case, how would you explain to your friend that a patient might be able to sense light but not perceive it? What other examples from the chapter could you use to illustrate the difference between sensation and perception?

2. In your philosophy class, the professor discusses the proposition that "perception is reality." From the point of view of philosophy, reality is the state of things that actually exists, whereas perception is how they appear to the observer. What does psychophysics have to say about this issue? What are three ways in which sensory transduction can alter perception, causing perceptions that may differ from absolute reality?

3. A friend comes across the story of an American soldier, Leroy Petry, who received the Medal of Honor for saving the lives of two of his men. The soldiers were in a firefight in Afghanistan when a live grenade landed at their feet; Petry picked up the grenade and tried to toss it away from the others, but it exploded, destroying his right hand. According to the news report, Petry didn't initially feel any pain; instead, he set about applying a tourniquet to his own arm while continuing to shout orders to his men as the firefight continued. "That's amazingly heroic," your friend says, "but that bit about not feeling the pain—that's crazy. He must just be so tough that he kept going despite the pain." What would you tell your friend? How can the perception of pain be altered?

ANSWERS TO SUMMARY QUIZZES

Summary Quiz 4.1: 1. b; 2. d; 3. b

Summary Quiz 4.2: 1. c; 2. b; 3. d

Summary Quiz 4.3: 1. a; 2. a; 3. c

Summary Quiz 4.4: 1. a; 2. a; 3. c

Summary Quiz 4.5: 1. b; 2. d

Summary Quiz 4.6: 1. a; 2. a

Need more help? Additional resources are located in LaunchPad at:

http://www.worthpublishers.com/launchpad/ schacterbrief3e

Consciousness

Unconsciousness is something you don't really appreciate until you need it. Belle Riskin needed it one day on an operating table, when she awoke just as doctors were pushing a breathing tube down her throat. She felt she was choking, but she couldn't see, breathe, scream, or move. Unable even to blink an eye, she couldn't signal to the surgeons that she was conscious. "I was terrified. Why is this happening to me? Why can't I feel my arms? I could feel my heart pounding in my head. It was like being buried alive, but with somebody shoving something down your throat," she explained later. "I knew I was conscious, that something was going on during the surgery. I had just enough awareness to know I was being intubated" (Groves, 2004).

How could this happen? Anesthesia for surgery is supposed to leave the patient unconscious, "feeling no pain," and yet in this case—and in about one in every 1,000–2,000 surgeries (Sandin et al., 2000)—the patient regains consciousness at some point and even remembers the experience. The problem arises because muscle-relaxing drugs are used to keep the patient from moving involuntarily and making unhelpful contributions to the operation. Then, when the drugs that are given to induce unconsciousness fail to do the job, the patient with extremely relaxed muscles is unable to show or tell doctors that there is a problem.

Fortunately, new methods of monitoring wakefulness by measuring the electrical activity of the brain are being developed. One system uses sensors attached to the patient's head and gives readings on a scale from 0 (*no electrical activity in the brain*) to 100 (*fully alert*), providing a kind of "consciousness meter." Anesthesiologists using this index deliver anesthetics to keep the patient in the recommended range of 40–60 for general anesthesia during surgery; they have found that this system reduces post-surgical reports of consciousness and memory of the surgical experience (Myles et al., 2004). One of these devices in the operating room might have helped Belle Riskin settle into the unconsciousness she so dearly needed.

When it's time for surgery, it's great to be unconscious.

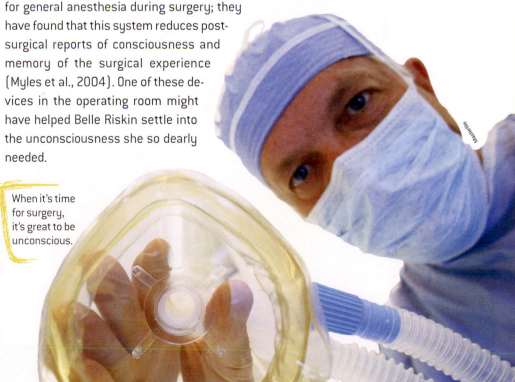

consciousness A person's subjective experience of the world and the mind.

phenomenology How things seem to the conscious person.

problem of other minds The fundamental difficulty we have in perceiving the consciousness of others.

MOST OF THE TIME, OF COURSE, CONSCIOUSNESS IS SOMETHING WE CHERISH. How else could we experience a favorite work of art; the familiar lyrics of an old song; the taste of a sweet, juicy peach; or the touch of a loved one's hand? **Consciousness** is *a person's subjective experience of the world and the mind.* Although you might think of consciousness as simply "being awake," the defining feature of consciousness is *experience,* which you have when you're awake or when having a vivid dream. Conscious experience is essential to what it means to be human. The anesthesiologist's dilemma in trying to monitor Belle Riskin's consciousness is a stark reminder, though, that it is impossible for one person to experience another's consciousness. Your consciousness is utterly private, a world of personal experience that only you can know.

How can this private world be studied? We'll begin by trying to understand what it is like and how it compares with the mind's *unconscious* processes. Then we'll examine altered states of consciousness: sleep and dreams, intoxication with alcohol and other drugs, and hypnosis. Like the traveler who learns the meaning of *home* by roaming far away, we can learn the meaning of *consciousness* by exploring its exotic variations.

Conscious and Unconscious: The Mind's Eye, Open and Closed

What does it feel like to be you right now? It probably feels as though you are somewhere inside your head, looking out at the world through your eyes. You can feel your hands on this book, perhaps, and notice the position of your body or the sounds in the room when you orient yourself toward them. If you shut your eyes, you may be able to imagine things in your mind, even though all the while thoughts and feelings come and go, passing through your imagination. But where are "you," really? And how is it that this theater of consciousness gives you a view of some things in your world and your mind but not others? The theater in your mind doesn't have seating for more than one, making it difficult to share what's on your mental screen with your friends, a researcher, or even yourself in precisely the same way a second time. We'll look first at the difficulty of studying consciousness directly, then examine the nature of consciousness (what it is that can be seen in this mental theater), and finally explore the unconscious mind (what is *not* visible to the mind's eye).

The Mysteries of Consciousness

Other sciences, such as physics, chemistry, and biology, have the great luxury of studying *objects,* things that we all can see. Psychology studies objects, too, looking at people and their brains and behaviors, but it has the unique challenge of trying to make sense of *subjects.* A physicist is not concerned with what it is like to be a neutron, but psychologists hope to understand what it is like to be a human; that is, they seek to understand the subjective perspectives of the people whom they study. Psychologists hope to include an understanding of **phenomenology,** *how things seem to the conscious person.* Let's look at two of the more vexing mysteries of consciousness: the problem of other minds and the mind–body problem.

The Problem of Other Minds

One great mystery is called the **problem of other minds,** *the fundamental difficulty we have in perceiving the consciousness of others.* How do you know that anyone else is conscious? People tell you that they are conscious, of course, and are often willing to describe in depth how they feel, what they are experiencing, and how good or how bad it all is. But perhaps they are just *saying* these things. There is no clear way to distinguish a conscious person from someone who might do and say all the same things as a conscious person but who is *not* conscious. Philosophers have called this hypothetical nonconscious person a *zombie*, in reference to the living-yet-dead creatures of horror films (Chalmers, 1996). A philosopher's zombie could talk about experiences ("The lights are so bright!") and could even seem to react to them (wincing and turning away) but might not be having any inner experience at all. No one knows whether there could be such a zombie, but then again, because of the problem of other minds, none of us will ever know for sure that another person is *not* a zombie.

Renee Keith/Getty Images

Luckily these zombies have the standard zombie look. But how do you know those around you are really conscious the same way that you are?

Even the consciousness meter used by anesthesiologists falls short. It certainly doesn't give the anesthesiologist any special insight into what it is like to be the patient on the operating table; it only predicts whether patients will *say* they were conscious. We simply lack the ability to directly perceive the consciousness of others. In short, *you* are the only thing in the universe you will ever truly know what it is like to be.

The problem of other minds also means there is no way you can tell if another person's experience of anything is at all like yours. Although you know what the color red looks like to you, for instance, you cannot know whether it looks the same to other people, or how their experience differs from yours. Of course, most people have come to trust each other in describing their inner lives, reaching the general assumption that other human minds are pretty much like their own. But they don't know this for a fact, and they can't know it directly.

How do people perceive other minds? Researchers conducting a large online survey asked people to compare the minds of 13 different targets, such as a baby, chimp, robot, man, and woman, on 18 different mental capacities, such as feeling pain, pleasure, hunger, and consciousness (Gray, Gray, & Wegner, 2007). Respondents compared pairs of targets: Is a frog or a dog more able to feel pain? Is a baby or a robot more able to feel pain? The researchers found that people judge minds according to two dimensions: the capacity for *experience* (such as the ability to feel pain, pleasure, hunger, consciousness, anger, or fear) and the capacity for *agency* (such as the ability for self-control, planning, memory, or thought). As shown in **FIGURE 5.1**, respondents rated some targets as having little experience or agency (the dead woman), others as having experiences but little agency (the baby), and yet others as having both experience and agency (adult humans). Still others were perceived to have agency without experiences (the robot, God). The perception of minds, then, involves more than just whether something has a mind. People appreciate that minds both have experiences and lead us to perform actions.

> **?** How does the capacity for experience differ from the capacity for agency?

As you'll remember from the Methods in Psychology chapter, the scientific method requires that any observation made by one scientist should, in principle, be available for observation by any other scientist. But if other minds aren't observable, how can consciousness be a topic of scientific study? One radical solution is to eliminate consciousness from psychology entirely and follow the other sciences into total objectivity by renouncing the study of *anything* mental. This was the solution offered by behaviorism, and it turned out to have its own shortcomings, as you saw in the Psychology: Evolution of a Science chapter. Despite the problem of other minds, modern psychology has embraced the study of consciousness. The astonishing richness of mental life simply cannot be ignored.

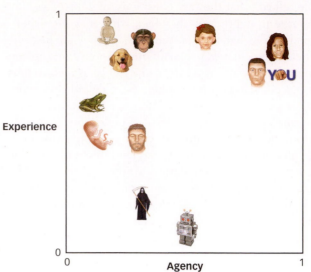

FIGURE 5.1 **Dimensions of Mind Perception**
When participants judged the mental capacities of 13 targets, two dimensions of mind perception were discovered (Gray, Gray, & Wegner, 2007). Participants perceived minds as varying in the capacity for experience (such as abilities to feel pain or pleasure) and in the capacity for agency (such as abilities to plan or exert self-control). They perceived normal adult humans (male, female, or "you," the respondent) to have minds on both dimensions, whereas other targets were perceived to have reduced experience or agency. The man in a persistent vegetative state ("PVS man"), for example, was judged to have only some experience and very little agency. (Information from Gray, Gray, & Wegner, 2007.)

The Mind–Body Problem

Another mystery of consciousness is the **mind–body problem,** *the issue of how the mind is related to the brain and body.* French philosopher and mathematician René Descartes (1596–1650) is famous for proposing, among other things, that the human body is a machine made of physical matter but that the human mind or soul is a separate entity made of a "thinking substance." We now know that the mind and brain are connected everywhere to each other. In other words, "the mind is what the brain does" (Minsky, 1986, p. 287).

But Descartes was right in pointing out the difficulty of reconciling the physical body with the mind. Most psychologists assume that mental events are intimately tied to brain events, such that every thought, perception, or feeling is associated with a particular pattern of activation of neurons in the brain (see the Neuroscience & Behavior chapter). Thinking about a particular person, for instance, occurs with a unique array of neural connections and activations. If the neurons repeat that pattern, then you must be thinking of the same person; conversely, if you think of the person, the brain activity occurs in that pattern.

One telling set of studies, however, suggests that the brain's activities *precede* the activities of the conscious mind. The electrical activity in the brains of volunteers was measured using sensors placed on their scalps as they repeatedly decided when to move a hand (Libet, 1985). Participants were also asked to indicate exactly when they consciously chose to move by reporting the position of a dot moving rapidly around the face of a clock just at the point of the decision (**FIGURE 5.2a**). As a rule, the brain begins to show electrical activity around half a second before a voluntary action (535 milliseconds, to be exact). This makes sense because brain activity certainly seems to be necessary to get an action started.

But, as shown in **FIGURE 5.2b**, the brain also started to show electrical activity before the person reported a conscious decision to move. Although your personal intuition is that you *think* of an action and *then* do it, these experiments suggest that your brain is getting started before *either* the thinking or the doing, preparing the way for both thought and action. Quite simply, it may appear to us that our minds are leading our brains and bodies, but the order of events may be the other way around (Haggard & Tsakiris, 2009; Wegner, 2002).

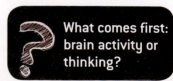

What comes first: brain activity or thinking?

mind-body problem The issue of how the mind is related to the brain and body.

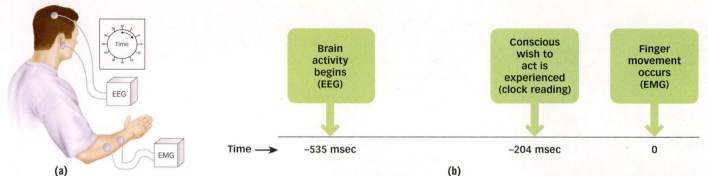

(a)

Time →   **Brain activity begins (EEG)** ↓ −535 msec   **Conscious wish to act is experienced (clock reading)** ↓ −204 msec   **Finger movement occurs (EMG)** ↓ 0

(b)

FIGURE 5.2 The Timing of Conscious Will (*a*) Participants were asked to move fingers at will while watching a dot move around the face of a clock to mark the moment at which the action was consciously willed. Meanwhile, EEG sensors timed the onset of brain activation and EMG sensors timed the muscle movement. (*b*) The experiment showed that brain activity (EEG) precedes the movement of the finger (EMG), but that the reported time of consciously willing the finger to move follows the brain activity. (Information from Libet, 1985.)

The Nature of Consciousness

How would you describe your own consciousness? Research suggests that consciousness has four basic properties (intentionality, unity, selectivity, and transience), that it occurs on different levels, and that it includes a range of different contents. Let's examine each of these points in turn.

Four Basic Properties

Researchers have identified four basic properties of consciousness, based on people's reports of conscious experience.

1. Consciousness has *intentionality*, which is the quality of being directed toward an object. Consciousness is always *about* something. Despite all the lush detail you see in your mind's eye, the kaleidoscope of sights and sounds and feelings and thoughts, the object of your consciousness at any one moment is just a small part of all of this (see **FIGURE 5.3**).

2. Consciousness has *unity*, which is resistance to division. As you read this book, your five senses are taking in a great deal of information. Your eyes are scanning lots of black squiggles on a page (or screen) while also sensing an enormous array of shapes, colors, depths, and textures in your periphery; your hands are gripping a heavy book (or computer); your butt and feet may sense pressure from gravity pulling you against a chair or floor; and you may be listening to music or talking in another room, while smelling the odor of your roommate's dirty laundry. Your brain—amazingly—integrates all of this information into the experience of one unified consciousness.

FIGURE 5.3 Bellotto's Dresden and Close-up (*left*) The people on the bridge in the distance look very finely detailed in *View of Dresden with the Frauenkirche* by Bernardo Bellotto (1720–1780). However, when you examine the detail closely (*right*), you discover that the people are made of brushstrokes merely *suggesting* people. Consciousness produces a similar impression of "filling in," as it seems to consist of extreme detail even in areas that are peripheral (Dennett, 1991).

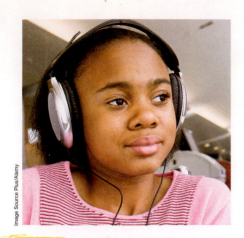

Participants in a dichotic listening experiment hear different messages played to the right and left ears.

FIGURE 5.4 The Necker Cube This cube has the property of reversible perspective in that you can bring one or the other of its two square faces to the front in your mind's eye. Although it may take a while to reverse the figure at first, once people have learned to do it, they can reverse it regularly, about once every 3 seconds (Gomez et al., 1995). The stream of consciousness flows even when the target is a constant object.

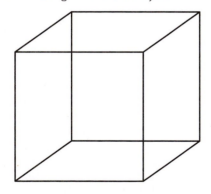

cocktail-party phenomenon A phenomenon in which people tune in one message even while they filter out others nearby.

dichotic listening A task in which people wearing headphones hear different messages presented to each ear.

minimal consciousness A low-level kind of sensory awareness and responsiveness that occurs when the mind inputs sensations and may output behavior.

full consciousness Consciousness in which you know and are able to report your mental state.

3. Consciousness has *selectivity*, the capacity to include some objects but not others. While binding the many sensations around you into a coherent whole, your mind must make decisions about which pieces of information to include—and which to exclude. For example, in what has come to be known as the **cocktail-party phenomenon,** *people tune in one message even while they filter out others nearby.* In **dichotic listening** situation tests, *in which people wearing headphones hear different messages in each ear*, participants directed to pay attention to messages in one ear are especially likely to notice if their own name is spoken into the unattended ear (Moray, 1959). Perhaps you, too, have noticed how abruptly your attention is diverted from whatever conversation you are having when someone else within earshot at the party mentions your name.

4. Consciousness has *transience*, or the tendency to change. The mind wanders not just sometimes, but incessantly, from one "right now" to the next "right now" and then on to the next (Wegner, 1997). William James, whom you met way back in the Psychology: Evolution of a Science chapter, famously described consciousness as a "stream" (James, 1890). The stream of consciousness may flow in this way partly because of the limited capacity of the conscious mind. We humans can hold only so much information in our minds at any one moment, so when more information is selected, some of what is currently there must disappear. As a result, our focus of attention keeps changing. The stream of consciousness flows so inevitably that it even changes our perspective when we view a constant object like a Necker cube (see **FIGURE 5.4**).

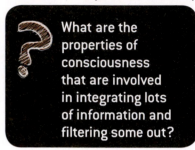

What are the properties of consciousness that are involved in integrating lots of information and filtering some out?

Levels of Consciousness

Consciousness can also be understood as having levels. The levels of consciousness are not a matter of degree of overall brain activity, and so they would probably all register as "conscious" on that wakefulness meter for surgery patients you read about at the beginning of the chapter. Instead, the levels of consciousness involve different qualities of awareness of the world and of the self.

1. **Minimal consciousness** is *a low-level kind of sensory awareness and responsiveness that occurs when the mind inputs sensations and may output behavior* (Armstrong, 1980). This kind of sensory awareness and responsiveness could even happen when someone pokes you during sleep and you turn over. Something seems to register in your mind, at least in the sense that you experience it, but you may not think at all about having had the experience. It could be that animals or, for that matter, even plants can have this minimal level of consciousness. But because of the problem of other minds and the notorious reluctance of animals and plants to talk to us, we can't know for sure that they *experience* the things that make them respond.

2. **Full consciousness** occurs when you *know and are able to report your mental state*. Being fully conscious means that you are aware of having a mental state while you are experiencing the mental state itself. When you have a hurt leg and mindlessly rub it, for instance, your pain may be minimally conscious. It is only when you realize that your leg hurts, though, that the pain becomes fully conscious. Have you ever been driving a car and suddenly realized that you don't remember the past 15 minutes of driving? Chances are that you were not unconscious but were instead minimally conscious.

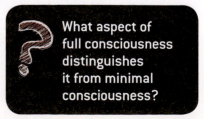

What aspect of full consciousness distinguishes it from minimal consciousness?

Hot Science

The Mind Wanders

Yes, the mind wanders. You've no doubt had experiences of reading and suddenly realizing that you have not even been processing what you've read. Even while your eyes are dutifully following the lines of print, at some point, you begin to think about something else—and only later catch yourself having wandered, perhaps thinking, "Where was I?" Or, "Why did I come into this room?"

Mind wandering, or the experience of "stimulus-independent thoughts," occurs most often when we are engaged in repetitive, undemanding tasks (Buckner, Andrews-Hanna, & Schacter, 2008). This happens a lot. A recent study revealed that we engage in mind wandering during nearly half of our daily activities (46.9%) (Killingsworth & Gilbert, 2010). Indeed, mind wandering occurred at least 30% of the time in every activity recorded (with the one exception being making love, during which it is apparently rare to have stimulus-independent thoughts). Although the mind often wanders, this study found that people are significantly less happy when mind wandering compared to when they are thinking about what they are currently doing.

Learning about the connection between mind wandering and unhappiness might lead you to feel . . . unhappy. But as it turns out, mind wandering may also have its benefits. For thousands of years, some of the world's greatest thinkers have noted that their most important breakthroughs came during periods of daydreaming or mind wandering. For instance, Einstein is said to have made major breakthroughs in his relativity theory while going for a walk (rather than sitting at his desk). In one recent study, participants completed a creative problem-solving test in which they were asked to generate as many uses as they could for everyday objects (e.g., brick, feather) both before and after engaging in either a demanding or undemanding task (Baird et al., 2012). The authors hypothesized—and found—that engagement in the undemanding task would facilitate higher levels of mind wandering (which it did), and also would in turn lead to improvements in their performance on the previously worked-on tests (which it did), but not on new tests (correct again). These findings suggest that allowing our minds to wander, while remaining active, can enhance our ability to think creatively and solve difficult problems.

Courtesy of the Leo Baeck Institute, New York

New research suggests that mind wandering can improve creative problem-solving. As a real-world example of this, Einstein is said to have come up with some of his greatest breakthroughs not while sitting at his desk, but while going for walks. Here he is hard at work.

When you are completely aware and thinking about your driving, you have moved into the realm of full consciousness. Full consciousness involves not only thinking about things but also thinking about the fact that you are thinking about things (Jaynes, 1976; see the Hot Science box).

3. **Self-consciousness** is yet another *distinct level of consciousness in which the person's attention is drawn to the self as an object* (Morin, 2006). Most people report experiencing such self-consciousness when they are embarrassed; when they find themselves the focus of attention in a group; when someone focuses a camera on them; or when they are deeply introspective about their thoughts, feelings, or personal qualities. Looking in a mirror, for example, is all it takes to make people evaluate themselves—thinking not just about their looks, but also about whether they are good or bad in other ways. People go out of their way to avoid mirrors when they've done something they are ashamed of (Duval & Wicklund, 1972). However, because it makes people self-critical, the self-consciousness that results when people see their own mirror images can make them briefly more helpful, more cooperative, and less aggressive (Gibbons, 1990).

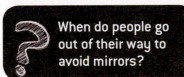
When do people go out of their way to avoid mirrors?

Most animals don't appear to have self-consciousness. The typical dog, cat, or bird seems mystified by a mirror, ignoring it or acting as though there is some other

Photomondo/Photodisc/Getty Images

Full consciousness involves a consciousness of oneself, such as thinking about the act of driving while driving a car. How is this different from self-consciousness?

self-consciousness A distinct level of consciousness in which the person's attention is drawn to the self as an object.

A chimpanzee tries to wipe off the red dye on its eyebrow, suggesting it can recognize itself in the mirror.

critter back there. However, chimpanzees that have spent time with mirrors sometimes behave in ways that suggest they recognize themselves in a mirror. To examine this phenomenon, researchers painted an odorless red dye over the eyebrow of an anesthetized chimp and then watched when the awakened chimp was presented with a mirror (Gallup, 1977). If the chimp interpreted the mirror image as a representation of some other chimp with an unusual approach to cosmetics, we would expect it just to look at the mirror or perhaps to reach toward it. But the chimp reached toward its *own eye* as it looked into the mirror, suggesting that it recognized the image as a reflection of itself. A few other animals, such as orangutans (Gallup, 1997), possibly dolphins (Reiss & Marino, 2001), and maybe even elephants (Plotnik, de Waal, & Reiss, 2006) and magpies (Prior, Schwartz, & Güntürkün, 2008) recognize their own mirror images. Dogs, cats, crows, monkeys, and gorillas have been tested, too, but they don't seem to know they are looking at themselves. Even humans don't have self-recognition right away. Infants don't recognize themselves in mirrors until they've reached about 18 months of age (Lewis & Brooks-Gunn, 1979). The experience of self-consciousness, as measured by self-recognition in mirrors, is limited to a few animals and to humans only after a certain stage of development.

Conscious Contents

What's on your mind? For that matter, what's on everybody's mind? One way to learn what is on people's minds is to ask them, and much research has called on people simply to *think aloud*. A more systematic approach is the *experience-sampling technique*, in which people are asked to report their conscious experiences at particular times. Equipped with electronic beepers or called on cell phones, for example, participants are asked to record their current thoughts when asked at random times throughout the day (Bolger, Davis, & Rafaeli, 2003).

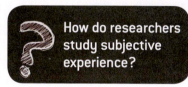

How do researchers study subjective experience?

Experience-sampling studies show that consciousness is dominated by the immediate environment—what is seen, felt, heard, tasted, and smelled—and that all are at the forefront of the mind. Much of consciousness beyond this orientation to the environment turns to the person's *current concerns*, or what the person is thinking about repeatedly (Klinger, 1975). **TABLE 5.1** shows the results of a study where 175 college students were asked to report their current concerns (Goetzman, Hughes, & Klinger, 1994). Keep in mind that these concerns are ones the students didn't mind reporting to psychologists; the private preoccupations of these students may have been different and probably far more interesting.

Although current concerns often dominate our thoughts, we also sometimes experience *daydreaming*, a state of consciousness in which a seemingly purposeless flow of thoughts comes to mind. The brain, however, is active even when there is no specific task at hand. Daydreaming was examined in an fMRI study of people resting in the scanner (Mason et al., 2007). Usually, people in brain-scanning studies don't have time to daydream much because they are kept busy with mental tasks—scans cost money, and researchers want to get as much data as possible for their bucks. But when people are *not* busy, they still show a widespread pattern of activation in many areas of the brain—now known as the *default network* (Gusnard & Raichle, 2001). This default network became activated whenever people worked on a mental task that they knew so well that they could daydream while doing it (see **FIGURE 5.5**). The areas of the default network are known to be involved in thinking about social life,

One concern on many students' minds is diet and exercise to keep in shape.

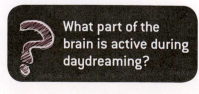

What part of the brain is active during daydreaming?

Table 5.1 What's on Your Mind? College Students' Current Concerns

Current Concern Category	Example	Frequency of Students Who Mentioned the Concern
Family	Gain better relations with immediate family	40%
Roommate	Change attitude or behavior of roommate	29%
Household	Clean room	52%
Friends	Make new friends	42%
Dating	Desire to date a certain person	24%
Sexual intimacy	Abstaining from sex	16%
Health	Diet and exercise	85%
Employment	Get a summer job	33%
Education	Go to graduate school	43%
Social activities	Gain acceptance into a campus organization	34%
Religious	Attend church more	51%
Financial	Pay rent or bills	8%
Government	Change government policy	14%

Source: Information from Goetzman, E.S., Hughes, T., & Klinger, E., 1994.

mental control The attempt to change conscious states of mind.

thought suppression The conscious avoidance of a thought.

rebound effect of thought suppression The tendency of a thought to return to consciousness with greater frequency following suppression.

about the self, and about the past and future—all the usual haunts of the daydreaming mind (Mitchell, 2006).

The current concerns that populate consciousness can sometimes get the upper hand, transforming daydreams or everyday thoughts into rumination and worry. When this happens, people may exert **mental control**, *the attempt to change conscious states of mind*. For example, someone troubled by a recurring worry about the future ("What if I can't get a decent job when I graduate?") might choose to try *not* to think about this because it causes too much anxiety and uncertainty. Whenever this thought comes to mind, the person engages in **thought suppression**, the *conscious avoidance of a thought*. This may seem like a perfectly sensible strategy because it eliminates the worry and allows the person to move on to think about something else.

Or does it? Daniel Wegner and his colleagues (1987) asked research participants to try *not* to think about a white bear for 5 minutes while they recorded each participant's thoughts aloud into a tape recorder. In addition, participants were asked to ring a bell if the thought of a white bear came to mind. On average, they mentioned the white bear or rang the bell (indicating the thought) more than once per minute. Thought suppression simply didn't work and instead produced a flurry of returns of the unwanted thought. What's more, when research participants were later asked to deliberately *think* about a white bear, they became oddly preoccupied with it. A graph of their bell rings in **FIGURE 5.6** shows that these participants had the white bear come to mind far more often than did people who had only been asked to think about the bear from the outset, with no prior suppression. This **rebound effect of thought suppression**, *the tendency of a thought to return to consciousness with greater frequency following suppression*, suggests that the act of trying to suppress a thought may itself cause that thought to return to consciousness in a robust way.

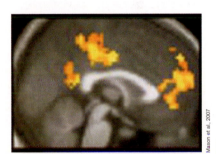

FIGURE 5.5 **The Default Network Activated during Daydreaming** An fMRI scan shows that many areas, known as the default network, are active when the person is not given a specific mental task to perform during the scan (Mason et al., 2007).

Go ahead, look away from the book for a minute and try not to think about a white bear.

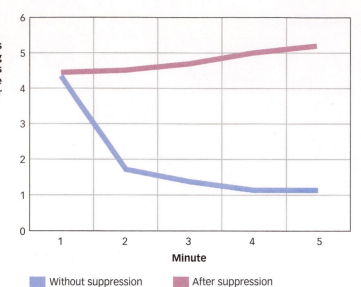

FIGURE 5.6 **Rebound Effect** Research participants were first asked to try not to think about a white bear, and then they were asked to think about it and to ring a bell whenever it came to mind. Compared to those who were simply asked to think about a bear without prior suppression, those people who *first* suppressed the thought showed a rebound of increased thinking. (Data from Wegner et al., 1987.)

ironic processes of mental control Mental processes that can produce ironic errors because monitoring for errors can itself produce them.

dynamic unconscious An active system encompassing a lifetime of hidden memories, the person's deepest instincts and desires, and the person's inner struggle to control these forces.

There are no conscious steps between hearing an easy problem (what's 4 + 5?) and thinking of the answer—unless you have to count on your fingers.

How ironic: Trying to consciously achieve one task may produce precisely the opposite outcome! These ironic effects seem most likely to occur when the person is distracted or under stress. People who are distracted while they are trying to get into a good mood, for example, tend to become sad (Wegner, Erber, & Zanakos, 1993), and those who are distracted while trying to relax actually become more anxious than those who are not trying to relax (Wegner, Broome, & Blumberg, 1997). Likewise, an attempt not to overshoot a golf putt, undertaken during distraction, often yields the unwanted overshot (Wegner, Ansfield, & Pilloff, 1998). The theory of **ironic processes of mental control** proposes that such *ironic errors occur because the mental process that monitors errors can itself produce them* (Wegner, 1994a, 2009). In the attempt not to think of a white bear, for instance, a small part of the mind is ironically *searching* for the white bear. As this unconscious monitoring whirs along in the background, it unfortunately increases the person's sensitivity to the very thought that is unwanted. Ironic processes are needed for effective mental control—they help in the process of banishing a thought from consciousness—but they can sometimes yield the very failure they seem designed to overcome. Ironic effects of mental control arise from processes that work outside of consciousness, so they remind us that much of the mind's machinery may be hidden from our view, lying outside the fringes of our experience.

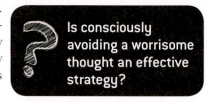
Is consciously avoiding a worrisome thought an effective strategy?

The Unconscious Mind

Many other mental processes are unconscious, too, in the sense that they occur without our experience of them. For example, think for a moment about the mental processes involved in simple addition. What happens in consciousness between hearing a problem (what's 4 + 5?) and thinking of the answer (9)? It may feel like nothing happens—the answer just appears in the mind. Nothing conscious seems to bridge the gap; rather, the answer comes from the unconscious mind.

Freudian Unconscious

As you read in the Psychology: Evolution of a Science chapter, Sigmund Freud's psychoanalytic theory viewed conscious thought as the surface of a much deeper mind made up of unconscious processes. Far more than just a collection of hidden processes, Freud described a **dynamic unconscious**—*an active system encompassing a lifetime of hidden memories, the person's deepest instincts and desires, and the person's inner struggle to control these forces.* The dynamic unconscious might contain hidden sexual thoughts about one's parents, for example, or destructive urges aimed at a helpless infant—the kinds of thoughts people keep secret from others and may not even acknowledge to themselves. According to Freud's theory, the unconscious is a force to be held in check by **repression**, *a mental process that removes unacceptable thoughts and memories from consciousness and keeps them in the unconscious.* Without repression, a person might think, do, or say every unconscious impulse or animal urge, no matter how selfish or immoral. With repression, these desires are held in the recesses of the dynamic unconscious.

Freud looked for evidence of the unconscious mind in speech errors and lapses of consciousness, or what are commonly called *Freudian slips*. Forgetting the name of someone you dislike, for example, is a slip that seems to have special meaning. Freud believed that errors are not random and instead have some surplus meaning that has been created by an intelligent unconscious mind, even though the person consciously disavows the thoughts and memories that caused the errors in the first place. For example, when reporting on the news that members of the U.S. military had killed Osama bin Laden, several reporters and commentators at Fox News, a conservative news outlet, independently reported that *Obama* bin Laden was dead. Did the Fox News slip mean anything? Many of the meaningful errors Freud attributed to the dynamic unconscious were not predicted in advance and so seem to depend on clever after-the-fact interpretations. Suggesting a pattern to a series of random events is not the same as scientifically predicting and explaining

After the death of Osama bin Laden, several staff members at the conservative Fox News channel slipped and reported on the death of *Obama* bin Laden.

What might Freudian slips tell us about the unconscious mind?

when and why an event should happen. Anyone can offer a reasonable, compelling explanation for an event after it has already happened, but the true work of science is to offer testable hypotheses that are evaluated based on reliable evidence.

A Modern View of the Cognitive Unconscious

Modern psychologists share Freud's interest in the impact of unconscious mental processes on consciousness and on behavior. However, rather than Freud's vision of the unconscious as a teeming menagerie of animal urges and repressed thoughts, the current study of the unconscious mind views it as the factory that builds the products of conscious thought and behavior (Kihlstrom, 1987; Wilson, 2002). The **cognitive unconscious** includes *all the mental processes that give rise to a person's thoughts, choices, emotions, and behavior even though they are not experienced by the person*.

One indication of the cognitive unconscious at work is when a person's thoughts or behaviors are changed by exposure to information outside of consciousness. This happens in **subliminal perception**, when *thought or behavior is influenced by stimuli that a person cannot consciously report perceiving*. Worries about the potential of subliminal influence were first provoked in 1957, when a marketer claimed he had increased concession sales at a movie theater by flashing the words "Eat Popcorn" and "Drink Coke" briefly on-screen during movies. It turns out his story was a hoax, and many attempts to increase sales using similar methods have failed. But the very idea of influencing behavior outside of consciousness created a wave of alarm about insidious "subliminal persuasion" that still concerns people (Epley, Savitsky, & Kachelski, 1999; Pratkanis, 1992).

Although the story above was a hoax, factors outside our conscious awareness can indeed influence our behavior. For example, one classic study had college students complete a survey that called for them to make sentences with various words (Bargh, Chen, & Burrows, 1996). The students were not informed that most of the words were commonly associated with aging (*Florida, gray, wrinkled*), and even afterward they didn't report being aware of this trend. In this case, the "aging" idea wasn't presented subliminally; instead, it was just not very noticeably presented. As these research participants left the experiment, they were clocked as

repression A mental process that removes unacceptable thoughts and memories from consciousness and keeps them in the unconscious.

cognitive unconscious All the mental processes that give rise to a person's thoughts, choices, emotions, and behavior even though they are not experienced by the person.

subliminal perception Thought or behavior that is influenced by stimuli that a person cannot consciously report perceiving.

Would subliminal messages make people in a movie theater more likely to eat popcorn? Maybe, but not much.

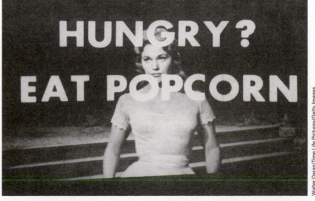

they walked down the hall. Compared with those not exposed to the aging-related words, the participants walked more slowly! Just as with subliminal perception, a passing exposure to ideas can influence actions without conscious awareness.

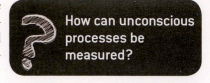

How can unconscious processes be measured?

SUMMARY QUIZ [5.1]

1. Which of the following is NOT a basic property of consciousness?
   a. intentionality
   b. disunity
   c. selectivity
   d. transience

2. Currently, unconscious processes are understood as
   a. a concentrated pattern of thought suppression.
   b. a hidden system of memories, instincts, and desires.
   c. a blank slate.
   d. unexperienced mental processes that give rise to thoughts and behavior.

3. The _____ unconscious is at work when subliminal and unconscious processes influence thought and behavior.
   a. minimal
   b. repressive
   c. dynamic
   d. cognitive

Sleep and Dreaming: Good Night, Mind

Sleep can produce a state of unconsciousness in which the mind and brain apparently turn off the functions that create experience: The theater in your mind is closed. But this is an oversimplification because the theater actually seems to reopen during the night for special shows of bizarre cult films—in other words, dreams. Dream consciousness involves a transformation of experience so radical that it is commonly considered an **altered state of consciousness**: *a form of experience that departs significantly from the normal subjective experience of the world and the mind.* Such altered states can be accompanied by changes in thinking, disturbances in the sense of time, feelings of the loss of control, changes in emotional expression, alterations in body image and sense of self, perceptual distortions, and changes in meaning or significance (Ludwig, 1966). Sleep and dreams provide two unique perspectives on consciousness: a view of the mind without consciousness and a view of consciousness in an altered state.

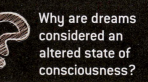

Why are dreams considered an altered state of consciousness?

Sleep

Consider a typical night. As you begin to fall asleep, the busy, task-oriented thoughts of the waking mind are replaced by wandering thoughts and images and odd juxtapositions, some of them almost dreamlike. This presleep consciousness is called the *hypnagogic state*. On some rare nights, you might experience a

altered state of consciousness A form of experience that departs significantly from the normal subjective experience of the world and the mind.

hypnic jerk, a sudden quiver or sensation of dropping, as though missing a step on a staircase. No one is quite sure why these jerks happen. Eventually, your presence of mind goes away entirely. Time and experience stop, you are unconscious, and in fact there seems to be no "you" there to have experiences. But then come dreams, whole vistas of a vivid and surrealistic consciousness you just don't get during the day, a set of experiences that occur with the odd prerequisite that there is nothing "out there" you are actually experiencing. More patches of unconsciousness may occur, with more dreams here and there. And finally, the glimmerings of waking consciousness return again in a foggy and imprecise form as you enter postsleep consciousness (the *hypnopompic state*) and then awaken, often with bad hair.

***Dreamers,* by Albert Joseph Moore (1879/1882).** Although their bodies are in the same room, their minds are probably worlds apart.

Sleep Cycle

The sequence of events that occurs during a night of sleep is part of one of the major rhythms of human life, the cycle of sleep and waking. This **circadian rhythm** is *a naturally occurring 24-hour cycle*, from the Latin *circa* (about) and *dies* (day). Even people sequestered in underground buildings without clocks who are allowed to sleep when they want tend to have a rest–activity cycle of about 25.1 hours (Aschoff, 1965).

The sleep cycle is far more than a simple on–off routine, however, as many bodily and psychological processes ebb and flow in this rhythm. EEG recordings reveal a regular pattern of changes in electrical activity in the brain accompanying the circadian cycle. During waking, these changes involve alternation between high-frequency activity (*beta waves*) during alertness and lower-frequency activity (*alpha waves*) during relaxation.

circadian rhythm A naturally occurring 24-hour cycle.

REM sleep A stage of sleep characterized by rapid eye movements and a high level of brain activity.

The largest changes in EEG occur during sleep. These changes show a regular pattern over the course of the night corresponding to five sleep stages (see **FIGURE 5.7**). In the first stage of sleep, the EEG moves to frequency patterns even lower than alpha waves (*theta waves*). In the second stage of sleep, these patterns

What do EEG recordings tell us about sleep?

are interrupted by short bursts of activity called *sleep spindles* and *K complexes*, and the sleeper becomes somewhat more difficult to awaken. The deepest stages of sleep are stages 3 and 4, known as slow-wave sleep, in which the EEG patterns show activity called *delta waves*.

During the fifth sleep stage, **REM sleep**, *a stage of sleep characterized by rapid eye movements and a high level of brain activity,* EEG patterns become high-frequency sawtooth waves, similar to beta waves, suggesting that the mind at this time is as active as it is during waking (see **FIGURE 5.7**). Sleepers wakened during REM periods reported having dreams much more often than those wakened during non-REM periods (Aserinsky & Kleitman, 1953). During REM sleep, the pulse quickens, blood pressure rises, and there are telltale signs of sexual arousal. At the same time, measurements of muscle movements indicate that the sleeper is very still, except for a rapid side-to-side movement of the eyes. (Watch someone sleeping, and you may be able to see the REMs through their closed eye-

Psychologists learn about what happens when we sleep by collecting EEG and other measurements from research volunteers while they sleep in sleep laboratories, like this one.

What are the stages in a typical night's sleep?

lids. But be careful doing this with strangers down at the bus station.) Although many people believe that they don't dream much (if at all), some 80% of people awakened during REM sleep report dreams,

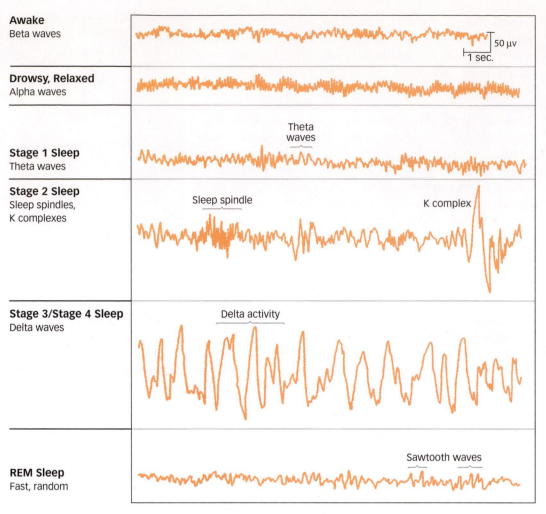

Awake
Beta waves

50 μv
1 sec.

Drowsy, Relaxed
Alpha waves

Stage 1 Sleep
Theta waves

Theta
waves

Stage 2 Sleep
Sleep spindles,
K complexes

Sleep spindle

K complex

Stage 3/Stage 4 Sleep
Delta waves

Delta activity

REM Sleep
Fast, random

Sawtooth waves

FIGURE 5.7 EEG Patterns during the Stages of Sleep The waking brain shows high-frequency beta wave activity, which changes during drowsiness and relaxation to lower-frequency alpha waves. Stage 1 sleep shows lower-frequency theta waves, whereas stage 2 includes irregular patterns called sleep spindles and K complexes. Stages 3 and 4 are marked by the lowest frequencies, delta waves. During REM sleep, EEG patterns return to higher-frequency sawtooth waves that resemble the beta waves of waking.

and most people's dreams appear to be experienced in real time. Some dreams are also reported in other sleep stages, but not as many—and the dreams that occur at those times are described as less wild than REM dreams and more like normal thinking.

Putting EEG and REM data together produces a picture of how a typical night's sleep progresses through cycles of sleep stages (see **FIGURE 5.8**). In the first hour of the night, you fall all the way from waking to the fourth and deepest stage of sleep, the stage marked by delta waves. These slow waves indicate a general synchronization of neural firing: the neuronal equivalent of "the wave" moving through the crowd at a stadium as lots of individuals move together in synchrony. You then return to lighter sleep stages, eventually reaching REM and dreamland. Note that although REM sleep is lighter than that of lower stages, it is deep enough that you may be difficult to awaken. You then continue to cycle between REM and slow-wave sleep stages every 90 minutes or so throughout the night. Periods of REM last longer as the night goes on, and lighter sleep stages predominate between these periods, with the deeper slow-wave stages 3 and 4 disappearing about halfway through the night. Although you're either unconscious or dream-conscious at the time, your brain and mind cycle through a remarkable array of different states each time you have a night's sleep.

Sleep Needs and Deprivation

How much do people sleep? The answer depends on the age of the sleeper (Dement, 1999). Newborns will sleep 6 to 8 times in 24 hours, often totaling more than 16 hours. Their napping cycle gets consolidated into "sleeping through the night,"

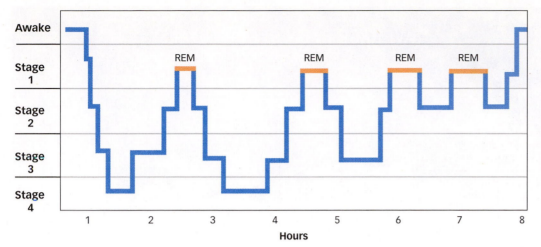

FIGURE 5.8 Stages of Sleep during the Night Over the course of the typical night, sleep cycles into deeper stages early on and then more shallow stages later. REM periods become longer in later cycles, and the deeper slow-wave sleep of stages 3 and 4 disappears about halfway through the night.

usually sometime between 9 and 18 months. The typical 6-year-old child might need 11 or 12 hours of sleep, and the average adult needs about 7 to 7.5 hours per night. With aging, people can get along with even a bit less sleep than that. Over a whole lifetime, we get about 1 hour of sleep for every 2 hours we are awake.

This is a lot of sleeping. Could we tolerate less? For a 1965 science project, 17-year-old Randy Gardner stayed up for 264 hours and 12 minutes. When he finally did go to sleep, he slept only 14 hours and 40 minutes and awakened essentially recovered (Dement, 1978).

Feats like this one suggest that sleep might be expendable. This is the theory behind the classic all-nighter that you may have tried on the way to a rough exam. But it turns out that this theory is mistaken. When people learning a difficult perceptual task are kept up all night after they have finished practicing the task, their learning of the task is wiped out (Stickgold et al., 2000). Sleep following learning appears to be essential for memory consolidation (see Hot Science: Sleep on It, p. 181, in the Memory chapter). It is as though memories normally deteriorate unless sleep occurs to help keep them in place. Studying all night may help you cram for the exam, but it won't make the material stick, which pretty much defeats the whole point.

What is the relationship between sleep and learning?

DATA VISUALIZATION

Consciousness
www.macmillanhighered.com/schacterbrief3e

Sleep turns out to be a necessity rather than a luxury in other ways as well. At the extreme, sleep loss can be fatal. When rats are forced to break Randy Gardner's human waking record and stay awake even longer, they have trouble regulating their body temperature and lose weight although they eat much more than normal. Their bodily systems break down and they die, on average, in 21 days (Rechtshaffen et al., 1983). Even for healthy young humans, a few hours of sleep deprivation each night can have a cumulative detrimental effect: reducing mental acuity and reaction time, increasing irritability and depression, and increasing the risk of accidents and injury (Coren, 1997).

Some studies have deprived people of different sleep stages selectively by waking them whenever certain stages are detected. Memory problems and excessive aggression are observed in both humans and rats after only a few days of being wakened whenever REM activity starts (Ellman et al., 1991). Such REM deprivation causes a rebound of more REM sleep the next night (Brunner et al., 1990). Deprivation from slow-wave sleep (in stages 3 and 4), in contrast, has more physical effects, with just a few nights of deprivation leaving people feeling tired, fatigued, and hypersensitive to muscle and bone pain (Lentz et al., 1999).

It's clearly dangerous to neglect the need for sleep. But why would we have such a need in the first place? All animals appear to sleep, although the amount of sleep

FIGURE 5.9 All animals and insects seem to require sleep, although in differing amounts. Next time you oversleep and someone accuses you of "sleeping like a baby," you might tell them instead that you were sleeping like a tiger, or a brown bat.

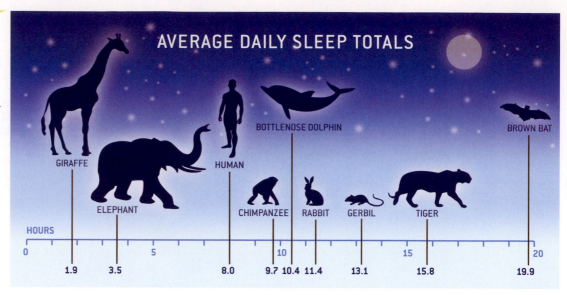

AVERAGE DAILY SLEEP TOTALS

BOTTLENOSE DOLPHIN

BROWN BAT

GIRAFFE

HUMAN

ELEPHANT

CHIMPANZEE   RABBIT   GERBIL   TIGER

HOURS

0   5   10   15   20

1.9   3.5   8.0   9.7 10.4 11.4   13.1   15.8   19.9

Sleep following learning is essential for memory consolidation. Sleep during class, on the other hand, not so much.

Sonda Dawes/The Image Works

insomnia Difficulty in falling asleep or staying asleep.

sleep apnea A disorder in which the person stops breathing for brief periods while asleep.

somnambulism (or sleepwalking) Occurs when a person arises and walks around while asleep.

narcolepsy A disorder in which sudden sleep attacks occur in the middle of waking activities.

sleep paralysis The experience of waking up unable to move.

required varies quite a bit from species to species (see **FIGURE 5.9**). Giraffes sleep less than 2 hours daily, whereas brown bats snooze for almost 20 hours. These variations in sleep needs—and the very existence of a need—are hard to explain. Is the restoration that happens during the unconsciousness of sleep something that simply can't be achieved during consciousness? Sleep is, after all, potentially costly in the course of evolution. The sleeping animal is easy prey, so the habit of sleep would not seem to have developed so widely across species unless it had significant benefits that made up for this vulnerability. Theories of sleep have not yet determined why the brain and body have evolved to need these recurring episodes of unconsciousness.

Sleep Disorders

In answer to the question, "Did you sleep well?," comedian Stephen Wright said, "No, I made a couple of mistakes." Sleeping well is something everyone would love to do, but for many people, sleep disorders are deeply troubling.

Insomnia, *difficulty in falling asleep or staying asleep,* is perhaps the most common sleep disorder. About 30–48% of people report symptoms of insomnia, and 6% of people meet criteria for a diagnosis of insomnia, a diagnosis that requires persistent and impairing sleep problems (Bootzin & Epstein, 2011; Ohayon, 2002). There are many potential causes of insomnia. In some instances, it results from lifestyle choices such as working night shifts (self-induced insomnia); sometimes it occurs in response to depression, anxiety, or some other condition (secondary insomnia); and in other cases, there are no obvious causal factors (primary insomnia). Regardless of type, insomnia can be exacerbated by worrying about insomnia (Borkevec, 1982). No doubt you've experienced some nights when sleeping was a high priority, such as before a class presentation or an important interview, and you've found that you were unable to fall asleep. The desire to sleep initiates an ironic process of mental control—a heightened sensitivity to signs of sleeplessness—and this sensitivity interferes with sleep. Although sedatives can be useful for brief sleep problems associated with emotional events, their long-term use is not effective. Not only are most sleeping pills addictive, but even in short-term use,

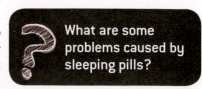

? **What are some problems caused by sleeping pills?**

sedatives can reduce the proportion of time spent in REM and slow-wave sleep (Qureshi & Lee-Chiong, 2004). As a result, the quality of sleep achieved with pills may not be as high as without, and there may be side effects such as grogginess and irritability during the day.

Sleep apnea is *a disorder in which the person stops breathing for brief periods while asleep.* A person with apnea usually snores because apnea involves an involuntary obstruction of the breathing passage. When episodes of apnea occur for over 10 seconds at a time and recur many times during the night, they may cause many awakenings and sleep loss or insomnia. Apnea occurs most often in middle-age overweight men (Punjabi, 2008) and may go undiagnosed because it is not easy for the sleeper to notice. Bed partners may be the ones who finally get tired of the snoring and noisy gasping for air when the sleeper's breathing restarts, or the sleeper may eventually seek treatment because of excessive sleepiness during the day. Therapies involving weight loss, drugs, sleep masks that push air into the nasal passage, or surgery may solve the problem.

Somnambulism (or **sleepwalking**) occurs when *a person arises and walks around while asleep.* Sleepwalking is more common in children, peaking between the ages of 4 and 8 years, with 15–40% of children experiencing at least one episode (Bhargava, 2011). Sleepwalking tends to happen early in the night, usually in slow-wave sleep, and sleepwalkers may awaken during their walks or return to bed without waking, in which case they will probably not remember the episode in the morning. The sleepwalker's eyes are usually open in a glassy stare. Walking with hands outstretched is uncommon except in cartoons. Sleepwalking is usually only problematic in that sleepwalkers sometimes engage in strange or unwise behaviors such as urinating in places other than the toilet and leaving the house while still sleeping. People who walk while they are sleeping do not tend to be very coordinated and can trip over furniture or fall down stairs. After all, they're sleeping. Contrary to popular belief, it is safe to wake sleepwalkers or lead them back to bed (but best to wait until after they finish their business).

There are other sleep disorders that are less common. **Narcolepsy** is *a disorder in which sudden sleep attacks occur in the middle of waking activities.* Narcolepsy involves the intrusion of a dreaming state of sleep into waking and is often accompanied by unrelenting excessive sleepiness and uncontrollable sleep attacks lasting from 30 seconds to 30 minutes. This disorder appears to have a genetic basis, as it runs in families, and it can be treated effectively with medication. **Sleep paralysis** is *the experience of waking up unable to move* and is sometimes associated with narcolepsy. This eerie experience usually happens as you are awakening from REM sleep but before you have regained motor control. This period typically lasts only a few seconds or minutes and can be accompanied by hypnopompic (when awakening) or hypnagogic (when falling asleep) hallucinations in which dream content may appear to occur in the waking world. A very clever series of recent studies suggests that sleep paralysis accompanied by hypnopompic hallucinations of figures in one's bedroom seems to explain many perceived instances of alien abductions and recovered memories of sexual abuse (aided by therapists who used hypnosis to help the sleepers [incorrectly] piece it

INSOMNIA JEOPARDY

WAYS IN WHICH PEOPLE HAVE WRONGED ME	STRANGE NOISES	DISEASES I PROBABLY HAVE	MONEY TROUBLES	WHY DID I SAY/DO THAT?	IDEAS FOR A SCREENPLAY
$10	$10	$10	$10	$10	$10
$20	$20	$20	$20	$20	$20
$30	$30	$30	$30	$30	$30
$40	$40	$40	$40	$40	$40
$50	$50	$50	$50	$50	$50

Is it safe to wake a sleepwalker?

Sleepwalkers in cartoons have their arms outstretched and eyes closed, but that's just for cartoons. A real-life sleepwalker usually walks normally with eyes open, sometimes with a glassy look.

night terrors (or sleep terrors) Abrupt awakenings with panic and intense emotional arousal.

all together; McNally & Clancy, 2005). **Night terrors** (or **sleep terrors**) are *abrupt awakenings with panic and intense emotional arousal.* These terrors, which occur most often in children and in only about 2% of adults (Ohayon, Guilleminault, & Priest, 1999), happen most often in non-REM sleep early in the sleep cycle and do not usually have dream content the sleeper can report.

To sum up, there is a lot going on when we close our eyes for the night. Humans follow a pretty regular sleep cycle, going through the five stages of sleep during the night. Disruptions to that cycle, either from sleep deprivation or sleep disorders, can produce consequences for waking consciousness. But something else happens during a night's sleep that affects our consciousness, both while asleep and when we wake up.

Dreams

Pioneering sleep researcher William C. Dement (1959) said, "Dreaming permits each and every one of us to be quietly and safely insane every night of our lives." Indeed, dreams do seem to have a touch of insanity about them. Even more bizarre is the fact that we are the writers, producers, and directors of the crazy things we experience in dreams. Just what are these experiences, and how can they be explained?

Dream Consciousness

Dreams depart dramatically from reality. You may dream of being naked in public, of falling from a great height, of sleeping through an important appointment, or of being chased (Holloway, 2001). These things don't happen much in reality unless you're having a very bad life. The quality of consciousness in dreaming is also altered significantly from waking consciousness. There are five major characteristics of dream consciousness that distinguish it from the waking state (Hobson, 1988).

1. We intensely feel *emotion*, whether it is bliss or terror or love or awe.
2. Dream *thought* is illogical: The continuities of time, place, and person don't apply. You may find you are in one place and then another, for example, without any travel in between—or people may change identity from one dream scene to the next.
3. *Sensation* is fully formed and meaningful; visual sensation is predominant, and you may also deeply experience sound, touch, and movement (although pain is very uncommon).
4. Dreaming occurs with *uncritical acceptance*, as though the images and events are perfectly normal rather than bizarre.
5. We have *difficulty remembering* the dream after it is over. People often remember dreams only if they are awakened during the dream and even then may lose recall for the dream within just a few minutes of waking. If waking memory were this bad, you'd be standing around half-naked in the street much of the time, having forgotten your destination, clothes, and lunch money.

> **?** What distinguishes dream consciousness from the waking state?

Not all of our dreams are fantastic and surreal, however. We often dream about mundane topics that reflect prior waking experiences or "day residue." Current conscious concerns pop up (Nikles et al., 1998), along with images from the recent past. The day residue does not usually include episodic memories—that is, complete daytime events replayed in the mind. Rather, dreams that reflect the day's experience tend to single out sensory experiences or objects from waking life and mix them together. For instance, after a fun day at the beach with your roommates, your dream that night might include cameo appearances by bouncing beach balls or a flock of seagulls. One study had research participants play the computer game Tetris and

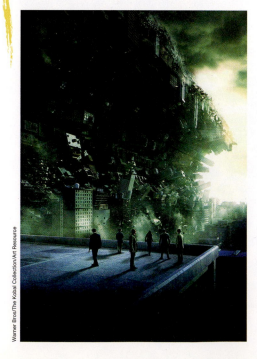

Dreams are often quite intense, vivid, and illogical. In this scene from the movie *Inception*, the dream sequence involves a city collapsing and moving in a vortex.

Warner Bros/The Kobal Collection/Art Resource

found that participants often reported dreaming about the Tetris geometrical figures falling down—even though they seldom reported dreams about being in the experiment or playing the game (Stickgold et al., 2001). The content of dreams takes snapshots from the day rather than retelling the stories of what you have done or seen. This means that dreams often come without clear plots or story lines, so they may not make a lot of sense.

Some of the most memorable dreams are nightmares. One set of daily dream logs from college undergraduates suggested that the average student has about 24 nightmares per year (Wood & Bootzin, 1990), although some people may have them as often as every night. Children have more nightmares than adults, and people who have experienced traumatic events are inclined to have nightmares that relive those events. Following the 1989 earthquake in the San Francisco Bay area, for example, college students who had experienced the quake reported more nightmares than those who had not, and they often reported that the dreams were about the quake (Wood et al., 1992).

The Nightmare, by Henry Fuseli (1790), depicts not only a mare in this painting but also an incubus—an imp perched on the dreamer's chest that is traditionally associated with especially horrifying nightmares.

Dream Theories

Dreams are puzzles that cry out to be solved. The search for dream meaning goes all the way back to biblical figures, who interpreted dreams and looked for prophecies in them. In the Old Testament, the prophet Daniel (a favorite of three of the authors of this book) curried favor with King Nebuchadnezzar of Babylon by interpreting the king's dream. Unfortunately, the meaning of dreams is usually far from obvious.

In the first psychological theory of dreams, Freud (1900/1965) proposed that dreams are confusing and obscure because the dynamic unconscious creates them precisely *to be* confusing and obscure. According to Freud's theory, dreams represent wishes, and some of these wishes are so unacceptable, taboo, and anxiety producing that the mind can only express them in disguised form. For example, a dream about a tree burning down in the park across the street from where a friend once lived might represent a camouflaged wish for the death of the friend. In this case, wishing for the death of a friend is unacceptable, so it is disguised as a tree on fire. The problem with Freud's approach is that there is an infinite number of potential interpretations of any dream, and finding the correct one is a matter of guesswork—and of convincing the dreamer that one interpretation is superior to the others.

Although dreams may not represent elaborately hidden wishes, there is evidence that they do feature the return of suppressed thoughts. Researchers asked volunteers to think of a personal acquaintance and then to spend 5 minutes before going to bed writing down whatever came to mind (Wegner, Wenzlaff, & Kozak, 2004). Some participants were asked to suppress thoughts of this person as they wrote, others were asked to focus on thoughts of the person, and yet others were asked just to write freely about anything. The next morning, participants wrote dream reports. Overall, all participants mentioned dreaming more about the person they had named than about other people. But they most often dreamed of the person they named if they were in the group that had been assigned to suppress thoughts of the person the night before. This finding suggests that Freud was right to suspect that dreams harbor unwanted thoughts. Perhaps this is why actors dream of forgetting their lines, travelers dream of getting lost, and football players dream of fumbling the ball.

Another key theory of dreaming is the **activation–synthesis model** (Hobson & McCarley, 1977). This theory proposes that *dreams are produced when the brain attempts to make sense of random neural activity that occurs during sleep.* During waking consciousness, the mind is devoted to interpreting lots of information that arrives through the senses. You figure out that the odd noise you're hearing during class is your cell phone vibrating, for example, or you

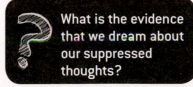

? What is the evidence that we dream about our suppressed thoughts?

activation–synthesis model The theory that dreams are produced when the brain attempts to make sense of random neural activity that occurs during sleep.

Barbara L. Salisbury/The Washington Times/Landov

Freud theorized that dreams represent unacceptable wishes that the mind can only express in disguised form. The activation–synthesis model proposes that dreams are produced when the mind attempts to make sense of random neural activity that occurs during sleep. Suppose a man is expecting a visit from his mother-in-law; the night before her arrival, he dreams that a bus is driven through the living room window of his house. How might Freud have interpreted such a dream? How might the activation–synthesis model interpret such a dream?

realize that the strange smell in the hall outside your room must be from burned popcorn. In the dream state, the mind doesn't have access to external sensations, but it keeps on doing what it usually does: interpreting information. Because that information now comes from neural activations that occur without the continuity provided by the perception of reality, the brain's interpretive mechanisms can run free. This might be why, for example, a person in a dream can sometimes change into someone else. There is no actual person being perceived to help the mind keep a stable view. In the mind's effort to perceive and give meaning to brain activation, the person you view in a dream about a grocery store might seem to be a clerk but then change to be your favorite teacher when the dream scene moves to your school. The great interest people have in interpreting their dreams the next morning may be an extension of the interpretive activity they've been doing all night.

The Freudian theory and the activation–synthesis model differ in the significance they place on the meaning of dreams. In Freud's theory, dreams begin with meaning, whereas in the activation–synthesis model, dreams begin randomly—but meaning can be added as the mind lends interpretations in the process of dreaming. Dream research has not yet sorted out whether one of these theories or yet another might be the best account of the meaning of dreams.

The Dreaming Brain

What happens in the brain when we dream? Several fMRI studies show that the brain changes that occur during REM sleep correspond clearly with certain alterations of consciousness that occur in dreaming. **FIGURE 5.10** shows some of the patterns of activation and deactivation found in the dreaming brain (Nir & Tononi, 2010; Schwartz & Maquet, 2002). Many dreams have emotional content—minor worries, the occasional monster, and sometimes that major exam you've forgotten about until you walk into class. And as it turns out, the amygdala, which is involved in response to threatening or stressful events, is quite active during REM sleep. However, even though the typical dream is a visual wonderland, the areas of the brain responsible for visual perception are *not* activated during dreaming. Instead, the visual association areas in the occipital lobe that are responsible for visual imagery *do* show activation (Braun et al., 1998). Your brain is smart enough to realize that it's not really seeing bizarre images but acts instead as though it's imagining bizarre images. Meanwhile, the prefrontal cortex—usually associated with planning

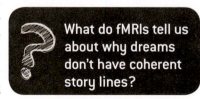

What do fMRIs tell us about why dreams don't have coherent story lines?

FIGURE 5.10 Brain Activation and Deactivation during REM Sleep Brain areas shaded red are activated during REM sleep; those shaded blue are deactivated. (a) The medial view shows activation of (starting at the top and going clockwise) the motor cortex, the visual association areas, the brain stem, and the amygdala and deactivation of the prefrontal cortex. (b) The ventral view shows activation of other visual association areas and deactivation of the prefrontal cortex (Schwartz & Maquet, 2002).

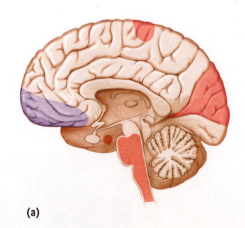
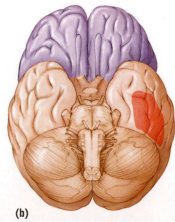

(a)　　　(b)

and executing actions—tends to show *less* activity during REM sleep than it does during waking consciousness, which may help explain why dreams often seem to be unplanned and rambling.

Another odd fact of dreaming is that while the eyes are moving rapidly, the body is otherwise very still. During REM sleep, the motor cortex is activated, but spinal neurons running through the brain stem inhibit the expression of this motor activation (Lai & Siegal, 1999). This turns out to be a useful property of brain activation in dreaming; otherwise, you might get up and act out every dream! People who are moving during sleep are probably not dreaming. The brain specifically inhibits movement during dreams, perhaps to keep us from hurting ourselves.

SUMMARY QUIZ [5.2]

1. The cycle of sleep and waking is one of the major patterns of human life called
   a. the circadian rhythm.
   b. the sleep stages.
   c. the altered state of consciousness.
   d. subliminal perception.

2. Sleep needs _____ over the life span.
   a. decrease
   b. increase
   c. fluctuate
   d. remain the same

3. Which explanation of dreams proposes that they are produced when the mind attempts to make sense of random neural activity that occurs in the brain during sleep?
   a. Freud's psychoanalytic theory
   b. the activation–synthesis model
   c. the cognitive unconscious model
   d. the manifest content framework

4. fMRI studies of the dreaming brain reveal all of the following EXCEPT
   a. increased sensitivity to emotions.
   b. activations associated with visual activity.
   c. increased capacity for planning.
   d. prevention of movement.

Drugs and Consciousness: Artificial Inspiration

The author of the dystopian novel *Brave New World*, Aldous Huxley (1932), once wrote of his experiences with the drug mescaline. *The Doors of Perception* described "a world where everything shone with the Inner Light, and was infinite in its significance. The legs, for example, of a chair—how miraculous their tubularity, how supernatural their polished smoothness! I spent several minutes—or was it several centuries?—not merely gazing at those bamboo legs, but actually *being* them" (Huxley, 1954, p. 22).

Being the legs of a chair? This probably is better than being the seat of a chair, but it still sounds like an odd experience. Still, many people seek out such experiences,

psychoactive drugs Chemicals that influence consciousness or behavior by altering the brain's chemical message system.

drug tolerance The tendency for larger doses of a drug to be required over time to achieve the same effect.

often through drug use. **Psychoactive drugs** are *chemicals that influence consciousness or behavior by altering the brain's chemical message system.* You read about several such drugs in the Neuroscience and Behavior chapter when we explored the brain's system of neurotransmitters. And you will read about them in a different light when we turn to their role in the treatment of psychological disorders in the Treatment chapter. Whether these drugs are used for entertainment, for treatment, or for other reasons, they each exert their influence by increasing the activity of a neurotransmitter (the agonists) or decreasing its activity (the antagonists). Like Huxley experiencing himself becoming the legs of a chair, people using drugs can have experiences unlike any they might find in normal waking consciousness or even in dreams. To understand these altered states, let's explore how people use and abuse drugs, and examine the major categories of psychoactive drugs.

Drug Use and Abuse

Why do children sometimes spin around until they get dizzy and fall down? There is something strangely attractive about altered states of consciousness, and people throughout history have sought out such states by dancing, fasting, chanting, meditating, and ingesting a bizarre assortment of chemicals to intoxicate themselves (Tart, 1969). People pursue altered consciousness even when there are costs—from the nausea that accompanies dizziness to the life-wrecking obsession with a drug that can come with addiction. In this regard, the pursuit of altered consciousness can be a fatal attraction.

In one study, researchers allowed rats to administer cocaine to themselves intravenously by pressing a lever (Bozarth & Wise, 1985). Over the course of the 30-day study, the rats not only continued to self-administer at a high rate but also occasionally binged to the point of giving themselves convulsions. They stopped grooming themselves and eating until they lost on average almost a third of their body weight. About 90% of the rats died by the end of the study. Other laboratory studies show that animals will work to obtain not only cocaine but also alcohol, amphetamines, barbiturates, caffeine, opiates (such as morphine and heroin), nicotine, phencyclidine (PCP), MDMA (Ecstasy), and THC (tetrahydrocannabinol, the active ingredient in marijuana). Rats are not tiny little humans, of course, so such research is not a firm basis for understanding human responses to cocaine. But these results do make it clear that cocaine is addictive and that the consequences of such addiction can be dire.

People usually do not become addicted to a psychoactive drug the first time they use it. They may experiment a few times, then try again, and eventually find that their tendency to use the drug increases over time due to several factors, including **drug tolerance,** *the tendency for larger drug doses to be required over time to achieve the same effect.* Physicians who prescribe morphine to control pain in their patients are faced with tolerance problems because steadily greater amounts of the drug may be needed to dampen the same pain. With increased tolerance comes the danger of drug overdose; recreational users find they need to use more and more of a drug to produce the same high. But then, if a new batch of heroin or cocaine is more concentrated than usual, the "normal" amount the user takes to achieve the same high can be fatal.

Self-administration of addictive drugs can also be prompted by withdrawal symptoms, which result when drug use is discontinued. Some withdrawal symptoms signal *physical dependence,* when pain, convulsions, hallucinations, or other unpleasant symptoms accompany withdrawal. A common example is the "caffeine headache" some people complain of when they haven't had their daily jolt of java. Other withdrawal symptoms result from *psychological dependence,* a strong desire to return

Matthew Nock

Why do kids enjoy spinning around until they get so dizzy that they fall down? Even from a young age, there seems to be something enjoyable about altering states of consciousness.

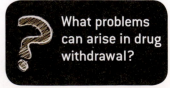

What problems can arise in drug withdrawal?

to the drug even when physical withdrawal symptoms are gone. For example, some exsmokers report longing wistfully for an after-dinner smoke even years after they've successfully quit the habit.

The psychological and social problems stemming from drug addiction are major. For many people, drug addiction becomes a way of life, and for some, it is a cause of death. But some people do overcome addictions. In one study, 64% of a sample of people who had a history of cigarette smoking had quit successfully, although many had to try again and again to achieve their success (Schachter, 1982). Indeed, large-scale studies consistently show that approximately 75% of those with substance use disorders overcome their addictions (Heyman, 2009). Although addiction is dangerous, it is not necessarily incurable.

It may not be accurate to view all recreational drug use under the umbrella of "addiction." Many people in the United States, for example, would not call the repeated use of caffeine an addiction, and some do not label the use of alcohol, tobacco, or marijuana in this way. In other times and places, however, the use of each of these drugs has been considered a terrifying addiction worthy of prohibition and public censure. In the early 17th century, for example, tobacco use was punishable by death in Germany, by castration in Russia, and by decapitation in China (Corti, 1931). Not a good time to be a smoker. By contrast, cocaine, heroin, marijuana, and amphetamines have each been popular and even recommended as medicines at several points throughout history (Inciardi, 2001). Societies react differently at different times, with some uses of drugs ignored, other uses encouraged, others simply taxed, and yet others subjected to intense prohibition (see the Real World box on p. 163). Rather than viewing *all* drug use as a problem, it is important to consider the costs and benefits of such use and to establish ways to help people choose behaviors that are informed by this knowledge (Parrott et al., 2005).

"Hi, my name is Barry, and I check my E-mail two to three hundred times a day."

David Sipress/The New Yorker Collection/Cartoonbank.com

Types of Psychoactive Drugs

Four in five North Americans use caffeine in some form every day, but not all psychoactive drugs are this familiar. To learn how both the well-known and lesser-known drugs influence the mind, let's consider several broad categories of drugs: depressants, stimulants, narcotics, hallucinogens, and marijuana. **TABLE 5.2** summarizes what is known about the potential dangers of these different types of drugs.

Depressants

Depressants are *substances that reduce the activity of the central nervous system.* Depressants have a sedative or calming effect, tend to induce sleep in high doses, and can produce both physical and psychological dependence.

The most commonly used depressant is *alcohol,* the "king of the depressants," with its worldwide use beginning in prehistory, its easy availability in most cultures, and its widespread acceptance as a socially approved substance. Fifty-two percent of Americans over 12 years of age report having had a drink in the past month, and 24% have binged on alcohol (over five drinks in succession) in that time. Young adults (ages 18–25) have even higher rates, with 62% reporting a drink the previous month and 42% reporting a binge (National Center for Health Statistics, 2012).

Alcohol's initial effects, euphoria and reduced anxiety, feel pretty positive. As it is consumed in greater quantities, drunkenness results, bringing slowed reactions, slurred speech, poor judgment, and other reductions in the effectiveness of thought

depressants Substances that reduce the activity of the central nervous system.

Table 5.2 Dangers of Drugs

Drug	Overdose (Can taking too much cause death or injury?)	Physical Dependence (Will stopping use make you sick?)	Psychological Dependence (Will you crave it when you stop using it?)
Depressants			
Alcohol	X	X	X
Benzodiazepines/Barbiturates	X	X	X
Toxic Inhalants	X	X	X
Stimulants			
Amphetamines	X	X	X
MDMA (Ecstasy)	X		?
Nicotine	X	X	X
Cocaine	X	X	X
Narcotics (opium, heroin, morphine, methadone, codeine)	X	X	X
Hallucinogens (LSD, mescaline, psilocybin, PCP, ketamine)	X		?
Marijuana		?	?

and action. The exact way in which alcohol influences neural mechanisms is still not understood, but like other depressants, alcohol increases activity of the neurotransmitter GABA (De Witte, 1996). As you read in the Neuroscience and Behavior chapter, GABA normally inhibits the transmission of neural impulses, and so one effect of alcohol is to stop the firing of other neurons. But there are many contradictions. Some people using alcohol become loud and aggressive, others become emotional and weepy, others become sullen, and still others turn giddy—and the same person can experience each of these effects in different circumstances. How can one drug do this? Two theories have been offered to account for these variable effects: *expectancy theory* and *alcohol myopia.*

Expectancy theory suggests that *alcohol effects can be produced by people's expectations of how alcohol will influence them in particular situations* (Marlatt & Rohsenow, 1980). So, for instance, if you've watched friends or family drink at weddings and notice that this often produces hilarity and gregariousness, you could well experience these effects yourself should you drink alcohol on a similarly festive occasion. Seeing people getting drunk and fighting in bars, in turn, might lead to aggression after drinking. Evidence for the expectancy theory has been obtained in studies where participants are given drinks containing alcohol or a substitute liquid. Some people in each group are led to believe they had alcohol, and others are led to believe they did not. These experiments often show that the belief that one has had alcohol can influence behavior as strongly as the ingestion of alcohol itself (Goldman, Brown, & Christiansen, 1987). You may have seen people at parties getting rowdy after only one beer—perhaps because they expected this effect rather than because the beer actually had this influence.

Another approach to the varied effects of alcohol is the theory of **alcohol myopia**, which proposes that *alcohol hampers attention, leading people to respond in simple ways to complex situations* (Steele & Josephs, 1990). This theory recognizes that life is filled with complicated pushes and pulls, and our behavior is often a balancing act.

Why do people experience being drunk differently?

expectancy theory The idea that alcohol effects can be produced by people's expectations of how alcohol will influence them in particular situations.

alcohol myopia A condition that results when alcohol hampers attention, leading people to respond in simple ways to complex situations.

Imagine that you are really attracted to someone who is dating your friend. Do you make your feelings known or focus on your friendship? The myopia theory holds that when you drink alcohol, your fine judgment is impaired. It becomes hard to appreciate the subtlety of these different options, and the inappropriate response is to veer full tilt one way or the other. So, alcohol might lead you to make a wild pass at your friend's date or perhaps just cry in your beer over your timidity—depending on which way you happened to tilt in your myopic state.

Both the expectancy and myopia theories suggest that people using alcohol will often go to extremes (Cooper, 2006). In fact, it seems that drinking is a major contributing factor to social problems that result from extreme behavior. Drinking while driving is a main cause of auto accidents. Approximately one-third of all traffic-related deaths in the U.S. involve an alcohol-impaired driver (Department of Transportation, 2012). A survey of undergraduate women revealed that alcohol contributes to approximately 76% of cases of incapacitated rape (rape after the victim is incapacitated by self-induced intoxication) and 72% of drug- or alcohol-facilitated rapes (in which the perpetrator deliberately intoxicates the victim prior to rape; McCauley et al., 2009).

Compared to alcohol, the other depressants are much less popular but still are widely used and abused. *Barbiturates* such as Seconal or Nembutal are prescribed as sleep aids and as anesthetics before surgery. *Benzodiazepines* such as Valium (diazepam) and Xanax are also called minor tranquilizers and are prescribed to treat anxiety or sleep problems. Physical dependence is possible because withdrawal from long-term use can produce severe symptoms (including convulsions), and psychological dependence is common as well. Finally, *toxic inhalants* are perhaps the most alarming substances in this category (Ridenour & Howard, 2012). These drugs are easily accessible even to children in the vapors of household products such as glue, hair spray, nail polish remover, or gasoline. Sniffing or "huffing" vapors from these products can promote temporary effects that resemble drunkenness, but overdoses can be lethal, and continued use holds the potential for permanent neurological damage (Howard et al., 2011).

Image Source/Getty Images

Which theory, expectancy theory or alcohol myopia, views a person's response to alcohol as being (at least partially) learned, through a process similar to observational learning?

Stimulants

Stimulants are *substances that excite the central nervous system, heightening arousal and activity levels.* They include caffeine, amphetamines, nicotine, and cocaine, and Ecstasy; and they sometimes have a legitimate pharmaceutical purpose. For example, *amphetamines* (also called *speed*) were originally prepared for medicinal uses and as diet drugs; however, some are widely abused, causing insomnia, aggression, and paranoia with long-term use. Stimulants increase the levels of dopamine and norepinephrine in the brain, inducing alertness and energy in the user, often producing a euphoric sense of confidence and a kind of agitated motivation to get things done. Stimulants produce physical and psychological dependence, and their withdrawal symptoms involve depressive effects such as fatigue and negative emotions.

? Do stimulants create dependence?

Ecstasy (also known as MDMA, "X," or "E") is an amphetamine derivative. Ecstasy is particularly known for making users feel empathic and close to those around them, but it has unpleasant side effects such as interfering with the regulation of body temperature, making users remain highly susceptible to heatstroke and exhaustion. Although Ecstasy is not as likely as some other drugs to cause physical or psychological dependence, it nonetheless can lead to some dependence. What's more, the impurities sometimes found in street pills are also dangerous (Parrott, 2001). Ecstasy's potentially toxic effect on serotonin neurons in the human brain is under debate,

stimulants Substances that excite the central nervous system, heightening arousal and activity levels.

narcotics (or opiates) Highly addictive drugs derived from opium that relieve pain.

although mounting evidence from animal and human studies suggests that sustained use is associated with damage to serotonergic neurons and potentially associated problems with mood, attention and memory, and impulse control (Cox et al., 2014; Urban et al., 2012).

Cocaine is derived from leaves of the coca plant, which has been cultivated by indigenous peoples of the Andes for millennia and chewed as a medication. Yes, the urban legend is true: Coca-Cola contained cocaine until 1903 and still may use coca leaves (with cocaine removed) as a flavoring—although the company's not telling (Pepsi-Cola never contained cocaine and is probably made from something brown). Sigmund Freud tried cocaine and wrote effusively about it for a while. Cocaine (usually snorted) and crack cocaine (smoked) produce exhilaration and euphoria and are seriously addictive, both for humans and the rats you read about earlier in this chapter. Withdrawal takes the form of an unpleasant crash, and dangerous side effects of cocaine use include both psychological problems such as insomnia, depression, aggression, and paranoia, as well as physical problems such as death from a heart attack or hyperthermia (Marzuk et al., 1998). Although cocaine has enjoyed popularity as a party drug, its extraordinary potential to create dependence and potentially lethal side effects should be taken very seriously.

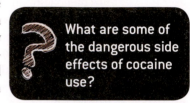
What are some of the dangerous side effects of cocaine use?

People will often endure significant inconveniences to maintain their addictions.

Smoking tobacco can be very difficult to quit. NPR reported that one interesting strategy being tried in Japan is filling ashtrays with soap and encouraging people to blow bubbles rather than smoke cigarettes.

Nicotine is something of a puzzle. This is a drug with almost nothing to recommend it to the newcomer. It usually involves inhaling smoke that doesn't smell that great, and there's not much in the way of a high either—at best, some dizziness or a queasy feeling. So why do people do it? Tobacco use is motivated far more by the unpleasantness of quitting than by the pleasantness of using. The positive effects people report from smoking—relaxation and improved concentration, for example—come chiefly from relief from withdrawal symptoms (Baker, Brandon, & Chassin, 2004). The best approach to nicotine is to never get started.

Narcotics

Opium, which comes from poppy seeds, and its derivatives heroin, morphine, methadone, and codeine (as well as prescription drugs such as Demerol and Oxycontin), are known as **narcotics** (or **opiates**), *highly addictive drugs derived from opium that relieve pain.* Narcotics induce a feeling of well-being and relaxation that is enjoyable but can also induce stupor and lethargy. The addictive properties of narcotics are powerful, and long-term use produces both tolerance and dependence. Because these drugs are often administered with hypodermic syringes, they also introduce the danger of diseases such as HIV when users share syringes. Unfortunately, these drugs are especially alluring because they mimic the brain's own internal relaxation and well-being system.

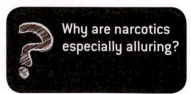
Why are narcotics especially alluring?

The brain produces endogenous opioids or endorphins, which are neurotransmitters closely related to opiates. As you learned in the Neuroscience & Behavior chapter, endorphins play a role in how the brain copes internally with pain and stress. These substances reduce the experience of pain naturally. When you exercise for a while and start to feel your muscles burning, for example, you may also find that there comes a time when the pain eases—sometimes even *during* exercise. Endorphins are secreted in the pituitary gland and other brain sites as response to injury or exertion, creating a kind of natural remedy (like the so-called runner's high) that subsequently reduces pain and increases feelings of well-being. When people use narcotics, the brain's endorphin receptors are artificially flooded, however, reducing receptor effectiveness and possibly also depressing the production of endorphins. When external administration of narcotics stops, withdrawal symptoms are likely to occur.

Hallucinogens

The drugs that produce the most extreme alterations of consciousness are the **hallucinogens**, *drugs that alter sensation and perception and that often cause visual and auditory hallucinations.* These include LSD (lysergic acid diethylamide, or acid), mescaline, psilocybin, PCP (phencyclidine), and ketamine (an animal anesthetic). Some of these drugs are derived from plants (mescaline from peyote cactus, psilocybin or "shrooms" from mushrooms) and have been used by people since ancient times. For example, the ingestion of peyote plays a prominent role in some Native American religious practices. The other hallucinogens are largely synthetic.

These drugs produce profound changes in perception. Sensations may seem unusually intense, stationary objects may seem to move or change, patterns or colors may appear, and these perceptions may be accompanied by exaggerated emotions ranging from blissful transcendence to abject terror. These are the "I've-become-the-legs-of-a-chair!" drugs. But the effects of hallucinogens are dramatic and unpredictable, creating a psychological roller-coaster ride that some people find intriguing and others find deeply disturbing. Hallucinogens are the main class of drugs that animals won't work to self-administer, so it is not surprising that in humans, these drugs are unlikely to be addictive. Hallucinogens do not induce significant tolerance or dependence, and overdose deaths are rare. Although hallucinogens still enjoy a marginal popularity with people interested in experimenting with their perceptions, they have been more a cultural trend than a dangerous attraction.

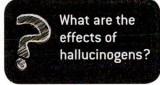
? What are the effects of hallucinogens?

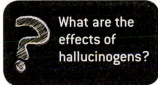
Andrew Herygers Creative/Superstock

Psychedelic art and music of the 1960s were inspired by some visual and auditory effects of drugs such as LSD.

Marijuana

Marijuana (or **cannabis**) *is a plant whose leaves and buds contain a psychoactive drug called tetrahydrocannabinol (THC).* When smoked or eaten, either as is or in concentrated form as *hashish*, this drug produces an intoxication that is mildly hallucinogenic. Users describe the experience as euphoric, with heightened senses of sight and sound and the perception of a rush of ideas. Marijuana affects judgment and short-term memory, and it impairs motor skills and coordination—making driving a car or operating heavy equipment a poor choice during its use ("Dude, where's my bulldozer?"). Researchers have found that receptors in the brain that respond to THC (Stephens, 1999) are normally activated by a neurotransmitter called *anandamide* that is naturally produced in the brain (Wiley, 1999). Anandamide is involved in the regulation of mood, memory, appetite, and pain perception and has been found temporarily to stimulate overeating in laboratory animals, much as marijuana does in humans (Williams & Kirkham, 1999). Some chemicals found in dark chocolate also mimic anandamide, although very weakly, perhaps accounting for the well-being some people claim they enjoy after a "dose" of chocolate.

The addiction potential of marijuana is not strong, as tolerance does not seem to develop, and physical withdrawal symptoms are minimal. Psychological dependence is possible, however, and some people do become chronic users. Marijuana use has been widespread around the world throughout recorded history, both as a medicine for pain

hallucinogens Drugs that alter sensation and perception and often cause visual and auditory hallucinations.

marijuana (or cannibis) The leaves and buds of the hemp plant, which contain a psychoactive drug called tetrahydrocannabinol (THC).

gateway drug A drug whose use increases the risk of the subsequent use of more harmful drugs.

and/or nausea and as a recreational drug, but its use remains controversial. Marijuana abuse and dependence have been linked with increased risk of depression, anxiety, and other forms of psychopathology. Many people also are concerned that marijuana (along with alcohol and tobacco) is a **gateway drug**, *a drug whose use increases the risk of the subsequent use of more harmful drugs*. The gateway theory has gained mixed support, with recent studies challenging this theory and suggesting that early-onset drug use in general, regardless of type of drug, increases the risk of later drug problems (Degenhardt et al., 2010). Despite the federal laws against the use of marijuana, approximately 42% of adults in the United States reported using it at some point in their lives—a rate much higher than that observed in most other countries (Degenhardt et al., 2008). Perhaps due to the perceived acceptability of marijuana among the general public, several states recently have taken steps to permit the sale of marijuana for medical purposes and decriminalize possession of marijuana (so violators pay a fine rather than go to jail). Two states, Colorado and Washington, have legalized its sale and possession for recreational purposes. The debate about the legal status of marijuana will likely take years to resolve. In the meantime, depending on where you live, the greatest risk of marijuana use may be incarceration (see The Real World: Drugs and the Regulation of Consciousness).

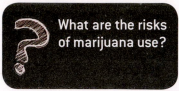

What are the risks of marijuana use?

SUMMARY QUIZ [5.3]

1. Psychoactive drugs influence consciousness by altering the effects of
   a. agonists.
   b. neurotransmitters.
   c. amphetamines.
   d. spinal neurons.

2. Tolerance for drugs involves
   a. larger doses being required over time to achieve the same effect.
   b. openness to new experiences.
   c. the initial attraction of drug use.
   d. the lessening of the painful symptoms that accompany withdrawal.

3. Drugs that heighten arousal and activity levels by affecting the central nervous system are
   a. depressants.
   b. stimulants.
   c. narcotics.
   d. hallucinogens.

4. Alcohol expectancy refers to
   a. alcohol's initial effects of euphoria and reduced anxiety.
   b. the widespread acceptance of alcohol as a socially approved substance.
   c. alcohol leading people to respond in simple ways to complex situations.
   d. people's beliefs about how alcohol will influence them in particular situations.

Drugs and the Regulation of Consciousness

Everyone has an opinion about drug use. Is consciousness something that governments should be able to legislate? Or should people be free to choose their own conscious states (McWilliams, 1993)?

Individuals and governments alike answer these questions by pointing to the costs of drug addiction, both to the addict and to the society that must "carry" unproductive people, pay for their welfare, and often even take care of their children. Drug users appear to be troublemakers and criminals, the culprits behind all those drug-related shootings, knifings, and robberies. Widespread anger about the drug problem surfaced in the form of the War on Drugs, a federal government program born in the 1970s that attempted to stop drug use through the imprisonment of users.

Drug use did not stop, though, and instead, prisons filled with people arrested for drug use. From 1990 to 2007, the number of drug offenders in state and federal prisons increased from 179,070 to 348,736—a jump of 94% (Bureau of Justice Statistics, 2008)—not because of a measurable increase in drug use, but because of the rapidly increasing use of imprisonment for drug offenses. The drug war seemed to be causing more harm than it was preventing.

What can be done? The policy of the Obama administration is to wind down the war mentality and instead focus on reducing the harm that drugs cause (Fields, 2009). This *harm reduction approach* focuses on reducing the harm that high-risk behaviors have on people's lives (Marlatt & Witkiewitz, 2010). Harm reduction originated in the Netherlands and England with tactics such as eliminating criminal penalties for some drug use or providing intravenous drug users with sterile syringes to help them avoid contracting HIV and other infections from shared needles (Des Jarlais et al., 2009). A harm reduction idea for alcoholics, in turn, is not to condemn drinking behavior but to allow moderate drinking while minimizing the harmful effects of heavy drinking (Marlatt & Witkiewitz, 2010). Harm reduction strategies do not always find public support because they challenge the popular idea that the solution to drug and alcohol problems must always be prohibition: stopping use entirely.

There are many reasons for the overcrowding in U.S. prisons—this country has the highest incarceration rate in the world. Treating drug abuse as a crime that requires imprisonment is one of the reasons.

There appears to be increasing support for the idea that people should be free to decide whether they want to use substances to alter their consciousness, especially when use of the substance carries a medical benefit, such as decreased nausea, decreased insomnia, and increased appetite. Since 1996, 21 states and the District of Columbia have enacted laws to legalize the use of marijuana for medical purposes. On November 6, 2012, Colorado and Washington became the first two states to legalize marijuana for purely recreational purposes. The fact that marijuana is still illegal under federal law complicates matters, and it may take years before the legal issues are fully resolved. Indeed, upon learning of the passing of the legalization initiative, Colorado governor John Hickenlooper warned citizens of Colorado: "Federal law still says marijuana is an illegal drug so don't break out the Cheetos or Goldfish too quickly" (Weiner, 2012).

In the Netherlands, marijuana use is not prosecuted. The drug is sold in "coffee shops" to those over 18.

Hypnosis: Open to Suggestion

When you think of hypnosis, you may envision people completely under the power of a hypnotist, who is ordering them to dance like a chicken or perhaps "regress" to early childhood and talk in childlike voices. Many common beliefs about hypnosis are false. **Hypnosis** refers to *a social interaction in which one person (the hypnotist) makes suggestions that lead to a change in another person's (the subject's) subjective experience of the world* (Kirsch et al., 2011). The essence of hypnosis is in leading people to expect that certain things will happen to them that are outside their conscious will (Wegner, 2002).

Induction and Susceptibility

To induce hypnosis, a hypnotist may ask the person to be hypnotized to sit quietly and focus on some item, such as a spot on the wall (or a swinging pocket watch), and then make suggestions to the person about what effects hypnosis will have (e.g., "your eyelids are slowly closing" or "your arms are getting heavy"). Even without hypnosis, some suggested behaviors might commonly happen just because a person is concentrating on them—just thinking about their eyelids slowly closing, for instance, may make many people shut their eyes briefly or at least blink. In hypnosis, however, suggestions may be made—and followed by people in a susceptible state of mind—for very unusual behavior that most people would not normally do, such as flapping their arms and making loud clucking sounds.

Not everyone is equally hypnotizable. Susceptibility varies greatly. Some highly suggestible people are very easily hypnotized, most people are only moderately influenced, and some people are entirely unaffected by attempts at hypnosis. One of the best indicators of a person's susceptibility is the person's own judgment. So, if you think you might be hypnotizable, you may well be (Hilgard, 1965). People with active, vivid imaginations or people who are easily absorbed in activities such as watching a movie are also somewhat more prone to be good candidates for hypnosis (Sheehan, 1979; Tellegen & Atkinson, 1974).

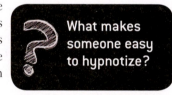

What makes someone easy to hypnotize?

Hypnotic Effects

From watching stage hypnotism, you might think that the major effect of hypnosis is making people do peculiar things. So what do we actually know to be true about hypnosis? There are some impressive demonstrations that suggest real changes occur in those under hypnosis. At the 1849 festivities for Prince Albert of England's birthday, for example, a hypnotized guest was asked to ignore any loud noises and then didn't even flinch when a pistol was fired near his face. Other stage hypnotists claim that their volunteers can perform feats of superhuman strength under hypnosis, such as becoming "stiff as a board" and lying unsupported with shoulders on one chair and feet on another while the hypnotist stands on the hypnotized person's body.

Studies have demonstrated that hypnosis can undermine memory, but with important limitations. People susceptible to hypnosis can be led to experience **posthypnotic amnesia**, *the failure to retrieve memories following hypnotic suggestions to forget.* Ernest Hilgard (1986) taught a hypnotized person the populations of some remote cities, for example, and then suggested that the participant forget the study session; the person was quite surprised after the session at being able to give the census figures correctly. Asked how he knew the answers, the individual decided he might have learned them from a TV program. Such amnesia can then be reversed in subsequent hypnosis.

Importantly, research has found that only memories that were lost under hypnosis can be retrieved through hypnosis. The false claim that hypnosis helps people

hypnosis A social interaction in which one person (the hypnotist) makes suggestions that lead to a change in another person's (the subject's) subjective experience of the world.

posthypnotic amnesia The failure to retrieve memories following hypnotic suggestions to forget.

to unearth memories that they are not able to retrieve in normal consciousness seems to have surfaced because hypnotized people often make up memories to satisfy the hypnotist's suggestions. For example, Paul Ingram, a sheriff's deputy accused of sexual abuse by his daughters in the 1980s, was asked by interrogators in session after session to relax and imagine having committed the crimes. He emerged from these sessions having confessed to dozens of horrendous acts of "satanic ritual abuse." These confessions were called into question, however, when independent investigator Richard Ofshe used the same technique to ask Ingram about a crime that Ofshe had simply made up out of thin air, something of which Ingram had never been accused. Ingram produced a three-page handwritten confession, complete with dialogue (Ofshe, 1992). Still, prosecutors in the case accepted Ingram's guilty plea, and he was only released in 2003 after a public outcry and years of work on his defense. After a person claims to remember something, even under hypnosis, it is difficult to convince others that the memory was false (Loftus & Ketchum, 1994).

Hypnosis can lead to measurable physical and behavioral changes in the body. One well-established effect is **hypnotic analgesia**, *the reduction of pain through hypnosis in people who are susceptible to hypnosis.* For example, one study (see **FIGURE 5.11**) found that for pain induced in volunteers in the laboratory, hypnosis was more effective than morphine, diazepam (Valium), aspirin, acupuncture, or placebos (Stern et al., 1977). For people who are hypnotically susceptible, hypnosis can be used to control pain in surgeries and dental procedures, in some cases more effectively than any form of anesthesia (Druckman & Bjork, 1994; Kihlstrom, 1985).

Hypnosis also has been shown to enable people to control mental processes previously believed to be beyond conscious control. For instance, the Stroop task (Stroop, 1935) is a classic psychological test in which a person is asked to name the color

Stage hypnotists often perform an induction on the whole audience and then bring some of the more susceptible members on stage for further demonstrations.

hypnotic analgesia The reduction of pain through hypnosis in people who are susceptible to hypnosis.

> **What evidence supports the idea that hypnosis leads to observable changes in the body?**

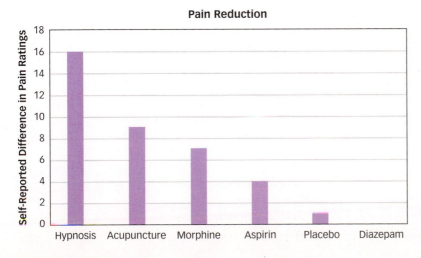

Pain Reduction

FIGURE 5.11 **Hypnotic Analgesia** The graph shows the degree of pain reduction reported by people using different techniques for the treatment of laboratory-induced pain. Hypnosis wins. (Data from Stern et al., 1977.)

Other Voices

A Judge's Plea for Pot

The Honorable Gustin L. Reichbach served as a New York State Supreme Court Justice from 1999 until 2012. He died of pancreatic cancer in July 2012.

Photo © Rick Kopstein

Should all drugs be illegal? Where should we draw the line between acceptable chemical alteration of one's own consciousness and criminal or pathological behavior? Let's take a specific example—think for a minute about where you stand on the legalization of marijuana. The Honorable Gustin L. Reichbach (2012, p. A27), a New York State Supreme Court Justice, wrote a strongly worded piece (slightly condensed here) on this issue, although his position surprised many people.

Three and a half years ago, on my 62nd birthday, doctors discovered a mass on my pancreas. It turned out to be Stage 3 pancreatic cancer. I was told I would be dead in four to six months. Today I am in that rare coterie of people who have survived this long with the disease. But I did not foresee that after having dedicated myself for 40 years to a life of the law, including more than two decades as a New York State judge, my quest for ameliorative and palliative care would lead me to marijuana.

My survival has demanded an enormous price, including months of chemotherapy, radiation hell and brutal surgery. For about a year, my cancer disappeared, only to return. About a month ago, I started a new and even more debilitating course of treatment. Every other week, after receiving an IV booster of chemotherapy drugs that takes three hours, I wear a pump that slowly injects more of the drugs over the next 48 hours.

Nausea and pain are constant companions. One struggles to eat enough to stave off the dramatic weight loss that is part of this disease. Eating, one of the great pleasures of life, has now become a daily battle, with each forkful a small victory. Every drug prescribed to treat one problem leads to one or two more drugs to offset its side effects. Pain medication leads to loss of appetite and constipation. Anti-nausea medication raises glucose levels, a serious problem for me with my pancreas so compromised. Sleep, which might bring respite from the miseries of the day, becomes increasingly elusive.

Inhaled marijuana is the only medicine that gives me some relief from nausea, stimulates my appetite, and makes it easier to fall asleep. The oral synthetic substitute, Marinol, prescribed by my doctors, was useless. Rather than watch the agony of my suffering, friends have chosen, at some personal risk, to provide the substance. I find a few puffs of marijuana before dinner gives me ammunition in the battle to eat. A few more puffs at bedtime permits desperately needed sleep.

This is not a law-and-order issue; it is a medical and a human rights issue. Being treated at Memorial Sloan Kettering Cancer Center, I am receiving the absolute gold standard of medical care. But doctors cannot be expected to do what the law prohibits, even when they know it is in the best interests of their patients. When palliative care is understood as a fundamental human and medical right, marijuana for medical use should be beyond controversy. . . .

Cancer is a nonpartisan disease, so ubiquitous that it's impossible to imagine that there are legislators whose families have not also been touched by this scourge. It is to help all who have been affected by cancer, and those who will come after, that I now speak. Given my position as a sitting judge still hearing cases, well-meaning friends question the wisdom of my coming out on this issue. But I recognize that fellow cancer sufferers may be unable, for a host of reasons, to give voice to our plight. It is another heartbreaking aporia in the world of cancer that the one drug that gives relief without deleterious side effects remains classified as a narcotic with no medicinal value.

Because criminalizing an effective medical technique affects the fair administration of justice, I feel obliged to speak out as both a judge and a cancer patient suffering with a fatal disease. . . . Medical science has not yet found a cure, but it is barbaric to deny us access to one substance that has proved to ameliorate our suffering.

How should we decide which consciousness-altering substances are OK for members of our society to use, and which should be made illegal? What criteria would you propose? Should this decision be based on negative health consequences associated with use of the substance? What weight should be given to positive consequences, such as those described by Justice Reichbach? Research described in this chapter tested—and failed to support—the gateway theory of drug use. If you had the opportunity to design and conduct one study to answer a key question in this area, what would you do?

of words on a page (appearing in ink that is red, blue, green, etc.). This is a simple task. However, sometimes the words themselves are the names of colors, but they are printed in a different color of the ink. It turns out that people are significantly slower and make more errors, when naming ink colors that don't match the content of the word (e.g., when the word "green" is written in red ink) than if the content is neutral or congruent (e.g., if the word "desk" or "red" is written in red ink). This effect is present no matter how hard we try. Amazingly, the effect is completely eliminated when highly suggestible people are hypnotized and told to respond to all words the same way (Raz et al., 2002). Importantly, though, follow-up studies have revealed that hypnotic induction is not required to eliminate the Stroop effect. It turns out that simply

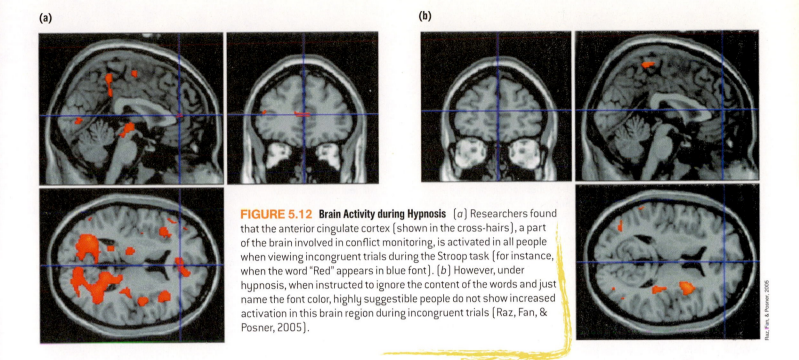

(a) (b)

FIGURE 5.12 Brain Activity during Hypnosis (*a*) Researchers found that the anterior cingulate cortex (shown in the cross-hairs), a part of the brain involved in conflict monitoring, is activated in all people when viewing incongruent trials during the Stroop task (for instance, when the word "Red" appears in blue font). (*b*) However, under hypnosis, when instructed to ignore the content of the words and just name the font color, highly suggestible people do not show increased activation in this brain region during incongruent trials (Raz, Fan, & Posner, 2005).

Raz, Fan, & Posner, 2005

suggesting to highly suggestible people that they should respond to all words the same has the same effect as hypnosis (Lifshitz et al., 2013). This suggests that hypnotic effects may be the result of highly suggestible people complying with the suggestions of others.

Nevertheless, people under hypnotic suggestion are not merely telling the hypnotist what the hypnotist wants to hear. Instead, they seem to be experiencing what they have been asked to experience. Under hypnotic suggestion, for example, regions of the brain responsible for color vision are activated in highly hypnotizable people when they are asked to perceive color, even when they are really shown gray stimuli (Kosslyn et al., 2000). While engaged in the Stroop task, people who can eliminate the Stroop effect under suggestion show decreased activity in the anterior cingulate cortex (ACC), the part of the brain involved in conflict monitoring (**FIGURE 5.12**; Raz, Fan, & Posner, 2005), consistent with the lack of conflict perceived between the color name and ink. Overall, hypnotic suggestion appears to change the subjective perception of those experiencing it, as reflected by changes in their self-report, behavior, and brain activity.

SUMMARY QUIZ [5.4]

1. Hypnosis has been proven to have
   a. an effect on physical strength.
   b. a positive effect on memory retrieval.
   c. an analgesic effect.
   d. an age-regression effect.

2. Which of the following four individuals is LEAST likely to be a good candidate for hypnosis?
   a. Jake, who spends lots of time watching movies
   b. Ava, who is convinced she is easily hypnotizable
   c. Evan, who has an active, vivid imagination
   d. Isabel, who loves to play sports

CHAPTER REVIEW

SUMMARY

Conscious and Unconscious: The Mind's Eye, Open and Closed

> Consciousness is a mystery of psychology because other people's minds cannot be perceived directly and because the relationship between mind and body is perplexing.

> Consciousness has four basic properties: intentionality, unity, selectivity, and transience. It can also be understood in terms of three levels: minimal consciousness, full consciousness, and self-consciousness.

> Conscious contents can include current concerns, daydreams, and unwanted thoughts.

> The cognitive unconscious is at work when subliminal perception and unconscious decision processes influence thought or behavior without the person's awareness.

Sleep and Dreaming: Good Night, Mind

> During a night's sleep, the brain passes in and out of five stages of sleep; most dreaming occurs in the REM sleep stage.

> Sleep needs decrease over the life span, but being deprived of sleep and dreams has psychological and physical costs.

> Sleep can be disrupted through disorders that include insomnia, sleep apnea, somnambulism, narcolepsy, sleep paralysis, and night terrors.

> fMRI studies of the brain in dreaming reveal increased activity in brain areas associated with visual imagery and emotions such as fear, and decreased activity in brain areas associated with planning and in suppression of movement.

Drugs and Consciousness: Artificial Inspiration

> Psychoactive drugs influence consciousness by altering the effects of neurotransmitters.

> Drug tolerance can result in overdose, and physical and psychological dependence can lead to addiction.

> Major types of psychoactive drugs include depressants, stimulants, narcotics, hallucinogens, and marijuana.

> The varying effects of alcohol, a depressant, are explained by theories of alcohol expectancy and alcohol myopia.

Hypnosis: Open to Suggestion

> Hypnosis is an altered state of consciousness characterized by suggestibility.

> Although many claims for hypnosis overstate its effects, hypnosis can create the experience that one's actions are occurring involuntarily, create analgesia, and even change brain activations in ways that suggest that hypnotic experiences are more than imagination.

KEY TERMS

consciousness (p. 136)
phenomenology (p. 136)
problem of other minds (p. 136)
mind–body problem (p. 138)
cocktail-party phenomenon (p. 140)
dichotic listening (p. 140)
minimal consciousness (p. 140)
full consciousness (p. 140)
self-consciousness (p. 141)
mental control (p. 143)
thought suppression (p. 143)

rebound effect of thought suppression (p. 143)
ironic processes of mental control (p. 144)
dynamic unconscious (p. 144)
repression (p. 144)
cognitive unconscious (p. 145)
subliminal perception (p. 145)
altered state of consciousness (p. 146)
circadian rhythm (p. 147)
REM sleep (p. 147)

insomnia (p. 150)
sleep apnea (p. 151)
somnambulism (or sleepwalking) (p. 151)
narcolepsy (p. 151)
sleep paralysis (p. 151)
night terrors (or sleep terrors) (p. 152)
activation–synthesis model (p. 153)
psychoactive drugs (p. 156)
drug tolerance (p. 156)

depressants (p. 157)
expectancy theory (p. 158)
alcohol myopia (p. 158)
stimulants (p. 159)
narcotics (or opiates) (p. 160)
hallucinogens (p. 161)
marijuana (or cannabis) (p. 161)
gateway drug (p. 162)
hypnosis (p. 164)
posthypnotic amnesia (p. 164)
hypnotic analgesia (p. 165)

CHANGING MINDS

1. "I had a really weird dream last night," your friend tells you. "I dreamed that I was trying to fly like a bird but I kept flying into clotheslines. I looked it up online, and dreams where you're struggling to fly mean that there is someone in your life who's standing in your way and preventing you from moving forward. I suppose that has to be my boyfriend, so maybe I'd better break up with him."

Based on what you've read in this chapter, what would you tell your friend about the reliability of dream interpretation?

2. During an early-morning class, you notice your friend yawning, and you ask if he slept well the night before. "On weekdays, I'm in class all day, and I work the night shift," he says. "So I don't sleep much during the week. But I figure it's okay because I make up for it by

sleeping in late on Saturday mornings." Is it realistic for your friend to assume that he can balance regular sleep deprivation with re-bound sleep on the weekends?

3. You and a friend are watching the 2010 movie *Inception*, starring Leonardo DiCaprio as a corporate spy. DiCaprio's character is hired by a businessman named Saito to plant an idea in the unconscious mind of a competitor while he sleeps. According to the plan, when the competitor awakens, he'll be compelled to act on the idea, to the secret benefit of Saito's company. "It's a cool idea," your friend says, "but it's pure science fiction. There's no such thing as an unconscious mind, and no way that unconscious ideas could influence the way you act when you're conscious." What would you tell your friend? What evidence do we have that the unconscious mind exists and can influence conscious behavior?

ANSWERS TO SUMMARY QUIZZES

Summary Quiz 5.1: 1. b; 2. d; 3. d
Summary Quiz 5.2: 1. a; 2. a; 3. b; 4. c
Summary Quiz 5.3: 1. b; 2. a; 3. b; 4. d
Summary Quiz 5.4: 1. c; 2. d

WWW

Need more help? Additional resources are located in LaunchPad at:
http://www.worthpublishers.com/launchpad/schacterbrief3e

6

Memory

JILL PRICE WAS 12 YEARS OLD WHEN SHE BEGAN TO SUSPECT THAT SHE POSSESSED AN UNUSUALLY GOOD MEMORY. Studying for a science test on May 30th, her mind drifted and she became aware that she could recall vividly everything she had been doing on May 30th of the previous year.

Remembering specifics of events that occurred a year ago may not seem so extraordinary—you can probably recall what you did for your last birthday or where you spent last Thanksgiving—but can you recall the details of what you did exactly 1 year ago today? Probably not, but Jill Price can.

Now turning 50, Jill can recall clearly and in great detail what has happened to her *every single day since early 1980* (Price & Davis, 2008). This is not just Jill's subjective impression. Memory researchers tested Jill's memory over a period of a few years and came up with some shocking results (Parker, Cahill, & McGaugh, 2006). For example, they asked Jill to recall the dates of each Easter from 1980 to 2003, which is a pretty tough task considering that Easter can fall on any day between March 22nd and April 15th. Nobody else the researchers tested came close. The researchers also asked Jill about the details of what she had been doing on various randomly chosen dates, and they checked Jill's recall against her personal diary. Again, Jill answered quickly and accurately: *July 1, 1986?*—"Tuesday. Went with (friend's name) to (restaurant name)." *October 3, 1987?*—"That was a Saturday. Hung out at the apartment all weekend, wearing a sling—hurt my elbow" (Parker et al., 2006, pp. 39–40).

Jill's memory is a gift we'd all love to have—right? Not necessarily. Here's what Jill has to say about her ability: "Most have called it a gift but I call it a burden. I run my entire life through my head every day and it drives me crazy!!!" (Parker et al., 2006, p. 35).

Jill Price can accurately remember just about everything that has happened to her during the past 35 years, as confirmed by her diary, but Jill's extraordinary memory is more of a curse than a blessing.

Dan Tuffs/Contributor; Getty Images

memory The ability to store and retrieve information over time.

encoding The process of transforming what we perceive, think, or feel into an enduring memory.

storage The process of maintaining information in memory over time.

retrieval The process of bringing to mind information that has been previously encoded and stored.

MEMORY *IS THE ABILITY TO STORE AND RETRIEVE INFORMATION OVER TIME.* Each of us has a unique identity that is intricately tied to the things we have thought, felt, done, and experienced. Memories are the residue of those events, the enduring changes that experience makes in our brains. If an experience passes without leaving a trace, it might just as well not have happened. But as Jill's story suggests, remembering all that has happened is not necessarily a good thing, either—a point we'll explore more fully later in the chapter.

The ease with which someone like Jill can remember her past shouldn't blind us from appreciating how complex that act of remembering really is. Because memory is so remarkably complex, it is also remarkably fragile (Schacter, 1996). We all have had the experience of forgetting something we desperately wanted to remember. Why does memory serve us so well in some situations and play such cruel tricks on us in other cases?

As you've seen in other chapters, the mind's mistakes provide key insights into its fundamental operation, and there is no better illustration of this than in the realm of memory. In this chapter, we will consider the three key functions of memory: **encoding**, *the process of transforming what we perceive, think, or feel into an enduring memory;* **storage**, *the process of maintaining information in memory over time;* and **retrieval**, *the process of bringing to mind information that has been previously encoded and stored.* We'll then examine several different kinds of memory and focus on the ways in which errors, distortions, and imperfections can reveal the nature of memory itself.

Encoding: Transforming Perceptions into Memories

Bubbles P., a professional gambler with no formal education, who spent most of his time shooting craps at local clubs or playing high-stakes poker, had no difficulty rattling off 20 numbers, in either forward or backward order, after just a single glance (Ceci, DeSimone, & Johnson, 1992). Most people can listen to a list of numbers and then repeat them from memory—as long as the list is no more than about seven items long (try it for yourself using **FIGURE 6.1**).

How did Bubbles accomplish his astounding feats of memory? For at least 2,000 years, people have thought of memory as a recording device that makes exact copies of information that comes in through our senses, after which it then stores those copies for later use. This idea is simple and intuitive. It is also completely incorrect. Memories are made by combining information we *already* have in our brains with new information that comes in through our senses. Memories are *constructed,* not recorded, and encoding is the process by which we transform what we perceive, think, or feel into an enduring memory. Let's look at three types of encoding processes—**semantic encoding, visual imagery encoding,** and **organizational encoding**—and then consider the possible survival value of encoding for our ancestors.

Semantic Encoding

Memories are a combination of old and new information, so the nature of any particular memory depends as much on the old information already in our memories as it does on the new information coming in through our senses. In other words, how we remember something depends on how we think about it at the time. For example, as a professional gambler, Bubbles found numbers unusually meaningful, so when he saw a string of digits, he tended to think about their meanings. To memorize the string 22061823, Bubbles would think about betting $220 at 6-to-1 odds on horse number 8 to place 2nd in the 3rd race. Indeed, when Bubbles was tested with materials

FIGURE 6.1 Digit Memory Test How many digits can you remember? Start on the first row and cover the rows below it with a piece of paper. Study the numbers in the row for 1 second, and then cover that row back up again. After a couple of seconds, try to repeat the numbers. Were you correct? If so, continue down to each row in turn until you can't recall all the numbers in a row. The number of digits in the last row you can remember correctly is your digit span. Bubbles P. could remember 20 random numbers. How did you do?

28
691
0473
87454
902481
5742296
64719304
356718485
1028834729
47208274264
731093435138

other than numbers—faces, words, objects, or locations—his memory performance was no better than average.

In one study, researchers presented participants with a series of words and asked them to make one of three types of judgments (Craik & Tulving, 1975): *semantic judgments* required the participants to think about the meaning of the words (Is *hat* a type of clothing?); *rhyme judgments* required the participants to think about the sound of the words (Does *hat* rhyme with *cat*?); and *visual judgments* required the partici- pants to think about the appearance of the words (Is *HAT* writ- ten uppercase or lowercase?). The type of judgment task had a powerful impact on the participants' memories. Those partici- pants who made semantic judgments (i.e., had thought about the meaning of the words) had much better memory

> **Which is most effective, semantic, rhyme, or visual judgment, and why?**

for the words than did participants who thought about how the word looked or sounded. The re- sults of these and many other studies have shown that long-term retention is greatly enhanced by **semantic encoding,** *the process of relating new information in a meaningful way to knowledge that is already stored in memory* (Brown & Craik, 2000).

So what's going on in the brain when this type of information processing occurs? Studies reveal that semantic encoding is uniquely associated with increased activity in the lower left part of the frontal lobe and the inner part of the left temporal lobe (**FIGURE 6.2a**; Demb et al., 1995; Kapur et al., 1994; Wagner et al., 1998). In fact, the amount of activity in each of these two regions during encoding is directly related to whether people later remember an item. The more activity there is in these areas, the more likely the person will remember the information.

Visual Imagery Encoding

In Ancient Athens, the poet Simonides had just left a banquet when the ceiling col- lapsed and killed all the people inside. Simonides was able to name every one of the dead simply by visualizing each chair around the banquet table and recalling the person who had been sitting there. Simonides wasn't the first to use ***visual imagery encoding,*** *the process of storing new information by converting it into mental pictures—* but he was among the most proficient.

If you wanted to use Simonides' method to create an enduring memory, you could simply convert the information that you wanted to remember into a visual image and then store it in a familiar location. For instance, if you were going to the grocery store

Have you ever wondered why you can remember 20 experiences (your favorite camping trip, your 16th birthday party, your first day at college, etc.) but not 20 digits? One reason is that we often think about the meaning behind our experiences, so we semantically encode them without even trying (Craik & Tulving, 1975).

semantic encoding The process of relating new information in a meaningful way to knowledge that is already in memory.

FIGURE 6.2 Brain Activity during Different Types of Judgments fMRI studies reveal that different parts of the brain are active during different types of judgments: (a) During semantic judgments, the lower left frontal lobe is active; (b) during visual judgments, the occipital lobe is active; and (c) during organizational judgments, the upper left frontal lobe is active.

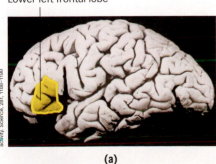

Lower left frontal lobe

(a)

Occipital lobe

(b)

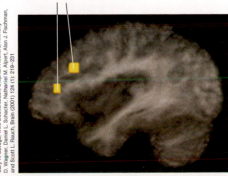

Upper left frontal lobe

(c)

Semantic encoding involves relating new information in a meaningful way to facts you already know; visual imagery encoding involves storing new information by converting it into mental pictures. How might you use both kinds of encoding to help store a new fact, such as the date of a friend's birthday that falls on, say, November 24th?

DATA VISUALIZATION

Gender Differences in Location Memory
www.macmillanhighered.com/schacterbrief3e

Ever wonder how a server remembers who ordered the pizza and who ordered the fries without writing anything down? Some have figured out how to use organizational encoding.

and wanted to remember to buy Coke, popcorn, and cheese dip, you could use the rooms in your house as locations and imagine your living room flooded in Coke, your bedroom pillows stuffed with popcorn, and your bathtub as a greasy pond of cheese dip. When you arrived at the store, you could then take a mental walk around your house and "look" into each room to remember the items you needed to purchase.

Numerous experiments have shown that visual imagery encoding can substantially improve memory. In one experiment, participants who studied lists of words by creating visual images of them later recalled twice as many items as participants who just mentally repeated the words (Schnorr & Atkinson, 1969). Why does visual imagery encoding work so well? First, visual imagery encoding does some of the same things that semantic encoding does: When you create a visual image, you relate incoming information to knowledge already in memory. For example, a visual image of a parked car might help you create a link to your memory of your first kiss.

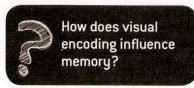

How does visual encoding influence memory?

Second, when you use visual imagery to encode words and other verbal information, you end up with two different mental *placeholders* for the items—a visual one and a verbal one—which gives you more ways to remember them than just a verbal placeholder alone (Paivio, 1971, 1986). Visual imagery encoding activates visual processing regions in the occipital lobe (see **FIGURE 6.2b**), which suggests that people actually enlist the visual system when forming memories based on mental images (Kosslyn et al., 1993).

Organizational Encoding

Have you ever ordered dinner with a group of friends and watched in amazement as your server took the order without writing anything down? To find out how this is done, one researcher spent 3 months working in a restaurant (Stevens, 1988). The researcher wired the servers with microphones and asked them to think aloud as they walked around all day doing their jobs. The researcher found that as soon as the server left a customer's table, he or she immediately began *grouping* or *categorizing* the orders into hot drinks, cold drinks, hot foods, and cold foods. The servers grouped the items into a sequence that matched the layout of the kitchen, first placing drink orders, then hot food orders, and finally cold food orders. The servers remembered their orders by relying on **organizational encoding,** *the process of categorizing information according to the relationships among a series of items.*

For example, suppose you had to memorize the words *peach, cow, chair, apple, table, cherry, lion, couch, horse, desk.* The task seems difficult, but if you organize the items into three categories—fruit (*peach, apple, cherry*), animals (*cow, lion, horse*), and furniture (*chair, table, couch, desk*)—the task becomes much easier. Studies have shown that instructing people to sort items into categories like this is an effective way to enhance their subsequent recall of those items (Mandler, 1967). Even more complex organizational schemes have been used, such as the hierarchy in **FIGURE 6.3** (Bower et al., 1969). People can improve their recall of individual items by organizing them into multiple-level categories, all the way from a general category such as *animals*, through intermediate categories such as *birds* and *songbirds*, down to specific examples such as *wren* and *sparrow*.

Just as semantic and visual imagery encoding activates distinct regions of the brain, so, too, does organizational encoding. As you can see in **FIGURE 6.2c**, organizational encoding activates

Why might mentally organizing the material for an exam enhance your retrieval of that material?

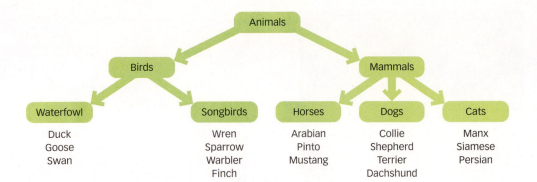

FIGURE 6.3 **Organizing Words into a Hierarchy** Organizing words into conceptual groups and relating them to one another—such as in this example of a hierarchy—makes it easier to reconstruct the items from memory later [Bower et al., 1969]. Keeping track of the 17 items in this example can be facilitated by remembering the hierarchical groupings they fall under.

the upper surface of the left frontal lobe (Fletcher, Shallice, & Dolan, 1998; Savage et al., 2001). Different types of encoding strategies appear to rely on different areas of brain activation.

Encoding of Survival-Related Information

Encoding new information is critical to many aspects of everyday life—prospects for attaining your degree would be pretty slim without this ability—and the survival of our ancestors likely depended on encoding and later remembering such things as the sources of food and water or where a predator appeared (Nairne & Pandeirada, 2008; Sherry & Schacter, 1987).

Recent experiments have addressed these ideas by examining encoding of survival-related information. The experiments were motivated by an evolutionary perspective based on Darwin's principle of natural selection: The features of an organism that help it survive and reproduce are more likely than other features to be passed on to subsequent generations (see the Psychology: Evolution of a Science chapter). Therefore, memory mechanisms that help us to survive and reproduce should be preserved by natural selection, and our memory systems should be built in a way that allows us to remember well-encoded information that is relevant to our survival.

To test this idea, some researchers gave participants three different encoding tasks (Nairne, Thompson, & Pandeirada, 2007). In the survival-encoding condition, participants were asked to imagine that they were stranded in the grasslands of a foreign land without any survival materials and that over the next few months, they would need supplies of food and water and also need to protect themselves from predators. The researchers then showed participants randomly chosen words (e.g., *stone, meadow, chair*) and asked them to rate on a 1–5 scale how relevant each item would be to survival in the hypothetical situation. In the moving-encoding condition, a second group of participants was asked to imagine that they were planning to move to a new home in a foreign land and to rate on a 1–5 scale how useful each item might be in helping them to set up a new home. Finally, in the pleasantness-encoding condition, a third group was shown the same words and asked to rate on a 1–5 scale the pleasantness of each word. The findings, displayed in **FIGURE 6.4**, show that participants recalled more words after the survival-encoding task than after either the moving or pleasantness tasks. Exactly what about survival encoding produces such high levels of memory?

Survival encoding draws on elements of semantic, visual imagery, and organizational encoding, which may give it an advantage over any one of the other three (Burns, Hwang, & Burns, 2011). Also, survival encoding encourages participants to engage in extensive planning, which in turn benefits memory and may account for much of the benefit of survival encoding. Of course, planning for the future is itself critical for our long-term survival, so these findings are broadly consistent with an evolutionary perspective in which memory is built to support planning and related forms of thinking about the future that enhance our chances of survival (Klein, Robertson, & Delton, 2011; Schacter, 2012; Suddendorf & Corballis, 2007).

FIGURE 6.4 **Survival Encoding Enhances Later Recall** What does a pouncing cougar that may threaten our survival have to do with recall? People recall more words after survival encoding . (Data from Nairne et al., 2007.)

Don Johnston/All Canada Photos/Getty Images

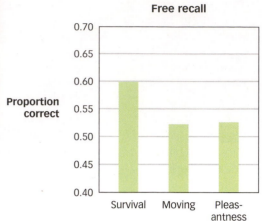

SUMMARY QUIZ [6.1]

1. Encoding is the process
   a. by which we transform what we perceive, think, or feel into an enduring memory.
   b. of maintaining information in memory over time.
   c. of bringing to mind information that has been previously stored.
   d. through which we recall information previously learned but forgotten.

2. What is the process of relating new information in a meaningful way to knowledge that is already in memory?
   a. spontaneous encoding
   b. organizational encoding
   c. semantic encoding
   d. visual imagery encoding

3. Our human ancestors depended on the encoding of
   a. organizational information.
   b. reproductive mechanisms.
   c. survival-related information.
   d. pleasantness conditions.

Storage: Maintaining Memories over Time

Encoding is the process of turning perceptions into memories; *storage is the process of maintaining information in memory over time*. There are three major kinds of memory storage: sensory, short-term, and long-term. As these names suggest, the three kinds of storage are distinguished primarily by the amount of time over which a memory is retained.

Sensory Storage

Sensory memory is *a type of storage that holds sensory information for a few seconds or less*. In a classic study, participants viewed three rows of four letters each, as shown in **FIGURE 6.5**. The researcher flashed the letters on a screen for just 1/20th of a second. When asked to remember all 12 of the letters they had just seen, participants recalled fewer than half (Sperling, 1960). There were two possible explanations for this: Either people simply couldn't encode all the letters in such a brief period of time, or they had encoded the letters but forgot them faster than they could recall them all.

To test the two ideas, the researcher relied on a clever trick. Just after the letters disappeared from the screen, a tone sounded that cued the participants to report the letters in a particular row. A *high* tone cued participants to report the contents of the top row, a *medium* tone cued participants to report the contents of the middle row, and a *low* tone cued participants to report the contents of the bottom row. When asked to report only a single row, people recalled almost all of the letters in that row! Because the tone sounded after the letters disappeared from the screen and because participants had no way of knowing which of the three rows would be cued, the researcher inferred that virtually all the letters had been encoded. In fact, if the tone was substantially delayed, participants couldn't perform the task because the information had slipped away from their sensory memories. Like the after image of a flashlight, the 12 letters flashed on a screen are visual icons, a lingering trace stored in memory for a very short period.

Because we have more than one sense, we have more than one kind of sensory memory. **Iconic memory** is *a fast-decaying store of visual information*. A similar storage area serves as a temporary warehouse for sounds. **Echoic memory** is *a fast-decaying store of auditory information*. When you have difficulty understanding what someone has just said, you probably find yourself replaying the last few words—listening to them echo in your "mind's ear," so to speak. When you do that, you are accessing information that is being held in your echoic memory store. The hallmark of both the iconic and echoic memory stores is that they hold information for a very short time. Iconic memories usually decay in about 1 second or less, and echoic memories usually decay in about 5 seconds (Darwin, Turvey, & Crowder, 1972). These two sensory memory stores are a bit like doughnut shops: The products come in, they sit briefly on the shelf, and then they are discarded. If you want one, you have to grab it fast.

> **How long is information held in iconic and echoic memory before it decays?**

```
X  L  W  F
J  B  O  V
K  C  Z  R
```

FIGURE 6.5 Iconic Memory Test When a grid of letters is flashed on screen for only 1/20th of a second, it is difficult to recall individual letters. But if prompted to remember a particular row immediately after the grid is shown, research participants will do so with high accuracy, indicating that although iconic memory stores the whole grid, the information fades away too quickly for a person to recall everything (Sperling, 1960).

Short-Term Storage and Working Memory

A second kind of memory storage is **short-term memory,** which *holds nonsensory information for more than a few seconds but less than a minute*. For example, if someone tells you a telephone number, you can usually repeat it back with ease—but only for a few seconds. In one study, research participants were given consonant strings to remember, such as DBX and HLM. After seeing each string, participants were asked to count backward from 100 by 3 for varying amounts of time and were then asked to recall the strings (Peterson & Peterson, 1959). As shown in **FIGURE 6.6**, memory for the consonant strings declined rapidly, from approximately 80% after a 3-second delay to less than 20% after a 20-second delay. These results suggest that information can be held in the short-term memory store for about 15 to 20 seconds.

What if 15 to 20 seconds isn't enough time? What if we need the information for a while longer? We can use a trick that allows us to get around the natural limitations of our short-term memories. **Rehearsal** is *the process of keeping information in short-term*

sensory memory A type of storage that holds sensory information for a few seconds or less.

iconic memory A fast-decaying store of visual information.

echoic memory A fast-decaying store of auditory information.

short-term memory A type of storage that holds nonsensory information for more than a few seconds but less than a minute.

rehearsal The process of keeping information in short-term memory by mentally repeating it.

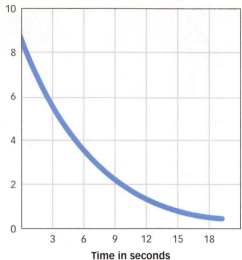

FIGURE 6.6 **The Decline of Short-Term Memory** Short-term memory fades quickly without rehearsal. On a test for memory of three-letter strings, participants were highly accurate when tested a few seconds after exposure to each string, but after 15 seconds, people barely recalled the strings at all. (Data from Peterson & Peterson, 1959.)

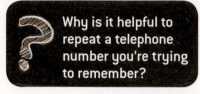

Why is it helpful to repeat a telephone number you're trying to remember?

memory by mentally repeating it. If someone gives you a telephone number and you can't put it immediately into your cell phone or write it down, you say it over and over to yourself until you can. Each time you repeat the number, you are reentering it into short-term memory, giving it another 15 to 20 seconds of shelf life.

Short-term memory is limited in how *long* it can hold information, and it is also limited in how *much* information it can hold. Most people can keep approximately seven items in short-term memory, but if they put more new items in, then old items begin to fall out (Miller, 1956). Those items can be numbers, letters, or even words or ideas. Therefore, one way to increase storage is to group several letters into a single meaningful item. **Chunking** involves *combining small pieces of information into larger clusters or chunks that are more easily held in short-term memory.* Waitresses who use organizational encoding (p. 174) to organize customer orders into groups are essentially chunking the information, giving themselves less to remember.

Short-term memory was originally conceived of as a kind of "place" where information is kept for a limited amount of time. More recently, researchers developed and refined a more dynamic model of a limited-capacity memory system, **working memory,** which refers to *active maintenance of information in short-term storage* (Baddeley & Hitch, 1974). Working memory includes subsystems that store and manipulate visual images or verbal information, as well as a central executive that coordinates the subsystems (Baddeley, 2001). If you wanted to keep the arrangement of pieces on a chessboard in mind as you contemplated your next move, you'd be relying on working memory. Working memory includes the visual representation of the positions of the pieces, your mental manipulation of the possible moves, and your awareness of the flow of information into and out of memory, all stored for a limited amount of time. Brain imaging studies indicate that the central executive component of working memory depends on regions within the frontal lobe that are important for controlling and manipulating information on a wide range of cognitive tasks (Baddeley, 2001).

Can working memory skills be trained? Some studies suggest yes. In one study, elementary school students who were trained on several working memory tasks (about 35 minutes/day for at least 20 days over a 5- to 7-week time period) showed improvement on other working memory tasks (Holmes, Gathercole, & Dunning, 2009). These gains were evident even when the children were tested 6 months after training. However, other studies suggest that working memory training improves performance—but only on the specific working memory task that was trained, not on other cognitive tasks (Redick et al., 2013). More research will be needed to determine whether working memory training produces any general improvements in cognitive performance (Shipstead, Redick, & Engle, 2012).

Long-Term Storage

In contrast to the time-limited sensory memory and short-term memory stores, **long-term memory** is *a type of storage that holds information for hours, days, weeks, or years.* In contrast to both sensory and short-term memory, long-term memory has no known capacity limits (see **FIGURE 6.7**). For example, most people can recall 10,000 to 15,000 words in their native language, tens of thousands of facts (The capital of France is Paris and 3 × 3 = 9), and an untold number of personal experiences. Just think of all the song lyrics you can recite by heart, and you'll understand that you've got a lot of information tucked away in long-term memory!

chunking Combining small pieces of information into larger clusters or chunks that are more easily held in short-term memory.

working memory Active maintenance of information in short-term storage.

long-term memory A type of storage that holds information for hours, days, weeks, or years.

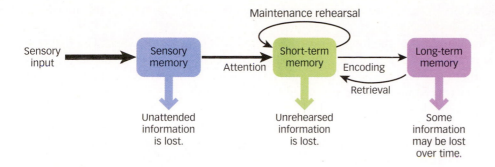

Maintenance rehearsal

Sensory input → Sensory memory → Attention → Short-term memory ⇄ (Encoding / Retrieval) → Long-term memory

Unattended information is lost.

Unrehearsed information is lost.

Some information may be lost over time.

FIGURE 6.7 **The Flow of Information through the Memory System** Information moves through several stages of memory as it gets encoded, stored, and made available for later retrieval.

The Role of the Hippocampus as Index

Where is long-term memory located in the brain? The clues to answering this question come from individuals who are unable to store long-term memories. In 1953, a young man, known then by the initials HM, suffered from intractable epilepsy (Scoville & Milner, 1957). In a desperate attempt to stop the seizures, HM's doctors removed parts of his temporal lobes, including the hippocampus and some surrounding regions (**FIGURE 6.8**). After the operation, HM could converse easily, use and understand language, and perform well on intelligence tests, but he could not remember anything that happened to him after the operation. HM could repeat a telephone number with no difficulty, suggesting that his short-term memory store was just fine (Corkin, 2002, 2013; Hilts, 1995; Squire, 2009). But after information left the short-term store, it was gone forever. For example, he would often forget that he had just eaten a meal or fail to recognize the hospital staff who helped him on a daily basis. Studies of HM and others have shown that the hippocampal region of the brain is critical for putting new information into the long-term store. When this region is damaged, individuals suffer from a condition known as **anterograde amnesia,** which is *the inability to transfer new information from the short-term store into the long-term store.*

Some individuals with amnesia also suffer from **retrograde amnesia,** which is *the inability to retrieve information that was acquired before a particular date, usually the date of an injury or surgery.* The fact that HM had much worse anterograde than retrograde amnesia suggests that the hippocampal region is not the site of long-term memory. Indeed, research has shown that different aspects of a single memory—its sights, sounds, smells, emotional content—are stored in different places in the cortex (Damasio, 1989; Schacter, 1996; Squire & Kandel, 1999). Some psychologists have argued that the hippocampal region acts as a kind of "index" that links together all of these otherwise separate bits and pieces so that we remember them as one memory

anterograde amnesia The inability to transfer new information from the short-term store into the long-term store.

retrograde amnesia The inability to retrieve information that was acquired before a particular date, usually the date of an injury or surgery.

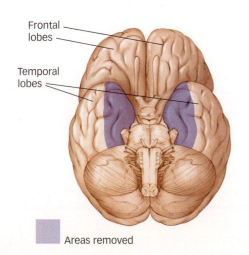

Frontal lobes

Temporal lobes

Areas removed

FIGURE 6.8 **The Hippocampus Patient** HM had his hippocampus and adjacent structures of the medial temporal lobe (indicated by the shaded area) surgically removed to stop his epileptic seizures (left). As a result, he could not remember things that happened after the surgery. Henry Molaison (right), better known to the world as patient HM, participated in countless memory experiments, and in so doing, he made fundamental contributions to our understanding of memory and the brain. He passed away on December 2, 2008, at the age of 82 at a nursing home near Hartford, Connecticut.

consolidation The process by which memories become stable in the brain.

reconsolidation The process that causes memories to become vulnerable to disruption when they are recalled, thus requiring them to become consolidated again.

(Schacter, 1996; Squire, 1992; Teyler & DiScenna, 1986). Over time, this index may become less necessary.

You can think of the hippocampal region index like a printed recipe. The first time you make a pie, you need the recipe to help you retrieve all the ingredients and then mix them together in the right amounts. As you bake more and more pies, though, you don't need to rely on the printed recipe anymore. Similarly, although the hippocampal region index is critical when a new memory is first formed, it may become less important as the memory ages. Scientists are still debating the extent to which the hippocampal region helps us to remember details of our old memories (Bayley et al., 2005; Kirwan et al., 2008; Moscovitch et al., 2006; Squire & Wixted, 2011; Winocur, Moscovitch, & Bontempi, 2010), but the notion of the hippocampus as an index explains why people like HM cannot make new memories and why they can remember old ones.

Memory Consolidation

The idea that the hippocampus becomes less important over time for maintaining memories is closely related to the concept of **consolidation,** *the process by which memories become stable in the brain* (McGaugh, 2000). Shortly after encoding, memories exist in a fragile state in which they can be easily disrupted; once consolidation has occurred, they are more resistant to disruption. One type of consolidation operates over seconds or minutes. For example, when someone experiences a head injury in a car crash and later cannot recall what happened during the few seconds or minutes before the crash—but can recall other events normally—the head injury probably prevented consolidation of short-term memory into long-term memory. Another type of consolidation occurs over much longer periods of time—days, weeks, months, and years—and likely involves transfer of information from the hippocampus to more permanent storage sites in the cortex. The operation of this longer-term consolidation process is why patients like HM can recall memories from childhood relatively normally, but they are impaired when recalling experiences that occurred just a few years prior to the time they became amnesic (Kirwan et al., 2008; Squire & Wixted, 2011).

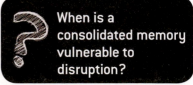

? How is using the hippocampal region index like learning a recipe?

How does a memory become consolidated? The act of recalling a memory, thinking about it, and talking about it with others probably contributes to consolidation (Moscovitch et al., 2006). As explained in the Hot Science box (p. 181), mounting evidence indicates that sleep also plays an important role in memory consolidation.

Many researchers have long believed that a fully consolidated memory becomes a permanent fixture in the brain, more difficult to get rid of than a computer virus. But even seemingly consolidated *memories can become vulnerable to disruption when they are recalled, thus requiring them to be consolidated again.* This process is called **reconsolidation** (Dudai, 2012; Nader & Hardt, 2009). Evidence for reconsolidation mainly comes from experiments with rats showing that when animals are cued to retrieve a new memory that was acquired a day earlier, giving the animal a drug (or an electrical shock) that prevents initial consolidation will cause forgetting (Nader, Shafe, & LeDoux, 2000; Sara, 2000). In fact, each time they are retrieved, memories become vulnerable to disruption and have to be reconsolidated.

? When is a consolidated memory vulnerable to disruption?

Might it be possible one day to eliminate painful memories by disrupting reconsolidation? Recent research with traumatized individuals suggests it could be: When a traumatic event was reactivated after administration of a drug that reduces anxiety, there was a subsequent reduction in traumatic symptoms (Brunet et al., 2008, 2011).

Has seeing too many shark movies left you afraid to swim in the ocean? What evidence is there that someday we might be able to erase painful memories?

PM Images/Photodisc/Getty Images

Hot Science

Sleep on It

Thinking about pulling an all-nighter before your next big test? Here's a reason to reconsider: Our minds don't simply shut off when we sleep (see the Consciousness chapter), and in fact, sleep may be as important to our memories as wakefulness.

Nearly a century ago, Jenkins and Dallenbach (1924) reported that recall of recently learned information is greater immediately after sleeping than after the same amount of time spent awake. They argued that being asleep passively protects us from encountering information that interferes with our ability to remember. As is explained by retroactive interference (p. 194), that's a valid argument. However, during the past few years, evidence has accumulated that sleep does more than simply protect us from waking interference (Diekelman & Born, 2010; Ellenbogen, Payne, & Stickgold, 2006). Sleep selectively enhances the consolidation of memories that reflect the meaning or gist of an experience (Payne et al., 2009), as well as emotionally important memories (Payne et al., 2008), suggesting that sleep helps us to remember what's important and to discard what's trivial.

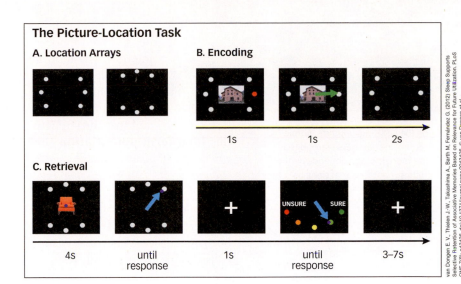

The Picture-Location Task
A. Location Arrays
B. Encoding
1s   1s   2s
C. Retrieval
4s   until response   1s   until response   3–7s
UNSURE   SURE

van Dongen E. V., Thielen J.-W., Takashima A., Barth M., Fernández G. (2012) Sleep Supports Selective Retention of Associative Memories Based on Relevance for Future Utilization. PLoS ONE 7(8): e43426. doi:10.1371/journal.pone.0043426 © van Dongen et al.

This idea is reinforced by recent evidence that shows that the beneficial effects of sleep on subsequent memory are observed only when people expect to be tested. In one study, Wilhelm et al. (2011) found that after studying a list of word pairs, participants who were informed that their memory would be tested later showed improved recall after sleep compared with an equivalent period of wakefulness. But a separate group that had not been informed of the memory test (and did not suspect it) showed no improvement in recall after sleep compared with wakefulness.

So, when you find yourself nodding off after hours of studying for your exam, the science is on the side of a good night's sleep.

Related work indicates that disrupting reconsolidation can seemingly eliminate a conditioned fear memory in a part of the brain called the *amygdala*, which we will learn, later in this chapter, plays a key role in emotional memory (Agren et al., 2012). Reconsolidation thus appears to be a key memory process with many important implications.

Memories, Neurons, and Synapses

We've already discussed parts of the brain that are related to memory storage, but we haven't said much about how memories are stored. Much of what we know about the neurological basis for long-term memory comes from the sea slug *Aplysia*, which has a simple nervous system consisting of only 20,000 neurons (compared to roughly 100 billion in the human brain). When an experimenter stimulates *Aplysia*'s tail with a mild electric shock, the slug immediately withdraws its gill, and if the experimenter does it again a moment later, *Aplysia* withdraws its gill even more quickly. If the experimenter comes back an hour later and shocks *Aplysia*, the withdrawal of the gill happens as slowly as it did the first time, as if *Aplysia* can't "remember" what happened an hour earlier (Abel et al., 1995). But if the experimenter shocks *Aplysia* over and over, it does develop an enduring "memory" that can last for days or even weeks. Research suggests that this long-term storage involves the growth of new synaptic connections between neurons (Abel et al., 1995; Kandel, 2006; Squire & Kandel, 1999). You'll recall from the Neuroscience and Behavior chapter that a *synapse* is the small space between the axon of one neuron and the dendrite of another, and neurons

By studying the sea slug *Aplysia's* simple nervous system, researchers learned that long-term memory storage depends on the growth of new synaptic connections between neurons.

long-term potentiation (LTP) A process whereby communication across the synapse between neurons strengthens the connection, making further communication easier.

communicate by sending neurotransmitters across these synapses. As it turns out, the act of sending actually *changes* the synapse. Specifically, it strengthens the connection between the two neurons, making it easier for them to transmit to each other the next time. This is why researchers sometimes say, "cells that fire together wire together" (Hebb, 1949).

If you're something more complex than a slug—say, a chimpanzee or your roommate—a similar process of synaptic strengthening happens in the hippocampus, which we've seen is an area crucial for storing new long-term memories. In the early 1970s, researchers applied a brief electrical stimulus to a neural pathway in a rat's hippocampus (Bliss & Lømo, 1973). They found that the electrical current produced a stronger connection between synapses that lay along the pathway and that the strengthening lasted for hours or even weeks. They called this **long-term potentiation** (more commonly known as **LTP**), *a process whereby communication across the synapse between neurons strengthens the connection, making further communication easier.* Drugs that block LTP can turn rats into rodent versions of patient HM: The animals have great difficulty remembering where they've been recently and become easily lost in a maze (Bliss, 1999; Morris et al., 1986).

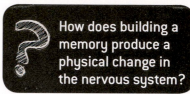

How does building a memory produce a physical change in the nervous system?

SUMMARY QUIZ [6.2]

1. What kind of memory storage holds information for a second or two?
   a. retrograde memory
   b. working memory
   c. short-term memory
   d. sensory memory

2. The process by which memories become stable in the brain is called
   a. consolidation.
   b. long-term memory.
   c. iconic memory.
   d. hippocampal indexing.

3. Long-term potentiation occurs through
   a. the interruption of communication between neurons.
   b. the strengthening of synaptic connections.
   c. the reconsolidation of disrupted memories.
   d. sleep.

Retrieval: Bringing Memories to Mind

There is something fiendishly frustrating about piggy banks. You can put money in them, you can shake them around to assure yourself that the money is there, but you can't easily get the money out. If memories were like pennies in a piggy bank, stored but inaccessible, what would be the point of saving them in the first place? Retrieval is the process of bringing to mind information that has been previously encoded and stored, and it is perhaps the most important of all memory processes (Roediger, 2000; Schacter, 2001a).

Retrieval Cues: Reinstating the Past

One of the best ways to retrieve information from *inside* your head is to encounter information *outside* your head that is somehow connected to it. The information outside your head is called a *retrieval cue,* external information that is associated with stored information and helps bring it to mind. Retrieval cues can be incredibly effective. How many times have you said something like, "I *know* who starred in *Trouble with the Curve,* but I just can't remember her name?" At such moments, did a friend give you a hint ("Wasn't she in *Julie & Julia*?"), which instantly brought the answer to mind ("Amy Adams!")? Such incidents suggest both that information is sometimes *available* in memory even when it is momentarily *inaccessible* and also that retrieval cues help us bring inaccessible information to mind.

Hints are one kind of retrieval cue, but they are not the only kind. The *encoding specificity principle* states that a retrieval cue can serve as an effective reminder when it helps re-create the specific way in which information was initially encoded (Tulving & Thomson, 1973). External contexts often make powerful retrieval cues (Hockley, 2008). For example, in one study, divers learned some words on land and some other words underwater; they recalled the words best when they were tested in the same dry or wet environment in which they had initially learned them because the environment itself served as a retrieval cue (Godden & Baddeley, 1975). Similarly, recovering alcoholics often experience a renewed urge to drink when visiting places in which they once drank because those places serve as retrieval cues. There may even be some wisdom to finding a seat in a classroom, sitting in it every day, and then sitting in it again when you take a test because the feel of the chair and the sights you see may help you remember the information you learned while you sat there.

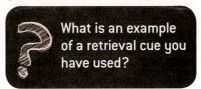

What is an example of a retrieval cue you have used?

Retrieval cues need not be external contexts—they can also be inner states. **State-dependent retrieval** is *the tendency for information to be better recalled when the person is in the same state during encoding and retrieval.* For example, retrieving information when you are in a sad or happy mood increases the likelihood that you will retrieve sad or happy episodes (Eich, 1995), which is part of the reason it is so hard to "look on the bright side" when you're feeling low. If the person's state at the time of retrieval matches the person's state at the time of encoding, the state itself serves as a retrieval cue—a bridge that connects the moment at which we experience something to the moment at which we remember it. Retrieval cues can even be thoughts themselves, as when one thought calls to mind another, related thought (Anderson et al., 1976).

The encoding specificity principle makes some unusual predictions. For example, you learned earlier that making semantic judgments about a word usually produces more durable memory for the word than does making rhyme judgments. So if you were shown a cue card of the word *brain* and if your friend were asked to think about what *brain* means while you were asked to think of a word that rhymes with *brain*, we would expect your friend to remember the word better the next day if we asked you both, "Hey, what was that word you saw yesterday?" However, suppose we asked you both, "What was that word that rhymed with *train*?" In this case, the retrieval cue would match your encoding context better than your friend's, and we would expect you to remember it better than your friend did (Fisher & Craik, 1977). The principle of **transfer-appropriate processing** is *the idea that memory is likely to transfer from one situation to another when the encoding and retrieval contexts of the situations match* (Morris, Bransford, & Franks, 1977; Roediger, Weldon, & Challis, 1989).

Consequences of Retrieval

Human memory differs substantially from computer memory. Simply retrieving a file from my computer doesn't have any effect on the likelihood that the file will open

Retrieval cues are hints that help bring stored information to mind. How does this explain the fact that most students prefer multiple-choice exams to fill-in-the-blank exams?

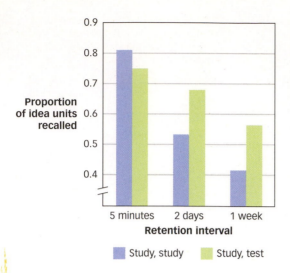

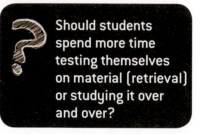

FIGURE 6.9 **Memory Testing Benefits Long-Term Retention** With a 5-minute retention interval, the study–study condition results in slightly higher recall. But with longer retention intervals of 2 days and 1 week, the study–test condition yields much higher levels of recall than the study–study condition . [Data from Roediger & Karpicke, 2006.]

again in the future. Not so with human memory. Retrieval doesn't merely provide a readout of what is in memory; it also changes the state of the memory system in important ways.

Retrieval Can Improve Subsequent Memory

The simple act of retrieval can strengthen a retrieved memory, making it easier to remember that information later (Bjork, 1975). For example, in one experiment, participants studied brief stories and then either studied them again or were given a test that required retrieving the stories (Roediger & Karpicke, 2006). Participants were then given a final recall test for the stories either 5 minutes, 2 days, or 1 week later. As shown in **FIGURE 6.9**, at the 5-minute delay, studying the stories twice resulted in slightly higher recall than studying and retrieving them. Critically, the opposite occurred at the 2-day and 1-week delays: Retrieval produced much higher levels of recall than did extra study exposure. These findings have potentially important implications for learning in educational contexts (Karpicke, 2012), which we will explore further in the Learning chapter (p. 239).

Should students spend more time testing themselves on material (retrieval) or studying it over and over?

Retrieval Can Impair Subsequent Memory

As much as retrieval can help memory, that's not always the case. *Retrieval-induced forgetting* is a process by which retrieving an item from long-term memory impairs subsequent recall of related items (Anderson, 2003; Anderson, Bjork, & Bjork, 1994). For example, when a speaker selectively talks about some aspects of memories shared with a listener and doesn't mention related information, both the speaker and the listener later have a harder time remembering the omitted events (Cuc, Koppel, & Hirst, 2007; Hirst & Echterhoff, 2012). Retrieval-induced forgetting can even affect eyewitness memory. When witnesses to a staged crime are questioned about some details of the crime scene, their ability to later recall related details that they were not asked about is impaired compared with witnesses who were not questioned at all initially (MacLeod, 2002; Shaw, Bjork, & Handal, 1995). These findings suggest that initial interviews with eyewitnesses should be as complete as possible in order to avoid potential retrieval-induced forgetting of significant details that are not probed during an interview (MacLeod & Saunders, 2008).

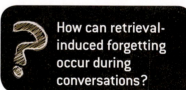

How can retrieval-induced forgetting occur during conversations?

Retrieval Can Change Subsequent Memory

In addition to improving and impairing subsequent memory, the act of retrieval can also change what we remember from an experience. In a recent experiment, participants went to a museum, where they took tours in which they viewed designated exhibits; each individual tour contained several different stops (St. Jacques & Schacter, 2013). The participants took a tour while wearing a camera that, every 15 seconds, automatically took pictures of what was in front of them. Two days later, participants visited the memory laboratory (in a separate building) for a "reactivation session." After memories of some of the stops were reactivated by looking at photos of them, participants were asked to rate, on a 1–5 scale, how vividly they reexperienced what had happened at each stop. Next, the participants were shown novel photos of *unvisited* stops within the exhibit; then they were asked to judge how closely these novel photos were related to the photos of the stops that they had actually seen in that exhibit. Finally, the participants were given a memory test 2 days after the reactivation session.

Participants sometimes incorrectly remembered that the stop shown in a novel photo had been part of the original tour. Most important, participants who tended to make this mistake also tended to have more vivid recollections during the reactivation session. In other words, retrieving and vividly reexperiencing memories of what participants actually did see at the museum led them to incorporate into their memories information that was not part of the original experience. This finding may be related to the phenomenon of reconsolidation that we discussed earlier (p. 180), where reactivating a memory temporarily makes it vulnerable to disruption and change. At the very least, this finding reinforces the idea that retrieving a memory involves far more than a simple readout of information.

As part of a recent experiment, participants wore cameras that took pictures every 15 seconds as they toured a museum.

Separating the Components of Retrieval

Before leaving the topic of retrieval, let's look at how the process actually works. There is reason to believe that *trying* to recall an incident and *successfully* recalling one are fundamentally different processes that occur in different parts of the brain (Moscovitch, 1994; Schacter, 1996). For example, regions in the left frontal lobe show heightened activity when people *try* to retrieve information that was presented to them earlier (Oztekin, Curtis, & McElree, 2009; Tulving et al., 1994). This activity may reflect the mental effort of struggling to dredge up the past event (Lepage et al., 2000). However, *successfully* remembering a past experience tends to be accompanied by activity in the hippocampal region (see **FIGURE 6.10**; Eldridge et al., 2000; Giovanello, Schnyer, & Verfaellie, 2004; Schacter, Alpert, et al., 1996). Furthermore, successful recall also activates parts of the brain that play a role in processing the sensory features of an experience. For instance, recall of previously heard sounds is accompanied by activity in the auditory cortex (the upper part of the temporal lobe), whereas recall of previously seen pictures is accompanied by activity in the visual cortex (in the occipital lobe; Wheeler, Petersen, & Buckner, 2000). Although retrieval may seem like a single process, brain studies suggest that separately identifiable processes are at work.

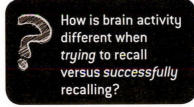

How is brain activity different when *trying* to recall versus *successfully* recalling?

This sheds some light on the phenomena we just discussed: retrieval-induced forgetting. Recent fMRI evidence indicates that during memory retrieval, regions within the frontal lobe that are involved in retrieval effort play a role in suppressing competitors (Benoit & Anderson, 2012; Kuhl et al., 2007; Wimber et al., 2009). When hippocampal activity during retrieval signals successful recall of an unwanted competitor,

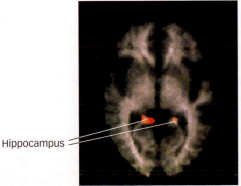

High recall minus baseline

Hippocampus

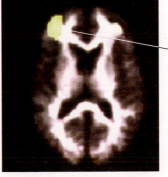

Low recall minus baseline

Left frontal lobe

Schacter DL, Alpert NM, Savage CR, Rauch SL, Albert MS. Conscious recollection and the human hippocampal formation: evidence from positron emission tomography. Proc Natl Acad Sci USA 1996; 93: 321-5

FIGURE 6.10 PET Scans of Successful and Unsuccessful Recall When people successfully remembered words they saw earlier in an experiment (achieving high levels of recall on a test), the hippocampus showed increased activity. When people tried but failed to recall words they had seen earlier (achieving low levels of recall on a test), the left frontal lobe showed increased activity (Schacter, Alpert, et al., 1996).

frontal lobe mechanisms are recruited that help to suppress the competitor. Once the competitor is suppressed, the frontal lobe no longer has to work as hard at controlling retrieval, ultimately making it easier to recall the target item (Kuhl et al., 2007). In addition, successful suppression of an unwanted memory causes reduced activity in the hippocampus (Anderson et al., 2004). These findings make sense once we understand the specific roles played by particular brain regions in the retrieval process.

SUMMARY QUIZ [6.3]

1. The increased likelihood of recalling a sad memory when you are in a sad mood is an illustration of
   a. the encoding specificity principle.
   b. state-dependent retrieval.
   c. transfer-appropriate processing.
   d. memory accessibility.

2. Which of the following statements regarding the consequences of memory retrieval is false?
   a. Retrieval-induced forgetting can affect eyewitness memory.
   b. The act of retrieval can strengthen a retrieved memory.
   c. Retrieval can impair subsequent memory.
   d. Retrieval boosts subsequent memory through the repetition of information.

3. Neuroimaging studies suggest that *trying* to remember activates the
   a. left frontal lobe.
   b. hippocampal region.
   c. occipital lobe.
   d. upper temporal lobe.

Multiple Forms of Memory: How the Past Returns

In 1977, neurologist Oliver Sacks interviewed a young man named Greg who had a tumor in his brain that wiped out his ability to remember day-to-day events. One thing Greg could remember was his life during the 1960s, when Greg's primary occupation seemed to be attending rock concerts by his favorite band, The Grateful Dead. Greg's memories of those concerts stuck with him over the following years, when he was living in a long-term care hospital. In 1991, Dr. Sacks took Greg to a Dead concert at New York's Madison Square Garden, wondering whether such a momentous event might jolt his memory into action. "That was fantastic," Greg told Dr. Sacks as they left the concert. "I will always remember it. I had the time of my life." But when Dr. Sacks saw Greg the next morning and asked him whether he recalled the previous night's concert, Greg drew a blank: "No, I've never been to the Garden" (Sacks, 1995, pp. 76–77).

Although Greg was unable to make new memories, some of the new things that happened to him seemed to leave a mark. For example, Greg did not recall learning that his father had died, but he did seem sad and withdrawn for years after hearing the news. Similarly, HM could not make new memories after his surgery, but if he played a game in which he had to track a moving target, his performance gradually improved

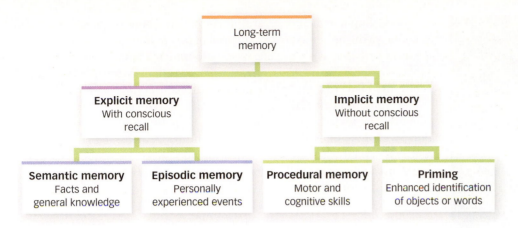

FIGURE 6.11 Multiple Forms of Memory Explicit and implicit memories are distinct from each other. Thus, a person with amnesia may lose explicit memory yet may display implicit memory for material that she or he cannot consciously recall learning.

with each round (Milner, 1962). Greg could not consciously remember hearing about his father's death, and HM could not consciously remember playing the tracking game, but both men showed clear signs of having been permanently changed by experiences that they so rapidly forgot. In other words, they *behaved* as though they were remembering things while claiming to remember nothing at all. This suggests that there must be several kinds of memory, some that are accessible to conscious recall, and some that we cannot consciously access (Eichenbaum & Cohen, 2001; Schacter & Tulving, 1994; Schacter, Wagner, & Buckner, 2000; Squire & Kandel, 1999).

Explicit and Implicit Memory

The fact that people can be changed by past experiences without having any awareness of those experiences suggests that there must be at least two different classes of memory (**FIGURE 6.11**). **Explicit memory** occurs *when people consciously or intentionally retrieve past experiences*. Recalling last summer's vacation, incidents from a novel you just read, or facts you studied for a test all involve explicit memory. Indeed, anytime you start a sentence with "I remember . . . ," you are talking about an explicit memory. **Implicit memory** occurs when *past experiences influence later behavior and performance, even without an effort to remember those experiences or an awareness of the recollection* (Graf & Schacter, 1985; Schacter, 1987). Implicit memories are not consciously recalled, but their presence is "implied" by our actions. Greg's persistent sadness after his father's death, even though he had no conscious knowledge of the event, is an example of implicit memory. So is HM's improved performance on a tracking task that he didn't consciously remember doing. So is the ability to ride a bike or tie your shoelaces or play guitar: You may know how to do these things, but you probably can't describe how to do them. Such knowledge reflects a particular kind of implicit memory called **procedural memory,** which refers to *the gradual acquisition of skills as a result of practice, or "knowing how" to do things*. The fact that people who have amnesia can acquire new procedural memories suggests that the hippocampal structures that are usually damaged in these individuals may be necessary for explicit memory, but they aren't needed for implicit procedural memory. In fact, it appears that brain regions outside the hippocampal area (including areas in the motor cortex) are involved in procedural memory. The Learning chapter discusses this evidence further, where you will also see that procedural memory is crucial for learning various kinds of motor, perceptual, and cognitive skills.

What type of memory is it when you just "know how" to do something?

explicit memory The act of consciously or intentionally retrieving past experiences.

implicit memory The influence of past experiences on later behavior and performance, even without an effort to remember them or an awareness of the recollection.

procedural memory The gradual acquisition of skills as a result of practice, or "knowing how" to do things.

Guitarists such as Jack White rely heavily on procedural memory to acquire and use the skills needed to play their music at a high level.

priming An enhanced ability to think of a stimulus, such as a word or object, as a result of a recent exposure to the stimulus.

Not all implicit memories are procedural or "how to" memories. For example, **priming** refers to *an enhanced ability to think of a stimulus, such as a word or object, as a result of a recent exposure to the stimulus* (Tulving & Schacter, 1990). In one experiment, college students were asked to study a long list of words, including items such as *avocado, mystery, climate, octopus,* and *assassin* (Tulving, Schacter, & Stark, 1982). Later, explicit memory was tested first by showing participants some of these words along with new ones they hadn't seen and then by asking them which words were on the list. To test implicit memory, participants received word fragments and were asked to come up with a word that fit the fragment. Try the test yourself:

ch – – – – nk   o – t – p – –   – o g – y – – –   – l – m – t e

You probably had difficulty coming up with the answers for the first and third fragments (*chipmunk, bogeyman*) but had little problem coming up with answers for the second and fourth (*octopus, climate*). Seeing *octopus* and *climate* on the original list made those words more accessible later during the fill-in-the-blanks test. Just as priming a pump makes water flow more easily, priming the memory system makes some information more accessible. In the fill-in-the-blanks experiment, people showed priming for studied words even when they failed to consciously remember that they had seen them earlier. This suggests that priming is an example of implicit, not explicit, memory.

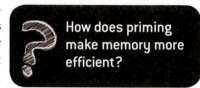

How does priming make memory more efficient?

A truly stunning example of this point comes from a study by Mitchell (2006), in which participants first studied black-and-white line drawings depicting everyday objects. Later, the participants were shown fragmented versions of the drawings that are difficult to identify; some of them depicted objects that had been studied earlier in the experiment, whereas others depicted new objects that had not been studied. Mitchell found that participants correctly identified more fragmented drawings of studied than new objects, and the participants also identified more studied objects than did participants in a control group who had never seen the pictures—a clear demonstration of priming (see **FIGURE 6.12**). Here's the stunning part: The fragmented drawing test was given 17 years after presentation of the study list! By that time, participants had little or no explicit memory of having seen the drawings, and some had no recollection that they had ever participated in the experiment! "I'm sorry—I really don't remember this experiment at all," said one 36-year-old man who showed a strong priming effect. A 36-year-old woman who showed even more priming stated simply, "Don't remember anything about it" (Mitchell, 2006, p. 929). These observations confirm both that priming is an example of implicit memory and also that priming can persist over very long periods of time.

As such, you'd expect amnesic individuals such as HM and Greg to show priming. In fact, many experiments have shown that amnesic individuals can show substantial priming effects—often as large as healthy, nonamnesic individuals—even though they have no explicit memory for the items they studied. Priming, like procedural memory, does not require the hippocampal structures that are damaged in cases of amnesia (Schacter & Curran, 2000).

If the hippocampal region isn't required for priming, what parts of the brain *are* involved? When research participants are shown the word stem *mot___* or *tab___* and are asked to provide the first word that comes to mind, parts of the occipital lobe involved in visual processing and parts of the frontal lobe involved in word retrieval become active. But if people perform the same task after being primed by seeing *motel* and *table*, there's less activity in these same regions (Buckner et al., 1995; Schott et al., 2005). Priming seems to make it easier for parts of the cortex that are involved in

FIGURE 6.12 Long-Term Priming of Visual Objects Participants who viewed drawings of common objects and then 17 years later were given a test in which they tried to identify the objects from fragmented drawings (longitudinal group) showed a strong priming effect; by contrast, participants who had not seen the drawings 17 years earlier (control group) showed nonsignificant priming. (Data from Mitchell, 2006.)

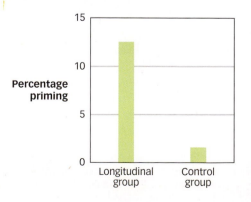

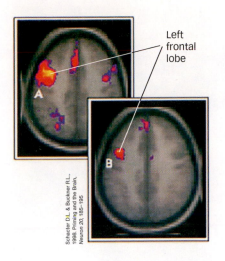

Left frontal lobe

A

B

Schacter D.L. & Buckner R.L.,
1998. Priming and the Brain,
Neuron 20, 185–195

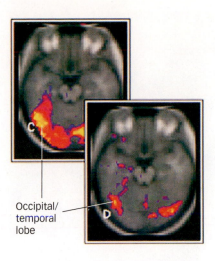

C

Occipital/ temporal lobe

D

FIGURE 6.13 **Primed and Unprimed Processing of Stimuli** Priming is associated with reduced levels of activation in the cortex. In each pair of fMRIs, the images on the upper left (A, C) show brain regions in the frontal lobe (A) and occipital/temporal lobe (C) that are active during an unprimed task (in this case, providing a word response to a visual word cue). The images on the lower right within each pair (B, D) show reduced activity in the same regions during the primed version of the task.

perceiving a word or object to identify the item after a recent exposure to it (Schacter, Dobbins, & Schnyer, 2004; Wiggs & Martin, 1998). This suggests that the brain saves a bit of processing time after priming (see **FIGURE 6.13**).

Semantic and Episodic Memory

Consider these two questions: (1) Why do Americans celebrate on July 4th? and (2) What is the most spectacular Fourth of July celebration you've ever seen? Every American knows the answer to the first question (we celebrate the signing of the Declaration of Independence on July 4, 1776), but we all have our own answers to the second. Although both of these questions require you to search your long-term memory and explicitly retrieve information that is stored there, one requires you to dredge up a fact that every American schoolchild knows and that is not part of your personal autobiography, and one requires you to revisit a particular time and place—or episode—from your personal past. These memories are called *semantic* and *episodic* memories, respectively (Tulving, 1972, 1983, 1998). **Semantic memory** is *a network of associated facts and concepts that make up our general knowledge of the world,* whereas **episodic memory** is *the collection of past personal experiences that occurred at a particular time and place.*

Episodic memory is special because it is the only form of memory that allows us to engage in mental time travel, projecting ourselves into the past and revisiting events that have happened to us. This ability allows us to connect our pasts and our presents and construct a cohesive story of our lives. People who have amnesia can usually travel back in time and revisit episodes that occurred before they became amnesic, but they are unable to revisit episodes that happened later. For example, Greg couldn't travel back to any time after 1969 because that's when he stopped being able to create new episodic memories. But can people with amnesia create new semantic memories?

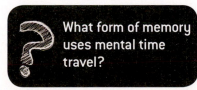

What form of memory uses mental time travel?

Researchers have studied three young adults who suffered damage to the hippocampus during birth as a result of difficult deliveries that interrupted oxygen supply to the brain (Brandt et al., 2009; Vargha-Khadem et al., 1997). Their parents noticed that the children could not recall what happened during a typical day, had to be constantly reminded of appointments, and often became lost and disoriented. In view of their hippocampal damage, you might also expect that these children would perform poorly in school. Remarkably, however, all three children learned to read, write, and spell; developed normal vocabularies; and acquired other kinds of semantic

semantic memory A network of associated facts and concepts that make up our general knowledge of the world.

episodic memory The collection of past personal experiences that occurred at a particular time and place.

These new Americans are taking the Oath of Allegiance after passing a citizenship test that would have required them to use their *semantic* memories.

EPA/Jim Lo Scalzo/Newscom

knowledge that allowed them to perform well in school. Based on this evidence, researchers have concluded that the hippocampus is not necessary for acquiring new *semantic* memories.

Episodic Memory and Imagining the Future

We've already seen that episodic memory allows us to travel backward in time, but it turns out that episodic memory also plays a role in allowing us to travel forward in time. An amnesic man known by the initials K.C. provided an early clue to this insight about traveling forward in time. K.C. could not recollect any specific episodes from his past, and when asked to imagine a future episode—such as what he might do tomorrow—he reported a complete "blank" (Tulving, 1985). Consistent with this observation, more recent findings from individuals with hippocampal amnesia reveal that some of them have difficulty imagining new experiences, such as sunbathing on a sandy beach (Hassabis et al., 2007), or events that might happen in their everyday lives (Race, Keane, & Verfaellie, 2011). Something similar happens with aging. When asked either to recall episodes that actually occurred in their pasts or imagine new episodes that might occur in their futures, older adults provided fewer details about what happened or what might happen than did college students (Addis, Wong, & Schacter, 2008; Schacter, Gaesser, & Addis, 2012). Consistent with these findings, neuroimaging studies reveal that a network of brain regions known to be involved in episodic memory—including the hippocampus—shows similarly increased activity when people remember the past and imagine the future (Addis, Wong, & Schacter, 2007; Okuda et al., 2003; Schacter, Addis, et al., 2012; Szpunar, Watson, & McDermott, 2007; see **FIGURE 6.14**).

Taken together, these observations strongly suggest that we rely heavily on episodic memory to envision our personal futures (Schacter, Addis, & Buckner, 2008; Szpunar, 2010). Episodic memory is well-suited to the task, because it is a flexible system that allows us to recombine elements of past experience in new ways so that we can mentally try out different versions of what might happen (Schacter, 2012; Schacter & Addis, 2007; Suddendorf & Corballis, 2007). For example,

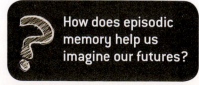

? How does episodic memory help us imagine our futures?

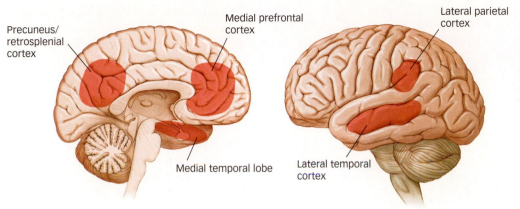

Precuneus/retrosplenial cortex

Medial prefrontal cortex

Lateral parietal cortex

Medial temporal lobe

Lateral temporal cortex

FIGURE 6.14 **Remembering the Past and Imagining the Future Depend on a Common Network of Brain Regions** A common brain network is activated when people remember episodes that actually occurred in their personal pasts and when they imagine episodes that might occur in their personal futures. This network includes the hippocampus, a part of the medial temporal lobe that plays an important role in episodic memory . [Information from Schacter, Addis, & Buckner, 2007.]

when you imagine having a difficult conversation with a friend that will take place in a couple of days, you can draw on past experiences to envisage different ways in which the conversation might unfold, and hopefully, you will then avoid saying things that, based on past experience, are likely to make the situation worse. As we'll discuss later, however, this flexibility of episodic memory might also be responsible for some kinds of memory errors (see p. 202).

Social Influences on Remembering: Collaborative Memory

So far, we've focused mainly on memory in individuals functioning on their own. But remembering also serves important social functions, which is why we get together with family to talk about old times or share our memories with friends by posting our vacation photos on Facebook. Sharing memories with others can strengthen those memories (Hirst & Echterhoff, 2012), but we've already seen that talking about some aspects of a memory but omitting other related events can also produce retrieval-induced forgetting (see p. 184; Coman, Manier, & Hirst, 2009; Cuc, Koppel, & Hirst, 2007). Psychologists have become increasingly interested in how people remember in groups, which is now referred to as *collaborative memory* (Rajaram, 2011).

In a typical collaborative memory experiment, participants first encode a set of target materials, such as a list of words, on their own (just like in the traditional memory experiments that we've already considered). Things start to get interesting at the time of retrieval when participants work together in small groups (usually two or three participants) to try to remember the target items. The number of items recalled by this group can then be compared with the number of items recalled by individuals who are trying to recall items on their own without any help from others. The collaborative group typically recalls more target items than any individual (Hirst & Echterhoff, 2012; Weldon, 2001), suggesting that collaboration benefits memory. For example, Tim might recall an item that Emily forgot, and Eric might remember items that neither Tim nor Emily recalled, so the sum total of the group will exceed what any one person can recall.

But things get really interesting when we compare the performance of the collaborative group to the performance of several individuals recalling target items on their own. For example, let's assume that after studying a list of eight words, and recalling the items on their own, Tim recalls items 1, 2, and 8; Emily recalls items 1, 4, and 7; and Eric recalls items 1, 5, 6, and 8. Adding them all together, Tim, Emily, and Eric recalled in combination seven of the eight items that were presented (nobody recalled item 3). The surprising finding is that when they remember together as a group, Tim, Emily, and Eric will typically come up with *fewer* total items than when they remember on their own (Basden et al., 1997; Hirst & Echterhoff, 2012; Rajaram, 2011;

Remembering as a collaborative group leads to greater recall than would be achieved by any single member of the group, but less than the total produced by all the individuals remembering on their own.

Rajaram & Pereira-Pasarin, 2010; Weldon, 2001). This negative effect of group recall on memory is known as *collaborative inhibition*: The same number of individuals working together recall fewer items than they would on their own.

What's going on here? One possibility is that the retrieval strategies used by some members of the group disrupt those used by others whenever the group members are recalling items together (Basden et al., 1997; Hirst & Echterhoff, 2012; Rajaram, 2011). For example, suppose that Tim goes first and recalls items in the order that they were presented. This retrieval strategy may be disruptive to Emily, who prefers to recall the last item first and then work backward through the list. So, next time you are sharing memories of a past activity with friends, you will be shaping your memories for both better and worse. (Can you rely on your computer for collaborative remembering? See The Real World: Is Google Hurting Our Memories?)

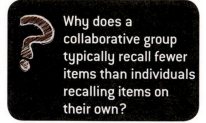

Why does a collaborative group typically recall fewer items than individuals recalling items on their own?

The Real World

Is Google Hurting Our Memories?

Take some time to try to answer a simple question before returning to reading this box: What country has a national flag that is not rectangular? Now let's discuss what went through your mind as you searched for an answer (the correct one is Nepal). There was probably a time not too long ago when most people would have tried to conjure up images of national flags or take a mental world tour to try to answer this question, but recent research conducted in the lab of one of your textbook authors indicates that nowadays, most of us think about computers and Google searches when confronted with questions of this kind (Sparrow, Liu, & Wegner, 2011).

Sparrow et al. found that after being given difficult general knowledge questions (like the one about nonrectangular flags), people were slower to name the color in which a computer word (e.g., Google, internet, Yahoo) was printed than the color in which a noncomputer word was printed (e.g., Nike, table, Yoplait). The slow-color-naming of computer words suggests that people were thinking about things related to computers after being given difficult questions, which interfered with their ability to name the color in which

the word was printed. The researchers concluded that we are now so used to searching for information on Google when we don't immediately know the answer to a question that we immediately think of computers rather than search our memories. This result also raises troubling questions: Is reliance on computers and the Internet having an adverse effect on human memory? If we rely on Google for answers, are we unknowingly making our memories obsolete?

What does your computer remember for you?

In follow-up studies, Sparrow et al. found that participants had a harder time remembering bits of trivia ("An ostrich's eye is bigger than its brain") that they typed into a computer when they were told that the computer would save their answers than when they were told that the answers would be erased. But when people saved information to one of several folders on a computer, they were often able to remember where they saved it even when they did not remember the information itself. People seemed to be using the computer in an efficient way to help remember facts, while relying on their own memories to recall where those facts could be found. Sparrow and colleagues suggested that people may be adapting their memories to the demands of new technology, relying on computers in a way that is similar to how we sometimes rely on other people (friends, family members, or colleagues) to remember things that we may not remember ourselves. This is similar to what we discussed as *collaborative memory*, and just as collaborative remembering with other people has both helpful and harmful effects, so does collaborative remembering with our computers.

SUMMARY QUIZ [6.4]

1. The act of consciously or intentionally retrieving past experiences is
   a. priming.
   b. procedural memory.
   c. implicit memory.
   d. explicit memory.

2. People who have amnesia are able to retain all of the following except
   a. explicit memory.
   b. implicit memory.
   c. procedural memory.
   d. priming.

3. Remembering a family reunion that you attended as a child illustrates
   a. semantic memory.
   b. procedural memory.
   c. episodic memory.
   d. perceptual priming.

Memory Failures: The Seven Sins of Memory

You probably haven't given much thought to breathing today, and the reason is that from the moment you woke up, you've been doing it effortlessly and well. But the moment breathing fails, you are reminded of just how important it is. Memory is like that. Every time we see, think, notice, imagine, or wonder, we are drawing on our ability to use information stored in our brains, but it isn't until this ability fails that we become acutely aware of just how much we should treasure it. Such memory errors—the "seven sins" of memory—cast similar illumination on how memory normally operates and how often it operates well (Schacter, 1999, 2001b). We'll discuss each of the seven sins in detail below.

1. Transience

On March 6, 2007, I. Lewis "Scooter" Libby, former Chief of Staff to Vice President Dick Cheney, was convicted of perjury during an FBI investigation into whether members of the Bush administration had unlawfully disclosed the identity of a CIA agent to the media. According to Libby's defense team, any misstatements he might have made in response to FBI questioning were the result of faulty memory, not an intention to deceive. How could Libby forget such important events? Research has shown that memories can and do degrade with time. The culprit here is **transience,** *forgetting what occurs with the passage of time.*

Transience occurs during the storage phase of memory after an experience has been encoded and before it is retrieved. This was first illustrated in the late 1870s by Hermann Ebbinghaus, a German philosopher who measured his own memory for lists of nonsense syllables at different delays after studying them (Ebbinghaus, 1885/1964). Ebbinghaus charted his recall of nonsense syllables over time, creating the forgetting curve shown in **FIGURE 6.15**. Ebbinghaus noted a rapid drop-off in retention during the first few tests, followed by a slower rate of forgetting on later tests—a general pattern confirmed by many subsequent memory researchers (Wixted & Ebbensen, 1991).

transience Forgetting what occurs with the passage of time.

I. Lewis "Scooter" Libby was convicted of perjury and obstructing justice, but he claimed that forgetting and related memory problems were responsible for any misstatements he made.

Alex Wong/Getty Images

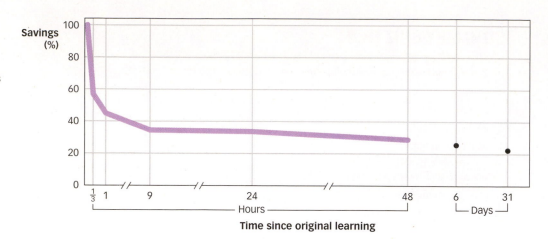

FIGURE 6.15 **The Curve of Forgetting** Ebbinghaus measured his retention at various delay intervals after he studied lists of nonsense syllables. Retention was measured in percent savings—that is, the percentage of time needed to relearn the list compared to the time needed to learn it initially. (Data from Ebbinghaus, 1885/1964.)

retroactive interference Situations in which later learning impairs memory for information acquired earlier.

proactive interference Situations in which earlier learning impairs memory for information acquired later.

absentmindedness A lapse in attention that results in memory failure.

So, for example, when English speakers were tested for memory of Spanish vocabulary acquired during high school or college courses 1 to 50 years earlier, there was a rapid drop-off in memory during the first 3 years after the students' last class, followed by tiny losses in later years (Bahrick, 1984, 2000). In all these studies, memories didn't fade at a constant rate as time passed; most forgetting happened soon after an event occurred, with increasingly less forgetting as more time passed.

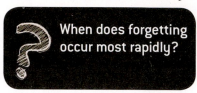

When does forgetting occur most rapidly?

Another way that memories can be distorted is by interference from other memories. For example, if you carry out the same activities at work each day, by the time Friday rolls around, it may be difficult to remember what you did on Monday because later activities blend in with earlier ones. This is an example of **retroactive interference,** *situations in which later learning impairs memory for information acquired earlier* (Postman & Underwood, 1973). **Proactive interference,** in contrast, refers to *situations in which earlier learning impairs memory for information acquired later.* If you use the same parking lot each day at work or at school, you've probably gone out to find your car and then stood there confused by the memories of having parked it on previous days.

2. Absentmindedness

The great cellist Yo-Yo Ma put his treasured $2.5 million instrument in the trunk of a taxicab in Manhattan. He rode to his destination, paid the driver and left the cab, forgetting his cello. Minutes later, Ma realized what he had done and called the police. Fortunately, they tracked down the taxi and recovered the instrument (Finkelstein, 1999). But how had the celebrated cellist forgotten about something so important that had occurred only 10 minutes earlier? Transience is not a likely culprit. As soon as Mr. Ma realized what he'd done with his instrument, he recalled where he had put it. This information had not disappeared from his memory (which is why he was able to tell the police where the cello was). Instead, Yo-Yo Ma was a victim of **absentmind-edness,** *a lapse in attention that results in memory failure.*

What makes people absentminded? One common cause is lack of attention. Attention plays a vital role in encoding information into long-term memory. Without proper attention, material is much less likely to be stored properly and recalled later. For example, in one study, participants listened to lists of 15 words for a later memory test (Craik et al., 1996). They were allowed to pay full attention to some of the lists, but while they heard other lists, they simultaneously performed another task that required them to press keys to indicate where an asterisk was appearing and disappearing. On a later test, participants recalled far fewer words from the list they had heard while their attention was divided.

What happens in the brain when attention is divided? As you saw earlier, greater activity in the lower left frontal region during encoding is associated with better memory. But participants showed less activity in the lower left frontal lobe when their attention was divided (Shallice et al., 1994). Dividing attention, then, prevents the lower left frontal lobe from playing its normal role in semantic encoding, and the result is absentminded forgetting. Divided attention also leads to less hippocampal involvement in encoding (Kensinger, Clarke, & Corkin, 2003; Uncapher & Rugg, 2008). Given the importance of the hippocampus to episodic memory, this finding may help to explain why absentminded forgetting is sometimes so extreme, as when we forget where we put our keys or glasses only moments earlier.

How is memory affected for someone whose attention is divided?

Another common cause of absentmindedness is forgetting to carry out actions that we planned to do in the future. On any given day, you need to remember the times and places that your classes meet, you need to remember with whom and where you are having lunch, and so on; this is called **prospective memory**, *remembering to do things in the future* (Einstein & McDaniel, 1990, 2005).

3. Blocking

Have you ever tried to recall the name of a famous movie actor or a book you've read—and felt that the answer was on the tip of your tongue, rolling around in your head *somewhere* but just out of reach at the moment? This tip-of-the-tongue experience is a classic example of **blocking**, *a failure to retrieve information that is available in memory even though you are trying to produce it.* The sought-after information has been encoded and stored, and a cue is available that would ordinarily trigger recall of it. The information has not faded from memory, and you aren't forgetting to retrieve it. Rather, you are experiencing a full-blown retrieval failure, which makes this memory breakdown especially frustrating. Researchers have described the tip-of-the-tongue state, in particular, as "a mild torment, something like [being] on the brink of a sneeze" (Brown & McNeill, 1966, p. 326).

Blocking occurs especially often for the names of people and places (Cohen, 1990; Semenza, 2009; Valentine, Brennen, & Brédart, 1996). Why? Because their links to related concepts and knowledge are weaker than for common names. That somebody's last name is Baker doesn't tell us much about the person, but saying that he *is* a baker does. To illustrate this point, researchers showed people pictures of cartoon and comic strip characters, some with descriptive names that highlight key features of the character (e.g., Grumpy, Snow White, Scrooge) and others with arbitrary names (e.g., Aladdin, Mary Poppins, Pinocchio; Brédart & Valentine, 1998). Even though the two types of names were equally familiar to participants in the experiment, they blocked less often on the descriptive names than on the arbitrary names.

Why is Snow White's name easier to remember than Mary Poppins' name?

Although it's frustrating when it occurs, blocking is a relatively infrequent event for most of us. However, it occurs more often as we grow older, and it is a very common complaint among people in their 60s and 70s (Burke et al., 1991; Schwartz, 2002). Even more striking, some individuals with brain damage live in a nearly perpetual tip-of-the-tongue state (Semenza, 2009). One such individual could recall the names of only 2 of 40 famous

Christina Kennedy/Getty Images

Talking on a cell phone while driving is a common occurrence of divided attention in everyday life; texting is even worse. Such activities can be dangerous, and an increasing number of states have banned the practice.

prospective memory Remembering to do things in the future.

blocking A failure to retrieve information that is available in memory even though you are trying to produce it.

stillfx/AgeFotostock

Suppose that, mentally consumed by planning for a psychology test the next day, you place your keys in an unusual spot and later forget where you put them. Is this more likely to reflect the memory sin of transience, absentmindedness, or blocking?

memory misattribution Assigning a recollection or an idea to the wrong source.

source memory Recall of when, where, and how information was acquired.

people when she saw their photographs, compared to 25 of 40 for healthy volunteers in the control group (Semenza & Zettin, 1989). Yet she could still recall correctly the occupations of 32 of these people—the same number that healthy people could recall. This case and similar ones have given researchers important clues about what parts of the brain are involved in retrieving proper names. Name blocking usually results from damage to parts of the left temporal lobe on the surface of the cortex, most often as a result of a stroke. In fact, studies that show strong activation of regions within the temporal lobe when people recall proper names support this idea (Damasio et al., 1996; Gorno-Tempini et al., 1998).

4. Memory Misattribution

Shortly after the 1995 bombing of the federal building in Oklahoma City, police set about searching for two suspects they called John Doe 1 and John Doe 2. John Doe 1 turned out to be Timothy McVeigh, who was quickly apprehended and later convicted of the crime and sentenced to death. John Doe 2, who had supposedly accompanied McVeigh when he rented a van two days before the bombing, was never found. In fact, John Doe 2 had never existed; he was a product of the memory of Tom Kessinger, a mechanic who was present when McVeigh rented the van. The day after, two other men had also rented a van in Kessinger's presence. The first man, like McVeigh, was tall and fair. The second man was shorter and stockier, was dark-haired, wore a blue and white cap, and had a tattoo beneath his left sleeve—a match to the description of John Doe 2. Tom Kessinger had confused his recollections of men he had seen on separate days in the same place. He was a victim of **memory misattribution**, *assigning a recollection or an idea to the wrong source* (see **FIGURE 6.16**).

Part of memory is knowing where our memories came from. This is known as **source memory**, *recall of when, where, and how information was acquired* (Johnson, Hashtroudi, & Lindsay, 1993; Mitchell & Johnson, 2009; Schacter, Harbluk, & McLachlan, 1984). People sometimes correctly recall a fact they learned earlier or accurately recognize a person or object they have seen before but misattribute the source of this knowledge—just as happened to Tom Kessinger (Davies, 1988). Such misattribution could be the cause of déjà vu experiences, where you suddenly feel that you have been in a situation before even though you can't recall any details. A present situation that is similar to a past experience may trigger a general sense of familiarity that is mistakenly attributed to having been in the exact situation previously (Brown, 2004; Reed, 1988).

What can explain a déjà vu experience?

FIGURE 6.16 Memory Misattribution In 1995, the Murrah Federal Building in Oklahoma City was bombed in an act of terrorism. The police sketch shows John Doe 2, who was originally thought to have been culprit Timothy McVeigh's partner in the bombing. It was later determined that the witness had confused his memories of different men whom he had encountered on different days.

Individuals with damage to the frontal lobes are especially prone to memory misattribution errors (Schacter et al., 1984; Shimamura & Squire, 1987). This is probably because the frontal lobes play a significant role in effortful retrieval processes, which are required to dredge up the correct source of a memory. But we are all vulnerable to memory misattribution. Take the following test and there is a good chance that you will experience it for yourself. First, study the two lists of words presented in **TABLE 6.1** by reading each word for about 1 second. When you are done, return to this paragraph for more instructions, but don't look back at the table! Now try to recognize which of the following words appeared on the list you just studied: *taste, bread, needle, king, sweet, thread*. If you think that *taste* and *thread* were on the lists you studied, you're right. And if you think that *bread* and *king* weren't on those lists, you're also right. But if you think that *needle* or *sweet* appeared on the lists, you're dead wrong.

Most people make exactly the same mistake, claiming with confidence that they saw *needle* and *sweet* on the list. This mistaken feeling of familiarity, called *false recognition*, occurs because all the words in the lists are associated with *needle* or *sweet*. Seeing each word in the study list activates related words. Because *needle* and *sweet* are related to all of the associates, they become more activated than other words—so highly activated that only minutes later, people swear that they actually studied the words (Deese, 1959; Gallo, 2006, 2010; Roediger & McDermott, 1995, 2000). In fact, brain scanning studies using PET and fMRI show that many of the same brain regions are active during false recognition and true recognition, including the hippocampus (Cabeza et al., 2001; Schacter et al., 1996; see **FIGURE 6.17**). Similar results are obtained when people view a series of common objects (e.g., cars, umbrellas) and then are later shown a new object that looks like one they saw earlier: They often falsely recognize the similar new item, and many of the same brain regions become active during this kind of false recognition as during true recognition (Gutchess & Schacter, 2012; Slotnick & Schacter, 2004).

However, false recognition can be reduced (Schacter, Israel, & Racine, 1999). For example, recent evidence shows that when participants are given a choice between an object that they actually saw (e.g., a car) and a visually similar new object (a different car that looks like the one they saw), they almost always choose the car that they actually saw and thus avoid making a false recognition error (Guerin et al., 2012a, 2012b). When people experience a strong sense of familiarity about a person, object, or event but lack specific recollections, a potentially dangerous recipe for memory misattribution is in place, both in the laboratory and also in real-world situations involving eyewitness memory. Understanding this point may be a key to reducing the dangerous consequences of misattribution in eyewitness testimony.

Table 6.1	False Recognition
Sour	Thread
Candy	Pin
Sugar	Eye
Bitter	Sewing
Good	Sharp
Taste	Point
Tooth	Prick
Nice	Thimble
Honey	Haystack
Soda	Pain
Chocolate	Hurt
Heart	Injection
Cake	Syringe
Tart	Cloth
Pie	Knitting

FIGURE 6.17 Hippocampal Activity during True and False Recognition Many brain regions show similar activation during true and false recognition, including the hippocampus. The figure shows results from an fMRI study of true and false recognition of visual shapes (Slotnick & Schacter, 2004). (*a*) A plot showing the activity level in the strength of the fMRI signal from the hippocampus over time. This shows that after a few seconds, there is comparable activation for true recognition of previously studied shapes (red line) and false recognition of similar shapes that were not presented (yellow line). Both true and false recognition show increased hippocampal activity compared with correctly classifying unrelated shapes as new (purple line). (*b*) A region of the left hippocampus. (Data from Slotnick & Schacter, 2004.)

Brain activity (% change)

0.1

0

−0.1

0   4   8   12   16

Time in seconds

(a)

(b)   Left hippocampus

Slotnick & Schacter, Nature Neuroscience, 2004, 7(61), p. 669

suggestibility The tendency to incorporate misleading information from external sources into personal recollections.

5. Suggestibility

On October 4, 1992, a cargo plane crashed into an apartment building in a suburb of Amsterdam, killing 39 residents and all 4 members of the airline crew. The disaster dominated news in the Netherlands for days as people viewed footage of the crash scene and read about the catastrophe. Ten months later, Dutch psychologists asked university students: "Did you see the television film of the moment the plane hit the apartment building?" Fifty-five percent answered yes (Crombag, Wagenaar, & Van Koppen, 1996). All of this might seem perfectly normal except for one key fact: There was no television film of the moment when the plane actually crashed. The researchers had asked a suggestive question that implied that television film of the crash had been shown. Respondents may have viewed television film of the postcrash scene, and they may have read, imagined, or talked about what might have happened when the plane hit the building, but they most definitely did not see the actual crash. The suggestive question led participants to misattribute information from these or other sources to a film that did not exist. **Suggestibility** is the *tendency to incorporate misleading information from external sources into personal recollections.*

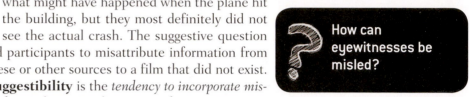

How can eyewitnesses be misled?

If misleading details can be implanted in people's memories, is it also possible to suggest entire episodes that never occurred? The answer seems to be yes (Loftus, 1993, 2003). In one study, the research participant, a teenager named Chris, was asked by his older brother, Jim, to try to remember the time Chris had been lost in a shopping mall at age 5. He initially recalled nothing, but after several days, Chris produced a detailed recollection of the event. He recalled that he "felt so scared I would never see my family again" and remembered that a kindly old man wearing a flannel shirt found him crying (Loftus, 1993, p. 532). But according to Jim and other family members, Chris was never lost in a shopping mall. Of 24 participants in a larger study on implanted memories, approximately 25% falsely remembered being lost as a child in a shopping mall or in a similar public place (Loftus & Pickrell, 1995).

People develop false memories in response to suggestions for some of the same reasons memory misattribution occurs. We do not store all the details of our experiences in memory, making us vulnerable to accepting suggestions about what might have happened or should have happened. In addition, visual imagery plays an important role

In 1992, a cargo plane crashed into an apartment building in a suburb of Amsterdam. When Dutch psychologists asked students if they had seen the television film of the plane crashing, a majority said they had. In fact, no such footage exists (Crombag et al., 1996).

in constructing false memories (Goff & Roediger, 1998). Asking people to imagine an event like spilling punch all over the bride's parents at a wedding increases the likelihood that they will develop a false memory of such a mishap (Hyman & Pentland, 1996).

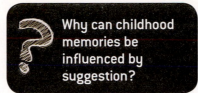

Why can childhood memories be influenced by suggestion?

Suggestibility played an important role in a controversy that arose during the 1980s and 1990s concerning the accuracy of childhood memories that people recalled during psychotherapy. One highly publicized example involved a woman named Diana Halbrooks (Schacter, 1996). After a few months in psychotherapy, she began recalling disturbing incidents from her childhood—for example, that her mother had tried to kill her and that her father had abused her sexually. Although her parents denied that these events had ever occurred, her therapist encouraged her to believe in the reality of her memories. Eventually, Diana Halbrooks stopped therapy and came to realize that the "memories" she had recovered were inaccurate.

How could this happen? A number of the techniques used by psychotherapists to try to pull up forgotten childhood memories are clearly suggestive (Poole et al., 1995). Specifically, research has shown that imagining past events and hypnosis can help create false memories (Garry et al., 1996; Hyman & Pentland, 1996; McConkey, Barnier, & Sheehan, 1998). More recent studies show that memories that people remember spontaneously on their own are corroborated by other people at about the same rate as the memories of individuals who never forgot their abuse, whereas memories recovered in response to suggestive therapeutic techniques are virtually never corroborated by others (McNally & Geraerts, 2009).

6. Bias

In 2000, the outcome of a very close presidential race between George W. Bush and Al Gore was decided by the Supreme Court 5 weeks after the election had taken place. The day after the election (when the result was still in doubt), supporters of Bush and Gore were asked to predict how happy they would be after the outcome of the election was determined (Wilson, Meyers, & Gilbert, 2003). These same respondents reported how happy they felt with the outcome on the day after Al Gore conceded. And 4 months later, the participants recalled how happy they had been right after the election was decided.

Bush supporters were understandably happy the day after the Supreme Court decision. However, their retrospective accounts *over*estimated how happy they were at the time. Conversely, Gore supporters were not pleased with the outcome. But when polled 4 months after the election was decided, Gore supporters *under*estimated how happy they actually were at the time of the result. In both groups, recollections of happiness were at odds with existing reports of their actual happiness at the time (Wilson et al., 2003).

These results illustrate the problem of **bias**, *the distorting influences of present knowledge, beliefs, and feelings on recollection of previous experiences.* Sometimes, what people remember from their pasts says less about what actually happened than about what they think, feel, or believe now. Researchers have also found that our current moods can bias our recall of past experiences (Bower, 1981; Buchanan, 2007; Eich, 1995). So, in addition to helping you recall actual sad memories (as you saw earlier in this chapter), a sad mood can also bias your recollections of experiences that may not have been so sad.

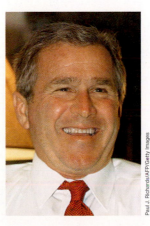

Memory bias can alter the recollection of previous happiness. Indeed, 4 months after they heard the outcome of the 2000 presidential election in which George W. Bush defeated Al Gore, Bush supporters overestimated how happy they were, whereas Gore supporters underestimated how happy they were.

How does your current outlook color your memory of a past event?

bias The distorting influences of present knowledge, beliefs, and feelings on recollection of previous experiences.

Sometimes, we exaggerate differences between what we feel or believe now and what we felt or believed in the past. For example, most of us would like to believe that our romantic attachments grow stronger over time. In one study, dating couples were asked, once a year for 4 years, to assess the present quality of their relationships and to recall how they felt in past years (Sprecher, 1999). Couples who stayed together for the 4 years recalled that the strength of their love had increased since they last reported on it. Yet their actual ratings over time did not show any increases in love and attachment. Objectively, the couples did not love each other more today than yesterday. But they did from the subjective perspective of memory. People were remembering the past as they wanted it to be rather than the way it was.

7. Persistence

The artist Melinda Stickney-Gibson awoke in her apartment to the smell of smoke. She jumped out of bed and saw black plumes rising through cracks in the floor. Raging flames had engulfed the entire building, and there was no chance to escape except by jumping from her third-floor window. Although she survived the fire and the fall, Melinda became overwhelmed by memories of the fire. When Melinda sat down in front of a blank canvas to start a new painting, her memories of that awful night intruded. Her paintings, which were previously bright, colorful abstractions, became dark meditations that included only black, orange, and ochre—the colors of the fire (Schacter, 1996).

Melinda Stickney-Gibson's experiences illustrate memory's seventh and most deadly sin, **persistence**: *the intrusive recollection of events that we wish we could forget*. Melinda's experience is far from unique; persistence frequently occurs after disturbing or traumatic incidents, such as the fire that destroyed her home. Although being able to recall memories quickly is usually considered a good thing, in the case of persistence, that ability mutates into an unwelcome burden.

Intrusive memories are undesirable consequences of emotional experiences because emotional experiences generally lead to more vivid and enduring recollections than nonemotional experiences do. One line of evidence comes from the study of **flashbulb memories**, which are *detailed recollections of when and where we heard about shocking events* (Brown & Kulik, 1977). For example, most Americans can recall exactly where they were and how they heard about the September 11, 2001, terrorist attacks on the World Trade Center and the Pentagon—almost as if a mental flashbulb had gone off automatically and recorded the event in long-lasting and

Andersen Ross/Photolibrary

The way each member of this happy couple recalls earlier feelings toward the other depends on how each currently views the relationship.

persistence The intrusive recollection of events that we wish we could forget.

flashbulb memories Detailed recollections of when and where we heard about shocking events.

Some events are so emotionally charged, such as President Kennedy's assassination and the terrorist attack on the World Trade Center, that we form unusually detailed memories of when and where we heard about them. These flashbulb memories generally persist much longer than memories for more ordinary events.

Bettman/Corbis

Kathy Willens/AP Photo

vivid detail (Kvavilashvili et al., 2009). Several studies have shown that flashbulb memories are not always entirely accurate, but they are generally better remembered than mundane news events from the same time (Larsen, 1992; Neisser & Harsch, 1992). Enhanced retention of flashbulb memories is partly attributable to the emotional arousal elicited by events such as the 9/11 terrorist attacks, and they are partly attributable to the fact that we tend to talk and think a lot about these experiences. Recall that semantic encoding enhances memory: When we talk about flashbulb experiences, we elaborate on them and thus further increase the memorability of those aspects of the experience that we discuss (Hirst et al., 2009).

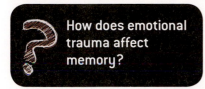
How does emotional trauma affect memory?

Why do our brains succumb to persistence? A key player in the brain's response to emotional events is the *amygdala*, shown in **FIGURE 6.18**. The amygdala influences hormonal systems that kick into high gear when we experience an arousing event; these stress-related hormones, such as adrenaline and cortisol, mobilize the body in the face of threat—and they also enhance memory for the experience. When people watch a slide show including emotional events (such as photos of a child being hit by a car) and also neutral events (a mother walking her child to school), there's a better chance that they will later recall the emotional rather than the neutral events, and the better recall is correlated with heightened activity in the amygdala as they watched the emotional events (Cahill et al., 1996; Kensinger & Schacter, 2005, 2006). When people are given a drug that interferes with the amygdala-mediated release of stress hormones, their memory for the emotional material is no better than their memory for neutral material. Similarly, patients with amygdala damage remember the emotional and neutral material equally well (Cahill & McGaugh, 1998).

In many cases, there are clear benefits to forming strong memories for highly emotional events, particularly those that are life-threatening. In the case of persistence, though, such memories may be too strong—strong enough to interfere with other aspects of daily life.

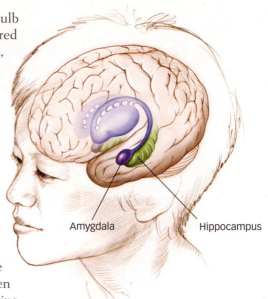
Amygdala   Hippocampus

FIGURE 6.18 **The Amygdala's Influence on Memory** The amygdala, located next to the hippocampus, responds strongly to emotional events. Individuals with amygdala damage are unable to remember emotional events any better than nonemotional ones (Cahill & McGaugh, 1998).

Are the Seven Sins Vices or Virtues?

You may have concluded that evolution has burdened us with an extremely inefficient memory system that is so prone to error that it often jeopardizes our well-being. Not so. The seven sins are the price we pay for the many benefits that memory provides, the occasional result of the normally efficient operation of the human memory system (Schacter, 2001b).

Consider transience, for example. Although it might sound great to remember all the details of every incident in your life, the fact is that it's helpful and sometimes important to forget information that isn't current, like an old phone number. If we didn't gradually forget information over time, our minds would be cluttered with details that we no longer need (Bjork, 2011; Bjork & Bjork, 1988). Memory, in essence, makes a bet that when we haven't used information recently, we probably won't need it in the future. We win this bet more often than we lose it, making transience an adaptive property of memory. But we are acutely aware of the losses—the frustrations of forgetting—and are never aware of the wins. This

How are we better off with imperfect memories?

is why people are often quick to complain about their memories: The drawbacks of forgetting are painfully evident, but the benefits of forgetting are hidden.

Similarly, absentmindedness and blocking can be frustrating, but they are side effects of our memory's usually successful attempt to sort through incoming information, preserving details that are worthy of attention and recall, and discarding those that are less worthy.

Memory misattribution and suggestibility both occur because we often fail to recall the details of exactly when and where we saw a face or learned a fact. Our memories carefully record such details only when we think they may be needed later, and most of the time, we are better off for it. Furthermore, we often use memories to anticipate possible future events. As discussed earlier, memory is flexible, allowing us to recombine elements of past experience in new ways so that we can mentally try out different versions of what might happen. But this very flexibility—a strength of memory—may sometimes produce misattribution errors in which elements of past experience are miscombined (Schacter & Addis, 2007; Schacter, Guerin, & St. Jacques, 2011). Bias skews our memories so that we depict ourselves in an overly favorable light, but it can produce the benefit of contributing to our overall sense of contentment, leading to greater psychological well-being (Taylor, 1989). Although persistence can cause us to be haunted by traumas that we'd be better off forgetting, overall, it is probably adaptive to remember threatening or traumatic events that could pose a threat to survival.

Although each of the seven sins can cause trouble in our lives, they have an adaptive side as well. You can think of the seven sins as costs we pay for benefits that allow memory to work as well as it does most of the time.

Other Voices

Early Memories

Charles Fernyhough is a psychologist at Durham University in England, and he is the author of several books, including *The Baby in the Mirror: A Child's World from Birth to Three* (2008).
LANN

In this eloquent passage from his recent book about memory, *Pieces of Light,* psychologist Charles Fernyhough (2012, pp. 1–2) described his attempt to remember the first fish that he ever caught. He comes up with what he thinks may be the answer, but how does he really know?

"Can you remember?"

It starts with a question from my 7-year-old son. We are in the grounds of our rented cottage in the Baixa Alentejo, killing time before we head to the Algarve coast for a boat trip. With his holiday money, Isaac has bought himself a hand-held toy that fires little foam rockets prodigious distances up into the air, and he has lost one of them on the graveled ground behind the swimming pool. As we search, he has been chattering away about how he wants to go fishing with me when we get home from Portugal. I have told him that I used to go fishing, as a child of about his age, with my uncle in the lake in the grounds of my grandparents' house in Essex. Then, out of the blue, he asks the question:

"Can you remember the first fish you ever caught?"

I stand straight and look out at the farmland that slopes away from our hillside vantage point. I have not been fishing in thirty-five years, but my thoughts have occasionally returned to my outings with my uncle. When they do, certain images rise out of the past. I can picture the greenish lake with its little island in the middle, how mysterious and unreachable that weeping willowed outcrop looked to my small-scale imaginings. I can sense my jocular young uncle next to me, his stretches of silence punctuated with kindly teasing. I remember the feel of the crustless bits of white bread soaked in pond water that we used to squidge on to the fishhooks as bait, and the excitement (for a keen young amateur naturalist) of an afternoon visitation from a stoat, scurrying along by the bullrushes with its black-tipped tail bobbing. I remember the weird, faintly gruesome exercise of extracting the hook from a rudd's mouth and then throwing the muscular sliver back into the lake to restart its perforated life. But I have never thought about the moment of feeling the tug on the line, the thrill that prefigured the landing of a fish. And I have certainly not had the question framed like this, narrowing my remembering down to the first time it ever happened.

"I don't know," I reply. "I *think* so."

What accounts for my uncertainty?

Try to recall your own earliest memory of a specific event from your life: How do you know when your recollection took place? How do you know that what you are remembering is the actual event? What kind of evidence would you require to be convinced that your memory is valid? Can you think of an experiment that might be conducted to provide that evidence?

One way to address this problem is to ask people about memories for events that have clearly definable dates, such as the birth of a younger sibling, the death of a loved one, or a family move. For example, one study found that individuals can recall events surrounding the birth of a sibling that occurred when they were about 2.4 years old (Eacott & Crawley, 1998).

Do you think that firm conclusions can be drawn from these kinds of studies? Isn't it still possible that memories of these early events are based on family conversations that took place long after the events occurred? An adult or a child who remembers having ice cream in the hospital as a 3-year-old when his baby sister was born may be recalling what his parents told him after the event. Carefully designed studies may bring us closer to answering the kinds of questions raised by Charles Fernyhough's response to his son's innocent question, but we still have a long way to go before we can provide convincing answers to the mysteries posed by our earliest memories.

SUMMARY QUIZ [6.5]

1. The rapid decline in memory, followed by more gradual forgetting, is reflected by
   a. chunking.
   b. blocking.
   c. absentmindedness.
   d. transience.

2. Eyewitness misidentification or false recognition is most likely a result of
   a. memory misattribution.
   b. suggestibility.
   c. bias.
   d. retroactive interference.

3. The fact that emotional arousal generally leads to enhanced memory is supported by
   a. bias.
   b. persistence.
   c. proactive interference.
   d. source memory.

CHAPTER REVIEW

SUMMARY

Encoding: Transforming Perceptions into Memories

> Encoding is the process of transforming into a lasting memory the information our senses take in.

> Memory is influenced by the type of encoding we perform regardless of whether we consciously intend to remember an event or a fact.

> Semantic encoding, visual imagery encoding, and organizational encoding all increase memory, but they use different parts of the brain to accomplish that task.

> Encoding information with respect to its survival value is a particularly effective method for increasing subsequent recall, perhaps because our memory systems have evolved in a way that allows us to remember especially well information that is relevant to our survival.

Storage: Maintaining Memories over Time

> Sensory memory holds information for a second or two. Short-term or working memory retains information for about 15 to 20 seconds. Long-term memory stores information anywhere from minutes to years or decades.

> The hippocampus and nearby structures play an important role in long-term memory storage. The hippocampus is also important for memory consolidation, the process that makes memories increasingly resistant to disruption over time.

> Memory storage depends on changes in synapses, and long-term potentiation (LTP) increases synaptic connections.

Retrieval: Bringing Memories to Mind

> Whether we remember a past experience depends on whether retrieval cues are available to trigger recall. Retrieval cues are effective when they are given in the same context as when we encoded an experience. Moods and inner states can serve as retrieval cues.

> Retrieving information from memory can improve subsequent memory of the retrieved information, as exemplified by the beneficial effect of testing on later recall, but it can also impair subsequent remembering of related information that is not retrieved.

> Neuroimaging studies suggest that trying to remember activates the left frontal lobe, whereas successful recovery of stored information activates the hippocampus and regions in the brain related to the sensory aspects of an experience.

Multiple Forms of Memory: How the Past Returns

> Long-term memory consists of explicit memory, the act of consciously or intentionally retrieving past experiences, and implicit memory, the unconscious influence of past experiences on later behavior and performance.

> Implicit memory in turn includes procedural memory, the acquisition of skills as a result of practice, and priming, a change in the ability to recognize or identify an object or a word as the result of past exposure to it.

> People who have amnesia are able to retain implicit memory, including procedural memory and priming, but they lack explicit memory.

> Episodic memory is the collection of personal experiences from a particular time and place; it allows us both to recollect the past and imagine the future. Semantic memory is a networked, general, impersonal knowledge of facts, associations, and concepts.

Memory Failures: The Seven Sins of Memory

> Memory's mistakes can be classified into seven sins, which are the price we pay for the benefits that allow memory to work as well as it does most of the time.

> Some of these "sins" reflect an inability to store or retrieve information we want. *Transience* is reflected by a rapid decline in memory followed by more gradual forgetting. *Absentmindedness* results from failures of attention, shallow encoding, and the influence of automatic behaviors. *Blocking* occurs when stored information is temporarily inaccessible, as when information is on the tip of the tongue. In contrast, *persistence* is the intrusive recollection of events we wish to forget.

> Other "sins" reflect errors in memory content. *Memory misattribution* happens when we experience a sense of familiarity but don't recall—or we mistakenly recall—the specifics of when and where an experience occurred. *Suggestibility* gives rise to implanted memories of small details or entire episodes. *Bias* reflects the influence of current knowledge, beliefs, and feelings on memory or past experiences.

KEY TERMS

memory (p. 172)
encoding (p. 172)
storage (p. 172)
retrieval (p. 172)
semantic encoding (p. 172)
sensory memory (p. 177)
iconic memory (p. 177)
echoic memory (p. 177)
short-term memory (p. 177)
rehearsal (p. 177)

chunking (p. 178)
working memory (p. 178)
long-term memory (p. 178)
anterograde amnesia (p. 179)
retrograde amnesia (p. 179)
consolidation (p. 180)
reconsolidation (p. 180)
long-term potentiation (LTP) (p. 182)
state-dependent retrieval (p. 183)

transfer-appropriate processing (p. 183)
explicit memory (p. 187)
implicit memory (p. 187)
procedural memory (p. 187)
priming (p. 188)
semantic memory (p. 189)
episodic memory (p. 189)
transience (p. 193)
retroactive interference (p. 194)
proactive interference (p. 194)

absentmindedness (p. 194)
prospective memory (p. 195)
blocking (p. 195)
memory misattribution (p. 196)
source memory (p. 196)
suggestibility (p. 198)
bias (p. 199)
persistence (p. 200)
flashbulb memories (p. 200)

CHANGING MINDS

1. A friend of yours lost her father to cancer when she was a very young child. "I really wish I remembered him better," she says. "I know all the memories are locked in my head. I'm thinking of trying hypnotism to unlock some of those memories." You explain that we don't, in fact, have stored memories of everything that ever happened to us locked in our heads. What examples could you give of ways in which memories can be lost over time?

2. Another friend of yours has a very vivid memory of sitting with his parents in the living room on September 11, 2001, watching live TV as the Twin Towers fell during the terrorist attacks. "I remember my mother was crying," he says, "and that scared me more than the pictures on the TV." Later, he goes home for a visit and discusses the events of 9/11 with his mother—and he is stunned when she assures him that he was actually in school on the morning of the attacks and was only sent home at lunchtime, after the towers had fallen. "I don't understand," he tells you afterward. "I think she must be confused, because I have a perfect memory of that morning." Assuming your friend's mother is recalling events correctly, how would you explain to your friend the ways in which his flashbulb memory could be wrong? What memory sin might be at fault?

3. You ask one of your psychology classmates if she wants to form a study group to prepare for an upcoming exam. "No offense," she says, "but I can study the material best by just reading the chapter eight or nine times, and I can do that without a study group." What's wrong with your classmate's study plan? In what ways might the members of a study group help one another learn more effectively?

4. You and a friend go to a party on campus where you meet a lot of new people. After the party, your friend says, "I liked a lot of the people we met, but I'll never remember all their names. Some people just have a good memory, and some don't, and there's nothing I can do about it." What advice could you give your friend to help him remember the names of people he meets at the next party?

5. A friend of yours who is taking a criminal justice class reads about a case in which the conviction of an accused murderer was later overturned, based on DNA evidence. "It's a travesty of justice," she

says. "An eyewitness clearly identified the man by picking him out of a lineup and then identified him again in court during the trial. No results from a chemistry lab should count more than eyewitness testimony." What is your friend failing to appreciate about eyewitness testimony? What sin of memory could lead an eyewitness to honestly believe she is identifying the correct man when she is actually making a false identification?

ANSWERS TO SUMMARY QUIZZES

Summary Quiz 6.1: 1. a; 2. c; 3. c.
Summary Quiz 6.2: 1. d; 2. a; 3. b.
Summary Quiz 6.3: 1. b; 2. d; 3. a.
Summary Quiz 6.4: 1. d; 2. a; 3. c.
Summary Quiz 6.5: 1. d; 2. a; 3. b.

Need more help? Additional resources are located in LaunchPad at:
http://www.worthpublishers.com/launchpad/
schacterbrief3e

7

Learning

J ENNIFER, A 45-YEAR-OLD CAREER MILITARY NURSE, served 19 months abroad during the Iraq war, including 4 months in a hospital near Baghdad, where she witnessed many horrifying events, including numerous deaths and serious casualties. Jennifer worked 12- to 14-hour shifts, trying to avoid incoming fire while tending to some of the most gruesomely wounded cases.

This repetitive trauma took a toll on Jennifer, and when she returned home, it became evident that she had not left behind her war experiences. Jennifer thought about them repeatedly, and they profoundly influenced her reactions to many aspects of everyday life. The previously innocent sound of a helicopter approaching, which in Iraq signaled that new wounded bodies were about to arrive, now created in Jennifer heightened feelings of fear and anxiety. She regularly awoke from nightmares concerning her Iraq experiences. Jennifer was "forever changed" by her Iraq experiences (Feczer & Bjorklund, 2009). And that is one reason why Jennifer's story is a compelling, though disturbing, introduction to the topic of learning.

Much of what happened to Jennifer after she returned home reflects the operation of a kind of learning based on association. Sights, sounds, and smells in Iraq had become associated with negative emotions in a way that created an enduring bond, so that encountering similar sights, sounds, and smells at home elicited similarly intense negative feelings.

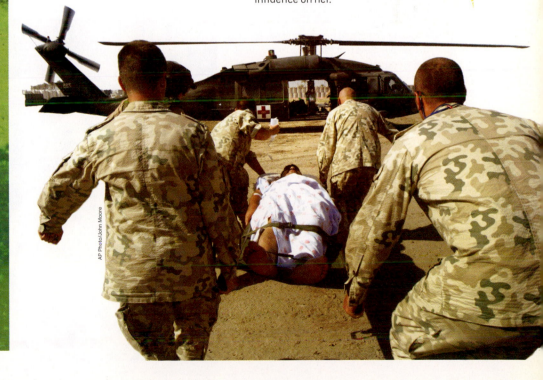

During the 4 months that she served at a prison hospital near Baghdad during the Iraq war, Jennifer learned to associate the sound of an arriving helicopter with wounded bodies. That learned association had a long-lasting influence on her.

AP Photo/John Moore

learning The acquisition of new knowledge, skills, or responses from experience that results in a relatively permanent change in the state of the learner.

habituation A general process in which repeated or prolonged exposure to a stimulus results in a gradual reduction in responding.

sensitization A simple form of learning that occurs when presentation of a stimulus leads to an increased response to a later stimulus.

Learning involves *the acquisition of new knowledge, skills, or responses from experience that results in a relatively permanent change in the state of the learner.* This definition emphasizes three key ideas: Learning is based on experience, learning produces changes in the organism, and these changes are relatively permanent.

Think about Jennifer's time in Iraq, and you'll see all of these elements: Experiences such as the association between the sound of an approaching helicopter and the arrival of wounded bodies changed the way Jennifer responded to certain situations in a way that lasted for years.

Learning can also occur in much simpler, nonassociative forms. You are probably familiar with the phenomenon of **habituation,** *a general process in which repeated or prolonged exposure to a stimulus results in a gradual reduction in responding.* If you've ever lived near a busy highway, you've probably noticed the sound of traffic when you first moved in. You probably also noticed that after a while, you ignored the sounds of the automobiles in your vicinity. This welcome reduction in responding reflects the operation of habituation.

Habituation occurs even in simple organisms, such as the sea slug *Aplysia* that you met in the Memory chapter: When lightly touched, the sea slug withdraws its gill, but the response gradually weakens after repeated light touches. *Aplysia* also exhibits another simple form of learning known as **sensitization,** which occurs when *presentation of a stimulus leads to an increased response to a later stimulus.* For example, after receiving a strong shock, *Aplysia* shows an increased gill withdrawal response to a light touch. In a similar manner, people whose houses have been broken into may later become hypersensitive to late-night sounds that wouldn't have bothered them previously.

Although these simple kinds of learning are important, in this chapter, we'll focus on more complex kinds of learning. As you'll recall from the Psychology: Evolution of a Science chapter, the behaviorists insisted on measuring only observable, quantifiable behavior and dismissed mental activity as irrelevant and unknowable. Behaviorists argued that learning's "permanent change in experience" could be demonstrated equally well in almost any organism: rats, dogs, pigeons, mice, pigs, or humans. But there are also some important cognitive considerations (i.e., elements of mental activity) that need to be addressed in order to

How might psychologists use the concept of habituation to explain the fact that today's action movies tend to show much more graphic violence than movies of the 1980s, which in turn tended to show more graphic violence than movies of the 1950s?

understand the learning process. In this chapter, we'll first discuss two major approaches to learning: classical conditioning and operant conditioning. We'll then see that some important kinds of learning occur simply by watching others and also that some kinds of learning can occur entirely outside of awareness. Finally, we'll discuss learning in a context that should matter a lot to you: the classroom.

Classical Conditioning: One Thing Leads to Another

American psychologist John B. Watson kick-started the behaviorist movement, arguing that psychologists should "never use the terms *consciousness, mental states, mind, content, introspectively verifiable, imagery,* and the like" (Watson, 1913, p. 166). Watson's firebrand stance was fueled in large part by the work of a Russian physiologist, Ivan Pavlov (1849–1936).

Pavlov studied the digestive processes of laboratory animals by surgically implanting test tubes into the cheeks of dogs to measure their salivary responses to different foods. Serendipitously, his explorations into spit and drool revealed a form of learning, which came to be called classical conditioning. **Classical conditioning** occurs *when a neutral stimulus produces a response after being paired with a stimulus that naturally produces a response.* Pavlov showed that dogs learned to salivate to a neutral stimulus, such as a bell or a tone, after that stimulus had been associated with another stimulus that naturally evokes salivation, such as food.

The Development of Classical Conditioning: Pavlov's Experiments

Pavlov's basic experimental setup involved cradling dogs in a harness to administer the foods and to measure the salivary response, as shown in **FIGURE 7.1**. He noticed that dogs that had previously been in the experiment began to produce a kind of "anticipatory" salivary response as soon as they were put in the harness, before any food was presented. Pavlov and his colleagues regarded these responses as annoyances at first because they interfered with collecting naturally occurring salivary secretions. In reality, the dogs were exhibiting classical conditioning. When the dogs were initially presented with a plate of food, they began to salivate. No surprise here. Pavlov called the presentation of food an **unconditioned stimulus (US)**, *something that reliably produces a naturally occurring reaction in an organism.* He called the dogs' salivation an **unconditioned response (UR)**, *a reflexive reaction that is reliably produced by an unconditioned stimulus.*

Pavlov soon discovered that he could make the dogs salivate to other stimuli, such as the ringing of a bell or the flash of a light (Pavlov, 1927). Each of these stimuli was a **conditioned stimulus (CS)**, *a previously neutral stimulus that produces a reliable response in an organism after being paired with a US* (see **FIGURE 7.2**). When the conditioned stimulus, such as the sound of a bell, is paired over time with the US (food), the animal will learn to associate food with the sound, and eventually, the CS is sufficient to produce a response (in this case, salivation). Pavlov called this response the **conditioned response (CR)**, *a reaction that resembles an unconditioned response but is produced by a conditioned stimulus.* In this example, the dogs' salivation (CR) was prompted by the sound of the bell (CS) because the bell and the food (US) had been associated so often in the past.

classical conditioning A type of learning that occurs when a neutral stimulus produces a response after being paired with a stimulus that naturally produces a response.

unconditioned stimulus (US) Something that reliably produces a naturally occurring reaction in an organism.

unconditioned response (UR) A reflexive reaction that is reliably produced by an unconditioned stimulus.

conditioned stimulus (CS) A previously neutral stimulus that produces a reliable response in an organism after being paired with a US.

conditioned response (CR) A reaction that resembles an unconditioned response but is produced by a conditioned stimulus.

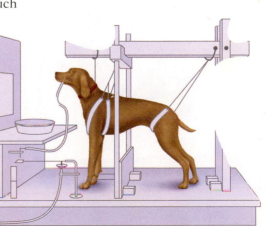

FIGURE 7.1 Pavlov's Apparatus for Studying Classical Conditioning Pavlov presented auditory stimuli to the animals using a bell or a tuning fork. Visual stimuli could be presented on the screen.

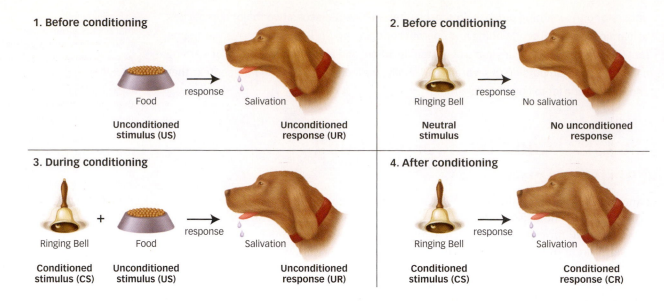

1. **Before conditioning**

Food → response → Salivation

Unconditioned stimulus (US) → Unconditioned response (UR)

2. **Before conditioning**

Ringing Bell → response → No salivation

Neutral stimulus → No unconditioned response

3. **During conditioning**

Ringing Bell + Food → response → Salivation

Conditioned stimulus (CS) | Unconditioned stimulus (US) → Unconditioned response (UR)

4. **After conditioning**

Ringing Bell → response → Salivation

Conditioned stimulus (CS) → Conditioned response (CR)

FIGURE 7.2 The Elements of Classical Conditioning In classical conditioning, a previously neutral stimulus (such as the sound of a bell) is paired with an unconditioned stimulus (such as the presentation of food). After several trials associating the two, the conditioned stimulus (the sound) alone can produce a conditioned response.

Consider your own dog (or cat). Does your dog always know when dinner's coming, as though she has one eye on the clock every day, waiting for the dinner hour? Alas, your dog is no clock-watching wonder hound. Instead, the presentation of food (the US) has become associated with a complex CS—your getting up, moving into the kitchen, opening the cabinet, working the can opener—such that the CS alone signals to your dog that food is on the way and therefore initiates the CR of her getting ready to eat.

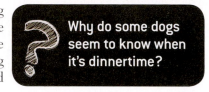

Why do some dogs seem to know when it's dinnertime?

The Basic Principles of Classical Conditioning

When Pavlov's findings first appeared (Pavlov, 1923a, 1923b), they produced a flurry of excitement. Classical conditioning was the kind of behaviorist psychology Watson was proposing: An organism experiences stimuli that are observable and measurable, and changes in that organism can be directly observed and measured. Dogs learned to salivate to the sound of a buzzer, and there was no need to resort to explanations about why it had happened, what the dog wanted, or how the animal thought about the situation. Pavlov also appreciated the significance of his discovery and embarked on a systematic investigation of the mechanisms of classical conditioning. Let's take a closer look at some of these principles. (As the Real World box shows, these principles help explain how drug overdoses occur.)

Acquisition

Remember when you first got your dog? Chances are she didn't seem too smart, especially the way she stared at you vacantly as you went into the kitchen, not anticipating that food was on the way. That's because learning through classical conditioning requires some period of association between the CS and US. This period is called **acquisition,** *the phase of classical conditioning when the CS and the US are presented together.* Typically, learning starts low, rises rapidly, and then slowly tapers off, as shown on the left side of **FIGURE 7.3.** Pavlov's dogs gradually increased their amount of salivation over several trials of pairing a tone with the presentation of food, and similarly, your dog eventually learned to associate your kitchen preparations with the subsequent appearance of food. After learning has been established, the CS by itself will reliably elicit the CR.

acquisition The phase of classical conditioning when the CS and the US are presented together.

"I THINK MOM'S USING THE CAN OPENER."

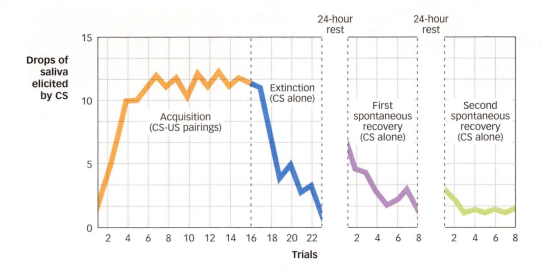

FIGURE 7.3 Acquisition, Extinction, and Spontaneous Recovery In classical conditioning, the CS is originally neutral and produces no specific response. After several trials pairing the CS with the US, the CS alone comes to elicit the CR. Learning tends to take place fairly rapidly and then levels off as stable responding develops. In extinction, the CR diminishes quickly. A rest period, however, is typically followed by spontaneous recovery of the CR. In fact, a well-learned CR may show spontaneous recovery after more than one rest period even though there have been no additional learning trials.

Second-Order Conditioning

After conditioning has been established, **second-order conditioning** can be demonstrated: *conditioning in which a CS is paired with a stimulus that became associated with the US in an earlier procedure.* For example, in an early study, Pavlov repeatedly paired a new CS, a black square, with the now reliable tone. After a number of training trials, his dogs produced a salivary response to the black square even though the square itself had never been directly associated with the food. Second-order conditioning helps explain why some people desire money to the point that they hoard it and value it even more than the objects it purchases. Money is initially used to purchase objects that produce gratifying outcomes, such as an expensive car. Although money is not directly associated with the thrill of a drive in a new sports car, through second-order conditioning, money can become linked with this type of desirable quality.

Extinction and Spontaneous Recovery

After Pavlov and his colleagues had explored the process of acquisition, they wondered what would happen if they continued to present the CS (tone) but stopped presenting the US (food). As shown on the right side of the first panel in Figure 7.3, behavior declines abruptly and continues to drop until eventually, the dog ceases to salivate at the sound of the tone. This process is called **extinction,** *the gradual elimination of a learned response that occurs when the CS is repeatedly presented without the US.* The term was introduced because the conditioned response is "extinguished" and no longer observed.

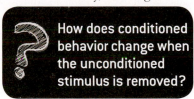

How does conditioned behavior change when the unconditioned stimulus is removed?

Pavlov next wondered if this elimination of conditioned behavior was permanent. When the dogs were brought back to the lab and presented with the CS again, they displayed **spontaneous recovery,** *the tendency of a learned behavior to recover from extinction after a rest period.* This phenomenon is shown in the middle panel in Figure 7.3. Notice that this recovery takes place even though there have not been any additional associations between the CS and US. Some spontaneous recovery of the conditioned response even takes place after a period of rest (see the right-hand panel in Figure 7.3). Clearly, extinction had not completely erased the learning that had been acquired.

Generalization and Discrimination

Do you think your dog will be stumped, unable to anticipate the presentation of her food, if you get a new can opener? Will a whole new round of conditioning need to be established with this modified CS?

second-order conditioning Conditioning in which a CS is paired with a stimulus that became associated with the US in an earlier procedure.

extinction The gradual elimination of a learned response that occurs when the CS is repeatedly presented without the US.

spontaneous recovery The tendency of a learned behavior to recover from extinction after a rest period.

GVictoria/Shutterstock

Your first electric can opener may cause your dog some confusion, but likely only for a little while.

Probably not. It wouldn't be very adaptive for an organism if each little change in the CS–US pairing required an extensive regimen of new learning. Rather, the phenomenon of **generalization** tends to take place: *The CR is observed even though the CS is slightly different from the CS used during acquisition.* This means that the conditioning generalizes to stimuli that are similar to the CS used during the original training. As you might expect, the more the new stimulus changes, the less conditioned responding is observed. If you replaced a manual can opener with an electric can opener, your dog would probably show a much weaker conditioned response (Pearce, 1987; Rescorla, 2006). Such *diminished* responding to the new stimulus indicates **discrimination,** *the capacity to distinguish between similar but distinct stimuli.* Generalization and discrimination are two sides of the same coin. The more organisms show one, the less they show the other, and training can modify the balance between the two.

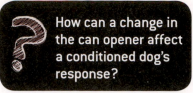

How can a change in the can opener affect a conditioned dog's response?

Conditioned Emotional Responses: The Case of Little Albert

Watson and his followers thought that it was possible to develop general explanations of pretty much *any* behavior of *any* organism based on classical conditioning principles. As a step in that direction, Watson embarked on a controversial study with his research

The Real World

Understanding Drug Overdoses

All too often, police are confronted with a perplexing problem: the sudden death of heroin addicts from a drug overdose. The victims are often experienced drug users; the dose taken is usually not larger than what they usually take; and the deaths tend to occur in unusual settings.

Classical conditioning provides some insight into how these deaths occur. First, when classical conditioning takes place, the CS is more than a simple bell or tone: It also includes the overall *context* within which the conditioning takes place. In the case of heroin, when the drug is injected, the entire setting (the drug paraphernalia, the room, the lighting, the addict's usual companions) functions as the CS. Second, many CRs are compensatory in nature, counteracting the anticipated effects of the US. Heroin, for example, causes many changes in the body, such as slower breathing, so the body responds by speeding up breathing in order to maintain a state of balance. Over time, this protective physiological response becomes part of the CR, and like all CRs, it occurs in the presence of the CS but prior to the actual administration of the US (in this case, the heroin). These compensatory physiological reactions are also what make drug abusers take increasingly larger doses to

achieve the same effect. Ultimately, these reactions produce *drug tolerance*, discussed in the Consciousness chapter.

Based on these principles of classical conditioning, taking drugs in a new environment can be fatal for a longtime drug user. If an addict injects the usual dose in a setting that is sufficiently novel or where heroin has never been taken before, the CS is now altered, so that the physiological compensatory CR that usually serves a protective function may not occur (Siegel et al., 2000). As a result, the addict's usual dose becomes an overdose, and death often results. Understanding these principles has led to treatments for drug addicts. For example,

the brain's compensatory response to a drug, when elicited by the familiar contextual cues ordinarily associated with drug taking that constitute the CS, can be experienced by the addict as withdrawal symptoms. In *cue exposure therapies*, an addict is exposed to drug-related cues without being given the usual dose of the drug itself, eventually resulting in extinction of the association between the contextual cues and the compensatory CR. After an addict has undergone such treatment, encountering familiar drug-related cues will no longer result in the CR, thereby making it easier for a recovering addict to remain abstinent (Siegel, 2005).

AP Photo/Chris Gardner

Although opium dens and crack houses may be considered blight, it is often safer for addicts to use drugs there. The environment becomes part of the addict's CS, so ironically, busting crack houses may contribute to more deaths from drug overdoses when addicts are pushed to use drugs in new situations.

assistant Rosalie Rayner (Watson & Rayner, 1920) to see if a healthy, well-developed child could be classically conditioned to experience a strong emotional reaction, namely, fear. To find out, Watson and Raynor enlisted the assistance of 9-month-old "Little Albert."

Watson presented Little Albert with a variety of stimuli: a white rat, a dog, a rabbit, various masks, and a burning newspaper. Albert's reactions in most cases were curiosity or indifference, and he showed no fear of any of the items. Watson also established that something *could* make Albert afraid. While Albert was watching Rayner, Watson unexpectedly struck a large steel bar with a hammer, producing a loud noise. Predictably, this caused Albert to cry, tremble, and be generally displeased.

Watson and Rayner then led Little Albert through the acquisition phase of classical conditioning. Albert was presented with a white rat. As soon as he reached out to touch it, the steel bar was

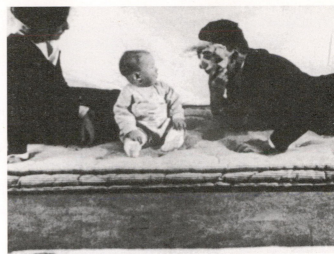

Watson & Rayner, 1920

struck. This pairing occurred again and again over several trials. Eventually, the sight of the rat alone caused Albert to recoil in terror. In this situation, a US (the loud sound) was paired with a CS (the presence of the rat) such that the CS all by itself was sufficient to produce the CR (a fearful reaction). Little Albert also showed stimulus generalization. The sight of a white rabbit, a seal-fur coat, and a Santa Claus mask produced the same kinds of fear reactions in the infant.

? Why did Albert fear the rat?

This study was controversial in its cavalier treatment of a young child. Modern ethical guidelines that govern the treatment of research participants make sure that this kind of study could not be conducted today. So, what was Watson's goal in all this? First, he wanted to show that a relatively complex reaction could be conditioned using Pavlovian techniques. Second, he wanted to show that emotional responses such as fear and anxiety could be produced by classical conditioning and therefore need not be the product of deeper unconscious processes. Instead, Watson proposed that fears could be learned, just like any other behavior.

The kind of conditioned fear responses that were at work in Little Albert's case were also important in the chapter-opening case of Jennifer, who experienced fear and anxiety when hearing the previously innocent sound of an approaching helicopter as a result of her experiences in Iraq. Indeed, a therapy that has proven effective in dealing with such trauma-induced fears is based directly on principles of classical conditioning: Individuals are repeatedly exposed to conditioned stimuli associated with their trauma in a safe setting in an attempt to extinguish the conditioned fear response (Bouton, 1988; Rothbaum & Schwartz, 2002). However, conditioned emotional responses are not limited to fear and anxiety responses. The warm and fuzzy feeling that envelops you when hearing a song on the radio that you used to listen to with a former boyfriend or girlfriend represents a type of conditioned emotional response.

A Deeper Understanding of Classical Conditioning

As a form of learning, classical conditioning has a simple set of principles and applications to real-life situations. It offered a good deal of utility for psychologists who sought to understand the mechanisms underlying learning, and it continues to do so today. Since Pavlov's day, classical conditioning has been subjected to deeper scrutiny in order to understand exactly how, when, and why it works. Let's examine three

John Watson and Rosalie Rayner show Little Albert an unusual bunny mask. Why doesn't the mere presence of these experimenters serve as a conditioned stimulus in itself?

generalization The CR is observed even though the CS is slightly different from the CS used during acquisition.

discrimination The capacity to distinguish between similar but distinct stimuli.

What response do you think the advertisers of Budweiser are looking for when they feature a Clydesdale horse in an ad?

AP Photo/ Kyle Ericson

areas that give us a closer look at the mechanisms of classical conditioning: the cognitive, neural, and evolutionary elements.

The Cognitive Elements of Classical Conditioning

Pavlov's work was a behaviorist's dream come true. In this view, conditioning is something that *happens* to a dog, a rat, or a person, apart from what the organism thinks about the conditioning situation. However, although the dogs salivated when their feeders approached (see the Psychology: Evolution of a Science chapter), they did not salivate when Pavlov did. Eventually, someone was bound to ask an important question: *Why not?* After all, Pavlov also delivered the food to the dogs, so why didn't he become a CS? Indeed, if Watson was present whenever the unpleasant US was sounded, why didn't Little Albert come to fear *him*?

Somehow, Pavlov's dogs were sensitive to the fact that Pavlov was not a *reliable* indicator of the arrival of food. Pavlov was linked with the arrival of food, but he was also linked with other activities that had nothing to do with food, including checking on the apparatus, bringing the dog from the kennel to the laboratory, and standing around and talking with his assistants.

Robert Rescorla and Allan Wagner (1972) were the first to theorize that classical conditioning occurs when an animal has an *expectation*. The bell, because of its systematic pairing with food, served to set up this cognitive state for the laboratory dogs; Pavlov, because of the lack of any reliable link with food, did not. The Rescorla–Wagner model introduced a cognitive component that accounted for a variety of classical conditioning phenomena that were difficult to understand from a simple behaviorist point of view. For example, the model predicted that conditioning would be easier when the CS was an *unfamiliar* event than when it was familiar. The reason is that familiar events, being familiar, already have expectations associated with them, making new conditioning difficult. In short, classical conditioning might appear to be a primitive process, but it is actually quite sophisticated and incorporates a significant cognitive element.

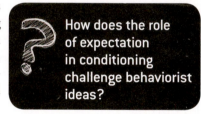

How does the role of expectation in conditioning challenge behaviorist ideas?

The Neural Elements of Classical Conditioning

Pavlov saw his research as providing insights into how the brain works. Recent research has clarified some of what Pavlov hoped to understand about conditioning and the brain.

Richard Thompson and his colleagues focused on classical conditioning of eyeblink responses in the rabbit, in which the CS (a tone) is immediately followed by the US (a puff of air), which elicits a reflexive eyeblink response. After many CS–US pairings, the eyeblink response occurs in response to the CS alone. Thompson and colleagues showed convincingly that the cerebellum is critical for the occurrence of eyeblink conditioning (Thompson, 2005). Studies of people with lesions to the cerebellum supported these findings by demonstrating impaired eyeblink conditioning (Daum et al., 1993). Rounding out the picture, more recent neuroimaging findings in healthy young adults show activation in the cerebellum during eyeblink conditioning (Cheng et al., 2008). As you learned in the Neuroscience and Behavior chapter, the cerebellum is part of the hindbrain and plays an important role in motor skills and learning.

Also in the Neuroscience and Behavior chapter, you saw that the amygdala plays an important role in the experience of emotion, including fear and anxiety. So, it should come as no surprise that the amygdala is also critical for emotional conditioning. Normal rats, trained so that a tone (CS) predicts a mild electric shock (US), show a defensive reaction (CR), known as *freezing*, where they crouch down

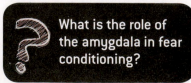

What is the role of the amygdala in fear conditioning?

and sit motionless. If connections linking the amygdala to the midbrain are disrupted, the rat does not exhibit the behavioral freezing response. The amygdala is involved in fear conditioning in people as well as rats and other animals (Olsson & Phelps, 2007; Phelps & LeDoux, 2005).

The Evolutionary Elements of Classical Conditioning

Evolutionary mechanisms also play an important role in classical conditioning. As you learned in the Psychology: Evolution of a Science chapter, evolution and natural selection go hand in hand with adaptiveness: Behaviors that are adaptive allow an organism to survive and thrive in its environment.

Consider this example: A psychology professor was once on a job interview in Southern California, and his hosts took him to lunch at a Middle Eastern restaurant. Suffering from a case of bad hummus, he was up all night long, and he developed a lifelong aversion to hummus. The hummus was the CS, a bacterium or some other source of toxicity was the US, and the resulting nausea was the UR. The UR (the nausea) became linked to the once-neutral CS (the hummus) and became a CR (an aversion to hummus).

This scenario makes sense from an evolutionary perspective. Any species that forages or consumes a variety of foods needs to develop a mechanism by which it can learn to avoid any food that once made it ill. To have adaptive value, this learning should be very rapid—occurring in perhaps one or two trials. If learning takes more trials than this, the animal could die from eating a toxic substance. Also, learned aversions should occur more often with novel foods than with familiar ones. It is not adaptive for an animal to develop an aversion to everything it has eaten on the particular day it got sick. Our psychologist friend didn't develop an aversion to the Coke he drank with lunch or the scrambled eggs he had for breakfast that day; however, the sight and smell of hummus do make him uneasy.

Classical conditioning of food aversions has been studied in rats, using USs such as injection or radiation that cause nausea and vomiting (Garcia & Koelling, 1966). Food aversions are relatively easy to produce in rats if the CS is an unfamiliar taste or smell, but they are difficult or impossible if the CS is a sight or sound. On the other hand, the taste and smell stimuli that produce food aversions in rats do not work with most species of birds. Birds depend primarily on visual cues for finding food and are relatively insensitive to taste and smell. However, it is relatively easy to produce a food aversion in birds using an unfamiliar visual stimulus as the CS, such as a brightly colored food (Wilcoxon, Dragoin, & Kral, 1971). Studies such as these suggest that evolution has provided each species with a kind of **biological preparedness,** *a propensity for learning particular kinds of associations over others*, so that some behaviors are relatively easy to condition in some species but not others.

This research had an interesting application. It led to the development of a technique for dealing with an unanticipated side effect of radiation and chemotherapy: Cancer patients who experience nausea from their treatments often develop aversions to foods they ate before the therapy. Broberg and Bernstein (1987) reasoned that if the findings with rats generalized to humans, a simple technique should minimize the negative consequences of this effect. The researchers gave the patients an unusual food (coconut- or root-beer–flavored candy) at the end of the last meal before undergoing treatment. Sure enough, the conditioned food aversions that the patients developed were overwhelmingly for one of the unusual flavors and not for any of the other foods in the meal. Other than any root beer or coconut fanatics among the sample, patients were spared developing aversions to common foods that they were more likely to eat.

biological preparedness A propensity for learning particular kinds of associations over others.

Under certain conditions, people may develop food aversions. This serving of hummus looks inviting and probably tastes delicious, but at least one psychologist avoids it like the plague.

Rats can be difficult to poison because of learned taste aversions, which are an evolutionarily adaptive element of classical conditioning. Here a worker tries his best in the sewers of Paris.

> **?** How has cancer patients' discomfort been eased by our understanding of food aversions?

SUMMARY QUIZ [7.1]

1. In classical conditioning, a conditioned stimulus is paired with an unconditioned stimulus to produce
   a. a neutral stimulus.
   b. a conditioned response.
   c. an unconditioned response.
   d. another conditioned stimulus.

2. What occurs when a conditioned stimulus is no longer paired with an unconditioned stimulus?
   a. generalization
   b. spontaneous recovery
   c. extinction
   d. acquisition

3. What did Watson and Rayner seek to demonstrate about behaviorism through the Little Albert experiment?
   a. Conditioning involves a degree of cognition.
   b. Classical conditioning has an evolutionary component.
   c. Behaviorism alone cannot explain human behavior.
   d. Even sophisticated behaviors such as emotion are subject to classical conditioning.

4. Which part of the brain is involved in the classical conditioning of fear?
   a. the amygdala
   b. the cerebellum
   c. the hippocampus
   d. the hypothalamus

Operant Conditioning: Reinforcements from the Environment

The study of classical conditioning is the study of behaviors that are *reactive*. Most animals don't voluntarily salivate or feel spasms of anxiety; rather, animals exhibit these responses involuntarily during the conditioning process. But we also engage in voluntary behaviors in order to obtain rewards and avoid punishment. **Operant conditioning** is *a type of learning in which the consequences of an organism's behavior determine whether it will be repeated in the future.* The study of operant conditioning is the exploration of behaviors that are *active*.

The Development of Operant Conditioning: The Law of Effect

The study of how active behavior affects the environment began at about the same time as classical conditioning. In the 1890s, Edward Thorndike studied *instrumental behaviors*—that is, behavior that required an organism to *do* something, solve a problem, or otherwise manipulate elements of its environment (Thorndike, 1898). Some of Thorndike's experiments used a puzzle box, which was a wooden crate with a door that

operant conditioning A type of learning in which the consequences of an organism's behavior determine whether it will be repeated in the future.

would open when a concealed lever was moved in the right way (see **FIGURE 7.4**). A hungry cat placed in a puzzle box would try various behaviors to get out—scratching at the door, meowing loudly, sniffing the inside of the box, putting its paw through the openings—but only one behavior opened the door and led to food: tripping the lever in just the right way. After this happened, Thorndike placed the cat back in the box for another round. Over time, the ineffective behaviors became less and less frequent, and the one instrumental behavior (going right for the latch) became more frequent (see **FIGURE 7.5**). From these observations, Thorndike developed the

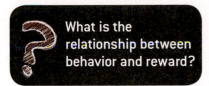

law of effect: *Behaviors that are followed by a "satisfying state of affairs" tend to be repeated and those that produce an "unpleasant state of affairs" are less likely to be repeated.*

FIGURE 7.4 Thorndike's Puzzle Box In Thorndike's original experiments, food was placed just outside the door of the puzzle box, where the cat could see it. If the cat triggered the appropriate lever, the door would open, letting the cat out.

Such learning is very different from classical conditioning. Remember that in classical conditioning experiments, the US occurred on every training trial no matter what the animal did. Pavlov delivered food to the dog whether it salivated or not. But in Thorndike's work, the behavior of the animal determined what happened next. If the behavior was "correct" (i.e., the latch was triggered), the animal was rewarded with food. Incorrect behaviors produced no results, and the animal was stuck in the box until it performed the correct behavior. Although different from classical conditioning, Thorndike's work resonated with most behaviorists at the time: It was still observable, quantifiable, and free from explanations involving the mind (Galef, 1998).

B. F. Skinner: The Role of Reinforcement and Punishment

Several decades after Thorndike's work, B. F. Skinner (1904–1990) coined the term **operant behavior** to refer to *behavior that an organism produces that has some impact on the environment.* In Skinner's system, all of these emitted behaviors "operated" on the environment in some manner, and the environment responded by providing events that either strengthened those behaviors (i.e., they *reinforced* them) or made them less likely to occur (i.e., they *punished* them). Skinner's elegantly simple observation was that most organisms do *not* behave like a dog in a harness, passively waiting to receive food no matter what the circumstances. Rather, most organisms are like cats in a box, actively engaging the environment in which they find themselves to reap rewards (Skinner, 1938, 1953). In order to study operant behavior scientifically, Skinner developed the *operant conditioning chamber,* or *Skinner box,* as it is commonly

law of effect Behaviors that are followed by a "satisfying state of affairs" tend to be repeated and those that produce an "unpleasant state of affairs" are less likely to be repeated.

operant behavior Behavior that an organism produces that has some impact on the environment.

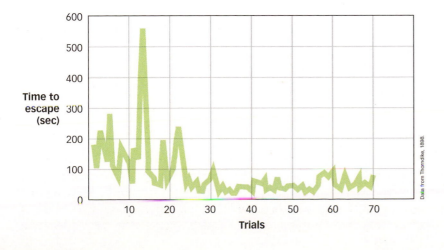

Time to escape (sec)

Data from Thorndike, 1898.

FIGURE 7.5 The Law of Effect Thorndike's cats displayed trial-and-error behavior when trying to escape from the puzzle box until, over time, they discovered the solution. Once they figured out what behavior was instrumental in opening the latch, they stopped all other ineffective behaviors and escaped from the box faster and faster.

B. F. Skinner with one of his many research participants.

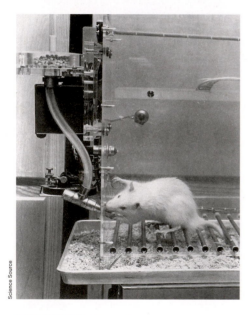

FIGURE 7.6 Skinner Box In a typical Skinner box, or *operant conditioning chamber*, a rat, pigeon, or other suitably sized animal is placed in this environment and observed during learning trials that use operant conditioning principles.

reinforcer Any stimulus or event that functions to increase the likelihood of the behavior that led to it.

punisher Any stimulus or event that functions to decrease the likelihood of the behavior that led to it.

called (shown in **FIGURE 7.6**), which allows a researcher to study the behavior of small organisms in a controlled environment.

Skinner's approach to the study of learning focused on *reinforcement* and *punishment*. These terms, which have commonsense connotations, have particular meanings in psychology, in terms of their effects on behavior. Therefore, a **reinforcer** is *any stimulus or event that functions to increase the likelihood of the behavior that led to it*, whereas a **punisher** is *any stimulus or event that functions to decrease the likelihood of the behavior that led to it*.

Whether a particular stimulus acts as a reinforcer or a punisher depends in part on whether it increases or decreases the likelihood of a behavior. Presenting food is usually reinforcing and produces an increase in the behavior that led to it; removing food is often punishing and leads to a decrease in the behavior. Turning on a device that causes an electric shock is typically punishing (and decreases the behavior that led to it); turning it off is rewarding (and increases the behavior that led to it).

To keep these possibilities distinct, Skinner used the term *positive* for situations in which a stimulus was presented and *negative* for situations in which it was removed. Consequently, there is *positive reinforcement* (where a rewarding stimulus is presented) and *negative reinforcement* (where an unpleasant stimulus is removed), as well as *positive punishment* (where an unpleasant stimulus is administered) and *negative punishment* (where a rewarding stimulus is removed). Here the words *positive* and *negative* mean, respectively, something that is *added* or something that is *taken away*, but the terms do not mean "good" or "bad" as they do in everyday speech. As you can see from **TABLE 7.1**, positive and negative reinforcement increase the likelihood of the behavior; positive and negative punishment decrease the likelihood of the behavior.

These distinctions can be confusing at first; after all, "negative reinforcement" and "punishment" both sound like they should be "bad" and produce the same type of behavior. However, negative reinforcement involves something pleasant; it's the *removal* of something unpleasant, like a shock, and the absence of a shock is indeed pleasant.

Reinforcement is generally more effective than punishment in promoting learning. There are many reasons (Gershoff, 2002), but one reason is this: Punishment signals that an unacceptable behavior has occurred, but it doesn't specify what should be done instead. Spanking a young child for starting to run into a busy street certainly stops the behavior, but it doesn't promote any kind of learning about the *desired* behavior.

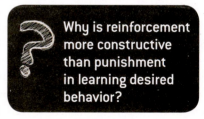

Why is reinforcement more constructive than punishment in learning desired behavior?

Primary and Secondary Reinforcement and Punishment

Reinforcers and punishers often gain their functions from basic biological mechanisms. A pigeon that pecks at a target in a Skinner box is usually reinforced with food pellets, just as an animal that learns to escape a mild electric shock has avoided the punishment of tingly paws. Food, comfort, shelter, or warmth are examples of *primary*

Table 7.1 **Reinforcement and Punishment**		
	Increases the Likelihood of Behavior	Decreases the Likelihood of Behavior
Stimulus is presented	Positive reinforcement	Positive punishment
Stimulus is removed	Negative reinforcement	Negative punishment

reinforcers because they help satisfy biological needs. However, the vast majority of reinforcers or punishers in our daily lives have little to do with biology: Verbal approval, a bronze trophy, or money all serve powerful reinforcing functions, yet none of them taste very good or help keep you warm at night.

These *secondary reinforcers* derive their effectiveness from their associations with primary reinforcers through classical conditioning. For example, money starts out as a neutral CS that, through its association with primary USs like acquiring food or shelter, takes on a conditioned emotional element. Flashing lights, originally a neutral CS, acquire powerful negative elements through association with a speeding ticket and a fine.

Immediate versus Delayed Reinforcement and Punishment

A key determinant of the effectiveness of a reinforcer is the amount of time between the occurrence of a behavior and the reinforcer: The more time that elapses, the less effective the reinforcer (Lattal, 2010; Renner, 1964). This was dramatically illustrated in experiments in which food reinforcers were given at varying times after the rat pressed the lever (Dickinson, Watt, & Griffiths, 1992). Delaying reinforcement by even a few seconds led to a reduction in the number of times the rat subsequently pressed the lever, and extending the delay to a minute rendered the food reinforcer completely ineffective (see **FIGURE 7.7**). The most likely explanation for this effect is that delaying the reinforcer made it difficult for the rats to figure out exactly what behavior they needed to perform in order to obtain it. In the same way, parents who wish to reinforce their children for playing quietly with a piece of candy should provide the candy while the child is still playing quietly; waiting until later when the child may be engaging in other behaviors—perhaps making a racket with pots and pans—will make it more difficult for the child to link the reinforcer with the behavior of playing quietly (Powell et al., 2009). Similar considerations apply to punishment: As a general rule, the longer the delay between a behavior and the administration of punishment, the less effective the punishment will be in suppressing the targeted behavior (Kamin, 1959; Lerman & Vorndran, 2002).

The greater potency of immediate versus delayed reinforcers may help us to appreciate why it can be difficult to engage in behaviors that have long-term benefits. The smoker who desperately

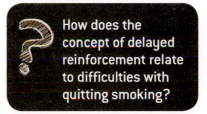

? How does the concept of delayed reinforcement relate to difficulties with quitting smoking?

Negative reinforcement involves the removal of something unpleasant from the environment. When Daddy stops the car, he gets a reward: His little monster stops screaming. However, from the perspective of the child, this is positive reinforcement. The child's tantrum results in something positive added to the environment—stopping for a snack.

Suppose you are the mayor of a suburban town and you want to institute some new policies to decrease the number of drivers who speed on residential streets. How might you use punishment to decrease the behavior you desire (speeding)? How might you use reinforcement to increase the behavior you desire (safe driving)? Based on the principles of operant conditioning you read about in this section, which approach do you think might be most fruitful?

FIGURE 7.7 **Delay of Reinforcement** Rats pressed a lever in order to obtain a food reward. The number of lever presses declined substantially with longer delays between the lever press and the delivery of food reinforcement. (Data from Dickinson, Watt, & Griffiths, 1992.)

wants to quit smoking will be reinforced immediately by the feeling of relaxation that results from lighting up, but he or she may have to wait years to be reinforced with better health that results from quitting; the dieter who sincerely wants to lose weight may easily succumb to the temptation of a chocolate sundae that provides reinforcement now, rather than wait for the reinforcement that would come weeks or months later, once the weight was lost.

The Basic Principles of Operant Conditioning

After establishing how reinforcement and punishment produced learned behavior, Skinner and other scientists began to expand the parameters of operant conditioning. Let's look at some of these basic principles of operant conditioning.

Culture & Community

Are there cultural differences in reinforcers? Operant approaches that use positive reinforcement have been applied extensively in everyday settings such as behavior therapy (see Treatment of Psychological Disorders, pp. 476–505). Surveys designed to assess what kinds of reinforcers are rewarding to individuals have revealed that there can be wide differences among various groups (Dewhurst & Cautela, 1980; Houlihan et al., 1991).

Recently, 750 high school students from America, Australia, Tanzania, Denmark, Honduras, Korea, and Spain were surveyed in order to evaluate possible cross-cultural differences among reinforcers (Homan et al., 2012). The survey asked students to rate how rewarding they found a range of activities, including listening to music, playing music, taking part in various kinds of sports, shopping, reading, spending time with friends, and so on. The researchers hypothesized that American high school students would differ most strongly from high school students in the third-world countries of Tanzania and Honduras, and that's what they found. The differences between American and Korean students were nearly as large, and somewhat surprisingly, so were the differences between American and Spanish students. There were much smaller differences between Americans and their Australian or Danish counterparts.

These results should be taken with a grain of salt because the researchers did not control for variables other than culture that could influence the results, such as economic status. Nonetheless, the study suggests that cultural differences should be considered in the design of programs or interventions that rely on the use of reinforcers to influence the behavior of individuals who come from different cultures.

Discrimination and Generalization

Operant conditioning shows both discrimination and generalization effects similar to those we saw with classical conditioning. For example, in one study, researchers presented either an Impressionist painting by Monet or a Cubist painting by Picasso (Watanabe, Sakamoto, & Wakita, 1995). Participants in the experiment were only reinforced if they responded when the appropriate painting was presented. After training, the participants discriminated appropriately; those trained with the Monet painting responded when other paintings by Monet were presented, but not when other Cubist paintings by Picasso were shown; those trained with a Picasso painting showed the opposite behavior. What's more, the research participants showed that they could generalize: Those trained with Monet responded appropriately when shown other Impressionist paintings, and the Picasso-trained participants responded to other Cubist artwork despite never having seen those paintings before. These results are particularly striking because the research participants were pigeons that were trained to key-peck to these various works of art.

Participants trained with Picasso paintings, such as the one on the left, responded to other paintings by Picasso or even to paintings by other Cubists. Participants trained with Monet paintings, such as the one on the right, responded to other paintings by Monet or by other French Impressionists. Interestingly, the participants in this study were pigeons.

Extinction

As in classical conditioning, operant behavior undergoes extinction when the reinforcements stop. Pigeons cease pecking at a key if food is no longer presented following the behavior. You wouldn't put more money into a vending machine if it failed to give you its promised candy bar or soda. On the surface, extinction of operant behavior looks like that of classical conditioning.

However, there is an important difference. As noted, in classical conditioning, the US occurs on every trial no matter what the organism does. In operant conditioning, the reinforcements only occur when the proper response has been made, and they don't always occur even then. Not every trip into the forest produces nuts for a squirrel, auto salespeople don't sell to everyone who takes a test drive, and researchers run many experiments that do not work out and never get published. Yet these behaviors don't weaken and gradually extinguish. Extinction is a bit more complicated in operant conditioning than in classical conditioning because it depends, in part, on how often reinforcement is received. In fact, this principle is an important cornerstone of operant conditioning that we'll examine next.

fixed-interval schedule (FI) An operant conditioning principle in which reinforcers are presented at fixed-time periods, provided that the appropriate response is made.

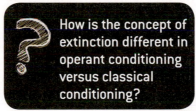

? How is the concept of extinction different in operant conditioning versus classical conditioning?

Schedules of Reinforcement

One day, Skinner was laboriously hand-rolling food pellets to reinforce the rats in his experiments. It occurred to him that perhaps he could save time and effort by not giving his rats a pellet for every bar press but instead delivering food on some intermittent schedule. The results of this hunch were dramatic. Not only did the rats continue bar pressing, but they also shifted the rate and pattern of bar pressing depending on the timing and frequency of the presentation of the reinforcers (Skinner, 1979). Unlike classical conditioning, where the sheer *number* of learning trials was important, in operant conditioning, the *pattern* with which reinforcements appeared was crucial. Skinner explored dozens of what came to be known as *schedules of reinforcement* (Ferster & Skinner, 1957; see **FIGURE 7.8**). We'll consider some of the most important next.

Interval Schedules. Under a **fixed-interval schedule (FI)**, *reinforcers are presented at fixed-time periods, provided that the appropriate response is made*. For example, on a 2-minute fixed-interval schedule, a response will be reinforced, but only after 2 minutes have expired

Students cramming for an exam often show the same kind of behavior as pigeons being reinforced under a fixed-interval schedule.

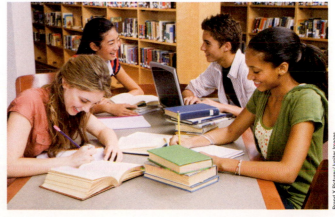

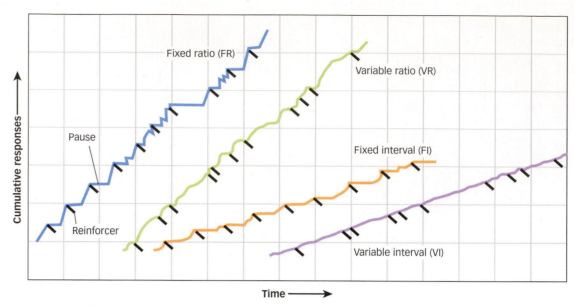

FIGURE 7.8 **Reinforcement Schedules** Different schedules of reinforcement produce different rates of responding. These lines represent the amount of responding that occurs under each type of reinforcement. The black slash marks indicate when reinforcement was administered. Notice that ratio schedules tend to produce higher rates of responding than do interval schedules, as shown by the steeper lines for fixed-ratio and variable-ratio reinforcement.

Radio station promotions and giveaways often follow a variable-interval schedule of reinforcement

variable-interval schedule (VI) An operant conditioning principle in which behavior is reinforced based on an average time that has expired since the last reinforcement.

fixed-ratio schedule (FR) An operant conditioning principle in which reinforcement is delivered after a specific number of responses have been made.

variable-ratio schedule (VR) An operant conditioning principle in which the delivery of reinforcement is based on a particular average number of responses.

intermittent reinforcement An operant conditioning principle in which only some of the responses made are followed by reinforcement.

These pieceworkers in a textile factory get paid following a fixed-ratio schedule: They receive payment after some set number of shirts have been sewn.

since the last reinforcement. Rats and pigeons in Skinner boxes produce predictable patterns of behavior under these schedules. They show little responding right after the presentation of the reinforcement, but as the next time interval draws to a close, they show a burst of responding. Many undergraduates behave exactly like this. They do relatively little work until just before the upcoming exam, and then they engage in a burst of reading and studying.

Under a **variable-interval schedule (VI),** *a behavior is reinforced based on an average time that has expired since the last reinforcement.* For example, on a 2-minute variable-interval schedule, responses will be reinforced every 2 minutes *on average.* Variable-interval schedules typically produce steady, consistent responding because the time until the next reinforcement is less predictable. One example of a VI schedule in real life might be radio promotional giveaways. The reinforcement—say, a ticket to a rock concert—might occur on average once an hour across the span of the broadcasting day, but it might come early in the 10:00 o'clock hour, later in the 11:00 o'clock hour, immediately into the 12:00 o'clock hour, and so on.

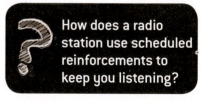

How does a radio station use scheduled reinforcements to keep you listening?

Both fixed-interval schedules and variable-interval schedules tend to produce slow, methodical responding because the reinforcements follow a time scale that is independent of how many responses occur. It doesn't matter if a rat on a fixed-interval schedule presses a bar 1 time during a 2-minute period or 100 times: The reinforcing food pellet won't drop out of the shoot until 2 minutes have elapsed, regardless of the number of responses.

Ratio Schedules. Under a **fixed-ratio schedule (FR),** *reinforcement is delivered after a specific number of responses have been made.* One schedule might present reinforcement after every fourth response, a different schedule might present reinforcement after every 20 responses; the special case of presenting reinforcement after *each* response is called *continuous reinforcement.* There are many situations in which people are reinforced on a fixed-ratio schedule: Book clubs often give you a freebie after a set number of regular purchases; pieceworkers get paid after making a fixed number of products; and some credit card companies return to their customers a percentage of the amount charged. When a fixed-ratio schedule is operating, it is possible, in principle, to know exactly when the next reinforcer is due. A laundry pieceworker on a 10-response, fixed-ratio schedule who has just washed and ironed the ninth shirt knows that payment is coming after the next shirt is done.

Under a **variable-ratio schedule (VR),** *the delivery of reinforcement is based on a particular average number of responses.* For example, slot machines in a modern casino pay off on variable-ratio schedules. A casino might advertise that it pays off on "every 100 pulls on average," but one player might hit a jackpot after 3 pulls on a slot machine, whereas another player might not hit a jackpot until after 80 pulls.

Not surprisingly, variable-ratio schedules produce slightly higher rates of responding than fixed-ratio schedules, primarily because the organism never knows when the next reinforcement is going to appear. What's more, the higher the ratio, the higher the response rate tends to be; a 20-response variable-ratio schedule will produce considerably more responding than a 2-response variable-ratio schedule.

When schedules of reinforcement provide **intermittent reinforcement,** *when only some of the responses made are followed by reinforcement,* they produce behavior that is much more resistant to extinction than a continuous reinforcement schedule. One way to think about this effect is to recognize that the more irregular and intermittent a schedule is, the more difficult it becomes for an organism to detect when the behavior has actually been placed on the road to extinction. For example, if you've just put a dollar into a soda machine that, unbeknownst to you, is broken, no soda comes out. Because you're used to getting your sodas on a continuous reinforcement schedule—one dollar produces one soda—this abrupt change in the environment is easily noticed, and you are unlikely to put additional money into the machine: You'd quickly show extinction. However, if you've put your dollar into a slot machine that, unbeknownst to you, is broken, do you stop after one or two plays? Almost certainly not. If you're a regular slot player, you're used to going for many plays in a row without winning anything, so it's difficult to tell that anything is out of the ordinary. The **intermittent reinforcement effect** refers to *the fact that operant behaviors that are maintained under intermittent reinforcement schedules resist extinction better than those maintained under continuous reinforcement.*

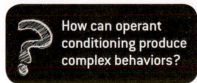
How do ratio schedules work to keep you spending your money?

Slot machines in casinos pay out following a variable-ratio schedule. This helps explain why some gamblers feel incredibly lucky, whereas others (like this chap) can't believe they can play a machine for so long without winning a thing.

intermittent reinforcement effect The fact that operant behaviors that are maintained under intermittent reinforcement schedules resist extinction better than those maintained under continuous reinforcement.

shaping Learning that results from the reinforcement of successive steps to a final desired behavior.

Imagine you own an insurance company and you want to encourage your salespeople to sell as many policies as possible. You decide to give them bonuses, based on the number of policies sold. How might you set up a system of bonuses using an FR schedule? Using a VR schedule? Which system do you think would encourage your salespeople to work harder, in terms of making more sales?

Shaping through Successive Approximations

Have you ever been to AquaLand and wondered how the dolphins learn to jump up in the air, twist around, splash back down, do a somersault, and then jump through a hoop, all in one smooth motion? Well, they don't. At least not all at once. Rather, elements of their behavior are shaped over time until the final product looks like one smooth motion.

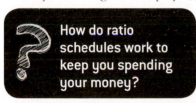
How can operant conditioning produce complex behaviors?

Behavior rarely occurs in fixed frameworks in which a stimulus is presented and then an organism has to engage in some activity or another. Most of our behaviors are the result of **shaping,** *learning that results from the reinforcement of successive steps to a final desired behavior.* The outcomes of one set of behaviors shape the next set of behaviors, whose outcomes shape the next set of behaviors, and so on.

Skinner noted that if you put a rat in a Skinner box and wait for it to press the bar, you could end up waiting a very long time: Bar pressing just isn't very high in a rat's natural hierarchy of responses. However, it is relatively easy to shape bar pressing. Wait

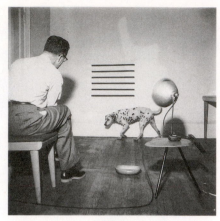

1 Minutes

4 Minutes

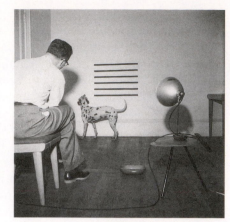

8 Minutes

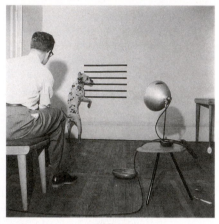

12 Minutes

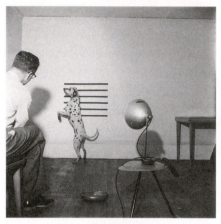

16 Minutes

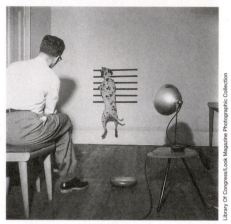

20 Minutes

Library Of Congress/Look Magazine Photographic Collection

B. F. Skinner shaping a dog named Agnes. In the span of 20 minutes, Skinner was able to use reinforcement of successive approximations to shape Agnes's behavior. The result was a pretty neat trick: to wander in, stand on hind legs, and jump.

until the rat turns in the direction of the bar, and then deliver a food reward. This will reinforce turning toward the bar, making such a movement more likely. Now wait for the rat to take a step toward the bar before delivering food; this will reinforce moving toward the bar. After the rat walks closer to the bar, wait until it touches the bar before presenting the food. Notice that none of these behaviors is the final desired behavior (reliably pressing the bar). Rather, each behavior is a *successive approximation* to the final product, or a behavior that gets incrementally closer to the overall desired behavior. In the dolphin example—and indeed, in many instances in which animals perform astoundingly complex behaviors—each smaller behavior is reinforced until the overall sequence of behavior is performed reliably.

Superstitious Behavior

Everything we've discussed so far suggests that one of the keys to establishing reliable operant behavior is the correlation between an organism's response and the occurrence of reinforcement. As you read in the Methods in Psychology chapter, however, just because two things are correlated (i.e., they tend to occur together in time and space) doesn't imply that there is causality (i.e., the presence of one reliably causes the other to occur).

Skinner (1948) designed an experiment that illustrates this distinction. He put several pigeons in Skinner boxes, set the food dispenser to deliver food every 15 seconds, and left the birds to their own devices. Later, he returned and found the birds engaging in odd, idiosyncratic behaviors, such as pecking aimlessly in a corner or turning in circles. He referred to these behaviors as "superstitious" and offered a behaviorist analysis of their occurrence. A pigeon that just happened to have pecked randomly in the corner when the food showed up had connected the delivery of food to that behavior.

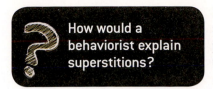

How would a behaviorist explain superstitions?

Because this pecking behavior was reinforced by the delivery of food, the pigeon was likely to repeat it. Now pecking in the corner was more likely to occur, and it was more likely to be reinforced 15 seconds later when the food appeared again. Skinner's pigeons acted as though there was a causal relationship between their behaviors and the appearance of food when it was merely an accidental correlation.

Although some researchers questioned Skinner's characterization of these behaviors as superstitious (Staddon & Simmelhag, 1971), later studies have shown that people, like pigeons, often behave as though there's a correlation between their responses and reward when in fact the connection is merely accidental (Bloom et al., 2007; Mellon, 2009; Ono, 1987; Wagner & Morris, 1987). For example, baseball players who hit several home runs on a day when they happened not to have showered are likely to continue that tradition, laboring under the belief that the accidental correlation between poor personal hygiene and a good day at bat is somehow causal. This "stench causes home runs" hypothesis is just one of many examples of human superstitions (Gilbert et al., 2000; Radford & Radford, 1949).

A Deeper Understanding of Operant Conditioning

To behaviorists such as Watson and Skinner, an organism behaved in a certain way as a response to stimuli in the environment, not because there was any wanting, wishing, or willing by the animal in question. However, some research on operant conditioning digs deeper into the underlying mechanisms that produce the familiar outcomes of reinforcement. Let's examine three elements that expand our view of operant conditioning: the cognitive, neural, and evolutionary elements of operant conditioning.

The Cognitive Elements of Operant Conditioning

Edward Chace Tolman (1886–1959) argued that there was more to learning than just knowing the circumstances in the environment (the properties of the stimulus) and being able to observe a particular outcome (the reinforced response). Instead, Tolman proposed that the conditioning experience produced knowledge or a belief that, in this particular situation, a specific reward will appear if a specific response is made.

Tolman's ideas may remind you of the Rescorla–Wagner model of classical conditioning. In both the Rescorla–Wagner model and Tolman's theories, the stimulus does not directly evoke a response; rather, it establishes an internal cognitive state, which then produces the behavior.

Latent Learning and Cognitive Maps. In **latent learning,** *something is learned, but it is not manifested as a behavioral change until sometime in the future.* Latent learning can easily be established in rats and occurs without any obvious reinforcement, a finding that posed a direct challenge to the then-dominant behaviorist position that all learning required some form of reinforcement (Tolman & Honzik, 1930a).

Tolman gave three groups of rats access to a complex maze every day for over 2 weeks. The rats in the control group never received any reinforcement for navigating the maze. They were simply allowed to run around until they reached the goal box at the end of the maze. In **FIGURE 7.9** you can see that over the 2 weeks of the study, the control group rats (in green) got a little better at finding their way through the maze, but not by much. A second group of rats (in blue) received regular reinforcements; when they reached the goal box, they found a small food reward there. Not surprisingly, these rats showed clear learning. A third group (orange) was treated exactly like the control group for the first 10 days and then rewarded for the last 7 days. For the first 10 days, these rats behaved like those in the control group. However, during the final 7 days, they behaved like the rats that had been reinforced every day. Clearly,

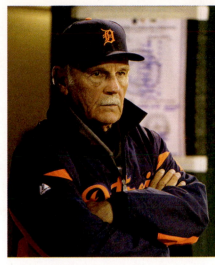

People engage in all kinds of superstitious behaviors. When the Detroit Tigers went on a winning streak in the summer of 2011, Tigers' manager Jim Leyland refused to change his underwear, wearing them to the park every day until the winning streak ended. Skinner thought superstitions resulted from the unintended reinforcement of inconsequential behavior.

latent learning Something is learned, but it is not manifested as a behavioral change until sometime in the future.

Edward Chace Tolman advocated a cognitive approach to operant learning and provided evidence that in maze-learning experiments, rats develop a mental picture of the maze, which he called a cognitive map.

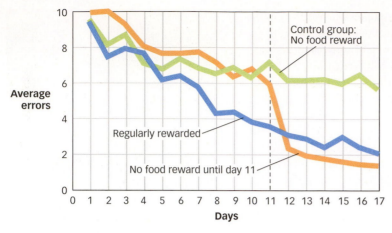

FIGURE 7.9 Latent Learning Rats in a control group that never received any reinforcement (in green) improved at finding their way through the maze over 17 days but not by much. Rats that received regular reinforcements (in blue) showed fairly clear learning; their error rate decreased steadily over time. Rats in the latent learning group (in orange) were treated exactly like the control group rats for the first 10 days and then like the regularly rewarded group for the last 7 days. Their dramatic improvement on day 12 shows that these rats had learned a lot about the maze and the location of the goal box even though they had never received reinforcements. (Data from Tolman & Honzik, 1930b.)

the rats in this third group had learned a lot about the maze and the location of the goal box during those first 10 days even though they had not received any reinforcements for their behavior. In other words, they showed evidence of latent learning.

These results suggested to Tolman that his rats had developed a **cognitive map,** *a mental representation of the physical features of the environment* (Tolman & Honzik, 1930b; Tolman, Ritchie, & Kalish, 1946). Support for this idea was obtained in a clever experiment, in which Tolman trained rats in a maze and then changed the maze—while keeping the start and goal locations in the same spot. Behaviorists would predict that the rats, finding the familiar route blocked, would be stymied. However, faced with a blocked path, the rats instead quickly navigated via a new pathway to the food. This behavior suggested that the rats had formed a sophisticated cognitive map of the environment and could use the map after conditions changed. Tolman's experiments strongly suggest that there is a cognitive component, even in rats, to operant learning.

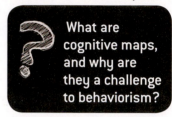

Learning to Trust: For Better or Worse. Cognitive factors also played a key role in an experiment examining learning and brain activity (using fMRI) in people who played a "trust" game with a fictional partner (Delgado, Frank, & Phelps, 2005). On each trial, a participant could either keep a $1 reward or transfer the reward to a partner, who would receive $3. The partner could then either keep the $3 or share half of it with the participant. When playing with a partner who was willing to share the reward, the participant would be better off transferring the money, but when playing with a partner who did not share, the participant would be better off keeping the $1. Participants in such experiments typically learn who is trustworthy on the basis of trial-and-error, and they give more money to partners who reinforce them by sharing.

In the study by Delgado et al., participants were given detailed descriptions of their partners that either portrayed the partners as trustworthy, neutral, or suspect. Even though during the game, all three of the partners shared equally often, the participants' cognitions about their partners had powerful effects. Participants transferred more money to the trustworthy partner than to the others, essentially ignoring the trial-by-trial feedback that would ordinarily shape their playing behavior, thus reducing the amount of reward they received. Highlighting the power of the cognitive effect, signals in a part of the brain that ordinarily distinguishes between positive and negative feedback were evident only when participants played with the neutral partner; these feedback signals were absent when participants played with the trustworthy partner and reduced when participants played with the suspect partner.

The Neural Elements of Operant Conditioning

The first hint of how specific brain structures might contribute to the process of reinforcement came from James Olds and his associates, who inserted tiny electrodes into different parts of a rat's brain and allowed the animal to control electric stimulation of its own brain by pressing a bar. They discovered that some brain areas produced what appeared to be intensely positive experiences: The rats would press the bar repeatedly to stimulate these structures, sometimes ignoring food, water, and other life-sustaining necessities for hours on end simply to receive stimulation directly in the brain. Olds and colleagues called these parts of the brain *pleasure centers* (Olds, 1956; see **FIGURE 7.10**).

In the years since these early studies, researchers have identified a number of structures and pathways in the brain that deliver rewards through stimulation (Wise,

cognitive map A mental representation of the physical features of the environment.

1989, 2005). The neurons in the *medial forebrain bundle*, a pathway that meanders its way from the midbrain through the *hypothalamus* into the *nucleus accumbens*, are the most susceptible to stimulation that produces pleasure. This is not surprising because psychologists have identified this bundle of cells as crucial to behaviors that clearly involve pleasure, such as eating, drinking, and engaging in sexual activity. Second, the neurons all along this pathway and especially those in the nucleus accumbens itself are all *dopaminergic* (i.e., they secrete the neurotransmitter *dopamine*). Remember from the Neuroscience and Behavior chapter that higher levels of dopamine in the brain are usually associated with positive emotions. In recent years, several competing hypotheses about the precise role of dopamine have emerged, including the idea that dopamine is more closely linked with the expectation of reward than with reward itself (Fiorillo, Newsome, & Schultz, 2008; Schultz, 2006, 2007), or that dopamine is more closely associated with wanting or even craving something rather than simply liking it (Berridge, 2007). Whichever view turns out to be correct, dopamine seems to play a key role in how we process reward. (For more on the relationship between dopamine and Parkinson's, see the Hot Science box: Dopamine and Reward Learning in Parkinson's Disease.)

How do specific brain structures contribute to the process of reinforcement?

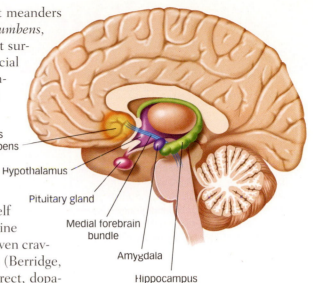

FIGURE 7.10 Pleasure Centers in the Brain The nucleus accumbens, medial forebrain bundle, and hypothalamus are all major pleasure centers in the brain.

Hot Science

Dopamine and Reward Learning in Parkinson's Disease

Many of us have relatives or friends who have been affected by Parkinson's disease, a movement disorder that involves loss of dopamine-producing neurons. As you learned in the Neuroscience and Behavior chapter, the drug L-dopa is often used to treat Parkinson's disease because it spurs surviving neurons to produce more dopamine. Dopamine also plays a key role in reward-related learning.

Research suggests that dopamine plays an important role in *prediction error*: the difference between the actual reward received versus the amount of predicted or expected reward. For example, when an animal presses a lever and receives an unexpected food reward, a *positive* prediction error occurs (a better than expected outcome), and the animal learns to press the lever again. By contrast, when an animal expects to receive a reward by pressing a lever but does not receive it, a *negative* prediction error occurs (a worse than expected outcome), and the animal will subsequently be less likely to press the lever again. Prediction error can thus serve as a kind of "teaching signal" that helps the animal to learn to behave in a way that maximizes reward. Intriguingly, dopamine neurons in the reward centers of a monkey's brain show

increased activity when the monkey receives unexpected juice rewards and decreased activity when the monkey does not receive expected juice rewards, suggesting that dopamine neurons play an important role in generating the prediction error (Schultz, 2006, 2007; Schultz, Dayan, & Montague, 1997). Neuroimaging studies show that human brain regions involved in reward-related learning also produce prediction error signals, and that dopamine is involved in generating those signals (O'Doherty et al., 2003; Pessiglione et al., 2006).

So, how do these findings relate to people with Parkinson's disease? Several studies re-

port that reward-related learning can be impaired in persons with Parkinson's (Dahger & Robbins, 2009). In one study of trial-and-error learning, participants with Parkinson's being treated with dopaminergic drugs had a higher learning rate than patients not on the drugs (Rutledge et al., 2009). However, there was greater learning for the positive prediction error (learning based on positive outcomes) than for the negative prediction error (learning based on negative outcomes). These results may relate to another intriguing feature of Parkinson's disease: Some individuals develop serious problems with compulsive gambling, shopping, and related impulsive behaviors. Such problems appear only after the individuals contract Parkinson's disease and receive treatment with certain types of dopaminergic drugs (Ahlskog, 2011; Weintraub, Papay, & Siderowf, 2013), and such problems may reflect an effect of the drug treatment on individuals who are susceptible to compulsive behaviors (Voon et al., 2011).

More studies will be needed to unravel the complex relations among dopamine, reward prediction error, learning, and Parkinson's disease, but the studies to date suggest that such research should have important practical as well as scientific implications.

The Evolutionary Elements of Operant Conditioning

As you'll recall, classical conditioning has an adaptive value that has been fine-tuned by evolution. Not surprisingly, operant conditioning does too. Several behaviorists who were using simple T mazes like the one shown in **FIGURE 7.11** to study learning in rats discovered that if a rat found food in one arm of the maze on the first trial of the day, it typically ran down the *other* arm on the very next trial. A staunch behaviorist wouldn't expect the rats to behave this way. According to operant conditioning, prior reinforcement in one arm should *increase* the likelihood of turning in that same direction next time, not reduce it. How can we explain this?

What was puzzling from a behaviorist perspective makes sense when viewed from an evolutionary perspective. Rats are foragers, and like all foraging species, they have evolved a highly adaptive strategy for survival. They move around in their environments looking for food. If they find it somewhere, they eat it (or store it) and then go look somewhere else for more. So, if the rat just found food in the *right* arm of a T maze, the obvious place to look next time is the *left* arm. The rat knows that there isn't any more food in the right arm because it just ate the food it found there! Indeed, given the opportunity to explore a complex environment like the multiarm maze shown in **FIGURE 7.12,** rats will systematically go from arm to arm collecting food, rarely returning to an arm they have previously visited (Olton & Samuelson, 1976).

FIGURE 7.11 **A Simple T Maze** When rats find food in the right arm of a typical T maze, on the next trial, they will often run to the left arm of the maze. This contradicts basic principles of operant conditioning: If the behavior of running to the right arm is reinforced, it should be more likely to occur again in the future. However, this behavior is perfectly consistent with a rat's evolutionary preparedness. Like most foraging animals, rats explore their environments in search of food and seldom return to where food has already been found. Quite sensibly, if food has already been found in the right arm of the T maze, the rat will search the left arm next to see if more food is there.

Start

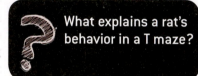

What explains a rat's behavior in a T maze?

FIGURE 7.12 **A Complex T Maze** Like many other foraging species, rats placed in a complex T maze such as this one show evidence of their evolutionary preparedness. These rats will systematically travel from arm to arm in search of food, never returning to arms they have already visited.

Start

Two of Skinner's former students, Keller Breland and Marian Breland, were among the first researchers to discover that it wasn't just rats in T mazes that presented a problem for behaviorists (Breland & Breland, 1961). The Brelands, who made a career out of training animals for commercials and movies, often used pigs because pigs are surprisingly good at learning all sorts of tricks. However, the Brelands discovered that it was extremely difficult to teach a pig the simple task of dropping coins in a box. Instead of depositing the coins, the pigs persisted in rooting with them as if they were digging them up in soil, tossing them in the air with their snouts, and pushing them around. The Brelands tried to train raccoons at the same task, with different but equally dismal results. The raccoons spent their time rubbing the coins between their paws instead of dropping them in the box. Having learned the association between the coins and food, the animals began to treat the coins as stand-ins for food. Pigs are biologically predisposed to root out their food, and raccoons have evolved to clean their food by rubbing it with their paws. That is exactly what each species of animal did with the coins. The Brelands' work shows that all species, including humans, are biologically predisposed to learn some things more readily than others and to respond to stimuli in ways that are consistent with their evolutionary histories (Gallistel, 2000).

The misbehavior of organisms: Pigs are biologically predisposed to root out their food, just as raccoons are predisposed to wash their food. Trying to train either species to behave differently can prove to be an exercise in futility.

SUMMARY QUIZ [7.2]

1. Which of the following is NOT an accurate statement concerning operant conditioning?
    a. Actions and outcomes are critical to operant conditioning.
    b. Operant conditioning involves the reinforcement of behavior.
    c. Complex behaviors cannot be accounted for by operant conditioning.
    d. Operant conditioning has roots in evolutionary behavior.

2. Which of the following mechanisms have no role in Skinner's approach to behavior?
    a. cognitive
    b. neural

c. evolutionary

d. all of the above

3. Latent learning provides evidence for a cognitive element in operant conditioning because

    a. it occurs without any obvious reinforcement.

    b. it requires both positive and negative reinforcement.

    c. it points toward the operation of a neural reward center.

    d. it depends on a stimulus–response relationship.

observational learning A condition in which learning takes place by watching the actions of others.

Observational Learning: Look at Me

Four-year-old Rodney and his 2-year-old sister Margie had always been told to keep away from the stove. Being a mischievous imp, however, Rodney decided one day to place his hand over a burner until the singeing of his flesh led him to recoil, shrieking in pain. Rodney was more scared than hurt, really—and he learned something important that day. But little Margie, who stood by watching these events unfold, *also* learned the same lesson. Rodney's story is a behaviorist's textbook example: The administration of punishment led to a learned change in the boy's behavior. But how can we explain Margie's learning? She received neither punishment nor reinforcement, and yet it's arguable that she's just as likely to keep her hands away from stoves in the future as Rodney is.

Margie's is a case of **observational learning,** in which *learning takes place by watching the actions of others*. In all societies, appropriate social behavior is passed on from generation to generation, not only through deliberate training of the young, but also through young people observing the patterns of behaviors of their elders and each other (Flynn & Whiten, 2008). Tasks such as using chopsticks or learning to operate a TV's remote control are more easily

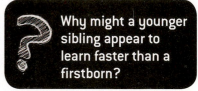
Why might a younger sibling appear to learn faster than a firstborn?

acquired if we watch these activities being carried out before we try ourselves. Even complex motor tasks, such as performing surgery, are learned in part through extensive observation and imitation of models. And anyone who is about to undergo surgery is grateful for observational learning. Just the thought of a generation of surgeons acquiring their surgical techniques using the trial-and-error techniques studied by Thorndike or the shaping of successive approximations that captivated Skinner would make any of us very nervous.

Observational Learning in Humans

In a series of studies that have become landmarks in psychology, Albert Bandura and his colleagues investigated the parameters of observational learning (Bandura, Ross, & Ross, 1961). The researchers escorted individual preschoolers into a play area filled with toys that 4-year-olds typically like. An adult *model*, someone whose behavior might serve as a guide for others, then entered the room and started playing with a Bobo doll, which is a large inflatable plastic toy with a weighted bottom that allows it to bounce back upright when knocked down. The adult played quietly for a bit but then started aggressing toward the Bobo doll,

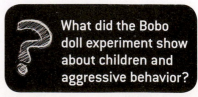
What did the Bobo doll experiment show about children and aggressive behavior?

Observational learning plays an important role in surgical training, as illustrated by the medical students observing a famed surgeon (beard and white gown) perform stomach surgery in 1901.

Stanley B. Burns, MD & The Burns Archive NY/Science Source

© Albert Bandura, Dept. of Psychology, Stanford University.

knocking it down, jumping on it, and kicking it around the room. When the children who observed these actions were later allowed to play with a variety of toys, including a child-size Bobo doll, they were more than twice as likely to interact with it in an aggressive manner as a group of children who hadn't observed the aggressive model (see **FIGURE 7.13**).

The children in these studies also showed that they were sensitive to the consequences of the actions they observed. When they saw the adult models being punished for behaving aggressively, the children showed considerably less aggression. When the children observed a model being rewarded and praised for aggressive behavior, they displayed an increase in aggression (Bandura, Ross, & Ross, 1963). The observational learning seen in Bandura's studies has implications for social learning and cultural transmission of behaviors, norms, and values (Bandura, 1977, 1994).

Observational learning is important in many domains of everyday life. Sports provide a good example. Coaches rely on observational learning when they demonstrate critical techniques and skills to players, and athletes also have numerous opportunities to observe other athletes perform. Studies of athletes in both team and individual sports indicate that all rely heavily on observational learning to improve their performance (Wesch, Law, & Hall, 2007). But can merely observing a skill result in an improvement in performing that skill without actually practicing it? A number of studies have shown that observing someone else perform a motor task, ranging from reaching for a target to pressing a sequence of keys, can produce robust learning in the observer. In fact, observational learning sometimes results in just as much learning as practicing the task itself (Heyes & Foster, 2002; Mattar & Gribble, 2005; Vinter & Perruchet, 2002).

FIGURE 7.13 Beating Up Bobo Children who were exposed to an adult model who behaved aggressively toward a Bobo doll were likely to behave aggressively themselves. This behavior occurred in the absence of any direct reinforcement. Observational learning was responsible for producing the children's behaviors.

Coaches rely on observational learning when they demonstrate techniques to athletes.

AP Photo/Robert F. Bukaty

Observational Learning in Animals

Humans aren't the only creatures capable of learning by observing. In one study, for example, pigeons watched other pigeons get reinforced for either pecking at the feeder or stepping on a bar. When placed in the box later, the pigeons tended to use whatever technique they had observed other pigeons using earlier (Zentall, Sutton, & Sherburne, 1996).

One of the most important questions about observational learning in animals concerns whether monkeys and chimpanzees can learn to use tools by observing tool use in others, the way young children can. In one of the first controlled studies to examine this issue, chimpanzees observed a model (the experimenter) use a metal bar shaped like a T to pull items of food toward him or her (Tomasello et al., 1987). Compared with a group that did not observe any tool use, these chimpanzees showed more learning when later performing the task themselves. In a later experiment, the researchers introduced a novel twist (Nagell, Olguin, & Tomasello, 1993). In one condition, a model used a rake in its normal position (with the teeth pointed to the ground) to capture a food reward, which was rather inefficient because the teeth were widely spaced and the food sometimes slipped between them. In a second condition, the model flipped over the rake so that the teeth were pointed up and the flat edge of the rake touched the ground—a more effective procedure for capturing the food. Both groups that observed tool use performed better when trying to obtain the food themselves than did a control group that did not observe a model using the tool. However, the chimpanzees that observed the more efficient procedure did not use it any more often than did those that observed the less efficient procedure. By contrast, 2-year-old children exposed to the same conditions used the rake in the exact same way that they had seen the model use it. The chimpanzees seemed only to be learning that the tool could be used to obtain food, whereas the children learned something specific about how to use the tool.

The chimpanzees in these studies had been raised by their mothers in the wild. Could chimpanzees that had been raised in environments that also included human contact learn to imitate the exact actions performed by a model? The answer is a resounding yes: Chimpanzees raised in a more humanlike environment showed more specific observational learning than did those that had been reared by their mothers, and thus they performed much like human children (Tomasello, Savage-Rumbaugh, & Kruger, 1993). This finding led Tomasello et al. (1993) to suggest that being raised in a human culture has a profound effect on the cognitive abilities of chimpanzees, especially their ability to understand the intentions of others when performing tasks such as using tools, which in turn increases their observational learning capacities.

More recent research has found something similar in capuchin monkeys that are known for their tool use in the wild, such as employing branches or stone hammers to crack open nuts (Boinski, Quatrone, & Swartz, 2000; Fragaszy et al., 2004) or using stones to dig up buried roots (Moura & Lee, 2004). Fredman and Whiten (2008) studied monkeys that had been reared in the wild by their mothers or by human families in Israel as part of a project to train the monkeys to aid quadriplegics. A model demonstrated two ways of using a screwdriver to gain access to a food reward hidden in a box. Some monkeys observed the model poke through a hole in the center of the box, whereas others watched him pry open the lid at the rim of the box (see **FIGURE 7.14**). Both mother-reared and human-reared monkeys showed evidence of observational learning, but the human-reared monkeys carried out the exact action they had observed more often than the mother-reared monkeys.

What are the cognitive differences between chimpanzees raised among humans versus raised in the wild?

Although this evidence implies that there is a cultural influence on the cognitive processes that support observational learning, the researchers noted that the effects on

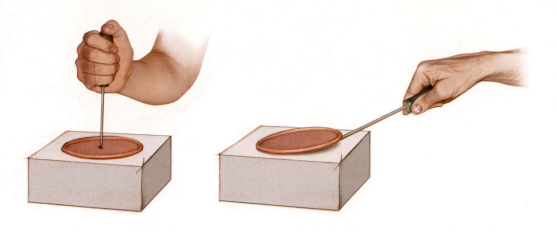

observational learning could be attributed to any number of influences on the human-reared monkeys, including more experience with tools, more attention to a model's behavior, or increased sensitivity to the intentions of others. Thus, more work is needed to understand the exact nature of those processes (Bering, 2004; Tomasello & Call, 2004).

Neural Elements of Observational Learning

Observational learning involves a neural component as well. As you read in the Neuroscience and Behavior chapter, *mirror neurons* are a type of cell found in the frontal and parietal lobes of primates (including humans). Mirror neurons fire when an animal performs an action, such as when a monkey reaches for a food item (**FIGURE 7.15**). Mirror neurons also fire when an animal watches someone *else* perform the same task (Rizzolatti & Craighero, 2004). For example, monkeys' mirror neurons fired when they observed humans grasping for a piece of food, either to eat it or to place it in a container (Fogassi et al., 2005). Although the exact functions of mirror neurons continue to be debated (Hickok, 2009), it seems likely that mirror neurons contribute to observational learning.

> **What do mirror neurons do?**

FIGURE 7.15 **Mirror Neuron System** Regions in the frontal lobe (area 44) and parietal lobe (area 40) are thought to be part of the mirror neuron system in humans.

Area 40

Area 44

Mirror neurons exist in humans too. Studies of observational learning in healthy adults have shown that watching someone else perform an action engages some of the same brain regions that are activated when people actually perform the action themselves. In one study, participants practiced dance sequences to unfamiliar songs and watched videos containing other dance sequences accompanied by unfamiliar songs (Cross et al., 2009). The participants were then given fMRI scans while viewing videos of sequences that they had previously danced or watched, as well as videos of untrained sequences.

Results showed differences between watching the untrained sequences and watching the previously danced or watched sequences. Viewing the previously danced or watched sequences caused activity in brain regions considered to be part of the mirror neuron system. The results of

Observing skilled dancers, such as Sugar Ray Leonard and Anna Trebunsyaya on *Dancing with the Stars*, engages many of the same brain regions as does actual dance practice, and such observing can produce significant learning.

AP Photo/ABC, Adam Larkey

a surprise dancing test given to participants after the conclusion of scanning showed that performance was better on sequences previously watched than on the untrained sequences, demonstrating significant observational learning, but it was best of all on the previously danced sequences (Cross et al., 2009). So, while watching *Dancing with the Stars* might indeed improve your dancing skills, practicing on the dance floor should help even more.

SUMMARY QUIZ [7.3]

1. Which is true of observational learning?
    a. Although humans learn by observing others, nonhuman animals seem to lack this capability.
    b. If a child sees an adult engaging in a certain behavior, the child is more likely to imitate the behavior.
    c. Humans learn complex behaviors more readily by trial and error than by observation.
    d. Observational learning is limited to transmission of information between individuals of the same species.

2. Which of the following mechanisms does NOT help form the basis of observational learning?
    a. attention
    b. perception
    c. punishment
    d. memory

3. Neural research indicates that observational learning is closely tied to brain areas that are involved in
    a. memory.
    b. vision.
    c. action.
    d. emotion.

Implicit Learning: Under the Wires

Most people are attuned to linguistic, social, emotional, or sensorimotor events in the world around them so much so that they gradually build up internal representations of those patterns that were acquired without explicit awareness. This process is often called **implicit learning,** or *learning that takes place largely independent of awareness of both the process and the products of information acquisition.* Because it occurs without awareness, implicit learning is knowledge that sneaks in "under the wires."

Habituation, which we discussed at the outset of the chapter, is a very simple kind of implicit learning in which repeated exposure to a stimulus results in a reduced response. In contrast, some forms of learning start out explicitly but become more implicit over time. When you first learned to drive a car, for example, you probably devoted a lot of attention to the many movements and sequences that needed to be carried out simultaneously ("step lightly on the

implicit learning Learning that takes place largely independent of awareness of both the process and the products of information acquisition.

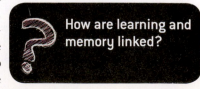
How are learning and memory linked?

accelerator while you push the turn indicator and look in the rearview mirror while you turn the steering wheel"). That complex interplay of motions is now probably quite effortless and automatic for you. Explicit learning has become implicit over time. These distinctions in learning might remind you of similar distinctions in memory and for good reason. In the Memory chapter, you read about the differences between *implicit* and *explicit* memories. Do implicit and explicit learning mirror implicit and explicit memory? It's not that simple, but it is true that learning and memory are inextricably linked. Learning produces memories, and conversely, the existence of memories implies that knowledge was acquired, that experience was registered and recorded in the brain, or that learning has taken place.

AP Photo/Mary Altaffer

Ten years ago, no one knew how to type using thumbs; now just about all teenagers do it automatically.

Cognitive Approaches to Implicit Learning

Most children, by the time they are 6 or 7 years old, are linguistically and socially fairly sophisticated. Yet most children have very little explicit awareness of when or how they learned a particular course of action and may not even be able to state the general principle underlying their behavior. Yet most kids have learned not to eat with their feet, to listen when they are spoken to, and not to kick the dog.

To investigate implicit learning in the laboratory, researchers in early studies showed participants 15 or 20 letter strings and asked them to memorize them. The letter strings, which at first glance look like nonsense syllables, were actually formed using a complex set of rules called an *artificial grammar* (see **FIGURE 7.16**). Participants were not told anything about the rules, but with experience, they gradually developed a vague, intuitive sense of the "correctness" of particular letter groupings, and they could get between 60–70% correct—but they were unable to provide much in the way of explicit awareness of the rules and regularities that they were using. The experience is similar to coming across a sentence with a grammatical error. You are immediately aware that something is wrong and you can certainly make the sentence grammatical, but unless you are a trained linguist, you'll probably find it difficult to articulate which rules of English grammar were violated.

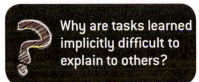

Why are tasks learned implicitly difficult to explain to others?

Other studies of implicit learning have used a *serial reaction time* task (Nissen & Bullemer, 1987). Here research participants are presented with five small boxes on a computer screen. Each box lights up briefly, and when it does, the participant is asked to press the button that is just underneath that box as quickly as possible. Like the artificial grammar task, the sequence of lights appears to be random, but in fact, it follows a pattern. Research participants eventually get faster with practice as they learn to anticipate which box is most likely to light up next. But, if asked, they are generally unaware that there is a pattern to the lights.

Implicit learning is remarkably resistant to disorders that are known to affect explicit learning. For example, profoundly amnesic patients display virtually normal implicit learning of artificial grammar (Knowlton, Ramus, & Squire, 1992), even though they have essentially no explicit memory of having been in the learning phase of the experiment! In contrast, several studies have shown that dyslexic children, who fail to acquire reading skills despite normal intelligence and good educational opportunities, exhibit deficits in implicit learning of artificial grammars (Pavlidou, Williams, & Kelly, 2009) and motor and spatial sequences on the serial reaction time task (Bennett et al., 2008; Orban, Lungu, & Doyon, 2008; Stoodley et al., 2008). These findings suggest that problems with implicit

FIGURE 7.16 Artificial Grammar and Implicit Learning These are examples of letter strings formed by an artificial grammar. Research participants are exposed to the rules of the grammar and are later tested on new letter strings. Participants show reliable accuracy at distinguishing the valid, grammatical strings from the invalid, nongrammatical strings even though they usually can't explicitly state the rule they are following when making such judgments. Using an artificial grammar is one way of studying implicit learning (Reber, 1996).

Grammatical Strings	Nongrammatical Strings
VXJJ	VXTJJ
XXVT	XVTVVJ
VJTVXJ	VJTTVTV
VJTVTV	VJTXXVJ
XXXXVX	XXXVTJJ

learning play an important role in developmental dyslexia and need to be taken into account when developing remedial programs (Stoodley et al., 2008).

Implicit and Explicit Learning Use Distinct Neural Pathways

The fact that individuals suffering amnesia show intact implicit learning strongly suggests that the brain structures that underlie implicit learning are distinct from those that underlie explicit learning. As we learned in the Memory chapter, amnesic individuals generally show signs of lesions in the hippocampus and nearby structures in the medial temporal lobe; accordingly, these regions are not necessary for implicit learning (Bayley, Frascino, & Squire, 2005).

For example, in one study, participants saw a series of dot patterns, each of which looked like an array of stars in the night sky (Reber et al., 2003). Actually, all the stimuli were constructed to conform to an underlying prototypical dot pattern. The dots, however, varied so much that it was virtually impossible for a viewer to guess that they all had this common structure. Before the experiment began, half of the participants were told about the existence of the prototype; in other words, they were given instructions that encouraged explicit processing. The others were given standard implicit learning instructions: They were told nothing other than to attend to the dot patterns.

The participants were then asked to categorize new dot patterns into those that conformed to the prototype and those that did not. Interestingly, both groups performed equally well on this task, correctly classifying about 65% of the new dot patterns. However, brain scans revealed that the two groups were making these decisions using very different parts of their brains (see **FIGURE 7.17**). Participants who were given the explicit instructions showed *increased* brain activity in the frontal cortex, parietal cortex, hippocampus, and a variety of other areas known to be associated with the processing of explicit memories. Those given the implicit instructions showed *decreased* brain activation primarily in the occipital region, which is involved in visual processing. This finding suggests that participants recruited distinct brain structures in different ways depending on whether they were approaching the task using explicit or implicit learning.

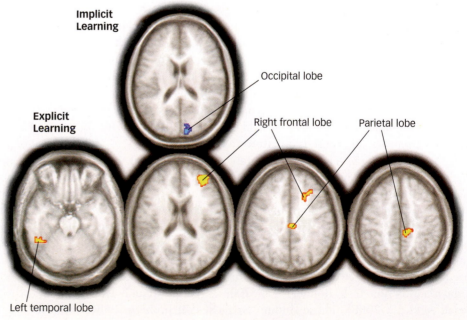

FIGURE 7.17 Implicit and Explicit Learning Activate Different Brain Areas Research participants were scanned with fMRI while engaged in either implicit or explicit learning about the categorization of dot patterns. The occipital region (in blue) showed decreased brain activity after implicit learning. The areas in yellow and orange showed increased brain activity during explicit learning, including the left temporal lobe, right frontal lobe, and parietal lobe (Reber et al., 2003).

©Reber, P. J., Gitelman, D. R., Parrish, T. B., & Mesulam, M. M. (2003). Dissociating explicit and implicit category knowledge with fMRI. Journal of Cognitive Neuroscience, 15, 574-583

SUMMARY QUIZ [7.4]

1. What kind of learning takes place largely independent of awareness of both the process and the products of information acquisition?
   a. latent learning
   b. implicit learning
   c. observational learning
   d. conscious learning

2. Which of the following statements about implicit learning is inaccurate?
   a. Some forms of learning start out as explicit but become more implicit over time.
   b. Implicit learning occurs even in the simplest organisms.
   c. People with amnesia tend to be severely impaired at implicit learning tasks.
   d. Children learn language and social conduct largely through implicit learning.

3. Responding to implicit instructions results in decreased brain activation in which part of the brain?
   a. the hippocampus
   b. the parietal cortex
   c. the prefrontal cortex
   d. the occipital region

Learning in the Classroom

In this chapter, we've considered several different types of learning from behavioral, cognitive, evolutionary, and neural perspectives. Yet it may seem strange to you that we haven't discussed the kind of learning to which you are currently devoting much of your life: learning in educational settings such as the classroom. Way back in the first chapter of this book (Psychology: Evolution of a Science), we reviewed some techniques that we think are useful for studying the material in this course and others (see The Real World, Improving Study Skills, p. 6). But we didn't say much about the actual research that supports these suggestions. Let's consider what recent research says about learning techniques, and then we will turn to the equally important topic of exerting control over learning processes.

Techniques for Learning

Students use a wide variety of study techniques in attempts to increase learning, including highlighting and underlining, rereading, summarizing, and visual imagery mnemonics (Annis & Annis, 1982; Wade, Trathen, & Schraw, 1990). How effective are such techniques? A comprehensive analysis of research concerning 10 learning techniques (Dunlosky et al., 2013) evaluated the overall usefulness of each technique and classified it as high, moderate, or low utility. **TABLE 7.2** provides a brief description of each of the 10 techniques and the overall utility assessment for each one.

Despite their popularity, highlighting, rereading, summarizing, and visual imagery mnemonics all received a low utility assessment. That doesn't mean that these techniques have no value whatsoever for improving learning, but it does indicate that each one has significant limitations and that time could be better spent using other approaches—a reason why none of these techniques appeared in the Improving Study Skills box. The Improving Study Skills box did highlight both of the techniques

Table 7.2 Rating the Effectiveness of Study Techniques

Technique	Description	Utility
Practice Testing	Using practice tests to self-test	High
Distributed practice	Spacing out over time your attempts to study the to-be-learned information.	High
Elaborative interrogation	Interpreting the information by thinking about its meaning and reflecting on its significance	Moderate
Self-explanation	Building new information on to information you've already learned	Moderate
Interleaved practice	Varying the types of materials studied during one study session	Moderate
Summarization	Writing notes of the key concepts	Low
Highlighting/underlining	Marking the key concepts so they stand out visually	Low
Keyword mnemonic	Pairing the concept's keywords with mental images	Low
Imagery for text	Forming mental images of the information	Low
Rereading	Repeatedly reading the material	Low

that received high utility assessments: distributed practice ("Rehearse") and practice testing ("Test"). Let's take a deeper look at some of the research that supports the beneficial effects of these two effective techniques, which have been intensively investigated during the past few years.

Distributed Practice

Cramming for exams (neglecting to study for an extended period of time and then studying intensively just before an exam; Vacha & McBride, 1993) is common in educational life. Surveys of undergraduates indicate that anywhere from about 25% to as many as 50% of students report relying on cramming (McIntyre & Munson, 2008). Though cramming is better than not studying at all, when students cram for an exam, they repeatedly study the to-be-learned information with little or no time between repetitions, a procedure known as *massed practice*. Such students are thus denying themselves the benefits of *distributed practice*, which involves spreading out study activities so that more time intervenes between repetitions of the to-be-learned information. (Students who rely on cramming are also inviting some of the health and performance problems associated with procrastination that we outlined in The Real World box on p. 4).

What's most impressive is just how widespread the benefits of distributed practice are: They have been observed for numerous different kinds of materials, including foreign vocabulary, definitions, and face–name pairs, and they have been demonstrated not only in undergraduates, but also in children, older adults, and individuals with memory problems due to brain damage (Dunlosky et al., 2013). A review of 254 separate studies involving more than 14,000 participants concluded that, on average, participants retained 47% of studied information after distributed practice compared with 37% after massed practice (Cepeda et al., 2006).

Despite all the evidence indicating that distributed practice is an effective learning strategy, we still don't fully understand why that is so. One promising idea is that when engaging in massed practice, retrieving recently studied information is relatively easy, whereas during distributed practice, it is more difficult to retrieve information that was studied less recently. More difficult retrievals benefit subsequent learning more than easy retrievals, in line with idea of "desirable difficulties" (Bjork & Bjork, 2011) introduced in the Improving Study Skills box. Whatever the explanation for the effects of distributed practice, there is no denying its benefits for students.

Practice Testing

Practice testing, like distributed practice, has proven useful across a wide range of materials, including the learning of stories, facts, vocabulary, and lectures (Dunlosky et al., 2013; Karpicke, 2012; see also the LearningCurve system associated with this text, which uses practice testing). As you learned in the Memory chapter, practice testing is effective, in part, because actively retrieving an item from memory on a test improves subsequent retention of that item more than simply studying it again (Roediger & Karpicke, 2006). Yet when asked about their preferred study strategies, students indicated by a wide margin that they prefer rereading materials to testing themselves (Karpicke, 2012). The benefits of testing tend to be greatest when the test is difficult and requires considerable retrieval effort (Pyc & Rawson, 2009), a finding that is also consistent with the desirable difficulties hypothesis (Bjork & Bjork, 2011). Not only does testing increase verbatim learning of the exact material that is tested, but it also enhances the *transfer* of learning from one situation to another (Carpenter, 2012). For example, if you are given practice tests with short-answer questions, such testing improves later performance on both short-answer and multiple-choice questions (Kang, McDermott, & Roediger, 2007). Testing also improves the ability to draw conclusions from the studied material, which is an important part of learning and often critical to performing well in the classroom (Karpicke & Blunt, 2011).

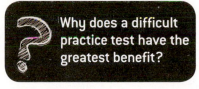

Why does a difficult practice test have the greatest benefit?

Studying well in advance of an exam, so that you can take breaks and distribute study time, will generally produce a better outcome than cramming at the last minute.

Testing Aids Attention

Recent research conducted in the laboratory of one of your textbook authors highlights yet another benefit of testing: Including brief tests during a lecture can improve learning by reducing the tendency to mind-wander (Szpunar, Khan, & Schacter, 2013). How often have you found your mind wandering—thinking about your evening plans, recalling a scene from a movie, or texting a friend—in the midst of a lecture that you know that you ought to be attending to carefully? It's probably happened more than once. Research indicates that students' minds wander frequently during classroom lectures (Bunce, Flens, & Neiles, 2011; Lindquist & McLean, 2011; Wilson & Korn, 2007). Critically, such mind wandering impairs learning of the lecture material (Risko et al., 2012). In the study by Szpunar et al. (2013), participants watched a videotaped lecture that was divided into four segments. All of the participants were told that they might or might not be tested after each segment; they were also encouraged to take notes during the lectures. However, some participants ("tested group") received brief tests on each segment, while others ("nontested group") did not receive a test until after the final segment. A third group of participants ("restudy group") were shown, but not tested on, the material after each segment.

At random times during the lectures, participants in all groups were probed about whether they were paying attention to the lecture or mind wandering off to other topics. Participants in the nontested and restudy groups indicated that they were mind wandering in response to about 40% of the probes, but the incidence of mind wandering was cut in half, to about 20%, in the tested group. Participants in the tested group took significantly more notes during the lectures, and they retained significantly more information from the lecture on a final test than did participants in the other two groups, who performed similarly. Participants in the tested group were also less anxious about the final test than those in the other groups. These results indicate that part of the value of testing comes from encouraging people to sustain attention to a lecture in a way that discourages task-irrelevant activities such as mind wandering, and it encourages task-relevant activities such as note taking. Because these benefits of testing were observed in response to a videotaped lecture, they apply most directly to online learning, where taped lectures are the norm, but there is every reason to believe that the results would apply in live classroom settings as well.

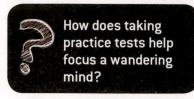

How does taking practice tests help focus a wandering mind?

Control of Learning

It's the night before the final exam in your introductory psychology course. You've put in a lot of time reviewing your course notes and the material in this textbook, and you feel that you have learned most of it pretty well. You are coming down the home stretch with little time left, and you've got to decide whether to devote those precious remaining minutes to studying psychological disorders or social psychology. How do you make that decision? What are the potential consequences of your decision? An important part of learning involves assessing how well we know something and how much more time we need to devote to studying it.

Experimental evidence reveals that people's judgments about what they have learned, which psychologists refer to as *judgments of learning* (JOLs), have a causal influence on learning: People typically devote more time to studying items that they judge they have not learned well (Metcalfe & Finn, 2008; Son & Metcalfe, 2000).

Unfortunately, JOLs are often inaccurate (Castel, McCabe, & Roediger, 2007). For example, after reading and rereading a chapter or article in preparation for a test, you may feel that the material is quite familiar, and that feeling may convince you that you've learned the material well enough that you don't need to study it further. However, the feeling of familiarity can be misleading: It may be the result of a low-level process such as perceptual priming (see the Memory chapter) and not the kind of learning that will be required to perform well on an exam (Bjork & Bjork, 2011). One way to avoid being fooled by such misleading subjective impressions is to test yourself from time to time when studying for an exam under examlike conditions and to carefully compare your responses to the actual answers.

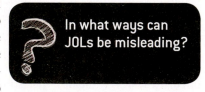

In what ways can JOLs be misleading?

So, if you are preparing for the final exam in this course and need to decide whether to devote more time to studying psychological disorders or social psychology, try to exert control over learning by testing yourself on material from the two chapters; you can use the results of those tests to help you decide which chapter requires further work. Heed the conclusion from researchers (Bjork, Dunlosky, and Kornell, 2013) that becoming a more sophisticated and effective learner requires understanding: (a) key features of learning and memory; (b) effective learning techniques; (c) how to monitor and control one's own learning; and (d) biases that can undermine judgments of learning.

DATA VISUALIZATION

Do "Learning Styles" Exist?
www.macmillanhighered.com/
schacterbrief3e

SUMMARY QUIZ [7.5]

1. Which study strategy has been shown to be the most effective?
   a. highlighting text
   b. rereading
   c. summarizing
   d. taking practice tests

2. Which of the following is true about judgments of learning (JOL)?
   a. People are generally good judges of how well they have learned new material.
   b. The feeling of familiarity with material is usually an indicator of whether the material is learned.
   c. Based on JOLs, people generally spend more time studying material they feel they know well.
   d. JOLs have a causal influence on learning.

3. Part of the value of self-testing as a study aid comes from:
   a. increasing feeling of familiarity with the material.
   b. helping to sustain attention during initial learning.
   c. passive re-exposure to the material.
   d. decreasing the need to take careful notes during the lecture.

CHAPTER REVIEW

SUMMARY

Classical Conditioning: One Thing Leads to Another

> Classical conditioning pairs a neutral stimulus (a conditioned stimulus or CS) with a meaningful event (an unconditioned stimulus or US); eventually, the CS, all by itself, elicits a response called a conditioned response (CR).

> Behaviorists viewed classical conditioning as providing a model in which no higher-level functions, such as thinking or awareness, needed to be invoked to understand behavior.

> Later researchers showed, however, that classical conditioning involves setting up expectations, is sensitive to the degree to which the CS functions as a genuine predictor of the US, and can involve some degree of cognition.

> The cerebellum plays an important role in eyeblink conditioning, whereas the amygdala is important for fear conditioning.

> Each species is biologically predisposed to acquire particular CS–US associations based on its evolutionary history, showing that classical conditioning is a sophisticated mechanism that evolved because it has adaptive value.

Operant Conditioning: Reinforcements from the Environment

> Operant conditioning is a process by which behaviors are reinforced and therefore become more likely to occur. The contingencies between actions and outcomes are critical in determining how an organism's behaviors will be displayed.

> The behaviorists tried to explain behavior without considering cognitive, neural, or evolutionary mechanisms. However, as with classical conditioning, this approach turned out to be incomplete.

> Operant conditioning has clear cognitive components: Organisms behave as though they have expectations about the outcomes of their actions and adjust their actions accordingly. Cognitive influences can sometimes override the trial-by-trial feedback that usually influences learning.

> The associative mechanisms that underlie operant conditioning have their roots in evolutionary biology. Some things are relatively easily learned and others are difficult; the history of a species is usually the best clue as to which will be which.

Observational Learning: Look at Me

> Observational learning is an important process by which species gather information about the world around them, and it has important social and cultural consequences.

> Chimpanzees and monkeys can benefit from observational learning, especially those reared in settings that include humans.

> The mirror neuron system becomes active during observational learning, and many of the same brain regions are active during observation and performance of a skill.

Implicit Learning: Under the Wires

> Implicit learning is a process that detects, learns, and stores patterns without the application of explicit awareness on the part of the learner.

> Implicit learning can produce simple behaviors such as habituation and also complex behaviors, such as language use or socialization.

> Neuroimaging studies indicate that implicit and explicit learning recruit distinct brain structures, sometimes in different ways.

Learning in the Classroom

> Research on learning techniques indicates that some popular study methods such as highlighting, underlining, and rereading have low utility, whereas other techniques such as practice testing and distributed practice have high utility.

> Practice testing improves retention and transfer of learning and can also enhance learning and reduce mind wandering during lectures.

> Judgments of learning (JOLs) play a causal role in determining what material to study, but they can be misleading.

KEY TERMS

learning (p. 208)

habituation (p. 208)

sensitization (p. 208)

classical conditioning (p. 209)

unconditioned stimulus (US) (p. 209)

unconditioned response (UR) (p. 209)

conditioned stimulus (CS) (p. 209)

conditioned response (CR) (p. 209)

acquisition (p. 210)

second-order conditioning (p. 211)

extinction (p. 211)

spontaneous recovery (p. 211)

generalization (p. 212)

discrimination (p. 212)

biological preparedness (p. 215)

operant conditioning (p. 216)

law of effect (p. 217)

operant behavior (p. 217)

reinforcer (p. 218)

punisher (p. 218)

fixed-interval schedule (FI) (p. 221)

variable-interval schedule (VI) (p. 222)

fixed-ratio schedule (FR) (p. 222)

variable-ratio schedule (VR) (p. 223)

intermittent reinforcement (p. 223)

intermittent reinforcement effect (p. 223)

shaping (p. 223)

latent learning (p. 225)

cognitive map (p. 226)

observational learning (p. 230)

implicit learning (p. 234)

CHANGING MINDS

1. A friend is taking a class in childhood education. "Back in the old days," she says, "teachers used physical punishment, but of course that's not allowed any more. Now, a good teacher should only use reinforcement. When children behave, teachers should provide positive reinforcement, like praise. When children misbehave, teachers should provide negative reinforcement, like scolding or withholding privileges." What is your friend misunderstanding about reinforcement? Can you give better examples of how negative reinforcement could be productively applied in an elementary school classroom?

2. A friend of your family is trying to train her daughter to make her bed every morning. You suggest she tries positive reinforcement. A month later, the woman reports back to you. "It's not working very well," she says. "Every time she makes her bed, I put a gold star on the calendar, and at the end of the week, if there are seven gold stars, I give Vicky a reward—a piece of licorice. But so far, she's only earned the licorice twice." How could you explain why the desired behavior—bed making—might not increase as a result of this reinforcement procedure?

3. While studying for the exam, you ask your study partner to provide a definition of classical conditioning. "In classical conditioning," she says, "there's a stimulus—the CS—that predicts an upcoming event, the US. Usually, it's something bad, like an electric shock, nausea, or a frightening loud noise. The learner makes a response, the CR, in order to prevent the US. Sometimes, the US is good, like food for Pavlov's dogs, and then the learner makes the response in order to earn the US." What's wrong with this definition?

4. One of your classmates announces that he liked the last chapter (on memory) better than the current chapter on learning. "I want to be a psychiatrist," he says, "so I mostly care about human learning. Conditioning might be a really powerful way to train animals to push levers or perform tricks, but it really doesn't have much relevance to how humans learn things." How similar is learning in humans and other animals? What real-world examples can you provide to show that conditioning does occur in humans?

ANSWERS TO SUMMARY QUIZZES

Answers to Summary Quiz 7.1: 1. b; 2. c; 3. d; 4. a.

Answers to Summary Quiz 7.2: 1. c; 2. d; 3. a.

Answers to Summary Quiz 7.3: 1. b; 2. c; 3. c.

Answers to Summary Quiz 7.4: 1. b; 2. c; 3. d.

Answers to Summary Quiz 7.5: 1. d; 2. d; 3. b.

www

Need more help? Additional resources are located in LaunchPad at:

http://www.worthpublishers.com/launchpad/ schacterbrief3e

Emotion and Motivation

EONARDO IS 5 YEARS OLD AND CUTE AS A BUTTON. He can do many of the things that other 5-year-olds can do: solve puzzles, build towers of blocks, and play guessing games with grown-ups. But unlike other 5-year-olds, Leonardo has never been proud of his abilities, angry at his mother, or bored with his lessons. He has never laughed or cried. That's because Leonardo has a condition that makes him unable to experience emotions of any kind.

In order to interact with people, Leonardo's mother spent years teaching him how to make the facial expressions that indicate emotions such as surprise and sadness, and how to detect those facial expressions in others. Leonardo now knows that he should smile when someone says something nice to him and that he should raise his eyebrow once in a while to show interest in what people are saying.

Leonardo is a quick learner, and he's gotten so good at this that when strangers interact with him, they find it hard to believe that deep down inside he is feeling nothing at all. When Leonardo's mother smiles at him, he always smiles back; and yet, she is keenly aware that Leonardo is merely making the faces he was taught to make and that he doesn't actually love her.

But that's okay. Even though Leonardo can't return her affection, Dr. Cynthia Breazeal still considers him one of the best robots she's ever designed (Breazeal, 2009).

A typical 5-year-old can experience emotions such as pride, anger, and boredom.

Alex Cao/Jupterimages

Leonardo and his "mom," MIT Professor Cynthia Breazeal.

YES, LEONARDO IS A MACHINE. HE CAN SEE AND HEAR, he can remember and reason. But despite his adorable smile and knowing wink, he can't feel a thing, and that makes him infinitely different from us. Our ability to love and to hate, to be amused and annoyed, to feel elated and devastated, is an essential element of our humanity, and a person who could not feel these emotions would seem a lot like a robot to the rest of us. But what exactly are these emotions and why are they so essential? In this chapter we will explore these questions. We'll start by discussing the nature of emotions and asking how they relate to the states of our bodies and our brains. Next we'll see how people express their emotions, and how they use those expressions to communicate with each other. Finally, we'll examine the essential role that emotions play in motivation—how they inform us, guide us, and compel us to do everything from making war to making love.

Emotional Experience: The Feeling Machine

Leonardo doesn't know what love feels like, and there's no way to teach him because trying to describe that feeling to someone who has never experienced it is a bit like trying to describe the color green to someone who was born blind. We could tell Leonardo what causes the feeling ("It happens whenever I see Marilynn"), and we could tell him about its consequences ("I breathe hard and say goofy stuff"), but in the end, these descriptions would miss the point because the essential feature of love—like the essential feature of all emotions—is the *experience*. It *feels* like something to love, and what it feels like is love's defining attribute (Heavey, Hurlburt, & Lefforge, 2012).

What Is Emotion?

"I never realized they had feelings."

How can we study something whose defining attribute defies description? Although people can't always say what an emotional experience feels like, they usually can say how similar or "close" one emotional experience is to another ("Love is more like happiness than like anger"). By asking people to rate the similarity of dozens of emotional experiences, psychologists have been able to use a technique known as *multidimensional scaling* to create a map of those experiences. The mathematics behind this technique is complex, but the logic is simple. Imagine that you had a list of the distances between a half-dozen U.S. cities and your job was to draw a map that reflected those distances. Whether you meant to or not, you would end up drawing a map of the United States because no other map would allow every city to be just the right distance from every other city (see **FIGURE 8.1**).

The same technique can be used to generate a map of the emotional landscape. If you had a list of the "distances" between a large number of emotional experiences (i.e., a list that showed how similar or "close" each was to the other) and tried to draw a map that reflected those distances, you would end up with a map like the one shown in **FIGURE 8.2**. What good would this map be? As it turns out, maps don't just show where things are; they also reveal the *dimensions* on which they vary. For example, the map in Figure 8.2 reveals that emotional experiences vary on a dimension called *valence* (how positive or negative the experience is) and a dimension called *arousal* (how active or passive the experience is). Research shows that all emotional experiences can

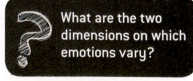

What are the two dimensions on which emotions vary?

It is almost impossible not to feel something when you look at this photograph, and it is almost impossible to say exactly what you are feeling.

be described by their unique coordinates on this two-dimensional map (Russell, 1980; Watson & Tellegen, 1985; Yik, Russell, & Steiger, 2011).

This map suggests that emotional experiences have two essential properties: they feel either good or bad, and they are associated with different degrees of bodily arousal. With these two facts in mind, we can define **emotion** as *a positive or negative experience that is associated with a particular pattern of physiological activity.* As you are about to see, the first step in understanding emotion involves understanding how the "experience" part and the "physiological activity" part of this definition are related.

The Emotional Body

You probably think that if you walked into your kitchen right now and saw a bear nosing through the cupboards, you would feel fear, your heart would start to pound, and the muscles in your legs would contract as you prepared to run. But in the late 19th century, William James suggested that the events might actually happen in the opposite order: First you'd see the bear, then your heart would start pounding and your leg muscles would contract, and *then* you would experience fear, which is simply your experience of your body's response to the sight of the bear. Psychologist Carl Lange

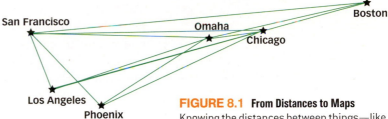

	Chicago	LA	SF	Omaha	Phoenix	Boston
Chicago	0	1749	1863	433	1447	856
LA	1749	0	344	1318	367	2605
SF	1863	344	0	1432	658	2708
Omaha	433	1318	1432	0	1029	1288
Phoenix	1447	367	658	1029	0	2290
Boston	856	2605	2708	1288	2299	0

FIGURE 8.1 From Distances to Maps Knowing the distances between things—like cities, for example—allows us to draw a map that reveals the dimensions on which they vary.

emotion A positive or negative experience that is associated with a particular pattern of physiological activity.

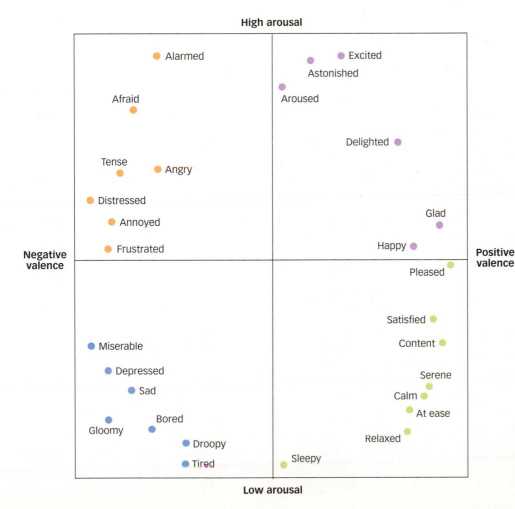

FIGURE 8.2 Two Dimensions of Emotion Just as cities vary on the dimensions of longitude and latitude, emotions vary on the dimensions of arousal and valence. [Data from Russell, 1980.]

James–Lange theory The theory that a stimulus triggers activity in the body, which in turn produces an emotional experience in the brain.

Cannon–Bard theory The theory that a stimulus simultaneously triggers activity in the body and emotional experience in the brain.

two-factor theory The theory that emotions are based on inferences about the causes of physiological arousal.

Did Princess Kate make Prince William blush by embarrassing him, or did she embarrass him by making him blush? The experience of embarrassment precedes blushing by up to 30 seconds, so it is unlikely that blushing is the cause of the emotional experience.

Andrew Milligan-WPA Pool/Getty Images

suggested something similar at about the same time, so the idea is now known as the **James–Lange theory** of emotion, which states that *stimuli trigger activity in the body, which in turn produces emotional experiences in the brain.* According to this theory, emotional experience is the consequence—not the cause—of our physiological reactions to objects and events in the world.

James's former student, Walter Cannon, didn't like this idea very much, and so together with *his* student, Philip Bard, he proposed an alternative. The **Cannon–Bard theory** of emotion suggests that *stimuli simultaneously trigger activity in the body and emotional experience in the brain* (Bard, 1934; Cannon, 1929). Cannon and Bard claimed that their theory was better than the James–Lange theory for several reasons. First, emotions happen quickly even though the body often reacts slowly. For example, a blush is a bodily response to embarrassment that takes 15 to 30 seconds to occur, and yet, people feel embarrassed within seconds of noticing that, oh say, their pants have fallen off in public. How could the blush be the cause of the feeling if it happened after the feeling? Second, people often have trouble accurately detecting their own bodily responses, such as changes in their heart rates. If people can't detect changes in their heart rates, then how can they experience those changes as an emotion? Third, environmental events, such as an increase in room temperature, cause the same bodily responses that an emotional stimulus does; so why don't people feel afraid when they get a fever? Finally, Cannon and Bard argued that there simply aren't enough unique patterns of bodily activity to account for all the unique emotional experiences people have. If many different emotional experiences are associated with the same pattern of bodily activity, then how could that pattern of activity be the sole determinant of the emotional experience?

These are all good questions, and about 30 years after Cannon and Bard asked them, psychologists Stanley Schachter and Jerome Singer supplied some answers (Schachter & Singer, 1962). Schachter and Singer thought that James and Lange were right to equate emotion with the perception of one's bodily reactions, and that Cannon and Bard were right to note that there are not nearly enough distinct bodily reactions to account for the wide variety of emotions that human beings can experience. Their **two-factor theory** of emotion suggested that *emotions are based on inferences about the causes of general physiological arousal* (see **FIGURE 8.3**). According to this theory, when you see a bear in your kitchen, your heart begins to pound. Your brain notices both the pounding and the bear, puts two and two together, and

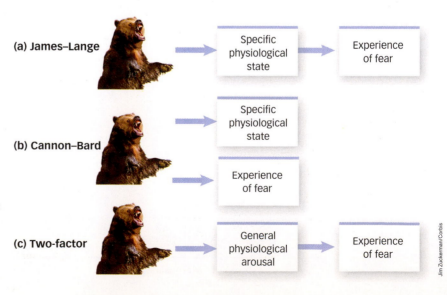

FIGURE 8.3 Classic Theories of Emotion The James–Lange theory suggests that stimuli trigger specific physiological states, which are then experienced as emotions (*a*). The Cannon–Bard theory suggests that stimuli trigger both specific physiological states and emotional experiences independently (*b*). The two-factor theory suggests that stimuli trigger general physiological arousal whose cause the brain interprets, and this interpretation leads to emotional experience (*c*).

(a) James–Lange → Specific physiological state → Experience of fear

(b) Cannon–Bard → Specific physiological state / Experience of fear

(c) Two-factor → General physiological arousal → Experience of fear

Jim Zuckerman/Corbis

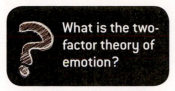

What is the two-factor theory of emotion?

interprets your bodily arousal as fear. According to the two-factor theory, people experience the same kind of bodily arousal in reaction to all emotional stimuli, but they interpret that arousal in different ways on different occasions. The feeling that your brain calls fear one day is exactly the same feeling that it might call excitement on another.

How has the two-factor model fared in the last half century? One of the model's claims has fared very well. For instance, participants in one study (Schachter & Singer, 1962) were injected with epinephrine, which causes physiological arousal, and then exposed to either a goofy or a nasty confederate. Just as the two-factor theory predicted, when the confederate acted goofy,

participants concluded that they were feeling *happy*, but when the confederate acted nasty, participants concluded that they were feeling *angry*. Subsequent research has shown that when people are made to feel aroused—say, by having them ride an exercise bike in the laboratory—they subsequently find attractive people more attractive, annoying people more annoying, and funny cartoons funnier, as if they were interpreting their exercise-induced arousal as attraction, annoyance, or amusement (Byrne et al., 1975; Dutton & Aron, 1974; Zillmann, Katcher, & Milavsky, 1972). In fact, these effects occur even when people merely *think* they're aroused—for example, when they hear an audiotape of a rapidly beating heart and are led to believe that the heartbeat they're hearing is their own (Valins, 1966). It appears that the two-factor model is right when it suggests that people make inferences about the causes of their arousal and that those inferences influence their emotional experience (Lindquist & Barrett, 2008).

But research has not been so kind to the model's claim that all emotional experiences are merely different interpretations of the same kind of bodily arousal. For example, researchers measured participants' physiological reactions as they experienced six different emotions and found that anger, fear, and sadness each produced a higher heart rate than disgust, and that anger produced a larger increase in finger temperature than did fear (Ekman, Levenson, & Friesen, 1983; see **FIGURE 8.4**). These findings have been replicated across different age groups, professions, genders, and cultures (Levenson, Ekman, & Friesen, 1990; Levenson et al., 1991, 1992). In fact,

The fact that people can mistake physical arousal for romantic attraction may help explain why so many first dates involve roller coasters. This couple—actress Brooke Shields and producer Chris Henchy—ended up getting married shortly after this photo was taken.

FIGURE 8.4 The Physiology of Emotion Contrary to the claims of the two-factor theory, different emotions do seem to have different underlying patterns of physiological arousal. Anger, fear, and sadness all produce higher heart rates compared to happiness, surprise, and disgust (a). Anger produces a much larger increase in finger temperature than any other emotion (b). (Data from Ekman, Levenson, & Friesen, 1983.)

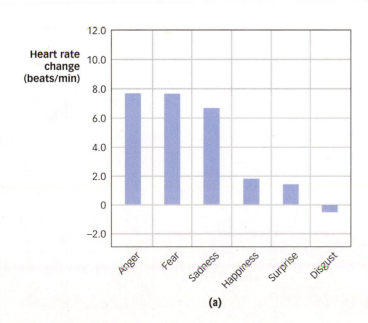

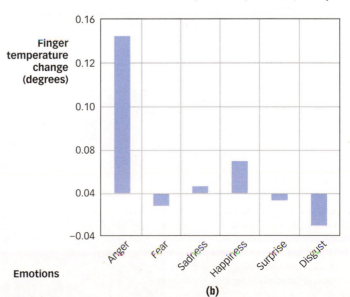

Emotions

(a)

(b)

some physiological responses seem unique to a single emotion. For example, a blush is the result of increased blood volume in the subcutaneous capillaries in the face, neck, and chest, and research suggests that people blush when they feel embarrassment but not when they feel any other emotion (Leary et al., 1992). Similarly, certain patterns of activity in the parasympathetic branch of the autonomic nervous system (which is responsible for slowing and calming rather than speeding and exciting) seem uniquely related to prosocial emotions such as compassion (Oately, Keltner, & Jenkins, 2006).

Where does all this leave us? James and Lange were right when they suggested that the patterns of physiological response are not the same for all emotions. But Cannon and Bard were also right when they suggested that people are not perfectly sensitive to these patterns of response, which is why people must sometimes make inferences about what they are feeling. Our bodily activity and our mental activity are, it seems, both the causes and the consequences of our emotional experience.

The Emotional Brain

In the late 1930s, psychologist Heinrich Klüver and physician Paul Bucy made an accidental discovery. A few days after performing brain surgery on a monkey named Aurora, they noticed that she was acting strangely. First, Aurora would eat just about

The tourist and the tiger have something in common: each has an amygdala that is working at lightning speed to decide whether the other is a threat.

anything and have sex with just about anyone—as though she could no longer distinguish between good and bad food, or between good and bad mates. Second, Aurora seemed absolutely fearless, remaining calm when she was handled by experimenters, and even when she was confronted by snakes (Klüver & Bucy, 1937). What had happened to her? As it turned out, during the surgery, Klüver and Bucy had accidentally damaged a structure in Aurora's brain called the *amygdala*. Subsequent studies confirmed that the amygdala plays a special role in producing emotions such as fear. For example, people normally have superior memory for emotionally evocative words such as *death* or *vomit*, but people whose amygdalae are damaged (LaBar & Phelps, 1998) or who take drugs that temporarily impair neurotransmission in the amygdala (van Stegeren et al., 1998) do not (see **FIGURE 8.5**).

What exactly does the amygdala do? Is it some sort of "fear center"? Not exactly (Cunningham & Brosch, 2012). Before an animal can feel fear, its brain must first decide that there is something to be afraid of. This decision

FIGURE 8.5 Emotion Recognition and the Amygdala Facial expressions of emotion were morphed into a continuum that ran from happiness to surprise to fear to sadness to disgust to anger and back to happiness. This sequence was shown to a patient with bilateral amygdala damage and to a control group of 10 people without brain damage. Although the patient's recognition of happiness, sadness, and surprise was generally in line with that of the control group, her recognition of anger, disgust, and fear was impaired (Calder et al., 1996).

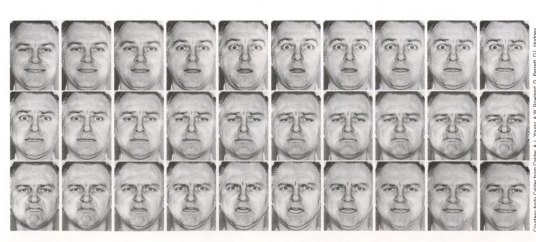

is called an **appraisal,** which is *an evaluation of the emotion-relevant aspects of a stimulus* (Arnold, 1960; Ellsworth & Scherer, 2003; Lazarus, 1984; Roseman, 1984; Roseman & Smith, 2001; Scherer, 1999, 2001). The amygdala is critical to making these appraisals. In essence, the amygdala is an extremely fast and sensitive threat detector (Whalen et al., 1998). Psychologist Joseph LeDoux (2000) found that information about a stimulus is transmitted through the brain simultaneously along two distinct routes. The thalamus is a kind of router that simultaneously sends information along a "fast pathway" (which goes directly from the thalamus to the amygdala) and a "slow pathway" (which goes from the thalamus to the cortex and *then* to the amygdala) (see **FIGURE 8.6**). This means that while the cortex is slowly using the information it received from the thalamus to conduct a full-scale investigation of the stimulus's identity and importance, the amygdala has already received the information directly from the thalamus and is making one very fast and very simple decision: "Is this a threat?" If the amygdala's answer to that question is yes, it initiates the neural processes that ultimately produce the bodily reactions and conscious experience that we call fear.

The cortex takes longer to process its information than the amygdala does. But when it's finished, it sends a signal to the amygdala telling it either to maintain the state of fear ("We've now analyzed all the data up here, and sure enough, that thing is a bear!") or to decrease it ("Relax, it's just some guy in a bear costume"). In a sense, the amygdala presses the emotional gas pedal and the cortex may or may not hit the brakes. When experimental subjects are instructed to *experience* emotions such as sadness, fear, and anger, they show increased activity in the amygdala and decreased activity in the cortex (Damasio et al., 2000), but when they are asked to *inhibit* these emotions, they show increased cortical activity and decreased amygdala activity (Ochsner et al., 2002). That's why adults with cortical damage and children (whose cortices are not well developed) have difficulty inhibiting their emotions (Stuss & Benson, 1986).

The conclusion is clear: emotion is part of a primitive brain system that prepares us to react rapidly and on the basis of little information to things that are relevant to our survival and well-being. While our evolutionarily new cortex works to identify a stimulus and make a reasoned decision about what to do, our evolutionarily ancient amygdala makes a split-second decision about whether that stimulus is a threat. If that decision is a yes, the amygdala gets our hearts pounding, our legs running, and our butts the heck out of the kitchen.

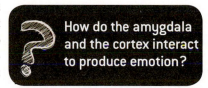

How do the amygdala and the cortex interact to produce emotion?

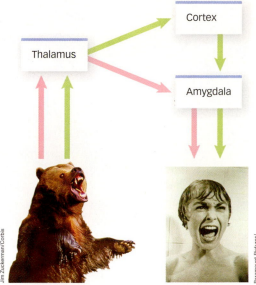

Stimulus   Experience of fear

FIGURE 8.6 The Fast and Slow Pathways of Fear According to Joseph LeDoux (2000), information about a stimulus takes two routes simultaneously: the "fast pathway" (shown in pink), which goes from the thalamus directly to the amygdala, and the "slow pathway" (shown in green), which goes from the thalamus to the cortex and then to the amygdala. Because the amygdala receives information from the thalamus before it receives information from the cortex, people can be afraid of something before they know what it is. Sometimes, as in the famous shower scene from the movie *Psycho,* neither is fast enough.

appraisal An evaluation of the emotion-relevant aspects of a stimulus.

emotion regulation The strategies people use to influence their own emotional experience.

The Regulation of Emotion

It will not surprise you to learn that people would usually rather feel good than bad. **Emotion regulation** refers to *the strategies people use to influence their own emotional experience*. Ninety percent of people report attempting to regulate their emotional experience at least once a day (Gross, 1998), and describe more than a thousand different strategies for doing so (Parkinson & Totterdell, 1999). Some of these are behavioral strategies (e.g., avoiding situations that trigger unwanted emotions), some are cognitive strategies (e.g., recruiting memories that trigger the desired emotion; Webb, Miles, & Sheeran, 2012), and research shows that people don't always know which of these strategies is most effective. For example, people tend to think that *suppression*, which involves inhibiting the outward signs of an emotion, is generally an effective strategy, but by and large, it isn't (Gross, 2002). Conversely, people tend to think that *affect labeling,* which involves putting one's feelings into words, will have little impact on their emotions, when in fact, it is actually an effective way to reduce the intensity of an emotional state (Lieberman et al., 2011).

AP Photo/Rick Bowmer

Emotion regulation can be difficult. In 2011, the city of Portland, Oregon, flushed 8 million gallons of drinking water simply because a man was seen urinating in this reservoir. Although the miniscule amount of urine posed no health threat, it made people feel disgusted—and the inability to regulate that emotion cost the citizens of Portland nearly $30,000.

reappraisal Changing one's emotional experience by changing the way one thinks about the emotion-eliciting stimulus.

One of the best strategies for emotion regulation is **reappraisal,** which involves *changing one's emotional experience by changing the way one thinks about the emotion-eliciting stimulus* (Ochsner et al., 2009). For example, in one study, participants' brains were scanned as they saw photos that induced negative emotions, such as a photo of a woman crying during a funeral. Some participants were then asked to reappraise the picture, for example, by imagining that the woman in the photo was at a wedding rather than a funeral. The results showed that when participants initially saw the photo, their amygdalae became active. But as they reappraised the picture, several key areas of the cortex became active, and moments later, their amygdalae were deactivated (Ochsner et al., 2002). In other words, participants were able to turn down the activity of their own amygdalae simply by thinking about the photo in a different way.

When it comes to reappraisal, some people do it better than others (Malooly, Genet, & Siemer, 2013), and those who do it best tend to be the most mentally and physically healthy (Davidson, Putnam, & Larson, 2000; Gross & Munoz, 1995). Indeed, as you will learn in the Stress and Health chapter, therapists often attempt to alleviate depression and distress by teaching people how to reappraise key events in their lives (Jamieson, Mendes, & Nock, 2013). About two thousand years ago, the Roman philosopher and emperor Marcus Aurelius wrote: "If you are distressed by anything external, the pain is not due to the thing itself, but to your estimate of it; and this you have the power to revoke at any moment." Modern science suggests that he was right.

? How, and how well, does reappraisal work?

SUMMARY QUIZ [8.1]

1. Emotions can be described by their location on the two dimensions of
   a. motivation and scaling.
   b. arousal and valence.
   c. stimulus and reaction.
   d. pain and pleasure.

2. Which theorists claimed that a stimulus simultaneously causes both an emotional experience and a physiological reaction?
   a. Cannon and Bard
   b. James and Lange
   c. Schacter and Singer
   d. Klüver and Bucy

3. Which brain structure is most directly involved in the rapid appraisal of a stimulus as good or bad?
   a. the cortex
   b. the hypothalamus
   c. the amygdala
   d. the thalamus

4. The act of changing an emotional experience by changing the meaning of the emotion-eliciting stimulus is called _____.

   a. deactivation

   b. appraisal

   c. valence

   d. reappraisal

emotional expression An observable sign of an emotional state.

Emotional Communication: Msgs w/o Wrds

Leonardo the robot may not be able to feel, but he sure can smile. And wink. And nod. Indeed, one of the reasons why people who interact with Leonardo find it so hard to think of him as a machine is that Leonardo *expresses* emotions that he doesn't actually have. An **emotional expression** is *an observable sign of an emotional state*, and both robots and people are programmed to make them.

Emotions can be expressed by the tone of our speech, the direction of our gaze, and even the rhythm of our gait. But no part of the body is more emotionally expressive than the face. The muscles of the human face can make 46 distinct patterns known as "action units" (Ekman, 1965; Ekman & Friesen, 1971), and combinations of different action units are reliably related to specific emotional states (Davidson et al., 1990). For example, when people feel happy, their *zygomatic major* muscles pull up their lip corners while their *obicularis oculi* muscles crinkle the outside edges of their eyes. Psychologists refer to the resulting expression as "Action Units 6+12" but the rest of the world just calls it smiling.

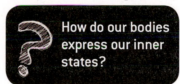

How do our bodies express our inner states?

Communicative Expression

Why do faces express emotion? In 1872, Charles Darwin published *The Expression of the Emotions in Man and Animals*, in which he speculated about the evolutionary significance of emotional expression. Darwin noticed that human and nonhuman animals share certain facial and postural expressions, and he suggested that these expressions were meant to communicate information about internal states. It's not

Fardad Faridi/Courtesy Personal Robots Group, M.I.T. Media Lab

Leonardo's face is capable of expressing a wide range of emotions (Breazeal, 2009).

According to Charles Darwin (1872/1998), both human and nonhuman animals use facial expressions to communicate information about their internal states.

In 2013, Nobuyuki Tsujii won the prestigious Van Cliburn International Piano competition. Although he was born blind and has never seen a facial expression, winning a million dollar prize immediately gave rise to a million dollar smile.

universality hypothesis Emotional expressions have the same meaning for everyone.

facial feedback hypothesis Emotional expressions can cause the emotional experiences they signify.

hard to see how such communications could be useful (Shariff & Tracy, 2011). For example, if a dominant animal can bare its teeth and communicate the message, "I am angry at you," and if a subordinate animal can lower its head and communicate the message, "I am afraid of you," then the two can establish a pecking order without actually spilling any blood. In this sense, emotional expressions are a bit like the words of a nonverbal language.

The Universality of Expression

Of course, a language only works if everybody speaks the same one, which is why Darwin advanced the **universality hypothesis,** which suggests that *all human beings naturally make and understand the same emotional expressions*. There is some evidence for this hypothesis. For example, people who have never seen a human face make the same facial expressions as those who have. Congenitally blind people smile when they are happy (Galati, Scherer, & Ricci-Bitt, 1997; Matsumoto & Willingham, 2009), and 2-day-old infants make a "disgust face" when bitter chemicals are put in their mouths (Steiner, 1973, 1979). In addition, people are fairly accurate when judging the emotional expressions of members of other cultures (Ekman & Friesen, 1971; Elfenbein & Ambady, 2002; Frank & Stennet, 2001; Haidt & Keltner, 1999). Not only do Chileans, Americans, and Japanese all recognize a smile as a sign of happiness and a frown as a sign of sadness, but so do members of preliterate cultures. In the 1950s, researchers took photographs of Westerners expressing anger, disgust, fear, happiness, sadness, and surprise (see **FIGURE 8.7**) and showed them to members of the South Fore, a people who lived a Stone Age existence in the highlands of Papua New Guinea and who at that point had had little contact with the modern world. Researchers asked these participants to match each photograph to a word (such as "happy" or "afraid") and discovered that the South Fore made matches that were essentially the same as those made by Americans. Evidence of this sort has convinced many psychologists that facial displays of at least six emotions—*anger, disgust, fear, happiness, sadness,* and *surprise*—are universal. And a few other emotions—*embarrassment, amusement, guilt, shame,* and *pride*—may have universal patterns of facial expression as well (Keltner, 1995; Keltner & Buswell, 1996; Keltner & Haidt, 1999; Keltner & Harker, 1998; Tracy et al., 2013).

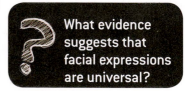

What evidence suggests that facial expressions are universal?

The Cause and Effect of Expression

It seems obvious that our emotional experiences cause our emotional expressions. What's less obvious is that it also works the other way around. The **facial feedback hypothesis** (Adelmann & Zajonc, 1989; Izard, 1971; Tomkins, 1981) suggests that *emotional expressions can cause emotional experiences*. And they can! People feel happier when they are asked to make the sound of a long *e* or to hold a pencil in their teeth (both of which cause contraction of the *zygomatic major* muscle) than when they are asked to make the sound of a long *u* or to hold a pencil in their lips (Strack, Martin, & Stepper, 1988; Zajonc, 1989; see **FIGURE 8.7**). Similarly, when people are instructed to arch their brows, they find facts more surprising; and when instructed to wrinkle their noses, they find odors less pleasant (Lewis, 2012). These things happen because facial expressions and emotional states become strongly associated with each other over time, and eventually, each can bring about the other. These effects are not limited to the face. For example, people feel more assertive when instructed to make a fist (Schubert & Koole, 2009) and rate

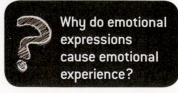

Why do emotional expressions cause emotional experience?

FIGURE 8.7 The Facial Feedback Hypothesis
Research shows that people who hold a pen with their teeth feel happier than those who hold a pen with their lips. These two postures cause contraction of the muscles associated with smiling and frowning, respectively.

Hot Science

The Body of Evidence

What can you tell from a face alone? Maybe less than you realize. Aviezer, Trope, and Todorov (2012) showed participants faces taken from pictures of tennis players who had either just won a point (Faces 2, 3, and 5 in the figure shown here) or lost a point (Faces 1, 4, and 6), and the researchers asked them to guess whether the athlete was experiencing a positive or negative emotion. As the leftmost bars of the graph show, participants couldn't tell. They guessed that the "winning faces" and the "losing faces" were experiencing equal amounts of somewhat negative emotion.

Next, the researchers showed a new group of participants bodies (without faces) taken from pictures of tennis players who had either just won a point (Body 1 in the figure) or lost a point (Body 2), and the researchers asked them to make the same judgment. As the middle bars show, participants were quite good at this. Participants guessed that "winning bodies" were experiencing positive emotions and that "losing bodies" were experiencing negative emotions.

Finally, the researchers showed a new group of participants the athletes' bodies *and* faces together. As the rightmost bars show, participants' ratings of the body–face combinations were identical to their ratings of the bodies alone, suggesting that when participants made their guesses, they relied entirely on the athletes' bodies and not on their faces. And yet, when they were later asked which information they had relied on most, more than half the participants said they had relied on the faces!

It seems that facial expressions of emotion are more ambiguous than most of us realize. When we see people expressing anger, fear, or joy, we are using information from their bodies, their voices, and their physical and social contexts to figure out what they are feeling. Yet, we mistakenly believe that we are getting most of our information from their facial expression.

The moral of the story? Next time you want to know how a losing athlete feels, concentrate more on defeat than deface. (Sorry.)

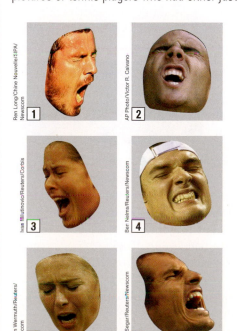

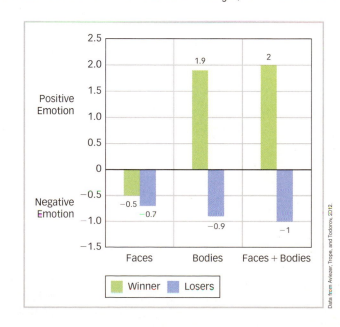

Data from Aviezer, Trope, and Todorov, 2012.

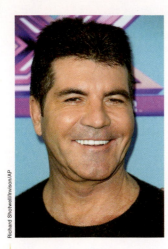

A popular form of cosmetic surgery is the Botox injection, which paralyzes certain facial muscles. Former *American Idol* judge Simon Cowell (quoted in Davis, 2008) gets them regularly and says, "Botox is no more unusual than toothpaste.... It works, you do it once a year—who cares?" Well, maybe he should. Some evidence suggests that Botox injections can impair both the experience of emotion (Davis et al., 2010) and the ability to process emotional information (Havas et al., 2010).

FIGURE 8.8 Crinkle Eyes Can you tell which of the two finalists in the 1986 Miss America pageant just won? Check out their eyes. Only one woman is showing the telltale "corner crinkle" that signifies genuine happiness. The winner is on the right, but don't feel too bad for the loser on the left. Her name is Halle Berry, and she went on to have a pretty good acting career.

others as more hostile when instructed to extend their middle fingers (Chandler & Schwarz, 2009).

The fact that emotional expressions can cause the emotional experiences they signify may help explain why people are generally so good at recognizing the emotional expressions of others. Many studies show that people unconsciously mimic other people's body postures and facial expressions (Chartrand & Bargh, 1999; Dimberg, 1982). When we see someone smile (or even when we read about someone smiling), our *zygomatic major* muscle contracts ever so slightly—as yours almost surely is right now (Foroni & Semin, 2009). Because facial expressions can cause the emotions they signify, mimicking another person's facial expression causes us to feel what they are feeling which allows us to identify their emotions. That's why people find it difficult to identify another person's emotions when they are unable to make facial expressions of their own, for example, if their facial muscles are paralyzed with Botox (Niedenthal et al., 2005). People also find it difficult to identify another person's emotions when they are unable to *experience* emotions of their own (Hussey & Safford, 2009; Pitcher et al., 2008). For example, people with amygdala damage don't normally feel fear and anger, and they are typically poor at recognizing the expressions of those emotions in others (Adolphs, Russell, & Tranel, 1999).

Deceptive Expression

Our emotional expressions can communicate our feelings truthfully—or not. When a friend makes a sarcastic remark about our haircut, we truthfully express our contempt with an arched brow and a reinforcing hand gesture; but when our boss makes the same remark, we swallow hard and fake a pained smile. Our knowledge that it is permissible to show contempt for a peer but not a superior is a **display rule,** which is a *norm for the appropriate expression of emotion* (Ekman, 1972; Ekman & Friesen, 1968).

People in different cultures have different display rules. For example, in one study, Japanese and American college students watched an unpleasant video of car accidents and amputations (Ekman, 1972; Friesen, 1972). When the students didn't know that the experimenters were observing them, Japanese and American students made similar expressions of disgust, but when they realized that they were being observed, the Japanese students (but not the American students) masked their disgust with pleasant expressions. In many Asian countries, it is considered rude to display negative emotions in the presence of a respected person, and so citizens of these countries tend to neutralize their expressions. The fact that different cultures have different display rules may help explain why we are good at recognizing the facial expressions of people from other cultures but *really really really* good at recognizing the facial expressions of people from our own cultures (Elfenbein & Ambady, 2002).

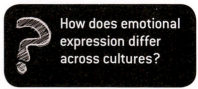
How does emotional expression differ across cultures?

Like most rules, display rules are sometimes difficult to obey. Anyone who has ever watched the loser of a beauty pageant congratulate the winner knows that no matter how hard they try, people can't always hide their emotional states. Even when people smile bravely to mask their disappointment, for example, their faces tend to express small bursts of disappointment that last just 1/25 to 1/5 of a second – so fast that they are almost impossible to detect with the naked eye (Porter & ten Brinke, 2008). In addition, some facial muscles resist conscious control. For example, people can easily control the *zygomatic major* muscle that raises the corners of their mouths to make a smile, but most can't easily control the *obicularis oculi* muscle that crinkles the corners of their eyes. This fact allows trained observers to tell when a smile is or isn't genuine (see **FIGURE 8.8**).

Our faces don't always tell the truth—and neither do our mouths! (DePaulo et al., 2003). When people tell lies, they tend to speak more slowly, take longer to respond to questions, and respond in less detail than they do when telling the truth. Liars are also less fluent, less engaging, more uncertain, more tense, and less pleasant than truth-tellers. Oddly enough, one of the telltale signs of a liar is that his or her performances tend to be just a bit too good. A liar's speech lacks the little imperfections that are typical of truthful speech, such as superfluous detail ("I noticed that the robber was wearing the same shoes that I saw on sale last week at Bloomingdale's and I found myself wondering what he paid for them"), spontaneous correction ("He was six feet tall . . . well, no, actually more like six-two"), and expressions of self-doubt ("I think he had blue eyes, but I'm really not sure").

Given the reliable differences between liars and truth-tellers, you might think that people would be quite good at detecting lies. In fact, under most circumstances, people are barely better than chance (DePaulo, Stone, & Lassiter, 1985; Ekman, 1992; Zuckerman, DePaulo, & Rosenthal, 1981; Zuckerman & Driver, 1985). One reason is that people have a strong bias toward believing that others are sincere, which explains why people tend to mistake liars for truth-tellers more often than they mistake truth-tellers for liars (Gilbert, 1991). A second reason is that people don't seem to know what information they should consider and what information they should ignore (Vrij et al., 2011). For instance, people think that fast talking is a sign of lying when actually it isn't, and that slow talking is not a sign of lying when actually it is. Not only are people bad lie detectors, but they don't even know how bad they are! The correlation between a person's ability to detect lies and the person's confidence in that ability is essentially zero (DePaulo et al., 1997).

When people can't do something well, such as adding large numbers or moving large rocks, they typically turn the job over to a machine (see **FIGURE 8.9**). Can machines detect lies better than we can? The answer is yes, though that's not saying very much. The most widely used lie detection machine is the *polygraph*, which measures the physiological responses that are associated with stress, which people often feel when they are afraid of being caught in a lie. A polygraph can detect lies at a rate that is better than chance, but its error rate is still remarkably high. The fact is that neither people nor machines are particularly good at lie detection, which is why lying remains such a popular sport among humans.

Alex Wong/Getty Images

Speaker of the House John Boehner wipes away tears he shed at a ceremony to award the Congressional Gold Medal. Crying is very difficult to control and thus provides reliable information about the intensity of a person's emotions.

display rule A norm for the appropriate expression of emotion.

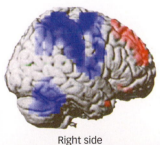
Langleben, D. D., Loughead, J. W., Bilker, W. B., Ruparel, K., Childress, A. R., Busch, S. I., & Gur, R. C. (2005) Telling Truth from Lie in Individual Subjects with Fast Event-Related fMRI. *Human Brain Mapping* 26, pp. 262–272. Courtesy of Daniel Langleben

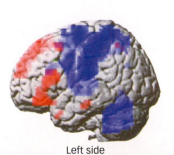

Right side   Left side   Anterior

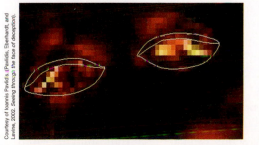
Courtesy of Ioannis Pavlidis (Pavlidis, Eberhardt, and Levine, 2002. *Seeing through the face of deception*).

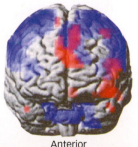
Courtesy of Ioannis Pavlidis (Pavlidis, Eberhardt, & Levine, 2002. *Seeing Through the Face of Deception*).

FIGURE 8.9 **Lie Detection Machines** Some researchers hope to replace the polygraph with accurate machines that measure changes in blood flow in the brain and the face. As the top panel shows, some areas of the brain are more active when people tell lies than when they tell the truth (shown in red), and some are less active (shown in blue; Langleben et al., 2005). The bottom panel shows images taken by a thermal camera that detects the heat caused by blood flow to different parts of the face. The images show a person's face before (*left*) and after (*right*) telling a lie (Pavlidis, Eberhardt, & Levine, 2002). Although neither of these new techniques is extremely accurate, that could soon change.

SUMMARY QUIZ [8.2]

1. Which of the following does NOT provide any support for the universality hypothesis?
   a. Congenitally blind people make the facial expressions associated with the basic emotions.
   b. Infants only days old react to bitter tastes with expressions of disgust.
   c. Robots have been engineered to exhibit emotional expressions.
   d. Researchers have discovered that isolated people living a Stone Age existence with little contact with the outside world recognize the emotional expressions of Westerners.

2. _____ is the idea that emotional expressions can cause emotional experiences.
   a. A display rule
   b. Expressional deception
   c. The universality hypothesis
   d. The facial feedback hypothesis

3. Which of the following statements is inaccurate?
   a. Certain facial muscles are reliably engaged by sincere facial expressions.
   b. Even when people smile bravely to mask disappointment, their faces tend to express small bursts of disappointment.
   c. Studies show that human lie detection ability is extremely good.
   d. Polygraph machines detect lies at a rate better than chance, but their error rate is still quite high.

Motivation: The Wanting Machine

Leonardo is a robot, so he does what he is programmed to do and nothing more. Because he doesn't have wants and urges—doesn't crave friendship or desire chocolate or hate homework—he doesn't initiate his own behavior. He can learn but not yearn. **Motivation** refers to *the purpose or goal of an action,* and human beings have two basic kinds of motivations: the biological and psychological. Let's explore each in turn.

Biological Motivations

Humans are animals, and all animals must survive and reproduce. It is not surprising, then, that two of our most powerful biological motivations are toward food and sex. We are driven to make lunch and driven to make love, but as you will see, neither of these motivations is as simple as it sounds.

Survival: The Motivation for Food

When a thermostat detects that a room is too cold, it sends a signal that initiates a corrective action, namely, turning up the furnace. Bodies are a bit like thermostats in this way. To survive, the body must maintain precise levels of nutrition, warmth, and so on, and when these levels depart from optimality, the body sends signals to the brain, asking it to take corrective action. That signal is called a **drive,** which is *an internal state that signals a physiological need.*

The most regular and familiar of your body's drives is what you call hunger. At every moment, your body is sending signals to your brain about the amount of energy it has available. If your body needs energy, it sends a signal to tell your brain to switch

motivation The purpose for or psychological cause of an action.

drive An internal state that signals a physiological need.

bulima nervosa An eating disorder characterized by binge eating followed by purging.

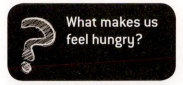
What makes us feel hungry?

hunger on, and if your body has sufficient energy, it sends a signal to tell your brain to switch hunger off (Gropp et al., 2005). No one knows precisely what these signals are or how they are sent and received, but research has identified a few candidates.

For example, *ghrelin* is a hormone that is produced in the stomach and appears to be one of the signals that tells the brain to switch hunger on (Inui, 2001; Nakazato et al., 2001). When people are injected with ghrelin, they become intensely hungry and eat about 30% more than usual (Wren et al., 2001). Another chemical called *leptin* is a secreted by fat cells, and it appears to be one of the signals that tells the brain to switch hunger off, which makes food less rewarding (Farooqi et al., 2007). People who are born with a leptin deficiency have trouble controlling their appetites (Montague et al., 1997). Some researchers think this story is far too simple. They argue that there is no general drive called *hunger*, but rather, that there are many different hungers, each of which is a response to a unique nutritional deficit and each of which is switched on by a unique chemical messenger (Rozin & Kalat, 1971). For example, rats that are deprived of proteins will gladly eat proteins but will turn down fats and carbohydrates, suggesting that they are experiencing a specific "protein hunger" and not a general hunger (Rozin, 1968).

Whether hunger is signaled by one chemical or many, the primary receiver of these signals is the hypothalamus (see **FIGURE 8.10**). The *lateral hypothalamus* receives the "hunger on" signals, and when it is destroyed, animals sitting in a cage full of food will starve themselves to death. The *ventromedial hypothalamus* receives the "hunger off" signals, and when it is destroyed, animals will gorge themselves to the point of illness and obesity (Miller, 1960; Steinbaum & Miller, 1965). These two structures were once thought to be the "hunger center" and "satiety center" of the brain, but it turns out to be much more complicated than that (Woods et al., 1998). These structures clearly play an important role in hunger, but no one yet knows exactly what the role is (Stellar & Stellar, 1985).

EATING DISORDERS. Feelings of hunger tell us when to start eating and when to stop. But for the 10 to 30 million Americans who have eating disorders, eating is a much more complicated affair (Hoek & van Hoeken, 2003). For instance, **bulimia nervosa** is *an eating disorder characterized by binge eating followed by purging.* People with bulimia typically ingest large quantities of food in a relatively short period and then take laxatives or induce vomiting to purge the food from their bodies. These people are caught in a cycle: They eat to ease negative emotions such as sadness and anxiety, but then concern about weight gain leads them to experience negative emotions such as guilt and self-loathing, and these emotions then lead them to purge (Sherry & Hall, 2009; cf. Haedt-Matt & Keel, 2011).

Anorexia nervosa is *an eating disorder characterized by an intense fear of being fat and severe restriction of food intake.* People with anorexia tend to have a distorted body image that leads them to believe they are fat when they are actually emaciated, and they tend to be high-achieving perfectionists who see their severe control of eating as a triumph of will over impulse. Remember ghrelin—the chemical that turns hunger on? Well, contrary to what you might expect, people with anorexia have extremely *high* levels of ghrelin in their blood, which suggests that their bodies are trying desperately to switch hunger on but that hunger's call is somehow being suppressed, ignored, or overridden (Ariyasu et al., 2001).

Anorexia may have both cultural and biological causes (Klump & Culbert, 2007). For example, women with anorexia typically believe that thinness equals beauty (which isn't a very surprising conclusion for women to draw when the average

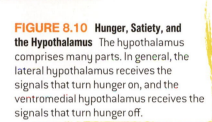

Lateral hypothalamus

Ventromedial hypothalamus

FIGURE 8.10 Hunger, Satiety, and the Hypothalamus The hypothalamus comprises many parts. In general, the lateral hypothalamus receives the signals that turn hunger on, and the ventromedial hypothalamus receives the signals that turn hunger off.

anorexia nervosa An eating disorder characterized by an intense fear of being fat and severe restriction of food intake.

Bar Refaeli is one of Israel's best known super-models. In 2012, Israel enacted a law banning models whose body mass index is under 18.5 from appearing in advertisements. So a 5'8" model must weigh at least 119 pounds.

Wireimage/Getty Images

Times have changed. People today are often astonished to see that ads once promised to help young women *gain* weight to become popular.

American fashion model is seven inches taller and 23 pounds lighter than the average American woman). But anorexia is not just "vanity run amok" (Striegel-Moore & Bulik, 2007, p. 193). Many researchers believe that there are as-yet-undiscovered biological and/or genetic components to the illness as well. For example, although anorexia primarily affects women, men have a sharply increased risk of becoming anorexic if they have a female twin who has the disorder (Procopio & Marriott, 2007), suggesting that anorexia may have something to do with prenatal exposure to female hormones.

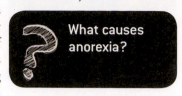

What causes anorexia?

OBESITY. America's most pervasive eating-related problem is obesity, which is defined as having a body mass index (BMI) of 30 or greater. **TABLE 8.1** allows you to compute your BMI, and the odds are that you won't like the number. Since 1999, Americans have collectively gained more than a billion pounds (Kolbert, 2009). In 2012, only one state (Colorado) had an obesity rate lower than 20% (see **FIGURE 8.11**).

Why should you care? Every year, obesity-related illnesses cost our nation about $147 billion (Finkelstein et al., 2009) and about 3 million lives (Allison et al., 1999). In addition to these financial and physical costs, obese people tend to be viewed negatively by others, have lower self-esteem, and have a lower quality of life (Hebl & Heatherton, 1997; Kolotkin, Meter, & Williams, 2001). The stigma of obesity is so

Table 8.1 Body Mass Index Table

	Normal								Overweight					Obese								Extreme Obesity															
BMI	19	20	21	22	23	24	25	26	27	28	29	30	31	32	33	34	35	36	37	38	39	40	41	42	43	44	45	46	47	48	49	50	51	52	53	54
Height (Inches)	Body Weight (pounds)																																			
58	91	96	100	105	110	115	119	124	129	134	138	143	148	153	158	162	167	172	177	181	186	191	196	201	205	210	215	220	224	229	234	239	244	248	253	258
59	94	99	104	109	114	119	124	128	133	138	143	148	153	158	163	169	173	178	183	188	193	198	203	308	212	217	222	227	232	237	242	247	252	257	262	267
60	97	102	107	112	116	123	128	133	138	143	148	153	156	163	168	174	179	184	189	194	199	204	209	215	220	225	230	235	240	245	250	256	261	266	271	278
61	100	108	111	116	122	127	132	137	143	148	153	156	164	169	174	180	186	190	195	201	206	211	217	222	227	232	238	243	248	254	259	264	269	275	280	285
62	104	109	115	120	126	131	138	142	147	153	158	164	169	175	180	186	191	196	202	207	213	218	224	229	235	240	248	251	258	262	267	273	278	264	289	295
63	107	113	118	124	130	135	141	148	152	158	163	169	175	180	188	191	197	203	208	214	220	225	231	237	242	248	254	260	265	270	278	282	287	293	299	304
64	110	118	122	128	134	140	145	151	157	163	169	174	180	188	192	197	204	209	215	221	227	232	238	244	250	258	262	267	273	279	285	291	298	302	308	314
65	114	120	128	132	138	144	150	156	162	168	174	180	186	192	193	204	210	218	222	228	234	240	246	252	258	264	270	278	282	288	294	300	308	312	318	324
66	118	124	130	138	142	148	155	161	167	173	179	186	192	198	204	210	216	223	229	235	241	247	253	260	266	272	278	284	291	297	303	309	315	322	328	334
67	121	127	134	140	146	153	159	166	172	178	185	191	198	204	211	217	223	230	238	242	249	256	261	268	274	280	287	293	299	308	312	319	325	331	338	344
68	125	131	138	144	151	158	164	171	177	184	190	197	203	210	216	223	230	236	243	249	256	262	269	278	282	289	295	302	303	315	322	328	335	341	348	354
69	128	135	142	149	155	162	169	178	182	189	195	203	209	218	223	230	236	243	250	257	263	270	277	284	291	297	304	311	318	324	331	338	345	351	358	365
70	132	139	146	153	160	167	174	181	188	195	202	209	216	222	229	236	243	250	257	264	271	278	285	292	299	308	313	320	327	334	341	348	355	362	369	378
71	138	143	150	157	166	172	179	186	193	200	208	215	222	229	235	243	250	257	265	272	279	288	293	301	308	315	322	329	338	343	351	358	365	372	379	388
72	140	147	154	162	169	177	184	191	199	208	213	221	228	235	242	250	258	265	272	279	287	294	302	309	316	324	331	338	346	353	361	368	375	383	390	397
73	144	151	159	166	174	182	189	197	204	212	219	227	236	242	250	257	266	272	280	288	295	302	310	318	326	333	340	348	355	363	371	378	388	393	401	408
74	148	155	163	171	179	188	194	202	210	218	225	233	241	249	258	264	272	280	287	295	303	311	319	328	334	342	350	358	365	373	381	389	398	404	412	420
75	152	160	166	178	184	192	200	208	216	224	232	240	248	256	264	272	279	287	295	303	311	319	327	335	343	351	359	367	375	383	391	399	407	415	423	431
76	158	164	172	180	189	197	205	213	221	230	238	246	254	263	271	279	287	295	304	312	320	328	338	344	353	361	369	377	385	394	402	410	418	428	436	443

Data from National Institutes of Health, 1998.

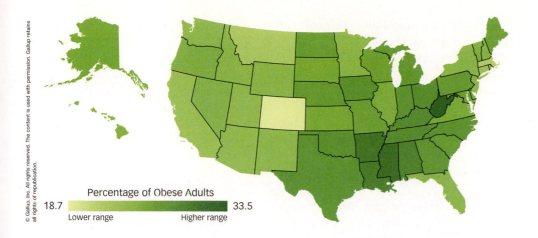

Percentage of Obese Adults

18.7   33.5

Lower range   Higher range

FIGURE 8.11 **The Geography of Obesity**
This 2013 map of U.S. obesity rates shows that obesity is a problem everywhere, but especially in the Southeast.

DATA VISUALIZATION

Historical BMI/Food Consumption Trends

www.macmillanhighered.com/schacterbrief3e

powerful that average-weight people are viewed negatively if they even have a relationship with someone who is obese (Hebl & Mannix, 2003).

What causes obesity? First, obesity is highly heritable (Allison et al., 1996) and may well have a genetic component. For example, obese people are often leptin-resistant, which is to say that their brains do not respond to the chemical message that shuts hunger off (Friedman & Halaas, 1998; Heymsfield et al., 1999). Second, obesity may have environmental causes. For example, some studies suggest that toxins in the environment can disrupt the functioning of the endocrine system and predispose people to obesity (Grün & Blumberg, 2006; Newbold et al., 2005), and other studies suggest that obesity can be caused by a dearth of "good bacteria" in the gut (Liou et al., 2013).

But in most cases, obesity is simply the result of eating too much. We don't breathe ourselves sick or sleep ourselves sick, so why do we eat ourselves sick? Blame the design. Hundreds of thousands of years ago, the main food-related problem facing

The Real World

Jeet Jet?

Does the amount of food placed in front of people influence how much they eat? Brian Wansink and colleagues (2005) sat research participants in front of a large bowl of tomato soup and told them to eat as much as they wanted. In one condition of the study, a server came to the table and refilled the participant's bowl whenever it got down to about a quarter full. In another condition, unbeknownst to the participants, the bottom of the bowl was connected by a long tube to a large vat of soup, so whenever the participant ate from the bowl, it would slowly and almost imperceptibly refill itself.

What the researchers found was sobering. Participants who unknowingly ate from a "bottomless bowl" consumed a whopping 73% more soup than those who ate from normal bowls—and yet,

Researcher Brian Wansink and his bottomless bowl of soup.

they didn't think they had consumed more and they didn't report feeling any more full.

It seems that we find it easier to keep track of what we are eating than how much, and this can cause us to overeat even when we are trying our best to do just the opposite. For instance, one study showed that diners at an Italian restaurant often chose to eat butter on their bread rather than dipping it in olive oil because they thought that doing so would reduce the number of calories per slice. And they were right. What they didn't realize, however, is that they would unconsciously compensate for this reduction in calories by eating 23% more bread during the meal (Wansink & Linder, 2003).

This and other research suggests that one of the best ways to reduce our waists is simply to count our bites.

metabolism The rate at which energy is used by the body.

our ancestors was starvation, and so our brains and bodies developed two strategies to avoid it. First, our brains developed a strong attraction to foods that provide large amounts of energy per bite (in other words, high calorie foods), which is why most of us prefer hamburgers and milkshakes to celery and water. Second, our bodies developed an ability to store excess food energy in the form of fat, which enabled us to eat more than we needed when food was plentiful and then live off our reserves when food was scarce. Our brains and bodies are beautifully engineered for a world in which high calorie foods are scarce, and the problem is that we don't live in that world anymore. Instead, we live in a world in which the fatty miracles of modern technology—from chocolate cupcakes to sausage pizzas—are inexpensive and readily available.

We are designed to gain weight easily—and to lose it with great difficulty. The human body resists weight loss in two ways. First, when we gain weight, we experience an increase in both the size and the number of fat cells in our bodies (usually in our abdomens if we are male and in our thighs and buttocks if we are female). But when we lose weight, we experience a decrease in the *size* of our fat cells but no decrease in their *number*. Once our bodies have added a fat cell, that cell is pretty much there to stay. It may become thinner when we diet, but it is unlikely to die. Second, our bodies respond to dieting by decreasing our **metabolism,** which is *the rate at which energy is used by the body.* When our bodies sense that we are living through a famine (which is what they conclude when we refuse to feed them), they find more efficient ways to turn food into fat, which was a great trick for our ancestors but a real nuisance for us. The bottom line is that avoiding obesity is easier than overcoming it (Casazza et al., 2013).

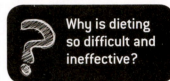

Why is dieting so difficult and ineffective?

And avoiding it isn't as difficult as you might think. People eat when they are hungry, of course, but they also eat when cues in the environment tell them to—for instance, when they see other people eating or when the clock says it is time for lunch (Herman, Roth, & Polivy, 2003; Rozin et al., 1998; see the Real World box). If environmental cues can make us eat, can they also make us stop? Research suggests the answer is yes. In one study, snacking students ate fewer Pringles when every seventh chip was colored red, presumably because the color coding allowed them to keep track of how much they were eating (Geier, Wansink, & Rozin, 2012). In another study, people ate 22% less pasta with tomato sauce when they used a white plate instead of a red plate, presumably because the white plate provided a stark contrast that allowed them to see what they were eating (van Ittersum & Wansink, 2012). These and dozens of other studies show that small changes in our environments can prevent big changes in our waistlines.

One reason why obesity rates are rising is that "normal portions" keep getting larger. When researchers analyzed 52 depictions of *The Last Supper* that were painted between the years 1000 and 1800, they found that the average plate size increased by 66% (Data from Wansink & Wansink, 2010).

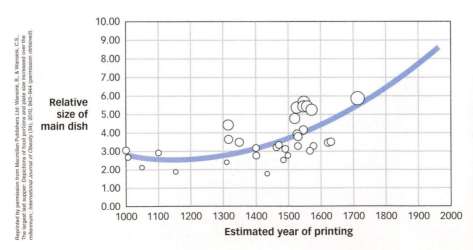

Reprinted by permission from Macmillan Publishers Ltd: Wansink, B. & Wansink, C.S., The largest last supper: Depictions of food portions and plate size increased over the millennium., International Journal of Obesity (34), 2010, 943–944 (permission obtained).

Scala/Art Resource, NY

Other Voices

Fat and Happy

Alice Randall is a novelist whose books include *The Wind Done Gone, Pushkin and the Queen of Spades, Rebel Yell,* and *Ada's Rules.*

© Sarah Krulwich/The New York Times/Redux Pictures

Nobody *wants* to be fat. At least that's what you might think. But as the novelist Alice Randall noted, in some cultures, being heavy isn't just acceptable—it is desirable.

Four out of five black women are seriously overweight. One out of four middle-aged black women has diabetes. With $174 billion a year spent on diabetes-related illness in America and obesity quickly overtaking smoking as a cause of cancer deaths, it is past time to try something new.

What we need is a body-culture revolution in black America. Why? Because too many experts who are involved in the discussion of obesity don't understand something crucial about black women and fat: many black women are fat because we want to be.

The black poet Lucille Clifton's 1987 poem "Homage to My Hips" begins with the boast, "These hips are big hips." She establishes big black hips as something a woman would want to have and a man would desire. She wasn't the first or the only one to reflect this community knowledge. Twenty years before, in 1967, Joe Tex, a black Texan, dominated the radio

airwaves across black America with a song he wrote and recorded, "Skinny Legs and All." One of his lines haunts me to this day: "some man, somewhere who'll take you baby, skinny legs and all." For me, it still seems almost an impossibility.

Chemically, in its ability to promote disease, black fat may be the same as white fat. Culturally it is not.

How many white girls in the '60s grew up praying for fat thighs? I know I did. I asked God to give me big thighs like my dancing teacher, Diane. There was no way I wanted to look like Twiggy, the white model whose boy-like build was the dream of white girls. Not with Joe Tex ringing in my ears.

How many middle-aged white women fear their husbands will find them less attractive if their weight drops to less than 200 pounds? I have yet to meet one.

But I know many black women whose sane, handsome, successful husbands worry when their women start losing weight. My lawyer husband is one.

Another friend, a woman of color who is a tenured professor, told me that her husband, also a tenured professor and of color, begged her not to lose "the sugar down below" when she embarked on a weight-loss program....

I live in Nashville. There is an ongoing rivalry between Nashville and Memphis. In black Nashville, we like to think of ourselves as the squeaky-clean brown town best known for our colleges and churches.

In contrast, black Memphis is known for its music and bars and churches. We often tease the city up the road by saying that in Nashville we have a church on every corner and in Memphis they have a church and a liquor store on every corner. Only now the saying goes, there's a church, a liquor store and a dialysis center on every corner in black Memphis.

The billions that we are spending to treat diabetes is money that we don't have for education reform or retirement benefits, and what's worse, it's estimated that the total cost of America's obesity epidemic could reach almost $1 trillion by 2030 if we keep on doing what we have been doing.

We have to change....

Randall suggests that if we really want to solve the obesity problem, we must first understand that some people don't see it as a problem at all. So what should society do? Should we try to change the belief that "fat is beautiful" through education and advertising? Would that alleviate the problem Randall identifies? Or would it just serve to stigmatize overweight people, who already suffer from prejudice and discrimination? How can you discourage obesity without hurting people who are obese?

Reproduction: The Motivation for Sex

Food motivates us because it is essential to our survival. But sex is also essential to our survival—or at least to the survival of our DNA—which is why evolution has wired a sex drive into almost every human brain.

The chemistry behind that drive is fairly well understood. The hormone dihydroepiandosterone (DHEA) seems to be involved in the initial onset of the sex drive. Both boys and girls begin producing this slow-acting hormone at about the age of 6, which may explain why boys and girls both experience their initial sexual interest at about the age of 10. Two other hormones have more gender-specific effects. Both males and females produce testosterone and estrogen, but males produce more of the former and females produce more of the latter. As you will learn in the Development chapter, these two hormones are largely responsible for the physical and psychological changes that characterize puberty.

"Come back, young man. He needs a booster shot."

The red coloration on the female gelada's chest (*left*) indicates that she is in estrus and amenable to sex. The sexual interest of a female human being (*right*) is not limited to a particular time in her monthly cycle.

intrinsic motivation A motivation to take actions that are themselves rewarding.

But are they also responsible for the waxing and waning of the sex drive in adults? The answer appears to be yes—as long as those adults are rats. Testosterone increases the sex drive of male rats, and estrogen increases the sex drive of female rats. But the story for human beings is far more interesting. The females of most mammalian species (e.g., dogs, cats, and rats) are only interested in sex when their estrogen levels are high, which happens when they are ovulating (i.e., when they are "in estrus" or "in heat"). But female humans can be interested in sex at any point in their monthly cycles. Although the level of estrogen in a woman's body changes dramatically over the course of her monthly menstrual cycle, studies suggest that sexual desire changes little, if at all.

If estrogen is not the chemical basis of women's sex drives, then what is? Two pieces of evidence suggest that the answer is testosterone—the same hormone that provides the chemical basis of men's sex drives. First, when women are given testosterone, their sex drives increase. Second, men naturally have more testosterone than women do, and they generally have stronger sex drives. Men are more likely than women to think about sex, have sexual fantasies, seek sex and sexual variety (whether positions or partners), masturbate, want sex at an early point in a relationship, and complain about low sex drive in their partners (Baumeister, Cantanese, & Vohs, 2001). All of this suggests that testosterone is the chemical basis of the sex drive in both men and women.

Although men and women have on average different levels of sex drive, they have sex for similar reasons. Sex is a prerequisite for reproduction, of course, but the vast majority of sexual acts are not meant to produce babies. College students, for example, are rarely aiming to get pregnant, but they often have sex, and when they do it is because of *physical attraction* ("The person had beautiful eyes"), as a *means to an end* ("I wanted to be popular"), to increase *emotional connection* ("I wanted to communicate at a deeper level"), and to *alleviate insecurity* ("It was the only way my partner would spend time with me"; Meston & Buss, 2007). Although men are more likely than women to report having sex for purely physical reasons, **TABLE 8.2** shows that men and women don't differ dramatically in this regard. We will have much more to say about sexual attraction and relationships in the Social Psychology chapter.

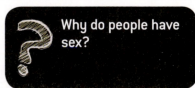

Why do people have sex?

Table 8.2 Reasons for Having Sex

Top Ten Reasons Why Men and Women Report Having Sex

	Women	Men
1	I was attracted to the person.	I was attracted to the person.
2	I wanted to experience the physical pleasure.	It feels good.
3	It feels good.	I wanted to experience the physical pleasure.
4	I wanted to show my affection to the person.	It's fun.
5	I wanted to express my love for the person.	I wanted to show my affection to the person.
6	I was sexually aroused and wanted the release.	I was sexually aroused and wanted the release.
7	I was "horny."	I was "horny."
8	It's fun.	I wanted to express my love for the person.
9	I realized I was in love.	I wanted to achieve an orgasm.
10	I was "in the heat of the moment."	I wanted to please my partner.

Source: Information from Meston & Buss, 2007.

Psychological Motivations

Survival and reproduction are every animal's first order of business, so it is no surprise that we are strongly motivated by food and sex. But we are motivated by other things too. Yes, we crave kisses of both the chocolate and romantic variety, but we also crave friendship and respect, security and certainty, wisdom and meaning, and a whole lot more. The psychologist Abraham Maslow (1954) argued that all human motivations (which he called needs) could be arranged in a hierarchy (see **FIGURE 8.12**) with biological motivations at the bottom and psychological motivations at the top. He suggested that until motivations at one level were satisfied, motivations at higher levels were ignored. In other words, when people are hungry or exhausted, they don't worry too much about intellectual fulfillment and moral clarity (see **FIGURE 8.13**).

Maslow was correct in observing that psychological motivations are usually more deferrable than biological motivations. But these two kinds of motivations differ in other ways as well. For example, although we share our biological motivations with most other animals, our psychological motivations are uniquely human. Chimps and rabbits and robins and turtles are all motivated to have sex, but only human beings are motivated to imbue the act with meaning. In addition, although our biological motivations are few—food, sex, oxygen, sleep, and a small handful of other things—our psychological motivations are so numerous and varied that no psychologist has ever been able to make a complete list (Hofmann, Vohs, & Baumeister, 2012). Nonetheless, even if you looked at an incomplete list, you'd quickly notice that psychological motivations vary on three key dimensions: extrinsic versus intrinsic, conscious versus unconscious, and approach versus avoidance. Let's examine each of these.

Need for self-actualization

Esteem needs

Belongingness and love needs

Safety and security needs

Physiological needs

FIGURE 8.12 Maslow's Hierarchy of Needs Human beings are motivated to satisfy a variety of needs. Psychologist Abraham Maslow thought these needs formed a hierarchy, with physiological needs forming a base and self-actualization needs forming a pinnacle. He suggested that people don't experience higher needs until the needs below them have been met.

Intrinsic vs. Extrinsic

Taking a psychology exam and eating a French fry are different in many ways. One makes you tired and the other makes you chubby, one requires that you move your lips and the other requires that you don't, and so on. But the key difference between these activities is that one is a means to an end and one is an end in itself. An **intrinsic motivation** is *a motivation to take actions that are themselves rewarding.* When we eat a French fry because it tastes good, dance because it feels good, or listen to music because it sounds good, we are intrinsically motivated. These activities don't *have* a

In 2010, Mohamed Bouazizi set himself on fire to protest his treatment by the Tunisian government, and his dramatic suicide ignited the revolution that came to be known as "Arab Spring." Clearly, psychological needs—such as the need for justice—can be powerful.

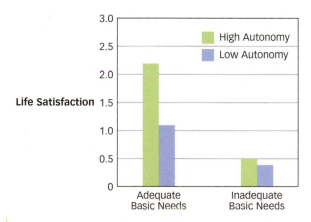

FIGURE 8.13 When Do Higher Needs Matter? Maslow was right. A recent study of 77,000 people in the world's 51 poorest nations (Martin & Hill, 2012) showed that if people have their basic needs met, then autonomy (i.e., freedom to make their own decisions) increases their satisfaction with their lives. But when people do not have their basic needs met, autonomy makes little difference. (Data from Martin & Hill, 2012.)

extrinsic motivation A motivation to take actions that lead to reward.

payoff: They *are* a payoff. Conversely, an **extrinsic motivation** is *a motivation to take actions that lead to reward*. When we floss our teeth so we can avoid gum disease (and get dates), when we work hard for money so we can pay our rent (and get dates), and when we take an exam so we can get a college degree (and get money to get dates), we are extrinsically motivated. None of these things directly brings pleasure, but all may lead to pleasure in the long run.

Extrinsic motivation gets a bad rap. Americans tend to believe that people should "follow their hearts" and "do what they love," and we feel sorry for students who choose courses just to please their parents and for parents who choose jobs just to make a living. But the fact is that our ability to engage in behaviors that are unrewarding in the present because we believe they will bring greater rewards in the future is one of our species' most significant talents, and no other species can do it quite as well as we can (Gilbert, 2006). In research on the ability to delay gratification (Ayduk et al., 2007; Mischel et al., 2004), people are typically faced with a choice between getting something they want right now (e.g., a scoop of ice cream) or waiting and getting more of what they want later (e.g., two scoops of ice cream). Waiting for ice cream is a lot like taking an exam or flossing: It isn't much fun, but you do it because you know you will reap greater rewards in the end. Studies show that 4-year-old children who can delay gratification are judged to be more intelligent and socially competent 10 years later and have higher SAT scores when they enter college (Mischel, Shoda, & Rodriguez, 1989). In fact, the ability to delay gratification is a better predictor of a child's grades in school than is the child's IQ (Duckworth & Seligman, 2005). Apparently there is something to be said for extrinsic motivation.

Why should people delay gratification?

There is a lot to be said for intrinsic motivation too (Patall, Cooper, & Robinson, 2008). People work harder when they are intrinsically motivated, they enjoy what they do more, and they do it more creatively. Both kinds of motivation have advantages, which is why many of us try to build lives in which we are both intrinsically and extrinsically motivated by the same activity—lives in which we are paid for doing exactly what we like to do best. Who hasn't fantasized about becoming an artist or an athlete or a wealthy celebrity's personal party planner? Alas, research suggests that it is difficult to get paid for doing what you love and still end up loving what you do because extrinsic rewards can undermine intrinsic interest (Deci, Koestner, & Ryan, 1999;

Why do rewards sometimes backfire?

Henderlong & Lepper, 2002). For example, in one study, college students who were intrinsically interested in a puzzle either were paid to complete it or completed it for free, and those who were paid were less likely to play with the puzzle later on (Deci, 1971). It appears that under some circumstances, people take rewards to indicate that an activity isn't inherently pleasurable ("If they had to pay me to do that puzzle, it couldn't have been very much fun"); thus rewards can cause people to lose their intrinsic motivation.

Just as the promise of rewards can undermine intrinsic motivation, the threat of punishment can create it. In one study, children who had no intrinsic interest in playing with a toy suddenly gained an interest when the experimenter threatened to punish them if they touched it (Aronson, 1963). And when a group of day care centers got fed up with parents who arrived late to pick up their children, some of them instituted a financial penalty for tardiness. As **FIGURE 8.14** shows, the financial penalty caused an *increase* in late arrivals (Gneezy & Rustichini, 2000).

FIGURE 8.14 When Threats Backfire Threats can cause behaviors that were once intrinsically motivated to become extrinsically motivated. Day care centers that instituted fines for late-arriving parents saw an increase in the number of parents who arrived late. (Data from Gneezy & Rustichini, 2000.)

Late arrivals

Week number

● Centers with fines   ● Centers without fines

Why? Because parents are intrinsically motivated to fetch their kids and they generally do their best to be on time. But when the day care centers imposed a fine for late arrival, the parents became extrinsically motivated to fetch their children—and because the fine wasn't particularly large, they decided to pay a small financial penalty in order to leave their children in day care for an extra hour. When punishments and rewards change intrinsic motivation into extrinsic motivation, unexpected consequences can follow.

Conscious versus Unconscious

When prizewinning artists or scientists are asked to explain their achievements, they typically say things like, "I wanted to liberate color from form" or "I wanted to cure diabetes." They almost never say, "I wanted to exceed my father's accomplishments, thereby proving to my mother that I was worthy of her love." People clearly have **conscious motivations,** which are *motivations of which people are aware,* but they also have **unconscious motivations,** which are *motivations of which people are not aware* (Aarts, Custers, & Marien, 2008; Bargh et al., 2001; Hassin, Bargh, & Zimerman, 2009).

For example, research suggests that people vary in their **need for achievement,** which is *the motivation to solve worthwhile problems* (McClelland et al., 1953). Some researchers have argued that this basic motivation is unconscious. For example, when words such as *achievement* are presented on a computer screen so rapidly that people cannot consciously perceive them, those people will work especially hard to solve a puzzle (Bargh et al., 2001) and will feel especially unhappy if they fail (Chartrand & Kay, 2006).

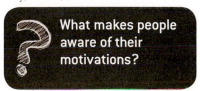

What makes people aware of their motivations?

What determines whether we are conscious of our motivations? Most actions have more than one motivation, and the ease or difficulty of performing the action may determine which of these motivations we will be aware of (Vallacher & Wegner, 1985, 1987). When actions are easy (e.g., screwing in a lightbulb), we are aware of our most *general motivations* (e.g., to be helpful), but when actions are difficult (e.g., wrestling with a lightbulb that is stuck in its socket), we are aware of our more *specific motivations* (e.g., to get the threads aligned). For example, participants in an experiment drank coffee either from a normal mug or from a mug that had a heavy weight attached to the bottom, which made the mug difficult to manipulate. When asked what they were doing, those who were drinking from the normal mug explained that they were "satisfying needs," whereas those who were drinking from the weighted mug explained that they were "swallowing" (Wegner et al., 1984).

Approach versus Avoidance

The poet James Thurber (1956) wrote, "All men should strive to learn before they die/What they are running from, and to, and why." The motivation to "run to" pleasure is called **approach motivation,** which is *a motivation to experience a positive outcome,* and the motivation to "run from" pain is called **avoidance motivation,** which is *a motivation not to experience a negative outcome.* Pleasure is not just the lack of pain, and pain is not just the lack of pleasure. They are independent experiences that occur in different parts of the brain (Davidson et al., 1990; Gray, 1990).

In most elections, only about a third of the eligible voters in Arizona bother to cast a ballot. That's what made Mark Osterloh (below) propose the Arizona Voter Reward Act, which would award $1 million to a randomly selected voter in every election. Given what you know about intrinsic and extrinsic motivation, what consequences might such an act have?

conscious motivations Motivations of which people are aware.

unconscious motivations Motivations of which people are not aware.

need for achievement The motivation to solve worthwhile problems.

approach motivation A motivation to experience a positive outcome.

avoidance motivation A motivation not to experience a negative outcome.

Michael Phelps is clearly high—in need for achievement, that is—which is one of the reasons why he ultimately became the most decorated Olympic athlete of all time.

terror management theory A theory about how people respond to knowledge of their own mortality.

Research suggests that, all else being equal, avoidance motivations tend to be more powerful than approach motivations. Most people will turn down a chance to bet on a coin flip that would pay them $10 if it came up heads but would require them to pay $8 if it came up tails, because they believe that the pain of losing $8 will be more intense than the pleasure of winning $10 (Kahneman & Tversky, 1979). On average, avoidance motivation is stronger than approach motivation, but the relative strength of these two tendencies does differ somewhat from person to person. **TABLE 8.3** shows the kind of question that has been used to measure the relative strength of a person's approach and avoidance tendencies (Carver & White, 1994). Research shows that people who are described by the high-approach items are happier when rewarded than those who are not, and that those who are described by the high-avoidance items are more anxious when threatened than those who are not (Carver, 2006). Just as some people seem to be more responsive to rewards

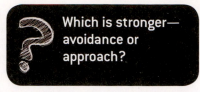

Which is stronger—avoidance or approach?

Table 8.3 Scale for Measuring the Behavioral Inhibition System and Behavioral Activation System
To what extent do each of these items describe you? The items in red measure the strength of your avoidance tendency, and the items in green measure the strength of your approach tendency.
• Even if something bad is about to happen to me, I rarely experience fear or nervousness. (LOW AVOIDANCE)
• I go out of my way to get things I want. (HIGH APPROACH)
• When I'm doing well at something, I love to keep at it. (HIGH APPROACH)
• I'm always willing to try something new if I think it will be fun. (HIGH APPROACH)
• When I get something I want, I feel excited and energized. (HIGH APPROACH)
• Criticism or scolding hurts me quite a bit. (HIGH AVOIDANCE)
• When I want something, I usually go all-out to get it. (HIGH APPROACH)
• I will often do things for no other reason than that they might be fun. (HIGH APPROACH)
• If I see a chance to get something I want, I move on it right away. (HIGH APPROACH)
• I feel pretty worried or upset when I think or know somebody is angry at me. (HIGH AVOIDANCE)
• When I see an opportunity for something I like, I get excited right away. (HIGH APPROACH)
• I often act on the spur of the moment. (HIGH APPROACH)
• If I think something unpleasant is going to happen, I usually get pretty "worked up." (HIGH AVOIDANCE)
• When good things happen to me, it affects me strongly. (HIGH APPROACH)
• I feel worried when I think I have done poorly at something important. (HIGH AVOIDANCE)
• I crave excitement and new sensations. (HIGH APPROACH)
• When I go after something, I use a "no holds barred" approach. (HIGH APPROACH)
• I have very few fears compared to my friends. (LOW AVOIDANCE)
• It would excite me to win a contest. (HIGH APPROACH)
• I worry about making mistakes. (HIGH AVOIDANCE)
Source: Information from Carver & White, 1994.

than to punishments (and vice versa), some people tend to think about their behaviors as attempts to get a reward rather than to avoid punishment (and vice versa; Higgins, 1997).

Avoidance motivation is powerful, and of all the things that people want to avoid, death is pretty high on everyone's list. All animals strive to avoid death, but only human beings realize that this striving is ultimately in vain. Some psychologists have suggested that our knowledge of death's inevitability creates a sense of "existential terror," and that much of our behavior is merely an attempt to manage it. **Terror Management Theory** is *a theory about how people respond to knowledge of their own mortality*, and it suggests that one of the ways that people cope with their existential terror is by developing a "cultural world-view"—a shared set of beliefs about what is good and right and true (Greenberg, Solomon, & Arndt, 2008; Solomon et al., 2004). These beliefs allow people to see themselves as more than mortal animals because they inhabit a world of meaning in which they can achieve symbolic immortality (e.g., by leaving a great legacy or having children) and perhaps even literal immortality (e.g., by being pious and earning a spot in the afterlife). According to this theory, our cultural worldview is a shield that buffers us against the anxiety that the knowledge of our own mortality creates.

imagebroker.net/Superstock

A "credit card surcharge" and a "cash discount" are precisely the same thing. But they sure don't feel that way! RyanAir customers were outraged in 2012 when the airline imposed a 2% surcharge on customers who paid with credit cards. Would the airline have been wiser to raise its ticket prices by 2% and then offer a 2% discount to customers who paid with cash?

SUMMARY QUIZ [8.3]

1. The hedonic principle states that
   a. emotions provide people with information.
   b. people are motivated to experience pleasure and avoid pain.
   c. people use their moods as information about the likelihood of succeeding at a task.
   d. motivations are acquired solely through experience.

2. According to the early psychologists, an unlearned tendency to seek a particular goal is called
   a. an instinct.
   b. a drive.
   c. a motivation.
   d. a corrective action.

3. According to Maslow, our most basic needs are
   a. self-actualization and self-esteem.
   b. biological.
   c. unimportant until other needs are met.
   d. belongingness and love.

4. Which of the following is NOT a dimension on which psychological motivations vary?
   a. intrinsic–extrinsic
   b. conscious–unconscious
   c. avoid–approach
   d. appraisal–reappraisal

5. Which of the following activities is most likely the result of extrinsic motivation?

   a. completing a crossword puzzle

   b. pursuing a career as a musician

   c. having ice cream for dessert

   d. flossing one's teeth

CHAPTER REVIEW

SUMMARY

Emotional Experience: The Feeling Machine

> Emotional experiences have two underlying dimensions: arousal and valence.

> The James–Lange theory suggests that a stimulus causes a physiological reaction, which leads to an emotional experience. The Cannon–Bard theory suggests that a stimulus causes both an emotional experience and a physiological reaction simultaneously. Schachter and Singer's two-factor theory suggests that a stimulus causes undifferentiated physiological arousal about which people draw inferences. Each theory has elements that are supported by research.

> Information about a stimulus is sent simultaneously to the amygdala (which makes a quick appraisal of the stimulus's goodness or badness) and the cortex (which does a slower and more comprehensive analysis of the stimulus).

> People use many strategies to regulate emotions, such as reappraisal, which involves changing the way one thinks about an object or event.

Emotional Communication: Msgs w/o Wrds

> Darwin suggested that emotional expressions are the same for all people and are universally understood, and research suggests that this is generally true.

> Emotions cause expressions, but expressions can also cause emotions.

> Not all emotional expressions are sincere because people use display rules to help them decide which emotions to express.

> Different cultures have different display rules, but people enact those rules using the same techniques.

> There are reliable differences between sincere and insincere emotional expressions, but people are generally poor at detecting them. The polygraph can distinguish true from false utterances with better-than-chance accuracy, but its error rate is troublingly high.

Motivation: The Wanting Machine

> The hedonic principle suggests that people approach pleasure and avoid pain and that this basic motivation underlies all others.

> Biological motivations, such as hunger and sexual interest, generally take precedence over psychological motivations.

> People have many psychological motivations that can be classified in many ways, such as intrinsic vs. extrinsic, conscious vs. unconscious, and approach vs. avoidance.

KEY TERMS

emotion (p. 247)
James–Lange theory (p. 248)
Cannon–Bard theory (p. 248)
two-factor theory (p. 248)
appraisal (p. 251)
emotion regulation (p. 251)
reappraisal (p. 252)

emotional expression (p. 253)
universality hypothesis (p. 254)
facial feedback hypothesis (p. 254)
display rule (p. 256)
motivation (p. 258)
drive (p. 258)

bulimia nervosa (p. 259)
anorexia nervosa (p. 259)
metabolism (p. 262)
intrinsic motivation (p. 265)
extrinsic motivation (p. 266)
conscious motivation (p. 267)
unconscious motivation (p. 267)

need for achievement (p. 267)
approach motivation (p. 267)
avoidance motivation (p. 267)
terror management theory (p. 269)

CHANGING MINDS

1. A friend is nearing graduation and has received a couple of job offers. "I went on the first interview," she says, "and I really liked the company, but I know you shouldn't go with your first impressions on difficult decisions. You should be completely rational and not let your emotions get in the way." Are emotions always barriers to rational decision making? In what ways can emotions help guide our decisions?

2. While watching TV, you and a friend hear about a celebrity who punched a fan in a restaurant. "I just lost it," the celebrity said. "I saw what I was doing, but I just couldn't control myself."

According to the TV report, the celebrity was sentenced to anger management classes. "I'm not excusing the violence," your friend says, "but I'm not sure anger management classes are any use either. You can't control your emotions; you just feel them." What example could you give your friend of ways in which we can attempt to control our emotions?

3. One of your friends has just been dumped by her boyfriend, and she's devastated. She's spent days in her room, crying and refusing to go out. You and your roommate decide to keep a close eye on her during this tough time. "Negative emotions are so destructive," your roommate says. "We'd all be better off without them." What would you tell your roommate? In what ways are negative emotions critical for our survival and success?

4. A friend is majoring in education. "We learned today about several cities, including New York and Chicago, that tried giving cash rewards to students who passed their classes or did well on achievement tests. That's bribing kids to get good grades, and as soon as you stop paying them, they'll stop studying." Your friend is assuming that extrinsic motivation undermines intrinsic motivation. In what ways is the picture more complicated?

5. One of your friends is a gym rat who spends all his free time working out and is very proud of his ripped abs. His roommate, though, is very overweight. "I keep telling him to diet and exercise," your friend says, "but he never loses any weight. If he just had a little more willpower, he could succeed." What would you tell your friend? When an individual has difficulty losing weight, what factors may contribute to this difficulty?

ANSWERS TO SUMMARY QUIZZES

Answers to Summary Quiz 8.1: 1. b; 2. a; 3. c; 4. d.
Answers to Summary Quiz 8.2: 1. c; 2. d; 3. c.
Answers to Summary Quiz 8.3: 1. b; 2. a; 3. b; 4. d; 5. d.

Need more help? Additional resources are located in LaunchPad at:
http://www.worthpublishers.com/launchpad/schacterbrief3e

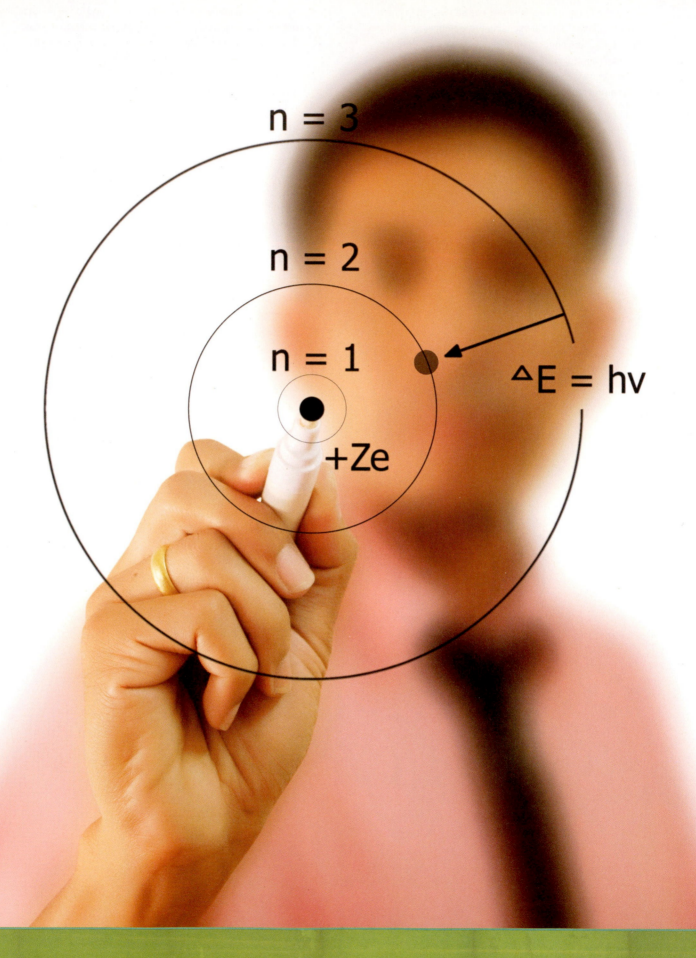

n = 3

n = 2

n = 1

+Ze

$\Delta E = h\nu$

9

Language, Thought, and Intelligence

HRISTOPHER SHOWED AN AMAZING TALENT FOR LANGUAGES. By the age of 6, he had learned French from his sister's schoolbooks; he acquired Greek from a textbook in only 3 months. His talent was so prodigious that grown-up Christopher could converse fluently in 16 languages. When tested on English–French translations, he scored as well as a native French speaker. Presented with a made-up language, he figured out the complex rules easily, even though advanced language students found them virtually impossible to decipher (Smith & Tsimpli, 1995).

If you've concluded that Christopher is extremely smart, perhaps even a genius, you're wrong. His scores on standard intelligence tests are far below normal. He fails simple cognitive tests that 4-year-old children pass with ease, and he cannot even learn the rules for simple games like tic-tac-toe. Despite his dazzling talent, Christopher lives in a halfway house because he does not have the cognitive capacity to make decisions, reason, or solve problems in a way that would allow him to live independently.

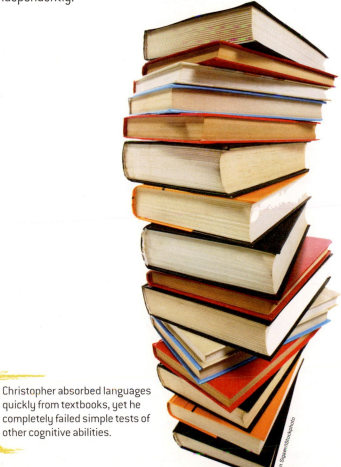

Christopher absorbed languages quickly from textbooks, yet he completely failed simple tests of other cognitive abilities.

Roman Sigaev/iStockphoto

CHRISTOPHER'S STRENGTHS AND WEAKNESSES offer compelling evidence that cognition is composed of distinct abilities. People who learn languages with lightning speed are not necessarily gifted at decision making or problem solving. People who excel at reasoning may have no special ability to master languages. In this chapter, you will learn about several key higher cognitive functions: acquiring and using language, forming concepts and categories, and making decisions: the components of intelligence itself. You'll also learn about where intelligence comes from, how it's measured, and whether it can be improved.

Language and Communication: From Rules to Meaning

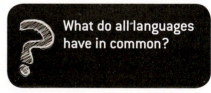

Don Farrall/Getty Images

Most social species have systems of communication that allow them to transmit messages to each other. Honeybees communicate the location of food sources by means of a "waggle dance" that indicates both the direction and distance of the food source from the hive (Kirchner & Towne, 1994; Von Frisch, 1974). Vervet monkeys have three different warning calls that uniquely signal the presence of their main predators: a leopard, an eagle, and a snake (Cheney & Seyfarth, 1990). A leopard call provokes them to climb into a tree; an eagle call makes them look up into the sky. Each different warning call conveys a particular meaning and functions like a word in a simple language.

Language is *a system for communicating with others using signals that are combined according to rules of grammar and convey meaning.* **Grammar** is *a set of rules that specify how the units of language can be combined to produce meaningful messages.* The complex structure of human language distinguishes it from simpler signaling systems used by other species; it also allows us to express a wide range of ideas and concepts, including intangible concepts, such as *unicorn* or *democracy*.

The Complex Structure of Human Language

Compared with other forms of communication, human language is a relatively recent evolutionary phenomenon, emerging as a spoken system no more than 1 to 3 million years ago and as a written system as recently as 6,000 years ago. There are approximately 4,000 human languages, which linguists have grouped into about 50 language families (Nadasdy, 1995). Despite their differences, all of these languages share a basic structure involving a set of sounds and rules for combining those sounds to produce meanings.

What do all languages have in common?

Basic Characteristics

The smallest units of sound that are recognizable as speech rather than as random noise are **phonemes.** These building blocks of spoken language differ in how they are produced. For example, when you say *ba,* your vocal cords start to vibrate as soon as you begin the *b* sound, but when you say *pa,* there is a 60-millisecond lag between the time you start the *p* sound and the time your vocal cords start to vibrate.

Every language has **phonological rules** that *indicate how phonemes can be combined to produce speech sounds.* For example, the initial sound *ts* is acceptable in German but not in English. Typically, people learn these phonological rules without

Honeybees communicate with each other about the location of food by doing a waggle dance that indicates the direction and distance of food from the hive.

Media Bakery

language A system for communicating with others using signals that are combined according to rules of grammar and convey meaning.

grammar A set of rules that specify how the units of language can be combined to produce meaningful messages.

phoneme The smallest unit of sound that is recognizable as speech rather than as random noise.

phonological rules A set of rules that indicate how phonemes can be combined to produce speech sounds.

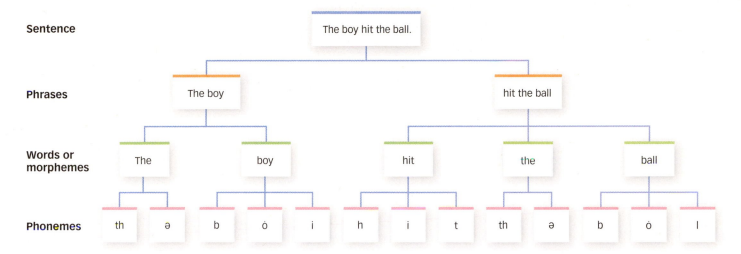

Sentence	The boy hit the ball.
Phrases	The boy · hit the ball
Words or morphemes	The · boy · hit · the · ball
Phonemes	th ə · b ȯ i · h i t · th ə · b ȯ l

FIGURE 9.1 Units of Language A sentence—the largest unit of language—can be broken down into progressively smaller units: phrases, morphemes, and phonemes. In all languages, phonemes and morphemes form words, which can be combined into phrases and ultimately into sentences.

instruction, and if the rules are violated, the resulting speech sounds so odd that we describe it as speaking with an accent.

Phonemes are combined to make **morphemes,** *the smallest meaningful units of language* (see **FIGURE 9.1**). For example, your brain recognizes the *p* sound you make at the beginning of *pat* as a speech *sound,* but it carries no particular meaning. The morpheme *pat,* on the other hand, is recognized as an element of speech that carries meaning. **Morphological rules** *are a set of rules that indicate how morphemes can be combined to form words.* Some morphemes—content morphemes and function morphemes—can stand alone as words. *Content morphemes* refer to things and events (e.g., "cat," "dog," "take"). *Function morphemes* serve grammatical functions, such as tying sentences together ("and," "or," "but") or indicating time ("when"). About half of the morphemes in human languages are function morphemes, and it is the function morphemes that make human language grammatically complex enough to permit us to express abstract ideas.

Words can be combined and recombined to form an infinite number of new sentences, which are governed by **syntactical rules,** *a set of rules that indicate how words can be combined to form phrases and sentences.* A simple syntactical rule in English is that every sentence must contain one or more nouns and one or more verbs (see **FIGURE 9.2**). So, the utterance "dogs bark" is a full sentence, but "the big gray dog over by the building" is not.

morphemes The smallest meaningful units of language.

morphological rules A set of rules that indicate how morphemes can be combined to form words.

syntactical rules A set of rules that indicate how words can be combined to form phrases and sentences.

deep structure The meaning of a sentence.

surface structure How a sentence is worded.

Meaning: Deep Structure versus Surface Structure

Language usually conveys meaning quite well, but everyday experience shows us that misunderstandings can occur. These errors sometimes result from differences between the deep structure of sentences and their surface structure (Chomsky, 1957). **Deep structure** refers to *the meaning of a sentence.* **Surface structure** refers to *how a sentence is worded.* "The dog chased the cat" and "The cat was chased by the dog" mean the same thing (they have the same deep structure) even though on the surface, their structures are different.

To generate a sentence, you begin with a deep structure (the meaning of the sentence) and create a surface structure (the particular words) to convey that meaning. When you comprehend a sentence, you do the reverse, processing the surface structure in order to extract the deep structure. After the deep structure is extracted, the surface structure is usually forgotten (Jarvella, 1970, 1971). In one study, researchers played tape-recorded stories to volunteers and then asked them to pick the sentences they had heard (Sachs, 1967). Participants frequently confused sentences they heard with sentences that had the same deep structure but a different surface structure. For example, if they heard the sentence "He struck John on the shoulder," they often

Why are we able to communicate effectively when we quickly forget the surface structure of sentences?

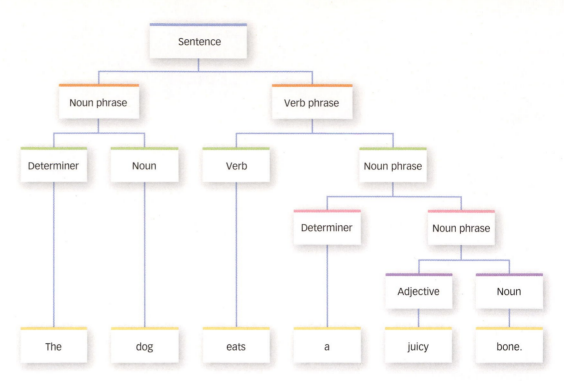

FIGURE 9.2 Syntactical Rules Syntactical rules indicate how words can be combined to form sentences. Every sentence must contain one or more nouns, which may be combined with adjectives or articles to create a noun phrase. A sentence also must contain one or more verbs, which may be combined with noun phrases, adverbs, or articles to create a verb phrase.

mistakenly claimed they had heard "John was struck on the shoulder by him." In contrast, they rarely misidentified "John struck him on the shoulder" because this sentence has a different deep structure from the original sentence.

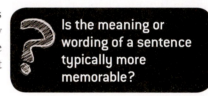

Is the meaning or wording of a sentence typically more memorable?

Language Development

Language is a complex cognitive skill, yet we can carry on complex conversations with playmates and family before we begin school. Three characteristics of language development are worth bearing in mind. First, children learn language at an astonishingly rapid rate. The average 1-year-old has a vocabulary of 10 words, which expands to more than *10,000* words in the next 4 years, requiring the child to learn, on average, about 6 or 7 new words *every day*. Second, children make few errors while learning to speak, and as we'll see shortly, the errors they do make usually result from applying, but overgeneralizing, grammatical rules they've learned. Third, children's *passive mastery* of language (ability to understand) develops faster than their *active mastery* (ability to speak). At every stage of language development, children understand language better than they speak.

Distinguishing Speech Sounds

At birth, infants can distinguish all the sounds that occur in all human languages. Within the first 6 months of life, they lose this ability, and, like their parents, can only distinguish among the contrasting sounds in the language they hear being spoken around them. For example, two distinct sounds in English are the *l* sound and the *r* sound, as in *lead* and *read*. These sounds are not distinguished in Japanese; instead, the *l* and *r* sounds fall within the same phoneme. Japanese adults cannot hear the difference between these two phonemes, but American adults can distinguish between them easily—and so can Japanese infants.

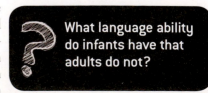

What language ability do infants have that adults do not?

Courtesy of Dr. Patricia K. Kuhl, UW Institute for Learning and Brain Sciences

In this test, the infant watches an animated toy animal while a speech sound is repeated. After a few repetitions, the sound changes, then the display changes, and then they both change again. If the infant switches her attention when the sound changes, she is anticipating the new display, showing that she can discriminate between the sounds.

In one study, researchers constructed a tape of a voice saying "la-la-la" or "ra-ra-ra" repeatedly (Eimas et al., 1971). They rigged a pacifier so that whenever an infant sucked on it, a tape player that broadcast the *la-la* tape was activated. When the *la-la* sound began playing in response to their sucking, the infants were delighted and kept sucking on the pacifier to keep the *la-la* sound playing. After a while, they began to lose interest, and sucking frequency declined to about half of its initial rate. At this point, the experimenters switched the tape so that *ra-ra* was repeatedly broadcast. The Japanese infants began sucking again with vigor, indicating that they could hear the difference between the old, boring *la* sound and the new, interesting *ra* sound.

Infants can distinguish among speech sounds, but they cannot produce them reliably, relying mostly on cries, laughs, and other vocalizations to communicate. Between the ages of about 4 and 6 months, they begin to babble speech sounds. Babbling involves combinations of vowels and consonants that sound like real syllables but are meaningless. Regardless of the language they hear spoken, all infants go through the same babbling sequence. For example, *d* and *t* appear in infant babbling before *m* and *n*. Even deaf infants babble sounds they've never heard, and they do so in the same order as hearing infants do (Ollers & Eilers, 1988). This is evidence that infants aren't simply imitating the sounds they hear and suggests that babbling is a natural part of the language development process. Recent research has shown that babbling serves as a signal that the infant is in a state of focused attention and ready to learn (Goldstein et al., 2010).

In order for vocal babbling to continue, however, infants must be able to hear themselves. In fact, delayed babbling or the cessation of babbling merits testing for possible hearing difficulties. Babbling problems can lead to speech impairments, but they do not necessarily prevent language acquisition. Deaf infants whose parents communicate using American Sign Language (ASL) begin to babble with their hands at the same age that hearing children begin to babble vocally—between 4 and 6 months (Petitto & Marentette, 1991). Their babbling consists of sign language syllables that are the fundamental components of ASL.

Deaf infants who learn sign language from their parents start babbling with their hands around the same time that hearing infants babble vocally.

Language Milestones

At about 10 to 12 months of age, infants begin to utter (or sign) their first words. By 18 months, they can say about 50 words and can understand several times more than that. Toddlers generally learn nouns before verbs, and the nouns they learn first are names for everyday, concrete objects (e.g., chair, table, milk) (see **TABLE 9.1**). At about this time, their vocabularies undergo explosive growth. By the time the average child begins school, a

Christina Kennedy/Alamy

fast mapping The fact that children can map a word onto an underlying concept after only a single exposure.

telegraphic speech Speech that is devoid of function morphemes and consists mostly of content words.

Table 9.1 Language Milestones

Average Age	Language Milestones
0–4 months	Can tell the difference between speech sounds (phonemes). Cooing, especially in response to speech.
4–6 months	Babbles consonants.
6–10 months	Understands some words and simple requests.
10–12 months	Begins to use single words.
12–18 months	Vocabulary of 30–50 words (simple nouns, adjectives, and action words).
18–24 months	Two-word phrases of about 1,000 words; production of phrases and incomplete sentences.
24–36 months	Vocabulary of about 1,000 words; production of phrases and incomplete sentences.
36–60 months	Vocabulary grows to more than 10,000 words; production of full sentences, mastery of grammatical morphemes (such as –*ed* for past tense) and function words (such as *the, and, but*). Can form questions and negations.

vocabulary of 5000 words is not unusual. By college, the average student's vocabulary is about 10,000–15,000 words. **Fast mapping,** in which children *map a word onto an underlying concept after only a single exposure,* enables them to learn at this rapid pace (Kan & Kohnert, 2008; Mervis & Bertrand, 1994). This astonishingly easy process contrasts dramatically with the effort required later to learn other concepts and skills, such as arithmetic or writing.

Around 24 months, children begin to form two-word sentences, such as "more milk" or "throw ball." Such sentences are referred to as **telegraphic speech** because they are *devoid of function morphemes and consist mostly of content words.* Yet despite the absence of function words, these two-word sentences tend to be grammatical; the words are ordered in a manner consistent with the syntactical rules of the language children are learning to speak. So, for example, toddlers will say, "throw ball" rather than "ball throw" when they want you to throw the ball to them, and they will say, "more milk" rather than "milk more" when they want you to give them more milk. With these seemingly primitive expressions, 2-year-olds show an appreciation of the syntactical rules of the language they are learning.

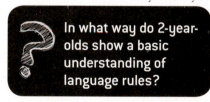
In what way do 2-year-olds show a basic understanding of language rules?

The Emergence of Grammatical Rules

If you listen to average 2- or 3-year-old children speaking, you may notice that they use the correct past-tense versions of common verbs, as in the expressions "I ran" and "you ate." By the age of 4 or 5, the same children will be using incorrect forms of these verbs, saying such things as "I runned" or "you eated," forms most children are unlikely to have ever heard (Prasada & Pinker, 1993). The reason is that very young children memorize the particular sounds (i.e., words) that express what they want to communicate. But as children acquire the grammatical rules of their language, they tend to *overgeneralize.* For example, if a child overgeneralizes the rule that past tense is indicated by -*ed,* then *run* becomes *runned* or even *ranned* instead of *ran.*

These errors show that language acquisition is not simply a matter of imitating adult speech. Instead, children acquire grammatical rules by listening to the speech around them and using the rules to create verbal forms they've never heard. They manage this without explicit

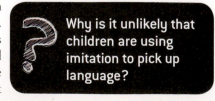
Why is it unlikely that children are using imitation to pick up language?

awareness of the grammatical rules they've learned. In fact, few children or adults can articulate the grammatical rules of their native language, yet the speech they produce obeys these rules.

By about 3 years of age, children begin to generate complete simple sentences that include function words (e.g., "Give me *the* ball" and "That belongs *to* me"). The sentences increase in complexity over the next 2 years. By 4 to 5 years of age, many aspects of the language acquisition process are complete. As children continue to mature, their language skills become more refined, with added appreciation of subtler communicative uses of language, such as humor, sarcasm, or irony.

Language Development and Cognitive Development

Language development typically unfolds as a sequence of steps in which one milestone is achieved before moving on to the next. Nearly all infants begin with one-word utterances before moving on to telegraphic speech and then to simple sentences that include function morphemes. This orderly progression could result from general cognitive development that is unrelated to experience with a specific language (Shore, 1986; Wexler, 1999). For example, perhaps infants begin with one- and then two-word utterances because their short-term memories are so limited that initially they can only hold in mind a word or two; additional cognitive development might be necessary before they have the capacity to put together a simple sentence. By contrast, the orderly progression might depend on experience with a specific language, reflecting a child's emerging knowledge of that language (Bates & Goodman, 1997; Gillette et al., 1999).

To tease apart these possibilities, researchers examined the acquisition of English by internationally adopted children who did not know any English prior to adoption (Snedeker, Geren, & Shafto, 2007, 2012). If the orderly sequence of milestones that characterizes the acquisition of English by infants is a by-product of general cognitive development, then different patterns should be observed in older internationally adopted children, who are more advanced cognitively than infants. However, if the milestones of language development are critically dependent on experience with a specific language—English—then language learning in older adopted children should show the same orderly progression as seen in infants. The main result was clear-cut: Language acquisition in preschool-aged adopted children showed the same orderly progression of milestones that characterizes infants. These children began with one-word utterances before moving on to simple word combinations. Furthermore, their vocabularies, just like those of infants, were initially dominated by nouns, and these children produced few function morphemes. These results indicate that some of the key milestones of language development depend on experience with English.

> **?** Why are studies of internationally adopted children especially useful?

Chinese preschoolers who are adopted by English-speaking parents progress through the same sequence of linguistic milestones as do infants born into English-speaking families, suggesting that these milestones reflect experience with English rather than general cognitive development.

Marvin Joseph/Washington Post/Getty Images

Theories of Language Development

We know a good deal about how language develops, but what underlies the process? The language acquisition process has been the subject of considerable controversy and (at times) angry exchanges among scientists coming from three different approaches: behaviorist, nativist, and interactionist.

Behaviorist Explanations

According to B. F. Skinner's behaviorist explanation of language learning, we learn to talk in the same way we learn any other skill: through reinforcement, shaping, extinction, and the other basic principles of

nativist theory The view that language development is best explained as an innate, biological capacity.

genetic dysphasia A syndrome characterized by an inability to learn the grammatical structure of language despite having otherwise normal intelligence.

operant conditioning that you learned about in the Learning chapter (Skinner, 1957). As infants mature, they begin to vocalize. Those vocalizations that are not reinforced gradually diminish, and those that are reinforced remain in the developing child's repertoire. So, for example, when an infant gurgles "prah," most parents are pretty indifferent. However, "da-da" is likely to be reinforced with smiles, whoops, and cackles of "Goooood baaaaaby!" by doting parents. Maturing children also imitate the speech patterns they hear. Then parents or other adults shape those speech patterns by reinforcing those that are grammatical and ignoring or punishing those that are ungrammatical. "I no want milk" is likely to be squelched by parental clucks and titters, whereas "No milk for me, thanks" will probably be reinforced.

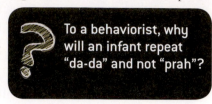
To a behaviorist, why will an infant repeat "da-da" and not "prah"?

The behavioral explanation is attractive because it offers a simple account of language development, but it cannot account for many fundamental characteristics of language development (Chomsky, 1986; Pinker, 1994; Pinker & Bloom, 1990).

> First, parents don't spend much time teaching their children to speak grammatically. So, for example, when a child says, "Nobody like me," his or her mother will respond with something like, "Why do you think that?" rather than "Now, listen carefully and repeat after me: Nobody likes me" (Brown & Hanlon, 1970).

> Second, children generate sentences that they've never heard before. This shows that children don't just imitate; they learn the rules for generating sentences.

> Third, as you read earlier, the errors children make when learning to speak tend to be overgeneralizations of grammatical rules. The behaviorist explanation would not predict these overgeneralizations if children were learning through trial and error or simply imitating what they hear.

Nativist Explanations

In a blistering reply to Skinner's behaviorist approach, linguist Noam Chomsky (1957, 1959) argued that language-learning capacities are built into the human brain and are separate from general intelligence. This **nativist theory** *is the view that language development is best explained as an innate, biological capacity.* According to the nativist view, studies of people with genetic dysphasia suggest that normal children learn the grammatical rules of human language with ease in part because they are "wired" to do so.

The story of Christopher, whom you met earlier in the chapter, is consistent with the nativist view of language development: His genius for language acquisition, despite his low overall intelligence, indicates that language capacity can be distinct from other mental capacities. Other individuals show the opposite pattern: People with normal or nearly normal intelligence can find certain aspects of human language difficult or impossible to learn. This condition is known as **genetic dysphasia,** *a syndrome characterized by an inability to learn the grammatical structure of language despite having otherwise normal intelligence.* For example, when asked to describe what she did over the weekend, one child wrote, "On Saturday I watch TV." Her teacher corrected the sentence to "On Saturday, I watch*ed* TV," drawing attention to the *-ed* rule for describing past events. The following week, the child was asked to write another account of what she did over the weekend. She wrote, "On Saturday I wash myself and I watched TV and I went to bed." Notice that although she had memorized the past-tense forms *watched* and *went,* she could not generalize the rule to form the past tense of another word (*washed*).

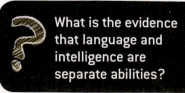
What is the evidence that language and intelligence are separate abilities?

"GOT IDEA. TALK BETTER. COMBINE WORDS. MAKE SENTENCES."

© Sidney Harris

Also consistent with the nativist view is evidence that language can be acquired only during a restricted period of development. This was dramatically illustrated by the tragic case of Genie (Curtiss, 1977). At the age of 20 months, Genie was tied to a chair by her parents and kept in virtual isolation. Her father forbade Genie's mother and brother to speak to her, and he himself only growled and barked at her. She remained in this brutal state until she was rescued at the age of 13. Genie's life improved substantially, and she received years of language instruction, but it was too late. Her language skills remained extremely primitive. She developed a basic vocabulary and could communicate her ideas, but she could not grasp the grammatical rules of English.

Less dramatic evidence for a restricted period in human learning comes from studies of language acquisition in immigrants. In one study, the proficiency with which immigrants spoke English depended not on how long they'd lived in the United States, but on their age at immigration, with those who had arrived as children being more proficient than those who arrived after puberty (Johnson & Newport, 1989). More recent work using fMRI shows that acquiring a second language early in childhood (between 1 and 5 years of age) results in very different representation of that language in the brain than does acquiring that language much later (after 9 years of age; Bloch et al., 2009).

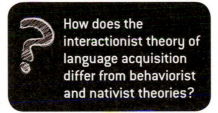

Immigrants who learn English as a second language are more proficient if they start to learn English before puberty rather than after.

Interactionist Explanations

Nativist theories are often criticized because they do not explain *how* language develops; they merely explain *why*. The interactionist approach holds that although infants are born with an innate ability to acquire language, social interactions also play a crucial role in language. Interactionists point out that parents tailor their verbal interactions with children in ways that simplify the language acquisition process: They speak slowly, enunciate clearly, and use simpler sentences than they do when speaking with adults (Bruner, 1983; Farrar, 1990).

? How does the interactionist theory of language acquisition differ from behaviorist and nativist theories?

Further evidence of the interaction of biology and experience comes from a fascinating study of deaf children's creation of a new language (Senghas, Kita, & Ozyurek, 2004). Prior to about 1980, deaf children in Nicaragua stayed at home and usually had little contact with other deaf individuals. In 1981, some deaf children began to attend a new school. At first, the school did not teach a formal sign language, and none of the children had learned to sign at home, but the children gradually began to communicate using hand signals that they invented. Initially, the gestures were simple, but over the past three decades, the Nicaraguan sign language has developed considerably, and it now contains many of the same features as more mature languages, including signs to describe separate components of complex concepts (Pyers et al., 2010). These acts of creation nicely illustrate the interplay of nativism (the predisposition to use language) and experience (growing up in an insulated deaf culture).

How does the evolution of the Nicaraguan deaf children's sign language support the interactionist explanation of language development?

Language Development and the Brain

In early infancy, language processing is distributed across many areas of the brain. But as the brain matures, language processing gradually becomes more and more concentrated in two areas, Broca's area

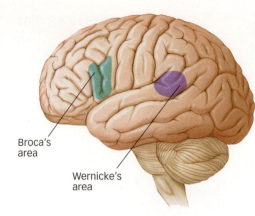

FIGURE 9.3 Broca's and Wernicke's Areas Neuroscientists study people with brain damage in order to better understand how the brain normally operates. When Broca's area is damaged, people have a hard time producing sentences. When Wernicke's area is damaged, people can produce sentences, but those sentences tend to be meaningless.

Japanese individuals who suffer from Wernicke's aphasia can still understand pictographs like this one, even though they have difficulty understanding speech sounds.

and Wernicke's area. *Broca's area* is located in the left frontal cortex and is involved in the production of the sequential patterns in vocal and sign languages (see **FIGURE 9.3**). *Wernicke's area,* located in the left temporal cortex, is involved in language comprehension (whether spoken or signed).

Together, Broca's area and Wernicke's area are sometimes referred to as the language centers of the brain; damage to them results in a serious condition called **aphasia,** *difficulty in producing or comprehending language.* As you saw in the Psychology: Evolution of a Science chapter, patients with damage to Broca's area understand language relatively well, although they have increasing comprehension difficulty as grammatical structures get more complex. But their real struggle is with speech production. Typically, they speak in short, staccato phrases that consist mostly of content morphemes: "Ah, Monday, uh, Casey park. Two, uh, friends, and, uh, 30 minutes." On the other hand, patients with damage to Wernicke's area can produce grammatical speech, but it tends to be meaningless: "Feel very well. In other words, I used to be able to work cigarettes. I don't know how. Things I couldn't hear from are here."

As important as Broca's and Wernicke's areas are for language, they are not the entire story. A number of neuroimaging studies have revealed evidence of right-hemisphere activation during language tasks, and individuals with damage to the right hemisphere sometimes have subtle problems with language comprehension. These studies indicate that not all language processing is limited to the left hemisphere.

Brain changes also appear to account for the fact that children who are fluent in two languages score higher than monolingual children on several measures of cognitive functioning, including executive control capacities such as the ability to prioritize information and flexibly focus attention (Bialystok, 1999, 2009; Bialystok, Craik, & Luk, 2012). The idea here is that bilingual individuals benefit from exerting executive control in their daily lives when they attempt to suppress the language that they don't want to use. Research shows that learning a second language produces lasting changes in the brain (Mechelli et al., 2004; Stein et al., 2009). For example, the gray matter in a part of the left parietal lobe that is involved in language is denser in bilingual than in monolingual individuals, and the increased density is most pronounced in those who are most proficient in using their second language (Mechelli et al., 2004). (Some other benefits of bilingualism are noted in the Other Voices box.)

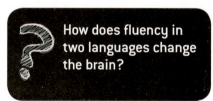

How does fluency in two languages change the brain?

SUMMARY QUIZ [9.1]

1. The combining of words to form phrases and sentences is governed by
   a. phonological rules.
   b. morphological rules.
   c. structural rules.
   d. syntactical rules.

2. Which of the following statements about language development is inaccurate?
   a. Language acquisition is largely a matter of children imitating adult speech.
   b. Deep structure refers to the meaning of a sentence, while surface structure refers to how it is constructed.
   c. By the time the average child begins school, a vocabulary of 10,000 words is not unusual.
   d. Children's passive mastery of language develops faster than their active mastery.

aphasia Difficulty in producing or comprehending language.

Other Voices

Americans' Future Has to Be Bilingual

Linda Moore is the founder and executive director of the Elsie Whitlow Stokes Community Freedom Public Charter School in Washington, DC.

Satsun Photography/Beverlie Lord

We discuss in the text some benefits of bilingualism that have been documented in recent research. Linda Moore (2012) noted several such benefits in the following article from *The Washington Diplomat* and argued that the American educational system should teach students foreign languages earlier than is commonly done.

We Americans must confront a stark disadvantage we face when it comes to the global economy. Some eight in 10 Americans speak only English, and the number of schools teaching a foreign language is in decline, according to a new study by the Council on Foreign Relations. But the opposite is true among our economic competitors.

While some 200 million Chinese students are learning English, only 24,000 Americans are studying Chinese, U.S. Department of Education statistics say. Foreign language degrees account for only 1 percent of all U.S. undergraduate degrees. And fewer than 2 percent of U.S. undergraduates study abroad in a given year, the Education Department says.

Our nation is largely monolingual but is entering an increasingly multilingual world. More than half of European Union citizens speak a language other than their mother tongue, and more than a quarter speak at least three languages. This is because additional languages are studied in European primary and secondary schools, and are taken up by European college students in much larger numbers than in the United States.

The Council on Foreign Relations-sponsored task force report, headed by former New York City Schools Chancellor Joel Klein and former Secretary of State Condoleezza Rice, concluded: "Education failure puts the United States' future economic prosperity, global position, and physical safety at risk." It warned that the country "will not be able to keep pace—

much less lead—globally unless it moves to fix the problems it has allowed to fester for too long."

For decades, our children were deprived of bilingual or multilingual education out of a mistaken belief that it took time away from other subjects, hindering students' academic development. But recent research has shown that learning another language is a wise investment, rather than a waste. Research from the University of Georgia found that bilingual school children perform better on standardized tests, including the Scholastic Aptitude Test (SAT) than their monolingual peers. A George Mason University study discovered that younger students who had enrolled in a second language immersion program outperformed those who did not in coursework, as well as on standardized tests, throughout their scholastic careers.

Educators now conclude that learning additional languages improves one's ability to focus, plan and solve problems. Among other benefits, this means that such students are better able to move efficiently from one subject to another. The D.C.-based Center for Applied Linguistics has ascertained that the earlier we learn a foreign language, the greater the benefits. Moreover, these benefits can last a lifetime. Learning another language can help people stave off the effects of aging, including preventing the onset of dementia and other age-related conditions like Alzheimer's, according to research done by University of California neuroscientists.

I believe that teaching students foreign languages in pre-kindergarten to sixth-grade classes is a worthwhile investment. Our school educates 350 students in Northeast Washington, D.C., to think, speak, read, write and learn in two languages, either English and French, or English and Spanish.

Exposure to a new language and the skills it helps develop is a key reason that our school, where 80 percent of our students come from low-income households, was ranked as high performing by D.C.'s Public Charter School Board in December. The ranking system was based on several factors, including test scores, attendance and re-enrollment rates.

The benefits of learning a new language go beyond the classroom. When students

graduate, being fluent in a second language improves their career prospects. The Bureau of Labor Statistics reports that a number of emerging occupations need workers who can speak and write in more than one language. A University of Florida study revealed that in large, linguistically diverse cities such as Miami and San Antonio, the ability to speak a second language translates into more than $7,000 of increased annual income. We want our students to have access to these opportunities and more.

The economic importance of being bilingual is highlighted by the fact that 31 percent of company executives can speak at least two languages, according to international executive search firm Korn/Ferry.

Using multilingualism, we are expanding the scope of children's learning at a time when public policy limits school accountability to math and reading. Most policymakers want their children to have global skill sets but do not encourage this in our public schools.

Other countries have learned this lesson and have made the necessary commitments to teach their students additional languages. Their students' exposure to additional languages is paying dividends. I would like to see the U.S. Department of Education encourage local education authorities to invest in bilingual and multilingual education. Given the global competition for good jobs, this is not a luxury, but a necessity. It will help our children, and our nation, to succeed in the economy of tomorrow.

Are you convinced by Moore's argument? If not, why not? And if so, how far do you think the educational system should go in promoting multilingual education? What about the possible impact of devoting more time in early grades to teaching languages on other subjects? What kinds of research would you want to see done to evaluate the effects of early instruction in foreign languages?

Moore, L. (August 31, 2012). America's Future Has to Be Bilingual. In *The Washington Diplomat*. Copyright 2012 The Washington Diplomat. Reproduced by permission. http://www.washdiplomat.com/index.php?option=com_content&view=article&id=8549:op-ed-americans-future-has-to-be-multilingual&catid=1492:september-2012&Itemid=504

concept A mental representation that groups or categorizes shared features of related objects, events, or other stimuli.

family resemblance theory Members of a category have features that appear to be characteristic of category members but may not be possessed by every member.

3. Language development as an innate, biological capacity is explained by

   a. fast mapping.

   b. behaviorism.

   c. nativist theory.

   d. interactionist explanations.

4. Damage to the brain region called Broca's area results in

   a. failure to comprehend language.

   b. difficulty in producing grammatical speech.

   c. the reintroduction of infant babbling.

   d. difficulties in writing.

Concepts and Categories: How We Think

In October 2000, a man known by the initials JB went for a neurological assessment because he was having difficulty understanding the meaning of words, even though he still performed well on many other perceptual and cognitive tasks. Over the next few years, his color language deteriorated dramatically; he had great difficulty naming colors and could not even match objects with their typical colors (e.g., strawberry and red, banana and yellow). Yet he could still classify colors normally, sorting color patches into groups of green, yellow, red, and blue. JB retained an intact concept of colors despite the decline of his language ability—a finding that suggests that we need to look at factors in addition to language in order to understand concepts (Haslam et al., 2007).

Concept refers to a *mental representation that groups or categorizes shared features of related objects, events, or other stimuli*. The brain organizes our concepts about the world, classifying them into categories based on shared similarities. Our category for *dog* may be something like "small, four-footed animal with fur that wags its tail and barks." Our category for *chair* may be something like "sturdy, flat-bottomed thing you can sit on." We form these categories in large part by noticing similarities among objects and events that we experience in everyday life. Concepts are fundamental to our ability to think and make sense of the world.

? Why are concepts useful to us?

Psychological Theories of Concepts and Categories

What is your definition of *dog*? Can you come up with a rule of "dogship" that includes all dogs and excludes all nondogs? Most people can't, but they still use the term *dog* intelligently, easily classifying objects as dogs or nondogs. Three theories seek to explain how people perform these acts of categorization.

Family Resemblance Theory

Eleanor Rosch developed a theory of concepts based on **family resemblance,** that is, *features that appear to be characteristic of category members but may not be possessed by every member* (Rosch, 1973, 1975; Rosch & Mervis, 1975; Wittgenstein, 1953/1999). For example, you and

"Attention, everyone! I'd like to introduce the newest member of our family."

Jeff Kaufman/The New Yorker Collection/cartoonbank.com

your brother may have your mother's eyes, although you and your sister may have your father's high cheekbones. There is a strong family resemblance between you, your parents, and your siblings despite the fact that there is no single defining feature that you all have in common. Similarly, many members of the *bird* category have feathers and wings, so these are the characteristic features. Anything that has these features is likely to be classified as a bird because of this "family resemblance" to other members of the *bird* category (see **FIGURE 9.4**).

Prototype Theory

Building on the idea of family resemblance, Rosch also proposed that categories are organized around a **prototype**, *the "best" or "most typical" member of a category.* A prototype possesses most (or all) of the most characteristic features of the category. For North Americans, the prototype of the *bird* category would be something like a wren: a small animal with feathers and wings that flies through the air, lays eggs, and migrates (see **FIGURE 9.5**). People make category judgments by comparing new instances to the category's prototype. According to *prototype theory,* if your prototypical bird is a robin, then a canary would be considered a better example of a bird than would an ostrich because a canary has more features in common with a robin than an ostrich does.

Exemplar Theory

In contrast to prototype theory, **exemplar theory** holds that *we make category judgments by comparing a new instance with stored memories for other instances of the category* (Medin & Schaffer, 1978). Imagine that you're out walking in the woods, and from the corner of your eye, you spot a four-legged animal that might be a wolf but reminds you of your cousin's German shepherd. You figure it must be a dog and continue to enjoy your walk rather than fleeing in panic. You probably categorized this new animal as a dog because it bore a striking resemblance to other dogs you've encountered; in other words, it was a good example (or an *exemplar*) of the category *dog*. Exemplar theory does a better job than prototype theory in accounting for certain aspects of categorization, especially in that we recall not only what a *prototypical* dog looks like but also what *specific* dogs look like. **FIGURE 9.6** illustrates the difference between prototype theory and exemplar theory.

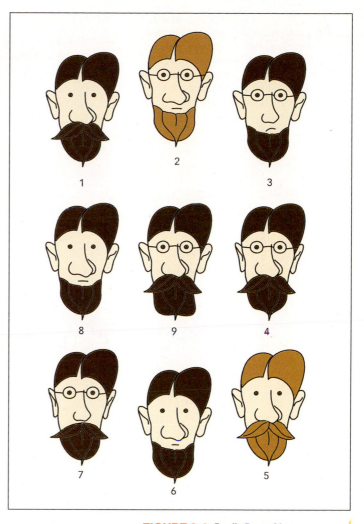

FIGURE 9.4 Family Resemblance Theory The family resemblance here is unmistakable, even though no two Smith brothers share all the family features. The prototype is brother 9. He has it all: brown hair, large ears, large nose, mustache, and glasses.

prototype The "best" or "most typical member" of a category.

exemplar theory A theory of categorization that argues that we make category judgments by comparing a new instance with stored memories for other instances of the category.

Properties	Generic bird	Wren	Blue heron	Golden eagle	Domestic goose	Penguin
Flies regularly	✓	✓	✓	✓		
Sings	✓	✓	✓			
Lays eggs	✓	✓		✓	✓	✓
Is small	✓	✓				
Nests in trees	✓	✓				

FIGURE 9.5 Critical Features of a Category We tend to think of a generic bird as possessing a number of critical features, but not every bird possesses all of those features. In North America, a wren is a better example of a bird than a penguin or an ostrich.

Exemplars

Prototype

Exemplar Theory

Prototype Theory

New stimulus

Concepts, Categories, and the Brain

Researchers using neuroimaging techniques have concluded that we use both prototypes and exemplars when forming concepts and categories. The visual cortex is involved in forming prototypes, whereas the prefrontal cortex and basal ganglia are involved in learning exemplars (Ashby & Ell, 2001; Ashby & O'Brien, 2005). This evidence suggests that exemplar-based learning involves analysis and decision making (prefrontal cortex), whereas prototype formation is a more holistic process involving image processing (visual cortex).

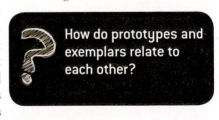

How do prototypes and exemplars relate to each other?

Some of the most striking evidence linking concepts with the brain comes from patients with brain damage. One such patient could not recognize a variety of human-made objects or retrieve any information about them, but his knowledge of living things and foods was perfectly normal (Warrington & McCarthy, 1983). Other patients exhibit the reverse pattern: They can recognize information about human-made objects, but their ability to recognize information about living things and foods is severely impaired (Martin & Caramazza, 2003; Warrington & Shallice, 1984). Such unusual cases became the basis for a syndrome called **category-specific deficit,** *a neurological syndrome characterized by an inability to recognize objects that belong to a particular category, although the ability to recognize objects outside the category is undisturbed.*

category-specific deficit A neurological syndrome that is characterized by an inability to recognize objects that belong to a particular category, although the ability to recognize objects outside the category is undisturbed.

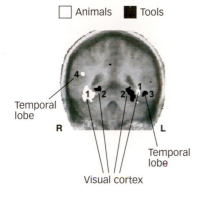
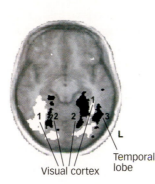
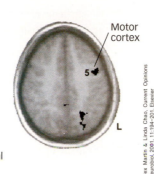

☐ Animals ■ Tools

Motor cortex

Temporal lobe

R   L

Visual cortex

Temporal lobe

Visual cortex

Temporal lobe

L

L

Alex Martin & Linda Chao, Current Opinions Neurobiol, 2001, 11:194–201, Elsevier

FIGURE 9.7 Brain Areas Involved in Category-Specific Processing Participants were asked to silently name pictures of animals and tools while they were scanned with fMRI. Areas in white, including parts of visual cortex and temporal lobe, labeled (1, 4), showed greater activity when participants named animals. Areas in black, including other parts of the visual cortex and temporal lobe (2, 3) and a region of the motor cortex (5), showed greater activity when participants named tools. Note that the images are left/right reversed.

The type of category-specific deficit suffered depends on where the brain is damaged. Deficits usually result when an individual suffers damage to areas in the left hemisphere of the cerebral cortex (Mahon & Caramazza, 2009). Damage to the front part of the left temporal lobe results in difficulty identifying humans; damage to the lower left temporal lobe results in difficulty identifying animals; and damage to the region where the temporal lobe meets the occipital and parietal lobes impairs the ability to retrieve names of tools (Damasio et al., 1996). Similarly, when healthy people undertake the same task, imaging studies have demonstrated that the same regions of the brain are more active during naming of tools than animals and vice versa, as shown in **FIGURE 9.7** (Martin, 2007; Martin & Chao, 2001).

How do particular brain regions develop category preferences for objects such as tools or animals? In one fMRI study, blind and sighted individuals each heard a series of words, including some words that referred to animals and others that referred to tools. Category-preferential regions showed highly similar patterns of activity in the blind and sighted individuals (Mahon et al., 2009). In both groups, for example, regions in the visual cortex and temporal lobe responded to animals and tools in much the same manner as shown in Figure 9.7. These results provide compelling evidence that category-specific organization of visual regions does not depend on an individual's visual experience. The simplest explanation may be that category-specific brain organization is innately determined (Bedny & Saxe, 2012; Mahon et al., 2009).

"Don't panic. It's only a prototype."

Robert Mankoff/The New Yorker Collection/cartoonbank.com

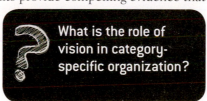

? What is the role of vision in category-specific organization?

SUMMARY QUIZ [9.2]

1. The "most typical" member of a category is a(n)

    a. prototype.

    b. exemplar.

    c. concept.

    d. definition.

2. Which theory of how we form concepts is based on our judgment of features that appear to be characteristic of category members but may not be possessed by every member?

   a. prototype theory

   b. family resemblance theory

   c. exemplar theory

   d. heuristic theory

3. The inability to recognize objects that belong to a particular category, although the ability to recognize objects outside the category is undisturbed, is called

   a. category-preferential organization.

   b. cognitive-visual deficit.

   c. a category-specific deficit.

   d. aphasia.

Decision Making: Rational and Otherwise

We use categories and concepts to guide the hundreds of decisions and judgments we make during the course of an average day. Some decisions are easy (what to wear, what to eat for breakfast, and whether to walk or drive to class) and some are more difficult (which car to buy, which apartment to rent, and even which job to take after graduation). Some decisions are made based on sound judgments. Others are not.

The Rational Ideal

Economists contend that if we are rational and are free to make our own decisions, we will behave as predicted by **rational choice theory:** *the classical view that we make decisions by determining how likely something is to happen, judging the value of the outcome, and then multiplying the two* (Edwards, 1955). This means that our judgments will vary depending on the value we assign to the possible outcomes. Suppose, for example, you were asked to choose between a 10% chance of gaining $500 and a 20% chance of gaining $2,000. The rational person would choose the second alternative because the expected payoff is $400 ($2,000 × 20%), whereas the first offers an expected gain of only $50 ($500 × 10%). Selecting the option with the highest expected value seems very straightforward. But how well does this theory describe decision making in our everyday lives? In many cases, the answer is not very well.

The Irrational Reality

Is the ability to classify new events and objects into categories always a useful skill? Alas, no. The same principles that allow cognition to occur easily and accurately can pop up to bedevil our decision making.

Judging Frequencies and Probabilities

Consider the following list of words:

> *block table block pen telephone block disk glass table block telephone block watch table candy*

You probably noticed that the words *block* and *table* occurred more frequently than the other words did. In fact, studies have shown that people are quite good at estimating *frequency,* or the number of times something will happen. In contrast, we

rational choice theory The classical view that we make decisions by determining how likely something is to happen, judging the value of the outcome, and then multiplying the two.

perform poorly on tasks that require us to think in terms of *probabilities,* or the likelihood that something will happen.

In one experiment, 100 physicians were asked to predict the incidence of breast cancer among women whose mammograms showed possible evidence of breast cancer. The physicians were told to take into consideration the rarity of breast cancer (1% of the population at the time the study was done) and radiologists' record in diagnosing the condition (correctly recognized only 79% of the time and falsely diagnosed almost 10% of the time). Of the 100 physicians, 95 estimated the probability of cancer at about 75%! The correct answer was 8% (Eddy, 1982). But dramatically different results were obtained when the study was repeated using *frequency* information instead of *probability* information. Stating the problem as "10 out of every 1,000 women actually have breast cancer" instead of "1% of women actually have breast cancer" led 46% of the physicians to derive the right answer (Hoffrage & Gigerenzer, 1998).

The **frequency format hypothesis** *is the proposal that our minds evolved to notice how frequently things occur, not how likely they are to occur* (Gigerenzer, 1996; Gigerenzer & Hoffrage, 1995). Thus, we interpret, process, and manipulate information about frequency with comparative ease because that's the way quantitative information usually occurs in natural circumstances. For example, the 20 men, 15 women, 5 dogs, 13 cars, and 2 bicycle accidents you encountered on the way to class came in the form of frequencies, not probabilities or percentages. Therefore, the frequency format provides an explanation for why physicians do so much better at predicting incidence of breast cancer when the relevant information is presented as frequencies rather than as probabilities.

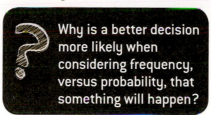

Why is a better decision more likely when considering frequency, versus probability, that something will happen?

People don't always make rational choices. When a lottery jackpot is larger than usual, more people will buy lottery tickets, thinking that they might well win big. However, more people buying lottery tickets reduces the likelihood of any one person winning the lottery. Ironically, people have a better chance at winning a lottery with a relatively small jackpot.

frequency format hypothesis The proposal that our minds evolved to notice how frequently things occur, not how likely they are to occur.

availability bias Items that are more readily available in memory are judged as having occurred more frequently.

Availability Bias

Take a look at the list of names in **FIGURE 9.8**. Now look away from the book and estimate the number of male names and female names in the figure. Did you notice that some of the women on the list are famous and none of the men are? Was your estimate off because you thought the list contained more women's than men's names (Tversky & Kahneman, 1973, 1974)? People typically fall prey to **availability bias:** *Items that are more readily available in memory are judged as having occurred more frequently.*

The availability bias affects our estimates because memory strength and frequency of occurrence are directly related. Frequently occurring items are remembered more easily than *in*frequently occurring items, so you naturally conclude that items for which you have better memory must also have been more frequent. Unfortunately, better memory in this case was not due to greater *frequency,* but to greater *familiarity.*

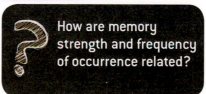

How are memory strength and frequency of occurrence related?

The Conjunction Fallacy

Consider the following description:

Linda is 31 years old, single, outspoken, and very bright. In college, she majored in philosophy. As a student, she was deeply concerned with issues of discrimination and social justice and also participated in antinuclear demonstrations.

Which state of affairs is more probable?
a. Linda is a bank teller.
b. Linda is a bank teller and is active in the feminist movement.

FIGURE 9.8 Availability Bias Looking at this list of names, estimate the number of women's and men's names.

Jennifer Aniston	Robert Kingston
Judy Smith	Gilbert Chapman
Frank Carson	Gwyneth Paltrow
Elizabeth Taylor	Martin Mitchell
Daniel Hunt	Thomas Hughes
Henry Vaughan	Michael Drayton
Agatha Christie	Julia Roberts
Arthur Hutchinson	Hillary Clinton
Jennifer Lopez	Jack Lindsay
Allan Nevins	Richard Gilder
Jane Austen	George Nathan
Joseph Litton	Britney Spears

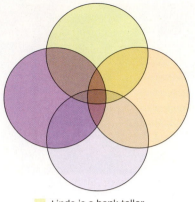

- Linda is a bank teller.
- Linda is a feminist.
- Linda writes poetry.
- Linda has endorsed a fair-housing petition.

FIGURE 9.9 The Conjunction Fallacy
People often think that with each additional bit of information, the probability that all the facts are simultaneously true of a person increases. In fact, the probability decreases dramatically. Notice how the intersection of all these possibilities is much smaller than the area of any one possibility alone.

In one study, 89% of participants rated option **b** as more probable than option **a** (Tversky & Kahneman, 1983).

This is called the **conjunction fallacy,** which is *when people think that two events are more likely to occur together than either individual event.* Actually, the reverse is true: The probability of two or more events occurring simultaneously (in conjunction) is always *less* than the probability of each event occurring alone, as you can see in **FIGURE 9.9.**

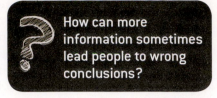
How can more information sometimes lead people to wrong conclusions?

Representativeness Heuristic

Think about the following situation:

A panel of psychologists wrote descriptions of 100 people, including 70 engineers and 30 lawyers. You will be shown a random selection of these descriptions. Read each and decide if it is more likely that the person is an engineer or a lawyer.

1. Jack enjoys reading books on social and political issues. During the interview, he displayed particular skill at argument.

2. Tom is a loner who enjoys working on mathematical puzzles during his spare time. During the interview, his speech remained fairly abstract, and his emotions were well controlled.

3. Harry is a bright man and an avid racquetball player. During the interview, he asked many insightful questions and was very well spoken.

The majority of research participants thought that Jack was more likely to be a lawyer and that Tom was more likely to be an engineer. Harry's description doesn't sound like a lawyer's or an engineer's, so most people said he was *equally likely* to hold either occupation (Kahneman & Tversky, 1973). But remember that the pool of descriptions contains more than twice as many engineers as lawyers, so based on this proportion, it is far *more* likely that Harry is an engineer. People seem to ignore information about *base rate,* or the probability of an event, and instead base their judg-

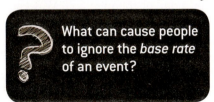
What can cause people to ignore the *base rate* of an event?

ments on similarities to categories. Researchers call this the **representativeness heuristic,** *a mental shortcut that involves making a probability judgment by comparing an object or event to a prototype of the object or event* (Kahneman & Tversky, 1973).

Framing Effects

If people are told that a particular drug has a 70% effectiveness rate, they're usually pretty impressed. Tell them instead that a drug has a 30% failure rate and they typically perceive it as risky and potentially harmful. Notice that the information is the same: A 70% effectiveness rate means that 30% of the time, it's ineffective. The way the information is presented, however, leads to substantially different conclusions (Tversky & Kahneman, 1981). This is called the **framing effect,** which occurs *when people give different answers to the same problem depending on how the problem is phrased (or framed).*

One of the most striking framing effects is the **sunk-cost fallacy,** *a framing effect in which people make decisions about a current situation based on what they have previously invested in the situation.* Imagine waiting in line for 3 hours, paying $100 for a ticket to the Warped Tour to

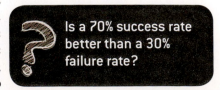
Is a 70% success rate better than a 30% failure rate?

conjunction fallacy When people think that two events are more likely to occur together than either individual event.

representativeness heuristic A mental shortcut that involves making a probability judgment by comparing an object or event to a prototype of the object or event.

framing effects When people give different answers to the same problem depending on how the problem is phrased (or framed).

sunk-cost fallacy A framing effect in which people make decisions about a current situation based on what they have previously invested in the situation.

see your favorite bands, and waking on the day of the outdoor concert to find that it's bitterly cold and rainy. If you go, you'll feel miserable. But you go anyway, reasoning that the $100 you paid for the ticket and the time you spent in line will have been wasted if you stay home.

Notice that you have two choices: (1) Stay comfortably at home or (2) endure many uncomfortable hours in the rain. The $100 is gone in either case: It's a sunk cost. But because you invested time and money, you feel obligated to follow through, even though it's something you no longer want.

Even the National Basketball Association (NBA) is guilty of a sunk-cost fallacy. The most *expensive* players are given more time on court and are kept on the team longer than cheaper players, even if the costly players are not performing up to par (Staw & Hoang, 1995). Coaches act to justify their team's investment in an expensive player rather than recognize the loss. Framing effects can be costly!

Another kind of framing effect occurs when information is presented in terms of losses instead of in terms of savings. For example, imagine you're renting a new apartment, and, as part of a promotion, you're given a choice between a $300 rebate on your first month's rent or spinning a wheel that offers an 80% chance of getting a $400 rebate. Which would you choose? If you're like most people, you'll choose the sure $300 over the risky $400.

But suppose the lease offers you a choice of penalty for damaging the apartment: either $300, or spin a wheel that offers an 80% chance of a $400 fine. Now which would you choose? Most people will choose to gamble by spinning the wheel, taking the chance of avoiding the fine altogether, even though the odds are they'll wind up paying more than the sure $300.

Prospect theory states that *people choose to take on risk when evaluating potential losses and avoid risks when evaluating potential gains* (Tversky & Kahneman, 1992). This asymmetry in risk preferences shows that we are willing to take on risk if we think it will ward off a loss, but we're risk-averse if we expect to lose some benefits.

Worth the cost? Sports teams sometimes try to justify their investment in an expensive player who is underperforming, an example of a sunk-cost effect. Hedo Turkoglu is a highly paid basketball player, but his recent performance has not lived up to his salary.

Culture & Community

Does culture influence optimism bias? In addition to the biases described in this chapter, human decision making often reflects the effects of *optimism bias*: People believe that they are more likely to experience positive events and less likely to experience negative events in the future, compared with other people (Sharot, 2011; Weinstein, 1980). Several studies have found that optimism bias is greater in North Americans than in individuals from Eastern cultures such as Japan (Heine & Lehman, 1995; Klein & Helweg-Larsen, 2002). One recent study examined optimism bias concerning the risk of natural disasters and terrorist attacks in American, Japanese, and Argentinean mental health workers who had received training in responding to such events (Gierlach, Blesher, & Beutler, 2010). Evidence for optimism bias was evident to some degree in all three samples: Participants in each country judged that they were at lower risk of experiencing a disaster than others in their country. However, optimism bias was strongest in the American sample. This bias was most clearly evident in responses across cultures to questions regarding vulnerability to terrorist attacks. Despite America's relatively recent experience with terrorist attacks, Americans judged themselves to be at lower risk of a terrorist attack than did Japanese or Argentineans.

Findings such as these may ultimately be helpful in attempting to understand *why* the optimism bias occurs. Although many possibilities have been suggested (Sharot, 2011), researchers haven't yet come up with a theory that explains all of the relevant evidence. Focusing on cultural similarities and differences in optimism bias may help to achieve that goal, although we shouldn't be unrealistically optimistic that we will achieve it anytime soon!

prospect theory People choose to take on risk when evaluating potential losses and avoid risks when evaluating potential gains.

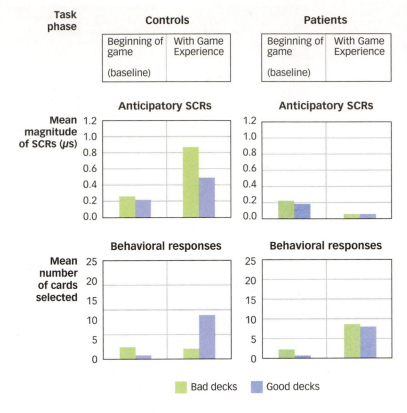

Task phase	Controls		Patients	
	Beginning of game (baseline)	With Game Experience	Beginning of game (baseline)	With Game Experience

FIGURE 9.10 **The Neuroscience of Risky Decision Making** In a study of risky decision making, participants played a game in which they selected a card from one of four decks. Two of the decks were made up of riskier cards, that is, "bad" cards that provided large payoffs or large losses. The other two contained safer cards—those with much smaller payoffs and losses. At the beginning of the game, both healthy controls and people with damage to prefrontal cortex chose cards from the two decks with equal frequency. Over the course of the game, the healthy controls avoided the bad decks and showed large emotional responses (SCRs, or skin conductance responses) when they even considered choosing a card from a risky deck. Participants with prefrontal brain damage, on the other hand, continued to choose cards from the two decks with equal frequency and showed no evidence of emotional learning and eventually went bankrupt. (Data from Bechara et al., 1997.)

Decision Making and the Brain

A man identified as Elliot (whom you met briefly in the Psychology: Evolution of a Science chapter) was a successful businessman, husband, and father prior to developing a brain tumor. After surgery, his intellectual abilities seemed intact, but he was unable to differentiate between important and unimportant activities. He lost his job and got involved in several risky financial ventures that bankrupted him. He had no difficulty discussing what had happened, but his descriptions were so detached and dispassionate that it seemed as though his abstract intellectual functions had become dissociated from his social and emotional abilities.

Research confirms that this interpretation of Elliot's downfall is right on track. In one study, researchers looked at how healthy volunteers differed from people with prefrontal lobe damage on a gambling task that involves risky decision making (Bechara et al., 1994, 1997). Participants were allowed to choose cards one-at-a-time from any of four decks; each card specified an amount of play money won or lost. Unbeknownst to the subjects, two of the decks had mostly cards with large payoffs and large losses (the "risky" decks). The other two decks had mostly cards with small payoffs and small losses (the "safe" decks). Early on, most healthy participants chose from each deck equally, but they gradually shifted to choosing primarily from the safe decks, where potential payoffs were smaller—but so were potential losses. In contrast, patients with prefrontal damage continued to select equally from the risky and safe decks, leading most to eventually go bankrupt in the game. This performance mirrors Elliot's real-life problems. The healthy participants also showed galvanic skin responses (GSR) that jumped dramatically when they were thinking about choosing a card from the risky deck—an anticipatory emotional response (Bechara et al., 1997). The participants with prefrontal damage didn't show these anticipatory feelings when they were thinking about selecting a card from the risky deck. Apparently, their emotional reactions did not guide their thinking, so they continued to make risky decisions, as shown in **FIGURE 9.10**.

Further studies of the participants with prefrontal damage suggest that risky decision making grows out of insensitivity to the future consequences of behavior (Naqvi, Shiv, & Bechara, 2006). Unable to think beyond immediate consequences, they cannot shift their choices in response to a rising rate of losses or a declining rate of rewards (Bechara, Tranel, & Damasio, 2000). Recent neuroimaging studies suggest that the area of prefrontal cortex that is typically damaged in these patients is also activated in healthy people who perform well on the gambling task (Fukui et al., 2005; Lawrence et al., 2009). Together, the neuroimaging and lesion studies show that aspects of risky decision making depend critically on the prefrontal cortex.

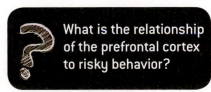

What is the relationship of the prefrontal cortex to risky behavior?

Interestingly, substance-dependent individuals, such as alcoholics, binge drinkers, and cocaine addicts often perform as poorly on the gambling task as do individuals with prefrontal damage (Bechara et al., 2001; Johnson et al., 2008). In one study, people who had been convicted of driving while impaired with alcohol (DWI or driving while intoxicated) were tested on the gambling task; those who performed poorly were much more likely to commit repeated DWI offenses than those who performed well (Bouchard, Brown, & Nadeau, 2012). Related recent work has documented gambling task impairments in binge eaters, another group in which there is an insensitivity to the future consequences of behavior (Danner et al., 2012).

intelligence The ability to direct one's thinking, adapt to one's circumstances, and learn from one's experiences.

SUMMARY QUIZ [9.3]

1. People give different answers to the same problem depending on how the problem is phrased because of
   a. the availability bias.
   b. the conjunction fallacy.
   c. the representativeness heuristic.
   d. framing effects.

2. The view that people choose to take on risk when evaluating potential losses and avoid risks when evaluating potential gains describes
   a. the conjunction fallacy.
   b. the frequency format hypothesis.
   c. prospect theory.
   d. the sunk-cost fallacy.

3. People with damage to the prefrontal cortex are prone to
   a. heightened anticipatory emotional reactions.
   b. risky decision making.
   c. galvanic skin response.
   d. extreme sensitivity to behavioral consequences.

Intelligence

Remember Christopher, the boy who could learn languages but not tic-tac-toe? Would you call him intelligent? It seems odd to say that someone is intelligent when he can't master a child's game, but it seems equally odd to say that someone is unintelligent when he can master 16 languages. In a world of Albert Einsteins and Homer Simpsons, we'd have no trouble distinguishing the geniuses from the dullards. But ours is a world of people like Christopher and people like us—people who are sometimes brilliant, often bright, usually competent, and occasionally dimmer than broccoli. Psychologists generally define **intelligence** as *the ability to direct one's thinking, adapt to one's circumstances, and learn from one's experiences* (Gottfredson, 1997), and as you will see, that definition captures much of what scientists and laypeople mean by that term.

When immigrants arrived at Ellis Island in the 1920s, they were given intelligence tests, which supposedly revealed whether they were "feebleminded."

©Bettmann/Corbis

The Intelligence Quotient

Few things are more dangerous than a man with a mission. In the 1920s, psychologist Henry Goddard administered intelligence tests to arriving immigrants at Ellis Island and concluded that the overwhelming majority of Jews, Hungarians, Italians, and Russians were "feebleminded." Goddard also used his tests to identify feebleminded American families (whom, he claimed, were largely responsible for the nation's social problems) and suggested that the

ratio IQ A statistic obtained by dividing a person's mental age by the person's physical age and then multiplying the quotient by 100 (see *deviation IQ*).

deviation IQ A statistic obtained by dividing a person's test score by the average test score of people in the same age group and then multiplying the quotient by 100 (see *ratio IQ*).

Alfred Binet (1857–1911; *left*) and Theodore Simon (1872–1961; *right*) developed the first intelligence test to identify children who needed remedial education.

In 2012, 4-year old Heidi Hankins became one of the youngest people ever admitted to Mensa, an organization for people with unusually high IQs. Heidi's IQ is 159—about the same as Albert Einstein's.

government should segregate them in isolated colonies and "take away from these people the power of procreation" (Goddard, 1913, p. 107). The United States subsequently passed laws restricting the immigration of people from southern and eastern Europe, and 27 states passed laws requiring the sterilization of "mental defectives."

From Goddard's day to our own, intelligence tests have been used to rationalize prejudice and discrimination against people of different races, religions, and nationalities. This is especially ironic because such tests were originally developed for the most noble of purposes: to help underprivileged children succeed in school. At the end of the 19th century, France instituted a sweeping set of education reforms that made a primary school education available to children of every social class, and suddenly French classrooms were filled with a diverse mix of children who differed dramatically in their readiness to learn. The French government called on Alfred Binet and Theodore Simon to create a test that would allow educators to develop remedial programs for those children who lagged behind their peers (Siegler, 1992). "Before these children could be educated," Binet (1909) wrote, "they had to be selected. How could this be done?"

Binet and Simon set out to develop an objective test that would provide an unbiased measure of a child's ability. They began, sensibly enough, by looking for tasks that the best students in a class could perform and that the worst students could not—in other words, tasks that could distinguish the best and worst students and thus predict a future child's success in school. The tasks they tried included solving logic problems, remembering words, copying pictures, distinguishing edible and inedible foods, making rhymes, and answering questions such as, "When anyone has offended you and asks you to excuse him, what ought you to do?" Binet and Simon settled on 30 of these tasks and assembled them into a test that they claimed could measure a child's "natural intelligence," meaning the *aptitude* for learning independent of the child's prior educational *achievement*. They suggested that teachers could use their test to estimate a particular child's "mental level" simply by computing the average test score of many children in different age groups and then finding the age group whose average test score was most like that of the particular child's. For example, a child who was 10 years old but whose score was about the same as the score of the average 8-year-old was considered to have the mental level of an 8-year-old and thus to need remedial education.

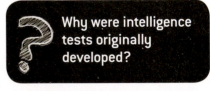

Why were intelligence tests originally developed?

This simple idea became the basis for what is now known as the *intelligence quotient* or *IQ score*. There are two ways to compute an IQ score. One is the **ratio IQ,** which is *a statistic obtained by dividing a person's mental age by the person's physical age and then multiplying the quotient by 100*. According to this formula, a 10-year-old child whose test score was about the same as the average 10-year-old child's test score would have a ratio IQ of 100 because $(10/10) \times 100 = 100$. But a 10-year-old child whose test score was about the same as the average 8-year-old child's test score would have a ratio IQ of 80 because $(8/10) \times 100 = 80$. Ratio IQ is a fine measure for children, but it doesn't work so well for adults. After all, there's nothing wrong with a 60-year-old who has the mental level of a 30-year-old, is there? That's why adult intelligence is usually measured using the **deviation IQ,** which is *a statistic obtained by dividing a person's test score by the average test score of people in the same age* *group and then multiplying the quotient by 100.* According to this formula, a person who scored the same as the average person his or her age would have a deviation IQ of 100.

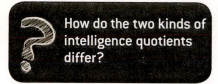

How do the two kinds of intelligence quotients differ?

The Intelligence Test

The most widely used modern intelligence test is the *Wechsler Adult Intelligence Scale* (WAIS), named after its originator, psychologist David Wechsler. Like Binet and Simon's original test, it measures intelligence by asking respondents to solve problems, to articulate the meaning of words, to recall general knowledge, to explain practical actions in everyday life, and so forth. Some sample problems from the WAIS are shown in **TABLE 9.2**. Decades of research show that a person's performance on tests like the WAIS predict a wide variety of important life outcomes, including

Intelligence is highly correlated with income. Ken Jennings won over three million dollars and was defeated just twice on *Jeopardy*: in 2004 by Nancy Zerg, and in 2011 by an IBM computer named Watson. In response to being beaten by a machine, Jennings graciously said, "I for one welcome our new computer overlords".

Table 9.2 The Tests and Core Subtests of the Wechsler Adult Intelligence Scale IV

WAIS-IV Test	Core Subtest	Questions and Tasks
Verbal Comprehension Test	Vocabulary	The test taker is asked to tell the examiner what certain words mean. For example: chair (easy), hesitant (medium), and presumptuous (hard).
	Similarities	The test taker is asked what 19 pairs of words have in common. For example: In what way are an apple and a pear alike? In what way are a painting and a symphony alike?
	Information	The test taker is asked several general knowledge questions. These cover people, places, and events. For example: How many days are in a week? What is the capital of France? Name three oceans. Who wrote The Inferno?
Perceptual Reasoning Test	Block Design	The test taker is shown 2-D patterns made up of red and white squares and triangles and is asked to reproduce these patterns using cubes with red and white faces.
	Matrix Reasoning	The test taker is asked to add a missing element to a pattern so that it progresses logically. For example: Which of the four symbols at the bottom goes in the empty cell of the table?
	Visual Puzzles	The test taker is asked to complete visual puzzles like this one: "Which three of these pictures go together to make this puzzle?"
Working Memory Test	Digit Span	The test taker is asked to repeat a sequence of numbers. Sequences run from two to nine numbers in length. In the second part of this test, the sequences must be repeated in reversed order. An easy example is to repeat 3-7-4. A harder one is 3-9-1-7-4-5-3-9.
	Arithmetic	The test taker is asked to solve arithmetic problems, progressing from easy to difficult ones.
Processing Speed Test	Symbol Search	The test taker is asked to indicate whether one of a pair of abstract symbols is contained in a list of abstract symbols. There are many of these lists, and the test taker does as many as he or she can in 2 minutes.
	Coding	The test taker is asked to write down the number that corresponds to a code for a given symbol (e.g., a cross, a circle, and an upside-down T) and does as many as he or she can in 90 seconds.

The Real World

Look Smart

Your interview is in 30 minutes. You've checked your hair twice, eaten your weight in breath mints, combed your résumé for typos, and rehearsed your answers to all the standard questions. Now you have to dazzle the interviewer with your intelligence whether you've got it or not. Because intelligence is one of the most valued of all human traits, we are often in the business of trying to make others think we're smart regardless of whether that's true. So we make clever jokes and drop the names of some of the longer books we've read in the hope that prospective employers, prospective dates, prospective customers, and prospective in-laws will be appropriately impressed.

But are we doing the right things, and if so, are we getting the credit we deserve? Research shows that ordinary people are, in fact, reasonably good judges of other people's intelligence (Borkenau & Liebler, 1995). For example, observers can look at a pair of photographs and reliably determine which of the two people in them is smarter (Zebrowitz et al., 2002). When observers watch 1-minute videotapes of different people engaged in social interactions, they can accurately estimate which person has the highest IQ—even if they see the videos without sound (Murphy, Hall, & Colvin, 2003).

People base their judgments of intelligence on a wide range of cues, from physical features (being tall and attractive) to dress (being well groomed and wearing glasses) to behavior (walking and talking quickly). And yet, none of these cues is actually a reliable indicator of a person's intelligence. The reason why people are such good judges of intelligence is that in addition to all these useless cues, they also take into account one very useful cue: eye gaze. As it turns out, intelligent people hold the gaze of their conversation partners both when they are speaking and when they are listening, and observers know this, which is what enables them to estimate a person's intelligence accurately, despite their mythical beliefs about the informational value of spectacles and neckties (Murphy et al., 2003). All of this is especially true when the observers are women (who tend to be better judges of intelligence) and the people being observed are men (whose intelligence tends to be easier to judge).

The bottom line? Breath mints are fine and a little gel on the cowlick certainly can't hurt, but when you get to the interview, don't forget to stare.

Wahad Mehood is interviewing for a job as a petroleum engineer with EPC Global. Studies show that when a job candidate holds an interviewer's gaze, the interviewer is more likely to consider the candidate to be intelligent. And the interviewer is right!

---

health, educational level, and income (Deary, Batty, & Gale, 2008; Deary et al., 2008; Der, Batty, & Deary, 2009; Gottfredson & Deary, 2004; Leon et al., 2009; Richards et al., 2009; Rushton & Templer, 2009; Whalley & Deary, 2001). One study compared siblings who had significantly different IQs and found that the less intelligent sibling earned roughly half of what the more intelligent sibling earned over the course of their lifetimes (Murray, 2002; see **FIGURE 9.11**). Perhaps that's because intelligent people perform better at their jobs (Hunter & Hunter, 1984; see the Real World box).

FIGURE 9.11 Income and Intelligence among Siblings This graph shows the average annual salary of a person who has an IQ of 90–109 (shown in pink) and of his or her siblings who have higher or lower IQs (shown in blue). (Data from Murray, 2002.)

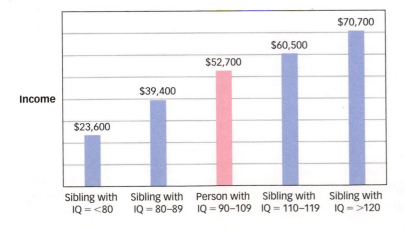

A Hierarchy of Abilities

During the 1990s, Michael Jordan won the National Basketball Association's Most Valuable Player award five times, led the Chicago Bulls to six league championships, and had the highest regular season scoring average in the history of the game. ESPN named him the greatest athlete of the century. So when Jordan quit professional basketball in 1993 to join professional baseball, he was as surprised as anyone else to find that he … well, sucked. One of his teammates lamented that Jordan "couldn't hit a curveball with an ironing board," and a major-league manager called him "a disgrace to the game" (Wulf, 1994).

Michael Jordan's brilliance on the basketball court and his mediocrity on the baseball field proved beyond all doubt that these two sports require different abilities that are not necessarily possessed by the same individual. But if basketball and baseball require different abilities, then what does it mean to say that someone is the greatest athlete of the century? Is *athleticism* a meaningless word? The science of intelligence has grappled with a similar question for more than a century. As we have seen, intelligence test scores predict important outcomes—from academic success to health. But is that because they measure a real ability that allows people to do well at everything?

To investigate this question, Charles Spearman (a student of Wilhelm Wundt, whom you met in the Psychology: Evolution of a Science chapter), measured how well school-age children could discriminate small differences in color, auditory pitch, and weight, and he then correlated these scores with the children's grades in different academic subjects (Spearman, 1904). Spearman's research revealed that these measures were positively correlated: that is, children who scored well on one measure (e.g., distinguishing the musical note C# from D) tended to score well on the other measures (e.g., solving algebraic equations). But, although these different measures were positively correlated, they were not *perfectly* correlated: that is, the child who had the best score on one measure didn't necessarily have the best score on *every* measure. Spearman combined these two facts into a **two-factor theory of intelligence,** which suggested that *every task requires a combination of a general ability (which he called* g) *and skills that are specific to the task (which he called* s).

As sensible as Spearman's conclusions were, not everyone agreed with them. Louis Thurstone (1938) noticed that although childrens' scores on different tests were indeed positively correlated with one another, scores on one kind of verbal test were more highly correlated with scores on another verbal test than they were with scores on other kinds of tests. Thurstone took this "clustering of correlations" to mean that there was actually no such thing as g and that there were, instead, a few stable and independent mental abilities such as perceptual ability, verbal ability, and numerical ability, which he called the *primary mental abilities*. In essence, Thurstone argued that just as we have games called *baseball* and *basketball* but no game called *athletics,* so we have abilities such as verbal ability and perceptual ability but no general ability called intelligence. **TABLE 9.3** shows the primary mental abilities that Thurstone identified.

The debate among Spearman, Thurstone, and other intelligence researchers raged for half a century as psychologists argued about the existence of g. But in the 1980s, new mathematical techniques brought the debate to a quiet close by revealing that Spearman and Thurstone had each been right in his own way. We now know that most intelligence test data are best described by a three-level hierarchy (see **FIGURE 9.12**). At the top is a *general factor* (like Spearman's g) called intelligence, which is made up of a small set of middle-level factors (like Thurstone's *primary mental abilities*), which in turn are made up of a large set of specific abilities that are unique to particular tasks (like Spearman's s). Although this resolution to 100 years of disagreement is not particularly thrilling, it appears to have the compensatory benefit of being true.

> **?** How was the debate between Spearman and Thurstone resolved?

So what are these middle level abilities, and how many are there? Psychologist John Carroll (1993) analyzed intelligence test scores from nearly 500 studies conducted over a half century, and he concluded that there are eight independent middle-level abilities: *memory and learning, visual perception, auditory perception, retrieval ability,*

Michael Jordan was an extraordinary basketball player and a mediocre baseball player. So was he or wasn't he a great athlete?

Dr. Jennifer Richeson received a so-called genius award from the MacArthur Foundation for her research in social psychology. Spearman's notion of general ability suggests that because she's *really* good at science, then she's probably at least *pretty* good at many other things, such as dancing. And, in fact, she is!

two-factor theory of intelligence Spearman's theory suggesting that every task requires a combination of a general ability (which he called *g*) and skills that are specific to the task (which he called *s*).

fluid intelligence The ability to see abstract relationships and draw logical inferences.

crystallized intelligence The ability to retain and use knowledge that was acquired through experience.

Table 9.3 Thurstone's Primary Mental Abilities

Primary Mental Ability	Description
Verbal Word Fluency	Ability to solve anagrams and to find rhymes, etc.
Verbal Comprehension	Ability to understand words and sentences
Numerical Ability	Ability to make mental and other numerical computations
Spatial Visualization	Ability to visualize a complex shape in various orientations
Associative Memory	Ability to recall verbal material, learn pairs of unrelated words, etc.
Perceptual Speed	Ability to detect visual details quickly
Reasoning	Ability to induce a general rule from a few instances

FIGURE 9.12 A Three-Level Hierarchy
Most intelligence test data are best described by a three-level hierarchy with general intelligence (*g*) at the top, specific abilities (*s*) at the bottom, and a small number of middle-level abilities (*m*) in the middle.

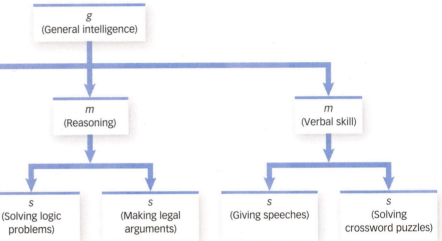

FIGURE 9.13 Raven's Progressive Matrices Test This item from Raven's Progressive Matrices Test measures fluid intelligence and is unlikely to be culturally biased.

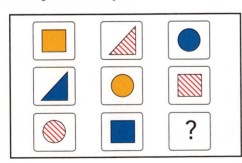

Which of these shapes correctly completes the above pattern?

cognitive speediness, processing speed, crystallized intelligence, and *fluid intelligence.* Although most of the abilities on this list are self-explanatory, the last two are not. **Fluid intelligence** is *the ability to see abstract relationships and draw logical inferences;* **crystallized intelligence** is *the ability to retain and use knowledge that was acquired through experience* (Horn & Cattell, 1966). Whereas crystallized intelligence is generally assessed by tests of vocabulary, factual information, and so on, fluid intelligence is generally assessed by tests that pose novel, abstract problems that must be solved under time pressure, such as Raven's Progressive Matrices Test (shown in **FIGURE 9.13**).

So was that the end of the debate? Not exactly, because some psychologists have argued that there are kinds of intelligence that traditional tests simply do not measure. For example, Robert Sternberg (1999) distinguishes between *analytic intelligence* (which is the ability to identify and define problems and to find strategies for solving them), *practical intelligence* (which is the ability to apply and implement these solutions in everyday settings), and *creative intelligence* (which is the ability to generate solutions that other people do not). According to Sternberg, standard intelligence tests measure analytic intelligence by giving people clearly defined problems that have one right answer. But everyday life confronts people with situations in which they must formulate the *problem,* find the information needed to solve it, and then choose among multiple acceptable solutions. These situations require practical and creative intelligence.

Another kind of intelligence that standard tests don't measure is **emotional intelligence,** which is *the ability to reason about emotions and to use emotions to enhance reasoning* (Mayer, Roberts, & Barsade, 2008; Salovey & Grewal, 2005). Emotionally intelligent people know what kinds of emotions a particular event will trigger; they can identify, describe, and manage their emotions; and they can identify other people's emotions from facial expressions and tones of voice. Emotionally intelligent people have better social skills and more friends (Eisenberg et al., 2000; Mestre et al., 2006; Schultz, Izard, & Bear, 2004), they are judged to be more competent in their interactions (Brackett et al., 2006), and they have better romantic relationships (Brackett, Warner, & Bosco, 2005). Given all this, it isn't surprising that emotionally intelligent people tend to be happier (Brackett & Mayer, 2003; Brackett et al., 2006) and more satisfied with their lives (Ciarrochi, Chan, & Caputi, 2000; Mayer, Caruso, & Salovey, 1999).

> **? What skills are particularly strong in emotionally intelligent people?**

Not only are there different kinds of intelligence, but the concept itself seems to differ across cultures. For instance, Westerners regard people as intelligent when they speak quickly and often, but Africans regard people as intelligent when they are deliberate and quiet (Irvine, 1978). The Confucian tradition emphasizes the ability to behave properly, the Taoist tradition emphasizes humility and self-knowledge, and the Buddhist tradition emphasizes determination and mental effort (Yang & Sternberg, 1997). Unlike Western societies, many African and Asian societies conceive of intelligence as including social responsibility and cooperativeness (Azuma & Kashiwagi, 1987; Serpell, 1974; White & Kirkpatrick, 1985), which is why the Mashona word for *intelligence, ngware,* means "to be wise in one's relationships." Definitions of intelligence may even differ within a culture: Californians of Latino ancestry are more likely to equate intelligence with social competence, whereas Californians of Asian ancestry are more likely to equate it with cognitive skill (Okagaki & Sternberg, 1993). Some researchers take all this to mean that different cultures have radically different conceptualizations of intelligence, but others are convinced that apparent differences in the conceptualization of intelligence are really just differences in ways of talking about it. They argue that every culture values the ability to solve important problems and that what really distinguishes cultures is the *kinds* of problems that are considered to be important.

> **? How does the concept of intelligence differ across cultures?**

"I don't have to be smart, because someday I'll just hire lots of smart people to work for me."

David Sipress/ The New Yorker Collection/cartoonbank.com

1.		

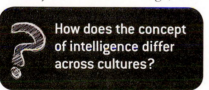

Courtesy of Daniel Gilbert

Emotion	Select one:
a. Happy	○
b. Angry	○
c. Fearful	○
d. Sad	○

2.

Scott felt worried when he thought about all the work he needed to do. He believed he could handle it—if only he had the time. When his supervisor brought him an additional project, he felt ____. (Select the best choice.)

Emotion	Select one:
a. Frustrated and anxious	○
b. Content and calm	○
c. Ashamed and accepting	○
d. Sad and guilty	○

Two items from a test of emotional intelligence. Item 1 measures the accuracy with which a person can read emotional expressions (*left*). Item 2 measures the ability to predict emotional responses to external events (*right*). The correct answer to both questions is A.

AP Photo/Francois Mori

Africans tend to think of intelligent people as deliberate and quiet. Nigerian poet Wole Soyinka spent nearly 2 years in solitary confinement for his radical writing, and a decade later was awarded the Nobel Prize in Literature. *Thought is hallowed in the lean oil of solitude,* he wrote.

emotional intelligence The ability to reason about emotions and to use emotions to enhance reasoning.

SUMMARY QUIZ [9.4]

1. Which of the following abilities is not an accepted feature of intelligence?
   a. the ability to direct one's thinking
   b. the ability to adapt to one's circumstances
   c. the ability to care for oneself
   d. the ability to learn from one's experiences

2. Intelligence tests
   a. were first developed to help children who lagged behind their peers.
   b. were developed to measure aptitude rather than educational achievement.
   c. have been used for detestable ends.
   d. all of the above

3. People who score well on one test of mental ability usually score well on others, suggesting that
   a. tests of mental ability are perfectly correlated.
   b. intelligence cannot be measured meaningfully.
   c. there is a general ability called intelligence.
   d. intelligence is genetic.

4. The two-factor theory suggests that intelligence is a combination of general ability and
   a. factor analysis.
   b. specific abilities.
   c. primary mental abilities.
   d. creative intelligence.

5. Most scientists now believe that intelligence is best described
   a. as a set of group factors.
   b. by a two-factor framework.
   c. as a single, general ability.
   d. by a three-level hierarchy.

fraternal twins (or dizygotic twins) Twins who develop from two different eggs that were fertilized by two different sperm (see *identical twins*).

identical twins (or monozygotic twins) Twins who develop from the splitting of a single egg that was fertilized by a single sperm (see *fraternal twins*).

shared environment Those environmental factors that are experienced by all relevant members of a household (see *nonshared environment*).

nonshared environment Those environmental factors that are not experienced by all relevant members of a household (see *shared environment*).

Where Does Intelligence Come From?

No one is born knowing calculus, and no one has to be taught how to yawn. Some things are learned, others are not. But almost all of the really *interesting* things about people are a joint product of the innate characteristics with which their genes have endowed them and of the experiences they have in the world. Intelligence is one of those really interesting things that is influenced both by nature and by nurture. Let's start by examining nature's influence.

Genetic Influences on Intelligence

The fact that intelligence appears to "run in families" isn't very good evidence of nature's influence. After all, brothers and sisters share genes, but they share many other things as well. They typically grow up in the same house, go to the same schools, read many of the same books, and have many of the same friends. Members of a family may have similar levels of intelligence because they share genes, environments, or both. To separate the influence of genes and environments, we need to examine the intelligence test scores of people who share genes but not environments (e.g., biological siblings who are separated at birth and raised by different families), people who share environments but not genes (e.g., adopted siblings who are raised together), and people who share both (e.g., biological siblings who are raised together).

To do this, it helps to understand that there are several kinds of siblings with different degrees of genetic relatedness. When siblings have the same biological parents but different birthdays, they share on average 50% of their genes. Twins have the same parents and the same birthdays, but there are two kinds of twins. **Fraternal twins** (or **dizygotic twins**) *develop from two different eggs that were fertilized by two different sperm*, and although they happen to have the same parents and birthdays, they are merely siblings who shared a womb, so like any siblings, they share on average 50% of their genes. **Identical twins** (or **monozygotic twins**) are special because they *develop from the splitting of a single egg that was fertilized by a single sperm*, so unlike any other siblings, they are genetic duplicates of each other who share 100% of their genes.

These different degrees of genetic relatedness allow psychologists to assess the influence that genes have on intelligence. Studies show that the IQs of identical twins are very strongly correlated when the twins are raised in the same household,

Small genetic differences can make a big difference. A single gene on chromosome 15 determines whether a dog will be too small for your pocket or too large for your garage.

Why are the intelligence test scores of relatives so similar?

but they are also strongly correlated when the twins are separated at birth and raised in different households. In fact, identical twins who are raised apart have more similar IQs than do fraternal twins who are raised together. What this means is that people who share all their genes have similar IQs regardless of whether they share their environments. By comparison, the intelligence test scores of unrelated people raised in the same household (e.g., two siblings, one or both of whom were adopted) are correlated only modestly (Bouchard & McGue, 2003). These patterns suggest that genes play an important role in determining intelligence and this shouldn't surprise us. Intelligence is, in part, a function of how the brain works, and given that brains are designed by genes, it would be quite remarkable if genes *didn't* play some role in determining a person's intelligence.

And yet, when identical twins who have identical genes are raised in the identical household, their IQ scores still differ. How come? The **shared environment** refers to *those environmental factors that are experienced by all relevant members of a household.* For example, siblings raised in the same household have about the same level of affluence, the same number and type of books, the same diet, and so on. The **nonshared environment** refers to *those environmental factors that are not experienced by all relevant members of a household.* Siblings raised in the same household may have different friends and teachers and may contract different illnesses. This may be why the correlation between the IQ scores of siblings is greater when they are close in age (Sundet, Eriksen, & Tambs, 2008).

Tamara Rabi and Adriana Scott were 20 years old when they met in a McDonald's parking lot in New York. "I'm just standing there looking at her," Adriana recalled. "It was a shock. I saw me" (Gootman, 2003). The two soon discovered that they were twins who had been separated at birth and adopted by different families.

First-born children tend to be more intelligent than their later-born siblings. But when a first-born child dies in infancy and the second-born child becomes the oldest child in the family, that second-born child ends up being just as intelligent as the average first-born child (Kristensen & Bjerkedal, 2007). This suggests that first-borns are smarter than their siblings because they experience a different family environment. So if Joe and Nick murdered Paul . . . um, never mind.

Like the Koreans, the Dutch have become much taller in the last century. The Dutch government recently passed a law requiring the doors of new buildings to be 7'6" tall, but that won't help this Dutchman, Pieter Gijselaar, because he's 7'9".

AP Photo/Peter Dejong

Environmental Influences on Intelligence

Americans believe that every individual should have an equal chance to succeed in life, and one of the reasons why some of us bristle when we first learn about genetic influences on intelligence is that we mistakenly believe that our genes are our destinies (Pinker, 2003). In fact, traits that are strongly influenced by genes may also be strongly influenced by the environment. Height is strongly influenced by genes, which is why tall parents tend to have tall children; and yet, the average height of Korean boys has increased by more than 7 inches in the last 50 years simply because of changes in nutrition (Nisbett, 2009). Genes may explain why two people who have the same diet differ in height—that is, why Chang-sun is taller than his brother Kwan-ho—but they do not dictate how tall either of these boys will actually grow up to be.

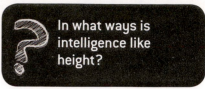

In what ways is intelligence like height?

Intelligence is definitely not something that is completely fixed and determined at birth. In fact, as **FIGURE 9.14** shows, intelligence changes over a person's lifespan (Owens, 1966; Schaie, 1996, 2005; Schwartzman, Gold, & Andres, 1987). For most people, intelligence increases between adolescence and middle age and then declines in old age (Kaufman, 2001; Salthouse, 1996a, 2000; Schaie, 2005), maybe due to a general slowing of the brain's processing speed (Salthouse, 1996b; Zimprich & Martin, 2002).

Not only does intelligence change over the life span, but it also changes over generations. The *Flynn effect* refers to the accidental discovery by James Flynn that the average IQ score is 30 points higher today than it was about a century ago (Dickens & Flynn, 2001; Flynn, 2012; cf. Lynn, 2013). In other words, the average person today is smarter than 95% of the people who were living in 1900! Why is each generation scoring higher than the

FIGURE 9.14 Absolute Intelligence Changes Over Time Data from Kaufman, 2001

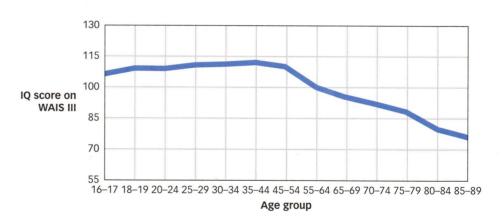

105-year-old Khatijah (front row, second from right) sits with five generations of her family. The Flynn Effect refers to the finding that intelligence is increasing across generations.

AP Photo/Binsar Bakkara

one before it? Some researchers give the credit to improved nutrition, schooling, and parenting (Lynn, 2009; Neisser, 1998), and some suggest that the least intelligent people are being left out of the mating game (Mingroni, 2007). But most (and that includes Flynn himself) believe that the industrial and technological revolutions have changed the nature of daily living such that people now spend more and more time solving precisely the kinds of abstract problems that intelligence tests include—and as we all know, practice makes perfect (Flynn, 2012). You are likely to score higher on an IQ test than your grandparents did in part because your daily life is more like an IQ test than theirs was!

But if intelligence changes over the lifespan, then why is a strong correlation between an individual's performance on intelligence tests that are taken at two different times (Deary, 2000; Deary et al., 2004; Deary, Batty, & Gale, 2008; Deary, Batty, Pattie, & Gale, 2008)? Well, consider two things you know about height: First, people get taller as they go from childhood to adulthood, and second, the tallest child in kindergarten is likely to be among the tallest adults in college. Height changes over the lifespan, but there is still a strong correlation between a person's height in childhood and their height in adulthood. Intelligence is just like that. Although a person's intelligence changes over their lifespan, the smartest youngsters tend to be the smartest oldsters.

The fact that intelligence changes over the life span and across generations suggests that our genes may determine the *range* in which our IQ is likely to fall, but our experiences determine the exact *point* in that range at which it does fall (Hunt, 2011; see **FIGURE 9.15**). Two of the most powerful experiential factors are economics and education.

Economics

Maybe money can't buy love, but it sure appears to buy intelligence. One of the best predictors of a person's intelligence is the material wealth of the family in which he or she was raised—what scientists call *socioeconomic status* (SES). Studies suggest that being raised in a high-SES family rather than a low-SES family is worth between 12 and 18 IQ points (Nisbett, 2009; van Ijzendoorn, Juffer, & Klein Poelhuis, 2005).

Exactly how does SES influence intelligence? One way is by influencing the brain itself. Low-SES children have poorer nutrition and medical care, they experience greater daily stress, and they are more likely to be exposed to environmental toxins such as air pollution and lead—all of which can impair brain development (Chen, Cohen, & Miller, 2010; Evans, 2004; Hackman & Farah, 2008).

SES also affects the environment in which the brain lives and learns. Intellectual stimulation increases intelligence (Nelson et al., 2007), and research shows that high-SES parents are more likely to provide it (Nisbett, 2009). For instance, high-SES parents are more likely to read to their children and to connect what they are reading to the outside world ("Billy has a rubber ducky. Who do you know who has a rubber ducky?"; Heath, 1983; Lareau, 2003). When high-SES parents talk to their children, they tend to ask stimulating questions ("Do you think a ducky likes to eat grass?"), whereas low-SES parents tend to give instructions ("Please put your ducky away"; Hart & Risley, 1995). By the age of 3, the average high-SES child has heard 30 million different words, while the average low-SES child has heard only 10 million different words, and as a result, the high-SES child knows 50% more words than his or her low-SES counterpart. Clearly, poverty is the enemy of intelligence (Evans & Kim, 2012).

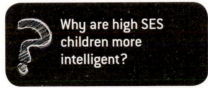

? Why are high SES children more intelligent?

Education

Alfred Binet believed that poverty was intelligence's enemy, and education was its friend. He was right on both counts. The correlation between the amount of formal education a person receives and his or her intelligence is quite large (Ceci, 1991; Neisser et al., 1996). One reason is that smart people tend to stay in school, but the other reason is that school makes people smarter (Ceci & Williams, 1997). When schooling is delayed because of war, political strife, or the simple lack of qualified teachers, children show a measurable decline in intelligence (Nisbett, 2009).

Does this mean that anyone can become a genius just by showing up for class? Unfortunately not. Although education reliably increases intelligence, its impact is small, and some studies suggest that it tends to enhance test-taking ability more than general cognitive ability and that

Josh

95   100   105

Jason

FIGURE 9.15 Genes and Environment
Genes may establish the range in which a person's intelligence *may* fall, but environment determines the point in that range at which the person's intelligence *will* fall. Although Jason's genes give him a better chance to be smart than Josh's genes do, differences in their educations or upbringings could easily cause Josh to have a higher IQ than Jason.

Education increases intelligence. But not everyone is in favor of that. In Afghanistan, for example, the Taliban attack young girls with acid, guns, and poison to keep them from attending school.

Dumb and Dumber?

For most of human history, the smartest people had the most children, and our species reaped the benefits. But in the middle of the 19th century, this effect began to reverse, and the smartest people began having fewer children, a trend that scientists call *dysgenic fertility*. That trend continues today.

But wait. If the smartest people are having the fewest children, and if IQ is largely heritable, then why—as James Flynn showed—is IQ rising over generations?

Some researchers suspect that two things are happening at once: Our inherited intelligence is going down over generations, but our acquired intelligence is going up! In other words, we were all born with a *slightly* less capable brain than our parents had, but this small effect is masked because we were born into a world that *greatly* boosted our intelligence with everything from nutrition to video games! How can we tell whether this hypothesis is right?

Francis Galton was the first to suggest that reaction time (the speed with which a person can respond to a stimulus) is a basic indicator of mental ability, and his suggestion has been confirmed by modern research (Deary, Der, & Ford, 2001). Recently, a group of researchers (Woodley, te Nijenhuis, & Murphy, 2013) went back and analyzed all available data on human reaction time collected between 1884 and 2004 (including data collected by Galton himself), and what they found was striking: The average reaction time has gotten slower since the Victorian era! The figure below shows the average reaction time of people in different studies conducted in different years.

Does this mean that we are innately less clever and that this fact is being obscured by the big IQ boost we get from our environments? Maybe, but maybe not. There are problems with using old data that were collected under unknown circumstances, and the participants in older studies were probably not representative of the entire population. Nonetheless, the finding is provocative because it suggests that modern life may be an even more powerful cognitive enhancer than we realize.

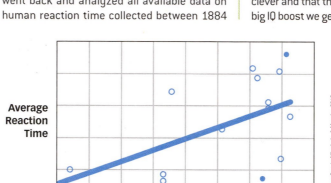

Average Reaction Time

Year — 1888, 1920, 1952, 1984, 2016

Data from Woodley, te Nijenhuis, & Murphy, 2013.

DATA VISUALIZATION

Nature vs. Nurture and the Correlates of Intelligence
www.macmillanhighered.com/schacterbrief3e

its effects vanish within a few years (Perkins & Grotzer, 1997). That might mean that education just can't change intelligence all that much, or it might mean that education is potentially very powerful but that modern schools aren't very good at providing it. Researchers lean toward the latter conclusion. Although most experiments in education—from magnet schools and charter schools to voucher systems and Head Start programs—have failed to produce substantial intellectual gains for students, a few have been quite successful (Nisbett, 2009), which shows that education *can* substantially increase intelligence even if it doesn't *usually* do so. No one knows just how big the impact of an optimal education could be, but it seems clear that our current educational system is less than optimal.

SUMMARY QUIZ [9.5]

1. Intelligence is influenced by
   a. genes alone.
   b. genes and environment.
   c. environment alone.
   d. neither genes nor environment.

2. Intelligence changes
   a. over the life span and across generations.
   b. over the life span but not across generations.

c. across generations but not over the life span.

d. neither across generations nor over the life span.

3. A person's socioeconomic status has a(n) _____ effect on intelligence.

a. powerful

b. negligible

c. unsubstantiated

d. unknown

Who Is Most Intelligent?

If everyone in the world were equally intelligent, we probably wouldn't even have a word for it. What makes intelligence such an interesting and important topic is that some individuals—and some groups of individuals—have more of it than others.

Individual Differences in Intelligence

The average IQ is 100, and the vast majority of us—about 70% in fact—have IQs between 85 and 115 (see **FIGURE 9.16**). The people who score well above this large middle range are said to be *intellectually gifted*, and the people who score well below it are said to be *intellectually disabled*. The people who live at opposite ends of this continuum have one thing in common: They are more likely to be male than female. Although males and females have the same average IQ, the distribution of males' IQ scores is more variable than the distribution of females' IQ scores, which means that there are more males than females at both the very top and the very bottom of the IQ range (Hedges & Nowell, 1995; Lakin, 2013; Wai, Putallaz, & Makel, 2012). Some of this difference is surely due to the different ways in which boys and girls are socialized. Whether some of this difference is also due to innate biological differences between males and females remains a hotly debated issue in psychology (Ceci, Williams, & Barnett, 2009; Nisbett et al., 2012; Spelke, 2005).

Those of us who occupy the large middle of the intelligence spectrum often embrace a number of myths about those who live at the extremes. For example, movies typically portray the "tortured genius" as a person (usually a male person) who is brilliant, creative, misunderstood, despondent, and more than a little weird. But for the most part, Hollywood has the relationship between intelligence and mental illness backwards: People with very high intelligence are *less* prone to mental illness than are people with very low intelligence (Dekker & Koot, 2003; Didden et al., 2012; Walker et al., 2002) and very high IQ children are about as well-adjusted as their peers (Garland & Zigler, 1999; Neihart, 1999). Another myth about geniuses is that they are brilliant at everything. In fact, gifted children are rarely gifted in all departments but instead have gifts in a single domain such as math, language, or music. More than 95% of gifted children show a sharp disparity between their mathematical

The artist Vincent van Gogh was the iconic "tortured genius." But data suggest that it is low intelligence and not high intelligence that is most strongly associated with mental illness.

Lee Foster/Alamy

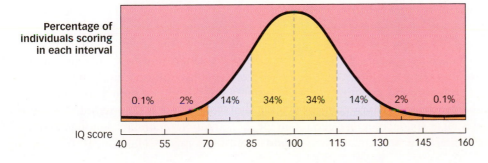

Percentage of individuals scoring in each interval

0.1% 2% 14% 34% 34% 14% 2% 0.1%

IQ score
40   55   70   85   100   115   130   145   160

FIGURE 9.16 The Normal Curve of Intelligence Deviation IQ scores produce a normal curve. This graph shows the percentage of people who score in each range of IQ.

Dustin Bean has Down syndrome, but that didn't prevent him from earning a black belt in Kung Fu. Or from showing off several of his swaggy moves to the widow of the martial arts movie icon, Bruce Lee.

Research suggests that men tend to outperform women in abstract mathematical and scientific domains and women tend to outperform men on production and comprehension of complex prose. Sonya Kovalevskaya (1850–1891), who was regarded as one of the greatest mathematicians of her time, wrote, "It seems to me that the poet must see what others do not see, must look deeper than others look. And the mathematician must do the same thing. As for myself, all my life I have been unable to decide for which I had the greater inclination, mathematics or literature" (Kovalevskaya, 1978, p. 35).

and verbal abilities (Achter, Lubinski, & Benbow, 1996). Because gifted children tend to be "single-gifted," they also tend to be single-minded. Indeed, some research suggests that the thing that most clearly distinguishes gifted children from their less gifted peers is the sheer amount of time they spend engaged in their domain of excellence (Ericsson & Charness, 1999).

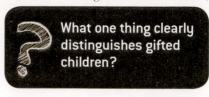

What one thing clearly distinguishes gifted children?

On the other end of the intelligence spectrum are people with intellectual disabilities, which is defined by an IQ of less than 70. About 70% of people with IQs in this range are male. Two of the most common causes of intellectual disability are *Down syndrome* (caused by the presence of a third copy of chromosome 21) and *fetal alcohol syndrome* (caused by a mother's alcohol use during pregnancy). Unlike intellectual gifts, intellectual disabilities tend to be quite general, and people who have them typically show impaired performance on most or all cognitive tasks. Perhaps the greatest myth about the intellectually disabled is that they are unhappy. A recent survey of people with Down syndrome (Skotko, Levine, & Goldstein, 2011) revealed that more than 96% are happy with their lives, like who they are, and like how they look. People with intellectual disabilities face many challenges, and being mistaken for miserable people is clearly one of them.

Group Differences in Intelligence

In the early 1900s, Stanford professor Lewis Terman improved on Binet and Simon's work and produced the intelligence test now known as the Stanford–Binet Intelligence Scale. Among the things his test revealed was that Whites performed better than non-Whites. "Are the inferior races really inferior, or are they merely unfortunate in their lack of opportunity to learn?" he asked. And, then he answered unequivocally: "Their dullness seems to be racial, or at least inherent in the family stocks from which they come" (Terman, 1916, pp. 91–92).

Was Terman right or wrong? Terman made three claims: First, he claimed that intelligence is influenced by genes; second, he claimed that members of some racial groups score better than others on intelligence tests; and third, he claimed that the difference in scores is due to a difference in genes. Virtually all modern scientists agree that Terman's first two claims are indeed true: Intelligence *is* influenced by genes and some groups *do* perform better than others on intelligence tests. However, Terman's third claim—that differences in genes are the *reason* why some groups outperform others—is not by any means a scientific fact Indeed, it is a provocative conjecture that has been the subject of both passionate and acrimonious debate. What does science have to say about it?

Before answering that question, we should be clear about one thing: Between-group differences in intelligence are not inherently troubling. No one is troubled by the possibility that Nobel laureates are on average more intelligent than shoe salesmen—and that includes most shoe salesmen. On the other hand, most of us *are* troubled by the possibility that people of one gender, race, or nationality may be more intelligent than people of another because intelligence is a valuable commodity and it doesn't seem fair for a few groups to corner the market by accidents of birth or geography.

But fair or not, they do. Whites routinely outscore Latinos, who routinely outscore Blacks (Neisser et al., 1996; Rushton, 1995). Women routinely outscore men on tests that require rapid access to and use of semantic information, production and comprehension of complex prose, fine motor skills, and perceptual speed of verbal intelligence, and men routinely outscore women on tests that require transformations in visual or spatial memory, certain motor skills, spatiotemporal responding, and fluid reasoning in abstract mathematical and scientific domains (Halpern, 1997; Halpern et al., 2007). Indeed, group differences in performance on intelligence tests "are among the most thoroughly documented findings in psychology" (Suzuki & Valencia, 1997, p. 1104). Although the average difference between groups is considerably less than the average difference within groups, Terman was right when he noted that some groups perform better than others on intelligence tests. The question is why?

"I don't know anything about the bell curve, but I say heredity is everything."

Tests and Test Takers

One possibility is that there is something wrong with the tests. In fact, the earliest intelligence tests asked questions whose answers were more likely to be known by members of one group (usually White Europeans) than by members of another. For example, when Binet and Simon asked students, "When anyone has offended you and asks you to excuse him, what ought you to do?," they were looking for answers such as "accept the apology graciously." Answers such as "demand three goats" would have been counted as wrong. But intelligence tests have come a long way in a century, and one would have to look hard to find questions on a modern intelligence test that have the same blatant cultural bias that Binet and Simon's test did (Suzuki & Valencia, 1997). It would be difficult to argue that the large differences between the average scores of different groups is due entirely—or even largely—to a cultural bias in IQ tests.

And yet, even when test *questions* are unbiased, testing *situations* may not be. For example, studies show that African American students perform more poorly on tests if they are asked to report their race at the top of the answer sheet, because doing so causes them to feel anxious about confirming racial stereotypes (Steele & Aronson, 1995) and anxiety naturally interferes with test performance (Reeve, Heggestad, & Lievens, 2009). European American students do not show the same effect when asked to report their race. When Asian American women are reminded of their gender, they perform unusually poorly on tests of mathematical skill, presumably because they are aware of stereotypes suggesting that women can't do math. But when the same women are instead reminded of their ethnicity, they perform unusually *well* on such tests, presumably because they are aware of stereotypes suggesting that Asians are especially good at math (Shih, Pittinsky, & Ambady, 1999). Findings such as these remind us that the situation in which intelligence tests are administered may cause group differences in performance that do not reflect group differences in actual intelligence.

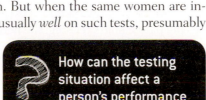

How can the testing situation affect a person's performance on an IQ test?

Environments and Genes

Biases in the testing situation may explain some of the between-group differences in intelligence test scores, but probably not all. There is broad agreement among scientists that environment also plays a major role. For example, African American children have on average lower birth weights, poorer diets, higher rates of chronic illness, and poorer medical care; and they attend worse schools and are three times more likely than European American children to live in single-parent households (Acevedo-Garcia et al., 2007; National Center for Health Statistics, 2004). Given the vast differences between the SES of European Americans and African Americans, it isn't very surprising that African Americans score on average 10 points lower on IQ tests than European Americans do.

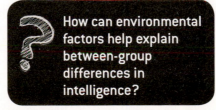

How can environmental factors help explain between-group differences in intelligence?

Do genes play any role in this difference? So far, there is no compelling evidence that they do. For example, the average African American has about 20%

AP Photo/Mary Ann Chastain

These high school juniors in South Carolina are taking the SAT. When people are anxious about the possibility of confirming a racial or gender stereotype, their test performance can suffer.

Millionaire Robert Graham opened the Repository for Germinal Choice in 1980 to collect sperm from Nobel laureates and mathematical prodigies and allow healthy young women to be inseminated with it. His so-called "genius factory" produced more than 200 children but closed after his death in 1999.

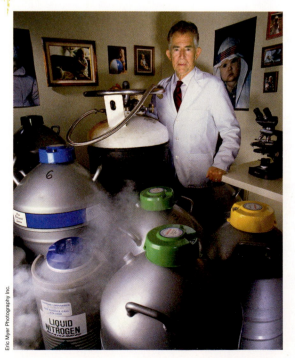

Eric Myer Photography Inc.

European genes, and yet those who have more are no smarter than those who have fewer, which is not what we'd expect if European genes made people smart (Loehlin, 1973; Scarr et al., 1977). Similarly, African American children and mixed-race children have different amounts of European genes, and yet, when they are adopted into middle-class families, their IQs don't differ (Moore, 1986). These facts do not definitively rule out the possibility that between-group differences in intelligence are caused by genetic differences, of course, but they do make that possibility less likely. Indeed, some experts, such as psychologist Richard Nisbett, believe the debate on this topic is all but over: "Genes account for none of the difference in IQ between blacks and whites; measurable environmental factors plausibly account for all of it" (Nisbett, 2009, p. 118).

Improving Intelligence

Intelligence can be improved—by money, for example, and by education. But most people can't just snap their fingers and become wealthier, and education takes time. Is there anything that parents can do to raise their child's IQ? Research suggests that four things reliably raise a child's intelligence (Protzko, Aronson, & Blair, 2013). First, supplementing the diets of pregnant women and neonates with long-chain polyunsaturated fatty acids (a substance found in breast milk) raises children's IQ by about 4 points. Second, enrolling low-SES infants in so-called early educational interventions raises their IQ by about 6 points (though surprisingly, enrolling them at a younger age seems to be no better than enrolling them at an older age). Third, reading to children in an interactive manner raises their IQ by about 6 points (and in this case, the earlier the parent starts reading, the better). Fourth and finally, sending children to preschool raises their IQ by about 6 points. Clearly, there are some things that parents can do to make their kids smarter.

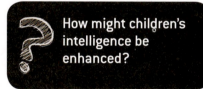

How might children's intelligence be enhanced?

Perhaps all this will be simpler in the future. *Cognitive enhancers* are drugs that produce improvements in the psychological processes that underlie intelligent behavior. For example, stimulants such as Ritalin (methylphenidate) and Adderall (mixed amphetamine salts) can enhance cognitive performance by improving people's ability to focus attention, manipulate information in working memory, and flexibly control responses (Sahakian & Morein-Zamir, 2007). Cognitive performance can also be enhanced by a class of drugs called ampakines (Ingvar et al., 1997). Modafinil is one such drug, and it has been shown to improve short-term memory and planning abilities in healthy, young volunteers (Turner et al., 2003).

Some scientists believe that cognitive enhancement will eventually be achieved by altering the brain's basic structure at birth. By manipulating the genes that guide hippocampal development, scientists have created a strain of "smart mice" that have extraordinary memory and learning abilities, leading the researchers to conclude that "genetic enhancement of mental and cognitive attributes such as intelligence and memory in mammals is feasible" (Tang et al., 1999, p. 64). Although no one has yet developed a safe and powerful "smart pill" or "smart gene therapy," many experts believe that this will happen in the next few years (Farah et al., 2004; Rose, 2002; Turner & Sahakian, 2006). When it does, we will need a whole lot of intelligence to know how to handle it.

SUMMARY QUIZ [9.6]

1. Which of the following statements is false?

   a. Modern intelligence tests have a very strong cultural bias.

   b. Testing situations can impair the performance of some groups more than others.

   c. Test performance can suffer if the test taker is concerned about confirming a racial or gender stereotype.

   d. Some ethnic groups perform better than others on intelligence tests.

2. On which of the following does broad agreement exist among scientists?

   a. Differences in the intelligence test scores of different ethnic groups are clearly due to genetic differences between those groups.

   b. Differences in the intelligence test scores of different ethnic groups are caused in part by factors such as low birth weight and poor diet that are more prevalent in some groups than in others.

   c. Differences in the intelligence test scores of different ethnic groups always reflect real differences in intelligence.

   d. Genes that are strongly associated with intelligence have been found to be more prevalent in some ethnic groups than in others.

3. Gifted children tend to

   a. be equally gifted in several domains.

   b. be gifted in a single domain.

   c. lose their special talent in adulthood.

   d. change the focus of their interests relatively quickly.

CHAPTER REVIEW

SUMMARY

Language and Communication: From Rules to Meaning

> Human language is organized at several levels, from phonemes to morphemes to phrases and finally to sentences.

> Grammatical rules are acquired early in development, even without being taught explicitly. Instead, children appear to be biologically predisposed to process language in ways that allow them to extract these grammatical rules from the language they hear.

> In the brain, Broca's area is critical for language production and Wernicke's area is critical for language comprehension.

> Some bilingual children show greater executive control capacities, such as the ability to prioritize information and flexibly focus attention.

Concepts and Categories: How We Think

> We organize knowledge about objects, events, or other stimuli by creating concepts, prototypes, and exemplars.

> Family resemblance theory states that items in the same category share certain, if not all, features; prototype theory states that we use the most typical member of a category to assess new items; exemplar theory states that we compare new items with stored memories of other members of the category.

> Neuroimaging studies have shown that prototypes and exemplars are processed in different parts of the brain and that the brain may be "prewired" to respond strongly to distinct categories, such as living things and human-made things.

Decision Making: Rational and Otherwise

> Human decision making often departs from a completely rational process, and the mistakes that accompany this departure tell us a lot about how the human mind works.

> We can make irrational decisions when we fail to estimate probabilities accurately or when we fall prey to the availability bias, the conjunction fallacy, the representativeness heuristic, or framing effects.

> The prefrontal cortex plays an important role in decision making, and patients with prefrontal damage make more risky decisions than do healthy individuals.

Intelligence

> *Intelligence* is a mental ability that enables people to direct their thinking, adapt to their circumstances, and learn from their experiences.

> Intelligence tests produce a score known as an *intelligence quotient* or IQ. *Ratio IQ* is the ratio of a person's mental to physical age, and *deviation IQ* is the deviation of a person's test score from the average score of his or her peers.

> Intelligence test scores predict a variety of important life outcomes, such as scholastic performance, job performance, health, and wealth.

> People who score well on one test of mental ability *usually* score well on others, which suggests that there is a property called *g* (general intelligence), but they don't *always* score well on others, which suggests that there are also properties called *s* (specific abilities). Research reveals that between *g* and *s* are several *middle-level abilities*.

Where Does Intelligence Come From?

> Both genes and environments influence intelligence.

> Relative intelligence is generally stable over time, but absolute intelligence changes.

> SES has a powerful influence on intelligence, and education has a moderate influence.

Who Is Most Intelligent?

> Some groups outscore others on intelligence tests because (a) testing situations impair the performance of some groups more than others, and (b) some groups live in less healthful and stimulating environments.

> There is no compelling evidence to suggest that between-group differences in intelligence are due to genetic differences.

> Human intelligence can be temporarily increased by cognitive enhancers such as Ritalin and Adderall, and nonhuman intelligence has been permanently increased by genetic manipulation.

KEY TERMS

language (p. 274)
grammar (p. 274)
phoneme (p. 274)
phonological rules (p. 274)
morphemes (p. 275)
morphological rules (p. 275)
syntactical rules (p. 275)
deep structure (p. 275)
surface structure (p. 275)
fast mapping (p. 278)
telegraphic speech (p. 278)

nativist theory (p. 280)
genetic dysphasia (p. 280)
aphasia (p. 282)
concept (p. 284)
family resemblance theory (p. 284)
prototype (p. 285)
exemplar theory (p. 285)
category-specific deficit (p. 286)
rational choice theory (p. 288)
frequency format hypothesis (p. 289)

availability bias (p. 289)
conjunction fallacy (p. 290)
representativeness heuristic (p. 290)
framing effects (p. 290)
sunk-cost fallacy (p. 290)
prospect theory (p. 291)
intelligence (p. 293)
ratio IQ (p. 294)
deviation IQ (p. 294)
two-factor theory of intelligence (p. 297)

fluid intelligence (p. 298)
crystallized intelligence (p. 298)
emotional intelligence (p. 299)
fraternal twins (or dizygotic twins) (p. 301)
identical twins (or monozygotic twins) (p. 301)
shared environment (p. 301)
nonshared environment (p. 301)

CHANGING MINDS

1. You mention to a friend that you've just learned that the primary language we learn can shape the way that we think. Your friend says that people are people everywhere and that this can't be true. What evidence could you describe to support your point?

2. In September 2011, *Wired* magazine ran an article discussing the fourth-down decisions of NFL coaches. On fourth down, a coach can choose to play aggressively and go for a first down (or even a touchdown), or the coach can settle for a punt or a field goal, which are safer options but result in fewer points than a touchdown. Statistically, the riskier play results in greater point gain, on average, than playing it safe. But in reality, coaches choose the safer plays over 90% of the time. Reading this article, one of your friends is incredulous. "Coaches aren't stupid, and they want to win," he says. "Why would they always make the wrong decision?" Your friend is assuming that humans are rational decision makers. In what ways is your friend wrong? What might be causing the irrational decision making by football coaches?

3. In biology class, the topic turns to genetics. The professor describes the "Doogie" mouse, named after a 1990s TV show starring Neil Patrick Harris as a child genius named Doogie Howser. Doogie mice have a genetic manipulation that makes them smarter than other, genetically normal mice. Your classmate turns to you. "I knew it," she said. "There's a 'smart gene' after all—some people have it, and some people don't, and that's why some people are intelligent and some people aren't." What would you tell her about the role genetics plays in intelligence? What other factors, besides genes, play an important role in determining an individual's intelligence?

4. One of your friends tells you about his sister. "We're very competitive," he says. "But she's smarter. We both took IQ tests when we were kids, and she scored 104, but I only scored 102." What would you tell your friend about the relationship between IQ scores and intelligence? What do IQ scores really measure?

5. A speaker visiting your university notes that there are still gender differences in academia; for example, in math departments across the country, women make up only about 26% of assistant professors and 10% of full professors. One of your classmates notes that the statistic isn't surprising: "Girls don't do as well as boys at math," he says. "So it's not surprising that fewer girls choose math-related careers." Based on what you've read in the text about group differences in intelligence, why might women perform more poorly then men on tests of math or science, even if the groups actually have similar ability?

ANSWERS TO SUMMARY QUIZZES

Answers to Summary Quiz 9.1: 1. d; 2. a; 3. c; 4. b.

Answers to Summary Quiz 9.2: 1. a; 2. b; 3. c.

Answers to Summary Quiz 9.3: 1. d; 2. c; 3. b.

Answers to Summary Quiz 9.4: 1. c; 2. d; 3. c; 4. b; 5. d.

Answers to Summary Quiz 9.5: 1. b; 2. a; 3. a.

Answers to Summary Quiz 9.6: 1. a; 2. b; 3. b.

Need more help? Additional resources are located in LaunchPad at:
http://www.worthpublishers.com/launchpad/schacterbrief3e

Development

His mother called him Adi and showered him with affection, but his father was not so kind. As his sister later recalled, "Adi challenged my father to extreme harshness and got his sound thrashing every day." Although his father wanted him to become a civil servant, Adi's true love was art, and his mother quietly encouraged that gentler interest. Adi was just 18 years old when his mother was diagnosed with terminal cancer, and he was heartbroken when she died.

But Adi had little time for grieving. As he later wrote, "Poverty and hard reality compelled me to make a quick decision. I was faced with the problem of somehow making my own living." Adi resolved to make that living as an artist. He applied to art school, but was flatly rejected. Motherless and penniless, Adi wandered the city streets for 5 long years, sleeping on park benches, living in homeless shelters, and eating in soup kitchens, while trying desperately to sell his sketches and watercolors.

Ten years later, Adi had achieved the fame he desired, and today collectors pay significant sums to acquire his paintings. In fact, just last year one of his paintings sold at auction for $40,000. But that isn't because Adi was a great artist; it is because his full name was Adolf Hitler.

Adi painted in many styles, including the precise and well-structured watercolor shown here.

(painting) Interfoto/Alamy; (easel) Maksym Bondarchuk/Shutterstock

developmental psychology The study of continuity and change across the life span.

WHY IS IT SO DIFFICULT TO IMAGINE THE GREATEST mass murderer of the 20th century as a gentle child who loved to draw, as a compassionate adolescent who cared for his ailing mother, or as a dedicated young adult who endured cold and hunger for the sake of art? After all, *you* didn't begin as the person you are today, and odds are that you aren't yet in finished form. From birth to infancy, from childhood to adolescence, from young adulthood to old age, human beings change over time. Their development includes both dramatic transformations and striking consistencies in the way they look, think, feel, and act. **Developmental psychology** is *the study of continuity and change across the life span*, and as you'll see, most human lives have plenty of both.

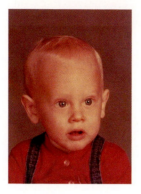   

From infancy to childhood to adolescence to adulthood, people exhibit both continuity and change.

We'll start by examining the 9-month period between conception and birth and see how prenatal events set the stage for everything to come. Then we'll examine childhood, during which children must learn how to think about the world and their relationship to it, to understand and bond with others, and to tell the difference between right and wrong. Next, we'll examine a relatively new invention called adolescence, which is the stage at which children become both independent and sexual creatures. Finally, we'll examine adulthood, the stage at which people typically leave their parents, find mates, have children, and watch Jeopardy.

Prenatality: A Womb with a View

You probably calculate your age by counting your birthdays, but the fact is that on the day you were born, you were already 9 months old. The *prenatal stage* of development ends with birth and begins 9 months earlier when about 200 million sperm make the journey from a woman's vagina, through her uterus, and on to her fallopian tubes. That journey is a perilous one. Many of the sperm have defects that prevent them from swimming vigorously enough to make any progress, and others get stuck in what is essentially a sperm traffic jam. Of those that do manage to make their way through the uterus, many will take a wrong turn and end up in the fallopian tube that does not contain an egg. In fact, a mere 200 or so of the original 200 million sperm will manage to get close enough to an egg to release digestive enzymes that erode the egg's protective outer layer. The moment the first sperm manages to penetrate the egg's coating, the egg will release a chemical that seals the coating and keeps all the other sperm from entering. After triumphing over 199,999,999 of its closest friends, this single successful sperm will shed its tail and fertilize the egg. About 12 hours later, the egg will merge with the nuclei of the sperm, and the prenatal development of a unique human being will begin.

Prenatal Development

A **zygote** is *a fertilized egg*. From the first moment of its existence, a zygote has one thing in common with the person it will someday become: sex. Each human sperm and each human egg contain 23 *chromosomes*, and one of these chromosomes (the 23rd) comes in two varieties known as X and Y. The egg's 23rd chromosome is always an X, but the sperm's can be an X or a Y. If the egg is fertilized by a sperm that has a Y chromosome, then the zygote is male (XY), and if it is fertilized by a sperm that has an X chromosome, then the zygote is female (XX).

The **germinal stage** is *the 2-week period of prenatal development that begins at conception.* During this stage, the one-celled zygote divides into two cells that then divide into four cells that then divide into eight, and so on. By the time an infant is born, its body contains trillions of cells, each of which came from the original zygote, and each of which contains exactly one set of 23 chromosomes from the sperm and one set of 23 chromosomes from the egg. During the germinal stage, the zygote migrates back down the fallopian tube and implants itself in the wall of the uterus. This too is a difficult journey, and about half of zygotes do not complete it, either because they are defective or because they implant themselves in an inhospitable part of the uterus.

If the zygote successfully implants itself in the uterine wall, it earns the right to be called an *embryo,* and a new stage of development begins. The **embryonic stage** is *a period of prenatal development that lasts from the 2nd week until about the 8th week* (see **FIGURE 10.1**). During this stage, the embryo continues to divide, and its cells begin to differentiate to build the structures of the body. The 1 inch long embryo has a beating heart and other body parts, such as arms and legs. Male embryos begin to produce a hormone called testosterone, which masculinizes their reproductive organs.

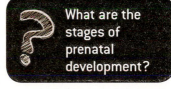

What are the stages of prenatal development?

At about 9 weeks, the embryo gets a new name: *fetus.* The **fetal stage** is *the period of prenatal development that lasts from the 9th week until birth.* The fetus has a skeleton and muscles that make it capable of movement. It develops a layer of insulating fat beneath its skin, and its digestive and respiratory systems mature. The cells that will ultimately become the brain divide and begin to generate axons and dendrites (which permit communication with other brain cells). They also begin to undergo a

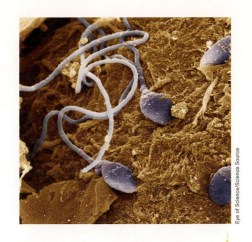

Eye of Science/Science Source

This electron micrograph shows several human sperm, one of which is fertilizing an egg. Contrary to what many people think, fertilization does not happen right away. It typically happens 1 to 2 days after intercourse, but it can happen as much as 5 days later.

zygote A fertilized egg that contains chromosomes from both a sperm and an egg.

germinal stage The 2-week period of prenatal development that begins at conception.

embryonic stage The period of prenatal development that lasts from the second week until about the eighth week.

fetal stage The period of prenatal development that lasts from the ninth week until birth.

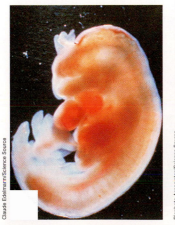

Claude Edelmann/Science Source

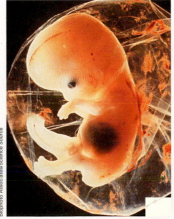

Biophoto Associates/Science Source

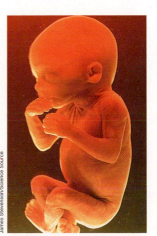

James Stevenson/Science Source

FIGURE 10.1 Prenatal Development
Human beings undergo amazing development in the 9 months of prenatal development. These images show an embryo at 30 days (about the size of a poppy seed), an embryo at 8 to 9 weeks (about the size of an olive), and a fetus at 5 months (about the size of a pomegranate).

This chimp and boy share a deep interest in dirt, bugs, and leaves. But one big difference between them is that the chimp was born with a nearly adult-sized brain, whereas the boy was born with a brain that will ultimately quadruple in size.

myelination The formation of a fatty sheath around the axons of a neuron.

teratogens Agents that damage the process of development.

fetal alcohol syndrome A developmental disorder caused by heavy alcohol use during pregnancy.

This child has some of the telltale facial features associated with FAS: short eye openings, a flat midface, a flat ridge under the nose, a thin upper lip, and an underdeveloped jaw.

process (described in the Neuroscience and Behavior chapter) known as **myelination,** which is *the formation of a fatty sheath around the axons of a neuron.* Just as plastic sheathing insulates a wire, myelin insulates a brain cell and prevents the leakage of neural signals that travel along the axon. This process starts during the fetal stage but doesn't end for years; the myelination of the cortex, for example, continues into adulthood.

Although the brain undergoes rapid and complex growth during the fetal period, at birth it is nowhere near its adult size. Whereas a newborn chimpanzee's brain is nearly 60% of its adult size, a newborn human's brain is only 25% of its adult size, which is to say that 75% of a person's brain development occurs outside the womb. There are two reasons for this. First, if a newborn human's head were 60% of its adult size (like a newborn chimp's head is) then that newborn could never pass through its mother's birth canal. Second, one of our species' greatest talents is its ability to adapt to a wide range of novel environments that differ in climate, social structure, and so on. Rather than arriving in the world with a fully developed brain, human brains do much of their developing *within* the very environments in which they ultimately must function. The fact that our brains are specifically shaped by the unique social and physical environment into which we are born is one of the main reasons why we are so adaptable.

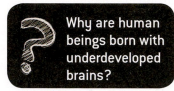

Why are human beings born with underdeveloped brains?

Prenatal Environment

The womb is an environment that has a powerful impact on development (Coe & Lubach, 2008; Glynn & Sandman, 2011; Wadhwa, Sandman, & Garite, 2001). For example, the *placenta* is the organ that physically links the bloodstreams of the mother and the embryo or fetus and permits the exchange of certain chemicals. That's why the foods a woman eats during pregnancy can affect her unborn child. The children of mothers who receive insufficient nutrition during pregnancy often have physical problems (Stein et al., 1975) and psychological problems, most notably an increased risk of schizophrenia and antisocial personality disorder (Neugebauer, Hoek, & Susser, 1999; Susser, Brown, & Matte, 1999). The foods a woman eats during pregnancy can also shape her child's food preferences: Studies show that infants tend to like the foods and spices that their mothers ate while they were in the womb (Mennella, Johnson, & Beauchamp, 1995).

But it isn't just food that affects the fetus. Almost anything a woman eats, drinks, inhales, injects, sniffs, snorts, or rubs on her skin can pass through the placenta. *Agents that impair development* are called **teratogens,** which literally means "monster makers." The most common teratogen is alcohol. **Fetal alcohol syndrome (FAS)** is *a developmental disorder caused by heavy alcohol use during pregnancy,* and children with FAS have a variety of brain abnormalities and cognitive deficits (Carmichael Olson et al., 1997; Streissguth et al., 1999). Some studies suggest that light drinking does not harm the fetus, but there is little consensus about how much drinking is light (Warren & Hewitt, 2009). Tobacco is another common teratogen. Babies whose mothers smoke have lower birth weights (Horta et al., 1997) and are more likely to have perceptual and attentional problems in childhood (Espy et al., 2011; Fried & Watkinson, 2000). Even secondhand smoke can lead to reduced birth weight and deficits in attention and learning (Makin, Fried, & Watkinson, 1991; Windham, Eaton, & Hopkins, 1999). Other teratogens include environmental poisons such as lead in the water, paint dust in the air, or mercury in fish.

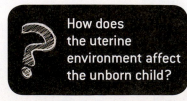

How does the uterine environment affect the unborn child?

The prenatal environment is rich with chemicals, but it is also rich with information. Wombs are dark because only the brightest light can filter through the mother's abdomen, but they are not quiet. The fetus can hear its mother's heartbeat, the gastrointestinal sounds associated with her digestion, and her voice. How do we know? Newborns will suck a nipple more vigorously when they hear the sound of their mother's voice than when they hear the voice of a female stranger (Querleu et al., 1984), demonstrating that they are more familiar with the former. Similarly, newborns whose mothers read aloud from *The Cat in the Hat* during their pregnancies react as though the story is familiar (DeCasper & Spence, 1986). Newborns who are presented with words from two languages prefer hearing their mother's native language—unless their mother is bilingual, in which case they are just as happy to hear both languages (Byers-Heinlein, Burns, & Werker, 2010). What newborns hear even influences the sounds they make at birth: French newborns cry with a rising melody and German newborns with a falling melody, mimicking the cadence of their mother's native tongue (Mampe et al., 2009). Clearly, the fetus is listening.

What can a fetus hear?

infancy The stage of development that begins at birth and lasts between 18 and 24 months.

SUMMARY QUIZ [10.1]

1. The sequence of prenatal development is
   a. fetus, embryo, zygote.
   b. zygote, embryo, fetus.
   c. embryo, zygote, fetus.
   d. zygote, fetus, embryo.

2. Learning begins
   a. in the womb.
   b. at birth.
   c. in the newborn stage.
   d. in infancy.

3. Which is true?
   a. Heavy alcohol use during the early stages of pregnancy will probably not damage the fetus because critical brain systems have not yet developed.
   b. Exposure of the mother to environmental poisons such as lead in the drinking water can interfere with the development of the fetus,
   c. The babies of women who smoke while pregnant may have impaired development, but exposure to secondhand smoke is okay
   d. All of the above

Infancy and Childhood: Becoming a Person

Infancy is *the stage of development that begins at birth and lasts between 18 and 24 months.* Although infants seem to be capable of little more than squalling and squirming, research shows that they are much more sophisticated than they appear.

motor development The emergence of the ability to execute physical action.

reflexes Specific patterns of motor response that are triggered by specific patterns of sensory stimulation.

cephalocaudal rule The "top-to-bottom" rule that describes the tendency for motor skills to emerge in sequence from the head to the feet.

proximodistal rule The "inside-to-outside" rule that describes the tendency for motor behavior to emerge in sequence from the center to the periphery.

Infants mimic the facial expressions of adults—and vice versa, of course!

Motor behaviors develop through practice, which infants get a lot of! In just 1 hour in a playroom, the average infant takes 2,368 steps, travels 0.4 miles, and falls 17 times (Adolph et al., 2012).

Perceptual and Motor Development

New parents like to stand around the crib and make goofy faces at the baby because they think the baby will be amused. What they don't know is that newborns have a rather limited range of vision. The level of detail that a newborn can see at a distance of 20 feet is roughly equivalent to the level of detail that an adult can see at 600 feet (Banks & Salapatek, 1983), which is to say that they are missing out on a lot of the cribside shenanigans. On the other hand, when stimuli are 8 to 12 inches away (about the distance between a nursing infant's eyes and its mother's face), newborns can see pretty well. How do we know? In one study, newborns were shown a circle with diagonal stripes over and over again. The infants stared a lot at first and then less and less on each subsequent presentation. Recall from the Learning chapter that *habituation* is the tendency for organisms to respond less intensely to a stimulus the more frequently they are exposed to it, and infants habituate just like the rest of us do. But when the researchers rotated the circle 90°, the newborns once again stared intently, indicating that they had noticed the change in the circle's orientation (Slater, Morison, & Somers, 1988).

What do newborns see?

Newborns are especially attentive to social stimuli. For example, in one study, researchers stood close to some newborns while sticking out their tongues and stood close to other newborns while pursing their lips. Newborns in the first group stuck out their own tongues more often than those in the second group did, and newborns in the second group pursed their lips more often than those in the first group did (Meltzoff & Moore, 1977). Indeed, newborns have been shown to mimic facial expressions in their very first *hour* of life (Reissland, 1988) and to mimic speech sounds as early as 12 weeks (Kuhl & Meltzoff, 1996).

Although infants can use their eyes right away, they must spend considerably more time learning how to use their other parts. **Motor development** is *the emergence of the ability to execute physical actions* such as reaching, grasping, crawling, and walking. Motor behavior starts with a small set of **reflexes,** which are *specific patterns of motor response that are triggered by specific patterns of sensory stimulation*. For example, the *rooting reflex* is the tendency for infants to move their mouths toward any object that touches their cheek, and the *sucking reflex* is the tendency to suck any object that enters their mouths. These two reflexes allow newborns to find their mother's nipple and begin feeding—a behavior so vitally important that nature took no chances and hardwired it into every one of us. Interestingly, these and other reflexes that are present at birth seem to disappear in the first few months.

Why are infants born with reflexes?

The development of more sophisticated motor behavior tends to obey two general rules. The first is the **cephalocaudal rule** (or the "top-to-bottom" rule), which describes *the tendency for motor behavior to emerge in sequence from the head to the feet*. Infants tend to gain control over their heads first, their arms and trunks next, and their legs last. A young infant who is placed on her stomach may lift her head and her chest by using her arms for support, but she typically has little control over her legs. The second rule is the **proximodistal rule** (or the "inside-to-outside"

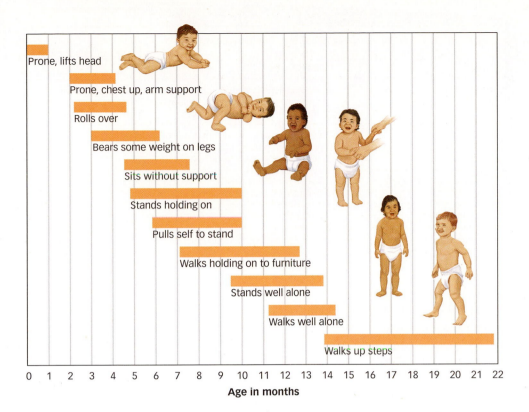

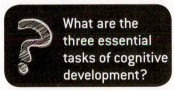

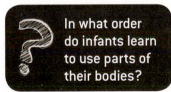

FIGURE 10.2 **Motor Development** Infants learn to control their bodies from head to feet and from center to periphery. These behaviors do not emerge on a strict timetable, but they do emerge in a strict sequence.

rule), which describes *the tendency for motor behavior to emerge in sequence from the center to the periphery.* Infants learn to control their trunks before their elbows and knees, which they learn to control before their hands and feet (see **FIGURE 10.2**). Motor behaviors generally emerge in an orderly sequence but not on a strict timetable. Rather, the timing of these behaviors is influenced by many factors, such as the infant's incentive for reaching, body weight, muscular development, and general level of activity. In one study, infants who had visually stimulating mobiles hanging above their cribs began reaching for objects 6 weeks earlier than infants who did not (White & Held, 1966).

? In what order do infants learn to use parts of their bodies?

cognitive development The emergence of the ability to think and understand.

Jean Piaget (1896–1980) was the father of modern developmental psychology, as well as the last man to look good in a beret.

Cognitive Development

In the first half of the 20th century, a Swiss biologist named Jean Piaget noticed that when asked certain kinds of questions (e.g., "Does the big glass have more liquid in it than the small glass? Can Billy see what you see?"), children of the same age gave the same wrong answers. And as they aged, they started giving the right answers at about the same time. This led Piaget to suggest that children move through discrete stages of **cognitive development,** which is *the emergence of the ability to think and understand.* Between infancy and adulthood, children must come to understand three important things: (a) how the world works, (b) how their minds represent that world, and (c) how other minds represent that world. Let's see how children accomplish these three essential tasks.

? What are the three essential tasks of cognitive development?

sensorimotor stage A stage of development that begins at birth and lasts through infancy.

schemas Theories about the way the world works.

assimilation The process by which infants apply their schemas in novel situations.

accommodation The process by which infants revise their schemas in light of new information.

object permanence The belief that objects exist even when they are not visible.

Table 10.1 Piaget's Four Stages of Cognitive Development

Stage	Characteristic
Sensorimotor (Birth–2 years)	Infant experiences world through movement and sense, develops schemas, begins to act intentionally, and shows evidence of understanding object permanence.
Preoperational (2–6 years)	Child acquires motor skills but does not understand conservation of physical properties. Child begins this stage of thinking egocentrically but ends with a basic understanding of other minds.
Concrete operational (6–11 years)	Child can think logically about physical objects and events and understands conservation of physical properties.
Formal operational (11 years and up)	Child can think logically about abstract propositions and hypotheticals.

Discovering the World

Piaget (1954) suggested that cognitive development occurs in four stages which he called the *sensorimotor* stage, the *preoperational* stage, the *concrete operational* stage, and the *formal operational* stage (see **TABLE 10.1**). The **sensorimotor stage** is *a period of development that begins at birth and lasts through infancy.* As its name suggests, infants at this stage are mainly busy using their ability to *sense* and their ability to *move* to acquire information about the world. By actively exploring their environments with their eyes, mouths, and fingers, infants begin to construct **schemas,** which are *theories about of the way the world works.*

What happens at the sensorimotor stage?

As every scientist knows, the key advantage of having a theory is that it can be used to predict what will happen in novel situations. If an infant learns that tugging at a stuffed animal causes the toy to come closer, then that observation is incorporated into the infant's theory about how physical objects behave when pulled, and the infant can later use that theory when he or she wants a different object to come closer, such as a rattle or a ball. Piaget called this **assimilation,** which is *the process by which infants apply their schemas in novel situations.* Of course, if the infant tugs the tail of the family cat, the cat is likely to sprint in the opposite direction. Because an infants' theories about the world ("Things come closer if I pull them") are occasionally disconfirmed, infants must occasionally adjust their schemas in light of new experiences ("Aha! Only *inanimate* things come closer when I pull them"). Piaget called this **accommodation,** which is *the process by which infants revise their schemas to take new information into account.*

Piaget suggested that infants lack some very basic understandings about the physical world and therefore must acquire them through experience. For example, when you put your shoes in the closet, you know that they exist even after you close the closet door, and you would be rather surprised if you opened the door a moment later and found the closet empty. But according to Piaget, this wouldn't surprise an infant because infants do not have a theory of **object permanence,** which is *the belief that objects exist even when they are not visible.* But modern research suggests that infants may acquire a sense of object permanence much earlier than Piaget realized (Shinskey & Munakata, 2005).

For instance, in one study, infants were shown a miniature drawbridge that flipped up and down (see **FIGURE 10.3**). Once the infants got used to this, they watched as a box was placed behind the drawbridge— in its path but out of their sight. Some infants then saw a *possible* event: The drawbridge began to flip and then suddenly stopped, as

During the sensorimotor stage, infants explore with their hands and mouths, learning important lessons about the physical world such as, "If you whack Jell-O hard enough, you can actually wear it."

© Michael Hagedorn/Corbis

(a)

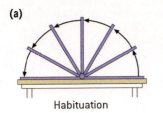

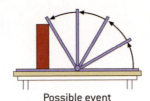
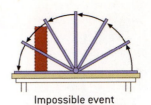

Habituation   Possible event   Impossible event

(b)

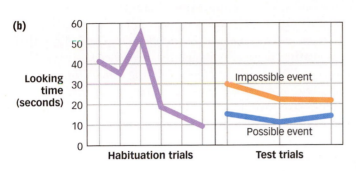
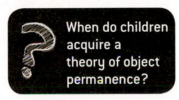

Looking time (seconds)

Impossible event

Possible event

Habituation trials   Test trials

FIGURE 10.3 The Impossible Event (*a*) In the habituation trials, infants watched a drawbridge flip back and forth with nothing in its path until they grew bored. Then a box was placed behind the drawbridge and the infants were shown one of two events: In the possible event, the box kept the drawbridge from flipping all the way over; in the impossible event, it did not. (*b*) The graph shows the infants' looking time during the habituation and the test trials. During the test trials, their interest was reawakened by the impossible event but not by the possible event (Baillargeon, Spelke, & Wasserman, 1985). [Data from Baillargeon, Spelke, & Wasserman, 1985.]

if impeded by the box that the infants could not see. Other infants saw an *impossible* event: The drawbridge began to flip and then continued, as if unimpeded by the box. Four-month-old infants stared longer at the impossible event than at the possible event, suggesting that they were puzzled by it (Baillargeon, Spelke, & Wasserman, 1985). The only thing that could have made it puzzling, of course, was the fact that the unseen box was not stopping the progress of the drawbridge (Fantz, 1964).

When do children acquire a theory of object permanence?

Hot Science

A Statistician in the Crib

A magician asks you to shuffle a deck of cards and then name your favorite. Then he dons a blindfold, reaches out his hand, and pulls your favorite card from the deck. You are astonished—and the reason you are astonished is that you know that when a magician reaches into a deck of 52 cards, the odds that he will pick your favorite by sheer chance alone is rather small.

Would that trick astonish an infant? That's pretty hard to imagine. After all, to appreciate the trick, one has to understand a basic rule of statistics—namely, that random samples look roughly like the populations from which they are drawn. But recent research (Denison, Reed, &Xu, 2013) suggests that infants as young as 24 weeks may understand just that.

In one study, researchers showed infants two boxes: One had mostly pink balls and just a few yellows; the other had mostly yellow balls with a few pinks. The infants then watched as an experimenter closed her eyes and reached into the mostly pink box, pulled out some balls, and deposited them in a little container in front of the infant. Sometimes she deposited four pinks and a yellow, and sometimes she deposited four yellows and a pink. What did the infants do?

When the experimenter pulled mainly pink balls from a mainly pink box, the infants glanced and then looked away. But when she pulled mainly yellow balls from a mainly pink box, they stared like bystanders at a train wreck. The fact that infants looked longer at the improbable sample than at the probable sample suggests that they found the former more astonishing; in other words, they had some basic understanding of how random sampling works.

Mostly pink   Mostly yellow

Probable sample   Probable sample

Improbable sample   Improbable sample

This study—like so many in developmental psychology—teaches us that infants know a lot more than anyone could guess from casual observation of their behavior.

Bianca Moscatelli/Worth Publishers

When preoperational children are shown two equal-size glasses filled with equal amounts of liquid, they correctly say that neither glass "has more." But when the contents of one glass are poured into a taller, thinner glass, they incorrectly say that the taller glass now "has more." Concrete operational children don't make this mistake because they recognize that operations such as pouring change the appearance of the liquid but not its actual volume.

childhood The stage of development that begins at about 18 to 24 months and lasts until about 11 or 14 years.

preoperational stage The stage of cognitive development that begins at about 2 years and ends at about 6 years, during which children develop a preliminary understanding of the physical world.

concrete operational stage The stage of cognitive development that begins at about 6 years and ends at about 11 years, during which children learn how actions or "operations" can transform the "concrete" objects of the physical world.

conservation The notion that the quantitative properties of an object are invariant despite changes in the object's appearance.

formal operational stage The final stage of cognitive development that begins around the age of 11, during which children learn to reason about abstract concepts.

Studies such as these suggest that infants may indeed have some understanding of object permanence by the time they are just 4 months old.

Discovering the Mind

The long period following infancy is called **childhood,** which is *the stage of development that begins at about 18 to 24 months and lasts until about 11 to 14 years.* According to Piaget, children enter childhood at the **preoperational stage,** which is *the stage of cognitive development that begins at about 2 years and ends at about 6 years, during which children develop a preliminary understanding of the physical world.* They then pass through the **concrete operational stage,** which is *the stage of cognitive development that begins at about 6 years and ends at about 11 years, during which children learn how actions or "operations" can transform the "concrete" objects of the physical world.*

The difference between these stages is nicely illustrated by one of Piaget's clever experiments in which he showed children a row of cups and asked them to place an egg in each. Preoperational children were able to do this, and afterward they readily agreed that there were just as many eggs as there were cups. Then Piaget removed the eggs and spread them out in a long line that extended beyond the row of cups. Preoperational children incorrectly claimed that there were now more eggs than cups, pointing out that the row of eggs was longer than the row of cups and hence there must be more of them. Concrete operational children, on the other hand, correctly reported that the number of eggs did not change when they were spread out in a longer line. They understood that *quantity* is a property of a set of concrete objects that does not change when an operation such as *spreading out* alters the set's appearance (Piaget, 1954). Piaget called the child's insight **conservation,** which is *the notion that basic properties of an object do not change despite changes in the object's appearance.*

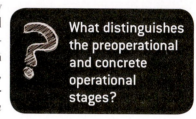

What distinguishes the preoperational and concrete operational stages?

The main reason why preoperational children do not fully grasp the notion of conservation is that they do not fully grasp the fact that they have *minds* and that these minds contain *mental representations* of the world. As adults, we naturally distinguish between appearances and realities. We realize that things aren't always as they seem: A wagon can *be* red but *look* gray at dusk, and a highway can *be* dry but *look* wet in the heat. Visual illusions delight us precisely because we know that things look like *this* but are really like *that.* Preoperational children don't make this distinction. When something *looks* gray or wet, they assume it *is* gray or wet.

But as children move from the preoperational to the concrete operational stage, they begin to realize that the way the world *appears* is not necessarily the way the world really *is.* For instance, concrete operational children can understand that when a ball of clay is rolled, stretched, or flattened, it is still the same amount of clay despite the fact that it looks larger in one form than in another. They can understand that when water is poured from a short, wide beaker into a tall, thin cylinder, it is still the same amount of water despite the fact that the water level in the cylinder is higher. Once children can make a distinction between objects and their mental representations of those objects, they begin to understand that certain operations—such as squishing, pouring, and spreading out—can change what an object *looks* like without changing what the object *is* like.

Once children are at the concrete operational stage, they can readily solve physical problems involving egg-spreading and clay squishing. They learn to solve nonphysical problems with equal ease at the **formal operational stage,** which is *the final stage of cognitive development that begins around the age of 11, during which children learn to reason about abstract concepts.* Childhood ends when formal operations begin, and people are able to reason systematically about abstract concepts such as *liberty*

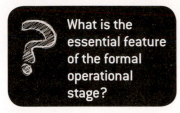

What is the essential feature of the formal operational stage?

and *love*, about events that have not yet happened, and about events that might have happened but didn't. The ability to generate, consider, reason about, or mentally "operate on" these abstract concepts, is the hallmark of formal operations.

Discovering Other Minds

As children develop, they discover their own minds, but they also discover the minds of others. Because preoperational children don't fully grasp the fact that they have minds that mentally represent objects, they also don't fully grasp the fact that other people have minds that often represent the same objects in different ways. As such, preoperational children generally expect others to see the world as they do. **Egocentrism** is *the failure to understand that the world appears different to different people.* Egocentrism is a hallmark of the preoperational stage, and it reveals itself in a variety of interesting ways. When 3-year-old children are asked what a person on the opposite side of a table is seeing, they typically claim that the other person sees what they see. They also think that others know what they know. For example, in a standard version of *the false-belief task* (Wimmer & Perner, 1983), children see a puppet named Maxi deposit some chocolate in a cupboard and then leave the room. A second puppet arrives a moment later, finds the chocolate, and moves it to a different cupboard. The children are then asked where Maxi will look for the chocolate when he returns: in the first cupboard where he initially put it, or in the second cupboard where the children know it currently is? Most 5-year-olds realize that Maxi will search the first cupboard because Maxi did not see the chocolate being moved. But 3-year-olds typically claim that Maxi will look in the second cupboard, because *the children* know that this is where the chocolate really is. Children are able to provide the right answer to this question somewhere between the ages of 4 to 6 (Callaghan et al., 2005), and children in some cultures are able to do it earlier than children in others (Liu et al., 2008).

What does the false-belief task show?

Although very young children do not fully understand that others have different perceptions or beliefs than they do, they do seem to understand that others have different desires. For example, a 2-year-old who likes dogs can understand that other children don't like dogs and can correctly predict that other children will avoid dogs that the child herself would approach. When 18-month-old toddlers see an adult express disgust while eating a food that the toddlers enjoy, they hand the adult a different food, as if they understand that different people have different tastes (Repacholi & Gopnik, 1997).

Eventually, the vast majority of children come to understand that they and others have minds and that these minds represent the world in different ways. Once children understand these things, they are said to have acquired a **theory of mind,** which is *the understanding that other people's mental representations guide their behavior.* The age at which children acquire a theory of mind appears to be influenced by a variety of factors, such as the number of siblings the child has, the frequency with which the child engages in pretend play, whether the child has an imaginary companion, and the socioeconomic status of the child's family. But of all the factors researchers have studied, language seems to be the

People who reach the formal operational stage can reason about abstract concepts such as freedom and justice. These two protesters are taking part in a demonstration in front of the White House, calling for the closing of the U.S. military prison at Guantanamo Bay, Cuba.

egocentrism The failure to understand that the world appears different to different observers.

theory of mind The understanding that other people's mental representations guide their behavior.

When small children are told to hide, they sometimes cover their eyes. Because they can't see you, they assume that you can't see them (Russell, Gee, & Bullard, 2012).

"You're five. How could you possibly understand the problems of a five-and-a-half-year-old?"

People with autism often have an unusual ability to concentrate on small details, words, and numbers for extended periods of time. Thorkil Sonne (*right*) started a company called Specialisterne.com, which places people with autism—like his son Lars (*left*)—at jobs that they can do better than more "neurotypical" people can.

Development is not the steplike progression that Piaget imagined. Children who are transitioning between stages may act more mature one day and less mature the next.

most important (Astington & Baird, 2005). Children's language skills are an excellent predictor of how well they perform on false-belief tasks (Happé, 1995). Language—and especially language about thoughts and feelings—is an important tool for helping children make sense of their own and others' minds (Harris, de Rosnay, & Pons, 2005).

Two groups of children lag far behind their peers in acquiring a theory of mind. Children with *autism* (a disorder we'll cover in more depth in the Disorders chapter) typically have difficulty communicating with other people and making friends, and some psychologists have suggested that this is because they have trouble acquiring a theory of mind (Frith, 2003). Although children with autism are typically normal on most intellectual dimensions—and sometimes far better than normal—they have difficulty understanding the inner lives of other people (Dawson et al., 2007). They do not seem to understand that other people can have false beliefs (Baron-Cohen, Leslie, & Frith, 1985; Senju et al., 2009), and they have special trouble understanding belief-based emotions such as embarrassment and shame (Baron-Cohen, 1991; Heerey, Keltner, & Capps, 2003). The second group of children who lag behind their peers in acquiring a theory of mind consists of deaf children whose parents do not know sign language. These children are slow to learn to communicate because they do not have ready access to any form of conventional language, and this restriction seems to slow the development of their understanding of other minds. Like children with autism, they display difficulties in understanding false beliefs even at 5 or 6 years of age (DeVilliers, 2005; Peterson & Siegal, 1999). Just as learning a spoken language seems to help hearing children acquire a theory of mind, so does learning a sign language help deaf children do the same (Pyers & Senghas, 2009).

Which children have special difficulty acquiring a theory of mind?

Cognitive development is a complex journey, and Piaget's ideas about it were nothing short of groundbreaking. Few psychologists have had such a profound impact on the field. Many of these ideas have held up quite well, but in the last few decades, psychologists have discovered two general ways in which Piaget got it wrong. First, Piaget thought that children graduated from one stage to another in the same way that they graduated from kindergarten to first grade: A child is in kindergarten *or* first grade, he is never in both, and there is an exact moment of transition to which everyone can point. Modern psychologists see development as more fluid and continuous—a less steplike progression than Piaget believed. Children who are transitioning between stages may perform more mature behaviors one day and less mature behaviors the next. Cognitive development is more like the change of seasons than it is like graduation. Second, children acquire many of the abilities that Piaget described much *earlier* than he realized (Gopnik, 2012). Every year, clever researchers find new ways of testing infants and children, and every year, textbook authors must lower the age at which cognitive milestones are achieved.

What did Piaget get wrong?

Discovering Our Cultures

Piaget saw the child as a lone scientist who made observations, developed theories, and then revised those theories in light of new observations. And yet, most scientists don't start from scratch. Rather, they receive training from more experienced scientists. According to Piaget's contemporary, the Russian psychologist Lev Vygotsky, children do much the same thing. Vygotsky believed that cognitive development was largely the result of the child's interaction with members of his or her own culture rather than his or her interaction with concrete objects (Vygotsky, 1978).

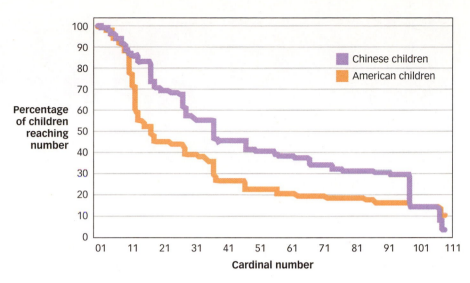

For example, in English, the names of numbers beyond 20 follow a logical pattern: twenty followed by a digit (twenty-one, twenty-two, twenty-three, etc.). In Chinese, the numbers from 11 to 19 follow the same rule (ten-one, ten-two, ten-three…), but in English they do not (eleven, twelve, thirteen…). The difference in the regularity of these two systems makes a big difference to the children who must learn them. It is obvious to a Chinese-speaking child that 12 is 10+2 because the number is actually called "ten-two," but this fact is not so obvious to an English-speaking child, who calls the number "twelve" (see **FIGURE 10.4**). In one study, children from many countries were asked to hand an experimenter a certain number of bricks. Some of the bricks were single, and some were glued together in strips of 10. When Asian children were asked to hand the experimenter 26 bricks, they tended to hand over 2 strips of 10 plus 6 singles. Non-Asian children tended to use the clumsier strategy of counting out 26 single bricks (Miura et al., 1994). Results such as these suggest that the regularity of the counting system that children inherit can promote or discourage their discovery of the fact that two-digit numbers can be broken down (Gordon, 2004; Imbo & LeFevre, 2009).

How does culture affect cognitive development?

FIGURE 10.4 Twelve or Two-Teen? The arbitrary English "twelve" versus the logical Chinese "ten-two" puts children learning counting in English at a disadvantage. The percentage of American children who can count through the cardinal numbers drops off suddenly when they hit the number 11, whereas the percentage of Chinese children shows a more gradual decline (Miller, Smith, & Zhu, 1995). (Data from Miller, Smith, & Zhu, 1995.)

Counting is just one of the many things that children learn from others. In fact, human beings are better than any other animal on earth at learning from other members of their own species, and that's because they have three important skills that most other animals lack (Meltzoff et al., 2009; Striano & Reid, 2006).

1. *Joint attention* is the ability to focus on what another person is focused on. If an adult turns her head to the left, both young infants (3 months) and older infants (9 months) will look to the left. But if the adult first closes her eyes and then looks to the left, the young infant will look to the left but the older infant will not (Brooks & Meltzoff, 2002). This suggests that older infants are not just following the adult's head movements, but are actually following her gaze—trying to see what they think she is seeing (see **FIGURE 10.5**).

2. *Imitation* is the tendency to do what another person does or is trying to do. Infants naturally mimic adults (Jones, 2007), but very early on, they begin to mimic adults' *intentions* rather than their actions per se. When an 18-month-old sees an adult's hand slip as the adult tries to pull the lid off a jar, the infant won't copy the slip, but will instead perform the *intended* action by removing the lid (Meltzoff, 1995, 2007).

3. *Social referencing* is the ability to use another person's reactions as information about the world (Kim, Walden, & Knieps, 2010; Walden & Ogan, 1988). As infants approach a new toy, they will often stop, look

Children are not lone explorers who discover the world for themselves but members of families, communities, and societies that teach them much of what they need to know.

A.N. Meltzoff, P. K. Kuhl, J. Movellan, & T. J. Sejnowski. "Foundations for a New Science of Learning." Published in Science, 2009, vol. 325, July 17, pp. 284–288.

(a)

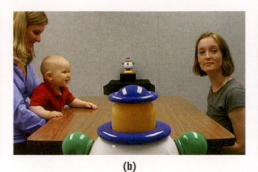
(b)

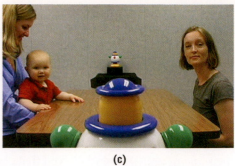
(c)

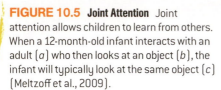

FIGURE 10.5 Joint Attention Joint attention allows children to learn from others. When a 12-month-old infant interacts with an adult (a) who then looks at an object (b), the infant will typically look at the same object (c) (Meltzoff et al., 2009).

back, and examine their mother's face for cues about whether she thinks the toy is or isn't dangerous. (You'll learn a lot more about how adults continue to use this skill when we discuss *informational influence* in the Social Psychology chapter).

Joint attention ("I see what you see"), imitation ("I do what you do"), and social referencing ("I think what you think") are three of the basic abilities that allow infants to learn from other members of their species.

The Real World

Walk This Way

Parents often complain that their children won't take their advice. But research shows that even 18-month-old infants know when to listen to mom and dad—and when to ignore them.

Researchers (Tamis-LeMonda et al., 2008) built an inclined plane whose steepness could be adjusted (as shown in the photo below), put some infants at the top and their moms at the bottom, and then watched to see whether the infants would attempt to walk down the plane and toward their mothers. Sometimes the plane was adjusted so that it was clearly flat and safe,

sometimes it was adjusted so that it was clearly steep and risky, and sometimes it was adjusted somewhere between these two extremes. Mothers were instructed either to encourage their infants to walk down the plane or to discourage them from doing so.

So what did the infants do? Did they trust their mothers or did they trust their eyes? As you can see in the figure below, when the inclined plane was clearly safe or clearly risky, infants ignored their mothers. They typically trotted down the flat plane even when mom advised against it and refused to try the risky plane even when

mom said it was okay. But when the plane was somewhere between safe and risky, the infants tended to follow mom's advice.

These data show that infants use social information in a very sophisticated way. When their senses provide unambiguous information about the world, they ignore what people tell them. But when their senses leave them unsure about what to do, they readily accept parental advice. It appears that from the moment children start to walk, they know when to listen to their parents and when to shake their heads, roll their eyes, and do what they darn well please.

Courtesy of Karen Adolph

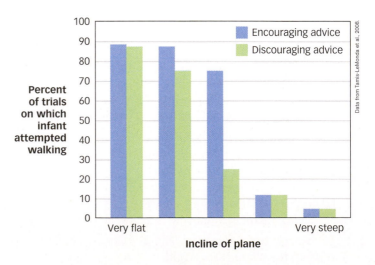
Data from Tamis-LeMonda et al., 2008.

Social Development

Unlike baby turtles, baby humans cannot survive without their caregivers. But what exactly do caregivers provide? Some obvious answers are warmth, safety, and food— and those obvious answers are right. But caregivers also provide something that is far less obvious but every bit as essential to an infant's development.

During World War II, psychologists studied infants who were living in orphanages while awaiting adoption. Although these children were warm, safe, and well-fed, many were developmentally impaired, both physically and psychologically (Spitz, 1949). A few years later, psychologist Harry Harlow (1958; Harlow & Harlow, 1965) discovered that infant rhesus monkeys that were warm, safe, and well fed but that were not allowed any social contact for the first 6 months of their lives developed a variety of behavioral abnormalities. They compulsively rocked back and forth while biting themselves, and if they were introduced to other monkeys, they avoided them entirely. These socially isolated monkeys turned out to be incapable of communicating with or learning from others of their kind, and when the females matured and became mothers, they ignored, rejected, and sometimes even attacked their own infants. Harlow also discovered that when socially isolated monkeys were put in a cage with two "artificial mothers"—one that was made of wire and dispensed food and one that was made of cloth and dispensed no food—they spent most of their time clinging to the soft cloth mother despite the fact that the wire mother was the source of their nourishment. Clearly, infants of both species require something more from their caregivers than mere sustenance. But what?

Becoming Attached

Few things are cuter than a string of ducklings following their mother. But how do they know who their mother is? In a series of studies, the biologist Konrad Lorenz discovered that ducklings don't actually know who their mothers are at all. Rather, they simply follow the first moving object they see after they are born—even if that object is a tennis ball or a biologist! Lorenz theorized that nature designed ducklings so that the first moving object they saw was *imprinted* on their brains and became "the thing I must always stay near" (Lorenz, 1952).

Psychiatrist John Bowlby was fascinated by Lorenz's work, as well as by Harlow's studies of rhesus monkeys reared in isolation and the work on children reared in orphanages, and he sought to understand how human infants form attachments to their caregivers (Bowlby, 1969, 1973, 1980). Bowlby began by noting that from the moment they are born, ducks waddle after their mothers and monkeys cling to their mothers' furry chests because the newborns of both species must stay close to their caregivers to survive. Human infants, he suggested, have a similar need, but because they are

Harlow's monkeys preferred the comfort and warmth of a soft cloth mother (*left*) to the wire mother (*right*) even when the wire mother was associated with food.

Like hatchlings, human infants need to stay close to their mothers to survive. Unlike hatchlings, human infants know how to get their mothers to come to them rather than the other way around.

attachment An emotional bond with a primary caregiver.

temperaments Characteristic patterns of emotional reactivity.

Children are naturally social creatures who readily develop relationships with caregivers and peers. Toddlers who spend time with a responsive robot will begin to treat it like a classmate instead of like a toy (Tanaka, Cicourel, & Movellan, 2007).

much less physically developed, they can't waddle or cling. So instead they smile and cry. When an infant cries, gurgles, coos, makes eye contact, or smiles, most adults reflexively move toward the infant, and Bowlby suggested that this is *why* infants have been designed to emit these signals.

According to Bowlby, infants initially send these signals to anyone within visual or auditory range. For the first 6 months or so, they keep a "mental tally" of who responds most promptly and often to their signals, and soon they begin to target the best and fastest responder, also known as the *primary caregiver*. This person quickly becomes the emotional center of the infant's universe. Infants feel secure in the primary caregiver's presence and will happily crawl around, exploring their environments with their eyes, ears, fingers, and mouths. But if their primary caregiver gets too far away, infants begin to feel insecure, and they take action to decrease the distance between themselves and their primary caregiver, perhaps by crawling toward their caregiver or perhaps by crying until their caregiver moves toward them. Human infants, Bowlby suggested, are predisposed to form an **attachment**—that is, *an emotional bond with a primary caregiver*.

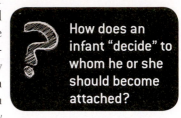

How does an infant "decide" to whom he or she should become attached?

Attachment Styles

Of course, not all emotional bonds are of the same kind. Research suggests that most infants show one of four basic patterns of attachment, known as *attachment styles* (Ainsworth et al., 1978), which can be inferred by watching how they respond when their caregivers leave them alone for a few minutes and then return:

1. *Secure attachment.* When the caregiver leaves, secure infants may or may not be distressed. When she returns, the distressed infants go to her and are calmed by her presence, while non-distressed infants acknowledge her with a glance or greeting.
2. *Avoidant attachment.* When the caregiver leaves, avoidant infants are not distressed, but when she returns, they don't acknowledge her.
3. *Ambivalent attachment.* When the caregiver leaves, ambivalent infants are distressed, and when she returns, they rebuff her, refusing any attempt at calming while arching their backs and squirming to get away.
4. *Disorganized attachment.* When their caregiver leaves and returns, disorganized infants show no consistent pattern of response.

Where do these attachment styles come from? Childrens' attachment styles are determined in part by their **temperament,** or *characteristic pattern of emotional reactivity* (Thomas & Chess, 1977). Whether measured by parents' reports or by physiological indices such as heart rate or cerebral blood flow, very young children vary in their tendency toward fearfulness, irritability, activity, positive affect, and other emotional traits (Rothbart & Bates, 1998). These temperamental differences among infants appear to result partly from innate biological differences (Baker et al., 2013). But culture also plays a role in determining attachment style. For example, although the secure attachment style is the most common one among infants of all cultures (van IJzendoorn & Kroonenberg, 1988), German children (whose parents tend to foster independence) are more likely to have avoidant than ambivalent attachment styles, and Japanese children (whose mothers typically stay home and do not leave them in the care of others) are more likely to have ambivalent than avoidant attachment styles (Takahashi, 1986).

Although biology and culture both play a role, for the most part a child's attachment style is determined by interactions with his or her primary caregiver. Studies have shown that mothers of securely attached

How do caregivers influence an infant's attachment style?

infants tend to be especially sensitive to signs of their child's emotional state, especially good at detecting their infant's "request" for reassurance, and especially responsive to that request (Ainsworth et al., 1978; De Wolff & van IJzendoorn, 1997). In contrast, mothers of infants with an ambivalent attachment style tend to respond inconsistently, only sometimes attending to infants who are showing signs of distress.

As a result of their interactions with their caregivers, infants develop an **internal working model of relationships,** which is *a set of beliefs about the self, the primary caregiver, and the relationship between them* (Bretherton & Munholland, 1999). Secure infants seem certain that their primary caregiver will respond when they feel distressed; avoidant infants seem certain that their primary caregiver will not respond when they are distressed; and ambivalent infants seem uncertain about whether their primary caregiver will respond. Infants with a disorganized attachment style seem to be confused about their caregivers, which has led some psychologists to speculate that this style primarily characterizes children who have been abused (Carolson, 1998; Cicchetti & Toth, 1998).

David Grossman/Alamy

Does spending time in day care impair the attachment process? A long-term study showed that attachment style is strongly influenced by maternal sensitivity and responsiveness, but not by the quality, amount, stability, or type of day care (Friedman & Boyle, 2008).

Differences in how caregivers respond are largely due to differences in their ability to read their infants' emotional states. Mothers who think of their infants as unique individuals with emotional lives and not just as creatures with urgent physical needs are more likely to have securely attached infants (Meins, 2003; Meins et al., 2001)? It appears so. Mothers whose infants were particularly irritable and difficult participated in a training program designed to sensitize them to their infants' emotional signals and to encourage them to be more responsive to their infants. A year or two later, those infants whose mothers had received the training were considerably more likely to have a secure attachment style than were those whose mothers did not receive the training (van den Boom, 1994, 1995).

This is potentially good news, because children and adults who were securely attached as infants have greater psychological well-being (Madigan et al., 2013) higher academic achievement (Jacobson & Hoffman, 1997), and better social relationships (McElwain, Booth-LaForce, & Wu, 2011; Schneider, Atkinson, & Tardif, 2001; Simpson, Collins, & Salvatore, 2011; Steele et al., 1999; Vondra et al., 2001). Some psychologists suggest that this is because people apply the working models they developed as infants to their later relationships with teachers, friends, and lovers (Sroufe, Egeland, & Kruetzer, 1990). But other psychologists argue that an infant's attachment style is correlated with later outcomes only because both the style and the outcome are caused by the same environment: In other words, sensitive and responsive caregivers cause both the infant's attachment style and his or her later adult outcomes (Lamb et al., 1985).

Moral Development

From the moment of birth, human beings can make one distinction quickly and well, and that's the distinction between pleasure and pain. Before they hit their very first diapers, infants can tell when something feels good or bad, and they can demonstrate to anyone within earshot that they strongly prefer the former. Over the next few years, they begin to notice that their pleasures ("Throwing food is fun") are often someone else's pains ("Throwing food makes Mom mad"), which is a bit of a problem because infants need these other people (and especially their caregivers) to survive. So they start to learn how to balance their needs and the needs of those around them, and they do this in part by developing the distinction between *right* and *wrong*.

internal working model of relationships A set of beliefs about the self, the primary caregiver, and the relationship between them.

preconventional stage A stage of moral development in which the morality of an action is primarily determined by its consequences for the actor.

conventional stage A stage of moral development in which the morality of an action is primarily determined by the extent to which it conforms to social rules.

According to Piaget, young children do not realize that moral rules can vary across persons and cultures. For instance, most Americans think it is immoral to eat a dog, but most Vietnamese disagree.

During WWII, many Albanian Muslims shielded their Jewish neighbors from the Nazis. Baba Haxhi Dede Reshatbardhi (pictured) was one of those who saved many Jewish lives.

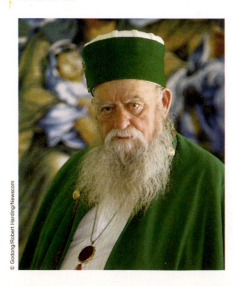

Knowing What's Right

How do children think about right and wrong? Piaget identified three ways in which children's moral thinking shifts as they grow and develop (Piaget, 1932/1965).

1. First, Piaget noticed that children's moral thinking tends to shift *from realism to relativism.* Very young children regard moral rules as real, inviolable truths about the world. For the young child, right and wrong are like day and night: They exist in the world and do not depend on what people think or say. That's why young children generally don't think that a bad action (such as hitting someone) can ever be good, even if everyone agreed to allow it. As they mature, children begin to realize that some moral rules (e.g., wives should obey their husbands) are inventions, not discoveries, and that people can therefore agree to adopt them, change them, or abandon them entirely.

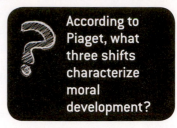

According to Piaget, what three shifts characterize moral development?

2. Second, Piaget noticed that children's moral thinking tends to shift *from prescriptions to principles.* Young children think of moral rules as guidelines for specific actions in specific situations ("Everyone gets a turn playing with the iPad"). As they mature, children come to see that specific rules are expressions of more general principles, such as fairness and equity, which means that specific rules can be abandoned or modified when they fail to uphold the general principle ("If Jason missed his turn last time then he should get two turns now").

3. Third and finally, Piaget noticed that children's moral thinking tends to shift from *outcomes* to *intentions.* For the young child, an unintentional action that causes great harm ("Josh accidentally broke Dad's iPad") seems "more wrong" than an intentional action that causes slight harm ("Josh got mad and broke Dad's pencil") because young children tend to judge the morality of an action by its outcome rather than by the actor's intentions. As they mature, children begin to see that the morality of an action is critically dependent on the actor's state of mind.

Psychologist Lawrence Kohlberg used Piaget's insights to produce a more detailed theory of the development of moral reasoning (Kohlberg, 1958, 1963, 1986). He based his theory on people's responses to a series of dilemmas like this one:

> A woman was near death from a special kind of cancer. The druggist in town had recently discovered a new drug that might save her. The druggist was charging $2,000 a dose, even though it only cost him $200 to make. The sick woman's husband, Heinz, only had $1,000. He told the druggist that his wife was dying and asked him to sell the drug cheaper. But the druggist said: "No, I discovered the drug and I'm going to make money from it." So Heinz got desperate and broke into the drugstore to steal the drug for his wife. Should Heinz have done that?

According to Kohlberg, people's answers to this question reveal that moral reasoning develops in three stages:

1. Most children are at the **preconventional stage,** which is *a stage of moral development in which the morality of an action is primarily determined by its consequences for the actor.* Immoral actions are simply those for which one is punished. For example, children at this stage often base their moral judgment of Heinz on the relative costs of one decision ("He would feel bad if he went to jail") and another ("But he'd feel even worse if his wife died, so he should steal the medicine").

2. Somewhere around adolescence, most people move to the **conventional stage,** which is *a stage of moral development in which the morality of an action is primarily*

determined by the extent to which it conforms to social rules. Immoral actions are those for which one is condemned by others. People at this stage argue that Heinz must weigh his duty to society, which suggests he should obey the law, against his duty to his family, which suggests he should break it.

3. Finally, most adults move to the **postconventional stage,** which is *a stage of moral development in which the morality of an action is determined by a set of general principles that reflect core values,* such as the right to life, liberty, and the pursuit of happiness. When a behavior violates these principles, it is immoral, and if a law requires these principles to be violated, then it should be disobeyed. For a person who has reached the postconventional stage, a woman's life is always more important than a shopkeeper's profits, and so stealing the drug is not only a moral behavior, but also a moral obligation.

Research supports Kohlberg's general claim that moral reasoning shifts from an emphasis on punishment to an emphasis on social rules and finally to an emphasis on ethical principles (Walker, 1988). But research also suggests that these stages are not quite as discrete as Kohlberg thought. For instance, a single person may use preconventional, conventional, and postconventional thinking in different circumstances, which suggests that the developing person does not "reach a stage" so much as "acquires a skill" that may or may not be used on a particular occasion. Others have criticized Kohlberg's theory on the grounds that it doesn't apply well to non-Westerners (Simpson, 1974). For example, some non-Western societies value obedience and community over liberty and individuality; thus, the moral reasoning of people in those societies may *appear* to reflect a conventional devotion to social norms when it *actually* reflects a postconventional consideration of ethical principles.

"You've been circling three days, and your prey won't die—what's your position, ethically speaking?"

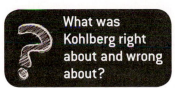

What was Kohlberg right about and wrong about?

Feeling What's Right

Research on moral reasoning suggests that people are like judges in a court of law, using rational analysis—sometimes simple and sometimes sophisticated—to distinguish between right and wrong. But moral dilemmas don't just make us think; they also make us *feel.* Consider this one:

> You are standing on a bridge. Below you see a runaway trolley hurtling down the track toward five people who will be killed if it remains on its present course. You can save these people by flipping a lever that will switch the trolley onto a different track, where it will kill just one person instead of five. Is it morally permissible to divert the trolley and prevent five deaths at the cost of one?

Now consider a slightly different version of this problem:

> You and a large man are standing on a bridge. Below you see a runaway trolley hurtling down the track toward five people who will be killed if it remains on its present course. You can save these people by pushing the large man onto the track, where his body will be caught up in the trolley's wheels and stop it before it kills the five people. Is it morally permissible to push the large man and prevent five deaths at the cost of one?

These scenarios are illustrated in **FIGURE 10.6**. If you are like most people, you are more likely to think it is morally permissible to pull a switch than to push a man (Greene et al., 2001). And yet, both cases involve killing one person to save five, so how did your moral reasoning lead you to reach such different conclusions? The answer is that you probably didn't reach these conclusions by moral reasoning at all. Rather, you simply had a strong negative emotional reaction to the thought of pushing

postconventional stage A stage of moral development at which the morality of an action is determined by a set of general principles that reflect core values.

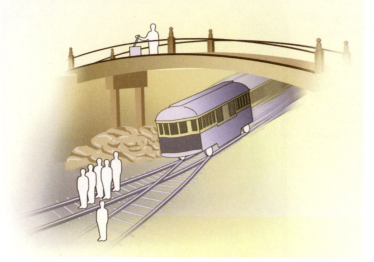 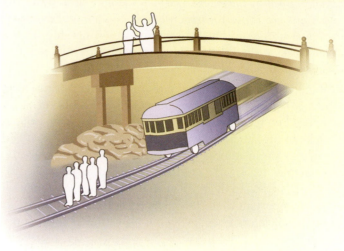

(a)   (b)

FIGURE 10.6 **The Trolley Problem** Why does it seem permissible to trade one life for five lives by pulling a switch but not by pushing a man from a bridge? Research suggests that the scenario shown in (b) elicits a more negative emotional response than does the scenario shown in (a), and this emotional response may be the basis for our moral intuitions.

Most people are upset by the suffering of others, and research suggests that even young children have this response, which may be the basis of their emerging morality.

another human being into the path of an oncoming trolley and watching him get sliced and diced, and that emotional reaction instantly led you to conclude that pushing him must be wrong. Sure, you came up with a few good arguments to support this conclusion ("What if he turned around and bit me?" or "I'd hate to get spleen all over my new shoes"), but those arguments probably followed your conclusion rather than preceding it (Greene, 2013).

The way people respond to cases such as these has convinced some psychologists that moral judgments are the consequences—and not the causes—of emotional reactions (Haidt, 2001). According to this *moral intuitionist* perspective, we have evolved to react emotionally to a small family of events that are particularly relevant to reproduction and survival, and we have developed the distinction between right and wrong as a way of labeling and explaining these emotional reactions (Hamlin, Wynn, & Bloom, 2007). Some research supports this view. For example, in one study (Wheatley & Haidt, 2005), participants were hypnotized and told that whenever they heard the word *take,* they would experience "a brief pang of disgust…a sickening feeling in your stomach." After they came out of the hypnotic state, the participants were asked to rate the morality of several actions. Sometimes the description of the action contained the word *take* ("How immoral is it for a police officer to *take* a bribe") and sometimes it did not ("How immoral is it for a police officer to *accept* a bribe?"). Participants rated the action as less moral when it contained the word *take,* suggesting that their negative feelings were causing—rather than being caused by—their moral reasoning.

Do moral judgments come before or after emotional reactions?

The moral intuitionist perspective suggests that we consider it immoral to push someone onto the tracks simply because the idea of watching someone suffer makes us feel bad (Greene et al., 2001). In fact, research has shown that watching someone suffer activates many of the same brain regions that are activated when we suffer ourselves (Carr et al., 2003; see the discussion of mirror neurons in the Neuroscience and Behavior chapter). In one study, women received a shock or watched their romantic partners receive a shock on different parts of their bodies. The regions of the women's brains that processed information about the location of the shock were activated only when the women experienced the shock themselves, but the regions that processed emotional information were activated whether the women received the shock or observed it (Singer et al.,

2004). The fact that we can actually *feel* another person's suffering may explain why even a small child who is incapable of sophisticated moral reasoning still considers it wrong when someone hurts someone else, especially when the person being hurt is similar to the child (Hamlin et al., 2013). Indeed, even very young children say that hitting is wrong even when an adult instructs someone to do it (Laupa & Turiel, 1986). It appears that from a very early age, other people's suffering can become our suffering, and this leads us to conclude that the actions that caused the suffering are immoral.

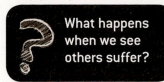

What happens when we see others suffer?

SUMMARY QUIZ [10.2]

1. Piaget believed that infants construct _____, which are theories about the way the world works.
   a. assimilations
   b. accommodations
   c. schemas
   d. habituations

2. Once children understand that human behavior is guided by mental representations, they are said to have acquired
   a. joint attention.
   b. a theory of mind.
   c. formal operational ability.
   d. egocentrism.

3. When infants in a new situation examine their mother's face for cues about what to do, they are demonstrating an ability known as
   a. joint attention.
   b. social referencing.
   c. imitation.
   d. all of the above.

4. The capacity for attachment may be innate, but the quality of attachment is influenced by
   a. the child's temperament.
   b. the ability of primary caregivers to read their child's emotional state.
   c. the interaction between the child and the primary caregiver.
   d. all of the above.

Adolescence: Minding the Gap

Between childhood and adulthood is an extended developmental stage that may not qualify for a hood of its own, but that is clearly distinct from the stages that come before and after. **Adolescence** is *the period of development that begins with the onset of sexual maturity (about 11 to 14 years of age) and lasts until the beginning of adulthood (about 18 to 21 years of age).* Unlike the transition from embryo to fetus or from infant to child, this transition is sudden and clearly marked. In just 3 or 4 years, the average adolescent gains about 40 pounds and grows about 10 inches. For girls, all this growing starts at about the age of 10 and ends when they reach their full heights at about the age of 15.5. For boys, it starts at about the age of 12 and ends at about the age of 17.5.

adolescence The period of development that begins with the onset of sexual maturity (about 11 to 14 years of age) and lasts until the beginning of adulthood (about 18 to 21 years of age).

Adolescents are often described as gawky because different parts of their faces and bodies mature at different rates. But as musician Justin Timberlake can attest, the gawkiness generally clears up.

puberty The bodily changes associated with sexual maturity.

primary sex characteristics Bodily structures that are directly involved in reproduction.

secondary sex characteristics Bodily structures that change dramatically with sexual maturity but that are not directly involved in reproduction.

The beginning of this growth spurt signals the onset of **puberty**, which refers to *the bodily changes associated with sexual maturity.* These changes involve **primary sex characteristics,** which are *bodily structures that are directly involved in reproduction*—for example, the onset of menstruation in girls and the enlargement of the testes, scrotum, and penis and the emergence of the capacity for ejaculation in boys. They also involve **secondary sex characteristics,** which are *bodily structures that change dramatically with sexual maturity but that are not directly involved in reproduction*—for example, the enlargement of the breasts and the widening of the hips in girls and the appearance of facial hair, pubic hair, underarm hair, and the lowering of the voice in both genders. This pattern of changes is caused by increased production of estrogen in girls and testosterone in boys.

Just as the body changes during adolescence, so too does the brain. Between the ages of 6 and 13, the connections between the temporal lobe (the brain region specialized for language) and the parietal lobe (the brain region specialized for understanding spatial relations) multiply rapidly and then stop—at just about the time that the critical period for learning a language ends (see **FIGURE 10.7**). There is also a massive increase in the number of new synapses in the prefrontal cortex before puberty, followed by a period of "synaptic pruning" after puberty, during which the synaptic connections that are not frequently used are eliminated (Giedd et al., 1999). Clearly, the adolescent brain is a work in progress.

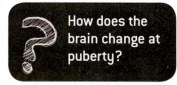

How does the brain change at puberty?

The Protraction of Adolescence

The age at which puberty begins varies across individuals (e.g., people tend to reach puberty at about the same age as their same-sexed parent did) and across cultures (e.g., African American girls tend to reach puberty before European American girls do). It also varies across generations (Malina, Bouchard, & Beunen, 1988). For example, in the United States, the age of first menstruation was between 16 and 17 years in the 19th century but was approximately 13 years in 1960. Puberty is accelerated by body fat (Kim & Smith, 1998), and the decrease in the age of its onset is largely due to improved diet and health (Ellis & Garber, 2000), though

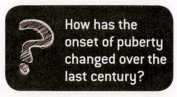

How has the onset of puberty changed over the last century?

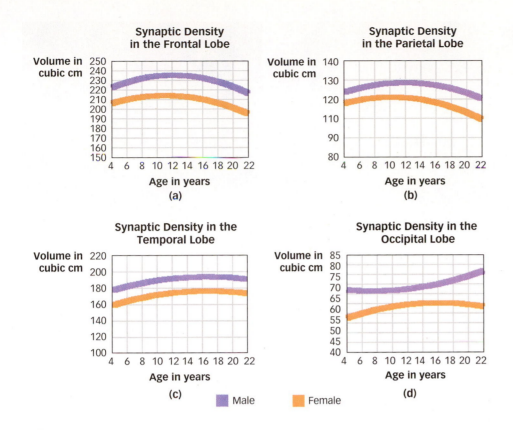

FIGURE 10.7 **Your Brain on Puberty** The development of neurons peaks in the frontal and parietal lobes at about age 12 (a, b), in the temporal lobe at about age 16 (c), and in the occipital lobe at about age 22 for males and age 14 for females (d). (Data from Giedd et al., 1999.)

some scientists believe it is also hastened by exposure to environmental toxins that mimic estrogen (Buck Louis et al., 2008) and by stressful family situations (Belsky, 2012).

The increasingly early onset of puberty has important psychological consequences. Just two centuries ago, the gap between childhood and adulthood was relatively brief because people became physically mature at roughly the same time that they were ready to accept adult roles in society, and these roles did not normally require them to have extensive schooling. But in modern societies, people typically spend 3 to 10 years in school after they reach puberty. Thus, while the age at which people become physically adult has decreased, the age at which they are prepared or allowed to take on adult responsibilities has increased, and so the period between childhood and adulthood has become extended or *protracted.*

Adolescence is often characterized as a time of internal turmoil and external recklessness, and some psychologists have speculated that the protraction of adolescence is partly to blame for its sorry reputation (Epstein, 2007a; Moffitt, 1993). In some sense, adolescents are adults who have temporarily been denied a place in adult society, so they try to demonstrate their adulthood by doing things like smoking, drinking, using drugs, having sex, and committing crimes. So yes, adolescence is rough, but it is not nearly as rough as television shows might lead you to believe (Steinberg & Morris, 2001). Research suggests that the "moody adolescent" who is a victim of "raging hormones" is largely a myth: Adolescents are no moodier than children (Buchanan, Eccles, & Becker, 1992), and fluctuations in their hormone levels have only a tiny impact on their moods (Brooks-Gunn, Graber, & Paikoff, 1994). Although they can be more impulsive and susceptible to peer influence than adults (see **FIGURE 10.8**), they are just as capable of making wise decisions based on good information (Steinberg, 2007). The fact is that the problems of adolescence

? Are adolescent problems inevitable?

About 60% of preindustrial societies don't even have a word for adolescence (Schlegel & Barry, 1991). When a Krobo female menstruates for the first time, older women take her into seclusion for 2 weeks and teach her about sex, birth control, and marriage. Afterward, a public ceremony called the *durbar* is held, and the young female who that morning was regarded as a child is thereafter regarded as an adult.

These students (*left*) may be experimenting with reckless behavior, but they are unlikely to become reckless adults. Of course, the state trooper (*right*) who is inspecting the car in which four teens died after a night of drinking would probably like to remind them that this rule only applies to those who live.

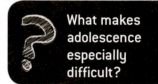

FIGURE 10.8 How Do Peers Affect Decision Making? Adolescents make better decisions when no one is around! Participants in one study played a video driving game with or without their peers in the room. The presence of peers greatly increased the number of risks taken and crashes experienced by adolescents, factor had little or no effect on adults. (Data from Gardner & Steinberg, 2005.)

are typically minor and temporary, and in some cultures, they barely occur at all (Epstein, 2007b; Sampson & Laub, 1995).

Sexuality

Puberty can be difficult, but it is especially difficult for girls who reach it earlier than their peers (Mendle, Turkheimer, & Emery, 2007; see **FIGURE 10.9**). Early blooming girls don't have as much time as their peers do to develop the skills necessary to cope with adolescence (Petersen & Grockett, 1985), but because they look mature, people expect them to act like adults. They also draw the attention of older men, who may lead them into a variety of unhealthy activities (Ge, Conger, & Elder, 1996). Some research suggests that for girls, the timing of puberty has a greater influence on emotional and behavioral problems than does the occurrence of puberty itself (Buchanan et al., 1992). The timing of puberty does not have such consistent effects on boys: Some studies suggest that early maturing boys do better than their peers, some suggest they do worse, and some suggest that there is no difference at all (Ge, Conger, & Elder, 2001).

> **What makes adolescence especially difficult?**

For a small minority of adolescents, puberty is additionally complicated by the fact that they are attracted to members of the same sex. Most gay men report having become aware of their sexual orientation between the ages of 6 and 18, and most gay women report having become aware between the ages of 11 and 26 (Calzo et al., 2011). Not only does their sexual orientation make gay adolescents different from the vast majority

FIGURE 10.9 Early Puberty Early puberty is a source of psychological distress for women. (Data from Ge, Conger, & Elder, 1996.)

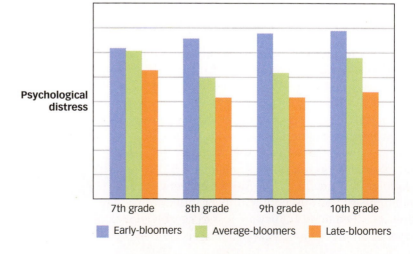

of their peers (a mere 3.5% of American adults identify themselves as lesbian, gay, or bisexual; Gates, 2011), but it can also subject them to disapproval from family, friends, and community. Americans are rapidly becoming more accepting of homosexuality (see **FIGURE 10.10**), but there are still plenty who disapprove. And in some nations, people do more than simply disapprove: They send gay citizens to prison or sentence them to death.

What determines whether a person's sexuality is primarily oriented toward the same or the opposite sex? For a long time, psychologists believed that a person's sexual orientation depended primarily on his or her upbringing. For example, psychoanalytic theorists claimed that boys who grow up with a domineering mother and a submissive father are less likely to identify with their father and are therefore more likely to become homosexual. But modern research has failed to identify *any* aspect of parenting that has a significant impact on a person's sexual orientation (Bell, Weinberg, & Hammersmith, 1981). Perhaps the most telling fact is that children raised by homosexual couples and children raised by heterosexual couples are equally likely to become heterosexual adults (Patterson, 1995). There is also little support for the idea that a person's early sexual encounters have a lasting impact on his or her sexual orientation (Bohan, 1996).

So what *does* determine a person's sexual orientation? There is now considerable evidence to suggest that biology plays the major role. The identical twin of a gay man (with whom he shares 100% of his genes) has a 50% chance of being gay, whereas the fraternal twin or nontwin brother of a gay man (with whom he shares 50% of his genes) has only a 15% chance (Bailey & Pillard, 1991; Gladue, 1994). A similar pattern has emerged in studies of women (Bailey et al., 1993). Some evidence suggests that the fetal environment may play a role in determining sexual orientation and that high levels of androgens in the womb may predispose both male and female fetuses later to develop a sexual preference for women (Ellis & Ames, 1987; Meyer-Bahlberg et al., 1995). Perhaps this is why the brains of gay people tend to look like the brains of opposite-gendered straight people (Savic & Lindstrom, 2008). For example, the brain's two hemispheres tend to be unequally sized among straight men and gay women (both of whom are attracted to women), but they are equally sized among straight women and gay men (both of whom are attracted to men). The science of sexual orientation is still young and fraught with conflicting findings, but one thing that seems abundantly clear is that sexual orientation is *not* simply a matter of choice. That's probably why so-called "conversion therapies" that attempt to change people's sexual orientation have proven so ineffective (American Psychological Association, 2009).

Sexual orientation may not be a matter of choice, but sexual behavior is, and many American teenagers choose it. Although the fraction of American teenagers who have had sex has declined in recent years (see **FIGURE 10.11**), it is still more than a third. Unfortunately, teenagers' interest in

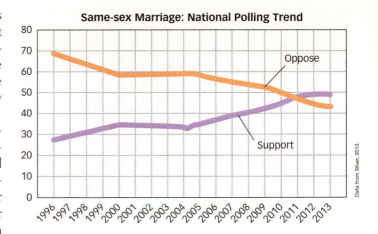

Same-sex Marriage: National Polling Trend

Oppose

Support

Data from Silver, 2013.

FIGURE 10.10 Polling Trends Americans' attitudes about homosexuality have changed dramatically in the last few years, as witnessed by their rapidly changing views on same-sex marriage.

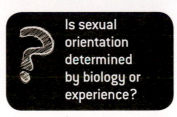

Reuters/Lee Celano/Landov

Jane Clementi's 18-year-old son Tyler committed suicide in 2010 after a college roommate videotaped him kissing another man. She later said, "I think some people think that sexual orientation can be changed or prayed over. But I know sexual orientation is not up for negotiation. I don't think my children need to be changed. I think that what needed changing is attitudes" (quoted in Zernike, 2012).

Is sexual orientation determined by biology or experience?

FIGURE 10.11 Teenage Sex The percentage of American teenagers who have had sex has declined in recent years. (Data from Martinez et al., 2011.)

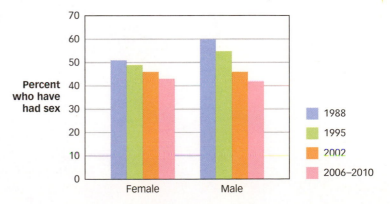

Percent who have had sex

Female   Male

1988
1995
2002
2006–2010

The human papilloma virus is a sexually transmitted disease that can lead to cervical cancer. Luckily, there is a vaccine that can prevent it. Some parents worry that being vaccinated will encourage their daughters to have sex early, but studies show that young women who have been vaccinated do not have sex earlier than those who have not been vaccinated (Bednarczyk et al., 2012).

sex typically surpasses their knowledge about it, and ignorance has consequences. A quarter of American teenagers have had four or more sexual partners by their senior year in high school, but only about half report using a condom during their last intercourse (Centers for Disease Control, 2002). Although teen birth rates have been falling in the United States for about 20 years, they are still the highest in the developed world, and consequently, so is the rate of abortion. That's too bad, because teenage mothers fare more poorly than teenage women without children on almost every measure of academic and economic achievement, and their children fare more poorly on most measures of educational success and emotional well-being than do the children of older mothers (Olausson et al., 2001).

Despite what some people believe, evidence suggests that sex education does not increase the likelihood that teenagers will have sex. Instead, sex education leads teens to delay having sex for the first time, increases the likelihood they will use birth control when they do have sex, and lowers the likelihood that they will get pregnant or catch a sexually transmitted disease (Mueller, Gavin, & Kulkarni, 2008; Satcher, 2001). Despite these documented benefits, sex education in American schools is often absent, sketchy, or based on the goal of abstinence rather than harm prevention. Alas, there is little evidence to suggest that abstinence-only programs are effective (Kohler, Manhart, & Lafferty, 2008), and some studies suggest that teens who take abstinence pledges are just as likely to have sex as those who don't, but that they are less likely to use birth control (Rosenbaum, 2009).

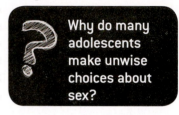

Why do many adolescents make unwise choices about sex?

Parents and Peers

Children define themselves almost entirely in terms of their relationships with parents and siblings, and adolescence marks a shift away from family relations and toward peer relations. Two things can make this shift difficult. First, although children cannot choose their parents, adolescents can choose their peers. As such, adolescents have the power to shape themselves

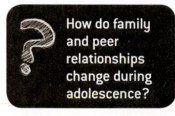

How do family and peer relationships change during adolescence?

by joining groups that will lead them to develop new values, attitudes, beliefs, and perspectives. The responsibility this opportunity entails can be overwhelming. Second, as adolescents strive for greater autonomy, their parents naturally rebel. For instance, parents and adolescents tend to disagree about the age at which certain adult behaviors—such as staying out late or having sex—are permissible (Holmbeck & O'Donnell, 1991). Because adolescents and parents often have different ideas about who should control the adolescent's behavior, their relationships become more conflictual and less close, and their interactions become briefer and less frequent (Larson & Richards, 1991).

Studies show that across a wide variety of cultures, historical epochs, and even species, peer relations evolve in a similar way (Dunphy, 1963; Weisfeld, 1999). Young adolescents initially form groups or "cliques" with same-sexed peers, many of whom were friends during childhood (Brown, Mory, & Kinney, 1994). Next, male cliques and female cliques begin to meet in public places, such as town squares or shopping malls, and they begin to interact—but only in groups and only in public. After a few years, the older members of these same-sex cliques peel off and form smaller, mixed-sex cliques, which may assemble in private as well as in public, but usually assemble as a group. Finally, couples peel off from the small, mixed-sex clique and begin romantic relationships.

"You're free-range when I say you're free-range."

Studies show that throughout adolescence, people spend increasing amounts of time with opposite-sex peers while maintaining the amount of time they spend with same-sex peers (Richards et al., 1998), and they do this by spending less time with their parents (Larson & Richards, 1991). Although peers exert considerable influence over the adolescent's beliefs and behaviors, studies suggest that this occurs mainly because adolescents respect, admire, and like their peers and not because their peers pressure them (Susman et al., 1994). In fact, as they age, adolescents show an increasing tendency to resist peer pressure (Steinberg & Monahan, 2007). Acceptance by peers is of tremendous importance to adolescents, and those who are rejected by their peers tend to be withdrawn, lonely, and depressed (Pope & Bierman, 1999). Fortunately for those of us who were seventh-grade nerds, individuals who are unpopular in early adolescence can become popular in later adolescence as their peers become less rigid and more tolerant (Kinney, 1993).

Jeff Greenberg/Alamy

Adolescents form same-sex cliques that meet opposite-sex cliques in public places. Eventually, these people will form mixed-sex cliques, pair off into romantic relationships, get married, have children, and then worry about their own children when they do all the same things that they did.

SUMMARY QUIZ [10.3]

1. Evidence indicates that American adolescents are
   a. moodier than children.
   b. victims of raging hormones.
   c. likely to develop drinking problems.
   d. living in a protracted gap between childhood and adulthood.

2. Scientific evidence suggests that _____ play(s) a key role in determining a person's sexual orientation.
   a. personal choices
   b. parenting styles
   c. sibling relationships
   d. biology

3. Adolescents place the greatest emphasis on relationships with
   a. peers.
   b. parents.
   c. siblings.
   d. nonparental authority figures.

Adulthood: Change We Can't Believe In

Adulthood is *the stage of development that begins around 18 to 21 years and ends at death*. Because physical change slows from a gallop to a crawl, many of us think of adulthood as the destination to which the process of development finally delivers us, and that once we've arrived, our journey is pretty much complete. Nothing could be further from the truth. A whole host of physical, cognitive, and emotional changes take place between our first legal beer and our last legal breath.

adulthood The stage of development that begins around 18 to 21 years and ends at death.

Changing Abilities

The early 20s are the peak years for health, stamina, vigor, and prowess, and because our psychology is so closely tied to our biology, these are also the years during which most cognitive abilities are sharpest. At this very moment, you probably see farther, hear better, and remember more accurately than you ever will again. Enjoy it. Somewhere between the ages of 26 and 30, you will begin the slow and steady decline that will not end until you do. Just 10 or 15 years after puberty, your body will begin to break down in almost every way. Your muscles will be replaced by fat, your skin will become less elastic, your hair will thin and your bones will weaken, your sensory abilities will become less acute, and your brain cells will die at an accelerated rate. Eventually, if you are a woman, your ovaries will stop producing eggs, and you will become infertile. Eventually, if you are a man, your erections will be softer and fewer and farther between. Indeed, other than being more resistant to colds and less sensitive to pain, your elderly body just won't work as well as your youthful body does.

But don't worry, the news gets worse. Because as these physical changes accumulate, they will begin to have measurable psychological consequences (Salthouse, 2006; see **FIGURE 10.12**). For instance, as you age, your prefrontal cortex will deteriorate more quickly than the other areas of your brain (Raz, 2000), and you will experience a noticeable decline on cognitive tasks that require effort, initiative, or strategy. Although your memory will worsen in general, you will experience more decline in working memory (the ability to hold information "in mind") than in long-term memory (the ability to retrieve information), and more decline in episodic memory (the ability to remember particular past events) than in semantic memory (the ability to remember general information such as the meanings of words).

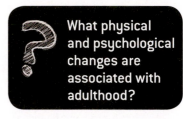

What physical and psychological changes are associated with adulthood?

But not all the news is bad. Even though your cognitive machinery will get rustier, research suggests that you will partially compensate by using it much more skillfully (Bäckman & Dixon, 1992; Salthouse, 1987). Older chess players *remember* chess positions much more poorly than younger players do, but they *play* just as well because they learn to search the board more efficiently (Charness, 1981). Older typists *react* more slowly than younger typists do, but they *type* just as quickly and accurately because they are better at anticipating the

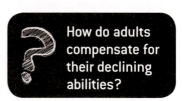

How do adults compensate for their declining abilities?

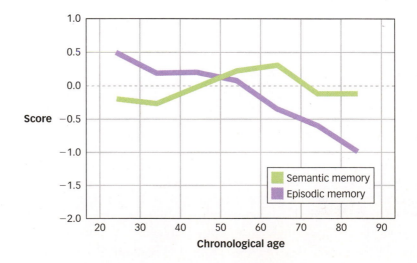

FIGURE 10.12 Cognitive Decline After the age of 20, people show dramatic declines on some measures of cognitive performance but not others (Salthouse, 2006). For example, the ability to recall past events (episodic memory) declines as we age, but the ability to recall the meanings of words (semantic memory) does not. (Data from Salthouse, 2006.)

AP Photo/Noah Berger

AP Photo/Steven Day

One week before his 58th birthday, US Airways pilot Chesley Sullenberger made a perfect emergency landing in the Hudson River and saved the lives of everyone on board. None of the passengers wished they'd had a younger pilot.

next word in spoken or written text (Salthouse, 1984). All of this suggests that older adults are using the skills they developed over a lifetime to compensate for the age-related declines they experience in memory and attention (Park & McDonough, 2013).

Even the brain changes the way it does business. As you know from the Neuroscience and Behavior chapter, brains are differentiated—that is, they have different parts that do different things. But as they age, brains become *de-differentiated* (Lindenberger & Baltes, 1994), and parts that once worked like independent specialists start to pull together as a team (Park & McDonough, 2013). For example, when young adults try to keep verbal information in working memory, the left prefrontal cortex is more strongly activated than the right, and when they try to keep spatial information in working memory, the right prefrontal cortex is more strongly activated than the left (Smith & Jonides, 1997). But this *bilateral asymmetry* pretty much disappears in older adults, which suggests that the older brain is compensating for the declining abilities of one half by calling on the other half to help out (Cabeza, 2002; see **FIGURE 10.13**). The physical machinery breaks down as time passes, and one of the ways in which the brain rises to that challenge is by changing its division of labor.

FIGURE 10.13 Information Processing in Older and Younger Brains Across a variety of tasks, young adult brains show bilateral asymmetry and older adult brains do not. One explanation for this is that older brains compensate for the declining abilities of one neural structure by calling on other neural structures for help (Cabeza, 2002).

Changing Goals

So one reason why Grandpa can't find his car keys is that his prefrontal cortex doesn't work as well as it used to. But another reason is that the location of car keys just isn't the sort of thing that grandpas spend their precious time memorizing (Haase, Heckhausen, & Wrosch, 2013). According to *socioemotional selectivity theory* (Carstensen & Turk-Charles, 1994), younger adults are largely oriented toward the acquisition of information that will be useful to them in the future (e.g., reading reviews of new technology), whereas older adults are generally oriented toward information that brings emotional satisfaction in the present (e.g., reading poems and novels). Because young people have such long futures, they invest their time attending to, thinking about, and remembering information that they may want to use tomorrow. Because older people have much shorter futures, they spend their

How do informational goals change in adulthood?

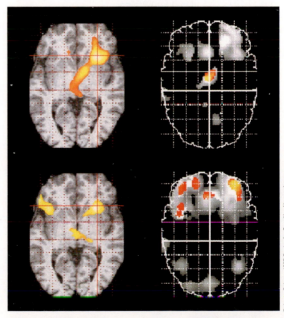

Young Adults

Old Adults

(a) Word-Pair Cued Recall

(b) Word Recognition

Roberto Cabeza, 1997 Center for Cognitive Neuroscience, Duke University; Madden, Gottlob, et al (1999)

Lucy Nicholson/Reuters/Newscom

Getting old isn't as bad as people think, and it even holds a few nice surprises. For example, one study of women aged 40 to 100 showed that the oldest women were nearly twice as likely as the youngest ones to report being "very satisfied" with their sex lives (Trompeter, Bettencourt, & Barrett-Connor, 2012).

FIGURE 10.14 Memory for Pictures
Memory generally declines with age, but the ability to remember negative information—such as unpleasant pictures—declines much more quickly than the ability to remember positive information. (Data from Carstensen et al., 2000.)

As people age, they prefer to spend time with family and a few close friends rather than with large circles of acquaintances.

Courtesy of Daniel Gilbert

FIGURE 10.15 Emotions and Age Older adults experience much lower levels of stress, worry, and anger than younger adults do. (Data from Walker, 1977.)

time attending to, thinking about, and remembering positive information that they can enjoy today.

That's one of the reasons why older people are *much* worse than younger people when they try to remember a series of unpleasant faces (see **FIGURE 10.14**), but only *slightly* worse when they try to remember a series of pleasant faces (Mather &Carstensen, 2003). Indeed, compared to younger adults, older adults are generally better at sustaining positive emotions and curtailing negative ones (Isaacowitz, 2012; Isaacowitz & Blanchard-Fields, 2012; Lawton et al., 1992; Mather & Carstensen, 2005). They also experience fewer negative emotions (Carstensen et al., 2000; Charles, Reynolds, & Gatz, 2001; Mroczek & Spiro, 2005; Schilling, Wahl, & Wiegering, 2013), and are more accepting of them when they do (Shallcross et al., 2013). Given all this, you shouldn't be surprised to learn that late adulthood is consistently reported to be one of the happiest and most satisfying periods of life (see **FIGURE 10.15**). You *shouldn't* be surprised, but you probably are because young adults vastly overestimate the problems of aging (Pew Research Center for People & the Press, 2009).

Is late adulthood a happy or unhappy time for most people?

Because having a short future orients people toward emotionally satisfying rather than intellectually profitable experiences, older adults become more selective about their interaction partners, choosing to spend time with family and a few close friends rather than with a large circle of acquaintances. One study monitored a group of people from the 1930s to the 1990s and found that the rate of interaction with acquaintances declined from early to middle adulthood, but the rate of interaction with spouses, parents, and siblings remained stable or increased (Carstensen, 1992). "Let's go meet some new people" isn't something that most 60-year-olds tend to say, but "Let's go hang out with some old friends" is. It is sad but instructive to note that many of the cognitive and emotional changes that characterize older adults are also observed among younger adults whose futures have been shortened by terminal illness (Carstensen & Fredrickson, 1998).

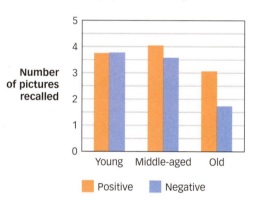

Number of pictures recalled

Young   Middle-aged   Old

■ Positive   ■ Negative

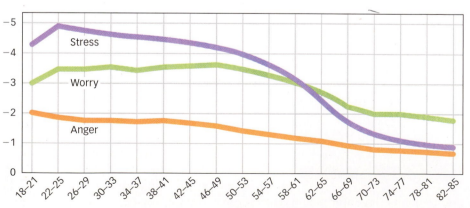

Stress

Worry

Anger

Age

Changing Roles

The psychological separation from parents that begins in adolescence usually becomes a physical separation in adulthood. In virtually all human societies, young adults leave home, get married, and have children of their own. The average college-age American is likely to get married at around the age of 27, have approximately 1.8 children, and consider both partner and children to be sources of great joy.

But do marriage and children really make us happy? Research shows that married people live longer, have more frequent sex (and enjoy that sex more), and earn several times as much money as unmarried people do (Waite, 1995). Given these differences, it is no surprise that married people report being happier than unmarried people—whether those unmarried people are single, widowed, divorced, or cohabiting (Johnson & Wu, 2002). That's why many researchers consider marriage one of the best investments individuals can make in their own happiness. But other researchers suggest that married people may be happier because happy people may

Does marriage make people happy or do happy people tend to get married?

What does research say about marriage, children, and happiness?

be more likely to get married and that marriage may be the consequence—and not the cause—of happiness (Lucas et al., 2003). The general consensus among scientists seems to be that both of these positions have merit: Even before marriage, people who end up married tend to be happier than those who never marry, but marriage does seem to confer further benefits.

Children are another story. In general, research suggests that children do not increase their parents' happiness, and may even decrease it (DiTella, MacCulloch, & Oswald, 2003; Simon, 2008; Senior, 2014). For example, parents typically report lower marital satisfaction than do nonparents—and the more children they have, the less satisfaction they report (Twenge, Campbell, & Foster, 2003). Studies suggest that marital satisfaction starts out high, dips down at about the time that the children are in diapers, begins to recover, dips again when the children are in adolescence, and returns to its premarital levels only when children leave home (see **FIGURE 10.16**). Given that mothers typically do more child care than fathers, it is little wonder that the negative impact of parenthood is stronger for women than for men. Women with young children are especially likely to experience role conflicts ("How am I supposed to manage being a full-time lawyer and a full-time mother?") and restrictions of freedom ("I never get to play tennis anymore"). One study found that American women were less happy when taking care of their children than when eating, exercising, shopping, napping, or watching television—and only slightly happier than when they were doing housework (Kahneman et al., 2004).

FIGURE 10.16 Marital Satisfaction over the Life Span Four independent studies of marital satisfaction among men and women all suggest that marital satisfaction is highest before children are born and after they leave home (Walker, 1977).

Satisfaction

(y-axis: 46–56)

(x-axis: Married without children | Childbearing | Preschool children, oldest 5 | School-children, oldest 5–12 | Teenagers, oldest 12–16 | First child gone to last leaving home | Empty nest to retirement | Empty nest to death of first spouse)

You Are Going to Die

Tim Kreider is an essayist and cartoonist whose newest book is *We Learn Nothing*.
Tim Kreider/Einstein Thompson Agency, NY, NY

Human development begins at conception and ends at death. Most of us would rather think about the conception part. Getting old seems scary and depressing, and one of the reasons why we send elderly people to retirement homes is so we don't have to watch as they wrinkle and wither and die. The essayist Tim Kreider (2013) thinks this is a terrible loss—not for older people, but for younger ones.

My sister and I recently toured the retirement community where my mother has announced she'll be moving. I have been in some bleak clinical facilities for the elderly where not one person was compos mentis and I had to politely suppress the urge to flee, but this was nothing like that. It was a very cushy modern complex housed in what used to be a seminary, with individual condominiums with big kitchens and sun rooms, equipped with fancy restaurants, grills and snack bars, a fitness center, a concert hall, a library, an art room, a couple of beauty salons, a bank and an ornate chapel of Italian marble. You could walk from any building in the complex to another without ever going outside, through underground corridors and glass-enclosed walkways through the woods. Mom described it as "like a college dorm, except the boys aren't as good-looking." Nonetheless I spent much of my day trying not to cry.

At all times of major life crisis, friends and family will crowd around and press upon you the false emotions appropriate to the occasion. "That's so great!" everyone said of my mother's decision to move to an assisted-living facility. "It's really impressive that she decided to do that herself." They cited their own stories of 90-year-old parents grimly clinging to drafty dilapidated houses, refusing to move until forced out by strokes or broken hips. "You should be really relieved and grateful." "She'll be much happier there." The overbearing unanimity of this chorus suggests to me that its real purpose is less to reassure than to suppress, to deny the most obvious and natural emotion that attends this occasion, which is sadness.

My sadness is purely selfish, I know. My friends are right; this was all Mom's idea,

she's looking forward to it, and she really will be happier there. But it also means losing the farm my father bought in 1976, where my sister and I grew up, where Dad died in 1991. We're losing *our old phone number*, the one we've had since the Ford administration, a number I know as well as my own middle name. However infrequently I go there, it is the place on earth that feels like home to me, the place I'll always have to go back to in case adulthood falls through. I hadn't realized, until I was forcibly divested of it, that I'd been harboring the idea that someday, when this whole crazy adventure was over, I would at some point be nine again, sitting around the dinner table with Mom and Dad and my sister. And beneath it all, even at age 45, there is the irrational, little-kid fear: Who's going to take care of me? I remember my mother telling me that when her own mother died, when Mom was in her 40s, her first thought was: *I'm an orphan*.

Plenty of people before me have lamented the way that we in industrialized countries regard our elderly as unproductive workers or obsolete products, and lock them away in institutions instead of taking them into our own homes out of devotion and duty. Most of these critiques are directed at the indifference and cruelty thus displayed to the elderly; what I wonder about is what it's doing to the rest of us.

Segregating the old and the sick enables a fantasy, as baseless as the fantasy of capitalism's endless expansion, of youth and health as eternal, in which old age can seem to be an inexplicably bad lifestyle choice, like eating junk food or buying a minivan, that you can avoid if you're well-educated or hip enough. So that when through absolutely no fault of your own your eyesight begins to blur and you can no longer eat whatever you want without consequence and the hangovers start lasting for days, you feel somehow ripped off, lied to. Aging feels grotesquely unfair. As if there ought to be someone to sue.

We don't see old or infirm people much in movies or on TV. We love explosive gory death onscreen, but we're not so enamored of the creeping, gray, incontinent kind. Aging and death are embarrassing medical conditions, like hemorrhoids or eczema, best kept out of sight. Survivors of serious illness or injuries have written that, once they were sick or disabled, they found themselves confined to a different world, a world of sick people, invisible to the rest of us. Denis Johnson writes in

his novel *Jesus' Son:* "You and I don't know about these diseases until we get them, in which case we also will be put out of sight."

My own father died at home, in what was once my childhood bedroom. He was, in this respect at least, a lucky man. Almost everyone dies in a hospital now, even though absolutely nobody wants to, because by the time we're dying all the decisions have been taken out of our hands by the well, and the well are without mercy. Of course we hospitalize the sick and the old for some good reasons (better care, pain relief), but I think we also segregate the elderly from the rest of society because we're afraid of them, as if age might be contagious. Which, it turns out, it is.

. . . You are older at this moment than you've ever been before, and it's the youngest you're ever going to get. The mortality rate is holding at a scandalous 100 percent. Pretending death can be indefinitely evaded with hot yoga or a gluten-free diet or antioxidants or just by refusing to look is craven denial. "Facing it, always facing it, that's the way to get through," Conrad wrote in *Typhoon*. "Face it." He was talking about more than storms. The sheltered prince Siddartha Gautama was supposedly set on the path to becoming the Buddha when he was out riding and happened to see an old man, a sick man and a dead man. Today he'd be spared the discomfiture, and the enlightenment, unless he were riding mass transit.

Just yesterday my mother sent me a poem she first read in college—Langston Hughes's "Mother to Son." She said she could still remember where she was, in her dorm room at Goshen College, when she came across it in her American Lit book. The title notwithstanding, it does not make for Hallmark-card copy. *Life for me ain't been no crystal stair*. It tells us that this life is not a story or an adventure or a journey of spiritual self-discovery; it's a slog. And it orders us to keep going, don't you dare give up, no matter what. Because I'm your mother, that's why.

Do you agree with Kreider: Do we do a disservice to the young when we segregate the old?

Does all of this mean that people would be happier if they didn't have children? Not necessarily. Because researchers cannot randomly assign people to be parents or nonparents, studies of the effects of parenthood are necessarily correlational. People who want children and have children may be somewhat less happy than people who neither want them nor have them, but it is possible that people who want children would be even less happy if they didn't have them. What does seem clear is that raising children is a challenging job that people find most rewarding when they're not in the middle of doing it.

SUMMARY QUIZ [10.4]

1. The peak years for health, stamina, vigor, and prowess are
   a. childhood.
   b. the early teens.
   c. the early 20s.
   d. the early 30s.

2. Data suggest that, for most people, the last decades of life are
   a. characterized by an increase in negative emotions.
   b. spent attending to the most useful information.
   c. extremely satisfying.
   d. a time during which they begin to interact with a much wider circle of people.

3. Which is true of marital satisfaction over the life span?
   a. It increases steadily.
   b. It decreases steadily.
   c. It is remarkably stable.
   d. It shows peaks and valleys, corresponding to the presence and ages of children.

CHAPTER REVIEW

SUMMARY

Prenatality: A Womb with a View

> Developmental psychology studies continuity and change across the life span.

> The prenatal stage of development begins when a sperm fertilizes an egg, producing a zygote, which contains chromosomes from both the egg and the sperm. The zygote develops into an embryo at 2 weeks and then into a fetus at 8 weeks.

> The fetal environment has important physical and psychological influences on the fetus. In addition to the food a pregnant woman eats, teratogens, or agents that impair fetal development, can affect the fetus. Some of the most common teratogens are tobacco and alcohol.

> In the womb, the fetus can hear sounds and become familiar with those it hears often, such as its mother's voice.

Infancy and Childhood: Becoming a Person

> Infants learn to control their bodies from the top down and from the center out.

> Infants slowly develop theories about how the world works. Piaget believed that these theories developin four stages, in which children learn basic facts about the world.

> Cognitive development also comes about through social interactions in which children are given tools for understanding that have been developed by members of their cultures.

> At a very early age, human beings develop strong emotional ties to their primary caregivers. The quality of these ties is determined both by the caregiver's behavior and the child's temperament.

> Children's reasoning about right and wrong is initially based on an action's consequences, but as they mature, children begin to

consider the actor's intentions as well as the extent to which the action obeys abstract moral principles.

Adolescence: Minding the Gap

> Adolescence is a stage of development that begins at puberty, which is the onset of sexual maturity of the human body.

> Adolescents are somewhat more prone to do things that are risky or illegal, but they rarely inflict serious or enduring harm on themselves or others.

> During adolescence, sexual interest intensifies, and in some cultures, sexual activity begins. Although most people are attracted to members of the opposite sex, some are not, and research suggests that biology plays a key role in determining a person's sexual orientation.

> As adolescents seek to develop their adult identities, they seek increasing autonomy from their parents and become more peer-oriented, forming single-sex cliques, followed by mixed-sex cliques, and finally pairing off as couples.

Adulthood: Change We Can't Believe In

> Gradual physical decline begins early in adulthood and has clear psychological consequences.

> Older adults show declines in working memory, episodic memory, and retrieval tasks, but they often develop strategies to compensate.

> Older people are more oriented toward emotionally satisfying information, which influences their basic cognitive performance, the size and structure of their social networks, and their general happiness.

> People who get married are typically happier, but children and the responsibilities that parenthood entails present a significant challenge, especially for women.

KEY TERMS

developmental psychology (p. 314)
zygote (p. 315)
germinal stage (p. 315)
embryonic stage (p. 315)
fetal stage (p. 315)
myelination (p. 316)
teratogens (p. 316)
fetal alcohol syndrome (FAS) (p. 316)
infancy (p. 317)

motor development (p. 318)
reflexes (p. 318)
cephalocaudal rule (p. 318)
proximodistal rule (p. 318)
cognitive development (p. 319)
sensorimotor stage (p. 320)
schemas (p. 320)
assimilation (p. 320)
accommodation (p. 320)
object permanence (p. 320)
childhood (p. 322)

preoperational stage (p. 322)
concrete operational stage (p. 322)
conservation (p. 322)
formal operational stage (p. 322)
egocentrism (p. 323)
theory of mind (p. 323)
attachment (p. 328)
temperaments (p. 328)
internal working model of relationships (p. 329)

preconventional stage (p. 330)
conventional stage (p. 330)
postconventional stage (p. 331)
adolescence (p. 333)
puberty (p. 334)
primary sex characteristics (p. 334)
secondary sex characteristics (p. 334)
adulthood (p. 339)

CHANGING MINDS

1. One of your friends recently got married, and she and her husband are planning to have children. You mention to your friend that once this happens, she should stop drinking. She scoffs. "They make it sound as though a pregnant woman who drinks alcohol is murdering her baby. Look, my mom drank wine every weekend when she was pregnant with me and I'm just fine." What is your friend failing to understand about the effects of alcohol on prenatal development? What other teratogens might you tell her about?

2. You are at the grocery store when you spot a crying child in a stroller. The mother picks up the child and cuddles it until it stops crying. A grocery clerk is standing next to you, stocking the shelves. He leans over and says, "Now, that's bad parenting. If you pick up and cuddle a child every time it cries, you're reinforcing the behavior, and the result will be a very spoiled child." Do you agree? What do studies of attachment tell us about the effects of picking up and holding children when they cry?

3. You and your roommate are watching a movie in which a young man tells his parents that he's gay. The parents react badly and decide to send him to a "camp" where he can learn to change his sexual orientation. Your roommate turns to you: "Do you know anything about this? Can people really be changed from gay to straight?" What would you tell your friend about the factors that determine sexual orientation?

4. One of your cousins has just turned 30 and, to his horror, has discovered a gray hair. "This is the end," he says. "Soon I'll start losing my eyesight, growing new chins, and forgetting how to use a cell phone. Aging is just one long, slow, agonizing decline." What could you tell your cousin to cheer him up? Does everything in life get worse as we get older?

ANSWERS TO SUMMARY QUIZZES

Answers to Summary Quiz 10.1: 1. b; 2. a; 3. b.

Answers to Summary Quiz 10.2: 1. c; 2. b; 3. b; 4. d.

Answers to Summary Quiz 10.3: 1. d; 2. d; 3. a.

Answers to Summary Quiz 10.4: 1. c; 2. c; 3. d.

Need more help? Additional resources are located in LaunchPad at:
http://www.worthpublishers.com/launchpad/schacterbrief3e

11

Personality

rowing up, Stefani Joanne Angelina Germanotta seemed to have personality. As a child, she was said to have shown up at the occasional family gathering naked. Now known as the pop star Lady Gaga, she continues the tradition of being different. Her first albums, *The Fame* and *The Fame Monster,* and the fact that she calls her fans "Little Monsters" and herself the "Mother Monster" hinted she might have issues. But she, like most of us, is not one-dimensional. Yes, her style is eccentric and seems silly to many (we're looking at you, raw meat dress), but she also is a serious supporter of humanitarian and personal causes, including equality for people who are gay, bisexual, lesbian, or transgendered (as in her song "Born This Way"). Lady Gaga is one of a kind. She has personality in an important sense—she has qualities that make her psychologically different from other people.

Singer Lady Gaga in her meat dress at the MTV Video Music Awards, September 2010.

Press Association Via Ap Images

Howard Stern

Hillary Clinton

Rihanna

How would you describe each of these personalities?

Cristiano Ronaldo

THE FORCES THAT CREATE ANY ONE PERSONALITY ARE SOMETHING OF A MYSTERY. Your personality is different from anyone else's and expresses itself pretty consistently across settings—at home, in the classroom, and elsewhere. But how and why do people differ psychologically? By studying many unique individuals, psychologists seek to gather enough information to answer these central questions of personality psychology scientifically.

Personality is *an individual's characteristic style of behaving, thinking, and feeling.* Whether Lady Gaga's quirks are real or merely for publicity, they are certainly hers, and they show her distinct personality. In this chapter, we will explore personality, first by looking at what it is and how it is measured, and then by focusing on each of four main approaches to understanding personality: trait—biological, psychodynamic, humanistic—existential, and social cognitive. At the end of the chapter, we discuss the psychology of self to see how our views of what we are like can shape and define our personality.

Personality: What It Is and How It Is Measured

If someone said, "You have no personality," how would you feel? Like a boring, grayish lump who should go out and get a personality as soon as possible? As a rule, people don't usually strive for a personality—one seems to develop naturally as we travel through life. As psychologists have tried to understand the process of personality development, they have pondered questions of description (*how* do people differ?), explanation (*why* do people differ?), and the more quantitative question of measurement (how can personality be *assessed*?).

Describing and Explaining Personality

As the first biologists earnestly attempted to classify all plants and animals, personality psychologists began by labeling and describing different personalities. Most personality psychologists focus on specific, psychologically meaningful individual differences, characteristics such as honesty, anxiousness, or moodiness. Still, personality is often in the eye of the beholder. When one person describes another as "a conceited jerk," for example, you may wonder whether you have just learned more about the describer or the person being described. Interestingly, studies that ask acquaintances to describe each other find a high degree of similarity among any one individual's descriptions of many different people ("Jason thinks that Carlos is considerate, Renata is kind, and Jean Paul is nice to others"). In contrast, resemblance is quite low when many people describe one person ("Carlos thinks Jason is smart, Renata thinks he is competitive, and Jean Paul thinks he has a good sense of humor"; Dornbusch et al., 1965).

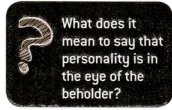

What does it mean to say that personality is in the eye of the beholder?

What leads Lady Gaga to all of her entertaining extremes? In general, explanations of personality differences are concerned with (1) *prior events* that can shape an individual's personality or (2) *anticipated events* that might motivate the person to reveal particular personality characteristics. In a biological prior event, Stefani Germanotta received genes from her parents that may have led her to develop into the sort of person who loves putting on a display (not to mention putting on raw meat) and stirring up controversy. Researchers interested in events that happen prior to our behavior study our genes, brains, and other aspects of our biological makeup, and these researchers also delve into our subconscious and into our circumstances and interpersonal surroundings. The consideration of *anticipated events* emphasizes the person's own, subjective perspective and often seems intimate and personal in its reflection of the person's inner life (hopes, fears, and aspirations).

Of course, our understanding of how the baby named Stefani Germanotta grew into the adult Lady Gaga (or the life of any woman or man) also depends on insights into the interaction between the prior and anticipated events: We need to know how her history may have shaped her motivations.

Measuring Personality

Of all the things psychologists have set out to measure, personality may be one of the toughest. How do you capture the uniqueness of a person? What aspects of people's personalities are important to know about, and how should we quantify them? The general personality measures can be classified broadly into personality inventories and projective techniques.

Personality Inventories

To learn about an individual's personality, you could follow the person around and, clipboard in hand, record every single thing the person does, says, thinks, and feels (including how long this goes on before the person calls the police). Some observations might involve your own impressions (Day 5: seems to be getting irritable); others would involve objectively observable events that anyone could verify (Day 7: grabbed my pencil and broke it in half, then bit my hand).

Psychologists have figured out ways to obtain objective data on personality without driving their subjects to violence. The most popular technique is **self-report,** *a method in which people provide subjective information about their own thoughts, feelings, or behaviors, typically via questionnaire or interview.* Scales based on the content of self-reports have been devised to assess a whole range of personality characteristics, all the way from general tendencies such as overall happiness (Lyubomirsky, 2008; Lyubomirsky & Lepper, 1999) to specific ones such as responding rapidly to insults (Swann & Rentfrow, 2001) or complaining about poor service (Lerman, 2006).

For example, the **Minnesota Multiphasic Personality Inventory (MMPI)** is *a well-researched, clinical questionnaire used to assess personality and psychological problems.* The MMPI was developed in 1939 and has been revised several times over the years, leading up to the current version, the MMPI–2–RF (restructured form; Ben-Porath & Tellegen, 2008). The MMPI–2–RF consists of 338 self-descriptive statements to which the respondent answers "true," "false," or "cannot say." The MMPI–2–RF measures a wide range of psychological constructs: clinical problems (e.g., antisocial behavior, thought dysfunction), somatic problems (e.g., head pain, cognitive complaints), internalizing problems (e.g., anxiety, self-doubt), externalizing problems (e.g., aggression, substance abuse), and interpersonal problems (e.g., family problems, avoidance). The MMPI–2–RF also includes *validity scales* that assess a person's attitudes toward test taking and any tendency to try to distort the results by faking answers.

Personality inventories such as the MMPI–2–RF are easy to administer: All that is needed is the test and a pencil (or a computer for the computer-based version). The respondent's scores are then calculated and compared with the average ratings of thousands of other test takers. Because no human interpretation of the responses is needed (i.e., "true" means true, "false" means false, etc.), any potential biases of the person giving the test are minimized. Of course, an accurate measurement of personality will only occur if people provide accurate responses. Although self-report test results are easy to obtain, critics of this approach highlight several limitations. One problem is that many people have a tendency to respond in a socially desirable way, such that they underreport things that are unflattering or embarrassing. Perhaps even more problematic is that there are many things we don't know about ourselves and so are unable to report! Studies show that people often are inaccurate in their self-report

What are some limitations of personality inventories?

personality An individual's characteristic style of behaving, thinking, and feeling.

self-report A method in which people provide subjective information about their own thoughts, feelings, or behaviors, typically via questionnaire or interview.

Minnesota Multiphasic Personality Inventory (MMPI) A well-researched, clinical questionnaire used to assess personality and psychological problems.

Personality inventories ask people to report what traits they possess; however, many psychologists believe that people do not always know what's in their mind. Can we rely on people to accurately report on their personality?

Jeff Greenberg/Getty Images

FIGURE 11.1 Sample Rorschach Inkblot Test takers are shown a card such as this sample and asked, "What might this be?" What they perceive, where they see it, and why it looks that way are assumed to reflect unconscious aspects of their personality.

projective tests Tests designed to reveal inner aspects of individuals' personalities by analysis of their responses to a standard series of ambiguous stimuli.

Rorschach Inkblot Test A projective technique in which respondents' inner thoughts and feelings are believed to be revealed by analysis of their responses to a set of unstructured inkblots.

FIGURE 11.2 Sample TAT Card Test takers are shown cards with ambiguous scenes and are asked to tell a story about what is happening in the picture. The main themes of the story, the thoughts and feelings of the characters, and how the story develops and resolves are considered useful indices of unconscious aspects of an individual's personality (Murray, 1943).

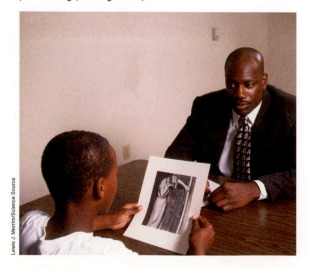

about what they have experienced in the past, what factors are motivating their behaviors in the present, or how they will feel or behave in the future (Wilson, 2009).

Projective Techniques

A second, somewhat controversial class of tools designed to circumvent the limitations of self-report mentioned above is **projective tests,** which are *tests designed to reveal inner aspects of individuals' personalities by analysis of their responses to a standard series of ambiguous stimuli.* The developers of projective tests assume that people will project personality factors that are below awareness—wishes, concerns, impulses, and ways of seeing the world—onto the ambiguous stimuli and will not censor these responses. Probably best known is the **Rorschach Inkblot Test,** *a projective technique in which respondents' inner thoughts and feelings are believed to be revealed by analysis of their responses to a set of unstructured inkblots.* An example inkblot is shown in **FIGURE 11.1**. Responses are scored according to complicated systems (derived in part from research with people with psychological disorders) that classify what people see (Exner, 1993; Rapaport, 1946). For example, most people who look at Figure 11.1 report seeing birds or people. Someone who reports seeing something very unusual (e.g., "I see two purple tigers eating a velvet cheeseburger") may be experiencing thoughts and feelings that are very different from those of most other people.

The **Thematic Apperception Test (TAT)** is *a projective technique in which respondents' underlying motives, concerns, and the way they see the social world are believed to be revealed through analysis of the stories they make up about ambiguous pictures of people.* To get a sense of the test, look at **FIGURE 11.2**. The test administrator shows the respondent the card and asks him or her to tell a story about the picture, asking questions such as: "Who are those people?" "What is happening?" "What will happen next?" Different people tell very different stories about the image. In creating the stories, the respondent is thought to identify with the main characters and to project his or her view of others and the world onto the other details in the drawing. Thus, any details that are not obviously drawn from the picture are believed to be projected onto the story from the respondent's own desires and internal conflicts.

For instance, one card that shows an older man standing over a child lying in bed tends to elicit themes regarding relationships that respondents have with an older man in their life, such as a father, teacher, boss, or therapist. The interviewer might be interested in learning whether respondents see the person lying down as a male or female, and whether they report that the man standing is trying to help or harm the person lying down. Consider a story proposed by a young man in response to this card: "The boy lying down had a hard day at school. He worked so hard studying for his exam that when he came home after taking the test, he fell asleep with his clothes on. No matter how hard the boy tries, he can never make his father happy. The father is sick and tired of the son not doing well in school and so he is going to kill him. He suffocates the boy and the boy dies." The test administrator might interpret this response as indicating that the respondent perceives that his father has high expectations that are not being met, and perhaps that the father is disappointed and angry with the young man.

The value of projective tests is debated by psychologists. A TAT story like the one above may *seem* revealing; however, the examiner must always add an interpretation (Was this about the respondent's actual father, about his own concerns about his academic failures, or about trying to be funny or provocative?), and that interpretation could well be the scorer's *own* projection into the mind of the test taker. Thus, despite the rich picture of a personality and the insights into an individual's motives that these tests offer,

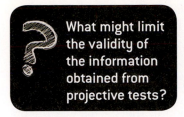
What might limit the validity of the information obtained from projective tests?

projective tests should be understood primarily as a way in which a psychologist can get to know someone personally and intuitively (McClelland et al., 1953). When measured by rigorous scientific criteria, projective tests such as the TAT and the Rorschach have not been found to be reliable or valid in predicting behavior (Lilienfeld, Lynn, & Lohr, 2003).

Newer personality measurement methods are moving beyond both self-report inventories and projective tests (Robins, Fraley, & Krueger, 2007). High-tech methods such as wireless communication, real-time computer analysis, and automated behavior identification open the door to personality measurements that are leaps and bounds beyond following the person around with a clipboard—and such methods can lead to surprising findings. The stereotype that women are more talkative than men, for example, was challenged by findings when 396 college students in the United States and Mexico each spent several days wearing an EAR (electronically activated recorder) that captured random snippets of their talk (Mehl et al., 2009). The result? Women and men were *equally* talkative, each averaging about 16,000 words per day. The advanced measurement of how people differ (and how they do not) is a key step in understanding personality.

Thanks to Stephanie Levitt; © Matthias Mehl, University of Arizona

The EAR (electronically activated recorder) sampled conversations of hundreds of participants and found that women and men are equally talkative (Mehl et al., 2009).

SUMMARY QUIZ [11.1]

1. From a psychological perspective, personality refers to
   a. a person's characteristic style of behaving, thinking, and feeling.
   b. physiological predispositions that manifest themselves psychologically.
   c. past events that have shaped a person's current behavior.
   d. choices people make in response to cultural norms.

2. Which of the following is *not* a drawback of self-report measures such as the MMPI-2-RF?
   a. People may respond in ways that put themselves in a flattering light.
   b. Some people tend to always agree or always disagree with the statements on the test.
   c. Interpretation is subject to the biases of the researcher.
   d. People are unaware of some of their personality characteristics and thus cannot answer accurately.

3. Projective techniques to assess personality involve
   a. personal inventories.
   b. self-reporting.
   c. responses to ambiguous stimuli.
   d. actuarial methodology.

Thematic Apperception Test (TAT) A projective technique in which respondents' underlying motives, concerns, and the way they see the social world are believed to be revealed through analysis of the stories they make up about ambiguous pictures of people.

The Trait Approach: Identifying Patterns of Behavior

Imagine writing a story about the people you know. To capture their special qualities, you might describe their traits: Keesha is *friendly, aggressive,* and *domineering;* Seth is *flaky, humorous,* and *superficial.* The trait approach to personality uses such trait terms to characterize differences among individuals. In attempting to create manageable and meaningful sets of descriptors, trait theorists face two significant challenges:

trait A relatively stable disposition to behave in a particular and consistent way.

narrowing down the almost infinite set of adjectives and answering the more basic question of why people have particular traits and whether they arise from biological or hereditary foundations.

Traits as Behavioral Dispositions and Motives

One way to think about personality is as a combination of traits. This was the approach of Gordon Allport (1937), one of the first trait theorists, who believed people could be described in terms of traits just as an object could be described in terms of its properties. He saw a **trait** as *a relatively stable disposition to behave in a particular and consistent way.* For example, a person who keeps his books organized alphabetically in bookshelves, hangs his clothing neatly in the closet, and keeps a clear agenda in a daily planner can be said to have the trait of *orderliness.* This trait consistently manifests itself in a variety of settings.

The orderliness trait *describes* a person but doesn't *explain* his or her behavior. Why does the person behave in this way? There are two basic ways in which a trait might serve as an explanation: The trait may be a preexisting disposition of the person that causes the person's behavior, or it may be a motivation that guides the person's behavior. Allport saw traits as preexisting dispositions, causes of behavior that reliably trigger the behavior. The person's orderliness, for example, is an inner property of the person that will cause the person to straighten things up and be tidy in a wide array of situations. Other personality theorists suggested instead that traits reflect motives. Just as a hunger motive might explain someone's many trips to the snack bar, a need for orderliness might explain the neat closet and alphabetically organized bookshelves (Murray & Kluckhohn, 1953). Researchers examining traits as causes have used personality inventories to measure them, whereas those examining traits as motives have more often used projective tests.

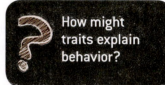
How might traits explain behavior?

The Search for Core Traits

Picking a single trait such as orderliness and studying it in depth doesn't get us very far in the search for the core of human character: the basic set of traits that defines how humans differ from one another. How have researchers tried to discover the core personality traits?

Classification Using Language

The study of core traits began with an exploration of how personality is represented in the store of wisdom we call *language*. Generation after generation, people have described people with words, so early psychologists proposed that core traits could be discerned by finding the main themes in all the adjectives used to describe personality. In one such analysis, a painstaking count of relevant words in a dictionary of English resulted in a list of over 18,000 potential traits (Allport & Odbert, 1936)! Attempts to narrow down the list to a more manageable set depend on the idea that traits might be related in a hierarchical pattern (see **FIGURE 11.3**), with more general or abstract traits at higher levels than more specific or concrete traits. The highest-level traits are sometimes called dimensions or *factors* of personality.

But how many factors are there? Different researchers have proposed different answers. Cattell (1950) proposed a 16-factor theory of personality (way down from 18,000, but still a lot), whereas Hans Eysenck (1967) simplified things nicely with a model of personality with only two major traits (although he later expanded it to three). Eysenck identified one dimension, Extraversion, that distinguished people who are sociable and active (extraverts) from those who are more introspective and

Big Five The traits of the five-factor personality model: openness to experience, conscientiousness, extraversion, agreeableness, and neuroticism.

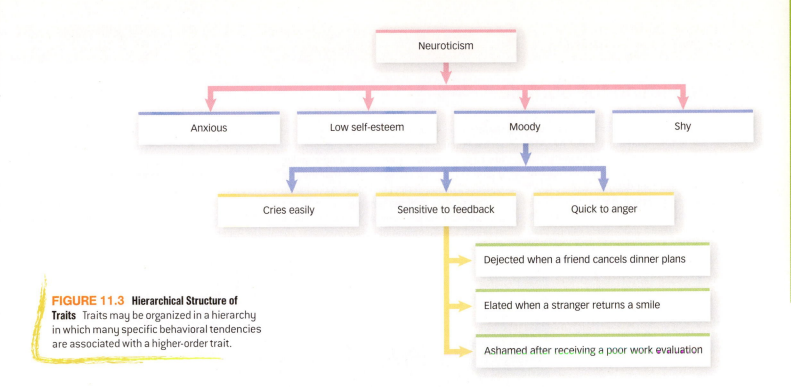

FIGURE 11.3 Hierarchical Structure of Traits Traits may be organized in a hierarchy in which many specific behavioral tendencies are associated with a higher-order trait.

quiet (introverts). He also identified a second dimension, Neuroticism, ranging from the tendency to be very neurotic or emotionally unstable to the tendency to be more emotionally stable. The third factor he proposed was Psychoticism, which refers to the extent to which a person is impulsive or hostile. (Notably, the term "psychotic" nowadays refers to an abnormal mental state marked by detachment from reality. This is discussed further in the Disorders chapter.)

The Big Five Dimensions of Personality

Today, most researchers agree that personality is best captured by 5 factors rather than by 2, 3, 16, or 18,000 (John & Srivastava, 1999; McCrae & Costa, 1999). The **Big Five,** as they are affectionately called, are *the traits of the five-factor personality model: openness to experience, conscientiousness, extraversion, agreeableness, and neuroticism* (see **TABLE 11.1**; remember them by the initials O.C.E.A.N.). The five-factor model, which overlaps with the pioneering work of Cattell and Eysenck, is now widely preferred for several reasons. First, this set of five factors strikes the right balance between accounting for as much variation in personality as possible while avoiding overlapping traits. Second, in a large number of studies using different kinds of data (people's descriptions of their own personalities, other people's descriptions of their personalities, interviewer checklists, and behavioral observation), the same five factors have emerged. Third, and perhaps most important, the basic five-factor structure seems to show up across a wide range of participants, including children, adults in other cultures, and even among those who use other languages, suggesting

Table 11.1 The Big Five Factor Model

	High on trait	Low on Trait
Openness to experience	imaginative.................down-to-earth	
	variety.............................routine	
	independent..................conforming	
Conscientiousness	organized.....................disorganized	
	careful...........................careless	
	self-disciplined...............weak-willed	
Extraversion	social.............................retiring	
	fun loving.........................sober	
	affectionate......................reserved	
Agreeableness	softhearted.......................ruthless	
	trusting.........................suspicious	
	helpful......................uncooperative	
Neuroticism	worried............................calm	
	insecure..........................secure	
	self-pitying..................self-satisfied	

Source: Data from McCrae & Costa, 1990, 1999.

Hot Science

Personality on the Surface

When you judge someone as friend or foe, interesting or boring, how do you do it? It's nice to think that your impressions of personality are based on solid foundations. You wouldn't judge personality based on something as shallow as someone's looks, or what's on his Facebook page, would you? These things may seem to be flimsy bases for understanding personality, but it turns out that some remarkably accurate personality judgments can be made from exactly such superficial cues.

Recent studies have shown that extraverts smile more than others and appear more stylish and healthy (Naumann et al., 2009), and people high in openness to experience are more likely to have tattoos and other body modifications (Nathanson, Paulhus, & Williams, 2006). Findings like these suggest that people can manipulate their surface identities to try to make desired impressions on others and that surface signs of personality might

therefore be false or misleading. However, one recent study of people's Facebook pages, which are clearly surface expressions of personality intended for others to see, found that the personalities people project online are more highly related to their real personalities than to the personalities they describe as their ideals (Back et al., 2010). The signs of personality that appear on the surface may be more than skin deep.

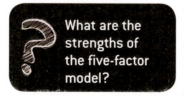

AP Photo/Pablo Martinez Monsivais

Going one step further, it turns out that people's Facebook activity is significantly associated with their self-reported personality traits. For instance, people high on extraversion report having more Facebook friends as well as making more status updates and comments. Posting updates and comments also is higher in Facebook users with elevated self-esteem. People high on agreeableness make more comments on their friends' posts, whereas those high on sensation seeking and openness to experience report playing a lot of games. And as you might have guessed, people high on narcissism post lots of comments, as well as lots of pictures of themselves (Seidman, 2013; Wang et al., 2012).

They say you can't judge a book by its cover, but some new research suggests you can judge people by their Facebook.

DATA VISUALIZATION

Stability of Personality Traits over Time

www.macmillanhighered.com/ schacterbrief3e

? What are the strengths of the five-factor model?

that the Big Five may be universal (John & Srivastava, 1999). It turns out that the Big Five personality traits also predict people's online behavior on social networking sites such as Facebook (see the Hot Science box).

Interestingly, research on the Big Five has shown that people's personalities tend to remain fairly stable through a lifetime: Scores at one time in life correlate strongly with scores at later dates, even decades later (Caspi, Roberts, & Shiner, 2005). William James offered the opinion that "in most of us, by the age of thirty, the character has set like plaster, and will never soften again" (James, 1890, p. 121), but this turns out to be too strong a view. Some variability is typical in childhood, and though there is less in adolescence, some personality change can even occur in adulthood for some people (Srivistava et al., 2003).

Traits as Biological Building Blocks

Can we explain *why* a person has a stable set of personality traits? Many trait theorists have argued that unchangeable brain and biological processes produce the remarkable stability of traits over the life span. Brain damage certainly can produce personality change, as the classic case of Phineas Gage so vividly demonstrates (see the Neuroscience and Behavior chapter). You may recall that after the blasting accident that blew an iron rod through his frontal lobes, Gage showed a dramatic loss of social appropriateness and conscientiousness (Damasio, 1994). In fact, when someone experiences a profound change in personality, testing often reveals the presence of such brain pathologies as Alzheimer's disease, stroke, or brain tumor (Feinberg, 2001). The administration of antidepressant medication and other pharmaceutical treatments that change brain chemistry also can trigger personality changes, making people, for example, somewhat more extraverted and less neurotic (Bagby et al., 1999; Knutson et al., 1998).

Genes, Traits, and Personality

Some of the most compelling evidence for the importance of biological factors in personality comes from the domain of behavioral genetics. Simply put, the more genes you have in common with someone, the more similar your personalities are likely

The Real World

Are There "Male" and "Female" Personalities?

Is there a typical female personality or a typical male personality? Researchers have found some reliable differences between men and women with respect to their self-reported traits, attitudes, and behaviors. Some of these findings conform to North American stereotypes of masculine and feminine. For example, researchers have found women to be more verbally expressive, more sensitive to nonverbal cues, and more nurturing than are men. Males are more physically aggressive than females, but females engage in more relational aggression (e.g., intentionally excluding someone from a social group) than do males (Crick & Grotpeter, 1995). On the Big Five, studies across dozens of cultures around the world show that women are higher on neuroticism, extraversion, agreeableness, and conscientiousness; in terms of openness, women report greater openness to feelings and men greater openness to ideas (Costa, Terracciano, & McCrae, 2001; Schmitt et al., 2008). On a variety of other personality characteristics, including helpfulness, men and women on average show no reliable differences. Overall, men and women seem to be far more similar in personality than they are different (Hyde, 2005).

An evolutionary perspective on gender differences in personality holds that men and women have evolved different personality characteristics in part because their reproductive success depends on different behaviors. For instance, aggressiveness in men may have an adaptive value in intimidating sexual rivals; women who are agreeable and nurturing may have evolved to protect and ensure the survival of their offspring (Campbell, 1999) as well as to secure a reliable mate and provider (Buss, 1989).

Gift of Jean and Francis Marshall/Berkeley Art Museum/Pacific Film Archive

Cultures differ in their appreciation of male and female characteristics, but the Hindu deity Ardhanarishwara represents the value of combining both parts of human nature. Male on one side and female on the other, this god is symbolic of the dual nature of the sacred. The only real problem with such side-by-side androgyny comes in finding clothes that fit.

In contrast, according to social role theory, personality differences between men and women result from cultural standards and expectations that assign the male and female roles (Eagly & Wood, 1999). Because of their physical size and their freedom from childbearing, men historically took roles of greater power—roles that in postindustrial society don't necessarily require physical strength. These differences then snowball, with men generally taking roles that require assertiveness and aggression (e.g., executive, school principal, surgeon) and women pursuing roles that emphasize greater supportiveness and nurturance (e.g., nurse, day care worker, teacher).

Regardless of the source of gender differences in personality, the degree to which people identify personally with masculine and feminine stereotypes may tell us about important personality differences between individuals. Sandra Bem (1974) designed a scale (the Bem Sex Role Inventory) that assesses the degree of identification with stereotypically masculine and feminine traits. Bem suggested that psychologically *androgynous* people (those who adopt the best of both worlds and identify with positive feminine traits such as kindness and positive masculine traits such as assertiveness) might be better adjusted than people who identify strongly with only one sex role.

Our genes influence our personality in various ways. For instance, genetic factors can impact how rigidly versus flexibly we think about things like religion and politics. This Tea Party advocate probably shares the same religious and political leanings as other members of his family.

Bill Clark/Roll Call/Getty Images

Extraverts pursue stimulation in the form of people, loud noise, and bright colors. Introverts tend to prefer softer, quieter settings. Pop quiz: Nikki Minaj: introvert or extrovert?

Dipasupil/Filmmagic/Getty Images

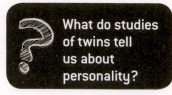

What do studies of twins tell us about personality?

to be. For example, in one review of studies involving over 24,000 twin pairs (Loehlin, 1992), identical twins (who share 100% of their genes) proved markedly more similar to each other in personality than did fraternal twins (who share on average only 50% of their genes). And identical twins reared apart in adoptive families end up at least as similar in personality as those who grew up together (McGue & Bouchard, 1998; Tellegen et al., 1988). These and other studies suggest that simply growing up in the same family does not make people very similar. Rather, when two siblings are similar, this is thought to be largely due to genetic similarities.

People who share genes often have striking similarities in behavior and attitude. One study that examined 3,000 pairs of identical and fraternal twins found evidence for the genetic transmission of conservative views regarding topics such as socialism, church authority, the death penalty, and mixed-race marriage (Martin et al., 1986). It is very unlikely that a specific gene is directly responsible for a complex psychological outcome such as beliefs about social or political issues. Rather, a set of genes (or, more likely, many sets of genes interacting) may produce specific characteristics or tendencies to think in a conservative versus liberal manner. One study examined the DNA of 13,000 people and measured the extent to which they reported conservative versus liberal attitudes, and the study found associations between conservatism–liberalism and chromosomal regions linked to mental flexibility, or the extent to which people change their thinking in response to shifts in their environment, which could be one of the factors influencing our views on social and political issues (Hatemi et al., 2011). Current research by psychological scientists is aimed at better understanding how variations in our genetic code may contribute to the development of personality.

Traits in the Brain

What neurophysiological mechanisms might influence the development of personality traits? Eysenck (1967) speculated that extraversion and introversion might arise from individual differences in cortical arousal. Eysenck suggested that extraverts pursue stimulation because their *reticular formation* (the part of the brain that regulates arousal or alertness, as described in the Neuroscience and Behavior chapter) is not easily stimulated. To achieve greater cortical arousal and feel fully alert, Eysenck argued, extraverts seek out social interaction, parties, and other activities to achieve mental stimulation. In contrast, introverts may prefer reading or quiet activities because their cortex is very easily stimulated to a point higher than optimal alertness.

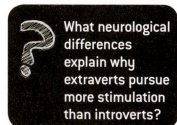

What neurological differences explain why extraverts pursue more stimulation than introverts?

Behavioral and physiological research generally supports Eysenck's view. When introverts and extraverts are presented with a range of intense stimuli, introverts respond more strongly, including salivating more when a drop of lemon juice is placed on their tongues and reacting more negatively to electric shocks or loud noises (Bartol & Costello, 1976; Stelmack, 1990). This reactivity has an impact on the ability to concentrate: Extraverts tend to perform well at tasks that are done in a noisy, arousing context (such as bartending or teaching), whereas introverts are better at tasks that require concentration in tranquil contexts (such as the work of a librarian or nighttime security guard; Geen, 1984; Lieberman & Rosenthal, 2001; Matthews & Gilliland, 1999).

In a refined version of Eysenck's ideas, Jeffrey Gray (1970) proposed that the dimensions of extraversion–introversion and neuroticism reflect two basic brain systems. The *behavioral activation system* (*BAS*), essentially a "go" system, activates approach behavior in response to the anticipation of reward. The extravert has a highly reactive BAS and will actively engage the environment, seeking social reinforcement and being on the go. The *behavioral inhibition system* (*BIS*), a "stop" system, inhibits behavior in response to stimuli signaling punishment. The anxious person, in turn, has a highly reactive BIS and will focus on negative outcomes and be on the lookout for stop signs.

Recent studies have suggested that the core personality traits may arise from individual differences in the brain. For instance, self-reported neuroticism is correlated with the volume of brain regions involved in sensitivity to threat; agreeableness with areas associated with processing information about the mental states of other people; conscientiousness with regions involved in self-regulation; and extraversion with areas associated with processing information about reward (DeYoung et al., 2010). Research aimed at understanding how the structure and activity of our brains can contribute to the formation of our personality traits is still in its early stages, but such research represents a growing area of the field that many believe holds great promise for helping us better understand how we each develop into the unique people that we are.

SUMMARY QUIZ [11.2]

1. A relatively stable disposition to behave in a particular and consistent way is a
   a. motive.
   b. goal.
   c. trait.
   d. reflex.

2. Which of the following is *not* one of the Big Five personality factors?
   a. conscientiousness
   b. agreeableness
   c. neuroticism
   d. orderliness

3. Compelling evidence for the importance of biological factors in personality is best seen in studies of
   a. parenting styles.
   b. identical twins reared apart.
   c. brain damage.
   d. factor analysis.

The Psychodynamic Approach: Forces That Lie beneath Awareness

Rather than trying to understand personality in terms of broad theories for describing individual differences, Freud looked for personality in the details: the meanings and insights revealed by careful analysis of the tiniest blemishes in a person's thought and

Sigmund Freud was the first psychologist to be honored with his own bobble-head doll. Let's hope he's not the last.

behavior. Working with patients who came to him with disorders that did not seem to have any physical basis, he began by interpreting the origins of their everyday mistakes and memory lapses, errors that have come to be called *Freudian slips*.

The theories of Freud and his followers (discussed in the Treatment chapter) are referred to as the **psychodynamic approach,** *an approach that regards personality as formed by needs, strivings, and desires largely operating outside of awareness—motives that can also produce emotional disorders.* The real engines of personality, in this view, are forces of which we are largely unaware.

The Structure of the Mind: Id, Superego, and Ego

To explain the emotional difficulties that beset his patients, Freud proposed that the mind consists of three independent, interacting, and often conflicting systems: the id, the superego, and the ego.

The most basic system, the **id,** is *the part of the mind containing the drives present at birth; it is the source of our bodily needs, wants, desires, and impulses, particularly our sexual and aggressive drives.* The id operates according to the *pleasure principle,* the psychic force that motivates the tendency to seek immediate gratification of any impulse. If governed by the id alone, you would never be able to tolerate the build-up of hunger while waiting to be served at a restaurant but would simply grab food from tables nearby.

Opposite the id is the **superego,** *the mental system that reflects the internalization of cultural rules, mainly learned as parents exercise their authority.* The superego acts as a kind of conscience, punishing us when it finds we are doing or thinking something wrong (by producing guilt or other painful feelings) and rewarding us (with feelings of pride or self-congratulation) for living up to ideal standards.

The final system of the mind, according to psychoanalytic theory, is the **ego,** *the component of personality, developed through contact with the external world, that enables us to deal with life's practical demands.* The ego is a regulating mechanism that enables the individual to delay gratifying immediate needs and function effectively in the real world. It is the mediator between the id and the superego. The ego helps you resist the impulse to snatch others' food and also chooses the restaurant and pays the check.

psychodynamic approach An approach that regards personality as formed by needs, strivings, and desires largely operating outside of awareness—motives that can also produce emotional disorders.

id The part of the mind containing the drives present at birth; it is the source of our bodily needs, wants, desires, and impulses, particularly our sexual and aggressive drives.

superego The mental system that reflects the internalization of cultural rules, mainly learned as parents exercise their authority.

ego The component of personality, developed through contact with the external world, that enables us to deal with life's practical demands.

"I'm sorry, I'm not speaking to anyone tonight. My defense mechanisms seem to be out of order."

Freud believed that the relative strength of the interactions among the three systems of mind (i.e., which system is usually dominant) determines an individual's basic personality structure. He believed that the dynamics among the id, superego, and ego are largely governed by *anxiety,* an unpleasant feeling that arises when unwanted thoughts or feelings occur, such as when the id seeks a gratification that the ego thinks will lead to real-world dangers or that the superego sees as leading to punishment. When the ego receives an "alert signal" in the form of anxiety, it launches into a defensive position in an attempt to ward off the anxiety. According to Freud, it does so using one of several different **defense mechanisms,** *unconscious coping mechanisms that reduce anxiety generated by threats from unacceptable impulses* (see **TABLE 11.2**). Psychodynamically oriented psychologists believe that defense mechanisms help us overcome anxiety and engage effectively with the outside world and that our characteristic style of defense becomes our signature in dealing with the world—and an essential aspect of our personality.

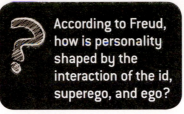

According to Freud, how is personality shaped by the interaction of the id, superego, and ego?

defense mechanisms Unconscious coping mechanisms that reduce anxiety generated by threats from unacceptable impulses.

Table 11.2 Defense Mechanisms

Repression is the first defense the ego tries, but if it is inadequate, then other defense mechanisms may come into play.

Defense Mechanism	Description	Example
Repression	Removing painful experiences and unacceptable impulses from the conscious mind: "motivated forgetting."	Not lashing out physically in anger; putting a bad experience out of your mind.
Rationalization	Supplying a reasonable sounding explanation for unacceptable feelings and behavior to conceal (mostly from oneself) one's underlying motives or feelings.	Dropping calculus "allegedly" because of poor ventilation in the classroom.
Reaction formation	Unconsciously replacing threatening inner wishes and fantasies with an exaggerated version of their opposite.	Being rude to someone you're attracted to.
Projection	Attributing one's own threatening feelings, motives, or impulses to another person or group.	Judging others as being dishonest because you believe that you are dishonest.
Regression	Reverting to an immature behavior or earlier stage of development, a time when things felt more secure, to deal with internal conflict and perceived threat.	Using baby talk, even though able to use appropriate speech, in response to distress.
Displacement	Shifting unacceptable wishes or drives to a neutral or less threatening alternative	Slamming a door; yelling at someone other than the person you're mad at.
Identification	Dealing with feelings of threat and anxiety by unconsciously taking on the characteristics of another person who seems more powerful or better able to cope.	A bullied child becoming a bully.
Sublimation	Channeling unacceptable sexual or aggressive drives into socially acceptable and culturally enhancing activities.	Diverting anger to the football or rugby field, or other contact sport.

psychosexual stages Distinct early life stages through which personality is formed as children experience sexual pleasures from specific body areas and caregivers redirect or interfere with those pleasures.

fixation A phenomenon in which a person's pleasure-seeking drives become psychologically stuck, or arrested, at a particular psychosexual stage.

oral stage The first psychosexual stage, in which experience centers on the pleasures and frustrations associated with the mouth, sucking, and being fed.

anal stage The second psychosexual stage, in which experience is dominated by the pleasures and frustrations associated with the anus, retention and expulsion of feces and urine, and toilet training.

phallic stage The third psychosexual stage, in which experience is dominated by the pleasure, conflict, and frustration associated with the phallic–genital region as well as coping with powerful incestuous feelings of love, hate, jealousy, and conflict.

Oedipus conflict A developmental experience in which a child's conflicting feelings toward the opposite-sex parent are (usually) resolved by identifying with the same-sex parent.

latency stage The fourth psychosexual stage, in which the primary focus is on the further development of intellectual, creative, interpersonal, and athletic skills.

One of the id's desires is to make a fine mess (a desire that is often frustrated early in life, perhaps during the anal stage). Famous painter Jackson Pollock found a way to make extraordinarily fine messes—behavior that at some level all of us envy.

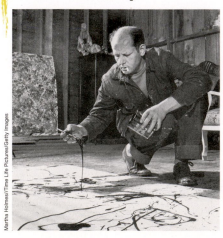

Martha Holmes/Time Life Pictures/Getty Images

Psychosexual Stages and the Development of Personality

Freud also proposed that a person's basic personality is formed before 6 years of age during a series of sensitive periods, or life stages, when experiences influence all that will follow. Freud called these periods **psychosexual stages,** *distinct early life stages through which personality is formed as children experience sexual pleasures from specific body areas and caregivers redirect or interfere with those pleasures.*

Problems and conflicts encountered at any psychosexual stage, Freud believed, will influence personality in adulthood. Conflict resulting from a person's being deprived or, paradoxically, overindulged at a given stage could result in **fixation,** *a phenomenon in which a person's pleasure-seeking drives become psychologically stuck, or arrested, at a particular psychosexual stage.* Here's how he explained each stage and the effects of fixation at each stage.

> In the 1st year and a half of life, the infant is in the **oral stage,** *the first psychosexual stage, in which experience centers on the pleasures and frustrations associated with the mouth, sucking, and being fed.* Infants who are deprived of pleasurable feeding or indulgently overfed are believed to have a personality style in which they are focused on issues related to fullness and emptiness and what they can "take in" from others.

> Between 2 and 3 years of age, the child moves on to the **anal stage,** *the second psychosexual stage, in which experience is dominated by the pleasures and frustrations associated with the anus, retention and expulsion of feces and urine, and toilet training.* Individuals who have had difficulty negotiating this conflict are believed to develop a rigid personality and remain preoccupied with issues of control.

> Between the ages of 3 and 5 years, the child is in the **phallic stage,** *the third psychosexual stage, in which experience is dominated by the pleasure, conflict, and frustration associated with the phallic–genital region as well as coping with powerful incestuous feelings of love, hate, jealousy, and conflict.* According to Freud, children in the phallic stage experience the **Oedipus conflict,** *a developmental experience in which a child's conflicting feelings toward the opposite-sex parent are (usually) resolved by identifying with the same-sex parent.*

> Between the ages of 5 and 13, children experience the **latency stage,** *the fourth psychosexual stage, in which the primary focus is on the further development of intellectual, creative, interpersonal, and athletic skills.* Because Freud believed that the most significant aspects of personality development occur before the age of 6 years, simply making it to the latency period relatively undisturbed by conflicts of the earlier stages is a sign of healthy personality development.

> At puberty and thereafter, the **genital stage** is *the fifth and final psychosexual stage, the time for the coming together of the mature adult personality with a capacity to love, work, and relate to others in a mutually satisfying and reciprocal manner.* Freud believed that people who are fixated in a prior stage fail to develop healthy adult sexuality and a well-adjusted adult personality.

What should we make of all this? On the one hand, the psychoanalytic theory of psychosexual stages offers an intriguing picture of early family relationships and the extent to which they allow the child to satisfy basic needs and wishes. On the other hand, critics argue that psychodynamic explanations lack any real evidence and tend to focus on provocative after-the-fact interpretation rather than testable

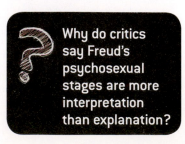

Why do critics say Freud's psychosexual stages are more interpretation than explanation?

prediction. The psychosexual stage theory offers a compelling set of story plots for interpreting lives once they have unfolded, but it has not generated clear-cut predictions supported by research.

genital stage The fifth and final psychosexual stage, the time for the coming together of the mature adult personality with a capacity to love, work, and relate to others in a mutually satisfying and reciprocal manner.

SUMMARY QUIZ [11.3]

1. Which of Freud's systems of the mind would impel you to, if hungry, start grabbing food off people's plates upon entering a restaurant?

   a. the id

   b. the reality principle

   c. the ego

   d. the pleasure principle

2. After performing poorly on an exam, you drop a class, saying that you and the professor are just a poor match. According to Freud, what defense mechanism are you employing?

   a. regression

   b. rationalization

   c. projection

   d. reaction formation

3. According to Freud, a person who is preoccupied with control over possessions, money, and people, as well as concerns about cleanliness versus messiness, is fixated at which psychosexual stage?

   a. the oral stage

   b. the anal stage

   c. the latency stage

   d. the genital stage

The Humanistic–Existential Approach: Personality as Choice

In the 1950s and 1960s, psychologists began to try to understand personality from a very different viewpoint. Humanistic and existential theorists turned their attention to how humans make *healthy choices* that create their personalities. *Humanistic psychologists* emphasized a positive, optimistic view of human nature that highlights people's inherent goodness and their potential for personal growth. *Existential psychologists* focused on the individual as a responsible agent who is free to create and live his or her life while negotiating the issue of meaning and the reality of death. The *humanistic–existential approach* integrates these insights with a focus on how a personality can become optimal.

Human Needs and Self-Actualization

Humanists see the **self-actualizing tendency,** *the human motive toward realizing our inner potential,* as a major factor in personality. The pursuit of knowledge, the expression of one's creativity, the quest for spiritual enlightenment, and the desire to give to society are all examples of self-actualization. As you saw in the Emotion and Motivation chapter, the noted humanistic theorist Abraham Maslow (1937) proposed a

self-actualizing tendency The human motive toward realizing our inner potential.

Decades of research have shown that growing up in a distressed neighborhood is associated with worse educational, occupational, and health outcomes. Humanistic psychologists would suggest that people in such settings must struggle to meet their basic daily needs and so do not have opportunities for self-actualization.

existential approach A school of thought that regards personality as governed by an individual's ongoing choices and decisions in the context of the realities of life and death.

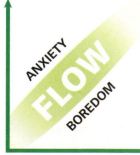

FIGURE 11.4 Flow Experience It feels good to do things that challenge your abilities but that don't challenge them too much. Csikszentmihalyi described this feeling between boredom and anxiety as the "flow experience." (Information from Csikszentmihalyi, 1990.)

hierarchy of needs, a model in which basic physiological and safety needs must be satisfied before a person can afford to focus on higher-level psychological needs, culminating in *self-actualization*: the need to be good, to be fully alive, and to find meaning in life.

Humanist psychologists explain individual personality differences as arising from the various ways that the environment facilitates—or blocks—attempts to satisfy psychological needs. For example, someone with the inherent potential to be a great scientist, artist, parent, or teacher might never realize these talents if his or her energies and resources are instead directed toward meeting basic needs of security, belongingness, and the like. Research indicates that when people shape their lives around goals that do not match their true nature and capabilities, they are less likely to be happy than those whose lives and goals do match (Ryan & Deci, 2000).

It feels great to be doing exactly what you are capable of doing. Mihaly Csikszentmihalyi (1990) found that engagement in tasks that exactly match one's abilities creates a mental state of energized focus that he called *flow* (see **FIGURE 11.4**). Tasks that are below our abilities cause boredom, those that are too challenging cause anxiety, and those that are "just right" lead to the experience of flow. If you know how to play the piano, for example, and are playing a Chopin prelude that you know well enough that it just matches your abilities, you are likely to experience this optimal state. People report being happier at these times than at any other times. Humanists believe that such peak experiences, or states of flow, reflect the realization of one's human potential and represent the height of personality development.

Personality as Existence

Existentialists agree with humanists about many of the features of personality but focus on challenges to the human condition that are more profound than the lack of a nurturing environment. For existentialists, specific aspects of the human condition, such as awareness of our own existence and the ability to make choices about how to behave, have a double-edged quality: They bring an extraordinary richness and dignity to human life, but they also force us to confront realities that are difficult to face, such as the prospect of our own death. The **existential approach** is *a school of thought that regards personality as governed by an individual's ongoing choices and decisions in the context of the realities of life and death.*

According to the existential perspective, the difficulties we face in finding meaning in life and in accepting the responsibility of making free choices provoke a type of anxiety existentialists call *angst* (the anxiety of fully being). The human ability to consider limitless numbers of goals and actions is exhilarating, but it can also open the door to profound questions such as: Why am I here? What is the meaning of my life?

Thinking about the meaning of existence also can evoke an awareness of the inevitability of death. What, then, is the purpose of living if life as we know it will end one day? Alternatively, does life have more meaning given that it is so temporary? Existential theorists do not suggest that people consider these profound existential issues on a day-to-day and moment-to-moment basis. Rather than ruminate about death and meaning, people typically pursue superficial answers that help them deal with the angst and dread they experience, and the defenses they construct form the basis of their personalities (Binswanger, 1958; May, 1983). Some people organize their lives around obtaining material possessions; others may immerse themselves in drugs or addictive behaviors such as compulsive web browsing, video gaming, or television watching in order to numb the mind to existential realities.

Challenge

ANXIETY

FLOW

BOREDOM

Abilities

For existentialists, a healthier solution is to face the issues head-on and learn to accept and tolerate the pain of existence. Indeed, being fully human means confronting existential realities rather than denying them or embracing comforting illusions. This approach requires the courage to accept the inherent anxiety and the dread of nonbeing that is part of being alive. Such courage may be bolstered by developing supportive relationships with others who can supply unconditional positive regard. There's something about being loved that helps take away the angst.

SUMMARY QUIZ [11.4]

1. Humanists see personality as directed toward the goal of
   a. existentialism.
   b. self-actualization.
   c. healthy adult sexuality.
   d. sublimation.

2. According to the existential perspective, the difficulties we face in finding meaning in life and in accepting the responsibility for making free choices provoke a type of anxiety called
   a. angst.
   b. flow.
   c. the self-actualizing tendency.
   d. mortality salience.

The Social-Cognitive Approach: Personalities in Situations

What is it like to be a person? The **social-cognitive approach** is *an approach that views personality in terms of how the person thinks about the situations encountered in daily life and behaves in response to them.* Bringing together insights from social psychology, cognitive psychology, and learning theory, this approach emphasizes how the person experiences and interprets situations (Bandura, 1986; Mischel & Shoda, 1999; Ross & Nisbett, 1991; Wegner & Gilbert, 2000).

social-cognitive approach An approach that views personality in terms of how the person thinks about the situations encountered in daily life and behaves in response to them.

Do researchers in social cognition think that personality arises from past experiences or from the current environment?

Researchers in social cognition believe that both the current situation and learning history are key determinants of behavior. These researchers focus on how people *perceive* their environments, how personality contributes to the way people construct situations in their own minds, and how people's goals and expectancies influence their responses to situations.

Consistency of Personality across Situations

At the core of the social-cognitive approach is a natural puzzle, the **person–situation controversy,** which focuses on *the question of whether behavior is caused more by personality or by situational factors.*

"He's not very exciting in social situations but on the net he's a wildman."

Mick Stevens © The New Yorker Collection/Cartoonbank.Com

Is a student who cheats on a test more likely than others to steal candy or lie to his grandmother? Social-cognitive research indicates that behavior in one situation does not necessarily predict behavior in a different situation.

person–situation controversy The question of whether behavior is caused more by personality or by situational factors.

This controversy began in earnest when Walter Mischel (1968) argued that measured personality traits often do a poor job of predicting individuals' behavior. Mischel also noted that knowing how a person will behave in one situation is not particularly helpful in predicting the person's behavior in another situation. For example, in classic studies, Hugh Hartshorne and M. A. May (1928) assessed children's honesty by examining their willingness to cheat on a test and found that such dishonesty was not consistent from one situation to another. The assessment of a child's trait of honesty in a cheating situation was of almost no use in predicting whether the child would act honestly in a different situation, such as when given the opportunity to steal money. Mischel proposed that measured traits do not predict behaviors very well because behaviors are determined more by situational factors than personality theorists were willing to acknowledge.

Is there no personality, then? Do we all just do what situations require? It turns out that information about both personality and situation are necessary to predict behavior accurately (Fleeson, 2004; Mischel, 2004). Some situations are particularly powerful, leading most everyone to behave similarly regardless of personality (Cooper & Withey, 2009). At a funeral, almost everyone looks somber, and during an earthquake, almost everyone shakes. But in more moderate situations, personality can come forward to influence behavior (Funder, 2001). Among the children in Hartshorne and May's (1928) studies, cheating versus not cheating on a test was actually a fairly good predictor of cheating on a test later—as long as the situation was similar. Personality consistency, then, appears to be a matter of when and where a certain kind of behavior tends to be shown (see the Culture & Community box).

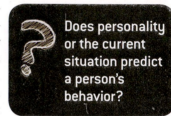

Does personality or the current situation predict a person's behavior?

Culture & Community

Does your personality change according to which language you're speaking? The personalities of people from different cultures often can diverge. For instance, in one study of personality tests taken by Americans and Mexicans, Americans reported being more extraverted, more agreeable, and more conscientious than Mexicans (Ramirez-Esparza et al., 2004). The authors suggested that this may be due to differences in how individualistic versus collectivistic people are in each culture. Individualistic cultures (like America's) emphasize personal achievement, whereas collectivistic cultures (like Mexico's) focus on the importance of family and community outcomes.

Interestingly, however, when the researchers tested Spanish–English bilinguals in Texas, California, and Mexico in both languages, scores of the bilingual participants were more extraverted, agreeable, and conscientious when they took the test in English than when they took it in Spanish! The authors proposed that this difference is the result of cultural frame switching, which refers to the tendency of bi- or multicultural people to adjust their style of thinking, feeling, and behaving to more closely match the group with which they are currently interacting. Most important, the changes are pretty subtle (more toning it up or down rather than total personality transplant), but the appearance of such changes highlights the importance of considering culture and context when thinking about personality.

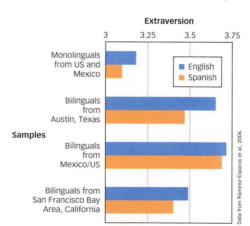

Personal Constructs

How can we understand differences in the way situations are interpreted? George Kelly (1955) long ago realized that these differences in perspective could be used to understand the *perceiver's* personality. He suggested that people view the social world from differing perspectives and that these different views arise through the application of **personal constructs,** *dimensions people use in making sense of their experiences.* Consider, for example, different individuals' personal constructs of a clown: One person may see him as a source of fun, another as a tragic figure, and yet another as so frightening that McDonald's must be avoided at all costs.

Kelly proposed that different personal constructs are the key to personality differences and lead people to engage in different behaviors. Taking a long break from work for a leisurely lunch might

Why doesn't everyone love clowns?

seem lazy to you. To your friend, the break might seem an ideal opportunity for catching up with friends and wonder why you always choose to eat at your desk. Social-cognitive theory explains different responses to situations with the idea that people experience and interpret the world in different ways.

Are two of these people taller and one shorter? Are two bareheaded while one wears a hood? Or are two the daughters and one the mom? George Kelly held that the personal constructs we use to distinguish among people in our lives are basic elements of our own personalities.

Personal Goals and Expectancies

Social-cognitive theories also recognize that a person's unique perspective on situations is reflected in his or her personal goals, which are often conscious. In fact, people can usually tell you their goals, whether they are to find a date for this weekend, get a good grade in psych, establish a fulfilling career, or just get this darn bag of chips open. These goals often reflect the tasks that are appropriate to the person's situation and stage of life (Cantor, 1990; Klinger, 1977; Little, 1983; Vallacher & Wegner, 1985). For instance, common goals for adolescents include being popular, achieving greater independence from parents and family, and getting into a good college. Common goals for adults include developing a meaningful career, finding a mate, securing financial stability, and starting a family.

People translate goals into behavior in part through **outcome expectancies,** *a person's assumptions about the likely consequences of a future behavior.* Just as a laboratory rat learns that pressing a bar releases a food pellet, we learn that "if I am friendly toward people, they will be friendly in return" and "if I ask people to pull my finger, they will withdraw from me." So we learn to perform behaviors that we expect will have the outcome of moving us closer to our goals. Outcome expectancies are learned through direct experience, both bitter and sweet, and through merely observing other people's actions and their consequences. Outcome expectancies combine with a person's goals to produce the person's characteristic style of behavior. We do not all want the same things from life, clearly, and our personalities largely reflect the goals we pursue and the expectancies we have about the best ways to pursue them.

People also differ in their expectancy for achieving goals. Some people seem to feel that they are fully in control of what happens to them in life, whereas others feel that the world doles out rewards and punishments to them irrespective of their actions. A person's **locus of control** is the *tendency to perceive the control of rewards as internal to the self or external in the environment* (Rotter, 1966). People who believe they control their own destinies are said to have an *internal* locus

What is the advantage of an internal locus of control?

of control, whereas those who believe that outcomes are random, determined by luck, or controlled by other people are described as having an *external* locus of control. These beliefs translate into individual differences in emotion and behavior. For example, people

personal constructs Dimensions people use in making sense of their experiences.

outcome expectancies A person's assumptions about the likely consequences of a future behavior.

locus of control A person's tendency to perceive the control of rewards as internal to the self or external in the environment.

Some days you feel like a puppet on a string. If you have an external locus of control, you may feel that way most days.

Table 11.3 Rotter's Locus-of-Control Scale

For each pair of items, choose the option that most closely reflects your personal belief. Then turn the book upside down to see if you have more of an internal or external locus of control.

1. a. Many of the unhappy things in people's lives are partly due to bad luck.
   b. People's misfortunes result from the mistakes they make.

2. a. I have often found that what is going to happen will happen.
   b. Trusting to fate has never turned out as well for me as making a decision to take a definite course of action.

3. a. Becoming a success is a matter of hard work; luck has little or nothing to do with it.
   b. Getting a good job depends mainly on being in the right place at the right time.

4. a. When I make plans, I am almost certain that I can make them work.
   b. It is not always wise to plan too far ahead because many things turn out to be a matter of good or bad fortune anyhow.

Source: Information from Rotter, 1966.

Answer: A more internal locus of control would be reflected in choosing options 1b, 2b, 3a, and 4a.

with an internal locus of control tend to be less anxious, achieve more, and cope better with stress than do people with an external orientation (Lefcourt, 1982). To get a sense of your standing on this trait dimension, choose one of the options for each of the sample items from the locus-of-control scale in **TABLE 11.3**.

SUMMARY QUIZ [11.5]

1. Which of the following is NOT an emphasis of the social-cognitive approach?
   a. how personality and situation interact to cause behavior
   b. how personality contributes to the way people construct situations in their own minds
   c. how people's goals and expectancies influence their responses to situations
   d. how people confront realities rather than embrace comforting illusions

2. According to social-cognitive theorists, _____ are the dimensions people use in making sense of their experiences.
   a. personal constructs
   b. outcome expectancies
   c. loci of control
   d. personal goals

3. Tyler has been getting poor evaluations at work. He attributes this to having a mean boss who always assigns him the hardest tasks. This suggests that Tyler has
   a. external locus of control
   b. internal locus of control
   c. high performance anxiety
   d. poorly developed personal constructs

The Self: Personality in the Mirror

Imagine that you wake up tomorrow morning, drag yourself into the bathroom, look into the mirror, and don't recognize the face looking back at you. This was the plight of a woman, married for 30 years and the mother of two grown children, who one day began to respond to her mirror image as if it were a different person (Feinberg, 2001).

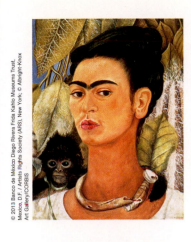

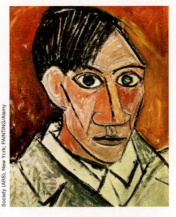

What do these self-portraits of Frida Kahlo, Vincent van Gogh, Pablo Picasso, Salvador Dalí, Wanda Wulz, and Jean-Michel Basquiat reveal about each artist's self-concept?

She talked to and challenged the person in the mirror. When there was no response, she tried to attack it as if it were an intruder. Her husband, shaken by this bizarre behavior, brought her to a neurologist, who was gradually able to convince her that the image in the mirror was in fact herself.

Most of us are pretty familiar with the face that looks back at us from every mirror. We develop the ability to recognize ourselves in mirrors by 18 months of age (as discussed in the Consciousness chapter). Self-recognition in mirrors signals our amazing capacity for reflexive thinking, for directing attention to our own thoughts, feelings, and actions—an ability that enables us to construct ideas about our own personalities. In contrast to a cow, which will never know that it has a poor sense of humor, or a cat, which will never know that it is awfully friendly, humans have rich and detailed self-knowledge.

Self-Concept

If asked to describe yourself, you might mention your physical characteristics (male or female, tall or short, dark-skinned or light), your activities (listening to hip-hop, alternative rock, jazz, or classical music), your personality traits (extraverted or introverted, agreeable or independent), or your social roles (student, son or daughter, member of a hiking club, krumper). These features make up the **self-concept,** *a person's explicit knowledge of his or her own behaviors, traits, and other personal characteristics.* A person's self-concept is an organized body of knowledge that develops from social experiences and has a profound effect on a person's behavior throughout life.

self-concept A person's explicit knowledge of his or her own behaviors, traits, and other personal characteristics.

Think about your own self-narrative (what you have done) and self-concept (how you view yourself). Are there areas that don't match up? Are there things that you've done, good or bad, that are not part of your self-concept? How might you explain that?

Self-Concept Organization

Our knowledge of ourselves seems to be organized in two ways: as narratives about episodes in our lives and in terms of traits (as would be suggested by the distinction between episodic and semantic memory discussed in the Memory chapter).

The aspect of the self-concept that is a *self-narrative* (a story that we tell about ourselves) can be brief or very lengthy. Your life story could start with your birth and upbringing, describe a series of defining moments, and end where you are today. Self-narrative organizes the highlights (and low blows) of your life into a story in which you are the leading character and binds them together into your self-concept (McAdams, 1993; McLean, 2008).

Self-concept is also organized in terms of personality traits— whether you are considerate or smart or lazy or active. Each person finds certain unique personality traits particularly important for conceptualizing the self (Markus, 1977). One person might define herself as independent, for example, whereas another might not care much about her level of independence but instead emphasizes her sense of style.

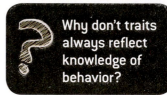

What is your life story as you see it—your self-narrative?

Our self-narratives and trait self-concepts don't always match up. You may think of yourself as an honest person, for example, but also may recall that time you nabbed a handful of change from your parents' dresser and conveniently forgot to replace it. The traits we use to describe ourselves are generalizations, and not every episode in our life stories may fit. In fact, research suggests that the stores of knowledge about our behaviors and traits are not very well integrated (Kihlstrom, Beer, & Klein, 2002). In people who develop amnesia, for example, memory for behaviors can be lost even though the trait self-concept remains stable (Klein, 2004). People can have a pretty strong sense of who they are even though they may not remember a single example of when they acted that way.

Why don't traits always reflect knowledge of behavior?

Causes and Effects of Self-Concept

How do self-concepts arise, and how do they affect us? Although we can gain self-knowledge in private moments of insight, we more often arrive at our self-concepts through interacting with others. Young children in particular receive plenty of feedback from their parents, teachers, siblings, and friends about their characteristics, and this helps them to form an idea of who they are. Even adults would find it difficult to hold a view of the self as "kind" or "smart" if no one else ever shared this impression. The sense of self, then, is largely developed and maintained in relationships with others.

Over the course of a lifetime, however, we become less and less impressed with what others have to say about us. All the things people have said about us accumulate after a while into what we see as a kind of consensus held by the "generalized other" (Mead, 1934). We typically adopt this general view of ourselves and hold on to it stubbornly. Just as we might argue vehemently with someone who tried to tell us a refrigerator is a pair of underpants, we are likely to defend our self-concept against anyone whose view of us departs from our own.

Because it is so stable, a major effect of the self-concept is to promote consistency in behavior across situations (Lecky, 1945). As existential theorists emphasize, people derive a comforting sense of familiarity

"I don't want to be defined by who I am."

and stability from knowing who they are. We tend to engage in **self-verification,** *the tendency to seek evidence to confirm the self-concept,* and we find it disconcerting if someone sees us quite differently from the way we see ourselves. For example, in one study, people who considered themselves submissive received feedback that they seemed very dominant and forceful (Swann, 1983). Rather than accepting this discrepant information, they went out of their way to act in an extremely submissive manner. Our tendency to project into the world our concept of the self contributes to personality coherence.

How does self-concept influence behavior?

self-verification The tendency to seek evidence to confirm the self-concept.

self-esteem The extent to which an individual likes, values, and accepts the self.

Self-Esteem

When you think about yourself, do you feel good and worthy? Do you like yourself, or do you feel bad and have negative, self-critical thoughts? **Self-esteem** is *the extent to which an individual likes, values, and accepts the self.* Researchers who study self-esteem typically ask participants to fill out a self-esteem questionnaire, such as one shown in **TABLE 11.4** (Rosenberg, 1965). People who strongly agree with the positive statements about themselves and strongly disagree with the negative statements are considered to have high self-esteem. In general, compared with people with low self-esteem, those with high self-esteem tend to live happier and healthier lives, cope better with stress, and be more likely to persist at difficult tasks (Baumeister et al., 2003). How does this aspect of personality develop, and why does everyone—whether high or low in self-esteem—seem to *want* high self-esteem?

Sources of Self-Esteem

An important factor in determining self-esteem is whom people choose for comparison. For example, James (1890) noted that an accomplished athlete who is the second best in the world should feel pretty proud, but this athlete might not feel that way if the standard of comparison involves being best in the world. In fact, athletes in

Table 11.4 Rosenberg Self-Esteem Scale				
Consider each statement and circle SA for strongly agree, A for agree, D for disagree, and SD for strongly disagree.				
1. On the whole, I am satisfied with myself.	SA	A	D	SD
2. At times, I think I am no good at all.	SA	A	D	SD
3. I feel that I have a number of good qualities.	SA	A	D	SD
4. I am able to do things as well as most other people.	SA	A	D	SD
5. I feel I do not have much to be proud of.	SA	A	D	SD
6. I certainly feel useless at times.	SA	A	D	SD
7. I feel that I'm a person of worth, at least on an equal plane with others.	SA	A	D	SD
8. I wish I could have more respect for myself.	SA	A	D	SD
9. All in all, I am inclined to feel that I am a failure.	SA	A	D	SD
10. I take a positive attitude toward myself.	SA	A	D	SD

Source: Rosenberg, *Society and the adolescent self-image,* Princeton University Press 1965.

Scoring: For items 1, 3, 4, 7, and 10, SA = 3, A = 2, D = 1, SD = 0; for items 2, 5, 6, 8, and 9, the scoring is reversed, with SA = 0, A = 1, D = 2, SD = 3. The higher the total score, the higher one's self-esteem.

Clive Rose/Getty Images

This is silver medalist Bo Qui of China, gold medalist David Boudia of the US, and bronze medalist Tom Daley of the UK following the 10m platform diving competition at the 2012 London Olympics. Notice the expression on Bo Qui's face compared to those of the gold and bronze medal winners.

the 1992 Olympics who had won silver medals looked less happy during the medal ceremony than those who had won bronze medals (Medvec, Madey, & Gilovich, 1995). If the actual self is seen as falling short of the ideal self, people tend to feel sad or dejected; when they become aware that the actual self is inconsistent with the self they have a duty to be, they are likely to feel anxious or agitated (Higgins, 1987).

Self-esteem is also affected by what kinds of domains we consider most important in our self-concept. One person's self-worth might be entirely contingent on, for example, how well she does in school, whereas another's self-worth might be based on her physical attractiveness (Crocker & Wolfe, 2001; Pelham, 1985). The first person's self-esteem might receive a big boost when she gets an A on an exam but much less of a boost when she's complimented on her new hairstyle, and this effect might be exactly reversed in the second person.

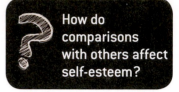

? How do comparisons with others affect self-esteem?

The Desire for Self-Esteem

What's so great about self-esteem? Why do people want to see themselves in a positive light? Three key theories on the benefits of self-esteem focus on status, belonging, and security.

1. *Social Status.* People with high self-esteem seem to carry themselves in a way that is similar to high-status animals of other social species. Dominant male gorillas, for example, appear confident and comfortable and not anxious or withdrawn. Perhaps high self-esteem in humans reflects high social status or suggests that the person is worthy of respect, and this perception triggers natural affective responses (Barkow, 1980; Maslow, 1937).

2. *Belongingness.* Evolutionary theory holds that early humans who managed to survive to pass on their genes were those who were able to maintain good relations with others rather than being cast out to fend for themselves. Thus, self-esteem could be an inner gauge of how much a person feels included

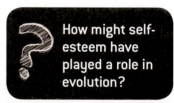

? How might self-esteem have played a role in evolution?

Survivor, The Bachelor, Big Brother. Why are shows in which everyone is fighting to remain a part of the group so popular today? Is it because they play on an evolutionary desire to belong? (Or do people just like to see other people get kicked out of the club?)

Monty Brinton/CBS via Getty Images

by others (Leary & Baumeister, 2000). According to evolutionary theory, then, we have evolved to seek out belongingness in our families, work groups, and culture, and higher self-esteem indicates that we are being accepted.

3. *Security.* Existential and psychodynamic approaches to personality suggest that the source of distress underlying negative self-esteem is ultimately the fear of death (Solomon, Greenberg, & Pyszczynski, 1991). In this view, humans find it terrifying to contemplate their own mortality, and so they try to defend against this awareness by immersing themselves in activities (such as earning money or dressing up to appear attractive) that their culture defines as meaningful and valuable. The desire for self-esteem may stem from a need to find value in ourselves as a way of escaping the anxiety associated with recognizing our mortality. The higher our self-esteem, the less anxious we feel with the knowledge that someday we will no longer exist.

Whatever the reason that low self-esteem feels so bad and high self-esteem feels so good, people are generally motivated to see themselves positively. In fact, we often process information in a biased manner in order to feel good about the self. The **self-serving bias** refers to *people's tendency to take credit for their successes but downplay responsibility for their failures.* You may have noticed this tendency in yourself, particularly in terms of the attributions you make about exams when you get a good grade ("I studied really intensely, and I'm good at that subject") or a bad grade ("The test was ridiculously tricky and the professor is unfair").

On the whole, most people satisfy the desire for high self-esteem and maintain a reasonably positive view of self by engaging in the self-serving bias (Miller & Ross, 1975; Shepperd, Malone, & Sweeny, 2008). In fact, if people are asked to rate themselves across a range of characteristics, they tend to see themselves as better than the average person in most domains (Alicke et al., 1995). For example, 90% of drivers describe their driving skills as better than average, and 86% of workers rate their performance on the job as above average. Even among university professors, 94% feel they are above average in teaching ability compared with other professors (Cross, 1977). These kinds of judgments simply cannot be accurate, statistically speaking, because the average of a group of people has to be the average, not better than

"I suffer from accurate self-esteem."

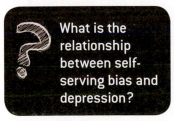

What is the relationship between self-serving bias and depression?

average! This particular error may be adaptive, however. People who do not engage in this self-serving bias to boost their self-esteem tend to be more at risk for depression, anxiety, and related health problems (Taylor & Brown, 1988).

On the other hand, a few people take positive self-esteem too far. **Narcissism** is *a trait that reflects a grandiose view of the self combined with a tendency to seek admiration from and exploit others.* At its extreme, narcissism is considered a personality disorder (see the Psychological Disorders chapter). Research has documented disadvantages of an overinflated view of self, most of which arise from the need to defend that grandiose view at all costs. For example, when highly narcissistic adolescents were given reasons to be ashamed of their performance on a task, their aggressiveness increased in the form of willingness to deliver loud blasts of noise to punish their opponent in a laboratory game (Thomaes et al., 2008).

Implicit Egotism

What's your favorite letter of the alphabet? About 30% of people answer by picking what just happens to be the first letter of their first name. Could this choice indicate

self-serving bias People's tendency to take credit for their successes but downplay responsibility for their failures.

narcissism A trait that reflects a grandiose view of the self combined with a tendency to seek admiration from and exploit others.

that some people think so highly of themselves that they base judgments of seemingly unrelated topics on how much it reminds them of themselves?

This *name-letter effect* was discovered some years ago (Nuttin, 1985), but more recently, researchers have gone on to discover how broad the egotistic bias in preferences can be, even influencing how people choose their home cities, streets, and even occupations (Pelham, Mirenberg, & Jones, 2002). For example, when researchers examined the rolls of people moving into several southern states, they found people named George were more likely than those with other names to move to Georgia. The same was true for Florences (Florida), Kenneths (Kentucky), and Louises (Louisiana). You can guess where the Virginias tended to relocate. People whose last name is Street seem biased toward addresses ending in *street,* whereas Lanes like lanes. The name effect seems to work for occupations as well: Slightly more people named Dennis and Denise chose dentistry and Lauras and Lawrences chose law compared with other occupations. Although the biases are small, they are consistent across many tests of the hypothesis. These biases have been called expressions of *implicit egotism* because people are not typically aware that they are influenced by the wonderful sound of their own names (Pelham, Carvallo, & Jones, 2005).

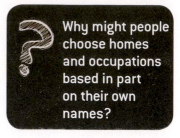

Why might people choose homes and occupations based in part on their own names?

At some level, of course, a bit of egotism is probably good for us. It's sad to meet someone who hates her own name or whose snap judgment of self is "I'm worthless." Yet in another sense, implicit egotism is a curiously subtle error: a tendency to make biased judgments of what we will do and where we will go in life just because we happen to have a certain name. Yes, the bias is only a small one. But your authors wonder: Could we have found better people to work with had we not fallen prey to this bias in our choice of colleagues? The first three authors (Dan, Dan, and Dan) thought they were breaking this cycle by adding a non-Dan author, only to realize that Matt was being added shortly after he decided to move his family (including children Matthew and Maya) to Massachusetts.

If you were trying to light up a room with a letter, would your first choice also be your initial?

© Maxstock/Alamy Images

The self is the part of personality that the person knows and can report about. Some of the personality measures we have seen in this chapter (such as personality inventories based on self-reports) are really no different from measures of self-concept. Both depend on the person's perceptions and memories of the self's behavior and traits. But personality runs deeper than this as well. The unconscious forces identified in psychodynamic approaches provide themes for behavior and sources of mental disorder that are not accessible for self-report. The humanistic and existential approaches remind us of the profound concerns we humans face and the difficulties we may have in understanding all of the forces that shape our self-views. Finally, in emphasizing how personality shapes our perceptions of social life, the social-cognitive approach brings the self back to center stage. The self, after all, is the hub of each person's social world.

SUMMARY QUIZ [11.6]

1. What we think about ourselves is referred to as our _____, and how we feel about ourselves is referred to as our _____.
   a. self-narrative; self-verification
   b. self-concept; self-esteem
   c. self-concept; self-verification
   d. self-esteem; self-concept

2. On what do the key theories on the benefits of self-esteem focus?
   a. status
   b. belonging
   c. security
   d. all of the above

3. When people take credit for their successes but downplay responsibility for their failures, they are exhibiting
   a. narcissism.
   b. implicit egotism.
   c. the self-serving bias.
   d. the name-letter effect.

CHAPTER REVIEW

SUMMARY

Personality: What It Is and How It Is Measured

> In psychology, personality refers to a person's characteristic style of behaving, thinking, and feeling.

> Personality psychologists attempt to find the best ways to describe personality, to explain how personalities come about, and to measure personality.

> Two general classes of personality tests are personality inventories, such as the MMPI–2–RF, and projective techniques, such as the Rorschach Inkblot Test and the TAT. Newer high-tech methods are proving to be even more effective.

The Trait Approach: Identifying Patterns of Behavior

> The trait approach tries to identify core personality dimensions that can be used to characterize an individual's behavior.

> Many personality psychologists currently focus on the Big Five personality factors: openness to experience, conscientiousness, extraversion, agreeableness, and neuroticism.

> Trait theorists often adopt a biological perspective, seeing personality largely as the result of genetic influences on brain functioning.

The Psychodynamic Approach: Forces That Lie beneath Awareness

> Freud believed that the personality results from forces that are largely unconscious, shaped by the interplay among id, superego, and ego.

> Defense mechanisms are methods the mind may use to reduce anxiety generated from unacceptable impulses.

> Freud believed that the developing person passes through a series of psychosexual stages and that failing to progress beyond one of the stages results in fixation, which is associated with corresponding personality traits.

The Humanistic–Existential Approach: Personality as Choice

> Humanists see personality as directed by an inherent striving toward self-actualization and development of our unique human potentials.

> Existentialists focus on angst and the defensive response people often have to questions about the meaning of life and the inevitability of death.

The Social-Cognitive Approach: Personalities in Situations

> The social-cognitive approach focuses on personality as arising from individuals' behavior in situations.

> According to social-cognitive personality theorists, the same person may behave differently in different situations but should behave consistently in similar situations.

> People translate their goals into behavior through outcome expectancies, their assumptions about the likely consequences of future behaviors.

The Self: Personality in the Mirror

> The self-concept is a person's knowledge of self, including both specific self-narratives and more abstract personality traits or personal characteristics.

> People's self-concept develops through social feedback, and people often act to try to confirm these views through a process of self-verification.

> Self-esteem is a person's evaluation of self; it is derived from being accepted by others, as well as by how we evaluate ourselves by comparison to others. Theories suggest that we seek positive self-esteem to achieve perceptions of status, or belonging, or of being symbolically protected against mortality.

> People strive for positive self-views through self-serving biases and implicit egotism.

KEY TERMS

personality (p. 350)
self-report (p. 351)
Minnesota Multiphasic Personality Inventory (MMPI) (p. 351)
projective tests (p. 352)
Rorschach Inkblot Test (p. 352)
Thematic Apperception Test (TAT) (p. 352)
trait (p. 354)

Big Five (p. 355)
psychodynamic approach (p. 360)
id (p. 360)
superego (p. 360)
ego (p. 360)
defense mechanisms (p. 361)
psychosexual stages (p. 362)
fixation (p. 362)
oral stage (p. 362)

anal stage (p. 362)
phallic stage (p. 362)
Oedipus conflict (p. 362)
latency stage (p. 362)
genital stage (p. 362)
self-actualizing tendency (p. 363)
existential approach (p. 364)
social-cognitive approach (p. 365)

person–situation controversy (p. 365)
personal constructs (p. 367)
outcome expectancies (p. 367)
locus of control (p. 367)
self-concept (p. 369)
self-verification (p. 371)
self-esteem (p. 371)
self-serving bias (p. 373)
narcissism (p. 373)

CHANGING MINDS

1. A presidential candidate makes a Freudian slip on live TV, calling his mother "petty"; he corrects himself quickly and says he meant to say "pretty." The next day, the video has gone viral, and the morning talk shows discuss the possibility that the candidate has an unresolved Oedipal conflict; if so, he's stuck in the phallic stage and is likely a relatively unstable person preoccupied with issues of seduction, power, and authority (which may be why he wants to be president). Your roommate knows you're taking a psychology class and asks for your opinion: "Can we really tell that a person is sexually repressed and may be in love with his own mother just because he stumbled over a single word?" How

would you reply? How widely are Freud's ideas about personality accepted by modern psychologists?

2. While reading a magazine, you come across an article on the nature–nurture controversy in personality. The magazine describes several adoption studies in which adopted children (who share no genes with each other but who grow up in the same household) are no more like each other than complete strangers. This suggests that family environment—and the influence of parental behavior—on personality is very weak. You show the article to a friend, who has trouble believing the results: "I always thought parents who don't show affection produce kids

who have trouble forming lasting relationships." How would you explain to your friend the relationship between nature, nurture, and personality?

3. One of your friends has found an online site that offers personality testing. He takes the test and reports that the results prove he's an "intuitive" rather than a "sensing" personality, someone who likes to look at the big picture rather than focus on tangible here-and-now experiences. "This explains a lot," he says, "like why I have trouble remembering details like other people's birthdays, and why it's hard for me to finish projects before the deadline." Aside from warning your friend about the dangers of self-diagnosis via Internet quizzes, what would you tell him

about the relationship between personality types and behavior? How well do scores on personality tests predict a person's actual behavior?

4. One of your friends tells you that her boyfriend cheated on her, so she will never date him or anyone who has ever been unfaithful because "once a cheat, always a cheat." She goes on to explain that personality and character are stable over time, so people will always make the same decisions and repeat the same mistakes over time. What do we know about the interaction between personality and situations that might confirm or deny her statements?

ANSWERS TO SUMMARY QUIZZES

Answers to Summary Quiz 11.1: 1. a; 2. c; 3. c.
Answers to Summary Quiz 11.2: 1. c; 2. d; 3. b.
Answers to Summary Quiz 11.3: 1. a; 2. b; 3. b.
Answers to Summary Quiz 11.4: 1. b; 2. a.
Answers to Summary Quiz 11.5: 1. d; 2. a; 3. a.
Answers to Summary Quiz 11.6: 1. b; 2. d; 3. c.

www

Need more help? Additional resources are located in LaunchPad at:
http://www.worthpublishers.com/launchpad/ schacterbrief3e

12

Social Psychology

TERRY, ROBERT, AND JOHN HAVE SOMETHING IN COMMON: They've all been tortured. Terry was an American journalist working in Lebanon when he was kidnapped by Hezbollah guerrillas; Robert was a semi-pro boxer living in Louisiana when he was arrested and sent to prison; and John was a naval aviator when he was shot down and captured by the North Vietnamese. All three men experienced a variety of tortures, and all agree about which was the worst.

John: It's an awful thing. It crushes your spirit and weakens your resistance more effectively than any other form of mistreatment.

Robert: It was a nightmare. I saw men so desperate that they ripped prison doors apart, starved and mutilated themselves . . . it takes every scrap of humanity to stay focused and sane.

Terry: I'm afraid I'm beginning to lose my mind, to lose control completely. I wish I could die. I ask God often to finish this, to end it any way that pleases Him.

The cruel technique that these three men are describing has nothing to do with electric shock or waterboarding. It does not require wax, rope, or razor blades. It is a remarkably simple technique that has been used for thousands of years to break the body and destroy the mind. It is called solitary confinement. John McCain spent 2 years in a cell by himself, Terry Anderson spent 7, and Robert King spent 29.

When we think of torture, we usually think of techniques designed to cause pain by depriving people of something they desperately need, such as oxygen, water, food, or sleep. But the need for social interaction is every bit as vital. Extensive periods of isolation can induce symptoms of psychosis (Grassian, 2006), and even in smaller doses, people who are socially isolated are more likely to become depressed, to become ill, and to die prematurely. In fact, social isolation is as bad for your health as being obese or smoking (Cacioppo & Patrick, 2008; House, Landis, & Umberson, 1988).

Terry Anderson, Robert King, and John McCain each spent years in isolation and described it as the worst form of torture.

social psychology The study of the causes and consequences of sociality.

aggression Behavior whose purpose is to harm another.

frustration–aggression hypothesis A principle stating that animals aggress when their desires are frustrated.

DATA VISUALIZATION

Dunbar's Number and the Size of Social Networks

www.macmillanhighered.com/schacterbrief3e

WHAT KIND OF ANIMAL GETS SICK OR GOES CRAZY when left alone? Our kind. Human beings are the most social species on the planet, and everything about us—from the structure of our brains to the structure of our societies—is influenced by that fact. **Social psychology** is *the study of the causes and consequences of sociality.* We'll start by examining *social behavior* (how people interact with each other), then we'll examine *social influence* (how people change each other), and finally we'll examine *social cognition* (how people think about each other).

Social Behavior: Interacting with People

Centipedes aren't social. Neither are snails or brown bears. In fact, most animals are loners that prefer solitude to company. So why don't we?

All animals must survive and reproduce, and being social is one strategy for accomplishing these two important goals. When it comes to finding food or fending off enemies, herds and packs and flocks can often do what individuals can't, and that's why over millions of years, many different species have found it useful to become social. But of the thousands and thousands of social species on our planet, only we form large-scale societies of genetically unrelated individuals. The ability to live in such large groups is one of the main reasons why we developed such large brains (Sallet et al., 2011; Shultz & Dunbar, 2010; Smith et al., 2010), and it has allowed our species to thrive. Consider this: If you had rounded up all the mammals on Earth 10,000 years ago and weighed them, human beings would have accounted for about 0.01% of the total weight. Today we would account for 98%. Being social has allowed us to become the heavyweight champions of survival and reproduction, and as you are about to see, much of our social behavior revolves around these two basic goals.

Survival: The Struggle for Resources

To survive, an animal must find resources such as food, water, and shelter. These resources are always scarce, because if they weren't, then the animal population would just keep increasing until they were. Animals solve the problem of scarce resources in two ways: by hurting each other and helping each other. *Hurting* and *helping* are antonyms, so you might expect them to have little in common. But as you will see, these seemingly antithetical behaviors are actually two solutions to the same problem (Hawley, 2002).

Aggression

The simplest way to solve the problem of scarce resources is simply to take what you want and kick the stuffing out of anyone who tries to stop you. **Aggression** is *behavior whose purpose is to harm another* (Anderson & Bushman, 2002; Bushman & Huesmann, 2010), and it is a strategy used by just about every animal on the planet. Aggression is not something that animals do for its own sake, but as a way of getting the resources they desire. The **frustration–aggression hypothesis** suggests *that animals aggress when their desires are frustrated* (Dollard et al., 1939), and it is pretty easy to see aggression through this lens. The chimp wants the banana (*desire*), but the pelican is about to take it (*frustration*), so the chimp threatens the pelican with its fist (*aggression*). The robber wants the money (*desire*), but

Human beings are the only animals that build large-scale societies of unrelated individuals. According to Facebook, Lady Gaga has more than 65 million friends who do not share her genes.

Erika Goldring/Filmmagic/Getty Images

the teller has it all locked up (*frustration*), so the robber threatens the teller with a gun (*aggression*).

The frustration–aggression hypothesis is right as far as it goes, but many scientists think it doesn't go far enough. They argue that the actual *cause* of aggressive behavior is negative affect (more commonly known as *feeling bad*) and that a frustrated desire is just one of many things that can induce it (Berkowitz, 1990). If it is true that animals aggress when they feel bad, then *anything* that makes them feel bad should increase aggression, and some evidence suggests it does. For example, laboratory rats that are given painful electric shocks will attack anything in their cage, including other animals, stuffed dolls, or even tennis balls (Kruk et al., 2004). People who are made to put their hands in ice water or to sit in a very hot room are more likely to blast others with noise weapons or punish others by making them eat hot chilis (Anderson, 1989; Anderson, Bushman, & Groom, 1997). The idea that aggression is a response to negative affect may even explain why so many acts of human aggression—from violent crime to athletic brawls—are more likely to occur on hot days when people are feeling irritated and uncomfortable (see **FIGURE 12.1**).

Of course, not everyone aggresses every time they feel bad. So who does and why? Research suggests that both biology and culture play important roles in determining if and when people who feel bad will aggress. Let's start by examining biology.

Biology and Aggression. If you wanted to know whether someone was likely to aggress and you could ask them only one question, it should be this: "Are you male or female?" (Wrangham & Peterson, 1997). Violent crimes such as assault, battery, and murder are almost exclusively perpetrated by men—and especially by young men (Strueber, Lueck, & Roth, 2006). Although most societies encourage males to be more aggressive than females (more on that shortly), male aggressiveness is not merely the product of socialization. Studies show that aggression is strongly correlated with the presence of a hormone called *testosterone*, which is typically much higher in men than in women, in younger men than in older men, and in violent criminals than in nonviolent criminals (Dabbs et al., 1995).

One of the most reliable ways to elicit aggression in males is to challenge their status or dominance. Indeed, three quarters of all murders can be classified as "status competitions" or "contests to save face" (Daly & Wilson, 1988). Contrary to popular wisdom, it isn't men with *low* self-esteem but men with unrealistically *high* self-esteem who are most prone to aggression, because such men are especially likely to perceive others' actions as a challenge to their inflated sense of their own status (Baumeister, Smart, & Boden, 1996). Men seem especially sensitive to these challenges when they are competing for the attention of women (Ainsworth & Maner, 2012).

FIGURE 12.1 Hot and Bothered
Professional pitchers have very good aim, so when they hit batters with the baseball, it's usually no accident. Data from nearly 60,000 major league baseball games shows that, as the temperature on the field increases, so does the likelihood that a pitcher will hit a batter. This effect becomes even stronger when members of the pitcher's own team have recently been hit by pitches, suggesting that the pitcher is seeking revenge. (Data from Larrick et al., 2011.)

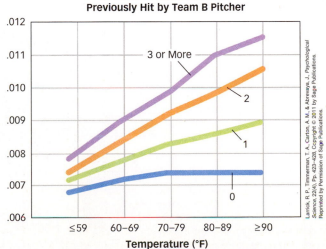

Number of Team A Batters Previously Hit by Team B Pitcher

Probability that Team A pitcher will hit Team B batter

3 or More

2

1

0

Temperature (°F)

≤59 60–69 70–79 80–89 ≥90

Larrick, R. P., Timmerman, T. A., Carton, A. M., & Abrevaya, J. Psychological Science, 22(4), Pp. 423–428. Copyright © 2011 by Sage Publications. Reprinted by Permission of Sage Publications.

Men often aggress in response to status threats. In 2005, John Anderson (*right*) called Russell Tavares (*left*) a "nerd" on a social networking site. So Tavares got in his car, drove 1,300 miles, and burned down Anderson's trailer. "I didn't think anybody was stupid enough to try to kill anybody over an Internet fight," said Anderson. Tavares was later sentenced to 7 years in prison.

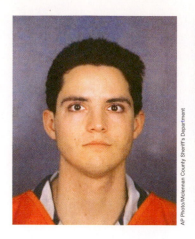

Women can be aggressive too, of course, but their aggression tends to be focused on challenges to their resources rather than to their status. Women are *much* less likely than men to aggress without provocation or to aggress in ways that cause physical injury, but they are only *slightly* less likely than men to aggress when provoked or to aggress in ways that cause psychological injury (Bettencourt & Miller, 1996; Eagly & Steffen, 1986). Indeed, women may even be *more* likely than men to aggress by causing social harm—for example, by ostracizing others (Benenson et al., 2011) or by spreading malicious rumors about them (Crick & Grotpeter, 1995).

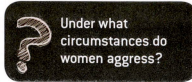
Under what circumstances do women aggress?

Pitchers born in Southern states are 40% more likely than those born in Northern states to hit batters with their pitches (Timmerman, 2007).

Culture and Aggression. Aggression has a biological basis, but it is also strongly influenced by culture (see **FIGURE 12.2**). For example, violent crime in the United States is more prevalent in the South, where traditional notions of honor require men to react aggressively when their status is challenged (Brown, Osterman, & Barnes, 2009; Nisbett & Cohen, 1996). In one set of experiments, researchers either did or did not insult American students from northern and southern states. When insulted, Southerners were more likely to experience a surge of testosterone and to feel that their status had been diminished by the insult (Cohen et al., 1996). And when a large man walked

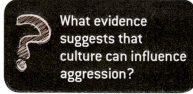
What evidence suggests that culture can influence aggression?

Culture influences aggression. In Iraq, where murder is a part of everyday life, children's games include mock executions. On the other hand, a Jainist teenager in India wears a mask at all times so that she will not harm insects or microbes by inhaling them.

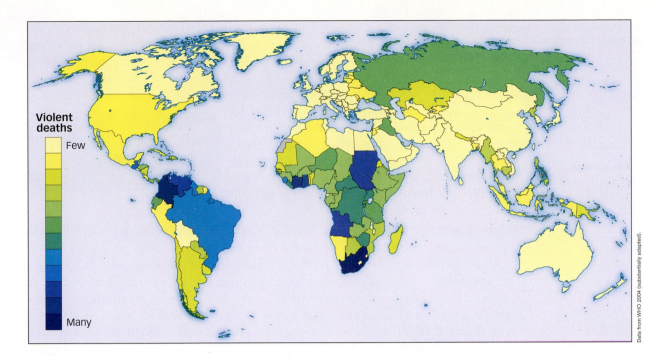

Data from WHO 2004 (substantially adapted).

Violent deaths

Few

Many

FIGURE 12.2 The Geography of Violence
When it comes to violence, culture matters a lot. One factor that distinguishes between more and less violent nations is gender equality (Caprioli, 2003; Melander, 2005). The better a nation's women are treated, the lower that nation's likelihood of going to war.

directly toward them as they were leaving the experiment, the insulted Southerners got "right up in his face" before giving way, whereas Northerners just stepped aside. On the other hand, when participants were *not* insulted, polite Southerners stepped aside *before* Northerners did. Clearly, culture plays an important role in determining whether our innate capacity for aggression will actually lead to aggressive behavior (Leung & Cohen, 2011).

Cooperation

Aggression is one way to solve the problem of scarce resources, but it is not the best way, because when individuals work together, they can often each get more resources than either could get alone. **Cooperation** is *behavior by two or more individuals that leads to mutual benefit* (Deutsch, 1949; Pruitt, 1998), and it is one of our species' greatest achievements—right up there with language, fire, and opposable thumbs (Axelrod, 1984; Axelrod & Hamilton, 1981; Nowak, 2006). Every roadway and supermarket, every robot and smartphone, every ballet and surgery is the result of cooperation, and it is difficult to think of an important human achievement that could have occurred without it.

Risk and Trust. So why don't we all cooperate all the time? Cooperation can be beneficial, but it can also be *risky,* and a simple game known as *the prisoner's dilemma* illustrates why. Imagine that you and your friend have been arrested for hacking into a bank's computer system and stealing a few million dollars. You are now being interrogated separately. The detectives tell you that if you and your friend both confess, you'll each get 10 years in prison for felony theft, and if you both refuse to confess, you'll each get 1 year in prison for disturbing the peace. However, if one of you confesses and the other doesn't, then the one who confesses will go free and the other will be put away for 30 years. What should you do? If you study **FIGURE 12.3**, you'll see that you and your friend would be wise to cooperate. If you both trust each other and both refuse to confess, then you will both get light sentences. But if you trust your friend and then your friend double-crosses you, your friend will go free and you will spend the next 30 years in a cell.

The prisoner's dilemma game illustrates a basic fact: Cooperation benefits everyone, but only if everyone cooperates. If someone doesn't cooperate, then everyone

cooperation Behavior by two or more individuals that leads to mutual benefit.

	COOPERATION (B does not confess)	NONCOOPERATION (B confesses)
COOPERATION (A does not confess)	A gets 1 year B gets 1 year	A gets 30 years B gets 0 years
NONCOOPERATION (A confesses)	A gets 0 years B gets 30 years	A gets 10 years B gets 10 years

FIGURE 12.3 **The Prisoner's Dilemma Game** The prisoner's dilemma game illustrates the benefits and costs of cooperation. Players A and B receive benefits whose size depends on whether they independently decide to cooperate. Mutual cooperation leads to a relatively moderate benefit to both players, but if only one player cooperates, then the cooperator gets no benefit, and the noncooperator gets a large benefit.

group A collection of people who have something in common that distinguishes them from others.

prejudice A positive or negative evaluation of another person based on the person's group membership.

discrimination Positive or negative behavior toward another person based on the person's group membership.

Kevin Hart owns the Gator Motel in Fargo, Georgia, which he runs on an honor system: Guests arrive, stay as long as they like, and leave their payment on the dresser. If just a few people cheated, it would not affect the room rates, but if too many cheated, then prices would have to rise. You don't have to be a prisoner to see the dilemma.

else pays a price. This fact makes it hard for us to decide whether we should or should not cooperate. We know that if everyone pays their taxes, then the tax rate stays low, and everyone enjoys the benefits of sturdy bridges and first-rate museums. But we also know that those who cheat and don't pay their taxes will get all the same benefits— and that we will have to pay for them! If we could be sure that everyone would pay their taxes we'd be happy to pay ours, but we don't want to pay ours if they aren't going to pay theirs. What to do? Is there any way to know whom we can trust?

What makes cooperation risky?

Groups and Favoritism. In fact, there is. A **group** is *a collection of people who have something in common that distinguishes them from others,* and every one of us is a member of many groups—from families and teams to religions and nations. Although groups differ in many ways, they all have one thing in common, which is that group members generally trust each other to be honest, fair, and nice. **Prejudice** is *a positive or negative evaluation of another person based on the person's group membership,* and **discrimination** is *positive or negative behavior toward another person based on the person's group membership* (Dovidio & Gaertner, 2010). One of the defining characteristics of groups is that members are positively prejudiced toward fellow members and tend to discriminate in their favor (DiDonato, Ullrich, & Krueger, 2011). Even when people are randomly assigned to be members of meaningless groups such as "Group 1" or "Group 2," they still give preferential treatment to members of their own group (Hodson & Sorrentino, 2001; Locksley, Ortiz, & Hepburn, 1980). Simply knowing that a person is one of *us* and not one of *them,* is sufficient to produce prejudice and discrimination (Tajfel et al., 1971). Because group members can be relied on to favor each other, group membership makes cooperation less risky.

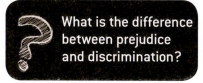
What is the difference between prejudice and discrimination?

The ability to trust and cooperate is one of the main benefits of being in a group. But groups also have costs. For example, when groups try to make decisions, they rarely do better than the best member would have done alone—and they quite often do worse (Minson & Mueller, 2012). One reason is that groups don't fully capitalize on the expertise of their members (Hackman & Katz, 2010). For instance, groups (such as a school board) often give too little weight to the opinions of members who are experts (the professor) and too much weight to the opinions of members who happen to be high in status (the mayor) or especially talkative (the mayor). Groups are also susceptible to the **common knowledge effect** which is *the tendency for group discussions to focus on information that all members share* (Gigone & Hastie, 1993). The problem with this is that the information everyone shares (the size of the gymnasium) is often relatively unimportant, whereas the truly important information (how a school in a different district solved its budget crisis) is known to just a few. In addition, group discussion often acts as an "amplifier" of initial opinions. **Group polarization** is *the tendency for groups to make decisions that are more extreme than any member would have made alone* (Myers & Lamm, 1975). A group whose members come to the table with moderate opinions ("We should probably just renovate the auditorium") can end up making an extreme decision ("We're going to build a new high school!") simply because, in the course of discussion, each member was exposed to many different arguments in favor of a single position (Isenberg, 1986). Finally, members of groups care about how other members feel and are sometimes reluctant to "rock the boat" even when it needs a good rocking. **Groupthink** is *the tendency for groups to reach consensus in order to facilitate interpersonal harmony* (Janis, 1982). Harmony is important (especially if the group is a choir), but studies show that groups often make poor decisions in order to achieve it (Turner & Pratkanis, 1998). For all of these reasons, groups underperform individuals in a wide variety of tasks.

The costs of groups go beyond bad decisions. People in groups sometimes do terrible things that they would never do alone, such as rioting, lynching, and gang-raping (Yzerbyt & Demoulin, 2010). Why do we sometimes behave badly when we assemble in groups?

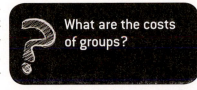

What are the costs of groups?

One reason is **deindividuation,** which *occurs when immersion in a group causes people to become less aware of their individual values.* We may wish we could grab the Rolex from the jeweler's window or plant a kiss on the attractive stranger in the library, but we don't do these things because they conflict with our personal values. Research shows that being assembled in groups draws our attention to others and *away* from ourselves, and as a result, we are less likely to consider our own personal values and instead adopt the group's values (Postmes & Spears, 1998).

A second reason why groups behave badly is **diffusion of responsibility,** which refers to *the tendency for individuals to feel diminished responsibility for their actions when they are surrounded by others who are acting the same way.* For example, studies of **bystander intervention**— which is *the act of helping strangers in an emergency situation*—reveal that people are less likely to help an innocent person in distress when there are many other bystanders present, because they assume that one of the other bystanders is more responsible than they are (Darley & Latané, 1968; Latané & Nida, 1981). If you saw a fellow student cheat on an exam, you'd probably feel more responsible for reporting the incident if you were taking the test in a group of 3 than in a group of 3,000 (see **FIGURE 12.4**).

If groups make bad decisions and foster bad behavior, then might we be better off without them? It seems unlikely. Not only do groups enable cooperation, which has extraordinary benefits, but one of the best predictors of a person's general well-being is the quality and extent of his or her group memberships (Myers & Diener, 1995). People who are excluded from groups are typically anxious, lonely, depressed, and at increased risk for illness and premature death (Cacioppo & Patrick, 2008; Cohen, 1988; Leary, 1990). Groups may cause us to misbehave, but they are also the key to our happiness and well-being.

common knowledge effect The tendency for group discussions to focus on information that all members share.

group polarization The tendency for groups to make decisions that are more extreme than any member would have made alone.

groupthink The tendency for groups to reach consensus in order to facilitate interpersonal harmony.

deindividuation A phenomenon that occurs when immersion in a group causes people to become less aware of their individual values.

diffusion of responsibility The tendency for individuals to feel diminished responsibility for their actions when they are surrounded by others who are acting the same way.

bystander intervention The act of helping strangers in an emergency situation.

"Hey, we're sheep. Everything seems like a good idea."

FIGURE 12.4 Mob Size and Level of Atrocity Groups are capable of horrible things. These two men were rescued by police just as residents of their town prepared to lynch them for stealing a car. Because larger groups provide more opportunity for deindividuation and diffusion of responsibility, their atrocities become more horrible as the ratio of mob members to victims becomes larger. (Data from Leader, Mullen, & Abrams, 2007.)

altruism Behavior that benefits another without benefiting oneself.

kin selection The process by which evolution selects for individuals who cooperate with their relatives.

reciprocal altruism Behavior that benefits another with the expectation that those benefits will be returned in the future.

Altruism

So far, the picture we've painted of human beings isn't all that rosy: People aggress against each other in order to get resources, and they cooperate when doing so provides them with greater benefits than aggression does. Okay, sure, we all like benefits. But aren't we ever just *nice* to each other?

Altruism is *behavior that benefits another without benefiting oneself,* and for centuries, scientists and philosophers have argued about whether people are ever truly altruistic. That might seem like an odd argument to have. After all, people give their blood to the injured, their food to the homeless, and their time to the elderly. We volunteer, we tithe, we donate. Isn't that evidence of altruism?

Not necessarily, because behaviors that appear to be altruistic often have hidden benefits for those who do them. For example, ground squirrels make a loud noise when they see a predator, which attracts the predator's attention and puts them at increased risk of being eaten, but which allows their fellow squirrels to escape. Although this behavior appears to be altruistic, it actually isn't because the helpers are *genetically related* to the helpees. Any animal that promotes the survival of its relatives is actually promoting the survival of its own genes (Hamilton, 1964). **Kin selection** is *the process by which evolution selects for individuals who cooperate with their relatives,* and cooperating with related individuals is not truly altruistic. Cooperating with unrelated individuals isn't necessarily altruistic either. Male baboons will risk injury to help an unrelated male baboon win a fight, and monkeys will spend time grooming unrelated monkeys when they could be doing something more interesting (which is just about anything). But as it turns out, the animals that give favors tend to get favors in return. **Reciprocal altruism** is *behavior that benefits another with the expectation that those benefits will be returned in the future,* and despite the second word in this term, it isn't truly altruistic (Trivers, 1972). Indeed, reciprocal altruism is merely cooperation extended over time.

Ground squirrels put themselves in danger when they warn others about predators, but those they warn share their genes, so the behavior is not truly altruistic. In contrast, Christine Karg-Palerio donated her kidney anonymously to someone she'd never even met. "If I had a spare, I'd do it again," she said.

The behavior of nonhuman animals provides little evidence of genuine altruism (cf. Bartal, Decety, & Mason, 2011). But what about us? Are we any different? Like other animals, we tend to help our kin more than we help strangers (Burnstein, Crandall, & Kitayama, 1994; Komter, 2010), and we tend to expect those we help to help us in return (Burger et al., 2009). But unlike other animals, we *do* sometimes provide benefits to complete strangers who have no chance of repaying us (Batson, 2002; Warneken & Tomasello, 2009). We hold the door for people who share precisely none of our genes and tip waiters in restaurants to which we will never return. And we do more than that. As the World Trade Center burned on the morning of September 11, 2001, civilians in sailboats headed *toward* the destruction rather than away from it, initiating the largest waterborne evacuation in U.S. history. As one observer remarked, "If you're out on the water in a pleasure craft and you see those buildings on fire, in a strictly rational sense you should head to New Jersey. Instead, people went into potential danger and rescued strangers" (Dreifus, 2003). Human beings can be truly altruistic, and some studies suggest that they are even more altruistic than they realize (Miller & Ratner, 1998).

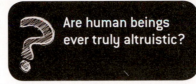

? Are human beings ever truly altruistic?

Reproduction: The Quest for Immortality

All animals must survive and reproduce, and social behavior is useful for survival. But it is an absolute prerequisite for reproduction, which doesn't happen until people get very, very social. The first step on the road to reproduction is finding someone who wants to travel that road with us. How do we do that?

Selectivity

With the exception of a few well-known celebrities, people don't mate randomly. Rather, they *select* their sexual partners, and as anyone who has lived on Earth for more than 7 full minutes knows, women tend to be more selective than men (Feingold, 1992; Fiore et al., 2010). When researchers asked an attractive person to approach strangers on a college campus and ask, "Would you go out with me?" they found that roughly half of the men and half of the women agreed to the request for a date. On the other hand, when the attractive person said to strangers, "Would you go to bed with me?" the researchers found that *none* of the women and *three quarters* of the men agreed to the request (Clark & Hatfield, 1989). There are many reasons why a woman in this particular situation might say no (Conley, 2011), but research suggests that women tend to be choosier than men in most other situations as well (Buss & Schmitt, 1993; Schmitt et al., 2012).

One reason for this is that our basic biology makes sex a riskier proposition for women than for men. Men produce billions of sperm in their lifetimes, their ability to conceive a child tomorrow is not inhibited by having conceived one today, and conception has no significant physical costs. On the other hand, women produce a small number of eggs in their lifetimes, conception eliminates their ability to conceive for at least 9 more months, and pregnancy produces physical changes that increase women's nutritional requirements and put them at risk of illness and death. Therefore, if a man mates with a woman who does not produce healthy offspring or who won't do her part to raise the children, he's lost nothing but 10 minutes and a teaspoon of bodily fluid. But if a woman makes the same mistake, she has lost a precious egg, borne the costs of pregnancy, risked her life in childbirth, and missed at least 9 months of other reproductive opportunities.

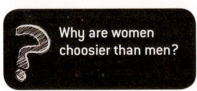

? Why are women choosier than men?

So basic biology pushes women to be choosier then men. But culture and experience can push equally hard, and in a different direction (Petersen & Hyde, 2010; Zentner, & Mitura, 2012). For example, women may be choosier than men simply because they are approached more often (Conley et al., 2011) or because the reputational costs of promiscuity are higher (Eagly & Wood, 1999; Kasser & Sharma, 1999). Indeed, when sex becomes expensive for men (e.g., when they are choosing a long-term mate

If men could become pregnant, how might their behavior change? Among sea horses, it is the male that carries the young, and not coincidentally, males are more selective than females are.

Creatas Images/Picturequest

Dr. Paul Zahl/Photo Researchers

The Real World

Making the Move

When it comes to selecting romantic partners, women tend to be choosier than men, and most scientists think that it has a lot to do with differences in their reproductive biology. But it might also have something to do with the nature of the courtship dance itself.

When it comes to approaching a potential romantic partner, the person with the most interest should be most inclined to "make the first move." Of course, in most cultures, men are *expected* to make the first move. Could it be that

making the first move *causes* men to think that they have more interest than women do?

To find out, researchers created two kinds of speed dating events (Finkel & Eastwick, 2009). In the traditional event, the women stayed in their seats, and the men moved around the room, stopping to spend a few minutes chatting with each woman. In the nontraditional event, the men stayed in their seats, and the women moved around the room, stopping to spend a few minutes chatting with each man. When the event was over, the researchers asked each man

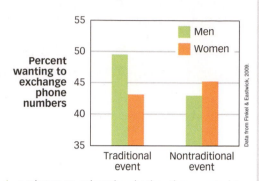

Data from Finkel & Eastwick, 2009.

and woman privately whether they wanted to exchange phone numbers with any of the potential partners they'd met.

The results were striking (see the accompanying figure). When men made the move (as they traditionally do), women were the choosier gender. That is, men wanted to get a lot more phone numbers than women wanted to give. But when women made the move, men were the choosier gender, and women asked for more numbers than men were willing to hand over. Apparently, approaching someone makes us eager, and being approached makes us cautious. One reason why women are typically the choosier gender may simply be that in most cultures, men are expected to make the first move.

Greg Gilbert KRT/Newscom

rather than a short-term date), they become every bit as choosey as women (Kenrick et al., 1990), and relatively minor changes in the courtship ritual can actually cause men to be *choosier* than women (see the Real World box). The point is that biology makes sex a riskier proposition for women than for men, but cultures can exaggerate, equalize, or even reverse those risks. The higher the risk, the more selective people of both genders tend to be.

Attraction

For most of us, there is a very small number of people with whom we are willing to have sex, an even smaller number of people with whom we are willing to have children, and a staggeringly large number of people with whom we are unwilling to have either. So when we meet someone new, how do we decide which of these categories the person belongs in? Many things go into choosing a date, a lover, or a partner for life, but perhaps none is more important than the simple feeling we call *attraction* (Berscheid & Reis, 1998). Research suggests that this feeling is caused by situational, physical, and psychological factors. Let's examine them in turn.

Situational Factors. We tend to think that we select our romantic partners on the basis of their personalities, appearances, and so on—and as you'll see in a moment, we do—but we only get to select from the pool of people we've met, which is why physical proximity is one of the best predictors of whether two people will end up in any kind of relationship (Festinger, Schachter, & Back, 1950; Nahemow & Lawton, 1975). Most of us end up marrying someone who lived or worked or went to school in the same places we did. Proximity not only provides the opportunity for attraction, but it also provides the motivation: People work especially hard to like those with whom they expect to have interaction (Darley & Berscheid, 1967). When you are assigned a roommate or an office mate, you know that your day-to-day existence will be a whole lot easier if you like the person than if you don't, and so you go out of your way to notice the person's good qualities and ignore the bad ones.

Proximity provides something else as well. Every time we encounter a person, that person becomes a bit more familiar to us, and people generally prefer familiar to novel stimuli. The **mere exposure effect** is *the tendency for liking to increase with the frequency of exposure* (Bornstein, 1989; Zajonc, 1968). For instance, in some experiments, geometric shapes, faces, or alphabetical characters were flashed on a computer screen so quickly that participants were unaware of having seen them. Participants were then shown some of the "old" stimuli that had been flashed on the screen as well as some "new" stimuli that had not. Although they could not reliably say which stimuli were old and which were new, the participants did tend to *like* the old stimuli better than the new ones (Monahan, Murphy, & Zajonc, 2000). Although there are some circumstances under which "familiarity breeds contempt" (Norton, Frost, & Ariely, 2007), for the most part, it tends to breed liking (Reis et al., 2011).

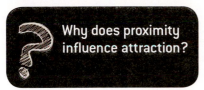

Why does proximity influence attraction?

Peter Kramer/NBC/NBC Newswire via Getty Images

"I'm a beast, I'm an animal, I'm that monster in the mirror." Like it or not, the mirror is the place where Usher most often sees himself. As a result, he probably prefers pictures of himself that are horizontally reversed (*left*), whereas his fans probably prefer pictures of him that are not (*right*). One consequence of the mere exposure effect is that people tend to like the photographic images with which they are most familiar (Mita, Dermer, & Knight, 1977).

mere exposure effect The tendency for liking to increase with the frequency of exposure.

Physical Factors. One of the strongest determinants of attraction is a person's physical appearance. One study found that a man's height and a woman's weight were among the best predictors of how many responses their personal ads received (Lynn & Shurgot, 1984), and another study found that physical attractiveness was the *only* factor that predicted the online dating choices of both women and men (Green, Buchanan, & Heuer, 1984). Good-looking

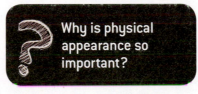

Why is physical appearance so important?

people have more sex, more friends, and more fun than the rest of us do (Curran & Lippold, 1975), and they even earn about 10% more money over the course of their lives (Hamermesh & Biddle, 1994; see **FIGURE 12.5**). Appearance is so powerful that it even influences non-romantic relationships: For example, mothers are more affectionate and playful when their children are more attractive (Langlois et al., 1995).

So yes, it pays to be beautiful. But what exactly constitutes beauty? The answer to that question varies across cultures. In the United States, for example, most women want to be slender, but in Mauritania, young girls are forced to drink up to 5 gallons of high-fat milk every day so that they will someday be obese enough to attract a husband. As one Mauritanian woman noted, "Men want women to be fat, and so they are fat. Women want men to be skinny, and so they are skinny" (LaFraniere, 2007). In the United States, most men want to be tall, but in Ghana, most men are short and consider height a curse. "To be a tall person can be quite embarrassing," said one particularly altitudinous Ghanaian man. "When you are standing in a crowd, the short people start to jeer at you," said another (French, 1997).

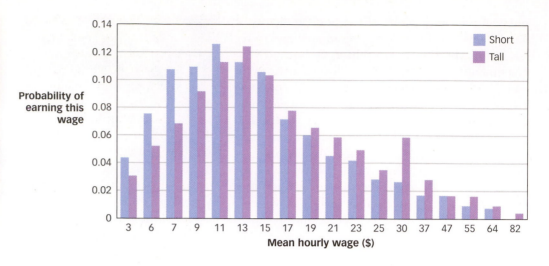

FIGURE 12.5 Height Matters NFL quarterback Tom Brady is 6'4", and his wife, supermodel Gisele Bunchen, is 5'10". Research shows that tall people earn $789 more per inch per year. The graph shows the average hourly wage of adult White men in the United States classified by height. (Data from Mankiw & Weinzierl, 2010.)

But while different cultures have somewhat different standards of beauty, those standards also have a lot in common (Cunningham et al., 1995). For example, in all cultures, faces are generally considered more attractive when they are bilaterally symmetrical—that is, when the left half is a mirror image of the right (Perrett et al., 1999). Symmetry is a sign of good genetic health (Jones et al., 2001; Thornhill & Gangestad, 1993), and so nature seems to have designed us to be attracted by it. Of course, attraction is one thing and action is another. Studies show that while everyone may desire the most beautiful person in the room, most people tend to approach, date, and marry someone who is about as attractive as they are (Berscheid et al., 1971; Lee et al., 2008).

Standards of beauty can vary across cultures. Mauritanian women long to be obese (*left*) and Ghanaian men are grateful to be short (*right*).

Psychological Factors. A person's physical appearance is often the first thing we know about them, so it isn't surprising that it determines our initial attraction (Lenton & Francesconi, 2010). But once people begin interacting, they quickly move beyond appearances (Cramer, Schaefer, & Reid, 1996; Regan, 1998). People's *inner* qualities—their personalities, points of view, attitudes, beliefs, values, ambitions, and abilities—play an important role in determining their sustained interest in each other, and there isn't much mystery about the kinds of inner qualities that most people find attractive. For example, intelligence, sense of humor, sensitivity, and ambition seem to be high on just about everybody's list, whereas "sadistic serial killer" typically ranks rather low (Daniel et al., 1985).

How much wit and wisdom do we want our mate to have? Research suggests that we are most attracted to those who are similar to us (Byrne, Ervin, & Lamberth, 1970;

passionate love An experience involving feelings of euphoria, intimacy, and intense sexual attraction.

Social Behavior: Interacting with People

Byrne & Nelson, 1965; Hatfield & Rapson, 1992; Neimeyer & Mitchell, 1988). Indeed, one of the best predictors of whether two people will marry is their similarity in terms of education, religious background, ethnicity, socioeconomic status, and personality (Botwin, Buss, & Shackelford, 1997; Buss, 1985; Caspi & Herbener, 1990).

Why is similarity so attractive? First, it's easy to interact with people who are similar to us because we can instantly agree on a wide range of issues, such as what to eat, where to live, how to raise children, and how to spend our money. Second, when someone shares our attitudes and beliefs, we feel more confident that those attitudes and beliefs are correct, and that's always a comfort (Byrne & Clore, 1970). Third, if we like people who share our attitudes and beliefs, then we can reasonably expect

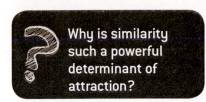

Why is similarity such a powerful determinant of attraction?

them to like us for the same reason, and *being liked* is a powerful source of attraction (Aronson & Worchel, 1966; Backman & Secord, 1959; Condon & Crano, 1988). Although we tend to like people who like us, it is worth noting that we *especially* like people who like us and who *don't* like anyone else (Eastwick et al., 2007).

Relationships

Once we have attracted a mate, we are ready to reproduce. (Note: It is perfectly fine to pause for dinner.) Human reproduction ordinarily happens in the context of committed, long-term relationships (Clark & Lemay, 2010). Only a few animals have such relationships, so why are we among them?

One answer is that we're born half-baked. Because human beings have large heads to house their large brains, a fully developed human infant could not pass

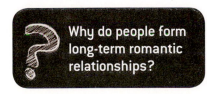

Why do people form long-term romantic relationships?

through its mother's birth canal. So human infants are *born before they are fully developed.* That means they need a lot more care than one parent can provide, and that's one reason why human adults tend to do their reproducing in the context of committed, long-term relationships.

In most cultures, committed, long-term relationships are signified by marriage, and ours is no exception. The probability of marrying by age 40 is about 81% for American men and 86% for American women (Goodwin, McGill, & Chandra, 2009). But when asked, people generally don't say that they got married in order to solve the big-headed baby problem; they say that they got married because they were in love. The fact that people marry for love is obvious, but it only became obvious in the past century or so (Brehm, 1992; Fisher, 1993; Hunt, 1959). Ancient Greeks and Romans got married, but they considered love a form of madness (Heine, 2010). Twelfth-century Europeans got married but thought of love as a game to be played by knights and ladies of the court (who happened to be married and not to the knights). Throughout history, marriage has traditionally served a variety of decidedly unromantic functions—ranging from cementing agreements between clans to paying back debts—and in many cultures, that's how it is still regarded. In fact, it wasn't until the 17th century that Westerners started to think that love might be a *reason* to get married.

But what exactly is love? Psychologists distinguish between two basic kinds: **passionate love,** which is *an experience involving feelings of euphoria, intimacy, and intense sexual attraction,* and **companionate love,** which is *an experience involving affection, trust, and concern for a partner's well-being* (Acevedo & Aron, 2009; Hatfield, 1988; Rubin, 1973; Sternberg, 1986). The ideal romantic relationship gives rise to both types of love, but the speeds, trajectories, and durations of the two experiences are markedly different (see **FIGURE 12.6**). Passionate love is what brings people

Similarity is a very strong source of attraction.

companionate love An experience involving affection, trust, and concern for a partner's well-being.

Humans and birds have something in common: Their offspring are utterly helpless at birth and require a lot of parental care. As a result, both humans and birds have enduring relationships. Though typically not with each other.

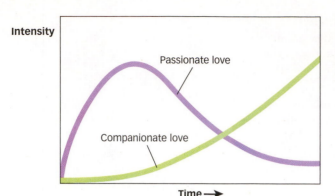

FIGURE 12.6 Passionate and Companionate Love Companionate and passionate love have different time courses and trajectories. Passionate love begins to cool within just a few months, but companionate love can grow slowly but steadily over years.

together: It has a rapid onset, reaches its peak quickly, and begins to diminish within just a few months (Aron et al., 2005). Companionate love is what keeps people together: It takes some time to get started, grows slowly, and need never stop growing (Gonzaga et al., 2001).

Divorce: When the Costs Outweigh the Benefits

The most recent U.S. government census statistics indicate that for every two couples that get married, roughly one couple gets divorced. But why? Marital satisfaction is only weakly correlated with marital stability (Karney & Bradbury, 1995), suggesting that relationships break up or remain intact for reasons other than the satisfaction of those involved (Drigotas & Rusbult, 1992; Rusbult & Van Lange, 2003). **Social exchange** is *the hypothesis that people remain in relationships only as long as they perceive a favorable ratio of costs to benefits* (Homans, 1961; Thibaut & Kelley, 1959). Relationships offer both benefits (love, sex, and financial security) and costs (responsibility, conflict, loss of freedom), and people maintain them as long as the ratio of the two is acceptable. Three things determine whether a person will find a particular cost-benefit ratio to be acceptable:

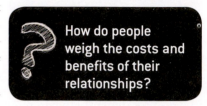

How do people weigh the costs and benefits of their relationships?

> The acceptableness of any cost–benefit ratio depends on the alternatives available. For example, a cost–benefit ratio that is acceptable to two people who are stranded on a desert island might not be acceptable to the same two people if they were living in a large city where each had access to other potential partners. A cost–benefit ratio is acceptable when we feel that it is the best we can or should do.

> People may want their cost–benefit ratios to be high, but they also want them to be roughly the same as their partner's. For example, spouses are more distressed when their respective cost–benefit ratios are *different* than when they are *unfavorable*, and this is true even when their cost–benefit ratio is *more* favorable than their partner's (Schafer & Keith, 1980).

> Relationships can be thought of as investments into which people pour resources such as time, money, and affection, and research suggests that once people have poured resources into a relationship, they are willing to settle for less favorable cost–benefit ratios (Kelley, 1983; Rusbult, 1983). This is one of the reasons why people are much more likely to end new marriages than old ones (Bramlett & Mosher, 2002; Cherlin, 1992).

"This next one goes out to all those who have ever been in love, then become engaged, gotten married, participated in the tragic deterioration of a relationship, suffered the pains and agonies of a bitter divorce, subjected themselves to the fruitless search for a new partner, and ultimately resigned themselves to remaining single in a world full of irresponsible jerks, noncommittal weirdos, and neurotic misfits."

social exchange The hypothesis that people remain in relationships only as long as they perceive a favorable ratio of costs to benefits.

SUMMARY QUIZ [12.1]

1. Why are acts of aggression—from violent crime to athletic brawls—more likely to occur on hot days when people are feeling irritated and uncomfortable?

   a. frustration

   b. negative affect

   c. resource scarcity

   d. biology and culture interaction

2. What is the single best predictor of aggression?
   a. temperament
   b. age
   c. gender
   d. status

3. The prisoner's dilemma game illustrates
   a. the hypothesis-confirming bias.
   b. the diffusion of responsibility.
   c. group polarization.
   d. the benefits and costs of cooperation.

4. Which of the following is NOT a downside of being in a group?
   a. Groups make cooperation less risky
   b. Groups make people less healthy and happy.
   c. Groups sometimes make poor decisions.
   d. Groups may take extreme actions an individual member would not take alone.

Social Influence: Controlling People

Those of us who grew up watching superhero cartoons have usually thought a bit about which of the standard superpowers we'd most like to have. Super strength and super speed have obvious benefits, invisibility could be interesting as well as lucrative, and there's always a lot to be said for flying. But when it comes right down to it, the ability to control other people would probably be the most useful. After all, who needs to change the course of mighty rivers or bend steel in his bare hands if someone else can be convinced to do it for them? The things we want from life—gourmet food, interesting jobs, big houses, fancy cars—can often be given to us by others, and the things we want most—loving families, loyal friends, admiring children, appreciative employers—cannot be had any other way. Getting others to do what we want them to do would be the ultimate super power.

Luckily, you've got it! **Social influence** is *the control of one person's behavior by another* (Cialdini & Goldstein, 2004) and it happens all the time. Every one of us influences other people, and every one of us is influenced by them. The techniques we use are numerous and varied, but in the end they all rely on the fact that human beings have three basic motivations: to experience pleasure and to avoid experiencing pain (the *hedonic motive*), to be accepted and to avoid being rejected (the *approval motive*), and to believe what is right and to avoid believing what is wrong (the *accuracy motive*; Bargh, Gollwitzer, & Oettingen, 2010; Fiske, 2010). As you will see, most attempts at social influence appeal to one or more of these three motivations.

The Hedonic Motive: Pleasure Is Better Than Pain

Pleasure seeking is the most basic of all motives, and social influence often involves creating situations in which others can achieve more pleasure by doing what we want them to do than by doing something else. Parents, teachers, governments, and businesses influence our behavior by offering rewards and threatening punishments (see **FIGURE 12.7**). There's nothing mysterious about how these influence attempts work, and they are often quite effective. When the Republic of Singapore warned its citizens that anyone caught chewing gum in public would face a year in prison and a $5,500 fine, the rest of the world was outraged; but when the outrage subsided, it was hard

social influence The control of one person's behavior by another.

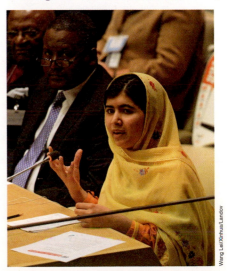

Malala Yousafzai, a 15-year-old Pakistani girl who stood up for women's rights despite being hunted by the Taliban, was named one of the world's 100 most influential people by *Time* magazine in both 2013 and 2014.

FIGURE 12.7 **The Cost of Speeding** The penalty for speeding in Massachusetts used to be a modest fine. In 2006, the law changed so that drivers under 18 who are caught speeding now lose their licenses for 90 days—and to get them back, they have to pay $500, attend 8 hours of training classes, and retake the state's driving exam. Guess what? Deaths among drivers under 18 fell by 38% in just 3 years. In other words, more than 8,000 young lives were saved by appealing to the hedonic motive. (Data from Moskowitz, 2010.)

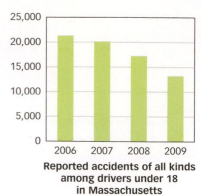

Reported accidents of all kinds among drivers under 18 in Massachusetts

Why would the ability to control others be the ultimate superpower? In a 2010 survey that asked Americans to identify the things that annoyed them most, 19 of the top 20 annoyances were caused by other people. The remaining annoyance was caused by other people's dogs. (Data from *Consumer Reports Magazine*, 2010.)

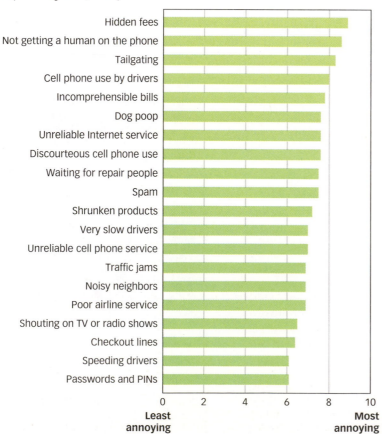

to ignore the fact that gum chewing in Singapore had fallen to an all-time low. A good caning will get your attention every time.

You'll recall from the Learning chapter that even a sea slug will repeat behaviors that are followed by rewards and avoid behaviors that are followed by punishments. Although the same is generally true of human beings, there are some instances in which rewards and punishments can backfire. For example, children in one study were allowed to draw with colored markers. Some were given a "Good Player Award" (the "rewarded" children) and some were not (the "unrewarded" children). The next day, all of the children were again given markers, but this time no awards were offered. The results showed that the previously rewarded children drew with the markers less than the previously unrewarded children did (Lepper, Greene, & Nisbett, 1973). Why? Because previously rewarded children had come to think of drawing as something one does to get a reward—and since they weren't going to receive a reward the second day, then why the heck should they draw a picture? (Deci, Koestner, & Ryan, 1999)? Rewards and punishments can also backfire because people resent being manipulated. Researchers placed signs in two restrooms on a college campus: "Please don't write on these walls" and "Do not write on these walls under any circumstances." Two weeks later, the walls in the second restroom had more graffiti on the walls, presumably because students didn't appreciate the threatening tone of the second sign and wrote on the walls just to prove that they could (Pennebaker & Sanders, 1976).

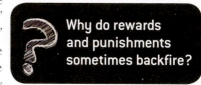

Why do rewards and punishments sometimes backfire?

The Approval Motive: Acceptance Is Better Than Rejection

Other people stand between us and starvation, predation, loneliness, and all the other things that make getting shipwrecked such an unpopular pastime. We depend on others for safety, sustenance, and solidarity, and so we are powerfully motivated to have others like us, accept us, and approve of us (Baumeister & Leary, 1995; Leary, 2010). Like the hedonic motive, the approval motive can be a lever for social influence.

Hidden fees
Not getting a human on the phone
Tailgating
Cell phone use by drivers
Incomprehensible bills
Dog poop
Unreliable Internet service
Discourteous cell phone use
Waiting for repair people
Spam
Shrunken products
Very slow drivers
Unreliable cell phone service
Traffic jams
Noisy neighbors
Poor airline service
Shouting on TV or radio shows
Checkout lines
Speeding drivers
Passwords and PINs

0   2   4   6   8   10
Least   Most
annoying   annoying

Culture & Community

Free parking. People don't like to be manipulated, and they get upset when someone threatens their freedom. Is this a uniquely Western reaction? To find out, psychologists asked college students for one of two favors and then measured how irritated the students felt (Jonas et al., 2009). In one case, the psychologists asked students if they would give up their right to park on campus for a week ("Would you mind if I used your parking card so I can participate in a research project in this building?"). In the other case, the psychologists asked students if they would give up *everyone's* right to park on campus for a week ("Would you mind if we closed the entire parking lot for a tennis tournament?"). How did students react to these requests?

It depended on culture. As the figure shows, European American students were more irritated by a request that limited their own freedom than by a request that limited everyone's freedom ("If nobody can park, that's inconvenient. But if everybody except *me* can park, that's unfair!"). But Latino and Asian American students had precisely the opposite reactions ("The needs of the requestor outweigh the needs of one student, but they don't outweigh the needs of all students"). It appears that all people value freedom—just not necessarily their own.

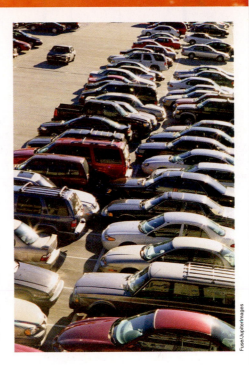

Data from Jonas et al., 2009.

How irritated? (chart, y-axis 0 to 7)

European Americans / Latinos and Asian Americans

■ Give up parking card ■ Close parking lot

Fuse/JupiterImages

Normative Influence

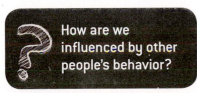

How are we influenced by other people's behavior?

When you get on an elevator, you are supposed to face forward and not talk to the person next to you even if you were talking to that person before you got on the elevator unless you are the only two people on the elevator in which case it's okay to talk and face sideways but still not backward. Although no one ever taught you this particularly long rule of elevator etiquette, you probably picked it up somewhere along the way. The unwritten rules that govern social behavior are called **norms,** which are *customary standards for behavior that are widely shared by members of a culture* (Cialdini, 2013; Miller & Prentice, 1996). We learn norms with exceptional ease and we obey them with exceptional fidelity because we know that if we don't, others won't approve of us. For example, every human culture has a **norm of reciprocity,** which is *the unwritten rule that people should benefit those who have benefited them* (Gouldner, 1960). When a friend buys you lunch, you must eventually return the favor; and if you don't, your friend will eventually get a new one. Indeed, the norm of reciprocity is so strong that when researchers randomly pulled the names of strangers from a telephone directory and sent them all Christmas cards, they received Christmas cards back from most (Kunz & Woolcott, 1976).

Norms can be a powerful tool for social influence. **Normative influence** is *a phenomenon that occurs when another person's behavior provides information about what is appropriate* (see **FIGURE 12.8**). For example, waiters and waitresses know all about the norm of reciprocity, and so they often give customers a piece of candy along with the bill, hoping that

norms Customary standards for behavior that are widely shared by members of a culture.

norm of reciprocity The unwritten rule that people should benefit those who have benefited them.

normative influence A phenomenon that occurs when another person's behavior provides information about what is appropriate.

FIGURE 12.8 The Perils of Connection Other people's behavior defines what is normal, which is one of the reasons why obesity spreads through social networks (Christakis & Fowler, 2007).

On average, your risk of becoming obese increases by ...

. . . **57%** if someone you consider a friend becomes obese.

. . . **171%** if a very close friend becomes obese.

. . . **100%** if you are a man and your male friend becomes obese.

. . . **38%** if you are a woman and your female friend becomes obese.

. . . **37%** if your spouse becomes obese.

. . . **40%** if one of your siblings becomes obese.

. . . **67%** if you are a woman and your sister becomes obese.

. . . **44%** if you are a man and your brother becomes obese.

© Francis Dean/Dean Pictures/The Image Works

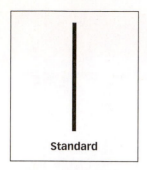 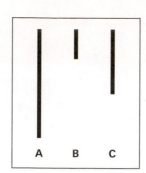

Standard   A   B   C

FIGURE 12.9 Asch's Conformity Study If you were asked which of the lines on the right (A, B, or C) matches the standard line on the left, what would you say? Research on conformity suggests that your answer would depend, in part, on how other people in the room answered the same question.

conformity The tendency to do what others do simply because others are doing it.

Have you ever wondered which big spender left the bill as a tip? In fact, the bills are often put there by the very people you are tipping because they know that the presence of paper money will suggest to you that others are leaving big tips and that it would be socially appropriate for you to do the same. By the way, the customary gratuity for someone who writes a textbook for you is 15%. But most students send us more.

customers who receive a free candy will feel obligated to do "a little extra" for the server who did "a little extra" for them. Research shows that this little trick works quite nicely (Strohmetz et al., 2002).

Conformity

People can influence us by invoking familiar norms, such as the norm of reciprocity. But if you've ever found yourself in a fancy restaurant, sneaking a peek at the person next to you in the hopes of discovering whether the little fork is meant to be used for shrimp or salad, then you know that other people can also influence us by defining *new* norms in ambiguous, confusing, or novel situations. **Conformity** is *the tendency to do what others do simply because others are doing it,* and it results in part from normative influence.

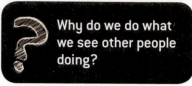

Why do we do what we see other people doing?

In a classic study, male participants sat in a room with seven other men who appeared to be ordinary participants but who were actually trained actors (Asch, 1951, 1956). An experimenter explained that the participants would be shown cards with three printed lines and that his job was simply to say which of the three lines matched a "standard line" that was printed on another card (see **FIGURE 12.9**). The experimenter held up a card and then asked each man to answer in turn. The real participant was among the last to be called on. Everything went well on the first two trials, but then on the third trial something really strange happened: The actors all began giving the same wrong answer! What did the real participants do? Seventy-five percent of them conformed and announced the wrong answer on at least one trial. Subsequent research has shown that these participants didn't actually misperceive the length of the lines, but were instead succumbing to normative influence (Asch, 1955; Nemeth & Chiles, 1988). Giving the wrong answer was apparently "the right thing to do," and so participants did it.

The behavior of others can tell us what is proper, appropriate, expected, and accepted—in other words, it can define a norm—and once a norm is defined, we feel obliged to honor it. This fact can be put to good use. When the Sacramento Municipal Utility District randomly selected 35,000 customers and sent them electric bills showing how their energy consumption compared to that of their neighbors, consumption fell by 2% (Kaufman, 2009).

A perplexed participant (center) is flanked by actors who have just given the wrong answer in one of Solomon Asch's class conformity experiments.

Other Voices

91% of All Students Read This Box and Love It

Tina Rosenberg is an editorial writer for the *New York Times*. Her 1995 book *The Haunted Land: Facing Europe's Ghosts After Communism* won both the Pulitzer Prize and the National Book Award.

Noah Greenberg Photography

Binge drinking is a problem on college campuses across America (Wechsler & Nelson, 2001). About half of all students report doing it, and those who do are much more likely to miss classes, get behind in their school work, drive drunk, and have unprotected sex. So what to do?

Colleges have tried a number of remedies—from education to abstinence—and none of them has worked particularly well. But lately, some schools have taken a new approach called "social norming." Although this approach is surprisingly effective, it is also controversial. Tina Rosenberg's recent book is titled *Join the Club: How Peer Pressure Can Transform the World*. In the following essay, she describes both the technique and the controversy.

… Like most universities, Northern Illinois University in DeKalb has a problem with heavy drinking. In the 1980s, the school was trying to cut down on student use of alcohol with the usual strategies. One campaign warned teenagers of the consequences of heavy drinking. "It was the 'don't run with a sharp stick you'll poke your eye out' theory of behavior change," said Michael Haines, who was the coordinator of the school's Health Enhancement Services. When that didn't work, Haines tried combining the scare approach with information on how to be well: "It's O.K. to drink if you don't drink too much—but if you do, bad things will happen to you."

That one failed, too. In 1989, 45 percent of students surveyed said they drank more than five drinks at parties. This percentage was slightly higher than when the campaigns began. And students thought heavy drinking was even more common; they believed that 69 percent of their peers drank that much at parties.

But by then Haines had something new to try. In 1987 he had attended a conference on alcohol in higher education sponsored by the United States Department of Education. There Wes Perkins, a professor of sociology at Hobart and William Smith Colleges, and Alan Berkowitz, a psychologist in the school's counseling center, presented a paper that they had just published on how student drinking is affected by peers. "There are decades of research on peer influence—that's nothing new," Perkins said at the meeting. What was new was their survey showing that when students were asked how much their peers drank, they grossly overestimated the amount. If the students were responding to peer pressure, the researchers said, it was coming from imaginary peers.

The "aha!" conclusion Perkins and Berkowitz drew was this: maybe students' drinking behavior could be changed by just telling them the truth.

Haines surveyed students at Northern Illinois University and found that they also had a distorted view of how much their peers drink. He decided to try a new campaign, with the theme "most students drink moderately." The centerpiece of the campaign was a series of ads in the *Northern Star*, the campus newspaper, with pictures of students and the caption "two thirds of Northern Illinois University students (72%) drink 5 or fewer drinks when they 'party'." …

Haines's staff also made posters with campus drinking facts and told students that if they had those posters on the wall when an inspector came around, they would earn $5. (35 percent of the students did have them posted when inspected.)

Later they [the staff members] made buttons for students in the fraternity and sorority system—these students drank more heavily—that said "Most of Us," and offered another $5 for being caught wearing one. The buttons were deliberately cryptic, to start a conversation.

After the first year of the social norming campaign, the perception of heavy drinking had fallen from 69 to 61 percent. Actual heavy drinking fell from 45 to 38 percent. The campaign went on for a decade, and at the end of it NIU students believed that 33 percent of their fellow students were episodic heavy drinkers, and only 25 percent really were—a decline in heavy drinking of 44 percent. …

Why isn't this idea more widely used? One reason is that it can be controversial. Telling college students "most of you drink moderately" is very different [from] saying "don't drink." (It's so different, in fact, that the National Social Norms Institute, with headquarters at the University of Virginia, gets its money from Anheuser Busch—a decision that has undercut support for the idea of social norming.) The approach angers people who lobby for a strong, unmuddied message of disapproval—even though, of course, disapproval doesn't reduce bad behavior, and social norming does….

Social norming is a powerful but controversial tool for changing behavior. When we tell students about drinking on campus, should we tell them what's true (even if the truth is a bit ugly) or should we tell them what's best (even if they are unlikely to do it)?

Obedience

In most situations, there are a few people whom we all recognize as having special authority both to define the norms and to enforce them. The guy who works at the movie theater may be some high school fanboy with a bad haircut and a 10:00 p.m. curfew, but in the theater he has authority. So when he asks you to stop texting in the middle of the movie, you do as you are told. **Obedience** is *the tendency to do what authorities tell us to do.*

obedience The tendency to do what powerful authorities tell us to do.

Why do we obey authorities? Well, yes, sometimes they have guns. But while authorities are often capable of rewarding and punishing us, research shows that much of their influence is *normative* (Tyler, 1990). Psychologist Stanley Milgram (1963) demonstrated this in one of psychology's most infamous experiments. The participants in this experiment met a middle-aged man who was introduced as another participant but who was actually a trained actor. An experimenter in a lab coat explained that the participant would play the role of *teacher* and the actor would play the role of *learner*. The teacher and learner would sit in different rooms, the teacher would read words to the learner over a microphone, and the learner would then repeat the words back to the teacher. If the learner made a mistake, the teacher would press a button that delivered an electric shock to the learner (see **FIGURE 12.10**). The shock-generating machine (which, by the way, was totally fake) offered 30 levels of shock, ranging from 15 volts (labeled *slight shock*) to 450 volts (labeled *Danger: severe shock*).

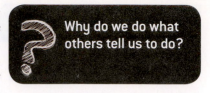

Why do we do what others tell us to do?

After the learner was strapped into his chair, the experiment began. When the learner made his first mistake, the participant dutifully delivered a 15-volt shock. As the learner made more mistakes, he received more shocks. When the participant delivered the 75-volt shock, the learner cried out in pain. At 150 volts, the learner screamed, "I refuse to go on. Let me out!" With every shock, the learner's screams became more agonized. Then, after receiving the 330-volt shock, the learner stopped responding altogether. Participants were naturally upset by all this and typically asked the experimenter to stop, but the experimenter simply replied, "You have no choice, you must go on." The experimenter never threatened the participant with punishment of any kind. Rather, he just stood there with his clipboard in hand and calmly instructed the participant to continue. So what did the participants do? Eighty percent of the participants continued to shock the learner even after he screamed, complained, pleaded, and then fell silent. And 62% went all the way, delivering the highest possible voltage. Although Milgram's study was conducted nearly half a century ago, a recent replication revealed about the same rate of obedience (Burger, 2009).

Would normal people electrocute a stranger just because some guy in a lab coat told them to? The answer, it seems, is *yes*—as long as *normal* means being sensitive to norms. The participants in this experiment knew that hurting others is not always wrong: Doctors give painful injections, and teachers give painful exams. There are many situations in which it is permissible to cause someone to suffer. The experimenter's calm demeanor and persistent instruction suggested that he—and not the participant—knew what was appropriate in this particular situation, and so the participant did what the authority ordered.

Philip G. Zimbardo, Inc.

In 1971, psychologist Philip Zimbardo built a mock prison in the basement of the Stanford Psychology Department and invited students to play the roles of either a prisoner or a guard. After 6 days, he was forced to halt his study because many of the guards had become so abusive toward the prisoners that he feared for the "prisoners'" safety (Haney, Banks, & Zimbardo, 1973).

FIGURE 12.10 Milgram's Obedience Studies The learner (*left*) is being hooked up to the shock generator (*right*) that was used in Stanley Milgram's obedience studies.

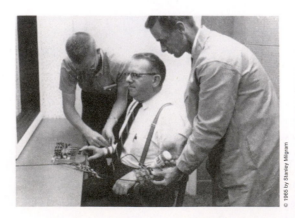

© 1965 by Stanley Milgram

© 1965 by Stanley Milgram

The Accuracy Motive: Right Is Better Than Wrong

If you know just two things—first, that apples taste good, and second, that there are apples in the refrigerator—then you know exactly what to do when you are hungry. Open the fridge! Actions rely on both an **attitude,** which is *an enduring positive or negative evaluation of an object or event,* and a **belief,** which is *an enduring piece of knowledge about an object or event.* Attitudes tell us what we should do (*eat an apple because they are good*), and beliefs tell us how to do it (*start by opening the fridge because that's where the apples are*). So if our attitudes or beliefs are inaccurate, then our actions are likely to be fruitless. Because we rely so much on our attitudes and beliefs, it isn't surprising that we are motivated to have the right ones. As you will see, social influence often appeals to this basic motivation.

Informational Influence

If everyone in the mall suddenly ran screaming for the exit, you'd probably join the stampede—not because you were afraid that the panicked people would disapprove of you if you didn't, but because their behavior would suggest to you that there was something worth running from. **Informational influence** is *a phenomenon that occurs when another person's behavior provides information about what is true.* You can observe the power of informational influence yourself just by standing in the middle of the sidewalk, tilting back your head, and staring at the top of a tall building. Research suggests that within just a few minutes, other people will stop and stare too (Milgram, Bickman, & Berkowitz, 1969). Why? They will assume that if you are staring, then there must be something worth staring at.

You are the constant target of informational influence. When a salesperson tells you that "most people buy the iPad with extra memory," she is artfully suggesting that you should take other people's behavior as information about the product. Advertisements that refer to soft drinks as "popular" or books as "best sellers" are reminding you that other people are buying these particular drinks and books, which suggests that they know something you don't and that you'd be wise to follow their example. Situation comedies provide laugh tracks because the producers know that when you hear other people laughing, you will mindlessly assume that something must be funny (Fein, Goethals, & Kugler, 2007; Nosanchuk & Lightstone, 1974). Bars and nightclubs make people stand in line even when there is plenty of room inside because the owners of these establishments know that passersby will see the line and assume that the club is worth waiting for. In short, the world is full of objects and events about which we know little, and we can often cure our ignorance by paying attention to the way in which others are acting toward them.

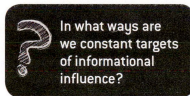

In what ways are we constant targets of informational influence?

Persuasion

Persuasion is *a phenomenon that occurs when a person's attitudes or beliefs are influenced by a communication from another person* (Albarracín & Vargas, 2010; Petty & Wegener, 1998). How does it work? When the next presidential election rolls around, the candidates will promise to persuade you to vote for them by demonstrating that their positions on the issues are the most practical, intelligent, fair, and beneficial. Having made that promise, they will then devote most of their financial resources to persuading you by other means—for example, by dressing nicely and smiling a lot, by surrounding themselves with famous athletes and movie stars, by repeatedly pairing their opponent's picture with Osama bin Laden's, and so on. The candidates will promise to engage in **systematic persuasion,** which refers to *the process by which attitudes or beliefs are changed by appeals to reason,* but they will spend most of their

attitude An enduring positive or negative evaluation of an object or event.

belief An enduring piece of knowledge about an object or event.

informational influence A phenomenon that occurs when another person's behavior provides information about what is true.

persuasion A phenomenon that occurs when a person's attitudes or beliefs are influenced by a communication from another person.

systematic persuasion The process by which attitudes or beliefs are changed by appeals to reason.

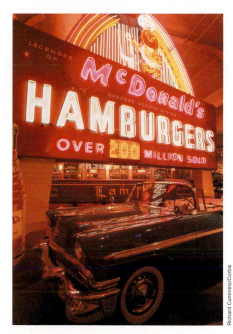

Richard Cummins/Corbis

Is McDonald's trying to keep track of sales from the parking lot? Probably not. Rather, it wants you to know that a lot of other people are buying its hamburgers, which suggests that you should too.

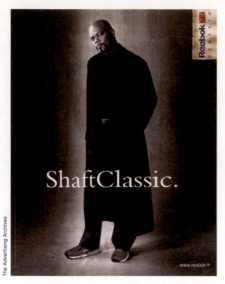

ShaftClassic.

Why do advertisers hire celebrities to endorse shoes but not cars? Cars are relatively expensive, so people are motivated to process information about them and are therefore persuaded by facts about quality and price. Shoes are relatively inexpensive, so people are not motivated to process information about them and are therefore persuaded by celebrity endorsements.

FIGURE 12.11 Systematic and Heuristic Persuasion (*a*) *Systematic persuasion.* When students were motivated to analyze arguments, their attitudes were influenced by the strength of the arguments (strong arguments were more persuasive than weak arguments), but not by the status of the communicator (the Princeton professor was not more persuasive than the high school student). (*b*) *Heuristic persuasion.* When students were not motivated to analyze arguments, their attitudes were influenced by the status of the communicator (the Princeton professor was more persuasive than the high school student), but not by the strength of the arguments (strong arguments were no more persuasive than weak arguments; data from Petty, Cacioppo, & Goldman, 1981).

time and money engaged in **heuristic persuasion,** which refers to *the process by which attitudes or beliefs are changed by appeals to habit or emotion* (Chaiken, 1980; Petty & Cacioppo, 1986). (You'll recall from the Language and Thought chapter that *heuristics* are simple shortcuts or "rules of thumb.")

Which form of persuasion will be more effective? That depends on whether you are willing and able to weigh evidence and analyze arguments. In one study, students heard a speech that contained either strong or weak arguments in favor of instituting comprehensive exams at their school (Petty, Cacioppo, & Goldman, 1981). Some students were told that the speaker was a Princeton University professor, and others were told that the speaker was a high school student—a bit of information that could be used as a shortcut to decide whether to believe the speech. Some students were told that their university was considering implementing these exams right away, thereby giving these students a strong motivation to analyze the evidence, and others were told that their university was considering implementing these exams long after they graduated, thereby giving these students little motivation to analyze the evidence. As **FIGURE 12.11** shows, when students were highly motivated to analyze the evidence, they were systematically persuaded—that is, their attitudes and beliefs were influenced by the strength of the arguments and not by the status of the speaker. But when students were not highly motivated to analyze the evidence, they were heuristically persuaded—that is, their attitudes and beliefs were influenced by the status of the speaker and not by the strength of the arguments.

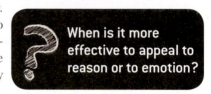

When is it more effective to appeal to reason or to emotion?

Consistency

If a friend told you that rabbits had just staged a coup in Antarctica and were halting all carrot exports, you probably wouldn't turn on CNN. You'd know right away that your friend must be joking (or on drugs) because the statement is logically inconsistent with other things that you know are true—for instance, that rabbits do not foment revolution and Antarctica does not export carrots. People evaluate the accuracy of new beliefs by assessing their *consistency* with old beliefs, and although this is

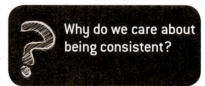

Why do we care about being consistent?

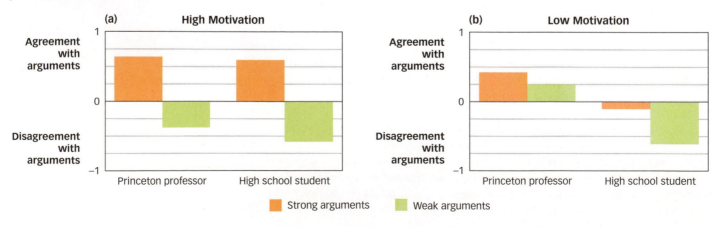

not a foolproof method for determining whether something is true, it provides a pretty good approximation. Because people are strongly motivated to have beliefs that are true, and because consistency is an indicator of truth, they are strongly motivated to have beliefs that are consistent as well.

The motivation to have consistent beliefs leaves people vulnerable to social influence. Consider the **foot-in-the-door technique,** which is *a social influence technique that involves making a small request before making a large request* (Burger, 1999). In one study (Freedman & Fraser, 1966), experimenters went to a neighborhood and knocked on doors to see if they could convince homeowners to let them install a big, ugly "Drive Carefully" sign in their front yards. One group of homeowners was simply asked if they would allow the ugly sign to be installed, and only 17% said yes. A second group of homeowners was first asked to sign a petition urging the state legislature to promote safe driving (which almost all agreed to do) and was *then* asked to allow the installation of the ugly sign. And 55% said yes! Why would homeowners be more likely to grant two requests than one?

Just imagine how the homeowners in the second group felt. They had just signed a petition stating that they thought safe driving was important, but they really didn't want an ugly sign in their front yards. And yet, saying yes to the petition and no to the sign would be obviously inconsistent. As they wrestled with this dilemma, they probably began to experience a feeling called **cognitive dissonance,** which is *an unpleasant state that arises when a person recognizes the inconsistency of his or her actions, attitudes, or beliefs* (Festinger, 1957). When people experience cognitive dissonance, they naturally try to alleviate it, and one way to alleviate cognitive dissonance is to restore consistency among one's actions, attitudes, and beliefs (Aronson, 1969; Cooper & Fazio, 1984). Allowing the ugly sign to be installed in their yards accomplished that goal. Recent research shows that this phenomenon can be used to good effect: Hotel guests who were asked at check-in to commit to being a "Friend of the Earth" were 25% more likely to reuse their towels during their stay (Baca-Motes et al., 2013).

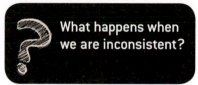

What happens when we are inconsistent?

We are motivated to be consistent, but there are inevitably times when we just can't be—for example, when we kindly tell a friend that her new hairstyle is "cutting edge" when we actually think it resembles a wet skunk after an unfortunate encounter with a snowblower. Why don't we experience cognitive dissonance under such circumstances? Because complementing a friend's hairstyle may be inconsistent with the belief that it is actually hideous, but it is consistent with the belief that one should be nice to one's friends. When small inconsistencies are *justified* by large consistencies, cognitive dissonance does not occur.

For example, participants in one study were asked to perform a dull task that involved turning knobs one way, then the other way, and then back again. After the participants were sufficiently bored, the experimenter explained that he desperately needed a few more people to volunteer for the study, and he asked the participants to go into the hallway, find another person, and tell that person that the knob-turning task was great fun. The experimenter offered some participants $1 to tell this lie, and offered other participants $20. All participants agreed to tell the lie, and after they did so, they were asked to report their true enjoyment of the knob-turning task. The results showed that participants liked the task *more* when they were paid $1 than when they were paid $20 to lie about it (Festinger & Carlsmith, 1959). Why? Because although the belief that *I said the task was fun* was inconsistent with the belief that *the task was really dull,* it was perfectly consistent with the belief that *$20 is a whole lot of money.* Because the large payment justified the lie, only those participants who received the small payment experienced cognitive dissonance, and then reduced it by changing their beliefs about the enjoyableness of the task.

heuristic persuasion The process by which attitudes or beliefs are changed by appeals to habit or emotion.

foot-in-the-door technique A social influence technique that involves making a small request before making a large request.

cognitive dissonance An unpleasant state that arises when a person recognizes the inconsistency of his or her actions, attitudes, or beliefs.

SUMMARY QUIZ [12.2]

1. The _____ motive describes how people are motivated to experience pleasure and to avoid experiencing pain.
   a. emotional
   b. accuracy
   c. approval
   d. hedonic

2. The tendency to do what authorities tell us to do is known as
   a. persuasion.
   b. obedience.
   c. conformity.
   d. the self-fulfilling prophecy.

3. Andrea and Jeff had to wait in line for over an hour to get into an exclusive restaurant. Despite being served a mediocre meal, they glowingly praised the restaurant to their friends. This behavior was probably a result of
   a. conformity
   b. the norm of reciprocity
   c. the foot in the door technique
   d. cognitive dissonance

social cognition The processes by which people come to understand others.

stereotyping The process by which people draw inferences about people based on their knowledge of the categories to which those people belong.

Shlomo Koenig does not fit most people's stereotype of a police officer or a rabbi, but he is both.

AP Photo/Gino Domenico

Social Cognition: Understanding People

Because other people are the source of most of our rewards and punishments, it isn't surprising that we spend a lot of our time trying to understand them. **Social cognition** is *the processes by which people come to understand others*. We are constantly making inferences about what other people think, feel, and want ("Ethan is angry because he thinks Abby really likes Jacob"), and about what kinds of people they are deep down inside ("Ethan is such a possessive person"). We base these inferences on two kinds of information: the social categories to which people belong, and the specific things that people say and do.

Stereotyping: Drawing Inferences from Categories

You'll recall from the Language and Thought chapter that categorization is the process by which people identify a stimulus as a member of a class of related stimuli. Once we have identified a novel stimulus as a member of a category ("That's a textbook"), we can then use our knowledge of the category to make educated guesses about the properties of the novel stimulus ("It's probably expensive") and act accordingly ("I think I'll download it illegally").

What we do with textbooks we also do with people. No, not the illegal downloading part. The educated guessing part. **Stereotyping** is *the process by which people draw inferences about people based on their knowledge of the categories to which those people belong*. The moment we categorize a person as an adult, a male, a baseball player, and a Russian, we can use our knowledge of those categories to make some educated guesses about him—for example, that he shaves his face but not his legs, that he understands the infield fly rule, and that he knows more about Moscow than we do. When we offer children candy instead of cigarettes or ask gas station attendants for directions instead of financial advice, we are making inferences about people based

Hot Science

The Wedding Planner

The human brain has nearly tripled in size in just 2 million years. The *social brain hypothesis* (Shultz & Dunbar, 2010) suggests that this happened primarily so that people could manage the everyday complexities of living in large social groups. What are those complexities?

Well, just think of what you'd need to know in order to seat people at a wedding. Does Uncle Jacob like Grandma Nora, does Grandma Nora hate Cousin Caleb, and if so, does Uncle Jacob hate Cousin Caleb too? With a guest list of just 150 people, there are more than 10,000 of these dyadic relationships to consider—and yet, people who can't balance a checkbook or solve a Sudoku somehow manage to do tasks like this one all the time. Are people social savants?

In a 2010 study, Mason et al. directly compared people's abilities to solve social and nonsocial problems. The nonsocial problem involved drawing inferences about metals. Participants were told that there were two basic groups of metals and that metals in the same group "attracted" each other, whereas metals in different groups "repelled" each other. Then,

participants were told about the relationships between particular metals and were asked to draw inferences about the missing relationship. For example, participants were told that *gold* and *tin* were both repelled by *platinum*, and they were then asked to infer the relationship between *gold* and *tin*. (The correct answer is "They are attracted to each other.")

The experimenters also gave participants a social version of this problem. Participants were told about two groups of people. People who were in the same group were said to be

attracted to each other, whereas people who were in different groups were said to be repelled by each other. Then participants learned about the relationships between particular people—for example, they learned that *Goldie* and *Tim* were both repelled by *Patrick*—and were then asked to infer the missing relationship between *Goldie* and *Tim*. (The correct answer is "They are attracted to each other.")

Although the social and nonsocial tasks were logically identical, results showed that participants were considerably faster *and* more accurate when drawing inferences about people than about metals. When the researchers replicated the study inside an MRI machine, they discovered that both tasks activated brain areas known to play a role in deductive reasoning but that only the social task activated brain regions known to play a role in understanding other minds.

It appears that our ability to think about people outshines our ability to think about most everything else, which is good news for the social brain hypothesis—as well as for wedding planners far and wide.

---

solely on their category membership. As these examples suggest, stereotyping can be useful (Allport, 1954). So why does the word have such a distasteful connotation? Because stereotyping is a useful process that often produces harmful

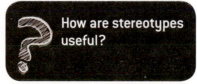

How are stereotypes useful?

results, and it does so because stereotypes have four properties: They can be (1) inaccurate, (2) overused, (3) self-perpetuating, and (4) unconscious and automatic.

1. Stereotypes Can Be Inaccurate

We draw inferences about individuals based on their groups, but some of the things we believe about those groups simply aren't true. For instance, there is no evidence to indicate that Jews are especially greedy or that African Americans are especially lazy. Nonetheless, many American college students hold those beliefs, and have done so for most of the last century (Gilbert, 1951; Karlins, Coffman, & Walters, 1969; Katz & Braly, 1933). We aren't born with beliefs like these, so how do we acquire them? We pay attention to what people say—in our homes and neighborhoods, on our televisions and computer screens. Many of the folks who believe that Jews are greedy or African Americans are lazy have never actually met a member of either group, and their mistaken beliefs are a result of listening too closely to what others tell them. In the process of inheriting the wisdom of our culture, it is inevitable that we also will inherit its ignorance.

"Great—now I'm gonna be suspicious of every poodle I meet."

2. Stereotypes Can Be Overused

Because all thumbtacks are pretty much alike, our stereotypes about thumbtacks (small, cheap, painful when chewed) are quite useful. We will rarely be mistaken if we generalize from one thumbtack to another. But human categories are so variable that our stereotypes may offer only vague clues about the individuals who populate those categories. You probably believe that men have greater upper body strength than women do, and that belief is correct—*on average*. But the upper body strength of individuals *within* each of these categories is so varied that you cannot easily predict how much weight a particular person can lift simply by knowing that person's gender. The inherent variability of human categories makes stereotypes less useful than they seem.

Alas, we don't always recognize this because the mere act of categorizing a stimulus tends to warp our perceptions of that category's variability. For instance, participants in some studies were shown a series of lines of different lengths (see **FIGURE 12.12**; McGarty & Turner, 1992; Tajfel & Wilkes, 1963). For one group of participants, the longest lines were labeled *Group A,* and the shortest lines were labeled *Group B,* as they are on the right side of Figure 12.12. For the second group of participants, the lines were shown without these category labels, as they are on the left side of Figure 12.12. When later asked to draw the lines from memory, those participants who had seen the category labels *overestimated* the similarity of the lines that shared a label and *underestimated* the similarity of lines that did not. What's true of lines is true of people as well. The mere act of categorizing people as Blacks or Whites, Jews or Gentiles, artists or accountants can cause us to underestimate the variability within those categories ("All artists are flaky") and to overestimate the variability between them ("Artists are much flakier than accountants"). When we underestimate the variability within a human category, we overestimate how useful our stereotypes about it will be (Park & Hastie, 1987; Rubin & Badea, 2012).

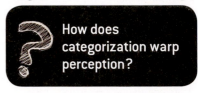

How does categorization warp perception?

perceptual confirmation The tendency for people to see what they expect to see.

FIGURE 12.12 How Categorization Warps Perception People who see the lines on the right tend to *overestimate the similarity* of lines 1 and 3 and *underestimate the similarity* of lines 3 and 4. Category labels cause the lines within a group to seem more similar to each other than they really are, and the lines in different groups to seem more different from each other than they really are.

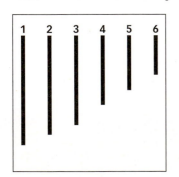

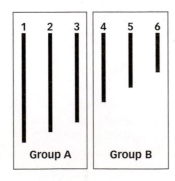

3. Stereotypes Can Be Self-Perpetuating

When we meet a truck driver who likes ballet more than football or a senior citizen who likes Eminem more than Bach, why don't we simply abandon our stereotypes of these groups? The answer is that stereotypes perpetuate themselves, and they do this in two ways.

First, stereotypes can bias our perceptions, leading us to believe that those stereotypes have been confirmed when actually they have not (Fiske, 1998). In one study, participants listened to a radio broadcast of a college basketball game and were asked to evaluate the performance of one of the players. Although all participants heard the same prerecorded game, some were led to believe that the player was African American, and others were led to believe that the player was White. Participants' stereotypes led them to expect different performances from Black and White athletes—and the participants perceived just what they expected: Those who believed the player was African American thought he had demonstrated greater athletic ability but less intelligence than did those who thought he was White (Stone, Perry, & Darley, 1997). **Perceptual confirmation** is *the tendency for people to see what they expect to see,* and this tendency helps perpetuate stereotypes.

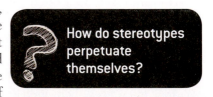

How do stereotypes perpetuate themselves?

Second, our stereotypes can cause other people to behave in ways that actually do confirm the stereotypes we hold about them. In one study (Steele & Aronson, 1995), African American and White students took a test, and half the students in each group were asked to list their race at the top of the exam. When students were not asked to list their races, they performed at their academic level, but when students were asked to list their races, African American students became anxious about confirming a negative stereotype of their group, and this anxiety led them to perform below their academic level (see **FIGURE 12.13**). **Self-fulfilling prophecy** is *the tendency for people to behave as they are expected to behave,* and it is one of the ways in which stereotypes perpetuate themselves. What's so troubling about this is that anyone who expected African-American students to perform poorly in this study would actually have seen evidence confirming their stereotype!

4. Stereotyping Can Be Unconscious and Automatic

If we recognize that stereotypes are inaccurate, overused, and self-perpetuating, then why don't we just stop using them? The answer is that stereotyping happens *unconsciously* (which means that we don't always know we are doing it) and *automatically* (which means that we often cannot avoid doing it even when we try; Banaji & Heiphetz, 2010; Greenwald, McGhee, & Schwartz, 1998; Greenwald & Nosek, 2001).

For example, in one study, participants played a video game in which photos of Black or White men holding either guns or cameras were briefly flashed on the screen. Participants earned money by shooting men with guns and lost money by shooting men with cameras. All participants made mistakes, but they tended to make two in particular, namely, they mistakenly shot Black men holding cameras and mistakenly failed to shoot White men holding guns (Correll et al., 2002). Although the photos appeared on the screen so quickly that participants did not have enough time to consciously consider their stereotypes, those stereotypes worked unconsciously, causing them to mistake a camera for a gun when it was in the hands of a Black man and a gun for a camera when it was in the hands of a White man. What's more, Black participants were just as likely to make this pattern of errors as were White participants!

Stereotyping is often unconscious and automatic, but that doesn't mean it is inevitable (Blair, 2002; Kawakami et al., 2000; Milne & Grafman, 2001; Rudman, Ashmore, & Gary, 2001). For instance, in one study, police officers received special training before playing the gun-and-camera video game (Correll et al., 2007). The results showed that just like ordinary people, the officers took a few milliseconds longer to decide not to shoot a Black man than a White man, indicating that their stereotypes were unconsciously and automatically influencing their thinking. But unlike ordinary people, the officers didn't actually *shoot* Black men more often than White men, indicating that they had learned how to keep those stereotypes from influencing their behavior. Other studies show that simple games and exercises can reduce the automatic influence of stereotypes among civilians too (Phills et al., 2011; Todd et al., 2011).

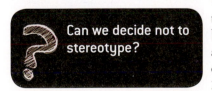
Can we decide not to stereotype?

Attribution: Drawing Inferences from Actions

In 1963, Dr. Martin Luther King Jr. gave a speech in which he described his vision for America: "I have a dream that my four children will one day live in a nation where they will not be judged by the color of their skin but by the content of their character." Research on stereotyping demonstrates that Dr. King's concerns are still justified. We do indeed judge others by the color of their skin—as well as by their gender,

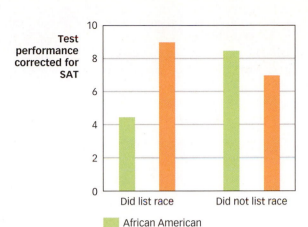

Test performance corrected for SAT

FIGURE 12.13 Self-fulfilling prophecy When asked to indicate their race before taking an exam, African American students performed below their academic level (as determined by their SAT scores). (Data from Steele & Aronson, 1995.)

self-fulfilling prophecy The tendency for people to behave as they are expected to behave.

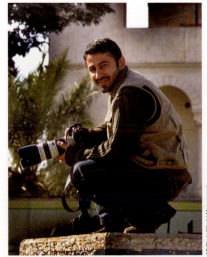

In 2007, Reuters news photographer Namir Noor-Eldeen was shot to death in Iraq by American soldiers in a helicopter who mistook his camera for a weapon. Would they have made the same mistake if Noor-Eldeen had been blonde or female?

attribution An inference about the cause of a person's behavior.

correspondence bias The tendency to make dispositional attributions instead of situational attributions.

actor–observer effect The tendency to make situational attributions for our own behaviors while making dispositional attributions for the identical behavior of others.

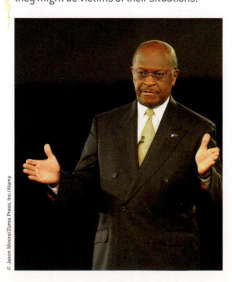

"For God's sake, think! Why is he being so nice to you?"

In 2011, presidential candidate Herman Cain said, "Don't blame Wall Street, don't blame the big banks. If you don't have a job and you are not rich, blame yourself!" Research on the correspondence bias suggests that it is easy to blame people's outcomes on their dispositions, such as stupidity and laziness, and difficult to consider the ways in which they might be victims of their situations.

nationality, religion, age, and occupation—and in so doing, we sometimes make mistakes. But are we any better at judging people by the content of their character? If we could somehow turn off our stereotypes and treat each person as an individual, would we judge these individuals accurately?

Probably not. Treating a person as an individual means judging that person by his or her own words and deeds, and this turns out to be a lot more difficult than it sounds because the relationship between what a person *is* and what a person *says or does* is neither simple nor straightforward. An honest person may lie to save a friend from embarrassment, and a dishonest person may tell the truth to bolster her credibility. Happy people have weepy moments, polite people can be rude in traffic, and those who despise us can be flattering when they need a favor. In short, people's behavior sometimes tells us about the kinds of people they are—about their characters, their traits, and their dispositions—but sometimes it simply tells us about the kinds of situations they happen to be in. Whenever we see a behavior, we must decide which of these two things—dispositions or situations—it is telling us about. How do we do that?

An **attribution** is *an inference about the cause of a person's behavior* (Epley & Waytz, 2010; Gilbert, 1998). We make *situational attributions* when we decide that a person's behavior was caused by some temporary aspect of the situation in which it occurred ("Sarah's crying because she just got some bad news"), and we make *dispositional attributions* when we decide that a person's behavior was caused by a relatively enduring tendency to think, feel, or act in a particular way ("Sarah's crying because she's just such a baby"). Research shows that this decision is quite difficult and that people often make the wrong one. Specifically, people are prone to **correspondence bias** which is *the tendency to make dispositional attributions instead of situational attributions* (Gilbert & Malone, 1995; Jones & Harris, 1967; Ross, 1977).

For example, volunteers in one experiment played a trivia game in which one participant acted as the quizmaster and made up a list of unusual questions, another participant acted as the contestant and tried to answer those questions, and a third participant acted as the observer and simply

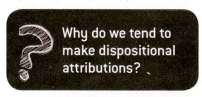

Why do we tend to make dispositional attributions?

watched the game. The quizmasters tended to ask tricky questions based on their own idiosyncratic knowledge, and contestants were generally unable to answer them. After watching the game, the observers were asked to decide how knowledgeable the quizmaster and the contestant were. Although the quizmasters had asked good questions and the contestants had given bad answers, it should have been clear to the observers that all this asking and answering was a product of the roles each person had been assigned to play and that the contestant would have asked equally good questions and the quizmaster would have given equally bad answers had their roles been reversed. And yet observers tended to rate the quizmaster as more knowledgeable than the contestant (Ross, Amabile, & Steinmetz, 1977) and were more likely to choose the quizmaster as their own partner in an upcoming game (Quattrone, 1982). Even when we know that a successful athlete had a home field advantage or that a successful entrepreneur had family connections, we tend to attribute the individual's success to talent and tenacity. Research shows that this happens because information about situations is often hard to get and hard to use (Gilbert, Pelham, & Krull, 1988). As a result, we tend to believe that other peoples' actions are caused by their dispositions even when there is a perfectly reasonable situational explanation.

The correspondence bias is stronger under some circumstances than others. For example, we seem to be more prone to correspondence bias when judging other people's behavior than when judging our own. The **actor–observer effect** is *the tendency to make situational attributions for our own behaviors while making*

The Kennedy brothers (Senator Robert, Senator Ted, and President John) and the Bush brothers (Governor Jeb and President George) were very successful men. Was their success due to the content of their characters, or to the money and fame that came with their family names?

dispositional attributions for the identical behavior of others (Jones & Nisbett, 1972). When college students are asked to explain why they and their friends chose their majors, they tend to explain their own choices in terms of situations ("I chose economics because my parents told me I have to support myself as soon as I'm done with college") and their friends' choices in terms of dispositions ("Leah chose economics because she's materialistic") (Nisbett et al., 1973). The actor–observer effect occurs because people typically have more information about the situations that caused their own behavior than about the situations that caused other people's behavior. We can remember getting the please-major-in-something-practical lecture from our parents, but we weren't at Leah's house to see her get the same lecture. Indeed, when people are shown videotapes of their conversations that allow them to see themselves from their partner's point of view, they tend to make dispositional attributions for their own behavior and situational attributions for their partner's (Storms, 1973; Taylor & Fiske, 1975).

SUMMARY QUIZ [12.3]

1. What is the process by which people come to understand others?
   a. dispositional attribution
   b. the accuracy motive
   c. social cognition
   d. cognitive dissonance

2. A common occupational stereotype is that lawyers are manipulative. Most people who subscribe to this stereotype
   a. believe that the stereotype applies to *all* lawyers.
   b. believe that the stereotype accurately applies to just a small percentage of lawyers.
   c. believe that lawyers are more likely than others to have this characteristic.
   d. would not be likely to misperceive lawyers when they actually meet.

3. The tendency to make a dispositional attribution even when another person's behavior was caused by the situation is referred to as
   a. the actor-observer effect.
   b. stereotyping.
   c. perceptual confirmation.
   d. correspondence bias.

CHAPTER REVIEW

SUMMARY

Social Behavior: Interacting with People

> Survival and reproduction require scarce resources, and aggression and cooperation are two ways to get them.

> Aggression often results from negative affect. The likelihood that people will aggress when they feel negative affect is determined both by biological factors (such as testosterone level) and cultural factors (such as geography).

> Cooperation is beneficial but risky, and one strategy for reducing its risks is to form groups whose members are biased in favor of each other. Unfortunately, groups often decide and behave badly.

> Both biology and culture tend to make the costs of reproduction higher for women than for men, which is one reason why women tend to be choosier when selecting potential mates.

> Attraction is determined by situational factors (such as proximity), physical factors (such as symmetry), and psychological factors (such as similarity).

> People weigh the costs and benefits of their relationships and tend to dissolve them when they think they can or should do better, when they and their partners have very different cost–benefit ratios, or when they have little invested in the relationship.

Social Influence: Controlling People

> People are motivated to experience pleasure and avoid pain (the hedonic motive), and thus can be influenced by rewards and punishments, although these can sometimes backfire.

> People are motivated to attain the approval of others (the approval motive) and thus can be influenced by social norms, such as the norm of reciprocity. People often look to the behavior of others to determine what's normative, and they often end up conforming or obeying, sometimes with disastrous results.

> People are motivated to know what is true (the accuracy motive) and thus can be influenced by other people's behaviors and communications. This motivation also causes them to seek consistency among their attitudes, beliefs, and actions.

Social Cognition: Understanding People

> People make inferences about others based on the categories to which they belong (stereotyping). This method can lead them to misjudge others because stereotypes can be inaccurate, overused, self-perpetuating, and unconscious and automatic.

> People make inferences about others based on others' behaviors. This method can lead to misjudgments because people tend to attribute actions to dispositions even when they should attribute them to situations.

KEY TERMS

social psychology (p. 380)

aggression (p. 380)

frustration–aggression hypothesis (p. 380)

cooperation (p. 383)

group (p. 384)

prejudice (p. 384)

discrimination (p. 384)

common knowledge effect (p. 384)

group polarization (p. 384)

groupthink (p. 385)

deindividuation (p. 385)

diffusion of responsibility (p. 385)

bystander intervention (p. 385)

altruism (p. 386)

kin selection (p. 386)

reciprocal altruism (p. 386)

mere exposure effect (p. 389)

passionate love (p. 391)

companionate love (p. 391)

social exchange (p. 392)

social influence (p. 393)

norms (p. 395)

norm of reciprocity (p. 395)

normative influence (p. 395)

conformity (p. 396)

obedience (p. 397)

attitude (p. 399)

belief (p. 399)

informational influence (p. 399)

persuasion (p. 399)

systematic persuasion (p. 399)

heuristic persuasion (p. 400)

foot-in-the-door technique (p. 401)

cognitive dissonance (p. 401)

social cognition (p. 402)

stereotyping (p. 402)

perceptual confirmation (p. 404)

self-fulfilling prophecy (p. 405)

attribution (p. 406)

correspondence bias (p. 406)

actor–observer effect (p. 406)

CHANGING MINDS

1. One of the senators from your state is supporting a bill that would impose heavy fines on aggressive drivers who run red lights. One of your classmates thinks this is a good idea. "The textbook taught us a lot about punishment and reward. It's simple. If we punish aggressive driving, its frequency will decline." Is your classmate right? Might the new law backfire? Might another policy be more effective in promoting safe driving?

2. One of your friends is outgoing, funny, and a star athlete on the women's basketball team. She has started to date a man who is introverted and prefers playing computer games to attending parties. You tease her about the contrast in personalities, and she replies, "Well, opposites attract." Is she right?

3. You and a friend read a news item about a Black job applicant who filed a racial discrimination lawsuit against a large law firm that

didn't hire him. Your friend says, "People are always so quick to claim racism. Sure, there are still a few racist people out there, but if you do surveys and ask people what they think about people of other races, they say they are fine with them." What would you tell your friend?

4. One of your friends has a very unique fashion sense and always wears clothes that are just a little bit different—for example, a neon orange track suit with a battered fedora. Most of the time, you appreciate your friend for his quirky personality. One day, he tells you that he chooses his clothes carefully to make a fashion statement. "Most people follow the crowd," he announces. "I don't. I'm an individual, and I make my own choices, without influence from anyone else." Could he be right? What examples might you provide for or against your friend's claim?

5. A classmate is shaken after learning about the Milgram (1963) study, in which participants were willing to obey orders to administer painful electric shocks to another human, even after he begged them to stop. "I know that you and I wouldn't behave like that." Is she right? What evidence would you give her to support or oppose her claim?

6. When your family gathers for Thanksgiving, your cousin Wendy brings her fiancée, Amanda. It's the first time Amanda has met the whole family, and she seems nervous. She talks too much, laughs too loud, and rubs everyone the wrong way. Later, when you're alone with your mother, she rolls her eyes. "It's hard to imagine Wendy wanting to spend the rest of her life married to someone that annoying." You decide to be more generous, because you think your mother might have fallen prey to correspondence bias. How could you change your mother's mind?

ANSWERS TO SUMMARY QUIZZES

Answers to Summary Quiz 12.1: 1. b; 2. c; 3. d; 4. a; 5. b.
Answers to Summary Quiz 12.2: 1. d; 2. b; 3. d.
Answers to Summary Quiz 12.3: 1. c; 2. c; 3. d.

Need more help? Additional resources are located in LaunchPad at:
http://www.worthpublishers.com/launchpad/schacterbrief3e

© Fotoarchiago fotostock

13

Stress and Health

 **HAVE A KNIFE TO YOUR NECK. DON'T MAKE A SOUND.** Get out of bed and come with me or I will kill you and your family." These are the words that awoke 14-year-old Elizabeth Smart in the middle of the night of June 5, 2002. Fearing for her own life and that of her family, she kept quiet and left with her abductor. Elizabeth was kidnapped by Brian David Mitchell, a man Elizabeth's parents had hired previously to do some roof work on their home. Mitchell and his wife Wanda Ileen Barzee held Elizabeth in captivity for 9 months, during which time Mitchell repeatedly raped her and threatened to kill her and her entire family. Mitchell, Barzee, and Smart were spotted walking down the street by a couple who recognized them from a recent airing of the television show *America's Most Wanted* and called the police. Mitchell and Barzee were apprehended, and Elizabeth was returned to her family.

Elizabeth suffered unimaginable circumstances for a prolonged period of time in what can be thought of as one of the most stressful situations possible, especially for a 14-year-old girl. Fortunately, Elizabeth is now safe and sound, happily married, and working as an activist and commentator for ABC News. She endured life-threatening stressors for months, and those experiences undoubtedly affected her in ways that will last her entire lifetime. Yet, despite the very difficult hand she was dealt, she appears to have bounced back and to be leading a happy, productive, and rewarding life. Hers is a story of both stress and health.

This smiling young face is that of Elizabeth Smart, who, between the times of these two photographs, was kidnapped, raped, and tortured for nearly a year. Stressful life events often affect us in ways that cannot be seen from the outside. Fortunately, there are things that we can do in response to even the most stressful of life events that can get us smiling again.

stressors Specific events or chronic pressures that place demands on a person or threaten the person's well-being.

stress The physical and psychological response to internal or external stressors.

health psychology The subfield of psychology concerned with ways psychological factors influence the causes and treatment of physical illness and the maintenance of health.

FORTUNATELY, VERY FEW OF US WILL EVER HAVE TO ENDURE the type of stress that Elizabeth Smart lived through. But life has its **stressors**, *specific events or chronic pressures that place demands on a person or threaten the person's well-being*. Although such stressors rarely involve threats of death, they do have both immediate and cumulative effects that can influence health.

In this chapter, we'll look at the kinds of life events that produce **stress**, *the physical and psychological response to internal or external stressors;* typical responses to such stressors; and ways to manage stress. Stress has such a profound influence on health that we consider stress and health together in this chapter. And because sickness and health are not merely features of the physical body, we then consider the more general topic of **health psychology**, *the subfield of psychology concerned with the ways psychological factors influence the causes and treatment of physical illness and the maintenance of health*. You will see how perceptions of illness can affect its course and how health-promoting behaviors can improve the quality of people's lives.

Sources of Stress: What Gets to You

First of all, what are the sources of stress? A natural catastrophe, such as a hurricane, earthquake, or volcanic eruption, is an obvious source. But for most of us, stressors are personal events that affect the comfortable pattern of our lives and little annoyances that bug us day after day. Let's look at the life events that can cause stress, chronic sources of stress, and the relationship between lack of perceived control and the impact of stressors.

Stressful Events

People often seem to get sick after major life events. In fact, simply adding up the stress ratings of each life change experienced is a significant indicator of a person's likelihood of future illness (Miller, 1996). Someone who becomes divorced, loses a job, and has a friend die all in the same year, for example, is more likely to get sick than someone who escapes the year with only a divorce.

A checklist adapted for the life events of college students (and sporting the snappy acronym CUSS, for College Undergraduate Stress Scale) is shown in **TABLE 13.1**. To assess your stressful events, check off any events that have happened to you in the past year and sum your point total. In a large sample of students in an introductory psychology class, the average was 1,247 points, ranging from 182 to 2,571 (Renner & Mackin, 1998).

Looking at the list, you may wonder why positive events are included. Stressful life events are unpleasant, right? Why would getting married be stressful? Isn't a wedding supposed to be fun? Research has shown that compared with negative events, positive events produce less psychological distress and fewer physical symptoms (McFarlane et al., 1980), and also that happiness can sometimes even counteract the effects of negative events (Fredrickson, 2000). However, positive events often require readjustment and preparedness that many people find extremely stressful (e.g., Brown & McGill, 1989), so these events are included in computing life-change scores.

As the movie *Bridesmaids* showcased perfectly, while weddings are positive events, they also can be stressful due to the often overwhelming amount of planning and decision making involved (and occasionally because of the difficulties managing the interactions of friends and family).

Universal Pictures/The Kobal Collection/Hanover, Suzanne

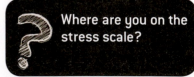

Where are you on the stress scale?

Chronic Stressors

Life would be simpler if an occasional stressful event such as a wedding or a lost job were the only pressures we faced. At least each event would

Table 13.1 College Undergraduate Stress Scale

Event	Stress Rating	Event	Stress Rating
Being raped	100	Lack of sleep	69
Finding out that you are HIV positive	100	Change in housing situation (hassles, moves)	69
Being accused of rape	98	Competing for performing in public	69
Death of a close friend	97	Getting in a physical fight	66
Death of a close family member	96	Difficulties with roommate	66
Contracting a sexually transmitted disease (other than AIDS)	94	Job changes (applying, new job, work hassles)	65
Concerns about being pregnant	91	Declaring your major or concerns about future plans	65
Finals week	90	A class you hate	62
Concerns about your partner being pregnant	90	Drinking or use of drugs	61
Oversleeping for an exam	89	Confrontations with professors	60
Flunking a class	89	Starting a new semester	58
Having a boyfriend or girlfriend cheat on you	85	Going on a first date	57
Ending a steady dating relationship	85	Registration	55
Serious illness in a close friend or family member	85	Maintaining a steady dating relationship	55
Financial difficulties	84	Commuting to campus or work or both	54
Writing a major term paper	83	Peer pressures	53
Being caught cheating on a test	83	Being away from home for the first time	53
Drunk driving	82	Getting sick	52
Sense of overload in school or work	82	Concerns about your appearance	52
Two exams in one day	80	Getting straight As	51
Cheating on your boyfriend or girlfriend	77	A difficult class that you love	48
Getting married	76	Making new friends, getting along with friends	47
Negative consequences of drinking or drug use	75	Fraternity or sorority rush	47
Depression or crisis in your best friend	73	Falling asleep in class	40
Difficulties with parents	73	Attending an athletic event	21
Talking in front of class	72		

Note: To compute your personal life score, sum the stress ratings for all events that have happened to you in the last year.
Source: Information from Renner and Mackin, 1998.

be limited in scope, with a beginning, a middle, and, ideally, an end. But unfortunately, life brings with it continued exposure to **chronic stressors,** *sources of stress that occur continuously or repeatedly*. Strained relationships, discrimination, bullying, overwork, money troubles—small stressors that may be easy to ignore if they happen only occasionally—can accumulate to produce distress and illness. People who report being affected by daily hassles also report more psychological symptoms (LaPierre et al., 2012) and physical symptoms (Piazza et al., 2013), and these effects often have a greater and longer-lasting impact than major life events.

Many chronic stressors are linked to social relationships. For instance, as described in the Social Psychology chapter, people often form different social groups based on

chronic stressors Sources of stress that occur continuously or repeatedly.

Shutterstock

City life can be fun, but the higher levels of noise, crowding, and violence can also be sources of chronic stress.

race, culture, interests, popularity, and so on. Being outside the in-group can be stressful. Being actively targeted by members of the in-group can be even more stressful, especially if this happens repeatedly over time (see Hot Science Box). Chronic stressors also can be linked to particular environments. For example, features of city life—noise, traffic, crowding, pollution, and even the threat of violence—provide particularly insistent sources of chronic stress (Evans, 2006). Rural areas have their own chronic stressors, of course, especially isolation and lack of access to amenities such as health care. The realization that chronic stressors are linked to environments has spawned the subfield of *environmental psychology*, the scientific study of environmental effects on behavior and health.

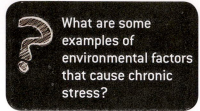

? What are some examples of environmental factors that cause chronic stress?

Perceived Control over Stressful Events

What do catastrophes, stressful life changes, and daily hassles have in common? Right off the bat, of course, their threat to the person or the status quo is easy to see. Stressors challenge you to *do something*—to take some action to eliminate or overcome the stressor.

Paradoxically, events are most stressful when there is *nothing to do*—no way to deal with the challenge. Expecting that you will have control over what happens to you is associated with greater effectiveness in dealing with stress. The stressful effects of

Hot Science

Can Discrimination Cause Stress and Illness?

Have you ever been discriminated against because of your race, gender, sexual orientation, or some other characteristic? If so, then you know that this can be a pretty stressful experience. But what exactly does it *do* to people?

Recent research has shown that there are a number of ways that discrimination can lead to elevated stress and negative health outcomes. People from socially disadvantaged groups who experience higher levels of stress as a result of discrimination engage more frequently in maladaptive behaviors (e.g., drinking, smoking, and overeating) in efforts to cope with stress. They also can experience difficulties in their interactions with health care professionals (e.g., clinician biases, patient suspiciousness about treatment; Major, Mendes, & Dovidio, 2013). Together, these factors may help to explain why members of socially disadvantaged groups

have significantly higher rates of health problems than do members of socially advantaged groups (Penner et al., 2010).

One recent study exposed Black and White participants to social rejection by either a person of the same race or a different race to test whether there is something particularly harmful about discrimination, versus social rejection in general (Jamieson et al., 2013). To test this idea, they had research participants deliver a speech to two confederates in different rooms via a video chat program, after which the confederates provided negative feedback about the participant's speech. The confederates were not seen by a participant but were represented by computer avatars that either matched each participant's race or did not. Interestingly, although the nature of the rejection was the same in all cases, participants responded very differently if the

people rejecting them were from a different race. Specifically, whereas being rejected by people from your own race was associated with greater displays of shame and physiological changes associated with an avoidance state (increased cortisol), being rejected by members of a different race was associated with displays of anger, greater vigilance for danger, physiological changes associated with an approach state (i.e., higher cardiac output and lower vascular resistance), and higher risk taking.

Studies like this one help to explain some of the health disparities that currently exist across different social groups. The results suggest that discrimination can lead to physiological, cognitive, and behavioral changes that in the short term prepare a person for action but that in the long-term could lead to negative health outcomes.

crowding, for example, appear to stem from the feeling that you can't control getting away from the crowded conditions (Evans & Stecker, 2004). Being jammed into a crowded dormitory room may be easier to handle, after all, the moment you realize you could take a walk and get away from it all.

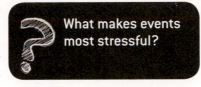

What makes events most stressful?

But what if you can't get up and walk away from a stressful situation? A classic study by Overmeir and Seligman (1967) showed that if dogs are repeatedly exposed to electric shocks with no way to escape, then they later don't even try to escape from shocks, even when escape is now possible. This **learned helplessness,** or *the belief that one has no control over one's situation based on past experience*, has been proposed to be a major contributor to the development of depression in humans who have experienced repeated stressful events (Abramson, Seligman, & Teasdale, 1978).

Some stressful life events, such as those associated with drunk driving, are within our power to control. We gain control when we give away the car keys to a designated driver.

SUMMARY QUIZ [13.1]

1. What kinds of stressors are you likely to be exposed to if you live in a dense urban area with considerable traffic, noise, and pollution?
   a. cultural stressors
   b. intermittent stressors
   c. chronic stressors
   d. positive stressors

2. In an experiment, two groups are subjected to loud noise while attempting to complete a task. The people in Group A are told they can turn off the noise by pushing a button. This information is withheld from Group B. Why will Group A's performance at the task likely be better than Group B's?
   a. Group B is working in a different environment.
   b. Group A has perceived control over the stress.
   c. Group B is less distracted than Group A.
   d. The distractions affecting Group B are now chronic.

3. According to the College Undergraduate Stress Scale, which of the following events is most stressful?
   a. concerns about your appearance
   b. lack of sleep
   c. getting sick
   d. confrontation with professors

Stress Reactions: All Shook Up

It was a regular Tuesday morning in New York City. College students were sitting in their morning classes. People were arriving at work and the streets were beginning to fill with shoppers and tourists. Then, at 8:46 a.m., American Airlines Flight 11 crashed into the North Tower of the World Trade Center. People watched in horror. This seemed like a terrible accident. Then at 9:03 a.m., United Airlines Flight 175 crashed into the South Tower of the World Trade Center. There were then reports of a plane crashing into the Pentagon. And another somewhere in Pennsylvania. America was under attack, and no one knew what would happen next on this terrifying morning

learned helplessness The belief that one has no control over one's situation based on past experience.

The threat of death or injury, such as that experienced by many in New York City at the time of the September 11 attacks, can cause significant and lasting physical and psychological stress reactions.

fight-or-flight response An emotional and physiological reaction to an emergency that increases readiness for action.

FIGURE 13.1 HPA Axis Just a few seconds after a fear-inducing stimulus is perceived, the hypothalamus activates the pituitary gland, which in turn activates the adrenal glands to release catecholamines and cortisol that energize the fight-or-flight response.

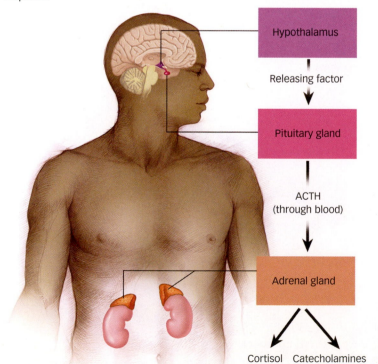

Hypothalamus

Releasing factor

Pituitary gland

ACTH
(through blood)

Adrenal gland

Cortisol   Catecholamines

of September 11, 2001. The terrorist attacks on the World Trade Center were an enormous stressor that had a lasting impact on many people, physically and psychologically. People living in close proximity to the World Trade Center (within 1.5 miles) during 9/11 were found to have less gray matter in the amygdala, hippocampus, insula, anterior cingulate, and medial prefrontal cortex relative to those living more than 200 miles away during the attacks, suggesting that the stress associated with the attacks may have reduced the size of these parts of the brain that play an important role in emotion, memory, and decision making (Ganzel et al., 2008). Children who watched more television coverage of 9/11 had higher symptoms of posttraumatic stress disorder than children who watched less coverage (Otto et al., 2007). Stress can produce changes in every system of the body and mind, stimulating both physical reactions and psychological reactions. Let's consider each in turn.

Physical Reactions

The **fight-or-flight response** is *an emotional and physiological reaction to an emergency that increases readiness for action.* The mind asks, "Should I stay and battle this somehow, or should I run like mad?" And the body prepares to react. If you're a cat at this time, your hair stands on end. If you're a human, your hair stands on end, too, but not as visibly.

Brain activation in response to threat occurs in the hypothalamus, initiating a cascade of bodily responses that include stimulation of the nearby pituitary gland, which in turn causes stimulation of the adrenal glands (see **FIGURE 13.1**). This pathway is sometimes called the HPA (hypothalamic–pituitary–adrenocortical) axis. The adrenal glands release hormones, including the *catecholamines* (epinephrine and norepinephrine), which increase sympathetic nervous system activation (and therefore increase heart rate, blood pressure, and respiration rate) and decrease parasympathetic activation (see the Neuroscience and Behavior chapter). The increased respiration and blood pressure make more oxygen available to the muscles to energize attack or to initiate escape. The adrenal glands also release *cortisol*, a hormone that increases the concentration of glucose in the blood to make fuel available to the muscles. Everything is prepared for a full-tilt response to the threat.

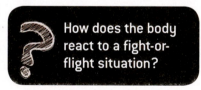

How does the body react to a fight-or-flight situation?

General Adaptation Syndrome

What might have happened if the terrorist attacks of 9/11 were spaced out over a period of days or weeks? In the 1930s, Canadian physician Hans Selye subjected rats to heat, cold, infection, trauma, hemorrhage, and other prolonged stressors, and he found that the stressed-out rats developed physiological responses that included an enlarged adrenal cortex, shrinking of the lymph glands, and ulceration of the stomach. Noting that many different kinds of stressors caused similar patterns of physiological change, he called the reaction the **general adaptation syndrome (GAS),** a *three-stage physiological stress response that appears regardless of the stressor that is encountered.* The GAS occurs in three phases (see **FIGURE 13.2**). First comes the *alarm phase* (equivalent to the fight-or-flight response),

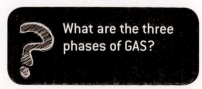

What are the three phases of GAS?

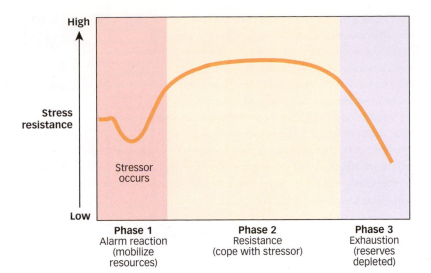

FIGURE 13.2 Selye's Three Phases of Stress Response
In Selye's theory, resistance to stress builds over time but then can only last so long before exhaustion sets in.

Hans Selye with rat. Given all the stress Selye put rats under, this one looks surprisingly calm.

in which the body rapidly mobilizes its resources to respond to the threat. Next, in the *resistance phase*, the body tries to adapt and cope with its stressor by shutting down unnecessary processes such as digestion, growth, and the sex drive. If the GAS continues long enough, the *exhaustion phase* sets in: the body's resistance collapses, creating damage that can include susceptibility to infection, tumor growth, aging, irreversible organ damage, or death.

Stress Effects on Health and Aging

As people age, the body slowly begins to break down (just ask any of the authors of this book). Interestingly, recent research has revealed that stress significantly accelerates the aging process. Elizabeth Smart's parents noted that, upon being reunited with her after 9 months of separation, they almost did not recognize her because she appeared to have aged so much (Smart, Smart, & Morton, 2003). More generally, people exposed to chronic stress, whether due to their relationships, job, or something else, experience actual wear and tear on their bodies and increased aging. Take a look at the pictures of the past three presidents before and after their terms as president of the United States (arguably, one of the most stressful jobs in the world). As you can see, they appear to have aged much more than the 4–8 years that passed between their first and second photographs.

Why does stress increase the aging process? The cells in our bodies are constantly dividing, and as part of this process, our chromosomes are repeatedly copied so that our genetic information is carried into the new cells. This process is facilitated by the presence of **telomeres,** *caps at the ends of each chromosome that protect the ends of chromosomes and prevent them from sticking to each other.* They are kind of like the tape at the end of your shoelaces that keeps them from being frayed and not working as efficiently. Each time a cell divides, the telomeres become slightly shorter. Over time, if the

general adaptation syndrome (GAS)
A three-stage physiological stress response that appears regardless of the stressor that is encountered.

telomeres Caps at the end of each chromosome that protect the ends of chromosomes and prevent them from sticking to each other.

Chronic stress can actually speed the aging process. Just look at how much each of our last three presidents aged while in office. College can be stressful too, but hopefully not so much so that you have white hair by graduation.

telomeres become too short, cells can no longer divide, and this can lead to the development of tumors and a range of diseases. The recent discovery of the function of telomeres and their relation to aging and disease has been one of the most exciting advances in science in the past several decades.

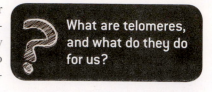

What are telomeres, and what do they do for us?

Interestingly, social stressors can play an important role in this process. People exposed to chronic stress have shorter telomere lengths (Epel et al., 2004). Laboratory studies suggest that increased cortisol can lead to shortened telomeres, which has downstream negative effects in the form of accelerated aging and increased risk of a wide range of diseases, including cancer, cardiovascular disease, diabetes, and depression (Blackburn & Epel, 2012). The good news is that activities like exercise and meditation seem to prevent chronic stress from shortening telomere length, providing a potential explanation of how these activities may convey health benefits such as longer life and lower risk of disease (Epel et al., 2009; Puterman et al., 2010).

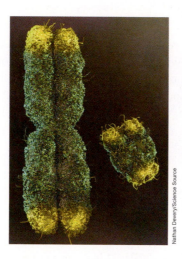

Dr. Elizabeth Blackburn was awarded a Nobel Prize in 2009 for her groundbreaking discoveries on the functions of telomeres (shown here in yellow).

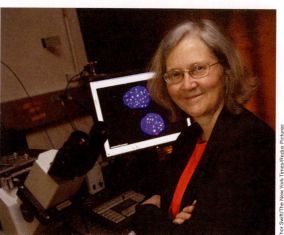

Stress Effects on the Immune Response

The **immune system** is *a complex response system that protects the body from bacteria, viruses, and other foreign substances.* The immune system is remarkably responsive to psychological influences. Stressors can cause hormones known as *glucocorticoids* to flood the brain (described in the Neuroscience and Behavior chapter), wearing down the immune system and making it less able to fight invaders (Webster Marketon & Glaser, 2008). For example, in one study, medical student volunteers agreed to receive small wounds to the roof of the mouth. Researchers observed that these wounds healed more slowly during exam periods than during summer vacation (Marucha, Kiecolt-Glaser, & Favagehi, 1998).

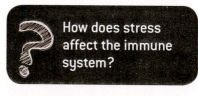

How does stress affect the immune system?

The effect of stress on immune response may help to explain why social status is related to health. Studies of British civil servants beginning in the 1960s found that mortality varied precisely with civil service grade: the higher the classification, the lower the death rate, regardless of cause (Marmot et al., 1991). One explanation is that people in lower-status jobs more often engage in unhealthy behavior such as smoking and drinking alcohol, and there is evidence of this. But there is also evidence that the stress of living life at the bottom levels of society may increase risk of infections by weakening the immune system. People who perceive themselves as low in social status are more prone to suffer from respiratory infections, for example, than those who do not bear this social burden—and the same holds true for low-status male monkeys (Cohen, 1999).

immune system A complex response system that protects the body from bacteria, viruses, and other foreign substances.

Stress and Cardiovascular Health

The heart and circulatory system are also sensitive to stress. Chronic stress is a major contributor to coronary heart disease (Krantz & McCeney, 2002), because prolonged stress-activated arousal of the sympathetic nervous system raises blood pressure and gradually damages the blood vessels. The damaged vessels accumulate plaque, and the more plaque, the greater the likelihood of coronary heart disease. In one study, men who exhibited elevated blood pressure in response to stress and who reported that their work environment was especially stressful showed progressive atherosclerosis during the 4-year study (Everson et al., 1997).

In the 1950s, cardiologists interviewed and tested 3,000 healthy middle-aged men and then tracked their subsequent cardiovascular health (Friedman & Rosenman, 1974). Some of the men displayed a **Type A behavior pattern,** *a tendency toward easily aroused hostility, impatience, a sense of time urgency, and competitive achievement strivings.* Other men displayed a less driven behavior pattern (sometimes called *Type B*). The Type A men were identified by their answers to questions in the interview (agreeing that they walk and talk fast, work late, set goals for themselves, work hard to win, and easily get frustrated and angry at others), and also by the pushy and impatient way in which they answered the questions. In the decade that followed, men who had been classified as Type A were twice as likely to have heart attacks as the Type B men.

Anywhere in the world, road rage starts to make sense when you believe that all the other drivers on the road are trying to kill you.

Type A behavior pattern The tendency toward easily aroused hostility, impatience, a sense of time urgency, and competitive achievement strivings.

Psychological Reactions

The body's response to stress is intertwined with responses of the mind. Perhaps the first thing the mind does is try to sort things out—to interpret whether an event is threatening or not—and if it is, whether something can be done about it.

Stress Interpretation

The interpretation of a stimulus as stressful or not is called *primary appraisal* (Lazarus & Folkman, 1984). Primary appraisal allows you to realize that a small dark spot on your shirt is a stressor (spider!) or that a 70-mile-per-hour drop from a great height in a small car full of screaming people may not be (roller coaster!).

The next step in interpretation is *secondary appraisal,* determining whether the stressor is something you can handle or not—that is, whether you have control over the event (Lazarus & Folkman, 1984). Interestingly, the body responds differently depending on whether the stressor is perceived as a *threat* (a stressor you believe you might *not* be able to overcome) or a *challenge* (a stressor you feel fairly confident you can control; Blascovich & Tomaka, 1996). The same midterm exam is seen as a challenge if you are well prepared, but it is a threat if you didn't study. Although both threats and challenges raise heart rate, threats increase vascular reactivity (such as constriction of the blood vessels, which can lead to high blood pressure; see the Hot Science box, p. 414).

? What is the difference between a threat and a challenge?

Changing your perception of a stressful situation from a "threat" to a "challenge" can actually modify your body's response to the situation and lead to better performance. This approach worked for Eminem's character (B. Rabbit) in the movie *8 Mile,* and it can work for you too.

Burnout

Did you ever take a class from an instructor who had lost interest in the job? The syndrome is easy to spot: The teacher looks distant and blank, almost robotic, giving predictable and humdrum lessons each day, as if it doesn't matter whether anyone is listening. Now imagine *being* this instructor. You decided to teach because you wanted to shape young minds. You worked hard, and for a while, things were great. But one day, you looked up to see a room full of miserable students

© STOCK4B GmbH/Alamy

burnout A state of physical, emotional, and mental exhaustion created by long-term involvement in an emotionally demanding situation and accompanied by lowered performance and motivation.

who were bored and didn't care about anything you had to say. They updated their Facebook pages while you talked and started putting things away long before the end of class. You're happy at work only when you're not in class. When people feel this way, especially about their careers, they are suffering from **burnout,** *a state of physical, emotional, and mental exhaustion created by long-term involvement in an emotionally demanding situation and accompanied by lowered performance and motivation.*

Burnout is a particular problem in the helping professions (Maslach, Schaufeli, & Leiter, 2001). Teachers, nurses, clergy, doctors, dentists, psychologists, social workers, police officers, and others who repeatedly encounter emotional turmoil on the job may only be able to work productively for a limited time before succumbing to burnout (Maslach, 2003). Their unhappiness can even spread to others; people with burnout tend to become disgruntled employees who revel in their co-workers' failures and ignore their co-workers' successes (Brenninkmeijer, Vanyperen, & Buunk, 2001).

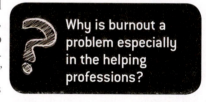

Why is burnout a problem especially in the helping professions?

What causes burnout? One theory suggests that the culprit is using your job to give meaning to your life (Pines, 1993). If you define yourself only by your career and gauge your self-worth by success at work, you risk having nothing left when work fails. For example, a teacher in danger of burnout might do well to invest time in family, hobbies, or other self-expressions. Others argue that some emotionally stressful jobs lead to burnout no matter how they are approached, and active efforts to overcome the stress before burnout occurs are important. The stress management techniques discussed in the next section may be lifesavers for people in such jobs.

Is there anything worse than taking a horribly boring class? How about being the teacher of that class? What techniques could be used to help people in helping professions (teachers, doctors, nurses, etc.) to prevent burnout from stress?

SUMMARY QUIZ [13.2]

1. The brain activation that occurs in response to a threat begins in the
   a. pituitary gland.
   b. hypothalamus.
   c. adrenal gland.
   d. corpus callosum.

2. According to the general adaptation syndrome, during the _____ phase, the body adapts to its high state of arousal as it tries to cope with a stressor.
   a. exhaustion
   b. alarm

c. resistance

d. energy

3. Which of the following statements is most accurate regarding the physiological response to stress?

a. Type A behavior patterns have psychological but not physiological ramifications.

b. The link between work-related stress and coronary heart disease is unfounded.

c. Stressors can cause hormones to flood the brain, strengthening the immune system.

d. The immune system is remarkably responsive to psychological influences.

Stress Management: Dealing with It

Most college students (92%) say they occasionally feel overwhelmed by the tasks they face, and over a third say they have dropped courses or received low grades in response to severe stress (Duenwald, 2002). No doubt you are among the lucky 8% who are entirely cool and report no stress. But just in case you're not, you may be interested in stress management techniques.

Mind Management

Stressful events are magnified in the mind. If you fear public speaking, for example, just the thought of an upcoming presentation to a group can create anxiety. And if you do break down during a presentation (going blank, for example, or blurting out something embarrassing), intrusive memories of this stressful event could echo in your mind afterward. A significant part of stress management, then, is control of the mind. Let's look at three specific strategies.

1. Repressive Coping

Controlling your thoughts is not easy, but some people do seem to be able to banish unpleasant thoughts from the mind. **Repressive coping** is characterized by *avoiding situations or thoughts that are reminders of a stressor and maintaining an artificially positive viewpoint.* Everyone has some problems, of course, but repressors are good at deliberately ignoring them (Barnier, Levin, & Maher, 2004). Like Elizabeth Smart, who for years after her rescue focused in interviews on what was happening in her life now rather than repeatedly discussing her past in captivity, people often rearrange their lives in order to avoid stressful situations. It may make sense to try to avoid stressful thoughts and situations if you're the kind of person who is good at putting unpleasant thoughts and emotions out of mind (Coifman et al., 2007). For some people, however, the avoidance of unpleasant thoughts and situations is so difficult that it can turn into a grim preoccupation (Parker & McNally, 2008; Wegner & Zanakos, 1994).

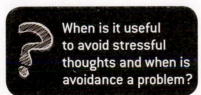

When is it useful to avoid stressful thoughts and when is avoidance a problem?

repressive coping Avoiding situations or thoughts that are reminders of a stressor and maintaining an artificially positive viewpoint.

Some people are good at deliberately ignoring negative events or thoughts after they occur, and their functioning may be improved as a result. However, those who are not as good at repressing this negative information may do better trying rational coping.

Cpl. Marco Mancha/Defense Video & Imagery Distribution System

This young woman is praying during a vigil held for the victim of a gang rape in New Delhi. Extremely stressful events, such as rape, are not only acute stressors but often have lasting psychological consequences. Fortunately, there are effective techniques for learning to cope with such events that can lead to improved psychological health.

rational coping Facing the stressor and working to overcome it.

reframing Finding a new or creative way to think about a stressor that reduces its threat.

meditation The practice of intentional contemplation.

Meditation is the practice of intentional contemplation, and it can also temporarily influence brain activity and enhance the sense of well-being.

2. Rational Coping

Rational coping involves *facing the stressor and working to overcome it.* This strategy is the opposite of repressive coping and so may seem to be the most unpleasant and unnerving thing you could do when faced with stress. It requires approaching, rather than avoiding, a stressor in order to lessen its longer-term negative impact (Hayes, Strosahl, & Wilson, 1999).

Rational coping is a three-step process. The first step is *acceptance,* coming to realize that the stressor exists and cannot be wished away. The second step is *exposure,* attending to the stressor, thinking about it, and even seeking it out. Psychological treatment may help during the exposure step by helping victims to confront and think about what happened. Using a technique called *prolonged exposure,* rape survivors relive the traumatic event in their imagination by recording a verbal account of the event and then listening to the recording daily. This sounds like bitter medicine indeed, but it is remarkably effective, producing significant reductions in anxiety and symptoms of posttraumatic stress disorder compared to no therapy and compared to other therapies that promote more gradual and subtle forms of exposure (Foa et al., 1999). The final step is *understanding,* working to find the meaning of the stressor in your life.

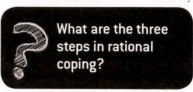

What are the three steps in rational coping?

3. Reframing

Changing the way you think is another way to cope with stressful thoughts. **Reframing** involves *finding a new or creative way to think about a stressor that reduces its threat.* If you experience anxiety at the thought of public speaking, for example, you might reframe by shifting from thinking of an audience as evaluating you to thinking of yourself as evaluating them, and this might make speech giving easier.

Reframing can take place spontaneously if people are given the opportunity to spend time thinking and writing about stressful events. In one study, the physical health of college students improved after they spent a few hours writing about their deepest thoughts and feelings. Compared with students who had written about something else, these students were less likely in subsequent months to visit the student health center; they also used less aspirin and achieved better grades (Pennebaker & Chung, 2007). In fact, engaging in such expressive writing was found to improve immune function (Pennebaker, Kiecolt-Glaser, & Glaser, 1988), whereas suppressing emotional topics weakened it (Petrie, Booth, & Pennebaker, 1998). The positive effect of self-disclosing writing may reflect its usefulness in reframing trauma and reducing stress.

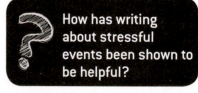

How has writing about stressful events been shown to be helpful?

Body Management

Stress can express itself as tension in your neck muscles, as back pain, as a knot in your stomach, as sweaty hands, or as the harried face you glimpse in the mirror. Because stress so often manifests itself through bodily symptoms, body management can reduce stress. Here are four techniques.

1. Meditation

Meditation is *the practice of intentional contemplation.* Techniques of meditation are associated with a variety of religious traditions and are also practiced outside religious contexts. Some forms of meditation call for attempts to clear the mind of thought, others involve focusing on a single thought (e.g., thinking about a candle flame), and still others involve concentration on breathing or on a *mantra* (a repetitive sound such as *om*). At a minimum, the techniques have in common a period of quiet.

Time spent meditating can be restful and revitalizing. Beyond these immediate benefits, many people also meditate in an effort to experience deeper or transformed consciousness. Whatever the reason, meditation does appear to have positive psychological effects (Hölzel et al., 2011). Many believe it does so, in part, by improving control over attention. Interestingly, experienced meditators show deactivation in the default mode network (which is associated with mind wandering; see Figure 5.5 in the Consciousness chapter) during meditation relative to nonmeditators (Brewer et al., 2011). Even short-term meditation training administered to college undergraduates has been shown to improve the connectivity between parts of the brain involved in conflict monitoring and cognitive and emotional control (Tang et al., 2012). These findings suggest that meditators may be better able to regulate their thoughts and emotions, which may translate to a better ability to manage interpersonal relations, anxiety, and a range of other activities that require conscious effort (Sedlmeier et al., 2012).

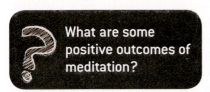

What are some positive outcomes of meditation?

Aung San Suu Kyi, the leader of the Myanmar opposition party who was awarded the Nobel Peace Prize in 1991, endured house arrest from 1989 until 2010. She has said that daily meditation helped her through this difficult time by improving her mood, awareness, and clarity.

2. Relaxation

Imagine for a moment that you are scratching your chin. Don't actually do it; just think about it and notice that your body participates by moving ever so slightly, tensing and relaxing in the sequence of the imagined action. Our bodies respond to all the things we think about doing every day. These thoughts create muscle tension even when we think we're doing nothing at all.

Relaxation therapy is *a technique for reducing tension by consciously relaxing muscles of the body.* A person in relaxation therapy may be asked to relax specific muscle groups one at a time or to imagine warmth flowing through the body or to think about a relaxing situation. This activity draws on a **relaxation response,** *a condition of reduced muscle tension, cortical activity, heart rate, breathing rate, and blood pressure* (Benson, 1990). Basically, as soon as you get in a comfortable position, quiet down, and focus on something repetitive or soothing that holds your attention, you relax.

Relaxing on a regular basis can reduce symptoms of stress (Carlson & Hoyle, 1993) and even reduce blood levels of cortisol, the biochemical marker of the stress response (McKinney et al., 1997). For example, in individuals who are suffering from a tension headache, relaxation reduces the tension that causes the headache; in people with cancer, relaxation makes it easier to cope with stressful treatments; in people with stress-related cardiovascular problems, relaxation can reduce the high blood pressure that puts the heart at risk (Mandle et al., 1996).

3. Biofeedback

Wouldn't it be nice if, instead of having to learn to relax, you could just flip a switch and relax as fast as possible? **Biofeedback,** *the use of an external monitoring device to obtain information about a bodily function and possibly gain control over that function,* was developed with this goal of high-tech relaxation in mind. You might not be aware right now of whether your fingers are warm or cold, for example, but with an electronic thermometer displayed before you, the ability to sense your temperature might allow you (with a bit of practice) to make your hands warmer or cooler at will (e.g., Roberts & McGrady, 1996).

Biofeedback can help people control physiological functions they are not otherwise aware of. For example, you probably have no idea right now what brain-wave patterns

relaxation therapy A technique for reducing tension by consciously relaxing muscles of the body.

relaxation response A condition of reduced muscle tension, cortical activity, heart rate, breathing rate, and blood pressure.

biofeedback The use of an external monitoring device to obtain information about a bodily function and possibly gain control over that function.

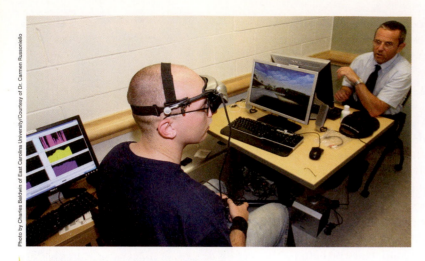

Photo by Charles Baldwin of East Carolina University/Courtesy of Dr. Carmen Russoniello

Biofeedback gives people access to visual or audio feedback showing levels of psychophysiological functions such as heart rate, breathing, brain electrical activity, or skin temperature that they would otherwise be unable to sense directly.

social support The aid gained through interacting with others.

Exercise is helpful for the reduction of stress, unless, like John Stibbard, your exercise involves carrying the Olympic torch on a wobbly suspension bridge over a 70-meter gorge.

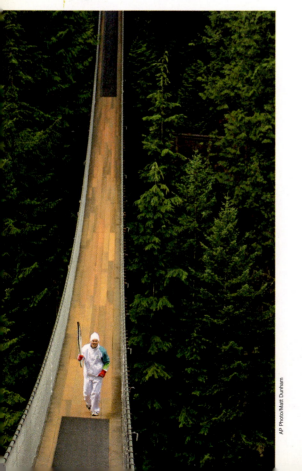

AP Photo/Matt Dunham

you are producing. But people can change their brain waves from alert beta patterns to relaxed alpha patterns and back again when they are permitted to monitor their brains using an electroencephalograph (also called an EEG and discussed in the Neuroscience and Behavior chapter). Often, however, the use of biofeedback to produce relaxation in the brain may not be much more effective than simply having a person stretch out in a hammock and hum a happy tune.

How does biofeedback work?

4. Aerobic Exercise

Studies indicate that *aerobic exercise* (exercise that increases heart rate and oxygen intake for a sustained period) is associated with psychological well-being (Hassmen, Koivula, & Uutela, 2000). In various studies, researchers have randomly assigned people to aerobic exercise activities and no-exercise comparison groups and have found that exercise actually does promote stress relief and happiness. One recent review compiled data from 90 studies, including over 10,000 people with chronic illness who were randomly assigned either to exercise or to a no-exercise condition, and the researchers found that people assigned to the aerobic exercise condition experienced a significant reduction in depressive symptoms (Herring et al., 2012). Another recent review showed that exercise is as effective as the most effective psychological interventions for depression (Rimer et al., 2012). Pretty good effects for a simple, timeless intervention with no side effects!

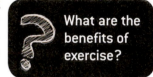

What are the benefits of exercise?

The reasons for these positive effects are unclear. Researchers have suggested that the effects result from increases in the body's production of neurotransmitters such as serotonin, which can have a positive effect on mood (as discussed in the Neuroscience and Behavior chapter) or from increases in the production of endorphins (the endogenous opioids discussed in the Neuroscience and Behavior and Consciousness chapters; Jacobs, 1994). Perhaps the simplest thing you can do to improve your happiness and health, then, is to participate regularly in an aerobic activity: Sign up for a dance class, get into a regular basketball game, or start paddling a canoe—just not all at once!

Situation Management

After you have tried to manage stress by managing your mind and managing your body, what's left to manage? Look around and you'll notice a whole world out there. Situation management involves changing your life situation as a way of reducing the impact of stress on your mind and body.

1. Social Support

The wisdom of the National Safety Council's first rule—"Always swim with a buddy"— is obvious when you're in water over your head, but people often don't realize that the same principle applies whenever danger threatens. Other people can offer help in times of stress. **Social support** is *aid gained through interacting with others*. Good ongoing relationships with friends and family and participation in social activities and religious groups can be as healthy for you as exercising and avoiding smoking (Umberson et al., 2006). Lonely people are more likely than others to be stressed and depressed (Baumeister & Leary, 1995), and they can be more susceptible to illness because of lower-than-normal levels of immune functioning (Kiecolt-Glaser et al., 1984).

Many first-year college students experience something of a crisis of social support. No matter how outgoing and popular they were in high school, newcomers typically find the task of developing satisfying new social relationships quite daunting. Not surprisingly, research shows that students reporting the greatest feelings of isolation also show reduced immune responses to flu vaccinations (Pressman et al., 2005). Time spent getting to know people in new social situations can be an investment in your own health.

The value of social support in protecting against stress may be very different for women and men. The fight-or-flight response to stress may be largely a male reaction; in contrast, the female response to stress is to *tend-and-befriend* by taking care of people and bringing them together (Taylor, 2002). Like men, women respond to stressors with sympathetic nervous system arousal and the release of epinephrine and norepinephrine; but unlike men, they also release *oxytocin,* a hormone secreted by the pituitary gland in pregnant and nursing mothers. In the presence of estrogen, oxytocin triggers social responses: a tendency to seek out social contacts, nurture others, and create and maintain cooperative groups. After a hard day at work, a man may come home frustrated and worried about his job and end up drinking a beer and fuming alone.

A woman under the same type of stress may instead play with her kids or talk to friends on the phone. The tend-and-befriend response to stress may help to explain why women are healthier and have a longer life span than do men. The typical male response amplifies the unhealthy effects of

Why is the hormone oxytocin a health advantage for women?

Women are more likely than men to respond to stress with a "tend-and-befriend" style in which they seek out social contact and cooperative relationships. The commonality of this response may partly explain the success of the television show *Sex and the City,* in which four young women helped one another through many difficult times (the fabulous outfits didn't hurt either).

Culture & Community

Land of the free, home of the . . . stressed? Chances are that you, your parents, grandparents, or someone further back in your family immigrated to the United States. Many families have moved to the United States in pursuit of a better life. Are things immediately better after the move to a new land, or does the process of picking up and moving to a strange land increase stress and lead to negative health consequences?

To answer these questions, researchers used survey data from large representative samples of English-speaking Mexicans residing in either the United States or Mexico to examine rates of anxiety and mood disorders throughout their lives (Breslau et al., 2007). The researchers found that the presence of an anxiety disorder while living in Mexico predicted immigration to the United States (i.e., if you are anxious in Mexico, you are more likely to move to the United States). In addition, moving to the United States increased the likelihood of developing an anxiety or mood disorder—and of having more persistent anxiety. The authors interpreted these results as support for the "acculturation stress" hypothesis, which suggests that living in a foreign culture increases stress (due to trouble with communication, knowledge of local customs, etc.) and decreases social support, which together increase the risk of negative health outcomes. The highest risk of experiencing a mental disorder after moving to the United States was observed for children ages 0–12 years old when they moved, suggesting that this early disruption can be especially difficult. Interestingly, U.S. immigrants have lower levels of mental disorders than people born in the United States (Borges et al., 2011; Breslau & Chang, 2006). So moving to a new country and culture can be very stressful, perhaps in part due to the stress and health levels of those in your new environment.

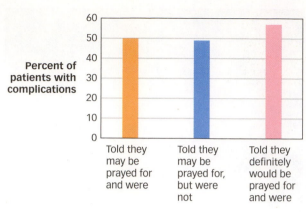

FIGURE 13.3 Pray for me? To test whether praying for individuals in their time of need actually helped them, researchers randomly assigned 1,802 patients about to undergo cardiac bypass surgery to one of three conditions: those told that they may be prayed for and were; those told that they may be prayed for and weren't; and those told that they definitely would be prayed for and were. Unfortunately, there were no differences in the presence of complications between those who were or were not prayed for. To make matters worse, those who knew they would be prayed for and were, in fact, prayed for experienced significantly more complications than the other two groups. [Data from Benson et al., 2006.]

When Andrew Mason, CEO of the Internet company Groupon, left his position, his resignation letter read: "After four and a half intense and wonderful years as CEO of Groupon, I've decided that I'd like to spend more time with my family. Just kidding—I was fired today." He went on to add, "I am so lucky to have had the opportunity to take the company this far with all of you. I'll now take some time to decompress (FYI I'm looking for a good fat camp to lose my Groupon 40, if anyone has a suggestion), and then maybe I'll figure out how to channel this experience into something productive." This seems like a textbook case of using humor to mitigate stress, which is why we put it, um, you know where.

stress, whereas the female response takes a lesser toll on her mind and body and provides social support for the people around her as well.

2. Religious Experiences

Polls indicate that over 90% of Americans believe in God, and most who do, pray at least once per day. Although many who believe in a higher power believe that their faith will be rewarded in an afterlife, it turns out that there may be some benefits here on Earth as well. An enormous body of research found associations between *religiosity* (affiliation with or engagement in the practices of a particular religion), *spirituality* (having a belief in and engagement with some higher power, not necessarily linked to any particular religion), and positive health outcomes, including lower rates of heart disease, decreases in chronic pain, and improved psychological health (Seybold & Hill, 2001).

Why do people who endorse religiosity or spirituality have better mental and physical health? Engagement in religious/spiritual practices, such as attendance at weekly religious services, may lead to the development of a stronger and more extensive social network, which has well-known health benefits. Those who are religious/spiritual also may fare better psychologically and physically as a result of following the healthy recommendations offered in many religious/spiritual teachings. That is, they may be more likely to follow dietary restrictions, restrain from the use of drugs or alcohol, and endorse a more hopeful and optimistic perspective of daily life events, all of which can lead to more positive health outcomes (Seeman, Dubin, & Seeman, 2003; Seybold & Hill, 2001). On balance, many claims made by some religious groups have not been supported, such as the beneficial effects of intercessory prayer (see FIGURE 13.3). Psychologists are actively testing the effectiveness of various religious and spiritual practices with the goal of better understanding how they might help to explain and improve the human condition.

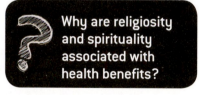
Why are religiosity and spirituality associated with health benefits?

3. Humor

Wouldn't it be nice to laugh at your troubles and move on? Most of us recognize that humor can diffuse unpleasant situations and reduce stress. Is laughter truly the best medicine? Should we close down the hospitals and send in the clowns?

There is a kernel of truth to the theory that humor can help us cope with stress. For example, humor can reduce sensitivity to pain and distress. In one study, participants were more tolerant of the pain from an over-inflated blood pressure cuff during a laughter-inducing comedy audiotape than during a neutral tape or instructed relaxation (Cogan et al., 1987).

Humor can also reduce the time needed to calm down after a stressful event. For example, men viewing a highly stressful film about three industrial accidents were asked to narrate the film aloud, either by describing the events seriously or by making their commentary as funny as possible. Although men in both groups reported feeling tense while watching the film and showed increased levels of sympathetic nervous arousal (increased heart rate and skin conductance, decreased

skin temperature), those looking for humor in the experience bounced back to normal arousal levels more quickly than did those in the serious story group (Newman & Stone, 1996).

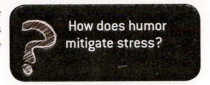

How does humor mitigate stress?

SUMMARY QUIZ [13.3]

1. Meditation is an altered state of consciousness that occurs
   a. with the aid of drugs.
   b. through hypnosis.
   c. naturally or through special practices.
   d. as a result of dreamlike brain activity.

2. Finding a new or creative way to think about a stressor that reduces its threat is called
   a. stress inoculation.
   b. repressive coping.
   c. reframing.
   d. rational coping.

3. The positive health outcomes associated with religiosity and spirituality are believed to be the result of all of the following except
   a. enhanced social support.
   b. engagement in healthier behavior.
   c. endorsement of hope and optimism.
   d. intercessory prayer.

The Psychology of Illness: Mind over Matter

One of the mind's main influences on the body's health and illness is the mind's sensitivity to bodily symptoms. Noticing what is wrong with the body can be helpful when it motivates a search for treatment, but sensitivity can also lead to further problems when it snowballs into a preoccupation with illness that itself can cause harm.

Psychological Effects of Illness

Why does it feel so bad to be sick? You notice scratchiness in your throat or the start of sniffles, and you think you might be coming down with something. And in just a few short hours, you're achy all over, energy gone, no appetite, feverish, feeling dull and listless. You're sick. The question is, why does it have to be like this? As long as you're going to have to stay at home and miss out on things anyway, couldn't sickness be less of a pain?

Sickness makes you miserable for good reason. Misery is part of the *sickness response*, a coordinated, adaptive set of reactions to illness organized by the brain (Hart, 1988; Watkins & Maier, 2005). Feeling sick keeps you home, where you'll spread germs to fewer people. More important, the sickness response makes you withdraw from activity and lie still, conserving the energy for fighting illness that you'd normally

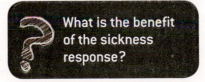

What is the benefit of the sickness response?

expend on other behavior. Appetite loss is similarly helpful: The energy spent on digestion is conserved. Thus, the behavioral changes that accompany illness are not random side effects; they help the body fight disease.

How does the brain know it should do this? The immune response to an infection begins with the activation of white blood cells that "eat" microbes and also release *cytokines,* proteins that circulate through the body (Maier & Watkins, 1998). Cytokines do not enter the brain, but they activate the vagus nerve that runs from the intestines, stomach, and chest to the brain carrying the "I am infected" message (Goehler et al., 2000). Perhaps this is why we often feel sickness in the "gut," a gnawing discomfort in the very center of the body.

Interestingly, the sickness response can be prompted without any infection at all, merely by the introduction of stress. The stressful presence of a predator's odor, for instance, can produce the sickness response of lethargy in an animal, along with symptoms of infection such as fever and increased white blood cell count (Maier & Watkins, 2000). In humans, the connection between sickness response, immune reaction, and stress is illustrated in depression, a condition in which all the sickness machinery runs at full speed. So, in addition to fatigue and malaise, depressed people show signs characteristic of infection, including high levels of cytokines circulating in the blood (Maes, 1995). Just as illness can make you feel a bit depressed, severe depression seems to recruit the brain's sickness response and make you feel ill (Watkins & Maier, 2005).

Recognizing Illness and Seeking Treatment

You probably weren't thinking about your breathing a minute ago, but now that you're reading this sentence, you notice it. Sometimes, we are very attentive to our bodies. At other times, the body seems to be on "automatic," running along unnoticed until specific symptoms announce themselves or are pointed out by an annoying textbook writer.

People differ substantially in the degree to which they attend to and report bodily symptoms. People who report many physical symptoms tend to be negative in other ways as well, describing themselves as anxious, depressed, and under stress (Watson & Pennebaker, 1989). Do people with many symptom complaints truly have a lot of problems, or are they just high-volume complainers? In one study, volunteers underwent several applications of heat (110–120° F) to the leg, and, as you might expect, some of the participants found it more painful than did others. fMRI brain scans during the painful events revealed that the anterior cingulate cortex, somatosensory cortex, and prefrontal cortex (areas known to respond to painful body stimulation) were particularly active in those participants who reported higher levels of pain experience (see **FIGURE 13.4**), suggesting that people can report accurately on the extent to which they experience pain (Coghill, McHaffie, & Yen, 2003).

> **?** What is the relationship between pain and activity in the brain?

In contrast to complainers are those who underreport symptoms and pain or ignore or deny the possibility that they are sick. Insensitivity to symptoms comes with costs: It can delay the search for treatment, sometimes with serious repercussions. Of 2,404 patients in one study who had been treated for a heart attack, 40% had delayed going to the hospital for over 6 hours from the time they first noticed suspicious symptoms (Gurwitz et al., 1997). These people often waited, just hoping the problem would go away, which is not a good idea because many of the treatments that can reduce the

How much does it hurt? Pain is a psychological state that can be difficult to measure. One way to put a number on a pain is to have people judge with reference to the external expression of the internal state.

Faces from Hockenberry MJ, Wilson D: Wong's essentials of pediatric nursing. Ed. 8, St. Louis, 2009, Mosby. Used with permission. Copyright Mosby.

0
No Hurt

1
Hurts
Little Bit

2
Hurts
Little More

3
Hurts
Even More

4
Hurts
Whole Lot

5
Hurts
Worst

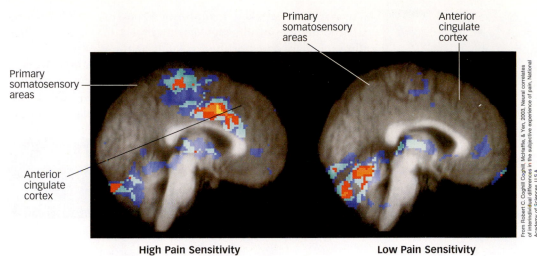

Primary somatosensory areas

Primary somatosensory areas

Anterior cingulate cortex

Anterior cingulate cortex

High Pain Sensitivity

Low Pain Sensitivity

From Robert C. Coghill Coghill, McHaffie, & Yen, 2003, Neural correlates of interindividual differences in the subjective experience of pain, National Academy of Sciences, U.S.A.

FIGURE 13.4 The Brain in Pain These are fMRI scans of brain activation in high- (*left*) and low-pain-sensitive (*right*) individuals during painful stimulation. The anterior cingulate cortex and primary somatosensory areas show greater activation in high-pain-sensitive individuals. Levels of activation are highest in yellow and red, then light blue and dark blue (Coghill, McHaffie, & Yen, 2003).

damage of a heart attack are most useful when provided early. When it comes to your own health, protecting your mind from distress through the denial of illness can result in exposing your body to great danger.

Somatic Symptom Disorders

The flip side of denial is excessive sensitivity to illness, and it turns out that sensitivity also has its perils. Indeed, hypersensitivity to symptoms or to the possibility of illness underlies a variety of psychological problems and can also undermine physical health. Psychologists studying **psychosomatic illness,** *an interaction between mind and body that can produce illness,* explore ways in which mind (*psyche*) can influence body (*soma*) and vice versa. The study of mind–body interactions focuses on psychological disorders called **somatic symptom disorders,** *the set of psychological disorders in which a person with at least one bodily symptom displays significant health-related anxiety, expresses disproportionate concerns about symptoms, and devotes excessive time and energy to symptoms or health concerns.* Such disorders will be discussed further in the Psychological Disorders chapter, but their association with symptoms in the body makes them relevant to this chapter's concern with stress and health.

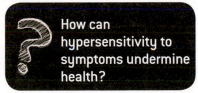

? How can hypersensitivity to symptoms undermine health?

psychosomatic illness An interaction between mind and body that can produce illness.

somatic symptom disorders The set of psychological disorders in which a person with at least one bodily symptom displays significant health-related anxiety, expresses disproportionate concerns about symptoms, and devotes excessive time and energy to symptoms or health concerns.

sick role A socially recognized set of rights and obligations linked with illness.

Have you ever ridden on public transportation while sitting next to a person with a hacking cough? We are bombarded by advertisements for medicines designed to suppress symptoms of illness so we can keep going. Is staying home with a cold socially acceptable or considered malingering? How does this jibe with the concept of the *sick role*?

On Being a Patient

Getting sick is more than a change in physical state: It can involve a transformation of identity. This change can be particularly profound with a serious illness: A kind of cloud settles over you, a feeling that you are now different, and this transformation can influence everything you feel and do in this new world of illness. You even take on a new role in life, a **sick role:** *a socially recognized set of rights and obligations linked with illness* (Parsons, 1975). The sick person is absolved of responsibility for many everyday obligations and enjoys exemption from normal activities. For example, in addition to skipping school and homework and staying on the couch all day, a sick child can watch TV and avoid eating anything unpleasant at dinner. In return for these exemptions, the sick role also incurs obligations. The properly "sick" individual cannot appear to enjoy the illness or reveal signs of wanting to be sick and must also take care to pursue treatment to end this "undesirable" condition.

Some people feign medical or psychological symptoms to achieve something they want, a type of behavior called *malingering.* Because many symptoms of

Image Source/Getty Source

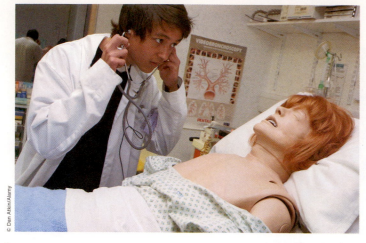

illness cannot be faked, malingering is possible only with a restricted number of illnesses. Faking illness is suspected when the secondary gains of illness, such as the ability to rest, to be freed from performing unpleasant tasks, or to be helped by others, outweigh the costs. Such gains can be very subtle, as when a child stays in bed because of the comfort provided by an otherwise distant parent, or they can be obvious, as when insurance benefits turn out to be a cash award for Best Actor. For this reason, malingering can be difficult to diagnose and treat (Feldman, 2004).

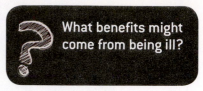

What benefits might come from being ill?

Doctor and patient have two modes of interaction, the technical and the interpersonal. Medical training with robot patients may help doctors learn the technical side of health care, but it is likely to do little to improve the interpersonal side.

Patient–Practitioner Interaction

Medical care usually occurs through a strange interaction. On one side is a patient, often miserable, who expects to be questioned and examined and possibly prodded, pained, or given bad news. On the other side is a health care provider, who hopes to quickly obtain information from the patient by asking lots of extremely personal questions (and examining extremely personal parts of the body); identify the problem and potential solution; help in some way; and achieve all of this as efficiently as possible because more patients are waiting. It seems less like a time for healing than an occasion for major awkwardness. One of the keys to an effective medical care interaction is physician empathy (Spiro et al., 1994). To offer successful treatment, the clinician must simultaneously understand the patient's physical state *and* psychological state. Physicians often err on the side of failing to acknowledge patients' emotions, focusing instead on technical issues of the case (Suchman et al., 1997). This is particularly unfortunate because a substantial percentage of patients who seek medical care do so for treatment of psychological and emotional problems (Taylor, 1986). The best physician treats the patient's mind as well as the patient's body.

Why is it important that a physician express empathy?

FIGURE 13.5 Antacid Intake This graph shows a scatterplot of antacid intake measured by bottle count plotted against patient's stated intake for 116 patients. When the actual and stated intakes are the same, the point lies on the diagonal line; when stated intake is greater than actual, the point lies above the line. Most patients exaggerated their intakes. (Data from Roth & Caron, 1978.)

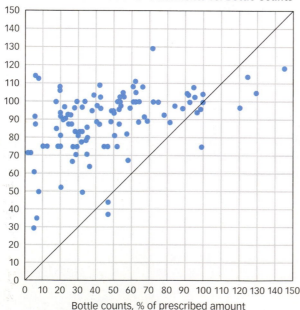

Antacid Intake: Patients' Statements vs. Bottle Counts

Patients' statements, % of prescribed doses

Bottle counts, % of prescribed amount

Another important part of the medical care interaction is motivating the patient to follow the prescribed regimen of care (Miller & Rollnick, 2012). When researchers check compliance by counting the pills remaining in a patient's bottle after a prescription has been underway, they find that patients often do an astonishingly poor job of following doctors' orders (see **FIGURE 13.5**). Compliance deteriorates when the treatment must be *frequent,* as when eyedrops for glaucoma are required every few hours, or *inconvenient* or *painful,* such as drawing blood or performing injections in managing diabetes. Finally, compliance decreases *as the number of treatments increases*. This is a worrisome problem, especially for older patients, who may have difficulty remembering when to take which pill. Failures in medical care may stem from the failure of health care providers to recognize the psychological challenges that are involved in self-care. Helping people to follow doctors' orders involves psychology, not medicine, and is an essential part of promoting health.

SUMMARY QUIZ [13.4]

1. A person who is preoccupied with minor symptoms and believes they signify a life-threatening illness is likely to be diagnosed with
   a. cytokines.
   b. repressive coping.
   c. burnout.
   d. a somatic symptom disorder.

2. Faking an illness is a violation of
   a. malingering.
   b. somatoform disorder.
   c. the sick role.
   d. the Type B pattern of behavior.

3. Which of the following describes a successful health care provider?
   a. displays empathy
   b. pays attention to both the physical and psychological state of the patient
   c. uses psychology to promote patient compliance
   d. all of the above

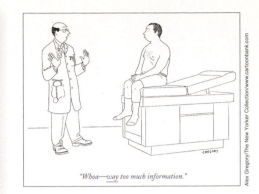

"Whoa—way too much information."

Alex Gregory/The New Yorker Collection/www.cartoonbank.com

The Psychology of Health: Feeling Good

Two kinds of psychological factors influence personal health: health-relevant personality traits and health behavior. Personality can influence health through relatively enduring traits that make some people particularly susceptible to health problems or stress while sparing or protecting others. The Type A behavior pattern is an example. Because personality is not typically something we choose ("I'd like a bit of that sense of humor and extraversion over there, please, but hold the whininess"), this source of health can be outside personal control. In contrast, engaging in positive health behaviors is something anyone can do, at least in principle.

Personality and Health

Different health problems seem to plague different social groups. For example, men are more susceptible to heart disease than are women, and African Americans are more susceptible to asthma than are Asian or European Americans. Beyond these general social categories, personality turns out to be a factor in wellness, with individual differences in optimism and hardiness important influences.

Optimism

An optimist who believes that "in uncertain times, I usually expect the best" is likely to be healthier than a pessimist who believes that "if something can go wrong for me, it will." One recent review of dozens of studies including tens of thousands of participants concluded that of all of the measures of psychological well-being examined, optimism is the one that most strongly predicted a positive outcome for cardiovascular health (Boehm & Kubzansky, 2012). Does just having positive thoughts about the future make it so? Unfortunately not.

Rather than improving physical health directly, optimism seems to aid in the maintenance of *psychological* health in the face of physical health problems. When sick, optimists are more likely than pessimists to maintain positive emotions, avoid negative emotions such as anxiety and depression, stick to medical regimens their

Adrianne Haslet-Davis was approximately four feet away from one of the bombs that exploded at the Boston Marathon in 2013. Although the explosion caused her to lose her left foot, Adrianne vowed that she will continue her career as a dancer. She is an optimist, and optimism can lead to positive health outcomes.

Donna Svennevik/ABC via Getty Images

caregivers have prescribed, and keep up their relationships with others. Optimism also seems to aid in the maintenance of physical health. For instance, optimism appears to be associated with cardiovascular health because optimistic people tend to engage in healthier behaviors like eating a balanced diet and exercising, which in turn decrease the risk of heart disease (Boehm et al., 2013). So being optimistic is a positive asset, but it takes more than just hope to obtain positive health benefits.

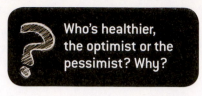

Who's healthier, the optimist or the pessimist? Why?

The benefits of optimism raise an important question: If the traits of optimism and pessimism are stable over time—even resistant to change—can pessimists ever hope to gain any of the advantages of optimism (Heatherton & Weinberger, 1994)? Research has shown that even die-hard pessimists can be trained to become significantly more optimistic and that this training can improve their psychosocial health outcomes. For example, pessimistic breast cancer patients who received 10 weeks of training in stress management techniques became more optimistic and were less likely than those who received only relaxation exercises to suffer distress and fatigue during their cancer treatments (Antoni et al., 2001).

Hardiness

Some people seem to be thick-skinned, somehow able to take stress or abuse that could be devastating to others. Are there personality traits that contribute to such resilience and offer protection from stress-induced illness? In one study, a group of stress-resistant business executives reported high levels of stressful life events but had histories of relatively few illnesses compared with a similar group of executives who succumbed to stress by getting sick (Kosaba, 1979). The stress-resistant group (labeled *hardy*) shared several traits, all conveniently beginning with the letter C. They showed a sense of *commitment,* an ability to become involved in life's tasks and encounters rather than just dabbling. They exhibited a belief in *control,* the expectation that their actions and words have a causal influence over their lives and environments. And they were willing to accept *challenge,* undertaking change and accepting opportunities for growth.

Can anyone develop hardiness? In one study, participants attended 10 weekly hardiness-training sessions, in which they were encouraged to examine their stresses, develop action plans for dealing with them, explore their bodily reactions to stress, and find ways to compensate for unchangeable situations without falling into self-pity. Compared with control groups (whose members engaged in relaxation and meditation training or in group discussions about stress), the participants in the hardiness-training group reported greater reductions in their perceived personal stress as well as fewer symptoms of illness (Maddi, Kahn, & Maddi, 1998). Hardiness training can have similar positive effects in college students—for some, even boosting their GPA (Maddi et al., 2009).

Sometimes, hardiness tips over the edge into foolhardiness. Members of the Coney Island Polar Bear Club take that plunge every Sunday in winter.

AP Photo/Kathy Willens

Health-Promoting Behaviors and Self-Regulation

Even without changing our personalities at all, we can do certain things to be healthy. The importance of healthy eating, safe sex, and giving up smoking are common knowledge. But we don't seem to be acting on the basis of this knowledge. At the turn of the 21st century, 69% of Americans over 20 are overweight or obese (National Center for Health Statistics, 2012). The prevalence of unsafe sex is difficult to estimate, but 20 million Americans contract one or more new sexually transmitted diseases (STDs) each year (Satterwhite et al., 2013). And despite endless warnings, 21% of Americans still smoke cigarettes (Pleis, Lucas, & Ward, 2009). What's going on?

Self-Regulation

Doing what is good for you is not necessarily easy. Engaging in health-promoting behaviors involves **self-regulation,** *the exercise of voluntary control over the self to bring the self into line with preferred standards.* When you decide on a salad rather than a cheeseburger, for instance, you control your impulse and behave in a way that will help to make you the kind of person you would prefer to be—a healthy one. Self-regulation often involves putting off immediate gratification for longer-term gains.

One theory suggests that self-control is a kind of strength that can be fatigued (Baumeister, Heatherton, & Tice, 1995; Baumeister, Vohs, & Tice, 2007). In other words, trying to exercise control in one area may exhaust self-control, leaving behavior in other areas unregulated. To test this theory, researchers seated hungry volunteers near a batch of fresh, hot, chocolate chip cookies. They asked some participants to leave the cookies alone but help themselves to a healthy snack of radishes, whereas others were allowed to indulge. When later challenged with an impossibly difficult figure-tracing task, the participants in the self-control group were more likely than those in the self-indulgent group to abandon the difficult task—suggesting that they had depleted their pool of self-control (Baumeister et al., 1998). The take-home message is that to control behavior successfully, we need to choose our battles, exercising self-control mainly on the personal weaknesses that are most harmful to health.

? Why is it difficult to achieve and maintain self-control?

Jean Sander/Featurepics

Nobody ever said self-control was easy. Probably the only reason you're able to keep yourself from eating this cookie is that it's just a picture of a cookie. Really. Don't eat it.

Eating Wisely

In many Western cultures, the weight of the average citizen is increasing alarmingly. One explanation is based on our evolutionary history: In order to ensure their survival, our ancestors found it useful to eat well in times of plenty in order to store calories for leaner times. In postindustrial societies in the 21st century, however, there are no leaner times, and people can't burn all of the calories they consume (Pinel, Assanand, & Lehman, 2000). But why, then, are people in France leaner on average than Americans even though their foods are high in fat? One reason has to do with the fact that activity level in France is greater. Another is that portion sizes in France are significantly smaller than in the United States, but at the same time, people in France take longer to finish their smaller meals. Right now, Americans seem to be involved in some kind of national eating contest, whereas in France, people are eating less food more slowly, perhaps leading them to be more conscious of what they are eating. This, ironically, probably leads to lower French fry consumption.

Short of moving to France, what can you do? Studies indicate that dieting doesn't always work because the process of conscious self-regulation can be easily undermined by stress, leading people who are trying to control themselves to lose control by overindulging in the very behavior they had been trying to overcome. This may remind you of a general principle discussed in the Consciousness chapter: Trying hard not to do something can often directly produce the unwanted behavior (Wegner, 1994a, 1994b). Rather than dieting, then, heading toward normal weight should involve a new emphasis on exercise and nutrition (Prochaska & Sallis, 2004). In emphasizing what is good to eat, the person can freely think about food rather than trying to suppress thoughts about it. Self-regulation is more effective when it focuses on what to do rather than on what *not* to do (Molden, Lee, & Higgins, 2009; Wegner & Wenzlaff, 1996).

? Why is exercise a more effective weight-loss choice than dieting?

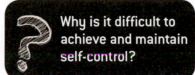

DATA VISUALIZATION

The Relationship Between Stress and Eating Habits
www.macmillanhighered.com/ schacterbrief3e

One of the reasons that people in France are leaner than people in the United States is because the average French diner spends 22 minutes to consume a fast-food meal, whereas the average American diner spends only 15 minutes. How could the length of the average meal influence an individual's body weight?

© Jeff Gilbert/Alamy

Avoiding Sexual Risks

People put themselves at risk when they have unprotected vaginal, oral, or anal intercourse. Sexually active adolescents and adults are usually aware of such risks, not to mention the risk of unwanted pregnancy, and yet many behave in risky ways nonetheless. Why doesn't awareness translate into avoidance? Risk takers harbor an *illusion of unique invulnerability,* a systematic bias toward believing that they are less likely to fall victim to the problem than are others (Perloff & Fetzer, 1986). For example, a study of sexually active female college students found that respondents judged their own likelihood of getting pregnant in the next year as less than 10%, but they estimated the average for other women at the university to be 27% (Burger & Burns, 1988).

Unprotected sex often is the impulsive result of last-minute emotions. When thought is further blurred by alcohol or recreational drugs, people often fail to use the latex condoms that can reduce their exposure to the risks of pregnancy, HIV, and many other STDs. One approach to reducing sexual risk taking, then, is simply finding ways to help people plan ahead. Sex education programs offer adolescents just such a chance by encouraging them, at a time when they have not had much sexual experience, to think about what they might do when they need to make decisions. Although sex education is sometimes criticized as increasing adolescents' awareness of and interest in sex, the research evidence is clear: Sex education reduces the likelihood that adolescents will engage in unprotected sexual activity and benefits their health (American Psychological Association, 2005). The same holds true for adults.

Why does planning ahead reduce sexual risk taking?

Not Smoking

One in two smokers dies prematurely from smoking-related diseases such as lung cancer, heart disease, emphysema, and cancer of the mouth and throat. Although the overall rate of smoking in the United States is declining, new smokers abound, and many can't seem to stop. College students are puffing away along with everyone else, with 20% of college students currently smoking (Thompson et al., 2007). In the face of all the devastating health consequences, why don't people quit?

Nicotine, the active ingredient in cigarettes, is addictive, so smoking is difficult to stop once the habit is established (discussed in the Consciousness chapter). As in other forms of self-regulation, the resolve to quit smoking is fragile and seems to break down under stress. In the months following 9/11, for example, cigarette sales jumped 13% in Massachusetts (Phillips, 2002). And for some time after quitting, ex-smokers remain sensitive to cues in the environment: Eating or drinking, a bad mood, anxiety, or just seeing someone else smoking is enough to make them want a cigarette (Shiffman et al., 1996). The good news is that the urge decreases and people become less likely to relapse the longer they've been away from nicotine.

Psychological programs and techniques to help people kick the habit include nicotine replacement systems such as gum and skin patches, counseling programs, and hypnosis, but these programs are not always successful. Trying again and again in different ways is apparently the best approach (Schachter, 1982). After all, to quit smoking forever, you only need to quit one more time than you start up. But like the self-regulation of eating and sexuality, the self-regulation of smoking can require effort and thought. Keeping healthy by behaving in healthy ways is one of the great challenges of life (see Other Voices box).

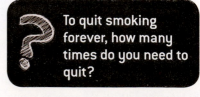

To quit smoking forever, how many times do you need to quit?

"Boy, I'm going to pay for this tomorrow at yoga class."

Freedom to Be Unhealthy?

Robert H. Frank is an economics professor at the Johnson Graduate School of Management at Cornell University.
Bloomberg via Getty Images

In the chapter on Emotion and Motivation, you learned about the health benefits and risks associated with what you eat. In this chapter, you learned that what you do (Do you exercise?) and what you think (Are you an optimist?) also can influence your experience of stress and health. The research is clear that people who eat right and exercise regularly have better mental and physical health outcomes. Is it our business, then, to try to get people to eat better and exercise more?

The former mayor of New York City, Michael Bloomberg, recently advocated for a tax on large, sugary drinks, which has been nick-named the "soda tax." Some have praised this idea, believing that it is our responsibility to structure society in a way that improves the health of our citizens—and especially our children. Others have criticized this initiative, arguing that we live in a free country and people should be free to drink all of the soda and avoid all of the exercise they want. Economist Robert Frank recently weighed in on this issue, considering the pros and cons of a soda tax.

On narrow technical grounds, a New York State court rejected Mayor Michael R. Bloomberg's proposed curbs on large sodas and other sugary drinks. The ruling is being appealed, but many people who viewed the proposal as a step down a slippery slope to a nanny state were quick to celebrate the court's move. Beyond questioning the mayor's legal authority to impose a 16-ounce limit on the size of sugary beverages sold in certain places, critics objected on philosophical grounds, arguing that people should be free to make such choices for themselves.

But while almost everyone celebrates freedom in the abstract, defending one cherished freedom often requires sacrificing another. Whatever the flaws in Mr. Bloomberg's proposal, it sprang from an entirely commendable concern: a desire to protect parents' freedom to raise healthy children.

Being free to do something doesn't just mean being legally permitted to do it. It also means having a reasonable prospect of being able to do it. Parents don't want their children to become obese, or to suffer the grave consequences of diet-induced diabetes. Yet our current social environment encourages heavy consumption of sugary soft drinks, making such outcomes much more likely. So that environment clearly limits parents' freedom to achieve an eminently laudable goal.

The mayor's critics want to protect their own freedom to consume soft drinks in 32-ounce containers. But pro-freedom slogans provide no guidance about what to do when specific freedoms are in conflict, as they are here. Nor do they alert us to the possibility that taxes or other alternative policies often render such tough choices unnecessary. Sensible policy decisions spring less reliably from slogans than from careful assessment of the pros and cons of the relevant alternatives.

Does frequent exposure to supersize sodas really limit parents' freedom to raise healthy children? There's room for skepticism, because people often believe that they're not much influenced by others' opinions and behavior. But believing doesn't make it so.

As an Illinois state legislator in 1842, Abraham Lincoln deftly illustrated the absurdity of this particular conceit: "Let me ask the man who could maintain this position most stiffly, what compensation he will accept to go to church some Sunday and sit during the sermon with his wife's bonnet upon his head?" Most men, Lincoln conjectured, would demand a considerable sum—not because wearing a woman's bonnet would be illegal or immoral, obviously, but just because it would be so unseemly.

Even those who concede the obvious power of the social environment have little reason to worry about how their own choices might alter it. Collectively, however, our choices can profoundly transform the environment, often in ways that cause serious problems. And that makes the social environment an object of legitimate public concern.

Imagine a society like the United States before 1964, where unregulated individual choices produced high percentages of smokers in the population—more than 50 percent among adult men. Not even the staunchest libertarians should deny that their children would be more likely to become smokers in such an environment.

Smokers harm not only themselves and those who inhale secondhand smoke but also those who simply want their children to grow up to be nonsmokers. People can urge their children to ignore peer influences, of course, but that's often a losing battle.

No rational deliberation about smoking policies can ignore the fact that smoking harms others in this way. Such considerations helped give rise to a variety of policies that discourage smoking. In New York City, for example, smoking is no longer permitted in many public places, and state and city taxes on a pack of cigarettes are now near $6.

Such policies have reduced the national smoking rate by more than half since 1965, making it much easier for parents to raise their children to be nonsmokers. That's an enormous benefit. Opponents of smoking restrictions must be prepared to show that those adversely affected by them suffer harm that outweighs that benefit. Given that the overwhelming majority of smokers themselves regret having taken up the habit, that's a tall order.

Parallel arguments apply to sugary drinks. Unless we're prepared to deny, against all evidence, that the environment powerfully influences children's choices, we're forced to conclude that rejecting Mr. Bloomberg's proposal significantly curtails parents' freedom to achieve the perfectly reasonable goal of raising healthy children. Why should opponents of the mayor's proposal be permitted to limit parents' freedom in this way, merely to spare themselves the trivial inconvenience of having to order a second 16-ounce soda?

Fortunately, society's legitimate interest in the social environment needn't be expressed by means of invasive prohibitions. The public policy goal that prompted the mayor's proposal could also be served in more direct and less intrusive ways.

For example, we could tax sugary soft drinks. In 2010, the mayor himself praised a proposal for a penny-per-ounce tax on soda in New York State; the idea was dropped after heavy opposition from the beverage industry.

The case for reintroducing such a proposal is strong. We have to tax something, after all, and taxing soft drinks would let us reduce taxes now imposed on manifestly useful activities. At the federal level, for example, a tax on soda would permit a reduction in the payroll tax, which would encourage businesses to hire more workers.

Just as few smokers are glad that they smoke, few people go to their graves wishing that they and their loved ones had drunk more sugary soft drinks. Evidence suggests that the current high volume of soft-drink consumption has generated enormous social costs. So to those who have lobbied successfully against a soda tax, I pose a simple

question: How do the benefits of your right to drink tax-free sodas outweigh the substantial costs of defending it?

Where do you stand? The research described in this textbook makes clear that healthier eating and behavior lead to better health outcomes—benefiting both the individual and society more generally in the form of greater productivity and lower health costs due to later illness. But does the government really have the right to penalize people for choosing to drink soda and other sugary drinks? On the other hand, does it

really impinge upon people's freedom to be charged a few more cents for drinks that are bad for them (and costlier to society in the form of health expenses)? How should the science of human health and behavior be used to influence actual human health and behavior?

SUMMARY QUIZ [13.5]

1. When sick, optimists are more likely than pessimists to
   a. maintain positive emotions.
   b. become depressed.
   c. ignore their caregiver's advice.
   d. avoid contact with others.

2. Which of the following is NOT a trait associated with hardiness?
   a. a sense of commitment
   b. an aversion to criticism
   c. a belief in control
   d. a willingness to accept challenge

3. Stress _____ the self-regulation of behaviors such as eating and smoking.
   a. strengthens
   b. has no effect on
   c. disrupts
   d. normalizes

CHAPTER REVIEW

SUMMARY

Sources of Stress: What Gets to You

> Stressors are events and threats that place specific demands on a person or threaten well-being.

> Sources of stress include major life events (even happy ones), catastrophic events, and chronic hassles, some of which can be traced to a particular environment.

> Events are most stressful when we perceive that there is no way to control or deal with the challenge.

Stress Reactions: All Shook Up

> The body responds to stress with an initial fight-or-flight reaction, which activates the hypothalamic–pituitary–adrenocortical (HPA) axis and prepares the body to face the threat or run away from it.

> Chronic stress can wear down the immune system, causing susceptibility to infection, aging, tumor growth, organ damage, and death.

> Response to stress varies if the stress is interpreted as something that can be overcome or not.

> The psychological response to stress can, if prolonged, lead to burnout.

Stress Management: Dealing with It

> The management of stress involves strategies for influencing the mind, the body, and the situation.

> Mind management strategies include repressing stressful thoughts or avoiding the situations that produce them, rationally coping with the stressor, and reframing.

> Body management strategies involve attempting to reduce stress symptoms through meditation, relaxation, biofeedback, and aerobic exercise.

> Situation management strategies can involve seeking out social support, engaging in religious experiences, or attempting to find humor in stressful events.

The Psychology of Illness: Mind over Matter

> The psychology of illness concerns how sensitivity to the body leads people to recognize illness and seek treatment.

> Somatic symptom disorders can stem from excessive sensitivity to physical problems.

> The sick role is a set of rights and obligations linked with illness; some people fake illness in order to accrue those rights.

> Successful health care providers interact with their patients to understand both the physical state and the psychological state.

The Psychology of Health: Feeling Good

> The personality traits of optimism and hardiness are associated with reduced risk for illnesses, perhaps because people with these traits can fend off stress.

> The self-regulation of behaviors such as eating, sexuality, and smoking is difficult for many people because self-regulation is easily disrupted by stress.

KEY TERMS

stressors (p. 412)

stress (p. 412)

health psychology (p. 412)

chronic stressor (p. 413)

learned helplessness (p. 415)

fight-or-flight response (p. 416)

general adaptation syndrome (GAS) (p. 416)

telomeres (p. 417)

immune system (p. 418)

Type A behavior pattern (p. 419)

burnout (p. 420)

repressive coping (p. 421)

rational coping (p. 422)

reframing (p. 422)

meditation (p. 422)

relaxation therapy (p. 423)

relaxation response (p. 423)

biofeedback (p. 423)

social support (p. 424)

psychosomatic illness (p. 429)

somatic symptom disorders (p. 429)

sick role (p. 429)

self-regulation (p. 433)

CHANGING MINDS

1. In 2002, researchers compared severe acne in college students during a relatively stress-free period and during a highly stressful exam period. After adjusting for other variables such as changes in sleep or diet, the researchers concluded that increased acne severity was strongly correlated with increased levels of stress. Learning about the study, your roommate is surprised. "Acne is a skin disease," your roommate says. "I don't see how it could have anything to do with your mental state." How would you weigh in on the role of stress in medical diseases? What other examples could you give of ways in which stress can affect health?

2. A friend of yours, who is taking a heavy course load, confides that he's feeling overwhelmed. "I can't take the stress," he says. "Sometimes, I daydream of living on an island somewhere, where I can just lie in the sun and have no stress at all." What would you tell your friend about stress? Is all stress bad? What would a life with no stress really be like?

3. One of your classmates spent the summer interning in a neurologist's office. "One of the most fascinating things," she says, "was the patients with psychosomatic illness. Some had seizures or partial paralysis of an arm, and there were no neurological causes—so it was all psychosomatic. The neurologist tried to refer these patients to psychiatrists, but a lot of the patients thought he was accusing them of faking their symptoms, and they were very insulted." What would you tell your friend about psychosomatic illness? Could a disease that's "all in the head" really produce symptoms such as seizures or partial paralysis, or are these patients definitely faking their symptoms?

ANSWERS TO SUMMARY QUIZZES

Answers to Summary Quiz 13.1: 1. c; 2. b; 3. b.

Answers to Summary Quiz 13.2: 1. b; 2. c; 3. d.

Answers to Summary Quiz 13.3: 1. c; 2. c; 3. d.

Answers to Summary Quiz 13.4: 1. d; 2. c; 3. d.

Answers to Summary Quiz 13.5: 1. a; 2. b; 3. c.

Need more help? Additional resources are located in LaunchPad at:
http://www.worthpublishers.com/launchpad/schacterbrief3e

Psychological Disorders

VIRGINIA WOOLF LEFT HER WALKING STICK ON THE BANK OF THE RIVER, put a large stone in the pocket of her coat, and made her way into the water. Her body was found 3 weeks later. She had written to her husband, "Dearest, I feel certain I am going mad again. . . . And I shan't recover this time. I begin to hear voices, and I can't concentrate. So I am doing what seems the best thing to do" (Dally, 1999, p. 182). Thus life ended for the prolific novelist and essayist, a victim of lifelong "breakdowns," with swings in mood between severe depression and unbridled mania.

The condition afflicting Woolf is now known as bipolar disorder. At one extreme were her episodes of depression: She was sullen and despondent, and she was sometimes bedridden for months. These periods alternated with mania, when, as her husband recounted, "She talked almost without stopping for 2 or 3 days, paying no attention to anyone in the room or anything said to her." Her language "became completely incoherent, a mere jumble of dissociated words." At the height of her spells, birds spoke to her in Greek, her dead mother reappeared and scolded her, and voices commanded her to "do wild things." She refused to eat, wrote pages of nonsense, and launched tirades of abuse at her husband and her companions (Dally, 1999, p. 240). Between these phases, Woolf somehow managed a brilliant literary life, producing nine novels, a play, five volumes of essays, and more than 14 volumes of diaries and letters. In a letter to a friend, she remarked, "As an experience, madness is terrific" (Dally, 1999, p. 240). The price that Woolf paid for her genius, of course, was a dear one. Disorders of the mind can create immense pain.

English novelist and critic, Virginia Woolf (1882–1941), in 1937. Her lifelong affliction with bipolar disorder ended in suicide, but the manic phases of her illness helped to fuel her prolific writing.

mental disorder A persistent disturbance or dysfunction in behavior, thoughts, or emotions that causes significant distress or impairment.

IN THIS CHAPTER, WE FIRST CONSIDER THIS QUESTION: What is abnormal? Virginia Woolf's bouts of depression and mania and her eventual suicide certainly are abnormal in the sense that most people do not have these experiences, but at times, she led a perfectly normal life. The enormously complicated human mind can produce thoughts, emotions, and behaviors that change radically from moment to moment. How do psychologists decide when a person's thoughts, emotions, and behaviors are "disordered?" We will first examine the key factors that must be weighed in making such a decision. We'll then focus on several of the most common *mental disorders*: anxiety, obsessive-compulsive, and trauma-related disorders; depressive and bipolar disorders; schizophrenia; disorders that begin in childhood and adolescence; and self-harm behaviors. As we view each type of disorder, we will examine in turn how it is manifested and what is known about its prevalence and causes. As we'll see in the next chapter, a scientific approach to understanding mental disorders offers some remarkably effective treatments, and for other disorders, it offers hope that pain and suffering can be alleviated in the future.

Defining Mental Disorders: What Is Abnormal?

The concept of a mental disorder seems simple at first glance, but it turns out to be very complex and quite tricky (similar to clearly defining "consciousness," "stress," or "personality"). Any extreme variation in your thoughts, feelings, or behaviors is not a mental disorder. For instance, severe anxiety before a test, sadness after the loss of a loved one, or a night of excessive alcohol consumption are not necessarily pathological. Similarly, a persistent pattern of deviating from the norm does not necessarily qualify a person for the diagnosis of a mental disorder. If it did, we would diagnose mental disorders in the most creative and visionary people—anyone whose ideas deviate from those around them.

So what *is* a mental disorder? Perhaps surprisingly, there is no universal agreement on a precise definition of the term "mental disorder." However, there is general agreement that a **mental disorder** can be defined as *a persistent disturbance or dysfunction in behavior, thoughts, or emotions that causes significant distress or impairment* (Stein et al., 2010; Wakefield, 2007). One way to think about mental disorders is as dysfunctions or deficits in the normal human psychological processes you have learned about throughout this book. People with mental disorders have problems with their perception, memory, learning, emotion, motivation, thinking, and social processes. You might ask: But this is still a broad definition, so what kinds of disturbances "count" as mental disorders? How long must they last to be considered "persistent?" And how much distress or impairment is required? These are all hotly debated questions in the field.

Conceptualizing Mental Disorders

Since ancient times, there have been reports of people acting strangely or reporting bizarre thoughts or emotions. Until fairly recently, such difficulties were interpreted as possession by spirits or demons, as enchantment by a witch or shaman, or as God's

According to the theory of physiognomy, mental disorders could be diagnosed from facial features. This theory is now considered superstition but was popular until the early 20th century.

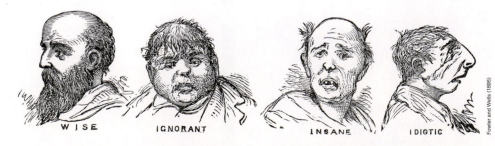

WISE   IGNORANT   INSANE   IDIOTIC

Fowler and Wells (1885)

punishment for wrongdoing. In many societies, including our own, people with psychological disorders have been feared and ridiculed, and often they were treated as criminals who were punished, imprisoned, or put to death for their "crime" of deviating from the normal.

Over the past 200 years, these ways of looking at psychological abnormalities have largely been replaced in most parts of the world by a **medical model,** in which *abnormal psychological experiences are conceptualized as illnesses that, like physical illnesses, have biological and environmental causes, defined symptoms, and possible cures.* Conceptualizing abnormal thoughts and behaviors as illness suggests that a first step is to determine the nature of the problem through *diagnosis.*

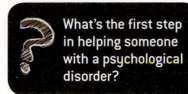

What's the first step in helping someone with a psychological disorder?

In diagnosis, clinicians seek to determine the nature of a person's mental disorder by assessing *signs* (objectively observed indicators of a disorder) and *symptoms* (subjectively reported behaviors, thoughts, and emotions) that suggest an underlying illness. So, for example, just as self-reported sniffles and cough are symptoms of a cold, Virginia Woolf's extreme moods, alternating between despondency and wild euphoria, can be seen as symptoms of her bipolar disorder. It is important to note the differences among three related general medical and classification terms:

> A *disorder* refers to a common set of signs and symptoms.

> A *disease* is a known pathological process affecting the body.

> A *diagnosis* is a determination as to whether a disorder or disease is present (Kraemer, Shrout, & Rubio-Stipec, 2007).

Importantly, knowing that a disorder is present (i.e., diagnosed) does not necessarily mean that we know the underlying disease process in the body that gives rise to the signs and symptoms of the disorder.

Viewing mental disorders as medical problems reminds us that people who are suffering deserve care and treatment, not condemnation. Nevertheless, there are some criticisms of the medical model. Some psychologists argue that it is inappropriate to use clients' subjective self-report, rather than physical tests of pathology (as in other areas of medical diagnostics), to determine underlying illness. Others argue that the

medical model Abnormal psychological experiences are conceptualized as illnesses that, like physical illnesses, have biological and environmental causes, defined symptoms, and possible cures.

Extreme shyness or social anxiety disorder? What are some of the criticisms of the medical model?

Simone Becchetti/Getty Images

Diagnostic and Statistical Manual of Mental Disorders (DSM) A classification system that describes the features used to diagnose each recognized mental disorder and indicates how the disorder can be distinguished from other, similar problems.

comorbidity The co-occurrence of two or more disorders in a single individual.

model often "medicalizes" or "pathologizes" normal human behavior. For instance, extreme sadness can be considered to be an illness called *major depressive disorder*, extreme shyness can be diagnosed as an illness called *social anxiety disorder*, and trouble concentrating in school can be *attention-deficit/hyperactivity disorder*. Although there are some valid concerns about the current method of defining and classifying mental disorders, the medical model inarguably is a huge advance over older alternatives, such as viewing mental disorders as the work of witchcraft or as punishment for sin.

Classifying Disorders: The DSM

So how is the medical model used to classify the wide range of abnormal behaviors that occur among humans? Most people working in the area of mental disorders use a standardized system for classifying mental disorders called the **Diagnostic and Statistical Manual of Mental Disorders (DSM)**, *a classification system that describes the features used to diagnose each recognized mental disorder and indicates how the disorder can be distinguished from other, similar problems.* Each disorder is named and classified as a distinct illness. The initial version of the *DSM*, published in 1952, provided a common language for talking about disorders. This was a major advance in the study of mental disorders; however, the diagnostic criteria listed in these early volumes were quite vague.

Over the decades, revised editions of the *DSM* have moved from vague descriptions of disorders to very detailed lists of symptoms (or *diagnostic criteria*) that had to be present in order for a disorder to be diagnosed. For instance, in addition to being extremely sad or depressed (for at least 2 weeks), a person must have at least five of nine agreed-upon symptoms of depression (e.g., diminished interest in normally enjoyable activities, significant weight loss or gain, significantly increased or decreased sleep, loss of energy, feelings of worthlessness or guilt, trouble concentrating). The use of these detailed lists of symptoms for each of more than 200 disorders listed led to a dramatic increase in the reliability, or consistency, in diagnosing mental disorders. Two clinicians interviewing the same individual were now much more likely to agree on what mental disorders were present, greatly increasing the credibility of the diagnostic process (and the fields of psychiatry and clinical psychology).

In May 2013, the American Psychiatric Association released the newest, fifth edition of the DSM, the *DSM–5*. The *DSM–5* describes 22 major categories containing more than 200 different mental disorders, along with the specific criteria that must be met in order for a person to be diagnosed with that disorder (see **TABLE 14.1**). In addition, there is a section devoted to cultural considerations in diagnosing mental disorders.

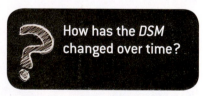
How has the *DSM* changed over time?

Studies of large, representative samples of the U.S. population reveal that approximately half of Americans report experiencing at least one mental disorder during the course of their lives (Kessler, Berglund, et al., 2005). And, most of those with a mental disorder (greater than 80%) report **comorbidity**, which refers to *the co-occurrence of two or more disorders in a single individual* (Gadermann et al., 2012).

Causation of Disorders

The medical model of mental disorder suggests that knowing a person's diagnosis is useful because any given category of mental illness is likely to have a distinctive cause. In other words, just as different viruses, bacteria, or genetic abnormalities cause different physical illnesses, so a specifiable pattern of causes (or *etiology*) may exist for different psychological disorders. The medical model also suggests that each category of mental disorder is likely to have a common *prognosis,* a typical course over time and susceptibility to treatment and cure. Unfortunately, this basic medical model is

DATA VISUALIZATION

Comorbidity: the Relationship Between Related Disorders
www.macmillanhighered.com/
schacterbrief3e

Table 14.1 Main *DSM-5* Categories of Mental Disorders

1. **Neurodevelopmental Disorders:** These are conditions that begin early in development and cause significant impairments in functioning, such as intellectual disability (formerly called "mental retardation"), autism spectrum disorder, and attention-deficient/hyperactivity disorder.

2. **Schizophrenia Spectrum and Other Psychotic Disorders:** This is a group of disorders characterized by major disturbances in perception, thought, language, emotion, and behavior.

3. **Bipolar and Related Disorders:** These disorders include major fluctuations in mood—from mania to depression—and can include psychotic experiences, which is why they are placed between the psychotic and depressive disorders in *DSM-5*.

4. **Depressive Disorders:** These are conditions characterized by extreme and persistent periods of depressive mood.

5. **Anxiety Disorders:** These are disorders characterized by excessive fear and anxiety that are extreme enough to impair a person's functioning, such as panic disorder, generalized anxiety disorder, and specific phobia.

6. **Obsessive-Compulsive and Related Disorders:** These are conditions characterized by the presence of obsessive thinking followed by compulsive behavior in response to that thinking.

7. **Trauma- and Stressor-Related Disorders:** These are disorders that develop in response to a traumatic event, such as posttraumatic stress disorder.

8. **Dissociative Disorders:** These are conditions characterized by disruptions or discontinuity in consciousness, memory, or identity, such as dissociative identity disorders (formerly called "multiple personality disorder").

9. **Somatic Symptom and Related Disorders:** These are conditions in which a person experiences bodily symptoms (e.g., pain or fatigue) associated with significant distress or impairment.

10. **Feeding and Eating Disorders:** These are problems with eating that impair health or functioning, such as anorexia nervosa or bulimia nervosa.

11. **Elimination Disorders:** These involve inappropriate elimination of urine or feces (e.g., bed-wetting).

12. **Sleep-Wake Disorders:** These are problems with the sleep-wake cycle, such as insomnia, narcolepsy, and sleep apnea.

13. **Sexual Dysfunctions:** These are problems related to unsatisfactory sexual activity, such as erectile disorder and premature ejaculation.

14. **Gender Dysphoria:** This is a single disorder characterized by incongruence between a person's experienced/expressed gender and assigned gender.

15. **Disruptive, Impulse-Control, and Conduct Disorders:** These are conditions involving problems controlling emotions and behaviors, such as conduct disorder, intermittent explosive disorder, and kleptomania.

16. **Substance-Related and Addictive Disorders:** This collection of disorders involves persistent use of substances or some other behavior (e.g., gambling) despite the fact that such behavior leads to significant problems.

17. **Neurocognitive Disorders:** These are disorders of thinking caused by conditions such as Alzheimer's disease or traumatic brain injury.

18. **Personality Disorders:** These are enduring patterns of thinking, feeling, and behaving that lead to significant life problems.

19. **Paraphilic Disorders:** These are conditions characterized by inappropriate sexual activity, such as pedophilic disorder.

20. **Other Mental Disorders:** This is a residual category for conditions that do not fit into one of the above categories but that are associated with significant distress or impairment, such as unspecified mental disorder due to a medical condition.

21. **Medication-Induced Movement Disorders and Other Adverse Effects of Medication:** These are problems with physical movement (e.g., tremors, rigidity) that are caused by medication.

22. **Other Conditions that May be the Focus of Clinical Attention:** These include problems related to abuse, neglect, relationship, or other problems.

Source: Information from American Psychiatric Association, 2013.

biopsychosocial perspective Explains mental disorders as the result of interactions among biological, psychological, and social factors.

diathesis–stress model Suggests that a person may be predisposed for a psychological disorder that remains unexpressed until triggered by stress.

Research Domain Criteria Project (RDoC) A new initiative that aims to guide the classification and understanding of mental disorders by revealing the basic processes that give rise to them.

usually an oversimplification; it is rarely useful to focus on a *single cause* that is *internal* to the person and that suggests a *single cure*.

Instead, most psychologists take an integrated **biopsychosocial perspective** that *explains mental disorders as the result of interactions among biological, psychological, and social factors.* On the biological side, the focus is on genetic and epigenetic influences, biochemical imbalances, and abnormalities in brain structure and function. The psychological perspective focuses on maladaptive learning and coping, cognitive biases, dysfunctional attitudes, and interpersonal problems. Social factors include poor socialization, stressful life experiences, and cultural and social inequities. The complexity of causation suggests that different individuals can experience a similar mental disorder (e.g., depression) for different reasons. A person might fall into depression as a result of biological causes (e.g., genetics, hormones), psychological causes (e.g., faulty beliefs, hopelessness, poor strategies for coping with loss), environmental causes (e.g., stress or loneliness), or more likely as a result of some combination of these factors. And, of course, multiple causes mean there may not be a single cure.

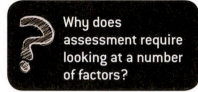

Why does assessment require looking at a number of factors?

Culture & Community

What do mental disorders look like in different parts of the world? Are the mental disorders that we see in the United States also experienced by people in other parts of the world? In an effort to find out, Ronald Kessler and colleagues launched the World Health Organization World Mental Health Surveys, a large-scale study in which people from nearly two dozen countries around the world were assessed for the presence of mental disorders (Kessler & Üstün, 2008). The study revealed that the major mental disorders seen in the United States—such as depression, anxiety, attention-deficit/hyperactivity disorder, and substance use—appear similarly in countries and cultures all around the world. Such disorders are reported at different rates in different countries (people in the United States reported the highest rates of mental disorders), but depression and anxiety are always the most common, followed by impulse-control and substance use disorders (Kessler et al., 2007).

Although all countries appear to have the common mental disorders described above, it is clear that cultural context can influence how mental disorders are experienced, described, assessed, and treated. To address this issue, the *DSM–5* includes a cultural formulation section that contains a Cultural Formulation Interview (CFI). The CFI includes 16 questions that the clinician asks a client during a mental health assessment in order to help the clinician understand how the client's culture might influence the experience, expression, and explanation of the person's mental disorder.

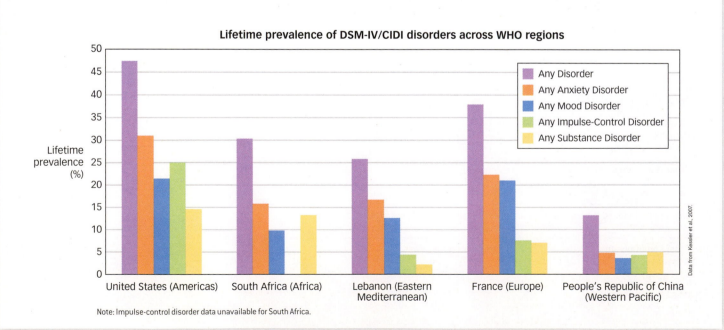

Lifetime prevalence of DSM-IV/CIDI disorders across WHO regions

Data from Kessler et al., 2007.

Note: Impulse-control disorder data unavailable for South Africa.

The observation that most disorders have both internal (biological and psychological) *and* external (environmental) causes has given rise to a theory known as the **diathesis–stress model,** which *suggests that a person may be predisposed for a psychological disorder that remains unexpressed until triggered by stress.* The diathesis is the internal predisposition, and the stress is the external trigger. For example, most people were able to cope with their strong emotional reactions to the terrorist attack of September 11, 2001. However, for some who had a predisposition to negative emotions, the horror of the events may have overwhelmed the person's ability to cope, thereby precipitating a psychological disorder. Although diatheses can be inherited, it's important to remember that heritability is not destiny. A person who inherits a diathesis may never encounter the precipitating stress, whereas someone with little genetic propensity to a disorder may still come to suffer from such a disorder given the right pattern of stress.

Terry Schmidbauer/Getty Images

Mental disorders can be caused by biological, psychological, and environmental factors. The diathesis–stress model suggests that a person may be predisposed for a psychological disorder that remains unexpressed until triggered by stress. Suppose that two identical twins (with the same genetic profile) grow up in the same household (sharing the same parents, the same basic diet, the same access to television, and so on). As a teenager, one twin but not the other develops a mental disorder such as schizophrenia. How could this be?

A New Approach to Understanding Mental Disorders: RDoC

Although the *DSM* provides a useful framework for classifying disorders, there has been a growing concern that the findings from scientific research on the factors that cause psychopathology do not map neatly onto individual *DSM* diagnoses. In order to better understand what actually causes mental disorders, researchers at the National Institutes of Mental Health (NIMH) have proposed a new framework for thinking about mental disorders, one that is focused not on the currently defined *DSM* categories of disorders, but on the basic biological, cognitive, and behavioral processes (or "constructs") that are believed to be the building blocks of mental disorders. This new system is called the **Research Domain Criteria Project (RDoC),** *a new initiative that aims to guide the classification and understanding of mental disorders by revealing the basic processes that give rise to them.* The RDoC is intended not to immediately replace the *DSM* but to inform future revisions to it in the coming years. Using the RDoC, researchers focus on biological domains, such as arousal and sleep patterns; and psychological domains, such as learning, attention, and memory; and social domains, such as attachment and self-perception (see **TABLE 14.2** for a list of domains). Each of these domains can be approached by studying various "units of analysis"— from genes, to cells, to behavior, as shown in the columns of the table.

Through the RDoC approach, the NIMH would like to shift researchers away from studying currently defined *DSM* categories and toward the study of the dimensional biopsychosocial processes believed, at the extreme end of the continuum, to lead to mental disorders. The long-term goal is to better understand what abnormalities cause different disorders, and to classify disorders based on those underlying causes, rather than on observed symptoms. This approach would bring the study of mental disorders in line with the study of other medical disorders. For example, if you are experiencing chest pain, severe headaches, fatigue, and difficulty breathing, it is unlikely that you are experiencing four separate disorders (*chest pain disorder, headache disorder,* etc.). Instead, we now know that these are all symptoms of an underlying disease process called hypertension. The RDoC approach similarly aims to shift the focus away from classifying based on surface symptoms and toward an understanding of the processes that give rise to disordered behavior. For instance, rather than studying cocaine addiction as a distinct disorder, from an RDoC perspective, researchers might try to understand what causes abnormalities in "responsiveness to reward," a factor seen in those with excessive cocaine use as well as those with other addictive behaviors. Indeed, recent research has shown that variations in a gene (*DRD2*) that codes for dopamine receptors are associated with abnormalities in connectivity between parts

The new Research Domain Criteria are trying to help us better understand why people seem to have "addictive personalities" in which they have trouble limiting their engagement in pleasurable experiences.

FStop/Superstock

Table 14.2 Draft Research Domain Criteria (RDoC) Matrix

Domain / construct	Units of Analysis							
	Genes	Molecules	Cells	Circuits	Physiology	Behavior	Self-reports	Paradigms
Negative Valence Systems								
Acute threat ("fear")								
Potential threat ("anxiety")								
Sustained threat								
Loss								
Frustrative nonreward								
Positive Valence Systems								
Approach motivation								
Initial responsiveness to reward								
Sustained responsiveness to reward								
Reward learning								
Habit								
Cognitive Systems								
Attention								
Perception								
Working memory								
Declarative memory								
Language behavior								
Cognitive (effortful) control								
Systems for Social Processes								
Affiliation and attachment								
Social communication								
Perception and understanding of self								
Perception and understanding of others								
Arousal and Regulatory Systems								
Arousal								
Circadian rhythms								
Sleep and wakefulness								

Gene Chromosome Chromatin DNA

Jeff Greenberg/Getty Images

of the frontal lobe and the striatum (described in the Neuroscience and Behavior chapter). This lack of connectivity is, in turn, related to the impulsiveness and responsiveness to rewards associated with a range of addictive behavior disorders (Buckholtz & Meyer-Lindenberg, 2012). This may help explain why some people seem to have addictive personalities in which they have trouble inhibiting their reward-seeking behavior, which in turn could predispose a person to develop drug addiction. Importantly, understanding what processes cause problems like addiction will help us to develop more effective treatments, a topic we address in more detail in the next chapter.

You might notice that the list of domains in Table 14.2 looks like a slightly more detailed version of the table of contents for this book! The RDoC approach has an overall emphasis on neuroscience (Chapter 3), with specific focuses on abnormalities in emotional and motivational systems (Chapter 8), cognitive systems such as memory (Chapter 6), learning (Chapter 7), language and cognition (Chapter 9), social processes (Chapter 12), and stress and arousal (Chapter 13). From the RDoC perspective, mental disorders can be thought of as the result of abnormalities or dysfunctions in normal psychological processes. By learning about many of these processes in this book, you will likely have a good understanding of new definitions of mental disorders as they are developed in the years ahead.

Dangers of Labeling

An important complication in the diagnosis and classification of psychological disorders is the effect of labeling. Psychiatric labels can have negative consequences because many labels carry the baggage of negative stereotypes and stigma, such as the idea that mental disorder is a sign of personal weakness or the idea that psychiatric patients are dangerous. The stigma associated with mental disorders may explain why most people with diagnosable psychological disorders (approximately 60%) do not seek treatment (Kessler, Demler, et al., 2005; Wang, Berglund, et al., 2005).

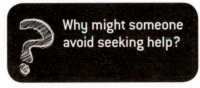
Why might someone avoid seeking help?

Unfortunately, educating people about mental disorders does not dispel the stigma borne by those with these conditions (Phelan et al., 1997). In fact, expectations created by psychiatric labels can sometimes even compromise the judgment of mental health professionals (Garb, 1998; Langer & Abelson, 1974; Temerlin & Trousdale, 1969). In a classic demonstration of this phenomenon, researchers reported to different mental hospitals complaining of "hearing voices," a symptom sometimes found in people with schizophrenia. Each was admitted to a hospital, and each promptly reported that the symptom had ceased. Even so, hospital staff were reluctant to identify these people as normal: It took an average of 19 days for these "patients" to secure their release, and even then they were released with the diagnosis of "schizophrenia in remission" (Rosenhan, 1973). Apparently, once hospital staff had labeled these patients as having a psychological disease, the label stuck.

Labeling may even affect how labeled individuals view themselves; persons given such a label may come to view themselves not just as mentally disordered, but as hopeless or worthless. Such a view may cause them to develop an attitude of defeat and, as a result, to fail to work toward their own recovery. As one small step toward counteracting such consequences, clinicians have adopted the important practice of applying labels to the disorder and not to the person with the disorder. For example, an individual might be described as "a person with schizophrenia," not as "a schizophrenic." You'll notice that we follow this convention in the text.

Although we label mental disorders, we should not apply those labels to people. For instance, rather than saying someone "is ADHD," we would say that the person currently meets diagnostic criteria for ADHD.

iStockphoto/Thinkstock

SUMMARY QUIZ [14.1]

1. The conception of psychological disorders as diseases that have symptoms and possible cures is referred to as
   a. the medical model.
   b. physiognomy.
   c. the root syndrome framework.
   d. a diagnostic system.

2. The *DSM–5* is best described as a

   a. medical model.

   b. classification system.

   c. set of theoretical assumptions.

   d. collection of physiological definitions.

3. Comorbidity of disorders refers to

   a. symptoms stemming from internal dysfunction.

   b. the relative risk of death arising from a disorder.

   c. the co-occurrence of two or more disorders in a single individual.

   d. the existence of disorders on a continuum from normal to abnormal.

4. The RDoC aims to

   a. provide evidence for the disorders currently listed in the *DSM-5*.

   b. shift researchers from focusing on a symptom-based classification of mental disorders to a focus on underlying processes that may lead to mental disorders.

   c. prevent the negative consequences of labeling individuals with mental disorders.

   d. help researchers better describe the observed symptoms of mental disorders.

anxiety disorder The class of mental disorder in which anxiety is the predominant feature.

phobic disorders Disorders characterized by marked, persistent, and excessive fear and avoidance of specific objects, activities, or situations.

specific phobia A disorder that involves an irrational fear of a particular object or situation that markedly interferes with an individual's ability to function.

social phobia A disorder that involves an irrational fear of being publicly humiliated or embarrassed.

preparedness theory The idea that people are instinctively predisposed toward certain fears.

Anxiety Disorders: When Fear Takes Over

"Okay, time for a pop quiz that will be half your grade for this class." If your instructor had actually said that, you would probably have experienced a wave of anxiety and dread. Your reaction would not be a sign that you have a mental disorder. In fact, situation-related anxiety is normal and adaptive: in this case, perhaps by reminding you to keep up with your textbook assignments so you are prepared for pop quizzes. But when anxiety arises that is out of proportion to real threats and challenges, it is maladaptive: It can take hold of people's lives, stealing their peace of mind and undermining their ability to function normally.

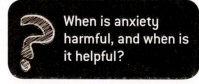 When is anxiety harmful, and when is it helpful?

Pathological anxiety is expressed as an **anxiety disorder,** *the class of mental disorder in which anxiety is the predominant feature.* Among the anxiety disorders recognized in the *DSM–5* are phobic disorders, panic disorder, and generalized anxiety disorder.

Phobic Disorders

Mary, a 47-year-old mother of three, sought treatment for *claustrophobia*—an intense fear of enclosed spaces. She traced her fear to childhood, when her older siblings would scare her by locking her in closets and confining her under blankets. She wanted to find a job but could not do so because of a terror of elevators and other confined places that, she felt, shackled her to her home (Carson, Butcher, & Mineka, 2000). Many people feel a little anxious in enclosed spaces, but Mary's fears were abnormal and dysfunctional because they were disproportionate to any actual risk and impaired her ability to carry out a normal life. The *DSM–5* describes **phobic disorders** as *disorders characterized by marked, persistent, and excessive fear and avoidance of specific objects, activities, or situations.* An individual with a phobic disorder recognizes that the fear is irrational but cannot prevent it from interfering with everyday functioning.

A **specific phobia** is *a disorder that involves an irrational fear of a particular object or situation that markedly interferes with an individual's ability to func-*

tion. Specific phobias fall into five categories: (1) animals (e.g., dogs, cats, rats, snakes, spiders); (2) natural environments (e.g., heights, darkness, water, storms); (3) situations (e.g., bridges, elevators, tunnels, enclosed places); (4) blood, injections, and injury; and (5) other phobias, including choking or vomiting; and in children, loud noises or costumed characters. Approximately 12% of people in the United States will develop a specific phobia during their lives (Kessler, Berglund, et al., 2005), with rates slightly higher among women than men (Kessler et al., 2012).

Social phobia is *a disorder that involves an irrational fear of being publicly humiliated or embarrassed.* Social phobia can be restricted to situations such as public speaking, eating in public, or urinating in a public bathroom or generalized to a variety of social situations that involve being observed or interacting with unfamiliar people. Individuals with social phobia try to avoid situations in which unfamiliar people might evaluate them, and such individuals experience intense anxiety and distress when public exposure is unavoidable. Social phobia can develop in childhood, but it typically emerges between early adolescence and early adulthood (Kessler, Berglund, et al., 2005). About 12% of men and 14% of women qualify for a diagnosis of social phobia at some time in their lives (Kessler et al., 2012).

Why are phobias so common? The high rates of both specific and social phobias suggest a predisposition to be fearful of certain objects and situations. Indeed, most of the situations and objects of people's phobias could pose a real threat—for example, falling from a high place or being attacked by a vicious dog or poisonous snake or spider. Social situations have their own dangers. A roomful of strangers could form impressions that affect your prospects for friends, jobs, or marriage. And of course, in some very rare cases, they could attack or bite.

Observations such as these are the basis for the **preparedness theory** of phobias, which is *the idea that people are instinctively predisposed toward certain fears* (Seligman, 1971). The preparedness theory is supported by research showing that

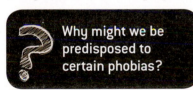

Why might we be predisposed to certain phobias?

both humans and monkeys can quickly be conditioned to have a fear response for stimuli such as snakes and spiders, but not for neutral stimuli such as flowers or toy rabbits (Cook & Mineka, 1989; Öhman, Dimberg, & Öst, 1985). Similarly, research on facial expressions has shown that people are more easily conditioned to fear angry facial expressions than other types of expressions (Öhman, 1996; Woody & Nosen, 2008). Phobias are particularly likely to form for objects that evolution has predisposed us to avoid.

Neurobiological factors may also play a role. Abnormalities in the neurotransmitters serotonin and dopamine are more common in individuals who report phobias than among people who don't (Stein, 1998). In addition, individuals with phobias sometimes show abnormally high levels of activity in the amygdala, an area of the brain linked with the development of emotional associations (discussed in the chapter on Emotion and Motivation and in Stein, Chavira, & Jang, 2001). Interestingly, although people with social phobia report feeling much more distressed than those without social phobia during tasks involving social evaluation (such as giving a speech), they are actually no more physiologically aroused than others (Jamieson, Nock, & Mendes, 2013). This suggests that social phobia may be due to a person's subjective

Phobias are anxiety disorders that involve excessive and persistent fear of a specific object, activity, or situation. Some phobias may be learned through classical conditioning, in which a conditioned stimulus (CS) that is paired with an anxiety-evoking unconditioned stimulus (US) itself comes to elicit a conditioned fear response (CR). Suppose your friend has a phobia of dogs that is so intense that he is afraid to go outside in case one of his neighbors' dogs barks at him. Using the principles of classical conditioning that you learned in the Learning chapter, how might you help him overcome his fear?

The preparedness theory explains why most merry-go-rounds carry children on beautiful horses. This mom might have some trouble getting her daughter to ride on a big spider or snake.

panic disorder A disorder characterized by the sudden occurrence of multiple psychological and physiological symptoms that contribute to a feeling of stark terror.

agoraphobia A specific phobia involving a fear of public places.

generalized anxiety disorder (GAD) A disorder characterized by chronic excessive worry accompanied by three or more of the following symptoms: restlessness, fatigue, concentration problems, irritability, muscle tension, and sleep disturbance.

experience of the situation rather than an abnormal physiological stress response to such situations.

This evidence does not rule out the influence of environments and upbringing on the development of phobic overreactions. As learning theorist John Watson (1924) demonstrated many years ago, phobias can be classically conditioned (see the discussion of Little Albert and the white rat in the Learning chapter). Similarly, the discomfort of a dog bite could create a conditioned association between dogs and pain, resulting in an irrational fear of all dogs. The idea that phobias are learned from emotional experiences with feared objects, however, is not a complete explanation for the occurrence of phobias. Most studies find that people with phobias are no more likely than people without phobias to recall personal experiences with the feared object that could have provided the basis for classical conditioning (Craske, 1999; McNally & Steketee, 1985). Moreover, many people are bitten by dogs, but few develop phobias. Despite its shortcomings, however, the idea that this is a matter of learning provides a useful model for therapy (see the Treatment chapter).

Panic Disorder

Wesley, a 20-year-old college student, began having panic attacks with increasing frequency, often two or three times a day. The attacks began with a sudden wave of "intense, terrifying fear" that seemed to come out of nowhere, often accompanied by dizziness, a tightening of the chest, and the thought that he was going to pass out or possibly die. Wesley finally decided to come in for treatment because he had begun to avoid buses, trains, and public places for fear that he would have an attack like this and not be able to escape.

Wesley's condition, called **panic disorder,** is *a disorder characterized by the sudden occurrence of multiple psychological and physiological symptoms that contribute to a feeling of stark terror.* The acute symptoms of a panic attack typically last only a few minutes and include shortness of breath, heart palpitations, sweating, dizziness, depersonalization (a feeling of being detached from one's body) or derealization (a feeling that the external world is strange or unreal), and a fear that one is going crazy or about to die. Not surprisingly, panic attacks often send people rushing to emergency rooms or their physicians' offices for what they believe are heart attacks. Unfortunately, because many of the symptoms mimic various medical disorders, a correct diagnosis may take years in spite of costly medical tests that produce normal results (Katon, 1994). According to the *DSM–5* diagnostic criteria, people should be diagnosed with panic disorder only if they experience recurrent unexpected attacks and report significant anxiety about having another attack.

A common complication of panic disorder is **agoraphobia,** *a specific phobia involving a fear of public places.* Many people with agoraphobia, including Wesley, are not frightened of public places in themselves; instead, such individuals are afraid of having a panic attack *in* a public place. In severe cases, people who have panic disorder with agoraphobia are unable to leave home, sometimes for years.

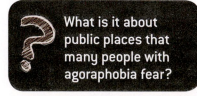

What is it about public places that many people with agoraphobia fear?

Approximately 22% of the U.S. population reports having had at least one panic attack (Kessler, Chiu, et al., 2006), typically during a period of intense stress (Telch, Lucas, & Nelson, 1989). An occasional episode is not sufficient for a diagnosis of panic disorder: The individual also has to experience significant dread and anxiety about having another attack. When this criterion is applied, approximately 5% of people will have diagnosable panic disorder sometime in their lives (Kessler, Berglund, et al., 2005). Panic disorder is more prevalent among women (7%) than men (3%; Kessler et al., 2012).

In panic disorder with agoraphobia, the fear of having a panic attack in public may prevent the person from going outside.

Barbara Stitzer/Photoedit

People who experience panic attacks may be hypersensitive to physiological signs of anxiety, which they interpret as having disastrous consequences for their well-being. Supporting this cognitive explanation is research showing that people who are high in anxiety sensitivity (i.e., they believe that bodily arousal and other symptoms of anxiety can have dire consequences) have an elevated risk for experiencing panic attacks (Olatunji & Wolitzky-Taylor, 2009). Thus, panic attacks may be conceptualized as a "fear of fear" itself.

Generalized Anxiety Disorder

Gina, a 24-year-old woman, began to experience debilitating anxiety during her first year of graduate school for clinical psychology. At first, she worried about whether she was sufficiently completing all of her assignments, then she worried about whether her clients were improving or if she was actually making them worse. Soon her concerns spread to focus on her health (did she have an undiagnosed medical problem?) as well as that of her boyfriend (he smokes cigarettes…is he giving himself cancer?). She worried incessantly for a year and ultimately took time off from school to get treatment for her worries, extreme agitation, fatigue, and feelings of sadness and depression.

Gina's symptoms are typical of **generalized anxiety disorder (GAD)**—called *generalized* because the unrelenting worries are not focused on any particular threat. GAD is *a disorder characterized by chronic excessive worry accompanied by three or more of the following symptoms: restlessness, fatigue, concentration problems, irritability, muscle tension, and sleep disturbance.* In people suffering from GAD, the uncontrollable worrying produces a sense of loss of control that can so erode self-confidence that simple decisions seem fraught with dire consequences. For example, Gina struggled to make everyday decisions as basic as which vegetables to buy at the market and how to prepare her dinner.

Approximately 6% of people in the United States suffer from GAD at some time in their lives (Kessler, Berglund, et al., 2005), with women experiencing GAD at higher rates (8%) than men (5%; Kessler et al., 2012). Biological explanations of GAD suggest that neurotransmitter imbalances may play a role in the disorder. Although the precise nature of this imbalance is not clear, *benzodiazepines* (a class of sedative drugs discussed in the Treatment chapter) that appear to stimulate the neurotransmitter *gamma-aminobutyric acid (GABA)* can sometimes reduce the symptoms of GAD, suggesting a potential role for this neurotransmitter in the occurrence of GAD. Psychological explanations focus on anxiety-provoking situations that produce high levels of GAD. The condition is especially prevalent among people who have low incomes, are living in large cities, and/or are in environments rendered unpredictable by political and economic strife. Research shows that unpredictable traumatic experiences in childhood increase the risk of developing GAD (Torgensen, 1986). Risk of GAD also increases following the experience of a loss, such as the loss of a home due to foreclosure (McLaughlin et al., 2012). Still, many people who might be expected to develop GAD don't, supporting the diathesis–stress notion that personal vulnerability must also be a key factor in this disorder.

What factors contribute to GAD?

The experience of major stressful life events, such as losing a job or home, can lead to generalized anxiety disorder, a condition characterized by chronic, excessive worry.

Sturti/Getty Images

SUMMARY QUIZ [14.2]

1. Irrational worries and fears that undermine one's ability to function normally are an indication of
   a. a genetic abnormality.
   b. dysthymia.
   c. diathesis.
   d. an anxiety disorder.

2. A(n) _____ disorder involves anxiety tied to a specific object or situation.
   a. generalized anxiety
   b. environmental
   c. panic
   d. phobic

3. Agoraphobia often develops as a result of
   a. preparedness theory.
   b. obsessive-compulsive disorder.
   c. panic disorder.
   d. social phobia.

Obsessive-Compulsive Disorder: Trapped in a Loop

You may have had the experience of having an irresistible urge to go back to check whether you actually locked the door or turned off the oven, even when you're pretty sure that you did. Or you may have been unable to resist engaging in some superstitious behavior, such as wearing your lucky shirt on a date or to a sporting event. In some people, such thoughts and actions spiral out of control and become a serious problem.

Karen, a 34-year-old with four children, sought treatment after several months of experiencing intrusive, repetitive thoughts in which she imagined that one or more of her children were having a serious accident. In addition, an extensive series of protective counting rituals hampered her daily routine. For example, when grocery shopping, Karen had the feeling that if she selected the first item (say, a box of cereal) on a shelf, something terrible would happen to her oldest child. If she selected the second item, some unknown disaster would befall her second child, and so on for the four children. For example, if she drank one cup of coffee, she felt compelled to drink four more to protect her children from harm. She acknowledged that her counting rituals were irrational, but she became extremely anxious when she tried to stop (Oltmanns, Neale, & Davison, 1991). Karen's preoccupation with numbers extended to other activities, most notably, the pattern in which she smoked cigarettes and drank coffee.

Karen's symptoms are typical of **obsessive-compulsive disorder (OCD),** a disorder *in which repetitive, intrusive thoughts (obsessions) and ritualistic behaviors (compulsions) designed to fend off those thoughts interfere significantly with an individual's functioning.* Anxiety plays a role in this disorder because the obsessive thoughts typically produce anxiety, and the compulsive behaviors are performed to reduce it. In OCD, these obsessions and compulsions are intense, frequent, and experienced as irrational and excessive. Attempts to cope with the obsessive thoughts by trying to suppress or ignore them are of little or no benefit. In fact (as discussed in the

obsessive-compulsive disorder (OCD)
A disorder in which repetitive, intrusive thoughts (obsessions) and ritualistic behaviors (compulsions) designed to fend off those thoughts interfere significantly with an individual's functioning.

Consciousness chapter), thought suppression can backfire, increasing the frequency and intensity of the obsessive thoughts (Wegner, 1989; Wenzlaff & Wegner, 2000). Despite anxiety's role, in *DSM–5*, OCD is classified separately from anxiety disorders because this disorder and the anxiety disorders are believed to have distinct causes and to be maintained via different neural circuitries in the brain.

> **?** How effective is willful effort at curing OCD?

Although 28% of adults in the United States report experiencing obsessions or compulsions at some point in their lives (Ruscio et al., 2010), only 2% will develop actual OCD (Kessler, Berglund, et al., 2005). Similar to anxiety disorders, rates of OCD are higher among women than men (Kessler et al., 2012). Although compulsive behavior is always excessive, it can vary considerably in intensity and frequency. For example, fear of contamination may lead to 15 minutes of hand washing in some individuals, whereas others may need to spend hours with disinfectants and extremely hot water, scrubbing their hands until they bleed.

The obsessions that plague individuals with OCD typically derive from concerns that could pose a real threat (such as contamination or disease), which supports preparedness theory. Thinking repeatedly about whether we've left a stove burner on when we leave the house makes sense, after all, if we want to return to a house that is not "well done." The concept of preparedness places OCD in the same evolutionary context as phobias (Szechtman & Woody, 2006). However, as with phobias, fears that may have served an evolutionary purpose become distorted and maladaptive.

Researchers have not determined the biological mechanisms that may contribute to OCD (Friedlander & Desrocher, 2006), but one hypothesis implicates heightened neural activity in the caudate nucleus of the brain, a portion of the basal ganglia (discussed in the Neuroscience and Behavior chapter) known to be involved in the initiation of intentional actions (Rappoport, 1990). Drugs that inhibit the activity of the caudate nucleus can relieve some of the symptoms of obsessive-compulsive disorder (Hansen et al., 2002). However, this finding does not indicate that overactivity of the caudate nucleus is the cause of OCD. It could also be an effect of the disorder: People with OCD often respond favorably to psychotherapy and show a corresponding reduction in activity in the caudate nucleus (Baxter et al., 1992).

AP Photo/Charles Sykes

Howie Mandel is a successful comedian, but his struggle with OCD is no laughing matter. Like approximately 2% of people in the United States, Mandel struggles with extreme fears of being contaminated by germs and engages in repeated checking and cleaning behaviors that often interfere with his daily life. He has spoken publicly about his struggles with OCD and about the importance of seeking effective treatment for this condition.

SUMMARY QUIZ [14.3]

1. Kelly's fear of germs leads her to wash her hands repeatedly throughout the day, often for a half hour or more, under extremely hot water. From which disorder does Kelly likely suffer?

   a. panic attacks

   b. obsessive-compulsive disorder

   c. phobia

   d. generalized anxiety disorder

Posttraumatic Stress Disorder: Troubles after a Trauma

Psychological reactions to stress can lead to a class of mental disorders that the *DSM-5* categorizes as "Trauma- and Stress-Related Disorders." For example, a person who lives through a terrifying and uncontrollable experience may develop **posttraumatic**

posttraumatic stress disorder (PTSD)
A disorder characterized by chronic physiological arousal, recurrent unwanted thoughts or images of the trauma, and avoidance of things that call the traumatic event to mind.

The traumatic events of war leave many debilitated by PTSD. But because PTSD is an invisible wound that is difficult to diagnose with certainty, the Pentagon has decided that psychological casualties of war are not eligible for the Purple Heart—the hallowed medal given to those wounded or killed by enemy action (Alvarez & Eckholm, 2009).

stress disorder (PTSD), *a disorder characterized by chronic physiological arousal, recurrent unwanted thoughts or images of the trauma, and avoidance of things that call the traumatic event to mind.*

Psychological scars left by traumatic events are nowhere more apparent than in war. Many soldiers returning from combat will experience symptoms including flashbacks of battle, exaggerated anxiety and startle reactions, and even medical conditions that do not arise from physical damage (e.g., paralysis or chronic fatigue). Most of these symptoms are normal, appropriate responses to horrifying events, and for most people, the symptoms subside with time. In PTSD, the symptoms can last much longer. For example, approximately 12% of U.S. veterans of recent operations in Iraq met criteria for PTSD after their deployment (Keane, Marshall, & Taft, 2006). The effects of PTSD are now recognized not only among the victims, witnesses, and perpetrators of war, but also among ordinary people who are traumatized by terrible events in civilian life. About 7% of Americans are estimated to suffer from PTSD at some time in their lives (Kessler, Berglund, et al., 2005).

Not everyone who is exposed to a traumatic event develops PTSD, suggesting that people differ in their degree of sensitivity to trauma. Research using brain imaging techniques has identified important neural correlates of PTSD. Specifically, those with PTSD show heightened activity in the amygdala (a region associated with the evaluation of threatening information and fear

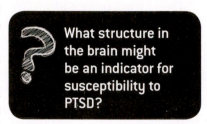

What structure in the brain might be an indicator for susceptibility to PTSD?

conditioning), decreased activity in the medial prefrontal cortex (a region important in the extinction of fear conditioning), and a smaller sized hippocampus (the part of the brain most linked with memory, as described in the Memory chapter; Shin, Rauch, & Pitman, 2006). Of course, an important question is whether people whose brains have these characteristics are at greater risk for PTSD if traumatized, or if these are the consequences of trauma in some people. For instance, does reduced hippocampal volume reflect a preexisting condition that makes the brain sensitive to stress, or does the traumatic stress itself somehow kill hippocampal cells? One important study suggests that although a group of combat veterans with PTSD showed reduced hippocampal volume, so did the identical (monozygotic) twins of those men (see **FIGURE 14.1**), even though the twins had never had any combat exposure or developed PTSD (Gilbertson et al., 2002). This suggests that the veterans' reduced hippocampal volumes weren't caused by the combat exposure; instead, both these veterans and their twin brothers might have had a smaller hippocampus to begin with, a preexisting condition that made them susceptible to developing PTSD when they were later exposed to trauma.

FIGURE 14.1 Hippocampal Volumes of Vietnam Veterans and Their Identical Twins Average hippocampal volumes for four groups of participants: (1) combat-exposed veterans who developed PTSD; (2) their combat-unexposed twins with no PTSD themselves; (3) combat-exposed veterans who never developed PTSD; and (4) their unexposed twins, also with no PTSD. Smaller hippocampal volumes were found both for the combat-exposed veterans with PTSD (Group 1) and their twins who had not been exposed to combat (Group 2) in comparison to veterans without PTSD (Group 3) and their twins (Group 4). This pattern of findings suggests that an inherited smaller hippocampus may make some people sensitive to conditions that cause PTSD (Gilbertson et al., 2002).

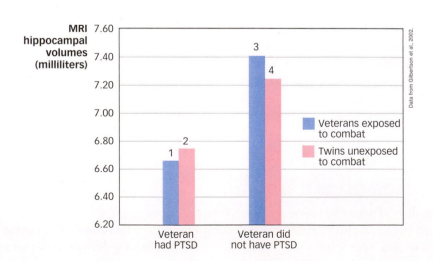

SUMMARY QUIZ [14.4]

1. Which of the below is not a symptom of PTSD?
   a. chronic physiological arousal
   b. avoidance of things or places that might serve as reminders of the traumatic event
   c. recurrent, intrusive thoughts about the traumatic event
   d. impaired acquisition of conditioned fear responses

mood disorders Mental disorders that have mood disturbance as their predominant feature.

major depressive disorder (or unipolar depression) A disorder characterized by a severely depressed mood and/or inability to experience pleasure that lasts 2 or more weeks and is accompanied by feelings of worthlessness, lethargy, and sleep and appetite disturbance.

seasonal affective disorder (SAD) Recurrent depressive episodes in a seasonal pattern.

Depressive and Bipolar Disorders: At the Mercy of Emotions

You're probably in a mood right now. Maybe you're happy that it's almost time to get a snack or saddened by something you heard from a friend. As you learned in the Emotion and Motivation chapter, moods are relatively long-lasting, nonspecific emotional states—and *nonspecific* means we often may have no idea what has caused a mood. Changing moods lend variety to our experiences. However, for Virginia Woolf and others with mood disorders, moods can become so intense that such individuals are pulled or pushed into life-threatening actions. **Mood disorders** are *mental disorders that have mood disturbance as their predominant feature* and take two main forms: *depression* (also called *unipolar depression*) and *bipolar disorder* (so named because people go from one end of the emotional pole [extreme depression] to the other [extreme mania]).

Depressive Disorders

Mark, a 34-year-old, visited his primary care physician complaining of difficulties falling asleep and staying asleep that left him chronically tired, so much so that he feared maybe he had some kind of medical problem. Over the past 6 months, he no longer had the energy to exercise and had gained 10 pounds. He also lost all interest in going out with his friends or even talking to other people. Nothing he normally enjoyed, even sexual activity, gave him pleasure anymore; he had trouble concentrating and was forgetful, irritable, impatient, and frustrated. Mark's change in mood and behavior as well as the sense of hopelessness and weariness he felt goes far beyond normal sadness. Instead, depressive disorders are dysfunctional, chronic, and fall outside the range of socially or culturally expected responses.

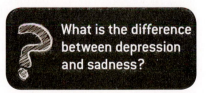

What is the difference between depression and sadness?

Major depressive disorder (or **unipolar depression),** which we refer to here simply as "depression," is *a disorder characterized by a severely depressed mood and/ or inability to experience pleasure that lasts 2 or more weeks and is accompanied by feelings of worthlessness, lethargy, and sleep and appetite disturbance.* Some people experience *recurrent depressive episodes in a seasonal pattern,* commonly known as **seasonal affective disorder (SAD)**. In most cases, the episodes begin in fall or winter and remit in spring, and this pattern is due to reduced levels of light over the colder seasons (Westrin & Lam, 2007). Nevertheless, recurrent summer depressive episodes have been reported. A winter-related pattern of depression appears to be more prevalent in higher latitudes.

Approximately 18% of people in the United States meet criteria for depression at some point in their lives (Kessler et al., 2012). On average, major depression lasts

Seasonal affective disorder is not merely having the blues because of the weather. It appears to be due to reduced exposure to light in the winter months.

© ARCTIC IMAGES/Alamy

Postpartum depression can strike women out of the blue, often causing new mothers to feel extreme sadness, guilt, and disconnection, and even to experience serious thoughts of suicide. Actress Brooke Shields wrote about her experience with postpartum depression in a popular book.

FIGURE 14.2 Gene × Environment Interactions in Depression Stressful life experiences are much more likely to lead to later depression among those with one short—and especially two short—alleles of the serotonin transporter gene. Those with two long alleles (long alleles are associated with more efficient serotonergic functioning) showed no increased risk of depression, even those who experienced severe maltreatment.

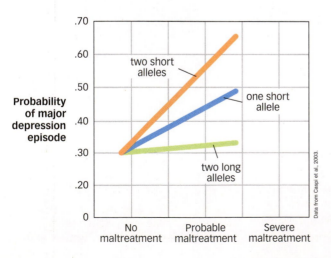

about 12 weeks (Eaton et al., 2008). However, without treatment, approximately 80% of individuals will experience at least one recurrence of the disorder (Judd, 1997; Mueller et al., 1999).

Much like the anxiety disorders, the rate of depression is much higher in women (22%) than in men (14%; Kessler et al., 2012). Socioeconomic standing has been invoked as an explanation for women's heightened risk: Their incomes are lower than those of men, and poverty could cause depression. Sex differences in hormones are another possibility: Estrogen, androgen, and progesterone influence depression; some women experience *postpartum depression* (depression following childbirth) due to changing hormone balances. It is also possible that the higher rate of depression in women reflects greater willingness by women to face their depression and seek out help, leading to higher rates of diagnosis (Nolen-Hoeksema, 2008).

Biological Factors

Beginning in the 1950s, researchers noticed that drugs that increased levels of the neurotransmitters norepinephrine and serotonin could sometimes reduce depression. This observation suggested that depression might be caused by depletion of these neurotransmitters (Schildkraut, 1965), leading to the development and widespread use of such prescription drugs as Prozac and Zoloft, which increase the availability of serotonin in the brain. Further research has shown, however, that reduced levels of these neurotransmitters cannot be the whole story regarding the causes of depression. For example, some studies have found *increases* in norepinephrine activity among depressed individuals (Thase & Howland, 1995). Moreover, even though the antidepressant medications change neurochemical transmission in less than a day, they typically take at least 2 weeks to relieve depressive symptoms and are not effective in decreasing depressive symptoms in many cases. A biochemical model of depression has yet to be developed that accounts for all the evidence.

Newer biological models of depression have tried to explain depression using a diathesis–stress framework. For instance, stressful life events are much more likely to lead to depression among those with a certain genetic trait (vulnerability) related to the activity of the neurotransmitter serotonin (Caspi et al., 2003): a finding showing that nature and nurture interact to influence brain structure, function, and chemistry in depression (see **FIGURE 14.2**).

Psychological Factors

If optimists see the world through rose-colored glasses, people who suffer with depression tend to view the world through dark gray lenses. Their negative cognitive style is remarkably consistent and, some argue, begins in childhood with experiences that create a pattern of negative self-thoughts (Blatt & Homann, 1992; Gibb, Alloy, & Tierney, 2001). One of the first theorists to emphasize the role of thought in depression, Aaron T. Beck (1967), noted that his depressed patients distorted perceptions of their experiences and embraced dysfunctional attitudes that promoted and maintained negative mood states. His observations led him to develop a *cognitive model of depression*, which states that biases in how information is attended to, processed, and remembered lead to and maintain depression.

Elaborating on this initial idea, researchers proposed a theory of depression that emphasizes the role of people's negative inferences about the causes of their experiences (Abramson, Seligman, & Teasdale, 1978). **Helplessness theory,** which is a part of the cognitive model of depression, is *the idea that individuals who are prone to depression automatically attribute negative experiences to causes that are internal (i.e., their own fault), stable (i.e., unlikely to change), and global (i.e., widespread).* For example, a student at risk for depression might view

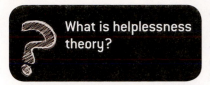

What is helplessness theory?

a bad grade on a math test as a sign of low intelligence (internal) that will never change (stable) and that will lead to failure in all his or her future endeavors (global). In contrast, a student without this tendency might have the opposite response, attributing the grade to something external (poor teaching), unstable (a missed study session), and/or specific (boring subject).

More recent research suggests that people with depression may have biases to interpret information negatively, coupled with better recall of negative information and trouble turning their attention away from negative information (Gotlib & Joormann, 2010). For example, a student at risk for depression who got a bad grade on a test might interpret a well-intentioned comment from the teacher ("Good job on the test") negatively ("She's being sarcastic!"), have trouble forgetting about both the test score and the perceived negative comment, and have a better memory about this test in the future ("Sure, I did well on my English exam, but don't forget about that bad math test last month"). These cognitive biases may reflect differences in brain structure and function. For instance, people with depression show abnormalities in parts of the brain involved in attention and memory, especially when presented with negative information (Disner et al., 2011). Although we don't fully understand the causes of depression, pieces of the puzzle are being discovered as you read this.

The cognitive model of depression is based on approaches used by Greek philosophers nearly 2,000 years ago. Epictetus's famous quote, "Men are disturbed not by things, but by the principles and notions which they form concerning things," is commonly cited as a guiding principle of the cognitive model of depression.

Bipolar Disorder

Julie, a 20-year-old college sophomore, had gone 5 days without sleep, was extremely active, and expressed bizarre thoughts and ideas. She proclaimed to friends that she did not menstruate because she was "of a third sex, a gender above the two human sexes." She claimed to be a "superwoman," capable of avoiding human sexuality and yet still able to give birth. She felt that she had switched souls with the senior senator from her state, had tapped into his thoughts and memories, and could save the world from nuclear destruction. She began to campaign for an elected position in the U.S. government (even though no elections were scheduled at that time). Worried that she would forget some of her thoughts, she had been leaving hundreds of notes about her ideas and activities everywhere, including on the walls and furniture of her dormitory room (Vitkus, 1999).

In addition to her manic episodes, Julie (like Woolf) had a history of depression. The diagnostic label for this constellation of symptoms is **bipolar disorder,** *a condition characterized by cycles of abnormal, persistent high mood (mania) and low mood (depression).* The depressive phase of bipolar disorder is often clinically indistinguishable from major depression (Johnson, Cuellar, & Miller, 2009). In the manic phase, which must last at least 1 week to meet *DSM* requirements, mood can be elevated, expansive, or irritable. Other prominent symptoms include grandiosity, decreased need for sleep, talkativeness, racing thoughts, distractibility, and reckless behavior (such as compulsive gambling, sexual indiscretions, and unrestrained spending sprees). Psychotic features such as hallucinations (erroneous perceptions) and delusions (erroneous beliefs) may be present, so the disorder can be misdiagnosed as schizophrenia (described in a later section).

Here's how Kay Redfield Jamison (1995, p. 67) described her own experience with bipolar disorder in *An Unquiet Mind: A Memoir of Moods and Madness.*

> There is a particular kind of pain, elation, loneliness, and terror involved in this kind of madness. When you're high it's tremendous. The ideas and feelings are fast and frequent like shooting stars, and you follow them until you find better and brighter ones . . . . But, somewhere, this changes. The fast ideas are far too fast, and there are far too many; overwhelming confusion replaces clarity. Memory goes. Humor and absorption on friends' faces are replaced by fear and concern. Everything previously moving with the grain is now against—you are irritable, angry, frightened, uncontrollable, and enmeshed totally

helplessness theory The idea that individuals who are prone to depression automatically attribute negative experiences to causes that are internal (i.e., their own fault), stable (i.e., unlikely to change), and global (i.e., widespread).

bipolar disorder A condition characterized by cycles of abnormal, persistent high mood (mania) and low mood (depression).

Basso Cannarsa / LUZphoto/Redux

Psychologist Kay Redfield Jamison has written several best-selling books about her own struggles with bipolar disorder.

in the blackest caves of the mind. You never knew those caves were there. It will never end, for madness carves its own reality.

The lifetime risk for bipolar disorder is about 2.5% and does not differ between men and women (Kessler et al., 2012). Bipolar disorder is typically a recurrent condition, with approximately 90% of afflicted people suffering from several episodes over a lifetime (Coryell et al., 1995). About 10% of people with bipolar disorder have *rapid cycling bipolar disorder,* characterized by at least four mood episodes (either manic or depressive) every year, and this form of the disorder is particularly difficult to treat (Post et al., 2008). Rapid cycling is more common in women than in men and is sometimes precipitated by taking certain kinds of antidepressant drugs (Liebenluft, 1996; Whybrow, 1997). Unfortunately, bipolar disorder tends to be persistent. In one study, 24% of the participants had relapsed within 6 months of recovery from an episode, and 77% had at least one new episode within 4 years of recovery (Coryell et al., 1995).

Some have suggested that people with psychotic and mood (especially bipolar) disorders have higher creativity and intellectual ability (Andreasen, 2011). In bipolar disorder, the suggestion goes, before the mania becomes too pronounced, the energy, grandiosity, and ambition that it supplies may help people achieve great things. In addition to Virginia Woolf, notable individuals thought to have had the disorder include Isaac Newton, Vincent Van Gogh, Abraham Lincoln, Ernest Hemingway, Winston Churchill, and Theodore Roosevelt.

Biological Factors

Like most other mental disorders, bipolar disorder is most likely *polygenic,* arising from the interaction of multiple genes that combine to create the symptoms observed in those with this disorder; however, these genes have been difficult to identify. Adding to the complexity, there also is evidence that common genetic risk factors are associated with bipolar disorder and schizophrenia, as well as with major depression, autism spectrum disorder, and attention-deficit/hyperactivity disorder. These disorders share overlapping symptoms such as problems with mood regulation, cognitive impairments, and social withdrawal (Cross-Disorder Group of the Psychiatric Genomics Consortium, 2013). Findings like these are exciting because they help us begin to understand why we see similar symptoms in people with what we previously thought were unrelated disorders. In RDoC terms, the genes identified in this study probably don't code for any specific mental disorder; instead they probably code for one or more of the traits that are common across these disorders. This is an example of focusing on the underlying mechanism, and associated psychological trait can be more useful than focusing on *DSM-5* defined disorders.

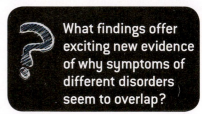

What findings offer exciting new evidence of why symptoms of different disorders seem to overlap?

There is growing evidence that the epigenetic changes you learned about in the Neuroscience and Behavior chapter can help to explain how genetic risk factors influence the development of bipolar and related disorders. Remember how rat pups whose moms spent less time licking and grooming them experienced epigenetic changes that led to a poorer stress response? These same kinds of epigenetic effects seem to occur in humans who develop symptoms of mental disorders. For instance, studies examining monozygotic twin pairs (identical twins who share 100% of their DNA) in which one develops bipolar disorder or schizophrenia and one doesn't, reveal significant epigenetic differences between the two, particularly at genetic locations known to be important in brain development and the occurrence of bipolar disorder and schizophrenia (Dempster et al., 2011; Labrie, Pai, & Petronis, 2012).

Psychological Factors

Stressful life experiences often precede manic and depressive episodes (Johnson, Cuellar, et al., 2008). One study found that severely stressed individuals took an average of three times longer to recover from an episode than did individuals not affected by stress (Johnson & Miller, 1997). Personality characteristics such as neuroticism and conscientiousness have also been found to predict increases in bipolar symptoms over time (Lozano & Johnson, 2001). Finally, people living with family members high on **expressed emotion,** which in this context is *a measure of how much hostility, criticism, and emotional overinvolvement are used when speaking about a family member with a mental disorder*, are more likely to relapse than people with supportive families (Miklowitz & Johnson, 2006). This is true not just of those with bipolar disorder: Expressed emotion is associated with higher rates of relapse across a wide range of mental disorders (Hooley, 2007).

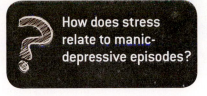

How does stress relate to manic-depressive episodes?

expressed emotion A measure of how much hostility, criticism, and emotional overinvolvement are used when speaking about a family member with a mental disorder.

SUMMARY QUIZ [14.5]

1. Major depression is characterized by a severely depressed mood that lasts at least

   a. 2 weeks.

   b. 1 week.

   c. 1 month.

   d. 6 months.

2. Extreme mood swings between _____ characterize bipolar disorder.

   a. depression and mania

   b. stress and lethargy

   c. anxiety and arousal

   d. obsessions and compulsions

Schizophrenia and Other Psychotic Disorders: Losing the Grasp on Reality

Margaret, a 39-year-old mother, believed that God was punishing her for marrying a man she did not love and bringing two children into the world. As her punishment, God had made her and her children immortal so that they would have to suffer in their unhappy home life forever—a realization that came to her one evening when she was washing dishes and saw a fork lying across a knife in the shape of a cross. Margaret found further support for her belief in two pieces of evidence: First, a local television station was rerunning old episodes of *The Honeymooners,* a 1950s situation comedy in which the main characters often argue and shout at each other. She saw this as a sign from God that her own marital conflict would go on forever. Second, she believed (falsely) that the pupils of her children's eyes were fixed in size and would neither dilate nor constrict—a sign of their immortality. At home, she would lock herself in her room for hours and sometimes days. The week before her diagnosis, she kept her 7-year-old son home from school so that he could join her and his 4-year-old sister in reading aloud from the Bible (Oltmanns, Neale, & Davison, 1991). Margaret was suffering from the most well-known and widely studied psychotic disorder: schizophrenia. Schizophrenia is one of the most mystifying and devastating of all the mental disorders.

Dreamworks/Universal/The Kobal Collection/Eli Reed

Those suffering from schizophrenia often experience hallucinations and delusions, and they are unable to determine what is real and what has been created by their own minds. The experience of John Nash, a Nobel Prize–winning economist with schizophrenia, was depicted in the book and movie *A Beautiful Mind*.

schizophrenia A psychotic disorder characterized by the profound disruption of basic psychological processes; a distorted perception of reality; altered or blunted emotion; and disturbances in thought, motivation, and behavior.

positive symptoms Thoughts and behaviors present in schizophrenia but not seen in those without the disorder, such as delusions and hallucinations.

hallucinations False perceptual experiences that have a compelling sense of being real despite the absence of external stimulation.

delusions Patently false beliefs, often bizarre and grandiose, that are maintained in spite of their irrationality.

disorganized speech A severe disruption of verbal communication in which ideas shift rapidly and incoherently among unrelated topics.

grossly disorganized behavior Behavior that is inappropriate for the situation or ineffective in attaining goals, often with specific motor disturbances.

catatonic behavior A marked decrease in all movement or an increase in muscular rigidity and overactivity.

Symptoms and Types of Schizophrenia

Schizophrenia is *a psychotic disorder* (*psychosis* is a break from reality) *characterized by the profound disruption of basic psychological processes; a distorted perception of reality; altered or blunted emotion; and disturbances in thought, motivation, and behavior.* Traditionally, schizophrenia was regarded primarily as a disturbance of thought and perception, in which the sense of reality becomes severely distorted and confused. However, this condition is now understood to take different forms affecting a wide range of functions. According to the *DSM–5*, schizophrenia is diagnosed when two or more symptoms emerge during a continuous period of at least 1 month with signs of the disorder persisting for at least 6 months. The symptoms of schizophrenia often are separated into *positive, negative,* and *cognitive symptoms.*

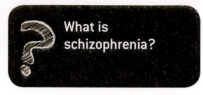

Positive symptoms of schizophrenia include *thoughts and behaviors not seen in those without the disorder,* such as:

> **Hallucinations** are *false perceptual experiences that have a compelling sense of being real despite the absence of external stimulation.* These can include hearing, seeing, smelling, or having a tactile sensation of things that are not there. Among people with schizophrenia, some 65% report hearing voices repeatedly (Frith & Fletcher, 1995). The voices typically command, scold, suggest bizarre actions, or offer snide comments. One individual reported a voice saying, "He's getting up now. He's going to wash. It's about time" (Frith & Fletcher, 1995).

> **Delusions** are *patently false beliefs, often bizarre and grandiose, that are maintained in spite of their irrationality.* For example, an individual with schizophrenia may believe that he or she is Jesus Christ, Napoleon, Joan of Arc, or some other well-known person. Such delusions of identity have helped foster the misconception that schizophrenia involves multiple personalities. However, adopted identities in schizophrenia do not alternate, exhibit amnesia for one another, or otherwise "split." Delusions of persecution are also common. Some individuals believe that the CIA, demons, extraterrestrials, or other malevolent forces are conspiring to harm them or control their minds, which may represent an attempt to make sense of the tormenting delusions (Roberts, 1991). People with schizophrenia have little or no insight into their disordered perceptual and thought processes (Karow et al., 2007). Without understanding that they have lost control of their own minds, they may develop unusual beliefs and theories that attribute control to external agents.

> **Disorganized speech** is *a severe disruption of verbal communication in which ideas shift rapidly and incoherently among unrelated topics.* The abnormal speech patterns in schizophrenia reflect difficulties in organizing thoughts and focusing attention. For example, asked by her doctor, "Can you tell me the name of this place?" one patient with schizophrenia responded, "I have not been a drinker for 16 years. I am taking a mental rest after a 'carter' assignment of 'quill.' You know, a 'penwrap.' I had contracts with Warner Brothers Studios and Eugene broke phonograph records but Mike protested" (Carson, Butcher, & Mineka, 2000, p. 474).

> **Grossly disorganized behavior** is *behavior that is inappropriate for the situation or ineffective in attaining goals, often with specific motor disturbances.* An individual might exhibit constant childlike silliness, improper sexual behavior (such as masturbating in public), disheveled appearance, or loud shouting or swearing. Specific motor disturbances might include strange movements, rigid posturing, odd mannerisms, bizarre grimacing, or hyperactivity. **Catatonic behavior** is *a marked decrease in all movement or an increase in muscular rigidity and overactivity.* Individuals with *catatonia* may actively resist movement (when

What is schizophrenia?

someone is trying to move them) or become completely unresponsive and un-aware of their surroundings in a *catatonic stupor*. In addition, individuals receiving drug therapy may exhibit motor symptoms (such as rigidity or spasm) as a side ef-fect of the medication. Indeed, the *DSM–5* includes a diagnostic category labeled *medication-induced movement disorders* that identifies motor disturbances arising from the use of medications of the sort commonly used to treat schizophrenia.

Negative symptoms of schizophrenia are *deficits or disruptions to normal emotions and behaviors*. They include emotional and social withdrawal; apathy; poverty of speech; and other indications of the absence or insufficiency of normal behavior, motivation, and emotion. These symptoms refer to things missing in people with schizophrenia. **Cognitive symptoms** of schizophrenia are *deficits in cognitive abilities, specifically in executive functioning, attention, and working memory*. These are the most difficult symptoms to notice because they are much less bizarre and public than the positive and negative symptoms. However, these cognitive deficits often play a large role in terms of preventing people with schizophrenia from achieving a high level of func-tioning, such as maintaining friendships and holding down a job (Green et al., 2000).

Schizophrenia occurs in about 1% of the population (Jablensky, 1997) and is slightly more common in men than in women (McGrath et al., 2008). Recent studies suggest that schizophrenia rarely develops before early adolescence (Rapoport et al., 2009). Despite its relatively low frequency, schizophrenia is the primary diagnosis for nearly 40% of all admissions to state and county mental hospitals (Rosenstein, Milazzo-Sayre, & Manderscheid, 1990). The disproportionate rate of hospitalization for schizophrenia is a testament to the devastation it causes in people's lives.

negative symptoms Deficits or disruptions to normal emotions and behaviors (e.g., emotional and social withdrawal; apathy; poverty of speech; and other indications of the absence or insufficiency of normal behavior, motivation, and emotion).

cognitive symptoms Deficits in cognitive abilities, specifically in executive functioning, attention, and working memory.

Biological Factors

Over the years, accumulating evidence for the role of biology in schizophrenia has come from studies of genetic factors, biochemical factors, and neuroanatomy. Fam-ily studies indicate that the closer a person's genetic relatedness to a person with schizophrenia, the greater the likelihood of developing the disor-der (Gottesman, 1991), as shown in **FIGURE 14.3**. Although genetics clearly have a strong predispos-ing role in schizophrenia, considerable evidence

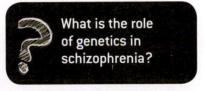

What is the role of genetics in schizophrenia?

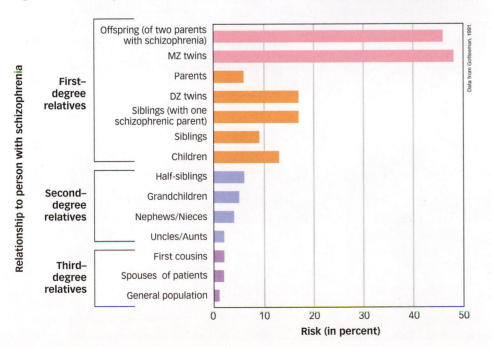

Data from Gottesman, 1991.

FIGURE 14.3 Average Risk of Developing Schizophrenia The risk of schizophrenia among biological relatives is greater for those with greater degrees of relatedness. An identical (MZ) twin of a twin with schizophrenia has a 48% risk of developing schizophrenia, for example, and offspring of two parents with schizophrenia have a 46% risk of developing the disorder.

dopamine hypothesis The idea that schizophrenia involves an excess of dopamine activity.

suggests that environmental factors also play a role (Jurewicz, Owen, & O'Donovan, 2001; Thaker, 2002; Torrey et al., 1994). For example, because approximately 70% of identical twins share the same prenatal blood supply, toxins in the mother's blood could contribute to the high concordance rate. More recent studies (discussed in the earlier section on bipolar disorder) are contributing to a better understanding of how environmental stressors can trigger epigenetic changes that increase susceptibility to this disorder.

Another advance came during the 1950s, when it was discovered that drugs that lower levels of the neurotransmitter dopamine could reduce the symptoms of schizophrenia. This finding suggested the **dopamine hypothesis,** *the idea that schizophrenia involves an excess of dopamine activity.* The hypothesis has been invoked to explain why amphetamines, which increase dopamine levels, often exacerbate symptoms of schizophrenia (Murray et al., 2013).

If only things were so simple. Considerable evidence suggests that this hypothesis is inadequate (Moncrieff, 2009). For example, many individuals with schizophrenia do not respond favorably to dopamine-blocking drugs, and those who do seldom show a complete remission of symptoms. Moreover, the drugs block dopamine receptors very rapidly, yet individuals with schizophrenia typically do not show a beneficial response for weeks. Finally, research has implicated other neurotransmitters in schizophrenia, suggesting that the disorder may involve a complex interaction among a host of different biochemicals (Risman et al., 2008; Sawa & Snyder, 2002). In sum, the precise role of neurotransmitters in schizophrenia has yet to be determined.

Finally, neuroimaging studies provide evidence of a variety of brain abnormalities in schizophrenia. One study examined changes in the brains of adolescents whose MRI scans could be traced sequentially from the onset of schizophrenia (Thompson et al., 2001). By morphing the images onto a standardized brain, the researchers were able to detect progressive tissue loss beginning in the parietal lobe and eventually encompassing much of the brain (see **FIGURE 14.4**). All adolescents lose some

FIGURE 14.4 Brain Tissue Loss in Adolescent Schizophrenia MRI scans of normal adolescent brains show some tissue loss due to "pruning" (*top*). Scans of adolescents recently diagnosed with schizophrenia reveal loss in the parietal areas (*middle*); individuals at this stage may experience symptoms such as hallucinations or bizarre thoughts. Scans 5 years later reveal extensive tissue loss over much of the cortex (*bottom*); individuals at this stage are likely to suffer from delusions, disorganized speech and behavior, and negative symptoms such as social withdrawal (Thompson et al., 2001).

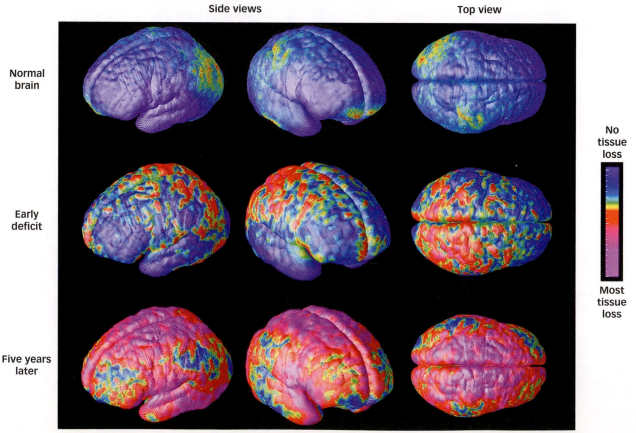

Thompson et al. (2001), National Academy of Sciences, USA

gray matter over time in a kind of normal "pruning" of the brain, but in the case of those developing schizophrenia, the loss was dramatic enough to seem pathological. Other studies suggest a clear relationship between biological changes in the brain and the progression of schizophrenia (Shenton et al., 2001).

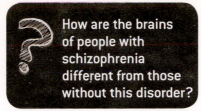

How are the brains of people with schizophrenia different from those without this disorder?

Psychological Factors

With all these potential biological contributors to schizophrenia, you might think there would be few psychological or social causes of the disorder. However, several studies do suggest that the family environment plays a role in the development of and recovery from the condition. One large-scale study compared the risk of schizophrenia in children adopted into healthy families and those adopted into severely disturbed families (Tienari et al., 2004). (Disturbed families were defined as those with extreme conflict, lack of communication, or chaotic relationships.) Among children whose biological mothers had schizophrenia, the disturbed environment increased the likelihood of developing schizophrenia—an outcome that was not found among children who were reared in disturbed families but whose biological mothers did *not* have schizophrenia. This finding provides support for the diathesis–stress model described earlier.

Other Voices

Successful and Schizophrenic

Elyn R. Saks is a law professor at the University of Southern California and the author of the memoir *The Center Cannot Hold: My Journey Through Madness.*

Mikel Healey, Courtesy of Elyn R. Saks

This chapter describes what we know about the characteristics and causes of mental disorders, and the next chapter describes how these disorders are commonly treated. For some of the more severe disorders, such as schizophrenia, the picture does not look good. People diagnosed with schizophrenia often are informed that it is a lifelong condition, and although current treatments show some effectiveness in decreasing the delusional thinking and hallucinations often present in those with schizophrenia, people with this disorder often are unable to hold down a full-time job, maintain healthy relationships, and achieve a high quality of life.

Elyn Saks is one such person who received a diagnosis of schizophrenia and was informed of this prognosis. She described what happened next in a longer version of the following article that appeared in the *New York Times* (2013).

Thirty years ago, I was given a diagnosis of schizophrenia. My prognosis was "grave": I would never live independently, hold a job, find a loving partner, get married. My home would be a board-and-care facility, my days spent watching TV in a day room with other people debilitated by mental illness. …

Then I made a decision. I would write the narrative of my life. Today I am a chaired professor at the University of Southern California Gould School of Law. I have an adjunct appointment in the department of psychiatry at the medical school of the University of California, San Diego. The MacArthur Foundation gave me a genius grant.

Although I fought my diagnosis for many years, I came to accept that I have schizophrenia and will be in treatment the rest of my life. …. What I refused to accept was my prognosis.

Conventional psychiatric thinking and its diagnostic categories say that people like me don't exist. Either I don't have schizophrenia (please tell that to the delusions crowding my mind), or I couldn't have accomplished what I have (please tell that to U.S.C.'s committee on faculty affairs). But I do, and I have. And I have undertaken research with colleagues at U.S.C. and U.C.L.A. to show that I am not alone. There are others with schizophrenia and such active symptoms as delusions and hallucinations who have significant academic and professional achievements.

Over the last few years, my colleagues … and I have gathered 20 research subjects with high-functioning schizophrenia in Los Angeles. They suffered from symptoms like mild delusions or hallucinatory behavior. Their average age was 40. Half were male, half female, and more than half were minorities. All had high school diplomas, and a majority either had or were working toward college or graduate degrees. They were graduate students, managers, technicians and professionals, including a doctor, lawyer, psychologist and chief executive of a nonprofit group. At the same time, most were unmarried and childless, which is consistent with their diagnoses. … More than three-quarters had been hospitalized between two and five times because of their illness, while three had never been admitted.

How had these people with schizophrenia managed to succeed in their studies and at such high-level jobs? We learned that, in addition to medication and therapy, all the participants had developed techniques to keep their schizophrenia at bay. For some, these techniques were cognitive. An educator with a master's degree said he had learned to face his hallucinations and ask, "What's the evidence for that? Or is it just a perception problem?" Another participant said, "I hear derogatory voices all the time. ... You just gotta blow them off." ...

Other techniques that our participants cited included controlling sensory inputs. For some, this meant keeping their living space simple (bare walls, no TV, only quiet music), while for others, it meant distracting music. "I'll listen to loud music if I don't want to hear things," said a participant who is a certified nurse's assistant. Still others mentioned exercise, a healthy diet, avoiding alcohol and getting enough sleep. ...

One of the most frequently mentioned techniques that helped our research participants manage their symptoms was work. "Work has been an important part of who I am," said an educator in our group. "When you become useful to an organization and feel respected in that organization, there's a certain value in belonging there." This person works on the weekends too because of "the distraction factor." In other words, by engaging in work, the crazy stuff often recedes to the sidelines. ....

THAT is why it is so distressing when doctors tell their patients not to expect or pursue fulfilling careers. Far too often, the conventional psychiatric approach to mental illness is to see clusters of symptoms that characterize people. Accordingly, many psychiatrists hold the view that treating symptoms with medication is treating mental illness. But this fails to take into account individuals' strengths and capabilities, leading mental health professionals to underestimate what their patients can hope to achieve in the world. ... A recent *New York Times Magazine* article described a new company that hires high-functioning adults with autism, taking advantage of their unusual memory skills and attention to detail. ...

An approach that looks for individual strengths, in addition to considering symptoms, could help dispel the pessimism surrounding mental illness. Finding "the wellness within the illness," as one person with schizophrenia said, should be a therapeutic goal. Doctors should urge their patients to develop relationships and engage in meaningful work. They should encourage patients to find their own repertory of techniques to manage their symptoms and aim for a quality of life as they define it.

And they should provide patients with the resources—therapy, medication and support—to make these things happen. ...

Elyn Saks's story is amazing and inspiring. It also is quite unusual. How should we incorporate stories like hers and the people in the research study she described? Are these people outliers—simply a carefully selected collection of people who had unusually favorable outcomes (given the large size of Los Angeles, it is reasonable to think one could amass a small sample of such cases)? Or has Professor Saks touched on an important limitation to the way in which the field currently conceptualizes, classifies, and treats mental disorders? Do we focus too much on what is wrong and on how professionalized health care can treat the pathology and not enough on what inherent strengths people have that can help them overcome their challenges, function at a high level, and achieve a high quality of life? These are all questions that are testable with the methods of psychological science, and the answers may help to improve the lives of many people.

SUMMARY QUIZ [14.6]

1. Schizophrenia is characterized by which of the following?
   a. hallucinations
   b. disorganized thoughts and behavior
   c. emotional and social withdrawal
   d. all of the above

2. Schizophrenia affects approximately _____ % of the population and accounts for approximately _____ % of admissions to state and county mental hospitals.
   a. 5; 20
   b. 5; 5
   c. 1; 1
   d. 1; 40

Neurodevelopmental Disorders: Starting Young

All of the disorders described above can have their onset during childhood, adolescence, or adulthood. Some often begin early in life (lots of adolescents develop anxiety disorders or depression), and in fact, half of all disorders begin by age 14, and three-quarters by age 24 (Kessler, Berglund, et al., 2005). But neurodevelopmental disorders *always*, by definition, begin in childhood or adolescence, and if they don't, you are never going to have them. These include autism spectrum disorder, attention-deficit/hyperactivity disorder, intellectual disability (formerly called *mental retardation*), learning disorders, communication disorders, and motor skill disorders, in addition to many others. The first two are among the most common and well known, so we will review them briefly here.

Autism Spectrum Disorder

Marco is a 4-year-old only child. Although his mother stays home with him all day and tries to play with him and talk with him, he still has not spoken a single word and he shows little interest in trying. He spends much of his time playing with his toy trains, sometimes sitting for hours staring at spinning train wheels or pushing a single train back and forth, seeming completely in his own world, uninterested in playing with anyone else. Marco's parents have become concerned about Marco's apparent inability to speak, disinterest in others, and development of some peculiar mannerisms, such as flapping his arms repeatedly for no apparent reason.

Autism spectrum disorder (ASD) is *a condition beginning in early childhood in which a person shows persistent communication deficits as well as restricted and repetitive patterns of behaviors, interests, or activities.* In DSM–5, ASD is considered a single disorder that includes autistic disorder, Asperger's disorder, childhood disintegrative disorder, and pervasive developmental disorder not otherwise specified.

The true rate of ASD is difficult to pinpoint. Estimates from the 1960s indicated that autism was fairly rare, occurring in 4 per 10,000 children, but current estimates range as high as 60 per 10,000 children (Newschaffer et al., 2007). It is unclear whether this increased rate is due to increased awareness and recognition of ASD, better screening and diagnostic tools, or to some other factor. Boys have higher rates of ASD than girls by a ratio of about 4:1.

One current model suggests that ASD can be understood as an impaired capacity for *empathizing,* knowing the mental states of others, combined with a superior ability for *systematizing,* understanding the rules that organize the structure and function of objects (Baron-Cohen & Belmonte, 2005). Consistent with this model, brain imaging studies show that people with autism have comparatively decreased activity in regions associated with understanding the minds of others and greater activation in regions related to basic object perception (Sigman, Spence, & Wang, 2006). At the same time, some people with ASD have remarkable abilities to perceive or remember details, or to master symbol systems such as mathematics or music (Happé & Vital, 2009).

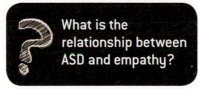

? What is the relationship between ASD and empathy?

Although many people with ASD experience impairments throughout their lives that prevent them from having relationships and holding down a job, many go on to very successful careers. The renowned behavioral scientist and author Temple Grandin (2006) was diagnosed with autism at age 3, started learning to talk late, and then suffered teasing for odd habits and "nerdy" behavior. Fortunately, she developed ways to cope and found a niche through her special talent—the ability to understand animal behavior (Sacks, 1996). She is now a professor, author, and the central character in an HBO movie based on her life. Temple Grandin's story lets us know that there are happy endings. Overall, those diagnosed with ASD as children have highly variable trajectories, with some achieving normal or better-than-normal functioning and others struggling with the profound disorder. Autism is a childhood disorder that in adulthood can turn out many ways (see the Hot Science box).

autism spectrum disorder (ASD) A condition beginning in early childhood in which a person shows persistent communication deficits as well as restricted and repetitive patterns of behaviors, interests, or activities.

Temple Grandin, Professor of Animal Sciences at Colorado State University, is living proof that people with Autism spectrum disorder are able to have very successful professional careers.

Wireimage/Getty Images

Hot Science

Optimal Outcomes in Autism Spectrum Disorder

What comes to mind when you think of the word *autism*? What kind of people do you imagine? As adults, can they hold a job? Can they care for themselves? Autism spectrum disorder (ASD) is considered by many to be a lifelong condition in which those affected will forever experience significant difficulties and disability in their interpersonal, educational, and occupational functioning. Several recent studies are helping to change this outlook.

For years, researchers have noticed that some children diagnosed with autism later fail to meet diagnostic criteria for ASD. One recent review suggested that 3 to 25% of children ultimately lose their ASD diagnosis over time (Helt et al., 2008). There are several potential explanations for this. The most obvious is that some portion of children diagnosed with ASD are misdiagnosed and don't really have this disorder. Perhaps they are overly shy, or quiet, or develop speech later than other children, and this is misinterpreted as ASD. Another possibility is that children who lose their ASD diagnosis had a milder form of the disorder and/or were identified and treated earlier. There is some support for this idea, as

Autism was once viewed as a condition with lifelong impairments. New research suggests that early intervention can help many of those in whom ASD is diagnosed to achieve normal levels of functioning and be like everyone else.

predictors of recovery from ASD include high IQ, stronger language abilities, and earlier age of identification and treatment (Helt et al., 2008).

Can ASD be effectively treated? In one study, researchers assigned 19 children with autism to an intensive behavioral intervention in which the children received over 40 hours per week of one-on-one behavior therapy for 2 years, and they assigned 40 children to control conditions in which they received fewer than 10 hours per

week of treatment (Lovaas, 1987). Amazingly, 47% of the children in the intensive behavior therapy condition obtained a normal level of intellectual and educational functioning—passing through a normal first grade class—compared to only 2% of those in the control conditions.

Extending this earlier work, Geraldine Dawson and colleagues (2010) are testing a program called the Early Start Denver Model (ESDM), an intensive behavioral intervention (20 hours per week for 2 years) similarly designed to improve outcomes among those with ASD. Dawson and colleagues found that toddlers with ASD who were randomly assigned to receive ESDM, compared to those assigned standard community treatment, showed significant improvements in IQ (a 17-point raise!), language, adaptive and social functioning, and ASD diagnosis. For at least some people diagnosed with ASD, intensive behavioral interventions can help them to reach the same levels as typically developing people in IQ, language, communication, or socialization (Fein et al., 2013). This is currently a very hot area of research, and one that could have implications for those in whom ASD is diagnosed.

---

attention-deficit/hyperactivity disorder (ADHD) A persistent pattern of severe problems with inattention and/or hyperactivity or impulsiveness that cause significant impairments in functioning.

Attention-Deficit/Hyperactivity Disorder

Chances are you have had the experience of being distracted during a lecture or while reading one of your *other* textbooks. We all have trouble focusing from time to time. Far beyond normal distraction, **attention-deficit/hyperactivity disorder (ADHD)** is *a persistent pattern of severe problems with inattention and/or hyperactivity or impulsiveness that cause significant impairments in functioning.* This is quite different from occasional mind wandering or bursts of activity. Meeting criteria for ADHD requires that a child have multiple symptoms of inattention (e.g., persistent problems with sustained attention, organization, memory, following instructions), hyperactivity–impulsiveness (e.g., persistent difficulties with remaining still, waiting for a turn, interrupting others), or both. Most children experience some of these behaviors at some point, but to meet criteria for ADHD, a child has to have many of these behaviors for at least 6 months in at least two settings (e.g., home and school) to the point where these behaviors impair the child's ability to perform at school or get along at home. Approximately 10% of boys and 4% of girls meet criteria for ADHD (Polzanczyk et al., 2007).

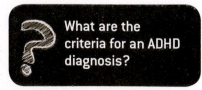

What are the criteria for an ADHD diagnosis?

For a long time, ADHD was thought of as a disorder that affects only children and adolescents and that people "age out" of the disorder. However, we now know that in many instances, this disorder persists into adulthood. The same symptoms are used to diagnose both children and adults (e.g., children with ADHD may struggle with attention and concentration in the classroom, whereas adults may experience the same problems in meetings). Approximately 4% of adults meet criteria for ADHD, and adults with this disorder are more likely to be male, divorced, and unemployed—and most did not receive any treatment for their ADHD (Kessler, Adler, et al., 2006).

Because ADHD, like most disorders, is defined by the presence of a wide range of symptoms, it is unlikely that it emerges from one single cause or dysfunction. The exact cause of ADHD is not known, but some studies suggest a strong genetic influence (Faraone et al., 2005). Brain imaging studies suggest that those with ADHD have smaller brain volumes (Castellanos et al., 2002) as well as structural and functional abnormalities in brain networks associated with attention and behavioral inhibition (Makris et al., 2009). The good news is that current drug treatments for ADHD are effective and appear to decrease the risk of later psychological and academic problems (Biederman et al., 2009).

SUMMARY QUIZ [14.7]

1. Autism spectrum disorder is characterized by which of the following?
   a. communication deficits and restricted, repetitive behavior
   b. hallucinations and delusions
   c. suicidal thoughts
   d. all of the above

2. Attention-deficit/hyperactivity disorder
   a. must begin before the age of 7.
   b. never persists into adulthood.
   c. sometimes persists into adulthood.
   d. affects only boys.

Disruptive, Impulse-Control, and Conduct Disorders: Acting Out

You already learned about how extreme fear, avoidance, and sadness can lead to the diagnosis of an anxiety or mood disorder. At the other end of the behavioral continuum, extreme anger, impulsiveness, and rule-breaking can lead to the diagnosis of a disruptive, impulse-control, or conduct disorder.

Michael is an 8-year-old boy whose mother brought him into a local clinic because his behavior had been getting out of control and his parents and teachers were no longer able to control him. At home, he routinely bullied his siblings, threw glasses and dishes at family members, and even punched and kicked his parents. Outside of the house, Michael had been getting into trouble for stealing from the local store and yelling at his teacher. Nothing his parents tried seemed to change his behavior.

Conduct disorder is a condition in which a child or adolescent engages in *a persistent pattern of deviant behavior involving aggression against people or animals, destruction of property, deceitfulness or theft, or serious rule violations.* Approximately 9% of people in the United States report a lifetime history of conduct disorder (12% of boys and 7% of girls; Nock et al., 2006). Meeting criteria for conduct disorder requires having any 3 of the 15 symptoms of conduct disorder. This means there are approximately 32,000 different combinations of symptoms that could lead to a diagnosis, which makes those with conduct disorder a pretty diverse group. This diversity makes

conduct disorder A persistent pattern of deviant behavior involving aggression against people or animals, destruction of property, deceitfulness or theft, or serious rule violations.

PhotoAlto/Laurence Mouton/Getty Images

Psychologists are attempting to identify the causes of conduct disorder with the hopes of being able to decrease the harmful behaviors, like bullying, that often accompany it.

Ever browse a copy of *Architectural Digest* and wonder who would live in one of those perfect homes? A person with obsessive-compulsive personality disorder might fit right in. This personality disorder (characterized by excessive perfectionism) should not be mistaken, by the way, for obsessive-compulsive disorder—the anxiety disorder in which the person suffers from repeated unwanted thoughts or actions.

Getty Images/Image Source

it difficult to pin down the causes of conduct disorder. Researchers currently are attempting to understand the pathways through which genetic factors interact with environmental stressors (e.g., childhood adversities) to lead to the behaviors that are characteristic of conduct disorder.

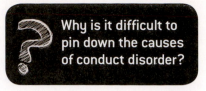

? Why is it difficult to pin down the causes of conduct disorder?

SUMMARY QUIZ [14.8]

1. Which of the following are NOT symptoms of conduct disorder?
   a. aggression toward people or animals
   b. property destruction
   c. childhood adversities
   d. stealing from others

Personality Disorders: Going to Extremes

Think for a minute about high school acquaintances whose personalities made them stand out. Was there an odd person who didn't seem to make sense, wore strange outfits, and sometimes wouldn't respond in conversation? Or perhaps a drama queen, whose theatrics and exaggerated emotions turned everything into a big deal? And don't forget the neat freak, who had the perfectly organized locker, precisely arranged hair, and sweater with zero lint balls. One way to describe such people is to say they simply have *personalities,* the unique patterns of traits we explored in the Personality chapter. But sometimes, personality traits can become so rigid and confining that they blend into mental disorders. **Personality disorders** are *enduring patterns of thinking, feeling, or relating to others or controlling impulses that deviate from cultural expectations and cause distress or impaired functioning.* Personality disorders begin in adolescence or early adulthood and are relatively stable over time.

The *DSM–5* lists 10 specific personality disorders (see **TABLE 14.3**). They fall into three clusters: (a) *odd/eccentric,* (b) *dramatic/erratic,* and (c) *anxious/inhibited.* The strange high school student, for example, could have *schizotypal personality disorder* (odd/eccentric cluster); the drama queen could have *histrionic personality disorder* (dramatic/erratic cluster); the neat freak could have *obsessive-compulsive personality disorder* (anxious/inhibited cluster). Don't rush to judgment, however. Most of those kids are probably quite healthy and fall far short of qualifying for a diagnosis. Still, the array of personality disorders suggests that there are multiple ways an individual's gift of a unique personality could become a problem.

Personality disorders have been a bit controversial for several reasons. First, critics question whether having a problematic personality is really a disorder. Given that approximately 15% of the U.S. population has a personality disorder according to the *DSM–5*, perhaps it might be better just to admit that a lot of people are difficult and leave it at that. Another question is whether personality problems correspond to "disorders" in that there are distinct *types* or whether such problems might be better understood as extreme values on trait *dimensions* such as the Big Five traits discussed in the Personality chapter (Trull & Durrett, 2005). Debate on these questions is ongoing.

One of the most well-studied of all personality disorders—and the one most likely to land someone in jail—is **antisocial personality disorder (APD),** *a pervasive pattern of disregard for and violation of the rights of others that begins in childhood or*

Table 14.3 Clusters of Personality Disorders

Cluster	Personality Disorder	Characteristics
A. Odd/ Eccentric	Paranoid	Distrust in others, suspicion that people have sinister motives. Apt to challenge the loyalties of friends and read hostile intentions into others' actions. Prone to anger and aggressive outbursts but otherwise emotionally cold. Often jealous, guarded, secretive, overly serious.
	Schizoid	Extreme introversion and withdrawal from relationships. Prefers to be alone, little interest in others. Humorless, distant, often absorbed with own thoughts and feelings, a daydreamer. Fearful of closeness, with poor social skills, often seen as a "loner."
	Schizotypal	Peculiar or eccentric manners of speaking or dressing. Strange beliefs. "Magical thinking" such as beliefs in ESP or telepathy. Difficulty forming relationships. May react oddly in conversation, not respond, or talk to self. Speech elaborate and difficult to follow. (Possibly a mild form of schizophrenia.)
B. Dramatic/ Erratic	Antisocial	Impoverished moral sense or "conscience." History of deception, crime, legal problems, impulsive and aggressive or violent behavior. Little emotional empathy or remorse for hurting others. Manipulative, careless, callous. At high risk for substance abuse and alcoholism
	Borderline	Unstable moods and intense, stormy personal relationships. Frequent mood changes and anger, unpredictable impulses. Self-mutilation or suicidal threats or gestures to get attention or manipulate others. Self-image fluctuation and a tendency to see others as "all good" or "all bad."
	Histrionic	Constant attention seeking. Grandiose language, provocative dress, exaggerated illness, all to gain attention. Believes that everyone loves them. Emotional, lively, overly dramatic, enthusiastic, and excessively flirtatious. Shallow and labile emotions. "Onstage."
	Narcissistic	Inflated sense of self-importance, absorbed by fantasies of self and success. Exaggerates own achievement, assumes others will recognize they are superior. Good first impressions but poor longer-term relationships. Exploitative of others.
C. Anxious/ Inhibited	Avoidant	Socially anxious and uncomfortable unless they are confident of being liked. In contrast with schizoid person, yearns for social contact. Fears criticism and worries about being embarrassed in front of others. Avoids social situations due to fear of rejection.
	Dependent	Submissive, dependent, requiring excessive approval, reassurance, and advice. Clings to people and fears losing them. Lacking self-confidence. Uncomfortable when alone. May be devastated by end of a close relationship or suicidal if breakup is threatened.
	Obsessive-compulsive	Conscientious, orderly, perfectionist. Excessive need to do everything "right." Inflexibly high standards and caution can interfere with their productivity. Fear of errors can make them strict and controlling. Poor expression of emotions. (Not the same as obsessive-compulsive disorder).

Source: Information from American Psychiatric Association, 2013.

early adolescence and continues into adulthood. The terms *sociopath* and *psychopath* describe people with APD who are especially coldhearted, manipulative, and ruthless—yet may be glib and charming (Cleckley, 1976; Hare, 1998). For example, consider the case of Henri Désiré Landru. In 1914, Landru began using personal ads to attract a woman "interested in matrimony," and he succeeded in seducing 10 of them. He bilked them of their savings, poisoned them, and cremated them in his stove. He recorded his murders in a notebook and maintained a marriage and a mistress all the while. The gruesome actions of serial killers such as Landru leave us frightened and wondering; however, bullies, compulsive liars, and even drivers who regularly speed

personality disorders Enduring patterns of thinking, feeling, or relating to others or controlling impulses that deviate from cultural expectations and cause distress or impaired functioning.

antisocial personality disorder (APD) A pervasive pattern of disregard for and violation of the rights of others that begins in childhood or early adolescence and continues into adulthood.

Three Lions/Getty Images

Henri Desiré Landru (1869–1922) was a serial killer who met widows through newspaper ads. After obtaining enough information to embezzle money from them, he murdered 10 women. He was executed for serial murder in 1922.

We all have an innate desire to keep ourselves alive. So why do some people purposely do things to harm themselves?

Piotr Powietrzynski/Getty Images

through a school zone share the same shocking blindness to human pain. Many people with APD do commit crimes, and many are caught because of the frequency and flagrancy of their infractions. Among 22,790 prisoners in one study, 47% of the men and 21% of the women were diagnosed with APD (Fazel & Danesh, 2002). Statistics such as these support the notion of a "criminal personality."

Adults with an APD diagnosis typically have a history of *conduct disorder* before the age of 15. In adulthood, a diagnosis of APD is given to individuals who show three or more of a set of seven diagnostic signs: illegal behavior, deception, impulsivity, physical aggression, recklessness, irresponsibility, and a lack of remorse for wrongdoing. About 3.6% of the general population has APD, and the rate of occurrence in men is 3 times the rate in women (Grant et al., 2004). Evidence of brain abnormalities in people with APD is also accumulating (Blair, Peschardt, & Mitchell, 2005). For example, criminal psychopaths who are shown negative emotional words such as *hate* or *corpse* exhibit less activity in the amygdala and hippocampus than do noncriminals (Kiehl et al., 2001). The two brain areas are involved in the process of fear conditioning (Patrick, Cuthbert, & Lang, 1994), so their relative inactivity suggests that psychopaths are less sensitive to fear than are other people. It might seem peaceful to go through life "without fear," but perhaps fear is useful in keeping people from the extremes of antisocial behavior.

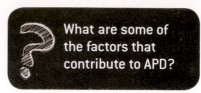

What are some of the factors that contribute to APD?

SUMMARY QUIZ [14.9]

1. Which of the following is a common feature of personality disorders?
   a. failure to take other people's perspectives
   b. excessive fear of rejection
   c. unstable moods
   d. overly dramatic attempts at attention seeking

2. Jim was diagnosed as having antisocial personality disorder based on the fact that he
   a. is emotionally distant, suspicious of others, and has an intense fear of rejection.
   b. avoids social interaction, has very poor social skills, and is often seen as a "loner."
   c. is very peculiar in his speech and dress and has difficulty forming relationships.
   d. is manipulative, impulsive, and coldhearted, showing little emotional empathy.

Self-Harm Behaviors: When the Mind Turns against Itself

We all have an innate drive to keep ourselves alive. We eat when we are hungry, get out of the way of fast-moving vehicles, and go to school so we can earn a living to keep ourselves and our families alive (see the discussion of evolutionary psychology in the Psychology: Evolution of a Science chapter). One of the most extreme manifestations of abnormal human behavior is when a person acts in direct opposition to this drive for self-preservation and engages in intentionally self-destructive behavior. Accounts of people intentionally harming themselves date back to the beginning of recorded history. However, it is only over the past several decades that we have begun to gain an understanding of why people purposely do things to hurt themselves. *DSM–5* includes two self-destructive behaviors in a special section on disorders in need of further study: suicide behavior disorder and nonsuicidal self-injury disorder.

Suicidal Behavior

Tim, a 35-year-old accountant, had by all appearances been living a pretty happy, successful life. He was married to his high school sweetheart and had two young children. Over the past several years, though, his workload had increased, and he started to experience severe job-related stress. At around the same time, he and his wife began to experience some financial problems, and his alcohol consumption increased, all of which put significant strain on the family and began to affect his work. One evening, after a heated argument with his wife, Tim went into the bathroom and swallowed a bottle full of prescription medicine in an effort to end his life. He was taken to the hospital and kept there to be treated for suicidal behavior.

Suicide, which refers to *intentional self-inflicted death*, is the 10th leading cause of death in the United States and the 2nd leading cause of death among people 15 to 24 years old. It takes the lives of more than 5 times as many people as HIV-AIDS each year in the United States, and more than twice as many people as homicide (Hoyert & Xu, 2012). Approximately 80% of all suicides occur among men, and in the United States, White people are much more likely to kill themselves than members of other racial and ethnic groups, accounting for 90% of all suicides (Centers for Disease Control and Prevention, 2013). Unfortunately, we currently do not have a good understanding of why these enormous sociodemographic differences exist.

A nonfatal **suicide attempt,** which refers to a *self-inflicted injury from which a person has at least some intention of dying*, occurs much more frequently than suicide deaths. In the United States, approximately 15% of adults report that they have seriously considered suicide at some point in their lives, 5% have made a plan to kill themselves, and 5% have actually made a suicide attempt. Although many more men than women die by suicide, women experience suicidal thoughts and (nonfatal) suicide attempts at significantly higher rates than do men (Nock et al., 2008). The rates of suicidal thoughts and attempts are virtually nonexistent before age 10, but then they increase dramatically from age 12 to 18 years (see **FIGURE 14.5**) before leveling off during early adulthood (Nock et al., 2013).

suicide Intentional self-inflicted death.

suicide attempt Self-inflicted injury from which a person has at least some intention of dying.

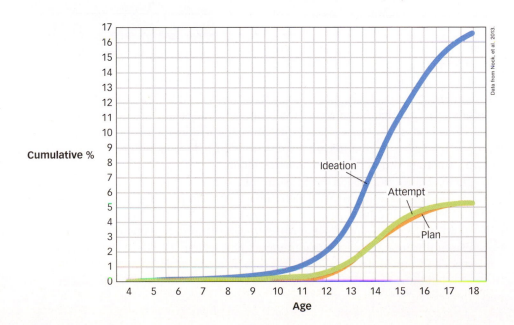

Data from Nock, et al. 2013.

FIGURE 14.5 **Age of Onset of Suicidal Behavior during Adolescence** A recent survey of a nationally representative sample of U.S. adolescents shows that although suicidal thoughts and behaviors are quite rare among children (the rate was 0.0 for ages 1–4), they increase dramatically starting at age 12 and continue to climb throughout adolescence.

nonsuicidal self-injury (NSSI) Direct, deliberate destruction of body tissue in the absence of any intent to die.

So the numbers are staggering, but *why* do people try to kill themselves? The short answer is: We do not yet know, and it's complicated. When interviewed in the hospital following a suicide attempt, most people who have tried to kill themselves report that they did so in order to escape from an intolerable state of mind or impossible situation (Boergers, Spirito, & Donaldson, 1998). Consistent with this explanation, research has documented that the risk of suicidal behavior is significantly increased if a person experiences distressing factors such as the presence of multiple mental disorders (more than 90% of people who die by suicide have at least one mental disorder); significant negative life events during childhood and adulthood (e.g., physical and sexual assault); and severe medical problems (Nock, Borges, & Ono, 2012). The search is ongoing for a more comprehensive understanding of how and why some people respond to negative life events with suicidal thoughts and behaviors, as well as on methods for better predicting and preventing these devastating outcomes.

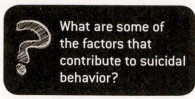

What are some of the factors that contribute to suicidal behavior?

Nonsuicidal Self-Injury

Louisa, an 18-year-old college student, secretly cuts her lower waist and upper thighs about once per week, typically when she is in the midst of feeling intense anger and hatred, either toward herself or someone else. She was 14 when she started using self-injury as a way to calm herself down. Louisa says that she actually feels a little ashamed after each episode of cutting, but she doesn't know how else to calm down when she gets really upset and so she has no plans of stopping this behavior.

Louisa is engaging in a behavior called **nonsuicidal self-injury (NSSI),** the *direct, deliberate destruction of body tissue in the absence of any intent to die*. NSSI has been reported since the beginning of recorded history; however, it appears to be on the rise over the past few decades. Recent studies suggest that as many as 15 to 20% of adolescents and 3 to 6% of adults report engaging in NSSI at some point in their lifetimes (Klonsky, 2011; Muehlenkamp et al., 2012). The rates appear to be even between males and females, and for people of different races and ethnicities. Like suicidal behavior, NSSI is virtually absent during childhood, increases dramatically during adolescence, and then appears to decrease across adulthood.

Although in the United States self-injury is considered to be pathological, in some parts of the world, scarification of the skin is viewed as a rite of passage into adulthood and a symbol of one's tribe, as in the case of this young man from the Republic of Benin in West Africa.

In some parts of the world, cutting or scarification of the skin is socially accepted, and in some cases, it is even encouraged as a rite of passage (Favazza, 2011). In parts of the world where self-cutting is not socially encouraged, why would a person purposely hurt him- or herself if not to die? Recent studies suggest that people who engage in self-injury have very strong emotional and physiological responses to negative events, that they perceive this response as intolerable, and that NSSI serves to diminish the intensity of this response (Nock, 2009). There also is some evidence that in many instances, people engage in self-injury as a means to communicate distress or elicit help from others (Nock, 2010).

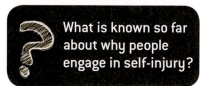

What is known so far about why people engage in self-injury?

Unfortunately, much like suicidal behavior, our understanding of the genetic and neurobiological influences on NSSI is limited, and there currently are no effective medications for these problems. There also is very limited evidence for behavioral interventions or prevention programs (Mann et al., 2005). So, whereas suicidal behavior and NSSI are some of the most disturbing and dangerous mental disorders, they also, unfortunately, are among the most perplexing. The field has made significant strides in our understanding of these behavior problems in recent years, but there is a long way to go before we are able to predict and prevent them accurately and effectively.

SUMMARY QUIZ [14.10]

1. In the United States, those at highest risk for suicide are
   a. men.
   b. White people.
   c. those with a mental disorder.
   d. all of the above

2. Nonsuicidal self-injury occurs among _____ % of adolescents.
   a. 1–2
   b. 3–5
   c. 15–20
   d. 50

CHAPTER REVIEW

SUMMARY

Defining Mental Disorders: What Is Abnormal?

> The *DSM–5* is a classification system that defines a mental disorder as occurring when the person experiences disturbances of thought, emotion, or behavior that produce distress or impairment and that arise from internal sources.

> According to the biopsychosocial perspective, mental disorders arise from an interaction of biological, psychological, and social factors, often thought of as a combination of a diathesis (internal predisposition) and stress (environmental life event).

> The RDoC is a new classification system that focuses on biological, cognitive, and behavioral aspects of mental disorders.

Anxiety Disorders: When Fear Takes Over

> People with anxiety disorders have irrational worries and fears that undermine their ability to function normally.

> Phobic disorders are characterized by excessive fear and avoidance of specific objects, activities, or situations, whereas generalized anxiety disorder (GAD) involves a chronic state of anxiety not focused on any particular threat.

> People who suffer from panic disorder experience a sudden and intense attack of anxiety that is terrifying and can lead them to become agoraphobic and housebound for fear of public humiliation.

Obsessive-Compulsive Disorder: Trapped in a Loop

> People with obsessive-compulsive disorder experience recurring, anxiety-provoking thoughts that compel them to engage in ritualistic, irrational behavior.

Posttraumatic Stress Disorder: Troubles after a Trauma

> In posttraumatic stress disorder (PTSD), a person experiences chronic physiological arousal, unwanted thoughts or images of the trauma, and avoidance of things that remind the person of a traumatic event.

Depressive and Bipolar Disorders: At the Mercy of Emotions

> Mood disorders are mental disorders in which a disturbance in mood is the predominant feature.

> Major depression (or unipolar depression) is characterized by a severely depressed mood; symptoms include an inability to experience pleasure, feelings of worthlessness, lethargy, and sleep and appetite disturbances.

> Bipolar disorder is an unstable emotional condition involving extreme mood swings of depression and mania, periods of abnormally and persistently elevated, expansive, or irritable mood.

Schizophrenia and Other Psychotic Disorders: Losing the Grasp on Reality

> Schizophrenia is a severe psychological disorder involving hallucinations, disorganized thoughts and behavior, and emotional and social withdrawal.

> Schizophrenia affects only 1% of the population, but it accounts for a disproportionate share of psychiatric hospitalizations.

> The first drugs that reduced the availability of dopamine sometimes reduced the symptoms of schizophrenia, suggesting that the disorder involved an excess of dopamine activity, but recent research suggests that schizophrenia may involve a complex interaction among a variety of neurotransmitters.

> Risks for developing schizophrenia include genetic factors, biochemical factors, brain abnormalities, and a stressful home environment.

Neurodevelopmental Disorders: Starting Young

> ASD emerges in early childhood and is a condition in which a person has persistent communication deficits as well as restricted and repetitive patterns of behavior, interests, or activities.

> ADHD begins by age 12 and involves persistent severe problems with inattention and/or hyperactivity or impulsiveness that cause significant impairments in functioning.

Disruptive, Impulse-Control, and Conduct Disorders: Acting Out

> Conduct disorder begins in childhood or adolescence and involves persistent behavior involving aggression against people or animals, destruction of property, deceitfulness or theft, or serious rule violations.

Personality Disorders: Going to Extremes

> Personality disorders are enduring patterns of thinking, feeling, relating to others, or controlling impulses that cause distress or impaired functioning.

> Antisocial personality disorder is associated with a lack of moral emotions and behavior; people with antisocial personality disorder can be manipulative, dangerous, and reckless, often hurting others and sometimes hurting themselves.

Self-Harm Behaviors: When the Mind Turns against Itself

> Suicide is among the leading causes of death in the United States and the world. Most people who die by suicide have a mental disorder, and suicide attempts are often motivated by an attempt to escape intolerable mental states or situations.

> Although NSSI is performed without suicidal intent, like suicidal behavior, it is most often motivated by an attempt to escape from painful mental states.

KEY TERMS

mental disorder (p. 440)

medical model (p. 441)

Diagnostic and Statistical Manual of Mental Disorders (DSM) (p. 442)

comorbidity (p. 442)

biopsychosocial perspective (p. 444)

diathesis–stress model (p. 445)

Research Domain Criteria Project (RDoC) (p. 445)

anxiety disorder (p. 448)

phobic disorders (p. 448)

specific phobia (p. 448)

social phobia (p. 449)

preparedness theory (p. 449)

panic disorder (p. 450)

agoraphobia (p. 450)

generalized anxiety disorder (GAD) (p. 451)

obsessive-compulsive disorder (OCD) (p. 452)

posttraumatic stress disorder (PTSD) (p. 453)

mood disorders (p. 455)

major depressive disorder (or unipolar depression) (p. 455)

seasonal affective disorder (SAD) (p. 455)

helplessness theory (p. 456)

bipolar disorder (p. 457)

expressed emotion (p. 459)

schizophrenia (p. 460)

positive symptoms (p. 460)

hallucinations (p. 460)

delusions (p. 460)

disorganized speech (p. 460)

grossly disorganized behavior (p. 460)

negative symptoms (p. 461)

cognitive symptoms (p. 461)

dopamine hypothesis (p. 462)

autism spectrum disorder (ASD) (p. 465)

attention-deficit/hyperactivity disorder (ADHD) (p. 466)

conduct disorder (p. 467)

personality disorders (p. 468)

antisocial personality disorder (APD) (p. 468)

suicide (p. 471)

suicide attempt (p. 471)

nonsuicidal self-injury (NSSI) (p. 472)

CHANGING MINDS

1. You catch a TV interview with a celebrity who describes his difficult childhood, living with a mother who suffered from major depression. "Sometimes my mother stayed in her bed for days, not even getting up to eat," he says. "At the time, the family hushed it up. My parents were immigrants, and they came from a culture where it was considered shameful to have mental problems. You are supposed to have enough strength of will to overcome your problems, without help from anyone else. So my mother never got treatment." How might the idea of a medical model of psychiatric disorders have helped the woman and her family in the decision whether to seek treatment?

2. A friend of yours has a family member who is experiencing severe mental problems, including delusions and loss of motivation. "We went to one psychiatrist," she says, "and got a diagnosis of schizophrenia. We went for a second opinion, and the other doctor said it was probably bipolar disorder. They're both good doctors, and they're both using the same *DSM*—how can they come up with different diagnoses?"

3. After reading the chapter, one of your classmates turns to you with a sigh of relief. "I finally figured it out. I have a deadbeat brother, who always gets himself into trouble and then blames other people for his problems. Even when he gets a ticket for speeding, he never thinks it's his fault—the police were picking on him, or his passengers were urging him to go too fast. I always thought he was just a loser, but now I realize he has a personality disorder!" Do you agree with your classmate's diagnosis of his brother? How would you caution your classmate about the dangers of self-diagnosis, or diagnosis of friends and family?

ANSWERS TO SUMMARY QUIZZES

Answers to Summary Quiz 14.1: 1. a; 2. b; 3. c; 4. b.

Answers to Summary Quiz 14.2: 1. d; 2. d; 3. c.

Answer to Summary Quiz 14.3: 1. b.

Answer to Summary Quiz 14.4: 1. d.

Answers to Summary Quiz 14.5: 1. a; 2. a.

Answers to Summary Quiz 14.6: 1. d; 2. d.

Answers to Summary Quiz 14.7: 1. a; 2. c.

Answer to Summary Quiz 14.8: 1. c

Answers to Summary Quiz 14.9: 1. a; 2. d.

Answers to Summary Quiz 14.10: 1. d; 2. c.

Need more help? Additional resources are located in LaunchPad at:
http://www.worthpublishers.com/launchpad/schacterbrief3e

15

Treatment of Psychological Disorders

"**T**ODAY WE'RE GOING TO BE TOUCHING A DEAD MOUSE I SAW IN THE ALLEY OUTSIDE MY OFFICE BUILDING," Dr. Jenkins said. "OK, let's do it, I'm ready," Christine responded. The pair walked down to the alley and spent the next 50 minutes touching, then stroking, the dead mouse. They then went back upstairs to plan out what other disgusting things Christine was going to touch over the next 7 days before coming back for her next therapy session. Yes, this is all part of the psychological treatment of Christine's obsessive-compulsive disorder (OCD). It is an approach called *exposure and response prevention* (ERP), in which people are gradually exposed to the content of their obsessions and prevented from engaging in their compulsions. Christine's obsession is that she is going to be contaminated by germs and die of cancer; her compulsive behavior involves several hours per day of washing her body and scrubbing everything around her with alcohol wipes. After dozens and dozens of exposures, without performing the behaviors that they believe have been keeping them safe, people eventually learn that their obsessive thoughts are not accurate and that they don't have to act out their compulsions. ERP can be a very scary treatment, but it has proven to be one of the most effective treatments available for this condition (Foa, 2010). ERP is just one of many approaches currently being used to help people overcome the mental disorders you learned about in the last chapter.

Exposure-based treatments, in which people learn to face the source of their fears and anxiety, have proven to be an effective way to treat anxiety disorders.

Keith Bitner/Getty Images

In this chapter, we will explore the most common approaches to psychological treatment. We will examine why people need to seek psychological help in the first place, and then we will explore how psychotherapy for individuals is built on the major theories of the causes and cures of disorders, including psychoanalytic, humanistic, existential, behavioral, and cognitive theories. We also will look into biological approaches to treatment that focus on directly modifying brain structure and function. We will discuss whether treatment works and also look to the future by exploring some exciting new directions in the assessment and treatment of disorders using innovative technologies.

Treatment: Getting Help to Those Who Need It

Estimates suggest that 46.4% of people in the United States suffer from a mental disorder at some point in their lifetimes (Kessler, Berglund, et al., 2005). The personal costs of these disorders involve anguish to the sufferers as well as interference in their ability to carry on the activities of daily life. Think about Christine from the example above. Her OCD was causing major problems in her life. She had to quit her job at the local coffee shop because she was no longer able to touch money or anything else that had been touched by other people without washing it first. Her relationship with her boyfriend was in trouble because he was growing tired of her constant reassurance-seeking regarding cleanliness (hers and his). She desperately wanted and needed some way to break out of this vicious cycle. She needed an effective treatment.

The personal and social burdens associated with mental disorders are enormous, and there are financial costs too. Depression is the fourth leading cause of disability worldwide, and it is expected to rise to the second leading cause of disability by 2020 (Murray & Lopez, 1996a, 1996b). People with severe depression often are unable to make it into work due to their disorder, and even when they do make it into work, they often suffer from poor work performance. Recent estimates suggest that depression-related lost work productivity costs somewhere from $30 to $50 billion per year (Kessler, 2012). If we add in similar figures for anxiety disorders, psychotic disorders, substance disorders, and all the other psychological problems, the overall costs are astronomical. In addition to the personal benefits of treatment, then, society also stands to benefit from the effective treatment of psychological disorders.

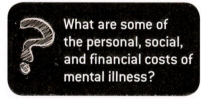

? What are some of the personal, social, and financial costs of mental illness?

Unfortunately, only about 18% of people in the United States with a mental disorder in the past 12 months received treatment. Treatment rates are even lower elsewhere around the world, especially in low-income or developing countries (Wang et al., 2007). Even among those with a mental disorder who do receive treatment, the average delay from onset until treatment is first received is over a decade (Wang et al., 2004)!

Why Many People Fail to Seek Treatment

A physical symptom such as a toothache would send most people to the dentist—a trip that usually results in a successful treatment. The clear source of pain and the obvious solution make for a quick and effective response. In contrast, the path from a mental disorder to a successful treatment is often far less clear. Here are three reasons why people may fail to get treatment for mental disorders:

1. *People may not realize that they have a mental disorder that could be effectively treated.* Approximately 45% of those with a mental disorder who do not seek treatment report that they did not do so because they didn't think that they needed to be treated (Mojtabai et al., 2011). Although most people know what a toothache

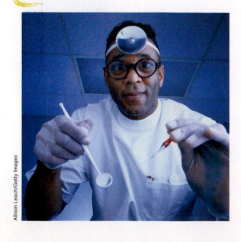

When your tooth hurts, you go to a dentist. But how do you know when to see a psychologist?

is and that it can be successfully treated, far fewer people know when they have a mental disorder and what treatments might be available.

2. *People's attitudes may keep them from getting help.* Individuals may believe that they should be able to handle things themselves. In fact, this is the primary reason that people with a mental disorder give for not seeking treatment (72.6%; Mojtabai et al., 2011). Other attitudinal barriers include perceived stigma from others (9.1%).

3. *Structural barriers prevent people from physically getting to treatment.* Like finding a good lawyer or plumber, finding the right psychologist can be difficult. This confusion is understandable given the plethora of different types of treatments available (see the Real World box, Types of Psychotherapists). Other structural barriers may include not being able to afford treatment (15.3% of nontreatment seekers), lack of clinician

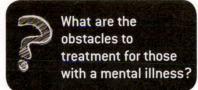
? What are the obstacles to treatment for those with a mental illness?

The Real World

Types of Psychotherapists

Therapists have widely varying backgrounds and training, and this affects the kinds of services they offer. There are several major "flavors."

> **Psychologist** A psychologist who practices psychotherapy holds a doctorate with specialization in clinical psychology (a PhD or PsyD) and has extensive training in therapy, the assessment of psychological disorders, and research. The psychologist will sometimes have a specialty, such as working with adolescents or helping people overcome sleep disorders, and he or she will usually conduct therapy that involves talking. Psychologists must be licensed by the state.

> **Psychiatrist** A psychiatrist is a medical doctor who has completed a M.D. with specialized training in assessing and treating mental disorders. Psychiatrists can prescribe medications, and some also practice psychotherapy. General practice physicians can also prescribe medications for mental disorders, but they do not typically receive much training in the diagnosis or treatment of mental disorders, and they do not practice psychotherapy.

> **Social worker** Social workers have a master's degree in social work and have training in working with people in dire life situations such as poverty, homelessness, or family conflict. Clinical or psychiatric social workers also receive training to help people in these situations who have mental disorders.

> **Counselor** In some states, a counselor must have a master's degree and extensive training in therapy; other states require minimal training or relevant education. Counselors who work in schools usually have a master's degree and specific training in counseling in educational settings.

Some people offer therapy under made-up terms that sound professional—"mind/body healing therapist," for example, or "marital adjustment adviser." Often these terms are simply invented to mislead clients and avoid licensing boards. To be safe, it is important to shop wisely for a therapist whose training and credentials inspire confidence.

People you know, such as your general practice physician, a school counselor, or a trusted friend or family member, might be able to recommend a good therapist. Or you can visit the American Psychological Association Web site for referrals to licensed mental health care providers.

Before you agree to see a therapist for treatment, you should ask questions to evaluate whether the therapist's style or background is a good match for your problem:

> What type of therapy do you practice?

> What types of problems do you usually treat?

> Will our work involve "talking" therapy, medications, or both?

> How effective is this type of therapy for the type of problem I'm having?

> What are your fees for therapy, and will health insurance cover them?

Zigy Kaluzny/Getty Images

Armed with the answers, you can make an informed decision about the type of service you need. The therapist's personality is also critically important. You should seek out someone who is willing and open to answer questions, and who shows general respect and empathy for you. You'll be entrusting the therapist with your mental health, and you should only enter into such a relationship when you and the therapist have good rapport.

availability (12.8%), inconvenience of attending treatment (9.8%), and trouble finding transportation to the clinic (5.7%; Mojtabai et al., 2011).

Even when people seek and find help, they sometimes do not receive the most effective treatments, which further complicates things. For starters, most of the treatment of mental disorders is not provided by mental health specialists, but by general medical practitioners (Wang et al., 2007). And even when people make it to a mental health specialist, they do not always receive the most effective treatment possible. In fact, only a small percentage of those with a mental disorder (< 40%) receive what would be considered minimally adequate treatment. Clearly, before choosing or prescribing a therapy, we need to know what kinds of treatments are available and understand which treatments are best for particular disorders.

Approaches to Treatment

Treatments can be divided broadly into two kinds: (a) psychological treatment, in which people interact with a clinician in order to use the environment to change their brain and behavior; and (b) biological treatment, in which the brain is treated directly with drugs, surgery, or some other direct intervention. In some cases, both psychological *and* biological treatments are used. Christine's OCD, for example, might be treated not only with ERP but also with medication that decreases her obsessive thoughts and compulsive urges. As we learn more about the biology and chemistry of the brain, approaches to mental health that begin with the brain are becoming increasingly widespread. As you'll see later in the chapter, many effective treatments combine both psychological and biological interventions.

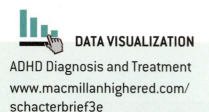

DATA VISUALIZATION

ADHD Diagnosis and Treatment
www.macmillanhighered.com/
schacterbrief3e

Culture & Community

Treatment of psychological disorders around the world Barriers that keep people from receiving treatment for mental disorders exist all around the world. However, they are greater in some places than in others. One recent study examined what percentage of people with a mental disorder in 17 different countries around the world received treatment for their disorder in the past year (Wang et al., 2007). Several different findings are interesting to note. First, people with a severe mental disorder are much more likely to be treated. This makes sense. For instance, if your disorder is so severe that it prevents you from going to school or work, you will probably seek treatment, but if it doesn't really interfere with your daily life you may not go for help. Second, people living in high-income countries (as defined by the World Bank) are much more likely to get treatment than those in middle- or low-income countries. This makes sense too. The more resources a country has, the more able it is to make psychological treatments available to its people. Third, most people with a mental disorder do not receive any treatment. This is true even in the countries with the highest income. This means that although we have a better understanding of mental disorders than we ever had before (as described in the last chapter) and also that we have better treatments than ever before (as described in this chapter), we still have to do a much better job removing the barriers that prevent those with mental disorders from getting help.

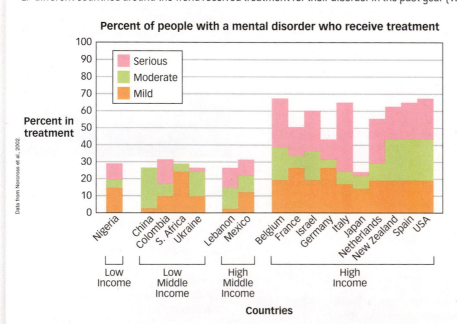

SUMMARY QUIZ [15.1]

1. One of the most effective treatments for obsessive-compulsive disorder is
   a. doing nothing because it will go away on its own.
   b. exposure and response prevention.
   c. bibliotherapy.
   d. Freudian psychoanalysis.

2. Which of the following is NOT a reason why people fail to get treatment for mental illness?
   a. People may not realize that their disorder needs to be treated.
   b. Levels of impairment for people with mental illness are not as high as those of people with chronic medical illnesses.
   c. There may be barriers to treatment, such as beliefs and circumstances that keep people from getting help.
   d. Even people who acknowledge they have a problem may not know where to look for services.

3. Which of the following statements is true?
   a. Mental illness is very rare, with only 1 person in 100 suffering from a psychological disorder.
   b. The majority of individuals with psychological disorders seek treatment.
   c. Women and men are equally likely to seek treatment for psychological disorders.
   d. Mental illness is often not taken as seriously as physical illness.

psychotherapy   An interaction between a socially sanctioned clinician and someone suffering from a psychological problem, with the goal of providing support or relief from the problem.

eclectic psychotherapy   A form of psychotherapy that involves drawing on techniques from different forms of therapy, depending on the client and the problem.

psychodynamic psychotherapies
Therapies that explore childhood events and encourage individuals to use the understanding that results to develop insight into their psychological problems.

Psychological Treatments: Healing the Mind through Interaction

Psychological therapy, or **psychotherapy,** is *an interaction between a socially sanctioned clinician and someone suffering from a psychological problem, with the goal of providing support or relief from the problem.* Currently, over 500 different forms of psychotherapy exist. A survey of 1,000 psychotherapists asked them to describe their main theoretical orientation (Norcross, Hedges, & Castle, 2002; see **FIGURE 15.1**). Over a third reported using **eclectic psychotherapy,** *a form of psychotherapy that involves drawing on techniques from different forms of therapy, depending on the client and the problem.* This allows therapists to apply an appropriate theoretical perspective suited to the problem at hand, rather than adhering to a single theoretical perspective for all clients and all types of problems. Nevertheless, as Figure 15.1 shows, the majority of psychotherapists use a single approach, such as psychodynamic therapy, humanistic and existential therapies, or behavioral and cognitive therapies. We'll examine each of those four major branches of psychotherapy in turn.

Psychodynamic Therapy

Psychodynamic psychotherapy has its roots in Freud's psychoanalytically oriented theory of personality. **Psychodynamic psychotherapies** are *therapies that explore childhood events and encourage individuals to use the understanding that results to develop insight into their psychological problems.* Psychoanalysis was the

FIGURE 15.1 Approaches to Psychotherapy in the 21st Century This chart shows the percentage of psychologists (from among 1,000 members of the American Psychological Association's Division of Psychotherapy) who have various primary psychotherapy orientations. (Data from Norcross et al., 2002.)

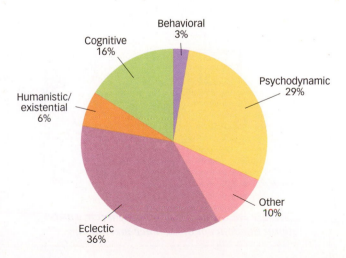

In traditional psychoanalysis, the client lies on a couch, with the therapist sitting behind, out of the client's view.

resistance   A reluctance to cooperate with treatment for fear of confronting unpleasant unconscious material.

transference   An event that occurs in psychoanalysis when the analyst begins to assume a major significance in the client's life and the client reacts to the analyst based on unconscious childhood fantasies.

interpersonal psychotherapy (IPT)   A form of psychotherapy that focuses on helping clients improve current relationships.

"Before we begin, I'd like to say a few words about the concept of 'defence mechanisms'."

first psychodynamic therapy to develop, but it has largely been replaced by modern psychodynamic therapies, such as interpersonal psychotherapy.

Psychoanalysis

As you saw in the Personality chapter, *psychoanalysis* assumes that people are born with aggressive and sexual urges that are repressed during childhood development through the use of defense mechanisms. Psychoanalysts encourage their clients to bring these repressed conflicts into consciousness so that the clients can understand them and reduce their unwanted influences.

Traditional psychoanalysis involves four or five sessions per week over an average of 3 to 6 years (Ursano & Silberman, 2003). During a session, the client reclines on a couch, facing away from the analyst, and is asked to express whatever thoughts and feelings come to mind. Occasionally, the therapist may comment on some of the information presented by the client but does not express his or her values and judgments. The stereotypic image you might have of psychological therapy—a person lying on a couch talking to a person sitting in a chair—springs from this approach.

The goal of psychoanalysis is for the client to understand the unconscious in a process Freud called *developing insight*. Some key techniques that psychoanalysts use to help the client develop insight include free association, in which the client reports every thought that enters the mind and the therapist looks for recurring themes, and dream analysis, in which the therapist looks for dream elements that might symbolize unconscious conflicts or wishes. Psychoanalysts also assess the client's **resistance,** or *a reluctance to cooperate with treatment for fear of confronting unpleasant unconscious material*. For example, the therapist might suggest that the client's problem with obsessive health worries could be traced to a childhood rivalry with her mother for her father's love and attention. The client could find the suggestion insulting and resist the interpretation, which might signal to the therapist that this is indeed an issue the client could be directed to confront in order to develop insight.

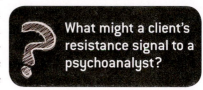

What might a client's resistance signal to a psychoanalyst?

Over time and many therapy sessions, the client and psychoanalyst often develop a close relationship. Freud believed that the development and resolution of this relationship was a key process of psychoanalysis. **Transference** is *an event that occurs when the analyst begins to assume a major significance in the client's life and the client reacts to the analyst based on unconscious childhood fantasies*. Successful psychoanalysis involves analyzing the transference so that the client understands this reaction and why it occurs.

Beyond Psychoanalysis

Although Freud's insights and techniques are fundamental, modern psychodynamic treatments differ from classic psychoanalysis in both their content and procedures. One of the most widely used psychodynamic treatments is **interpersonal psychotherapy (IPT),** *a form of psychotherapy that focuses on helping clients improve current relationships* (Weissman, Markowitz, & Klerman, 2000). Rather than using free association, therapists using IPT talk to clients about their interpersonal behaviors and feelings. The therapists pay particular attention to the client's grief (an exaggerated reaction to the loss of a loved one), role disputes (conflicts with a significant other), role transitions (changes in life status, such as starting a new job, getting married, or retiring), or interpersonal deficits (lack of the necessary skills to start or maintain a relationship). The treatment assumes that, as interpersonal relations improve, symptoms will subside.

Modern psychodynamic psychotherapies such as IPT also differ from classical psychoanalysis in the procedures used. For starters, in modern psychodynamic therapy, the therapist and client typically sit face-to-face. In addition, therapy is less intensive, with meetings often occurring only once a week and therapy lasting months rather than years. In contrast to classical psychoanalysis, modern psychodynamic therapists are more likely to offer support or advice in addition to interpretation (Barber et al., 2013). Therapists are also now less likely to interpret a client's statements as a sign of unconscious sexual or aggressive impulses.

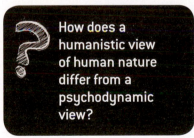

In the movie *Good Will Hunting*, the lead character, played by actor Matt Damon, forms a strong bond with his therapist, played by Robin Williams. As in psychodynamic therapy, the therapist uses their relationship to help break down the patient's defense mechanisms and resolve an inner conflict. The amazing bond that was formed between therapist and patient as well as the life-changing treatment delivered is the stuff of therapists' dreams (and Hollywood scripts).

> **In what ways do modern psychodynamic treatments differ from Freudian analysis?**

Although psychodynamic therapy has been around for a long time and continues to be widely practiced, there is relatively little evidence for its effectiveness. Moreover, there is some evidence that some aspects of psychodynamic therapy may actually be harmful. For instance, research suggests that the more a therapist makes interpretations about perceived transference in the client, the worse the therapeutic alliance and the worse the clinical outcome (Henry et al., 1994). Psychodynamic therapy is not as widely used as it once was, but many psychologists still use it in practice, and many people say that they find it helpful.

Humanistic and Existential Therapies

Humanistic and existential therapies emerged in part as a reaction to the negative views that psychoanalysis holds about human nature. Humanistic and existential therapies share the assumption that psychological problems stem from feelings of alienation and loneliness, and that those feelings can be traced to failures to reach one's potential (in the humanistic approach) or from failures to find meaning in life (in the existential approach). Although interest in these approaches peaked in the 1960s and 1970s, some therapists continue to use these approaches today. Two well-known types are person-centered therapy (a humanistic approach) and gestalt therapy (an existential approach).

> **How does a humanistic view of human nature differ from a psychodynamic view?**

Person-Centered Therapy

Person-centered therapy (or **client-centered therapy**) *assumes that all individuals have a tendency toward growth and that this growth can be facilitated by acceptance and genuine reactions from the therapist.* Psychologist Carl Rogers (1902–1987) developed person-centered therapy in the 1940s and 1950s (Rogers, 1951). Person-centered therapy assumes that each person is qualified to determine his or her own goals for therapy, such as feeling more confident or making a career decision, and even the frequency and length of therapy. In this type of treatment, the therapist tends not to provide advice or suggestions about what the client should be doing, but instead paraphrases the client's words, mirroring the client's thoughts and sentiments (e.g., "I think I hear you saying . . ."). Person-centered therapists believe that with adequate support, the client will recognize the right things to do.

person-centered therapy (or client-centered therapy) Assume that individuals have a tendency toward growth and that this growth can be facilitated by acceptance and genuine reactions from the therapist.

gestalt therapy Has the goal of helping the client become aware of his or her thoughts, behaviors, experiences, and feelings and to "own" or take responsibility for them.

Person-centered therapists should demonstrate three basic qualities. The first is *congruence,* which refers to openness and honesty in the therapeutic relationship. For example, the same message must be communicated in the therapist's words, the therapist's facial expression, and the therapist's body language. Saying "I think your concerns are valid" while smirking would simply not do. The second quality, *empathy,* refers to trying to understand the client by seeing the world from the client's perspective, which enables the therapist to better appreciate the client's apprehensions, worries, or fears. The third quality is *unconditional positive regard,* which entails providing a nonjudgmental, warm, and accepting environment in which the client can feel safe expressing his or her thoughts and feelings.

The goal is not to uncover repressed conflicts, as in psychodynamic therapy, but instead to try to understand the client's experience and reflect that experience back to the client in a supportive way, encouraging the client's natural tendency toward growth. This style of therapy is reminiscent of psychoanalysis in its way of encouraging the client toward the free expression of thoughts and feelings.

Gestalt Therapy

Gestalt therapy was founded by Frederick "Fritz" Perls (1893–1970) and colleagues in the 1940s and 1950s (Perls, Hefferkine, & Goodman, 1951). **Gestalt therapy** *has the goal of helping the client become aware of his or her thoughts, behaviors, experiences, and feelings and to "own" or take responsibility for them.* Gestalt therapists are encouraged to be enthusiastic and warm toward their clients, an approach they share with person-centered therapists. To help facilitate the client's awareness, gestalt therapists also reflect back to the client their impressions of the client.

PhotoAlto/Alamy

As part of gestalt therapy, clients may be encouraged to imagine that another person is sitting across from them in a chair. The client then moves from chair to chair, role-playing what he or she would say to the imagined person and what that person would answer.

Gestalt therapy emphasizes the experiences and behaviors that are occurring at that particular moment in the therapy session. For example, if a client is talking about something stressful that occurred during the previous week, the therapist might ask, "How do you feel now as you describe what happened to you?" Clients are also encouraged to put their feelings into action. One way to do this is the empty chair technique, in which the client imagines that another person (e.g., a spouse, a parent, or a co-worker) is in an empty chair, sitting directly across from the client. The client then moves from chair to chair, alternating from role-playing what he or she would say to the other person and how he or she imagines the other person would respond. Gestalt techniques are often used in counseling or "life coaching" to help people prepare for new job or family situations (Grant, 2008).

Behavioral and Cognitive Therapies

Unlike the talk therapies described earlier, behavioral and cognitive treatments emphasize actively changing a person's current thoughts and behaviors as a way to decrease or eliminate the patient's psychopathology. In the evolution of psychological treatments, clients started out lying down in psychoanalysis, then sitting in psychodynamic and related approaches, but they are often standing and engaging in behavior-change homework assignments in their everyday lives in behavioral and cognitive therapies.

Behavior Therapy

behavior therapy A type of therapy that assumes that disordered behavior is learned and that symptom relief is achieved through changing overt maladaptive behaviors into more constructive behaviors.

token economy A form of behavior therapy in which clients are given "tokens" for desired behaviors, which they can later trade for rewards.

Whereas Freud developed psychoanalysis as an offshoot of hypnosis and other techniques used by other clinicians before him, behavior therapy was developed based on laboratory findings from earlier behavioral psychologists. As you read in the Psychology: Evolution of a Science chapter, behaviorists rejected theories that were based on "invisible" mental properties that were difficult to test and impossible to observe directly. Behaviorists found psychoanalytic ideas particularly hard to test: How do you know whether a person has an unconscious conflict? Behavioral principles, in contrast, focused solely on behaviors that could be observed (e.g., avoidance of a feared object, such as refusing to get on an airplane). **Behavior therapy** is *a type of therapy that assumes that disordered behavior is learned and that symptom relief is achieved through changing overt maladaptive behaviors into more constructive behaviors.* A variety of behavior therapy techniques have been developed for many disorders, based on the learning principles you encountered in the Learning chapter, including operant conditioning

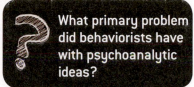

What primary problem did behaviorists have with psychoanalytic ideas?

procedures (which focus on reinforcement and punishment) and classical conditioning procedures (which focus on extinction). Here are three examples of behavior therapy techniques in action:

A behavioral psychologist might treat a temper tantrum using a time-out from reinforcement, which is based on the behavioral principle of operant conditioning and ensures that a child will not be rewarded for her undesired behavior.

1. **Eliminating Unwanted Behaviors.** How would you change a 3-year-old boy's habit of throwing tantrums at the grocery store? A behavior therapist might investigate what happens immediately before and after the tantrum: Did the child get candy to "shut him up?" The study of operant conditioning shows that behavior can be influenced by its *consequences* (the reinforcing or punishing events that follow). Adjusting these consequences might help change the behavior. Making them less reinforcing (no candy!) and more punishing (a period of time-out facing the wall in the grocery store while the parent watches from nearby rather than providing a rush of attention) could eliminate the problem behavior.

2. **Promoting Desired Behaviors.** Candy and a time-out can have a strong influence on child behavior, but they work less well with adults. How might you get an individual with schizophrenia to engage in activities of daily living? How would you get a cocaine addict to stop using drugs? A behavior therapy technique that has proven to be quite effective in such cases is the **token economy,** *a form of behavior therapy in which clients are given "tokens" for desired behaviors, which they can later trade for rewards.* For instance, in the case of cocaine dependence, the desired behavior is not using cocaine. Programs that reward nonuse (verified by urine samples) with vouchers that can be exchanged for rewards such as money, bus passes, clothes, and so on, have shown an ability to significantly reduce cocaine use and associated psychological problems (Petry, Alessi, & Rash, 2013). Similar systems are used to promote desired behaviors in classrooms, the workplace, and commercial advertising (e.g., airline and credit card rewards programs).

exposure therapy An approach to treatment that involves confronting an emotion-arousing stimulus directly and repeatedly, ultimately leading to a decrease in the emotional response.

An exposure therapy client with obsessive-compulsive disorder who fears contamination in public restrooms might be given "homework" to visit three such restrooms in a week, touch the toilets, and then *not* wash up.

3. **Reducing Unwanted Emotional Responses.** One of the most powerful ways to reduce fear is by gradual exposure to the feared object or situation. **Exposure therapy** is *an approach to treatment that involves confronting an emotion-arousing stimulus directly and repeatedly, ultimately leading to a decrease in the emotional response.* This technique depends on the processes of habituation and response extinction. For example, in Christine's case, her clinician gradually exposed her to the content of her obsessions (dirt and germs), which became less and less distressing with repeated exposure. Similarly, for clients who are afraid of social interaction and are unable to function at school or work, a behavioral treatment might involve exposure first to imagined situations in which they talk briefly with one person, then a bit longer talk to a medium-sized group, and finally, giving a speech to a large group. It's now known that *in vivo* (live) exposure is more effective than imaginary exposure (Choy, Fyer, & Lipsitz, 2007). In other words, if a person fears social situations, it is better for that person to practice social interaction than merely to imagine it. Behavioral therapists use an exposure hierarchy to expose

Table 15.1 Exposure Hierarchy for Social Phobia

Item	Fear (0–100)
1. Have a party and invite everyone from work	99
2. Go to a holiday party for 1 hour without drinking	90
3. Invite Cindy to have dinner and see a movie	85
4. Go for a job interview	80
5. Ask boss for a day off from work	65
6. Ask questions in a meeting at work	65
7. Eat lunch with co-workers	60
8. Talk to a stranger on a bus	50
9. Talk to cousin on the telephone for 10 minutes	40
10. Ask for directions at a gas station	35

Source: Information from Ellis, 1991.

the client gradually to the feared object or situation. Easier situations are practiced first, and as fear decreases, the client progresses to more difficult or frightening situations (see **TABLE 15.1**).

Cognitive Therapy

Whereas behavior therapy focuses primarily on changing a person's behavior, **cognitive therapy** *focuses on helping a client identify and correct any distorted thinking about self, others, or the world* (Beck, 2005). For example, behaviorists might explain a phobia as the outcome of a classical conditioning experience such as being bitten by a dog, where the dog bite leads to the development of a dog phobia through the association of the dog with the experience of pain. Cognitive theorists might instead emphasize the *interpretation* of the event and focus on a person's new or strengthened belief that dogs are dangerous to explain the fear.

Cognitive therapies use a technique called **cognitive restructuring**, *a therapeutic approach that teaches clients to question the automatic beliefs, assumptions, and predictions that often lead to negative emotions and to replace negative thinking with more realistic and positive beliefs.* Specifically, clients are taught to examine the evidence for and against a particular belief or to be more accepting of outcomes that may be undesirable yet still manageable. For example, a depressed client may believe that she is stupid and will never pass her college courses—all on the basis of one poor grade. In this situation, the therapist would work with the client to examine the validity of this belief. The therapist would consider relevant evidence such as grades on previous exams, performance in other coursework, and examples of intelligence outside school. In therapy sessions, the cognitive therapist will help the client to identify evidence that supports—and fails to support—each negative thought in order to help the client generate more balanced thoughts that accurately reflect the true state of affairs. In other words, the clinician tries to remove the dark lens through which the client views the world, not with the goal of replacing it with rose-colored glasses, but instead with clear glasses. Here is a brief sample transcript of what part of a cognitive therapy session might sound like.

cognitive therapy Focuses on helping a client identify and correct any distorted thinking about self, others, or the world.

cognitive restructuring A therapeutic approach that teaches clients to question the automatic beliefs, assumptions, and predictions that often lead to negative emotions and to replace negative thinking with more realistic and positive beliefs.

Clinician	Last week, I asked you to keep a thought record of both the situations that made you feel very depressed and the automatic thoughts that popped into your mind. Were you able to do that?
Client	Yes.
Clinician	Wonderful, I'm glad you were able to complete this assignment. Let's take a look at this together. What's the first situation that you recorded?
Client	Well . . . I went out on Friday night with my friends, which I thought would be fun. But I was feeling kind of down about things and I ended up not really talking to anyone. Instead I just sat in the corner and drank all night. I got so drunk that I passed out at the party. I woke up the next day feeling embarrassed and more depressed than ever.
Clinician	OK, and what thoughts automatically popped into your head?
Client	My friends think I'm a loser and will never want to hang out with me again.
Clinician	What evidence can you think of that supports this thought?
Client	Well . . . um . . . I got really drunk and so they *have* to think I'm a loser. I mean, who does that?
Clinician	Is there any other evidence you can think of that supports those thoughts?

Client	No.
Clinician	All right. Now let's take a moment to think about whether there is any evidence that doesn't support those thoughts. Did anything happen that suggests that your friends do want to keep hanging out with you?
Client	Well . . . my friends brought me home safely and then called the next day and joked about what happened and my one friend Tommy said something like, "we've all been there," and that he wants to hang out again this weekend.
Clinician	This is very interesting. So on one hand, you feel depressed and have thoughts that you are a loser and your friends don't like you. But on the other hand, you have some pretty real-world evidence that even though you drank too much, they were still there for you and they do in fact want to hang out with you again, yes?
Client	Yeah, I guess you're right if you put it that way. I didn't think about it like that.
Clinician	So now if we were going to replace your first thoughts, which don't seem to have a lot of real-world evidence, with a more balanced thought based on the evidence, what would that new thought be?
Client	Probably something like, my friends probably weren't happy about the fact that I got so drunk because then they had to take care of me, but they are my friends and were there for me and want to keep hanging out with me.
Clinician	Excellent job. I think that sounds just right based on the evidence.

mindfulness meditation Teaches an individual to be fully present in each moment; to be aware of his or her thoughts, feelings, and sensations; and to detect symptoms before they become a problem.

cognitive behavioral therapy (CBT) A blend of cognitive and behavioral therapeutic strategies.

In addition to cognitive restructuring techniques, which try to change a person's thoughts to be more balanced or accurate, some forms of cognitive therapy also include techniques for coping with unwanted thoughts and feelings, techniques that resemble meditation (see the Consciousness chapter). One such technique, called **mindfulness meditation,** *teaches an individual to be fully present in each moment; to be aware of his or her thoughts, feelings, and sensations; and to detect symptoms before they become a problem.* In one study, people recovering from depression were about half as likely to relapse during a 60-week assessment period if they received mindfulness meditation-based cognitive therapy than if they received treatment as usual (Teasdale, Segal, & Williams, 2000).

> **How might a client restructure a negative self-image into a positive one?**

> How might the use of behavior-change homework improve the effectiveness of behavior therapy?

Cognitive Behavioral Therapy

Historically, cognitive and behavioral therapies were considered distinct systems of therapy. Today, most therapists working with anxiety and depression use *a blend of cognitive and behavioral therapeutic strategies,* often referred to as **cognitive behavioral therapy** (**CBT**). In contrast to traditional behavior therapy and cognitive therapy, CBT is *problem focused,* meaning that it is undertaken for specific problems (e.g., reducing the frequency of panic attacks or returning to work after a bout of depression), and *action oriented,* meaning that the therapist tries to assist the client in selecting specific strategies to help address those problems. The client is expected to *do* things, such as engage in exposure exercises, practice behavior change skills or use a diary to monitor relevant symptoms (e.g., the severity of a depressed mood or panic attack symptoms). This is in contrast to psychodynamic or other therapies in which goals may not be explicitly discussed or agreed on and the client's only necessary action is to attend the therapy session.

> **How does cognitive behavioral therapy differ from psychodynamic therapy?**

©Bonnie Kamin/Photoedit

"Rebooting" Psychological Treatment

Modern psychotherapy has advanced far beyond the days of Freud and his free-associating patients. We now have more sophisticated treatments that have been developed based on recent advances in psychological science and supported in experimental studies showing that they actually do decrease peoples' psychological suffering. However, psychological treatment is still pretty primitive in many ways. It usually involves weekly meetings in which a clinician attempts to talk a patient out of a psychological disorder—just as in Freud's day. In a recent paper, Alan Kazdin (and his student Stacey Blase) called for a "rebooting" of psychotherapy research and practice to take advantage of recent advances in technology (Kazdin & Blase, 2011).

For example, research suggests that biases in the ways that people process information cause psychological disorders. Cognitive bias modification (CBM) is a computerized intervention that focuses on eliminating these biases (MacLeod & Mathews, 2012). Specifically, people with social anxiety show selective attention for threatening information (e.g., when shown several faces, they have an automatic tendency to look at the angrier one). In one form of CBM for social anxiety, the patient completes a computerized training program in which he or she

Courtesy Philip M. Enock

is repeatedly shown pairs of faces, one angry and one neutral, that flash on the screen very quickly (for 500 milliseconds), after which a letter appears behind one of them and the patient's task is to name that letter. In CBM, the letter nearly always appears behind the neutral face, which over time teaches the person to ignore the angry face and attend to the neutral face, thus reducing the tendency to attend to threatening faces. The training is intended to generalize beyond faces to reduce attention to threatening stimuli in general. CBM has been tested for the treatment of a range of different psychological disorders (Beard, Sawyer, & Hofmann, 2012) and represents an exciting

new direction in treatment development. However, it is important to note that in CBM, as with many novel treatments, several nonreplications followed the initial successful trials (e.g., Enock & McNally, 2013), suggesting that the jury is still out regarding the effectiveness of this new type of treatment.

In addition to new forms of treatment that can be administered in clinics, advances in technology are allowing psychologists to bring the clinic into people's everyday lives. Psychologists are now using computers, cellular phones, and wearable biosensors to measure patients' experiences in the real world in real time, and also to administer interventions well beyond the clinic walls (e.g., using text messages to remind patients not to smoke or to practice the skills they learned during their last therapy session). The development of "mobile health" or "mHealth" interventions has been extremely exciting; however, one recent review found that more than half of interventions that used mobile technologies fail to show any benefit (Kaplan & Stone, 2013). So although the development of portable technological devices has opened up lots of new opportunities for intervention, it is important that psychologists carefully evaluate which can help improve health outcomes and which are simply fancier ways of providing ineffective treatment.

Cognitive behavioral therapies have been found to be effective for a number of disorders (Butler et al., 2006), including unipolar depression, generalized anxiety disorder, panic disorder, social phobia, posttraumatic stress disorder, and childhood depressive and anxiety disorders (see the Hot Science box).

Group Treatments: Healing Multiple Minds at the Same Time

It is natural to think of psychopathology as an illness that affects only the individual. Yet each person lives in a world of other people, and interactions with others may intensify and even create disorders. A depressed person may be lonely after moving away from friends and loved ones, or an anxious person could be worried about pressures from parents. These ideas suggest that people might be able to recover from disorders in the same way they got into them—not just as an individual effort, but through social processes.

Couples and Family Therapy

When a couple is "having problems," neither individual may be suffering from any psychopathology. Rather, it may be the relationship itself that is disordered. *Couples therapy* is when a married, cohabitating, or dating couple is seen together in therapy to work on problems usually arising within the relationship. For example, a couple might seek help because they are unhappy with their relationship. In this scenario, both members of the couple are expected to attend therapy sessions, and the problem is seen as arising from their interaction rather than from the problems of one half of the couple. Treatment strategies would target changes in *both* parties, focusing on ways to break their repetitive dysfunctional pattern.

There are cases in which therapy with even larger groups is warranted. An individual may be having a problem—say, an adolescent is abusing alcohol—but the source of the problem is the individual's relationships with family members; perhaps the mother is herself an alcoholic who subtly encourages the adolescent to drink and the father travels and neglects the family. In this case, it could be useful for the therapist to work with the whole group at once in *family therapy*—psychotherapy involving members of a family. As in couples therapy, the problems and solutions are seen as arising from the *interaction* of individuals in the family rather than simply from any one individual.

Anna Goldbergs/AgeFotostock

Families enter therapy for many reasons, sometimes to help particular members and other times because there are problems in one or more of the relationships in the family.

Group Therapy

Taking these ideas one step further, if individuals (or families) can benefit from talking with a psychotherapist, perhaps they can also benefit from talking with other clients who are talking with the therapist. This is **group therapy,** *a technique in which multiple participants (who often do not know one another at the outset) work on their individual problems in a group atmosphere.* The therapist in group therapy serves more as a discussion leader than as a personal therapist, conducting the sessions both by talking with individuals and by encouraging them to talk with one another.

Why do people choose group therapy? One advantage is that attending a group with others who have similar problems shows clients that they are not alone in their suffering. In addition, group members model appropriate behaviors for one another and share their insights about how to deal with their problems. Group therapy is often just as effective as individual therapy (e.g., Jonsson & Hougaard, 2008). So, from a societal perspective, group therapy is much more efficient.

Group therapy also has disadvantages. It may be difficult to assemble a group of individuals who have similar needs. This is particularly an issue with CBT, which tends to focus on specific problems such as depression or panic disorder. Group therapy may become a problem if one or more members undermine the treatment of other group members—for example, by dominating the discussions or by making others in the group uncomfortable (e.g., attempting to date other members). Finally, clients in group therapy get less attention than they might in individual psychotherapy.

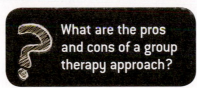

What are the pros and cons of a group therapy approach?

Self-Help and Support Groups

An important offshoot of group therapy is the concept of *self-help groups* and *support groups,* which are discussion groups that are often run by peers who have themselves struggled with the same issues. The most famous self-help and support groups are Alcoholics Anonymous (AA), Gamblers Anonymous, and Al-Anon (a program for the family and friends of those with alcohol problems). Other self-help groups offer support to people with mood disorders, eating disorders, and substance abuse problems. In fact, self-help and support groups exist for just about every psychological disorder. In addition to being cost-effective, self-help and support groups allow people to realize that they are not the only ones with a particular problem and give them the opportunity to offer guidance and support to each other based on personal experiences of success.

group therapy A technique in which multiple participants (who often do not know one another at the outset) work on their individual problems in a group atmosphere.

Self-help groups are a cost-effective, time-effective, and treatment-effective solution for dealing with some types of psychological problems. Many people like self-help groups, but are they effective? How could you test this?

© Richard T. Nowitz/CORBIS

In some cases, though, self-help and support groups can do more harm than good. Some members may be disruptive or aggressive or encourage one another to engage in behaviors that are countertherapeutic (e.g., avoiding feared situations or using alcohol to cope). People with moderate problems may be exposed to others with severe problems and may become oversensitized to symptoms they might not otherwise have found disturbing. Because self-help and support groups are usually not led by trained therapists, mechanisms to evaluate these groups or to ensure their quality are rarely in place.

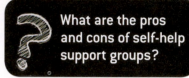

What are the pros and cons of self-help support groups?

AA has more than two million members in the United States, with 185,000 group meetings that occur around the world (Mack, Franklin, & Frances, 2003). Members are encouraged to follow "12 steps" to reach the goal of lifelong abstinence from all drinking, and the steps include believing in a higher power, practicing prayer and meditation, and making amends for harm to others. A few studies examining the effectiveness of AA have been conducted, and it appears that individuals who participate tend to overcome problem drinking with greater success than those who do not participate in AA (Fiorentine, 1999; Morgenstern et al., 1997). However, several tenets of the AA philosophy are not supported by the research. We know that the general AA program is useful, but questions about which parts of this program are most helpful have yet to be studied.

Considered together, the many social approaches to psychotherapy reveal how important interpersonal relationships are for each of us. It may not always be clear how psychotherapy works, whether one approach is better than another, or what particular theory should be used to understand how problems have developed. What is clear, however, is that social interactions between people—both in individual therapy and in all the different forms of therapy in groups—can be useful in treating psychological disorders.

SUMMARY QUIZ [15.2]

1. The different psychodynamic therapies all share an emphasis on
   a. the influence of the collective unconscious.
   b. the importance of taking responsibility for psychological problems.
   c. combining behavioral and cognitive approaches.
   d. developing insight into the unconscious sources of psychological disorders.

2. Which type of therapy would likely work best for someone with an irrational fear of heights?

    a. psychodynamic

    b. gestalt

    c. behavioral

    d. humanistic

3. Self-help groups are an important offshoot of

    a. cognitive behavioral therapy.

    b. support groups.

    c. person-centered therapy.

    d. group therapy.

Medical and Biological Treatments: Healing the Mind by Physically Altering the Brain

Ever since someone discovered that a whack to the head can affect the mind, people have suspected that direct brain interventions might hold the keys to a cure for psychological disorders. Archaeological evidence, for example, indicates that the occasional human thousands of years ago was "treated" for some malady by the practice of *trephining* (drilling a hole in the skull), perhaps in the belief that this would release evil spirits that were affecting the mind (Alt et al., 1997). Surgery for psychological disorders is a last resort nowadays, and treatments that focus on the brain usually involve interventions that are less dramatic. The use of drugs to influence the brain was also discovered in prehistory (alcohol, for example, has been around for a long time). Since then, drug treatments have grown in variety, effectiveness, and popularity, and they are now the most common medical approach in treating psychological disorders (see **FIGURE 15.2**).

This is a trephined skull from a Stone Age burial site (about 5900–6200 BCE) in the Alsace region of France. Two holes were drilled in the skull, and the individual survived, as shown by the regrowth of bone covering the holes (from Alt et al., 1997). Don't try this at home.

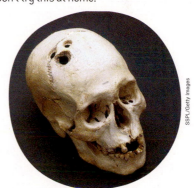

SSPL/Getty Images

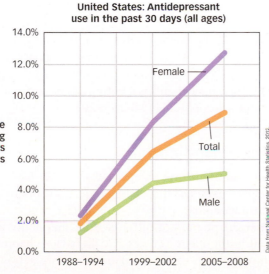

United States: Antidepressant use in the past 30 days (all ages)

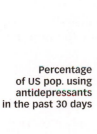

Percentage of US pop. using antidepressants in the past 30 days

Data from National Center for Health Statistics, 2012.

FIGURE 15.2 Antidepressant Use A recent report showed that the use of antidepressant medications increased 400% over the period of 1988 to 2008 (National Center for Health Statistics, 2012). This rise may be due to a number of factors, including new data on the effectiveness of these medications and also the enhanced efforts to market these drugs directly to consumers. The higher rates of use shown here for females may be due in part to the fact that women have higher rates of both depression and treatment use, compared to men.

antipsychotic drugs Medications that are used to treat schizophrenia and related psychotic disorders.

psychopharmacology The study of drug effects on psychological states and symptoms.

antianxiety medications Drugs that help reduce a person's experience of fear or anxiety.

Antipsychotic Medications

Antipsychotic drugs are *medications that are used to treat schizophrenia and related psychotic disorders*. The first antipsychotic drug, back in the 1950s, was chlorpromazine (brand name Thorazine), which was originally developed as a sedative. Other related medications, such as thioridazine (Mellaril) and haloperidol (Haldol), followed. Before the introduction of antipsychotic drugs, people with schizophrenia often exhibited bizarre symptoms and were sometimes so disruptive and difficult to manage that the only way to protect them (and other people) was to keep them in hospitals for people with mental disorders, which were initially called *asylums* but now are referred to as *psychiatric hospitals*. In the period following the introduction of these drugs, the number of people in psychiatric hospitals decreased by more than two thirds. Antipsychotic drugs made possible the deinstitutionalization of hundreds of thousands of people and gave a major boost to the field of **psychopharmacology,** *the study of drug effects on psychological states and symptoms.*

Antipsychotic medications are believed to block dopamine receptors. As you read in the Psychological Disorders chapter, the effectiveness of schizophrenia medications led to the dopamine hypothesis, suggesting that schizophrenia may be caused by excess dopamine in the brain. Research has indeed found that dopamine overactivity in some areas of the brain is related to the more bizarre positive symptoms of schizophrenia, such as hallucinations and delusions (Marangell et al., 2003). Unfortunately, the negative symptoms of schizophrenia, such as emotional numbing and social withdrawal, may be related to dopamine *underactivity* in other areas of the brain. This may explain why antipsychotic medications do not relieve negative symptoms well.

After the introduction of antipsychotic medications, there was little change in the available treatments for schizophrenia for more than a quarter of a century. However, in the 1990s, a new class of antipsychotic drugs was introduced. These newer drugs, which include clozapine (Clozaril), risperidone (Risperdal), and olanzapine (Zyprexa), have become known as *atypical* antipsychotics (the older drugs are now often referred to as *conventional* or *typical* antipsychotics). Unlike the older antipsychotic medications, these newer drugs appear to block both dopamine and serotonin receptors.

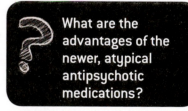

What are the advantages of the newer, atypical antipsychotic medications?

Serotonin has been implicated in some of the core difficulties in schizophrenia, such as cognitive and perceptual disruptions, as well as mood disturbances, which may explain why atypical antipsychotics can provide relief for both the positive and negative symptoms of schizophrenia (Bradford, Stroup, & Lieberman, 2002).

Like most medications, antipsychotic drugs have side effects. These can include motor disturbances such as involuntary movements of the face, mouth, and extremities. In fact, people often need to take another medication to treat the unwanted side effects of the conventional antipsychotic drugs. Side effects of the newer medications tend to be different and sometimes milder than those of the older antipsychotics. For that reason, the atypical antipsychotics are now usually the front-line treatments for schizophrenia (Meltzer, 2013).

Antianxiety Medications

Antianxiety medications are *drugs that help reduce a person's experience of fear or anxiety*. The most commonly used antianxiety medications are the benzodiazepines, a type of tranquilizer that works by facilitating the action of the neurotransmitter gamma-aminobutyric acid (GABA). As you read in the Neuroscience and Behavior chapter, GABA inhibits certain neurons in the brain. This inhibitory action can produce a

"The drug has, however, proved more effective than traditional psychoanalysis."

calming effect for the person. Commonly prescribed benzodiazepines include diazepam (Valium), lorazepam (Ativan), and alprazolam (Xanax). The benzodiazepines typically take effect in a matter of minutes and are effective for reducing symptoms of anxiety disorders (Roy-Byrne & Cowley, 2002).

Nonetheless, these days, doctors are relatively cautious when prescribing benzodiazepines. One concern is that these drugs can be highly addictive. They also have side effects, especially drowsiness, but also negative effects on coordination and memory. And benzodiazepines combined with alcohol can depress respiration, potentially causing accidental death.

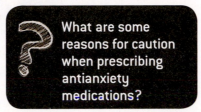

? What are some reasons for caution when prescribing antianxiety medications?

antidepressants A class of drugs that help lift people's moods.

Antidepressants and Mood Stabilizers

Antidepressants are *a class of drugs that help lift people's moods.* Two classes of antidepressants were introduced in the 1950s, the *monoamine oxidase inhibitors (MAOIs)* and the *tricyclic antidepressants.* MAOIs prevent the enzyme monoamine oxidase from breaking down neurotransmitters such as norepinephrine, serotonin, and dopamine. However, despite their effectiveness, MAOIs are rarely prescribed anymore due to side effects such as dizziness and loss of sexual interest, as well as potentially dangerous interactions with other common medications. Tricyclic antidepressants are still sometimes used, but they also have serious side effects, including dry mouth, constipation, difficulty urinating, blurred vision, and racing heart (Marangell et al., 2003).

Thinkstock

Today, the most commonly used antidepressants are the *selective serotonin reuptake inhibitors,* or SSRIs, which include drugs such as fluoxetine (Prozac), citalopram (Celexa), and paroxetine (Paxil). The SSRIs work by blocking the reuptake of serotonin in the brain, which makes more serotonin available in the synaptic space between neurons. The greater availability of serotonin in the synapse gives the neuron a better chance of "recognizing" and using this neurotransmitter in sending the desired signal. The SSRIs were developed based on hypotheses that low levels of serotonin are a causal factor in depression. Supporting this hypothesis, SSRIs are effective for depression, as well as for a wide range of other problems. SSRIs are called *selective* because, unlike the tricyclic antidepressants, which work on the serotonin and norepinephrine systems, SSRIs work more specifically on the serotonin system (see **FIGURE 15.3**).

? What are the most common antidepressants used today? How do they work?

If you watch television, you have seen advertisements for specific drugs. Does this direct-to-consumer advertising really work? Sure does! One recent study sent people acting as patients to physicians' offices asking for specific drugs and found that patient requests had a huge impact on doctors' behavior: Those "patients" asking about specific drugs were much more likely to receive a prescription than those who did not make a request (Kravitz et al., 2005).

Finally, antidepressants such as Effexor (venlafaxine) and Wellbutrin (ibupropion) offer other alternatives. Effexor is an example of a serotonin and norepinephrine reuptake inhibitor (SNRI), whereas SSRIs act only upon serotonin, SNRIs act on both serotonin and norepinephrine. Wellbutrin, in contrast, is a norepinephrine and dopamine reuptake inhibitor. These and other newly developed antidepressants appear to have fewer (or at least different) side effects than the tricyclic antidepressants and MAOIs.

Most antidepressants can take up to a month before they start to have an effect on mood. Besides relieving symptoms of depression, almost all of the antidepressants effectively treat anxiety disorders, and many of them can resolve other problems, such as eating disorders. In fact, several companies that manufacture SSRIs have marketed their drugs as treatments for anxiety disorders rather than for their antidepressant effects. Although antidepressants can be effective in treating major depression, they

FIGURE 15.3 **Antidepressant Drug Actions**
Antidepressant drugs, such as MAOIs, SSRIs, and tricyclic antidepressants, act on neurotransmitters such as serotonin, dopamine, and norepinephrine by inhibiting their breakdown and blocking reuptake. These actions leave more of the neurotransmitter in the synaptic gap to activate the receptor sites on the postsynaptic neuron. These drugs relieve depression and often alleviate anxiety and other disorders.

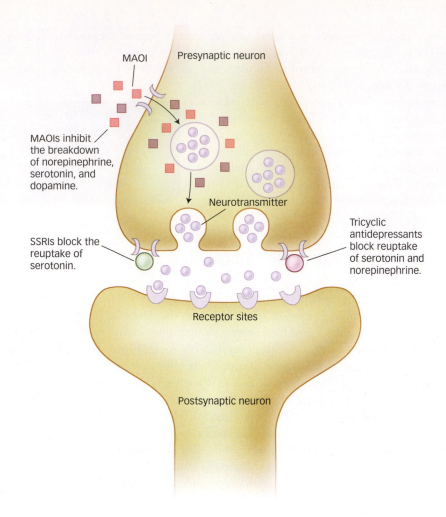

are not recommended for treating bipolar disorder because, in the process of lifting one's mood, they might actually trigger a manic episode in a person with bipolar disorder. Instead, bipolar disorder is commonly treated with *mood stabilizers,* which are medications used to suppress swings between mania and depression. Commonly used mood stabilizers include lithium and valproate.

Herbal and Natural Products

In a survey of more than 2,000 Americans, 7% of those suffering from anxiety disorders and 9% of those suffering from severe depression reported using alternative "medications" such as herbal medicines, megavitamins, homeopathic remedies, or naturopathic remedies to treat these problems (Kessler et al., 2001). Major reasons people use these products are that they are easily available over the counter, are less expensive, and are perceived as "natural" alternatives to synthetic or manmade "drugs." Are herbal and natural products effective in treating mental health problems, or are they just "snake oil?"

The answer to this question isn't simple. Herbal products are not considered medications by regulatory agencies like the U.S. Food and Drug Administration, so they are exempt from rigorous research to establish their safety and effectiveness. Instead, herbal products are classified as nutritional supplements and regulated in the same way as food. There is little scientific information about herbal products, including possible interactions with other medications, possible tolerance and withdrawal symptoms, side effects, appropriate dosages, how they work, or even *whether* they work—and the purity of these products often varies from brand to brand (Jordan, Cunningham, & Marles, 2010).

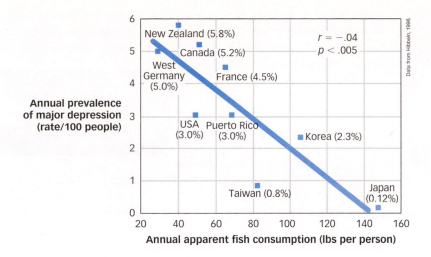

FIGURE 15.4 Omega-3 Fatty Acids and Depression Recent studies have shown that consumption of omega-3 fatty acids is associated with a wide range of positive mental health outcomes. For instance, Joe Hibbeln (1998) showed that countries that consume more fish (a main dietary source of omega-3s) have significantly lower rates of depression.

There is research support for the effectiveness of some herbal and natural products, but the evidence is not overwhelming (Lake, 2009). For example, some studies have shown that St. John's wort (a wort, it turns out, is an herb) has an advantage over a placebo condition for the treatment of depression (e.g., Lecrubier et al., 2002), whereas other studies show no advantage (e.g., Hypericum Depression Trial Study Group, 2002). Omega-3 fatty acids have been linked with lower rates of depression and suicide, and several treatment studies have repeatedly shown that omega-3s are superior to a placebo at decreasing depression (see **FIGURE 15.4**) (Lewis et al., 2011; Parker et al., 2006). Overall, although herbal medications and treatments are worthy of continued research, these products should be closely monitored and used judiciously until more is known about their safety and effectiveness.

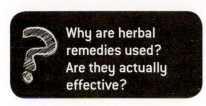

Why are herbal remedies used? Are they actually effective?

Combining Medication and Psychotherapy

Given that psychological treatments and medications both have shown an ability to treat mental disorders effectively, some natural next questions are: Which is more effective? Is the combination of psychological and medicinal treatments better than either by itself? The answer often depends on the particular problem being considered. For example, in the cases of schizophrenia and bipolar disorder, researchers have found that medication is more effective than psychological treatment and so is considered a necessary part of treatment. But in the case of mood and anxiety disorders, medication and psychological treatments are equally effective. One study compared cognitive behavior therapy, imipramine (an antidepressant), and the combination of these treatments (CBT plus imipramine) with a placebo (administration of an inert medication) for the treatment of panic disorder (Barlow et al., 2000). After 12 weeks of treatment, either CBT alone or imipramine alone was found to be superior to a placebo. But the combination of CBT plus imipramine was not significantly better than that for either CBT or imipramine alone. In other words, either treatment was better than nothing, but the combination of treatments was not significantly more effective than one or the other (see **FIGURE 15.5**). More is not always better.

Given that both therapy and medications are effective, one question is whether they work through similar

FIGURE 15.5 The Effectiveness of Medication and Psychotherapy for Panic Disorder One study of CBT and medication (imipramine) for panic disorder found that the effects of CBT, medication, and combined CBT and medication were not significantly different over the short term, though all three were superior to the placebo condition (Barlow et al., 2000).

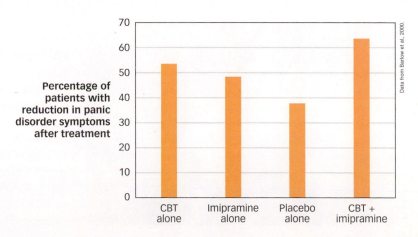

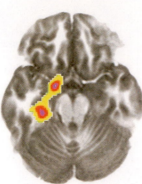

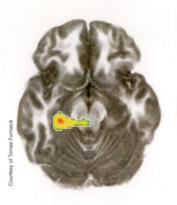

Courtesy of Tomas Furmark

FIGURE 15.6 The Effects of Medication and Therapy in the Brain PET scans of individuals with social phobia showed similar reductions in activation of the amygdala–hippocampus region after they received treatment with CBT (*left*) or the SSRI citalopram (*right*) (from Furmark et al., 2002).

electroconvulsive therapy (ECT) A treatment that involves inducing a brief seizure by delivering an electrical shock to the brain.

transcranial magnetic stimulation (TMS) A treatment that involves placing a powerful pulsed magnet over a person's scalp, which alters neuronal activity in the brain.

Electroconvulsive therapy (ECT) can be an effective treatment for severe depression. To reduce the side effects, it is administered under general anesthesia.

Richard Perry/The New York Times/Redux

mechanisms. A study of people with social phobia examined patterns of cerebral blood flow following treatment using either citalopram (an SSRI) or CBT (Furmark et al., 2002). Participants in both groups were alerted to the possibility that they would soon have to speak in public. In both groups, those who responded to treatment showed similar reductions in activation in the amygdala, hippocampus, and neighboring cortical areas during this challenge (see **FIGURE 15.6**). The amygdala, located next to the hippocampus (see Figure 6.18) plays a significant role in memory for emotional information. These findings suggest that both therapy and medication affect the brain in regions associated with a reaction to threat.

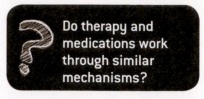

Do therapy and medications work through similar mechanisms?

One complication in combining medication and psychotherapy is that these treatments are often provided by different people. Psychiatrists are trained in the administration of medication in medical school (and they may also provide psychological treatment), whereas psychologists provide psychological treatment but cannot prescribe medication. This means that the coordination of treatment often requires cooperation between psychologists and psychiatrists.

The question of whether psychologists should be licensed to prescribe medications has been a source of debate (Fox et al., 2009). Only Illinois, Louisiana, and New Mexico currently allow licensed and specially trained psychologists prescription privileges, but other states are considering it (Munsey, 2008). Opponents argue that psychologists do not have the medical training to understand how medications interact with other drugs. Proponents argue that patient safety would not be compromised as long as rigorous training procedures were established. At present, the coordination of medication and psychological treatment usually involves a team effort of psychiatry and psychology.

Biological Treatments beyond Medications

Medication can be an effective biological treatment, but for some people, medications do not work or side effects are intolerable. If this group of people doesn't respond to psychotherapy either, what other options do they have to achieve symptom relief? Some additional avenues of help are available, but some are risky or poorly understood.

Electroconvulsive therapy (ECT), sometimes referred to as *shock therapy*, is *a treatment that involves inducing a brief seizure by delivering an electrical shock to the brain.* The shock is applied to the person's scalp for less than a second. ECT is primarily used to treat severe depression that has not responded to antidepressant medications, although it may also be useful for treating bipolar disorder (Khalid et al., 2008; Poon et al., 2012). Patients are pretreated with muscle relaxants and are under general anesthesia so they are not conscious of the procedure. The main side effect of ECT is impaired short-term memory, which usually improves over the first month or two after the end of treatment. In addition, patients undergoing this procedure sometimes report headaches and muscle aches afterward (Marangell et al., 2003). Despite these side effects, the treatment can be effective: ECT is more effective than simulated ECT, placebos, and antidepressant drugs such as tricyclic antidepressants and MAOIs (Pagnin et al., 2008).

Transcranial magnetic stimulation (TMS) is *a treatment that involves placing a powerful pulsed magnet over a person's scalp, which alters neuronal activity in the brain* (see the Neuroscience and Behavior chapter). Unlike ECT, TMS is noninvasive, and side effects are minimal: They include mild headaches and a small risk of seizure, but

Other Voices

Diagnosis: Human

Ted Gup is an author and fellow of the Edmond J. Safra Center for Ethics at Harvard University.
Susan Symones/Infinity Portrait Design

Should more people receive psychological treatment or medications? Or should fewer? On one hand, data indicate that most people with a mental disorder do not receive treatment and that untreated mental disorders are an enormous source of pain and suffering. On the other hand, some argue that we have become too quick to label normal human behavior as "disordered" and too willing to medicate any behavior, thought, or feeling that makes us uncomfortable. Ted Gup is one of these people. The following is a version of his op-ed piece that appeared in *The New York Times* on April 3, 2013 under the headline "Diagnosis: Human."

The news that 11 percent of school-age children now receive a diagnosis of attention deficit hyperactivity disorder—some 6.4 million—gave me a chill. My son David was one of those who received that diagnosis.

In his case, he was in the first grade. Indeed, there were psychiatrists who prescribed medication for him even before they met him. One psychiatrist said he would not even see him until he was medicated. For a year I refused to fill the prescription at the pharmacy. Finally, I relented. And so David went on Ritalin, then Adderall, and other drugs that were said to be helpful in combating the condition.

In another age, David might have been called "rambunctious." His battery was a little too large for his body. And so he would leap over the couch, spring to reach the ceiling and show an exuberance for life that came in brilliant microbursts.

As a 21-year-old college senior, he was found on the floor of his room, dead from a fatal mix of alcohol and drugs. The date was Oct. 18, 2011. No one made him take the heroin and alcohol, and yet I cannot help but hold myself and others to account.

I had unknowingly colluded with a system that devalues talking therapy and rushes to medicate, inadvertently sending a message that self-medication, too, is perfectly acceptable.

My son was no angel (though he was to us) and he was known to trade in Adderall, to create a submarket in the drug among his classmates who were themselves all too eager to get their hands on it. What he did cannot be excused, but it should be understood. What he did was to create a market that perfectly mirrored the society in which he grew up, a culture where Big Pharma itself prospers from the off-label uses of drugs, often not tested in children and not approved for the many uses to which they are put.

And so a generation of students, raised in an environment that encourages medication, are emulating the professionals by using drugs in the classroom as performance enhancers. And we wonder why it is that they use drugs with such abandon. As all parents learn—at times to their chagrin—our children go to school not only in the classroom but also at home, and the culture they construct for themselves as teenagers and young adults is but a tiny village imitating that to which they were introduced as children.

The issue of permissive drug use and over-diagnosis goes well beyond hyperactivity. In May, the American Psychiatric Association will publish its *DSM–5*, the *Diagnostic and Statistical Manual of Mental Disorders*. It is called the bible of the profession. Its latest iteration, like those before, is not merely a window on the profession but on the culture it serves, both reflecting and shaping societal norms. (For instance, until the 1970s, it categorized homosexuality as a mental illness.)

One of the new, more controversial provisions expands depression to include some forms of grief. On its face it makes sense. The grieving often display all the common indicators of depression—loss of interest in life, loss of appetite, irregular sleep patterns, low functionality, etc. But as others have observed, those same symptoms are the very hallmarks of grief itself.

Ours is an age in which the airwaves and media are one large drug emporium that claims to fix everything from sleep to sex. I fear that being human is itself fast becoming a condition. It's as if we are trying to contain grief, and the absolute pain of a loss like mine. We have become increasingly disassociated and estranged from the patterns of life and death, uncomfortable with the messiness of our own humanity, aging and, ultimately, mortality.

Challenge and hardship have become pathologized and monetized. Instead of enhancing our coping skills, we undermine them and seek shortcuts where there are none, eroding the resilience upon which each of us, at some point in our lives, must rely. Diagnosing grief as a part of depression runs the very real risk of delegitimizing that which is most human—the bonds of our love and attachment to one another. The new entry in the *DSM* cannot tame grief by giving it a name or a subsection, nor render it less frightening or more manageable.

The *DSM* would do well to recognize that a broken heart is not a medical condition, and that medication is ill-suited to repair some tears. Time does not heal all wounds, closure is a fiction, and so too is the notion that God never asks of us more than we can bear. Enduring the unbearable is sometimes exactly what life asks of us.

But there is a sweetness even to the intensity of this pain I feel. It is the thing that holds me still to my son. And yes, there is a balm even in the pain. I shall let it go when it is time, without reference to the *DSM*, and without the aid of a pill.

Have we gone too far in labeling and treatment of mental disorders? Or have we not gone far enough? How can we make sure that we are not medicating normal behavior, while at the same time ensuring that we provide help to those who are suffering with a true mental disorder?

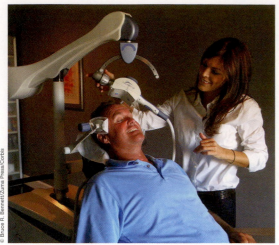

Transcranial magnetic stimulation (TMS) is an exciting new technique that allows researchers and clinicians to change brain activity using a magnetic wand—no surgery is required.

phototherapy   A therapy that involves repeated exposure to bright light.

psychosurgery   Surgical destruction of specific brain areas.

Deep brain stimulation involves the insertion of battery-powered electrodes that deliver electrical pulses to specific areas of the brain believed to be causing a person's mental disorder.

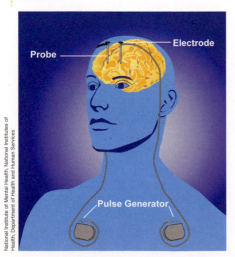

TMS has no impact on memory or concentration. TMS may be particularly useful in treating depression that is unresponsive to medication (Avery et al., 2009). In fact, a study comparing TMS to ECT found that both procedures were effective, with no significant differences between them (Janicak et al., 2002). Other studies have found that TMS can also be used to treat auditory hallucinations in schizophrenia (Aleman, Sommer, & Kahn, 2007).

Phototherapy, *a therapy that involves repeated exposure to bright light,* may be helpful to people who have a seasonal pattern to their depression. This could include people suffering from seasonal affective disorder (SAD; see the Psychological Disorders chapter). Typically, people are exposed to bright light in the morning, using a lamp designed for this purpose. Phototherapy has not been as well researched as psychological treatment or medication, but the handful of studies available suggest it is approximately as effective as antidepressant medication in the treatment of SAD (Thaler et al., 2011).

In very rare cases, **psychosurgery,** *the surgical destruction of specific brain areas,* may be used to treat psychological disorders. Psychosurgery has a controversial history, beginning in the 1930s with the invention of the lobotomy by Portuguese physician Egas Moniz (1874–1955). After discovering that certain surgical procedures on animal brains calmed behavior, Moniz began to use similar techniques on violent or agitated human patients. Lobotomies involved inserting an instrument into the brain through the patient's eye socket or through holes drilled in the side of the head. The objective was to sever connections between the frontal lobes and inner brain structures such as the thalamus, known to be involved in emotion. Although some lobotomies produced highly successful results and Moniz received the 1949 Nobel Prize for his work, significant side effects such as extreme lethargy or childlike impulsiveness detracted from these benefits. Lobotomy was used widely for years, leaving many people devastated by these permanent side effects, and because of this, there is an ongoing movement challenging the awarding of the Nobel Prize to Moniz. The development of antipsychotic drugs in the 1950s provided a safer way to treat violent individuals and brought the practice of lobotomy to an end (Swayze, 1995).

Today, psychosurgery is reserved only for extremely severe cases for which both no other interventions have been effective and the symptoms of the disorder are intolerable to the patient. Modern psychosurgery involves a very precise destruction of brain tissue in order to disrupt the brain circuits known to be involved in the generation of symptoms. For example, people suffering from OCD who fail to respond to treatment (including several trials of medications and cognitive behavioral treatment) may benefit from specific surgical procedures to destroy part of the corpus callosum (see Figure 3.16) and cingulate gyrus (the ridge just above the corpus collosum), two brain areas known to be involved in the generation of obsessions and compulsions. Because of the relatively small number of cases of psychosurgery, there are not as many studies of these techniques as there are for other treatments; however, available studies have shown that psychosurgery typically leads to substantial improvements in both the short and long term for people with severe OCD (Csigó et al., 2010; van Vliet et al., 2013).

A final approach, called *deep brain stimulation* (DBS), combines the use of psychosurgery with the use of electric currents (as in ECT and TMS). In DBS, a treatment pioneered only recently, a small, battery-powered device is implanted in the body to deliver electrical stimulation to specific areas of the brain known to be involved in the disorder being targeted. This technique has been successful for OCD treatment (Abelson et al., 2009) and can provide benefits for people with a variety of neurologic conditions. The tremor that accompanies Parkinson's disease has proven to be treatable in this way (Perlmutter & Mink, 2006), as have some cases of severe depression that are otherwise untreatable (Mayberg et al., 2005). The early view of psychosurgery as a

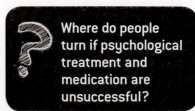

Where do people turn if psychological treatment and medication are unsuccessful?

treatment of last resort is being replaced by a cautious hope that newer, focused treatments that target brain circuits known to be functioning abnormally in those with certain mental disorders can have beneficial effects (Ressler & Mayberg, 2007).

SUMMARY QUIZ [15.3]

1. Antipsychotic drugs are used to treat
   a. depression.
   b. schizophrenia.
   c. anxiety.
   d. mood disorders.

2. Which of the following statements is NOT accurate regarding antidepressants?
   a. Current antidepressants act on combinations of different neurotransmitter systems.
   b. Antidepressants have had significantly positive results in the treatment of bipolar disorder.
   c. Antidepressants are also prescribed to treat anxiety.
   d. Most antidepressants can take up to a month before they start to have an effect on mood.

3. What do electroconvulsive therapy, transcranial magnetic stimulation, and phototherapy all have in common?
   a. They incorporate herbal remedies in their treatment regimens.
   b. They may result in the surgical destruction of certain brain areas.
   c. They are considered biological treatments beyond medication.
   d. They are typically used in conjunction with psychotherapy.

Treatment Effectiveness: For Better or for Worse

Think back to Christine and the dead mouse at the beginning of the chapter. What if, instead of exposure and response prevention, Christine had been assigned psychoanalysis or psychosurgery? Could these alternatives have been just as effective (and justified) for treating her OCD? Throughout this chapter, we have explored various psychological and biological treatments that may help people with psychological disorders. But do these treatments actually work, and which ones work better than the others?

As you learned in the Methods in Psychology chapter, pinning down a specific cause for an effect can be a difficult detective exercise. The detection is made even more difficult because people may approach treatment evaluation very unscientifically, often by simply noticing an improvement (or no improvement) and reaching a conclusion based on that sole observation. Determination of a treatment's effectiveness can be misdirected by illusions that can only be overcome by careful, scientific evaluation.

Treatment Illusions

Imagine you're sick and the doctor says, "Take a pill." You follow the doctor's orders, and you get better. To what do you attribute your improvement? If you're like most people, you reach the conclusion that the pill cured you. That's one possible explanation, but you might have fallen victim to an illusion of treatment. Such illusions can be produced by natural improvement, by placebo effects, and by reconstructive memory. Let's look more closely at each.

1. Natural Improvement

Natural improvement is the tendency of symptoms to return to their mean or average level. The illusion in this case happens when you conclude mistakenly that a treatment has made you better when you would have gotten better anyway. People typically turn to therapy or medication when their symptoms are at their worst. When this is the case, the client's symptoms will often improve regardless of whether there was any treatment at all; when you're at rock bottom, there's nowhere to move but up. In most cases, for example, depression that becomes severe enough to make individuals candidates for treatment will tend to lift in several months *no matter what they do*. A person who enters therapy for depression may develop an illusion that the therapy works because the therapy coincides with the typical course of the illness and the person's natural return to health. How can we know if change was caused by the treatment or by natural improvement? As discussed in the Methods in Psychology chapter, we could do an experiment in which we assign half of the people who are depressed to receive treatment and the other half to receive no treatment, and then we could monitor them over time to see if the ones who got treatment actually show greater improvement. This is precisely how researchers test out different interventions, as described in more detail below.

placebo An inert substance or procedure that has been applied with the expectation that a healing response will be produced.

2. Placebo Effects

Recovery could be produced by *nonspecific treatment effects* that are not related to the specific mechanisms by which treatment is supposed to be working. For example, simply knowing that you are getting a treatment can be a nonspecific treatment effect. These instances include the positive influences that can be produced by a **placebo,** *an inert substance or procedure that has been applied with the expectation that a healing response will be produced.* Research shows that a large percentage of individuals with anxiety, depression, and other emotional and medical problems experi-

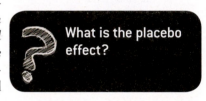

What is the placebo effect?

ence significant improvement after a placebo treatment. One recent study considered 718 patients with depression who were randomly assigned to receive either antidepressant medication or pill placebo (Fournier et al., 2010). For those participants with mild or moderate depression symptoms, a placebo was just as effective as antidepressant medication, and it was only in instances of severe depression that antidepressants seem to work better than placebos (see **FIGURE 15.7**).

3. Reconstructive Memory

A third treatment illusion can come about when the client's motivation to get well causes errors in *reconstructive memory* for the original symptoms. You might think that you've improved because of a treatment when in fact you're simply misremembering: You mistakenly believe that your symptoms before treatment were worse than they actually were. For example, a client who forms a strong expectation of success in therapy might conclude later that even a useless treatment had worked wonders by recalling past symptoms and troubles as worse than they were and thereby making the treatment seem effective.

Treatment Studies

How can we make sure that we are using treatments that actually work and not wasting time with procedures that may be useless or even harmful? Research

"If this doesn't help you don't worry, it's a placebo."

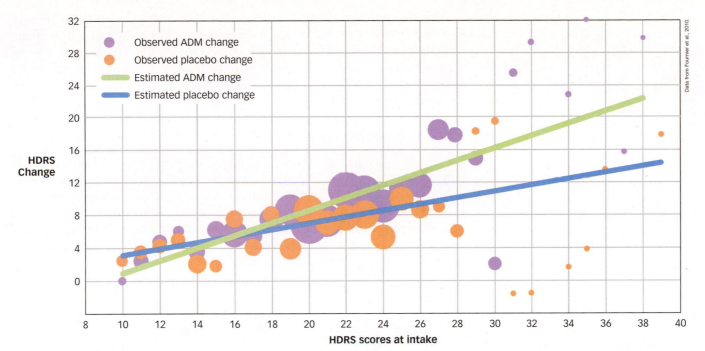

Data from Fournier et al., 2010.

FIGURE 15.7 Antidepressants versus Placebos for Depression A total of 718 depressed individuals from six different studies were given pills to treat their depression. Half were randomly assigned to receive an antidepressant medication (ADM) and half to receive a pill placebo. Importantly, the participants did not know if they were taking an antidepressant or simply a placebo. For those with mild or moderate depression, as measured by the Hamilton Depression Rating Scale (HDRS), antidepressants did not work any better than placebos. However, those with severe depression showed much greater improvement on antidepressants than on placebos. The circle size represents the number of people with data at each point.

psychologists use the approaches covered in the Methods in Psychology chapter to create experiments that test whether treatments are effective for the different mental disorders described in the previous chapter.

Treatment outcome studies are designed to evaluate whether a particular treatment works, often in relation to some other treatment or a control condition. For example, to study the outcome of treatment for depression, researchers might compare the self-reported symptoms of two groups of people who were initially depressed: those who received treatment for 6 weeks and a control group that had also been selected for the study but were assigned to a waiting list for later treatment and were simply tested 6 weeks after their selection. The study could determine whether this treatment had any benefit.

Researchers use a range of methods to ensure that any observed effects are not due to the treatment illusions described earlier. For example, the treatment illusions caused by natural improvement and reconstructive memory happen when people compare their symptoms before treatment to their symptoms after treatment. To avoid this, a treatment (or experimental) group and a control group need to be randomly assigned to each condition and then compared at the end of treatment. That way, natural improvement or motivated reconstructive memory can't cause illusions of effective treatment.

But what should happen to the control group during the treatment? If its members simply stay home, waiting until they can get treatment later (a wait-list control group), they won't receive the placebo effects. So, ideally, a treatment should be assessed in a *double-blind experiment*, a study in which both the participant and the researcher/therapist are uninformed about which treatment the participant is receiving. In the case of drug studies, this isn't hard to arrange because active drugs and placebos can be made to look alike to both the participants and the researchers during the study. Keeping both participants and researchers "in the dark" is much harder in the study of psychological treatments; in fact, in most cases, it is not possible. Both the participant and the therapist can easily notice the differences in treatments such as psychoanalysis

Why is a double-blind experiment so important in assessing treatment effectiveness?

and behavior therapy, for example, so there's no way to keep the beliefs and expectations of both participant and therapist completely out of the picture in evaluating psychotherapy effectiveness. Nevertheless, by comparing treatments either to no treatment or to other active interventions (such as other psychological treatments or medications), researchers can determine which treatments work and which are most effective for different disorders.

Which Treatments Work?

The distinguished psychologist Hans Eysenck (1916–1997) reviewed the relatively few studies of psychotherapy effectiveness available in 1957 and raised a furor among therapists by concluding that psychotherapy—particularly psychoanalysis—not only was ineffective but seemed to *impede* recovery (Eysenck, 1957). Since then, studies support a more optimistic conclusion: The typical psychotherapy client is better off than three quarters of untreated individuals (Seligman, 1995; Smith, Glass, & Miller, 1980), and strong evidence generally supports the effectiveness of many treatments (Nathan & Gorman, 2007). Still, some psychologists have argued that most psychotherapies work about equally well. In this view, common factors shared by all forms of psychotherapy, such as contact with and empathy from a professional, contribute to change (Luborsky et al., 2002; Luborsky & Singer, 1975). In contrast, others have argued that there are important differences among therapies and that certain treatments are more effective than others, especially for treating particular types of problems (Beutler, 2002; Hunsley & Di Giulio, 2002). How can we make sense of these differing perspectives? A recent review highlighted several specific psychological treatments that have been shown to work as well as—or even better than—other available treatments, including medication (Barlow et al., 2013). **TABLE 15.2** lists several of these treatments.

Some have questioned whether treatments shown to work in treatment studies conducted at university clinics will work in the real world. For instance, most treatment studies reported in the literature do not have large numbers of participants who are of ethnic minority status, and so it is unclear if these treatments will work with ethnically and culturally diverse groups. One recent, comprehensive review of all

Table 15.2 Selected List of Specific Psychological Treatments Compared to Medication or Other Treatments

Disorder	Treatment	Results
Depression	CBT	PT = meds; PT + meds > either alone
Panic disorder	CBT	PT > meds at follow-up; PT = meds at end of treatment; both > placebo
Posttraumatic stress disorder	CBT	PT > present-centered therapy
Tourette's disorder	Habit reversal training	PT > supportive therapy
Insomnia	CBT	PT > medication or placebo
Depression and physical health in Alzheimer's patients	Exercise and behavioral management	PT > routine medical care
Gulf War Veterans' illnesses	CBT and exercise	PT > usual care or alternative treatments

Note: CBT = cognitive behavior therapy; PT = psychological treatment; Meds = medication.
Source: Information from Barlow et al., 2013.

available data suggests that although there are gaps in the literature, results suggest that current evidence-based psychological treatments work as well with ethnic minority clients as with White clients (Miranda et al., 2005).

Even trickier than the question of establishing whether a treatment works is whether a psychotherapy or medication might actually do harm. The dangers of drug treatment should be clear to anyone who has read a magazine ad for a drug and studied the fine print with its list of side effects, potential drug interactions, and complications. Many drugs used for psychological treatment may be addictive, creating long-term dependency with serious withdrawal symptoms. The strongest critics of drug treatment claim that drugs do no more than trade one unwanted symptom for another: depression for sexual disinterest, anxiety for intoxication, or agitation for lethargy and dulled emotion (e.g., see Breggin, 2000).

How do psychologists know which treatments work and which might be harmful?

The dangers of psychotherapy are more subtle, but one is clear enough in some cases that there is actually a name for it. **Iatrogenic illness** is *a disorder or symptom that occurs as a result of a medical or psychotherapeutic treatment itself* (e.g., Boisvert & Faust, 2002). Such an illness might arise, for example, when a psychotherapist becomes convinced that a client has a disorder that in fact the client does not have. As a result, the therapist works to help the client accept that diagnosis and participate in psychotherapy to treat that disorder. Being treated for a disorder can, under certain conditions, make a person show signs of that very disorder—and so an iatrogenic illness is born. For example, there are cases of patients who have been influenced through hypnosis and repeated suggestions in therapy to "recover" memories of traumatic childhood events when investigation reveals no evidence for these problems prior to therapy (Acocella, 1999; McNally, 2003; Ofshe & Watters, 1994).

Just as psychologists have created lists of treatments that work, they also have begun to establish lists of treatments that *harm*. The purpose of doing so is to inform other researchers, clinicians, and the public which treatments they should avoid. Many are under the impression that although every psychological treatment may not be effective, some treatment is better than no treatment. However, it turns out that a number of interventions intended to help alleviate people's symptoms actually make them worse! Did your high school have a D.A.R.E. (Drug Abuse and Resistance Education) program? Have you heard of critical-incident stress debriefing (CISD), scared straight, and boot-camp programs? They all sound like they might work, but careful scientific experiments have determined that people who participate in these interventions are actually worse off after doing so (see **TABLE 15.3**); Lilienfeld, 2007)!

To regulate the potentially powerful influence of therapies, psychologists hold themselves to a set of ethical standards for the treatment of people with mental disorders (American Psychological Association, 2002). Adherence to these standards is required for membership in the American Psychological Association, and state licensing boards also monitor adherence to ethical principles in therapy. These ethical standards include (a) striving to benefit clients and taking care to do no harm; (b) establishing relationships of trust with clients; (c) promoting accuracy, honesty, and truthfulness; (d) seeking fairness in treatment and taking precautions to avoid biases; and (e) respecting the dignity and worth of all people. When

iatrogenic illness A disorder or symptom that occurs as a result of a medical or psychotherapeutic treatment itself.

Mary Kate Denny/Photoedit

Treatments that are shown to be effective in research studies (which often include only a small percentage of ethnic minority patients) have been found to work equally well with people of different ethnicities (Miranda et al., 2005).

Table 15.3 Some Psychological Treatments that Cause Harm

Type of Treatment	Potential Harm	Source of Evidence
CISD	Increased risk of PTSD	RCTs
Scared straight	Worsening of conduct problems	RCTs
Boot-camp interventions for conduct problems	Worsening of conduct problems	Meta-analysis (review of studies)
D.A.R.E. programs	Increased use of alcohol and drugs	RCTs

Note: CISD = critical-incident stress debriefing; PTSD = posttraumatic stress disorder; RCTs = randomized controlled trials
Source: Information from Lilienfeld, 2007.

people suffering from mental disorders come to psychologists for help, adhering to these guidelines is the least that psychologists can do. Ideally, in the hope of relieving this suffering, they can do much more.

SUMMARY QUIZ [15.4]

1. Which treatment illusion occurs when a client or therapist attributes the client's improvement to a feature of treatment, although that feature wasn't really the active element that caused improvement?
   a. nonspecific treatment effects
   b. natural improvement
   c. error in reconstructive memory
   d. regression to the mean

2. Current studies indicate that the typical psychotherapy client is better off than _____ of untreated individuals.
   a. one half
   b. the same number
   c. one fourth
   d. three fourths

CHAPTER REVIEW

SUMMARY

Treatment: Getting Help to Those Who Need It

> Mental illness is often misunderstood and too often goes untreated, affecting an individual's ability to function and also causing social and financial burdens.

> Many people who suffer from mental illness do not get the help they need; they may be unaware that they have a problem, they may be uninterested in getting help for their problem, or they may face structural barriers to getting treatment.

> Treatments include psychotherapy, which focuses on the mind, and medical and biological methods, which focus on the brain and body.

Psychological Treatments: Healing the Mind through Interaction

> Psychodynamic therapies, including psychoanalysis, emphasize helping clients gain insight into their unconscious conflicts.

> Humanistic approaches (e.g., person-centered therapy) and existential approaches (e.g., gestalt therapy) focus on helping people develop a sense of personal worth.

> Behavior therapy applies learning principles to specific behavior problems; cognitive therapy is focused on teaching people to challenge irrational thoughts. Cognitive behavior therapy (CBT) merges these two approaches.

> Group therapies target couples, families, or groups of clients brought together for the purpose of working together to solve their problems.

Medical and Biological Treatments: Healing the Mind by Physically Altering the Brain

> Medications have been developed to treat many psychological disorders, including antipsychotic medications (used to treat schizophrenia and psychotic disorders), antianxiety medications (used to treat anxiety disorders), and antidepressants (used to treat depression and related disorders).

> Medications are often combined with psychotherapy.

> Other biomedical treatments include electroconvulsive therapy (ECT), transcranial magnetic stimulation (TMS), and psychosurgery—this last one used in extreme cases, when other methods of treatment have been exhausted.

Treatment Effectiveness: For Better or for Worse

> Observing improvement during treatment does not necessarily mean that the treatment was effective; it might instead reflect natural improvement, nonspecific treatment effects (e.g., the placebo effect), and reconstructive memory processes.

> Scientific research methods such as double-blind techniques and placebo controls can help establish whether a treatment is really causing improvement.

> Some treatments for psychological disorders are more effective than others for certain disorders, and both medication and psychotherapy have dangers that ethical practitioners must consider carefully.

KEY TERMS

psychotherapy (p. 481)

eclectic psychotherapy (p. 481)

psychodynamic psychotherapies (p. 481)

resistance (p. 482)

transference (p. 482)

interpersonal psychotherapy (IPT) (p. 482)

person-centered therapy (or client-centered therapy) (p. 483)

gestalt therapy (p. 484)

behavior therapy (p. 485)

token economy (p. 485)

exposure therapy (p. 485)

cognitive therapy (p. 486)

cognitive restructuring (p. 486)

mindfulness meditation (p. 487)

cognitive behavioral therapy (CBT) (p. 487)

group therapy (p. 489)

antipsychotic drugs (p. 492)

psychopharmacology (p. 492)

antianxiety medications (p. 492)

antidepressants (p. 493)

electroconvulsive therapy (ECT) (p. 496)

transcranial magnetic stimulation (TMS) (p. 496)

phototherapy (p. 498)

psychosurgery (p. 498)

placebo (p. 500)

iatrogenic illness (p. 503)

CHANGING MINDS

1. One of your friends recently lost a close family member in a tragic car accident, and he's devastated. He's not been attending classes, and when you check up on him, you learn that he's not sleeping well or eating regularly. You want to help him but feel a little out of your depth, so you suggest he visit the campus counseling center and talk to a therapist. "Only crazy people go to therapy," he says. What could you tell your friend to dispel his assumption?

2. While you're talking to your bereaved friend, his roommate comes in. The roommate agrees with your suggestion about therapy but takes it further. "I'll give you the name of my therapist. He helped me quit smoking—he'll be able to cure your depression in no time." Why is it dangerous to assume that a good therapist can cure any-one and anything?

3. In the Methods in Psychology chapter you read about Louise Hay, whose best-selling book, *You Can Heal Your Life*, promotes a kind of psychotherapy: teaching readers how to change their thoughts and thereby improve not only their inner lives but also their physi-cal health. The chapter quotes Hay as saying that scientific evi-dence is unnecessary to validate her claims. Is there a scientific basis for the major types of psychotherapy described in this chapter? How is scientific experimentation used to assess their effectiveness?

4. In June 2009, pop icon Michael Jackson died after receiving a fatal dose of the anesthetic propofol, which is sometimes used off-label as an antianxiety drug; autopsy confirmed that his body contained a cocktail of prescription drugs, including the benzodiazepines lorazepam and diazepam. (Jackson's cardiologist, Dr. Conrad Murray, was later convicted of involuntary manslaughter for administering the fatal dose.) Other celebrities whose deaths have been attributed to medications commonly prescribed for anxiety and depression include Heath Ledger in 2008 and Anna Nicole Smith in 2007. "These drugs are dangerous," your roommate notes. "People who have psychological problems should seek out talk therapy for their problems and stay away from the medications, even if they're prescribed by a responsible doctor." You agree that medications can be dangerous if misused, but how would you justify the use of drug treatment for serious mental disorders?

ANSWERS TO SUMMARY QUIZZES

Answers to Summary Quiz 15.1: 1. b; 2. b; 3. d.

Answers to Summary Quiz 15.2: 1. d; 2. c; 3. d.

Answers to Summary Quiz 15.3: 1. b; 2. b; 3. c.

Answers to Summary Quiz 15.4: 1. a; 2. d.

Need more help? Additional resources are located in LaunchPad at:
http://www.worthpublishers.com/launchpad/schacterbrief3e

APPENDIX

Essentials of Statistics for Psychological Science

Graphic Representations

In Chapter 2, you learned how to generate a valid operational definition, how to design a reliable and powerful instrument, and how to use that instrument while avoiding demand characteristics and observer bias. So where does that leave you? With a big page filled with numbers—and if you are like most people, a big page filled with numbers just doesn't seem very informative. Don't worry, most psychologists feel the same way, and that's why they have techniques for making sense of big pages full of numbers. One such technique is graphic representation.

The most common kind of graphic representation is the **frequency distribution,** which is *a graphic representation of measurements arranged by the number of times each measurement was made.* **FIGURE A.1** shows a pair of frequency distributions that represent the hypothetical performances of a group of men and women who took a test of fine motor skills (i.e., the ability to manipulate things with their hands). Every possible test score is shown on the horizontal axis. The number of times (or the *frequency* with which) each score was observed is shown on the vertical axis. Although frequency distributions can have many shapes, the shape of the frequency distribution shown below is a very common one. It is often called the *bell curve,* but is technically known as the *Gaussian distribution* or the **normal distribution,** which is *a mathematically defined frequency distribution in which the frequency of measurements is highest in the middle and decreases symmetrically in both directions.* When we say that the normal distribution is *symmetrical,* we mean that the left half is a mirror image of the right half.

The picture in Figure A.1 reveals in a single optical gulp what a page full of numbers never can. For instance, the shapes of the two distributions instantly tell you that most people have moderate motor skills and that only a few have exceptionally good or exceptionally bad motor skills. You can also see that the distribution of men's scores is to the left of the distribution of women's scores, which instantly tells you that women tend to have better motor skills than men on average. And finally, you can see that the

frequency distribution A graphical representation of measurements arranged by the number of times each measurement was made.

normal distribution A mathematically defined distribution in which the frequency of measurements is highest in the middle and decreases symmetrically in both directions.

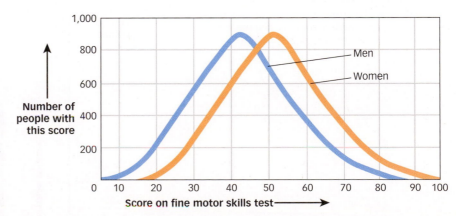

FIGURE A.1 Frequency Distributions This graph shows how a hypothetical group of men and women scored on a test of fine motor skills. Test scores are listed along the horizontal axis, and the frequency with which each score was obtained is represented along the vertical axis.

A-1

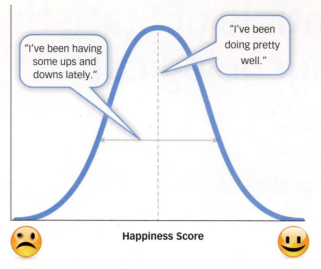

FIGURE A.2 Two Kinds of Descriptive Statistics Descriptive statistics are used to describe two important features of a frequency distribution: central tendency (where do most of the scores lie?) and variability (how much do the scores differ from one another?).

mode The value of the most frequently observed measurement.

mean The average value of all the measurements.

median The value that is in the middle; that is, greater than or equal to half the measurements and less than or equal to half the measurements.

two distributions have a great deal of overlap, which tells you that although women tend to have better motor skills than men on average, there are still many men who have better motor skills than many women.

Descriptive Statistics

A frequency distribution depicts every measurement and thus provides a full and complete picture of those measurements. But sometimes a full and complete picture is just too much information. When we ask a friend how she's been, we don't want her to show us a frequency distribution of her happiness scores; we want a brief summary statement such as "I've been doing pretty well" or "I've been having some ups and downs lately." In psychology, brief summary statements that capture the essential information from a frequency distribution are called *descriptive statistics*. There are two important kinds of descriptive statistics: those that describe the *central tendency* of a frequency distribution and those that describe the *variability* in a frequency distribution.

Central Tendency

Descriptions of *central tendency* are statements about the value of the measurements that *tend* to lie near the *center* or midpoint of the frequency distribution. When a friend says "I've been doing pretty well," she is describing the central tendency (or approximate location of the midpoint) of the frequency distribution of her happiness over time (see **FIGURE A.2**). The three most common descriptions of central tendency are: the **mode** (*the value of the most frequently observed measurement*), the **mean** (*the average value of all the measurements*), and the **median** (*the value that is in the middle; i.e., greater than or equal to half the measurements and less than or equal to half the measurements*). **FIGURE A.3** shows how each of these descriptive statistics is calculated.

FIGURE A.3 Some Descriptive Statistics This frequency distribution shows the scores of 15 individuals on a 7-point test. Descriptive statistics include measures of central tendency (such as the mean, median, and mode) and measures of variability (such as the range and the standard deviation).

- Mode = 3 because there are five 3s and only three 2s, two 1s, two 4s, one 5, one 6, and one 7.
- Mean = 3.27 because (1 + 1 + 2 + 2 + 2 + 3 + 3 + 3 + 3 + 3 + 4 + 4 + 5 + 6 + 7)/15 = 3.27
- Median = 3 because 10 scores are ≥ 3 and 10 scores are ≤ 3

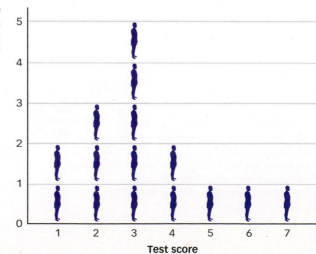

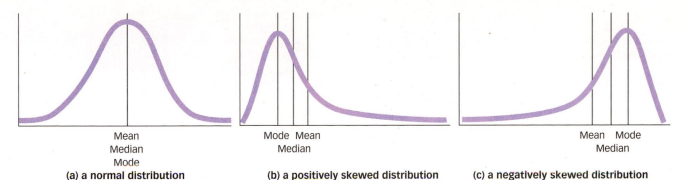

(a) a normal distribution — Mean / Median / Mode

(b) a positively skewed distribution — Mode Mean / Median

(c) a negatively skewed distribution — Mean Mode / Median

FIGURE A.4 Skewed Distributions When a frequency distribution is normal (*a*) the mean, median, and mode are all the same, but when it is positively skewed (*b*) or negatively skewed (*c*), these three measures of central tendency are quite different.

In a normal distribution, the mean, median, and mode all have the same value, but when the distribution is not normal, these three descriptive statistics can differ. For example, imagine that you measured the net worth of 40 college professors and Facebook founder Mark Zuckerberg. The frequency distribution of your measurements would not be normal, but would instead be *positively skewed*. As you can see in **FIGURE A.4**, the mode and the median of positively skewed distribution (*b*) are lower than the mean because the mean is more strongly influenced by the value of a single extreme measurement (which, in case you've been sleeping for the last few years, would be the net worth of Mark Zuckerberg). When distributions become skewed, the mean gets dragged off toward the tail, the mode stays home at the hump, and the median goes to live between the two.

When distributions are skewed, a single measure of central tendency can paint a misleading picture of the measurements. For example, the mean net worth of the people you measured is probably about a billion dollars each, but that statement makes the college professors sound a whole lot richer than they are. You could provide a much better description of the net worth of the people you measured if you also mentioned that the median net worth is $300,000 and that the modal net worth is $288,000. Indeed, you should always be suspicious when you hear some new fact about "the average person" but don't hear anything about the shape of the frequency distribution.

Variability

Whereas descriptions of central tendency are statements about the location of the measurements in a frequency distribution, descriptions of variability are statements about the extent to which the measurements differ from each other. When a friend says "I've been having some ups and downs lately," she is offering a brief summary statement that describes how measurements of her happiness taken at different times tend to differ from one another. The simplest description of variability is the **range,** which is *the value of the largest measurement in a frequency distribution minus the value of the smallest measurement*. The range is easy to compute, but like the mean, it can be dramatically affected by a single measurement. If you said that the net worth of people you had measured in the previous example ranged from $40,000 to $14 billion, a listener might get the impression that these people were all remarkably different from each other when, in fact, they were all quite similar save for one very rich guy.

Other descriptions of variability aren't quite as susceptible to this problem. For example, the **standard deviation** is *a statistic that describes the average difference between the mean of a frequency distribution and each of the measurements in that distribution*. In other words, how different are the measurements from each other on average? As **FIGURE A.5** shows, two frequency distributions that have the same central tendencies can have very different ranges and standard deviations. For example, many

range The value of the largest measurement in a frequency distribution minus the value of the smallest measurement.

standard deviation A statistic that describes the average difference between the measurements in a frequency distribution and the mean of that distribution.

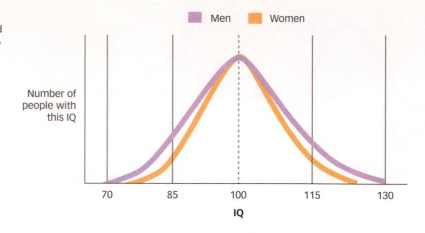

FIGURE A.5 IQ of Men and Women Men and women have the same average IQ, but men are more variable than women.

correlation coefficient A mathematical measure of both the direction and strength of a correlation, which is symbolized by the letter *r*.

studies suggest that men and women have about the same mean IQ, but that men have a larger range and standard deviation, which is to say that a man is more likely than a woman to be either extremely intelligent or extremely unintelligent.

Measuring Correlation

Most of us have learned from experience that memory works better when we've had a good night's sleep. So if you were to predict that well-rested students will score better on a memory test than sleep-deprived students will, you will be right more often than wrong. But you won't be right in every single instance. *Some* sleepy students will outscore *some* well-rested students. How often your prediction will be right depends on the strength of the correlation on which it is based: If the correlation between sleep and test performance is strong, then the prediction will be right almost all of the time, and if it is weak, then the prediction will be right less often. The **correlation coefficient** is *a mathematical measure of the strength of a correlation*, and it is symbolized by the letter *r* (as in "relationship"). The value of *r* can range from −1 to 1, and numbers outside that range are meaningless. What, then, do the numbers *inside* that range mean?

> If every time the value of one variable increases by a fixed amount the value of the second variable also increases by a fixed amount, then the relationship between the variables is called a *perfect positive correlation* and *r* = 1 (see Figure A.6). For example, if every 30-minute increase in sleep were associated with a 10% increase in memory, then sleep and memory would be *perfectly positively correlated*.

> If every time the value of one variable increases by a fixed amount the value of the second variable *decreases* by a fixed amount, then the relationship between the variables is called a *perfect negative correlation* and *r* = −1 (see Figure A.6). For example, if every 30-minute increase in sleep were associated with a 10% decrease in memory, then sleep and memory would be *perfectly negatively correlated*.

> If every time the value of one variable increases by a fixed amount the value of the second variable neither increases nor decreases systematically, then the two variables are said to be *uncorrelated* and *r* = 0 (see Figure A.6). For example, if a 30-minute increase in sleep were sometimes associated with an increase in memory, sometimes associated with a decrease in memory, and sometimes associated with no change in memory at all, then sleep and memory would be uncorrelated.

Perfect correlations are extremely rare. In the real world, sleep and memory performance are *positively* correlated (i.e., as one increases, the other usually increases), but

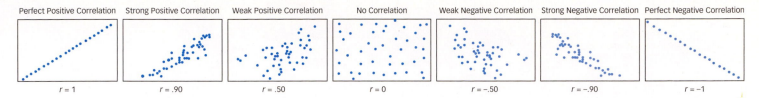

FIGURE A.6 **Examples of Correlations**
This figure shows correlations of different signs and strengths. Notice how the pattern of data changes as r moves from 1 to −1.

they are *imperfectly* correlated (i.e., every 1-minute increase in sleep does not lead to exactly one extra point on a memory test). When variables are imperfectly correlated, then the absolute value of *r* will lie somewhere between 0 and 1. **FIGURE A.6** shows a variety of different correlations. The sign of *r* (plus or minus) tells us whether the correlation is positive or negative, and the absolute value of *r* (which varies from 0 to 1) tells us about its strength.

KEY TERMS

frequency distribution (p. A-1)
normal distribution (p. A-1)

mode (p. A-2)
mean (p. A-2)

median (p. A-2)
range (p. A-3)

standard deviation (p. A-3)
correlation coefficient (p. A-4)

GLOSSARY

absentmindedness A lapse in attention that results in memory failure. (p. 194)

absolute threshold The minimal intensity needed to just barely detect a stimulus in 50% of the trials. (p. 99)

accommodation The process by which the eye maintains a clear image on the retina. (p. 102)

accommodation The process by which infants revise their schemas in light of new information. (p. 320)

acquisition The phase of classical conditioning when the CS and the US are presented together. (p. 210)

action potential An electric signal that is conducted along a neuron's axon to a synapse. (p. 61)

activation–synthesis model The theory that dreams are produced when the brain attempts to make sense of random neural activity that occurs during sleep. (p. 153)

actor–observer effect The tendency to make situational attributions for our own behaviors while making dispositional attributions for the identical behavior of others. (p. 406)

adolescence The period of development that begins with the onset of sexual maturity (about 11 to 14 years of age) and lasts until the beginning of adulthood (about 18 to 21 years of age). (p. 333)

adulthood The stage of development that begins around 18 to 21 years and ends at death. (p. 339)

aggression Behavior whose purpose is to harm another. (p. 380)

agonists Drugs that increase the action of a neurotransmitter. (p. 62)

agoraphobia A specific phobia involving a fear of public places. (p. 450)

alcohol myopia A condition that results when alcohol hampers attention, leading people to respond in simple ways to complex situations. (p. 158)

altered state of consciousness A form of experience that departs significantly from the normal subjective experience of the world and the mind. (p. 146)

altruism Behavior that benefits another without benefiting oneself. (p. 386)

amygdala A part of the limbic system that plays a central role in many emotional processes, particularly the formation of emotional memories. (p. 71)

anal stage The second psychosexual stage, in which experience is dominated by the pleasures and frustrations associated with the anus, retention and expulsion of feces and urine, and toilet training. (p. 362)

anorexia nervosa An eating disorder characterized by an intense fear of being fat and severe restriction of food intake. (p. 259)

antagonists Drugs that block the function of a neurotransmitter (p. 62)

anterograde amnesia The inability to transfer new information from the short-term store into the long-term store. (p. 179)

antianxiety medications Drugs that help reduce a person's experience of fear or anxiety. (p. 492)

antidepressants A class of drugs that help lift people's moods. (p. 493)

antipsychotic drugs Medications that are used to treat schizophrenia and related psychotic disorders. (p. 492)

antisocial personality disorder (APD) A pervasive pattern of disregard for and violation of the rights of others that begins in childhood or early adolescence and continues into adulthood. (p. 469)

anxiety disorder The class of mental disorder in which anxiety is the predominant feature. (p. 448)

aphasia Difficulty in producing or comprehending language. (p. 282)

apparent motion The perception of movement as a result of alternating signals appearing in rapid succession in different locations. (p. 115)

appraisal An evaluation of the emotion-relevant aspects of a stimulus. (p. 251)

approach motivation A motivation to experience a positive outcome. (p. 267)

area A1 A portion of the temporal lobe that contains the primary auditory cortex. (p. 121)

area V1 The part of the occipital lobe that contains the primary visual cortex. (p. 107)

assimilation The process by which infants apply their schemas in novel situations. (p. 320)

association areas Areas of the cerebral cortex that are composed of neurons that help provide sense and meaning to information registered in the cortex. (p. 74)

attachment An emotional bond with a primary caregiver. (p. 328)

attention deficit/hyperactivity disorder (ADHD) A persistent pattern of severe problems with inattention and/or hyperactivity or impulsiveness that cause significant impairments in functioning. (p. 466)

attitude An enduring positive or negative evaluation of an object or event. (p. 399)

attribution An inference about the cause of a person's behavior. (p. 406)

autism spectrum disorder (ASD) A condition beginning in early childhood in which a person shows persistent communication deficits as well as restricted and repetitive patterns of behaviors, interests, or activities. (p. 465)

autonomic nervous system (ANS) A set of nerves that carries involuntary and automatic commands that control blood vessels, body organs, and glands. (p. 65)

availability bias Items that are more readily available in memory are judged as having occurred more frequently. (p. 289)

avoidance motivation A motivation not to experience a negative outcome. (p. 267)

axon The part of a neuron that carries information to other neurons, muscles, or glands. (p. 56)

basal ganglia A set of subcortical structures that directs intentional movements. (p. 72)

basilar membrane A structure in the inner ear that undulates when vibrations from the ossicles reach the cochlear fluid. (p. 119)

behavior Observable actions of human beings and nonhuman animals. (p. 2)

behavior therapy A type of therapy that assumes that disordered behavior is learned and that symptom relief is achieved through changing overt maladaptive behaviors into more constructive behaviors. (p. 484)

behavioral neuroscience An approach to psychology that links psychological processes to activities in the nervous system and other bodily processes. (p. 14)

behaviorism An approach that advocates that psychologists restrict themselves to the scientific study of objectively observable behavior. (p. 10)

belief An enduring piece of knowledge about an object or event. (p. 399)

bias The distorting influences of present knowledge, beliefs, and feelings on recollection of previous experiences. (p. 199)

Big Five The traits of the five-factor personality model: openness to experience, conscientiousness, extraversion, agreeableness, and neuroticism. (p. 354)

binding problem How features are linked together so that we see unified objects in our visual world rather than free-floating or miscombined features. (p. 109)

binocular disparity The difference in the retinal images of the two eyes that provides information about depth. (p. 114)

biofeedback The use of an external monitoring device to obtain information about a bodily function and possibly gain control over that function. (p. 423)

biological preparedness A propensity for learning particular kinds of associations over others. (p. 215)

biopsychosocial perspective Explains mental disorders as the result of interactions among biological, psychological, and social factors. (p. 444)

bipolar disorder A condition characterized by cycles of abnormal, persistent high mood (mania) and low mood (depression). (p. 457)

blind spot A location in the visual field that produces no sensation on the retina. (p. 104)

blocking A failure to retrieve information that is available in memory even though you are trying to produce it. (p. 195)

bulima nervosa An eating disorder characterized by binge eating followed by purging. (p. 259)

burnout A state of physical, emotional, and mental exhaustion created by long-term involvement in an emotionally demanding situation and accompanied by lowered performance and motivation. (p. 420)

bystander intervention The act of helping strangers in an emergency situation (p. 385)

Cannon–Bard theory The theory that a stimulus simultaneously triggers activity in the body and emotional experience in the brain. (p. 248)

case method A procedure for gathering scientific information by studying a single individual. (p. 43)

catatonic behavior A marked decrease in all movement or an increase in muscular rigidity and overactivity. (p. 460)

category-specific deficit A neurological syndrome that is characterized by an inability to recognize objects that belong to a particular category, although the ability to recognize objects outside the category is undisturbed. (p. 286)

cell body (or soma) The part of a neuron that coordinates information-processing tasks and keeps the cell alive. (p. 56)

central nervous system (CNS) The part of the nervous system that is composed of the brain and spinal cord. (p. 65)

cephalocaudal rule The "top-to-bottom" rule that describes the tendency for motor skills to emerge in sequence from the head to the feet. (p. 318)

cerebellum A large structure of the hindbrain that controls fine motor skills. (p. 69)

cerebral cortex The outermost layer of the brain, visible to the naked eye and divided into two hemispheres. (p. 72)

change blindness When people fail to detect changes to the visual details of a scene. (p. 116)

childhood The stage of development that begins at about 18 to 24 months and lasts until about 11 or 14 years. (p. 322)

chromosomes Strands of DNA wound around each other in a double-helix configuration. (p. 79)

chronic stressors Sources of stress that occur continuously or repeatedly. (p. 413)

chunking Combining small pieces of information into larger clusters or chunks that are more easily held in short-term memory. (p. 178)

circadian rhythm A naturally occurring 24-hour cycle. (p. 147)

classical conditioning A type of learning that occurs when a neutral stimulus produces a response after being paired with a stimulus that naturally produces a response. (p. 209)

cochlea A fluid-filled tube that is the organ of auditory transduction. (p. 119)

cocktail-party phenomenon A phenomenon in which people tune in one message even while they filter out others nearby. (p. 140)

cognitive behavioral therapy (CBT) A blend of cognitive and behavioral therapeutic strategies. (p. 487)

cognitive development The emergence of the ability to think and understand. (p. 319)

cognitive dissonance An unpleasant state that arises when a person recognizes the inconsistency of his or her actions, attitudes, or beliefs. (p. 401)

cognitive map A mental representation of the physical features of the environment. (p. 226)

cognitive neuroscience The field of study that attempts to understand the links between cognitive processes and brain activity. (p. 15)

cognitive psychology The scientific study of mental processes, including perception, thought, memory, and reasoning. (p. 12)

cognitive restructuring A therapeutic approach that teaches clients to question the automatic beliefs, assumptions, and predictions that often lead to negative emotions and to replace negative thinking with more realistic and positive beliefs. (p. 486)

cognitive symptoms Deficits in cognitive abilities, specifically in executive functioning, attention, and working memory. (p. 461)

cognitive therapy Focuses on helping a client identify and correct any distorted thinking about self, others, or the world. (p. 486)

cognitive unconscious All the mental processes that give rise to a person's thoughts, choices, emotions, and behavior even though they are not experienced by the person. (p. 145)

common knowledge effect The tendency for group discussions to focus on information that all members share. (p. 385)

comorbidity The co-occurrence of two or more disorders in a single individual. (p. 442)

companionate love An experience involving affection, trust, and concern for a partner's well-being. (p. 391)

concept A mental representation that groups or categorizes shared features of related objects, events, or other stimuli. (p. 284)

concrete operational stage The stage of cognitive development that begins at about 6 years and ends at about 11 years, during which children learn how actions or "operations" can transform the "concrete" objects of the physical world. (p. 322)

conditioned response (CR) A reaction that resembles an unconditioned response but is produced by a conditioned stimulus. (p. 209)

conditioned stimulus (CS) A previously neutral stimulus that produces a reliable response in an organism after being paired with a US. (p. 209)

conduct disorder A persistent pattern of deviant behavior involving aggression against people or animals, destruction of property, deceitfulness or theft, or serious rule violations. (p. 467)

cones Photoreceptors that detect color, operate under normal daylight conditions, and allow us to focus on fine detail. (p. 102)

conformity The tendency to do what others do simply because others are doing it. (p. 396)

conjunction fallacy When people think that two events are more likely to occur together than either individual event. (p. 290)

conscious motivations Motivations of which people are aware. (p. 267)

consciousness A person's subjective experience of the world and the mind. (pp. 5, 136)

conservation The notion that the quantitative properties of an object are invariant despite changes in the object's appearance. (p. 322)

consolidation The process by which memories become stable in the brain. (p. 180)

control group The group of people who are not exposed to the particular manipulation, as compared to the experimental group, in an experiment. (p. 38)

conventional stage A stage of moral development in which the morality of an action is primarily determined by the extent to which it conforms to social rules. (p. 330)

cooperation Behavior by two or more individuals that leads to mutual benefit. (p. 383)

corpus callosum A thick band of nerve fibers that connects large areas of the cerebral cortex on each side of the brain and supports communication of information across the hemispheres. (p. 72)

correlation Two variables are said to "be correlated" when variations in the value of one variable are synchronized with variations in the value of the other. (p. 34)

correlation coefficient A mathematical measure of both the direction and strength of a correlation, which is symbolized by the letter *r*. (p. A–3)

correspondence bias The tendency to make dispositional attributions instead of situational attributions. (p. 406)

crystallized intelligence The ability to retain and use knowledge that was acquired through experience. (p. 298)

cultural psychology The study of how cultures reflect and shape the psychological processes of their members. (p. 18)

debriefing A verbal description of the true nature and purpose of a study. (p. 48)

deep structure The meaning of a sentence. (p. 275)

defense mechanisms Unconscious coping mechanisms that reduce anxiety generated by threats from unacceptable impulses. (p. 361)

deindividuation A phenomenon that occurs when immersion in a group causes people to become less aware of their individual values. (p. 385)

delusions Patently false beliefs, often bizarre and grandiose, that are maintained in spite of their irrationality. (p. 460)

demand characteristics Those aspects of an observational setting that cause people to behave as they think someone else wants or expects. (p. 31)

dendrites The part of a neuron that receives information from other neurons and relays it to the cell body. (p. 56)

dependent variable The variable that is measured in a study. (p. 38)

depressants Substances that reduce the activity of the central nervous system. (p. 157)

developmental psychology The study of continuity and change across the life span. (p. 314)

deviation IQ A statistic obtained by dividing a person's test score by the average test score of people in the same age group and then multiplying the quotient by 100 (see *ratio IQ*). (p. 294)

Diagnostic and Statistical Manual of Mental Disorders (DSM) A classification system that describes the features used to diagnose each recognized mental disorder and indicates how the disorder can be distinguished from other, similar problems. (p. 442)

diathesis–stress model Suggests that a person may be predisposed for a psychological disorder that remains unexpressed until triggered by stress. (p. 444)

dichotic listening A task in which people wearing headphones hear different messages presented to each ear. (p. 140)

diffusion of responsibility The tendency for individuals to feel diminished responsibility for their actions when they are surrounded by others who are acting the same way. (p. 385)

discrimination The capacity to distinguish between similar but distinct stimuli. (p. 213)

discrimination Positive or negative behavior toward another person based on the person's group membership. (p. 384)

disorganized speech A severe disruption of verbal communication in which ideas shift rapidly and incoherently among unrelated topics. (p. 460)

display rule A norm for the appropriate expression of emotion. (p. 257)

dopamine hypothesis The idea that schizophrenia involves an excess of dopamine activity. (p. 462)

double-blind An observation whose true purpose is hidden from both the observer and the person being observed. (p. 32)

drive An internal state that signals a physiological need. (p. 258)

drug tolerance The tendency for larger doses of a drug to be required over time to achieve the same effect. (p. 156)

dynamic unconscious An active system encompassing a lifetime of hidden memories, the person's deepest instincts and desires, and the person's inner struggle to control these forces. (p. 144)

echoic memory A fast-decaying store of auditory information. (p. 177)

eclectic psychotherapy A form of psychotherapy that involves drawing on techniques from different forms of therapy, depending on the client and the problem. (p. 481)

egocentrism The failure to understand that the world appears different to different observers. (p. 323)

ego The component of personality, developed through contact with the external world, that enables us to deal with life's practical demands. (p. 360)

electroconvulsive therapy (ECT) A treatment that involves inducing a brief seizure by delivering an electrical shock to the brain. (p. 496)

embryonic stage The period of prenatal development that lasts from the second week until about the eighth week. (p. 315)

emotion A positive or negative experience that is associated with a particular pattern of physiological activity. (p. 247)

emotion regulation The strategies people use to influence their own emotional experience. (p. 251)

emotional expression An observable sign of an emotional state. (p. 253)

emotional intelligence The ability to reason about emotions and to use emotions to enhance reasoning. (p. 299)

empirical method A set of rules and techniques for observation. (p. 28)

empiricism The belief that accurate knowledge can be acquired through observation. (p. 28)

encoding The process of transforming what we perceive, think, or feel into an enduring memory. (p. 172)

epigenetics Environmental influences that determine whether or not genes are expressed, or the degree to which they are expressed, without altering the basic DNA sequences that constitute the genes themselves. (p. 81)

episodic memory The collection of past personal experiences that occurred at a particular time and place. (p. 189)

evolutionary psychology A psychological approach that explains mind and behavior in terms of the adaptive value of abilities that are preserved over time by natural selection. (p. 17)

exemplar theory A theory of categorization that argues that we make category judgments by comparing a new instance with stored memories for other instances of the category. (p. 285)

existential approach A school of thought that regards personality as governed by an individual's ongoing choices and decisions in the context of the realities of life and death. (p. 364)

expectancy theory The idea that alcohol effects can be produced by people's expectations of how alcohol will influence them in particular situations. (p. 158)

experiment A technique for establishing the causal relationship between variables. (p. 37)

experimental group The group of people who are exposed to a particular manipulation, as compared to the control group, in an experiment. (p. 38)

explicit memory The act of consciously or intentionally retrieving past experiences. (p. 187)

exposure therapy An approach to treatment that involves confronting an emotion-arousing stimulus directly and repeatedly, ultimately leading to a decrease in the emotional response. (p. 485)

expressed emotion A measure of how much hostility, criticism, and emotional overinvolvement are used when speaking about a family member with a mental disorder. (p. 459)

external validity An attribute of an experiment in which variables have been defined in a normal, typical, or realistic way. (p. 40)

extinction The gradual elimination of a learned response that occurs when the CS is repeatedly presented without the US. (p. 211)

extrinsic motivation A motivation to take actions that lead to reward. (p. 266)

facial feedback hypothesis Emotional expressions can cause the emotional experiences they signify. (p. 254)

family resemblance theory Members of a category have features that appear to be characteristic of category members but may not be possessed by every member. (p. 284)

fast mapping The fact that children can map a word onto an underlying concept after only a single exposure. (p. 278)

feature-integration theory The idea that focused attention is not required to detect the individual features that comprise a stimulus, but is required to bind those individual features together. (p. 111)

fetal alcohol syndrome A developmental disorder caused by heavy alcohol use during pregnancy. (p. 316)

fetal stage The period of prenatal development that lasts from the ninth week until birth. (p. 315)

fight-or-flight response An emotional and physiological reaction to an emergency that increases readiness for action. (p. 416)

fixation A phenomenon in which a person's pleasure-seeking drives become psychologically stuck, or arrested, at a particular psychosexual stage. (p. 362)

fixed-interval schedule (FI) An operant conditioning principle in which reinforcers are presented at fixed-time periods, provided that the appropriate response is made. (p. 221)

fixed-ratio schedule (FR) An operant conditioning principle in which reinforcement is delivered after a specific number of responses have been made. (p. 222)

flashbulb memories Detailed recollections of when and where we heard about shocking events. (p. 200)

fluid intelligence The ability to see abstract relationships and draw logical inferences. (p. 298)

foot-in-the-door technique A social influence technique that involves making a small request before making a large request. (p. 401)

formal operational stage The final stage of cognitive development that begins around the age of 11, during which children learn to reason about abstract concepts. (p. 322)

fovea An area of the retina where vision is the clearest and there are no rods at all. (p. 102)

framing effects When people give different answers to the same problem depending on how the problem is phrased (or framed). (p. 290)

fraternal twins (or dizygotic twins) Twins who develop from two different eggs that were fertilized by two different sperm (see *identical twins*). (p. 300)

frequency format hypothesis The proposal that our minds evolved to notice how frequently things occur, not how likely they are to occur. (p. 289)

frequency distribution A graphical representation of measurements arranged by the number of times each measurement was made. (p. A–1)

frontal lobe A region of the cerebral cortex that has specialized areas for movement, abstract thinking, planning, memory, and judgment. (p. 73)

frustration–aggression hypothesis A principle stating that animals aggress when their desires are frustrated. (p. 380)

full consciousness Consciousness in which you know and are able to report your mental state. (p. 140)

functionalism The study of the purpose mental processes serve in enabling people to adapt to their environment. (p. 7)

gate-control theory of pain A theory of pain perception based on the idea that signals arriving from pain receptors in the body can be stopped, or gated, by interneurons in the spinal cord via feedback from two directions. (p. 125)

gateway drug A drug whose use increases the risk of the subsequent use of more harmful drugs. (p. 162)

general adaptation syndrome (GAS) A three-stage physiological stress response that appears regardless of the stressor that is encountered. (p. 417)

generalization The CR is observed even though the CS is slightly different from the CS used during acquisition. (p. 213)

generalized anxiety disorder (GAD) A disorder characterized by chronic excessive worry accompanied by three or more of the following symptoms: restlessness, fatigue, concentration problems, irritability, muscle tension, and sleep disturbance. (p. 450)

genetic dysphasia A syndrome characterized by an inability to learn the grammatical structure of language despite having otherwise normal intelligence. (p. 280)

gene The major unit of hereditary transmission. (p. 79)

genital stage The fifth and final psychosexual stage, the time for the coming together of the mature adult personality with a capacity to love, work, and relate to others in a mutually satisfying and reciprocal manner. (p. 363)

germinal stage The 2-week period of prenatal development that begins at conception. (p. 315)

Gestalt psychology A psychological approach that emphasizes that we often perceive the whole rather than the sum of the parts. (p. 12)

gestalt therapy Has the goal of helping the client become aware of his or her thoughts, behaviors, experiences, and feelings and to "own" or take responsibility for them. (p. 484)

glial cells Support cells found in the nervous system (p. 56)

grammar A set of rules that specify how the units of language can be combined to produce meaningful messages. (p. 274)

grossly disorganized behavior Behavior that is inappropriate for the situation or ineffective in attaining goals, often with specific motor disturbances. (p. 460)

group A collection of people who have something in common that distinguishes them from others. (p. 384)

group polarization The tendency for groups to make decisions that are more extreme than any member would have made alone. (p. 385)

group therapy A technique in which multiple participants (who often do not know one another at the outset) work on their individual problems in a group atmosphere. (p. 489)

groupthink The tendency for groups to reach consensus in order to facilitate interpersonal harmony. (p. 385)

habituation A general process in which repeated or prolonged exposure to a stimulus results in a gradual reduction in responding. (p. 208)

hair cells Specialized auditory receptor neurons embedded in the basilar membrane. (p. 121)

hallucinogens Drugs that alter sensation and perception and often cause visual and auditory hallucinations. (p. 161)

hallucinations False perceptual experiences that have a compelling sense of being real despite the absence of external stimulation. (p. 460)

haptic perception The active exploration of the environment by touching and grasping objects with our hands. (p. 122)

health psychology The subfield of psychology concerned with ways psychological factors influence the causes and treatment of physical illness and the maintenance of health. (p. 412)

helplessness theory The idea that individuals who are prone to depression automatically attribute negative experiences to causes that are internal (i.e., their own fault), stable (i.e., unlikely to change), and global (i.e., widespread). (p. 457)

heuristic persuasion The process by which attitudes or beliefs are changed by appeals to habit or emotion. (p. 401)

hindbrain An area of the brain that coordinates information coming into and out of the spinal cord. (p. 69)

hippocampus A structure critical for creating new memories and integrating them into a network of knowledge so that they can be stored indefinitely in other parts of the cerebral cortex. (p. 71)

humanistic psychology An approach to understanding human nature that emphasizes the positive potential of human beings. (p. 9)

hypnosis A social interaction in which one person (the hypnotist) makes suggestions that lead to a change in another person's (the subject's) subjective experience of the world. (p. 164)

hypnotic analgesia The reduction of pain through hypnosis in people who are susceptible to hypnosis. (p. 165)

hypothalamus A subcortical structure that regulates body temperature, hunger, thirst, and sexual behavior. (p. 71)

hypothesis A falsifiable prediction made by a theory. (p. 28)

hysteria A temporary loss of cognitive or motor functions, usually as a result of emotionally upsetting experiences. (p. 8)

iatrogenic illness A disorder or symptom that occurs as a result of a medical or psychotherapeutic treatment itself. (p. 503)

iconic memory A fast-decaying store of visual information. (p. 177)

id The part of the mind containing the drives present at birth; it is the source of our bodily needs, wants, desires, and impulses, particularly our sexual and aggressive drives. (p. 360)

identical twins (or monozygotic twins) Twins who develop from the splitting of a single egg that was fertilized by a single sperm (see *fraternal twins*). (p. 300)

illusions Errors of perception, memory, or judgment in which subjective experience differs from objective reality. (p. 12)

illusory conjunction A perceptual mistake where features from multiple objects are incorrectly combined. (p. 109)

immune system A complex response system that protects the body from bacteria, viruses, and other foreign substances. (p. 418)

implicit learning Learning that takes place largely independent of awareness of both the process and the products of information acquisition. (p. 234)

implicit memory The influence of past experiences on later behavior and performance, even without an effort to remember them or an awareness of the recollection. (p. 187)

inattentional blindness A failure to perceive objects that are not the focus of attention. (p. 116)

independent variable The variable that is manipulated in an experiment. (p. 38)

infancy The stage of development that begins at birth and lasts between 18 and 24 months. (p. 317)

informational influence A phenomenon that occurs when another person's behavior provides information about what is true. (p. 399)

informed consent A written agreement to participate in a study made by an adult who has been informed of all the risks that participation may entail. (p. 48)

insomnia Difficulty in falling asleep or staying asleep. (p. 150)

instrument Anything that can detect the condition to which an operational definition refers. (p. 31)

intelligence The ability to direct one's thinking, adapt to one's circumstances, and learn from one's experiences. (p. 293)

intermittent reinforcement An operant conditioning principle in which only some of the responses made are followed by reinforcement. (p. 223)

intermittent reinforcement effect The fact that operant behaviors that are maintained under intermittent reinforcement schedules resist extinction better than those maintained under continuous reinforcement. (p. 223)

internal validity An attribute of an experiment that allows it to establish causal relationships. (p. 40)

internal working model of relationships A set of beliefs about the self, the primary caregiver, and the relationship between them. (p. 329)

interneurons Neurons that connect sensory neurons, motor neurons, or other interneurons. (p. 58)

interpersonal psychotherapy (IPT) A form of psychotherapy that focuses on helping clients improve current relationships. (p. 482)

intrinsic motivation A motivation to take actions that are themselves rewarding. (p. 264)

introspection The subjective observation of one's own experience. (p. 7)

ironic processes of mental control Mental processes that can produce ironic errors because monitoring for errors can itself produce them. (p. 144)

James–Lange theory The theory that a stimulus triggers activity in the body, which in turn produces an emotional experience in the brain. (p. 248)

just noticeable difference (JND) The minimal change in a stimulus that can just barely be detected. (p. 99)

kin selection The process by which evolution selects for individuals who cooperate with their relatives. (p. 386)

language A system for communicating with others using signals that are combined according to rules of grammar and convey meaning. (p. 274)

latency stage The fourth psychosexual stage, in which the primary focus is on the further development of intellectual, creative, interpersonal, and athletic skills. (p. 362)

latent learning Something is learned, but it is not manifested as a behavioral change until sometime in the future. (p. 225)

law of effect Behaviors that are followed by a "satisfying state of affairs" tend to be repeated and those that produce an "unpleasant state of affairs" are less likely to be repeated. (p. 217)

learned helplessness The belief that one has no control over one's situation based on past experience. (p. 415)

learning The acquisition of new knowledge, skills, or responses from experience that results in a relatively permanent change in the state of the learner. (p. 208)

locus of control A person's tendency to perceive the control of rewards as internal to the self or external in the environment. (p. 367)

long-term memory A type of storage that holds information for hours, days, weeks, or years. (p. 178)

long-term potentiation (LTP) A process whereby communication across the synapse between neurons strengthens the connection, making further communication easier. (p. 182)

loudness A sound's intensity. (p. 118)

major depressive disorder (or unipolar depression) A disorder characterized by a severely depressed mood and/or inability to experience pleasure that lasts 2 or more weeks and is accompanied by feelings of worthlessness, lethargy, and sleep and appetite disturbance. (p. 455)

manipulation Changing a variable in order to determine its causal power. (p. 37)

marijuana (or cannibis) The leaves and buds of the hemp plant, which contain a psychoactive drug called tetrahydrocannabinol (THC). (p. 161)

mean The average value of all the measurements. (p. A–3)

median The value that is in the middle; that is, greater than or equal to half the measurements and less than or equal to half the measurements. (p. A-2)

medical model Abnormal psychological experiences are conceptualized as illnesses that, like physical illnesses, have biological and environmental causes, defined symptoms, and possible cures. (p. 441)

meditation The practice of intentional contemplation. (p. 422)

medulla An extension of the spinal cord into the skull that coordinates heart rate, circulation, and respiration. (p. 69)

memory misattribution Assigning a recollection or an idea to the wrong source. (p. 196)

memory The ability to store and retrieve information over time. (p. 172)

mental control The attempt to change conscious states of mind. (p. 143)

mental disorder A persistent disturbance or dysfunction in behavior, thoughts, or emotions that causes significant distress or impairment. (p. 440)

mere exposure effect The tendency for liking to increase with the frequency of exposure. (p. 389)

metabolism The rate at which energy is used by the body. (p. 262)

mindfulness meditation Teaches an individual to be fully present in each moment; to be aware of his or her thoughts, feelings, and sensations; and to detect symptoms before they become a problem. (p. 487)

mind The private inner experience of perceptions, thoughts, memories, and feelings. (p. 2)

mind–body problem The issue of how the mind is related to the brain and body. (p. 138)

minimal consciousness A low-level kind of sensory awareness and responsiveness that occurs when the mind inputs sensations and may output behavior. (p. 140)

Minnesota Multiphasic Personality Inventory (MMPI) A well-researched, clinical questionnaire used to assess personality and psychological problems. (p. 351)

mirror neurons Neurons that are active when an animal performs a behavior, such as reaching for or manipulating an object, and are also activated when another animal observes that animal performing the same behavior. (p. 74)

mode The value of the most frequently observed measurement. (p. A–2)

monocular depth cues Aspects of a scene that yield information about depth when viewed with only one eye. (p. 113)

mood disorders Mental disorders that have mood disturbance as their predominant feature. (p. 455)

morphemes The smallest meaningful units of language. (p. 275)

morphological rules A set of rules that indicate how morphemes can be combined to form words. (p. 275)

motivation The purpose for or psychological cause of an action. (p. 258)

motor development The emergence of the ability to execute physical action. (p. 318)

motor neurons Neurons that carry signals from the spinal cord to the muscles to produce movement. (p. 58)

myelin sheath An insulating layer of fatty material. (p. 56)

myelination The formation of a fatty sheath around the axons of a neuron. (p. 316)

narcissism A trait that reflects a grandiose view of the self combined with a tendency to seek admiration from and exploit others. (p. 373)

narcolepsy A disorder in which sudden sleep attacks occur in the middle of waking activities. (p. 150)

narcotics (or opiates) Highly addictive drugs derived from opium that relieve pain. (p. 160)

nativism The philosophical view that certain kinds of knowledge are innate or inborn. (p. 3)

nativist theory The view that language development is best explained as an innate, biological capacity. (p. 280)

natural selection Charles Darwin's theory that the features of an organism that help it survive and reproduce are more likely than other features to be passed on to subsequent generations. (p. 7)

natural correlations A correlation observed in the world around us. (p. 34)

naturalistic observation A technique for gathering scientific information by unobtrusively observing people in their natural environments. (p. 32)

need for achievement The motivation to solve worthwhile problems. (p. 267)

negative symptoms Deficits or disruptions to normal emotions and behaviors (e.g., emotional and social withdrawal; apathy; poverty of speech; and other indications of the absence or insufficiency of normal behavior, motivation, and emotion). (p. 461)

nervous system An interacting network of neurons that conveys electrochemical information throughout the body. (p. 65)

neurons Cells in the nervous system that communicate with one another to perform information-processing tasks. (p. 56)

neurotransmitters Chemicals that transmit information across the synapse to a receiving neuron's dendrites. (p. 61)

night terrors (or sleep terrors) Abrupt awakenings with panic and intense emotional arousal. (p. 152)

nonshared environment Those environmental factors that are not experienced by all relevant members of a household (see *shared environment*). (p. 300)

nonsuicidal self-injury (NSSI) Direct, deliberate destruction of body tissue in the absence of any intent to die. (p. 472)

norm of reciprocity The unwritten rule that people should benefit those who have benefited them. (p. 395)

normal distribution A mathematically defined distribution in which the frequency of measurements is highest in the middle and decreases symmetrically in both directions. (p. A–1)

normative influence A phenomenon that occurs when another person's behavior provides information about what is appropriate. (p. 395)

norms Customary standards for behavior that are widely shared by members of a culture. (p. 395)

obedience The tendency to do what powerful authorities tell us to do. (p. 397)

object permanence The belief that objects exist even when they are not visible. (p. 320)

observational learning A condition in which learning takes place by watching the actions of others. (p. 230)

obsessive-compulsive disorder (OCD) A disorder in which repetitive, intrusive thoughts (obsessions) and ritualistic behaviors (compulsions) designed to fend off those thoughts interfere significantly with an individual's functioning. (p. 452)

occipital lobe A region of the cerebral cortex that processes visual information. (p. 72)

Oedipus conflict A developmental experience in which a child's conflicting feelings toward the opposite-sex parent are (usually) resolved by identifying with the same-sex parent. (p. 362)

olfactory bulb A brain structure located above the nasal cavity beneath the frontal lobes. (p. 128)

olfactory receptor neurons (ORNs) Receptor cells that initiate the sense of smell. (p. 127)

operant behavior Behavior that an organism produces that has some impact on the environment. (p. 217)

operant conditioning A type of learning in which the consequences of an organism's behavior determine whether it will be repeated in the future. (p. 216)

operational definition A description of a property in concrete, measurable terms. (p. 30)

oral stage The first psychosexual stage, in which experience centers on the pleasures and frustrations associated with the mouth, sucking, and being fed. (p. 362)

outcome expectancies A person's assumptions about the likely consequences of a future behavior. (p. 367)

panic disorder A disorder characterized by the sudden occurrence of multiple psychological and physiological symptoms that contribute to a feeling of stark terror. (p. 450)

parasympathetic nervous system A set of nerves that helps the body return to a normal resting state. (p. 66)

parietal lobe A region of the cerebral cortex whose functions include processing information about touch. (p. 72)

passionate love An experience involving feelings of euphoria, intimacy, and intense sexual attraction. (p. 390)

perception The organization, identification, and interpretation of a sensation in order to form a mental representation. (p. 96)

perceptual confirmation The tendency for people to see what they expect to see. (p. 404)

peripheral nervous system (PNS) The part of the nervous system that connects the central nervous system to the body's organs and muscles. (p. 65)

persistence The intrusive recollection of events that we wish we could forget. (p. 200)

person-centered therapy (or client-centered therapy) Assumes all individuals have a tendency toward growth and that this growth can be facilitated by acceptance and genuine reactions from the therapist. (p. 483)

personal constructs Dimensions people use in making sense of their experiences. (p. 367)

personality An individual's characteristic style of behaving, thinking, and feeling. (p. 351)

personality disorders Enduring patterns of thinking, feeling, or relating to others or controlling impulses that deviate from cultural expectations and cause distress or impaired functioning. (p. 469)

person–situation controversy The question of whether behavior is caused more by personality or by situational factors. (p. 366)

persuasion A phenomenon that occurs when a person's attitudes or beliefs are influenced by a communication from another person. (p. 399)

phallic stage The third psychosexual stage, in which experience is dominated by the pleasure, conflict, and frustration associated with the phallic-genital region as well as coping with powerful incestuous feelings of love, hate, jealousy, and conflict. (p. 362)

phenomenology How things seem to the conscious person. (p. 136)

pheromones Biochemical odorants emitted by other members of its species that can affect an animal's behavior or physiology. (p. 128)

philosophical empiricism The view that all knowledge is acquired through experience. (p. 4)

phobic disorders Disorders characterized by marked, persistent, and excessive fear and avoidance of specific objects, activities, or situations. (p. 448)

phoneme The smallest unit of sound that is recognizable as speech rather than as random noise. (p. 274)

phonological rules A set of rules that indicate how phonemes can be combined to produce speech sounds. (p. 274)

phototherapy A therapy that involves repeated exposure to bright light. (p. 498)

pitch How high or low a sound is. (p. 118)

pituitary gland The "master gland" of the body's hormone-producing system, which releases hormones that direct the functions of many other glands in the body. (p. 71)

place code The process by which different frequencies stimulate neural signals at specific places along the basilar membrane, from which the brain determines pitch. (p. 121)

placebo An inert substance or procedure that has been applied with the expectation that a healing response will be produced. (p. 500)

pons A brain structure that relays information from the cerebellum to the rest of the brain. (p. 69)

population A complete collection of participants who might possibly be measured. (p. 42)

positive symptoms Thoughts and behaviors present in schizophrenia but not seen in those without the disorder, such as delusions and hallucinations. (p. 460)

postconventional stage A stage of moral development at which the morality of an action is determined by a set of general principles that reflect core values. (p. 331)

posthypnotic amnesia The failure to retrieve memories following hypnotic suggestions to forget. (p. 164)

posttraumatic stress disorder (PTSD) A disorder characterized by chronic physiological arousal, recurrent unwanted thoughts or images of the trauma, and avoidance of things that call the traumatic event to mind. (p. 453)

power An instrument's ability to detect small magnitudes of the property. (p. 31)

preconventional stage A stage of moral development in which the morality of an action is primarily determined by its consequences for the actor. (p. 330)

prejudice A positive or negative evaluation of another person based on the person's group membership. (p. 384)

preoperational stage The stage of cognitive development that begins at about 2 years and ends at about 6 years, during which children develop a preliminary understanding of the physical world. (p. 322)

preparedness theory The idea that people are instinctively predisposed toward certain fears. (p. 448)

primary sex characteristics Bodily structures that are directly involved in reproduction. (p. 334)

priming An enhanced ability to think of a stimulus, such as a word or object, as a result of a recent exposure to the stimulus. (p. 188)

proactive interference Situations in which earlier learning impairs memory for information acquired later. (p. 194)

problem of other minds The fundamental difficulty we have in perceiving the consciousness of others. (p. 136)

procedural memory The gradual acquisition of skills as a result of practice, or "knowing how" to do things. (p. 187)

projective tests Tests designed to reveal inner aspects of individuals' personalities by analysis of their responses to a standard series of ambiguous stimuli. (p. 352)

prospect theory People choose to take on risk when evaluating potential losses and avoid risks when evaluating potential gains. (p. 291)

prospective memory Remembering to do things in the future. (p. 195)

prototype The "best" or "most typical member" of a category. (p. 285)

proximodistal rule The "inside-to-outside" rule that describes the tendency for motor behavior to emerge in sequence from the center to the periphery. (p. 318)

psychoactive drugs Chemicals that influence consciousness or behavior by altering the brain's chemical message system. (p. 156)

psychoanalysis A therapeutic approach that focuses on bringing unconscious material into conscious awareness to better understand psychological disorders. (p. 8)

psychoanalytic theory An approach that emphasizes the importance of unconscious mental processes in shaping feelings, thoughts, and behavior. (p. 8)

psychodynamic approach An approach that regards personality as formed by needs, strivings, and desires largely operating outside of awareness—motives that can also produce emotional disorders. (p. 360)

psychodynamic psychotherapies Therapies that explore childhood events and encourage individuals to use the understanding that results to develop insight into their psychological problems. (p. 481)

psychology The scientific study of mind and behavior. (p. 2)

psychopharmacology The study of drug effects on psychological states and symptoms. (p. 492)

psychophysics Methods that measure the strength of a stimulus and the observer's sensitivity to that stimulus. (p. 97)

psychosexual stages Distinct early life stages through which personality is formed as children experience sexual pleasures from specific body areas and caregivers redirect or interfere with those pleasures. (p. 362)

psychosomatic illness An interaction between mind and body that can produce illness. (p. 429)

psychosurgery Surgical destruction of specific brain areas. (p. 498)

psychotherapy An interaction between a socially sanctioned clinician and someone suffering from a psychological problem, with the goal of providing support or relief from the problem. (p. 481)

puberty The bodily changes associated with sexual maturity. (p. 334)

punisher Any stimulus or event that functions to decrease the likelihood of the behavior that led to it. (p. 218)

random assignment A procedure that lets chance assign people to the experimental or control group. (p. 39)

random sampling A technique for choosing participants that ensures that every member of a population has an equal chance of being included in the sample. (p. 43)

range The value of the largest measurement in a frequency distribution minus the value of the smallest measurement. (p. A-3)

ratio IQ A statistic obtained by dividing a person's mental age by the person's physical age and then multiplying the quotient by 100 (see *deviation IQ*). (p. 294)

rational choice theory The classical view that we make decisions by determining how likely something is to happen, judging the value of the outcome, and then multiplying the two. (p. 288)

rational coping Facing the stressor and working to overcome it. (p. 422)

reaction time The amount of time taken to respond to a specific stimulus. (p. 5)

reappraisal Changing one's emotional experience by changing the way one thinks about the emotion-eliciting stimulus. (p. 252)

rebound effect of thought suppression The tendency of a thought to return to consciousness with greater frequency following suppression. (p. 143)

receptors Parts of the cell membrane that receive the neurotransmitter and initiate or prevent a new electric signal. (p. 62)

reciprocal altruism Behavior that benefits another with the expectation that those benefits will be returned in the future. (p. 386)

reconsolidation The process that causes memories to become vulnerable to disruption when they are recalled, thus requiring them to become consolidated again. (p. 180)

referred pain Feeling of pain when sensory information from internal and external areas converges on the same nerve cells in the spinal cord. (p. 125)

reflexes Specific patterns of motor response that are triggered by specific patterns of sensory stimulation. (p. 318)

reframing Finding a new or creative way to think about a stressor that reduces its threat. (p. 422)

rehearsal The process of keeping information in short-term memory by mentally repeating it. (p. 177)

reinforcement The consequences of a behavior determine whether it will be more or less likely to occur again. (p. 10)

reinforcer Any stimulus or event that functions to increase the likelihood of the behavior that led to it. (p. 218)

relaxation response A condition of reduced muscle tension, cortical activity, heart rate, breathing rate, and blood pressure. (p. 423)

relaxation therapy A technique for reducing tension by consciously relaxing muscles of the body. (p. 423)

reliability The tendency for an instrument to produce the same measurement whenever it is used to measure the same thing. (p. 31)

REM sleep A stage of sleep characterized by rapid eye movements and a high level of brain activity. (p. 147)

representativeness heuristic A mental shortcut that involves making a probability judgment by comparing an object or event to a prototype of the object or event. (p. 290)

repression A mental process that removes unacceptable thoughts and memories from consciousness and keeps them in the unconscious. (p. 145)

repressive coping Avoiding situations or thoughts that are reminders of a stressor and maintaining an artificially positive viewpoint. (p. 421)

Research Domain Criteria Project (RDoC) A new initiative that aims to guide the classification and understanding of mental disorders by revealing the basic processes that give rise to them. (p. 444)

resistance A reluctance to cooperate with treatment for fear of confronting unpleasant unconscious material. (p. 482)

response An action or physiological change elicited by a stimulus. (p. 10)

resting potential The difference in electric charge between the inside and outside of a neuron's cell membrane. (p. 59)

reticular formation A brain structure that regulates sleep, wakefulness, and levels of arousal. (p. 69)

retina Light-sensitive tissue lining the back of the eyeball. (p. 102)

retrieval The process of bringing to mind information that has been previously encoded and stored. (p. 172)

retroactive interference Situations in which later learning impairs memory for information acquired earlier. (p. 194)

retrograde amnesia The inability to retrieve information that was acquired before a particular date, usually the date of an injury or surgery. (p. 179)

rods Photoreceptors that become active under low-light conditions for night vision. (p. 102)

Rorschach Inkblot Test A projective technique in which respondents' inner thoughts and feelings are believed to be revealed by analysis of their responses to a set of unstructured inkblots. (p. 352)

sample A partial collection of people drawn from a population. (p. 43)

schemas Theories about the way the world works. (p. 320)

schizophrenia A psychotic disorder characterized by the profound disruption of basic psychological processes; a distorted perception of reality; altered or blunted emotion; and disturbances in thought, motivation, and behavior. (p. 460)

scientific method A procedure for finding truth by using empirical evidence. (p. 28)

seasonal affective disorder (SAD) Recurrent depressive episodes in a seasonal pattern. (p. 455)

second-order conditioning Conditioning in which a CS is paired with a stimulus that became associated with the US in an earlier procedure. (p. 211)

secondary sex characteristics Bodily structures that change dramatically with sexual maturity but that are not directly involved in reproduction. (p. 334)

self-actualizing tendency The human motive toward realizing our inner potential. (p. 363)

self-concept A person's explicit knowledge of his or her own behaviors, traits, and other personal characteristics. (p. 369)

self-consciousness A distinct level of consciousness in which the person's attention is drawn to the self as an object. (p. 141)

self-esteem The extent to which an individual likes, values, and accepts the self. (p. 371)

self-fulfilling prophecy The tendency for people to behave as they are expected to behave. (p. 405)

self-regulation The exercise of voluntary control over the self to bring the self into line with preferred standards. (p. 433)

self-report A method in which people provide subjective information about their own thoughts, feelings, or behaviors, typically via questionnaire or interview. (p. 351)

self-selection A problem that occurs when anything about a person determines whether he or she will be included in the experimental or control group. (p. 39)

self-serving bias People's tendency to take credit for their successes but to downplay responsibility for their failures. (p. 373)

self-verification The tendency to seek evidence to confirm the self-concept. (p. 371)

semantic encoding The process of relating new information in a meaningful way to knowledge that is already in memory. (p. 173)

semantic memory A network of associated facts and concepts that make up our general knowledge of the world. (p. 189)

sensation Simple stimulation of a sense organ. (p. 96)

sensitization A simple form of learning that occurs when presentation of a stimulus leads to an increased response to a later stimulus. (p. 208)

sensorimotor stage A stage of development that begins at birth and lasts through infancy. (p. 320)

sensory adaptation Sensitivity to prolonged stimulation tends to decline over time as an organism adapts to current conditions. (p. 100)

sensory memory A type of storage that holds sensory information for a few seconds or less. (p. 177)

sensory neurons Neurons that receive information from the external world and convey this information to the brain via the spinal cord. (p. 58)

shaping Learning that results from the reinforcement of successive steps to a final desired behavior. (p. 223)

shared environment Those environmental factors that are experienced by all relevant members of a household (see *nonshared environment*). (p. 300)

short-term memory A type of storage that holds nonsensory information for more than a few seconds but less than a minute. (p. 177)

sick role A socially recognized set of rights and obligations linked with illness. (p. 429)

signal detection theory The response to a stimulus depends both on a person's sensitivity to the stimulus in the presence of noise and on a person's response criterion. (p. 99)

sleep apnea A disorder in which the person stops breathing for brief periods while asleep. (p. 150)

sleep paralysis The experience of waking up unable to move. (p. 150)

social cognition The processes by which people come to understand others. (p. 402)

social-cognitive approach An approach that views personality in terms of how the person thinks about the situations encountered in daily life and behaves in response to them. (p. 365)

social exchange The hypothesis that people remain in relationships only as long as they perceive a favorable ratio of costs to benefits. (p. 392)

social influence The control of one person's behavior by another. (p. 393)

social phobia A disorder that involves an irrational fear of being publicly humiliated or embarrassed. (p. 448)

social psychology The study of the causes and consequences of sociality. (pp. 17, 380)

social support The aid gained through interacting with others. (p. 424)

somatic nervous system A set of nerves that conveys information between voluntary muscles and the central nervous system. (p. 65)

somatic symptom disorders The set of psychological disorders in which a person with at least one bodily symptom displays significant health-related anxiety, expresses disproportionate concerns about symptoms, and devotes excessive time and energy to symptoms or health concerns. (p. 429)

somnambulism (or sleepwalking) Occurs when a person arises and walks around while asleep. (p. 150)

source memory Recall of when, where, and how information was acquired. (p. 196)

specific phobia A disorder that involves an irrational fear of a particular object or situation that markedly interferes with an individual's ability to function. (p. 448)

spinal reflexes Simple pathways in the nervous system that rapidly generate muscle contractions. (p. 66)

spontaneous recovery The tendency of a learned behavior to recover from extinction after a rest period. (p. 211)

standard deviation A statistic that describes the average difference between the measurements in a frequency distribution and the mean of that distribution. (p. A–3)

state-dependent retrieval The tendency for information to be better recalled when the person is in the same state during encoding and retrieval. (p. 183)

stereotyping The process by which people draw inferences about people based on their knowledge of the categories to which those people belong. (p. 402)

stimulants Substances that excite the central nervous system, heightening arousal and activity levels. (p. 159)

stimulus Sensory input from the environment. (p. 10)

storage The process of maintaining information in memory over time. (p. 172)

stress The physical and psychological response to internal or external stressors. (p. 412)

stressors Specific events or chronic pressures that place demands on a person or threaten the person's well-being. (p. 412)

structuralism The analysis of the basic elements that constitute the mind. (p. 5)

subcortical structures Areas of the forebrain housed under the cerebral cortex near the very center of the brain. (p. 70)

subliminal perception Thought or behavior that is influenced by stimuli that a person cannot consciously report perceiving. (p. 145)

suggestibility The tendency to incorporate misleading information from external sources into personal recollections. (p. 198)

suicide attempt self-inflicted injury from which a person has at least some intention of dying. (p. 471)

suicide Intentional self-inflicted death. (p. 471)

sunk-cost fallacy A framing effect in which people make decisions about a current situation based on what they have previously invested in the situation. (p. 290)

superego The mental system that reflects the internalization of cultural rules, mainly learned as parents exercise their authority. (p. 360)

surface structure How a sentence is worded. (p. 275)

sympathetic nervous system A set of nerves that prepares the body for action in challenging or threatening situations. (p. 66)

synapse The junction or region between the axon of one neuron and the dendrites or cell body of another. (p. 56)

syntactical rules A set of rules that indicate how words can be combined to form phrases and sentences. (p. 275)

systematic persuasion The process by which attitudes or beliefs are changed by appeals to reason. (p. 399)

taste buds The organ of taste transduction. (p. 128)

telegraphic speech Speech that is devoid of function morphemes and consists mostly of content words. (p. 278)

telomeres Caps at the end of each chromosome that protect the ends of chromosomes and prevent them from sticking to each other. (p. 417)

temperaments Characteristic patterns of emotional reactivity. (p. 328)

temporal code The cochlea registers low frequencies via the firing rate of action potentials entering the auditory nerve. (p. 121)

temporal lobe A region of the cerebral cortex responsible for hearing and language. (p. 73)

teratogens Agents that damage the process of development. (p. 316)

terminal buttons Knoblike structures that branch out from an axon. (p. 61)

terror management theory A theory about how people respond to knowledge of their own mortality. (p. 268)

thalamus A subcortical structure that relays and filters information from the senses and transmits the information to the cerebral cortex. (p. 70)

Thematic Apperception Test (TAT) A projective technique in which respondents' underlying motives, concerns, and the way they see the social world are believed to be revealed through analysis of the stories they make up about ambiguous pictures of people. (p. 353)

theory of mind The understanding that other people's mental representations guide their behavior. (p. 323)

theory A hypothetical explanation of a natural phenomenon. (p. 28)

third-variable correlation Two variables are correlated only because each is causally related to a third variable. (p. 36)

third-variable problem The fact that a causal relationship between two variables cannot be inferred from the naturally occurring correlation between them because of the ever-present possibility of third-variable correlation. (p. 37)

thought suppression The conscious avoidance of a thought. (p. 143)

timbre A listener's experience of sound quality or resonance. (p. 118)

token economy A form of behavior therapy in which clients are given "tokens" for desired behaviors, which they can later trade for rewards. (p. 484)

trait A relatively stable disposition to behave in a particular and consistent way. (p. 354)

transcranial magnetic stimulation (TMS) A treatment that involves placing a powerful pulsed magnet over a person's scalp, which alters neuronal activity in the brain. (p. 496)

transduction What takes place when many sensors in the body convert physical signals from the environment into encoded neural signals sent to the central nervous system. (p. 96)

transfer-appropriate processing The idea that memory is likely to transfer from one situation to another when the encoding and retrieval contexts of the situations match. (p. 183)

transference An event that occurs in psychoanalysis when the analyst begins to assume a major significance in the client's life and the client reacts to the analyst based on unconscious childhood fantasies. (p. 482)

transience Forgetting what occurs with the passage of time. (p. 193)

two-factor theory The theory that emotions are based on inferences about the causes of physiological arousal. (p. 248)

two-factor theory of intelligence Spearman's theory suggesting that every task requires a combination of a general ability (which he called *g*) and skills that are specific to the task (which he called *s*). (p. 297)

Type A behavior pattern The tendency toward easily aroused hostility, impatience, a sense of time urgency, and competitive achievement strivings. (p. 419)

unconditioned response (UR) A reflexive reaction that is reliably produced by an unconditioned stimulus. (p. 209)

unconditioned stimulus (US) Something that reliably produces a naturally occurring reaction in an organism. (p. 209)

unconscious The part of the mind that operates outside of conscious awareness but influences conscious thoughts, feelings, and actions. (p. 8)

unconscious motivations Motivations of which people are not aware. (p. 267)

universality hypothesis Emotional expressions have the same meaning for everyone. (p. 254)

validity The goodness with which a concrete event defines a property. (p. 31)

variable A property whose value can vary across individuals or over time. (p. 34)

variable-interval schedule (VI) An operant conditioning principle in which behavior is reinforced based on an average time that has expired since the last reinforcement. (p. 222)

variable-ratio schedule (VR) An operant conditioning principle in which the delivery of reinforcement is based on a particular average number of responses. (p. 222)

vestibular system The three fluid-filled semicircular canals and adjacent organs located next to the cochlea in each inner ear. (p. 126)

visual acuity The ability to see fine detail. (p. 100)

visual form agnosia The inability to recognize objects by sight. (p. 108)

Weber's law The just noticeable difference of a stimulus is a constant proportion despite variations in intensity. (p. 99)

working memory Active maintenance of information in short-term storage. (p. 178)

zygote A fertilized egg that contains chromosomes from both a sperm and an egg. (p. 315)

REFERENCES

Aarts, H., Custers, R., & Marien, H. (2008). Preparing and motivating behavior outside of awareness. *Science, 319,* 1639.

Abel, T., Alberini, C., Ghirardi, M., Huang, Y.-Y., Nguyen, P., & Kandel, E. R. (1995). Steps toward a molecular definition of memory consolidation. In D. L. Schacter (Ed.), *Memory distortion: How minds, brains and societies reconstruct the past* (pp. 298–328). Cambridge, MA: Harvard University Press.

Abelson, J., Curtis, G., Sagher, O., Albucher, R., Harrigan, M., Taylor, S., . . . Giordani, B. (2009). Deep brain stimulation for refractory obsessive-compulsive disorder. *Biological Psychiatry, 57,* 510–516.

Abramson, L. Y., Seligman, M. E. P., & Teasdale, J. D. (1978). Learned helplessness in humans: Critique and reformulation. *Journal of Abnormal Psychology, 87,* 49–74.

Acevedo, B. P., & Aron, A. (2009). Does a long-term relationship kill romantic love? *Review of General Psychology, 13,* 59–65.

Acevedo-Garcia, D., McArdle, N., Osypuk, T. L., Lefkowitz, B., & Krimgold, B. K. (2007). *Children left behind: How metropolitan areas are failing America's children.* Boston: Harvard School of Public Health.

Achter, J. A., Lubinski, D., & Benbow, C. P. (1996). Multipotentiality among the intellectually gifted: "It was never there and already it's vanishing." *Journal of Counseling Psychology, 43,* 65–76.

Acocella, J. (1999). *Creating hysteria: Women and multiple personality disorder.* San Francisco: Jossey-Bass.

Addis, D. R., Wong, A. T., & Schacter, D. L. (2007). Remembering the past and imagining the future: Common and distinct neural substrates during event construction and elaboration. *Neuropsychologia, 45,* 1363–1377.

Addis, D. R., Wong, A. T., & Schacter, D. L. (2008). Age-related changes in the episodic simulation of future events. *Psychological Science, 19,* 33–41.

Adelmann, P. K., & Zajonc, R. B. (1989). Facial efference and the experience of emotion. *Annual Review of Psychology, 40,* 249–280.

Adolph, K. E., Cole, W. G., Komati, M., Garciaguirre, J. S., Badaly, D., Lingeman, J. M., . . . Sotsky, R. B. (2012). How do you learn to walk? Thousands of steps and dozens of falls per day. *Psychological Science, 23*(11), 1387–1394. doi:10.1177/0956797612446346

Adolphs, R., Russell, J. A., & Tranel, D. (1999). A role for the human amygdala in recognizing emotional arousal from unpleasant stimuli. *Psychological Science, 10,* 167–171.

Aggleton, J. (Ed.). (1992). *The amygdala: Neurobiological aspects of emotion, memory and mental dysfunction.* New York: Wiley-Liss.

Agin, D. (2007). *Junk science: An overdue indictment of government, industry, and faith groups that twist science for their own gain.* New York: Macmillan.

Agren, T., Engman, J., Frick, A., Björkstrand, J., Larsson, E. M., Furmark, T., & Fredrikson, M. (2012). Disruption of reconsolidation erases a fear memory trace in the human amygdala. *Science, 337,* 1550–1552.

Ahlskog, J. E. (2011). Pathological behaviors provoked by dopamine agonist therapy of Parkinson's disease. *Physiology & Behavior, 104,* 168–172.

Ainsworth, M. D. S., Blehar, M. C., Waters, E., & Wall, S. (1978). *Patterns of attachment: A psychological study of the strange situation.* Hillsdale, NJ: Erlbaum.

Ainsworth, S. E., & Maner, J. K. (2012). Sex begets violence: Mating motives, social dominance, and physical aggression in men. *Journal of Personality and Social Psychology, 103*(5), 819–829. doi: 10.1037/a0029428

Albarracín, D., & Vargas, P. (2010). Attitudes and persuasion: From biology to social responses to persuasive intent. In S. T. Fiske, D. T. Gilbert, & G. Lindzey (Eds.), *The handbook of social psychology* (5th ed., Vol. 1, pp. 389–422). New York: Wiley.

Aleman, A., Sommer, I. E., & Kahn, R. S. (2007). Efficacy of slow repetitive transcranial magnetic stimulation in the treatment of resistant auditory hallucinations in schizophrenia: A meta-analysis. *Journal of Clinical Psychiatry, 68,* 416–421.

Alicke, M. D., Klotz, M. L., Breitenbecher, D. L., Yurak, T. J., & Vredenburg, D. S. (1995). Personal contact, individuation, and the better-than-average effect. *Journal of Personality and Social Psychology, 68,* 804–824.

Allison, D. B., Fontaine, K. R., Manson, J. E., Stevens, J., & VanItallie, T. B. (1999). Annual deaths attributable to obesity in the United States. *Journal of the American Medical Association, 282,* 1530–1538.

Allison, D. B., Kaprio, J., Korkeila, M., Koskenvuo, M., Neale, M. C., & Hayakawa, K. (1996). The heritability of body mass index among an international sample of monozygotic twins reared apart. *International Journal of Obesity, 20*(6), 501–506.

Allport, G. W. (1937). *Personality: A psychological interpretation.* New York: Holt.

Allport, G. W. (1954). *The nature of prejudice.* Cambridge, MA: Addison-Wesley.

Allport, G. W., & Odbert, H. S. (1936). Trait-names: A psycholexical study. *Psychological Monographs, 47,* 592.

Alt, K. W., Jeunesse, C., Buitrago-Téllez, C. H., Wächter, R., Boës, E., & Pichler, S. L. (1997). Evidence for stone age cranial surgery. *Nature, 387,* 360.

Alvarez, K., & Eckholm, E. (2009, January 8). Purple heart is ruled out for traumatic stress. *New York Times,* p. A1.

Alvarez, L. W. (1965). A pseudo experience in parapsychology. *Science, 148,* 1541.

American Academy of Pediatrics. (2000, July 26). *The impact of entertainment violence on children.* Joint statement issued at a meeting of the Congressional Public Health Summit. Retrieved from http://www.aap.org/advocacy/releases/jstmtevc.htm

American Psychiatric Association. (2013). *Diagnostic and statistical manual of mental disorders* (5th ed.). Washington, DC: Author.

American Psychological Association. (2002). *Ethical principles of psychologists and code of conduct.* Washington, DC: Author. Retrieved from apa.org/code/ethics/index.aspx [includes 2010 amendments].

American Psychological Association. (2005). *Resolution in favor of empirically supported sex education and HIV prevention programs for adolescents.* Washington, DC: Author.

American Psychological Association. (2009). *Report of the American Psychological Association task force on appropriate therapeutic responses to sexual orientation.* Washington, DC: Author.

Anand, S., & Hotson, J. (2002). Transcranial magnetic stimulation: Neurophysiological applications and safety. *Brain and Cognition, 50,* 366–386.

Anderson, C. A. (1989). Temperature and aggression: Ubiquitous effects of heat on occurrence of human violence. *Psychological Bulletin, 106,* 74–96.

Anderson, C. A., Berkowitz, L., Donnerstein, E., Huesmann, L. R., Johnson, J. D., Linz, D., . . . Wartella, E. (2003). The influence of media violence on youth. *Psychological Science in the Public Interest, 4,* 81–110.

Anderson, C. A., & Bushman, B. J. (2001). Effects of violent video games on aggressive behavior, aggressive cognition, aggressive affect, physiological arousal, and prosocial behavior: A metaanalytic review of the scientific literature. *Psychological Science, 12*(5), 353–359.

Anderson, C. A., & Bushman, B. J. (2002). Human aggression. *Annual Review of Psychology, 53,* 27–51.

Anderson, C. A., Bushman, B. J., & Groom, R. W. (1997). Hot years and serious and deadly assault: Empirical tests of the heat hypothesis. *Journal of Personality and Social Psychology, 73,* 1213–1223.

Anderson, M. C. (2003). Rethinking interference theory: Executive control and the mechanisms of forgetting. *Journal of Memory and Language, 49,* 415–445.

Anderson, M. C., Bjork, R. A., & Bjork, E. L. (1994). Remembering can cause forgetting: Retrieval dynamics in long-term memory. *Journal of Experimental Psychology: Learning, Memory, and Cognition, 20,* 1063–1087.

Anderson, M. C., Ochsner, K. N., Kuhl, B., Cooper, J., Robertson, E., Gabrieli, S. W., . . . Gabrieli, J. D. E. (2004). Neural systems underlying the suppression of unwanted memories. *Science, 303,* 232–235.

Anderson, R. C., Pichert, J. W., Goetz, E. T., Schallert, D. L., Stevens, K. V., & Trollip, S. R. (1976). Instantiation of general terms. *Journal of Verbal Learning and Verbal Behavior, 15,* 667–679.

Andreasen, N. C. (2011). A journey into chaos: Creativity and the unconscious. *Mens Sana Monographs, 9,* 42–53.

Andrewes, D. (2001). *Neuropsychology: From theory to practice.* Hove, England: Psychology Press.

Andrews-Hanna, J. R. (2012). The brain's default network and its adaptive role in internal mentation. *Neuroscientist, 18,* 251–270.

Annis, L. F., & Annis, D. B. (1982). A normative study of students' reported preferred study techniques. *Literacy Research and Instruction, 21,* 201–207.

Antoni, M. H., Lehman, J. M., Klibourn, K. M., Boyers, A. E., Culver, J. L., Alferi, S. M., . . . Carver, C. S. (2001). Cognitive-behavioral stress management intervention decreases the prevalence of depression and enhances benefit finding among women under treatment for early-stage breast cancer. *Health Psychology, 20,* 20–32.

Apicella, C. L., Feinberg, D. R., & Marlowe, F. W. (2007). Voice pitch predicts reproductive success in male hunter-gatherers. *Biology Letters, 3*(6), 682–684. doi:10.1098/rsbl.2007.0410

Arellano, D., Varona, J., & Perales, F. (2008). Generation and visualization of emotional states in virtual characters. *Computer Animation and Virtual Worlds, 19*(3–4), 259–270.

Ariyasu, H., Takaya, K., Tagami, T., Ogawa, Y., Hosoda, K., Akamizu, T., . . . Hosoda, H. (2001). Stomach is a major source of circulating ghrelin, and feeding state determines plasma ghrelin-like immunoreactivity levels in humans. *Journal of Clinical Endocrinology and Metabolism, 86,* 4753–4758.

Armstrong, D. M. (1980). *The nature of mind.* Ithaca, NY: Cornell University Press.

Arnold, M. B. (Ed.). (1960). *Emotion and personality: Psychological aspects* (Vol. 1). New York: Columbia University Press.

Aron, A., Fisher, H., Mashek, D., Strong, G., Li, H., & Brown, L. (2005). Reward, motivation, and emotion systems associated with early-stage intense romantic love. *Journal of Neurophysiology, 93,* 327–337.

Aronson, E. (1963). Effect of the severity of threat on the devaluation of forbidden behavior. *Journal of Abnormal and Social Psychology, 66,* 584–588.

Aronson, E. (1969). The theory of cognitive dissonance: A current perspective. In L. Berkowitz (Ed.), *Advances in experimental social psychology* (Vol. 4, pp. 1–34): Academic Press.

Aronson, E., & Worchel, P. (1966). Similarity versus liking as determinants of interpersonal attractiveness. *Psychonomic Science, 5,* 157–158.

Asch, S. E. (1951). Effects of group pressure on the modification and distortion of judgments. In H. Guetzkow (Ed.), *Groups, leadership, and men* (pp. 177–190). Pittsburgh, PA: Carnegie Press.

Asch, S. E. (1955). Opinions and social pressure. *Scientific American, 193,* 31–35.

Asch, S. E. (1956). Studies of independence and conformity: 1. A minority of one against a unanimous majority. *Psychological Monographs: General and Applied, 70,* 1–70.

Aschoff, J. (1965). Circadian rhythms in man. *Science, 148,* 1427–1432.

Aserinsky, E., & Kleitman, N. (1953). Regularly occurring periods of eye motility, and concomitant phenomena, during sleep. *Science, 118,* 273–274.

Ashby, F. G., & Ell, S. W. (2001). The neurobiology of human category learning. *Trends in Cognitive Sciences, 5,* 204–210.

Ashby, F. G., & O'Brien, J. B. (2005). Category learning and multiple memory systems. *Trends in Cognitive Sciences, 9,* 83–89.

Ashcraft, M. H. (1998). *Fundamentals of cognition.* New York: Longman.

Astington, J. W., & Baird, J. (2005). *Why language matters for theory of mind.* Oxford, England: Oxford University Press.

Avery, D., Holtzheimer, P., III, Fawaz, W., Russo, J., Naumeier, J., Dunner, D., . . . Roy-Byrne, P. (2009). A controlled study of repetitive transcranial magnetic stimulation in medication-resistant major depression. *Biological Psychiatry, 59,* 187–194.

Aviezer, H., Hassin, R. R., Ryan, J., Grady, C., Susskind, J., Anderson, A., . . . Bentin, S. (2008). Angry, disgusted, or afraid? Studies on the malleability of emotion perception. *Psychological Science, 19,* 724–732.

Aviezer, H., Trope, Y., & Todorov, A. (2012). Body cues, not facial expressions, discriminate between intense positive and negative emotions. *Science, 338,* 1225–1229.

Axelrod, R. (1984). *The evolution of cooperation.* New York: Basic Books.

Axelrod, R., & Hamilton, W. D. (1981). The evolution of cooperation. *Science, 211,* 1390–1396.

Ayduk, O., Shoda, Y., Cervone, D., & Downey, G. (2007). Delay of gratification in children: Contributions to social–personality psychology. In G. Downey, Y. Shoda, & C. Cervone (Eds.), *Persons in context: Building a science of the individual* (pp. 97–109). New York: Guilford Press.

Azuma, H., & Kashiwagi, K. (1987). Descriptors for an intelligent person: A Japanese study. *Japanese Psychological Research, 29,* 17–26.

Baars, B. J. (1986). *The cognitive revolution in psychology.* New York: Guilford Press.

Baca-Motes, K., Brown, A., Gneezy, A., Keenan, E. A., & Nelson, L. D. (2013). Commitment and behavior change: Evidence from the field. *Journal of Consumer Research, 39*(5), 1070–1084. doi:10.1086/667226

Back, M. D., Stopfer, J. M., Vazire, S., Gaddis, S., Schmukle, S. C., Egloff, B., & Gosling, S. (2010). Facebook profiles reflect actual personality not self-idealization. *Psychological Science, 21,* 372–374.

Backman, C. W., & Secord, P. F. (1959). The effect of perceived liking on interpersonal attraction. *Human Relations, 12,* 379–384.

Bäckman, L., Almkvist, O., Andersson, J., Nordberg, A., Winblad, B., Reineck, R., & Långström, B. (1997). Brain activation in young and older adults during implicit and explicit retrieval. *Journal of Cognitive Neuroscience, 9,* 378–391.

Bäckman, L., & Dixon, R. A. (1992). Psychological compensation: A theoretical framework. *Psychological Bulletin, 112,* 259–283.

Baddeley, A. D. (2001). Is working memory still working? *American Psychologist, 56,* 851–864.

Baddeley, A. D., & Hitch, G. J. (1974). Working memory. In S. Dornic (Ed.), *Attention and performance* (Vol. 6, pp. 647–667). Hillsdale, NJ: Erlbaum.

Bagby, R. M., Levitan, R. D., Kennedy, S. H., Levitt, A. J., & Joffe, R. T. (1999). Selective alteration of personality in response to noradrenergic and serotonergic antidepressant medication in depressed sample: Evidence of non-specificity. *Psychiatry Research, 86,* 211–216.

Bahrick, H. P. (1984). Semantic memory content in permastore: 50 years of memory for Spanish learned in school. *Journal of Experimental Psychology: General, 113,* 1–29.

Bahrick, H. P. (2000). Long-term maintenance of knowledge. In E. Tulving & F. I. M. Craik (Eds.), *The Oxford handbook of memory* (pp. 347–362). New York: Oxford University Press.

Bailey, J. M., & Pillard, R. C. (1991). A genetic study of male sexual orientation. *Archives of General Psychiatry, 48,* 1089–1096.

Bailey, J. M., Pillard, R. C., Dawood, K., Miller, M. B., Farrer, L. A., Trivedi, S., . . . Murphy, R. L. (1999). A family history study of male sexual orientation using three independent samples. *Behavior Genetics, 29,* 79–86.

Bailey, J. M., Pillard, R. C., Neale, M. C., & Agyes, Y. (1993). Heritable factors influence sexual orientation in women. *Archives of General Psychiatry, 50,* 217–223.

Baillargeon, R., Spelke, E. S., & Wasserman, S. (1985). Object permanence in 5-month-old infants. *Cognition, 20,* 191–208.

Baird, B., Smallwood, J., Mrazek, M. D., Kam, J. W. Y., Franklin, M. S., & Schooler, J. W. (2012). Inspired by distraction: Mind wandering facilitates creative incubation. *Psychological Science, 23,* 1117–1122.

Baker, E., Shelton, K. H., Baibazarova, E., Hay, D. F., & van Goozen, S. H. M. (2013). Low skin conductance activity in infancy predicts aggression in toddlers 2 years later. *Psychological Science, 24*(6), 1051–1056. doi:10.1177/0956797612465198

Baker, T. B., Brandon, T. H., & Chassin, L. (2004). Motivational influences on cigarette smoking. *Annual Review of Psychology, 55,* 463–491.

Baler, R. D., & Volkow, N. D. (2006). Drug addiction: The neurobiology of disrupted self-control. *Trends in Molecular Medicine, 12,* 559–566.

Banaji, M. R., & Heiphetz, L. (2010). Attitudes. In S. T. Fiske, D. T. Gilbert, & G. Lindzey (Eds.), *The handbook of social psychology* (5th ed., Vol. 1, pp. 348–388). New York: Wiley.

Bandura, A. (1977). *Social learning theory.* Englewood Cliffs, NJ: Prentice Hall.

Bandura, A. (1986). *Social foundations of thought and action: A social cognitive theory.* Englewood Cliffs, NJ: Prentice Hall.

Bandura, A. (1994). Social cognitive theory of mass communication. In J. Bryant & D. Zillmann (Eds.), *Media effects: Advances in theory and research* (pp. 61–90). Hillsdale, NJ: Erlbaum.

Bandura, A., Ross, D., & Ross, S. (1961). Transmission of aggression through imitation of adult models. *Journal of Abnormal and Social Psychology, 63,* 575–582.

Bandura, A., Ross, D., & Ross, S. (1963). Vicarious reinforcement and imitative learning. *Journal of Abnormal and Social Psychology, 67,* 601–607.

Banks, M. S., & Salapatek, P. (1983). Infant visual perception. In M. Haith & J. Campos (Eds.), *Handbook of child psychology: Biology and infancy* (pp. 435–572). New York: Wiley.

Barber, J. P., Muran, J. C., McCarthy, K. S., & Keefe, J. R. (2013). Research on dynamic therapies. In M. Lambert (Ed.), *Bergin and Garfield's handbook of psychotherapy and behavior change* (6th ed., pp. 443–494). Hoboken, NJ: Wiley.

Bard, P. (1934). On emotional experience after decortication with some remarks on theoretical views. *Psychological Review, 41,* 309–329.

Bargh, J. A., Chen, M., & Burrows, L. (1996). The automaticity of social behavior: Direct effects of trait concept and stereotype activation on action. *Journal of Personality and Social Psychology, 71,* 230–244.

Bargh, J. A., Gollwitzer, P. M., Lee-Chai, A., Barndollar, K., & Trötschel, R. (2001). The automated will: Nonconscious activation and pursuit of behavioral goals. *Journal of Personality and Social Psychology, 81,* 1014–1027.

Bargh, J. A., Gollwitzer, P. M., & Oettingen, G. (2010). Motivation. In S. T. Fiske, D. T. Gilbert, & G. Lindzey (Eds.), *The handbook of social psychology* (5th ed., Vol. 1, pp. 263–311). New York: Wiley.

Barker, A. T., Jalinous, R., & Freeston, I. L. (1985). Noninvasive magnetic stimulation of the human motor cortex. *Lancet, 2,* 1106–1107.

Barkow, J. (1980). Prestige and self-esteem: A biosocial interpretation. In D. R. Omark, F. F. Stayer, & D. G. Freedman (Eds.), *Dominance relations* (pp. 319–322). New York: Garland.

Barlow, D. H., Bullis, J. R., Comer, J. S., & Ametaj, A. A. (2013). Evidence-based psychological treatments: An update and a way forward. *Annual Review of Clinical Psychology, 9,* 1–27.

Barlow, D. H., Gorman, J. M., Shear, M. K., & Woods, S. W. (2000). Cognitive-behavioral therapy, imipramine, or their combination for panic disorder: A randomized controlled trial. *Journal of the American Medical Association, 283*(19), 2529–2536.

Barnier, A. J., Levin, K., & Maher, A. (2004). Suppressing thoughts of past events: Are repressive copers good suppressors? *Cognition and Emotion, 18,* 457–477.

Baron-Cohen, S. (1991). Do people with autism understand what causes emotion? *Child Development, 62,* 385–395.

Baron-Cohen, S., & Belmonte, M. K. (2005). Autism: A window onto the development of the social and analytic brain. *Annual Review of Neuroscience, 28,* 109–126.

Baron-Cohen, S., Leslie, A., & Frith, U. (1985). Does the autistic child have a "theory of mind"? *Cognition, 21,* 37–46.

Barrett, L. F., Mesquita, B., & Gendron, M. (2011). Context in emotion perception. *Current Directions in Psychological Science, 20*(5), 286–290. doi:10.1177/0963721411422522

Bartal, I. B.-A., Decety, J., & Mason, P. (2011). Empathy and prosocial behavior in rats. *Science, 334*(6061), 1427–1430.

Bartol, C. R., & Costello, N. (1976). Extraversion as a function of temporal duration of electric shock: An exploratory study. *Perceptual and Motor Skills, 42,* 1174.

Bartoshuk, L. M. (2000). Comparing sensory experiences across individuals: Recent psychophysical advances illuminate genetic variation in taste perception. *Chemical Senses, 25,* 447–460.

Bartoshuk, L. M., & Beauchamp, G. K. (1994). Chemical senses. *Annual Review of Psychology, 45,* 419–445.

Basden, B. H., Basden, D. R., Bryner, S., & Thomas, R. L. (1997). A comparison of group and individual remembering: Does collaboration disrupt retrieval strategies? *Journal of Experimental Psychology: Learning, Memory, and Cognition, 23,* 1176–1191.

Bates, E., & Goodman, J. C. (1997). On the inseparability of grammar and the lexicon: Evidence from acquisition, aphasia, and real-time processing. *Language and Cognitive Processes, 12,* 507–584.

Batson, C. D. (2002). Addressing the altruism question experimentally. In S. G. Post & L. G. Underwood (Eds.), *Altruism & altruistic love: Science, philosophy, & religion in dialogue* (pp. 89–105). London: Oxford University Press.

Baumeister, R. F., Bratslavsky, E., Muraven, M., & Tice, D. M. (1998). Ego depletion: Is the active self a limited resource? *Journal of Personality and Social Psychology, 74,* 1252–1265.

Baumeister, R. F., Campbell, J. D., Krueger, J. I., & Vohs, K. D. (2003). Does high self-esteem cause better performance, interpersonal success, happiness, or healthier lifestyles? *Psychological Science in the Public Interest, 4,* 1–44.

Baumeister, R. F., Cantanese, K. R., & Vohs, K. D. (2001). Is there a gender difference in strength of sex drive? Theoretical views, conceptual distinctions, and a review of relevant evidence. *Personality and Social Psychology Review, 5,* 242–273.

Baumeister, R. F., Heatherton, T. F., & Tice, D. M. (1995). *Losing control.* San Diego, CA: Academic Press.

Baumeister, R. F., & Leary, M. R. (1995). The need to belong: Desire for interpersonal attachments as a fundamental human motivation. *Psychological Bulletin, 117,* 497–529.

Baumeister, R. F., Smart, L., & Boden, J. M. (1996). Relation of threatened egotism to violence and aggression: The dark side of high self-esteem. *Psychological Review, 103,* 5–33.

Baumeister, R. F., Vohs, K. D., & Tice, D. M. (2007). The strength model of self-control. *Current Directions in Psychological Science, 16,* 351–355.

Baxter, L. R., Schwartz, J. M., Bergman, K. S., Szuba, M. P., Guze, B. H., Mazziotta, J. C., Alazraki, A., . . . Munford, P. (1992). Caudate glucose metabolic rate changes with both drug behavior therapy for obsessive-compulsive disorder. *Archives of General Psychiatry, 49,* 681–689.

Bayley, P. J., Frascino, J. C., & Squire, L. R. (2005). Robust habit learning in the absence of awareness and independent of the medial temporal lobe. *Nature, 436,* 550–553.

Bayley, P. J., Gold, J. J., Hopkins, R. O., & Squire, L. R. (2005). The neuroanatomy of remote memory. *Neuron, 46,* 799–810.

Beard, C., Sawyer, A. T., & Hoffmann, S. G. (2012). Efficacy of attention bias modification using threat and appetitive stimuli: A meta-analytic review. *Behavior Therapy, 43,* 724–740.

Bechara, A., Damasio, A. R., Damasio, H., & Anderson, S. W. (1994). Insensitivity to future consequences following damage to human prefrontal cortex. *Cognition, 50,* 7–15.

Bechara, A., Damasio, H., Tranel, D., & Damasio, A. R. (1997). Deciding advantageously before knowing the advantageous strategy. *Science, 275,* 1293–1295.

Bechara, A., Dolan, S., Denburg, N., Hindes, A., & Anderson, S. W. (2001). Decision-making deficits, linked to a dysfunctional ventromedial prefrontal cortex, revealed in alcohol and stimulant abusers. *Neuropsychologia, 39,* 376–389.

Bechara, A., Tranel, D., & Damasio, H. (2000). Characterization of the decision-making deficit of patients with ventromedial prefrontal cortex lesions. *Brain, 123,* 2189–2202.

Beck, A. T. (1967). *Depression: Causes and treatment.* Philadelphia: University of Pennsylvania Press.

Beck, A. T. (2005). The current state of cognitive therapy: A 40-year retrospective. *Archives of General Psychiatry, 62,* 953–959.

Beckers, G., & Zeki, S. (1995). The consequences of inactivating areas V1 and V5 on visual motion perception. *Brain, 118,* 49–60.

Bednarczyk, R. A., Davis, R., Ault, K., Orenstein, W., & Omer, S. B. (2012). Sexual activity-related outcomes after human papillomavirus vaccination of 11- to 12-year-olds. *Pediatrics, 130*(5), 798–805. doi:10.1542/peds.2912-1516

Bedny, M., & Saxe, R. (2012). Insights into the origins of knowledge from the cognitive neuroscience of blindness. *Cognitive Neuropsychology, 29,* 56–84.

Bell, A. P., Weinberg, M. S., & Hammersmith, S. K. (1981). *Sexual preference: Its development in men and women.* Bloomington: Indiana University Press.

Belsky, J. (2012). The development of human reproductive strategies: Progress and prospects. *Current Directions in Psychological Science, 21*(5), 310–316. doi:10.1177/0963721412453588

Bem, S. L. (1974). The measure of psychological androgyny. *Journal of Consulting and Clinical Psychology, 42,* 155–162.

Benenson, J. F., Markovits, H., Thompson, M. E., & Wrangham, R. W. (2011). Under threat of social exclusion, females exclude more than males. *Psychological Science, 22*(4), 538–544. doi: 10.1177/0956797611402511

Bennett, I. J., Romano, J. C., Howard, J. H., & Howard, D. V. (2008). Two forms of implicit learning in young adults with dyslexia. *Annals of the New York Academy of Sciences, 1145,* 184–198.

Benoit, R. G., & Anderson, M. C. (2012). Opposing mechanisms support the voluntary forgetting of unwanted memories. *Neuron, 76,* 450–460.

Ben-Porath, Y. S., & Tellegen, A. (2008). *Minnesota Multiphasic Personality Inventory–2–Restructured Form: Manual for administration, scoring, and interpretation.* Minneapolis: University of Minnesota Press.

Benson, H. (Ed.). (1990). *The relaxation response.* New York: Harper Torch.

Benson, H., Dusek, J. A., Sherwood, J. B., Lam, P., Bethea, C. F., Carpenter, W., . . . Hibberd, P. L. (2006). Study of the therapeutic effects of intercessory prayer (STEP) in cardiac bypass patients: A multi-center randomized trial of uncertainty and certainty of receiving intercessory prayer. *American Heart Journal, 151,* 934–942.

Bering, J. (2004). A critical review of the "enculturation hypothesis": The effects of human rearing on great ape social cognition. *Animal Cognition, 7,* 201–212.

Berkowitz, L. (1990). On the formation and regulation of anger and aggression: A cognitive-neoassociationistic analysis. *American Psychologist, 45,* 494–503.

Berscheid, E., Dion, K., Walster, E., & Walster, G. W. (1971). Physical attractiveness and dating choice: A test of the matching hypothesis. *Journal of Experimental Social Psychology, 7*(2), 173–189.

Berscheid, E., & Reis, H. T. (1998). Interpersonal attraction and close relationships. In D. T. Gilbert, S. T. Fiske, & G. Lindzey (Eds.), *The handbook of social psychology* (4th ed., Vol. 2, pp. 193–281). New York: McGraw-Hill.

Bertenthal, B. I., Rose, J. L., & Bai, D. L. (1997). Perception–action coupling in the development of visual control of posture. *Journal of Experimental Psychology: Human Perception & Performance, 23,* 1631–1643.

Berthoud, H.-R., & Morrison, C. (2008). The brain, appetite, and obesity. *Annual Review of Psychology, 59,* 55–92.

Best, J. B. (1992). *Cognitive psychology* (3rd ed.). New York: West Publishing.

Bettencourt, B. A., & Miller, N. (1996). Gender differences in aggression as a function of provocation: A meta-analysis. *Psychological Bulletin, 119,* 422–447.

Beutler, L. E. (2002). The dodo bird is extinct. *Clinical Psychology: Science and Practice, 9,* 30–34.

Bhargava, S. (2011). Diagnosis and management of common sleep problems in children. *Pediatrics in Review, 32,* 91.

Bialystok, E. (1999). Cognitive complexity and attentional control in the bilingual mind. *Child Development, 70,* 636–644.

Bialystok, E. (2009). Bilingualism: The good, the bad, and the indifferent. *Bilingualism: Language and Cognitive Processes, 12,* 3–11.

Bialystok, E., Craik, F. I. M., & Luk, G. (2012). Bilingualism: Consequences for mind and brain. *Trends in Cognitive Sciences, 16,* 240–250.

Biederman, J., Monuteaux, M. C., Spencer, T., Wilens, T. E., & Faraone, S. V. (2009). Do stimulants protect against psychiatric disorders in youth with ADHD? A 10-year follow-up study. *Pediatrics, 124,* 71–78.

Binet, A. (1909). *Les idées modernes sur les enfants* [Modern ideas about children]. Paris: Flammarion.

Binswanger, L. (1958). The existential analysis school of thought. In R. May (Ed.), *Existence: A new dimension in psychiatry and psychology* (pp. 191–213). New York: Basic Books.

Bjork, E. L., & Bjork, R. A. (2011). Making things hard on yourself, but in a good way: Creating desirable difficulties to enhance learning. In M. A. Gernsbacher, R. W. Pewe, L. M. Hough, & J. R. Pomerantz (Eds.), *Psychology and the real world: Essays illustrating fundamental contributions to society* (pp. 56–64). New York: Worth Publishers.

Bjork, D. W. (1983). *The compromised scientist: William James in the development of American psychology.* New York: Columbia University Press.

Bjork, D. W. (1993). *B. F. Skinner: A life.* New York: Basic Books.

Bjork, R. A. (1975). Retrieval as a memory modifier. In R. Solso (Ed.), *Information processing and cognition: The Loyola symposium* (pp. 123–144). Hillsdale, NJ: Lawrence Erlbaum Associates.

Bjork, R. A. (2011). On the symbiosis of remembering, forgetting, and learning. In A. S. Benjamin (Ed.), *Successful remembering and successful forgetting: A festschrift in honor of Robert A. Bjork* (pp. 1–22). London: Psychology Press.

Bjork, R. A., & Bjork, E. L. (1988). On the adaptive aspects of retrieval failure in autobiographical memory. In M. M. Gruneberg, P. E. Morris,

& R. N. Sykes (Eds.), *Practical aspects of memory: Current research and issues* (pp. 283–288). Chichester, England: Wiley.

Bjork, R. A., Dunlosky, J., & Kornell, N. (2013). Self-regulated learning: Beliefs, techniques, and illusions. *Annual Review of Psychology, 64,* 417–444.

Blackburn, E. H., & Epel, E. S. (2012). Too toxic to ignore. *Nature, 490,* 169–171.

Blair, I. V. (2002). The malleability of automatic stereotypes and prejudice. *Personality and Social Psychology Review, 6,* 242–261.

Blair, J., Peschardt, K., & Mitchell, D. R. (2005). *Psychopath: Emotion and the brain.* Oxford, England: Blackwell.

Blascovich, J., & Tomaka, J. (1996). The biopsychosocial model of arousal regulation. In M. P. Zanna (Ed.), *Advances in experimental social psychology* (Vol. 28, pp. 1–51). San Diego, CA: Academic Press.

Blatt, S. J., & Homann, E. (1992). Parent–child interaction in the etiology of dependent and self-critical depression. *Clinical Psychology Review, 12,* 47–91.

Blesch, A., & Tuszynski, M. H. (2009). Spinal cord injury: Plasticity, regeneration and the challenge of translational drug development. *Trends in Neurosciences, 32,* 41–47.

Bliss, T. V. P. (1999). Young receptors make smart mice. *Nature, 401,* 25–27.

Bliss, T. V. P., & Lømo, W. T. (1973). Long-lasting potentiation of synaptic transmission in the dentate area of the anesthetized rabbit following stimulation of the perforant path. *Journal of Physiology, 232,* 331–356.

Bloch, C., Kaiser, A., Kuenzli, E., Zappatore, D., Haller, S., Franceschini, R., . . . Nitsch, C. (2009). The age of second language acquisition determines the variability in activation elicited by narration in three languages in Broca's and Wernicke's area. *Neuropsychologia, 47,* 625–633.

Bloom, C. M., Venard, J., Harden, M., & Seetharaman, S. (2007). Non-contingent positive and negative reinforcement schedules of superstitious behaviors. *Behavioural Process, 75,* 8–13.

Boecker, H., Sprenger, T., Spilker, M. E., Henriksen, G., Koppenhoefer, M., Wagner, K. J., . . . Tolle, T. R. (2008). The runner's high: Opioidergic mechanisms in the human brain. *Cerebral Cortex, 18,* 2523–2531.

Boehm, J. K., & Kubzansky, L. D. (2012). The heart's content: The association between positive psychological well-being and cardiovascular health. *Psychological Bulletin, 138,* 655–691.

Boehm, J. K., Williams, D. R., Rimm, E. B., Ryff, C., & Kubzansky, L. D. (2013). Relation between optimism and lipids in midlife. *American Journal of Cardiology, 111,* 1425–1431.

Boergers, J., Spirito, A., & Donaldson, D. (1998). Reasons for adolescent suicide attempts: Associations with psychological functioning. *Journal of the American Academy of Child and Adolescent Psychiatry, 37,* 1287–1293.

Bohan, J. S. (1996). *Psychology and sexual orientation: Coming to terms.* New York: Routledge.

Boinski, S., Quatrone, R. P., & Swartz, H. (2000). Substrate and tool use by brown capuchins in Suriname: Ecological contexts and cognitive bases. *American Anthropologist, 102,* 741–761.

Boisvert, C. M., & Faust, D. (2002). Iatrogenic symptoms in psychotherapy: A theoretical exploration of the potential impact of labels, language, and belief systems. *American Journal of Psychotherapy, 56,* 244–259.

Bolger, N., Davis, A., & Rafaeli, E. (2003). Diary methods: Capturing life as it is lived. *Annual Review of Psychology, 54,* 579–616.

Boomsma, D., Busjahn, A., & Peltonen, L. (2002). Classical twin studies and beyond. *Nature Reviews Genetics, 3,* 872–882.

Bootzin, R. R., & Epstein, D. R. (2011). Understanding and treating insomnia. *Annual Review of Clinical Psychology, 7,* 435–458.

Borges, G., Breslau, J., Orozco, R., Tancredi, D. J., Anderson, H., Aguilar-Gaxiola, S., & Medina-Mora, M.-E. (2011). A cross-national study on Mexico–US migration, substance use and substance use disorders. *Drug and Alcohol Dependence, 117,* 16–23.

Borghol, N., Suderman, M., McArdle, W., Racine, A., Hallett, M., Pembrey, M., . . . Szyf, M. (2012). Associations with early-life socioeconomic position in adult DNA methylation. *International Journal of Epidemiology, 41,* 62–74.

Borkenau, P., & Liebler, A. (1995). Observable attributes as manifestations and cues of personality and intelligence. *Journal of Personality, 63,* 1–25.

Borkevec, T. D. (1982). Insomnia. *Journal of Consulting and Clinical Psychology, 50,* 880–895.

Born, R. T., & Bradley, D. C. (2005). Structure and function of visual area MT. *Annual Review of Neuroscience, 28,* 157–189.

Börner, K., Klavans, R., Patek, M., Zoss, A. M., Biberstine, J. R., Light, R. P., Larivière, V., & Boyack, K. W. (2012). Design and update of a classification system: The UCSD map of science. *PLoS ONE, 7,* e39464.

Bornstein, R. F. (1989). Exposure and affect: Overview and meta-analysis of research, 1968–1987. *Psychological Bulletin, 106,* 265–289.

Botwin, M. D., Buss, D. M., & Shackelford, T. K. (1997). Personality and mate preferences: Five factors in mate selection and marital satisfaction. *Journal of Personality, 65,* 107–136.

Bouchard, S. M., Brown, T. G., & Nadeau, L. (2012). Decision making capacities and affective reward anticipation in DWI recidivists compared to non-offenders: A preliminary study. *Accident Analysis and Prevention, 45,* 580–587.

Bouchard, T. J., & McGue, M. (2003). Genetic and environmental influences on human psychological differences. *Journal of Neurobiology, 54,* 4–45.

Bouton, M. E. (1988). Context and ambiguity in the extinction of emotional learning: Implications for exposure therapy. *Behaviour Research and Therapy, 26,* 137–149.

Bower, G. H. (1981). Mood and memory. *American Psychologist, 36,* 129–148.

Bower, G. H., Clark, M. C., Lesgold, A. M., & Winzenz, D. (1969). Hierarchical retrieval schemes in recall of categorical word lists. *Journal of Verbal Learning and Verbal Behavior, 8,* 323–343.

Bowlby, J. (1969). *Attachment and loss: Vol. 1. Attachment.* New York: Basic Books.

Bowlby, J. (1973). *Attachment and loss: Vol. 2. Separation.* New York: Basic Books.

Bowlby, J. (1980). *Attachment and loss: Vol. 3. Loss: Sadness and depression.* New York: Basic Books.

Boyack, K. W., Klavans, R., & Börner, K. (2005). Mapping the backbone of science. *Scientometrics, 64,* 351–374.

Boyd, R. (2008, February 7). Do people use only 10 percent of their brains? *Scientific American.* Retrieved from http://www.scientificamerican.com/article.cfm?id=people-only-use-10-percent-of-brain&page=2

Bozarth, M. A., & Wise, R. A. (1985). Toxicity associated with long-term intravenous heroin and cocaine self-administration in the rat. *Journal of the American Medical Association, 254,* 81–83.

Brackett, M. A., & Mayer, J. D. (2003). Convergent, discriminant, and incremental validity of competing measures of emotional intelligence. *Personality and Social Psychology Bulletin, 29,* 1147.

Brackett, M. A., Rivers, S. E., Shiffman, S., Lerner, N., & Salovey, P. (2006). Relating emotional abilities to social functioning: A comparison of self-report and performance measures of emotional intelligence. *Journal of Personality and Social Psychology, 91,* 780.

Brackett, M. A., Warner, R. M., & Bosco, J. (2005). Emotional intelligence and relationship quality among couples. *Personal Relationships, 12*(2), 197–212.

Bradford, D., Stroup, S., & Lieberman, J. (2002). Pharmacological treatments for schizophrenia. In P. E. Nathan & J. M. Gorman (Eds.), *A guide to treatments that work* (2nd ed., pp. 169–199). New York: Oxford University Press.

Bramlett, M. D., & Mosher, W. D. (2002). *Cohabitation, marriage, divorce, and remarriage in the United States* (Vital and Health Statistics Series 23, No. 22). Hyattsville, MD: National Center for Health Statistics.

Brandt, K. R., Gardiner, J. M., Vargha-Khadem, F., Baddeley, A. D., & Mishkin, M. (2009). Impairment of recollection but not familiarity in a case of developmental amnesia. *Neurocase, 15,* 60–65.

Braun, A. R., Balkin, T. J., Wesensten, N. J., Gwadry, F., Carson, R. E., Varga, M., . . . Herscovitch, P. (1998). Dissociated pattern of activity in visual cortices and their projections during rapid eye movement sleep. *Science, 279,* 91–95.

Breazeal, C. (2009, December 12). The role of expression in robots that learn from people. *Philosophical Transactions of the Royal Society B, 364*(1535), 3527–3538.

Brédart, S., & Valentine, T. (1998). Descriptiveness and proper name retrieval. *Memory, 6,* 199–206.

Bredy, T. W., Wu, H., Crego, C., Zellhoefer, J., Sun, Y. E., & Barad, M. (2007). Histone modifications around individual BDNF gene promoters in prefrontal cortex are associated with extinction of conditioned fear. *Learning and Memory, 14,* 268–276.

Breggin, P. R. (1990). Brain damage, dementia, and persistent cognitive dysfunction associated with neuroleptic drugs: Evidence, etiology, implications. *Journal of Mind and Behavior, 11,* 425–463.

Breggin, P. R. (2000). *Reclaiming our children.* Cambridge, MA: Perseus Books.

Brehm, S. S. (1992). *Intimate relationships* (2nd ed.). New York: McGraw-Hill.

Breland, K., & Breland, M. (1961). The misbehavior of organisms. *American Psychologist, 16,* 681–684.

Brennan, P. A., & Zufall, F. (2006). Pheromonal communication in vertebrates. *Nature, 444,* 308–315.

Brenninkmeijer, V., Vanyperen, N. W., & Buunk, B. P. (2001). I am not a better teacher, but others are doing worse: Burnout and perceptions of superiority among teachers. *Social Psychology of Education, 4*(3–4), 259–274.

Breslau, J., Aguilar-Gaxiola, S., Borges, G., Castilla-Puentes, R. C., Kendler, K. S., Medina-Mora, M.-E., . . . Kessler, R. C. (2007). Mental disorders among English-speaking Mexican immigrants to the US compared to a national sample of Mexicans. *Psychiatry Research, 151,* 115–122.

Breslau, J., & Chang, D. F. (2006). Psychiatric disorders among foreign-born and US-born Asian-Americans in a US national survey. *Social Psychiatry & Psychiatric Epidemiology, 41,* 943–950.

Bretherton, I., & Munholland, K. A. (1999). Internal working models in attachment relationships: A construct revisited. In J. Cassidy & P. R. Shaver (Eds.), *Handbook of attachment: Theory, research and clinical applications* (pp. 89–114). New York: Guilford Press.

Brewer, J. A., Worhunsky, P. D., Gray, J. R., Tang, Y.-Y., Weber, J., & Kober, H. (2011). Meditation experience is associated with differences in default mode network activity and connectivity. *Proceedings of the National Academy of Sciences, 108,* 20254–20259.

Broadbent, D. E. (1958). *Perception and communication.* London: Pergamon Press.

Broberg, D. J., & Bernstein, I. L. (1987). Candy as a scapegoat in the prevention of food aversions in children receiving chemotherapy. *Cancer, 60,* 2344–2347.

Brooks, R., & Meltzoff, A. N. (2002). The importance of eyes: How infants interpret adult looking behavior. *Developmental Psychology, 38,* 958–966.

Brooks-Gunn, J., Graber, J. A., & Paikoff, R. L. (1994). Studying links between hormones and negative affect: Models and measures. *Journal of Research on Adolescence, 4,* 469–486.

Brown, A. S. (2004). *The déjà vu experience.* New York: Psychology Press.

Brown, B. B., Mory, M., & Kinney, D. (1994). Casting crowds in a relational perspective: Caricature, channel, and context. In G. A. R. Montemayor & T. Gullotta (Eds.), *Advances in adolescent development: Personal relationships during adolescence* (Vol. 5, pp. 123–167). Newbury Park, CA: Sage.

Brown, J. D., & McGill, K. L. (1989). The cost of good fortune: When positive life events produce negative health consequences. *Journal of Personality and Social Psychology, 57,* 1103–1110.

Brown, R., & Hanlon, C. (1970). Derivational complexity and order of acquisition in child speech. In J. R. Hayes (Ed.), *Cognition and the development of language* (pp. 11–53). New York: Wiley.

Brown, R., & Kulik, J. (1977). Flashbulb memories. *Cognition, 5,* 73–99.

Brown, R., & McNeill, D. (1966). The "tip-of-the-tongue" phenomenon. *Journal of Verbal Learning and Verbal Behavior, 5,* 325–337.

Brown, R. P., Osterman, L. L., & Barnes, C. D. (2009). School violence and the culture of honor. *Psychological Science, 20*(11), 1400–1405.

Brown, S. C., & Craik, F. I. M. (2000). Encoding and retrieval of information. In E. Tulving & F. I. M. Craik (Eds.), *The Oxford handbook of memory* (pp. 93–107). New York: Oxford University Press.

Bruner, J. S. (1983). Education as social invention. *Journal of Social Issues, 39,* 129–141.

Brunet, A., Orr, S. P., Tremblay, J., Robertson, K., Nader, K., & Pitman, R. K. (2008). Effects of post-retrieval propranolol on psychophysiologic responding during subsequent script-driven traumatic imagery in posttraumatic stress disorder. *Journal of Psychiatric Research, 42,* 503–506.

Brunet, A., Poundjia, J., Tremblay, J., Bui, E., Thomas, E., Orr, S. P., . . . Pitman, R. K. (2011). Trauma reactivation under the influence of propranolol decreases posttraumatic stress symptoms and disorder. *Journal of Clinical Psychopharmacology, 31,* 547–550.

Brunner, D. P., Dijk, D. J., Tobler, I., & Borbely, A. A. (1990). Effect of partial sleep deprivation on sleep stages and EEG power spectra. *Electroencephalography and Clinical Neurophysiology, 75,* 492–499.

Bryck, R. L., & Fisher, P. A. (2012). Training the brain: Practical applications of neural plasticity from the intersection of cognitive neuroscience, developmental psychology, and prevention science. *American Psychologist, 67,* 87–100.

Buchanan, C. M., Eccles, J. S., & Becker, J. B. (1992). Are adolescents the victims of raging hormones? Evidence for activational effects of hormones on moods and behavior at adolescence. *Psychological Bulletin, 111,* 62–107.

Buchanan, T. W. (2007). Retrieval of emotional memories. *Psychological Bulletin, 133,* 761–779.

Buckholtz, J. W., & Meyer-Lindenberg, A. (2012). Psychopathology and the human connectome: Toward a transdiagnostic model of risk for mental illness. *Neuron, 74,* 990–1003.

Buck Louis, G. M., Gray, L. E., Marcus, M., Ojeda, S. R., Pescovitz, O. H., Witchel, S. F., . . . Euling, S. Y. (2008). Environmental factors and puberty timing: Expert panel research. *Pediatrics, 121*(Suppl. 3), S192–S207. doi:10.1542/peds1813E

Buckner, R. L., Andrews-Hanna, J. R., & Schacter, D. L. (2008). The brain's default network: Anatomy, function, and relevance to disease. *Annals of the New York Academy of Sciences, 1124,* 1–38.

Buckner, R. L., Petersen, S. E., Ojemann, J. G., Miezin, F. M., Squire, L. R., & Raichle, M. E. (1995). Functional anatomical studies of explicit and implicit memory retrieval tasks. *The Journal of Neuroscience, 15,* 12–29.

Bunce, D. M., Flens, E. A., & Neiles, K. Y. (2011). How long can students pay attention in class? A study of student attention decline using clickers. *Journal of Chemical Education, 87,* 1438–1443.

Bureau of Justice Statistics. (2008). *Prisoners in 2007* (No. NCJ224280 by H. C. West & W. J. Sabol). Washington, DC: U.S. Department of Justice.

Burger, J. M. (1999). The foot-in-the-door compliance procedure: A multiple-process analysis and review. *Personality and Social Psychology Review, 3*, 303–325.

Burger, J. M. (2009). Replicating Milgram: Would people still obey today? *American Psychologist, 64*, 1–11.

Burger, J. M., & Burns, L. (1988). The illusion of unique invulnerability and the use of effective contraception. *Personality and Social Psychology Bulletin, 14*, 264–270.

Burger, J. M., Sanchez, J., Imberi, J. E., & Grande, L. R. (2009). The norm of reciprocity as an internalized social norm: Returning favors even when no one finds out. *Social Influence, 4*(1), 11–17.

Burke, D., MacKay, D. G., Worthley, J. S., & Wade, E. (1991). On the tip of the tongue: What causes word failure in young and older adults? *Journal of Memory and Language, 30*, 237–246.

Burns, D. J., Hwang, A. J., & Burns, S. A. (2011). Adaptive memory: Determining the proximate mechanisms responsible for the memorial advantages of survival processing. *Journal of Experimental Psychology: Learning, Memory, and Cognition, 37*, 206–218.

Burnstein, E., Crandall, C., & Kitayama, S. (1994). Some neo-Darwinian decision rules for altruism: Weighing cues for inclusive fitness as a function of the biological importance of the decision. *Journal of Personality and Social Psychology, 67*, 773–789.

Bushman, B. J., & Huesmann, L. R. (2010). Aggression. In S. T. Fiske, D. T. Gilbert, & G. Lindzey (Eds.), *The handbook of social psychology* (5th ed., Vol. 2, pp. 833–863). New York: Wiley.

Buss, D. M. (1985). Human mate selection. *American Scientist, 73*, 47–51.

Buss, D. M. (1989). Sex differences in human mate preferences: Evolutionary hypotheses tested in 37 cultures. *Behavioral and Brain Sciences, 12*, 1–49.

Buss, D. M. (2000). *The dangerous passion: Why jealousy is as necessary as love and sex.* New York: Free Press.

Buss, D. M. (2007). The evolution of human mating. *Acta Psychologica Sinica, 39*, 502–512.

Buss, D. M., & Schmitt, D. P. (1993). Sexual strategies theory: An evolutionary perspective on human mating. *Psychological Review, 100*, 204–232.

Buss, D. M., & Haselton, M. G. (2005). The evolution of jealousy. *Trends in Cognitive Sciences, 9*, 506–507.

Buss, D. M., Haselton, M. G., Shackelford, T. K., Bleske, A. L., & Wakefield, J. C. (1998). Adaptations, exaptations, and spandrels. *American Psychologist, 53*, 533–548.

Butler, A. C., Chapman, J. E., Forman, E. M., & Beck, A. T. (2006). The empirical status of cognitive-behavioral therapy: A review of meta-analyses. *Clinical Psychology Review, 26*, 17–31.

Butler, M. A., Corboy, J. R., & Filley, C. M. (2009). How the conflict between American psychiatry and neurology delayed the appreciation of cognitive dysfunction in multiple sclerosis. *Neuropsychology Review, 19*, 399–410.

Byers-Heinlein, K., Burns, T. C., & Werker, J. F. (2010). The roots of bilingualism in newborns. *Psychological Science, 21*(3), 343–348. doi:10.1177/0956797609360758

Byrne, D., Allgeier, A. R., Winslow, L., & Buckman, J. (1975). The situational facilitation of interpersonal attraction: A three-factor hypothesis. *Journal of Applied Social Psychology, 5*, 1–15.

Byrne, D., & Clore, G. L. (1970). A reinforcement model of evaluative responses. *Personality: An International Journal, 1*, 103–128.

Byrne, D., Ervin, C. R., & Lamberth, J. (1970). Continuity between the experimental study of attraction and real-life computer dating. *Journal of Personality and Social Psychology, 16*, 157–165.

Byrne, D., & Nelson, D. (1965). Attraction as a linear function of proportion of positive reinforcements. *Journal of Personality and Social Psychology, 1*, 659–663.

Cabeza, R. (2002). Hemispheric asymmetry reduction in older adults: The HAROLD model. *Psychology and Aging, 17*, 85–100.

Cabeza, R., Grady, C. L., Nyberg, L., McIntosh, A. R., Tulving, E., Kapur, S., . . . Craik, F. I. M. (1997). Age-related differences in neural activity during memory encoding and retrieval: A positron emission tomography study. *The Journal of Neuroscience, 17*, 391–400.

Cabeza, R., Rao, S., Wagner, A. D., Mayer, A., & Schacter, D. L. (2001). Can medial temporal lobe regions distinguish true from false? An event-related fMRI study of veridical and illusory recognition memory. *Proceedings of the National Academy of Sciences, USA, 98*, 4805–4810.

Cacioppo, J. T., & Patrick, B. (2008). *Loneliness: Human nature and the need for social connection.* New York: Norton.

Cahill, L., Haier, R. J., Fallon, J., Alkire, M. T., Tang, C., Keator, D., . . . McGaugh, J. L. (1996). Amygdala activity at encoding correlated with long-term, free recall of emotional information. *Proceedings of the National Academy of Sciences, USA, 93*, 8016–8021.

Cahill, L., & McGaugh, J. L. (1998). Mechanisms of emotional arousal and lasting declarative memory. *Trends in Neurosciences, 21*, 294–299.

Calder, A. J., Young, A. W., Rowland, D., Perrett, D. I., Hodges, J. R., & Etcoff, N. L. (1996). Facial emotion recognition after bilateral amygdala damage: Differentially severe impairment of fear. *Cognitive Neuropsychology, 13*, 699–745.

Callaghan, T., Rochat, P., Lillard, A., Claux, M. L., Odden, H., Itakura, S., . . . Singh, S. (2005). Synchrony in the onset of mental-state reasoning: Evidence from five cultures. *Psychological Science, 16*, 378–384.

Calkins, M. W. (Ed.). (1930). *Mary Whiton Calkins* (Vol. 1). Worcester, MA: Clark University Press.

Calzo, J. P., Antonucci, T. C., Mays, V. M., & Cochran, S. D. (2011). Retrospective recall of sexual orientation identity development among gay, lesbian, and bisexual adults. *Developmental Psychology, 47*(6), 1658–1673. doi:10.1037/a0025508

Cameron, C. D., & Payne, B. K. (2011). Escaping affect: How motivated emotion regulation creates insensitivity to mass suffering. *Journal of Personality and Social Psychology, 100*(1), 1–15.

Campbell, A. (1999). Staying alive: Evolution, culture, and women's intrasexual aggression. *Behavioral & Brain Sciences, 22*, 203–252.

Cannon, W. B. (1929). *Bodily changes in pain, hunger, fear, and rage: An account of recent research into the function of emotional excitement* (2nd ed.). New York: Appleton-Century-Crofts.

Cantor, N. (1990). From thought to behavior: "Having" and "doing" in the study of personality and cognition. *American Psychologist, 45*, 735–750.

Caparelli, E. C. (2007). TMS & fMRI: A new neuroimaging combinational tool to study brain function. *Current Medical Imaging Review, 3*, 109–115.

Caprioli, M. (2003). Gender equality and state aggression: The impact of domestic gender equality on state first use of force. *International Interactions, 29*(3), 195–214. doi:10.1080/03050620304595

Carey, N. (2012). *The epigenetics revolution: How modern biology is rewriting our understanding of genetics, disease, and inheritance.* New York: Columbia University Press.

Carlson, C., & Hoyle, R. (1993). Efficacy of abbreviated progressive muscle relaxation training: A quantitative review of behavioral medicine research. *Journal of Consulting and Clinical Psychology, 61*, 1059–1067.

Carmichael Olson, H., Streissguth, A. P., Sampson, P. D., Barr, H. M., Bookstein, F. L., & Thiede, K. (1997). Association of prenatal alcohol exposure with behavioral and learning problems in early adolescence. *Journal of the American Academy of Child & Adolescent Psychiatry, 36*(9), 1187–1194.

Carolson, E. A. (1998). A prospective longitudinal study of attachment disorganization/disorientation. *Child Development, 69*, 1107–1128.

Carpenter, S. K. (2012). Testing enhances the transfer of learning. *Current Directions in Psychological Science, 21,* 279–283.

Carr, L., Iacoboni, M., Dubeau, M., Mazziotta, J. C., & Lenzi, G. L. (2003). Neural mechanisms of empathy in humans: A relay from neural systems for imitation to limbic areas. *Proceedings of the National Academy of Sciences, USA, 100,* 5497–5502.

Carroll, J. B. (1993). *Human cognitive abilities.* Cambridge, England: Cambridge University Press.

Carson, R. C., Butcher, J. N., & Mineka, S. (2000). *Abnormal psychology and modern life* (11th ed.). Boston: Allyn & Bacon.

Carstensen, L. L. (1992). Social and emotional patterns in adulthood: Support for socioemotional selectivity theory. *Psychology and Aging, 7,* 331–338.

Carstensen, L. L., & Fredrickson, B. L. (1998). Influence of HIV status and age on cognitive representations of others. *Health Psychology, 17,* 1–10.

Carstensen, L. L., Pasupathi, M., Mayr, U., & Nesselroade, J. R. (2000). Emotional experience in everyday life across the adult life span. *Journal of Personality and Social Psychology, 79,* 644–655.

Carstensen, L. L., & Turk-Charles, S. (1994). The salience of emotion across the adult life span. *Psychology and Aging, 9,* 259–264.

Carver, C. S. (2006). Approach, avoidance, and the self-regulation of affect and action. *Motivation and Emotion, 30,* 105–110.

Carver, C. S., & White, T. L. (1994). Behavioral inhibition, behavioral activation, and affective responses to impending reward and punishment: The bis/bas scales. *Journal of Personality and Social Psychology, 67*(2), 319–333.

Casazza, K., Fontaine, K. R., Astrup, A., Birch, L. L., Brown, A. W., Bohan Brown, M. M., . . . Allison, D. B. (2013). Myths, presumptions, and facts about obesity. *New England Journal of Medicine, 368*(5), 446–454.

Caspi, A., & Herbener, E. S. (1990). Continuity and change: Assortative marriage and the consistency of personality in adulthood. *Journal of Personality and Social Psychology, 58,* 250–258.

Caspi, A., Roberts, B. W., & Shiner, R. L. (2005). Personality development: Stability and change. *Annual Review of Psychology, 56,* 453–484.

Caspi, A., Sugden, K., Moffitt, T. E., Taylor, A., Craig, I. W., Harrington, H., . . . Poulton, R. (2003). Influence of life stress on depression: Moderation by a polymorphism in the 5-HTT gene. *Science, 301,* 386–389.

Castel, A. D., McCabe, D. P., & Roediger, H. L. III. (2007). Illusions of competence and overestimation of associate memory for identical items: Evidence from judgments of learning. *Psychonomic Bulletin & Review, 14,* 107–111.

Castellanos, F. X., Patti, P. L., Sharp, W., Jeffries, N. O., Greenstein, D. K., Clasen, L. S., . . . Rapoport, J. L. (2002). Developmental trajectories of brain volume abnormalities in children and adolescents with attention-deficit/hyperactivity disorder. *Journal of the American Medical Association, 288,* 1740–1748. doi: 10.1001/jama.288.14.1740

Cattell, R. B. (1950). *Personality: A systematic, theoretical, and factual study.* New York: McGraw-Hill.

Ceci, S. J. (1991). How much does schooling influence general intelligence and its cognitive components? A reassessment of the evidence. *Developmental Psychology, 27,* 703–722.

Ceci, S. J., DeSimone, M., & Johnson, S. (1992). Memory in context: A case study of "Bubbles P.," a gifted but uneven memorizer. In D. J. Herrmann, H. Weingartner, A. Searleman, & C. McEvoy (Eds.), *Memory improvement: Implications for memory theory* (pp. 169–186). New York: Springer-Verlag.

Ceci, S. J., & Williams, W. M. (1997). Schooling, intelligence, and income. *American Psychologist, 52,* 1051–1058.

Ceci, S. J., Williams, W. M., & Barnett, S. M. (2009). Women's underrepresentation in science: Sociocultural and biological considerations. *Psychological Bulletin, 135*(2), 218–261. doi:10.1037/a0014412

Centers for Disease Control and Prevention (CDC). (2002, June 28). Youth risk behavior surveillance. *Surveillance Summary, 51*(SS-4), 1–64. Washington, DC: Author.

Centers for Disease Control and Prevention. (2013). *Injury prevention and control: Data and statistics (WISQARS).* Retrieved from http://www.cdc.gov/injury/wisqars/index.html

Cepeda, N. J., Pashler, H., Vul, E., Wixted, J. T., & Rohrer, D. (2006). Distributed practice in verbal recall tests: A review and quantitative synthesis. *Psychological Bulletin, 132,* 354–380.

Chabris, C., & Simons, D. (2012, November 16). Using just 10% of your brains? Think again. *Wall Street Journal Online.* Retrieved from http://online.wsj.com/article/SB1000142412788732455630457811935187421218.html

Chaiken, S. (1980). Heuristic versus systematic information processing and the use of source versus message cues in persuasion. *Journal of Personality and Social Psychology, 39,* 752–766.

Chalmers, D. (1996). *The conscious mind: In search of a fundamental theory.* New York: Oxford University Press.

Chandler, J., & Schwarz, N. (2009). How extending your middle finger affects your perception of others: Learned movements influence concept accessibility. *Journal of Experimental Social Psychology, 45,* 123–128.

Charles, S. T., Reynolds, C. A., & Gatz, M. (2001). Age-related differences and change in positive and negative affect over 23 years. *Journal of Personality and Social Psychology, 80,* 136–151.

Charness, N. (1981). Aging and skilled problem solving. *Journal of Experimental Psychology: General, 110,* 21–38.

Chartrand, T. L., & Bargh, J. A. (1999). The chameleon effect: The perception-behavior link and social interaction. *Journal of Personality and Social Psychology, 76,* 893–910.

Chartrand, T. L., & Kay, A. (2006). *Mystery moods and perplexing performance: Consequences of succeeding and failing at a nonconscious goal.* Unpublished manuscript.

Chen, E., Cohen, S., & Miller, G. E. (2010). How low socioeconomic status affects 2-year hormonal trajectories in children. *Psychological Science, 21*(1), 31–37.

Cheney, D. L., & Seyfarth, R. M. (1990). *How monkeys see the world.* Chicago: University of Chicago Press.

Cheng, D. T., Disterhoft, J. F., Power, J. M., Ellis, D. A., & Desmond, J. E. (2008). Neural substrates underlying human delay and trace eyeblink conditioning. *Proceedings of the National Academy of Sciences, USA, 105,* 8108–8113.

Cherlin, A. J. (Ed.). (1992). *Marriage, divorce, remarriage* (2nd ed.). Cambridge, MA: Harvard University Press.

Chomsky, N. (1957). *Syntactic structures.* The Hague: Mouton.

Chomsky, N. (1959). A review of *Verbal Behavior* by B. F. Skinner. *Language, 35,* 26–58.

Chomsky, N. (1986). *Knowledge of language: Its nature, origin, and use.* New York: Praeger.

Choy, Y., Fyer, A. J., & Lipsitz, J. D. (2007). Treatment of specific phobia in adults. *Clinical Psychology Review, 27,* 266–286.

Christakis, N. A., & Fowler, J. H. (2007). The spread of obesity in a large social network over 32 years. *New England Journal of Medicine, 357*(4), 370–379.

Cialdini, R. B. (2013). The focus theory of normative conduct. In P. A. M. van Lange, A. W. Kruglanski, & E. T. Higgins (Eds.), *Handbook of theories of social psychology* (Vol. 3, pp. 295–312). New York: Sage.

Cialdini, R. B., & Goldstein, N. J. (2004). Social influence: Compliance and conformity. *Annual Review of Psychology, 55*(1), 591–621. doi: 10.1146/annurev.psych.55.090902.142015

Ciarrochi, J. V., Chan, A. Y., & Caputi, P. (2000). A critical evaluation of the emotional intelligence concept. *Personality & Individual Differences, 28,* 539.

Cicchetti, D., & Toth, S. L. (1998). Perspectives on research and practice in developmental psychopathology. In I. E. Sigel & K. A. Renninger (Eds.), *Handbook of child psychology: Vol. 4. Child psychology in practice* (5th ed., pp. 479–583). New York: Wiley.

Clark, M. S., & Lemay, E. P. (2010). Close relationships. In S. T. Fiske, D. T. Gilbert, & G. Lindzey (Eds.), *The handbook of social psychology* (5th ed., Vol. 2). New York: Wiley.

Clark, R. D., & Hatfield, E. (1989). Gender differences in receptivity to sexual offers. *Journal of Psychology and Human Sexuality, 2,* 39–55.

Cleckley, H. M. (1976). *The mask of sanity* (5th ed.). St. Louis: Mosby.

Coe, C. L., & Lubach, G. R. (2008). Fetal programming prenatal origins of health and illness. *Current Directions in Psychological Science, 17,* 36–41.

Cogan, R., Cogan, D., Waltz, W., & McCue, M. (1987). Effects of laughter and relaxation on discomfort thresholds. *Journal of Behavioral Medicine, 10,* 139–144.

Coghill, R. C., McHaffie, J. G., & Yen, Y. (2003). Neural correlates of individual differences in the subjective experience of pain. *Proceedings of the National Academy of Sciences, USA, 100,* 8538–8542.

Cohen, D., Nisbett, R. E., Bowdle, B. F., & Schwarz, N. (1996). Insult, aggression, and the southern culture of honor: An "experimental ethnography." *Journal of Personality and Social Psychology, 70,* 945–960.

Cohen, G. (1990). Why is it difficult to put names to faces? *British Journal of Psychology, 81,* 287–297.

Cohen, S. (1988). Psychosocial models of the role of social support in the etiology of physical disease. *Health Psychology, 7,* 269–297.

Cohen, S. (1999). Social status and susceptibility to respiratory infections. *New York Academy of Sciences, 896,* 246–253.

Cohen, S., Frank, E., Doyle, W. J., Skoner, D. P., Rabin, B. S., & Gwaltney, J. M., Jr. (1998). Types of stressors that increase susceptibility to the common cold in healthy adults. *Health Psychology, 17,* 214–223.

Coifman, K. G., Bonanno, G. A., Ray, R. D., & Gross, J. J. (2007). Does repressive coping promote resilience? Affective-autonomic response discrepancy during bereavement. *Journal of Personality and Social Psychology, 92,* 745–758.

Colcombe, S. J., Erickson, K. I., Scalf, P. E., Kim, J. S., Prakesh, R., McAuley, E., . . . Kramer, A. F. (2006). Aerobic exercise training increases brain volume in aging humans. *Journals of Gerontology Series A: Biological Sciences and Medical Sciences, 61,* 1166–1170.

Colcombe, S. J., Kramer, A. F., Erickson, K. I., Scalf, P., McAuley, E., Cohen, N. J., . . . Elavsky, S. (2004). Cardiovascular fitness, cortical plasticity, and aging. *Proceedings of the National Academy of Sciences, USA, 101,* 3316–3321.

Cole, M. (1996). *Cultural psychology: A once and future discipline.* Cambridge, MA: Belknap Press of Harvard University Press.

Coman, A., Manier, D., & Hirst, W. (2009). Forgetting the unforgettable through conversation: Social shared retrieval-induced forgetting of September 11 memories. *Psychological Science, 20,* 627–633.

Condon, J. W., & Crano, W. D. (1988). Inferred evaluation and the relation between attitude similarity and interpersonal attraction. *Journal of Personality and Social Psychology, 54,* 789–797.

Conley, T. D. (2011). Perceived proposer personality characteristics and gender differences in acceptance of casual sex offers. *Journal of Personality and Social Psychology, 100*(2), 309–329. doi: 10.1037/a0022152

Conley, T. D., Moors, A. C., Matsick, J. L., Ziegler, A., & Valentine, B. A. (2011). Women, men, and the bedroom: Methodological and conceptual insights that narrow, reframe, and eliminate gender differences in sexuality. *Current Directions in Psychological Science, 20*(5), 296–300. doi: 10.1177/0963721411418467

Cook, M., & Mineka, S. (1989). Observational conditioning of fear to fear-relevant versus fear-irrelevant stimuli in rhesus monkeys. *Journal of Abnormal Psychology, 98*(4), 448–459.

Coontz, P. (2008). The responsible conduct of social research. In K. Yang & G. J. Miller (Eds.), *Handbook of research methods in public administration* (pp. 129–139). Boca Raton, FL: Taylor & Francis.

Cooper, J., & Fazio, R. H. (1984). A new look at dissonance theory. In L. Berkowitz (Ed.), *Advances in experimental social psychology* (Vol. 17, pp. 229–266). New York: Academic Press.

Cooper, J. R., Bloom, F. E., & Roth, R. H. (2003). *Biochemical basis of neuropharmacology.* New York: Oxford University Press.

Cooper, M. L. (2006). Does drinking promote risky sexual behavior? A complex answer to a simple question. *Current Directions in Psychological Science, 15,* 19–23.

Cooper, W. H., & Withey, W. J. (2009). The strong situation hypothesis. *Personality and Social Psychology Review, 13,* 62–72.

Coren, S. (1997). *Sleep thieves.* New York: Free Press.

Corkin, S. (2002). What's new with the amnesic patient HM? *Nature Reviews Neuroscience, 3,* 153–160.

Corkin, S. (2013). *Permanent present tense: The unforgettable life of the amnesic patient, H.M.* New York: Basic Books.

Correll, J., Park, B., Judd, C. M., & Wittenbrink, B. (2002). The police officer's dilemma: Using ethnicity to disambiguate potentially threatening individuals. *Journal of Personality and Social Psychology, 83,* 1314–1329.

Correll, J., Park, B., Judd, C. M., Wittenbrink, B., Sadler, M. S., & Keesee, T. (2007). Across the thin blue line: Police officers and racial bias in the decision to shoot. *Journal of Personality and Social Psychology, 92,* 1006–1023.

Corti, E. (1931). *A history of smoking* (P. England, Trans.). London: Harrap.

Coryell, W., Endicott, J., Maser, J. D., Mueller, T., Lavori, P., & Keller, M. (1995). The likelihood of recurrence in bipolar affective disorder: The importance of episode recency. *Journal of Affective Disorders, 33,* 201–206.

Costa, P. T., Terracciano, A., & McCrae, R. R. (2001). Gender differences in personality traits across cultures: Robust and surprising findings. *Journal of Personality and Social Psychology, 81,* 322–331.

Costanza, A., Weber, K., Gandy, S., Bouras, C., Hof, P. R., Giannakopoulos, G., & Canuto, A. (2011). Contact sport-related chronic traumatic encephalopathy in the elderly: Clinical expression and structural substrates. *Neuropathology and Applied Neurobiology, 37,* 570–584.

Cottrell, C. A., Neuberg, S. L., & Li, N. P. (2007). What do people desire in others? A sociofunctional perspective on the importance of different valued characteristics. *Journal of Personality and Social Psychology, 92,* 208–231.

Cox, B. M., Shah, M. M., Cichon, T., Tancer, M. E., Galloway, M. P., Thomas, D. M., & Perrine, S. A. (2014). Behavioral and neurochemical effects of repeated MDMA administration during late adolescence in the rat. *Progress in Neuropsychopharmacology & Biological Psychiatry, 48,* 229–235.

Coyne, J. A. (2000, April 3). Of vice and men: Review of R. Tornhill and C. Palmer, *A natural history of rape. The New Republic,* pp. 27–34.

Craik, F. I. M., Govoni, R., Naveh-Benjamin, M., & Anderson, N. D. (1996). The effects of divided attention on encoding and retrieval processes in human memory. *Journal of Experimental Psychology: General, 125,* 159–180.

Craik, F. I. M., & Tulving, E. (1975). Depth of processing and the retention of words in episodic memory. *Journal of Experimental Psychology: General, 104,* 268–294.

Cramer, R. E., Schaefer, J. T., & Reid, S. (1996). Identifying the ideal mate: More evidence for male–female convergence. *Current Psychology, 15,* 157–166.

Craske, M. G. (1999). *Anxiety disorders: Psychological approaches to theory and treatment.* Boulder, CO: Westview Press.

Crick, N. R., & Grotpeter, J. K. (1995). Relational aggression, gender, and social-psychological adjustment. *Child Development, 66,* 710–722.

Crocker, J., & Wolfe, C. T. (2001). Contingencies of self-worth. *Psychological Review, 108*(3), 593–623.

Crombag, H. F. M., Wagenaar, W. A., & Van Koppen, P. J. (1996). Crashing memories and the problem of "source monitoring." *Applied Cognitive Psychology, 10,* 95–104.

Cross, E. S., Kraemer, D. J. M., Hamilton, A. F. de C., Kelley, W. M., & Grafton, S. T. (2009). Sensitivity of the action observation network to physical and observational learning. *Cerebral Cortex, 19,* 315–326.

Cross, P. (1977). Not can but will college teachers be improved? *New Directions for Higher Education, 17,* 1–15.

Cross-Disorder Group of the Psychiatric Genomics Consortium. (2013). Identification of risk loci with shared effects on five major psychiatric disorders: A genome-wide analysis. *Lancet, 381,* 1371–1379.

Csigó, K., Harsányi, A., Demeter, G., Rajkai, C., Németh, A., & Racsmány, M. (2010). Long-term follow-up of patients with obsessive-compulsive disorder treated by anterior capsulotomy: A neuropsychological study. *Journal of Affective Disorders, 126,* 198–205.

Csikszentmihalyi, M. (1990). *Flow: The psychology of optimal experience.* New York: Harper & Row.

Cuc, A., Koppel, J., & Hirst, W. (2007). Silence is not golden: A case of socially shared retrieval-induced forgetting. *Psychological Science, 18,* 727–733.

Cunningham, M. R., Roberts, A. R., Barbee, A. P., Druen, P. B., & Wu, C.-H. (1995). "Their ideas of beauty are, on the whole, the same as ours": Consistency and variability in the cross-cultural perception of female physical attractiveness. *Journal of Personality and Social Psychology, 68,* 261–279.

Cunningham, W. A., & Brosch, T. (2012). Motivational salience: Amygdala tuning from traits, needs, values, and goals. *Current Directions in Psychological Science, 21*(1), 54–59.

Curran, J. P., & Lippold, S. (1975). The effects of physical attraction and attitude similarity on attraction in dating dyads. *Journal of Personality, 43,* 528–539.

Curtiss, S. (1977). *Genie: A psycholinguistic study of a modern-day "wild-child."* New York: Academic Press.

Dabbs, J. M., Carr, T. S., Frady, R. L., & Riad, J. K. (1995). Testosterone, crime, and misbehavior among 692 male prison inmates. *Personality and Individual Differences, 18,* 627–633.

Dahger, A., & Robbins, T. W. (2009). Personality, addiction, dopamine: Insights from Parkinson's disease. *Neuron, 61,* 502–510.

Dahl, G., & Della Vigna, S. (2009). Does movie violence increase violent crime? *The Quarterly Journal of Economics, 124,* 677–734.

Dally, P. (1999). *The marriage of heaven and hell: Manic depression and the life of Virginia Woolf.* New York: St. Martin's Griffin.

Dalton, P. (2003). Olfaction. In H. Pashler & S. Yantis (Eds.), *Stevens' handbook of experimental psychology: Vol. 1. Sensation and perception* (3rd ed., pp. 691–746). New York: Wiley.

Daly, M., & Wilson, M. (1988). Evolutionary social psychology and family homicide. *Science, 242,* 519–524.

Damasio, A. R. (1989). Time-locked multiregional retroactivation: A systems-level proposal for the neural substrates of recall and recognition. *Cognition, 33,* 25–62.

Damasio, A. R. (1994). *Descartes' error: Emotion, reason, and the human brain.* New York: Putnam.

Damasio, A. R. (2005). *Descartes' error: Emotion, reason, and the human Brain.* New York: Penguin.

Damasio, A. R., Grabowski, T. J., Bechara, A., Damasio, H., Ponto, L. L. B., Parvisi, J., & Hichwa, R. D. (2000). Subcortical and cortical brain activity during the feeling of self-generated emotions. *Nature Neuroscience, 3,* 1049–1056.

Damasio, H., Grabowski, T. J., Tranel, D., Hichwa, R. D., & Damasio, A. R. (1996). A neural basis for lexical retrieval. *Nature, 380,* 499–505.

Daneshvar, D. H., Nowinski, C. J., McKee, A. C., & Cantu, R. C. (2011). The epidemiology of sport-related concussion. *Clinical Sports Medicine, 30,* 1–17.

Daniel, H. J., O'Brien, K. F., McCabe, R. B., & Quinter, V. E. (1985). Values in mate selection: A 1984 campus survey. *College Student Journal, 19,* 44–50.

Danner, U. N., Ouwehand, C., van Haastert, N. L., Homsveld, H., & de Ridder, D. T. (2012). Decision-making impairments in women with binge eating disorder in comparison with obese and normal weight women. *European Eating Disorders Review, 20,* e56–e62.

Darley, J. M., & Berscheid, E. (1967). Increased liking caused by the anticipation of interpersonal contact. *Human Relations, 10,* 29–40.

Darley, J. M., & Gross, P. H. (1983). A hypothesis-confirming bias in labeling effects. *Journal of Personality and Social Psychology, 44,* 20–33.

Darley, J. M., & Latané, B. (1968). Bystander intervention in emergencies: Diffusion of responsibility. *Journal of Personality and Social Psychology, 8,* 377–383.

Darwin, C. (1998). *The expression of the emotions in man and animals* (P. Ekman, Ed.). New York: Oxford University Press. (Original work published 1872)

Darwin, C. J., Turvey, M. T., & Crowder, R. G. (1972). An auditory analogue of the Sperling partial report procedure: Evidence for brief auditory storage. *Cognitive Psychology, 3,* 255–267.

Dauer, W., & Przedborski, S. (2003). Parkinson's disease: Mechanisms and models. *Neuron, 39,* 889–909.

Daum, I., Schugens, M. M., Ackermann, H., Lutzenberger, W., Dichgans, J., & Birbaumer, N. (1993). Classical conditioning after cerebellar lesions in humans. *Behavioral Neuroscience, 107,* 748–756.

Davidson, R. J., Ekman, P., Saron, C., Senulis, J., & Friesen, W. V. (1990). Emotional expression and brain physiology I: Approach/withdrawal and cerebral asymmetry. *Journal of Personality and Social Psychology, 58,* 330–341.

Davidson, R. J., Putnam, K. M., & Larson, C. L. (2000). Dysfunction in the neural circuitry of emotion regulation—a possible prelude to violence. *Science, 289,* 591–594.

Davies, G. (1988). Faces and places: Laboratory research on context and face recognition. In G. M. Davies & D. M. Thomson (Eds.), *Memory in context: Context in memory* (pp. 35–53). New York: Wiley.

Davis, C. (2008, March 30). Simon Cowell admits to using Botox. *People Magazine.* Retrieved from http://www.people.com/people/article/0,20181478,00.html

Davis, J. L., Senghas, A., Brandt, F., & Ochsner, K. N. (2010). The effects of BOTOX injections on emotional experience. *Emotion, 10*(3), 433–440. doi: 10.1037/a0018690

Dawson, G., Rogers, S., Munson, J., Smith, M., Winter, J., Greenson, J., . . . Varley, J. (2010). Randomized, controlled trial of an intervention for toddlers with autism: The Early Start Denver Model. *Pediatrics, 125,* e17–e23.

Dawson, M., Soulieres, I., Gernsbacher, M. A., & Mottron, L. (2007). The level and nature of autistic intelligence. *Psychological Science, 18,* 657–662.

Day, J. J., & Sweatt, J. D. (2011). Epigenetic mechanisms in cognition. *Neuron, 70,* 813–829.

Dayan, P., & Huys, Q. J. M. (2009). Serotonin in affective control. *Annual Review of Neuroscience, 32,* 95–126.

de Araujo, I. E., Rolls, E. T., Velazco, M. I., Margot, C., & Cayeux, I. (2005). Cognitive modulation of olfactory processing. *Neuron, 46,* 671–679.

Deary, I. J. (2000). *Looking down on human intelligence: From psychometrics to the brain.* New York: Oxford University Press.

Deary, I. J., Batty, G. D., & Gale, C. R. (2008). Bright children become enlightened adults. *Psychological Science, 19*(1), 1–6.

Deary, I. J., Batty, G. D., Pattie, A., & Gale, C. R. (2008). More intelligent, more dependable children live longer: A 55-year longitudinal study of a representative sample of the Scottish nation. *Psychological Science, 19,* 874.

Deary, I. J., Der, G., & Ford, G. (2001). Reaction time and intelligence differences: A population based cohort study. *Intelligence, 29*(5), 389–399.

Deary, I. J., Whiteman, M. C., Starr, J. M., Whalley, L. J., & Fox, H. C. (2004). The impact of childhood intelligence on later life: Following up the Scottish mental surveys of 1932 and 1947. *Journal of Personality and Social Psychology, 86,* 130–147.

DeCasper, A. J., & Spence, M. J. (1986). Prenatal maternal speech influences newborns' perception of speech sounds. *Infant Behavior and Development, 9,* 133–150.

Deci, E. L. (1971). Effects of externally mediated rewards on intrinsic motivation. *Journal of Personality and Social Psychology, 18,* 105–115.

Deci, E. L., Koestner, R., & Ryan, R. M. (1999). A meta-analytic review of experiments examining the effects of extrinsic rewards on intrinsic motivation. *Psychological Bulletin, 125,* 627–668.

Deese, J. (1959). On the prediction of occurrence of particular verbal intrusions in immediate recall. *Journal of Experimental Psychology, 58,* 17–22.

Degenhardt, L., Chiu, W. T., Sampson, N., Kessler, R. C., Anthony, J. C., Angermeyer, M., . . . Wells, J. E. (2008). Toward a global view of alcohol, tobacco, cannabis, and cocaine use: Findings from the WHO World Mental Health surveys. *PLoS Medicine, 5,* e141.

Degenhardt, L., Dierker, L., Chiu, W. T., Medina-Mora, M. E., Neumark, Y., Sampson, N., . . . Kessler, R. C. (2010). Evaluating the drug use "gateway" theory using cross-national data: Consistency and associations of the order of initiation of drug use among participants in the WHO World Mental Health surveys. *Drug and Alcohol Dependence, 108,* 84–97.

Dekker, M. C., & Koot, H. M. (2003). DSM–IV disorders in children with borderline to moderate intellectual disability: I. Prevalence and impact. *Journal of the American Academy of Child and Adolescent Psychiatry, 42*(8), 915–922. doi:10.1097/01.CHI.0000046892.27264.1A

Dekker, S., Lee, N. C., Howard-Jones, P., & Jolles, J. (2012). Neuromyths in education: Prevalence and predictors of misconceptions among teachers. *Frontiers in Psychology 3: 429.* doi:10.3389/fpsyg.2012.00429

Delgado, M. R., Frank, R. H., & Phelps, E. A. (2005). Perceptions of moral character modulate the neural systems of reward during the trust game. *Nature Neuroscience, 8,* 1611–1618.

Demb, J. B., Desmond, J. E., Wagner, A. D., Vaidya, C. J., Glover, G. H., & Gabrieli, J. D. E. (1995). Semantic encoding and retrieval in the left inferior prefrontal cortex: A functional MRI study of task difficulty and process specificity. *The Journal of Neuroscience, 15,* 5870–5878.

Dement, W. C. (1959, November 30). Dreams. *Newsweek.*

Dement, W. C. (1978). *Some must watch while some must sleep.* New York: Norton.

Dement, W. C. (1999). *The promise of sleep.* New York: Delacorte Press.

Dement, W. C., & Wolpert, E. (1958). Relation of eye movements, body motility, and external stimuli to dream content. *Journal of Experimental Psychology, 55,* 543–553.

Dempster, E. L., Pidsley, R., Schalkwyk, L. C., Owens, S., Georgiades, A., Kane, F., . . . Mill, J. (2011). Disease-associated epigenetic changes in monozygotic twins discordant for schizophrenia and bipolar disorder. *Human Molecular Genetics, 20,* 4786–4796.

Denison, S., Reed, C., & Xu, F. (2013). The emergence of probabilistic reasoning in very young infants: Evidence from 4.5- and 6-month-olds. *Developmental Psychology, 49*(2), 243–249. doi:10.1037/a0028278

Dennett, D. (1991). *Consciousness explained.* New York: Basic Books.

Department of Transportation (U.S.), National Highway Traffic Safety Administration (NHTSA). *Traffic safety facts 2010: Alcohol-impaired driving.* Washington (DC): NHTSA; 2012 [cited 2012 Sep 28]. Available at http://www-nrd.nhtsa.dot.gov/Pubs/811606.PDF

DePaulo, B. M., Charlton, K., Cooper, H., Lindsay, J. J., & Muhlenbruck, L. (1997). The accuracy–confidence correlation in the detection of deception. *Personality and Social Psychology Review, 1,* 346–357.

DePaulo, B. M., Lindsay, J. J., Malone, B. E., Muhlenbruck, L., Charlton, K., & Cooper, H. (2003). Cues to deception. *Psychological Bulletin, 129,* 74–118.

DePaulo, B. M., Stone, J. I., & Lassiter, G. D. (1985). Deceiving and detecting deceit. In B. R. Schlenker (Ed.), *The self and social life* (pp. 323–370). New York: McGraw-Hill.

Der, G., Batty, G. D., & Deary, I. J. (2009). The association between IQ in adolescence and a range of health outcomes at 40 in the 1979 U.S. national longitudinal study of youth. *Intelligence, 37*(6), 573–580.

DesJardin, J. L., Eisenberg, L. S., & Hodapp, R. M. (2006). Sound beginnings: Supporting families of young deaf children with cochlear implants. *Infants and Young Children, 19,* 179–189.

Des Jarlais, D. C., McKnight, C., Goldblatt, C., & Purchase, D. (2009). Doing harm reduction better: Syringe exchange in the United States. *Addiction, 104*(9), 1331–1446.

Deutsch, M. (1949). A theory of cooperation and competition. *Human Relations, 2,* 129–152.

DeVilliers, P. (2005). The role of language in theory-of-mind development: What deaf children tell us. In J. W. Astington & J. A. Baird (Eds.), *Why language matters for theory of mind* (pp. 266–297). Oxford, England: Oxford University Press.

Dewhurst, D. L., & Cautela, J. R. (1980). A proposed reinforcement survey schedule for special needs children. *Journal of Behavior Therapy and Experimental Psychiatry, 11,* 109–112.

De Witte, P. (1996). The role of neurotransmitters in alcohol dependency. *Alcohol & Alcoholism, 31*(Suppl. 1), 13–16.

De Wolff, M., & van IJzendoorn, M. H. (1997). Sensitivity and attachment: A meta-analysis on parental antecedents of infant attachment. *Child Development, 68,* 571–591.

DeYoung, C. G., Hirsh, J. B., Shane, M. S., Papademetris, X., Rajeevan, N., & Gray, J. R. (2010). Testing predictions from personality neuroscience: Brain structure and the Big Five. *Psychological Science, 21,* 820–828.

Diaconis, P., & Mosteller, F. (1989). Methods for studying coincidences. *Journal of the American Statistical Association, 84,* 853–861.

Dickens, W. T., & Flynn, J. R. (2001). Heritability estimates versus large environmental effects: The IQ paradox resolved. *Psychological Review, 108,* 346–369.

Dickinson, A., Watt, A., & Griffiths, J. H. (1992). Free-operant acquisition with delayed reinforcement. *Quarterly Journal of Experimental Psychology Section B: Comparative and Physiological Psychology, 45,* 241–258.

Didden, R., Sigafoos, J., Lang, R., O'Reilly, M., Drieschner, K., & Lancioni, G. E. (2012). Intellectual disabilities. In P. Sturmey & M. Hersen (Eds.), *Handbook of evidence-based practice in clinical psychology.* Hoboken, NJ: Wiley. Retrieved from http://doi.wiley.com/10.1002/9781118156391.ebcp001006

DiDonato, T. E., Ullrich, J., & Krueger, J. I. (2011). Social perception as induction and inference: An integrative model of intergroup differentiation, ingroup favoritism, and differential accuracy. *Journal of Personality and Social Psychology, 100*(1), 66–83. doi: 10.1037/a0021051

Diekelmann, S., & Born, J. (2010). The memory function of sleep. *Nature Reviews Neuroscience, 11,* 114–126.

Dimberg, U. (1982). Facial reactions to facial expressions. *Psychophysiology, 19,* 643–647.

Disner, S. G., Beevers, C. G., Haigh, E. A., & Beck, A. T. (2011). Neural mechanisms of the cognitive model of depression. *Nature Reviews Neuroscience, 12,* 467–477.

DiTella, R., MacCulloch, R. J., & Oswald, A. J. (2003). The macroeconomics of happiness. *Review of Economics and Statistics, 85,* 809–827.

Dollard, J., Doob, L. W., Miller, N. E., Mowrer, O. H., & Sears, R. R. (1939). *Frustration and aggression.* Oxford, England: Yale University Press.

Dornbusch, S. M., Hastorf, A. H., Richardson, S. A., Muzzy, R. E., & Vreeland, R. S. (1965). The perceiver and perceived: Their relative influence on categories of interpersonal perception. *Journal of Personality and Social Psychology, 1,* 434–440.

Dovidio, J. F., & Gaertner, S. L. (2010). Intergroup bias. In S. T. Fiske, D. T. Gilbert, & G. Lindzey (Eds.), *The handbook of social psychology* (5th ed., Vol. 2, pp. 1085–1121). New York: Wiley.

Downing, P. E., Chan, A. W. Y., Peelen, M. V., Dodds, C. M., & Kanwisher, N. (2006). Domain specificity in visual cortex. *Cerebral Cortex, 16,* 1453–1461.

Dreifus, C. (2003, May 20). Living one disaster after another, and then sharing the experience. *New York Times,* p. D2.

Drigotas, S. M., & Rusbult, C. E. (1992). Should I stay or should I go? A dependence model of breakups. *Journal of Personality and Social Psychology, 62,* 62–87.

Druckman, D., & Bjork, R. A. (1994). *Learning, remembering, believing: Enhancing human performance.* Washington, DC: National Academy Press.

Duckworth, A. L., & Seligman, M. E. P. (2005). Self-discipline outdoes IQ in predicting academic performance of adolescents. *Psychological Science, 16,* 939–944.

Dudai, Y. (2012). The restless engram: Consolidations never end. *Annual Review of Neuroscience, 35,* 227–247.

Duenwald, M. (2002, September 12). Students find another staple of campus life: Stress. *New York Times.* Retrieved from http://www.nytimes.com/2002/09/17/health/students-find-another-staple-of-campus-life-stress.html?pagewanted=all&src=pm

Dunlop, S. A. (2008). Activity-dependent plasticity: Implications for recovery after spinal cord injury. *Trends in Neurosciences, 31,* 410–418.

Dunlosky, J., Rawson, K. A., Marsh, E. J., Nathan, M. J., & Willingham, D. T. (2013). Improving students' learning with effective learning techniques: Promising directions from cognitive and educational psychology. *Psychological Science in the Public Interest, 14(1),* 4–58.

Dunphy, D. C. (1963). The social structure of urban adolescent peer groups. *Sociometry, 26,* 230–246.

Dutton, D. G., & Aron, A. P. (1974). Some evidence for heightened sexual attraction under conditions of high anxiety. *Journal of Personality and Social Psychology, 30,* 510–517.

Duval, S., & Wicklund, R. A. (1972). *A theory of objective self awareness.* New York: Academic Press.

Dyer, D., Dalzell, F., & Olegario, F. (2004). *Rising Tide: Lessons from 165 years of brand building at Procter & Gamble.* Cambridge, MA: Harvard Business School Press.

Eacott, M. J., & Crawley, R. A. (1998). The offset of childhood amnesia: Memory for events that occurred before age 3. *Journal of Experimental Psychology: General, 127,* 22–33.

Eagly, A. H., & Steffen, V. J. (1986). Gender and aggressive behavior: A meta-analytic review of the social psychological literature. *Psychological Bulletin, 100,* 309–330.

Eagly, A. H., & Wood, W. (1999). The origins of sex differences in human behavior: Evolved dispositions versus social roles. *American Psychologist, 54,* 408–423.

Eastwick, P. W., Finkel, E. J., Mochon, D., & Ariely, D. (2007). Selective versus unselective romantic desire: Not all reciprocity is created equal. *Psychological Science, 18,* 317–319.

Eaton, W. W., Shao, H., Nestadt, G., Lee, B. H., Bienvenu, O. J., & Zandi, P. (2008). Population-based study of first onset and chronicity of major depressive disorder. *Archives of General Psychiatry, 65,* 513–520.

Ebbinghaus, H. (1964). *Memory: A contribution to experimental psychology.* New York: Dover. (Original work published 1885)

Eddy, D. M. (1982). Probabilistic reasoning in clinical medicine: Problems and opportunities. In D. Kahneman, P. Slovic, & A. Tversky (Eds.), *Judgments under uncertainty: Heuristics and biases* (pp. 249–267). New York: Cambridge University Press.

Edwards, W. (1955). The theory of decision making. *Psychological Bulletin, 51,* 201–214.

Eich, J. E. (1995). Searching for mood dependent memory. *Psychological Science, 6,* 67–75.

Eichenbaum, H., & Cohen, N. J. (2001). *From conditioning to conscious recollection: Memory systems of the brain.* New York: Oxford University Press.

Eimas, P. D., Siqueland, E. R., Jusczyk, P., & Vigorito, J. (1971). Speech perception in infants. *Science, 171,* 303–306.

Einstein, G. O., & McDaniel, M. A. (1990). Normal aging and prospective memory. *Journal of Experimental Psychology: Learning, Memory, and Cognition, 16,* 717–726.

Einstein, G. O., & McDaniel, M. A. (2005). Prospective memory: Multiple retrieval processes. *Current Direction in Psychological Science, 14,* 286–290.

Eisenberg, N., Fabes, R. A., Guthrie, I. K., & Reiser, M. (2000). Dispositional emotionality and regulation: Their role in predicting quality of social functioning. *Journal of Personality and Social Psychology, 78,* 136.

Ekman, P. (1965). Differential communication of affect by head and body cues. *Journal of Personality and Social Psychology, 2,* 726–735.

Ekman, P. (1972). Universals and cultural differences in facial expressions of emotion. In J. K. Cole (Ed.), *Nebraska Symposium on Motivation, 1971* (pp. 207–283). Lincoln: University of Nebraska Press.

Ekman, P. (1992). *Telling lies.* New York: Norton.

Ekman, P., & Friesen, W. V. (1968). Nonverbal behavior in psychotherapy research. In J. M. Shlien (Ed.), *Research in psychotherapy* (Vol. 3, pp. 179–216). Washington, DC: American Psychological Association.

Ekman, P., & Friesen, W. V. (1971). Constants across cultures in the face and emotion. *Journal of Personality and Social Psychology, 17,* 124–129.

Ekman, P., & Friesen, W. V. (1982). Felt, false, and miserable smiles. *Journal of Nonverbal Behavior, 6,* 238–252.

Ekman, P., Levenson, R. W., & Friesen, W. V. (1983). Autonomic nervous system activity distinguishes among emotions. *Science, 221,* 1208–1210.

Eldridge, L. L., Knowlton, B. J., Furmanski, C. S., Bookheimer, S. Y., & Engel, S. A. (2000). Remembering episodes: A selective role for the hippocampus during retrieval. *Nature Neuroscience, 3,* 1149–1152.

Elfenbein, H. A., & Ambady, N. (2002). On the universality and cultural specificity of emotion recognition: A meta-analysis. *Psychological Bulletin, 128,* 203–235.

Ellenbogen, J. M., Payne, J. D., & Stickgold, R. (2006). The role of sleep in declarative memory consolidation: Passive, permissive, or none? *Current Opinion in Neurobiology, 16,* 716–722.

Ellis, A. (1991). *Reason and emotion in psychotherapy.* New York: Carol.

Ellis, B. J., & Garber, J. (2000). Psychosocial antecedents of variation in girls' pubertal timing: Maternal depression, stepfather presence, and marital and family stress. *Child Development, 71,* 485–501.

Ellis, L., & Ames, M. A. (1987). Neurohormonal functioning in sexual orientation: A theory of homosexuality–heterosexuality. *Psychological Bulletin, 101,* 233–258.

Ellman, S. J., Spielman, A. J., Luck, D., Steiner, S. S., & Halperin, R. (1991). REM deprivation: A review. In S. J. Ellman & J. S. Antrobus (Eds.), *The mind in sleep: Psychology and psychophysiology* (2nd ed., pp. 329–376). New York: Wiley.

Ellsworth, P. C., & Scherer, K. R. (2003). Appraisal processes in emotion. In R. J. Davidson, K. R. Scherer, & H. H. Goldsmith (Eds.), *The handbook of affective science* (pp. 572–595). New York: Oxford University Press.

Emerson, R. C., Bergen, J. R., & Adelson, E. H. (1992). Directionally selective complex cells and the computation of motion energy in cat visual cortex. *Vision Research, 32,* 203–218.

Enock, P. M., & McNally, R. J. (2013). How mobile apps and other web-based interventions can transform psychological treatment and the treatment development cycle. *Behavior Therapist, 36*(3), 56, 58, 60, 62–66.

Epel, E. S., Blackburn, E. H., Lin, J., Dhabhar, F. S., Adler, N.E., Morrow, J. D., & Cawthorn, R. M. (2004). Accelerated telomere shortening in response to life stress. *Proceedings of the National Academy of Sciences, 101,* 17312–17315.

Epel, E. S., Daubenmier, J., Moskowitz, J. T., Foldman, S., & Blackburn, E. H. (2009). Can meditation slow rate of cellular aging? Cognitive stress, mindfulness, and telomerase. *Annals of the New York Academy of Sciences, 1172,* 34–53.

Epley, N., Savitsky, K., & Kachelski, R. A. (1999). What every skeptic should know about subliminal persuasion. *Skeptical Inquirer, 23,* 40–45, 58.

Epley, N., & Waytz, A. (2010). Mind perception. In S. T. Fiske, D. T. Gilbert, & G. Lindzey (Eds.), *The handbook of social psychology* (5th ed., Vol. 1, pp. 498–541). New York: Wiley.

Epstein, R. (2007a). *The case against adolescence: Rediscovering the adult in every teen.* New York: Quill Driver.

Epstein, R. (2007b). The myth of the teen brain. *Scientific American Mind, 18,* 27–31.

Ericsson, K. A., & Charness, N. (1999). Expert performance: Its structure and acquisition. In S. J. Ceci & W. M. Williams (Eds.), *The nature–nurture debate: The essential readings* (pp. 200–256). Oxford, England: Blackwell.

Espy, K. A., Fang, H., Johnson, C., Stopp, C., Wiebe, S. A., & Respass, J. (2011). Prenatal tobacco exposure: Developmental outcomes in the neonatal period. *Developmental Psychology, 47*(1), 153–169. doi:10.1037/a0020724

Evans, G. W. (2004). The environment of childhood poverty. *American Psychologist, 59*(2), 77–92.

Evans, G. W. (2006). Child development and the physical environment. *Annual Review of Psychology, 57,* 423–451.

Evans, S. W., & Kim, P. (2012). Childhood poverty and young adults' allostatic load: The mediating role of childhood cumulative risk exposure. *Psychological Science, 23*(9), 979–983. doi:10.1177/0956797612441218

Evans, G. W., & Stecker, R. (2004). Motivational consequences of environmental stress. *Journal of Environmental Psychology, 24,* 143–165.

Everson, S. A., Lynch, J. W., Chesney, M. A., Kaplan, G. A., Goldberg, D. E., Shade, S. B., . . . Salonen, J. T. (1997). Interaction of workplace demands and cardiovascular reactivity in progression of carotid atherosclerosis: Population based study. *British Medical Journal, 314,* 553–558.

Exner, J. E. (1993). *The Rorschach: A comprehensive system: Vol. 1. Basic Foundations.* New York: Wiley.

Eysenck, H. J. (1957). The effects of psychotherapy: An evaluation. *Journal of Consulting Psychology, 16,* 319–324.

Eysenck, H. J. (1967). *The biological basis of personality.* Springfield, IL: Charles C Thomas.

Falk, R., & McGregor, D. (1983). The surprisingness of coincidences. In P. Humphreys, O. Svenson, & A. Vari (Eds.), *Analysing and aiding decision processes* (pp. 489–502). New York: North Holland.

Fancher, R. E. (1979). *Pioneers in psychology.* New York: Norton.

Fantz, R. L. (1964). Visual experience in infants: Decreased attention to familiar patterns relative to novel ones. *Science, 164,* 668–670.

Farah, M. J., Illes, J., Cook-Deegan, R., Gardner, H., Kandel, E., King, P., . . . Wolpe, P. R. (2004). Neurocognitive enhancement: What can we do and what should we do? *Nature Reviews Neuroscience, 5,* 421–426.

Faraone, S. V., Perlis, R. H., Doyle, A. E., Smoller, J. W., Goralnick, J. J., Holmgren, M. A., & Sklar, P. (2005). Molecular genetics of attention-deficit/hyperactivity disorder. *Biological Psychiatry, 57,* 1313–1323.

Farooqi, I. S., Bullmore, E., Keogh, J., Gillard, J., O'Rahilly, S., & Fletcher, P. C. (2007). Leptin regulates striatal regions and human eating behavior. *Science, 317,* 1355.

Farrar, M. J. (1990). Discourse and the acquisition of grammatical morphemes. *Journal of Child Language, 17,* 607–624.

Favazza, A. (2011). *Bodies under siege: Self-mutilation, nonsuicidal self-injury, and body modification in culture and psychiatry.* Baltimore, MD: Johns Hopkins University Press.

Fazel, S., & Danesh, J. (2002). Serious mental disorder in 23,000 prisoners: A review of 62 surveys. *Lancet, 359,* 545–550.

Fechner, G. T. (1966). *Elements of psychophysics* (H. E. Alder, Trans.). New York: Holt, Rinehart, & Winston. (Original work published 1860)

Feczer, D., & Bjorklund, P. (2009). Forever changed: Posttraumatic stress disorder in female military veterans, a case report. *Perspectives in Psychiatric Care, 45,* 278–291.

Fehr, E., & Gaechter, S. (2002). Altruistic punishment in humans. *Nature, 415,* 137–140.

Fein, D., Barton, M., Eigsti, I.-M., Kelley, E., Naigles, L., Schultz, R. T., . . . Tyson, K. (2013). Optimal outcome in individuals with a history of autism. *Journal of Child Psychology and Psychiatry, 54,* 195–205.

Fein, S., Goethals, G. R., & Kugler, M. B. (2007). Social influence on political judgments: The case of presidential debates. *Political Psychology, 28,* 165–192.

Feinberg, T. E. (2001). *Altered egos: How the brain creates the self.* New York: Oxford University Press.

Feingold, A. (1992). Gender differences in mate selection preferences: A test of the parental investment model. *Psychological Bulletin, 112,* 125–139.

Feldman, D. E. (2009). Synaptic mechanisms for plasticity in neocortex. *Annual Review of Neuroscience, 32,* 33–55.

Feldman, M. D. (2004). *Playing sick.* New York: Brunner-Routledge.

Fernyhough, C. (2012). *Pieces of light: The new science of memory.* London: Profile Books.

Ferster, C. B., & Skinner, B. F. (1957). *Schedules of reinforcement.* New York: Appleton-Century-Crofts.

Festinger, L. (1957). *A theory of cognitive dissonance.* Stanford, CA: Stanford University Press.

Festinger, L., & Carlsmith, J. M. (1959). Cognitive consequences of forced compliance. *Journal of Abnormal and Social Psychology, 58,* 203–210.

Festinger, L., Schachter, S., & Back, K. (1950). *Social pressures in informal groups: A study of human factors in housing.* Oxford, England: Harper & Row.

Fields, G. (2009, May 14). White House czar calls for end to "War on Drugs." *Wall Street Journal,* p. A3. Retrieved May 14, 2009, from http://online.wsj.com/article/SB124225891527617397.html

Finkel, E. J., & Eastwick, P. W. (2009). Arbitrary social norms influence sex differences in romantic selectivity. *Psychological Science, 20,* 1290–1295.

Finkelstein, E. A., Trogdon, J. G., Cohen, J. W., & Dietz, W. (2009). Annual medical spending attributable to obesity: Payer- and service-specific estimates. *Health Affairs, 28*(5), w822–w831.

Finkelstein, K. E. (1999, October 17). Yo-Yo Ma's lost Stradivarius is found after wild search. *New York Times*, p. 34.

Fiore, A. T., Taylor, L. S., Zhong, X., Mendelsohn, G. A., & Cheshire, C. (2010). Who's right and who writes: People, profiles, contacts, and replies in online dating. *Proceedings of Hawaii International Conferences on Systems Science, 43*, Persistent Conversation minitrack.

Fiorentine, R. (1999). After drug treatment: Are 12-step programs effective in maintaining abstinence? *American Journal of Drug and Alcohol Abuse, 25*, 93–116.

Fiorillo, C. D., Newsome, W. T., & Schultz, W. (2008). The temporal precision of reward prediction in dopamine neurons. *Nature Neuroscience, 11*, 966–973.

Fisher, H. E. (1993). *Anatomy of love: The mysteries of mating, marriage, and why we stray.* New York: Fawcett.

Fisher, R. P., & Craik, F. I. M. (1977). The interaction between encoding and retrieval operations in cued recall. *Journal of Experimental Psychology: Human Learning and Perception, 3*, 153–171.

Fiske, S. T. (1998). Stereotyping, prejudice, and discrimination. In D. T. Gilbert, S. T. Fiske, & G. Lindzey (Eds.), *The handbook of social psychology* (4th ed., Vol. 2, pp. 357–411). New York: McGraw-Hill.

Fiske, S. T. (2010). *Social beings: A core motives approach to social psychology.* Hoboken, NJ: Wiley.

Fleeson, W. (2004). Moving personality beyond the person-situation debate: The challenge and opportunity of within-person variability. *Current Directions in Psychological Science, 13*, 83–87.

Fletcher, P. C., Shallice, T., & Dolan, R. J. (1998). The functional roles of prefrontal cortex in episodic memory. I. Encoding. *Brain, 121*, 1239–1248.

Flynn, E., & Whiten, A. (2008). Cultural transmission of tool-use in young children: A diffusion chain study. *Social Development, 17*, 699–718.

Flynn, J. R. (2012). *Are we getting smarter? Rising IQ in the twenty-first century.* New York: Cambridge University Press.

Foa, E. B. (2010). Cognitive behavioral therapy of obsessive-compulsive disorder. *Dialogues in Clinical Neuroscience, 12*, 199–207.

Foa, E. B., Dancu, C. V., Hembree, E. A., Jaycox, L. H., Meadows, E. A., & Street, G. P. (1999). A comparison of exposure therapy, stress inoculation training, and their combination for reducing posttraumatic stress disorder in female assault victims. *Journal of Consulting and Clinical Psychology, 67*, 194–200.

Fogassi, L., Ferrari, P. F., Gesierich, B., Rozzi, S., Chersi, F., & Rizzolatti, G. (2005). Parietal lobe: From action organization to intention understanding. *Science, 308*, 662–667.

Foroni, F., & Semin, G. R. (2009). Language that puts you in touch with your bodily feelings: The multimodal responsiveness of affective expressions. *Psychological Science, 20*(8), 974–980.

Fournier, J. C., DeRubeis, R., Hollon, S. D., Dimidjian, S., Amsterdam, J. D., Shelton, R. C., & Fawcett, J. (2010). Antidepressant drug effects and depression severity. *Journal of the American Medical Association, 303*, 47–53.

Fox, R. E., DeLeon, P. H., Newman, R., Sammons, M. T., Dunivin, D. L., & Baker, D. C. (2009). Prescriptive authority and psychology: A status report. *American Psychologist, 64*, 257–268.

Fragaszy, D. M., Izar, P., Visalberghi, E., Ottoni, E. B., & de Oliveria, M. G. (2004). Wild capuchin monkeys (*Cebus libidinosus*) use anvils and stone pounding tools. *American Journal of Primatology, 64*, 359–366.

Francis, D., Diorio, J., Liu, D., & Meaney, M. J. (1999). Nongenomic transmission across generations of maternal behavior and stress responses in the rat. *Science, 286*, 1155–1158.

Frank, M. G., Ekman, P., & Friesen, W. V. (1993). Behavioral markers and recognizability of the smile of enjoyment. *Journal of Personality and Social Psychology, 64*, 83–93.

Frank, M. G., & Stennet, J. (2001). The forced-choice paradigm and the perception of facial expressions of emotion. *Journal of Personality and Social Psychology, 80*, 75–85.

Fredman, T., & Whiten, A. (2008). Observational learning from tool using models by human-reared and mother-reared capuchin monkeys (*Cebus apella*). *Animal Cognition, 11*, 295–309.

Fredrickson, B. L. (2000). Cultivating positive emotions to optimize health and well-being. *Prevention and Treatment, 3*, Article 0001a. doi:10.1037/1522-3736.3.1.31a. Retrieved September 21, 2013 from http://psycnet.apa.org

Freedman, J. L., & Fraser, S. C. (1966). Compliance without pressure: The foot-in-the-door technique. *Journal of Personality and Social Psychology, 4*, 195–202.

Freeman, S., Walker, M. R., Borden, R., & Latané, B. (1975). Diffusion of responsibility and restaurant tipping: Cheaper by the bunch. *Personality and Social Psychology Bulletin, 1*, 584–587.

French, H. W. (1997, February 26). In the land of the small it isn't easy being tall. *New York Times.* Retrieved from http://www.nytimes.com/1997/02/26/world/in-the-land-of-the-small-it-isn-t-easy-being-tall.html

Freud, S. (1965). *The interpretation of dreams* (J. Strachey, Trans.). New York: Avon. (Original work published 1900)

Fried, P. A., & Watkinson, B. (2000). Visuoperceptual functioning differs in 9- to 12-year-olds prenatally exposed to cigarettes and marijuana. *Neurotoxicology and Teratology, 22*, 11–20.

Friedlander, L., & Desrocher, M. (2006). Neuroimaging studies of obsessive-compulsive disorder in adults and children. *Clinical Psychology Review, 26*, 32–49.

Friedman, J. M. (2003). A war on obesity, not the obese. *Science, 299*(5608), 856–858.

Friedman, J. M., & Halaas, J. L. (1998). Leptin and the regulation of body weight in mammals. *Nature, 395*(6704), 763–770.

Friedman, M., & Rosenman, R. H. (1974). *Type A behavior and your heart.* New York: Knopf.

Friedman, S. L., & Boyle, D. E. (2008). Attachment in U.S. children experiencing nonmaternal care in the early 1990s. *Attachment & Human Development, 10*(3), 225–261.

Friedman-Hill, S. R., Robertson, L. C., & Treisman, A. (1995). Parietal contributions to visual feature binding: Evidence from a patient with bilateral lesions. *Science, 269*, 853–855.

Friesen, W. V. (1972). *Cultural differences in facial expressions in a social situation: An experimental test of the concept of display rules.* Unpublished doctoral dissertation, University of California, San Francisco.

Frith, C. D., & Fletcher, P. (1995). Voices from nowhere. *Critical Quarterly, 37*, 71–83.

Frith, U. (2003). *Autism: Explaining the enigma.* Oxford, England: Blackwell.

Fukui, H., Murai, T., Fukuyama, H., Hayashi, T., & Hanakawa, T. (2005). Functional activity related to risk anticipation during performance of the Iowa gambling task. *NeuroImage, 24*, 253–259.

Funder, D. C. (2001). Personality. *Annual Review of Psychology, 52*, 197–221.

Furmark, T., Tillfors, M., Marteinsdottir, I., Fischer, H., Pissiota, A., Långström, B., & Fredrikson, M. (2002). Common changes in cerebral blood flow in patients with social phobia treated with citalopram or cognitive behavioral therapy. *Archives of General Psychiatry, 59*(5), 425–433.

Fuster, J. M. (2003). *Cortex and mind.* New York: Oxford University Press.

Gadermann, A. M., Alonso, J., Vilagut, G., Zaslavsky, A. M., & Kessler, R. C. (2012). Comorbidity and disease burden in the National

Comorbidity Survey Replication (NCS-R). *Depression and Anxiety, 29,* 797–806.

Gais, S., & Born, J. (2004). Low acetylcholine during slow-wave sleep is critical for declarative memory consolidation. *Proceedings of the National Academy of Sciences, USA, 101,* 2140–2144.

Galati, D., Scherer, K. R., & Ricci-Bitt, P. E. (1997). Voluntary facial expression of emotion: Comparing congenitally blind with normally sighted encoders. *Journal of Personality and Social Psychology, 73,* 1363–1379.

Galef, B. (1998). Edward Thorndike: Revolutionary psychologist, ambiguous biologist. *American Psychologist, 53,* 1128–1134.

Gallistel, C. R. (2000). The replacement of general-purpose learning models with adaptively specialized learning modules. In M. S. Gazzaniga (Ed.), *The new cognitive neurosciences* (pp. 1179–1191). Cambridge, MA: MIT Press.

Gallo, D. A. (2006). *Associative illusions of memory.* New York: Psychology Press.

Gallo, D. A. (2010). False memories and fantastic beliefs: 15 years of the DRM illusion. *Memory & Cognition, 38,* 833–848.

Gallup, G. G. (1977). Self-recognition in primates: A comparative approach to the bidirectional properties of consciousness. *American Psychologist, 32,* 329–338.

Ganzel, B. L., Kim, P., Glover, G. H., & Temple, E. (2008). Resilience after 9/11: Multimodal neuroimaging evidence for stress-related change in the healthy adult brain. *NeuroImage, 40,* 788–795.

Garb, H. N. (1998). *Studying the clinician: Judgment research and psychological assessment.* Washington, DC: American Psychological Association.

Garcia, J. (1981). Tilting at the windmills of academe. *American Psychologist, 36,* 149–158.

Garcia, J., & Koelling, R. A. (1966). Relation of cue to consequence in avoidance learning. *Psychonomic Science, 4,* 123–124.

Gardner, M., & Steinberg, L. (2005). Peer influence on risk taking, risk preference, and risky decision making in adolescence and adulthood: An experimental study. *Developmental Psychology, 41*(4), 625–635. doi:10.1037/0012-1649.41.4.625

Garland, A. F., & Zigler, E. (1999). Emotional and behavioral problems among highly intellectually gifted youth. *Roeper Review, 22*(1), 41.

Garry, M., Manning, C., Loftus, E. F., & Sherman, S. J. (1996). Imagination inflation: Imagining a childhood event inflates confidence that it occurred. *Psychonomic Bulletin & Review, 3,* 208–214.

Gaser, C., & Schlaug, G. (2003). Brain structures differ between musicians and nonmusicians. *Journal of Neuroscience, 23,* 9240–9245.

Gates, F. J. (2011). *How many people are lesbian, gay, bisexual, and transgender?* Los Angeles: UCLA School of Law, Williams Institute. Retrieved from http://williamsinstitute.law.ucla.edu/wp-content/uploads/Gates-How-Many-People-LGBT-Apr-2011.pdf

Gazzaniga, M. S. (Ed.). (2000). *The new cognitive neurosciences.* Cambridge, MA: MIT Press.

Gazzaniga, M. S. (2006). Forty-five years of split brain research and still going strong. *Nature Reviews Neuroscience, 6,* 653–659.

Ge, X. J., Conger, R. D., & Elder, G. H. (1996). Coming of age too early: Pubertal influences on girls' vulnerability to psychological distress. *Child Development, 67,* 3386–3400.

Ge, X. J., Conger, R. D., & Elder, G. H., Jr. (2001). Pubertal transition, stressful life events, and the emergence of gender differences in adolescent depressive symptoms. *Developmental Psychology, 37*(3), 404–417. doi:10.1037/0012-1649.37.3.404

Geen, R. G. (1984). Preferred stimulation levels in introverts and extraverts: Effects on arousal and performance. *Journal of Personality and Social Psychology, 46,* 1303–1312.

Geier, A., Wansink, B., & Rozin, P. (2012). Red potato chips: Segmentation cues substantially decrease food intake. *Health Psychology, 31,* 398–401.

Gershoff, E. T. (2002). Corporal punishment by parents and associated child behaviors and experiences: A meta-analytic and theoretical review. *Psychological Bulletin, 128,* 539–579.

Gibb, B. E., Alloy, L. B., & Tierney, S. (2001). History of childhood maltreatment, negative cognitive styles, and episodes of depression in adulthood. *Cognitive Therapy and Research, 25,* 425–446.

Gibbons, F. X. (1990). Self-attention and behavior: A review and theoretical update. In M. P. Zanna (Ed.), *Advances in experimental social psychology* (Vol. 23, pp. 249–303). San Diego, CA: Academic Press.

Giedd, J. N., Blumenthal, J., Jeffries, N. O., Castellanos, F. X., Liu, H., Zijdenbos, A., . . . Rapoport, J. L. (1999). Brain development during childhood and adolescence: A longitudinal MRI study. *Nature Neuroscience, 2,* 861–863.

Gierlach, E., Blesher, B. E., & Beutler, L. E. (2010). Cross-cultural differences in risk perceptions of disasters. *Risk Analysis, 30,* 1539–1549.

Gigerenzer, G. (1996). The psychology of good judgment: Frequency formats and simple algorithms. *Journal of Medical Decision Making, 16,* 273–280.

Gigerenzer, G., & Hoffrage, U. (1995). How to improve Bayesian reasoning without instruction: Frequency formats. *Psychological Review, 102,* 684–704.

Gigone, D., & Hastie, R. (1993). The common knowledge effect: Information sharing and group judgment. *Journal of Personality and Social Psychology, 54,* 959–974.

Gilbert, D. T. (1991). How mental systems believe. *American Psychologist, 46,* 107–119.

Gilbert, D. T. (1998). Ordinary personology. In D. T. Gilbert, S. T. Fiske, & G. Lindzey (Eds.), *The handbook of social psychology* (4th ed., Vol. 2, pp. 89–150). New York: McGraw-Hill.

Gilbert, D. T. (2006). *Stumbling on happiness.* New York: Knopf.

Gilbert, D. T., Brown, R. P., Pinel, E. C., & Wilson, T. D. (2000). The illusion of external agency. *Journal of Personality and Social Psychology, 79,* 690–700.

Gilbert, D. T., Gill, M. J., & Wilson, T. D. (2002). The future is now: Temporal correction in affective forecasting. *Organizational Behavior and Human Decision Processes, 88,* 430–444.

Gilbert, D. T., & Malone, P. S. (1995). The correspondence bias. *Psychological Bulletin, 117,* 21–38.

Gilbert, D. T., Pelham, B. W., & Krull, D. S. (1988). On cognitive busyness: When persons perceive meet persons perceived. *Journal of Personality and Social Psychology, 54,* 733–740.

Gilbert, G. M. (1951). Stereotype persistence and change among college students. *Journal of Abnormal and Social Psychology, 46,* 245–254.

Gilbertson, M. W., Shenton, M. E., Ciszewski, A., Kasai, K., Lasko, N. B., Orr, S. P., & Pitman, R. K. (2002). Smaller hippocampal volume predicts pathological vulnerability to psychological trauma. *Nature Neuroscience, 5,* 1242–1247.

Gillette, J., Gleitman, H., Gleitman, L., & Lederer, A. (1999). Human simulation of vocabulary learning. *Cognition, 73,* 135–176.

Gilovich, T. (1991). *How we know what isn't so: The fallibility of human reason in everyday life.* New York: Free Press.

Giovanello, K. S., Schnyer, D. M., & Verfaellie, M. (2004). A critical role for the anterior hippocampus in relational memory: Evidence from an fMRI study comparing associative and item recognition. *Hippocampus, 14,* 5–8.

Gladue, B. A. (1994). The biopsychology of sexual orientation. *Current Directions in Psychological Science, 3,* 150–154.

Glenwick, D. S., Jason, L. A., & Elman, D. (1978). Physical attractiveness and social contact in the singles bar. *Journal of Social Psychology, 105,* 311–312.

Glynn, L. M., & Sandman, C. A. (2011). Prenatal origins of neurological development: A critical period for fetus and mother. *Current Directions in Psychological Science, 20*(6), 384–389. doi:10.1177/0963721411422056

Gneezy, U., & Rustichini, A. (2000). A fine is a price. *Journal of Legal Studies, 29*, 1–17.

Goddard, H. H. (1913). *The Kallikak family: A study in the heredity of feeble-mindedness.* New York: Macmillan.

Godden, D. R., & Baddeley, A. D. (1975). Context-dependent memory in two natural environments: On land and underwater. *British Journal of Psychology, 66*, 325–331.

Goehler, L. E., Gaykema, R. P. A., Hansen, M. K., Anderson, K., Maier, S. F., & Watkins, L. R. (2000). Vagal immune-to-brain communication: A visceral chemosensory pathway. *Autonomic Neuroscience: Basic and Clinical, 85*, 49–59.

Goetzman, E. S., Hughes, T., & Klinger, E. (1994). *Current concerns of college students in a midwestern sample.* Unpublished report, University of Minnesota, Morris.

Goff, L. M., & Roediger, H. L., III. (1998). Imagination inflation for action events—repeated imaginings lead to illusory recollections. *Memory & Cognition, 26*, 20–33.

Goldman, M. S., Brown, S. A., & Christiansen, B. A. (1987). Expectancy theory: Thinking about drinking. In H. T. Blane & K. E. Leonard (Eds.), *Psychological theories of drinking and alcoholism* (pp. 181–266). New York: Guilford Press.

Goldstein, M. H., Schwade, J. A., Briesch, J., & Syal, S. (2010). Learning while babbling: Prelinguistic object-directed vocalizations signal a readiness to learn. *Infancy, 15*, 362–391.

Gomez, C., Argandota, E. D., Solier, R. G., Angulo, J. C., & Vazquez, M. (1995). Timing and competition in networks representing ambiguous figures. *Brain and Cognition, 29*, 103–114.

Gonzaga, G. C., Keltner, D., Londahl, E. A., & Smith, M. D. (2001). Love and the commitment problem in romantic relations and friendship. *Journal of Personality and Social Psychology, 81*, 247–262.

Goodale, M. A., & Milner, A. D. (1992). Separate visual pathways for perception and action. *Trends in Neurosciences, 15*, 20–25.

Goodale, M. A., & Milner, A. D. (2004). *Sight unseen.* Oxford, England: Oxford University Press.

Goodale, M. A., Milner, A. D., Jakobson, L. S., & Carey, D. P. (1991). A neurological dissociation between perceiving objects and grasping them. *Nature, 349*, 154–156.

Goodwin, P., McGill, B., & Chandra, A. (2009). *Who marries and when? Age at first marriage in the United States, 2002* (Data Brief 19). Hyattsville, MD: National Center for Health Statistics.

Gootman, E. (2003, March 3). Separated at birth in Mexico, united at campuses on Long Island. *New York Times*, p. A25.

Gopnik, A. (2012). Scientific thinking in young children: Theoretical advances, empirical research, and policy implications. *Science, 337*(6102), 1623–1627. doi:10.1126/science.1223416

Gordon, P. (2004). Numerical cognition without words: Evidence from Amazonia. *Science, 306*, 496–499.

Gorno-Tempini, M. L., Price, C. J., Josephs, O., Vandenberghe, R., Cappa, S. F., Kapur, N., & Frackowiak, R. S. (1998). The neural systems sustaining face and proper-name processing. *Brain, 121*, 2103–2118.

Gotlib, I. H., & Joormann, J. (2010). Cognition and depression: Current status and future directions. *Annual Review of Clinical Psychology, 6*, 285–312.

Gottesman, I. I. (1991). *Schizophrenia genesis: The origins of madness.* New York: Freeman.

Gottesman, I. I., & Hanson, D. R. (2005). Human development: Biological and genetic processes. *Annual Review of Psychology, 56*, 263–286.

Gottfredson, L. S. (1997). Mainstream science on intelligence: An editorial with 52 signatories, history, and bibliography. *Intelligence, 24*, 13–23.

Gottfredson, L. S., & Deary, I. J. (2004). Intelligence predicts health and longevity, but why? *Current Directions in Psychological Science, 13*, 1–4.

Gottfried, J. A. (2008). Perceptual and neural plasticity of odor quality coding in the human brain. *Chemosensory Perception, 1*, 127–135.

Gouldner, A. W. (1960). The norm of reciprocity. *American Sociological Review, 25*, 161–178.

Graf, P., & Schacter, D. L. (1985). Implicit and explicit memory for new associations in normal subjects and amnesic patients. *Journal of Experimental Psychology: Learning, Memory, and Cognition, 11*, 501–518.

Grandin, T. (2006). *Thinking in pictures: My life with autism* (expanded edition). Visalia, CA: Vintage.

Grant, A. M. (2008). Personal life coaching for coaches-in-training enhances goal attainment, insight, and learning. *Coaching, 1*(1), 54–70.

Grant, B. F., Hasin, D. S., Stinson, F. S., Dawson, D. A., Chou, S. P., & Ruan, W. J. (2004). Prevalence, correlates, and disability of personality disorders in the U.S.: Results from the National Epidemiologic Survey on Alcohol and Related Conditions. *Journal of Clinical Psychiatry, 65*, 948–958.

Grassian, S. (2006). Psychiatric effects of solitary confinement. *Washington University Journal of Law and Policy, 22*, 325–383.

Gray, H. M., Gray, K., & Wegner, D. M. (2007). Dimensions of mind perception. *Science, 315*, 619.

Gray, J. A. (1970). The psychophysiological basis of introversion–extraversion. *Behavior Research and Therapy, 8*, 249–266.

Gray, J. A. (1990). Brain systems that mediate both emotion and cognition. *Cognition and Emotion, 4*, 269–288.

Green, C. S., & Bavelier, D. (2007). Action video-game experience alters the spatial resolution of vision. *Psychological Science, 18*, 88–94.

Green, D. A., & Swets, J. A. (1966). *Signal detection theory and psychophysics.* New York: Wiley.

Green, M. F., Kern, R. S., Braff, D. L., & Mintz, J. (2000). Neurocognitive deficits and functional outcome in schizophrenia: Are we measuring the "right stuff"? *Schizophrenia Bulletin, 26*, 119–136.

Green, S. K., Buchanan, D. R., & Heuer, S. K. (1984). Winners, losers, and choosers: A field investigation of dating initiation. *Personality and Social Psychology Bulletin, 10*, 502–511.

Greenberg, J., Solomon, S., & Arndt, J. (2008). A basic but uniquely human motivation: Terror management. In J. Y. Shah & W. L. Gardner (Eds.), *Handbook of motivation science* (pp. 114–134). New York: Guilford Press.

Greene, J. (2013). *Moral tribes: Emotion, reason, and the gap between us and them.* New York: Penguin.

Greene, J. D., Sommerville, R. B., Nystrom, L. E., Darley, J. M., & Cohen, J. D. (2001). An fMRI investigation of emotional engagement in moral judgment. *Science, 293*, 2105–2108.

Greenwald, A. G., McGhee, D. E., & Schwartz, J. L. K. (1998). Measuring individual differences in implicit cognition: The implicit association test. *Journal of Personality and Social Psychology, 74*, 1464–1480.

Greenwald, A. G., & Nosek, B. A. (2001). Health of the Implicit Association Test at age 3. *Zeitschrift für Experimentelle Psychologie, 48*, 85–93.

Gropp, E., Shanabrough, M., Borok, E., Xu, A. W., Janoschek, R., Buch, T., . . . Brüning, J. C. (2005). Agouti-related peptide-expressing neurons are mandatory for feeding. *Nature Neuroscience, 8*, 1289–1291.

Gross, J. J. (1998). Antecedent- and response-focused emotion regulation: Divergent consequences for experience, expression, and physiology. *Journal of Personality and Social Psychology, 74*, 224–237.

Gross, J. J. (2002). Emotion regulation: Affective, cognitive, and social consequences. *Psychophysiology, 39*, 281–291.

Gross, J. J., & Munoz, R. F. (1995). Emotion regulation and mental health. *Clinical Psychology: Science and Practice, 2*, 151–164.

Groves, B. (2004, August 2). Unwelcome awareness. *The San Diego Union-Tribune*, p. 24.

Grün, F., & Blumberg, B. (2006). Environmental obesogens: Organotins and endocrine disruption via nuclear receptor signaling. *Endocrinology, 147,* s50–s55.

Guerin, S. A., Robbins, C. A., Gilmore, A. W., & Schacter, D. L. (2012a). Interactions between visual attention and episodic retrieval: Dissociable contributions of parietal regions during gist-based false recognition. *Neuron, 75,* 1122–1134.

Guerin, S. A., Robbins, C. A., Gilmore, A. W., & Schacter, D. L. (2012b). Retrieval failure contributes to gist-based false recognition. *Journal of Memory and Language, 66,* 68–78.

Guillery, R. W., & Sherman, S. M. (2002). Thalamic relay functions and their role in corticocortical communication: Generalizations from the visual system. *Neuron, 33,* 163–175.

Gurwitz, J. H., McLaughlin, T. J., Willison, D. J., Guadagnoli, E., Hauptman, P. J., Gao, X., & Soumerai, S. B. (1997). Delayed hospital presentation in patients who have had acute myocardial infarction. *Annals of Internal Medicine, 126,* 593–599.

Gusnard, D. A., & Raichle, M. E. (2001). Searching for a baseline: Functional imaging and the resting human brain. *Nature Reviews: Neuroscience, 2,* 685–694.

Gutchess, A. H., & Schacter, D. L. (2012). The neural correlates of gist-based true and false recognition. *NeuroImage, 59,* 3418–3426.

Guthrie, R. V. (2000). Kenneth Bancroft Clark (1914–). In A. E. Kazdin (Ed.), *Encyclopedia of Psychology* (Vol. 2, p. 91). Washington, DC: American Psychological Association.

Haase, C. M., Heckhausen, J., & Wrosch, C. (2013). Developmental regulation across the life span: Toward a new synthesis. *Developmental Psychology, 49*(5), 964–972. doi:10.1037/a0029231

Hackman, D. A., & Farah, M. J. (2008). Socioeconomic status and the developing brain. *Trends in Cognitive Sciences, 13,* 65–73.

Hackman, J. R., & Katz, N. (2010). Group behavior and performance. In S. T. Fiske, D. T. Gilbert, & G. Lindzey (Eds.), *The handbook of social psychology* (5th ed., Vol. 2, pp. 1208–1251). New York: Wiley.

Haedt-Matt, A. A., & Keel, P. K. (2011). Revisiting the affect regulation model of binge eating: A meta-analysis of studies using ecological momentary assessment. *Psychological Bulletin, 137*(4), 660–681.

Haggard, P., & Tsakiris, M. (2009). The experience of agency: Feelings, judgments, and responsibility. *Current Directions in Psychological Science, 18,* 242–246.

Haidt, J. (2001). The emotional dog and its rational tail: A social intuitionist approach to moral judgment. *Psychological Review, 108,* 814–834.

Haidt, J. (2006). *The happiness hypothesis: Finding modern truth in ancient wisdom.* New York: Basic Books.

Haidt, J., & Keltner, D. (1999). Culture and facial expression: Open-ended methods find more expressions and a gradient of recognition. *Cognition and Emotion, 13,* 225–266.

Hallett, M. (2000). Transcranial magnetic stimulation and the human brain. *Nature, 406,* 147–150.

Halpern, B. (2002). Taste. In H. Pashler & S. Yantis (Eds.), *Stevens' handbook of experimental psychology: Vol. 1. Sensation and perception* (3rd ed., pp. 653–690). New York: Wiley.

Halpern, D. F. (1997). Sex differences in intelligence: Implications for education. *American Psychologist, 52,* 1091–1102.

Halpern, D. F., Benbow, C. P., Geary, D. C., Gur, R. C., Hyde, J. S., & Gernsbacher, M. A. (2007). The science of sex differences in science and mathematics. *Psychological Science in the Public Interest, 8,* 1–51.

Hamermesh, D. S., & Biddle, J. E. (1994). Beauty and the labor market. *American Economic Review, 84,* 1174–1195.

Hamilton, A. F., & Grafton, S. T. (2006). Goal representation in human anterior intraparietal sulcus. *The Journal of Neuroscience, 26,* 1133–1137.

Hamilton, A. F., & Grafton, S. T. (2008). Action outcomes are represented in human inferior frontoparietal cortex. *Cerebral Cortex, 18,* 1160–1168.

Hamilton, W. D. (1964). The genetical evolution of social behaviour. *Journal of Theoretical Biology, 7,* 1–16.

Hamlin, J. K., Mahajan, N., Liberman, Z., & Wynn, K. (2013). Not like me = bad: Infants prefer those who harm dissimilar others. *Psychological Science, 24*(4), 589–594. doi:10.1177/0956797612457785

Hamlin, J. K., Wynn, K., & Bloom, P. (2007). Social evaluation by preverbal infants. *Nature, 450*(7169), 557–559.

Haney, C., Banks, W. C., & Zimbardo, P. G. (1973). Study of prisoners and guards in a simulated prison. *Naval Research Reviews, 9,* 1–17.

Hannon, E. E., & Trainor, L. J. (2007). Music acquisition: Effects of enculturation and formal training on development. *Trends in Cognitive Sciences, 11,* 466–472.

Hansen, E. S., Hasselbalch, S., Law, I., & Bolwig, T. G. (2002). The caudate nucleus in obsessive-compulsive disorder. Reduced metabolism following treatment with paroxetine: A PET study. *International Journal of Neuropsychopharmacology, 5,* 1–10.

Happé, F. G. E. (1995). The role of age and verbal ability in the theory of mind performance of subjects with autism. *Child Development, 66,* 843–855.

Happé, F. G. E., & Vital, P. (2009). What aspects of autism predispose to talent? *Philosophical Transactions of the Royal Society B: Biological Science, 364,* 1369–1375.

Harlow, H. F. (1958). The nature of love. *American Psychologist, 13,* 573–685.

Harlow, H. F., & Harlow, M. L. (1965). The affectional systems. In A. M. Schrier, H. F. Harlow, & F. Stollnitz (Eds.), *Behavior of nonhuman primates* (Vol. 2, pp. 287–334). New York: Academic Press.

Harlow, J. M. (1848). Passage of an iron rod through the head. *Boston Medical and Surgical Journal, 39,* 389–393.

Harris, P. L., de Rosnay, M., & Pons, F. (2005). Language and children's understanding of mental states. *Current Directions in Psychological Science, 14,* 69–73.

Hart, B., & Risley, T. R. (1995). *Meaningful differences in the everyday experience of young American children.* Baltimore, MD: Brookes.

Hart, B. L. (1988). Biological basis of the behavior of sick animals. *Neuroscience and Biobehavioral Reviews, 12,* 123–137.

Hart, W., Albarracin, D., Eagly, A. H., Lindberg, M. J., Merrill, L., & Brechan, I. (2009). Feeling validated versus being correct: A meta-analysis of selective exposure to information. *Psychological Bulletin, 135,* 555–588.

Hartshorne, H., & May, M. (1928). *Studies in deceit.* New York: Macmillan.

Haslam, C., Wills, A. J., Haslam, S. A., Kay, J., Baron, R., & McNab, F. (2007). Does maintenance of colour categories rely on language? Evidence to the contrary from a case of semantic dementia. *Brain and Language, 103,* 251–263.

Hassabis, D., Kumaran, D., Vann, S. D., & Maguire, E. A. (2007). Patients with hippocampal amnesia cannot imagine new experiences. *Proceedings of the National Academy of Sciences, USA, 104,* 1726–1731.

Hasselmo, M. E. (2006). The role of acetylcholine in learning and memory. *Current Opinion in Neurobiology, 16,* 710–715.

Hassin, R. R., Bargh, J. A., & Zimerman, S. (2009). Automatic and flexible: The case of non-conscious goal pursuit. *Social Cognition, 27,* 20–36.

Hassmen, P., Koivula, N., & Uutela, A. (2000). Physical exercise and psychological well-being: A population study in Finland. *Preventive Medicine, 30,* 17–25.

Hasson, U., Hendler, T., Bashat, D. B., & Malach, R. (2001). Vase or face? A neural correlate of shape-selective grouping processes in the human brain. *Journal of Cognitive Neuroscience, 13,* 744–753.

Hatemi, P. K., Gillespie, N. A., Eaves, L. J., Maher, B. S., Webb, B. T., Heath, A. C., . . . Martin, N. G. (2011). A genome-wide analysis of liberal and conservative political attitudes. *The Journal of Politics, 73,* 271–285.

Hatfield, E. (1988). Passionate and companionate love. In R. J. Sternberg & M. L. Barnes (Eds.), *The psychology of love* (pp. 191–217). New Haven, CT: Yale University Press.

Hatfield, E., & Rapson, R. L. (1992). Similarity and attraction in close relationships. *Communication Monographs, 59,* 209–212.

Hausser, M. (2000). The Hodgkin-Huxley theory of the action potential. *Nature Neuroscience, 3,* 1165.

Havas, D. A., Glenberg, A. M., Gutowski, K. A., Lucarelli, M. J., & Davidson, R. J. (2010). Cosmetic use of botulinum toxin-A affects processing of emotional language. *Psychological Science, 21*(7), 895–900. doi:10.1177/0956797610374742

Hawley, P. H. (2002). Social dominance and prosocial and coercive strategies of resource control in preschoolers. *International Journal of Behavioral Development, 26,* 167–176.

Haxby, J. V., Gobbini, M. I., Furey, M. L., Ishai, A., Schouten, J. L., & Pietrini, P. (2001). Distributed and overlapping representations of faces and objects in ventral temporal cortex. *Science, 293,* 2425–2430.

Hayes, J. E., Bartoshuk, L. M., Kidd, J. R., & Duffy, V. B. (2008). Supertasting and PROP bitterness depends on more than the TAS2R38 gene. *Chemical Senses, 23,* 255–265.

Hayes, S. C., Strosahl, K., & Wilson, K. G. (1999). *Acceptance and commitment therapy: An experiential approach to behavior change.* New York: Guilford Press.

Hay-McCutcheon, M. J., Kirk, K. I., Henning, S. C., Gao, S. J., & Qi, R. (2008). Using early outcomes to predict later language ability in children with cochlear implants. *Audiology and Neuro-Otology, 13,* 370–378.

Heath, S. B. (1983). *Way with words: Language, life and work in communities and classrooms.* Cambridge, England: Cambridge University Press.

Heatherton, T. F., & Weinberger, J. L. (Eds.). (1994). *Can personality change?* Washington, DC: American Psychological Association.

Heavey, C. L., Hurlburt, R. T., & Lefforge, N. L. (2012). Toward a phenomenology of feelings. *Emotion, 12*(4), 763–777.

Hebb, D. O. (1949). *The organization of behavior.* New York: Wiley.

Hebl, M. R., & Heatherton, T. F. (1997). The stigma of obesity in women: The difference is Black and White. *Personality and Social Psychology Bulletin, 24,* 417–426.

Hebl, M. R., & Mannix, L. M. (2003). The weight of obesity in evaluating others: A mere proximity effect. *Personality and Social Psychology Bulletin, 29,* 28–38.

Hedges, L. V., & Nowell, A. (1995). Sex differences in mental test scores, variability, and numbers of high-scoring individuals. *Science, 269*(5220), 41–45.

Heerey, E. A., Keltner, D., & Capps, L. M. (2003). Making sense of self-conscious emotion: Linking theory of mind and emotion in children with autism. *Emotion, 3,* 394–400.

Heine, S. J. (2010). Cultural psychology. In S. T. Fiske, D. T. Gilbert, & G. Lindzey (Eds.), *The handbook of social psychology* (5th ed., Vol. 2, pp. 1423–1464). New York: Wiley.

Heine, S. J., & Lehman, D. R. (1995). Cultural variation in unrealistic optimism: Does the West feel more invulnerable than the East? *Journal of Peronality and Social Psychology, 68,* 595–607.

Helt, M., Kelley, E., Kinsbourne, M., Pandey, J., Boorstein, H., Herbert, M., & Fein, D. (2008). Can children with autism recover? If so, how? *Neuropsychology Review, 18,* 339–366.

Henderlong, J., & Lepper, M. R. (2002). The effects of praise on children's intrinsic motivation: A review and synthesis. *Psychological Bulletin, 128,* 774–795.

Henrich, J., Heine, S. J., & Norenzayan, A. (2010). Most people are not WEIRD. *Nature, 466,* 29.

Henry, W. P., Strupp, H. H., Schacht, T. E., & Gaston, L. (1994). Psychodynamic approaches. In A. E. Bergin & S. L. Garfield (Eds.), *Handbook of psychotherapy and behavior change* (pp. 467–508). New York: Wiley.

Herman, C. P., Roth, D. A., & Polivy, J. (2003). Effects of the presence of others on food intake: A normative interpretation. *Psychological Bulletin, 129,* 873–886.

Herring, M. P., Puetz, T. W., O'Connor, P. J., & Dishman, R. K. (2012). Effect of exercise training on depressive symptoms among patients with chronic illness: A systematic review and meta-analysis of randomized controlled trials. *Archives of Internal Medicine, 172,* 101–111.

Herrnstein, R. J. (1977). The evolution of behaviorism. *American Psychologist, 32,* 593–603.

Herz, R. S., & von Clef, J. (2001). The influence of verbal labeling on the perception of odors. *Perception, 30,* 381–391.

Heyes, C. M., & Foster, C. L. (2002). Motor learning by observation: Evidence from a serial reaction time task. *Quarterly Journal of Experimental Psychology (A), 55,* 593–607.

Heyman, G. M. (2009). *Addiction: A disorder of choice.* Cambridge, MA: Harvard University Press.

Heymsfield, S. B., Greenberg, A. S., Fujioka, K., Dixon, R. M., Kushner, R., Hunt, T., . . . McCarnish, M. (1999). Recombinant leptin for weight loss in obese and lean adults: A randomized, controlled, dose-escalation trial. *Journal of the American Medical Association, 282*(16), 1568–1575.

Hibbeln, J. R. (1998). Fish consumption and major depression. *Lancet, 351,* 1213.

Hickok, G. (2009). Eight problems for the mirror neuron theory of action understanding in monkeys and humans. *Journal of Cognitive Neuroscience, 21,* 1229–1243.

Higgins, E. T. (1987). Self-discrepancy theory: A theory relating self and affect. *Psychological Review, 94,* 319–340.

Higgins, E. T. (1997). Beyond pleasure and pain. *American Psychologist, 52,* 1280–1300.

Hilgard, E. R. (1965). *Hypnotic susceptibility.* New York: Harcourt, Brace and World.

Hilgard, E. R. (1986). *Divided consciousness: Multiple controls in human thought and action.* New York: Wiley-Interscience.

Hillman, C. H., Erickson, K. I., & Kramer, A. F. (2008). Be smart, exercise your heart: Exercise effects on brain and cognition. *Nature Reviews Neuroscience, 9,* 58–65.

Hilts, P. (1995). *Memory's ghost: The strange tale of Mr. M and the nature of memory.* New York: Simon & Schuster.

Hine, T. (1995). *The total package: The evolution and secret meanings of boxes, bottles, cans, and tubes.* Boston: Little, Brown.

Hintzman, D. L., Asher, S. J., & Stern, L. D. (1978). Incidental retrieval and memory for coincidences. In M. M. Gruneberg, P. E. Morris, & R. N. Sykes (Eds.), *Practical aspects of memory* (pp. 61–68). New York: Academic Press.

Hirst, W., & Echterhoff, G. (2012). Remembering in conversations: The social sharing and reshaping of memory. *Annual Review of Psychology, 63,* 55–79.

Hirst, W., Phelps, E. A., Buckner, R. L., Budson, A. E., Cuc, A., Gabrieli, J. D. E., . . . Vaidya, C. J. (2009). Long-term memory for the terrorist attack of September 11: Flashbulb memories, event memories, and the factors that influence their retention. *Journal of Experimental Psychology: General, 138,* 161–176.

Hobson, J. A. (1988). *The dreaming brain.* New York: Basic Books.

Hobson, J. A., & McCarley, R. W. (1977). The brain as a dream-state generator: An activation–synthesis hypothesis of the dream process. *American Journal of Psychiatry, 134,* 1335–1368.

Hockley, W. E. (2008). The effects of environmental context on recognition memory and claims of remembering. *Journal of Experimental Psychology: Learning, Memory, and Cognition, 34,* 1412–1429.

Hodgkin, A. L., & Huxley, A. F. (1939). Action potential recorded from inside a nerve fibre. *Nature, 144,* 710–712.

Hodson, G., & Sorrentino, R. M. (2001). Just who favors the ingroup? Personality differences in reactions to uncertainty in the minimal group paradigm. *Group Dynamics, 5,* 92–101.

Hoek, H. W., & van Hoeken, D. (2003). Review of the prevalence and incidence of eating disorders. *International Journal of Eating Disorders, 34,* 383–396.

Hoffrage, U., & Gigerenzer, G. (1998). Using natural frequencies to improve diagnostic inferences. *Academic Medicine, 73,* 538–540.

Hofmann, W., Vohs, K. D., & Baumeister, R. F. (2012). What people desire, feel conflicted about, and try to resist in everyday life. *Psychological Science, 23,* 582–588.

Hollins, M. (2010). Somesthetic senses. *Annual Review of Psychology, 61,* 243–271.

Holloway, G. (2001). *The complete dream book: What your dreams tell about you and your life.* Naperville, IL: Sourcebooks.

Holman, M. A., Carlson, M. L., Driscoll, C. L. W., Grim, K. J., Petersson, R., Sladen, D. P., & Flick, R. P. (2013). Cochlear implantation in children 12 months of age or younger. *Otology & Neurology, 34,* 251–258.

Holmbeck, G. N., & O'Donnell, K. (1991). Discrepancies between perceptions of decision making and behavioral autonomy. In R. L. Paikoff (Ed.), *New directions for child development: Shared views in the family during* adolescence (no. 51, pp. 51–69). San Francisco: Jossey-Bass.

Holmes, J., Gathercole, S. E., & Dunning, D. L. (2009). Adaptive training leads to sustained enhancement of poor working memory in children. *Developmental Science, 12,* F9-F15.

Hölzel, B. K., Carmody, J., Vangel, M., Congleton, C., Yerramsetti, S. M., Gard, T., & Lazar, S. W. (2011). Mindfulness practice leads to increases in regained gray matter density. *Psychiatry Research: Neuroimaging, 191*(1), 36–43.

Homan, K. J., Houlihan, D., Ek, K., & Wanzek, J. (2012). Cultural differences in the level of rewards between adolescents from America, Tanzania, Denmark, Honduras, Korea, and Spain. *International Journal of Psychological Studies, 4,* 264–272.

Homans, G. C. (1961). *Social behavior.* New York: Harcourt, Brace and World.

Hooley, J. M. (2007). Expressed emotion and relapse of psychopathology. *Annual Review of Clinical Psychology, 3,* 329–352.

Horn, J. L., & Cattell, R. B. (1966). Refinement and test of the theory of fluid and crystallized general intelligences. *Journal of Educational Psychology, 5,* 253–270.

Horrey, W. J., & Wickens, C. D. (2006). Examining the impact of cell phone conversation on driving using meta-analytic techniques. *Human Factors, 48,* 196–205.

Horta, B. L., Victoria, C. G., Menezes, A. M., Halpern, R., & Barros, F. C. (1997). Low birthweight, preterm births and intrauterine growth retardation in relation to maternal smoking. *Pediatrics and Perinatal Epidemiology, 11,* 140–151.

Hosking, S. G., Young, K. L., & Regan, M. A. (2009). The effects of text messaging on young drivers. *Human Factors, 51,* 582–592.

Houlihan, D., Jesse, V. C., Levine, H. D., & Sombke, C. (1991). A survey of rewards for use with teenage children. *Child & Family Behavior Therapy, 13,* 1–12.

House, J. S., Landis, K. R., & Umberson, D. (1988). Social relationships and health. *Science, 241,* 540–545.

Howard, I. P. (2002). Depth perception. In S. Yantis & H. Pashler (Eds.), *Stevens' handbook of experimental psychology: Vol. 1. Sensation and perception* (3rd ed., pp. 77–120). New York: Wiley.

Howard, M. O., Brown, S. E., Garland, E. L., Perron, B. E., & Vaughn, M. G. (2011). Inhalant use and inhalant use disorders in the United States. *Addiction Science & Clinical Practice, 6,* 18–31.

Hoyert, D. L., & Xu, J. (2012). Deaths: Preliminary data for 2011. *National Vital Statistics Reports, 61,* 1–51.

Hubel, D. H. (1988). *Eye, brain, and vision.* New York: Freeman.

Hubel, D. H., & Wiesel, T. N. (1962). Receptive fields, binocular interaction and functional architecture in the cat's visual cortex. *Journal of Physiology, 160,* 106–154.

Hubel, D. H., & Wiesel, T. N. (1998). Early exploration of the visual cortex. *Neuron, 20,* 401–412.

Huesmann, L. R., Moise-Titus, J., Podolski, C.-L., & Eron, L. D. (2003). Longitudinal relations between children's exposure to TV violence and their aggressive and violent behavior in young adulthood: 1977–1992. *Developmental Psychology, 39,* 201–221.

Hull, C. L. (1930). Knowledge and purpose as habit mechanisms. *Psychological Review, 37,* 511–525.

Hunsley, J., & Di Giulio, G. (2002). Dodo bird, phoenix, or urban legend? The question of psychotherapy equivalence. *Scientific Review of Mental Health Practice, 1,* 13–24.

Hunt, E. B. (2011). *Human intelligence.* New York: Cambridge University Press.

Hunt, M. (1959). *The natural history of love.* New York: Knopf.

Hunter, J. E., & Hunter, R. F. (1984). Validity and utility of alternative predictors of job performance. *Psychological Bulletin, 96,* 72–98.

Hussey, E., & Safford, A. (2009). Perception of facial expression in somatosensory cortex supports simulationist models. *The Journal of Neuroscience, 29*(2), 301–302.

Huxley, A. (1932). *Brave new world.* London: Chatto and Windus.

Huxley, A. (1954). *The doors of perception.* New York: Harper & Row.

Hyde, J. S. (2005). The gender similarities hypothesis. *American Psychologist, 60*(6), 581–592.

Hyman, I. E., Jr., Boss, S. M., Wise, B. M., McKenzie, K. E., & Caggiano, J. M. (2010). Did you see the unicycling clown? Inattentional blindness while walking and talking on a cell phone. *Applied Cognitive Psychology, 24*(5), 597–607.

Hyman, I. E., Jr., & Pentland, J. (1996). The role of mental imagery in the creation of false childhood memories. *Journal of Memory and Language, 35,* 101–117.

Hypericum Depression Trial Study Group. (2002). Effect of *Hypericum perforatum* (St. John's wort) in major depressive disorder: A randomized controlled trial. *Journal of the American Medical Association, 287,* 1807–1814.

Iacoboni, M. (2009). Imitation, empathy, and mirror neurons. *Annual Review of Psychology, 60,* 653–670.

Imbo, I., & LeFevre, J.-A. (2009). Cultural differences in complex addition: Efficient Chinese versus adaptive Belgians and Canadians. *Journal of Experimental Psychology: Learning, Memory, and Cognition, 35,* 1465–1476.

Inciardi, J. A. (2001). *The war on drugs III.* New York: Allyn & Bacon.

Ingvar, M., Ambros-Ingerson, J., Davis, M., Granger, R., Kessler, M., Rogers, G. A., . . . Lynch, G. (1997). Enhancement by an ampakine of memory encoding in humans. *Experimental Neurology, 146,* 553–559.

Inui, A. (2001). Ghrelin: An orexigenic and somatotrophic signal from the stomach. *Nature Reviews Neuroscience, 2,* 551–560.

Irvine, J. T. (1978). Wolof "magical thinking": Culture and conservation revisited. *Journal of Cross-Cultural Psychology, 9,* 300–310.

Isaacowitz, D. M. (2012). Mood regulation in real time: Age differences in the role of looking. *Current Directions in Psychological Science, 21*(4), 237–242. doi:10.1177/0963721412448651

Isaacowitz, D. M., & Blanchard-Fields, F. (2012). Linking process and outcome in the study of emotion and aging. *Perspectives on Psychological Science, 7*(1), 3–17. doi:10.1177/1745691611424750

Isenberg, D. J. (1986). Group polarization: A critical review and meta-analysis. *Journal of Personality and Social Psychology, 50*(6), 1141–1151. doi:10.1037/0022-3514.50.6.1141

Ittelson, W. H. (1952). *The Ames demonstrations in perception.* Princeton, NJ: Princeton University Press.

Izard, C. E. (1971). *The face of emotion.* New York: Appleton-Century-Crofts.

Jablensky, A. (1997). The 100-year epidemiology of schizophrenia. *Schizophrenia Research, 28,* 111–125.

Jacobs, B. L. (1994). Serotonin, motor activity, and depression-related disorders. *American Scientist, 82,* 456–463.

Jacobson, T., & Hoffman, V. (1997). Children's attachment representations: Longitudinal relations to school behavior and academic competency in middle childhood and adolescence. *Developmental Psychology, 33,* 703–710.

James, W. (1890). *The principles of psychology.* Cambridge, MA: Harvard University Press.

Jamieson, J. P., Koslov, K., Nock, M. K., & Mendes, W. B. (2013). Experiencing discrimination increases risk-taking. *Psychological Science, 24,* 131–139.

Jamieson, J. P., Mendes, W. B., & Nock, M. K. (2013). Improving acute stress responses: The power of reappraisal. *Current Directions in Psychological Science, 22*(1), 51–56.

Jamieson, J. P., Nock, M. K., & Mendes, W. B. (2013). Changing the conceptualization of stress in social anxiety disorder: Affective and physiological consequences. *Clinical Psychological Science.* Advance online publication. doi:10.1177/2167702613482119

Jamison, K. R. (1995). *An unquiet mind: A memoir of moods and madness.* New York: Random House.

Janicak, P. G., Dowd, S. M., Martis, B., Alam, D., Beedle, D., Krasuski, J., . . . Viana, M. (2002). Repetitive transcranial magnetic stimulation versus electroconvulsive therapy for major depression: Preliminary results of a randomized trial. *Biological Psychiatry, 51,* 659–667.

Janis, I. L. (1982). *Groupthink: Scientific studies of policy decisions and fiascoes.* Boston: Houghton-Mifflin.

Jarvella, R. J. (1970). Effects of syntax on running memory span for connected discourse. *Psychonomic Science, 19,* 235–236.

Jarvella, R. J. (1971). Syntactic processing of connected speech. *Journal of Verbal Learning and Verbal Behavior, 10,* 409–416.

Jaynes, J. (1976). *The origin of consciousness in the breakdown of the bicameral mind.* London: Allen Lane.

Jenkins, J. G., & Dallenbach, K. M. (1924). Obliviscence during sleep and waking. *American Journal of Psychology, 35,* 605–612.

John, O. P., & Srivastava, S. (1999). The Big Five trait taxonomy: History, measurement, and theoretical perspectives. In L. A. Pervin & O. P. John (Eds.), *Handbook of personality: Theory and research* (2nd ed., pp. 102–138). New York: Guilford Press.

Johnson, C. A., Xiao, L., Palmer, P., Sun, P., Wang, Q., Wei, Y. L., . . . Bechara, A. (2008). Affective decision-making deficits, linked to dysfunctional ventromedial prefrontal cortex, revealed in 10th grade Chinese adolescent binge drinkers. *Neuropsychologia, 46,* 714–726.

Johnson, D. H. (1980). The relationship between spike rate and synchrony in responses of auditory-nerve fibers to single tones. *Journal of the Acoustical Society of America, 68,* 1115–1122.

Johnson, D. R., & Wu, J. (2002). An empirical test of crisis, social selection, and role explanations of the relationship between marital disruption and psychological distress: A pooled time-series analysis of four-wave panel data. *Journal of Marriage and the Family, 64,* 211–224.

Johnson, J. S., & Newport, E. L. (1989). Critical period effects in second language learning: The influence of maturational state on the acquisition of English as a second language. *Cognitive Psychology, 21,* 60–99.

Johnson, K. (2002). Neural basis of haptic perception. In H. Pashler & S. Yantis (Eds.), *Stevens' handbook of experimental psychology: Vol. 1. Sensation and perception* (3rd ed., pp. 537–583). New York: Wiley.

Johnson, M. K., Hashtroudi, S., & Lindsay, D. S. (1993). Source monitoring. *Psychological Bulletin, 114,* 3–28.

Johnson, S. L., Cuellar, A. K., & Miller, C. (2009). Unipolar and bipolar depression: A comparison of clinical phenomenology, biological vulnerability, and psychosocial predictors. In I. H. Gottlib & C. L. Hammen (Eds.), *Handbook of depression* (2nd ed., pp. 142–162). New York: Guilford Press.

Johnson, S. L., Cuellar, A. K., Ruggiero, C., Winnett-Perman, C., Goodnick, P., White, R., & Miller, I. (2008). Life events as predictors of mania and depression in bipolar 1 disorder. *Journal of Abnormal Psychology, 117,* 268–277.

Johnson, S. L., & Miller, I. (1997). Negative life events and time to recover from episodes of bipolar disorder. *Journal of Abnormal Psychology, 106,* 449–457.

Jonas, E., Graupmann, V., Kayser, D. N., Zanna, M., Traut-Mattausch, E., & Frey, D. (2009). Culture, self, and the emergence of reactance: Is there a "universal" freedom? *Journal of Experimental Social Psychology, 45,* 1068–1080.

Jones, B. C., Little, A. C., Penton-Voak, I. S., Tiddeman, B. P., Burt, D. M., & Perrett, D. I. (2001). Facial symmetry and judgements of apparent health: Support for a "good genes" explanation of the attractiveness–symmetry relationship. *Evolution and Human Behavior, 22,* 417–429.

Jones, E. E., & Harris, V. A. (1967). The attribution of attitudes. *Journal of Experimental Social Psychology, 3,* 1–24.

Jones, E. E., & Nisbett, R. E. (1972). The actor and the observer: Divergent perceptions of the causes of behavior. In E. E. Jones, D. E. Kanouse, H. H. Kelley, R. E. Nisbett, S. Valins, & B. Weiner (Eds.), *Attribution: Perceiving the causes of behavior* (pp. 79–94). Morristown, NJ: General Learning Press.

Jones, S. S. (2007). Imitation in infancy. *Psychological Science, 18*(7), 593–599.

Jonsson, H., & Hougaard, E. (2008). Group cognitive behavioural therapy for obsessive-compulsive disorder: A systematic review and meta-analysis. *Acta Psychiatrica Scandinavica, 117,* 1–9.

Jordan, S. A., Cunningham, D. G., & Marles, R. J. (2010). Assessment of herbal medicinal products: Challenges and opportunities to increase the knowledge base for safety assessment. *Toxicology and Applied Pharmacology, 243,* 198–216.

Judd, L. L. (1997). The clinical course of unipolar major depressive disorders. *Archives of General Psychiatry, 54,* 989–991.

Jurewicz, I., Owen, R. J., & O'Donovan, M. C. (2001). Searching for susceptibility genes in schizophrenia. *European Neuropsychopharmacology, 11,* 395–398.

Kaas, J. H. (1991). Plasticity of sensory and motor maps in adult mammals. *Annual Review of Neuroscience, 14,* 137–167.

Kahneman, D., Krueger, A. B., Schkade, D. A., Schwarz, N., & Stone, A. A. (2004). A survey method for characterizing daily life experience: The day reconstruction method. *Science, 306,* 1776–1780.

Kahneman, D., & Tversky, A. (1973). On the psychology of prediction. *Psychological Review, 80,* 237–251.

Kamin, L. J. (1959). The delay-of-punishment gradient. *Journal of Comparative and Physiological Psychology, 52,* 434–437.

Kan, P. F., & Kohnert, K. (2008). Fast mapping by bilingual preschool children. *Journal of Child Language, 35,* 495–514.

Kandel, E. R. (2000). Nerve cells and behavior. In E. R. Kandel, G. H. Schwartz, & T. M. Jessell (Eds.), *Principles of neural science* (pp. 19–35). New York. McGraw-Hill.

Kandel, E. R. (2006). *In search of memory: The emergence of a new science of mind.* New York: Norton.

Kang, S. H. K., McDermott, K. B., & Roediger, H. L. III. (2007). Test format and corrective feedback modify the effect of testing on long-term retention. *European Journal of Cognitive Psychology, 19,* 528–558.

Kanwisher, N., McDermott, J., & Chun, M. M. (1997). The fusiform face area: A module in human extrastriate cortex specialized for face perception. *The Journal of Neuroscience, 17,* 4302–4311.

Kanwisher, N., & Yovel, G. (2006). The fusiform face area: A cortical region specialized for the perception of faces. *Philosophical Transactions of the Royal Society (B), 361,* 2109–2128.

Kaplan, R. M., & Stone, A. A. (2013). Bringing the laboratory and clinic to the community: Mobile technologies for health promotion and disease prevention. *Annual Review of Psychology, 64,* 471–498.

Kapur, S., Craik, F. I. M., Tulving, E., Wilson, A. A., Houle, S., & Brown, G. M. (1994). Neuroanatomical correlates of encoding in episodic memory: Levels of processing effects. *Proceedings of the National Academy of Sciences, USA, 91,* 2008–2011.

Karlins, M., Coffman, T. L., & Walters, G. (1969). On the fading of social stereotypes: Studies in three generations of college students. *Journal of Personality and Social Psychology, 13,* 1–16.

Karney, B. R., & Bradbury, T. N. (1995). The longitudinal course of marital quality and stability: A review of theory, methods, and research. *Psychological Bulletin, 118,* 3–34.

Karow, A., Pajonk, F. G., Reimer, J., Hirdes, F., Osterwald, C., Naber, D., & Moritz, S. (2007). The dilemma of insight into illness in schizophrenia: Self- and expert-rated insight and quality of life. *European Archives of Psychiatry and Clinical Neuroscience, 258,* 152–159.

Karpicke, J. D. (2012). Retrieval-based learning: Active retrieval promotes meaningful learning. *Current Directions in Psychological Science, 21,* 157–163.

Karpicke, J. D., & Blunt, J. R. (2011). Retrieval practice produces more learning than elaborative studying with concept mapping. *Science, 331,* 772–775.

Kasser, T., & Sharma, Y. S. (1999). Reproductive freedom, educational equality, and females' preference for resource-acquisition characteristics in mates. *Psychological Science, 10,* 374–377.

Katon, W. (1994). Primary care—psychiatry panic disorder management. In B. E. Wolfe & J. D. Maser (Eds.), *Treatment of panic disorder: A consensus development conference* (pp. 41–56). Washington, DC: American Psychiatric Press.

Katz, D., & Braly, K. (1933). Racial stereotypes of one hundred college students. *Journal of Abnormal and Social Psychology, 28,* 280–290.

Kaufman, A. S. (2001). WAIS-III IQs, Horn's theory, and generational changes from young adulthood to old age. *Intelligence, 29,* 131–167.

Kaufman, L. (2009, January 30). Utilities turn their customers green, with envy. *New York Times.* Retrieved from http://www.nytimes.com/2009/01/31/science/earth/31compete.html

Kawakami, K., Dovidio, J. F., Moll, J., Hermsen, S., & Russin, A. (2000). Just say no (to stereotyping): Effects of training in the negation of stereotypic associations on stereotype activation. *Journal of Personality and Social Psychology, 78,* 871–888.

Kazdin, A. E., & Blasé, S. L. (2011). Rebooting psychotherapy research and practice to reduce the burden of mental illness. *Perspectives on Psychological Science, 6,* 21–37.

Keane, T. M., Marshall, A. D., & Taft, C. T. (2006). Posttraumatic stress disorder: Etiology, epidemiology, and treatment outcome. *Annual Review of Clinical Psychology, 2,* 161–197.

Keefe, F. J., Lumley, M., Anderson, T., Lynch, T., & Carson, K. L. (2001). Pain and emotion: New research directions. *Journal of Clinical Psychology, 57,* 587–607.

Kelley, H. H. (1983). Love and commitment. In H. H. Kelley, E. Berscheid, A. Christensen, & J. H. Harvey (Eds.), *Close relationships* (pp. 265–314). New York: W. H. Freeman and Company.

Kelly, G. (1955). *The psychology of personal constructs.* New York: Norton.

Keltner, D. (1995). Signs of appeasement: Evidence for the distinct displays of embarrassment, amusement, and shame. *Journal of Personality and Social Psychology, 68,* 441–454.

Keltner, D., & Buswell, B. N. (1996). Evidence for the distinctness of embarrassment, shame, and guilt: A study of recalled antecedents and facial expressions of emotion. *Cognition and Emotion, 10,* 155–171.

Keltner, D., & Haidt, J. (1999). Social functions of emotions at four levels of analysis. *Cognition and Emotion, 13,* 505–521.

Keltner, D., & Harker, L. A. (1998). The forms and functions of the nonverbal signal of shame. In P. Gilbert & B. Andrews (Eds.), *Shame: Interpersonal behavior, psychopathology, and culture* (pp. 78–98). New York: Oxford University Press.

Kenrick, D. T., Sadalla, E. K., Groth, G., & Trost, M. R. (1990). Evolution, traits, and the stages of human courtship: Qualifying the parental investment model. *Journal of Personality, 58,* 97–116.

Kensinger, E. A., Clarke, R. J., & Corkin, S. (2003). What neural correlates underlie successful encoding and retrieval? A functional magnetic resonance imaging study using a divided attention paradigm. *The Journal of Neuroscience, 23,* 2407–2415.

Kensinger, E. A., & Schacter, D. L. (2005). Emotional content and reality monitoring ability: fMRI evidence for the influence of encoding processes. *Neuropsychologia, 43,* 1429–1443.

Kensinger, E. A., & Schacter, D. L. (2006). Amygdala activity is associated with the successful encoding of item, but not source, information for positive and negative stimuli. *The Journal of Neuroscience, 26,* 2564–2570.

Kessler, R. C. (2012). The costs of depression. *Psychiatric Clinics of North America, 35,* 1–14.

Kessler, R. C., Adler, L., Barkley, R., Biederman, J., Connors, C. K., Demler, O., . . . Zaslavsky, A. M. (2006). The prevalence and correlates of adult ADHD in the United States: Results from the National Comorbidity Study Replication. *American Journal of Psychiatry, 163,* 716–723.

Kessler, R. C., Angermeyer, M., Anthony, J. C., deGraaf, R., Demyittenaere, K., Gasquet, I., . . . Üstün, T. B. (2007). Lifetime prevalence and age-of-onset distributions of mental disorders in the World Health Organization World Mental Health Survey Initiative. *World Psychiatry, 6,* 168–176.

Kessler, R. C., Berglund, P., Demler, M. A., Jin, R., Merikangas, K. R., & Walters, E. E. (2005). Lifetime prevalence and age-of-onset distributions of *DSM–IV* disorders in the National Comorbidity Survey replication. *Archives of General Psychiatry, 62,* 593–602.

Kessler, R. C., Chiu, W. T., Jin, R., Ruscio, A. M., Shear, K., & Walters, E. E. (2006). The epidemiology of panic attacks, panic disorder, and agoraphobia in the National Comorbidity Survey Replication. *Archives of General Psychiatry, 63,* 415–424.

Kessler, R. C., Demler, O., Frank, R. G., Olfson, M., Pincus, H. A., Walters, E. E., . . . Zaslavsky, A. M. (2005). Prevalence and treatment of mental disorders, 1990 to 2003. *New England Journal of Medicine, 352*(24), 2515–2523.

Kessler, R. C., Petukhova, M., Sampson, N. A., Zaslavsky, A. M., & Wittchen, H. U. (2012). Twelve-month and lifetime prevalence and lifetime morbid risk of anxiety and mood disorders in the United States. *International Journal of Methods in Psychiatric Research, 21*(3), 169–184.

Kessler, R. C., Soukup, J., Davis, R. B., Foster, D. F., Wilkey, S. A., Van Rompay, M. I., & Eisenberg, D. M. (2001). The use of complementary and alternative therapies to treat anxiety and depression in the United States. *American Journal of Psychiatry, 158,* 289–294.

Kessler, R. C., & Üstün, T. B. (Eds.) (2008). *The WHO Mental Health surveys: Global perspectives on the epidemiology of mental health.* Cambridge, England: Cambridge University Press.

Khalid, N., Atkins, M., Tredget, J., Giles, M., Champney-Smith, K., & Kirov, G. (2008). The effectiveness of electroconvulsive therapy in treatment-resistant depression: A naturalistic study. *The Journal of ECT, 24,* 141–145.

Khan, R. M., Luk, C.-H., Flinker, A., Aggarwal, A., Lapid, H., Haddad, R., & Sobel, N. (2007). Predicting odor pleasantness from odorant structure: Pleasantness as a reflection of the physical world. *Journal of Neuroscience, 27,* 10015–10023.

Kiecolt-Glaser, J. K., Garner, W., Speicher, C., Penn, G., & Glaser, R. (1984). Psychosocial modifiers of immunocompetence in medical students. *Psychosomatic Medicine, 46,* 7–14.

Kiefer, H. M. (2004). *Americans unruffled by animal testing.* Retrieved August 8, 2009, from http://www.gallup.com/poll/11767/Americans-Unruffled-Animal-Testing.aspx

Kiehl, K. A., Smith, A. M., Hare, R. D., Mendrek, A., Forster, B. B., Brink, J., & Liddle, P. F. (2001). Limbic abnormalities in affective processing by criminal psychopaths as revealed by functional magnetic resonance imaging. *Biological Psychiatry, 50,* 677–684.

Kihlstrom, J. F. (1985). Hypnosis. *Annual Review of Psychology, 36,* 385–418.

Kihlstrom, J. F. (1987). The cognitive unconscious. *Science, 237,* 1445–1452.

Kihlstrom, J. F., Beer, J. S., & Klein, S. B. (2002). Self and identity as memory. In M. R. Leary & J. P. Tangney (Eds.), *Handbook of self and identity* (pp. 68–90). New York: Guilford Press.

Killingsworth, M. A., & Gilbert, D. T. (2010). A wandering mind is an unhappy mind. *Science, 330,* 932.

Kim, G., Walden, T. A., & Knieps, L. J. (2010). Impact and characteristics of positive and fearful emotional messages during infant social referencing. *Infant Behavior and Development, 33,* 189–195.

Kim, K., & Smith, P. K. (1998). Childhood stress, behavioural symptoms and mother–daughter pubertal development. *Journal of Adolescence, 21,* 231–240.

Kim, U. K., Jorgenson, E., Coon, H., Leppert, M., Risch, N., & Drayna, D. (2003). Positional cloning of the human quantitive trait locus underlying taste sensitivity to phenylthiocarbamide. *Science, 299,* 1221–1225.

Kinney, D. A. (1993). From nerds to normals—the recovery of identity among adolescents from middle school to high school. *Sociology of Education, 66,* 21–40.

Kirchner, W. H., & Towne, W. F. (1994). The sensory basis of the honeybee's dance language. *Scientific American, 270*(6), 74–80.

Kirsch, I., Cardena, E., Derbyshire, S., Dienes, Z., Heap, M., Kallio, S., . . . Whalley, M. (2011). Definitions of hypnosis and hypnotizability and their relation to suggestion and suggestibility: A consensus statement. *Contemporary Hypnosis and Integrative Therapy, 28,* 107–115.

Kirwan, C. B., Bayley, P. J., Galvan, V. V., & Squire, L. R. (2008). Detailed recollection of remote autobiographical memory after damage to the medial temporal lobe. *Proceedings of the National Academy of Sciences, USA, 105,* 2676–2680.

Kitayama, S., Duffy, S., Kawamura, T., & Larsen, J. T. (2003). Perceiving an object and its context in different cultures: A cultural look at the new look. *Psychological Science, 14,* 201–206.

Kitayama, S., & Uskul, A. K. (2011). Culture, mind, and the brain: Current evidence and future directions. *Annual Review of Psychology, 62,* 419–449.

Klein, C. T. F., & Helweg-Larsen, M. (2002). Perceived control and the optimistic bias: A meta-analytic review. *Psychology and Health, 17,* 437–446.

Klein, S. B. (2004). The cognitive neuroscience of knowing one's self. In M. Gazzaniga (Ed.), *The cognitive neurosciences* (3rd ed., pp. 1007–1089). Cambridge, MA: MIT Press.

Klein, S. B., Robertson, T. E., & Delton, A. W. (2011). The future-orientation of memory: Planning as a key component mediating the high levels of recall found with survival processing. *Memory, 19,* 121–139.

Klinger, E. (1975). Consequences of commitment to and disengagement from incentives. *Psychological Review, 82,* 1–25.

Klinger, E. (1977). *Meaning and void.* Minneapolis: University of Minnesota Press.

Klonsky, E. D. (2011). Non-suicidal self-injury in United States adults: Prevalence, sociodemographics, topography, and functions. *Psychological Medicine, 41,* 1981–1986.

Klump, K. L., & Culbert, K. M. (2007). Molecular genetic studies of eating disorders: Current status and future directions. *Current Directions in Psychological Science, 16*(1), 37–41.

Klüver, H., & Bucy, P. C. (1937). "Psychic blindness" and other symptoms following bilateral temporary lobectomy in rhesus monkeys. *American Journal of Physiology, 119,* 352–353.

Knowlton, B. J., Ramus, S. J., & Squire, L. R. (1992). Intact artificial grammar learning in amnesia: Dissociation of classification learning and explicit memory for specific instances. *Psychological Science, 3,* 173–179.

Knutson, B., Wolkowitz, O. M., Cole, S. W., Chan, T., Moore, E. A., Johnson, R. C., & Reus, V. I. (1998). Selective alteration of personality and social behavior by serotonergic intervention. *American Journal of Psychiatry, 155,* 373–379.

Koffka, K. (1935). *Principles of Gestalt psychology.* New York: Harcourt, Brace and World.

Kohlberg, L. (1958). *The development of modes of thinking and choices in years 10 to 16.* Unpublished doctoral dissertation, University of Chicago.

Kohlberg, L. (1963). Development of children's orientation towards a moral order (Part I). Sequencing in the development of moral thought. *Vita Humana, 6,* 11–36.

Kohlberg, L. (1986). A current statement on some theoretical issues. In S. Modgil & C. Modgil (Eds.), *Lawrence Kohlberg: Concensus and controversy* (pp. 485–546). Philadelphia: Falmer.

Kohler, P. K., Manhart, L. E., & Lafferty, E. (2008). Abstinence-only and comprehensive sex education and the initiation of sexual activity and teen pregnancy. *Journal of Adolescent Health, 42,* 344–351.

Kolb, B., & Whishaw, I. Q. (2003). *Fundamentals of human neuropsychology* (5th ed.). New York: Worth Publishers.

Kolbert, E. (2009, July 20). XXXL. *The New Yorker,* pp. 73–77.

Kolotkin, R. L., Meter, K., & Williams, G. R. (2001). Quality of life and obesity. *Obesity Reviews, 2,* 219–229.

Komter, A. (2010). The evolutionary origins of human generosity. *International Sociology, 25*(3), 443–464.

Kosaba, S. C., Maddi, S. R., & Kahn, S. (1979). Hardiness and health: A prospective study. *Journal of Personality and Social Psychology, 42,* 168–177.

Kosslyn, S. M., Alpert, N. M., Thompson, W. L., Chabris, C. F., Rauch, S. L., & Anderson, A. K. (1993). Visual mental imagery activates topographically organized visual cortex: PET investigations. *Journal of Cognitive Neuroscience, 5,* 263–287.

Kosslyn, S. M., Thompson, W. L., Constantini-Ferrando, M. F., Alpert, N. M., & Spiegel, D. (2000). Hypnotic visual illusion alters color processing in the brain. *American Journal of Psychiatry, 157,* 1279–1284.

Kovalevskaya, S. (1978). *A Russian childhood*. New York: Springer-Verlag.

Kraemer, H. C., Shrout, P. E., & Rubio-Stipec, M. (2007). Developing the *Diagnostic and Statistical Manual–V*: What will "statistical" mean in *DSM–V*? *Social Psychiatry and Psychiatric Epidemiology, 42*, 259–267.

Krantz, D. S., & McCeney, M. K. (2002). Effects of psychological and social factors on organic disease: A critical assessment of research on coronary heart disease. *Annual Review of Psychology, 53*, 341–369.

Kraus, N., & Chandrasekaran, B. (2010). Music training for the development of auditory skills. *Nature Reviews Neuroscience, 11*, 599–605.

Kravitz, D. J., Saleem, K. S., Baker, C. I., & Mishkin, M. (2011). A new neural framework for visuospatial processing. *Nature Reviews Neuroscience, 12*, 217–230.

Kravitz, D. J., Saleem, K. S., Baker, C. I., Ungerleider, L. G., & Mishkin, M. (2013). The ventral visual pathway: An expanded neural framework for the processing of object quality. *Trends in Cognitive Sciences, 17*, 26–49.

Kravitz, R. L., Epstein, R. M., Feldman, M. D., Franz, C. E., Azari, R., Wilkes, M. S., . . . Franks, P. (2005). Influence of patients' requests for direct-to-consumer advertised antidepressants: A randomized controlled trial. *Journal of the American Medical Association, 293*, 1995–2002.

Kreider, T. (2013, January 20). You are going to die. *New York Times*. Retrieved from http://opinionator.blogs.nytimes.com/2013/01/20/you-are-going-to-die/

Krings, T., Topper, R., Foltys, H., Erberich, S., Sparing, R., Willmes, K., & Thron, A. (2000). Cortical activation patterns during complex motor tasks in piano players and control subjects. A functional magnetic resonance imaging study. *Neuroscience Letters, 278*, 189–193.

Kristensen, P., & Bjerkedal, T. (2007). Explaining the relation between birth order and intelligence. *Science, 316*, 1717.

Kroeze, W. K., & Roth, B. L. (1998). The molecular biology of serotonin receptors: Therapeutic implications for the interface of mood and psychosis. *Biological Psychiatry, 44*, 1128–1142.

Kruk, M. R., Halasz, J., Meelis, W., & Haller, J. (2004). Fast positive feedback between the adrenocortical stress response and a brain mechanism involved in aggressive behavior. *Behavioral Neuroscience, 118*, 1062–1070.

Kubovy, M. (1981). Concurrent-pitch segregation and the theory of indispensable attributes. In M. Kubovy & J. R. Pomerantz (Eds.), *Perceptual organization* (pp. 55–96). Hillsdale, NJ: Erlbaum.

Kuhl, B. A., Dudukovic, N. M., Kahn, I., & Wagner, A. D. (2007). Decreased demands on cognitive control reveal the neural processing benefits of forgetting. *Nature Neuroscience, 10*, 908–917.

Kuhl, P. K., & Meltzoff, A. N. (1996). Infant vocalizations in response to speech: Vocal imitation and developmental change. *The Journal of the Acoustical Society of America, 100*(4), 2425. doi:10.1121/1.417951

Kunda, Z. (1990). The case for motivated reasoning. *Psychological Bulletin, 108*, 480–498.

Kunz, P. R., & Woolcott, M. (1976). Season's greetings: From my status to yours. *Social Science Research, 5*, 269–278.

Kvavilashvili, L., Mirani, J., Schlagman, S., Foley, K., & Kornbrot, D. E. (2009). Consistency of flashbulb memories of September 11 over long delays: Implications for consolidation and wrong time slice hypotheses. *Journal of Memory and Language, 61*, 556–572.

LaBar, K. S., & Phelps, E. A. (1998). Arousal-mediated memory consolidation: Role of the medial temporal lobe in humans. *Psychological Science, 9*, 490–493.

Labrie, V., Pai, S., & Petronis, A. (2012). Epigenetics of major psychosis: Progress, problems, and perspectives. *Trends in Genetics, 28*, 427–435.

Lachman, R., Lachman, J. L., & Butterfield, E. C. (1979). *Cognitive psychology and information processing: An introduction*. Hillsdale, NJ: Erlbaum.

Lackner, J. R., & DiZio, P. (2005). Vestibular, proprioceptive, and haptic contributions to spatial orientation. *Annual Review of Psychology, 56*, 115–147.

LaFraniere, S. (2007, July 4). In Mauritania, seeking to end an overfed ideal. *New York Times*. Retrieved from http://www.nytimes.com/2007/07/04/world/africa/04mauritania.html?pagewanted=all

Lahkan, S. E., & Kirchgessner, A. (2012, March 12). Chronic traumatic encephalopathy: The dangers of getting "dinged." *Springer Plus, 1*(2) doi:10.1186/2193-1801-1-2

Lai, Y., & Siegal, J. (1999). Muscle atonia in REM sleep. In B. Mallick & S. Inoue (Eds.), *Rapid eye movement sleep* (pp. 69–90). New Delhi, India: Narosa Publishing House.

Lake, J. (2009). Natural products used to treat depressed mood as monotherapies and adjuvants to antidepressants: A review of the evidence. *Psychiatric Times, 26*, 1–6.

Lakin, J. M. (2013). Sex differences in reasoning abilities: Surprising evidence that male–female ratios in the tails of the quantitative reasoning distribution have increased. *Intelligence, 41*(4), 263–274. doi:10.1016/j.intell.2013.04.004

Lam, L. L., Emberly, E., Fraser, H. B., Neumann, S. M., Chen, E., Miller, G. E., . . . Kobor, M. S. (2012). Factors underlying variable DNA methylation in a human community cohort. *Proceedings of the National Academy of Sciences, USA, 109*(Suppl. 2), 17253–17260.

Lamb, M. E., Thompson, R. A., Gardner, W., & Charnov, E. L. (1985). *Infant–mother attachment: The origins and developmental significance of individual differences in Strange Situation behavior*. Hillsdale, NJ: Erlbaum.

Landauer, T. K., & Bjork, R. A. (1978). Optimum rehearsal patterns and name learning. In M. M. Gruneberg, P. E. Morris, & R. N. Sykes (Eds.), *Practical aspects of memory* (pp. 625–632). New York: Academic Press.

Langer, E. J., & Abelson, R. P. (1974). A patient by any other name. . . . Clinician group difference in labeling bias. *Journal of Consulting and Clinical Psychology, 42*, 4–9.

Langleben, D. D., Loughead, J. W., Bilker, W. B., Ruparel, K., Childress, A. R., Busch, S. I., & Gur, R. C. (2005). Telling truth from lie in individual subjects with fast event-related fMRI. *Human Brain Mapping, 26*, 262–272.

Langlois, J. H., Ritter, J. M., Casey, R. J., & Sawin, D. B. (1995). Infant attractiveness predicts maternal behaviors and attitudes. *Developmental Psychology, 31*, 464–472.

LaPierre, S., Boyer, R., Desjardins, S., Dubé, M., Lorrain, D., Préville, M., & Brassard, J. (2012). Daily hassles, physical illness, and sleep problems in older adults with wishes to die. *International Psychogeriatrics, 24*, 243–252.

Lareau, A. (2003). *Unequal childhoods: Class, race, and family life*. Berkeley: University of California Press.

Larrick, R. P., Timmerman, T. A., Carton, A. M., & Abrevaya, J. (2011). Temper, temperature, and temptation: Heat-related retaliation in baseball. *Psychological Science, 22*(4), 423–428. doi:10.1177/0956797611399292

Larsen, S. F. (1992). Potential flashbulbs: Memories of ordinary news as baseline. In E. Winograd & U. Neisser (Eds.), *Affect and accuracy in recall: Studies of "flashbulb memories"* (pp. 32–64). New York: Cambridge University Press.

Larson, R., & Richards, M. H. (1991). Daily companionship in late childhood and early adolescence—changing developmental contexts. *Child Development, 62*, 284–300.

Latané, B., & Nida, S. (1981). Ten years of research on group size and helping. *Psychological Bulletin, 89*(2), 308–324.

Lattal, K. A. (2010). Delayed reinforcement of operant behavior. *Journal of the Experimental Analysis of Behavior, 93*, 129–139.

Lashley, K. S. (1960). In search of the engram. In F. A. Beach, D. O. Hebb, C. T. Morgan, & H. W. Nissen (Eds.), *The neuropsychology of Lashley* (pp. 478–505). New York: McGraw-Hill.

Laupa, M., & Turiel, E. (1986). Children's conceptions of adult and peer authority. *Child Development, 57*, 405–412.

Lawrence, N. S., Jollant, F., O'Daly, O., Zelaya, F., & Phillips, M. L. (2009). Distinct roles of prefrontal cortical subregions in the Iowa Gambling Task. *Cerebral Cortex, 19*, 1134–1143.

Lawton, M. P., Kleban, M. H., Rajagopal, D., & Dean, J. (1992). The dimensions of affective experience in three age groups. *Psychology and Aging, 7*, 171–184.

Lazarus, R. S. (1984). On the primacy of cognition. *American Psychologist, 39*, 124–129.

Lazarus, R. S., & Folkman, S. (1984). *Stress, appraisal, and coping.* New York: Springer.

Leader, T., Mullen, B., & Abrams, D. (2007). Without mercy: The immediate impact of group size on lynch mob atrocity. *Personality and Social Psychology Bulletin, 33*(10), 1340–1352.

Leary, M. R. (1990). Responses to social exclusion: Social anxiety, jealousy, loneliness, depression, and low self-esteem. *Journal of Social and Clinical Psychology, 9*, 221–229.

Leary, M. R. (2010). Affiliation, acceptance, and belonging: The pursuit of interpersonal connection. In S. T. Fiske, D. T. Gilbert, & G. Lindzey (Eds.), *The handbook of social psychology* (5th ed., Vol. 2, pp. 864–897). New York: Wiley.

Leary, M. R., & Baumeister, R. F. (2000). The nature and function of self-esteem: Sociometer theory. In M. P. Zanna (Ed.), *Advances in experimental social psychology* (Vol. 32, pp. 1–62). San Diego: Academic Press.

Leary, M. R., Britt, T. W., Cutlip, W. D., & Templeton, J. L. (1992). Social blushing. *Psychological Bulletin, 112*, 446–460.

Lecky, P. (1945). *Self-consistency: A theory of personality.* New York: Island Press.

Lecrubier, Y., Clerc, G., Didi, R., & Kieser, M. (2002). Efficacy of St. John's wort extract WS 5570 in major depression: A double-blind, placebo-controlled trial. *American Journal of Psychiatry, 159*, 1361–1366.

Lederman, S. J., & Klatzky, R. L. (2009). Haptic perception: A tutorial. *Attention, Perception, & Psychophysics, 71*, 1439–1459.

LeDoux, J. E. (2000). Emotion circuits in the brain. *Annual Review of Neuroscience, 23*, 155–184.

Lee, D. N., & Aronson, E. (1974). Visual proprioceptive control of standing in human infants. *Perception & Psychophysics, 15*, 529–532.

Lee, L., Loewenstein, G., Ariely, D., Hong, J., & Young, J. (2008). If I'm not hot, are you hot or not? Physical-attractiveness evaluations and dating preferences as a function of one's own attractiveness. *Psychological Science, 19*, 669–677.

Lee, M. H., Smyser, C. D., & Shimoy, J. S. (2013). Resting-state fMRI: A review of methods and clinical applications. *American Journal of Neuroradiology, 34*, 1866–1872. doi: 10.3174/ajnr.A3263

Lefcourt, H. M. (1982). *Locus of control: Current trends in theory and research* (2nd ed.). Hillsdale, NJ: Erlbaum.

Lenton, A. P., & Francesconi, M. (2010). How humans cognitively manage an abundance of mate options. *Psychological Science, 21*(4), 528–533. doi: 10.1177/0956797610364958

Lentz, M. J., Landis, C. A., Rothermel, J., & Shaver, J. L. (1999). Effects of selective slow wave sleep disruption on musculoskeletal pain and fatigue in middle aged women. *Journal of Rheumatology, 26*, 1586–1592.

Leon, D. A., Lawlor, D. A., Clark, H., Batty, G. D., & Macintyre, S. (2009). The association of childhood intelligence with mortality risk from adolescence to middle age: Findings from the Aberdeen children of the 1950s cohort study. *Intelligence, 37*(6), 520–528.

Lepage, M., Ghaffar, O., Nyberg, L., & Tulving, E. (2000). Prefrontal cortex and episodic memory retrieval mode. *Proceedings of the National Academy of Sciences, USA, 97*, 506–511.

Lepper, M. R., Greene, D., & Nisbett, R. E. (1973). Undermining children's intrinsic interest with extrinsic rewards: A test of the "overjustification" hypothesis. *Journal of Personality and Social Psychology, 28*, 129–137.

Lerman, D. (2006). Consumer politeness and complaining behavior. *Journal of Services Marketing, 20*, 92–100.

Lerman, D. C., & Vorndran, C. M. (2002). On the status of knowledge for using punishment: Implications for treating behavior disorders. *Journal of Applied Behavior Analysis, 35*, 4312–4464.

Leung, A. K.-Y., & Cohen, D. (2011). Within- and between-culture variation: Individual differences and the cultural logics of honor, face, and dignity cultures. *Journal of Personality and Social Psychology, 100*(3), 507–526. doi:10.1037/a0022151

Levenson, J. M., & Sweatt, J. D. (2005). Epigenetic mechanisms in memory formation. *Nature Reviews Neuroscience, 6*, 108–118.

Levenson, R. W., Cartensen, L. L., Friesen, W. V., & Ekman, P. (1991). Emotion physiology, and expression in old age. *Psychology and Aging, 6*, 28–35.

Levenson, R. W., Ekman, P., & Friesen, W. V. (1990). Voluntary facial action generates emotion-specific autonomic nervous system activity. *Psychophysiology, 27*, 363–384.

Levenson, R. W., Ekman, P., Heider, K., & Friesen, W. V. (1992). Emotion and automatic nervous system activity in the Minangkabau of West Sumatra. *Journal of Personality and Social Psychology, 62*, 972–988.

Levine, R. V., Norenzayan, A., & Philbrick, K. (2001). Cross-cultural differences in helping strangers. *Journal of Cross-Cultural Psychology, 32*, 543–560.

Lewis, M., & Brooks-Gunn, J. (1979). *Social cognition and the acquisition of self.* New York: Plenum Press.

Lewis, M. B. (2012). Exploring the positive and negative implications of facial feedback. *Emotion, 12*(4), 852–859.

Lewis, M. D., Hibbeln, J. R., Johnson, J. E., Lin, Y. H., Hyun, D. Y., & Loewke, J. D. (2011). Suicide deaths of active duty U. S. military and omega-3 fatty acid status: A case control comparison. *Journal of Clinical Psychiatry, 72*, 1585–1590.

Li, R., Polat, U., Makous, W., & Bavelier, D. (2009). Enhancing the contrast sensitivity function through action video game training. *Nature Neuroscience, 12*, 549–551.

Libet, B. (1985). Unconscious cerebral initiative and the role of conscious will in voluntary action. *Behavioral and Brain Sciences, 8*, 529–566.

Liebenluft, E. (1996). Women with bipolar illness: Clinical and research issues. *American Journal of Psychiatry, 153*, 163–173.

Lieberman, M. D., Inagaki, T. K., Tabibnia, G., & Crockett, M. J. (2011). Subjective responses to emotional stimuli during labeling, reappraisal, and distraction. *Emotion, 11*, 468–480.

Lieberman, M. D., & Rosenthal, R. (2001). Why introverts can't always tell who likes them: Multitasking and nonverbal decoding. *Journal of Personality and Social Psychology, 80*, 294–310.

Lifshitz, M., Aubert Bonn, N., Fischer, A., Kashem, I. R., & Raz, A. (2013). Using suggestion to modulate automatic processes: From Stroop to McGurk and beyond. *Cortex, 49*(2), 463–473. doi:10.1016/j.cortex.2012.08.007

Lilienfeld, S. O. (2007). Psychological treatments that cause harm. *Perspectives on Psychological Science, 2*, 53–70.

Lilienfeld, S. O., Lynn, S. J., & Lohr, J. M. (Eds.) (2003). *Science and pseudoscience in clinical psychology.* New York: Guilford Press.

Lindenberger, U., & Baltes, P. B. (1994). Sensory functioning and intelligence in old age: A strong connection. *Psychology and Aging, 9*(3), 339–355. doi:10.1037/0882-7974.9.3.339

Lindquist, K., & Barrett, L. F. (2008). Constructing emotion: The experience of fear as a conceptual act. *Psychological Science, 19,* 898–903.

Lindquist, S. I., & McLean, J. P. (2011). Daydreaming and its correlates in an educational environment. *Learning and Individual Differences, 21,* 158–167.

Lindstrom, M. (2005). *Brand sense: How to build powerful brands through touch, taste, smell, sight and sound.* London: Kogan Page.

Liou, A. P., Paziuk, M., Luevano, J.-M., Machineni, S., Turnbaugh, P. J., & Kaplan, L. M. (2013). Conserved shifts in the gut microbiota due to gastric bypass reduce host weight and adiposity. *Science Translational Medicine, 5*(178), 178ra41–178ra41.

Little, B. R. (1983). Personal projects: A rationale and method for investigation. *Environment and Behavior, 15,* 273–309.

Liu, D., Diorio, J., Tannenbaum, B., Caldji, C., Francis, D., Freedman, A., . . . Meaney, M. J. (1997). Maternal care, hippocampal glucocorticoid receptors, and hypothalamic–pituitary–adrenal responses to stress. *Science, 277,* 1659–1662.

Liu, D., Wellman, H. M., Tardif, T., & Sabbagh, M. A. (2008). Theory of mind development in Chinese children: A meta-analysis of false belief understanding across cultures and languages. *Developmental Psychology, 44,* 523–531.

Livingstone, M., & Hubel, D. (1988). Segregation of form, color, movement, and depth: Anatomy, physiology, and perception. *Science, 240,* 740–749.

Locksley, A., Ortiz, V., & Hepburn, C. (1980). Social categorization and discriminatory behavior: Extinguishing the minimal intergroup discrimination effect. *Journal of Personality and Social Psychology, 39,* 773–783.

Loehlin, J. C. (1973). Blood group genes and Negro–White ability differences. *Behavior Genetics, 3*(3), 263–270.

Loehlin, J. C. (1992). *Genes and environment in personality development.* Newbury Park, CA: Sage.

Loftus, E. F. (1993). The reality of repressed memories. *American Psychologist, 48,* 518–537.

Loftus, E. F. (2003). Make-believe memories. *American Psychologist, 58,* 867–873.

Loftus, E. F., & Ketchum, K. (1994). *The myth of repressed memory.* New York: St. Martin's Press.

Loftus, E. F., & Pickrell, J. E. (1995). The formation of false memories. *Psychiatric Annals, 25,* 720–725.

Lorenz, K. (1952). *King Solomon's ring.* New York: Crowell.

Lovaas, O. I. (1987). Behavioral treatment and normal educational and intellectual functioning in young autistic children. *Journal of Consulting and Clinical Psychology, 55,* 3–9.

Lozano, B. E., & Johnson, S. L. (2001). Can personality traits predict increases in manic and depressive symptoms? *Journal of Affective Disorders, 63,* 103–111.

Luborsky, L., Rosenthal, R., Diguer, L., Andrusyna, T. P., Berman, J. S., Levitt, J. T., . . . Krause, E. D. (2002). The dodo bird verdict is alive and well—mostly. *Clinical Psychology: Science and Practice, 9,* 2–12.

Luborsky, L., & Singer, B. (1975). Comparative studies of psychotherapies: Is it true that "everyone has won and all must have prizes"? *Archives of General Psychiatry, 32*(8), 995–1008.

Lucas, R. E., Clark, A. E., Georgellis, Y., & Diener, E. (2003). Reexamining adaptation and the set point model of happiness: Reactions to changes in marital status. *Journal of Personality and Social Psychology, 84,* 527–539.

Ludwig, A. M. (1966). Altered states of consciousness. *Archives of General Psychiatry, 15,* 225–234.

Lynn, M., & Shurgot, B. A. (1984). Responses to lonely hearts advertisements: Effects of reported physical attractiveness, physique, and coloration. *Personality and Social Psychology Bulletin, 10,* 349–357.

Lynn, R. (2009). What has caused the Flynn effect? Secular increases in the development quotients of infants. *Intelligence, 37*(1), 16–24.

Lynn, R. (2013). Who discovered the Flynn effect? A review of early studies of the secular increase of intelligence. *Intelligence.* Advance online publication. doi:10.1016/j.intell.2013.03.008

Lyubomirsky, S. (2008). *The how of happiness: A scientific approach to getting the life you want.* New York: Penguin.

Lyubomirsky, S., & Lepper, H. S. (1999). A measure of subjective happiness: Preliminary reliability and construct validation. *Social Indicators Research, 46,* 137–155.

MacDonald, S., Uesiliana, K., & Hayne, H. (2000). Cross-cultural and gender differences in childhood amnesia. *Memory, 8,* 365–376.

Mack, A. H., Franklin, J. E., Jr., & Frances, R. J. (2003). Substance use disorders. In R. E. Hales & S. C. Yudofsky (Eds.), *The American Psychiatric Publishing textbook of clinical psychiatry* (4th ed., pp. 309–377). Washington, DC: American Psychiatric Publishing.

MacLeod, C., & Mathews, A. (2012). Cognitive bias modification approaches to anxiety. *Annual Review of Clinical Psychology, 8,* 189–217.

MacLeod, M. D. (2002). Retrieval-induced forgetting in eyewitness memory: Forgetting as a consequence of remembering. *Applied Cognitive Psychology, 16,* 135–149.

MacLeod, M. D., & Saunders, J. (2008). Retrieval inhibition and memory distortion: Negative consequences of an adaptive process. *Current Directions in Psychological Science, 17,* 26–30.

Macmillan, M. (2000). *An odd kind of fame: Stories of Phineas Gage.* Cambridge, MA: MIT Press.

Macmillan, N. A., & Creelman, C. D. (2005). *Detection theory.* Mahwah, NJ: Erlbaum.

Maddi, S. R., Harvey, R. H., Khoshaba, D. M., Fazel, M., & Resurreccion, N. (2009). Hardiness training facilitates performance in college. *The Journal of Positive Psychology, 4,* 566–577.

Maddi, S. R., Kahn, S., & Maddi, K. L. (1998). The effectiveness of hardiness training. *Consulting Psychology Journal: Practice and Research, 50,* 78–86.

Madigan, S., Atkinson, L., Laurin, K., & Benoit, D. (2013). Attachment and internalizing behavior in early childhood: A meta-analysis. *Developmental Psychology, 49*(4), 672–689. doi:10.1037/a0028793

Maes, M. (1995). Evidence for an immune response in major depression: A review and hypothesis. *Progress in Neuro-Psychopharmacology and Biological Psychiatry, 19,* 11–38.

Mahon, B. Z., Anzellotti, S., Schwarzbach, J., Zampini, M., & Caramazza, A. (2009). Category-specific organization in the human brain does not require visual experience. *Neuron, 63,* 397–405.

Mahon, B. Z., & Caramazza, A. (2009). Concepts and categories: A cognitive neuropsychological perspective. *Cognitive Neuropsychology, 60,* 27–51.

Maier, S. F., & Watkins, L. R. (1998). Cytokines for psychologists: Implications of bidirectional immune-to-brain communication for understanding behavior, mood, and cognition. *Psychological Review, 105,* 83–107.

Maier, S. F., & Watkins, L. R. (2000). The immune system as a sensory system: Implications for psychology. *Current Directions in Psychological Science, 9,* 98–102.

Major, B., Mendes, W. B., & Dovidio, J. F. (2013). Intergroup relations and health disparities: A social psychological perspective. *Health Psychology, 32,* 514–524.

Makin, J. E., Fried, P. A., & Watkinson, B. (1991). A comparison of active and passive smoking during pregnancy: Long-term effects. *Neurotoxicology and Teratology, 16,* 5–12.

Makris, N. , Biederman, J., Monuteaux, M. C., & Seidman, L. J. (2009). Towards conceptualizing a neural systems-based anatomy of attention-deficit/hyperactivity disorder. *Developmental Neuroscience, 31,* 36–49.

Malina, R. M., Bouchard, C., & Beunen, G. (1988). Human growth: Selected aspects of current research on well-nourished children. *Annual Review of Anthropology, 17,* 187–219.

Malooly, A. M., Genet, J. J., & Siemer, M. (2013). Individual differences in reappraisal effectiveness: The role of affective flexibility. *Emotion, 13*(2), 302–313. doi:10.1037/a0029980

Mampe, B., Friederici, A. D., Christophe, A., & Wermke, K. (2009). Newborns' cry melody is shaped by their native language. *Current Biology, 19,* 1–4.

Mandle, C. L., Jacobs, S. C., Arcari, P. M., & Domar, A. D. (1996). The efficacy of relaxation response interventions with adult patients: A review of the literature. *Journal of Cardiovascular Nursing, 10,* 4–26.

Mandler, G. (1967). Organization and memory. In K. W. Spence & J. T. Spence (Eds.), *The psychology of learning and motivation* (Vol. 1, pp. 327–372). New York: Academic Press.

Mankiw, N. G., & Weinzierl, M. (2010). The optimal taxation of height: A case study of utilitarian income redistribution. *American Economic Journal: Economic Policy, 2,* 155–176.

Mann, J. J., Apter, A., Bertolote, J., Beautrais, A., Currier, D., Haas, A., . . . Hendin, H. (2005). Suicide prevention strategies: A systematic review. *Journal of the American Medical Association, 294*(16), 2064–2074. doi:10.1001/jama.294.16.2064

Marangell, L. B., Silver, J. M., Goff, D. M., & Yudofsky, S. C. (2003). Psychopharmacology and electroconvulsive therapy. In R. E. Hales & S. C. Yudofsky (Eds.), *The American Psychiatric Publishing textbook of clinical psychiatry* (4th ed., pp. 1047–1149). Washington, DC: American Psychiatric Publishing.

Markus, H. (1977). Self-schemata and processing information about the self. *Journal of Personality and Social Psychology, 35,* 63–78.

Marlatt, G. A., & Rohsenow, D. (1980). Cognitive processes in alcohol use: Expectancy and the balanced placebo design. In N. K. Mello (Ed.), *Advances in substance abuse: Behavioral and biological research* (pp. 159–199). Greenwich, CT: JAI Press.

Marlatt, G. A., & Witkiewitz, K. (2010). Update on harm reduction policy and intervention research. *Annual Review of Clinical Psychology, 6,* 591–606.

Marmot, M. G., Stansfeld, S., Patel, C., North, F., Head, J., White, L., . . . Feeney, A. (1991). Health inequalities among British civil servants: The Whitehall II study. *Lancet, 337,* 1387–1393.

Martin, A. (2007). The representation of object concepts in the brain. *Annual Review of Psychology, 58,* 25–45.

Martin, A., & Caramazza, A. (2003). Neuropsychological and neuroimaging perspectives on conceptual knowledge: An introduction. *Cognitive Neuropsychology, 20,* 195–212.

Martin, A., & Chao, L. L. (2001). Semantic memory and the brain: Structure and processes. *Current Opinion in Neurobiology, 11,* 194–201.

Martin, K. D., & Hill, R. P. (2012). Life satisfaction, self-determination, and consumption adequacy at the bottom of the pyramid. *Journal of Consumer Research, 38,* 1155–1168.

Martin, N. G., Eaves, L. J., Geath, A. R., Jarding, R., Feingold, L. M., & Eysenck, H. J. (1986). Transmission of social attitudes. *Proceedings of the National Academy of Sciences, USA, 83,* 4364–4368.

Martinez, G., Copen, C. E., & Abma, J. C. (2011). Teenagers in the United States: Sexual activity, contraceptive use, and childbearing, 2006–2010: National Survey of Family Growth. *Vital Health Statistics, 23*(31).

Marucha, P. T., Kiecolt-Glaser, J. K., & Favagehi, M. (1998). Mucosal wound healing is impaired by examination stress. *Psychosomatic Medicine, 60,* 362–365.

Marzuk, P. M., Tardiff, K., Leon, A. C., Hirsch, C., Portera, L., Iqbal, M. I., . . . Hartwell, N. (1998). Ambient temperature and mortality from unintentional cocaine overdose. *Journal of the American Medical Association, 279,* 1795–1800.

Maslach, C. (2003). Job burnout: New directions in research and intervention. *Current Directions in Psychological Science, 12,* 189–192.

Maslach, C., Schaufeli, W. B., & Leiter, M. P. (2001). Job burnout. *Annual Review of Psychology, 52,* 397–422.

Maslow, A. H. (1937). Dominance-feeling, behavior, and status. In R. J. Lowry (Ed.), *Dominance, self-esteem, self-actualization: Germinal papers by A. H. Maslow* (pp. 49–70). Monterey, CA: Brooks-Cole.

Maslow, A. H. (1954). *Motivation and personality.* New York: Harper & Row.

Mason, M. F., Magee, J. C., Kuwabara, K., & Nind, L. (2010). Specialization in relational reasoning: The efficiency, accuracy, and neural substrates of social versus nonsocial inferences. *Social Psychological and Personality Science, 1*(4), 318–326. doi:10.1177/1948550610366166

Mason, M. F., Norton, M. I., Van Horn, J. D., Wegner, D. M., Grafton, S. T., & Macrae, C. N. (2007). Wandering minds: The default network and stimulus-independent thought. *Science, 3154,* 393–395.

Masuda, T., & Nisbett, R. E. (2006). Culture and change blindness. *Cognitive Science, 30,* 381–399.

Mather, M., & Carstensen, L. L. (2003). Aging and attentional biases for emotional faces. *Psychological Science, 14,* 409–415.

Mather, M., & Carstensen, L. L. (2005). Aging and motivated cognition: The positivity effect in attention and memory. *Trends in Cognitive Sciences, 9*(10), 496–502.

Matsumoto, D., & Willingham, B. (2009). Spontaneous facial expressions of emotion of congenitally and noncongenitally blind individuals. *Journal of Personality and Social Psychology, 96,* 1–10.

Mattar, A. A. G., & Gribble, P. L. (2005). Motor learning by observing. *Neuron, 46,* 153–160.

Matthews, G., & Gilliland, K. (1999). The personality theories of H. J. Eysenck and J. A. Gray: A comparative review. *Personality and Individual Differences, 26,* 583–626.

May, R. (1983). *The discovery of being: Writings in existential psychology.* New York: Norton.

Mayberg, H., Lozano, A., Voon, V., McNeely, H., Seminowicz, D., Hamani, C., . . . Kennedy, S. H. (2005). Deep brain stimulation for treatment-resistant depression. *Neuron, 45,* 651–660.

Mayer, J. D., Caruso, D. R., & Salovey, P. (1999). Emotional intelligence meets traditional standards for an intelligence. *Intelligence, 27,* 267.

Mayer, J. D., Roberts, R. D., & Barsade, S. G. (2008). Human abilities: Emotional intelligence. *Annual Review of Psychology, 59,* 507–536.

McAdams, D. (1993). *The stories we live by: Personal myths and the making of the self.* New York: Morrow.

McCauley, J., Ruggiero, K. J., Resnick, H. S., Conoscenti, L. M., & Kilpatrick, D. G. (2009). Forcible, drug-facilitated, and incapacitated rape in relation to substance use problems: Results from a national sample of college women. *Addictive Behaviors, 34,* 458–462.

McClelland, D. C., Atkinson, J. W., Clark, R. A., & Lowell, E. L. (1953). *The achievement motive.* New York: Appleton-Century-Crofts.

McConkey, K. M., Barnier, A. J., & Sheehan, P. W. (1998). Hypnosis and pseudomemory: Understanding the findings and their implications. In S. J. Lynn & K. M. McConkey (Eds.), *Truth in memory* (pp. 227–259). New York: Guilford Press.

McCrae, R. R., & Costa, P. T. (1990). *Personality in adulthood.* New York: Guilford Press.

McCrae, R. R., & Costa, P. T. (1999). A five-factor theory of personality. In L. A. Pervin & O. P. John (Eds.), *Handbook of personality: Theory and research* (pp. 139–153). New York: Guilford Press.

McElwain, N. L., Booth-LaForce, C., & Wu, X. (2011). Infant–mother attachment and children's friendship quality: Maternal mental state talk as an intervening mechanism. *Developmental Psychology, 47*(5), 1295–1311. doi:10.1037/a0024094

McEvoy, S. P., Stevenson, M. R., McCartt, A. T., Woodward, M., Haworth, C., Palamara, P., & Circarelli, R. (2005). Role of mobile phones in motor vehicle crashes resulting in hospital attendance: A case-crossover study. *British Medical Journal, 331,* 428–430.

McFarlane, A. H., Norman, G. R., Streiner, D. L., Roy, R., & Scott, D. J. (1980). A longitudinal study of the influence of the psychosocial environment on health status: A preliminary report. *Journal of Health and Social Behavior, 21,* 124–133.

McGarty, C., & Turner, J. C. (1992). The effects of categorization on social judgement. *British Journal of Social Psychology, 31,* 253–268.

McGaugh, J. L. (2000). Memory: A century of consolidation. *Science, 287,* 248–251.

McGowan, P. O., Sasaki, A., D., Alessio, A. D., Dymov, S., Labonté, B., Szyf, M., . . . Meaney, M. J. (2009). Epigenetic regulation of the glucocorticoid receptor in human brain associates with childhood abuse. *Nature Neuroscience, 12,* 342–348.

McGrath, J., Saha, S., Chant, D., & Welham, J. (2008). Schizophrenia: A concise overview of incidence, prevalence, and mortality. *Epidemiologic Reviews, 30,* 67–76.

McGue, M., & Bouchard, T. J. (1998). Genetic and environmental influences on human behavioral differences. *Annual Review of Neuroscience, 21,* 1–24.

McIntyre, S. H., & Munson, J. M. (2008). Exploring cramming: Student behaviors, beliefs, and learning retention in the principles of marketing course. *Journal of Marketing Education, 30,* 226–243.

McKee, A. C., Cantu, R. C., Nowinski, C. J., Hedley-Whyte, E. T., Gavett, B. E., Budson, A. E., . . . Stern, R. A. (2009). Chronic traumatic encephalopathy in athletes: Progressive tauopathy after repetitive head injury. *Journal of Neuropathology and Experimental Neurology, 68,* 709–735.

McKee, A. C., Stein, T. D., Nowinski, C. J., Stern, R. A., Daneshvar, D. H., Alvarez, V. E., . . . Cantu, R. (2012). The spectrum of disease in chronic traumatic encephalopathy. *Brain, 136*(1), 43–64. doi:10.1093/brain/aws307

McKinney, C. H., Antoni, M. H., Kumar, M., Tims, F. C., & McCabe, P. M. (1997). Effects of guided imagery and music (GIM) therapy on mood and cortisol in healthy adults. *Health Psychology, 16,* 390–400.

McLaughlin, K. A., Nandi, A., Keyes, K. M., Uddin, M., Aiello, A. E., Galea, S., & Koenen, K. C. (2012). Home foreclosure and risk of psychiatric morbidity during the recent financial crisis. *Psychological Medicine, 42,* 1441–1448.

McLean, K. C. (2008). The emergence of narrative identity. *Social and Personality Psychology Compass, 2*(4), 1685–1702.

McNally, R. J. (2003). *Remembering trauma.* Cambridge, MA: Belknap Press of Harvard University Press.

McNally, R. J., & Clancy, S. A. (2005). Sleep paralysis, sexual abuse, and space alien abduction. *Transcultural Psychiatry, 42,* 113–122.

McNally, R. J., & Geraerts, E. (2009). A new solution to the recovered memory debate. *Perspective on Psychological Science, 4,* 126–134.

McNally, R. J., & Steketee, G. S. (1985). Etiology and maintenance of severe animal phobias. *Behavioral Research and Therapy, 23,* 431–435.

McWilliams, P. (1993). *Ain't nobody's business if you do: The absurdity of consensual crimes in a free society.* Los Angeles: Prelude Press.

Mead, G. H. (1934). *Mind, self, and society.* Chicago: University of Chicago Press.

Meaney, M. J., & Ferguson-Smith, A. C. (2010). Epigenetic regulation of the neural transcriptome: The meaning of the marks. *Nature Neuroscience, 13,* 1313–1318.

Mechelli, A., Crinion, J. T., Noppeney, U., O'Doherty, J., Ashburner, J., Frackowiak, R. S., & Price, C. J. (2004). Neurolinguistics: Structural plasticity in the bilingual brain. *Nature, 431,* 757.

Medin, D. L., & Schaffer, M. M. (1978). Context theory of classification learning. *Psychological Review, 85,* 207–238.

Medvec, V. H., Madey, S. F., & Gilovich, T. (1995). When less is more: Counterfactual thinking and satisfaction among Olympic medalists. *Journal of Personality and Social Psychology, 69,* 603–610.

Meeren, H. K. M., van Heijnsbergen, C. C. R. J., & de Gelder, B. (2005). Rapid perceptual integration of facial expression and emotional body language. *Proceedings of the National Academy of Sciences, USA, 102*(45), 16518–16523.

Mehl, M. R., Vazire, S., Ramirez-Esparza, N., Slatcher, R. B., & Pennebaker, J. W. (2009). Are women really more talkative than men? *Science, 317,* 82.

Meins, E. (2003). Emotional development and attachment relationships. In A. Slater & G. Bremner (Eds.), *An introduction to developmental psychology* (pp. 141–164). Malden, MA: Blackwell.

Meins, E., Fernyhough, C., Fradley, E., & Tuckey, M. (2001). Rethinking maternal sensitivity: Mothers' comments on infants' mental processes predict security of attachment at 12 months. *Journal of Child Psychology & Psychiatry & Allied Disciplines, 42,* 637–648.

Melander, E. (2005). Gender equality and intrastate armed conflict. *International Studies Quarterly, 49*(4), 695–714. doi:10.1111/j.1468-2478.2005.00384.x

Mellon, R. C. (2009). Superstitious perception: Response-independent reinforcement and punishment as determinants of recurring eccentric interpretations. *Behaviour Research and Therapy, 47,* 868–875.

Meltzer, H. Y. (2013). Update on typical and atypical antipsychotic drugs. *Annual Review of Medicine, 64,* 393–406.

Meltzoff, A. N. (1995). Understanding the intentions of others: Reenactment of intended acts by 18-month-old children. *Developmental Psychology, 31,* 838–850.

Meltzoff, A. N. (2007). "Like me": A foundation for social cognition. *Developmental Science, 10*(1), 126–134. doi:10.1111/j.1467-7687.2007.00574x

Meltzoff, A. N., Kuhl, P. K., Movellan, J., & Sejnowski, T. J. (2009). Foundations for a new science of learning. *Science, 325,* 284–288.

Meltzoff, A. N., & Moore, M. K. (1977). Imitation of facial and manual gestures by human neonates. *Science, 198,* 75–78.

Melzack, R., & Wall, P. D. (1965). Pain mechanisms: A new theory. *Science, 150,* 971–979.

Mendle, J., Turkheimer, E., & Emery, R. E. (2007). Detrimental psychological outcomes associated with early pubertal timing in adolescent girls. *Developmental Review, 27,* 151–171.

Mennella, J. A., Johnson, A., & Beauchamp, G. K. (1995). Garlic ingestion by pregnant women alters the odor of amniotic fluid. *Chemical Senses, 20,* 207–209.

Mervis, C. B., & Bertrand, J. (1994). Acquisition of the "Novel Name" Nameless Category (N3C) principle. *Child Development, 65,* 1646–1662.

Merzenich, M. M., Recanzone, G. H., Jenkins, W. M., & Grajski, K. A. (1990). Adaptive mechanisms in cortical networks underlying cortical contributions to learning and nondeclarative memory. *Cold Spring Harbor Symposia on Quantitative Biology, 55,* 873–887.

Meston, C. M., & Buss, D. M. (2007). Why humans have sex. *Archives of Sexual Behavior, 36,* 477–507.

Mestre, J. M., Guil, R., Lopes, P. N., Salovey, P., & Gil-Olarte, P. (2006). Emotional intelligence and social and academic adaptation to school. *Psicothema, 18,* 112.

Mestry, N., Donnelly, N., Meneer, T., & McCarthy, R. A. (2012). Discriminating Thatcherised from typical faces in a case of prosopagnosia. *Neuropsychologia, 50,* 3410–3418.

Metcalfe, J., & Finn, B. (2008). Evidence that judgments of learning are causally related to study choice. *Psychonomic Bulletin & Review, 15,* 174–179.

Methven, L., Allen, V. J., Withers, G. A., & Gosney, M. A. (2012). Ageing and taste. *Proceedings of the Nutrition Society, 71,* 556–565.

Meyer-Bahlberg, H. F. L., Ehrhardt, A. A., Rosen, L. R., & Gruen, R. S. (1995). Prenatal estrogens and the development of homosexual orientation. *Developmental Psychology, 31,* 12–21.

Mikels, J. A., Maglio, S. J., Reed, A. E., & Kaplowitz, L. J. (2011). Should I go with my gut? Investigating the benefits of emotion-focused decision making. *Emotion, 11*(4), 743–753.

Miklowitz, D. J., & Johnson, S. L. (2006). The psychopathology and treatment of bipolar disorder. *Annual Review of Clinical Psychology, 2,* 199–235.

Milgram, S. (1963). Behavioral study of obedience. *Journal of Abnormal and Social Psychology, 67,* 371–378.

Milgram, S. (1974). *Obedience to authority.* New York: Harper & Row.

Milgram, S., Bickman, L., & Berkowitz, O. (1969). Note on the drawing power of crowds of different size. *Journal of Personality and Social Psychology, 13,* 79–82.

Miller, C., Seckel, E., & Ramachandran, V. S. (2012). Using mirror box therapy to treat phantom pain in Haitian earthquake victims. *Journal of Vision, 12,* article 1323. doi:10.1167/12.9.1323

Miller, D. T., & Prentice, D. A. (1996). The construction of social norms and standards. In E. T. Higgins & A. W. Kruglanski (Ed.), *Social psychology: Handbook of basic principles* (pp. 799–829). New York: Guilford Press.

Miller, D. T., & Ratner, R. K. (1998). The disparity between the actual and assumed power of self-interest. *Journal of Personality and Social Psychology, 74,* 53–62.

Miller, D. T., & Ross, M. (1975). Self-serving biases in the attribution of causality: Fact or fiction? *Psychological Bulletin, 82,* 213–225.

Miller, G. A. (1956). The magical number seven, plus or minus two: Some limits on our capacity for processing information. *Psychological Review, 63,* 81–96.

Miller, K. F., Smith, C. M., & Zhu, J. (1995). Preschool origins of cross-national differences in mathematical competence: The role of number-naming systems. *Psychological Science, 6,* 56–60.

Miller, N. E. (1960). Motivational effects of brain stimulation and drugs. *Federation Proceedings, 19,* 846–854.

Miller, T. W. (Ed.). (1996). *Theory and assessment of stressful life events.* Madison, CT: International Universities Press.

Miller, W. R., & Rollnick, S. (2012). *Motivational interviewing: Helping people change* (3rd ed.). New York: Guilford Press.

Milne, E., & Grafman, J. (2001). Ventromedial prefrontal cortex lesions in humans eliminate implicit gender stereotyping. *Journal of Neuroscience, 21,* 1–6.

Milner, A. D., & Goodale, M. A. (1995). *The visual brain in action.* Oxford, England: Oxford University Press.

Milner, B. (1962). Laterality effects in audition. In V. B. Mountcastle (Ed.), *Interhemispheric relations and cerebral dominance* (pp. 177–195). Baltimore: Johns Hopkins University Press.

Mingroni, M. A. (2007). Resolving the IQ paradox: Heterosis as a cause of the Flynn effect and other trends. *Psychological Review, 114,* 806–829.

Minsky, M. (1986). *The society of mind.* New York: Simon & Schuster.

Minson, J. A., & Mueller, J. S. (2012). The cost of collaboration: Why joint decision making exacerbates rejection of outside information. *Psychological Science, 23*(3), 219–224. doi:10.1177/0956797611429132

Miranda, J., Bernal, G., Lau, A., Kihn, L., Hwang, W. C., & LaFromboise, T. (2005). State of the science on psychological interventions for ethnic minorities. *Annual Review of Clinical Psychology, 1,* 113–142.

Mischel, W. (1968). *Personality and assessment.* New York: Wiley.

Mischel, W. (2004). Toward an integrative science of the person. *Annual Review of Psychology, 55,* 1–22.

Mischel, W., Ayduk, O., Baumeister, R. F., & Vohs, K. D. (2004). Willpower in a cognitive-affective processing system: The dynamics of delay of gratification. In *Handbook of self-regulation: Research, theory, and applications* (pp. 99–129). New York: Guilford Press.

Mischel, W., & Shoda, Y. (1999). Integrating dispositions and processing dynamics within a unified theory of personality: The cognitive affective personality system. In L. A. Pervin & O. P. John (Eds.), *Handbook of personality: Theory and research.* New York: Guilford Press.

Mischel, W., Shoda, Y., & Rodriguez, M. L. (1989). Delay of gratification in children. *Science, 244,* 933–938.

Mita, T. H., Dermer, M., & Knight, J. (1977). Reversed facial images and the mere-exposure hypothesis. *Journal of Personality and Social Psychology, 35,* 597–601.

Mitchell, J. P. (2006). Mentalizing and Marr: An information processing approach to the study of social cognition. *Brain Research, 1079,* 66–75.

Mitchell, K. J., & Johnson, M. K. (2009). Source monitoring 15 years later: What have we learned from fMRI about the neural mechanisms of source memory? *Psychological Bulletin, 135,* 638–677.

Miura, I. T., Okamoto, Y., Kim, C. C., & Chang, C. M. (1994). Comparisons of children's cognitive representation of number: China, France, Japan, Korea, Sweden and the United States. *International Journal of Behavioral Development, 17,* 401–411.

Moffitt, T. E. (1993). Adolescence-limited and life-course-persistent antisocial behavior: A developmental taxonomy. *Psychological Review, 100,* 674–701.

Mojtabai, R., Olfson, M., Sampson, N. A., Jin, R., Druss, B., Wang, P. S., . . . Kessler, R. C. (2011). Barriers to mental health treatment: Results from the National Comorbidity Survey replication. *Psychological Medicine, 41*(8), 1751–1761.

Molden, D., Lee, A. Y., & Higgins, E. T. (2009). Motivations for promotion and prevention. In J. Shah & W. Gardner (Eds.), *Handbook of motivation science* (pp. 169–187). New York: Guilford Press.

Monahan, J. L., Murphy, S. T., & Zajonc, R. B. (2000). Subliminal mere exposure: Specific, general, and diffuse effects. *Psychological Science, 11,* 462–466.

Moncrieff, J. (2009). A critique of the dopamine hypothesis of schizophrenia and psychosis. *Harvard Review of Psychiatry, 17,* 214–225.

Montague, C. T., Farooqi, I. S., Whitehead, J. P., Soos, M. A., Rau, H., Wareham, N. J., . . . O'Rahilly, S. (1997). Congenital leptin deficiency is associated with severe early-onset obesity in humans. *Nature, 387*(6636), 903–908.

Mook, D. G. (1983). In defense of external invalidity. *American Psychologist, 38,* 379–387.

Moon, S. M., & Illingworth, A. J. (2005). Exploring the dynamic nature of procrastination: A latent growth curve analysis of academic procrastination. *Personality and Individual Differences, 38,* 297–309.

Moore, D. W. (2003). *Public lukewarm on animal rights.* Retrieved June 22, 2010, from http://www.gallup.com/poll/8461/publiclukewarm-animal-rights.aspx

Moore, E. G. J. (1986). Family socialization and the IQ test performance of traditionally and transracially adopted Black children. *Developmental Psychology, 22,* 317–326.

Moore, K. L. (1977). *The developing human* (2nd ed.). Philadelphia: Saunders.

Moore, L. (2012, August 31). American's future has to be multilingual. *The Washington Diplomat.* Retrieved from http://www.washdiplomat.com/index.php?option=com_content&view=article&id=8549:op-ed-americans-future-has-to-be-multilingual&catid=1492:september-2012&Itemid=504

Moray, N. (1959). Attention in dichotic listening: Affective cues and the influence of instructions. *Quarterly Journal of Experimental Psychology, 11,* 56–60.

Moreno, S., Marques, C., Santos, A., Santos, M., Castro, S. L., & Besson, M. (2009). Musical training influences linguistic abilities in 8-year-old children: More evidence for brain plasticity. *Cerebral Cortex, 19,* 712–723.

Morewedge, C. K., & Norton, M. I. (2009). When dreaming is believing: The (motivated) interpretation of dreams. *Journal of Personality and Social Psychology, 96,* 249–264.

Morgenstern, J., Labouvie, E., McCrady, B. S., Kahler, C. W., & Frey, R. M. (1997). Affiliation with Alcoholics Anonymous after treatment: A study of its therapeutic effects and mechanisms of action. *Journal of Consulting and Clinical Psychology, 65,* 768–777.

Morin, A. (2006). Levels of consciousness and self-awareness: A comparison of various neurocognitive views. *Consciousness & Cognition, 15,* 358–371.

Morris, C. D., Bransford, J. D., & Franks, J. J. (1977). Levels of processing versus transfer-appropriate processing. *Journal of Verbal Learning and Verbal Behavior, 16,* 519–533.

Morris, R. G., Anderson, E., Lynch, G. S., & Baudry, M. (1986). Selective impairment of learning and blockade of long-term potentiation by an N-methyl-D-aspartate receptor antagonist, AP5. *Nature, 319,* 774–776.

Moruzzi, G., & Magoun, H. W. (1949). Brain stem reticular formation and activation of the EEG. *Electroencephalography and Clinical Neurophysiology, 1,* 455–473.

Moscovitch, M. (1994). Memory and working-with-memory: Evaluation of a component process model and comparisons with other models. In D. L. Schacter & E. Tulving (Eds.), *Memory systems 1994* (pp. 269–310). Cambridge, MA: MIT Press.

Moscovitch, M., Nadel, L., Winocur, G., Gilboa, A., & Rosenbaum, R. S. (2006). The cognitive neuroscience of remote episodic, semantic and spatial memory. *Current Opinion in Neurobiology, 16,* 179–190.

Mroczek, D. K., & Spiro, A. (2005). Change in life satisfaction during adulthood: Findings from the Veterans Affairs Normative Aging Study. *Journal of Personality and Social Psychology, 88,* 189.

Muehlenkamp, J. J., Claes, L., Havertape, L., & Plener, P. L. (2012). International prevalence of adolescent non-suicidal self-injury and deliberate self-harm. *Child and Adolescent Psychiatry and Mental Health, 6*(10). doi:10.1156/1753-2000-6-10

Mueller, T. E., Gavin, L. E., & Kulkarni, A. (2008). The association between sex education and youth's engagement in sexual intercourse, age at first intercourse, and birth control use at first sex. *The Journal of Adolescent Health, 42*(1), 89–96.

Mueller, T. I., Leon, A. C., Keller, M. B., Solomon, D. A., Endicott, J., Coryell, W., . . . Maser, J. D. (1999). Recurrence after recovery from major depressive disorder during 15 years of observational follow-up. *American Journal of Psychiatry, 156,* 1000–1006.

Muenter, M. D., & Tyce, G. M. (1971). L-dopa therapy of Parkinson's disease: Plasma L-dopa concentration, therapeutic response, and side effects. *Mayo Clinic Proceedings, 46,* 231–239.

Munsey, C. (2008, February). Prescriptive authority in the states. *Monitor on Psychology, 39,* 60.

Murphy, N. A., Hall, J. A., & Colvin, C. R. (2003). Accurate intelligence assessments in social interactions: Mediators and gender effects. *Journal of Personality, 71,* 465–493.

Murray, C. (2002). *IQ and income inequality in a sample of sibling pairs from advantaged family backgrounds.* Paper presented at the 114th Annual Meeting of the American Economic Association.

Murray, C. J. L., & Lopez, A. D. (1996a). Evidence-based health policy—Lessons from the Global Burden of Disease study. *Science, 274,* 740–743.

Murray, C. J. L., & Lopez, A. D. (1996b). *The Global Burden of Disease: A comprehensive assessment of mortality and disability from diseases, injuries, and risk factors in 1990 and projected to 2020.* Cambridge, MA: Harvard University Press.

Murray, H. A. (1943). *Thematic Apperception Test manual.* Cambridge, MA: Harvard University Press.

Murray, H. A., & Kluckhohn, C. (1953). Outline of a conception of personality. In C. Kluckhohn, H. A. Murray, & D. M. Schneider (Eds.), *Personality in nature, society, and culture* (2nd ed., pp. 3–52). New York: Knopf.

Murray, R. M., Paparelli, A, Morrison, P. D., Marconia, A., & Di Forti, M. (2013). What can we learn about schizophrenia from studying the human model, drug-induced psychosis? *American Journal of Medical Genetics Part B, 162B,* 661-670.

Myers, D. G., & Diener, E. (1995). Who is happy? *Psychological Science, 6,* 10–19.

Myers, D. G., & Lamm, H. (1975). The polarizing effect of group discussion. *American Scientist, 63*(3), 297–303.

Myles, P. S., Leslie, K., McNeil, J., Forbes, A., & Chan, M. T. V. (2004). Bispectral index monitoring to prevent awareness during anaesthesia: The B-Aware randomized controlled trial. *Lancet, 363,* 1757–1763.

Nadasdy, A. (1995). Phonetics, phonology, and applied linguistics. *Annual Review of Applied Linguistics, 15,* 68–77.

Nader, K., & Hardt, O. (2009). A single standard for memory: The case of reconsolidation. *Nature Reviews Neuroscience, 10,* 224–234.

Nader, K., Shafe, G., & LeDoux, J. E. (2000). Fear memories require protein synthesis in the amygdala for reconsolidation after retrieval. *Nature, 406,* 722–726.

Nagasako, E. M., Oaklander, A. L., & Dworkin, R. H. (2003). Congenital insensitivity to pain: An update. *Pain, 101,* 213–219.

Nagell, K., Olguin, R. S., & Tomasello, M. (1993). Processes of social learning in the tool use of chimpanzees (*Pan troglodytes*) and human children (*Homo sapiens*). *Journal of Comparative Psychology, 107,* 174–186.

Nahemow, L., & Lawton, M. P. (1975). Similarity and propinquity in friendship formation. *Journal of Personality and Social Psychology, 32,* 205–213.

Nairne, J. S., & Pandeirada, J. N. S. (2008). Adaptive memory: Remembering with a stone age brain. *Current Directions in Psychological Science, 17,* 239–243.

Nairne, J. S., Thompson, S. R., & Pandeirada, J. N. S. (2007). Adaptive memory: Survival processing enhances retention. *Journal of Experimental Psychology: Learning, Memory, and Cognition, 33,* 263–273.

Nakazato, M., Murakami, N., Date, Y., Kojima, M., Matsuo, H., Kangawa, K., & Matsukura, S. (2001). A role for ghrelin in the central regulation of feeding. *Nature, 409,* 194–198.

Naqvi, N., Shiv, B., & Bechara, A. (2006). The role of emotion in decision making: A cognitive neuroscience perspective. *Current Directions in Psychological Science, 15,* 260–264.

Nathan, P. E., & Gorman, J. M. (2007). *A guide to treatments that work* (3rd ed.). New York: Oxford University Press.

Nathanson, C., Paulhus, D. L., & Williams, K. M. (2006). Personality and misconduct correlates of body modification and other cultural deviance markers. *Journal of Research in Personality, 40,* 779–802.

National Center for Health Statistics. (2004). *Health, United States, 2004 (with chartbook on trends in the health of Americans).* Hyattsville, MD: Author.

National Center for Health Statistics. (2012). *Health, United States, 2011 (with special feature on socioeconomic status and health).* Hyattsville, MD: Author.

National Institutes of Health. (1998). *Clinical Guidelines on the Identification, Evaluation, and Treatment of Overweight and Obesity in Adults: The Evidence Report.*

Naumann, L. P., Vazire, S., Rentfrow, P. J., & Gosling, S. D. (2009). Personality judgments based on physical appearance. *Personality & Social Psychology Bulletin, 35,* 1661–1671.

Neihart, M. (1999). The impact of giftedness on psychological well-being: What does the empirical literature say? *Roeper Review, 22*(1), 10.

Neimark, J. (2004; July/August). The power of coincidence. *Psychology Today,* pp. 47–52.

Neimeyer, R. A., & Mitchell, K. A. (1988). Similarity and attraction: A longitudinal study. *Journal of Social and Personal Relationships, 5,* 131–148.

Neisser, U. (Ed.) (1998). *The rising curve: Long-term gains in IQ and related measures.* Washington, DC: American Psychological Association.

Neisser, U., Boodoo, G., Bouchard, T. J., Jr., Boykin, A. W., Brody, N., Ceci, S. J., . . . Loehlin, J. C. (1996). Intelligence: Knowns and unknowns. *American Psychologist, 51,* 77–101.

Neisser, U., & Harsch, N. (1992). Phantom flashbulbs: False recollections of hearing the news about Challenger. In E. Winograd & U. Neisser (Eds.), *Affect and accuracy in recall: Studies of "flashbulb memories"* (pp. 9–31). Cambridge, England: Cambridge University Press.

Nelson, C. A., Zeanah, C. H., Fox, N. A., Marshall, P. J., Smyke, A. T., & Guthrie, D. (2007). Cognitive recovery in socially deprived young children: The Bucharest early intervention project. *Science, 318,* 1937–1940.

Neugebauer, R., Hoek, H. W., & Susser, E. (1999). Prenatal exposure to wartime famine and development of antisocial personality in early adulthood. *Journal of the American Medical Association, 282,* 455–462.

Newbold, R. R., Padilla-Banks, E., Snyder, R. J., & Jefferson, W. N. (2005). Developmental exposure to estrogenic compounds and obesity. *Birth Defects Research Part A: Clinical and Molecular Teratology, 73,* 478–480.

Newman, J. P., Wolff, W. T., & Hearst, E. (1980). The feature-positive effect in adult human subjects. *Journal of Experimental Psychology: Human Learning and Memory, 6,* 630–650.

Newman, M. G., & Stone, A. A. (1996). Does humor moderate the effects of experimentally induced stress? *Annals of Behavioral Medicine, 18,* 101–109.

Newschaffer, C. J., Croen, L. A., Daniels, J., Giarelli, E., Grether, J. K., Levy, S. E., . . . Windham, G. C. (2007). The epidemiology of autism spectrum disorders. *Annual Review of Public Health, 28,* 235–258.

Newsome, W. T., & Paré, E. B. (1988). A selective impairment of motion perception following lesions of the middle temporal visual area (MT). *Journal of Neuroscience, 8,* 2201–2211.

Niedenthal, P. M., Barsalou, L. W., Winkielman, P., Krauth-Gruber, S., & Ric, F. (2005). Embodiment in attitudes, social perception, and emotion. *Personality and Social Psychology Review, 9*(3), 184–211.

Nikles, C. D., II, Brecht, D. L., Klinger, E., & Bursell, A. L. (1998). The effects of current concern- and nonconcern-related waking suggestions on nocturnal dream content. *Journal of Personality and Social Psychology, 75,* 242–255.

Nir, Y., & Tononi, G. (2010). Dreaming and the brain: From phenomenology to neurophysiology. *Trends in Cognitive Sciences, 14*(2), 88–100.

Nisbett, R. E. (2009). *Intelligence and how to get it.* New York: Norton.

Nisbett, R. E., Aronson, J., Blair, C., Dickens, W., Flynn, J., Halpern, D. F., & Turkheimer, E. (2012). Intelligence: New findings and theoretical developments. *American Psychologist, 67*(2), 130–159. doi:10.1037/a0026699

Nisbett, R. E., Caputo, C., Legant, P., & Maracek, J. (1973). Behavior as seen by the actor and as seen by the observer. *Journal of Personality and Social Psychology, 27,* 154–164.

Nisbett, R. E., & Cohen, D. (1996). *Culture of honor: The psychology of violence in the South.* Boulder, CO: Westview Press.

Nisbett, R. E., & Miyamoto, Y. (2005). The influence of culture: Holistic versus analytic perception. *Trends in Cognitive Sciences, 9,* 467–473.

Nissen, M. J., & Bullemer, P. (1987). Attentional requirements of learning: Evidence from performance measures. *Cognitive Psychology, 19,* 1–32.

Nock, M. K. (2009). Why do people hurt themselves? New insights into the nature and functions of self-injury. *Current Directions in Psychological Science, 18,* 78–83. doi:10.1111/j.1467-8721.2009.01613.x

Nock, M. K. (2010). Self-injury. *Annual Review of Clinical Psychology, 6,* 339–363. doi: 10.1146/annurev.clinpsy.121208.131258

Nock, M. K., Borges, G., Bromet, E. J., Alonso, J., Angermeyer, M., Beautrais, A., . . . Williams, D. (2008). Cross-national prevalence and risk factors for suicidal ideation, plans, and attempts. *British Journal of Psychiatry, 192,* 98–105.

Nock, M. K., Borges, G., & Ono, Y. (Eds.) (2012). *Suicide: Global perspectives from the WHO World Mental Health Surveys.* New York: Cambridge University Press.

Nock, M. K., Green, J. G., Hwang, I., McLaughlin, K. A., Sampson, N. A., Zaslavsky, A. M., & Kessler, R. C. (2013). Prevalence, correlates and treatment of lifetime suicidal behavior among adolescents: Results from the National Comorbidity Survey Replication–Adolescent Supplement (NCSA–A). *Journal of the American Medical Association Psychiatry, 70*(3), 300–310. doi:10.1001/2013.jamapsychiatry.55

Nock, M. K., Kazdin, A. E., Hiripi, E., & Kessler, R. C. (2006). Prevalence, subtypes, and correlates of *DSM–IV* conduct disorder in the National Comorbidity Survey Replication. *Psychological Medicine, 36,* 699–710.

Nolen-Hoeksema, S. (2008). Gender differences in coping with depression across the lifespan. *Depression, 3,* 81–90.

Norcross, J. C., Hedges, M., & Castle, P. H. (2002). Psychologists conducting psychotherapy in 2001: A study of the Division 29 membership. *Psychotherapy: Theory/Research/Practice/Training, 39,* 97–102.

Norton, M. I., Frost, J. H., & Ariely, D. (2007). Less is more: The lure of ambiguity, or why familiarity breeds contempt. *Journal of Personality and Social Psychology, 92*(1), 97–105. doi:10.1037/0022-3514.92.1.97

Nosanchuk, T. A., & Lightstone, J. (1974). Canned laughter and public and private conformity. *Journal of Personality and Social Psychology, 29,* 153–156.

Nowak, M. A. (2006). Five rules for the evolution of cooperation. *Science, 314,* 1560–1563.

Nuttin, J. M. (1985). Narcissism beyond Gestalt and awareness: The name letter effect. *European Journal of Social Psychology, 15,* 353–361.

Oately, K., Keltner, D., & Jenkins, J. M. (2006). *Understanding emotions* (2nd ed.). Malden, MA: Blackwell.

Ochsner, K. N., Bunge, S. A., Gross, J. J., & Gabrieli, J. D. E. (2002). Rethinking feelings: An fMRI study of the cognitive regulation of emotion. *Journal of Cognitive Neuroscience, 14,* 1215–1229.

Ochsner, K. N., Ray, R. R., Hughes, B., McRae, K., Cooper, J. C., Weber, J., . . . Gross, J. J. (2009). Bottom-up and top-down processes in emotion generation: Common and distinct neural mechanisms. *Psychological Science, 20,* 1322–1331.

O'Doherty, J. P., Dayan, P., Friston, K., Critchley, H., & Dolan, R. J. (2003). Temporal difference models and reward-related learning in the human brain. *Neuron, 38*, 329–337.

Ofshe, R. J. (1992). Inadvertent hypnosis during interrogation: False confession due to dissociative state, misidentified multiple personality, and the satanic cult hypothesis. *International Journal of Clinical and Experimental Hypnosis, 40*, 125–126.

Ofshe, R., & Watters, E. (1994). *Making monsters: False memories, psychotherapy, and sexual hysteria.* New York: Scribner/Macmillan.

Ohayon, M. M., Guilleminault, C., & Priest, R. G. (1999). Night terrors, sleepwalking, and confusional arousals in the general population: Their frequency and relationship to other sleep and mental disorders. *Journal of Clinical Psychiatry, 60*, 268–276.

Öhman, A. (1996). Preferential preattentive processing of threat in anxiety: Preparedness and attentional biases. In R. M. Rapee (Ed.), *Current controversies in the anxiety disorders.* New York: Guilford Press.

Öhman, A., Dimberg, U., & Öst, L. G. (1985). Animal and social phobias: Biological constraints on learned fear responses. In S. Reiss & R. Bootzin (Eds.), *Theoretical issues in behavior therapy* (pp. 123–175). New York: Academic Press.

Okagaki, L., & Sternberg, R. J. (1993). Parental beliefs and children's school performance. *Child Development, 64*, 36–56.

Okuda, J., Fujii, T., Ohtake, H., Tsukiura, T., Tanji, K., Suzuki, K., . . . Yamadori, A. (2003). Thinking of the future and the past: The roles of the frontal pole and the medial temporal lobes. *NeuroImage, 19*, 1369–1380.

Okulicz-Kozaryn, A. (2011). Europeans work to live and Americans live to work (Who is happy to work more: Americans or Europeans?). *Journal of Happiness Studies, 12*(2), 225–243.

Olatunji, B. O., & Wolitzky-Taylor, K. B. (2009). Anxiety sensitivity and the anxiety disorders: A meta-analytic review and synthesis. *Psychological Bulletin, 135*, 974–999.

Olausson, P. O., Haglund, B., Weitoft, G. R., & Cnattingius, S. (2001). Teenage child-bearing and long-term socioeconomic consequences: A case study in Sweden. *Family Planning Perspectives, 33*, 70–74.

Olds, J. (1956, October). Pleasure center in the brain. *Scientific American, 195*, 105–116.

Ollers, D. K., & Eilers, R. E. (1988). The role of audition in infant babbling. *Child Development, 59*, 441–449.

Olsson, A., & Phelps, E. A. (2007). Social learning of fear. *Nature Neuroscience, 10*, 1095–1102.

Oltmanns, T. F., Neale, J. M., & Davison, G. C. (1991). *Case studies in abnormal psychology* (3rd ed.). New York: Wiley.

Olton, D. S., & Samuelson, R. J. (1976). Remembrance of places passed: Spatial memory in rats. *Journal of Experimental Psychology: Animal Behavior Processes, 2*, 97–116.

Ono, K. (1987). Superstitious behavior in humans. *Journal of the Experimental Analysis of Behavior, 47*, 261–271.

Orban, P., Lungu, O., & Doyon, J. (2008). Motor sequence learning and developmental dyslexia. *Annals of the New York Academy of Sciences, 1145*, 151–172.

Otto, M. W., Henin, A., Hirshfeld-Becker, D. R., Pollack, M. H., Biederman, J., & Rosenbaum, J. F. (2007). Posttraumatic stress disorder symptoms following media exposure to tragic events: Impact of 9/11 on children at risk for anxiety disorders. *Journal of Anxiety Disorders, 21*, 888–902.

Overmier, J. B., & Seligman, M. E. P. (1967). Effects of inescapable shock upon subsequent escape and avoidance learning. *Journal of Comparative and Physiological Psychology, 63*, 28–33.

Owens, W. A. (1966). Age and mental abilities: A second adult follow-up. *Journal of Educational Psychology, 57*, 311–325.

Oztekin, I., Curtis, C. E., & McElree, B. (2009). The medial temporal lobe and left inferior prefrontal cortex jointly support interference resolution in verbal working memory. *Journal of Cognitive Neuroscience, 21*, 1967–1979.

Pagnin, D., de Queiroz, V., Pini, S., & Cassano, G. B. (2008). Efficacy of ECT in depression: A meta-analytic review. *Focus, 6*, 155–162.

Paivio, A. (1971). *Imagery and verbal processes.* New York: Holt, Rinehart and Winston.

Paivio, A. (1986). *Mental representations: A dual coding approach.* New York: Oxford University Press.

Parbery-Clark, A., Skoe, E., & Kraus, N. (2009). Musical experience limits the degradative effects of background noise on the neural processing of sound. *Journal of Neuroscience, 11*, 14100–14107.

Parbery-Clark, A., Tierney, A., Strait, D. L., & Kraus, N. (2012). Musicians have fine-tuned neural distinction of speech syllables. *Neuroscience, 219*, 111–119.

Park, B., & Hastie, R. (1987). Perception of variability in category development: Instance- versus abstraction-based stereotypes. *Journal of Personality and Social Psychology, 53*(4), 621–635. doi:10.1037/0022-3514.53.4.621

Park, D. C., & McDonough, I. M. (2013). The dynamic aging mind: Revelations from functional neuroimaging research. *Perspectives on Psychological Science, 8*(1), 62–67. doi:10.1177/1745691612469034

Parker, E. S., Cahill, L. S., & McGaugh, J. L. (2006). A case of unusual autobiographical remembering. *Neurocase, 12*, 35–49.

Parker, G., Gibson, N. A., Brotchie, H., Heruc, G., Rees, A. M., & Hadzi-Pavlovic, D. (2006). Omega-3 fatty acids and mood disorders. *American Journal of Psychiatry, 163*, 969–978.

Parker, H. A., & McNally, R. J. (2008). Repressive coping, emotional adjustment, and cognition in people who have lost loved ones to suicide. *Suicide and Life-Threatening Behavior, 38*, 676–687.

Parkinson, B., & Totterdell, P. (1999). Classifying affect-regulation strategies. *Cognition and Emotion, 13*, 277–303.

Parrott, A. C. (2001). Human psychopharmacology of Ecstasy (MDMA): A review of 15 years of empirical research. *Human Psychopharmacology, 16*, 557–577.

Parrott, A. C., Morinan, A., Moss, M., & Scholey, A. (2005). *Understanding drugs and behavior.* Chichester, England: Wiley.

Parsons, T. (1975). The sick role and the role of the physician reconsidered. *Milbank Memorial Fund Quarterly, Health and Society, 53*(3), 257–278.

Pascual-Ferrá, P., Liu, Y., & Beatty, M. J. (2012). A meta-analytic comparison of the effects of text messaging to substance-induced impairment on driving performance. *Communication Research Reports, 29*, 229–238.

Pascual-Leone, A., Amedi, A., Fregni, F., & Merabet, L. B. (2005). The plastic human brain cortex. *Annual Review of Neuroscience, 28*, 377–401.

Pascual-Leone, A., Houser, C. M., Reese, K., Shotland, L. I., Grafman, J., Sato, S., . . . Cohen, L. G. (1993). Safety of rapid-rate transcranial magnetic stimulation in normal volunteers. *Electroencephalography and Clinical Neurophysiology, 89*, 120–130.

Patall, E. A., Cooper, H., & Robinson, J. C. (2008). The effects of choice on intrinsic motivation and related outcomes: A meta-analysis of research findings. *Psychological Bulletin, 134*(2), 270–300.

Patrick, C. J., Cuthbert, B. N., & Lang, P. J. (1994). Emotion in the criminal psychopath: Fear image processing. *Journal of Abnormal Psychology, 103*, 523–534.

Patterson, C. J. (1995). Lesbian mothers, gay fathers, and their children. In A. R. D'Augelli & C. J. Patterson (Eds.), *Lesbian, gay and bisexual identities across the lifespan: Psychological perspectives* (pp. 262–290). New York: Oxford University Press.

Pavlidis, I., Eberhardt, N. L., & Levine, J. A. (2002). Human behaviour: Seeing through the face of deception. *Nature, 415*, 35.

Pavlidou, E. V., Williams, J. M., & Kelly, L. M. (2009). Artificial grammar learning in primary school children with and without developmental dyslexia. *Annals of Dyslexia, 59,* 55–77.

Pavlov, I. P. (1923a). New researches on conditioned reflexes. *Science, 58,* 359–361.

Pavlov, I. P. (1923b, July 23). Pavloff. *Time, 1*(21), 20–21.

Pavlov, I. P. (1927). *Conditioned reflexes.* Oxford, England: Oxford University Press.

Payne, J. D., Schacter, D. L., Propper, R., Huang, L., Wamsley, E., Tucker, M. A., . . . Stickgold, R. (2009). The role of sleep in false memory formation. *Neurobiology of Learning and Memory, 92,* 327–334.

Payne, J. D., Stickgold, R., Swanberg, K., & Kensinger, E. A. (2008). Sleep preferentially enhances memory for emotional components of scenes. *Psychological Science, 19,* 781–788.

Pearce, J. M. (1987). A model of stimulus generalization for Pavlovian conditioning. *Psychological Review, 84,* 61–73.

Peck, J., & Shu, S. B. (2009). The effect of mere touch on perceived ownership. *Journal of Consumer Research, 36,* 434–447.

Pelham, B. W. (1985). Self-investment and self-esteem: Evidence for a Jamesian model of self-worth. *Journal of Personality and Social Psychology, 69,* 1141–1150.

Pelham, B. W., Carvallo, M., & Jones, J. T. (2005). Implicit egotism. *Current Directions in Psychological Science, 14,* 106–110.

Pelham, B. W., Mirenberg, M. C., & Jones, J. T. (2002). Why Susie sells seashells by the seashore: Implicit egotism and major life decisions. *Journal of Personality and Social Psychology, 82,* 469–487.

Penfield, W., & Rasmussen, T. (1950). *The cerebral cortex of man: A clinical study of localization of function.* New York: Macmillan.

Pennebaker, J. W., & Chung, C. K. (2007). Expressive writing, emotional upheavals, and health. In H. Friedman & R. Silver (Eds.), *Handbook of health psychology* (pp. 263–284). New York: Oxford University Press.

Pennebaker, J. W., Kiecolt-Glaser, J. K., & Glaser, R. (1988). Disclosure of traumas and immune function: Health implications for psychotherapy. *Journal of Consulting and Clinical Psychology, 56,* 239–245.

Pennebaker, J. W., & Sanders, D. Y. (1976). American graffiti: Effects of authority and reactance arousal. *Personality and Social Psychology Bulletin, 2,* 264–267.

Penner, L. A., Albrecht, T. L., Orom, H., Coleman, D. K., & Underwood, W. (2010). Health and health care disparities. In J. F. Dovidio, M. Hewstone, P. Glick, & V. M. Esses (Eds.), *The Sage handbook of prejudice, stereotyping and discrimination* (pp. 472–489). Thousand Oaks, CA: Sage.

Perenin, M.-T., & Vighetto, A. (1988). Optic ataxia: A specific disruption in visuomotor mechanisms. I. Different aspects of the deficit in reaching for objects. *Brain, 111,* 643–674.

Perkins, D. N., & Grotzer, T. A. (1997). Teaching intelligence. *American Psychologist, 52,* 1125–1133.

Perlmutter, J. S., & Mink, J. W. (2006). Deep brain stimulation. *Annual Review of Neuroscience, 29,* 229–257.

Perloff, L. S., & Fetzer, B. K. (1986). Self-other judgments and perceived vulnerability to victimization. *Journal of Personality and Social Psychology, 50,* 502–510.

Perls, F. S., Hefferkine, R., & Goodman, P. (1951). *Gestalt therapy: Excitement and growth in the human personality.* New York: Julian Press.

Perrett, D. I., Burt, D. M., Penton-Voak, I. S., Lee, K. J., Rowland, D. A., & Edwards, R. (1999). Symmetry and human facial attractiveness. *Evolution and Human Behavior, 20,* 295–307.

Perry, R. B. (1996). *The thought and character of William James.* Nashville: Vanderbilt University Press.

Pessiglione, M., Seymour, B., Flandin, G., Dolan, R. J., & Frith, C. D. (2006). Dopamine-dependent prediction errors underpin reward-seeking behavior in humans. *Nature, 442,* 1042–1045.

Petersen, A. C., & Grockett, L. (1985). Pubertal timing and grade effects on adjustment. *Journal of Youth and Adolescence, 14,* 191–206.

Petersen, J. L., & Hyde, J. S. (2010). A meta-analytic review of research on gender differences in sexuality, 1993–2007. *Psychological Bulletin, 136*(1), 21–38. doi:10.1037/a0017504

Peterson, C., & Siegal, M. (1999). Representing inner worlds: Theory of mind in autistic, deaf and normal hearing children. *Psychological Science, 10,* 126–129.

Peterson, L. R., & Peterson, M. J. (1959). Short-term retention of individual verbal items. *Journal of Experimental Psychology, 58,* 193–198.

Petitto, L. A., & Marentette, P. F. (1991). Babbling in the manual mode: Evidence for the ontogeny of language. *Science, 251,* 1493–1496.

Petrie, K. P., Booth, R. J., & Pennebaker, J. W. (1998). The immunological effects of thought suppression. *Journal of Personality and Social Psychology, 75,* 1264–1272.

Petry, N. M., Alessi, S. M., & Rash, C. J. (2013). Contingency management treatments decrease psychiatric symptoms. *Journal of Consulting and Clinical Psychology, 81*(5), 926–931. doi:10.1037/a0032499

Petty, R. E., & Cacioppo, J. T. (1986). The elaboration likelihood model of persuasion. In L. Berkowitz (Ed.), *Advances in experimental social psychology* (Vol. 19, pp. 123–205). New York: Academic Press.

Petty, R. E., Cacioppo, J. T., & Goldman, R. (1981). Personal involvement as a determinant of argument-based persuasion. *Journal of Personality and Social Psychology, 41,* 847–855.

Petty, R. E., & Wegener, D. T. (1998). Attitude change: Multiple roles for persuasion variables. In D. T. Gilbert, S. T. Fiske, & G. Lindzey (Eds.), *The handbook of social psychology* (4th ed., Vol. 1, pp. 323–390). Boston: McGraw-Hill.

Pham, M. T., Lee, L., & Stephen, A. T. (2012). Feeling the future: The emotional oracle effect. *Journal of Consumer Research, 39*(3), 461–477.

Phelan, J., Link, B., Stueve, A., & Pescosolido, B. (1997, August). *Public conceptions of mental illness in 1950 in 1996: Has sophistication increased? Has stigma declined?* Paper presented at the American Sociological Association, Toronto, Ontario.

Phelps, E. A. (2006). Emotion and cognition: Insights from studies of the human amygdala. *Annual Review of Psychology, 24,* 27–53.

Phelps, E. A., & LeDoux, J. L. (2005). Contributions of the amygdala to emotion processing: From animal models to human behavior. *Neuron, 48,* 175–187.

Phillips, F. (2002, January 24). Jump in cigarette sales tied to Sept. 11 attacks. *Boston Globe,* p. B1.

Phills, C. E., Kawakami, K., Tabi, E., Nadolny, D., & Inzlicht, M. (2011). Mind the gap: Increasing associations between the self and Blacks with approach behaviors. *Journal of Personality and Social Psychology, 100*(2), 197–210. doi:10.1037/a0022159

Piaget, J. (1954). *The child's conception of number.* New York: Norton.

Piaget, J. (1965). *The moral judgment of the child.* New York: Free Press. (Original work published 1932)

Piazza, J. R., Charles, S. T., Sliwinski, M. J., Mogle, J., & Almeida, D. M. (2013). Affective reactivity to daily stressors and long-term risk of reporting a chronic physical health condition. *Annals of Behavioral Medicine, 45,* 110–120.

Pinel, J. P. J., Assanand, S., & Lehman, D. R. (2000). Hunger, eating, and ill health. *American Psychologist, 55,* 1105–1116.

Pines, A. M. (1993). Burnout: An existential perspective. In W. B. Schaufeli, C. Maslach, & T. Marek (Eds.), *Professional burnout: Recent developments in theory and research* (pp. 33–51). Washington, DC: Taylor & Francis.

Pinker, S. (1994). *The language instinct.* New York: Morrow.

Pinker, S. (1997a). Evolutionary psychology: An exchange. *New York Review of Books, 44,* 55–58.

Pinker, S. (1997b). *How the mind works.* New York: Norton.

Pinker, S. (2003). *The blank slate: The modern denial of human nature.* New York: Viking.

Pinker, S. (2007, March 19). A history of violence. *The New Republic Online.*

Pinker, S., & Bloom, P. (1990). Natural language and natural selection. *Behavioral and Brain Sciences, 13,* 707–784.

Pitcher, D., Garrido, L., Walsh, V., & Duchaine, B. C. (2008). Transcranial magnetic stimulation disrupts the perception and embodiment of facial expressions. *Journal of Neuroscience, 28*(36), 8929–8933.

Pleis, J. R., Lucas, J. W., & Ward, B. W. (2009). Summary of health statistics for U.S. adults: National health interview survey, 2008, *Vital Health Stat 10*(242). National Center for Health Statistics.

Plotnik, J. M., de Waal, F. B. M., & Reiss, D. (2006). Self-recognition in an Asian elephant. *Proceedings of the National Academy of Sciences, USA, 103,* 17053–17057.

Poliak, S., & Pelas, E. (2003). The local differentiation of myelinated axons at nodes of Ranvier. *Nature Reviews Neuroscience, 4,* 968–980.

Polzanczyk, G., de Lima, M. S., Horta, B. L., Biederman, J., & Rohde, L. A. (2007). The worldwide prevalence of ADHD: A systematic review and metaregression analysis. *American Journal of Psychiatry, 164,* 942–948.

Poole, D. A., Lindsay, S. D., Memon, A., & Bull, R. (1995). Psychotherapy and the recovery of memories of childhood sexual abuse: U.S. and British practitioners' opinions, practices, and experiences. *Journal of Consulting and Clinical Psychology, 63,* 426–487.

Poon, S. H., Sim, K., Sum, M. Y., Kuswanto, C. N., & Baldessarini, R. J. (2012). Evidence-based options for treatment-resistant adult bipolar disorder patients. *Bipolar Disorders, 14,* 573–584.

Pope, A. W., & Bierman, K. L. (1999). Predicting adolescent peer problems and antisocial activities: The relative roles of aggression and dysregulation. *Developmental Psychology, 35,* 335–346.

Porter, S., & ten Brinke, L. (2008). Reading between the lies: Identifying concealed and falsified emotions in universal facial expressions. *Psychological Science, 19,* 508–514.

Posner, M. I., & Raichle, M. E. (1994). *Images of mind.* New York: W. H. Freeman and Company.

Post, R. M., Frye, M. A., Denicoff, G. S., Leverich, G. S., Dunn, R. T., Osuch, E. A., . . . Jajodia, K. (2008). Emerging trends in the treatment of rapid cycling bipolar disorder: A selected review. *Bipolar Disorders, 2,* 305–315.

Postman, L., & Underwood, B. J. (1973). Critical issues in interference theory. *Memory & Cognition, 1,* 19–40.

Postmes, T., & Spears, R. (1998). Deindividuation and anti-normative behavior: A meta-analysis. *Psychological Bulletin, 123,* 238–259.

Powell, R. A., Symbaluk, D. G., MacDonald, S. E., & Honey, P. L. (2009). *Introduction to learning and behavior* (3rd ed.). Belmont, CA: Wadsworth Cengage Learning.

Prasada, S., & Pinker, S. (1993). Generalizations of regular and irregular morphology. *Language and Cognitive Processes, 8,* 1–56.

Pratkanis, A. R. (1992). The cargo-cult science of subliminal persuasion. *Skeptical Inquirer, 16,* 260–272.

Pressman, S. D., Cohen, S., Miller, G. E., Barkin, A., Rabin, B. S., & Treanor, J. J. (2005). Loneliness, social network size, and immune response to influenza vaccination in college freshmen. *Health Psychology, 24,* 297–306.

Price, J. L., & Davis, B. (2008). *The woman who can't forget: The extraordinary story of living with the most remarkable memory known to science.* New York: Free Press.

Prior, H., Schwartz, A., & Güntürkün, O. (2008). Mirror-induced behavior in the magpie (*Pica pica*): Evidence of self-recognition. *PLoS Biology, 6,* e202.

Prochaska, J. J., & Sallis, J. F. (2004). A randomized controlled trial of single versus multiple health behavior change: Promoting physical activity and nutrition among adolescents. *Health Psychology, 23,* 314–318.

Procopio, M., & Marriott, P. (2007). Intrauterine hormonal environment and risk of developing anorexia nervosa. *Archives of General Psychiatry, 64*(12), 1402–1407.

Protzko, J., Aronson, J., & Blair, C. (2013). How to make a young child smarter: Evidence from the database of raising intelligence. *Perspectives on Psychological Science, 8*(1), 25–40. doi:10.1177/1745691612462585

Pruitt, D. G. (1998). Social conflict. In D. T. Gilbert, S. T. Fiske, & G. Lindzey (Eds.), *The handbook of social psychology* (4th ed., Vol. 2, pp. 470–503). New York: McGraw-Hill.

Punjabi, N. M. (2008). The epidemiology of adult obstructive sleep apnea. *Proceedings of the American Thoracic Society, 5,* 136–143.

Puterman, E., Lin, J., Blackburn, E. H., O'Donovan, A., Adler, N., & Epel, E. (2010). The power of exercise: Buffering the effect of chronic stress on telomere length. *PLoS ONE, 5,* e10837.

Pyc, M. A., & Rawson, K. A. (2009). Testing the retrieval effort hypothesis: Does greater difficulty correctly recalling information lead to higher levels of memory? *Journal of Memory and Language, 60,* 437–447.

Pyers, J. E., & Senghas, A. (2009). Language promotes false-belief understanding: Evidence from learners of a new sign language. *Psychological Science, 20*(7), 805–812.

Pyers, J. E., Shusterman, A., Senghas, A., Spelke, E. S., & Emmorey, K. (2010). Evidence from an emerging sign language reveals that language supports spatial cognition. *Proceedings of the National Academy of Sciences, USA, 107,* 12116–12120.

Quattrone, G. A. (1982). Behavioral consequences of attributional bias. *Social Cognition, 1,* 358–378.

Querleu, D., Lefebvre, C., Titran, M., Renard, X., Morillon, M., & Crepin, G. (1984). Réactivité de nouveau-né de moins de deux heures de vie á la voix maternelle [Reactivity of a newborn at less than two hours of life to the mother's voice]. *Journal de Gynécologie Obstétrique et de Biologie de la Reproduction, 13,* 125–134.

Qureshi, A., & Lee-Chiong, T. (2004). Medications and their effects on sleep. *Medical Clinics of North America, 88,* 751–766.

Race, E., Keane, M. M., & Verfaellie, M. (2011). Medial temporal lobe damage causes deficits in episodic memory and episodic future thinking not attributable to deficits in narrative construction. *Journal of Neuroscience, 31,* 10262–10269.

Radford, E., & Radford, M. A. (1949). *Encyclopedia of superstitions.* New York: Philosophical Library.

Raichle, M. E., & Mintun, M. A. (2006). Brain work and brain imaging. *Annual Review of Neuroscience, 29,* 449–476.

Rajaram, S. (2011). Collaboration both hurts and helps memory: A cognitive perspective. *Current Directions in Psychological Science, 20,* 76–81.

Rajaram, S., & Pereira-Pasarin, L. P. (2010). Collaborative memory: Cognitive research and theory. *Perspectives on Psychological Science, 6,* 649–663.

Ramachandran, V. S., & Altschuler, E. L. (2009). The use of visual feedback, in particular mirror visual feedback, in restoring brain function. *Brain, 132,* 1693–1710.

Ramachandran, V. S., & Blakeslee, S. (1998). *Phantoms in the brain: Probing the mysteries of the human mind.* New York: Morrow.

Ramachandran, V. S., Brang, D., & McGeoch, P. D. (2010). Dynamic reorganization of referred sensations by movements of phantom limbs. *NeuroReport, 21,* 727–730.

Ramachandran, V. S., Rodgers-Ramachandran, D., & Stewart, M. (1992). Perceptual correlates of massive cortical reorganization. *Science, 258,* 1159–1160.

Ramirez-Esparza, N., Gosling, S. D., Benet-Martinez, V., & Potter, J. P. (2004). Do bilinguals have two personalities? A special case of cultural frame-switching. *Journal of Research in Personality, 40,* 99–120.

Randall, A. (2012, May 5). Black women and fat. *New York Times.* Retrieved from http:// www.nytimes.com/2012/05/06/opinion/sunday/why-black-women-are-fat.html?_r=0

Rapaport, D. (1946). *Diagnostic psychological testing: The theory, statistical evaluation, and diagnostic application of a battery of tests.* Chicago: Year Book Publishers.

Rapoport, J., Chavez, A., Greenstein, D., Addington, A., & Gogtay, N. (2009). Autism-spectrum disorders and childhood onset schizophrenia: Clinical and biological contributions to a relationship revisited. *Journal of the American Academy of Child and Adolescent Psychiatry, 48,* 10–18.

Rappoport, J. L. (1990). Obsessive-compulsive disorder and basal ganglia dysfunction. *Psychological Medicine, 20,* 465–469.

Rauschecker, J. P., & Scott, S. K. (2009). Maps and streams in the auditory cortex: Nonhuman primates illuminate human speech processing. *Nature Neuroscience, 12,* 718–724.

Raz, A., Shapiro, T., Fan, J., & Posner, M. I. (2002). Hypnotic suggestion and the modulation of Stroop interference. *Archives of General Psychiatry, 59,* 1155–1161.

Raz, A., Fan, J., & Posner, M. I. (2005). Hypnotic suggestion reduces conflict in the brain. *Proceedings of the National Academy of Sciences, 102,* 9978–9983.

Raz, N. (2000). Aging of the brain and its impact on cognitive performance: Integration of structural and functional findings. In F. I. M. Craik & T. A. Salthouse (Eds.), *The handbook of aging and cognition* (pp. 1–90). Mahwah, NJ: Erlbaum.

Reason, J., & Mycielska, K. (1982). *Absent-minded?: The psychology of mental lapses and everyday errors.* Englewood Cliffs, NJ: Prentice-Hall.

Reber, A. S. (1996). *Implicit learning and tacit knowledge: An essay on the cognitive unconscious.* New York: Oxford University Press.

Reber, P. J., Gitelman, D. R., Parrish, T. B., & Mesulam, M. M. (2003). Dissociating explicit and implicit category knowledge with fMRI. *Journal of Cognitive Neuroscience, 15,* 574–583.

Recanzone, G. H., & Sutter, M. L. (2008). The biological basis of audition. *Annual Review of Psychology, 59,* 119–142.

Rechsthaffen, A., Gilliland, M. A., Bergmann, B. M., & Winter, J. B. (1983). Physiological correlates of prolonged sleep deprivation in rats. *Science, 221,* 182–184.

Redick, T. S., Shipstead, Z., Harrison, T. L., Hicks, K. L., Fried, D. E., Hambrick, D. Z., . . . Engle, R. W. (2013). No evidence of intelligence improvement after working memory training: A randomized, placebo-controlled study. *Journal of Experimental Psychology: General, 142,* 359–379. doi:10.1037/a002908

Reed, C. L., Klatzky, R. L., & Halgren, E. (2005). What vs. where in touch: An fMRI study. *NeuroImage, 25,* 718–726.

Reed, D. R. (2008). Birth of a new breed of supertaster. *Chemical Senses, 33,* 489–491.

Reed, G. (1988). *The psychology of anomalous experience* (rev. ed.). Buffalo, NY: Prometheus Books.

Reeve, C. L., Heggestad, E. D., & Lievens, F. (2009). Modeling the impact of test anxiety and test familiarity on the criterion-related validity of cognitive ability tests. *Intelligence, 37*(1), 34–41.

Regan, P. C. (1998). What if you can't get what you want? Willingness to compromise ideal mate selection standards as a function of sex, mate value, and relationship context. *Personality and Social Psychology Bulletin, 24,* 1294–1303.

Reichbach, G. L. (2012, May 16). A judge's plea for pot [op-ed article]. *New York Times,* p. A27.

Reis, H. T., Maniaci, M. R., Caprariello, P. S., Eastwick, P. W., & Finkel, E. J. (2011). Familiarity does indeed promote attraction in live interaction. *Journal of Personality and Social Psychology, 101*(3), 557–570. doi:10.1037/a0022885

Reiss, D., & Marino, L. (2001). Mirror self-recognition in the bottlenose dolphin: A case of cognitive convergence. *Proceedings of the National Academy of Sciences, USA, 98,* 5937–5942.

Reissland, N. (1988). Neonatal imitation in the first hour of life: Observations in rural Nepal. *Developmental Psychology, 24,* 464–469.

Renner, K. E. (1964). Delay of reinforcement: A historical review. *Psychological Review, 61,* 341–361.

Renner, M. J., & Mackin, R. (1998). A life stress instrument for classroom use. *Teaching of Psychology, 25,* 46–48.

Rensink, R. A. (2002). Change detection. *Annual Review of Psychology, 53,* 245–277.

Rensink, R. A., O'Regan, J. K., & Clark, J. J. (1997). To see or not to see: The need for attention to perceive changes in scenes. *Psychological Science, 8,* 368–373.

Repacholi, B. M., & Gopnik, A. (1997). Early reasoning about desires: Evidence from 14- and 18-month-olds. *Developmental Psychology, 33,* 12–21.

Rescorla, R. A. (2006). Stimulus generalization of excitation and inhibition. *Quarterly Journal of Experimental Psychology, 59,* 53–67.

Rescorla, R. A., & Wagner, A. R. (1972). A theory of Pavlovian conditioning: Variations in effectiveness of reinforcement and nonreinforcement. In A. Black & W. F. Prokasky, Jr. (Eds.), *Classical conditioning II* (pp. 64–99). New York: Appleton-Century-Crofts.

Ressler, K. J., & Mayberg, H. S. (2007). Targeting abnormal neural circuits in mood and anxiety disorders: From the laboratory to the clinic. *Nature Neuroscience, 10,* 1116–1124.

Ressler, K. J., & Nemeroff, C. B. (1999). Role of norepinephrine in the pathophysiology and treatment of mood disorders. *Biological Psychiatry, 46,* 1219–1233.

Rice, K. G., Richardson, C. M. E., & Clark, D. (2012). Perfectionism, procrastination, and psychological distress. *Journal of Counseling Psychology, 39,* 288–302.

Richards, M., Black, S., Mishra, G., Gale, C. R., Deary, I. J., & Batty, D. G. (2009). IQ in childhood and the metabolic syndrome in middle age: Extended follow-up of the 1946 British birth cohort study. *Intelligence, 37*(6), 567–572.

Richards, M. H., Crowe, P. A., Larson, R., & Swarr, A. (1998). Developmental patterns and gender differences in the experience of peer companionship during adolescence. *Child Development, 69,* 154–163.

Ridenour, T. A., & Howard, M. O. (2012). Inhalants abuse: Status of etiology and intervention. In J. C. Verster, K. Brady, M. Galanter, & P. Conrod (Eds.), *Drug abuse and addiction in medical illness: Causes, consequences, and treatment* (pp. 189–199). New York: Springer.

Rimer, J., Dwan, K., Lawlor, D. A., Greig, C. A., McMurdo, M., Morley, W., & Mead, G. E. (2012). Exercise for depression. *Cochrane Database of Systematic Reviews, 7,* CD004366.

Risko, E. F., Anderson, N., Sarwal, A., Engelhardt, M., & Kingstone, A. (2012). Every attention: Variation in mind wandering and memory in a lecture. *Applied Cognitive Psychology, 26,* 234–242.

Risman, J. E., Coyle, J. T., Green, R. W., Javitt, D. C., Benes, F. M., Heckers, S., & Grace, A. A. (2008). Circuit-based framework for understanding neurotransmitter and risk gene interactions in schizophrenia. *Trends in Neurosciences, 31,* 234–242.

Rizzolatti, G., & Craighero, L. (2004). The mirror-neuron system. *Annual Review of Neuroscience, 27,* 169–192.

Rizzolatti, G., & Sinigaglia, C. (2012). The functional role of the parieto-frontal mirror circuit. *Nature Reviews Neuroscience, 11,* 264–274.

Roberts, G. A. (1991). Delusional belief and meaning in life: A preferred reality? *British Journal of Psychiatry, 159,* 20–29.

Roberts, G. A., & McGrady, A. (1996). Racial and gender effects on the relaxation response: Implications for the development of hypertension. *Biofeedback and Self-Regulation, 21,* 51–62.

Robertson, L. C. (1999). What can spatial deficits teach us about feature binding and spatial maps? *Visual Cognition, 6,* 409–430.

Robertson, L. C. (2003). Binding, spatial attention and perceptual awareness. *Nature Reviews Neuroscience, 4,* 93–102.

Robins, R. W., Fraley, R. C., & Krueger, R. F. (Eds.). (2007). *Handbook of research methods in personality psychology.* New York: Guilford Press.

Robinson, D. N. (1995). *An intellectual history of psychology.* Madison: University of Wisconsin Press.

Roediger, H. L., III. (2000). Why retrieval is the key process to understanding human memory. In E. Tulving (Ed.), *Memory, consciousness, and the brain: The Tallinn conference* (pp. 52–75). Philadelphia: Psychology Press.

Roediger, H. L., III, & Karpicke, J. D. (2006). Test-enhanced learning: Taking memory tests improves long-term retention. *Psychological Science, 17,* 249–255.

Roediger, H. L., III, & McDermott, K. B. (1995). Creating false memories: Remembering words not presented in lists. *Journal of Experimental Psychology: Learning, Memory, and Cognition, 21,* 803–814.

Roediger, H. L., III, & McDermott, K. B. (2000). Tricks of memory. *Current Directions in Psychological Science, 9,* 123–127.

Roediger, H. L., III, Weldon, M. S., & Challis, B. H. (1989). Explaining dissociations between implicit and explicit measures of retention: A processing account. In H. L. Roediger, III & F. I. M. Craik (Eds.), *Varieties of memory and consciousness: Essays in honor of Endel Tulving* (pp. 3–41). Hillsdale, NJ: Erlbaum.

Rogers, C. R. (1951). *Client-centered therapy: Its current practice, implications, and theory.* Boston: Houghton Mifflin.

Rosch, E. H. (1973). Natural categories. *Cognitive Psychology, 4,* 328–350.

Rosch, E. H. (1975). Cognitive representations of semantic categories. *Journal of Experimental Psychology: General, 104,* 192–233.

Rosch, E. H., & Mervis, C. B. (1975). Family resemblances: Studies in the internal structure of categories. *Cognitive Psychology, 7,* 573–605.

Rose, S. P. R. (2002). Smart drugs: Do they work? Are they ethical? Will they be legal? *Nature Reviews Neuroscience, 3,* 975–979.

Roseman, I. J. (1984). Cognitive determinants of emotion: A structural theory. *Review of Personality and Social Psychology, 5,* 11–36.

Roseman, I. J., & Smith, C. A. (2001). Appraisal theory: Overview, assumptions, varieties and controversies. In K. R. Scherer, A. Schorr, & T. Johnstone (Eds.), *Appraisal processes in emotion: Theory, methods, research* (pp. 3–19). New York: Oxford University Press.

Rosenbaum, J. E. (2009). Patient teenagers? A comparison of the sexual behavior of virginity pledgers and matched nonpledgers. *Pediatrics, 123*(1), e110–e120.

Rosenberg, M. (1965). *Society and the adolescent self-image.* Princeton, NJ: Princeton University Press.

Rosenhan, D. (1973). On being sane in insane places. *Science, 179,* 250–258.

Rosenkranz, K., Williamon, A., & Rothwell, J. C. (2007). Motorcortical excitability and synaptic plasticity is enhanced in professional musicians. *The Journal of Neuroscience, 27,* 5200–5206.

Rosenstein, M. J., Milazzo-Sayre, L. J., & Manderscheid, R. W. (1990). Characteristics of persons using specifically inpatient, outpatient, and partial care programs in 1986. In M. A. Sonnenschein (Ed.), *Mental health in the United States* (pp. 139–172). Washington, DC: U.S. Government Printing Office.

Rosenthal, R., & Fode, K. L. (1963). The effect of experimenter bias on the performance of the albino rat. *Behavioral Science, 8,* 183–189.

Ross, L. (1977). The intuitive psychologist and his shortcomings: Distortions in the attribution process. *Advances in Experimental Social Psychology, 10,* 173–220.

Ross, L., Amabile, T. M., & Steinmetz, J. L. (1977). Social roles, social control, and biases in social-perception processes. *Journal of Personality and Social Psychology, 35,* 485–494.

Ross, L., Lepper, M. R., & Hubbard, M. (1975). Perseverance in self-perception and social perception: Biased attributional processing the debriefing paradigm. *Journal of Personality and Social Psychology, 32,* 880–892.

Ross, L., & Nisbett, R. E. (1991). *The person and the situation.* New York: McGraw-Hill.

Rosvall, M., & Bergstrom, C. T. (2008). Maps of random walks on complex networks reveal community structure. *Proceedings of the National Academy of Sciences, USA, 105,* 1118–1123.

Roth, H. P., & Caron, H. S. (1978). Accuracy of doctors' estimates and patients' statements on adherence to a drug regimen. *Clinical Pharmacology and Therapeutics, 23,* 361–370.

Rothbart, M. K., & Bates, J. E. (1998). Temperament. In W. Damon (Series Ed.) & N. Eisenberg (Vol. Ed.), *Handbook of child psychology: Vol. 3. Social, emotional and personality development* (5th ed., pp. 105–176). New York: Wiley.

Rothbaum, B. O., & Schwartz, A. C. (2002). Exposure therapy for post-traumatic stress disorder. *American Journal of Psychotherapy, 56,* 59–75.

Rotter, J. B. (1966). Generalized expectancies for internal versus external locus of control of reinforcement. *Psychological Monographs: General and Applied, 80,* 1–28.

Roy-Byrne, P. P., & Cowley, D. S. (2002). Pharmacological treatments for panic disorder, generalized anxiety disorder, specific phobia, and social anxiety disorder. In P. E. Nathan & J. M. Gorman (Eds.), *A guide to treatments that work* (2nd ed., pp. 337–365). New York: Oxford University Press.

Rozin, P. (1968). Are carbohydrate and protein intakes separately regulated? *Journal of Comparative and Physiological Psychology, 65,* 23–29.

Rozin, P., Dow, S., Moscovitch, M., & Rajaram, S. (1998). What causes humans to begin and end a meal? A role for memory for what has been eaten, as evidenced by a study of multiple meal eating in amnesic patients. *Psychological Science, 9,* 392–396.

Rozin, P., & Kalat, J. W. (1971). Specific hungers and poison avoidance as adaptive specializations of learning. *Psychological Review, 78,* 459–486.

Rubin, M., & Badea, C. (2012). They're all the same! . . . but for several different reasons: A review of the multicausal nature of perceived group variability. *Current Directions in Psychological Science, 21*(6), 367–372. doi:10.1177/0963721412457363

Rubin, Z. (1973). *Liking and loving.* New York: Holt, Rinehart & Winston.

Rudman, L. A., Ashmore, R. D., & Gary, M. L. (2001). "Unlearning" automatic biases: The malleability of implicit prejudice and stereotypes. *Journal of Personality and Social Psychology, 81,* 856–868.

Rusbult, C. E. (1983). A longitudinal test of the investment model: The development (and deterioration) of satisfaction and commitment in heterosexual involvements. *Journal of Personality and Social Psychology, 45,* 101–117.

Rusbult, C. E., & Van Lange, P. A. M. (2003). Interdependence, interaction and relationships. *Annual Review of Psychology, 54,* 351–375.

Ruscio, A. M., Stein, D. J., Chiu, W. T., Kessler, R. C. (2010). The epidemiology of obsessive-compulsive disorder in the National Comorbidity Survey Replication. *Molecular Psychiatry, 15,* 53–63.

Rushton, J. P. (1995). Asian achievement, brain size, and evolution: Comment on A. H. Yee. *Educational Psychology Review, 7,* 373–380.

Rushton, J. P., & Templer, D. I. (2009). National differences in intelligence, crime, income, and skin color. *Intelligence, 37*(4), 341–346.

Russell, B. (1945). *A history of Western philosophy.* New York: Simon & Schuster.

Russell, J., Gee, B., & Bullard, C. (2012). Why do young children hide by closing their eyes? Self-visibility and the developing concept of self. *Journal of Cognition and Development, 13*(4), 550–576. doi:10.1080/15248372.2011.594826

Rutledge, R. B., Lazzaro, S. C., Lau, B., Myers, C. E., Gluck, M. A., & Glimcher, P. W. (2009). Dopaminergic drugs modulate learning rates and perseveration in Parkinson's patients in a dynamic foraging task. *Journal of Neuroscience, 29,* 15104–15114.

Rutter, M., & Silberg, J. (2002). Gene–environment interplay in relation to emotional and behavioral disturbance. *Annual Review of Psychology, 53,* 463–490.

Ryan, R. M., & Deci, E. L. (2000). Self-determination theory and the facilitation of intrinsic motivation, social development, and well-being. *American Psychologist, 55,* 68–78.

Ryle, G. (1949). *The Concept of Mind.* Hutchinson, London.

Sachs, J. S. (1967). Recognition of semantic, syntactic, and lexical changes in sentences. *Psychonomic Bulletin & Review, 1,* 17–18.

Sacks, O. (1995). *An anthropologist on Mars.* New York: Knopf.

Sacks, O. (1996). *An anthropologist on Mars* (pbk). Visalia, CA: Vintage.

Saks, E. R. (2013, January 25). Successful and schizophrenic. *New York Times.* Retrieved from http://www.nytimes.com/2013/01/27/opinion/sunday/schizophrenic-not-stupid.html

Sahakian, B., & Morein-Zamir, S. (2007). Professor's little helper. *Nature, 450*(7173), 1157–1159.

Sallet, J., Mars, R. B., Noonan, M. P., Andersson, J. L., O'Reilly, J. X., Jbabdi, S., . . . Rushworth, M. F. S. (2011). Social network size affects neural circuits in macaques. *Science, 334*(6056), 697–700. doi:10.1126/science.1210027

Salmon, D. P., & Bondi, M. W. (2009). Neuropsychological assessment of dementia. *Annual Review of Psychology, 60,* 257–282.

Salovey, P., & Grewal, D. (2005). The science of emotional intelligence. *Current Directions in Psychological Science, 14*(6), 281–285.

Salthouse, T. A. (1984). Effects of age and skill in typing. *Journal of Experimental Psychology: General, 113,* 345–371.

Salthouse, T. A. (1987). Age, experience, and compensation. In C. Schooler & K. W. Schaie (Eds.), *Cognitive functioning and social structure over the life course* (pp. 142–150). Norwood, NJ: Ablex.

Salthouse, T. A. (1996a). General and specific mediation of adult age differences in memory. *Journal of Gerontology: Series B: Psychological Sciences and Social Sciences, 51B,* P30–P42.

Salthouse, T. A. (1996b). The processing-speed theory of adult age differences in cognition. *Psychological Review, 103,* 403–428.

Salthouse, T. A. (2000). Pressing issues in cognitive aging. In D. Park & N. Schwartz (Eds.), *Cognitive aging: A primer* (pp. 43–54). Philadelphia: Psychology Press.

Salthouse, T. A. (2006). Mental exercise and mental aging. *Perspectives on Psychological Science, 1*(1), 68–87.

Sampson, R. J., & Laub, J. H. (1995). Understanding variability in lives through time: Contributions of life-course criminology. *Studies of Crime Prevention, 4,* 143–158.

Sandin, R. H., Enlund, G., Samuelsson, P., & Lenmarken, C. (2000). Awareness during anesthesia: A prospective case study. *Lancet, 355,* 707–711.

Sara, S. J. (2000). Retrieval and reconsolidation: Toward a neurobiology of remembering. *Learning & Memory, 7,* 73–84.

Sarris, V. (1989). Max Wertheimer on seen motion: Theory and evidence. *Psychological Research, 51,* 58–68.

Sarter, M. (2006). Preclinical research into cognition enhancers. *Trends in Pharmacological Sciences, 27,* 602–608.

Satcher, D. (2001). *The Surgeon General's call to action to promote sexual health and responsible sexual behavior.* Washington, DC: U.S. Government Printing Office.

Satterwhite, C. L., Torrone, E., Meites, E., Dunne, E. F., Mahajan, R., Ocfernia, M. C., . . . Weinstock, H. (2013). Sexually transmitted infections among U. S. women and men: Prevalence and incidence estimates, 2008. *Sexually Transmitted Diseases, 40*(3), 187–193.

Savage, C. R., Deckersbach, T., Heckers, S., Wagner, A. D., Schacter, D. L., Alpert, N. M., . . . Rauch, S. L. (2001). Prefrontal regions supporting spontaneous and directed application of verbal learning strategies: Evidence from PET. *Brain, 124,* 219–231.

Savic, I., Berglund, H., & Lindstrom, P. (2005). Brain response to putative pheromones in homosexual men. *Proceedings of the National Academy of Sciences, USA, 102,* 7356–7361.

Savic, I., & Lindstrom, P. (2008). PET and MRI show differences in cerebral asymmetry and functional connectivity between homo- and heterosexual subjects. *Proceedings of the National Academy of Sciences, USA, 105*(27), 9403–9408.

Sawa, A., & Snyder, S. H. (2002). Schizophrenia: Diverse approaches to a complex disease. *Science, 295,* 692–695.

Sawyer, T. F. (2000). Francis Cecil Sumner: His views and influence on African American higher education. *History of Psychology, 3*(2), 122–141.

Scarborough, E., & Furumoto, L. (1987). *Untold lives: The first generation of American women psychologists.* New York: Columbia University Press.

Scarr, S., Pakstis, A. J., Katz, S. H., & Barker, W. B. (1977). Absence of a relationship between degree of White ancestry and intellectual skills within a Black population. *Human Genetics, 39*(1), 69–86.

Schachter, S. (1982). Recidivism and self-cure of smoking and obesity. *American Psychologist, 37,* 436–444.

Schachter, S., & Singer, J. E. (1962). Cognitive, social, and physiological determinants of emotional state. *Psychological Review, 69,* 379–399.

Schacter, D. L. (1987). Implicit memory: History and current status. *Journal of Experimental Psychology: Learning, Memory, and Cognition, 13,* 501–518.

Schacter, D. L. (1996). *Searching for memory: The brain, the mind, and the past.* New York: Basic Books.

Schacter, D. L. (1999). The seven sins of memory: Insights from psychology and cognitive neuroscience. *American Psychologist, 54*(3), 182–203.

Schacter, D. L. (2001a). *Forgotten ideas, neglected pioneers: Richard Semon and the story of memory.* Philadelphia: Psychology Press.

Schacter, D. L. (2001b). *The seven sins of memory: How the mind forgets and remembers.* Boston: Houghton Mifflin.

Schacter, D. L. (2012). Adaptive constructive processes and the future of memory. *American Psychologist, 67,* 603–613.

Schacter, D. L., & Addis, D. R. (2007). The cognitive neuroscience of constructive memory: Remembering the past and imagining the future. *Philosophical Transactions of the Royal Society of London. Series B: Biological Sciences, 362,* 773–786.

Schacter, D. L., Addis, D. R., & Buckner, R. L. (2007). Remembering the past to imagine the future: The prospective brain. *Nature Reviews Neuroscience, 8,* 657-661.

Schacter, D. L., Addis, D. R., & Buckner, R. L. (2008). Episodic simulation of future events: Concepts, data, and applications. *Annals of the New York Academy of Sciences, 1124,* 39–60.

Schacter, D. L., Addis, D. R., Hassabis, D., Martin, V. C., Spreng, R. N., & Szpunar, K. K. (2012). The future of memory: Remembering, imagining, and the brain. *Neuron, 16,* 582–583.

Schacter, D. L., Alpert, N. M., Savage, C. R., Rauch, S. L., & Albert, M. S. (1996). Conscious recollection and the human hippocampal formation: Evidence from positron emission tomography. *Proceedings of the National Academy of Sciences, USA, 93,* 321–325.

Schacter, D. L., & Curran, T. (2000). Memory without remembering and remembering without memory: Implicit and false memories. In M. S. Gazzaniga (Ed.), *The new cognitive neurosciences* (2nd ed., pp. 829–840). Cambridge, MA: MIT Press.

Schacter, D. L., Dobbins, I. G., & Schnyer, D. M. (2004). Specificity of priming: A cognitive neuroscience perspective. *Nature Reviews Neuroscience, 5,* 853–862.

Schacter, D. L., Gaesser, B., & Addis, D. R. (2012). Remembering the past and imagining the future in the elderly. *Gerontologist, 59*(2), 143–151. doi:10.1159/000342198

Schacter, D. L., Guerin, S. A., & St. Jacques, P. L. (2011). Memory distortion: An adaptive perspective. *Trends in Cognitive Sciences, 15,* 467–474.

Schacter, D. L., Harbluk, J. L., & McLachlan, D. R. (1984). Retrieval without recollection: An experimental analysis of source amnesia. *Journal of Verbal Learning and Verbal Behavior, 23,* 593–611.

Schacter, D. L., Israel, L., & Racine, C. A. (1999). Suppressing false recognition in younger and older adults: The distinctiveness heuristic. *Journal of Memory and Language, 40,* 1–24.

Schacter, D. L., Reiman, E., Curran, T., Yun, L. S., Bandy, D., McDermott, K. B., & Roediger, H. L., III. (1996). Neuroanatomical correlates of veridical and illusory recognition memory: Evidence from positron emission tomography. *Neuron, 17,* 267–274.

Schacter, D. L., & Tulving, E. (1994). *Memory systems 1994.* Cambridge, MA: MIT Press.

Schacter, D. L., Wagner, A. D., & Buckner, R. L. (2000). Memory systems of 1999. In E. Tulving & F. I. M. Craik (Eds.), *The Oxford handbook of memory* (pp. 627–643). New York: Oxford University Press.

Schafer, R. B., & Keith, P. M. (1980). Equity and depression among married couples. *Social Psychology Quarterly, 43,* 430–435.

Schaie, K. W. (1996). *Intellectual development in adulthood: The Seattle Longitudinal Study.* New York: Cambridge University Press.

Schaie, K. W. (2005). *Developmental influences on adult intelligence: The Seattle Longitudinal Study.* New York: Oxford University Press.

Schenk, T., Ellison, A., Rice, N., & Milner, A. D. (2005). The role of V5/MT+ in the control of catching movements: An rTMS study. *Neuropsychologia, 43,* 189–198.

Scherer, K. R. (1999). Appraisal theory. In T. Dalgleish & M. Power (Eds.), *Handbook of cognition and emotion* (pp. 637–663). New York: Wiley.

Scherer, K. R. (2001). The nature and study of appraisal: A review of the issues. In K. R. Scherer, A. Schorr, & T. Johnstone (Eds.), *Appraisal processes in emotion: Theory, methods, research* (pp. 369–391). New York: Oxford University Press.

Schildkraut, J. J. (1965). The catecholamine hypothesis of affective disorders: A review of supporting evidence. *American Journal of Psychiatry, 122,* 509–522.

Schilling, O. K., Wahl, H.-W., & Wiegering, S. (2013). Affective development in advanced old age: Analyses of terminal change in positive and negative affect. *Developmental Psychology, 49*(5), 1011–1020. doi:10.1037/a0028775

Schlegel, A., & Barry, H., III. (1991). *Adolescence: An anthropological inquiry.* New York: Free Press.

Schmitt, D. P., Jonason, P. K., Byerley, G. J., Flores, S. D., Illbeck, B. E., O'Leary, K. N., & Qudrat, A. (2012). A reexamination of sex differences in sexuality: New studies reveal old truths. *Current Directions in Psychological Science, 21*(2), 135–139. doi:10.1177/0963721412436808

Schmitt, D. P., Realo, A., Voracek, M., & Allik, J. (2008). Why can't a man be more like a woman? Sex differences in personality traits across 55 cultures. *Journal of Personality and Social Psychology, 94,* 168–182.

Schneider, B. H., Atkinson, L., & Tardif, C. (2001). Child–parent attachment and children's peer relations: A quantitative review. *Developmental Psychology, 37,* 86–100.

Schnorr, J. A., & Atkinson, R. C. (1969). Repetition versus imagery instructions in the short- and long-term retention of paired associates. *Psychonomic Science, 15,* 183–184.

Schoenemann, P. T., Sheenan, M. J., & Glotzer, L. D. (2005). Prefrontal white matter volume is disproportionately larger in humans than in other primates. *Nature Neuroscience, 8,* 242–252.

Schott, B. J., Henson, R. N., Richardson-Klavehn, A., Becker, C., Thoma, V., Heinze, H. J., & Duzel, E. (2005). Redefining implicit and explicit memory: The functional neuroanatomy of priming, remembering, and control of retrieval. *Proceedings of the National Academy of Sciences, USA, 102,* 1257–1262.

Schreiner, C. E., Read, H. L., & Sutter, M. L. (2000). Modular organization of frequency integration in primary auditory cortex. *Annual Review of Neuroscience, 23,* 501–529.

Schreiner, C. E., & Winer, J. A. (2007). Auditory cortex mapmaking: Principles, projections, and plasticity. *Neuron, 56,* 356–365.

Schubert, T. W., & Koole, S. L. (2009). The embodied self: Making a fist enhances men's power-related self-conceptions. *Journal of Experimental Social Psychology, 45,* 828–834.

Schultz, D., Izard, C. E., & Bear, G. (2004). Children's emotion processing: Relations to emotionality and aggression. *Development and Psychopathology, 16*(2), 371–387.

Schultz, W. (2006). Behavioral theories and the neurophysiology of reward. *Annual Review of Psychology, 57,* 87–115.

Schultz, W. (2007). Behavioral dopamine signals. *Trends in Neurosciences, 30,* 203–210.

Schultz, W., Dayan, P., & Montague, P. R. (1997). A neural substrate of prediction and reward. *Science, 275,* 1593–1599.

Schwartz, B. L. (2002). *Tip-of-the-tongue states: Phenomenology, mechanisms, and lexical retrieval.* Mahwah, NJ: Erlbaum.

Schwartz, J. H., & Westbrook, G. L. (2000). The cytology of neurons. In E. R. Kandel, G. H. Schwartz, & T. M. Jessell (Eds.), *Principles of neural science* (pp. 67–104). New York: McGraw-Hill.

Schwartz, S., & Maquet, P. (2002). Sleep imaging and the neuropsychological assessment of dreams. *Trends in Cognitive Sciences, 6,* 23–30.

Schwartzman, A. E., Gold, D., & Andres, D. (1987). Stability of intelligence: A 40-year follow-up. *Canadian Journal of Psychology, 41,* 244–256.

Schwarz, N., & Clore, G. L. (1983). Mood, misattribution, and judgments of well-being: Informative and directive functions of affective states. *Journal of Personality and Social Psychology, 45,* 513–523.

Schwarz, N., Mannheim, Z., & Clore, G. L. (1988). How do I feel about it? The informative function of affective states. In K. Fiedler & J. Forgas (Eds.), *Affect cognition and social behavior: New evidence and integrative attempts* (pp. 44–62). Toronto: C. J. Hogrefe.

Scoville, W. B., & Milner, B. (1957). Loss of recent memory after bilateral hippocampal lesions. *Journal of Neurology, Neurosurgery, and Psychiatry, 20,* 11–21.

Sedlmeier, P., Eberth, J., Schwarz, M., Zimmermann, D., Haarig, F., Jaeger, S., & Kunze, S. (2012). The psychological effects of meditation: A meta-analysis. *Psychological Bulletin, 138,* 1139–1171.

Seeman, T. E., Dubin, L. F., & Seeman, M. (2003). Religiosity/spirituality and health: A critical review of the evidence for biological pathways. *American Psychologist, 58,* 53–63.

Segall, M. H., Lonner, W. J., & Berry, J. W. (1998). Cross-cultural psychology as a scholarly discipline: On the flowering of culture in behavioral research. *American Psychologist, 53*(10), 1101–1110.

Seidman, G. (2013). Self-presentation and belonging on Facebook: How personality influences social media use and motivations. *Personality and Individual Differences, 54,* 402–407.

Seligman, M. E. P. (1971). Phobias and preparedness. *Behavior Therapy, 2,* 307–320.

Seligman, M. E. P. (1995). The effectiveness of psychotherapy: The Consumer Reports study. *American Psychologist, 48,* 966–971.

Selye, H., & Fortier, C. (1950). Adaptive reaction to stress. *Psychosomatic Medicine, 12,* 149–157.

Semenza, C. (2009). The neuropsychology of proper names. *Mind & Language, 24,* 347–369.

Semenza, C., & Zettin, M. (1989). Evidence from aphasia from proper names as pure referring expressions. *Nature, 342,* 678–679.

Senghas, A., Kita, S., & Ozyurek, A. (2004). Children create core properties of language: Evidence from an emerging sign language in Nicaragua. *Science, 305,* 1782.

Senior, J. (2014). *All joy and no fun: The paradox of modern parenthood.* New York: Harper-Collins.

Senju, A., Southgate, V., White, S., & Frith, U. (2009). Mindblind eyes: An absence of spontaneous theory of mind in Asperger syndrome. *Science, 325,* 883–885.

Serpell, R. (1974). Aspects of intelligence in a developing country. *African Social Research, 17,* 578–596.

Seybold, K. S., & Hill, P. C. (2001). The role of religion and spirituality in mental and physical health. *Current Directions in Psychological Science, 10,* 21–23.

Seymour, K., Clifford, C. W. G., Logothetis, N. K., & Bartels, A. (2010). Coding and binding of color and form in visual cortex. *Cerebral Cortex.* doi:10.1093/cercor/bhp265

Shallcross, A. J., Ford, B. Q, Floerke, V. A., & Mauss, I. B. (2013). Getting better with age: The relationship between age, acceptance, and negative affect. *Journal of Personality and Social Psychology, 104*(4), 734–749. doi:10.1037/a0031180

Shallice, T., Fletcher, P., Frith, C. D., Grasby, P., Frackowiak, R. S. J., & Dolan, R. J. (1994). Brain regions associated with acquisition and retrieval of verbal episodic memory. *Nature, 368,* 633–635.

Shariff, A. F., & Tracy, J. L. (2011). What are emotion expressions for? *Current Directions in Psychological Science, 20*(6), 395–399.

Sharot, T. (2011). *The optimism bias: A tour of the irrationally positive brain.* New York: Pantheon Books.

Shaw, J. S., Bjork, R. A., & Handal, A. (1995). Retrieval-induced forgetting in an eyewitness paradigm. *Psychonomic Bulletin & Review, 13,* 1023–1027.

Sheehan, P. (1979). Hypnosis and the process of imagination. In E. Fromm & R. S. Shor (Eds.), *Hypnosis: Developments in research and new perspectives* (pp. 293–319). Chicago: Aldine.

Shenton, M. E., Dickey, C. C., Frumin, M., & McCarley, R. W. (2001). A review of MRI findings in schizophrenia. *Schizophrenia Research, 49,* 1–52.

Shepherd, G. M. (1988). *Neurobiology.* New York: Oxford University Press.

Shepperd, J., Malone, W., & Sweeny, K. (2008). Exploring the causes of the self-serving bias. *Social and Personality Psychology Compass, 2*(2), 895–908.

Sherry, D. F., & Schacter, D. L. (1987). The evolution of multiple memory systems. *Psychological Review, 94,* 439–454.

Sherry, S. B., & Hall, P. A. (2009). The perfectionism model of binge eating: Tests of an integrative model. *Journal of Personality and Social Psychology, 96*(3), 690–709.

Shiffman, S., Gnys, M., Richards, T. J., Paty, J. A., & Hickcox, M. (1996). Temptations to smoke after quitting: A comparison of lapsers and maintainers. *Health Psychology, 15,* 455–461.

Shih, M., Pittinsky, T. L., & Ambady, N. (1999). Stereotype susceptibility: Identity salience and shifts in quantitative performance. *Psychological Science, 10,* 80–83.

Shimamura, A. P., & Squire, L. R. (1987). A neuropsychological study of fact memory and source amnesia. *Journal of Experimental Psychology: Learning, Memory, and Cognition, 13,* 464–473.

Shin, L. M., Rauch, S. L., & Pitman, R. K. (2006). Amygdala, medial prefrontal cortex, and hippocampal function in PTSD. *Annals of the New York Academy of Science, 1071,* 67–79.

Shinskey, J. L., & Munakata, Y. (2005). Familiarity breeds searching. *Psychological Science, 16*(8), 596–600.

Shipstead, Z., Redick, T. S., & Engle, R. W. (2012). Is working memory training effective? *Psychological Bulletin, 138,* 628–654.

Shiv, B., Loewenstein, G., Bechara, A., Damasio, H., & Damasio, A. R. (2005). Investment behavior and the negative side of emotion. *Psychological Science, 16,* 435–439.

Shomstein, S., & Yantis, S. (2004). Control of attention shifts between vision and audition in human cortex. *Journal of Neuroscience, 24,* 10702–10706.

Shore, C. (1986). Combinatorial play: Conceptual development and early multiword speech. *Developmental Psychology, 22,* 184–190.

Shultz, S., & Dunbar, R. (2010). Encephalization is not a universal macroevolutionary phenomenon in mammals but is associated with sociality. *Proceedings of the National Academy of Sciences,107,* 21582–21586.

Shweder, R. A., & Sullivan, M. A. (1993). Cultural psychology: Who needs it? *Annual Review of Psychology, 44,* 497–523.

Siegel, S., Baptista, M. A. S., Kim, J. A., McDonald, R. V., & Weise-Kelly, L. (2000). Pavlovian psychopharmacology: The associative basis of tolerance. *Experimental and Clinical Psychopharmacology, 8,* 276–293.

Siegler, R. S. (1992). The other Alfred Binet. *Developmental Psychology, 28*(2), 179–190. doi:10.1037/0012-1649.28.2.179

Sigman, M., Spence, S. J., & Wang, T. (2006). Autism from developmental and neuropsychological perspectives. *Annual Review of Clinical Psychology, 2,* 327–355.

Silver, N. (2013, March 26). How opinion on same-sex marriage is changing, and what it means. *New York Times.* Retrieved from http://fivethirtyeightblogs.nytimes.com/2013/03/26/how-opinion-on-same-sex-marriage-is-changing-and-what-it-means/

Simon, R. W. (2008). The joys of parenthood reconsidered. *Contexts, 7,* 40–45.

Simons, D. J., & Levin, D. T. (1998). Failure to detect changes to people during a real-world interaction. *Psychonomic Bulletin & Review, 5,* 644–649.

Simons, D. J., & Rensink, R. A. (2005). Change blindness: Past, present, and future. *Trends in Cognitive Sciences, 9,* 16–20.

Simpson, E. L. (1974). Moral development research: A case study of scientific cultural bias. *Human Development, 17,* 81–106.

Simpson, J. A., Collins, W. A., & Salvatore, J. E. (2011). The impact of early interpersonal experience on adult romantic relationship functioning: Recent findings from the Minnesota Longitudinal Study of Risk and Adaptation. *Current Directions in Psychological Science, 20*(6), 355–359. doi:10.1177/0963721411418468

Singer, P. (1975). *Animal liberation: A new ethics for our treatment of animals.* New York: Random House.

Singer, T., Seymour, B., O'Doherty, J., Kaube, H., Dolan, R. J., & Frith, C. D. (2004). Empathy for pain involves the affective but not sensory components of pain. *Science, 303,* 1157–1162.

Skinner, B. F. (1938). *The behavior of organisms: An experimental analysis.* New York: Appleton-Century-Crofts.

Skinner, B. F. (1948). "Superstition" in the pigeon. *Journal of Experimental Psychology, 38,* 168–172.

Skinner, B. F. (1953). *Science and human behavior.* New York: Macmillan.

Skinner, B. F. (1957). *Verbal behavior.* New York: Appleton-Century- Crofts.

Skinner, B. F. (1971). *Beyond freedom and dignity.* New York: Bantam Books.

Skinner, B. F. (1979). *The shaping of a behaviorist: Part two of an autobiography*. New York: Knopf.

Skinner, B. F. (1986). *Walden II*. Englewood Cliffs, NJ: Prentice Hall. (Original work published 1948)

Skoe, E., & Kraus, N. (2012). A little goes a long way: How the adult brain is shaped by musical training in adulthood. *Journal of Neuroscience, 32,* 11507–11510.

Skotko, B. G., Levine, S. P., & Goldstein, R. (2011). Self-perceptions from people with Down syndrome. *American Journal of Medical Genetics Part A, 155*(10), 2360–2369. doi:10.1002/ajmg.a.34235

Slater, A., Morison, V., & Somers, M. (1988). Orientation discrimination and cortical function in the human newborn. *Perception, 17,* 597–602.

Slotnick, S. D., & Schacter, D. L. (2004). A sensory signature that distinguished true from false memories. *Nature Neuroscience, 7,* 664–672.

Smart, E., Smart, L, & Morton, L. (2003). *Bringing Elizabeth home: A journey of faith and hope*. New York: Doubleday.

Smetacek, V. (2002). Balance: Mind-grasping gravity. *Nature, 415,* 481.

Smith, A. R., Seid, M. A., Jimanez, L. C., & Wcislo, W. T. (2010). Socially induced brain development in a facultatively eusocial sweat bee *Megalopta genalis* (Halictidae). *Proceedings of the Royal Society B: Biological Sciences.*

Smith, E. E., & Jonides, J. (1997). Working memory: A view from neuroimaging. *Cognitive Psychology, 33,* 5–42.

Smith, M. L., Glass, G. V., & Miller, T. I. (1980). *The benefits of psychotherapy*. Baltimore: Johns Hopkins University Press.

Smith, N., & Tsimpli, I.-M. (1995). *The mind of a savant*. Oxford, England: Oxford University Press.

Snedeker, J., Geren, J., & Shafto, C. (2007). Starting over: International adoption as a natural experiment in language development. *Psychological Science, 18,* 79–87.

Snedeker, J., Geren, J., & Shafto, C. (2012). Disentangling the effects of cognitive development and linguistic expertise: A longitudinal study of the acquisition of English in internationally adopted children. *Cognitive Psychology, 65,* 39–76.

Snyder, M., & Swann, W. B. (1978). Hypothesis testing processes in social interaction. *Journal of Personality and Social Psychology, 36,* 1202–1212.

Solomon, S., Greenberg, J., & Pyszczynski, T. (1991). A terror management theory of social behavior: The psychological functions of self-esteem and cultural worldviews. In M. P. Zanna (Ed.), *Advances in experimental social psychology* (Vol. 24, pp. 93–159). New York: Academic Press.

Solomon, S., Greenberg, J., Pyszczynski, T., Greenberg, J., Koole, S. L., & Pyszczynski, T. (2004). The cultural animal: Twenty years of terror management theory and research. In J. Greenberg, S. L. Koole, & T. Pyszczynski (Eds.), *Handbook of experimental existential psychology* (pp. 13–34). New York: Guilford Press.

Son, L. K., & Metcalfe, J. (2000). Metacognitive and control strategies in study-time allocation. *Journal of Experimental Psychology: Learning, Memory, and Cognition, 26,* 204–221.

Sparrow, B., Liu, J., & Wegner, D. M. (2011). Google effects on memory: Cognitive consequence of having information at our fingertips. *Science, 333,* 776–778.

Spearman, C. (1904). "General intelligence," objectively determined and measured. *American Journal of Psychology, 15,* 201–293.

Spelke, E. S. (2005). Sex differences in intrinsic aptitude for mathematics and science: A critical review. *The American Psychologist, 60*(9), 950–958. doi:10.1037/0003-066X.60.9.950

Spence, K. W. (1936). The nature of discrimination learning in animals. *Psychological Review, 43,* 427–449.

Sperling, G. (1960). The information available in brief visual presentations. *Psychological Monographs, 74* (Whole No. 48).

Spiro, H. M., McCrea Curnan, M. G., Peschel, E., & St. James, D. (1994). *Empathy and the practice of medicine: Beyond pills and the scalpel*. New Haven, CT: Yale University Press.

Sprecher, S. (1999). "I love you more today than yesterday": Romantic partners' perceptions of changes in love and related affect over time. *Journal of Personality and Social Psychology, 76,* 46–53.

Squire, L. R. (1992). Memory and the hippocampus: A synthesis from findings with rats, monkeys, and humans. *Psychological Review, 99,* 195–231.

Squire, L. R. (2009). The legacy of patient HM for neuroscience. *Neuron, 61,* 6–9.

Squire, L. R., & Kandel, E. R. (1999). *Memory: From mind to molecules*. New York: Scientific American Library.

Squire, L. R., Knowlton, B., & Musen, G. (1993). The structure and organization of memory. *Annual Review of Psychology, 44,* 453–495.

Squire, L. R., & Wixted, J. T. (2011). The cognitive neuroscience of memory since HM. *Annual Review of Neuroscience, 34,* 259–288.

Srivistava, S., John, O. P., Gosling, S. D., & Potter, J. (2003). Development of personality in early and middle adulthood: Set like plaster or persistent change? *Journal of Personality and Social Psychology, 84,* 1041–1053.

Sroufe, L. A., Egeland, B., & Kruetzer, T. (1990). The fate of early experience following developmental change: Longitudinal approaches to individual adaptation in childhood. *Child Development, 61,* 1363–1373.

Staddon, J. E. R., & Simmelhag, V. L. (1971). The "superstition" experiment: A reexamination of its implications for the principles of adaptive behavior. *Psychological Review, 78,* 3–43.

Staw, B. M., & Hoang, H. (1995). Sunk costs in the NBA: Why draft order affects playing time and survival in professional basketball. *Administrative Science Quarterly, 40,* 474–494.

Steele, C. M., & Aronson, J. (1995). Stereotype threat and the intellectual test performance of African Americans. *Journal of Personality and Social Psychology, 69,* 797–811.

Steele, C. M., & Josephs, R. A. (1990). Alcohol myopia: Its prized and dangerous effects. *American Psychologist, 45,* 921–933.

Steele, H., Steele, M., Croft, C., & Fonagy, P. (1999). Infant-mother attachment at one year predicts children's understanding of mixed emotions at six years. *Social Development, 8,* 161–178.

Stein, D. J., Phillips, K. A., Bolton, D., Fulford, K. W. M., Sadler, J. Z., & Kendler, K. S. (2010). What is a mental/psychiatric disorder? From DSM–IV to DSM–V. *Psychological Medicine, 40*(11), 1759–1765. doi:10.1017/S0033291709992261.

Stein, M., Federspiel, A., Koenig, T., Wirth, M., Lehmann, C., Wiest, R, . . . Dierks, T. (2009). Reduced frontal activation with increasing second language proficiency. *Neuropsychologia, 47,* 2712–2720.

Stein, M. B. (1998). Neurobiological perspectives on social phobia: From affiliation to zoology. *Biological Psychiatry, 44,* 1277–1285.

Stein, M. B., Chavira, D. A., & Jang, K. L. (2001). Bringing up bashful baby: Developmental pathways to social phobia. *Psychiatric Clinics of North America, 24,* 661–675.

Stein, Z., Susser, M., Saenger, G., & Marolla, F. (1975). *Famine and development: The Dutch hunger winter of 1944–1945*. Oxford, England: Oxford University Press.

Steinbaum, E. A., & Miller, N. E. (1965). Obesity from eating elicited by daily stimulation of hypothalamus. *American Journal of Physiology, 208,* 1–5.

Steinberg, L. (2007). Risk taking in adolescence: New perspectives from brain and behavioral science. *Current Directions in Psychological Science, 16*(2), 55–59. doi:10.1111/j.1467-8721.2007.00475x

Steinberg, L., & Monahan, K. C. (2007). Age differences in resistance to peer influence. *Developmental Psychology, 43,* 1531–1543.

Steinberg, L., & Morris, A. S. (2001). Adolescent development. *Annual Review of Psychology, 52,* 83–110.

Steiner, F. (1986). Differentiating smiles. In E. Branniger-Huber & F. Steiner (Eds.), *FACS in psychotherapy research* (pp.139–148). Zurich: Universität Zürich, Department of Clinical Psychology.

Steiner, J. E. (1973). The gustofacial response: Observation on normal and anencephalic newborn infants. In J. F. Bosma (Ed.), *Fourth symposium on oral sensation and perception: Development in the fetus and infant* (DHEW 73–546; pp. 254–278). Bethesda, MD: U.S. Department of Heath, Education, and Welfare.

Steiner, J. E. (1979). Human facial expressions in response to taste and smell stimulation. *Advances in Child Development and Behavior, 13,* 257–295.

Stellar, J. R., & Stellar, E. (1985). *The neurobiology of motivation and reward.* New York: Springer-Verlag.

Stelmack, R. M. (1990). Biological bases of extraversion: Psychophysiological evidence. *Journal of Personality, 58,* 293–311.

Stephens, R. S. (1999). Cannabis and hallucinogens. In B. S. McCrady & E. E. Epstein (Eds.), *Addictions: A comprehensive guidebook* (pp. 121–140). New York: Oxford University Press.

Sterelny, K., & Griffiths, P. E. (1999). *Sex and death: An introduction to philosophy of biology.* Chicago: University of Chicago Press.

Stern, J. A., Brown, M., Ulett, A., & Sletten, I. (1977). A comparison of hypnosis, acupuncture, morphine, Valium, aspirin, and placebo in the management of experimentally induced pain. In W. E. Edmonston (Ed.), *Conceptual and investigative approaches to hypnosis and hypnotic phenomena* (Vol. 296, pp. 175–193). New York: Annals of the New York Academy of Sciences.

Sternberg, R. J. (1986). A triangular theory of love. *Psychological Review, 93,* 119–135.

Sternberg, R. J. (1999). The theory of successful intelligence. *Review of General Psychology, 3*(4), 292–316. doi:10.1037/1089-2680.3.4.292

Stevens, G., & Gardner, S. (1982). *The women of psychology* (Vol. 1). Rochester: Schenkman Books.

Stevens, J. (1988). An activity approach to practical memory. In M. M. Gruneberg, P. E. Morris, & R. N. Sykes (Eds.), *Practical aspects of memory: Current research and issues* (Vol. 1, pp. 335–341). New York: Wiley.

Stevenson, R. J., & Boakes, R. A. (2003). A mnemonic theory of odor perception. *Psychological Review, 110,* 340–364.

Stickgold, R., Hobson, J. A., Fosse, R., & Fosse, M. (2001). Sleep, learning, and dreams: Off-line memory reprocessing. *Science, 294,* 1052–1057.

Stickgold, R., Malia, A., Maguire, D., Roddenberry, D., & O'Connor, M. (2000). Replaying the game: Hypnagogic images in normals and amnesics. *Science, 290,* 350–353.

St. Jacques, P. L., & Schacter, D. L. (2013). Modifying memory: Selectively enhancing and updating personal memories for a museum tour by reactivating them. *Psychological Science, 24,* 537–543.

Stone, A. A., Schwartz, J. E., Broderick, J. E., & Deaton, A. (2010). A snapshot of the age distribution of psychological well-being in the United States. *Proceedings of the National Academy of Sciences, USA, 107*(22), 9985–9990. doi:10.1073/pnas.1003744107

Stone, J., Perry, Z. W., & Darley, J. M. (1997). "White men can't jump": Evidence for the perceptual confirmation of racial stereotypes following a basketball game. *Basic and Applied Social Psychology, 19,* 291–306.

Stoodley, C. J., Ray, N. J., Jack, A., & Stein, J. F. (2008). Implicit learning in control, dyslexic, and garden-variety poor readers. *Annals of the New York Academy of Sciences, 1145,* 173–183.

Storms, M. D. (1973). Videotape and the attribution process: Reversing actors' and observers' points of view. *Journal of Personality and Social Psychology, 27,* 165–175.

Strack, F., Martin, L. L., & Stepper, S. (1988). Inhibiting and facilitating conditions of the human smile: A nonobtrusive test of the facial feedback hypothesis. *Journal of Personality and Social Psychology, 54,* 768–777.

Strayer, D. L., Drews, F. A., & Johnston, W. A. (2003). Cell phone induced failures of visual attention during simulated driving. *Journal of Experimental Psychology: Applied, 9,* 23–32.

Streissguth, A. P., Barr, H. M., Bookstein, F. L., Sampson, P. D., & Carmichael Olson, H. (1999). The long-term neurocognitive consequences of prenatal alcohol exposure: A 14-year study. *Psychological Science, 10,* 186–190.

Striano, T., & Reid, V. M. (2006). Social cognition in the first year. *Trends in Cognitive Sciences, 10*(10), 471–476.

Striegel-Moore, R. H., & Bulik, C. M. (2007). Risk factors for eating disorders. *American Psychologist, 62,* 181–198.

Strohmetz, D. B., Rind, B., Fisher, R., & Lynn, M. (2002). Sweetening the till: The use of candy to increase restaurant tipping. *Journal of Applied Social Psychology, 32,* 300–309.

Stroop, J. P. (1935). Studies of interference in serial verbal reactions. *Journal of Experimental Psychology, 18,* 643–661.

Strueber, D., Lueck, M., & Roth, G. (2006). The violent brain. *Scientific American Mind, 17,* 20–27.

Stuss, D. T., & Benson, D. F. (1986). *The frontal lobes.* New York: Raven Press.

Suchman, A. L., Markakis, K., Beckman, H. B., & Frankel, R. (1997). A model of empathic communication in the medical interview. *Journal of the American Medical Association, 277,* 678–682.

Suddendorf, T., & Corballis, M. C. (2007). The evolution of foresight: What is mental time travel and is it unique to humans? *Behavioral and Brain Sciences, 30,* 299–313.

Sundet, J. M., Eriksen, W., & Tambs, K. (2008). Intelligence correlations between brothers decrease with increasing age difference: Evidence for shared environmental effects in young adults. *Psychological Science, 19,* 843–847.

Susman, S., Dent, C., McAdams, L., Stacy, A., Burton, D., & Flay, B. (1994). Group self-identification and adolescent cigarette smoking: A 1-year prospective study. *Journal of Abnormal Psychology, 103,* 576–580.

Susser, E. B., Brown, A., & Matte, T. D. (1999). Prenatal factors and adult mental and physical health. *Canadian Journal of Psychiatry, 44*(4), 326–334.

Suzuki, L. A., & Valencia, R. R. (1997). Race-ethnicity and measured intelligence: Educational implications. *American Psychologist, 52,* 1103–1114.

Swann, W. B., Jr. (1983). Self-verification: Bringing social reality into harmony with the self. In J. M. Suls & A. G. Greenwald (Ed.), *Psychological perspectives on the self* (Vol. 2, pp. 33–66). Hillsdale, NJ: Erlbaum.

Swann, W. B., Jr., & Rentfrow, P. J. (2001). Blirtatiousness: Cognitive, behavioral, and physiological consequences of rapid responding. *Journal of Personality and Social Psychology, 181*(6), 1160–1175.

Swayze, V. W., II. (1995). Frontal leukotomy and related psychosurgical procedures before antipsychotics (1935–1954): A historical overview. *American Journal of Psychiatry, 152,* 505–515.

Szechtman, H., & Woody, E. Z. (2006). Obsessive-compulsive disorder as a disturbance of security motivation: Constraints on comorbidity. *Neurotoxicity Research, 10,* 103–112.

Szpunar, K. K. (2010). Episodic future thought: An emerging concept. *Perspectives on Psychological Science, 5,* 142–162.

Szpunar, K. K., Khan, N. Y., & Schacter, D. L. (2013). Interpolated memory tests reduce mind wandering and improve learning of online lectures. *Proceedings of the National Academy of Sciences, USA, 110,* 6313–6317.

Szpunar, K. K., Watson, J. M., & McDermott, K. B. (2007). Neural substrates of envisioning the future. *Proceedings of the National Academy of Sciences, USA, 104,* 642–647.

Tajfel, H., Billig, M. G., Bundy, R. P., & Flament, C. (1971). Social categorization and intergroup behaviour. *European Journal of Social Psychology, 1*, 149–178.

Tajfel, H., & Wilkes, A. L. (1963). Classification and quantitative judgement. *British Journal of Psychology, 54*, 101–114.

Takahashi, K. (1986). Examining the Strange Situation procedure with Japanese mothers and 12-month-old infants. *Developmental Psychology, 22*, 265–270.

Tamis-LeMonda, C. S., Adolph, K. E., Lobo, S. A., Karasik, L. B., Ishak, S., & Dimitropoulou, K. A. (2008). When infants take mothers' advice: 18-month-olds integrate perceptual and social information to guide motor action. *Developmental Psychology, 44*, 734–746.

Tamminga, C. A., Nemeroff, C. B., Blakely, R. D., Brady, L., Carter, C. S., Davis, K. L., . . . Suppes, T. (2002). Developing novel treatments for mood disorders: Accelerating discovery. *Biological Psychiatry, 52*, 589–609.

Tanaka, F., Cicourel, A., & Movellan, J. R. (2007). Socialization between toddlers and robots at an early childhood education center. *Proceedings of the National Academy of Sciences, USA, 104*(46), 17954–17958.

Tang, Y.-P., Shimizu, E., Dube, G. R., Rampon, C., Kerchner, G. A., Zhuo, M., . . . Tsien, J. Z. (1999). Genetic enhancement of learning and memory in mice. *Nature, 401*, 63–69.

Tang, Y. Y., Lu, Q., Fan, M., Yang, Y., & Posner, M. I. (2012). Mechanisms of white matter changes induced by meditation. *Proceedings of the National Academy of Sciences, 109*, 10570–10574.

Tart, C. T. (Ed.). (1969). *Altered states of consciousness.* New York: Wiley.

Taylor, S. E. (1986). *Health psychology.* New York: Random House.

Taylor, S. E. (1989). *Positive illusions.* New York: Basic Books.

Taylor, S. E. (2002). *The tending instinct: How nurturing is essential to who we are and how we live.* New York: Times Books.

Taylor, S. E., & Brown, J. D. (1988). Illusion and well-being: A social psychological perspective on mental health. *Psychological Bulletin, 103*, 193–210.

Taylor, S. E., & Fiske, S. T. (1975). Point-of-view and perceptions of causality. *Journal of Personality and Social Psychology, 32*, 439–445.

Teasdale, J. D., Segal, Z. V., & Williams, J. M. G. (2000). Prevention of relapse/recurrence in major depression by mindfulness-based cognitive therapy. *Journal of Consulting and Clinical Psychology, 68*, 615–623.

Telch, M. J., Lucas, J. A., & Nelson, P. (1989). Non-clinical panic in college students: An investigation of prevalence and symptomology. *Journal of Abnormal Psychology, 98*, 300–306.

Tellegen, A., & Atkinson, G. (1974). Openness to absorbing and self-altering experiences ("absorption"), a trait related to hypnotic susceptibility. *Journal of Abnormal Psychology, 83*, 268–277.

Tellegen, A., Lykken, D. T., Bouchard, T. J., Wilcox, K., Segal, N., & Rich, A. (1988). Personality similarity in twins reared together and apart. *Journal of Personality and Social Psychology, 54*, 1031–1039.

Temerlin, M. K., & Trousdale, W. W. (1969). The social psychology of clinical diagnosis. *Psychotherapy: Theory, Research & Practice, 6*, 24–29.

Terman, L. M. (1916). *The measurement of intelligence.* Boston: Houghton Mifflin.

Teyler, T. J., & DiScenna, P. (1986). The hippocampal memory indexing theory. *Behavioral Neuroscience, 100*, 147–154.

Thaker, G. K. (2002). Current progress in schizophrenia research. Search for genes of schizophrenia: Back to defining valid phenes. *Journal of Nervous and Mental Disease, 190*, 411–412.

Thaler, K., Delivuk, M., Chapman, A., Gaynes, B. N., Kaminski, A., & Gartlehner, G. (2011). Second-generation antidepressants for seasonal affective disorder. *Cochrane Database of Systematic Reviews,* CD008591.

Thaler, R. H. (1988). The ultimatum game. *Journal of Economic Perspectives, 2*, 195–206.

Thase, M. E., & Howland, R. H. (1995). Biological processes in depression: An updated review and integration. In E. E. Beckham & W. R. Leber (Eds.), *Handbook of depression* (2nd ed., pp. 213–279). New York: Guilford Press.

Thibaut, J. W., & Kelley, H. H. (1959). *The social psychology of groups.* New Brunswick, NJ: Transaction Publishers.

Thomaes, S., Bushman, B. J., Stegge, H., & Olthof, T. (2008). Trumping shame by blasts of noise: Narcissism, self-esteem, shame, and aggression in young adolescents. *Child Development, 79*(6), 1792–1801.

Thomas, A., & Chess, S. (1977). *Temperament and development.* New York: Brunner/Mazel.

Thomason, M., & Thompson, P. M. (2011). Diffusion imaging, white matter, and psychopathology. *Annual Review of Clinical Psychology, 7*, 63–85.

Thompson, B., Coronado, G., Chen, L., Thompson, L. A., Halperin, A., Jaffe, R., . . . Zbikowski, S. M. (2007). Prevalence and characteristics of smokers at 30 Pacific Northwest colleges and universities. *Nicotine & Tobacco Research, 9*, 429–438.

Thompson, P. M., Vidal, C., Giedd, J. N., Gochman, P., Blumenthal, J., Nicolson, R., . . . Rapoport, J. L. (2001). Accelerated gray matter loss in very early-onset schizophrenia. *Proceedings of the National Academy of Sciences, USA, 98*, 11650–11655.

Thompson, R. F. (2005). In search of memory traces. *Annual Review of Psychology, 56*, 1–23.

Thorndike, E. L. (1898). Animal intelligence: An experimental study of associative processes in animals. *Psychological Review Monograph Supplements, 2*, 4–160.

Thornhill, R., & Gangestad, S. W. (1993). Human facial beauty: Averageness, symmetry, and parasite resistance. *Human Nature, 4*, 237–269.

Thurber, J. (1956). *Further fables of our time.* New York: Simon & Schuster.

Thurstone, L. L. (1938). *Primary mental abilities.* Chicago: University of Chicago Press.

Tice, D. M., & Baumeister, R. F. (1997). Longitudinal study of procrastination, performance, stress, and health: The costs and benefits of dawdling. *Psychological Science, 8*(6), 454–458.

Tienari, P., Wynne, L. C., Sorri, A., Lahti, I., Läksy, K., Moring, J., . . . Wahlberg, K. E. (2004). Genotype–environment interaction in schizophrenia spectrum disorder: Long-term follow-up study of Finnish adoptees. *British Journal of Psychiatry, 184*, 216–222.

Timmerman, T. A. (2007). "It was a thought pitch": Personal, situational, and target influences on hit-by-pitch events across time. *Journal of Applied Psychology, 92*, 876–884.

Todd, A. R., Bodenhausen, G. V., Richeson, J. A., & Galinsky, A. D. (2011). Perspective taking combats automatic expressions of racial bias. *Journal of Personality and Social Psychology, 100*(6), 1027–1042. doi:10.1037/a0022308

Toga, A. W., Clark, K. A., Thompson, P. M., Shattuck, D. W., & Van Horn, J. D. (2012). Mapping the human connectome. *Neurosurgery, 71*, 1–5.

Tolman, E. C., & Honzik, C. H. (1930a). "Insight" in rats. *University of California Publications in Psychology, 4*, 215–232.

Tolman, E. C., & Honzik, C. H. (1930b). Introduction and removal of reward and maze performance in rats. *University of California Publications in Psychology, 4*, 257–275.

Tolman, E. C., Ritchie, B. F., & Kalish, D. (1946). Studies in spatial learning: I: Orientation and short cut. *Journal of Experimental Psychology, 36*, 13–24.

Tomasello, M., & Call, J. (2004). The role of humans in the cognitive development of apes revisited. *Animal Cognition, 7*, 213–215.

Tomasello, M., Davis-Dasilva, M., Camak, L., & Bard, K. (1987). Observational learning of tool use by young chimpanzees. *Human Evolution, 2*, 175–183.

Tomasello, M., Savage-Rumbaugh, S., & Kruger, A. C. (1993). Imitative learning of actions on objects by children, chimpanzees, and enculturated chimpanzees. *Child Development, 64*, 1688–1705.

Tomkins, S. S. (1981). The role of facial response in the experience of emotion. *Journal of Personality and Social Psychology, 40*, 351–357.

Torgensen, S. (1986). Childhood and family characteristics in panic and generalized anxiety disorder. *American Journal of Psychiatry, 143*, 630–639.

Torrey, E. F., Bower, A. E., Taylor, E. H., & Gottesman, I. I. (1994). *Schizophrenia and manic-depressive disorder: The biological roots of mental illness as revealed by the landmark study of identical twins.* New York: Basic Books.

Tracy, J. L., Shariff, A. F., Zhao, W., & Henrich, J. (2013). Cross-cultural evidence that the noverbal expression of pride is an automatic status signal. *Journal of Experimental Psychology: General, 142*(1), 163–180.

Treede, R. D., Kenshalo, D. R., Gracely, R. H., & Jones, A. K. (1999). The cortical representation of pain. *Pain, 79*, 105–111.

Treisman, A. (1998). Feature binding, attention and object perception. *Philosophical Transactions of the Royal Society (B), 353*, 1295–1306.

Treisman, A. (2006). How the deployment of attention determines what we see. *Visual Cognition, 14*, 411–443.

Treisman, A., & Gelade, G. (1980). A feature integration theory of attention. *Cognitive Psychology, 12*, 97–136.

Treisman, A., & Schmidt, H. (1982). Illusory conjunctions in the perception of objects. *Cognitive Psychology, 14*, 107–141.

Trivers, R. L. (1972). Parental investment and sexual selection. In B. Campbell (Ed.), *Sexual selection and the descent of man, 1871–1971* (pp. 139–179). Chicago: Aldine.

Trompeter, S. E., Bettencourt, R., & Barrett-Connor, E. (2012). Sexual activity and satisfaction in healthy community-dwelling older women. *American Journal of Medicine, 125*(1), 37–43. doi:10.1016/j.amjmed.2011.07.036

Trull, T. J., & Durrett, C. A. (2005). Categorical and dimensional models of personality disorder. *Annual Review of Clinical Psychology, 1*, 355–380.

Tulving, E. (1972). Episodic and semantic memory. In E. Tulving & W. Donaldson (Eds.), *Organization of memory* (pp. 381–403). New York: Academic Press.

Tulving, E. (1983). *Elements of episodic memory.* Oxford, England: Clarendon Press.

Tulving, E. (1985). Memory and consciousness. *Canadian Psychologist, 25*, 1–12.

Tulving, E. (1998). Neurocognitive processes of human memory. In C. von Euler, I. Lundberg, & R. Llins (Eds.), *Basic mechanisms in cognition and language* (pp. 261–281). Amsterdam: Elsevier.

Tulving, E., Kapur, S., Craik, F. I. M., Moscovitch, M., & Houle, S. (1994). Hemispheric encoding/retrieval asymmetry in episodic memory: Positron emission tomography findings. *Proceedings of the National Academy of Sciences, USA, 91*, 2016–2020.

Tulving, E., & Schacter, D. L. (1990). Priming and human memory systems. *Science, 247*, 301–306.

Tulving, E., Schacter, D. L., & Stark, H. (1982). Priming effects in word fragment completion are independent of recognition memory. *Journal of Experimental Psychology: Learning, Memory, and Cognition, 8*, 336–342.

Tulving, E., & Thompson, D. M. (1973). Encoding specificity and retrieval processes in episodic memory. *Psychological Review, 80*, 352–373.

Turkheimer, E. (2000). Three laws of behavior genetics and what they mean. *Current Directions in Psychological Science, 9*, 160–164.

Turner, D. C., Robbins, T. W., Clark, L., Aron, A. R., Dowson, J., & Sahakian, B. J. (2003). Cognitive enhancing effects of modafinil in healthy volunteers. *Psychopharmacology, 165*, 260–269.

Turner, D. C., & Sahakian, B. J. (2006). Neuroethics of cognitive enhancement. *BioSocieties, 1*, 113–123.

Turner, M. E., & Pratkanis, A. R. (1998). Twenty-five years of group-think theory and research: Lessons from the evaluation of a theory. *Organizational Behavior and Human Decision Processes, 73*(2–3), 105–115. doi:10.1006/obhd.1998.2756

Tversky, A., & Kahneman, D. (1973). Availability: A heuristic for judging frequency and probability. *Cognitive Psychology, 5*, 207–232.

Tversky, A., & Kahneman, D. (1974). Judgment under uncertainty: Heuristics and biases. *Science, 185*, 1124–1131.

Tversky, A., & Kahneman, D. (1981). The framing of decisions and the psychology of choice. *Science, 211*, 453–458.

Tversky, A., & Kahneman, D. (1983). Extensional versus intuitive reasoning: The conjunction fallacy in probability judgment. *Psychological Review, 90*, 293–315.

Tversky, A., & Kahneman, D. (1992). Advances in prospect theory: Cumulative representation of uncertainty. *Journal of Risk and Uncertainty, 5*, 297–323.

Twenge, J. M., Campbell, W. K., & Foster, C. A. (2003). Parenthood and marital satisfaction: A meta-analytic review. *Journal of Marriage and Family, 65*, 574–583.

Tyler, T. R. (1990). *Why people obey the law.* New Haven, CT: Yale University Press.

Umberson, D., Williams, K., Powers, D. A., Liu, H., & Needham, B. (2006). You make me sick: Marital quality and health over the life course. *Journal of Health and Social Behavior, 47*, 1–16.

Uncapher, M. R., & Rugg, M. D. (2008). Fractionation of the component processes underlying successful episodic encoding: A combined fMRI and divided-attention study. *Journal of Cognitive Neuroscience, 20*, 240–254.

Ungerleider, L. G., & Mishkin, M. (1982). Two cortical visual systems. In D. J. Ingle, M. A. Goodale, & R. J. W. Mansfield (Eds.), *Analysis of visual behavior* (pp. 549–586). Cambridge, MA: MIT Press.

Urban, N. B. L., Girgis, R. R., Talbot, P. S., Kegeles, L. S., Xu, X., Frankie, W. G., . . . Laruelle, M. (2012). Sustained recreational use of ecstasy is associated with altered pre- and postsynaptic markers of serotonin transmission in neocortical areas: A PET study with [11c] DASB and [11c] MDL 100907. *Neuropsychopharmacology, 37*, 1465–1473.

Ursano, R. J., & Silberman, E. K. (2003). Psychoanalysis, psychoanalytic psychotherapy, and supportive psychotherapy. In R. E. Hales & S. C. Yudofsky (Eds.), *The American Psychiatric Publishing textbook of clinical psychiatry* (4th ed., pp. 1177–1203). Washington, DC: American Psychiatric Publishing.

U.S. Census Bureau. (2012). *The 2012 statistical abstract: National data book.* Washington, DC: Author.

Vacha, E., & McBride, M. (1993). Cramming: A barrier to student success, a way to beat the system, or an effective strategy? *College Student Journal, 27*, 2–11.

Valentine, T., Brennen, T., & Brédart, S. (1996). *The cognitive psychology of proper names: On the importance of being Ernest.* London: Routledge.

Valins, S. (1966). Cognitive effects of false heart-rate feedback. *Journal of Personality and Social Psychology, 4*, 400–408.

Vallacher, R. R., & Wegner, D. M. (1985). *A theory of action identification.* Hillsdale, NJ: Erlbaum.

Vallacher, R. R., & Wegner, D. M. (1987). What do people think they're doing? Action identification and human behavior. *Psychological Review, 94*, 3–15.

van den Boom, D. C. (1994). The influence of temperament and mothering on attachment and exploration: An experimental manipulation of sensitive responsiveness among lower-class mothers with irritable infants. *Child Development, 65*, 1457–1477.

van den Boom, D. C. (1995). Do first year intervention effects endure? Follow-up during toddlerhood of a sample of Dutch irritable infants. *Child Development, 66,* 1798–1816.

van IJzendoorn, M. H., Juffer, F., & Klein Poelhuis, C. W. (2005). Adoption and cognitive development: A meta-analytic comparison of adopted and nonadopted children's IQ and school performance. *Psychological Bulletin, 131,* 301–316.

van IJzendoorn, M. H., & Kroonenberg, P. M. (1988). Cross-cultural patterns of attachment: A meta-analysis of the strange situation. *Child Development, 59,* 147–156.

van Ittersum, K., & Wansink, B. (2012). Plate size and color suggestibility: The Delboeuf illusion's bias on serving and eating behavior. *Journal of Consumer Research, 39,* 121–130.

van Praag, H. (2009). Exercise and the brain: Something to chew on. *Trends in Neuroscience, 32,* 283–290.

van Stegeren, A. H., Everaerd, W., Cahill, L., McGaugh, J. L., & Gooren, L. J. G. (1998). Memory for emotional events: Differential effects of centrally versus peripherally acting blocking agents. *Psychopharmacology, 138,* 305–310.

Van Vliet, I. M., van Well, E. P., Bruggeman, R., Campo, J. A., Hijman, R., Van Megen, H. J., . . . Van Rijen, P. C. (2013). An evaluation of irreversible psychosurgical treatment of patients with obsessive-compulsive disorder in the Netherlands, 2001–2008. *Journal of Nervous and Mental Disease, 201,* 226–228.

Vargha-Khadem, F., Gadian, D. G., Watkins, K. E., Connelly, A., Van Paesschen, W., & Mishkin, M. (1997). Differential effects of early hippocampal pathology on episodic and semantic memory. *Science, 277,* 376–380.

Vinter, A., & Perruchet, P. (2002). Implicit motor learning through observational training in adults and children. *Memory & Cognition, 30,* 256–261.

Vitkus, J. (1999). *Casebook in abnormal psychology* (4th ed.). New York: McGraw-Hill.

Vondra, J. I., Shaw, D. S., Swearingen, L., Cohen, M., & Owens, E. B. (2001). Attachment stability and emotional and behavioral regulation from infancy to preschool age. *Development and Psychopathology, 13,* 13–33.

Von Frisch, K. (1974). Decoding the language of the bee. *Science, 185,* 663–668.

Voon, V., Pessiglione, M., Brezing, C., Gallea, C., Fernandez, H. H., Dolan, R. J., & Hallett, M. (2011). Mechanisms underlying dopamine-mediated reward bias in compulsive behaviors. *Neuron, 65,* 135–142.

Vrij, A., Granhag, P. A., Mann, S., & Leal, S. (2011). Outsmarting the liars: Toward a cognitive lie detection approach. *Current Directions in Psychological Science, 20*(1), 28–32.

Vygotsky, L. S. (1978). *Mind in society: The development of higher psychological processes.* Cambridge, MA: Harvard University Press.

Wade, N. J. (2005). *Perception and illusion: Historical perspectives.* New York: Springer.

Wade, S. E., Trathen, W., & Schraw, G. (1990). An analysis of spontaneous study strategies. *Reading Research Quarterly, 25,* 147–166.

Wadhwa, P. D., Sandman, C. A., & Garite, T. J. (2001). The neurobiology of stress in human pregnancy: Implications for prematurity and development of the fetal central nervous system. *Progress in Brain Research, 133,* 131–142.

Wagner, A. D., Schacter, D. L., Rotte, M., Koutstaal, W., Maril, A., Dale, A. M., . . . Buckner, R. L. (1998). Remembering and forgetting of verbal experiences as predicted by brain activity. *Science, 281,* 1188–1190.

Wagner, G., & Morris, E. (1987). Superstitious behavior in children. *Psychological Record, 37,* 471–488.

Wai, J., Putallaz, M., & Makel, M. C. (2012). Studying intellectual outliers: Are there sex differences, and are the smart getting smarter? *Current Directions in Psychological Science, 21*(6), 382–390. doi:10.1177/0963721412455052

Waite, L. J. (1995). Does marriage matter? *Demography, 32,* 483–507.

Wakefield, J. C. (2007). The concept of mental disorder: Diagnostic implications of the harmful dysfunction analysis. *World Psychiatry, 6,* 149–156.

Walden, T. A., & Ogan, T. A. (1988). The development of social referencing. *Child Development, 59,* 1230–1240.

Walker, C. (1977). Some variations in marital satisfaction. In R. C. J. Peel (Ed.), *Equalities and inequalities in family life* (pp. 127–139). London: Academic Press.

Walker, L. J. (1988). The development of moral reasoning. *Annals of Child Development, 55,* 677–691.

Walker, N. P., McConville, P. M., Hunter, D., Deary, I. J., & Whalley, L. J. (2002). Childhood mental ability and lifetime psychiatric contact. *Intelligence, 30*(3), 233–245. doi:10.1016/S0160-2896(01)00098-8

Waltzman, S. B. (2006). Cochlear implants: Current status. *Expert Review of Medical Devices, 3,* 647–655.

Wang, J. L., Jackson, L. A., Zhang, D. J., & Su, Z. Q. (2012). The relationships among the Big Five personality factors, self-esteem, narcissism, and sensation seeking to Chinese university students' uses of social networking sites (SNSs). *Computers in Human Behavior, 28,* 2313–2319.

Wang, L. H., McCarthy, G., Song, A. W., & LaBar, K. S. (2005). Amygdala activation to sad pictures during high-field (4 tesla) functional magnetic resonance imaging. *Emotion, 5,* 12–22.

Wang, P. S., Aguilar-Gaxiola, S., Alonso, J., Angermeyer, M. C., Borges, G., Bromet, E. J., . . . Wells, J. E. (2007). Use of mental health services for anxiety, mood, and substance disorders in 17 countries in the WHO World Mental Health Surveys. *Lancet, 370,* 841–850.

Wang, P. S., Berglund, P. A., Olfson, M., & Kessler, R. C. (2004). Delays in initial treatment contact after first onset of a mental disorder. *Health Services Research, 39,* 393–415.

Wang, P. S., Berglund, P., Olfson, M., Pincus, H. A., Wells, K. B., & Kessler, R. C. (2005). Failure and delay in initial treatment contact after first onset of mental disorders in the National Comorbidity Survey Replication. *Archives of General Psychiatry, 62*(6), 629–640.

Wansink, B., & Linder, L. R. (2003). Interactions between forms of fat consumption and restaurant bread consumption. *International Journal of Obesity, 27,* 866–868.

Wansink, B., Painter, J. E., & North, J. (2005). Bottomless bowls: Why visual cues of portion size may influence intake. *Obesity Research, 13,* 93–100.

Wansink, B., & Wansink, C. S. (2010). The largest last supper: Depictions of food portions and plate size increased over the millennium. *International Journal of Obesity, 34,* 943–944.

Warneken, F., & Tomasello, M. (2009). Varieties of altruism in children and chimpanzees. *Trends in Cognitive Sciences, 13,* 397–402.

Warren, K. R., & Hewitt, B. G. (2009). Fetal alcohol spectrum disorders: When science, medicine, public policy, and laws collide. *Developmental Disabilities Research Reviews, 15,* 170–175.

Warrington, E. K., & McCarthy, R. A. (1983). Category specific access dysphasia. *Brain, 106,* 859–878.

Warrington, E. K., & Shallice, T. (1984). Category specific semantic impairments. *Brain, 107,* 829–854.

Watanabe, S., Sakamoto, J., & Wakita, M. (1995). Pigeons' discrimination of painting by Monet and Picasso. *Journal of the Experimental Analysis of Behavior, 63,* 165–174.

Watkins, L. R., & Maier, S. F. (2005). Immune regulation of central nervous system functions: From sickness responses to pathological pain. *Journal of Internal Medicine, 257,* 139–155.

Watson, D., & Pennebaker, J. W. (1989). Health complaints, stress, and distress: Exploring the central role of negative affectivity. *Psychological Review, 96,* 234–254.

Watson, D., & Tellegen, A. (1985). Toward a consensual structure of mood. *Psychological Bulletin, 98,* 219–235.

Watson, J. B. (1913). Psychology as the behaviorist views it. *Psychological Review, 20,* 158–177.

Watson, J. B. (1924). *Behaviorism.* New York: People's Institute.

Watson, J. B. (1928). *Psychological care of infant and child.* New York: Norton.

Watson, J. B., & Rayner, R. (1920). Conditioned emotional reactions. *Journal of Experimental Psychology, 3,* 1–14.

Watson, R. I. (1978). *The great psychologists.* New York: Lippincott.

Weaver, I. C. G., Cervoni, N., Champagne, F. A., D'Alessio, A. C., Sharma, S., Seckl, J. R., . . . Meaney, M. J. (2004). Epigenetic programming by maternal behavior. *Nature Neuroscience, 7,* 847–854.

Webb, T. L., Miles, E., & Sheeran, P. (2012). Dealing with feeling: A meta-analysis of the effectiveness of strategies derived from the process model of emotion regulation. *Psychological Bulletin, 138*(4), 775–808.

Webster Marketon, J. I., & Glaser, R. (2008). Stress hormones and immune function. *Cellular Immunology, 252,* 16–26.

Wechsler, H., & Nelson, T. F. (2001). Binge drinking and the American college student: What's five drinks? *Psychology of Addictive Behaviors, 15*(4), 287–291. doi:10.1037/0893-164X.15.4.287

Wegner, D. M. (1989). *White bears and other unwanted thoughts.* New York: Viking.

Wegner, D. M. (1994a). Ironic processes of mental control. *Psychological Review, 101,* 34–52.

Wegner, D. M. (1994b). *White bears and other unwanted thoughts: Suppression, obsession, and the psychology of mental control.* New York: Guilford Press.

Wegner, D. M. (1997). Why the mind wanders. In J. D. Cohen & J. W. Schooler (Eds.), *Scientific approaches to consciousness* (pp. 295–315). Mahwah, NJ: Erlbaum.

Wegner, D. M. (2002). *The illusion of conscious will.* Cambridge, MA: MIT Press.

Wegner, D. M. (2009). How to think, say, or do precisely the worst thing for any occasion. *Science, 325,* 48–51.

Wegner, D. M., Ansfield, M., & Pilloff, D. (1998). The putt and the pendulum: Ironic effects of the mental control of action. *Psychological Science, 9,* 196–199.

Wegner, D. M., Broome, A., & Blumberg, S. J. (1997). Ironic effects of trying to relax under stress. *Behavior Research and Therapy, 35,* 11–21.

Wegner, D. M., Erber, R. E., & Zanakos, S. (1993). Ironic processes in the mental control of mood and mood-related thought. *Journal of Personality and Social Psychology, 65,* 1093–1104.

Wegner, D. M., & Gilbert, D. T. (2000). Social psychology: The science of human experience. In H. Bless & J. Forgas (Eds.), *The message within: Subjective experience in social cognition and behavior* (pp. 1–9). Philadelphia: Psychology Press.

Wegner, D. M., Schneider, D. J., Carter, S. R., & White, T. L. (1987). Paradoxical effects of thought suppression. *Journal of Personality and Social Psychology, 53,* 5–13.

Wegner, D. M., Vallacher, R. R., Macomber, G., Wood, R., & Arps, K. (1984). The emergence of action. *Journal of Personality and Social Psychology, 46,* 269–279.

Wegner, D. M., & Wenzlaff, R. M. (1996). Mental control. In E. T. Higgins & A. Kruglanski (Eds.), *Social psychology: Handbook of basic mechanisms and processes* (pp. 466–492). New York: Guilford Press.

Wegner, D. M., Wenzlaff, R. M., & Kozak, M. (2004). Dream rebound: The return of suppressed thoughts in dreams. *Psychological Science, 15,* 232–236.

Wegner, D. M., & Zanakos, S. (1994). Chronic thought suppression. *Journal of Personality, 62,* 615–640.

Weiner, R. (2012, November 7). Hickenlooper on Colorado pot vote: 'Don't break out the Cheetos.' *Washington Post.* Retrieved from http://www.washingtonpost.com/blogs/post-politics/wp/2012/11/07/hickenlooper-on-amendment-64-dont-break-out-the-cheetos/?tid=up_next.

Weinstein, N. D. (1980). Unrealistic optimism about future life events. *Journal of Personality and Social Psychology, 39,* 806–820.

Weintraub, D., Papay, K., & Siderowf, A. (2013). Screening for impulse control symptoms in patients with de novo Parkinson disease: A case-control study. *Neurology, 80,* 176–180.

Weisfeld, G. (1999). *Evolutionary principles of human adolescence.* New York: Basic Books.

Weissman, M. M., Markowitz, J. C., & Klerman, G. L. (2000). *Comprehensive guide to interpersonal psychotherapy.* New York: Basic Books.

Weldon, M. S. (2001). Remembering as a social process. In D. L. Medin (Ed.), *The psychology of learning and motivation: Advances in research and theory* (Vol. 40, pp. 67–120). San Diego, CA: Academic Press.

Wenzlaff, R. M., & Wegner, D. M. (2000). Thought suppression. In S. T. Fiske (Ed.), *Annual review of psychology* (Vol. 51, pp. 51–91). Palo Alto, CA: Annual Reviews.

Wesch, N. N., Law, B., & Hall, C. R. (2007). The use of observational learning by athletes. *Journal of Sport Behavior, 30,* 219–231.

Westrin, A., & Lam, R. W. (2007). Seasonal affective disorder: A clinical update. *Journal of Clinical Psychiatry, 19,* 239–246.

Wexler, K. (1999). Maturation and growth of grammar. In W. C. Ritchie & T. K. Bhatia (Eds.), *Handbook of child language acquisition* (pp. 55–110). San Diego: Academic Press.

Whalen, P. J., Rauch, S. L., Etcoff, N. L., McInerney, S. C., Lee, M. B., & Jenike, M. A. (1998). Masked presentations of emotional facial expressions modulate amygdala activity without explicit knowledge. *The Journal of Neuroscience, 18,* 411–418.

Whalley, L. J., & Deary, I. J. (2001). Longitudinal cohort study of childhood IQ and survival up to age 76. *British Medical Journal, 322,* 1–5.

Wheatley, T., & Haidt, J. (2005). Hypnotic disgust makes moral judgments more severe. *Psychological Science, 16,* 780–784.

Wheeler, M. A., Petersen, S. E., & Buckner, R. L. (2000). Memory's echo: Vivid recollection activates modality-specific cortex. *Proceedings of the National Academy of Sciences, USA, 97,* 11125–11129.

White, B. L., & Held, R. (1966). Plasticity of motor development in the human infant. In J. F. Rosenblith & W. Allinsmith (Eds.), *The cause of behavior* (pp. 60–70). Boston: Allyn & Bacon.

White, G. M., & Kirkpatrick, J. (Eds.) (1985). *Person, self, and experience: Exploring pacific ethnopsychologies.* Berkeley: University of California Press.

Whitney, D., Ellison, A., Rice, N. J., Arnold, D., Goodale, M., Walsh, V., & Milner, D. (2007). Visually guided reaching depends on motion area MT+. *Cerebral Cortex, 17,* 2644–2649.

Whybrow, P. C. (1997). *A mood apart.* New York: Basic Books.

Wiggs, C. L., & Martin, A. (1998). Properties and mechanisms of perceptual priming. *Current Opinion in Neurobiology, 8,* 227–233.

Wilcoxon, H. C., Dragoin, W. B., & Kral, P. A. (1971). Illness-induced aversions in rats and quail: Relative salience of visual and gustatory cues. *Science, 171,* 826–828.

Wiley, J. L. (1999). Cannabis: Discrimination of "internal bliss"? *Pharmacology, Biochemistry, & Behavior, 64,* 257–260.

Wilhelm, I., Dieckelmann, S., Molzow, I., Ayoub, A., Molle, M., & Born, J. (2011). Sleep selectively enhances memories expected to be of future relevance. *Journal of Neuroscience, 31,* 1563–1569.

Williams, C. M., & Kirkham, T. C. (1999). Anandamide induces overeating: Mediation by central cannabinoid (CB1) receptors. *Psychopharmacology, 143,* 315–317.

Willingham, D. T. (2007). Critical thinking: Why is it so hard to teach? *American Educator, 31*(2), 8–19.

Wilson, K., & Korn, J. H. (2007). Attention during lectures: Beyond ten minutes. *Teaching of Psychology, 34,* 85–89.

Wilson, T. D. (2002). *Strangers to ourselves: Discovering the adaptive unconscious.* Cambridge, MA: Harvard University Press.

Wilson, T. D. (2009). Know thyself. *Perspectives on Psychological Science, 4,* 384–389.

Wilson, T. D. (2011). *Redirect: The surprising new science of psychological change.* New York: Little Brown.

Wilson, T. D. (2012, July 12). Stop bullying the "soft" sciences. *Los Angeles Times.* Available from http://articles.latimes.com/2012/jul/12/opinion/la-oe-wilson-social-sciences-20120712

Wilson, T. D., Meyers, J., & Gilbert, D. T. (2003). "How happy was I, anyway?" A retrospective impact bias. *Social Cognition, 21,* 421–446.

Wimber, M., Rutschmann, R. N., Greenlee, M. W., & Bauml, K.-H. (2009). Retrieval from episodic memory: Neural mechanisms of interference resolution. *Journal of Cognitive Neuroscience, 21,* 538–549.

Wimmer, H., & Perner, J. (1983). Beliefs about beliefs: Representations and constraining function of wrong beliefs in young children's understanding of deception. *Cognition, 13,* 103–128.

Windham, G. C., Eaton, A., & Hopkins, B. (1999). Evidence for an association between environmental tobacco smoke exposure and birthweight: A meta-analysis and new data. *Pediatrics and Perinatal Epidemiology, 13,* 35–57.

Winocur, G., Moscovitch, M., & Bontempi, B. (2010). Memory formation and long-term retention in humans and animals: Convergence towards a transformation account of hippocampal–neocortical interactions. *Neuropsychologia, 48,* 2339–2356.

Winterer, G., & Weinberger, D. R. (2004). Genes, dopamine and cortical signal-to-noise ratio in schizophrenia. *Trends in Neuroscience, 27,* 683–690.

Wise, R. A. (1989). Brain dopamine and reward. *Annual Review of Psychology, 40,* 191–225.

Wise, R. A. (2005). Forebrain substrates of reward and motivation. *Journal of Comparative Neurology, 493,* 115–121.

Wittgenstein, L. (1999). *Philosophical investigations.* Upper Saddle River, NJ: Prentice Hall. (Originally published 1953)

Wixted, J. T., & Ebbensen, E. (1991). On the form of forgetting. *Psychological Science, 2,* 409–415.

Wolf, J. R., Arkes, H. R., & Muhanna, W. A. (2008). The power of touch: An examination of the effect of duration of physical contact on the valuation of objects. *Judgment and Decision Making, 3,* 476–482.

Wood, J. M., & Bootzin, R. R. (1990). Prevalence of nightmares and their independence from anxiety. *Journal of Abnormal Psychology, 99,* 64–68.

Wood, J. M., Bootzin, R. R., Rosenhan, D., Nolen-Hoeksema, S., & Jourden, F. (1992). Effects of the 1989 San Francisco earthquake on frequency and content of nightmares. *Journal of Abnormal Psychology, 101,* 219–224.

Woodley, M. A., te Nijenhuis, J., & Murphy, R. (2013). Were the Victorians cleverer than us? The decline in general intelligence estimated from a meta-analysis of the slowing of simple reaction time. *Intelligence.* Advance online publication. doi:10.1016/j.intell.2013.04.006

Woods, S. C., Seeley, R. J., Porte, D., Jr., & Schwartz, M. W. (1998). Signals that regulate food intake and energy homeostasis. *Science, 280,* 1378–1383.

Woody, S. R., & Nosen, E. (2008). Psychological models of phobic disorders and panic. In M. M. Anthony & M. B. Stein (Eds.), *Oxford handbook of anxiety and related disorders* (pp. 209–224). New York: Oxford University Press.

Wrangham, R., & Peterson, D. (1997). *Demonic males: Apes and the origin of human violence.* New York: Mariner.

Wren, A. M., Seal, L. J., Cohen, M. A., Brynes, A. E., Frost, G. S., Murphy, K. G., . . . Bloom, S. R. (2001). Ghrelin enhances appetite and increases food intake in humans. *Journal of Clinical Endocrinology and Metabolism, 86,* 5992–5995.

Wrenn, C. C., Turchi, J. N., Schlosser, S., Dreiling, J. L., Stephenson, D. A., & Crawley, J. N. (2006). Performance of galanin transgenic mice in the 5-choice serial reaction time attentional task. *Pharmacology Biochemistry and Behavior, 83,* 428–440.

Wulf, S. (1994, March 14). Err Jordan. *Sports Illustrated.*

Yamaguchi, S. (1998). Basic properties of umami and its effects in humans. *Physiology and Behavior, 49,* 833–841.

Yang, S., & Sternberg, R. J. (1997). Conceptions of intelligence in ancient Chinese philosophy. *Journal of Theoretical and Philosophical Psychology, 17,* 101–119.

Yeo, B. T. T., Krienen, F. M., Sepulcre, J., Sabuncu, M. R., Lashkari, D., Hollinshead, M., . . . Buckner, R. L. (2011). The organization of the human cerebral cortex estimated by intrinsic functional connectivity. *Journal of Neurophysiology, 106,* 1125–1165.

Yik, M., Russell, J. A., & Steiger, J. H. (2011). A 12-point circumplex structure of core affect. *Emotion, 11*(4), 705–731.

Yzerbyt, V., & Demoulin, S. (2010). Intergroup relations. In S. T. Fiske, D. T. Gilbert, & G. Lindzey (Eds.), *The handbook of social psychology* (5th ed., Vol. 2, pp. 1024–1083). New York: Wiley.

Zajonc, R. B. (1968). Attitudinal effects of mere exposure. *Journal of Personality and Social Psychology, 9,* 1–27.

Zajonc, R. B. (1989). Feeling the facial efference: Implications of the vascular theory of emotion. *Psychological Review, 96,* 395–416.

Zebrowitz, L. A., Hall, J. A., Murphy, N. A., & Rhodes, G. (2002). Looking smart and looking good: Facial cues to intelligence and their origins. *Personality and Social Psychology Bulletin, 28,* 238–249.

Zeki, S. (1993). *A vision of the brain.* London: Blackwell Scientific.

Zeki, S. (2001). Localization and globalization in conscious vision. *Annual Review of Neuroscience, 24,* 57–86.

Zentall, T. R., Sutton, J. E., & Sherburne, L. M. (1996). True imitative learning in pigeons. *Psychological Science, 7,* 343–346.

Zentner, M., & Mitura, K. (2012). Stepping out of the caveman's shadow: Nations' gender gap predicts degree of sex differentiation in mate preferences. *Psychological Science, 23*(10), 1176–1185. doi:10.1177/0956797612441004

Zernike, K. (2012, August 25). After gay son's suicide, mother finds blame in herself and in her church. *New York Times, p. A14.*

Zhang, T. Y., & Meaney, M. J. (2010). Epigenetics and the environmental regulation of the genome and its function. *Annual Review of Psychology, 61,* 439–466.

Zihl, J., von Cramon, D., & Mai, N. (1983). Selective disturbance of movement vision after bilateral brain damage. *Brain, 106,* 313–340.

Zillmann, D., Katcher, A. H., & Milavsky, B. (1972). Excitation transfer from physical exercise to subsequent aggressive behavior. *Journal of Experimental Psychology, 8,* 247–259.

Zimprich, D., & Martin, M. (2002). Can longitudinal changes in processing speed explain longitudinal age changes in fluid intelligence? *Psychology and Aging, 17,* 690–695.

Zuckerman, M., DePaulo, B. M., & Rosenthal, R. (1981). Verbal and nonverbal communication of deception. In L. Berkowitz (Ed.), *Advances in experimental social psychology* (Vol. 14, pp. 1–59). New York: Academic Press.

Zuckerman, M., & Driver, R. E. (1985). Telling lies: Verbal and nonverbal correlates of deception. In W. Seigman & S. Feldstein (Eds.), *Multichannel integrations of nonverbal behavior* (pp. 129–147). Hillsdale, NJ: Erlbaum.

NAME INDEX

Note: Page numbers followed by f indicate figures.

SUBJECT INDEX

Note: Page numbers followed by f indicate figures; those followed by t indicate tables.